CASSELL'S
LATIN and ENGLISH
DICTIONARY

Other Cassell's Dictionaries

Cassell's French and English Dictionary
Cassell's German and English Dictionary
Cassell's Spanish and English Dictionary

CASSELL'S
LATIN and ENGLISH
DICTIONARY

Compiled by

D. P. Simpson

Houghton Mifflin Harcourt
Boston • New York

Copyright © 2002 by Houghton Mifflin Harcourt Publishing Company

For information about permission to reproduce selections from this book,
write to trade.permissions@hmhco.com or to Permissions, Houghton Mifflin
Harcourt Publishing Company, 3 Park Avenue, 19th Floor, New York, NY 10016.

www.hmhco.com

Library of Congress Cataloging-in-Publication Data:
    Cassell's Latin and English dictionary.
    Reprint. Originally published: Cassell's new compact Latin-English,
English-Latin dictionary. New York : Funk & Wagnalls, 1963.
        1. Latin language—Dictionaries—English.
2. English language—Dictionaries—Latin.
I. Title.
PA2365.E5C33   1987   473'.21   87-12237
ISBN 978-0-02-013340-7

Manufactured in the United States of America

OPM 40 39
4500603522

CONTENTS

INTRODUCTION

This dictionary is concerned primarily with classical Latin as used from about 200 B.C. to 100 A.D. In prehistoric times Italy was settled by speakers of a variety of Indo-European dialects. Classical Latin developed from the dialect of the Latins, who inhabited the region near Rome. The Latin alphabet was derived from Greek via the Etruscans. As the Roman state developed, Latin was enriched through borrowings from the various languages with which Rome came into contact. The Roman armies moved throughout the Mediterranean lands, carrying Latin to the outlying regions of the known world. Over time, the colloquial language, influenced by the native tongues in different areas, evolved into a group of new languages. These "Romance" languages today include Italian, French, Provençal, Catalan, Spanish, Portuguese, Romanian, and Romansh. Other languages, such as English, have absorbed many Latin elements, as will be apparent from even a cursory examination of this dictionary.

The first *Cassell's Latin Dictionary*, by J. R. Beard and Charles Beard, was published in England in 1854. It consisted of Latin-English and English-Latin sections, of about equal length. An enlarged version of the Latin-English section, by J. R. V. Marchant, appeared in 1886. By 1892 the English-Latin section had been revised and shortened by J. F. Charles, with help from Marchant. During the next 60 years the combined dictionary was reprinted in this form numerous times. A compact version, prepared by Millicent Thomas, was published in 1927; Thomas considerably reduced the number of entries and omitted rare forms and quotations from Latin authors. In 1959 there was published a complete revision of the Latin-English and English-Latin dictionary of Marchant and Charles. It was the work of D. P. Simpson, assistant master, and formerly head of the Classical Department, at Eton College. Simpson subsequently condensed his dictionary, following much the same process of selection and simplification as Millicent Thomas had. The present edition adds to Simpson's compact dictionary supplementary material prepared by Sharon R. Gibson, Latin teacher at Brownsburg High School in Brownsburg, Indiana, and former visiting instructor of Latin at Butler University. This material is intended to aid the user by providing quick reference to key elements of Latin pronunciation and grammar and Roman culture; for more complete information on these subjects the reader should consult standard textbooks and specialized reference works.

ADVICE TO THE USER

LATIN-ENGLISH SECTION

ORDER OF WORDS Entries are arranged in alphabetical order. However, adverbs generally appear under the corresponding adjectives, and participial adjectives under the parent verbs; related proper names are grouped together. Cross-references are provided where helpful.

SPELLING Classical Latin did not have the letter **J, j,** and this "consonantal *i*" is rendered in the dictionary by **I, i.** The letter **V, v** is retained for "consonantal *u*." Compound words are generally given in their unassimilated form; e.g., **adsiduus** instead of **assiduus.**

STRUCTURE OF ENTRIES The Latin head word being defined is printed in boldface type, followed by notable alternative spellings. If the word is a noun, or substantive, the genitive singular ending and gender are indicated. If the word is an adjective, nonmasculine endings are noted for the nominative singular; if the adjective does not have separate nominative singular forms, the genitive singular ending is shown. If the word is a verb, the ending for the present active infinitive (or present passive infinitive in the case of deponents) is indicated, along with the endings for other principal parts needed to insure correct spelling.

VOWEL QUANTITY Where helpful, short vowels are indicated by the symbol ˘ , and long vowels by the symbol ¯ ; e.g., **dēbĕo**, *owe*. Vowels are in most instances not marked for length in the final syllable of words that follow a regular conjugation or declension.

ENGLISH-LATIN SECTION

This section is intended primarily for students of Latin prose composition. Grammatical details for Latin words, as well as indications of vowel quantity, are provided sparingly, and the user should refer to the Latin-English section for fuller information. Parentheses are used in the English-Latin section not only for explanatory or supplementary material (such as a genitive ending for a noun) but also to indicate a portion of a Latin word or phrase that is in some instances omissible: e.g., **exchange,** v. (*per*)*mutare* means that both the verb *mutare* and the verb *permutare* may be found in the meaning "exchange."

KEY TO PRONUNCIATION

SOUNDS

The sounds of classical Latin were spoken approximately as follows:

Vowels

Short	Long
ă as in *a*gain	ā as in f*a*ther
ĕ as in m*e*t	ē as in g*a*te
ĭ as in h*i*nt	ī as in *ea*t
ŏ as in *o*ffer	ō as in *o*pen
ŭ as in f*oo*t	ū as in f*oo*d

y was pronounced like French *u*

Diphthongs

ae as in k*i*te
au as in *ou*t
ei as in str*ay*
oe as in c*oil*

Consonants

Consonants were pronounced as in English, with a few exceptions:

c always hard as in *c*ar
g always hard as in *g*ate
i ("consonantal i," later written **j**) pronounced like *y* in *y*et
r trilled
s always as in *s*ign, never as in ea*s*e
t pronounced without aspiration
v always like *w* in *w*in
bs always like *ps* in a*ps*e
bt always like *pt* in a*pt*
ch always like *ch* in *ch*aotic
ph always like *ph* in to*p h*eavy
th always like *t* in *t*ake

SYLLABLE DIVISION

Every Latin word has as many syllables as it has vowels or diphthongs.

When a word is divided into syllables, a single consonant that lies between two vowels is pronounced with the second vowel. If two or more consonants come between two vowels, the last consonant is pronounced with the second vowel. The consonant groups **ch, ph, th,** and **qu** each count as a single consonant, as do "blends"—groups consisting of a stop (**p, b, t, d, c, g**) plus **l** or **r**.

The prefix in a compound word, however, is pronounced as a separate syllable; e.g., **abest** is pronounced **ab—est**.

QUANTITY

A vowel or syllable may be either long or short according to the time required to pronounce it.

A vowel is short
    —if it is followed by another vowel or **h**
    —if it is followed by **nd** or **nt**.
A vowel is long
    —if it is derived from a diphthong
    —if it is followed by **ns, nf,** or sometimes **gn**
    —if it is formed by contraction (e.g., **nīl,** *nothing,* from **nihil**).
A diphthong is long.
A syllable is long
    —if it contains a long vowel or diphthong
    —if it contains a short vowel followed by two or more consonants (not a blend) or by **x**, which is regarded as a double consonant (**ks**).
A syllable is short
    —if it contains a short vowel followed by another vowel or a single consonant
    —if it contains a short vowel followed by a consonant blend (in verse, however, such a syllable may be long).

ACCENT

In words of two syllables the 1st syllable is accented. In words of three or more syllables the accent falls on the penult (the next–to–last syllable) if it is long; the accent falls on the antepenult (the syllable before the penult) if the penult is short.

GRAMMATICAL NOTES

VERBS

PRINCIPAL PARTS The various forms of a verb can generally be deduced from four key forms called principal parts. These are, for **porto,** *carry*:

(1)	1st person singular, present active indicative	**porto**
(2)	present active infinitive	**portare**
(3)	1st person singular, perfect active indicative	**portavi**
(4)	supine (or a participial form)	**portatum**

STEMS The present stem is what remains when the infinitive ending –**re** is subtracted from the 2nd principal part. The final vowel in the stem is called the stem vowel. For **porto**, the present stem is **porta–**, and the stem vowel is –**a**–.

The perfect stem is what remains when the perfect active personal ending is subtracted from the 3rd principal part: **portav**–.

The participial stem is what remains when the ending is subtracted from the 4th principal part (or the 3rd in the case of deponent verbs): **portat**–.

Regular verbs are divided into four different conjugations according to their stem vowels:

–**a**–	1st conjugation
–**e**– $\begin{cases} \text{2nd conjugation if long } (-\bar{e}-) \\ \text{3rd conjugation if short } (-\breve{e}-) \end{cases}$	
–**i**–	4th conjugation

PERSONAL ENDINGS

Active—for indicative present, imperfect, future, pluperfect, and future perfect and for subjunctive present, imperfect, perfect, and pluperfect.

	Singular			Plural	
1st person	–**o**, –**m**	*I*		–**mus**	*we*
2nd person	–**s**	*you*		–**tis**	*you*
3rd person	–**t**	*he, she, it*		–**nt**	*they*

Passive—for indicative present, imperfect, and future and for subjunctive present and imperfect.

	Singular		Plural	
1st	–r	*I*	–mur	*we*
2nd	–ris	*you*	–mini	*you*
3rd	–tur	*he, she, it*	–ntur	*they*

Perfect active—for perfect indicative only.

	Singular		Plural	
1st	–i	*I*	–imus	*we*
2nd	–isti	*you*	–istis	*you*
3rd	–it	*he, she, it*	–erunt	*they*

CONJUGATIONS IN BRIEF

Present Indicative

The 1st principal part tells the 1st person singular. The other present indicative forms are constructed as follows:

1ST AND 2ND CONJUGATIONS

present stem + personal endings

portare, *to carry*

Active		Passive	
porto	portamus	portor	portamur
portas	portatis	portaris	portamini
portat	portant	portatur	portantur

docere, *to teach*

doceo	doceor
doces, etc.	doceris, etc.

3RD CONJUGATION (non–**io** verbs)

> present stem (stem vowel –**e**– becomes –**i**–) + personal endings
> *exceptions* 3rd person plural changes –**e**– to –**u**–;
> in passive, 2nd person singular retains –**e**–

regere, *to rule*

Active		Passive	
rego	regimus	regor	regimur
regis	regitis	regeris	regimini
regit	regunt	regitur	reguntur

3rd conjugation verbs in –**io**, like **capio**, *take*, are conjugated like 4th conjugation verbs.

4TH CONJUGATION

> present stem + personal endings
> *exception* 3rd person plural has –**u**– between the stem vowel and ending

audire, *to hear*

Active		Passive	
audio	audimus	audior	audimur
audis	auditis	audiris	audimini
audit	audiunt	auditur	audiuntur

Imperfect Indicative

ALL REGULAR VERBS EXCEPT THOSE IN –**io**

> present stem + –**ba**– + personal endings

Active		Passive	
portabam	portabamus	portabar	portabamur
portabas	portabatis	portabaris	portabamini
portabat	portabant	portabatur	portabantur
docebam, etc.		docebar, etc.	
regebam, etc.		regebar, etc.	

VERBS IN –**io**

> same as above, but with –**ie**– before the –**ba**–

audiebam, etc.   audiebar, etc.

Future Indicative

1ST AND 2ND CONJUGATIONS

present stem + –**bi**– + personal endings

exceptions 1st person singular adds simply –**bo** (–**bor** for passive) to the stem;

3rd person plural uses –**bu**– instead of –**bi**–;

in passive, 2nd person singular uses –**be**– instead of –**bi**–

Active		Passive	
portabo	portabimus	portabor	portabimur
portabis	portabitis	portaberis	portabimini
portabit	portabunt	portabitur	portabuntur

docebo, etc.   **docebor**, etc.

3RD CONJUGATION (non–**io** verbs)

present stem + personal endings

exception 1st person singular changes the stem vowel –**e**– to –**a**–

Active		Passive	
regam	regemus	regar	regemur
reges	regetis	regeris	regemini
reget	regent	regetur	regentur

VERBS IN –**io**

same as for **rego** except that there is an –**i**– before the –**a**– or –**e**– preceding the personal endings

     audiam   **audiar**

     audies, etc.   **audieris**, etc.

Perfect Indicative

ACTIVE

perfect stem + perfect active endings

     portavi   **portavimus**

     portavisti   **portavistis**

     portavit   **portaverunt**

PASSIVE

participial stem + adjective endings –us –a –um and the present tense of **sum**

portatus –a –um sum	portati –ae –a sumus
portatus –a –um es	portati –ae –a estis
portatus –a –um est	portati –ae –a sunt

Pluperfect Indicative

ACTIVE

perfect stem + imperfect of **sum**

portaveram	portaveramus
portaveras	portaveratis
portaverat	portaverant

PASSIVE

participial stem + adjective endings –us –a –um and the imperfect tense of **sum**

portatus –a –um eram	portati –ae –a eramus
portatus –a –um eras	portati –ae –a eratis
portatus –a –um erat	portati –ae –a erant

Future Perfect Indicative

ACTIVE

perfect stem + future of **sum**
exception 3rd person plural ending is –**erint**

portavero	portaverimus
portaveris	portaveritis
portaverit	portaverint

PASSIVE

participial stem + adjective endings –us –a –um and the future of **sum**

portatus –a –um ero	portati –ae –a erimus
portatus –a –um eris	portati –ae –a eritis
portatus –a –um erit	portati –ae –a erunt

Present Subjunctive

1ST CONJUGATION

present stem (stem vowel –a– becomes –e–) + personal endings

Active		Passive	
portem	portemus	porter	portemur
portes	portetis	porteris	portemini
portet	portent	portetur	portentur

2ND CONJUGATION

present stem (stem vowel –e– becomes –ea–) + personal endings

doceam, etc.   **docear,** etc.

3RD CONJUGATION

present stem (stem vowel –e– becomes –a–) + personal endings

regam, etc.   **regar,** etc.

Verbs in –io use –ia– instead of –a–.

4TH CONJUGATION

present stem (stem vowel –i– becomes –ia–) + personal endings

audiam, etc.   **audiar,** etc.

Imperfect Subjunctive

present active infinitive + personal endings

Active		Passive	
portarem	portaremus	portarer	portaremur
portares	portaretis	portareris	portaremini
portaret	portarent	portaretur	portarentur

Perfect Subjunctive

ACTIVE

perfect stem + –eri– + personal endings

portaverim	portaverimus
portaveris	portaveritis
portaverit	portaverint

PASSIVE

participial stem + adjective endings –us –a –um and the present subjunctive of **sum**

portatus –a –um sim	portati –ae –a simus
portatus –a –um sis	portati –ae –a sitis
portatus –a –um sit	portati –ae –a sint

Pluperfect Subjunctive

ACTIVE

perfect active infinitive + personal endings

portavissem	portavissemus
portavisses	portavissetis
portavisset	portavissent

PASSIVE

participial stem + adjective endings –us –a –um and the imperfect subjunctive of **sum**

portatus –a –um essem	portati –ae –a essemus
portatus –a –um esses	portati –ae –a essetis
portatus –a –um esset	portati –ae –a essent

Imperative

SINGULAR PRESENT ACTIVE IMPERATIVE

present stem

porta	**rege**
doce	**audi**

PLURAL PRESENT ACTIVE IMPERATIVE

present stem + **–te**
exception in 3rd conjugation, the stem vowel **–e–** changes to **–i–**

portate	**regite**
docete	**audite**

Infinitives

PRESENT ACTIVE INFINITIVE

2nd principal part

portare	**regere**
docere	**audire**

PRESENT PASSIVE INFINITIVE

present active infinitive with the final **–e** changed to **–i**
exception in 3rd conjugation verbs, the final **–ere** changes to **–i**

portari	**regi**
doceri	**audiri**

PERFECT ACTIVE INFINITIVE

perfect stem + **–isse**

portavisse	**rexisse**
docuisse	**audivisse**

PERFECT PASSIVE INFINITIVE

participial stem + adjective endings **–us –a –um** and **esse**

portatus –a –um esse	**rectus –a –um esse**
doctus –a –um esse	**auditus –a –um esse**

FUTURE ACTIVE INFINITIVE

participial stem + –ur– + adjective endings –us –a –um and esse

portaturus –a –um esse   **recturus –a –um esse**
docturus –a –um esse   **auditurus –a –um esse**

Participles

PRESENT ACTIVE PARTICIPLE

present stem + –ns –ntis (with 3rd declension adjective endings)
exception –io verbs have –ie– before the –n–

portans, portantis   **regens, regentis**
docens, docentis   **audiens, audientis**

PERFECT PASSIVE PARTICIPLE

participial stem + adjective endings –us –a –um

portatus –a –um   **rectus –a –um**
doctus –a –um   **auditus –a –um**

FUTURE ACTIVE PARTICIPLE

participial stem + –ur– + adjective endings –us –a –um

portaturus –a –um   **recturus –a –um**
docturus –a –um   **auditurus –a –um**

FUTURE PASSIVE PARTICIPLE (gerundive)

present stem + –nd– + adjective endings –us –a –um
exception –io verbs have –ie– before the –nd–

portandus –a –um   **regendus –a –um**
docendus –a –um   **audiendus –a –um**

Gerund

present stem + **–ndi –ndo –ndum –ndo** (for genitive, dative, accusative, ablative, respectively)
exception **–io** verbs have **–ie–** before the **–nd–**

portandi, portando, portandum, portando
docendi, etc.
regendi, etc.
audiendi, etc.

IRREGULAR VERBS

sum, esse, fui, futurus, *to be*

Indicative (active only)

Present		Imperfect		Future	
sum	sumus	eram	eramus	ero	erimus
es	estis	eras	eratis	eris	eritis
est	sunt	erat	erant	erit	erunt

Perfect, pluperfect, and future perfect are regular.

Subjunctive (active only)

Present	
sim	simus
sis	sitis
sit	sint

Imperfect, perfect, and pluperfect are regular.

Imperative   singular **es**
                     plural **este**

Infinitives   regular

Participles   future only, **futurus –a –um**

Gerund   none

possum, posse, potui, *to be able*

Indicative (active only)

Present		Imperfect		Future	
possum	possumus	poteram	poteramus	potero	poterimus
potes	potestis	poteras	poteratis	poteris	poteritis
potest	possunt	poterat	poterant	poterit	poterunt

Perfect, pluperfect, and future perfect are regular.

Subjunctive (active only)

Present	
possim	possimus
possis	possitis
possit	possint

Imperfect, perfect, and pluperfect are regular.

Imperative   none

Infinitives   present and perfect only, **posse** and **potuisse**

Participles   present only, **potens, potentis**

Gerund   none

eo, ire, ivi or **ii, itum,** *to go*

Indicative (active only)

Present		Imperfect	Future
eo	imus	ibam	ibo
is	itis	ibas, etc.	ibis, etc.
it	eunt		

Perfect, pluperfect, and future perfect are regular.

eo (continued)

Subjunctive (active only)

Present

eam	eamus
eas	eatis
eat	eant

Imperfect, perfect, and pluperfect are regular.

Imperative   singular **i**
                 plural **ite**

Infinitives   regular

Participles   present active **iens, ientis**
               future active regular

Gerund **eundi,** etc.

fero, ferre, tuli, latum, *to bear*

Present stem is **fere–**; **fero** is a regular 3rd conjugation verb in all forms except the present indicative and the imperatives.

Present Indicative

Active		Passive	
fero	ferimus	feror	ferimur
fers	fertis	ferris	ferimini
fert	ferunt	fertur	feruntur

Imperative   singular **fer**
                 plural **ferte**

volo, velle, volui, *to be willing*   present stem, **vole–**
nolo, nolle, nolui, *to be unwilling*   present stem, **nole–**
malo, malle, malui, *to prefer*   present stem, **male–**

These are regular 3rd conjugation verbs except in the present and have only active forms.

Present Indicative		*Present Subjunctive*	
volo	volumus	velim	velimus
vis	vultis	velis	velitis
vult	volunt	velit	velint
nolo	nolumus	nolim	nolimus
non vis	non vultis	nolis	nolitis
non vult	nolunt	nolit	nolint
malo	malumus	malim	malimus
mavis	mavultis	malis	malitis
mavult	malunt	malit	malint

DEPONENT VERBS

Deponent verbs end in **–or** in the 1st principal part. They follow regular verb conjugations except that they have for the most part only passive endings and active meanings.

Examples, with principal parts

1st conjugation:	**conor, conari, conatus**
	present stem: **cona–**
2nd conjugation:	**vereor, vereri, veritus**
	present stem: **vere–**
3rd conjugation:	**loquor, loqui, locutus**
	present stem: **loque–**
4th conjugation:	**potior, potiri, potitus**
	present stem; **poti–**

Deponent verbs have three active forms with active meanings: the present active participle, future active participle, and future active infinitive. The gerundive is a passive form with a passive meaning.

DECLENSIONS IN BRIEF

Nouns

The genitive singular ending of a noun indicates to which of the five declensions the noun belongs:

1st declension	–ae
2nd declension	–i
3rd declension	–is
4th declension	–us
5th declension	–ei

1st Declension

	Singular	Plural
Nominative	–a	–ae
Genitive	–ae	–arum
Dative	–ae	–is
Accusative	–am	–as
Ablative	–a	–is

2nd Declension

	Singular		Plural	
	M.	N.	M.	N.
Nom.	–us, –er	–um	–i	–a
Gen.	–i	–i	–orum	–orum
Dat.	–o	–o	–is	–is
Acc.	–um	–um	–os	–a
Abl.	–o	–o	–is	–is

3rd Declension

	Singular		Plural	
	M. & F.	N.	M. & F.	N.
Nom.	(various)		–es	–a (–ia*)
Gen.	–is	–is	–um (–ium*)	–um (–ium*)
Dat.	–i	–i	–ibus	–ibus
Acc.	–em	(various)	–es	–a (–ia*)
Abl.	–e	–e (–i*)	–ibus	–ibus

*for i–stem nouns

4th Declension

	Singular		Plural	
	M. & F.	N.	M. & F.	N.
Nom.	–us	–u	–us	–ua
Gen.	–us	–us	–uum	–uum
Dat.	–ui	–u	–ibus	–ibus
Acc.	–um	–u	–us	–ua
Abl.	–u	–u	–ibus	–ibus

5th Declension

	Singular	Plural
Nom.	–es	–es
Gen.	–ei	–erum
Dat.	–ei	–ebus
Acc.	–em	–es
Abl.	–e	–ebus

Adjectives

1st and 2nd Declensions

	Singular			Plural		
	M.	F.	N.	M.	F.	N.
Nom.	–us, –er	–a	–um	–i	–ae	–a
Gen.	–i	–ae	–i	–orum	–arum	–orum
	(–ius*)	(–ius*)	(–ius*)			
Dat.	–o (–i*)	–ae (–i*)	–o (–i*)	–is	–is	–is
Acc.	–um	–am	–um	–os	–as	–a
Abl.	–o	–a	–o	–is	–is	–is

* for adjectives like **unus**

3rd Declension

	Singular			Plural	
	M.	F.	N.	M. & F.	N.
Nom.	–er	–is	–e (3–ending)	–es	–ia
	–is	–is	–e (2–ending)		
		(various)	(1–ending)		
Gen.	–is	–is	–is	–ium	–ium
Dat.	–i	–i	–i	–ibus	–ibus
Acc.	–em	–em	(= nominative)	–es	–ia
Abl.	–i	–i	–i	–ibus	–ibus

Pronouns

	1st Person Personal & Reflexive		2nd Person Personal & Reflexive	
	Singular	Plural	Singular	Plural
Nom.	ego, *I*	nos, *we*	tu, *you*	vos, *you*
Gen.	mei	nostri, nostrum	tui	vestri, vestrum
Dat.	mihi	nobis	tibi	vobis
Acc.	me	nos	te	vos
Abl.	me	nobis	te	vobis

3rd Person

	Personal Singular			Reflexive, *himself, herself, itself*
	M.	F.	N.	
Nom.	is, *he*	ea, *she*	id, *it*	—
Gen.	eius	eius	eius	sui
Dat.	ei	ei	ei	sibi
Acc.	eum	eam	id	se, sese
Abl.	eo	ea	eo	se, sese

Personal Plural

	M.	F.	N.
Nom.	ei, ii	eae	ea
Gen.	eorum	earum	eorum
Dat.	eis, iis	eis, iis	eis, iis
Acc.	eos	eas	ea
Abl.	eis	eis	eis

PREFIXES

In the following list of common Latin prefixes, the forms in parentheses are variations that may occur both in Latin and in English.

ab– (a–, abs–) *from, away*
ad– (ac–, an–, ap–) *to, toward, near*
ambi– *both, around*
ante– *before*
bene– *well*
bis– (bi–) *two, twice*
circum– *around*
con– (co–, col–, com–, cor–) *with, together, deeply*
contra– *against*
de– *from, down, not*
dis– (di–, dif–) *apart, away, not*
ex– (e–, ef–) *out of*
extra– *outside, beyond*
in– (il–, im–, ir–) *in, into, upon, on, against*
in– (il–, im–, ir–) *not*
inter– *between, among*
intra– (intro–) *within, inside*
male– (mal–) *badly, ill*
multi– *many*
non– *not, without*
ob– (oc–, of–, op–) *against, toward*
per– *through, thoroughly, very*
prae– *ahead, before, very, in front of*
pro– *forth, for, forward*
quadri– (quadr–, quadru–) *four*
re– (red–) *back, again*
retro– *backward, back*
se– (sed–) *apart, away, from*
semi– *half, partly*
sub– (suf–, sug–, sup–) *under, up from under*
super– *over, beyond, above*
trans– (tra–) *across, over, through*
ultra– *extremely*
un– (uni–) *one*

NUMERALS

Arabic	Roman	Cardinal	Ordinal
1	I	unus –a –um	primus –a –um
2	II	duo, duae, duo	secundus –a –um
3	III	tres, tria	tertius –a –um
4	IV	quattuor	quartus –a –um
5	V	quinque	quintus –a –um
6	VI	sex	sextus –a –um
7	VII	septem	septimus –a –um
8	VIII	octo	octavus –a –um
9	IX	novem	nonus –a –um
10	X	decem	decimus –a –um
11	XI	undecim	undecimus –a –um
12	XII	duodecim	duodecimus –a –um
13	XIII	tredecim	tertius decimus –a –um
14	XIV	quattuordecim	quartus decimus –a –um
15	XV	quindecim	quintus decimus –a –um
16	XVI	sedecim	sextus decimus –a –um
17	XVII	septendecim	septimus decimus –a –um
18	XVIII	duodeviginti	duodevice(n)simus –a –um
19	XIX	undeviginti	undevice(n)simus –a –um
20	XX	viginti	vice(n)simus –a –um
30	XXX	triginta	trice(n)simus –a –um
40	XL	quadraginta	quadrage(n)simus –a –um
50	L	quinquaginta	quinquage(n)simus –a –um
60	LX	sexaginta	sexage(n)simus –a –um
70	LXX	septuaginta	septuage(n)simus –a –um
80	LXXX	octoginta	octoge(n)simus –a –um
90	XC	nonaginta	nonage(n)simus –a –um
100	C	centum	cente(n)simus –a –um
500	D	quingenti	quingente(n)simus –a –um
1,000	M	mille	mille(n)simus –a –um

CULTURAL NOTES

ROMAN CALENDAR

During the Roman Republic years were recorded under the name of the consuls in office. Dates were also figured from the founding of the city of Rome (traditionally thought to be in 753 B.C.), **ab urbe condita**, or A.U.C. The Romans always counted both the starting number and the ending number in figuring time. Therefore 596 A.U.C. would be 158 B.C.

From the time of Julius Caesar the Roman calendar was divided into 12 months, with 365 days a year. There was an extra day every 4 years, with February 24 counted twice. All the dates during a given month were reckoned from three days:

Kalendae, *Calends*	the 1st day of the month
Nonae, *Nones*	the 5th day (except in March, May, July, and October when it was the 7th)
Idus, *Ides*	the 13th day (except in March, May, July, and October when it was the 15th)

To figure a particular date, the Romans counted the number of days before the next Calends, Nones, or Ides. Thus, June 9 would be the 5th day before the Ides of June, since both the 9th and 13th of June are counted. This date, then, would be **ante diem quintum Idus Iunias** or **a.d. V Id. Iun.**

ROMAN HISTORY TO THE REIGN OF TRAJAN
(some dates approximate)

Key Dates

753 B.C.	Founding of Rome
509	Expulsion of the kings
450	Twelve Tables of Roman law
390	Gauls capture Rome
343–341	1st Samnite War
326–304	2nd Samnite War
298–290	3rd Samnite War
280–275	War with Pyrrhus
264–241	1st Punic War
219–202	2nd Punic War
149–146	3rd Punic War
73–71	Revolt led by Spartacus
63	Catilinarian conspiracy
60	1st Triumvirate
58–51	Gallic Wars
44	Julius Caesar assassinated
43	2nd Triumvirate
30	Death of Mark Antony
27	Octavian assumes title "Augustus"
9 A.D.	Battle of Teutoburg Forest
64	Fire associated with Nero
70	Destruction of Jerusalem
72–73	Siege of Masada
79	Eruption of Vesuvius
80	Great fire at Rome

Major Writers

Plautus (254–184 B.C.)
Terence (195–159 B.C.)
Varro (116–27 B.C.)
Cicero (106–43 B.C.)
Julius Caesar (100–44 B.C.)
Sallust (86–34 B.C.)
Catullus (85–55 B.C.)
Virgil (70–19 B.C.)
Horace (65–8 B.C.)
Livy (59 B.C.–17 A.D.)
Ovid (43 B.C.–17 A.D.)
Seneca (4 B.C.–65 A.D.)
Pliny the Elder (23–79 A.D.)
Quintilian (35–97 A.D.)
Martial (40–104 A.D.)
Tacitus (55–120 A.D.)
Juvenal (55–127 A.D.)
Pliny the Younger (61–113 A.D.)

Emperors and Their Reigns

Augustus (27 B.C.–14 A.D.)
Tiberius (14–37 A.D.)
Caligula (37–41)
Claudius (41–54)
Nero (54–68)
Galba (68–69)
Otho (69)
Vitellius (69)
Vespasian (69–79)
Titus (79–81)
Domitian (81–96)
Nerva (96–98)
Trajan (98–117)

MAJOR GODS AND GODDESSES IN CLASSICAL MYTHOLOGY

A Simplified View of the Greek Divinities and
Their Roman Counterparts   (Greek/*Roman*)

Offspring of Cronus/*Saturn* and Rhea/*Ops*

Hades, Pluto/*Dis*   Demeter/*Ceres*
Poseidon/*Neptune*   Hera/*Juno*
Zeus/*Jupiter, Jove*   Hestia/*Vesta*

Offspring of Zeus/*Jupiter*

by Demeter/*Ceres:* Persephone/*Proserpina*
by Dione: Aphrodite/*Venus*
by Hera/*Juno:* Ares/*Mars* and Hephaestus/*Vulcan*
by Leto/*Latona:* Apollo and Artemis/*Diana*
by Maia: Hermes/*Mercury*
by Metis: Athena/*Minerva*
by Semele: Dionysus/*Bacchus*

LIST OF ABBREVIATIONS USED IN THE DICTIONARY

abbrev. *abbreviated, abbreviation*
abl. *ablative*
absol. *absolute*
abstr. *abstract*
acc. *accusative*
act. *active*
adj. *adjective*
adv. *adverb*
adversat. *adversative*
architect. *architectural*
c. *common (both male and female)*
class. *classical*
coll. *collective*
colloq. *colloquial*
commerc. *commercial*
compar. *comparative*
concr. *concrete*
conj. *conjunction*
dat. *dative*
dep. *deponent*
dim. *diminutive*
distrib. *distributive*
e.g. *exempli gratia (for example)*
esp. *especially*
etc. *et cetera*
exclam. *exclamatory*
f. *feminine*
fig. *figure, figurative*
foll. *followed*
fut. *future*
gen. *general, generally*
genit. *genitive*
gram., grammat. *grammatical*
i.e. *id est (that is)*
imperf. *imperfect*
impers. *impersonal*
indecl. *indeclinable*
indef. *indefinite*
indic. *indicative*
infin. *infinitive*
interj. *interjection*
interrog. *interrogative*
intransit. *intransitive*
logic. *logical*

m. *masculine*
medic. *medical*
meton. *by metonymy*
milit. *military*
myth. *mythological*
n. *neuter*
naut. *nautical*
neg. *negative*
nom. *nominative*
num. *numeral*
obs. *obsolete*
occ. *occasionally*
opp. *opposite (to)*
part., partic. *participle*
pass. *passive*
perf. *perfect*
pers. *person*
personif. *personified*
philosoph. *philosophy, philosophical*
phr. *phrase*
pl., plur. *plural*
poet. *poetical*
polit. *political*
posit. *positive*
prep. *preposition*
pres. *present*
pron. *pronoun*
q.v. *quod vide, quae vide (i.e., see article concerned)*
reflex. *reflexive*
relat. *relative*
relig. *religious*
rhet. *rhetoric, rhetorical*
sc. *scilicet (that is to say)*
sing. *singular*
subj. *subjunctive*
subst. *substantive*
superl. *superlative*
t.t. *technical term*
transf. *transferred (i.e., used in altered sense)*
transit. *transitive*
v. *verb*
voc. *vocative*

CASSELL'S LATIN-ENGLISH DICTIONARY

A

A, a, the first letter of the Latin Alphabet.

a, ah, interj. *Ah!*

a, ab, abs, prep. with abl. (1) of motion or measurement in space, *from, away from*. (2) of time, *from, after*. (3) of separation, difference, change, *from*; so of position or number, *counting from*; and of the relation of part to whole, *out of, of*. (4) of origin and agency; especially with passive verbs, *by, at the hands of, because of*. (5) viewed *from, on the side of*: a tergo, *in the rear*; hence *in connexion with, as regards*.

ăbăcus -i, m. *a square board*; hence *sideboard, counting-board, gaming-board, ceiling panel*.

ăbăliēnātio -ōnis, f. *transfer of property*.

ăbăliēno -are, *to make alien, separate, estrange*.

ăbăvus -i, m. *great-great-grandfather*.

Abdēra -orum, n. pl., also -ae, f., *a town in Thrace, noted for the stupidity of its inhabitants*.

abdĭcātĭo -ōnis, f. *disowning, renunciation*.

¹abdĭco -are, *to renounce, reject*; esp. of magistracies, *to abdicate*, often with reflex. and ablative of office.

²abdĭco -dicĕre -dixi -dictum, in augury, *to disapprove of*.

abdo -dĕre -dĭdi -dĭtum, *to put away, withdraw, remove*; esp. *to secrete, hide*.

    Hence partic. **abdĭtus** -a -um, *concealed, secret*. Adv. **abdĭtē**.

abdōmen -ĭnis, n. *belly*; hence *gluttony*.

abdūco -dūcĕre -duxi -ductum, *to lead* or *take away, detach, withdraw*.

ăbĕo -ire -ĭi -ĭtum, *to go away*; abi, *be off with you*; abi in malam rem, *go to the devil*. Transf., *to retire from office*; *to depart from life, die*; in discussion, *to digress*; in form, *to change*; of things, *to pass away, disappear, vanish*; *to pass over from owner to owner*.

ăbĕquĭto -are, *to ride off*.

ăberrātĭo ōnis, f. *escape, relief*.

ăberro -are, *to wander, deviate, escape*.

abhinc. (1) *hereafter*. (2) *ago*: abhinc annos tres, or annis tribus *three years ago*.

ăbhorrĕo -ēre, *to shrink back from*; hence *to be inconsistent with* or *opposed to*; a fide, *to be incredible*. Pres. part., as adj., *unseasonable, inappropriate*.

abĭcĭo -icĕre -iēci -iectum, *to throw down* or *away*. Transf., *to pronounce carelessly, break off abruptly*; *to get rid of, give up*; *to dash to the ground, weaken, dishearten*.

    Hence partic. **abiectus** -a -um; of position, *low, common*; of character, *cowardly, mean*; of style, *without force, prosaic*. Adv. **abiectē**, *without spirit, meanly*.

abiectĭo -ōnis, f. *throwing away*; animi, *despondency, despair*.

ăbiegnus -a -um, *of fir wood* or *deal*.

ăbiēs ĕtis, f. *the silver fir*; meton., *anything made of deal*, such as *a ship* or *spear*.

ăbĭgo -ĕre -ēgi -actum, *to drive away*; of cattle, *to remove, steal*. Transf., *to banish, be rid of*: uxorem, *to divorce*.

ăbĭtĭo -ōnis, f. and **ăbĭtus** -ūs, m., *going away, departure*; *place of egress*.

ăbiūdĭco -are, *to take away by a judgment*.

abiungo -iungĕre -iunxi -iunctum, *to unharness*; hence *to estrange, detach*.

abiūro -are, *to abjure, deny on oath*.

ablātīvus -a -um, *ablative*.

ablēgātĭo -onis, f. *sending away, banishment*.

ablēgo -are, *to send away, remove to a distance*.

ablĭgūrĭo -ire, *to lick away*; hence *to squander*.

ablūdo -ĕre, *to be out of tune*.

ăblŭo -lŭĕre -lŭi -lūtum. *to wash clean*; *to wash away*.

abnĕgo -are, *to deny, refuse*.

abnĕpōs -ōtis, m. *great-great-grandson*.

abneptis -is, f. *great-great-granddaughter*.

abnocto -are, *to stay out all night*.

abnormis -e, *irregular, unconventional*.

abnŭo -nŭĕre -nŭi, fut. partic. -nūitūrus, *to refuse by a gesture, to deny*.

ăbŏlĕo -ēre -ēvi -itum, *to destroy, do away with*.

ăbŏlesco -ĕre -ēvi, *to perish*.

ăbŏlĭtĭo -ōnis, f. *removing, annulling, abolition*.

ăbolla -ae, f. *a cloak of thick woollen cloth*.

ăbōmĭno -are, and **ăbōmĭnor** -ari, dep. (1) *to deprecate*: quod abominor, *God forbid*. (2) *to hate, detest*.

ăbŏrĭor -ōrĭri -ortus, dep.: of heavenly bodies, *to set*; poet., of the voice, *to fail*.

ăbŏriscor -i = aborior: q.v.

ăbortĭo -ōnis, f. *untimely birth, miscarriage*.

ăbortīvus -a -um, *prematurely born*.

ăbortus -ūs, m. *miscarriage*.

abrādo -radĕre -rāsi -rāsum, *to scrape off, shave*. Transf., *to squeeze out, to extort*.

abrĭpĭo -rĭpĕre -rĭpŭi -reptum *to, snatch away, drag off, remove, detach*.

abrōdo -rōdĕre -rōsi -rōsum, *to gnaw off*.

abrŏgātĭo -ōnis, f. *annulling, repealing*.

abrŏgo -are. *to repeal, annul, remove, take away*.

abrŏtŏnum -i, n. and **abrŏtŏnus** -i, m. *southern-wood.*

abrumpo -rumpĕre -rūpi -ruptum, *to break off, sever; to remove, dissociate; to break off prematurely, destroy.* Hence partic. **abruptus** -a -um, *steep, precipitous, abrupt, rough.* N. as subst., *a steep place.* Adv. **abruptē.**

abruptĭo -ōnis, f. *tearing away;* hence *divorce.*

abscēdo -cēdĕre -cessi -cessum, *to go away, depart, retire, desert.*

abscessĭo -ōnis, f. *going away, separation.*

abscessus -ūs, m. *going away, withdrawal.*

abscīdo -cīdĕre -cīdi -cīsum, *to cut off; to separate or take away.* Hence partic. **abscīsus** -a -um, *precipitous, abrupt, short.*

abscindo -scindĕre -scĭdi -scissum, *to tear off, wrench away; venas, to cut open the veins;* poet., abscissa comas, *with her hair torn.* Transf., *to divide or separate.*

abscondo -condĕre -condi (-condidi) -condĭtum (-consum), *to conceal; to lose sight of;* pass., of stars, *to set.* Adv. from partic., **absconditē,** *obscurely.*

absens -entis, *absent;* see also **absum.**

absentĭa -ae, f. *absence.*

absĭlĭo -ire, -li or -ŭi, *to spring forth or away.*

absĭmĭlis -e, *unlike.*

absinthĭum -i, n. *wormwood.*

absisto -sistĕre -stĭti. *to go away from a place or person; to desist from an action.*

absŏlūtĭo -ōnis, f. (1) *acquittal.* (2) *perfection.*

absŏlūtōrĭus -a -um, *relating to acquittal.*

absolvo -solvĕre -solvi -sŏlūtum, *to loosen, to free:* of an accused person, *to acquit;* of a subject, *to dispose of, relate in full;* in gen. *to complete.* Hence partic. **absŏlūtus** -a -um, *perfect, complete; unfettered, unconditional.* Adv. **absŏlūtē,** *perfectly, completely.*

absŏnus -a -um, *inharmonious, discordant, disagreeing.*

absorbĕo -ēre -ŭi, *to swallow, gulp down;* hence *to carry away, engross.*

absque, prep. with abl. *without.*

abstēmĭus -a -um, *temperate, abstemious.*

abstergĕo -tergēre -tersi -tersum. *to wipe off, clean away.*

absterrĕo -ēre. *to frighten away.*

abstĭnentĭa -ae, f. *self-denial, temperance;* sometimes *fasting.*

abstĭnĕo -tĭnēre -tĭnŭi -tentum: transit., *to hold back;* intransit., *to abstain.* Hence present partic. **abstĭnens** -entis, *temperate.* Adv. **abstĭnenter.**

absto -are, *to stand aloof.*

abstrăho -trăhĕre -traxi -tractum *to drag away;* hence *to remove, exclude, restrain.*

abstrūdo -trūdĕre -trūsi -trūsum, *to push away, hide.*

Hence partic. **abstrūsus** -a -um, *concealed, secret, abstruse;* of character, *reserved.*

absum, ăbesse, āfŭi. (1) *to be away, be absent or missing;* hence *to take no part* in a thing, *fail to help.* (2) *to be far away, be distant;* hence *to be far from* doing a thing, *to be free from* a fault.

absūmo -sūmĕre -sumpsi -sumptum, *to reduce, consume, waste, destroy.*

absurdus -a -um, *unmelodious, harsh.* Transf., *foolish, unreasonable, out of place;* of persons, *incapable.* Hence adv. **absurdē,** *harshly, discordantly; foolishly.*

ăbundantĭa -ae, f. *abundance, plenty; riches, wealth.*

ăbundē, *copiously, abundantly;* with est and genit., *there is plenty of* a thing.

ăbundo -are, *to overflow; to grow in abundance; to abound, be rich in* esp. with abl. Hence partic. **ăbundans** -antis, *overflowing; abundant, numerous; abounding in;* adv. **ăbundanter,** *abundantly, copiously.*

ăbusquĕ, prep. with abl., *from.*

ăbūsus -ūs, m. *using up, wasting.*

ăbūtor -ūti -ūsus, dep., with abl. (1) *to make full use of.* (2) *to abuse, waste;* esp. *to use a word wrongly.*

ac; see **atque.**

Ăcădēmĭa -ae, f., *the Academy, a grove near Athens where Plato taught;* meton., *the Academic school of philosophy.* Hence adj. **Ăcădēmĭcus** -a -um; n. pl. **Ăcădēmĭca,** *Cicero's treatise on the Academic philosophy.*

ăcălanthis and **ăcanthis** -idis, f., *a small bird, perhaps siskin.*

ăcanthus -i, m. (1) *bear's foot, a plant.* (2) *a thorny evergreen tree.*

Ăcarnānĭa -ae, *Acarnania, a country in western Greece.*

Acca Lārentĭa, *a Roman goddess;* **Lārentālĭa** or **Accālĭa** -ium, n. pl. *her festival at Rome in December.*

accēdo -cēdĕre -cessi -cessum, *to approach, come near;* of persons, *to enter upon a course;* ad rem publicam, *to begin public life;* of things, *to be added;* huc accedit ut, *it is also true that, moreover.*

accĕlĕro -are: transit., *to quicken, accelerate;* intransit., *to hasten.*

accendo -cendĕre -cendi -censum, *to kindle, set alight, set on fire.* Transf., *to fire, inflame, excite.*

accensĕo -censēre -censum, *to reckon in addition.* Hence partic. **accensus** -a -um, *reckoned with;* m. as subst., *an attendant;* in plural, **accensi,** *reserve troops, supernumeraries.*

acceptĭo -ōnis, f. *reception, acceptance.*

accepto -are, *to receive.*

acceptus -a -um, partic. from accipio; q.v.

accerso = arcesso; q.v.

accessio -ōnis, f. *a going or coming to; increase; a thing added, appendage.*

accessus -ūs, m. *approach, access; means of approach, entrance.*

¹accido -cīdĕre -cīdi -cīsum, *to hew or hack at*; hence *to weaken, ruin.*

²accido -cīdĕre -cīdi, *to fall down*; ad pedes, *to fall at a person's feet.* Transf., *to happen, fall out.*

acciĕo -ēre, obs. form of accio; q.v.

accingo -cingĕre -cinxi -cinctum, *to gird on a weapon; to equip, arm a person*; with reflex., or in pass., *to arm oneself,* hence *to make oneself ready.*

accio -īre -īvi (-ii) -ītum, *to call, summon.*

accipio -cĭpĕre -cēpi -ceptum, *to take, receive, accept.* Esp. with the senses, *to hear, feel,* etc.; with the understanding, *to grasp, to learn*; also *to take, interpret in a certain sense*; of persons, *to receive hospitably,* or *to treat in any particular manner*; in business, acceptum referre, *to enter on the credit side of an account book,* hence *to consider oneself indebted to someone for a thing.*
    Hence partic. **acceptus** -a -um, *welcome, pleasant, agreeable.*

accipiter -tris, m. *a hawk.*

accītus -ūs, m. *a summons.*

Accius -a -um, *name of a Roman gens*; esp. of L. Accius, tragic poet (170-c. 85 B.C.).

acclāmātio -ōnis, f. *a loud cry.*

acclāmo -are, *to cry out* (in approval or otherwise); with acc. of person, *to name by acclamation.*

acclāro -are, *to make clear, reveal.*

acclīnis -e, *leaning towards, inclined to.*

acclīno -are, *to lean towards, incline to.*

acclīvis -e, *inclined upwards.*

acclīvitās -ātis, f. *upward slope.*

acclīvus -a -um, = acclivis; q.v.

accŏla -ae, m. or f. *neighbour*; as adj. *living near, neighbouring.*

accŏlo -cŏlĕre -cŏlŭi -cultum, *to live near.*

accommŏdātio -ōnis, f. (1) *proportion or adjusting.* (2) *courteousness, complaisance.*

accommŏdātus -a -um, partic. from accommodo; q.v.

accommŏdo -are, *to fit, put on equipment,* etc.; *to make suitable, adjust, adapt.*
    Hence partic. **accommŏdātus** -a -um, *adapted, suitable*; adv. **accommŏdātē**, *agreeably.*

accommŏdus -a -um, *fit, adapted.*

accrēdo -crēdĕre -crēdĭdi -crēdĭtum, *to believe* (with dat.).

accresco -crescĕre -crēvi -crētum, *to grow, increase*; with dat., *to be joined to a thing.*

accŭbĭtio -ōnis, f. and **accŭbĭtus** -ūs, m. *the act of reclining at table.*

accŭbo -are, *to lie,* or *recline beside,* esp. at table; apud hominem, *to dine at a man's house.*

accumbo -cumbĕre -cŭbŭi -cŭbĭtum, *to lie down* or *recline,* esp. at table.

accŭmŭlātor -ōris, m. *one who heaps together.*

accŭmŭlo -are, *to heap up, accumulate*; *to heap things on a person, give in abundance*; *to ply, overwhelm a person with things*; *to increase.* Adv. from partic. **accŭmŭlātē**, *abundantly, copiously.*

accūrātio -ōnis, f. *accuracy, carefulness.*

accūro -are, *to take care of, prepare with care.*
    Hence partic. **accūrātus** -a -um, *done with care, careful, exact, accurate.* Adv. **accūrātē**.

accurro -currere -curri (-cŭcurri) -cursum, *to run to*; of ideas, *to occur.*

accursus -ūs, m. *running, concourse.*

accūsābilis -e, *blameworthy.*

accūsātio -ōnis, f. *an accusation, indictment.*

accūsātor -ōris, m. *an accuser*; hence *an informer.*

accūsātōrius -a -um, *of* or *like an accuser*; adv. **accūsātōriē**.

accūsatrix -īcis, f. *a female accuser.*

accūso -are, *to accuse*; in gen., *to blame, find fault with.*

¹acer -ĕris, n. *the maple tree* or *maple wood.*

²acer -cris -cre, *sharp, cutting, keen.* Hence, to taste, *biting*; to touch, *sharp*; of sounds, *shrill*; of smells, *penetrating*; of sight, *keen*; of emotions, *painful*; of understanding or character, *quick, vigorous, energetic.* Adv. **ācriter**, *sharply, keenly.*

ācerbĭtās -ātis, f. *bitterness, harshness, painfulness*; in plur., *calamities.*

ācerbo -are, *to make bitter, to aggravate.*

ācerbus -a -um, *bitter.* Hence, of sounds, *harsh*; of looks, *dark, gloomy*; of speech or writing, *bitter*; of events, etc., *painful, severe*; of persons, *morose*; from the notion of unripeness, *premature.* Adv. **ācerbē**, *bitterly, harshly.*

ācernus -a -um, *made of maple wood.*

ācerra -ae, f. *a casket for incense.*

ācervatim, *by accumulation*; dicere, *to sum up.*

ācervo -are, *to heap up.*

ācervus -i, m. *a heap, mass*; in logic, *argument by accumulation.*

ācesco ācescĕre ācŭi, *to grow sour.*

ācētum -i, n. *vinegar.*

Āchāia or **Āchāja** -ae, f., *the Greek country of Achaia, in the Peloponnese,* or in gen. *Greece*; after 146 B.C., *the Roman province of Achaea.* Hence adj. and subst. **Āchaeus** and **Āchīvus**, *Achaean,* an *Achaean* (or *Greek).*

Āchātes -ae, m. *friend of Aeneas.*

Āchĕron -ontis, m. (older form **Āchĕruns** -untis) *mythol. river in the lower world; the lower world itself.*

Āchillēs s, and **Āchillēŭs** -ei, m. *a Greek hero, son of Peleus and Thetis.* Adj. **Āchillēus** -a -um.

Āchīvus -a -um; see Āchāia.

ācĭdus -a -um, *sharp, sour.*

ăcĭēs -ei, f. *keenness, edge*; of the mind, *penetration, insight*; of the eye, *a piercing look* or *keen vision*; sometimes *the pupil of the eye*, or *the eye* itself. Milit., *battle-line*; hence *battle, battlefield.*

ăcīnācēs -is, m. *a Persian sabre.*

ăcīnus -i, m. and **ăcīnum** -i, n. *a berry; the seed of a berry.*

ăcĭpenser -eris, also **ăcĭpensis** -is, m. *the sturgeon.*

ăclys -ӯdis, f. *a small javelin.*

ăcŏnītum -i, n. *monk's hood, aconite*; in gen., *strong poison.*

acq- = adq-; q.v.

ăcrătŏphŏrum -i, n. *a vessel for unmixed wine.*

ăcrēdŭla -ae, f. *a bird*, perhaps *thrush, owl*, or *nightingale.*

ăcrĭcŭlus -a -um, *somewhat sharp in temper.*

ăcrĭmōnĭa -ae, f. *sharpness, keenness.*

ăcrĭtĕr, adv. from acer; q.v.

ăcrŏāma -ătis, n. *an entertainment*, esp. *musical; an entertainer*, i.e. *reader, actor*, or *singer.*

ăcrŏāsis -is, f. *reading aloud, recitation.*

Ăcrŏcĕraunĭa -orum, n. pl. *part of the Ceraunian mountains*; hence *any dangerous place.*

¹acta -ae, f. *sea-shore, beach*; meton., *life at the seaside.*

²acta -orum, from partic. of ago; q.v.

Actaeon -ōnis, m. *a hunter turned into a stag by Diana, and killed by his hounds.*

actio -ōnis, f. *action, doing*; gratiarum, *giving of thanks.* Esp. *the action of a magistrate, a proposal*; in the theatre, *a plot*; at law, *an action* or *the bringing of it* or *right to bring it*; also a legal *formula* or *speech on an indictment.*

actĭto -are, *to be busy, in law-court* or *theatre.*

Actĭum -i, n. *a promontory in Acarnania*, near which Augustus conquered Antony and Cleopatra (31 B.C.). Adj. **Actĭăcus** and **Actĭus** -a -um.

actor -ōris, m. (1) *a driver.* (2) *a doer*; esp. *a dramatic actor, player; a public speaker; the plaintiff in an action; a manager of property.*

actŭărĭŏlum -i, n. *a small skiff.*

actŭārĭus -a -um *swift*; actuaria (navis), *a fast-sailing vessel.*

actŭōsus -a -um, *active*; adv. **actŭōsē.**

actus -ūs, m. (1) *driving, movement*; esp. of cattle; hence *right of way for driving cattle*, etc. (2) *doing, action*, esp. on the stage; hence *the presentation of a piece on the stage*; also *a division of a piece, an act.*

actūtum, adv. *immediately, directly.*

ăcŭlĕātus -a -um, *provided with prickles* or *stings*; hence *pointed, stinging; hair-splitting, subtle.*

ăcŭlĕus -i, m. *sting, point*; fig., esp. in plur., *painful thoughts, cutting remarks.*

ăcūmen -ĭnis, n. *sharp point*; hence *the point of remarks*, etc.; *sharpness of intellect; cunning, trickery.*

ăcŭo -ŭĕre -ŭi -ūtum, *to sharpen, whet*;

to quicken, make expert; to inflame, encourage, incite.

Hence partic. **ăcūtus** -a ᵗ-um, *sharpened, pointed, acute*; to the hearing, *shrill*; to touch, *piercing*; of events, etc., *sharp, painful*; of minds, *sharp, keen, intelligent*; of orators, *effective.* Adv. **acūtē**, *keenly, sharply.*

ăcus -ūs, f. *a needle, bodkin*; acu pingere, *to embroider*; acu rem tangere, *to hit the nail on the head.*

ăcūtŭlus -a -um *rather subtle.*

ăcūtus; see acuo.

ad, prep. with acc. (1) of motion, *towards*, to a person or place; ad Dianae (sc. aedem) *to Diana's temple*; ad me, *to my house*; often strengthened by usque. (2) of rest, *at* or *near.* (3) of time: either *to, until*, or *at, about.* (4) of other relations: *towards*, for a purpose; *concerning, bearing on; compared with, in addition to; in conformity with; approximating to, about; in consequence of an event; as far as, up to a certain degree*; ad summam, *on the whole*; ad verbum, *literally.*

ădactio -ōnis, f. *driving, compulsion.*

ădactus -ūs, m. *bringing to, application.*

ădaeque, *in like manner.*

ădaequo -are: transit., *to make equal*; hence *to compare*; intransit., *to match, come near to.*

ădămantēus -a -um, *hard as steel.*

ădămantĭnus -a -um, *made of steel.*

ădămas -antis, m. *the hardest steel, adamant*; poet., *anything firm, unyielding, durable.*

ădambŭlo -are, *to walk by* or *near.*

ădămo -are, *to fall in love with, find pleasure in.*

ădăpĕrĭo -ăpĕrīre -ăpĕrui -ăpertum, *to open fully.*

ădauctus -ūs, m. *increase.*

ădaugĕo -ēre -auxi -auctum, *to increase, augment.*

ădaugesco -ĕre, *to begin to increase.*

adbĭbo -bĭbĕre -bĭbi -bĭbĭtum, *to drink in.*

addenseo -ēre, and **addenso** -are, *to make thick* or *compact.*

addīco -dīcĕre -dixi -dictum, *to assent to; in augury, to promise well*; of a judge (especially the praetor), *to award*; of an auctioneer, *to knock down a lot*; of an owner, *to put up for sale.* Hence in gen., *to give up* or *over, doom, dedicate, surrender*; partic. **addictus**, *bound, pledged.*

addictio -ōnis, f. *a judge's award.*

addisco -discĕre -dĭdĭci, *to learn in addition.*

addĭtāmentum -i, n. *an addition.*

addo **addĕre** **addĭdi** **addĭtum.** (1) *to give, bring, place*; of feelings, *to inspire, cause.* (2) *to add, join*; esp. in speech or writing; adde, or adde huc, or eo, *add to this, take also into consideration.*

addŏcĕo -ēre, *to teach in addition.*

addŭbĭto -are, *to begin to doubt.*

addūco -dūcĕre -duxi -ductum. (1) *to bring* or *lead to a person, place, or* condition; of persons, *to bring to a certain state of mind, to influence, induce.* (2) *to draw to oneself, pull in;* hence *to contract;* partic. **adductus** -a -um, *contracted, taut;* of persons, *strict.* Compar. adv. **adductius**.

ădĕdo -esse -ēdi -ēsum, *to nibble, gnaw; to consume, waste away.*

ădemptio -ōnis, f. *taking away.*

ădĕō, adv., *to that point, so far;* often strengthened by usque; of space, *so far;* of time, *so long;* of degree, *so much, so, to such an extent;* sometimes, *even, what is more;* enclitically, with pron. or conjunction, *just.*

ădĕo -ire -ii -itum, *to go or come to, approach, visit;* in ius, *to go to law;* of business, etc., *to undertake, undergo, incur;* adire hereditatem, *to enter on an inheritance.*

ădeps -ipis, c. *soft fat.*

ădeptio -ōnis, f. *attainment, obtaining.*

ădĕquito -are, *to ride to.*

ădesdum, or **ades dum**, *come hither.*

adfābilis -e, *easy to speak to, affable.*

adfābilitās -ātis, f. *affability.*

adfabrē, *in a workmanlike way.*

adfătim, *sufficiently, enough.*

adfātus -ūs, m. *address, speech.*

adfectātio -onis, f. *striving, eagerness.*

adfectātor -ōris, m. *a striver.*

adfectio -ōnis, f. *manner of being affected;* hence *relation to a thing or person, or change, or state, condition;* sometimes *favourable state of mind, good-will.*

adfecto -are, *to strive after, grasp at, aim at, aspire to;* polit. *to try to win over;* in literary style, *to affect;* partic. **adfectatus** -a -um, *studied.*

adfectus -ūs, m. *condition, disposition;* esp. of the mind, *a feeling;* often *friendly feeling, good-will.*

adfectus -a -um, partic. from adficio; q.v.

adfero adferre attŭli adlātum, *to carry to, bring to;* esp. of messages, and news; absol., *to bring news, report.* Transf., *to apply, bring to bear;* vim, *to offer violence; to cause, bring about; to bring forward* by way of excuse or reason; *to bring* by way of help, *contribute.*

adficio -ficĕre -fēci -fectum, *to influence, work upon;* with adverbs, *to affect;* with abl. of nouns, *to treat with, present with;* nominem sepultura, *to bury;* poena, *to punish,* beneficio adfici, *to be benefited;* absol., of the body, *to affect adversely, weaken.* Hence partic. **adfectus** -a -um, *affected, influenced;* with abl. *furnished with, treated with;* absol., of the body, *weakened, sick;* of undertakings, *worked upon,* and so *nearly finished.*

adfigo -figĕre -fixi -fixum, *to fasten to, affix;* litteram ad caput, *to brand;* adfigi animis, *to be imprinted.*

adfingo -fingĕre -finxi -fictum, *to form or invent in addition.*

adfīnis -e *neighbouring;* hence *connected with, privy to;* also *related by marriage;* as subst., *a relative.*

adfīnitās -ātis, f., *relationship by marriage;* meton., *relations by marriage;* in gen., *union.*

adfirmatio -ōnis, f. *positive assertion.*

adfirmo -are *to strengthen; to support a statement, to prove; to assert as true.* Adv. from partic., **adfirmatē**, *positively.*

adflatus -ūs, m. *blowing or breathing on, breath;* maris, *sea breeze.* Transf. *inspiration.*

adflĕo -flēre -flēvi -flētum, *to weep at.*

adflictātio -ōnis, f. *pain, torture.*

adflicto -are, *to agitate, knock about harass, distress.*

adflictor -ōris, m., *a subverter.*

adfligo -fligĕre -flixi -flictum, *to dash, knock down, knock about; to weaken, discourage, injure;* causam susceptam, *to drop.* Hence partic. **adflictus** -a -um, *damaged, shattered;* of spirits, *broken down, desponding;* of character, *vile, contemptible.*

adflo -are, *to blow on or breathe on.*

adfluentia -ae, f. *overflow, abundance.*

adflŭo -fluĕre -fluxi -fluxum. *to flow to, flow near;* of men, *to stream, to flock together.* Transf., *to flow freely, to be abundant,* with abl., *to abound in.* Hence partic. **adflŭens** -entis, *rich, abounding.* Compar. adv. **adflŭentius**.

adfor -ari, dep. *to accost, address;* esp. *to say farewell* to the dead, and *to pray to gods.*

adfulgĕo -fulgēre -fulsi *to shine, glitter; to shine upon, favour,* with dat.

adfundo -fundĕre -fūdi -fusum, *to pour upon;* colonia amne adfusa, *washed by a river;* adfundere se, or adfundi, *to prostrate oneself.* Transf., *to throw in, add.*

adgĕmo -ĕre, *to groan at,* with dat.

adgĕro -gĕrĕre -gessi -gestum, *to carry to, bring up.*

adgestus -ūs, m. *carrying to, accumulation.*

adglŏmĕro -are, *to wind on a ball;* hence *to add.*

adglūtino -are, *to glue to, fasten to.*

adgrăvesco -ĕre, *to grow worse (of sickness).*

adgrăvo -are, *to make heavier;* hence, *to make worse.*

adgrĕdĭor -grĕdi -gressus, dep. *to go to, approach;* with words, *to address;* of enemies, *to attack;* of business, etc., *to begin, undertake, attempt.*

adgrĕgo -are, *to add to the flock; so to attach, associate.*

adgressio -ōnis, f. *the introduction to a speech.*

ădhaerĕo -haerēre -haesi -haesum, *to hang to, stick to, adhere;* of places, *to border on, be near;* fig., *to depend on, cling to.*

adhaeresco -haerescĕre -haesi -haesum, *to hang to, adhere.* Transf., *to*

cling to, hang on, attach oneself; in
speaking, to stick fast, stop.

adhaesio -ōnis, f. and **adhaesus** -ūs, m.
adhering, clinging.

ădhĭbĕo -ēre -ŭi -ĭtum, to bring up to,
apply, bring to bear; of persons, to
invite, call in, employ for a purpose;
with adv., to treat.

ădhinnio -ire, to neigh after, neigh at.

ădhortātĭo -ōnis, f. exhortation.

ădhortātor -ōris, m. one who exhorts.

ădhortor -ari, dep. to exhort, encourage
(esp. of soldiers).

ădhūc, of time, hitherto, till now, till
then; still, even now; in gen.,
besides, also; with comparatives, even,
still.

adiăcĕo -ēre, to lie by the side of, be
adjacent. N. pl. of partic. as subst.
adiăcentia, the neighbourhood.

adicio -icĕre -iēci -iectum, to throw to;
hence to cast, direct, apply; also to
add; at an auction, to outbid.

adiectĭo -ōnis, f. addition, advance.

adiectus -ūs, m. addition.

ădigo -ĭgĕre -ēgi -actum, to drive, force,
compel; hominem ad iusiurandum, or
iureiurando, to put a man on his oath.

ădĭmo -imĕre -ēmi -emptum, to take
away.
Hence partic. **ădemptus** -a -um,
poet., dead.

ădĭpatus -a -um, fatty, greasy; n. pl. as
subst., pastry. Transf., o style,
bombastic.

ădĭpiscor -ĭpisci -eptus, dep. to come
up to, overtake; hence to obtain. Perf.
partic. adeptus, used passively, =
obtained.

ădĭtĭo -ōnis, f. approach.

ădĭtus -ūs, m. approach, access; hence
also right or possibility of entrance;
homo rari aditus, difficult of access;
concr., an entrance to a place, approach.
Transf., opportunity of obtaining.

adiūdĭco -are, to award as a judge,
assign, grant.

adiūmentum -i, n. help, assistance.

adiunctĭo -ōnis, f. joining, addition,
union; rhet. a limitation, or repetition.

adiunctor -ōris, m., one who joins.

adiungo -iungĕre -iunxi -iunctum, to
join to, connect; adiunctus fundus,
neighbouring; of immaterial things, to
associate, impart; of persons, to
attach, esp. as partner, friend, etc.
Hence partic. **adiunctus** -a -um,
bound to, belonging to; n. pl. as subst.
collateral circumstances.

adiūro, -are, to swear in addition;
to swear to a thing, promise on oath.

adiūto -are, to be serviceable, help.

adiūtor -ōris, m., a helper, assistant,
deputy.

adiūtrix -ĭcis, f., of females and f.
nouns, an assistant, aid; used of
reserve legions under the empire.

adiŭvo -iŭvāre -iūvi -iūtum, to help,
assist, support.

adlăbor -lābi -lapsus, dep. to glide to,
flow to, with dat or acc.

adlăbōro -are, to labour at; also to
add to by labour.

adlacrĭmo -are, to weep at.

adlapsus -ūs, m., a gliding approach.

adlatro -are, to bark at, rail at.

adlaudābilis -e, praiseworthy.

adlecto -are, to entice.

adlēgātĭo -ōnis, f. the sending of a
person on a mission.

adlēgo -are., to send on private business,
to commission; adlegati, deputies.
Transf., to instigate, suborn; to
adduce or allege in excuse.

adlēgo -lēgĕre -lēgi -lectum, to choose,
elect.

adlĕvāmentum -i, n., a means of
alleviation.

adlĕvātĭo -ōnis, f., a lifting up; hence
alleviation.

adlĕvo -are, to lift up, erect; hence to
lighten, alleviate; pass., adlevari, to
be cheered.

adlicio -lĭcĕre -lexi -lectum, to allure,
entice.

adlīdo -līdĕre -līsi -līsum, to strike
against, dash against; pass., adlidi, to
suffer damage.

adlĭgo -are, to tie to, bind to; of wounds,
to bind up. Transf., in gen., to fetter,
bind, confine; esp. to bind by friendship, obligations, promise, etc.; pass.,
to become an accomplice in, make
oneself responsible for; perf. partic.
adligatus, implicated, involved.

adlĭno -linĕre -lēvi -litum, to smear on,
bedaub.

adlŏcūtĭo -ōnis, f. an address; esp. a
word of comfort.

adlŏquium -i, n., exhortation, encouragement, consolation.

adlŏquor -lŏqui -lŏcūtus, dep. to
address; esp. to encourage, appeal to.

adlūcĕo -lūcēre -luxi, to shine at, or
upon.

adlūdo -lūdĕre -lūsi -lūsum, to jest at,
sport with; of waves, to play or
dash upon.

adluo -lŭĕre -lŭi, to wash, of the sea.

adlŭvĭēs -ēi, f., a pool caused by
flooding.

adlŭvĭo -ōnis, f., alluvial land.

admātūro -are, to hasten.

admētĭor mētiri -mensus, dep. to
measure out to.

Admētus -i, m. husband of Alcestis.

admĭnĭcŭlor -ari, dep. to support, prop.

admĭnĭcŭlum -i, n. prop, support; in
gen., aid, help.

admĭnister -stri, m. attendant, assistant.

admĭnistra -ae, f. a (female) helper.

admĭnistrātĭo -ōnis, f. the giving of
help; direction, government.

admĭnistrātor -ōris, m. administrator,
manager.

admĭnistro -are. to help, assist; to
manage, direct, administer: navem,
to steer.

admīrābĭlis -e. admirable; astonishing,
strange. Adv., **admīrābĭliter**.

admīrābĭlĭtās -ātis, f. admirableness;
admiration.

admīrātĭo -ōnis, f. admiration; plur.
outbursts of admiration; wonder,
astonishment.

admīror -ari, dep. *to admire; to be astonished, to wonder.* Hence gerundive **admīrandus** -a -um, *admirable.*

admiscĕo -miscēre -miscŭi -mixtum (-mistum), *to mix with, to join;* admisceri novis sermonibus *to become familiar with.*

admissārius -i, m. *stallion.*

admissio -onis, f. *audience,* esp. with kings, etc.

admitto -mittĕre -mīsi -missum, *to send to, admit;* esp. of horses, *to let go, put to a gallop.* Transf., *to allow; to admit a crime to one's record,* so *to commit;* hence n. of partic. as subst. **admissum** -i, *a crime.*

admixtio -ōnis, f. *an admixture.*

admŏdĕrātē, *appropriately.*

admŏdum, *up to the measure, up to the mark;* hence, *completely.* With adjectives and other parts of speech, *wholly, quite;* puer admodum, *a mere boy;* with numbers, *just about;* in affirmative answers, *certainly.*

admŏnĕo -ēre -ŭi -itum, *to admonish, remind,* of a fact or duty. N. of partic. as subst. **admŏnĭtum** -i, *an admonition.*

admŏnĭtio -ōnis, f. *a reminding;* esp. *a friendly admonition.*

admŏnĭtor -ōris, m. *one who reminds.*

admŏnĭtū, abl. sing. m., *by reminding, by warning.*

admordĕo -mordēre -morsum, *to bite at, gnaw;* fig. *to fleece.*

admōtio -ōnis, f. *moving to, application.*

admŏvĕo -mŏvēre -mōvi -mōtum, *to move to, bring up, apply;* manum operi, *to engage in a work;* manus nocentibus, *to lay hands on the guilty;* milit. *to bring up war-machines or soldiers.*

admūgio -ire, *to bellow after.*

admurmŭrātio -ōnis, f. *murmuring.*

admurmŭro -are, *to murmur at.*

adnāto -are, *to swim to or beside.*

adnecto -nectĕre -nexŭi -nexum, *to bind to, connect with.*

adnexus -ūs, m. *binding, connexion.*

adnītor -niti -nisus or -nixus, dep. *to press against, lean upon.* Transf., *to strive after.*

adno -are, *to swim to, or near, or beside.*

adnŏto -are, *to note, remark on.*

adnŭmĕro -are, *to count out, pay; to reckon in with,* with acc. and dat.

adnŭo -nŭĕre -nŭi -nūtum, *to nod to; to indicate by nodding; to nod assent to;* in gen., *to agree;* also *to agree to give or do a thing.*

¹**ădŏlĕo** -ēre -ŭi, *to worship, offer sacrifice, burn a sacrifice; to sacrifice on an altar;* in gen., *to burn.*

²**ădŏlĕo** -ēre, *to smell.*

ădŏlescens = adulescens; q.v.

ădŏlesco -ŏlescĕre -ŏlēvi. (1) *to grow up, come to maturity.* (2) *to be heaped up,* or perhaps *to burn* (cf. adoleo). Hence partic. **ădultus** -a -um, *grown up, adult, mature.*

Ădōnis -is or -Idis, *a beautiful young man, beloved of Venus.*

ădŏpĕrĭo -ŏpĕrīre -ŏpĕrŭi -ŏpertum, *to cover or close.*

ădŏpīnor -ari, dep. *to guess.*

ădoptātio -ōnis, f. *adopting.*

ădoptio -ōnis, f. *the adoption of a child.*

ădoptīvus -a -um, *adopted, connected with adoption;* of plants, *grafted.*

ădopto -are, *to choose for oneself;* esp. *to adopt,* as child or grandchild; of plants, *to graft.*

ădŏr -oris, n. *a species of grain, spelt.*

ădōrātio -ōnis, f. *praying to, adoration.*

ădōrĕus -a -um, *of spelt;* f. as subst. *a reward for valour* (originally a gift of corn).

ădŏrior -ŏriri -ortus, dep. *to rise up at;* hence *to attack, set about, attempt, undertake.*

ădorno -are, *to prepare, furnish, provide; to adorn.*

ădōro -are, *to speak to;* esp. *to address* a deity, in worship or entreaty; sometimes *to ask* a deity for a thing.

adp-; see under app-.

adquiesco -quiescĕre -quiēvi quiētum, *to rest, repose, be undisturbed, find comfort.*

adquiro -quirĕre -quisīvi -quisītum, *to acquire, get,* esp. in addition to previous possessions.

adrādo -rādĕre -rāsi -rāsum, *to scrape, shave.*

adrectus -a -um, partic. from adrigo; q.v.

adrēpo -rēpĕre -repsi -reptum, *to creep up, glide gently to.*

Adria = Hadria; q.v.

adrīdĕo -ridēre -risi -risum, *to laugh to, to smile upon.* Transf., *to be favourable to; to please.*

adrigo rigĕre -rexi -rectum, *to erect, lift up;* hence *to excite, arouse.*

adrĭpĭo -rĭpĕre -rĭpŭi -reptum, *to seize, snatch, appropriate;* poet., terram velis, *to sail quickly to;* mentally, *to grasp, comprehend quickly;* legal, *to arrest, bring to court, accuse;* hence perhaps *to satirize.*

adrīsor -ōris, m. *a flatterer.*

adrōdo -rōdĕre -rōsi -rōsum, *to gnaw at.*

adrŏgans, partic. from adrogo; q.v.

adrŏgantia -ae, f. *assumption,* hence *pride, haughtiness.*

adrŏgo -are, polit., *to associate in office;* in gen., either *to take to oneself* (sibi), *to claim, assume,* or *to adjudge, grant to another* (dat.). Hence partic. **adrŏgans** -antis, *assuming, arrogant, haughty;* adv. **adrŏganter.**

adsc-; see under asc-.

adsectātio -ōnis, f. *respectful attendance.*

adsectātor -ōris, m. *a companion, follower.*

adsector -ari, dep. *to follow, attend respectfully.*

adsēcŭla (adsecla) -ae, m. *follower, servant, sycophant.*

adsensio -ōnis, f. *assent, agreement, applause;* philosoph. *belief in the reality of sensible appearances.*

adsensor -ōris, m. *one who assents or agrees.*

adsensus -ūs, m. *assent, agreement;* philosoph. *belief in the reality of sensible appearances;* poet., *echo.*

adsentātio -ōnis, f. *flattering assent or applause, flattery.*

adsentātiuncŭla -ae, f. *trivial flattery.*

adsentātor -oris, m. *a flatterer.*

adsentātōriē, *flatteringly.*

adsentio -sentire -sensi -sensum, and **adsentior** -sentiri, -sensus, dep. *to assent to, agree with.*

adsentor -ari, dep. *to assent constantly; hence to flatter.*

adsēquor -sēqui -sēcūtus, dep. *to follow after; to reach by following, to come up to, attain;* mentally, *to grasp.*

¹**adsĕro** -sĕrĕre -sĕvi -situm, *to plant at or near.*

²**adsĕro** -sĕrĕre -sĕrui -sertum, *to lay hold of a slave, and thereby either claim him or declare him free;* in gen. *to set free, protect, or to claim.*

adsertor -ōris, m. *one who asserts the freedom of another person or claims him as his own.*

adservio -ire, *to assist, help.*

adservo -are, *to preserve, watch.*

adsessio -ōnis, f. *a sitting by the side of one* (to console).

adsessor -ōris, m. *one who sits by, or assists.*

adsĕvērātio -ōnis, f. *earnestness, vehemence;* esp. *vehement assertion, asseveration.*

adsĕvēro -are, *to be earnest;* esp. *to assert confidently or strongly.* Adv. from partic. **adsĕvēranter,** *earnestly.*

adsĭdĕo -sĭdēre -sēdi -sessum, *to sit near, sit beside,* esp. *beside a person, to give comfort, advice,* etc.; usually with dat. Hence, *to devote oneself to; to approximate to;* milit., *to besiege, blockade.*

adsido -sidĕre -sēdi -sessum, *to sit down.*

adsĭdŭĭtās -atis, f. *continual presence, regular attention.* Hence *constancy; constant repetition;* epistularum, *regular correspondence.*

¹**adsĭdŭus** -a -um, *continuously in one place, or one occupation,* in gen. *constant, persistent.* Adv. **adsĭdŭē** and **adsĭdŭō,** *continuously, without remission.*

²**adsĭdŭus** -i, m. *a taxpaying citizen.*

adsignātio -ōnis, f. *assignment, allotment.*

adsigno -are. (1) *to assign, allot;* hence *to impute, ascribe.* (2) *to seal;* hence *to impress upon.*

adsĭlio -silire -silŭi, *to leap to, or on.*

adsĭmĭlis -e, *like, similar.*

adsĭmŭlo -are, *to make like; to compare.*

Hence partic. **adsĭmŭlatus** -a -um, *similar, pretended, simulated.*

adsisto adsistĕre adstĭti or astĭti, *to place oneself at, to stand by;* at law, *to defend.*

adsŏlĕo -ēre, *to be accustomed;* ut adsolet, *as is usual.*

adsŏno -are, *to answer with a sound.*

adsp-; see under asp-.

adsterno -ĕre, *to strew or spread upon.*

adstĭpŭlātor -ōris, m. *a supporter.*

adstĭpŭlor -ari, dep. *to agree with.*

adsto -stare -stĭti, *to stand up, stand by* esp. *to stand by to help, to assist.*

adstrĕpo -ĕre, *to make a noise at;* esp. *to applaud.*

adstringo -stringĕre -strinxi -strictum, *to tighten, draw together, contract, make fast;* in writing or speech, *to compress;* of persons, *to bind, oblige;* with reflex., se adstringere, *to commit oneself to, become guilty of.*

Hence partic. **adstrictus** -a -um, *tight, compressed, drawn together, close-fisted, avaricious;* of oratory, *concise;* adv. **adstrictē.**

adstrŭo -strŭĕre -struxi -structum, *to build to or near;* hence *to add to.*

adstŭpĕo -ēre, *to be astonished at,* with dat.

adsuēfăcio -făcĕre -fēci -factum, *to accustom a person to a thing.*

adsuesco -suescĕre -suēvi -suētum: intransit., *to grow accustomed:* adsuevi, *I am accustomed;* transit., *to accustom;* poet., of things, *to make familiar.*

Hence partic. **adsuētus** -a -um, *customary, usual; accustomed to.*

adsuētūdo -ĭnis, f. *custom, use.*

adsuētus -a -um, partic. from adsuesco; q.v.

adsulto -are, *to leap violently upon; to attack, assault.*

adsultus -u, m. *leaping up, assault.*

adsum ădesse adfŭi, *to be present, to be at or near;* esp. *to be present and ready, to stand by;* hence, *to support, be favourable to;* sometimes *to be present for a special purpose,* esp. political or legal; of the mind, adesse animo or animis, *to attend;* of things, *to be near, at hand.*

adsūmo -sūmĕre -sumpsi -sumptum, *to take to oneself, or take in addition a person or thing;* hence *to claim, appropriate, call in;* in logic, *to state the minor premises of a syllogism.*

adsumptio -ōnis, f. *choice, adoption;* in logic, *the minor premise of a syllogism.*

adsumptīvus -a -um, *deriving its defence from an extraneous cause.*

adsŭo -ĕre, *to sew on.*

adsurgo -surgĕre -surrexi -surrectum, *to rise up, stand up;* with dat., *to rise in the presence of a person,* as a sign of respect: of feelings, *to rise, be aroused;* of style, *to become elevated;* of material things, *to rise up.*

adt-; see under att-.

ădŭlātio -ōnis, f. *fawning, cringing, flattery.*

ădŭlātor -ōris, m. *flatterer.*

ădŭlescens (ădŏlescens) -entis: as adj., *young, growing;* as subst., *a young man or young woman.*

ădŭlescentĭa -ae, f. *youth.*

ădŭlescentŭlus -i, m. *a young man.*

ădŭlo -are, *to fawn (upon).*

ădŭlor -ari, dep. *to fawn;* with acc. or dat., *to flatter, cringe before.*

ădulter -eri, m., **ădultĕra** -ae, f. *an adulterer, adulteress.*

ădulter -era -erum, adj. *adulterous.*

ădultĕrinus -a -um, *adulterous; not genuine, forged.*

ădultĕrium -i, n. *adultery.*

ădultĕro -are, *to commit adultery, to defile.* Transf. *to falsify, defile, corrupt.*

ădultus -a -um, partic. from adolesco; q.v.

ădumbrātim, *in outline.*

ădumbrātio -ōnis, f. *a sketch.*

ădumbro -are, *to shade in, to sketch,* esp. in words. Partic. **ădumbrātus** -a -um, *sketched;* hence *imperfect, shadowy, unreal.*

ăduncĭtās -ātis, f. *a bending, curvature.*

ăduncus -a -um, *bent in, crooked.*

ădurgĕo -ēre, *to press against;* poet., *to pursue closely.*

ădūro -ūrĕre -ussi -ustum, *to set fire to, kindle, singe;* of frost or wind, *to nip.* Hence partic. **ădustus** -a -um, *burnt:* hominum color, *sunburnt.*

ădusquĕ: prep. with acc., *as far as;* adv. *thoroughly, entirely.*

advectīcius -a -um, *brought from a distance, foreign.*

advecto -are, *to convey often.*

advectus -us, m. *conveying, carrying.*

advĕho -vĕhĕre -vexi -vectum, *to carry, bring, convey to a place;* pass., *to ride up, sail to,* etc.

advēlo -are, *to veil.*

advĕna -ae, c. *a stranger, foreigner.*

advĕnio -vĕnire -vēni -ventum, *to come to, arrive.* Transf., of time, *to come;* of events, *to happen, come near, break out;* of property, *to come to* an owner.

adventīcius -a -um, *coming from without;* esp. *coming from abroad, foreign.*

advento -are, *to approach, come near.*

adventor -ōris, m. *a visitor, guest.*

adventus -ūs, m. *an arrival.*

adversārius -a -um. (1) *turned towards;* n. pl. as subst. *a day-book, journal, memorandum.* (2) *turned against, opposed, contrary;* as subst., m. and f. *an antagonist, rival;* n. pl., *the assertions of an opponent.*

adversor -ari, dep. *to oppose, resist.*

adversus -a -um, partic. from adverto; q.v.

adversus, adversum. Adv., *against, opposite;* adversum ire or venire, *go to meet.* Prep. with acc.: of place, *towards, opposite;* of action, etc., *against, in answer to;* of behaviour, *towards;* of comparison, *compared with.*

adverto (advorto) -vertĕre -verti -versum, *to turn towards;* of the senses, etc. *to direct towards an object;* esp. of the mind, animum (or mentem) advertere, *to direct one's attention to, to perceive,* and of offences, *to punish;* of the object of attention, *to attract.*

Hence partic. **adversus** -a -um, *turned towards, fronting, opposite;* solem adversum intueri, *to look straight at the sun;* adverso flumine, *against the stream;* venti adversi, *contrary winds;* hence, in gen., of persons and things, *opposed, unfavourable;* adversa valetudo, *ill health;* proelium, *unsuccessful;* n. as subst. *misfortune.*

advespĕrascit -avit, *evening approaches.*

advĭgĭlo -are, *to watch by, guard, be vigilant.*

advŏcātio -ōnis, f. *a calling to one's aid;* hence *legal assistance;* concr., *the bar.*

advŏco -are, *to summon, call;* esp. *to call to one's aid:* as legal t. t., *to call in as adviser, to consult an advocate.* M. of partic. as subst. **advŏcātus** -i, m. *one called in to help,* esp. in court as *witness* or *advocate.*

advŏlo -are, *to fly to;* hence *to hasten* or *rush to.*

advolvo -volvĕre -volvi -vŏlūtum, *to roll to;* of suppliants, advolvi, *or* se advolvere, *to throw oneself down* before a person.

advors- advort- = advers-, advert-; q.v.

ădўtum -i, n. *shrine;* poet., ex adyto cordis, *from the bottom of the heart.*

Aeăcus -i, m. *king of Aegina, grandfather of Achilles; after death a judge in the infernal regions.* Hence subst. **Aeăcĭdes** -ae, m. *a male descendant of Aeacus.*

aedēs (aedis) -is, f. *a building;* in sing., usually *a temple;* plur., *rooms,* or *a house;* of bees, *cells.*

aedīcŭla -ae, f. *a small building,* esp. *a small temple* or *shrine;* in plur., *a little house.*

aedĭfĭcātio -ōnis. f.: abstr., *the act of building;* concr., *a building, structure.*

aedĭfĭcātor -ōris, m. *a builder, architect.*

aedĭfĭcium -i, n. *a building.*

aedĭfĭco -are, *to build, erect, establish; to create, frame.*

aedīlĭcius -a -um, *relating to the aediles;* m. as subst. *an ex-aedile.*

aedīlis -is, m. *an aedile, a public officer at Rome, in charge of streets, markets and public games.*

aedīlĭtās -ātis, f. *aedileship.*

aedītĭmus -i, and **aedītŭens** -entis, and **aedītŭus** -i, m. *keeper of a temple, sacristan.*

Aeēta and **Aeētēs** -ae, m., *king of Colchis, father of Medea.* Hence f. subst. **Aeētĭas** -ādis, and **Aeētĭne** -es, = *Medea.*

Aegaeus -a -um, *Aegean;* n. as subst. **Aegaeum** -i, *the Aegean Sea.*

Aegātes -um, f. pl. *three islands off the west coast of Sicily.*

aeger -gra -grum, *sick, ill,* physically or mentally; aeger consilii, *infirm of purpose;* aegris oculis, *with envious eyes;* politically *unsound, mutinous.* M. as subst. *an invalid.* Adv. **aegrē** *with pain, regret* or *difficulty;* hence *hardly, scarcely* (cf. vix).

Aegeus -ĕi, m., *king of Athens, father of Theseus.*

Aegīna -ae, f. *an island near Athens.*

aegis -ĭdis, f. *an aegis, or shield, esp. that of Jupiter or Minerva.* Transf., *a protection, bulwark.*

Aegisthus -i, m. *murderer of Agamemnon, afterwards husband of Clytemnestra.*

aegrē, adv. from aeger; q.v.

aegreo -ēre, *to be sick.*

aegresco -ĕre, *to fall ill;* mentally, *to become troubled;* of bad things, *to become worse.*

aegrĭmōnĭa -ae, f., *grief, trouble of mind.*

aegrĭtūdo -ĭnis, f. *sickness,* esp. of the mind.

aegrōtātĭo -ōnis, f. *sickness,* of body or mind.

aegrōto -are *to be sick or ill,* in body or mind.

aegrōtus -a -um, *sick, ill,* in body or mind.

Aegyptus -i. (1) m., *a king of Egypt, brother of Danaus.* (2) f. *Egypt;* adj. **Aegyptĭus** and **Aegyptĭăcus** -a -um, *Egyptian.*

aelinos -i, m. *a dirge.*

Aemilĭus -a -um, *name of an old patrician family at Rome.* Hence adj. **Aemĭlĭānus** -a -um, *relating to the gens Aemilia; a surname of Scipio Africanus minor.*

Aemōnĭa = Haemonia; q.v.

aemŭlātĭo -ōnis, f., *a striving after, emulation;* in bad sense, *jealousy, rivalry.*

aemŭlātor -ōris, m., *a rival, imitator.*

aemŭlor -ari, dep., *to rival, emulate;* with dat., *to envy.*

aemŭlus -a -um, *emulous, rivalling;* in bad sense, *jealous.* M. or f. as subst., *a rival,* esp. in love.

Aemus = Haemus; q.v.

Aenēās -ae, m., *son of Venus and Anchises, hero of Vergil's Aeneid.* Hence subst. **Aenĕădēs** -ae, m., *a male descendant of Aeneas;* **Aenēis** -idos, f. *Vergil's Aeneid.*

ăhēnĕus and **ăhēnĕus** -a -um, *made of copper or bronze; hard as bronze, brazen.*

aenigma -ătis, n., *a riddle, mystery.*

ăēnĭpēs -pĕdĭs, *brazen-footed.*

ăēnus (**ăhēnus**) -a -um, *made of copper or bronze;* poet., *hard as bronze.* N. as subst., *a brazen vessel.*

Aeŏles -um, m. *the Aeolians, Greeks living in Greece and Asia Minor.* Hence adj. **Aeŏlĭcus** and **Aeŏlĭus** -a -um, *Aeolic.*

Aeŏlĭa -ae, f. *north part of the coast of Asia Minor.*

Aeŏlus -i, m. *ruler of the Aeolian islands and of the winds.*

aequābĭlis -e, *like, similar, equal.* Transf., *equal to itself, uniform, consistent; fair, impartial.* Hence adv. **aequābĭlĭter,***equably,uniformly,fairly.*

aequābĭlĭtās -ātis, f., *uniformity, equability;* hence *evenness in style, impartiality in law.*

aequaevus -a -um, *of equal age.*

aequālis -e, *even;* of places, *level.* Transf., *equal;* esp. of time, *of the same age, contemporary, coexistent.* M. or f. as subst., *a comrade, person of the same age.* Adv. **aequālĭtĕr**, *evenly, equally.*

aequālĭtās -ātis, f., *evenness;* of places, *smoothness.* Transf., *equality,* esp. *equality of age.*

aequănĭmĭtās -ātis, f. *impartiality.*

aequātĭo -ōnis, f. *making equal;* bonorum, *communism.*

Aequi -orum, m. *a people of central Italy.*

aequĭlībrĭtās -ātis, f. *equal distribution of natural forces.*

aequĭnoctĭālis -e, *equinoctial.*

aequĭnoctĭum -i, n., *the equinox.*

aequĭpăro (**aequĭpĕro**) -are, *to compare; to equal.*

aequĭtās -ātis, f., *uniformity, evenness.* Transf., *equanimity;* also *impartiality, fairness, justice.*

aequo -are. (1) *to make level or equal.* (2) *to compare.* (3) *to equal, come up to.*

aequor -ōris, n., *a flat level surface;* esp. *of a plain, or of the sea;* rarely *of a river.*

aequŏrĕus -a -um, *belonging to the sea.*

aequus -a -um, adj. *equal.* (1) *equal in itself, even, level;* ex aequo loco loqui, *to speak in the senate;* milit., aequa frons, *a straight line.* (2) *equal to something else:* ex aequo, in aequo, *on even terms.* Transf., of places or times, *favourable, advantageous;* of battles, *even,* and so *indecisive;* of temper, *even, contented, easy;* aequo animo, *patiently, with resignation;* of behaviour, etc., *equal, impartial;* of persons, *fair;* aequum est, *it is just.* N. as subst. aequum -i, *level ground; fairness, equity.* Adv. **aequē**, *in like manner, equally; fairly, justly.*

ăēr ăĕris, m., *the lower air, the atmosphere.*

aerārĭus -a -um, *of or belonging to bronze or copper;* hence *belonging to (copper) money;* tribuni, *paymasters.* M. as subst. *a copper-smith;* in plur., aerarii, *the citizens of the lowest class in Rome.* N. as subst. *a treasury,* esp. *the public treasury at Rome.*

aerātus -a -um, *made of or fitted with copper or bronze;* hence *provided with money, rich.*

aerĕus -a -um, *made of or fitted with copper or bronze.*

aerĭfer -fĕra -fĕrum, *bearing brazen cymbals.*

aerĭpēs -pĕdis, *brazen-footed.*

ăērĭus (**ăērĕus**) -a -um, *belonging to the air, airy;* hence *high in the air, lofty.*

aerūgo -ĭnis, f., *the rust of copper, verdigris; rusty money.* Transf., *envy or avarice.*

aerumna -ae, f. *labour, toil, hardship.*

aerumnōsus -a -um, adj., *full of hardship.*

aes, aeris, n. *copper ore, and the alloy of copper, bronze.* Transf., *anything made of bronze; a vessel, statue,* trumpet, kettle; aera aere repulsa, cymbals; aes publicum, public inscriptions. Esp. copper or bronze money; aes grave, the as; aes signatum, coined money; also money generally, pay; aes alienum, debt.

Aeschฤlus -i, m. an Athenian tragic poet.

Aescŭlāpĭus -i, m. the god of medicine. Hence subst. **Aescŭlāpĭum** -i, n. a temple of Aesculapius.

aescŭlētum -i, n., an oak forest.

aescŭlĕus -a -um, relating to the (winter) oak.

aescŭlus -i, f. the winter or Italian oak.

Aesōn -ōnis, m., a Thessalian prince, father of Jason. Hence subst. **Aesōnĭdēs** -ae, m. a male descendant of Aeson, = Jason; adj. **Aesōnĭus** -a -um.

Aesōpus -i, m. a Greek fabulist of Phrygia.

aestās -ātis, f. summer; hence summer weather, summer heat.

aestĭfer -fĕra -fĕrum, heatbringing.

aestĭmābĭlis -e, valuable.

aestĭmātĭo -ōnis, f. an appraising in terms of money; litis, assessment of damages. Transf., in gen., valuation, worth, value.

aestĭmātor -ōris, m. one who estimates, an appraiser.

aestĭmo (aestŭmo) -are, to appraise, rate, estimate the value of; litem, to assess the damages in a law-suit; in a wider sense, to value a thing or person; hence, in gen., to judge.

aestīvus -a -um, relating to summer. N. pl. as subst. **aestīva** -orum, a summer camp, and hence, a campaign; summer pastures for cattle.

aestŭārĭum -i, n., low ground covered by the sea at high water; a firth, creek.

aestŭo -are, to be agitated or hot; of liquids, to boil, seethe; fig., of emotional excitement, to burn; of perplexity, to waver.

aestŭōsus -a -um, hot, agitated; adv. **aestŭōsē**.

aestus -ūs, m., agitation, heat; of liquids, esp. of the sea, seething, raging; also of the sea's tide, and spray; fig., of persons, dizziness; also emotional excitement, heat, fury, and perplexity, anxiety.

aetās -ātis, f., age: of human life, either a lifetime or a time of life, age; id aetatis, of that age; bona (or iniens) aetas, flos aetatis, youth; aetas ingravescens, or provecta, old age. Meton., the persons of a particular age: aetas puerilis, boys. In gen., time, age, a period of time, epoch.

aetātŭla -ae, f., youth.

aeternĭtas -ātis, f., eternity, immortality.

aeterno -are, to make eternal, immortalize.

aeternus -a -um, eternal, everlasting: aeternum, or in aeternum, for ever.

aether -ĕris, acc. -ĕra, m., the upper air; poet., heaven, or the upper world.

aethĕrĭus -a -um, of the air or upper air; aqua, rain; poet., heavenly, or belonging to the upper world.

Aethĭōpĭa -ae, f., Ethiopia; adj. **Aethĭōpĭcus** -a -um. and **Aethĭops** -ōpis, Ethiopian, Negro.

aethra -ae, f., the upper air, clear sky.

Aetna -ae and **Aetnē** -ēs, f. Etna, a volcano in Sicily; adj. **Aetnaeus** -a -um.

Aetōlĭa -ae, f., Aetolia, a country in the west of Greece; adj. **Aetōlus**, **Aetōlĭcus**, **Aetōlĭus** -a -um.

aevĭtās -ātis, f. = aetas; q.v.

aevum -in, n., also **aevus** -i, m., eternity. Transf., time, lifetime, or time of life; flos aevi, youth; in gen., a period of time.

Āfer -fra -frum, adj. and subst., African, from Africa; esp. from Carthage. Hence subst. **Āfrĭca** -ae, f. the continent of Africa; esp. either the country round Carthage or the Roman province of Africa. Adj. **Āfrĭcānus** -a -um, African, belonging to Africa; esp. as a surname, conferred upon two of the Scipios. Also adj. **Āfrĭcus** -a -um; ventus Africus, or simply Africus, the S.W. wind (bringing rain and storms).

aff-; see under adf-.

Ăgămemnon -ŏnis, m. leader of the Greek expedition to Troy.

Ăgănippē -ēs, f. a fountain in Boeotia, sacred to the Muses; adj. **Ăgănippēus** -a -um, sacred to the Muses.

ăgāso -ōnis, m. a groom. lockey.

ăgellus -i, m. a little field.

ăgēma -ătis, n. a corps in the Macedonian army.

Ăgēnor -ōris, m. father of Cadmus and Europa; hence adj. **Ăgēnŏrēus** -a -um, and subst. **Ăgēnŏrĭdēs** -ae, m. a male descendant of Agenor.

ăger, agri, m. land, territory; as cultivated, a field; open country (opp. towns); land, (opp. sea).

agg- (except agger and aggero); see adg-.

agger -ĕris, m. heap, mound; milit., rampart; poet., any high place.

aggĕro -are, to form a mound, heap up, increase.

ăgĭlis -e, easily moved, light, nimble, active.

ăgĭlĭtās -ātis, f. quickness, agility.

ăgĭtābĭlis -e, easily moved, light.

ăgĭtātĭo -ōnis, f., movement, agitation, activity; rerum magnarum, management.

ăgĭtātor -ōris, m. driver; esp. charioteer.

ăgĭto -are, to put in motion, drive about (cf. ago); of animals, to drive or hunt; of water, to toss. Transf. (1) to vex, harry, trouble persons, etc. (2) to deal with, be engaged upon, argue, discuss, consider a subject; to maintain a state of affairs; to conduct a business; to keep a holiday; to spend time; so, absol., to live.

Ăglāĭa -ae or **Ăglāĭē** -ēs, f. one of the Graces.

agmĕn -ĭnis, n. *a driving movement or a mass in (orderly)movement, a stream, band, train*; esp. milit., *an army on the march.*

agna -ae, f. *a ewe lamb.*

agnascor -nasci, -nātus, dep., *of children, to be born after their father's will.* M. of partic. as subst. **agnātus** -i, *a relation descended from a common ancestor in the male line; a child born into a family where a regular heir already exists.*

agnātio -ōnis, f. *relationship reckoned through males only.*

agnellus -i, m. *a little lamb.*

agninus -a -um, *of a lamb*; f. as subst., *lamb's flesh.*

agnitio -ōnis, f. *recognition*; in gen., *knowledge.*

agnōmen -ĭnis, n., *surname.*

agnosco -noscĕre -nōvi -nĭtum, *to know again, recognise; to know by inference or report, understand; to express knowledge, admit, acknowledge.*

agnus -i, m. *lamb.*

ăgo ăgĕre ĕgi actum, *to set in motion, drive; of animals, to drive or hunt;* se agere, *to go;* animam, *to give up the ghost;* radices, *to strike root.* Transf., *to incite to action; to deal with, be engaged upon; to treat of a subject;* hoc agere, *to attend to the matter in hand;* pass., *to be concerned, be at stake;* actum est de, *it is settled about, so it is all over with;* bene agere cum homine, *to treat a person well;* grates, gratias, *to express thanks;* pacem, *to keep the peace;* of time, *to spend;* so absol., *to spend time, live;* on the stage, *to act, play;* primas partes, *to play the leading part;* legal and polit., *to take a matter up publicly;* agere (iure, or lege), *to go to law;* agere causam, *to plead a cause.* Pres. partic. **ăgens** -entis, as adj. *effective.*

ăgōn -ōnis, m. *a contest in the public games.*

ăgōnālia -ium and -orum, n. *a festival of Janus.*

agrārĭus -a -um, *relating to land*; m. pl. as subst., *the agrarian party,* aiming at a general distribution of public land.

agrestis -e, *belonging to the field or country; wild, rustic;* hence, *countrified, boorish, clownish.* M. as subst. agrestis -is, *a countryman.*

'agricŏla -ae, m. *farmer.*

'Agricŏla -ae, m. Gnaeus Julius, *governor of Britain, and father-in-law of Tacitus.*

agricult-; see under cult-.

Agrigentum -i, n.; also **Acrăgās** -antis, m.; *a Doric town in S.W. Sicily.*

agripĕta -ae, m. *a land-grabber, squatter.*

Agrippa -ae, m. *a Roman family name.*

Agrippīna -ae, f. *the name of several Roman women,* esp. Nero's mother. Hence Colonia Agrippinensis (now Cologne).

ah or **a**, *ah! oh!*

Ăhāla -ae, m., C. Servilius, *master of the horse under the dictator Cincinnatus,* 439 B.C.

ai, *ah!,* interjection of grief.

Aiax -ācis, m. *name of two Homeric heroes, sons of Telamon and of Oileus.*

āio, defective verb. *to say yes, to affirm, assert, state;* ain tu? *you don't say?* Hence pres. partic. aiens -entis, *affirmative.*

āla -ae, f. *a wing;* poet., *of the sails or oars of a ship;* of a man, *the armpit;* milit., *a wing, squadron.*

ălăbaster -stri, m., with pl. **ălăbastra,** *a perfume casket.*

ălăcer -cris -cre, and **ălăcris** -e, *quick, lively, animated.*

ălăcrĭtās -ātis, f. *quickness, eagerness, animation.*

ălăpa -ae, f. *a box on the ear,* given by a master to his slave when freeing him.

ālārĭus -a -um, and **ālāris** -e, *belonging to the wings of an army;* m. pl. as subst., *allied troops.*

ālātus -a -um, *winged.*

ălauda -ae, f. *a lark;* also *the name of a legion formed by Caesar in Gaul;* in pl. **Ălaudae** -arum, *the soldiers of this legion.*

Alba -ae, *Alba Longa,* the oldest Latin town; hence adj. **Albānus** -a -um.

albātus -a -um, *clothed in white.*

albĕo -ēre, *to be white.*

albesco -ĕre, *to become white.*

albico -are, *to be white.*

albĭdus -a -um, *whitish.*

Albĭon -ōnis, f. *old name of Great Britain.*

Albis -is, m. *the Elbe.*

albŭlus -a -um, *whitish;* f. as subst. **Albŭla** -ae (sc. aqua), *old name of the Tiber.*

album -i; *see* albus.

albus -a -um, *white, dead white;* hence *pale* or *bright;* sometimes *making bright;* fig., *fortunate.* N. as subst. **album** -i, *white colour;* a white writing-tablet, a list.

Alcaeus -i, m. *a Greek lyric poet (about* 600 B.C.).

alcēdo -inis and **alcўōn** -onis, f. *the kingfisher.* Hence n. pl. **alcēdŏnia** -orum, *the kingfisher's time, quietness, calm.*

alces -is, f. *the elk.*

Alcestis -is, and **Alcestē** -ēs, f. *wife of Admetus, who saved her husband by dying for him.*

Alcēūs -ēi and -ĕos, m. *grandfather of Hercules.* Hence subst. **Alcīdes** -ae, m. esp. *of Hercules.*

Alcĭbĭădēs -is, m. *an Athenian general, pupil of Socrates.*

Alcĭnŏūs -i, m. *king of the Phaeacians, host of Odysseus.*

Alcmēna -ae, also **Alcmēnē** -ēs, f. *mother of Hercules.*

alcўōn = alcedo; q.v.

ālĕa -ae, f. *a game of dice, game of hazard;* hence *chance, risk, uncertainty.*

ălĕātor -ōris, m. *dicer, gambler.*

alĕātōrĭus -um, *of a gambler.*

ālec = allec; q.v.

ālēs alĭtis, *winged;* hence *swift;* as subst., *a bird,* esp. *a large bird* or *bird of omen;* poet., *an omen, sign.*

ălesco -ĕre, *to grow up.*

Ālexander -dri, m. (1) = *Paris, son of Priam, king of Troy.* (2) *Alexander the Great* (356-323 B.C.), *king of Macedonia.* Hence **Alexandrīa** or **ēa** -ae, f. *a city founded by Alexander,* esp. *Alexandria in Egypt;* adj. **Ālexandrīnus** -a -um, *of Alexandria.*

alga -ae, f. *sea-weed.*

algĕo algēre alsi, *to be cold;* partic. **algens** -entis, *cold.*

algesco algescĕre alsi, *to catch cold.*

¹**algĭdus** -a -um, *cold.*

²**Algĭdus** -i, m. *a mountain in Latium;* adj. **Algīdus** -a -um, *of Algidus.*

algor -ōris, m. *cold.*

algus -ūs, = algor; q.v.

ălĭās, see under alius.

ălĭbī. (1) *elsewhere, at another place;* alibi . . . alibi, *here . . . there.* (2) *otherwise, in other respects.*

ălĭca -ae, f. *spelt,* or *a drink prepared from spelt.*

ălĭcŭbi, *anywhere, somewhere.*

ălĭcundĕ, *from anywhere, from somewhere.*

ălĭēnātĭo -ōnis, f. *a transference, alienation;* mentis, *aberration of mind.*

ălĭēnĭgĕna -ae, m. *strange, foreign;* as subst., *a foreigner.*

ălĭēnĭgĕnus -a -um, *of different elements, heterogeneous.*

ălĭēno -are, *to make something another's, let go, transfer; to estrange one person from another; to put a thing out of one's mind, forget;* with mentem, etc., *to cause a person to lose his reason;* pass., alienari, *to go out of one's mind.*

ălĭēnus -a -um, *belonging to another;* aes, *another's money, and so debt;* in gen., *strange, foreign, unrelated;* esp. of persons, *not at home, unfamiliar,* or *estranged, unfriendly;* of things, *unfavourable.* M. as subst., alienus, *a stranger;* n. as subst. alienum, *another person's property.*

ālĭger -gĕra -gĕrum, *winged.*

ălĭmentārĭus -a -um, *relating to food.*

ălĭmentum -i, n. (1) *food.* (2) *maintenance.*

ălĭmōnĭum -i, n. *nourishment.*

ălĭo; see under alius.

ălĭōquī and **ălĭōquĭn.** (1) *otherwise, in other respects.* (2) *in general, in most respects.* (3) *else, in other conditions.*

ălĭorsum and **ălĭorsus.** (1) *in another direction, elsewhere.* (2) *in another manner.*

ălĭpēs -pĕdis, *having wings on the feet;* hence *swift;* m. pl. as subst., *horses.*

ălĭpta and **ălĭptēs** -ae, m. *the anointer in the wrestling-school* or *the baths.*

aliqua, aliquamdiu, aliquammultus; see under aliquis.

ălĭquando, *at any time, once; sometimes, occasionally; at last.*

ălĭquantŭlus -a -um, *little, small;* n. as adv. *a little.*

ălĭquantus -a -um, *of some size, moderate.* N. as subst. **ălĭquantum** -i, *a good deal;* acc. aliquantum, and (with compar.) abl. aliquanto, *somewhat, considerably.*

ălĭquātĕnus, *to a certain degree.*

ălĭqui, aliquae, or aliqua, aliquod, adj. *some.*

ălĭquis aliquid, pron. *someone, something; anyone, anything.* N. aliquid often with partitive genit., *a certain amount or number of;* as adv., *in any respect.* Transf., *somebody* or *something great* or *significant.* Hence adv. **ălĭquō,** *some whither, in some direction;* adv. **ălĭquā,** *by some road, in some way;* adv. **ălĭquamdĭu,** *for some time;* adj. **ălĭquammultus,** *considerable* in number or quantity.

ălĭquot, indecl., *some, several.*

ălĭquŏtĭē(n)s, *several times.*

ălĭs, alid, old form of alius, aliud; q.v.

ălĭter; see under alius.

ālĭum or **allium** -i, *garlic.*

ălĭundĕ, *from some other direction:* alii aliunde, *from various directions.*

ălĭus -a -ud, adj. and pronoun, *another, other, different.* Distributively, *one, another:* alii alii . . . alii, *some . . . others;* alii alia censent, *some think one thing, some another.* In comparison, *other than,* followed by atque, quam, etc. Rarely, in plur., *all other, the rest;* in sing. = alter, *one of two.* Hence adv. **ălĭās,** (1) *at another time;* alius alias, *one person at one time, another at another.* (2) *otherwise.* Adv. **ălĭō,** *to another place;* alius alio *in various directions.* Transf., *to another person* or *object; for another end.* Adv. **ălĭtĕr.** (1) *otherwise, in another way;* alius aliter, *in different ways.* (2) *else, in other conditions.*

ălĭusmŏdi, *of another kind.*

all-, v. also under adl-.

allec or **ălec** -ēcis, n. *fish-pickle.*

Allecto or **Alecto,** *one of the three Furies.*

Allĭa (Alia) -ae, f. *river in Latium;* adj. **Alliensis** -e.

Allobrox -ŏgis, and pl. **Allobrŏges** -um, m. *the Allobroges, a Gallic people.*

almus -a -um, *nourishing, kind.*

alnus -i, f. *the alder;* meton, *a ship of alderwood.*

ălo ălĕre ălŭi altum (or ălĭtum), *to nourish, support, rear, feed;* hence in gen., *to strengthen, increase, promote, advance.*

Hence partic. **altus** -a -um, *grown, great.* As seen from below, *high,* hence, of the voice, *shrill;* of character, *dignity, rank, lofty, noble.* As seen from above, *deep;* hence of quiet, *deep;* of thoughts, *secret, deep-seated;* of time, *reaching far back, ancient.* N. as subst. **altum** -i,

either *height* or *depth.* Adv. **alte,**
highly or *deeply.*

ălŏē -ēs, f., *the aloe; bitterness.*

Alpēs -ium, f. *the Alps;* adj. **Alpīnus**
and **Alpīcus** -a -um, *Alpine.*

Alphēus or **Alphēos** -i, m. *the chief
river of the Peloponnese.*

alsius -a -um, *frosty, cold.*

altāria -ium, n. pl. *an erection upon an
altar;* hence *high altars,* or *a high
altar.*

alter -těra -těrum, *one of two, the one,
the other;* as a numeral, *second;* unus
et alter, *one or two;* in pl., *of a second
set.* Hence *of quality, second, next
best;* of similarity, *another, a second;*
alter idem, *a second self;* of difference,
other, changed.

altercātio -ōnis, f., *dispute, wrangling;*
legal, *cross-examination.*

altercor -ari, dep. *to dispute, contend,
quarrel;* legal, *to cross-examine, cross-
question.*

alterno -are, *to do first one thing, then
another;* transit, *to interchange;*
intransit., *to alternate, waver.*

alternus -a -um, *one after the other, by
turns, alternate, interchanging;* sermones, *dialogue;* of metre, *elegiac*
(with hexameter and pentameter
alternating).

altěrūter -utra -utrum, *one of two.*

altilis -e, *fattened, fed;* f. as subst.
(sc. avis), *a fowl.*

altĭsŏnus -a -um, *sounding from on
high; high-sounding, sublime.*

altĭtūdo -īnis, f. (1) *height;* hence
sublimity. (2) *depth;* animi, *secrecy,
reserve.*

altor -ōris, m, *nourisher, foster-father.*

altrix -īcis, f. *nurse, foster-mother.*

altus -a -um, **alte,** etc.; see under alo.

ălūcĭnor -ari, dep. *to wander in mind,
dream, talk idly.*

ălumnus -a -um, adj. used as noun,
nursling, foster-child; hence *pupil.*

ălūta -ae, f. *soft leather; a shoe, purse*
or *patch.*

alvĕārium -i, n. *beehive.*

alvĕŏlus -i, m. *tray, trough, bucket;
gaming-board.*

alvĕus -i, m. *a hollow, cavity, trough;*
hence *boat;* also *the hold of a ship;
bath-tub; bed of a stream; beehive;
gaming-table.*

alvus -i, f. *belly, womb, stomach; hold
of a ship, beehive.*

ămābĭlis -e, *amiable, lovely;* adv.
ămābĭlĭter.

Ămalthēa -ae, f. either *a nymph, the
nurse of Jupiter in Crete* or *the goat
on the milk of which Jupiter was
reared.*

ămandātio -ōnis, f. *a sending away.*

ămando -are, *to send away.*

ămans = partic. of amo; q.v.

ămānŭensis -is, m. *secretary, clerk.*

ămārācĭnus -a -um, *made of marjoram;*
n. as subst. *marjoram ointment.*

ămārăcus -i, c. and **ămārăcum** -i, n.
marjoram.

ămārantus -i, m., *the amaranth.*

ămārĭtiēs -ēi, f., *bitterness.*

ămārĭtūdo -ĭnis, f. *bitterness;* vocis,
harshness of voice.

ămāror -ōris, m., *bitterness.*

ămārus -a -um, *bitter, pungent.*
Hence, of things, *disagreeable, unpleasant;* of persons, *irritable;* of
speech, *biting, acrimonious.* Adv.
ămārē, *bitterly.*

ămātor -ōris, m. *a lover, friend,
admirer;* esp. *the lover of a woman.*

ămātōrius -a -um, *loving, amorous;*
n. as subst. *a love philtre.* Adv.
ămātōriē.

ămātrix -īcis, f. *mistress, sweet-heart.*

Ămāzon -ōnis, f.; gen. in plur.
Ămāzŏnes -um, myth., *nation of
female warriors.* Hence subst.
Ămāzŏnis -ĭdis, f. = Amazon; adj.
Ămāzŏnĭcus, Ămāzŏnius -a -um.

ambactus -i, m. *vassal.*

ambāges, abl. -e, f. (of sing. only abl.
found) *a roundabout way, winding.*
Hence, in speech, etc., either *circumlocution* or *obscurity, ambiguity.*

ambēdo -esse -ēdi -ēsum, *to eat round,
consume.*

ambĭgo -ēre, *to go about* or *round.*
Transf., (1) *to doubt, hesitate;* am-
bigitur, impers., *it is in doubt;*
(2) *to dispute, contend.*

ambĭgŭĭtās -ātis, f. *ambiguity.*

ambĭgŭus -a -um, *moving from side to
side, doubtful, uncertain, insecure,
unreliable;* of speech, *ambiguous,
obscure;* n. as subst. *uncertainty,
doubt, ambiguity.* Adv. **ambĭgŭē,**
ambiguously, indecisively.

ambĭo -ire -ivi -or -ii -itum *to go round.*
Hence (1) *to surround.* (2) *to go round
from person to person, to approach,
entreat, canvass* (for votes, help, etc.).

Ambĭorix -rigis, m. *chief of the Eburones
in Gallia Belgica.*

ambĭtio -ōnis, f. *canvassing for office*
(in a lawful manner); in gen., *desire
for office, popularity* or *fame.*

ambĭtiōsus -a -um, *going round;* esp.
active in seeking office, popularity or
fame; ambitious, ostentatious. Adv.
ambĭtiōsē, *ambitiously, ostentatiously.*

ambĭtus -ūs, m. *a going round, circuit,
revolution.* Hence, of things, *border,
edge* or *extent;* in speech, *circumlocution;* in relation to persons, *illegal
canvassing for office, bribery, striving
after popularity* or *effect.*

ambō -ae -ō, *both, two together.*

ambrŏsia -ae, f. *ambrosia, the food* or
unguent of the gods.

ambrŏsius -a -um, *divine, immortal,
ambrosial.*

ambūbāia -ae, f., *a Syrian flute-girl.*

ambūlātĭo -ōnis, f. *a walk* or *place for
walking.*

ambūlātiuncŭla -ae, f. *a little walk* or
place for walking, promenade.

ambŭlo -are, *to walk, go for a walk,
travel, march:* bene ambula, " *bon
voyage*"; with acc., *to traverse.*

ambūro -ūrēre -ussi -ustum, *to burn*

round, scorch; of cold, *to nip, numb*; in gen., *to injure*.

āmellus -i, m. *the purple Italian starwort*.

āmens -entis, *mad, insane, senseless*.

āmentia -ae, f. *madness, senselessness*.

āmento -are, *to furnish with a strap*.

āmentum -i, n. *a strap, thong*.

āmēs -ĭtis, m. *a forked pole*.

āmĕthystinus -a -um, *amethyst-coloured*; n. pl. as subst., *dresses of amethyst colour*.

āmĕthystus -i, f. *an amethyst*.

amfractus = anfractus; q.v.

āmĭcĭo -ĭcīre -ĭcŭi or -ixi -ictum, *to clothe, wrap round, wrap up, cover, conceal*.

āmĭcĭtĭa -ae, f. *friendship*; in plur., concrete, = *friends*.

āmĭcĭtĭēs -ēi, f. = amicitia; q.v.

āmictus -ūs, m., *the putting on of a garment, esp. the toga*. Transf., *a garment, covering*.

āmīcŭla -ae, f. *a little mistress*.

āmīcŭlum -i, n. *a mantle, cloak*.

āmīcŭlus -i, m. *a dear friend*.

āmīcus -a -um, *friendly, well-wishing, favourable*. M. as subst., **āmīcus** -i, *a friend*; in plur., *retinue*; f. as subst., **āmīca** -ae, *a friend or mistress*. Adv. **āmīcē** and **āmīcĭter**, *in a friendly manner*.

āmissĭo -ōnis, f. *loss*.

āmissus -ūs, m. = amissio; q.v.

āmĭta -ae, f. *a father's sister, aunt*.

āmitto -mittĕre -mīsi -missum, *to send away, let go, let slip*; hence, in gen., *to lose*.

Ammōn (Hammōn) (ōnis, m. *a Libyan deity, worshipped at Rome under the name of Jupiter Ammon*.

amnĭcŏla -ae, c. *dwelling by the riverside*.

amnĭcŭlus -i, m. *a little river*.

amnis -is, m. *a stream, river, torrent*; poet., *current, river water*.

āmo -are, *to love (passionately), be fond of*; amare se, *to be selfish or pleased with oneself*; amabo te, or amabo, *please, be so good*; with infin., *to like to do a thing, also to be wont, be accustomed*.

Hence partic. **āmans** -antis, *loving, fond*; as subst., *a lover*. Adv. **āmanter**, *lovingly*.

āmoenĭtās -ātis, f. *pleasantness, esp. of places*.

āmoenus -a -um, *pleasant, delightful, esp. of places*.

āmōlĭor -iri, dep. *to remove by an effort, set aside, get rid of*; amoliri se, *to take oneself off*.

āmōmum -i, n. *a shrub*.

āmor -ōris, m. *love, passion, fondness, desire*; meton., *an object of love, darling*; personified, *Love, Cupid*.

āmōtĭo -ōnis, f. *removal*.

āmŏvĕo -mŏvēre -mōvi -mōtum, *to move away, withdraw; se amovere, to depart*; in insulam, *to banish to an island*; of ideas or feelings, *to put aside*.

amphĭbŏlĭa -ae, f. *ambiguity, double meaning*.

Amphictўŏnes -aum, m. plur., *the Amphictyons, religious representatives of the Greek states*.

Amphīŏn -ōnis, m. *king of Thebes, husband of Niobe*.

amphĭthĕātrum -i, n. *amphitheatre*.

Amphĭtrītē -ēs, f. *wife of Neptune, goddess of the sea*.

amphŏra -ae, f. (1) *a two-handled jar*. (2) *a measure: liquid*, = about 7 gallons; *of shipping*, = about 1/40 of our ton.

amplector -plecti -plexus, dep., *to embrace, twine round, enclose, surround*. Transf., *to welcome, love, esteem*; in thought or speech, *to take in, consider, deal with*; *to include, comprise*.

amplexor -ari, dep. *to embrace; to welcome, love*.

amplexus -ūs, m. *encircling, embrace*.

amplĭfĭcātĭo -ōnis, f. *enlarging, heightening, amplification*.

amplĭfĭcātor -ōris, m. *one who enlarges*.

amplĭfĭco -are, *to enlarge, heighten, increase, magnify*.

amplĭo -are, *to enlarge, increase, magnify*; legal, *to adjourn a case*.

amplĭtūdo -ĭnis, f. *breadth, size; greatness, dignity, grandeur*.

amplus -a -um, *large, spacious, ample*. Transf., *great, important, honourable; eminent, distinguished*; amplissimi viri, *men of the highest position*; rhet., *grand, full*. Adv. **amplē** and **amplĭter** *fully, grandly*. Compar. adv. and n. subst., **amplĭus**, *more, further, besides*; with numerals, often = *more than*.

ampulla -ae, f. *flask, bottle*. Transf., *bombast*.

ampullor -ari, dep. *to speak bombastically*.

ampŭtātĭo -ōnis, f. *cutting off, pruning*.

ampŭto -are, *to cut off, esp. of trees, to lop, prune*; of limbs, *to amputate*; hence, in gen., *to remove, diminish*; amputata loqui, *to speak disconnectedly*.

Āmūlĭus -i, m. *king of Alba Longa, brother of Numitor*.

āmurca -ae, f. *oil-lees*.

āmygdălum -i, n., *almond*.

Āmyntas -ae, m., *name of several Macedonian kings*.

āmystis -ĭdis, f., *the emptying of a goblet at a draught*.

ăn, conj.: in direct questions, *or*; in indirect questions, *or whether*.

ănăbathrum -i, n. *a raised seat*.

ănădēma -ătis, n. *a head ornament, fillet*.

ănagnostēs -ae, m. *reader*.

ănălecta -ae, m. *a dining-room slave*.

ănălŏgĭa -ae, f. *proportion, comparison, analogy*.

ănăpaestus -a -um: pes, *a metrical foot, anapaest*. n. as subst. *a poem in anapaestic verse*.

ănăphŏra -ae, f. in rhetoric, *the repetition of a word at the beginning of several sentences*.

ănas ănătis, f. *duck.*

ănătĭcŭla -ae, f. *little duck.*

ănătŏcismus -i, m. *compound interest.*

Ănaxagoras -ae, m. *a Greek philosopher of the fifth century B.C.*

anceps -cĭpĭtis, *two-headed; hence with two peaks or edges.* Transf., *coming on or from both sides; of two natures; ambiguous, uncertain, undecided;* hence *dangerous;* n. as subst., *danger.*

Anchīsēs -ae, m. *father of Aeneas.* Hence subst. **Anchīsĭădēs** -ae. m. *a male descendant of Anchises, Aeneas.*

ancīle -is, n., *a sacred shield, supposed to have fallen from heaven.*

ancilla -ae, f. *maid-servant, female slave.*

ancillāris -e *of a maid-servant.*

ancillor -ari, dep. *to serve (as a maid).*

ancillŭla -ae, f. *a little maid-servant.*

ancīsus -a -um, *cut round.*

Ancōn -onis, and **Ancōna** -ae. f. *a town on the Adriatic coast of Italy.*

ancŏra -ae, f. *an anchor;* ancoram tollere, *to weigh anchor.*

ancŏrāle -is, n. *a cable.*

ancŏrārius -a -um, *belonging to an anchor.*

Ancus (Marcius) -i, *fourth king of Rome.*

Ancȳra -ae, f. *capital of Galatia, in Asia Minor.*

andrŏgȳnus -i, m. or **andrŏgȳne** -es, f. *hermaphrodite.*

Andrŏmăchē -ēs and -cha -ae, f. *wife of Hector.*

Andrŏmĕdē -ēs, f. and -da -ae, f. *wife of Perseus.*

andrōn -ōnis, m., *corridor.*

Andrŏnicus -i, m. L. Livius, *Roman dramatic and epic poet of the third century B.C.*

ānellus -i, m. *a little ring.*

ănēthum -i, n. *dill, anise.*

anfractus -ūs, m. *a turning, a bend;* solis, *revolution;* vallis, *winding.* Transf., *legal intricacies, circumlocution, digression.*

angellus -i, m. *a little corner.*

angĭportum -i, n. and **angĭportus** -ūs, m. *a narrow street.*

ango -ĕre, *to press tightly;* of the throat, *to strangle, throttle;* in gen., *to hurt, distress;* of the mind, *to torment, make anxious.*

angor -ōris, m. *compression of the throat, suffocation;* of the mind, *distress, anguish, trouble.*

anguĭcŏmus -a -um, *having snaky hair.*

anguĭfer -fĕra -fĕrum, *snake-bearing.*

anguĭgĕna -ae, m. *snake-born.*

anguilla -ae, f. *an eel.*

anguĭmānus -a -um, *snake-handed.*

anguĭnĕus -a -um, *of a snake, snaky.*

anguīnus -a -um, *snaky.*

anguĭpēs -pēdis, *snake-footed.*

anguis -is, c. *a snake;* in astronomy, *the constellation Draco, or Hydra, or the Serpent.*

Anguĭtĕnens -entis, m., *the Snake-holder,* i.e. *the constellation Ophiuchus.*

angŭlātus -a -um, *angular, cornered.*

angŭlus -i, m. *a corner, angle;* esp.

either *a quiet corner, retired spot,* or, fig., *an awkward corner, strait.*

angustĭae -arum, f. pl. *narrowness;* hence, of space, *a strait, narrow place;* spiritūs, *shortness of breath;* of time, *shortness;* of supplies, *shortness, poverty;* of circumstances, *difficulty, distress;* of disposition, *narrow-mindedness;* of reasoning, *subtlety.*

angustus -a -um, *narrow, confined;* habenae, *tightly-drawn reins;* spiritus angustior, *constricted breath;* of time, *short;* of supplies, *short, scarce;* of circumstances, *precarious, critical;* of mind or speech, *narrow, petty, limited;* of style, *brief, simple.* N. as subst. **angustum** -i, *a narrow space.* Adv. **angustē**, *narrowly, sparingly,* in a *narrow, confined manner;* of speech, *briefly.*

ănhēlĭtus -ūs, m. *puffing, panting.* Transf., in gen., *breath; exhalation, vapour.*

ănhēlo -are, *to puff, pant;* transit., *to pant out words;* also *to pant for a thing, desire eagerly.*

ănhēlus -a -um, *puffing, panting;* febris, *causing to pant.*

ănĭcŭla -ae, f. *a little old woman.*

ănīlis -e *belonging to or like an old woman.* Adv. **ănīlĭter.**

ănīlĭtās -ātis, f. *old age (of women).*

ănĭma -ae, f. *breath, wind, air.* Transf., *the breath of life, vital principle, soul;* animam edere, *to give up the ghost;* poet., *life-blood;* meton., *a living being;* sometimes = animus, *rational soul.*

ănĭmadversio -ōnis, f. *perception, observation, notice;* esp. *unfavourable notice; censure, blame, punishment.*

ănĭmadversor -ōris, m. *an observer.*

ănĭmadverto (**ănĭmadvorto**) -vertĕre -verti -versum *to turn or give the mind to.* Hence *to take notice of, attend to; to perceive, observe.* Esp. *to take notice of a fault, blame, censure, punish.*

ănĭmăl -ālis, n. *a living being, animal.*

ănĭmālis -e. (1) *consisting of air, airy.* (2) *living.*

ănĭmans -antis, *living;* as subst., *a living being, animal.*

ănĭmātio -ōnis, f. *animating;* hence, *a living being.*

ănĭmo -are. (1) (anima), *to animate, give life to.* (2) (animus), *to endow with a particular disposition.* Hence partic. **ănĭmātus** -a -um. (1) *having life, alive.* (2) *having a disposition, inclined, disposed;* esp. *having courage, spirited.*

ănĭmōsus -a -um. (1) (anima), *full of breath, airy.* (2) (animus), *full of spirit or courage.* Adv. **ănĭmōsē,** *courageously.*

ănĭmŭla -ae, f. *a little soul, little life.*

ănĭmus -i, m. *the spiritual or rational principle of life in man.* More specifically: (1) *the seat of feeling, the heart;* animi causa, *for pleasure;* loc. (or genit.) animi, *at heart.* (2)

character, disposition: as a trait of character (esp. in plur.) *courage, spirit, vivacity*; also *pride, arrogance*. (3) *the seat of the will, intention*: habeo in animo, *I am resolved*. (4) *the seat of thought, intellect, mind, memory, consciousness.*

Ănio -ēnis, and poet. **Ănĭēnus** -i, m. *the Anio, a tributary of the Tiber.*

Anna -ae, f., *sister of Dido*; Anna Perenna, *an Italian goddess.*

annālis -e *lasting a year, or relating to a year.* M. as subst., usually plur. **annālēs** -ium, *yearly records, annals.*

anniversārius -a -um, *recurring every year.*

annōna -ae, f. *yearly produce, crop*, esp. of grain; *the price of provisions* (esp. corn), *the cost of living.*

annōsus -a -um, *full of years, long-lived.*

annōtīnus -a -um, *a year old, belonging to last year.*

annus -i, m. *a circuit of the sun, year*; exeunte anno, *at the end of the year*; annos LXX natus, *seventy years old*; habere annos viginti, *to be twenty*; esp. *year of office, or of eligibility for office*; poet., *time of year, season.*

annŭus -a -um, *lasting for a year*; *returning every year, annual.* N. plur. as subst. *a salary, pension.*

anquiro -quirĕre -quisivi -quisitum, *to seek carefully, inquire after, investigate*; legal, *to set an inquiry on foot.*

ansa -ae, f. *a handle*; hence, *occasion, opportunity.*

ansātus -a -um, *with a handle*; homo, *a man with arms akimbo.*

anser -ĕris, m. *goose.*

Antaeus -i, m. *a giant killed by Hercules.*

ante. Adv., *before*, of place or time. Prep., *before*, of place or time; ante urbem conditam, *before the founding of the city*; of preference, *sooner than, above.*

antĕā, *before, formerly.*

antĕambŭlo -ōnis, m. *a footman to clear the way ahead.*

antĕcăpĭo -căpĕre -cēpi -ceptum, *to seize beforehand*; hence *to anticipate, not to wait for*; philosoph., antecepta informatio, *an innate idea.*

antĕcēdo -cēdĕre -cessi -cessum, *to go before, precede*, in space or time; *to excel* (with dat. or acc.). Hence partic. **antĕcēdens** -entis, *preceding, antecedent.*

antĕcello -ĕre, *to be outstanding, excel* (with dat. or acc.).

antĕcessĭo -ōnis, f. *a preceding or going before*; philosoph., *the antecedent cause.*

antĕcursor -ōris, m. *a forerunner*; in pl., *pioneers.*

antĕĕo -ire -ii *to go before*, in space or time; hence *to excel* (with dat. or acc.).

antĕfĕro -ferre -tŭli -lātum, *to carry before.* Transf., *to prefer*; *to anticipate, consider before.*

antĕfixus -a -um, *astened in front*; n. as subst. *ornaments fixed on roofs.*

antĕgrĕdior -grĕdi -gressus, dep. *to*

go before; philosoph., *of antecedent causes.*

antehăbĕo -ēre, *to prefer.*

antĕhāc, *before this time, formerly.*

antĕlūcānus -a -um, *happening before daybreak.*

antĕmērĭdĭānus -a -um, *before noon.*

antemitto -mittĕre -mīsi -missum, *to send before.*

antemna or **antenna** -ae, f. *a sail-yard.*

anteoccŭpātĭo -ōnis, f. *an exception.*

antĕpēs -pĕdis, m. *the forefoot.*

antĕpīlāni -orum, m. *front line soldiers* (i.e. *the* hastati *and* principes).

antĕpōno -pōnĕre -pōsŭi -pōsĭtum. *to place before, to prefer.*

antĕquam, conjunction, *before.*

antēs -ium, m. pl. *rows or ranks.*

antesignanus -i, m. usually plur., *soldiers chosen for a place in front of the standards*; hence, sing., *a leader.*

antesto (antisto) -stare -stĕti, *to stand before*; *to excel, surpass.*

antestor -ari, dep. legal, *to call as a witness.*

antĕvĕnio -vĕnire -vēni -ventum. *to come before, get the start of.* Transf., *to anticipate, prevent*; *to excel.*

antĕverto (-vorto) -vertĕre -verti -versum, *to come or go before, precede.* Transf., *to anticipate, prevent*; *to prefer.*

anticĭpātĭo -ōnis, f. *a preconception, innate idea.*

anticĭpo -are *to receive before, anticipate*; viam, *to travel over before.*

anticus -a -um, *forward, in front.*

antidea, antideo, antidhac; see antea, anteeo, antehac, of which they are old forms.

Antĭgŏnē -ēs, f. and **Antĭgŏna** -ae, f. *daughter of Oedipus, put to death for burying her brother.*

Antĭgŏnus -i, m., *name of several of the successors of Alexander the Great.*

Antĭochĭa or **Antĭŏchēa** -ae, f. *Antioch, name of several Asiatic towns.*

Antĭpăter -tri, m. *name of several kings of Macedonia.*

antīquārĭus -a -um *belonging to antiquity*; m. or f. as subst. *an antiquary.*

antīquĭtās -ātis, f. *antiquity, ancient times*; *the history of ancient times*; in plur., *the ancients.*

antīquĭtus v. antiquus.

antīquo -are, *to leave in its former state*; legem, *to reject a bill.*

antīquus -a -um, *coming before*; *previous, earlier*; absol., *old, ancient, primitive.* In compar. and superl., *preferred, more important.* M. pl. as subst. **antīqui** -orum, *the people of old time*, esp. *ancient authors.* Hence adv. **antīquē,** *in the ancient manner*; also **antīquĭtus,** *from of old or long ago.*

antistēs -stĭtis, c. *a presiding priest or priestess.*

antistĭta -ae, f., *a presiding priestess.*

antisto, v. antesto.

antĭthĕton -i, n. *antithesis, opposition.*

Antīum -i, n. *an old town of Latium on the sea-coast.*

antlīa -ae, f., *a pump.*

Antōnīnus -i, m. *name of several Roman emperors.*

Antōnīus -a -um, *the name of a Roman gens.*

antrum -i, n. *a cave, hollow.*

Ănūbis -bis or -bĭdis, m. *an Egyptian god.*

ānŭlārīus -a -um, *of a ring*: m. as subst. *a ring-maker.*

ānŭlus -i, m. *a ring*; anulus equestris, *the badge of knighthood at Rome.*

¹ānus -i, m. *the fundament.*

²ānus -ūs, f. *an old woman*; also used like adj., *old.*

anxĭětās -ātis, f., *anxiety, grief, anguish.*

anxĭfer -fěra -fěrum, *causing anxiety.*

anxĭtūdo -ĭnis, f. *anxiousness.*

anxĭus -a -um, *anxious, uneasy.* Transf., *causing anxiety.* Adv. **anxĭē.**

Anxŭr -ūris, n. *an old town of the Volsci.*

Ăōnes -um, *the Boeotians*; **Ăŏnia** -ae, f. *part of Boeotia, resort of the Muses*; hence **Ăŏnĭdēs** -um, f. *the Muses*; adj. **Ăŏnĭus** -a -um.

Ăornos -i, m., *the lake of Avernus.*

ăpăgĕ, interj. *away! be off!*

Ăpellēs -is, m., *a Greek painter, friend of Alexander the Great.* Adj. **Ăpellēus** -a -um.

ăper apri, m. *a wild boar.*

ăpĕrio ăpĕrire ăpĕrŭi ăpertum. (1) *to uncover, lay bare*; hence in gen. *to reveal.* (2) *to open what was shut, open up*; ludum, *to open a school*; annum, *to begin the year.*
    Hence partic. **ăpertus** -a -um. (1) *uncovered, clear, unconcealed, manifest*; of speech, *clear, intelligible, frank*; of character, *frank, straightforward, open.* (2) *unclosed, accessible, exposed.* N. as subst., *an open space.* Adv. **ăpertē**, *openly, frankly.*

ăpex -ĭcis, m. *the top*; esp. *the top of the conical cap of the Roman flamines, or the cap itself*; hence any *crown, tiara, helmet*; fig., *highest honour, crown*; gram., *the long mark over a vowel.*

aphractus -i, f. *a long undecked boat.*

ăpĭcātus -a -um, *wearing the priest's cap.*

ăpīnae -arum, f. pl. *trifles.*

ăpis or **ăpes** -is, f. *a bee.*

Ăpis -is, m., *Apis, the ox-god of the Egyptians.*

ăpiscor apisci aptus, dep., *to attain, come to, come by.*

ăpium -i, n. *parsley or celery.*

ăplustre -is, n. generally plur. aplustria -ĭum; and aplustra -orum, *the carved stern of a ship.*

ăpŏdȳtērĭum -i, n. *the undressing-room in a bath.*

Ăpollo -ĭnis, m. *Apollo, god of the sun, born at Delos*; ad Apollinis (sc. aedem), *to the temple of Apollo.* Adj. **Ăpollĭnāris** -e, and **Ăpollĭnēus** -a -um.

ăpŏlŏgus -i, m. *a narrative, fable.*

ăpŏphŏrēta -orum, n. *presents given to guests.*

ăpŏthēca -ae, f. *store-room.*

appărātē, adv. from apparo; q.v.

appărātĭo -ōnis, f. *preparation.*

appărātus -ūs, m.: abstr., *preparation, preparing*; concr., *provision, equipment, apparatus*, esp. on a pretentious scale; hence *splendour, magnificence, pomp, parade.*

appărĕo -ēre -ŭi -ĭtum, *to become visible, appear, be manifest*; apparet, *it is clear*; sometimes *to appear as a servant, to serve* (with dat.).

appārĭo -ēre, *to get, obtain.*

appărĭtĭo -ōnis, f. *waiting upon, serving*; meton., plur. *servants.*

appărĭtor -ōris, m. *a servant*; esp. *a public servant*, e.g. lictor.

appăro -are, *to prepare, get ready, provide.*
    Hence partic. **appărātus** -a -um, *prepared, well supplied or sumptuous.* Adv. **appărātē**, *sumptuously.*

appellātĭo -ōnis, f. *addressing, speech*; legal, *an appeal*; *a naming, name, title; pronunciation.*

appellātor -ōris, m. *an appellant.*

appellito -are, *to be accustomed to name.*

¹appello -are. (1) *to address, accost, speak to*; esp. *of asking favours, to approach, entreat, sue*; legal, *to appeal to.* (2) *to name, entitle*; hence, *to mention by name, make known.* (3) *to pronounce.*

²appello -pellěre -pŭli -pulsum, *to drive to, bring to, apply*; nautical, *to bring to land*; huc appelle, *put in here.*

appendix -ĭcis, f. *appendage, addition.*

appendo -penděre -pendi -pensum, *to weigh to, deal out by weight.*

Appennīnus -i, m. *the chain of the Appennines.*

appĕtentĭa -ae, f. and **appĕtītĭo** -ōnis, f. *desire, longing.*

appĕtītus -ūs, m. *longing, appetite*; plur., *the passions.*

appĕto -ēre -ivi or -ii -ītum, *to make for, grasp at, seek*; of places, *to make for or go to*; in hostile sense, *to attack*: intransit., of time, *to draw near.*
    Hence partic. **appĕtens** -entis, *eager, desirous, avaricious.* Adv. **appĕtenter**, *greedily.*

appingo -pingěre -pinxi -pictum, *to paint to, or upon*; *to write in addition.*

Appĭus -i, m., **Appĭa** -ae, f. *a Roman praenomen common in the gens Claudia*; as adj. **Appĭus** -a -um, *Appian*: via, *the Appian Way, a road from Rome to Capua, afterwards extended to Brundisium*; also adj. **Appĭānus** -a -um, *belonging to an Appius, Appian.*

applaudo -plauděre -plausi -plausum, *to strike upon, clap.*

applĭcātĭo -ōnis, f. *attachment, application.*

applĭco -are -avi -atum, and -ŭi -ĭtum, *to apply to, place to or near*; corpora corporibus, *to close up the ranks*; naut., *to lay a ship to or beside*;

absol., *to land.* Transf. in gen., *to attach, connect;* with reflex. *to attach oneself, devote oneself.* Perf. partic. pass. **applicātus** -a -um, *situated near, built near.*

applōro -are, *to lament, deplore.*

appōno -pōnĕre -pōsŭi -pōsĭtum, *to place near, put to;* esp. *to serve, put on table; to appoint a person, to add a thing;* appone lucro, *reckon as gain.* Hence partic. **appŏsĭtus** -a -um, *placed near, lying near; approaching, near to; fit appropriate, apposite;* adv. **appŏsĭtē,** *appropriately.*

apporrectus -a -um, *extended near.*

apporto -are, *to carry, bring to.*

apposco -ĕre, *to ask in addition.*

apprecor -ari, dep. *to worship, pray to.*

apprĕhendo -prehendĕre -prĕhendi -prehensum, and poet. **apprendo,** *to seize, lay hold of.*

apprimē, *above all, exceedingly.*

apprimo -primĕre -pressi -pressum, *to press to.*

approbatio -ōnis, f. *approval, assent;* in philosophy, *proof.*

approbātor -ōris, m. *one who approves or assents.*

approbo -are, *to approve of, assent to; to prove, establish; to make acceptable to another.*

apprōmitto -mittĕre -misi -missum, *to promise in addition.*

apprōpĕro -are, *to hasten, hasten on.*

apprŏpinquātio -ōnis, f. *approach.*

apprŏpinquo -are, *to approach, draw near.*

appugno -are, *to assault, fight against.*

Appulia v. Apulia.

appulsus -ūs, m. *a driving towards;* hence *approach, influence;* naut. *landing.*

aprīcātio -ōnis, f. *sun-bathing.*

apricor -ari, dep. *to sun oneself.*

aprīcus -a -um, adj. *open to the sun, sunny; loving the sun.*

Aprīlis -e *of April;* m. as subst. *the month of April.*

apto -are, *to fit, adapt, adjust; to make ready or fit.*

aptus -a -um. (1) as partic. *fitted, fastened, connected.* Transf., *depending on;* also *prepared, fitted out; fitted up with, equipped with,* with abl. (2) as adj. *suitable, appropriate, fitting.* Adv. **aptē.**

ăpŭd, prep. with acc. *at, near, by, with;* apud me, *at my house.* Of other relations; apud se, *in one's senses;* apud me valet, *it weighs with me;* apud patres *in our fathers' time;* apud Ciceronem, *in the works of Cicero.*

Ăpūlia or **Appūlia** -ae, f. *Apulia, a region in S. Italy.* Adj. **Ăpūlicus** and **Ăpūlus** -a -um.

ăqua -ae, f. *water;* aqua et ignis, *the necessaries of life;* aqua et igni interdicere homini, *to banish a person;* aquam terramque poscere, *to demand submission.* Esp. *the water of the sea, a lake, a river, or rain;* in

plur. *(medicinal) springs;* often *water in the water-clock.*

aquaeductus -ūs, m. *an aqueduct; the right of conveying water.*

ăquārius -a -um, *belonging to water;* m. as subst. *a water-carrier* or *an inspector of conduits.*

ăquāticus -a -um, *living in water,* or *full of water, watery.*

ăquātilis -e, *living in water.*

ăquātio -ōnis, f. *a fetching of water;* meton., *a watering-place.*

ăquātor -ōris, m. *a water-carrier.*

ăquila -ae, f. *an eagle;* milit., *an eagle as the standard of a Roman legion;* architect, *gable* or *pediment.*

ăquilifer -fĕri m. *an eagle-* or *standard-bearer.*

ăquilo -ōnis, m. *the north wind; the north.*

ăquilōnius -a -um, *northern.*

ăquilus -a -um, *dark-coloured, blackish.*

Ăquitānia -ae, f. *Aquitania, the south-west part of Gaul.* Adj. **Ăquitānus** -a -um.

ăquor -ari, dep. *to fetch water.*

ăquōsus -a -um, *full of water, watery.*

ăquŭla -ae, f. *a little water, small stream.*

āra -ae, f. *altar;* hence *refuge, protection;* arae, plur., *name of certain rocks at sea.*

Ărăbĭă -ae, f. *Arabia.* Adj. **Ărăbĭus** and **Ărăbĭcus** -a -um, *Arabian;* adj. and subst. **Ărabs** -ăbis and **Ărăbus** -a -um *Arabian, an Arabian.*

Ărachnē -ēs, f. *a Lydian maiden turned into a spider by Minerva.*

ărānĕa -ae, f. *a spider;* menton., *the spider's web.*

ărānĕŏla -ae, f. and **ărānĕŏlus** -i, m. *a little spider.*

ărānĕōsus -a -um, *full of cobwebs.*

¹ărānĕus -i, m. *a spider.*

²ărānĕus -a -um, *of a spider;* n. as subst. *a cobweb.*

ărātio -ōnis, f. *ploughing, agriculture;* meton., *a ploughed field.*

ărātor -ōris, m. *ploughman, husband-man.*

ărātrum -i, n. *plough.*

arbĭter -tri, m. *a witness, spectator;* legal, *an umpire, arbitrator;* hence *any judge, ruler, master.*

arbĭtra -ae, f. *a female witness.*

arbĭtrārius -a -um, *arbitrary, uncertain.*

arbĭtrātus -ūs, m. *will, choice, decision.*

arbĭtrĭum -i, n. (1) *the presence of witnesses.* (2) *the decision of an umpire;* hence *any decision, judgment, authority;* arbitrio suo, *under his own control.*

arbĭtro -are, and **arbĭtror** -ari, dep. (1) *to witness; to bear witness.* (2) *to arbitrate, judge, decide.*

arbŏr (arbōs) -ŏris, f. *a tree;* also any wooden object, such as an *oar, mast, ship;* arbor infelix, *the gallows.*

arbŏrĕus -a -um, *relating to trees; treelike.*

arbustus -a -um, *planted with trees.*

N. as subst. **arbustum** -i, *a plantation, vineyard planted with trees.*

arbŭtĕus -a -um, *of the arbutus.*

arbŭtum -i, n. *the fruit, leaves, etc., of
the wild strawberry or arbutus tree.*

arbŭtus -i, f. *the wild strawberry or
arbutus tree.*

arca -ae, f. *a chest, box; esp. a money-
box or coffin; also a cell.*

Arcădĭa -ae, f. *part of the Peloponnesus.*
adj. **Arcădĭus** and **Arcădĭcus** -a -um.

arcānus -a -um, *shut, closed; hence
silent, secret.* N. as subst. *a secret.*
Adv. **arcāno**, *secretly.*

Arcăs -ădis, m. adj. and subst.,
Arcadian, an Arcadian.

arcĕo -ēre -ŭi. (1) *to shut in.* (2) *to
keep at a distance, hinder, prevent, keep
away.*

accessĭtor -ōris, m. *a summoner.*

accessĭtū abl. sing. m. *at the summons
(of a person).*

arcesso (accerso) -ĕre -īvi -ītum, *to
fetch, call, summon; legal, to summon,
bring before a court of justice; in gen.,
to fetch, derive, obtain.*
Hence partic. **accessĭtus**, *strained,
far-fetched.*

archĕtўpus -a -um *original.*

Archĭās -ae, m., Aulus Licinius, *a
Greek poet defended by Cicero.*

archĭmăgĭrus -i, m. *head cook.*

Archĭmēdes -is, m. *a mathematician
and inventor, killed at the capture of
Syracuse (212 B.C.).*

archĭpīrāta -ae, m. *chief pirate.*

architectōn -ōnis, m. *master-builder.*

architector -ari, dep. *to build, devise.*

architectūra -ae, f. *architecture.*

architectus -i, m. *an architect, master-
builder, inventor, maker.*

archōn -ontis, m. *an archon, an Athenian
magistrate.*

arcĭtēnens -entis, *holding the bow.*

Arctŏs -i, f. *the Great and Little Bear;
hence the north.*

arctōus -a -um, *belonging to the Bear;
hence, northern.*

Arctūrus -i, m. *the brightest star of
Bootes.*

arcŭla -ae, f. *a casket.* Transf.,
rhetorical ornament.

arcŭo -are, *to bend or shape like a bow.*

arcus -ūs, m. *a bow, arch, arc; esp. the
rainbow.*

ardĕa -ae, f. *a heron.*

ardēlĭo -ōnis, m. *a busybody.*

ardĕo ardēre arsi, *to burn, glow, be on
fire; of bright objects, to gleam; of
feeling (esp. of love), to burn, smart;
of political disorder, to be ablaze.*
Hence partic. **ardens** -entis, *hot,
glowing, burning, fiery, eager;* adv.
ardenter.

ardesco -ĕre *to take fire; of bright
objects, to glitter; of passions, to
become inflamed; of strife, to blaze up.*

ardor -ōris, m. *flame, burning, heat; of
bright objects, gleam; of feelings
(esp. of love), heat, eagerness; meton.,
an object of love, loved one.*

ardŭus -a -um, *steep, towering, lofty.*

Transf., *difficult to undertake or
reach;* n. as subst., *difficulty.*

ārĕa -ae, f. *a level or open space, site,
court-yard, threshing floor; esp. a
playground;* hence, in gen., *play.
scope.*

ārĕfăcĭo -făcĕre -fēci -factum, *to make
dry.*

ārĕna = harena; q.v.

ārĕo -ēre, *to be dry;* partic. **ārens**
-entis, *dry, thirsty.*

Ārĕŏpăgus -i, m. *Mars' hill at Athens,
where a court sat.* Hence **Ārĕŏpăgītes**
-ae, m. *a member of the court.*

Ārēs -is, m. *the Greek god of war,
Latin Mars.*

āresco -ĕre *to become dry.*

ārĕtălŏgus -i, m. *a babbler about virtue.*

Ārĕthūsa -ae, f. *a fountain at Syracuse;
myth. a nymph chased by the river
Alpheus under the sea to Sicily.*

argentārĭus -a -um *relating to silver or
money; taberna, a banker's stall.*
M. as subst. *a money-changer, banker;*
f. as subst., *the office or trade of a
banker; also a silver mine.*

argentātus -a -um *ornamented with
silver.*

argentĕus -a -um, *of silver.* Transf.,
*ornamented with silver; of the colour
of silver; belonging to the Silver Age.*

argentum -i, n. *silver; esp. silver plate
or silver coin; hence, in gen., money.*

Argīlētum -i, n. *the booksellers' district
in Rome.*

argilla -ae, f. *white clay, potter's clay.*

Argō, Argūs, f. *the ship Argo.*

Argŏnautae -arum, m. pl. *the
Argonauts, the heroes who sailed in the
Argo.*

Argŏs, n. and **Argi** -orum, m. pl.
*Argos, capital of Argolis in the
Peloponnese.* Adj. **Argēus** and
Argīvus -a -um; plur. subst.
Argivi, m. *the Argives or Greeks.*
Hence f. subst. **Argŏlis** -ĭdis, *the
district Argolis;* adj. **Argŏlĭcus** -a
-um.

argūmentātĭo -ōnis, f. *the bringing
forward of a proof.*

argūmentor -ari, dep. *to bring forward
a proof, allege as a proof.*

argūmentum -i, n. *argument, proof;
subject, contents, matter.*

argŭo -ŭĕre -ŭi -ūtum, *to put in clear
light; to declare, prove; to accuse,
blame, expose, convict.*
Hence partic. **argūtus** -a -um: *to
the eye, expressive, lively; to the ear,
piercing, shrill, noisy; of omens,
clear, significant; of persons, sagacious,
cunning.* Adv. **argūtē**, *sagaciously.*

Argus -i, m. *the hundred-eyed guardian
of Io.*

argūtĭae -arum, f. pl. *liveliness, animation; of the mind, cleverness, sagacity,
cunning.*

argūtŭlus -a -um, *somewhat acute.*

Ărĭadna -ae and **Ărĭadnē** -ēs, f.
daughter of Minos of Crete.

ārĭdŭlus -a -um *somewhat dry.*

ārĭdus -a -um, adj. *dry, arid, thirsty;*

febris, *parching*; crura, *shrivelled*; of living conditions, *meagre*; intellectually *dry, jejune*; of character, *avaricious.* N. as subst., *dry ground.*

ăriēs -iĕtis, m. *a ram; a battering ram; a prop, beam.*

ăriĕto -are, *to butt like a ram.*

Ăriŏn -ŏnis, m. *a cithara player, saved from drowning by a dolphin.*

Ariovistus -i, m. *a Germanic prince.*

ărista -ae, f. *the beard of an ear of grain;* hence *the ear itself;* also *a harvest.*

Ăristŏphănēs -is, m. *the Athenian comic dramatist.* Adj. **Ăristŏphănĕus** -a -um.

Ăristŏtĕlēs -is and -i, m. *the Greek philosopher, pupil of Plato, founder of the Peripatetic school.* Adj. **Ăristŏtĕlēus** and **Ăristŏtĕlīus** -a -um.

ărithmĕtĭca -ae and -e -ēs, f.; also **ărithmĕtica** -orum, n. pl.; *arithmetic.*

arma -orum, n. pl. *defensive arms, armour, weapons of war;* hence *war; soldiers, military power; protection, defence;* in gen., *tools, equipment.*

armāmenta -orum, n. pl. *implements, tackle,* esp. of a ship.

armāmentārium -i, n. *an armoury.*

armārium -i, n. *a cupboard, chest.*

armātū, abl. sing. m. *with armour;* gravi armatu, *with heavy-armed troops.*

armātūra -ae, f. *equipment, armour;* meton., *armed soldiers.*

armentālis -e, *belonging to a herd.*

armentārius -i, m. *herdsman.*

armentum -i, n. *cattle for ploughing;* coll., *a herd.*

armĭfer -fĕra -fĕrum *bearing arms, warlike.*

armĭger -gĕra -gĕrum *bearing arms;* as subst., m. or f., *an armour-bearer.*

armilla -ae, f. *bracelet.*

armillātus -a -um *adorned with a bracelet.*

armĭpŏtens -entis *mighty in arms, warlike.*

armĭsŏnus -a -um *resounding with arms.*

armo -are, *to provide with arms, arm, equip, fit out.*

armus -i, m. *shoulder* or *shoulder-blade;* also, of an animal, *the side.*

Arnus -i, m. *chief river of Etruria (now Arno).*

ăro -are, *to plough, farm, cultivate.* Transf., *to furrow, wrinkle;* of ships, *to plough the sea.*

Arpīnum -i, n. *a Volscian hill-town, birthplace of Cicero;* adj. and subst. **Arpīnas** -atis; adj. **Arpīnus** -a -um.

arquātus -a -um, *relating to jaundice;* m. as subst., *a sufferer from jaundice.*

arr -; see also adr-.

arrha -ae, f. and **arrhăbo** -ōnis, m. *earnest money.*

ars -tis, f. (1) *skill, method, technique;* ex arte, *according to the rules of art.* (2) *an occupation, profession.* (3) *concrete,* in pl., *works of art.* (4) *con-*

duct, character, method of acting; bonae artes, *good qualities.*

Artaxerxēs -is, m. *name of several Persian kings.*

artēria -ae, f. *the wind-pipe; an artery.*

arthrītĭcus -a -um *gouty.*

artĭcŭlāris -e *of the joints;* morbus, *gout.*

artĭcŭlātim, *piecemeal, joint by joint, distinctly.*

artĭcŭlo -are, *to articulate, speak distinctly.*

artĭcŭlus -i, m.: in the body, *a small joint;* in plants, *a knob, knot;* of time, *a moment, crisis;* in gen., *a part, division, point.*

artĭfex -fĭcis, m. As adj.: act., *skilled, clever;* pass., *skilfully made.* As subst., *worker, craftsman, maker, creator, expert.*

artĭfĭcĭōsus -a- -um. *skilful, accomplished; skilfully made;* hence *artificial.* Adv. **artĭfĭcĭōsē,** *skilfully.*

artĭfĭcĭum -i, n. *occupation, craft, art;* also *the theory, system of an art;* concr., *work of art;* in gen., *cleverness, skill, cunning.*

arto -are *to press together, reduce, abridge.*

artŏlăgănus -i, m. *a cake made of meal, wine, milk, etc.*

artopta -ae, m. *a baker; a bread pan.*

¹artus (arctus) -a -um, *narrow, tight, close;* somnus, *fast, sound;* of supplies, *small, meagre;* of circumstances, *difficult, distressing.* N. as subst. *a narrow space;* in gen., *difficulty, constraint.* Adv. **artē,** *narrowly, tightly, closely;* dormire, *soundly, fast:* artius appellare. *to cut a name short.*

²artus -ūs, m. normally plur., *the joints;* dolor artuum, *gout:* poet., *limbs.*

ărŭla -ae, f. *a little altar.*

ărund-; see harund-.

Aruns, *an Etruscan name for a younger son.*

arvīna -ae, f. *fat, lard.*

arvus -a -um, *ploughed.* N. as subst. **arvum** -i, *ploughed land, a field;* in gen., *a region.*

arx -cis, f. *fortress, citadel, stronghold, height;* fig., *bulwark, protection, headquarters.*

as, assis, m. *a whole, a unit,* divided into 12 parts (unciae); heres ex asse, *sole heir;* as a small coin, *the as;* as a weight, *a pound.*

Ascănĭus -i, m. *son of Aeneas.*

ascendo -scendĕre -scendi -scensum *to mount, ascend, rise.*

ascensĭo -ōnis, f. *ascent;* oratorum *lofty flight.*

ascensus -ūs, m. *a going up, ascent;* meton., *a way up.*

ascia -ae, f. *a carpenter's axe; a mason's trowel.*

ascĭo -scire, *to take to oneself, adopt as one's own.*

ascisco asciscĕre ascivi ascitum, *to receive, admit;* of persons, *to adopt;* of things, *to take up, to approve.*

Hence partic. **ascītus** -a -um, *foreign, acquired.*

Ascra -ae, f. *town in Boeotia, home of Hesiod;* adj. **Ascraeus** -a -um.

ascribo -scribĕre -scripsi -scriptum: of things, *to write in, add in writing;* hence *to attribute, impute;* of persons, *to enrol, include, put on a list.*

ascriptīcius - . -um, *enrolled as member of a community.*

ascriptio -ōnis, f. *addition in writing.*

ascriptor -ōris, m. *one who approves.*

ăsella -ae, f. *she-ass.*

ăsellus -i, m. *ass.*

Āsia -ae, f. (1) *a town and district in Lydia.* (2) *the continent of Asia.* (3) *the peninsula of Asia Minor.* (4) *the Roman province of Asia, formed in* 133 B.C. Hence adj. **Asiānus, Asiāticus** and **Asius** -a -um; subst. **Asis** -ĭdis, f., poet., *Asia.*

ăsilus -i, m. *gad-fly.*

ăsina -ae, f. *she-ass.*

ăsinus -i, m. *ass.*

ăsōtus -i, m. *sensualist, libertine.*

aspărăgus -i, m. *asparagus.*

aspargo, v. aspergo.

aspectābilis -e, *visible.*

aspecto -are, *to look at earnestly, look towards, observe, attend to.*

aspectus -ūs, m.: act., *looking, sight, range* or *power of vision;* pass., *sight, power of being seen, look, aspect, appearance.*

aspello -ĕre, *to drive away.*

asper -ĕra -ĕrum, *rough, uneven;* to the taste, *pungent, sour;* to the hearing, *harsh, grating;* of weather, *rough, stormy;* of character or circumstances, *rough, wild, harsh, difficult, severe.* N. as subst. *roughness, a rough place.* Adv. **aspĕrē,** *roughly.*

¹**aspergo (aspargo)** -spergĕre -spersi -spersum, *to sprinkle upon* or *besprinkle with.*

²**aspergo (aspargo)** -ĭnis, f. *sprinkling, spray.*

aspĕrĭtās -ātis, f. *roughness, unevenness;* to the taste, *sourness;* to the ear, *harshness;* of character or circumstances, *harshness, fierceness, severity, difficulty.*

aspernātio -ōnis, f. *contempt.*

aspernor -ari, dep. *to despise, reject, spurn.*

aspĕro -are, *to make rough* or *sharp; to excite, arouse.*

aspersio -ōnis, f. *sprinkling.*

aspicio -spicĕre -spexi -spectum, *to look at, behold, survey, inspect, confront.* Transf., mentally, *to investigate, consider;* of places, *to look towards, face.*

aspīrātio -ōnis, f. *breathing, exhalation;* in speech, *pronunciation of the letter H, aspiration.*

aspīro -are: intransit., *to breathe, blow, exhale:* fig. *to be favourable, assist;* also *to climb up, reach towards a thing;* transit., *to blow air;* fig. *to infuse spirit,* etc.

aspis -ĭdis, f. *an adder, asp.*

asportātio -ōnis, f. *a taking away carrying off.*

asporto -are, *to carry off, take away.*

asprēta -orum, n. pl. *rough, uneven places.*

asser -ĕris, m. *a stake, pole.*

assŭla -ae, f. *a shaving, chip.*

assus -a -um *dried, roasted;* n. pl. as subst. *a sweating bath.*

ast = at; q. v.

ast -; see also adst -.

astrŏlŏgia -ae, f. *astronomy.*

astrŏlŏgus -i, m. *an astronomer* or *astrologer.*

astrum -i, n. *a star,* or *constellation.* Transf., esp. plur., *the heights, glory, immortality.*

astu, n. *a city,* esp. *Athens.*

astus -ūs, m. *cleverness, cunning.*

astūtia -ae, f. *adroitness, craft;* in pl. *tricks.*

astūtus -a -um, *adroit, clever, crafty;* adv. **astūtē.**

āsylum -i, n. *a sanctuary, place of refuge.*

ăsymbŏlus -a -um, *contributing nothing to the cost of an entertainment.*

at (ast), *but, yet, moreover;* sometimes introducing an imaginary objection, *but, you may say.*

ătăt, attat, attatae, attattatae, etc. interj. *oh! ah! alas!*

ătăvus -i, m. *a great-great-great-grandfather;* in gen., *an ancestor.*

Ătella -ae, f. *a city in Campania;* adj. **Ătellānus** -a -um; f. as subst. (sc. fabella) *a kind of popular farce;* m. as subst., *a player in these farces;* adj. **Ātellānius** or **Ătellānĭcus** -a -um, *of Atellane farces.*

āter atra atrum, *dead black, dark;* poet. *clothed in black.* Transf., *dark, gloomy, sad; malicious, poisonous.*

Ăthēnae -arum, f. pl. *Athens;* meton., *leaning.* Adj. **Ăthēnaeus** -a -um, *Athenian;* adj. and subst. **Ăthēnĭensis** -e, *Athenian, an Athenian.*

ătheos and **ăthĕus** -i, m. *an atheist.*

athlēta -ae, m. *wrestler, athlete.*

athlēticus -a -um, *relating to an athlete;* adv. **athlētĭcē,** *athletically.*

Atlās -antis, m. (1) *a mountain in Mauretania.* (2) *a mythical king and giant, changed into Mount Atlas.* Hence **Atlantĭădes** -ae, m. *a male descendant of Atlas;* **Atlantis** -ĭdis, f. *a female descendant of Atlas;* adj. **Atlanticus, Atlantĕus** -a -um.

ătŏmus -i, f. *an atom.*

atque and **ac,** *and, and also, and indeed* In comparisons: of similarity, with such words as aequus or idem, *as;* of difference, with such words as alius or secus, *than, from.*

atquī, *nevertheless, but in fact;* sometimes confirmatory, *indeed, certainly.*

ătrāmentum -i, n. *black fluid,* such as *ink* or *shoemaker's black.*

ătrātus -a -um, *clothed in black, in mourning.*

Atreus -ei, m. *son of Pelops, father of*

Agamemnon and Menelaus. Hence **Atrĭdēs** or **Atrīda** -ae, m. *a son of Atreus.*

ātriensis -is, m. *head slave, steward.*

ātrĭŏlum -i, n. *a little atrium, an antechamber.*

ātrĭum -i, n. *the hall* or *entrance room in a Roman house temple* or *public building.*

atrōcĭtās -ātis, f. *frightfulness, cruelty, harshness, barbarity.*

Atrŏpŏs -i, f. *one of the three Parcae* or *Fates.*

atrox -ŏcis, *terrible cruel, horrible;* of human character, *harsh, fierce, severe.* Adv. **atrōcĭtĕr.**

attactū abl. sing. m., *by touch, by contact.*

attāgēn -ēnis, m. and **attāgēna** -ae, f. *the black partridge.*

Attălus -i, m. *name of several kings of Pergamum:* adj. **Attălĭcus** -a -um.

attāmen or **at tămen**, *but yet.*

attempĕro -are *to fit, adjust to;* adv. from partic., **attempĕrātē**, *appropriately.*

attendo -tendĕre -tendi -tentum, *to stretch to;* usually with animum (animos) or absol., *to direct the attention towards, attend to.*
  Hence partic. **attentus**, *attentive, careful:* adv. **attentē.**

attentĭo -ōnis, f. *attentiveness, attention.*

attento or **attempto** -are, *to try, test, essay; to tamper with, try to corrupt,* or *to attack.*

attĕnŭo -are, *to make thin, reduce, weaken.*
  Hence partic. **attĕnŭātus**, *made weak;* of style, *abbreviated, overrefined,* or *unadorned;* adv. **attĕnŭātē**, *simply, without ornament.*

attĕro -tĕrĕre -trīvi (-tĕrŭi) -trītum, *to rub against, rub away;* in gen., *to weaken, ruin.*
  Hence partic. **attrītus** -a -um, *rubbed away, worn out;* fig., *frons, shameless.*

attestor -ari, dep. *to attest, bear witness to.*

attexo -texĕre -texŭi -textum, *to weave* or *plait on* or *to;* hence, in gen., *to add.*

Atthis -ĭdis, f. adj., *Attic, Athenian.*

Attĭca -ae, f. *Attica, the district of Greece containing Athens.*

¹**Attĭcus** -a -um, *belonging to Attica* or *Athens, Attic, Athenian;* adv. **Attĭcē**, *in the Attic* or *Athenian manner.*

²**Attĭcus**, T. Pomponius, *the friend of Cicero.*

attĭnĕo -tĭnēre -tĭnŭi -tentum: transit., *to hold, keep, detain;* intransit., *to pertain to,* or *concern,* only in third person: quod ad me attinet, *as far as I am concerned;* nihil attinet, *it is pointless.*

attingo -tingĕre -tĭgi -tactum, *to touch, to reach;* of places, *to border upon;* of enemies, *to attack, to strike.* Transf., *to handle, manage, be concerned* or *connected with;* of feelings,

to affect a person; in writing or speech, *to touch upon, to mention.*

attollo -tollĕre, *to raise, lift up.* Transf., *to elevate, excite, exalt.*

attondĕo -tondēre -tondi -tonsum, *to cut, clip, prune;* in gen., *to diminish.*

attŏno -tŏnare -tŏnŭi -tŏnĭtum, *to strike with thunder, stun.*
  Hence partic. **attŏnĭtus** -a -urn, *struck by thunder; stunned, senseless; inspired, frantic.*

attorquĕo -ēre, *to whirl, swing upward.*

attrăho -trăhĕre -traxi -tractum, *to draw, drag, attract.*

attrecto -are, *to touch, handle, lay hands on.*

attrĭbŭo -ŭĕre -ŭi -ūtum, *to allot, assign, hand over.* Transf., in gen., *to give, ascribe, add;* of taxes, *to impose.* N. of partic. as subst. **attrĭbūtum** -i, *a predicate, attribute.*

attrĭbūtĭo -ōnis, f. *the assignment of a debt;* rhet. *an attribute.*

attrītus -a -um, partic. from attero; q.v.

au, interj., *oh!*

auceps -cŭpis, m. *a fowler, bird-catcher; a spy, eavesdropper,* or *caviller.*

auctĭficus -a -um, *increasing.*

auctĭo -ōnis, f. *an increasing;* hence, *from the bidding, an auction.*

auctĭōnārĭus -a -um, *relating to an auction.*

auctĭōnor -ari, dep. *to hold an auction.*

auctĭto -are and **aucto** -are, *to increase very much.*

auctŏr -ōris, m. *one that gives increase.* Hence (1) *an originator, causer, doer; founder* of a family; *architect* of a building; *author* of a book; *originator* of or *leader* in an enterprise; *source* of or *warrant for* a piece of information. (2) *a backer, supporter, approver, surety.*

auctōrāmentum -i, n. *a contract; wages.*

auctōrĭtās -ātis, f. (1) *support, backing, lead, warrant* ; polit., *sanction* (esp. of the senate). (2) *power conferred, rights, command; legal title.* (3) in gen., *influence, authority, prestige;* meton., *an influential person.*

auctŏro -are, *to bind* or *hire for money.*

auctumnus = autumnus; q.v.

auctus -ūs, m. *increase, enlargement, growth.*

aucŭpātĭo -ōnis, f. *fowling, bird-catching.*

aucŭpĭum -i, n. *bird-catching, fowling;* hence, in gen., *hunting, watching, eavesdropping;* aucupia verborum, *cavilling, quibbling.*

aucŭpor -ari, dep. *to catch birds;* in gen., *to watch out for, lie in wait for.*

audācĭa -ae, f. *courage, daring;* in bad sense, *audacity, impudence, temerity;* in plur., *audacious deeds.*

audax -ācis, *bold* (in good or bad sense); adv. **audactĕr** or **audācĭtĕr.**

audentĭa -ae, f. *boldness, courage.*

audĕo audēre ausus sum, *to be daring to dare, venture, bring oneself to.*

Hence partic. **audens** -entis, *daring, bold*; compar. adv. **audentius**.

audientia -ae, f. *hearing, attention*.

audio -ire, *to hear, listen; to learn a thing by hearing*; sometimes *to listen to and believe* (or *obey*); rarely *to be called*; bene audire, *to be well spoken of*. Hence partic. **audiens** -entis, as adj., *obedient*; as subst., *a hearer*.

auditio -ōnis, f. *hearing, listening*; concr., *hearsay report*.

auditor -ōris, m. *a hearer, auditor, scholar*.

auditōrium -i, n. *a place of audience, lecture-room, court of justice, etc.*

auditus -ūs, m. *hearing, sense of hearing*; concr., *a report*.

aufero auferre abstŭli ablātum, *to carry away, remove*: in bad sense, *to make away with, carry off, steal*.

Aufidus -i, m. *a river in Apulia*.

aufugio fŭgĕre -fŭgi, *to flee, escape*.

augeo augēre auxi auctum, *to enlarge, increase*; of rivers, in pass., *to be swollen*; in speech, *to extol, set forth*; with abl., *to enrich with, furnish with*; in transit. (rare), *to grow*. Hence partic. **auctus** -a -um, *increased, enriched*.

augesco -ĕre, *to increase, begin to grow*.

augmen -ĭnis, n. *increase, growth*.

augur -ŭris, c. *augur, soothsayer, seer*.

augŭrālis -e, *relating to an augur or augury*; n. as subst. **augŭrāle** -is, *part of the Roman camp, where auspices were taken*.

augŭrātio -ōnis, f. *divining, soothsaying*.

augŭrātus -ūs, m. *the office of augur*.

augŭrium -i, n., *the office and work of an augur, observation and interpretation of omens, augury*; in gen., *an omen, prophecy, presentiment*.

augŭrius -a -um, *relating to an augur*.

augŭro -are, *to act as an augur, take auguries*; locus auguratur, *the place is consecrated by auguries*; in gen., *to have a foreboding or presentiment*.

augŭror -ari, dep. *to act as an augur, foretell by auguries*; hence, in gen., *to foretell or to guess*.

Augusta -ae, f. *a name for any female elative of the Roman emperor, or town named after him*.

Augustālis -e, *belonging to or in honour of the Emperor Augustus*.

¹**augustus** -a -um, *consecrated, holy; majestic, dignified*. Adv. **augustē**, *reverently*.

²**Augustus** -i, m. *a name assumed by all Roman emperors*.

³**Augustus** -a -um, *relating to Augustus*; mensis, *August*.

aula -ae, f. *fore-court, court-yard*; poet = atrium, *an inner court*. Transf., *a palace, royal court*; meton., *courtiers*.

aula = olla; q.v.

aulaeum -i, n. usually plur., *embroidered work, tapestry curtains* (esp. of a theatre).

aulicus -a -um, *of the court, princely*.

auloedus -i, m. *one who sings to the flute*.

aura -ae, *air, esp. air breathed or blowing, breath, wind*; poet., esp. plur., *upper air, heaven*; superas ad auras, *to the light of day*; ferre sub auras, *to make known*; poet. (rarely), *smell, glitter or echo*.

aurārius -a -um, *golden, of gold*; f. as subst., *a gold-mine*.

aurātus -a -um, *golden or adorned with gold*.

Aurēlius -a -um, *name of a Roman plebeian gens*.

aureŏlus -a -um, *golden, glittering, splendid*.

aureus -a -um, *golden, made of gold or adorned with gold*; poet., *of the colour of gold*, and, in gen., *excellent, beautiful*.

aurichalchum = orichalchum; q.v.

auricŏmus -a -um, *with golden hair or leaves*.

auricŭla -ae, f. *the lobe of the ear*; in gen., *the ear*.

aurifer -fĕra -fĕrum, *gold-bearing, gold-producing*.

aurifex -fĭcis, m. *a goldsmith*.

auriga -ae, c. *charioteer, driver*; of a ship, *helmsman*; as a constellation *the Waggoner*.

auriger -gĕra -gĕrum, *gold-bearing*.

aurigo -are, *to drive a chariot*.

auris -is, f. *the ear*; hence *hearing*; of a plough, *the earth- or mould-board*.

auritus -a -um, *long-eared*; hence *attentive*.

aurōra -ae, f. *dawn, break of day*; personified, *Aurora, goddess of morning*; meton., *the east*.

aurum -i, n. *gold; anything made of gold, gold plate, coin, a cup, ring, etc.*; *the golden age*.

Aurunca -ae, f. *a town in Campania*.

auscultātor -ōris, m. *a listener*.

ausculto -are, *to hear attentively, listen to*; sometimes also *to obey*; of servants, *to attend, wait*.

ausim, as subjunctive of audeo; q.v.

Ausōnia -ae, f. *Ausonia, Lower Italy*, and in gen., *Italy*; adj. **Ausōnius** -a -um.

auspex -ĭcis, c. *one who watches birds and divines from them*; esp. *an official witness of marriage contracts*: poet., in gen., *a leader*.

auspicium -i, n. *divination by means of birds, the taking of or right to take auspices*. Transf., *any omen or sign*; poet. *leadership, guidance*.

auspico -are, *to take the auspices*. Hence partic. **auspicātus** -a -um, *consecrated by auguries*; as adj., *favourable, auspicious*. Abl. abs. **auspicāto**, *after taking auspices*; hence *in a fortunate hour*.

auspicor -ari, dep., *to take the auspices*; hence *to begin favourably*.

auster -stri, m. *the south wind*; meton. *the south*.

austērĭtās -ātis, f., *harshness, strictness, severity*.

austērus -a -um, *sour, harsh, strict, severe, gloomy.* Adv. **austērē.**

austrālis -e, *southern.*

austrīnus -a -um, *southern.*

ausum -i, n. *a daring deed, undertaking.*

aut, *or, or else*; repeated, aut . . . aut . . ., *either . . . or . . .*

autem, *but, on the other hand, however, moreover, now.*

authepsa -ae, f. *a cooking-stove.*

Autŏmĕdōn -ontis, m. *charioteer of Achilles.*

autumnālis -e, *autumnal.*

¹autumnus -i, m. *autumn.*

²autumnus -a -um, adj., *autumnal.*

autŭmo -are, *to say, assert.*

auxiliāris -e, *giving help, assisting*: m. pl. as subst., *auxiliary or allied troops.*

auxiliārius -a -um, *helping*; milites, *auxiliary troops.*

auxiliātŏr -ōris, m. *a helper.*

auxiliātus -ūs, m. *help, assistance.*

auxilior -ari, dep., *to help, assist, support.*

auxilium -i, n. *help, aid, assistance*; milit., often plur., *auxiliary troops, or in gen., military power.*

ăvāritia -ae and **ăvārītiēs** -ēi f. *avarice, covetousness.*

ăvārus -a -um, *covetous, greedy*; adv. **ăvārē** and **ăvārĭtēr.**

ăvĕho -vĕhĕre -vexi -vectum, *to carry off, bear away*; pass., *to ride or sail off.*

ăvello -vellĕre -velli and -vulsi (-volsi) -vulsum (-volsum), *to tear away, pluck away* (esp. with violence).

ăvēna -ae, f. *oats or wild oats*; hence *oaten pipe, shepherd's pipe*; in gen., *any stalk, straw.*

Aventīnum -i, n. and **Aventīnus** -i, m. *the Aventine, one of the seven hills of Rome.*

¹ăvĕo -ēre, *to long for, desire.*

²ăvĕo (hăvĕo) -ēre, *to be well*; found only in imperat. and infin.; ave, *hail!* or *farewell!*

Avernus -i, m. *a lake near Puteoli, said to be an entrance to the infernal regions*; meton., *the infernal regions*; adj **Avernus** -a -um, **Avernālis** -e.

ăverrunco -are, *to turn away, avert.*

ăversābilis, *from which one must turn away, horrible.*

¹āversor -ari, dep. *to turn away* (in shame, disgust, etc.); with acc., *to turn away from, avoid, shun.*

²āversŏr -ōris, m. *an embezzler.*

averto (avorto) -vertĕre -verti (-vorti) -versum (-vorsum), *to turn away, remove*: flumina, *to divert*; of feelings, *to estrange*; of property, *to carry off, appropriate embezzle*; poet., intransit., *to retire.*
Hence partic. **āversus** -a -um, *turned away, backward, behind*; of feeling, *disinclined, unfavourable, hostile.*

ăvia -ae. f. *a grandmother.*

ăviārium -i, *an aviary*; also *the haunts of wild birds.*

ăvidĭtās -ātis, f. *desire, longing*; esp. *desire for money, avarice.*

ăvidus -a -um, *desiring, longing for*; esp. *greedy for money, avaricious*; adv. **ăvidē.**

ăvis -is, f. *a bird*; often *a bird of omen, and in gen., an omen.*

ăvītus -a -um, *of a grandfather, ancestral.*

ăvīus -a -um: of places, *out of the way, untrodden*; of persons, *wandering, astray, lost.*

ăvŏcātio -ōnis, f. *a calling away, diversion.*

ăvŏco -are, *to call away, or off, to withdraw, remove, divert.*

ăvŏlo -are, *to fly away, hasten away.*

ăvunculus -i, m. *a mother's brother, uncle.*

ăvus -i, m. *a grandfather*; poet., in gen., *an ancestor.*

axis (or assis) -is, m. *an axle.* Hence (1) *a wheel*; meton., *a chariot, waggon.* (2) *the axis of the earth*; meton. *the north pole or the heavens*; sub axe, *in the open air.* (3) *a board, plank.*

B

B, b, *the second letter of the Latin Alphabet.*

băbae or **păpae**, interj. *wonderful!*

Băbȳlōn -ōnis, f. *a city on the Euphrates*; **Băbȳlōnia** -ae, f. *Babylonia, between the Euphrates and the Tigris*; adj. **Băbȳlōnicus** and **Băbȳlōnius** -a -um.

băca (bacca) -ae, f. *a berry, fruit*; *a pearl.*

băcātus -a -um, *set with pearls.*

baccar (bacchar) -āris, n. and **baccaris** -is, f. *a plant*, perhaps *sowbread.*

Baccha -ae, f. *a Bacchante, female worshipper of Bacchus.*

Bacchānal -is, n. *the place where Bacchus was worshipped*; plur. **Bacchānālia** -ium, *the (Greek) festival of Dionysus or Bacchus.*

bacchātio -ōnis, f. *revelling in Bacchanalian fashion.*

bacchor -ari, dep. *to celebrate the festival of Bacchus*: as passive, of places, *to be made the scene of Bacchic revels*; in gen., *to rage, rave like a Bacchante.* Partic. **bacchantes** = Bacchae; see Baccha.

Bacchus -i, m. *the god of wine*: meton., *the vine., or wine, or the Bacchic cry* (Io Bacche). Adj. **Bacchēus, Bacchicus,** and **Bacchius** -a -um.

bacifer -fĕra -fĕrum, *bearing berries.*

băcillum -i, n. *a little staff*; esp. *the lictor's staff.*

băculum -i, n. and **băculus** -i, m. *a staff, walking-stick.*

Baetis -is, m. *a river in Spain*; adj. **Baeticus** -a -um, *relating to the Baetis*; f. subst. **Baetica** -ae, f. *the*

Roman province of Baetica on the Baetis.

Baiae -arum, f. pl. *a holiday-resort on the coast of Campania*; adj. **Baiānus** -a -um.

bāiŭlo -are, *to carry a burden.*

bāiŭlus -i, m. *a porter.*

bālaena -ae, f. *a whale.*

bālǎnus -i, f. rarely m. *an acorn, bennut, chestnut or date.*

bālatro -ōnis, m. *buffoon, jester.*

bālātus -ūs, m. *the bleating of sheep or goats.*

balbus -a -um, *stammering*; adv. **balbē.**

balbūtio -ire, *to stammer, stutter*; hence in gen., *to speak obscurely.*

Bāliāres (Bāleāres) -ium, f. pl. *the Balearic Islands*; adj. **Bāliāris** -e, **Bāliāricus** -a -um.

bālǐnĕum or balnĕum -i, n. esp. in pl.; also heteroclite pl. **bālǐnĕae or balnĕae** -arum; *a bath, bathing place.*

ballista -ae, f. *a military engine for throwing large stones.*

balnĕae, v. balineum.

balnĕārius -a -um, *belonging to the bath*; n. pl. as subst. *baths, bathing-rooms.*

balnĕātor -ōris, m. *the keeper of a bath.*

balnĕŏlum -i, n. *a little bathroom.*

balnĕum, v. balineum.

bālo -are, *to bleat.*

balsāmum -i, n. *the balsam-tree, or its gum.*

baltĕus -i, m. and **baltĕum** -i, n. *a girdle.*

bărathrum -i, n. *a pit, abyss*; esp. *of the lower world.*

barba -ae, f. *beard;* promittere barbam, *to let the beard grow.*

barbăria -ae and **barbărĭēs,** f. *a foreign country, as opposed to Greece and Rome; want of culture, rudeness, savagery.*

barbārǐcus -a -um, *foreign, i.e., not Greek or Roman.*

barbărus -a -um, *foreign, strange; uncultivated, rough, savage;* as subst., *a foreigner.* Adv. **barbārē,** *like a foreigner; roughly, barbarously.*

barbātŭlus -a -um, *with a slight beard.*

barbātus -a -um, *bearded.*

barbĭger -gĕra -gĕrum, *wearing a beard.*

barbĭtōs, m. and f. *a lyre.*

barbŭla -ae, f. *a little beard.*

bardŏcŭcullus -i, m. *a Gallic overcoat.*

bardus -a -um, *stupid, slow, dull.*

bāris -idos, f. *an Egyptian barge.*

barītus (barrītus) -ūs, m. *a German war-cry.*

bāro -ōnis, m. *a blockhead, simpleton.*

barrus -i, m. *elephant.*

bascauda -ae, f. *a basket.*

bāsiātio -ōnis, f. *kissing, a kiss.*

bāsǐātor -ōris, m. *a kisser.*

bāsĭlǐcus -a -um, *royal, kingly, princely.* M. as subst., *the best cast of the dice;* n. as subst., *a royal robe;* f. as subst., **bāsĭlǐca** -ae, *a basilica, a building with double colonnades, where merchants met and courts were held.* Adv. **bāsǐlǐcē,** *royally.*

bāsǐo -are, *to kiss.*

bāsis -is and **ĕos,** f. *a pedestal, base;* villae, *foundation-wall; trianguli, base.*

bāsǐum -i, n. *a kiss.*

Bassāreus -ei, m. *a name of Bacchus.*

bătillum (or vătillum) -i, n. *a chafing-dish or shovel.*

battŭo (bātŭo) -ĕre, *to beat, knock.*

baubor -ari, dep., *to bark gently.*

bĕātĭtās -ātis, f. and **bĕātĭtūdo** -īnis, f. *happiness, blessedness.*

bĕātus -a -um, partic. from beo; q.v.

Belgae -arum, m. *the Belgae, a warlike people in the north of Gaul.*

bellāria -orum, n. pl. *dessert.*

bellātor -ōris, m. and **bellatrix** -īcis, f., *a warrior;* as adj. *warlike, courageous.*

bellātōrius -a -um, *warlike.*

bellǐcōsus -a -um, *warlike.*

bellǐcus -a -um, *of war, warlike.* N. as subst. **bellicum** -i, *the signal for march or attack.*

belliger -gĕra -gĕrum, *waging war, warlike.*

bellǐgĕro -are, *to wage war.*

bellĭpŏtens -entis, *mighty in war.*

bello -are and **bellor** -ari, dep. *to wage war, fight.*

Bellōna -ae, f. *the goddess of war.*

bellŭa, v. belua.

bellŭlus -a -um, *pretty, elegant.*

bellum -i, n. (old form, **duellum**), *war, fighting;* in bello, or loc., belli, *in time of war.*

bellus -a -um, colloq., *pretty, handsome;* adv. **bellē.**

bēlŭa -ae, f. *a beast, large animal;* as a term of reproach, *monster, brute, beast.*

bēlŭōsus -a -um, *full of monsters.*

Bēlus -i, m. *a king, founder of Babylon.* Hence f. pl. subst., **Bēlĭdes** -um, *the granddaughters of Belus, the Danaides.*

bĕnĕ, adv.; comp. **mĕlĭus;** superl. **optĭmē;** *well, rightly, properly;* bene rem gerere, *to succeed;* with adj. or adv., *thoroughly, very;* as an exclamation, *good, excellent;* bene facis, *I am obliged to you;* bene facta (or **benefacta**), *good deeds, benefits.*

bĕnĕfǐcentia -ae, f. *kindness.*

bĕnĕfǐcĭārius -a -um, *of a favour;* m. pl. as subst., *privileged soldiers.*

bĕnĕfǐcĭum -i, n. *a kindness, favour, service;* in political life, *favour, distinction, promotion, also privilege, exemption.*

bĕnĕfǐcus -a -um, comp. -entior, superl. -entissimus, f. *kind, generous, obliging.*

Bĕnĕventum -i, n. *a town in Samnium.*

bĕnĕvŏlens -entis, *well-wishing, obliging.*

bĕnĕvŏlentia -ae, f. *good-will, kindness.*

bĕnĕvŏlus -a -um, *kind, obliging, well disposed;* adv. **bĕnĕvŏlē.**

bĕnignĭtās -ātis, f. *kindness, generosity.*

bĕnignus -a -um, *kind, friendly, generous;* of things, *abundant, fruitful.* Adv. **bĕnignē,** *kindly, generously;* colloq., benigne dicis, or benigne, *much obliged (accepting or refusing an offer).*

běo -are, *to bless, enrich, make happy.*
  Hence partic. **běātus** -a -um,
  happy, blessed, prosperous; well off;
  n. as subst. *happiness.* Adv. **běātē,**
  happily.

běryllus -i, c. *a beryl.*

běs bessis, m. *two-thirds.*

bestia -ae, f. *an animal without reason,
  a brute, beast.*

bestiārius -a -um, *belonging to animals;*
  m. as subst., *one who fought with wild
  beasts at the public shows.*

bestĭŏla -ae, f. *a small animal.*

¹**běta** -ae, f. *a vegetable, beet.*

²**běta**, n. indecl. *beta, the second letter in
  the Greek alphabet.*

bibliŏpŏla -ae, m. *a book-seller.*

bibliŏthēca -ae, f. and **bibliŏthēcē** -es,
  f. *a collection of books, library.*

bibo bibĕre bibi bibitum, *to drink, drink
  in.*

Bibracte -is, n. *a town in Gaul.*

bĭbŭlus -a -um, *fond of drinking,
  thirsty;* charta, *blotting paper.*

biceps -cĭpĭtis, *two-headed.*

bĭcŏlor -ōris, *of two colours.*

bĭcorniger -gĕri, m. *two-horned.*

bĭcornis -e, *two-horned, two-pronged;*
  luna, *the new moon;* Rhenus, *with
  two mouths.*

bĭcorpor -ōris, *having two bodies.*

bĭdens -entis, *having two teeth.* As
  subst.: m., *a hoe with two crooked
  teeth;* f., *a sheep.*

bĭdental -ālis, n. *a sacred enclosure.*

bĭdŭum -i, n. *a space of two days;*
  abl., biduo, *in the course of two days.*

biennium -i, n. *a space of two years.*

bĭfăriam, *in two parts.*

bĭfer -fĕra -fĕrum, *of a tree, bearing
  fruit twice a year.*

bĭfĭdus -a -um, *split into two parts.*

bĭfŏris -e, *having two doors or openings.*

bĭformātus -a -um and **bĭformis** -e, *of
  double form.*

bĭfrons -frontis, *with double forehead or
  countenance.*

bĭfurcus -a -um, *having two prongs or
  forks.*

bīgae -arum, f. pl. (and sing. **bīga**
  -ae) *a pair of horses, or a chariot
  drawn by a pair.*

bīgātus -a -um, *stamped with the
  effigy of a pair of horses;* m. as subst.,
  a silver coin so marked.

bĭiŭgis -e and **bĭiŭgus** -a -um,
  yoked two together; m. pl. as subst.,
  *a pair of horses or a chariot drawn by
  a pair.*

bĭlibra -ae, f. *two pounds weight.*

bĭlibris -e, *weighing or containing two
  pounds.*

bĭlinguis -e, *having two tongues, or
  speaking two languages;* hence *double-
  tongued, treacherous.*

bīlis -is, f. *gall, bile, anger, displeasure;*
  atra (*or* nigra) bilis, *black bile,* i.e.
  melancholy, madness.

bĭlix -īcis, *having a double thread.*

bĭlustris -e, *lasting ten years.*

bĭmāris -e, *lying on two seas.*

bĭmārĭtus, m. *the husband of two wives.*

bĭmāter -tris, *having two mothers.*

bĭmembris -e, *having two kinds of
  limbs;* m. pl. as subst., *Centaurs.*

bĭmestris -e, *lasting two months:* porcus,
  a pig two months old.

bīmŭlus -a -um, *two years old.*

bīmus -a -um, *two years old or lasting
  two years.*

bīni -ae, -a, *twofold.* Hence *two
  apiece,* sometimes simply *two;* of
  things that match, *a pair;* findi in
  bina, *to be cleft in twain;* bis bina,
  twice two.

bĭnoctium -i, n. *a space of two nights.*

bĭnōminis -e, *having two names.*

bĭpalmis -e, *two palms or spans long
  or broad.*

bĭpartitus *or* **bĭpertitus** -a -um,
  divided in two; abl. as adv., bipartito
  or bipertito, *in two parts, in two
  ways.*

bĭpătens -entis, *doubly open, open in
  two directions.*

bĭpĕdālis -e, *two feet long, broad,
  thick or high.*

bĭpennifer -fĕra -fĕrum, *armed with a
  two-edged axe.*

bĭpennis -e, *having two wings or edges;*
  f. as subst., *a double-edged axe.*

bĭpēs -ēdis, *having two feet;* as subst.
  biped.

birēmis -e, *two-oared;* f. as subst.,
  *a boat with two oars or a ship with two
  banks of oars.*

bis, *twice.*

Bistōnes -um, m. *a Thracian people;*
  adj. **Bistōnius** -a -um, *Bistonian or
  Thracian.*

bĭsulcus -a -um, *split into two parts,
  forked.*

Bĭthȳnia -ae, f. *a country in north-west
  Asia.Minor.*

bito -ĕre, *to go.*

bĭtūmen -ĭnis, n. *asphalt, bitumen.*

bĭtūminĕus -a -um, *bituminous.*

bĭvius -a -um, *having two ways or
  passages;* n. as subst. **bivium,** *a
  place where two roads meet.*

blaesus -a -um, *lisping, indistinct.*

blandimentum -i, n. *flattery, allurement.*

blandior -iri, dep. *to flatter, caress,
  coax,* with dat.
  Hence partic. **blanditus** -a -um,
  charming.

blanditia -ae, f. *flattery, allurement,
  attraction, charm.*

blandus -a -um, adj. *flattering, caressing,
  alluring, tempting.* Adv. **blandē** and
  blanditĕr, *flatteringly.*

blătĕro -are, *to chatter, babble.*

blatta -ae, f. *a cockroach.*

bŏārius and **bŏvārius** -a -um, *relating
  to cattle.*

Boeōti -orum *or* -um, and **Boeōtii,** m.
  *the inhabitants of Boeotia, a district in
  Greece to the west of Attica.*

Bŏii -orum, m. pl. *a Celtic people of
  north Italy, Germany and Gaul.*

bōlētus -i, m. *a mushroom.*

bŏlus -i, m. *a throw;* hence *the haul
  or catch of a fishing net.*

bombus -i, m. *a boom, deep hollow noise.*

bombȳcĭnus -a -um, *silken.*

bombyx -ỹcis, m. and f. *the silkworm,* or *silk.*

bŏnĭtās -ātis, f. *goodness, excellence;* esp. *moral goodness, kindness, integrity.*

bŏnus -a -um; compar. **mělĭor** -ius; superl. **optĭmus** -a -um; *good:* in gen., *good of its kind;* nummi boni, *genuine coin;* bona aetas, *youth;* bona verba, *words of good omen;* bona pars, *a good* (i.e. *considerable) proportion;* in a particular respect of tools, workmen, etc. *useful, efficient;* morally *good, virtuous, honest, kind;* polit., *patriotic, loyal.* N. as subst. **bŏnum** -i, *good;* in gen., *profit, advantage;* bonum publicum, *the common weal;* cui bono fuisset, *for whose advantage;* materially, usually pl., *goods, property;* morally, *the good:* summum bonum, *the supreme good.*

bŏo -are, *to shout, roar, echo.*

Bŏŏtēs -ae, m. *a constellation in the northern hemisphere.*

Bŏrĕās -ae, m. *the north wind;* meton., *the north.* Adj. **Bŏrĕus** -a -um, *northern.*

bōs, bŏvis, c. (1) *ox, bullock, cow;* bos Lucas, *elephant.* (2) *a kind of flat fish.*

Bospŏrus (Bosphŏrus), -i, m. *name of various straits,* esp. *those between Thrace and Asia Minor.*

bŏtŭlus -i, m. *a sausage.*

bŏvĭle = bubile, q.v.

Bŏvĭllae -ārum, f. pl. *a town in Latium.*

bŏvillus -a -um, *relating to oxen.*

brābeuta -ae, m. *a judge, umpire.*

brācae (braccae) -arum, f. pl. *breeches, trousers.*

brācātus (braccātus) -a -um, *wearing breeches;* Gallia Bracata, *Gaul on the north side of the Alps.*

brācchĭum -i, n. *the forearm, arm from elbow to wrist;* *any limb of a living creature;* *any other thing like an arm,* e.g. *branch, spur, yard, outwork of a fortification, mole.*

bractĕa (brattĕa) -ae, f. *a thin plate of metal; gold leaf.*

brassĭca -ae, f. *cabbage.*

brĕvĭārĭum -i, n. *a summary, epitome.*

brĕvĭlŏquens -entis, *brief in speech.*

brĕvĭlŏquentĭa -ae f. *brevity of speech.*

brĕvis -e, *short,* in space or time; of water, *shallow;* of living things, conditions, etc., *short-lived;* of style, *concise;* n. abl. **brĕvĭ,** *shortly, soon, briefly;* n. pl. as subst. **brĕvĭa** -ium, *shallows, shoals.* Adv. **brĕvĭtĕr,** *shortly, briefly.*

brĕvĭtās ātis, f. *shortness,* in space or time; of style, *brevity, conciseness.*

Brĭārĕus -ei, m. *a giant with a hundred arms.*

Brĭtanni -orum, m. pl. *the Britons;* **Brĭtannĭa** -ae, f. *Britain;* adj. **Brĭtannĭcus** -a -um, *British;* m. sing. as a title commemorating *successes in Britain.*

Brŏmĭus -i, m. *a surname of Bacchus.*

brūma -ae, f. *the winter solstice;* in gen., *winter, wintry cold.*

brūmālis -e, *relating to the shortest day;* in gen., *wintry.*

Brundĭsĭum -i, n. *a seaport in Calabria;* adj. **Brundĭsīnus** -a -um.

Bruttĭi (Brūtĭi, Brittĭi) -orum, m. *the inhabitants of the southern extremity of Italy.*

¹brūtus -a -um, *heavy, immoveable; dull, without feeling or reason.*

²Brūtus -i, m. *a cognomen of the Roman Gens Iunia.*

bŭbĭle -is, n. *an ox-stall.*

bŭbo -ōnis, m., *the owl.*

bŭbulcus -i m. *one who ploughs with oxen.*

bŭbŭlus -a -um, *relating to cows or oxen;* f. as subst. (sc. caro), *beef.*

bucca -ae, f. *the cheek,* esp. *when puffed out.* Transf., *a declaimer, bawler; a parasite; a mouthful.*

buccĭna, buccĭnātor, etc.; v. bucina, etc.

buccŭla -ae, f. *a small cheek;* of a helmet, *beaver, visor.*

būcĕrus and **būcĕrĭus** -a -um, *having ox's horns.*

būcĭna -ae, f. *a crooked trumpet or horn.*

būcĭnātor -ōris, m. *a trumpeter.*

būcŏlica -orum, n. pl. *pastoral poems.*

būcŭla -ae, f. *a heifer.*

būfo -ōnis, m. *a toad.*

bulbus -i, m. *an onion.*

būleutērĭon -i, n. *the place of meeting of a Greek council.*

bulla -ae, f. *a round swelling;* in water, *a bubble;* on furniture or equipment, *a boss, stud;* bulla aurea, *a golden ornament, an amulet.*

bullātus -a -um. (1) *inflated, bombastic,* or perhaps *transitory.* (2) *wearing the bulla* (q.v.).

būmastus -i, m. *a kind of vine.*

būris -is, m. *the crooked hinder part of the plough.*

bustŭārĭus -a -um, *belonging to the place where corpses were burned.*

bustum -i, n. *the place where corpses were burned and buried; hence grave, sepulchre.*

buxĭfer -fĕra -fĕrum, *producing the box-tree.*

buxus -i, f. and **buxum** -i, n. *the evergreen box-tree; box-wood;* an *article made of box-wood.*

Byzantĭum -i, n. *Byzantium, a Greek city on the Bosphorus.*

C

C, c, *the third letter of the Latin Alphabet.*

căballus -i, m. *pack-horse, nag, hack.*

căchinnātĭo -ōnis, f. *violent laughter.*

¹căchinno -are, *to laugh aloud.*

²căchinno -ōnis, m. *jester, scoffer.*

căchinnus -i m. *loud laughter.*

căcŏēthēs -is, n. *an obstinate disease.*

căcūmen -ĭnis, n. *the extreme point, top, tip, zenith.*

căcūmĭno -are, *to point, make pointed.*

cădāver -ĕris, n. *dead body, carcass.*

cădāvĕrōsus -a -um, *corpse-like.*

Cadmus -i, m. *the founder of Thebes;* adj. **Cadmēus** -a -um, *Theban.*

cădo cădĕre cĕcidi, *to fall, sink, drop;* vela cadunt, *are furled;* iuxta solem cadentem, *in the west;* of living beings, often *to fall in death, die;* hence *to be destroyed, to subside, sink, flag, fail;* cadere animis, *to lose heart;* with in or sub, *to come under, be subject to;* with in, *to agree with, be consistent with;* of events, *to fall out, happen;* of payments, *to fall due.*

cădūcĕātor -ōris, m. *herald.*

cădūcĕus -i, m. and **cădūcĕum** -i, n. *a herald's staff.*

cădūcifer -fĕra -fĕrum, *bearing the caduceus* (of Mercury).

cădūcus -a -um. (1) *fallen or falling.* (2) *inclined or ready to fall;* esp. *destined to die, devoted to death;* in gen., *frail, perishable, transitory.*

cădus -i, m. *jar or urn.*

caecigĕnus -a -um, *born blind.*

Caecilius -a -um, *name of a plebeian gens.*

cuecĭtās -ātis, f. *blindness.*

caeco -are, *to make blind or dark.*

Caecŭbum -i, n. and **Caecŭbus ager**, *a marshy district in Latium, famous for its wine;* (vinum) Caecubum, *Caecuban wine.*

caecus -a -um: act., *blind, not seeing;* *intellectually or morally blind; uncertain, objectless;* pass., *unseen, hidden, obscure, dark.*

caedēs -is, f. *cutting down, killing, slaughter.* Transf., *persons slain; blood shed in slaughter.*

caedo caedĕre cĕcidi caesum. (1) *to cut.* (2) *to beat, knock about.* (3) *to kill, slay.*

caelāmen -ĭnis, n. *bas-relief.*

caelātor -ōris, m. *chaser, graver, carver.*

caelātūra -ae, f. *the art of engraving or chasing; an engraving.*

caelebs -lĭbis, *unmarried, single* (of men); of trees, *to which no vine is trained.*

caelĕs -ĭtis, *heavenly;* as subst., *a dweller in heaven, god.*

caelestis -e, *belonging to heaven, coming from heaven;* n. pl. as subst. *things in heaven, heavenly bodies.* Transf., *belonging to the gods, celestial, divine, superhuman;* as subst., esp. plur., *the gods.*

caelĭcŏla -ae, *dwelling in heaven;* as subst. *a god.*

caelifer -fĕra -fĕrum, *bearing the heavens.*

Caelius -a -um, *name of a Roman plebeian gens;* Caelius Mons, *a hill in Rome.*

caelo -are, *to engrave or chase, to carve in bas-relief, to fashion.*

¹caelum -i, n. *the burin or engraving tool.*

²caelum -i, n. *the heavens, sky, air, climate.* Esp. *heaven as the home of the gods;* fig., *heaven as the height of joy, renown, etc.*

caementum -i, n. *rough stone from the quarry.*

caenōsus -a -um, *muddy.*

caenum -i, n. *mud, dirt, filth.*

caepa (cēpa) -ae, f. and **caepe** (cēpe) -is, n. *onion.*

Caerē, n. *a very old city of Etruria;* adj. **Caerēs** -ĭtis and -ētis.

caerĭmōnia -ae, f. *holiness, sanctity; holy awe, reverence; religious usage, sacred ceremony.*

caerŭlĕus (poet. also **caerŭlus**) -a -um, *blue, dark blue* (esp. of the sea or sky).

Caesar -ăris, m. *a Roman family name of the gens Iulia;* esp. of C. Iulius Caesar, *the general and dictator, and later of all the emperors.*

caesărĭēs -ēi, f. *hair, a head of hair.*

caesim, *with cutting;* fig. of style, *in short sentences.*

caesius -a -um, *bluish grey* (esp. of eyes).

caespĕs (cespĕs) -ĭtis, m. *a turf, sod.* Transf., *a hut or altar of turf.*

caestus -ūs, m. *gauntlet for boxers.*

caetra (cetra) -ae, f. *short Spanish shield.*

caetrātus -a -um, *armed with the caetra.*

Caius = Gaius; q.v.

Călăbrĭa -ae, f. *the peninsula at the south-east extremity of Italy;* adj. and subst. **Călăber** -bra -brum, *Calabrian, a Calabrian.*

călămister -tri, m. and **călămistrum** -tri, n. *a curling-iron for the hair.* Transf., *excessive ornament or flourish in style.*

călămistrātus -a -um, *curled with the curling-iron.*

călămĭtās -ātis, f. *loss, failure, misfortune, damage, a reverse.*

călămĭtōsus -a -um: act., *causing loss, destructive;* pass., *suffering loss, miserable.* Adv. **călămĭtōsē**, *disastrously.*

călămus -i, m. *reed;* hence *anything made of reed, e.g. a pen, a reed pipe, an arrow.*

călăthiscus -i, m. *a small wicker basket.*

călăthus -i, m. *a wicker basket;* and of other containers, e.g. *a milk-pail, wine-bowl.*

călător -ōris, m. *attendant.*

calcar -āris, n. *spur.*

calcĕāmentum -ī, n. *covering for the foot.*

calcĕo -are, *to shoe, provide with shoes.*

calcĕus -i, m. *shoe.*

calcitro -are, *to kick; to resist obstinately.*

calco -are, *to tread, trample on.*

calcŭlus -i, m. *a little stone, pebble.* Esp. *a piece used in the Roman game of draughts; a voting pebble; a counter for reckoning;* hence *a calculation.*

caldus = calidus; q.v.

Călēdōnia -ae, f. *the highlands of Scotland;* adj. **Călēdōnius** -a -um,

călĕfăcio (calfăcio) -făcĕre -fēci -factum, pass. călĕfīo, etc., *to make warm, heat; to disturb, excite.*

călĕfacto -are, *to make warm, heat.*

Cālendae = Kalendae; q.v.

cālĕo -ēre -ŭi, *to be warm, to glow*; of feeling, etc. *to be inflamed, aroused, excited.*

cālesco -ĕre, *to become warm, grow hot.*

cālĭdus (caldus) -a -um, *warm, hot; fiery, passionate.* F. sing. as subst., **cālĭda (calda)** -ae, *warm water*; n. sing. **cālĭdum** -i, *warm wine and water.*

cāliendrum -i, n. *a lady's wig.*

cālĭga -ae, f. *a stout shoe or boot* (esp. a soldier's).

cālĭgātus -a -um, *wearing heavy boots*; m. as subst., *a private soldier.*

cālĭgĭnōsus -a -um, *foggy, misty, dark.*

¹**cālīgo** -ĭnis, f. *fog, mist, darkness.* Transf., *mental darkness, dullness; calamity, affliction, gloom.*

²**cālīgo** -are: transit., *to spread a dark mist around, to make dizzy*; intransit., *to be dark, misty.*

Cālĭgŭla -ae, m. *a little soldier's shoe; nickname given by the soldiers to the emperor Gaius.*

călix -ĭcis, m. *a drinking or cooking vessel.*

callĕo -ēre, *to be thick-skinned.* Transf.: intransit., *to be practised, experienced*; transit., *to know by experience, understand.*

callĭdĭtas -ātis, f. *expertness, cleverness*; in bad sense, *cunning, craft, artifice.*

callĭdus -a -um, *experienced, clever, dexterous, skilful*; in bad sense, *cunning, subtle, sly.* Adv. **callĭdē.**

Calliŏpē -ēs and **Calliŏpēa** -ae, f. *Calliope, the Muse of epic poetry.*

callis -is, m. or f. *narrow track, footpath, cattle track.*

callōsus -a -um, *hard-skinned, solid.*

callum -i, n. *hard skin or flesh; toughness, insensibility.*

¹**cālo (kălo)** -are, *to call, summon.*

²**cālo** -ōnis, m. *a soldier's servant*; in gen., *a drudge.*

cālor -ōris, m. *warmth, heat, glow; passion, excitement.*

Calpurnĭus -a -um, *name of a Roman plebeian gens.*

caltha -ae, f. *a plant, prob. marigold.*

călumnĭa -ae, f. *trick, artifice, chicanery, craft*; at law, *a false accusation,* or *an action for false accusation.*

călumnĭātor -ōris, m. *a false accuser, pettifogger.*

călumnĭor -ari, dep. *to accuse falsely, misrepresent*; in gen., *to practise trickery.*

calva -ae, f. *the bald scalp of the head.*

calvĭtĭēs -ēi, f. and **calvĭtĭum** -i, n. *baldness.*

calvus -a -um, *bald, without hair.*

¹**calx** -cis, f. *the heel.*

²**calx** -cis, f. rarely m. *a stone, pebble*; collectively, *lime; chalk*; meton., *a goal* (marked with chalk), *an end.*

Călypsŏ -ūs, *a nymph who entertained Ulysses.*

cămella -ae, f. *a goblet.*

cămēlus -i, m. and f. *a camel or dromedary.*

Cămēna -ae, f. usually pl., *Latin goddesses of poetry,* identified with the Greek *Muses.*

cămĕra (cămăra) -ae, f. *a vaulted chamber, vault; a flat covered boat.*

Cămillus -i, m. *cognomen of several members of the gens Furia.*

cămīnus -i, m. *a forge, fire-place, fire.*

cammărus -i, m. *a crustacean,* perhaps *crayfish.*

Campānĭa -ae, f. *a district of Central Italy.*

campester -tris -tre: in gen., *on level ground, flat*; esp. *relating to the Campus Martius and its exercises and elections.* N. sing. as subst., *a loin-cloth worn by wrestlers*; n. pl. as subst., *a plain.*

campus -i, m. *a level space, plain, field*; esp. *of the Campus Martius at Rome, as a place for various exercises, and for meetings of the comitia.* Transf., *any free space, field,* or *theatre of action; any level surface*; poet., *the sea.*

Camulŏdūnum -i n. *a town in Britain* (now *Colchester*).

cămŭr -a -um, *hooked, curved.*

cănālis -is. m. *waterpipe, channel canal.*

cancelli -orum, m. pl. *lattice, railing, grating.* Transf., *bounds, limits.*

cancer -cri, m. *crab; a sign of the Zodiac*; meton., *the south,* or *summer heat; the disease cancer.*

candēla -ae, f. *a wax or tallow candle, taper; a cord coated with wax.*

candēlābrum -i, n. *a candle-stick.*

candĕo -ēre -ŭi, *to shine, white, glitter or glow with heat.*

candesco -ĕre -ŭi, *to begin to shine or glow.*

candĭdātōrĭus -a -um, *relating to a candidate.*

candĭdātus -a -um, *clothed in white*; as subst. *a candidate for office.*

candĭdŭlus -a -um, *shining, dazzling.*

candĭdus -a -um, *shining white*; of persons, with the suggestion of beauty, *fair.* Transf., of time or fortune, *happy*; of writing, *clear, lucid*; of character, *honest, straight-forward*; of dress, *clothed in white*; **sententia candida,** *a vote for acquittal.* N. as subst. **candĭdum** -i, *white colour.* Adv. **candĭdē,** *in white; clearly candidly.*

candor -ōris, m. *shining whiteness, lustre*; of character, *sincerity, candour*; of writing, *clarity, simplicity.*

cănĕo -ēre -ŭi, *to be white,* or *hoary.*

cănesco -ĕre, *to become white or hoary*; hence *to become old.*

cănĭcŭla -ae, f. *little bitch*; sometimes a term of abuse. Transf., *Dog-star, Sirius; the worst throw at dice.*

cănīnus -a -um, *of a dog, canine.* Transf., *snarling, spiteful*; **littera,** *the letter R.*

cănis -is, c. *dog, hound*; of persons, as a term of abuse; in dice, *the worst throw.*

cănistra -orum, n. pl. *baskets.*

cānĭtĭēs, acc. -em. *whitish-grey colour,* esp. of the hair; meton., *grey hair, old age.*

canna -ae, f. *reed.* Transf., *a reed-pipe; a small boat.*

cannăbis -is, and **cannăbum** -i, n. *hemp.*

Cannae -arum, f. pl. *town in Apulia, where Hannibal defeated the Romans* (216 B.C.). Adj. **Cannensis** -e.

căno cănĕre cĕcĭni cantum, *to sing or play.* Intransit. *to sing;* of cocks, *to crow;* of frogs, *to croak;* also (with abl.), *to play on an instrument;* canere receptui, *to sound the signal for retreat;* of instruments, *to sound.* Transit.: (1) *to sing with the voice.* (2) *to sing of, celebrate in song.* (3) *to sound or play an instrument.* (4) *to prophesy.*

cănor -ōris, m. *melody, song, sound.*

cănōrus -a -um, *melodious, harmonious, sweet-sounding;* n. as subst., *harmonious sound.*

Cantăbrĭa -ae, f. *a region in north-west Spain.*

cantāmen -ĭnis, n. *incantation.*

canthăris -ĭdis, f. *a beetle:* esp. *the Spanish fly.*

canthărus -i, m. *a tankard; a sea-fish, the black bream.*

canthērĭus -i, m. *a gelding, nag.*

canthus -i, m. *the tire of a wheel.*

cantĭcum -i, n. *a scene in Roman comedy, accompanied by music and dancing; a song; sing-song delivery in an orator.*

cantĭlēna -ae, f. *an old song, twaddle, chatter.*

cantĭo -ōnis, f. *a song; an incantation, enchantment.*

cantĭto -are, *to sing or play often.*

Cantĭum -i, n. *a district in Britain* (now Kent).

cantĭuncŭla -ae, f. *a flattering song.*

canto -are -avi -atum, *to sing or play.* Intransit., of persons, *to sing;* of cocks, *to crow;* also *to play on an instrument;* of instruments, *to sound.* Transit. (1) *to sing.* (2) *to sing of, celebrate, continually mention.* (3) *to predict.*

cantor -ōris, m. *a singer, poet, musician; an actor.*

cantus -ūs, m. *song, melody music, poetry; prophecy; incantation.*

cānus -a -um, *whitish-grey;* hence *aged;* m. pl. as subst., *grey hair.*

căpācĭtās -ātis, f. *breadth, capacity.*

căpax -ācis, *able to hold, broad, wide, roomy.* Transf., *receptive, able to grasp, capable, fit for.*

căpēdo -ĭnis, f. *a bowl used in sacrifices.*

căpella -ae, f. *a she-goat; a star in the constellation Auriga.*

Căpēna -ae, f. *a town in Etruria;* adj. **Căpēnus** -a -um; porta Capena, *a gate in Rome at the beginning of the Via Appia.*

căper -ri, m. *he-goat.*

căpesso -ĕre -ivi and -ii -ītum, *to seize, grasp eagerly;* of places, *to strive to reach, to make for;* of

business, etc., *to take up, undertake;* rempublicam *to enter public life.*

căpillātus -a -um, *hairy, having hair.*

căpillus -i, m. *a hair;* usually pl., or collect. sing., *the hair of the head or beard.*

căpĭo căpĕre cēpi captum, *to take.* (1) in gen. *to take, seize;* of places, *to choose, reach,* or *take possession of;* of business, opportunities, etc. *to take up, take in hand, adopt;* of persons, *to choose.* (2) *to catch, take in a violent or hostile manner;* hence, *to attack, injure;* pass. capi, *to be injured or diseased;* oculis et auribus captus, *blind and deaf;* also *to charm, captivate, take in;* at law, *to convict.* (3) *to receive,* esp. of money; in gen., *to suffer, undergo, take on.* (4) *to take in, hold, contain, keep in;* mentally, *to grasp, comprehend.*

căpis -ĭdis, f. *a one-handled vessel.*

căpistro -are, *to fasten with a halter.*

căpistrum -i, n. *a halter.*

căpĭtālis -e, *relating to the head,* or *to life.* Transf., *deadly, mortal; first, chief, distinguished.* N. as subst. căpital and căpitāle, *a capital crime.*

căpĭto -onis, m. *a man with a large head.*

Căpĭtōlĭum -i, n. *the temple of Jupiter at Rome, the Capitol;* adj. **Căpĭtōlīnus** -a -um; m. pl. as subst., *superintendents of games in honour of Jupiter Capitolinus.*

căpĭtŭlum -i, n. *a little head.*

Cappădŏcĭa -ae, f. *a district in Asia Minor.*

capra -ae, f. *a she-goat;* also *a star in the constellation Auriga.*

caprĕa -ae, f. *a roe.*

Caprĕae -arum, f. *small island off the Campanian coast* (now Capri).

caprĕŏlus -i, m. *a roebuck;* in plur., *props, supports.*

Caprĭcornus -i, m. *Capricorn, a sign of the Zodiac.*

caprĭfĭcus -i, f. *the wild fig-tree,* and *its fruit.*

caprĭgĕnus -a -um, *born of goats.*

caprĭmulgus -i, m. *goat-milker*—i.e. *a countryman.*

caprīnus -a -um, *relating to a goat.*

caprĭpēs -pĕdis, *goat-footed.*

capsa -ae, f. *a box or case,* esp. *for books.*

capsārĭus -i, m. *a slave who carried his young master's satchel.*

capsŭla -ae, f. *a little chest.*

captātĭo -ōnis, f. *an eager seizing;* verborum, *quibbling.*

captātor -ōris, m. *one who eagerly seizes;* esp. *a legacy-hunter.*

captĭo -ōnis, f. (1) *a cheat, deception.* (2) *harm, loss.* (3) *a fallacy, sophism.*

captĭōsus -a -um, *deceitful; captious;* n. pl. as subst. *sophistries.* Adv. captĭōsē.

captĭuncŭla -ae, f. *fallacy, quibble.*

captīvĭtās -ātis, f. *captivity, capture;* collectively, *a number of captives.*

captīvus -a -um, *captured, taken,* esp. *in war.* Transf., *of a prisoner.*

M. and f. as subst., *a prisoner, captive.*

capto -are, *to seize, catch at*; in gen., *to strive after, desire, seek.*

captus -ūs, m. *catching, taking*; hence *power or manner of comprehension, idea.*

Capŭa -ae, f. *chief town of Campania.*

căpŭlus -i, m. (1) *a coffin.* (2) *a handle*; esp. *the hilt of a sword.*

căput -ĭtis, n. *the head*; meton., *a living individual*, esp. of human beings, *a person*; also of a person's life, existence, esp., in Rome, *a man's political and social rights.* Transf., of lifeless things, *the top, summit, extremity*; of rivers, etc., *the source*; of persons and things, *the head, leader, chief, headquarters, chief point*; of places, *the capital.*

carbāsĕus -a -um, *made of canvas.*

carbāsus -i, f.; heteroclite pl. **carbăsa** -orum, n.; *flax*; meton., *anything made of flax*, e.g. *garments, curtains, sails.*

carbo -ōnis, m. *burning or burnt wood.*

carbōnārīus -i, m. *a charcoal burner.*

carcer -ēris, m. *prison, cell*; in plur., **carceres**, *the starting-place of a race-course.*

carchēsīum -i, n. *a goblet with handles.* Transf., *the top of a mast, scuttle.*

cardĭăcus -a -um, *pertaining to the stomach*; m. as subst., *one who suffers from a disease of the stomach.*

cardo -ĭnis, m. *a hinge*; *any pole or pivot*: cardo duplex, *the ends of the earth's axis; a cardinal point, main consideration.*

cardŭus -i, m. *thistle.*

cărectum -i, n. *a sedgy spot.*

cărĕo -ēre -ŭi, *to be without* (with abl) *of a place, to absent oneself from.*

cărex -icis, f. *rush, sedge.*

cărĭēs, acc. -em. abl. -e, f. *rottenness, decay.*

cărīna -ae, f. *the keel of a ship*; meton., *a ship, vessel.*

cărĭōsus -a -um, *rotten, decayed.*

căris -ĭdis, f. *a kind of crab.*

cărĭtās -ātis, f. *dearness, high price*; esp. *high cost of living.* Transf., *affection, love, esteem.*

carmen -ĭnis, n. *a song, tune, vocal or instrumental*; *a poem, poetry, verse; a prediction; an incantation; a religious or legal formula.*

Carmentis -is, and **Carmenta** -ae, f. *a prophetess, mother of Evander*; adj. **Carmentālis** -e.

carnĭfex -fĭcis, m. *an executioner, hangman.*

carnĭfĭcīna -ae, f. *the work of a hang-man; execution, torture.*

carnĭfĭco -are, *to behead, or mangle.*

¹**cāro** -ēre, *to card.*

²**cāro** carnis, f. *flesh.*

carpentum -i, n. *a two-wheeled carriage.*

carpo carpĕre carpsi carptum, *to pluck, pull off, select, choose out*; and so *to enjoy*; of animals, *to graze.* Transf., *to proceed on a journey; to pass over a place; to carp at, slander a person;*

to weaken, annoy, harass an enemy; to break up, separate, divide forces.

carptim, *in pieces, in small parts; in different places; at different times.*

carptor -ōris, m. *one who carves food.*

carrūca -ae, f. *a four-wheeled carriage.*

carrus -i, m. *a four-wheeled baggage-waggon.*

Carthāgo (Karthāgo) -ĭnis, f. (1) *the city of Carthage in N. Africa.* (2) Carthago (Nova), *a colony of the Carthaginians in Spain* (now Cartagena). Adj. **Carthāginiensis** -e.

căruncŭla -ae, f. *a small piece of flesh.*

cārus -a -um, adj. *high-priced, dear costly.* Transf., *dear, beloved.*

căsa -ae, f. *hut, cottage, cabin.*

căsĕŏlus -i, m. *a little cheese.*

căsĕus -i, m. *cheese.*

căsia -ae, f. (1) *a tree with an aromatic bark, like cinnamon.* (2) *the sweet-smelling mezereon.*

Cassandra -ae, f. *a prophetess, daughter of Priam.*

cassēs -ĭum, m. pl. *a net; a trap :nare; also a spider's web.*

cassĭda -ae, f. = cassis; q.v.

Cassĭŏpē -ēs, f. *mother of Andromeda.*

cassĭs -ĭdis and **cassĭda** -ae, f. *a metal helmet.*

Cassĭus -a -um, *name of a Roman* gens; adj. **Cassĭānus** -a -um.

cassus -a -um, *empty, hollow*; with abl., *devoid of.* Transf., *worthless, useless, vain*; **in cassum** or **in-cassum** as adv., *in vain.*

Castālĭa -ae, f. *a spring on Mount Parnassus, sacred to Apollo and the Muses.*

castănĕa -ae f. *a chestnut or chestnut-tree.*

castellānus -a -um, *relating to a fort-ress*; m. pl. as subst., *the garrison of a fortress.*

castellātim, *in single fortresses.*

castellum -i, n. *a castle, fortress, fort; a shelter, refuge.*

castigātĭo -ōnis, f. *punishment, reproof.*

castigātor -ōris, m. *one who reproves or corrects.*

castigo -are, *to reprove, chasten, punish; to check, restrain.* Hence partic. **castigātus** -a -um, *restrained, orderly, neat.*

castimōnĭa -ae, f. *purity.*

castĭtās -ātis, f. *chastity.*

¹**castor** -ōris, m. *the beaver.*

²**Castor** -ōris, m. *twin-brother of Pollux.* Hence **ecastor** and **mecastor**, *By Castor!*

castŏrĕum -i, n. *an aromatic secretion obtained from the beaver.*

castrensis -e, *pertaining to a camp.*

castro -are, *to castrate, enervate, weaken.*

castrum -i, n.: sing., *a castle, fort, fortress*; plur. **castra** -orum, *a camp, encampment*; aestiva, *summer quarters;* hiberna, *winter quarters.* Transf.: *a day's march; martial service; a party, faction.*

castus -a -um, *clean, pure, chaste; with reference to religion, pious,* *religious, holy.* Adv. **castē,** *purely piously, religiously.*

căsŭla -ae, f. *a little hut, cottage.*

căsus -ūs, m. *a falling, fall.* Transf.: (1) *what befalls, an accident, event, occurrence.* (2) *occasion, opportunity.* (3) *destruction, downfall, collapse;* and, in gen., *end.* (4) in grammar, *a case.*

cătăphractēs -ae, m. *a breastplate of iron scales.*

cătăphractus -a -um, *mail-clad.*

cătăplūs -i, m. *the arrival of a ship; a ship that is arriving.*

cătăpulta -ae, f. *an engine of war, a catapult.*

cătăracta (cătarracta) -ae, f. and **cătăractēs** -ae, m. *a waterfall; a sluice or flood-gate; a portcullis.*

cătasta -ae, f. *a stage upon which slaves were exposed in the market.*

cătēla -ae, f. *a kind of spear.*

¹**cătellus** -i, m. and **cătella** -ae, f. *a little dog, puppy.*

²**cătellus** -i, m. and **cătella** -ae, f. *a little chain.*

cătēna -ae, f. *a chain, fetter.* Transf., (1) *restraint.* (2) *a series.*

cătēnātus -a -um, *chained, bound, linked together;* labores, *continuous.*

cătĕrva -ae, f. *crowd, troop, flock.*

cătervātim, *in troops, in masses.*

căthedra -ae, f. *a chair;* esp. *a soft one for ladies, or one occupied by a professor.*

Cătilīna -ae, m. L. Sergius, *a Roman noble, killed at the head of a conspiracy in 62 B.C.* Hence adj. **Cătilīnārius** -a -um.

cătillus -i, m. *a small dish or plate.*

cătinus -i, m. *a deep dish or bowl.*

Căto -ōnis, m. *a cognomen belonging to members of the gens Porcia;* adj. **Cătōniānus** -a -um; subst. **Cătōnīni** -orum, m. *the party of* M. Porcius Cato Uticensis, *the younger Cato.*

Cătōnium -i, n. *the lower world* (with a play on the word Cato).

Cătullus -i, m. C. Valerius (c. 85-55 B.C.) *the Roman lyric and epigrammatic poet.*

cătŭlus -i, m. *a young animal,* esp. *a whelp, puppy.*

cătus -a -um, *sharp, cunning;* adv. **cătē.**

cauda (cōda) -ae, f. *the tail of an animal.*

caudex = codex; q.v.

Caudium -i, n. *an old city in Samnium, near the pass of the Caudine Forks.* Adj. **Caudīnus** -a -um.

caulae -arum, f. pl. *a hole, opening; a sheep-fold.*

caulis -is, m. *the stalk of a plant;* esp. *of a cabbage.*

caupo -ōnis, m. *a small shopkeeper or inn-keeper.*

caupōna -ae, f. *a tavern, inn.*

caupōnor -ari, dep. *to trade.*

caupōnŭla -ae, f. *a little inn.*

Caurus (Cōrus) -i, m. *the north-west wind.*

causa (caussa) -ae, f. *a cause,* in all senses of the English word. (1) *a*

reason, motive, pretext. (2) *interest;* abl., causā, *on account of, for the sake of.* with genit., meā, etc. (3) *a case at law, law-suit, claim, contention;* causam dicere, *to plead.* (4) *situation, condition, case.*

causārius -a -um, *sickly, diseased;* m. pl., milit., *men invalided out of the army.*

causidĭcus -i, m. *an advocate, barrister* (often used contemptuously).

causor -ari, dep. *to give as a reason, or pretext; to plead, pretend.*

causŭla -ae, f. *a little cause or case.*

cautēs -is, f. *a rough sharp rock.*

cautĭo -ōnis, f. *caution, care, fore-sight, precaution;* legal, *security, bail, bond.*

cautor -ōris, m. *one who is on his guard, or who gives bail for another.*

cautus -a -um, partic. from caveo; q.v.

căvaedĭum -i, n. *an inner quadrangle.*

căvĕa -ae, f. *a hollow place, cavity.* Esp. *an enclosure, den, cage; the seats in a theatre.*

căvĕo căvēre cāvi cautum, *to be on one's guard;* with acc. *to be on one's guard against:* cave ignoscas, *take care not to forgive;* with ut and the subj., *to take care that;* with dat. of person, *to take care for, provide for.* Commercial and legal, *to give security or to get security;* also *to provide, order,* in a will, treaty or law.

Hence partic. **cautus** -a -um: of persons, etc., *cautious, wary, careful;* of property, *made safe, secured.* Adv. **cautē, cautim,** *cautiously or with security.*

căverna -ae, f. *a hollow place, cavern;* navis, *the hold;* caeli, *the vault of heaven.*

căvillātĭo -ōnis, f. *raillery, jesting, irony.* Transf., *sophistry.*

căvillātor -ōris, m. *a jester 'oker.* Transf., *a quibbler.*

căvillor -ari, dep. *to jest, joke, satirize.* Transf., *to quibble.*

căvo -are, *to hollow out, excavate, pierce.*

căvum -i, n. and **căvus** -i, m. *a hollow, hole, cavity.*

căvus -a -um, *hollow, concave.*

-cĕ, *a demonstrative particle joined on to pronouns and adverbs*—e.g. hisce.

Cecrops -ōpis, m. *the mythical first king of Athens;* adj. **Cecrōpĭus** -a -um, *Cecropian, Athenian.*

¹**cēdo** cēdĕre cessi cessum, *to go, proceed:* of things, *to turn out, happen; to fall to the lot of a person; to change into something else; to go away, withdraw, retire;* with dat., *to give ground to, submit to, hence to be inferior to;* transit., *to grant, yield.*

²**cēdŏ** and plur. **cettĕ,** colloquial imperat., *give, hand over, out with it!*

cedrus -i, f. *the cedar;* meton. *cedar-wood or cedar oil.*

cēlător -ōris, m. *a concealer.*

cĕlĕber -bris -bre, *filled, crowded;* of places, *frequented;* of occasions, *well attended;* of sayings, *often repeated;*

of persons and things, *celebrated, famous, renowned.*

cĕlĕbrātĭo -ōnis, f. *a numerous assembly or attendance.*

cĕlĕbrātŏr -ōris, m. *one who praises.*

cĕlĕbrĭtās -ātis, f. *a crowd, multitude, numerous attendance;* of a festival, *celebration;* in gen., *fame, renown.*

cĕlĕbro -are, *to visit frequently, or in large numbers; to fill; to celebrate, solemnize; to publish, make known; to sing the praises of, to honour; to practise often, repeat, exercise.* Hence partic. **cĕlĕbrātus** -a -um: of places, *much frequented:* of festivals, *kept solemn, festive;* in gen., *famous, celebrated.*

cĕlĕr -ĕris -ĕre, *swift, quick, rapid;* in a bad sense, *hasty, rash.* Adv. **cĕlĕrĕ** and **cĕlĕrĭtĕr.**

Cĕlĕres -um, m. *early name for Roman nobles,* esp. *the body-guard of the kings.*

cĕlĕrĭpēs -pĕdis, *swift-footed.*

cĕlĕrĭtās -ātis, f. *quickness, swiftness.*

cĕlĕro -are: transit., *to make quick, accelerate;* intransit., *to hasten.*

cella -ae, f. *a room:* esp. *a store-room or a garret, mean apartment;* in a temple, *the shrine of the god's image.*

cellārĭus -a -um, *of a store-room;* as subst. *a cellarer.*

cēlo -are, *to hide, conceal, keep secret.*

cēlōx -ōcis, *swift, quick;* f. as subst. *a swift vessel, yacht.*

celsus -a -um, *upraised, high, lofty, elevated;* in bad sense, *proud, haughty.*

Celtae -arum, m. pl. *the Celts,* esp. those of Central Gaul. Adj. **Celtĭcus** -a -um.

Celtibĕri -orum, m. *the Celtiberians, a people in the middle of Spain.*

cēna -ae, f. *dinner, the main Roman meal;* meton., *a dish or course at a dinner.*

cēnācŭlum -i, n. *a garret, attic.*

cēnātĭo -ōnis, f. *a dining-hall.*

cēnātŏrĭus -a -um, *relating to dinner;* n. pl. as subst. *clothes to dine in.*

cēnĭto -are, *to dine often.*

cēno -are: intransit., *to dine, sup;* transit, *to dine on, to eat.* Perf. partic., with middle meaning, **cēnātus,** *having dined, after dinner.*

cēnsĕo censēre censŭi censum, *to estimate, to form or express an opinion or valuation of a person or thing;* esp. of the censor at Rome, *to take an account of the names and property of Roman citizens.* In gen., *to express an opinion, be of opinion, vote, advise, recommend;* of the senate, *to resolve.*

censŏr -ōris, m. *the sensor, a Roman magistrate.* Transf., *a severe judge, rigid moralist.*

censōrĭus -a -um, *relating to the censor; homo, an ex-censor;* tabulae, *the censor's lists.* Transf., *rigid, severe.*

censūra -ae, f. *the censor's office, censorship.* Transf., *judgment.*

census -ūs, m. *the census, an enrolment*

of names and assessment of property. Transf., *the censor's list; the amount of property necessary for enrolment in a certain rank;* in gen., *property, wealth.*

centaurĕum and **centaurĭum** -i, n. *the plant centaury.*

Centaurus -i, m. *a centaur,* i.e. *a monster of Thessaly, half man and half horse.*

centēni -ae -a (poet. also sing.), *a hundred together, a hundred each.*

centēsĭmus -a -um, *the hundredth.* F. sing. as subst. *the hundredth part;* hence *a tax of one per cent,* or as *interest on money, one per cent,* (reckoned at Rome by the month, therefore = 12 *per cent. per annum*).

centĭceps -cĭpĭtis, *hundred-headed.*

centĭens or **centĭes,** *a hundred times.*

centĭmānus -a -um, *hundred-handed.*

cento -ōnis, m. *patchwork;* in war, *coverings to ward off missiles or extinguish fires.*

centum, *a hundred;* also *any indefinitely large number.*

centumgĕmĭnus -a -um, *hundred-fold.*

centumvĭrālis -e, *relating to the centumviri.*

centum vĭri or **centumvĭri** -orum, *a bench of judges dealing with civil suits.*

centuncŭlus -i, m. *a little piece of patchwork or a saddle-cloth.*

centuplex -lcis, *a hundred-fold.*

centurĭa -ae, f. *a division of 100; a company of soldiers; a century, a part of the Roman people, as divided by Servius Tullius.*

centurĭātim, *by centuries or companies.*

centurĭātus -ūs, m. *a division into companies or centuries; the centurion's office.*

¹centurĭo -are, *to divide into centuries;* comitia centuriata, *the assembly in which the whole Roman people voted in their centuries.*

²centurĭo -ōnis, m. *commander of a century, centurion.*

centurĭōnātus -ūs, m. *an election of centurions.*

cēnŭla -ae, f. *a little meal.*

cenum, see caenum.

cēra -ae, f. *wax; a waxen writing-tablet, wax seal, or waxen image.*

cērārĭum -i, n. *a fee for sealing a document.*

cērastēs -ae, m. *the horned snake.*

cĕrăsus -i, f. *a cherry-tree or a cherry.*

Cerbĕrus -i, m. *the dog guarding Hades.*

cercōpĭthēcus -i, m. *a kind of ape.*

cercūrus -i, m. *a species of vessel peculiar to Cyprus; a sea-fish.*

cerdo -ōnis, m. *a workman, artisan.*

cĕrebrōsus -a -um, *hot-tempered.*

cĕrebrum -i, n. *the brain; the understanding; hot temper.*

Cĕrēs -ĕris, m. *the Roman goddess of agriculture.* Transf., *bread, grain, corn.* Adj. **Cĕrĕālis** -e; n. pl. as subst. *the festival of Ceres on April 10.*

cērĕus -a -um, *waxen, or of resembling wax;* m. as subst., *a wax taper.*

cērintha -ae, f. *the wax flower.*

cērīnus -a -um, *wax-coloured:* n. pl. as subst. *wax-coloured garments.*

cerno cernĕre crēvi crētum, *to separate, sift.* Transf., *to distinguish,* with the senses or with the mind; *to decide, resolve, determine.*

cernŭus -a -um, *falling headlong.*

cēro -are, *to smear or cover with wax.*

cērōma -ātis, n. *an ointment of oil and wax used by wrestlers.*

cērōmăticus -a -um, *anointed with the* ceroma.

cerrītus -a -um, *frantic, mad.*

certāmen -ĭnis, n. *contest, struggle.*

certātim, adv. *emulously, eagerly.*

certātĭo -ōnis, f. *contest, rivalry.*

certē and certŏ, adv. from certus; q.v.

certo -are, *to settle by contest;* hence *to contend, struggle, dispute.*

certus -a -um, adj. *settled, resolved, decided,* of projects and persons; *definite, certain, fixed; sure,* to be *depended on;* of things as known, *undoubted, sure;* certum scio, *I know for certain;* pro certo habeo, *I feel sure;* of persons knowing, *sure, certain;* certiorem facere, *to inform.* Adv. certē and certŏ, *certainly, assuredly.*

cērŭla -ae, f. *a little piece of wax.*

cērussa -ae, f. *white lead.*

cērussātus -a -um, *painted with white lead.*

cerva -ae, f. *hind;* poet., *deer.*

cervīcal -ālis, n. *cushion, pillow.*

cervīcŭla -ae, f. *a little neck.*

cervīnus -a -um, *relating to a stag.*

cervix -īcis, f. *the nape of the neck, the neck;* dare cervices, *to submit to the executioner.*

cervus -i, m. *stag, deer;* pl., milit., *stakes stuck in the ground as a palisade.*

cespes; see caespes.

cessātĭo -ōnis, f. *delaying, inactivity, laziness.*

cessātor -ōris, m. *one who loiters.*

cessĭo -ōnis, f. *a giving up, a cession.*

cesso -are, *to leave off, cease work, be idle, rest;* of things, *to be left alone, do nothing;* so of land, *to lie fallow.*

cestrosphendŏnē -ēs, f. *engine for hurling stones.*

¹cestus and cestos -i, m. *a girdle.*

²cēstus -us, m; see caestus.

cētārĭum -i, n. *a fish-pond.*

cētārĭus -i, m. *a fishmonger.*

cētĕrōqui or cētĕrōquin, *otherwise, else.*

cētĕrus -a -um, *the other, the rest;* usually plur., cētĕri -ae, -a; et cetera, *and so on.* Acc. n. sing. as adv. cētĕrum, *otherwise, moreover, but.*

Cēthēgus -i, m. C. Cornelius, *a conspirator with Catiline, put to death by Cicero in* 63 B.C.

cētra; see caetra.

cette; see cedo.

cētus -i, m. and cētos n.; plur. cete; *any large sea-creature, such as whale, seal, dolphin.*

ceu, adv., *as, like as;* sometimes *as if.*

Chalcis -ĭdis or -ĭdos, f. *the chief city of Euboea.*

Chaldaei -orum, m. pl. *the Chaldaeans, famous as astrologers.*

chălўbēĭus -a -um, *of steel.*

chălўbs -ўbis, m. *steel;* an article made of steel, such as *a sword, a horse's bit, the tip of an arrow.*

chănē or channē -ēs, f. *the sea perch.*

Chăos, acc. Chaos, abl. Chao, n. *boundless empty space.* Hence *the lower world;* personified, Chaos, the *father of Night and Erebus; the shapeless mass out of which the universe was made.*

chara -ae, f. *an edible root.*

Chărĭtes -um, f. pl. *the Graces,* i.e. *Aglaia, Euphrosyne, and Thalia.*

Chăron -ontis, m. *Charon, who ferried souls over the Styx.*

charta -ae, f. *a leaf of Egyptian papyrus, paper; anything written on paper, a letter, poem,* etc.

chartŭla -ae, f. *a little paper, small piece of writing.*

Chărybdis -is, f. *a whirlpool opposite the rock Scylla.*

Chatti (Catti) -orum, m. *a Germanic people.*

Chauci -orum. m. *a Germanic people on the coast of the North Sea.*

chēlўdrus -i, m. *an amphibious snake.*

chēlys, acc. -yn, f. *the tortoise;* hence, *the lyre made of its shell.*

chēragra and chiragra -ae, f. *the gout in the hands.*

Cherrōnēsus and Chersŏnēsus -i, f. *a peninsula;* esp. *of Gallipoli or the Crimea.*

chĭlĭarchēs -ae, and chĭlĭarchus -i, m. *a commander of* 1,000 *soldiers;* among Persians, *chancellor, or prime minister.*

Chĭmaera -ae, f. *a monster killed by Bellerophon.*

chĭmaerĭfer -fĕra -fĕrum, *producing the Chimaera.*

Chios or Chĭus -i, f. *an island in the Aegean Sea, famous for wine and marble.*

chīrŏgrăphum -i, n. *an autograph, a person's own handwriting.*

chīrŏnŏmos -i, and chīrŏnŏmōn -ontis, m. *a gesticulator, a mime.*

chīrurgĭa -ae, f. *surgery.*

chlămўdātus -a -um, *dressed in a* chlamys.

chlămys -ўdis, f. *a large upper garment of wool.*

chŏrăgĭum -i, n. *the training and production of a chorus.*

chŏrăgus -i, m. *he who pays for a chorus.*

chŏraulēs -ae, m. *a flute-player, accompanying the chorus.*

chorda -ae, f. *cat-gut;* usually as the *string* of a musical instrument.

chŏrēa -ae, f. *a dance in a ring.*

chŏrēus and chŏrĭus -i, m. *the metrical foot afterwards called a trochee.*

chŏrus -i, m. *dance in a circle, choral dance.* Transf., *the persons singing and dancing, the chorus;* hence *a crowd, troop.*

Christus -i, m. *Christ;* **Christiānus** -i, m. *a Christian.*

chrŏmis -is, c. *a sea-fish.*

chrȳsanthus -i, m. *a flower,* perhaps *marigold.*

chrȳsŏlithos -i, m. and f. *chrysolite,* or *topaz.*

chrȳsophrys, acc. -yn. f. *a sea-fish.*

cĭbārĭus -a -um, *relating to food;* n. pl. as subst., *food, rations.* Transf. (from the food of slaves), *ordinary, common.*

cĭbātus -ūs, m. *food, nourishment.*

cĭbŏrĭum -i, n. *a large drinking-vessel.*

cĭbus -i, m. *food, fodder, nourishment, sustenance.*

cĭcāda -ae, f. *a cicada,* or *tree cricket.*

cĭcātrix -īcis, f. *a scar;* on plants, *a mark of incision;* also *a patch on an old shoe.*

cĭcer -eris, n. *a chick-pea.*

Cĭcĕro -onis, M. Tullius, *Roman Statesman, orator, and writer* (106-43 B.C.); adj. **Cĭcĕrōnĭānus** -a -um.

cĭchŏrēum -i, n. *succory* or *endive.*

cĭcōnĭa -ae, f. *a stork.*

cĭcur -ŭris, *tame.*

cĭcūta -ae, f. *hemlock; poison extracted from the hemlock; a shepherd's pipe, made of hemlock stalk.*

cĭĕo cĭēre civi cĭtum, *to move, stir, agitate.* Transf., *to give rise to, excite, arouse; to summon; to call by name.*
    Hence partic. **cĭtus** -a -um, *quick, speedy.* Adv. **cĭtō,** *quickly;* citius quam, *sooner than, rather than.*

Cĭlĭcĭa -ae, f. *a region in Asia Minor.*

Cimber -bri, m.; usually pl. **Cimbri,** *the Cimbrians, a German tribe;* adj. **Cimbrĭcus** -a -um.

cīmex -ĭcis, m. *a bug.*

Cimmĕrĭi -orum, m. pl. (1) *a Thracian people, living on the Dnieper.* (2) *a mythical people, living in eternal darkness.*

cĭnaedus -i, m. *a wanton* or *shameless person.*

¹cincinnātus -a -um, *having curled hair.*

²Cincinnātus -i, m. *a cognomen in the gens Quinctia.*

cincinnus -i, m. *curled hair, a lock of hair.* Transf., *artificial rhetorical ornament.*

Cincĭus -a -um, *name of a Roman gens.*

cinctūra -ae, f. *a girdle.*

cinctus -ūs, m. *a girding, a way of wearing the toga.* Transf., *a girdle.*

cinctūtus -a -um, *girded.*

cĭnĕfactus -a -um, *turned to ashes.*

cingo cingĕre cinxi cinctum, *to surround* or *equip the head* or *body;* pass., cingi, *to gird oneself;* in gen., *to surround;* esp. *to surround with hostile intent,* or *for protection;* of persons, *to escort, accompany.*

cingŭla -ae, f. *a girdle.*

cingŭlum -i, n. *a girdle, sword-belt.*

cingŭlus -i, m. *a girdle of the earth, zone.*

cĭnĭflo -onis, m. = cinerarius.

cĭnis -ĕris, m. rarely f. *ashes.*

Cinna -ae, m. *a Roman cognomen,* esp. of L. Cornelius Cinna, *supporter of Marius, noted for his cruelty.* Adj. **Cinnānus** -a -um.

cinnămōmum or **cinnămum** -i, n. *cinnamon.*

cippus -i, m. *a pale, stake;* esp. *a tombstone;* plur., milit., *palisades.*

circā. Adv., *around, round about.* Prep. with acc.: of space, *around, near;* of persons, *around* or *with;* of time or number, *about.*

circāmoerĭum -i, n. = pomerium; q.v.

Circē -ēs and -ae, f. *an enchantress, daughter of the Sun;* adj. **Circaeus** -a -um.

Circēĭi -orum, m. pl. *a town in Latium.*

circensis -e, *belonging to the circus;* m. pl. as subst. (sc. ludi), *the circus games.*

circĭno -are, *to form into a circle* hence *to fly round.*

circĭnus -i, m. *a pair of compasses.*

circĭter, adv., and prep. with acc., *about.*

circlus = circulus; q.v.

circŭeo; see circumeo.

circŭĭtĭo and **circŭmĭtĭo** -ōnis, f. *a going round, patrol.* Transf., *a roundabout way of speaking.*

circŭĭtus -ūs, m. *a going round in a circle, circuit.* Hence *a roundabout way, circuitous course;* also *compass, circumference, extent;* rhet., *a period.*

circŭlor -ari, dep. *to gather in groups,* or *collect a group around oneself.*

circŭlus (**circlus**) -i, m. *a circle, circular figure, circuit; any circular body; a circle* or *group for conversation.*

circum. Adv. *roundabout, around.* Prep. with acc. *round, around, round about, near.*

circŭmăgo -ăgĕre -ēgi -actum. (1) *to turn round;* esp. in the ceremonial manumission of a slave; of time, circumagi or circumagere se, *to pass away, be spent;* of the feelings, *to influence, bring round.* (2) *to drive about from one place to another; to distract.*

circŭmăro -are, *to plough round.*

circumcaesūra -ae, f. *the external outline of a body.*

circumcīdo -cīdĕre cīdi -cisum, *to cut round, to cut, trim.* Transf., *to make less, by cutting, diminish.*
    Hence partic. **circumcīsus** -a -um, of places, *abrupt, steep, inaccessible;* of style, *abridged, brief.*

circumcircā, *all round about.*

circumclūdo -clūdĕre -clūsi -clūsum, *to shut in, enclose, surround.*

circumcŏlo -ere, *to dwell around, dwell near.*

circumcurso -are, *to run round.*

circumdo -dăre -dĕdi -dătum, *surround.* (1) *to put something round,* with acc. of the thing placed, and dat. of that round which it is placed. (2)

to surround with something, with acc. and abl. (rarely double acc.).

circumdŭco -dŭcĕre -duxi -ductum, *to lead round, move or drive round.* Transf., *to cheat; to extend, amplify.*

circŭmĕo (**circŭĕo**) -ire, -ii or -ivi, circŭĭtum, *to go round*; milit., *to surround; to go the rounds of, to visit*; hence *to canvass or solicit.* Transf., *to cheat, circumvent.*

circumĕquĭto -are, *to ride round.*

circumfĕro -ferre -tŭli -lātum, *to carry round, take round*; esp. of the eyes, *to turn all round*; in religion, *to lustrate, purify*, by carrying round consecrated objects. Transf., *to spread*, esp. *to spread news.*

circumflecto -flectĕre -flexi -flexum, *to bend round, turn about.*

circumflo -are, *to blow round.*

circumflŭo -flŭĕre -fluxi -fluxum, *to flow round.* Transf., *to overflow, abound*; with abl., *to abound in.*

circumflŭus -a -um: act., *flowing round, circumfluent*; pass., *flowed round, surrounded by water.*

circumfŏrānĕus -a -um. (1) *round the forum*: aes, *money borrowed from bankers.* (2) *attending at markets.*

circumfundo -fundĕre -fūdi -fūsum. (1) *to pour around*; in pass., or with reflexive, *to be poured round = to surround.* (2) act., *to surround, encompass*, and pass., *to be surrounded*; usually with instrumental abl.

circumgĕmo -ĕre, *to growl round.*

circumgesto -are, *to carry round.*

circumgrĕdĭor -grĕdi -gressus, dep., *to go round, travel round.*

circumiăcĕo -ēre, *to lie round about, adjoin.*

circumicio -icĕre -iēci -iectum. (1) *to throw round, put round.* (2) *to surround* one thing with another.
Hence partic. **circumiectus** -a -um, *thrown round, so surrounding adjacent.*

circumiectus -ūs, m. *a surrounding, enclosing.*

circumĭtĭo = circuitio; q.v.

circumlĭgo -are. (1) *to bind round, bind to.* (2) *to bind round with* something.

circumlĭno -lĭnĕre -lĭtum. (1) *to smear one thing over another.* (2) *to besmear with, bedaub*; hence poet., *to cover.*

circumlŭo -lŭĕre, *to wash round, flow round.*

circumlŭvĭo -ōnis, f. *alluvial land.*

circummitto -mittĕre -misi -missum, *to send round.*

circummūnĭo -ire, *to wall round, to shut in by lines of circumvallation.*

circummūnītĭo -ōnis, f. *circumvallation.*

circumpădānus -a -um, *near the river Po.*

circumplector -plecti -plexus, dep. *to embrace, enclose, surround.*

circumplĭco -are, *to fold round, wind round.*

circumpono -pōnĕre -pŏsŭi -pŏsĭtum, *to place or put round.*

circumrētĭo -ire, *to enclose in a net, ensnare.*

circumrōdo -rōdĕre -rōsi, *to gnaw round.* Transf., *to slander.*

circumsaepĭo -saepire -saeptum, *to hedge round, enclose.*

circumscindo -ĕre, *to tear off, round, to strip.*

circumscrībo -scrībĕre -scripsi -scriptum, *to describe a circle round, to enclose in a circular line.* Transf., (1) *to confine, define, limit, restrict.* (2) *to set aside, exclude.* (3) *to take in, ensnare, defraud*; vectigalia, *to embezzle.*
Hence partic. **circumscriptus** -a -um, as rhet. t. t. *rounded, periodic*; also *concise.* Adv. **circumscriptē**. *in rhetorical periods, fully.*

circumscriptĭo -ōnis, f. *an encircling*; hence *circumference.* Transf., (1) *outline, boundary, limit*; in rhetoric, *a period.* (2) *swindling, defrauding.*

circumscriptor -ōris, m. *a cheat, swindler.*

circumsĕco -sĕcare -sectum *to cut round.*

circumsĕdĕo -sĕdĕre -sēdi -sessum, *to sit round*; esp. *to besiege, beleaguer.*

circumsessĭo -ōnis, f. *encircling, beleaguering.*

circumsĭdo -ĕre, *to besiege.*

circumsĭlĭo -ire, *to leap or jump round.*

circumsisto -sistĕre -stĕti or -stĭti, *to stand round, surround.*

circumsŏno -sonare -sonui: transit., *to sound all around or to make to resound*; intransit., *to resound, to echo.*

circumsŏnus -a -um, *sounding all around.*

circumspectĭo -ōnis, f. *looking about, circumspection, caution.*

circumspecto -are: intransit., *to look round repeatedly*; transit., *to look round at or for.*

¹**circumspectus** -a -um; see circumspicio.

²**circumspectus** -ūs, m. *looking round at*; hence *attention to; prospect, view all round.*

circumspĭcĭo -spĭcĕre -spexi -spectum: intransit., *to look round, esp. anxiously*; hence *to consider*; transit., *to look round at, survey*; hence *to consider carefully*; also *to look about for, seek for.*
Hence partic. **circumspectus** -a -um: pass., of things, *deliberate, well considered*; act., of persons, *circumspect, cautious.*

circumsto -stare -stĕti: intransit., *to stand round or in a circle*; partic. as subst., circumstantes, *the bystanders*; transit., *to surround, beleaguer.*

circumstrĕpo -ĕre, *to make a loud noise around.*

circumsurgens -entis, *rising round.*

circumtĕro -tĕrĕre, *to rub against on all sides.*

circumtextus -a -um, *woven all round.*

circumtŏno -tonare -tŏnŭi, *to thunder round.*

circumtonsus -a -um, *shorn all round; of discourse, artificial.*

circumvādo -vădĕre -văsi, *to attack from every side, to surround.*

circumvăgus -a -um, *wandering round, flowing round.*

circumvallo -are, *to blockade, beleaguer.*

circumvectio -ŏnis, f. *a carrying round of merchandise:* portorium circumvectionis, *transit dues;* in gen., *circuit, revolution.*

circumvector -ari, *to ride or sail round;* poet, *to go through, describe.*

circumvĕhor -vĕhi -vectus, *to ride or sail round;* poet., *to describe.*

circumvēlo -are, *to veil round, envelop.*

circumvĕnio -vĕnire -vĕni -ventum, *to come round, surround, encircle.* Transf., *to beset, assail; to cheat, defraud.*

circumvertor (-vortor) -verti, *to turn oneself round.*

circumvestio -ire, *to clothe all round.*

circumvŏlito -are, *to fly round, rove about.*

circumvŏlo -are, *to fly round.*

circumvolvo -volvĕre -volvi -vŏlūtum, *to roll round;* usually pass., *to revolve.*

circus -i, m. *a ring, circle, orbit:* candens, *the milky way;* also *an oval course for races.*

ciris -is, f. *a bird, into which Scylla was transformed.*

cirrātus -a -um, *curly-haired.*

Cirrha -ae, f. *a city near Delphi, sacred to Apollo;* adj. Cirrhaeus -a -um.

cirrus -i, m. *a lock, or ringlet of hair; the fringe of a garment.*

cis, prep., with acc., *on this side of, within.*

Cisalpinus -a -um, *on this (the Roman) side of the Alps.*

cisium -i, n. *a light two-wheeled vehicle.*

Cisrhenānus -a -um, *on this (the Roman) side of the Rhine.*

cista -ae, f. *a chest, box.*

cistella -ae, f. *a little chest or box.*

cisterna -ae, f. *reservoir, cistern.*

cistŏphŏrus -i, m. *an Asiatic coin.*

cistŭla -ae, f. *a little chest or box.*

citātus -a -um, partic. from ²cito; q.v.

citĕr -tra -trum, *on this side;* usually compar., citĕrior -us, genit. -oris, *on this side, nearer;* superl. citimus -a -um, *nearest.*

cithăra -ae, f. *a stringed instrument, lyre, lute.*

cithărista -ae, m. *a player on the cithara.*

cithăristria -ae, f. *a female player on the cithara.*

cithărizo -are, *to play the cithara.*

cithăroedus -i, m. *one who plays the cithara with voice accompanying.*

¹cĭtŏ, adv. from cieo; q.v.

²cĭto -are (1) *to put in motion, excite, start up.* (2) *to summon, call forward;* esp. for legal, political or military purposes; hence *to appeal to, point to authorities,* etc.

Hence partic. citātus -a -um,

quick, speedy: citato equo, *at full gallop.* Adv. cītātim.

cĭtrā (abl. f. from citer). Adv. *on this side, nearer.* Prep. with acc., *on this side of, nearer than;* of time, *since;* hence, in gen., *short of, without.*

citrĕus -a -um, *belonging to the citrus-tree or citron-tree.*

citrō, adv. *found only with ultro:* ultro (et) citro, *up and down, hither and thither.*

citrus -i, m. (1) *the citrus, a kind of African cypress.* (2) *the citron-tree.*

citus -a -um, partic. from cieo; q.v.

cīvicus -a -um, *relating to a citizen, civic;* civica (corona), *the civic crown, awarded to one who had saved the life of a Roman in war.*

cīvilis -e, *relating to a citizen, civic, civil;* esp. ius civile, *the Roman civil law or civil rights; befitting a citizen;* hence, *popular, affable, courteous; relating to public life or the state.* Adv. cīviliter, *like a citizen; politely.*

cīvilitās -ātis, f. (1) *the science of politics.* (2) *politeness, civility.*

cīvis -is, c. *citizen;* also *a fellow citizen:* under a king, *a subject.*

cīvitās -ātis, f.: abstr., *citizenship;* concr., *a union of citizens, state, commonwealth; the inhabitants of a city, townsfolk;* (rarely) *a city, town.*

clādēs -is, f. *destruction;* in gen. *disaster, injury, defeat.*

clam. Adv., *secretly, in secret:* esse, *to remain unknown.* Prep. with acc. or abl., *unknown to, without the knowledge of.*

clāmātor -ŏris, m. *a shouter, noisy speaker.*

clāmito -are, *to cry aloud, shout violently.*

clāmo -are, *to call, shout, cry aloud;* with object, *to call to or upon a person, to shout something;* sometimes *to proclaim, declare.*

clāmor -ōris, m. *a loud shouting, cry;* poet., *of lifeless things, echo, reverberation.*

clāmōsus -a -um: act., *noisy, clamorous;* pass., *filled with noise.*

clanculum. Adv. *secretly, in secret.* Prep. with acc., *unknown to.*

clandestīnus -a -um, *secret, clandestine;* Adv. clandestīnō.

clangor -ōris, m. *sound, clang, noise.*

clārĕo -ēre, *to be bright, to shine.* Transf., *to be evident; to be distinguished.*

clāresco clārescĕre clārŭi, *to become clear to the senses.* Transf., *to become evident; to become illustrious.*

clārigo -are, *to demand satisfaction,* used of the Fetialis.

clārisŏnus -a -um, *clearly sounding.*

clāritās -ātis, f. *clearness, brightness.* Transf., *clearness to the mind, plainness; fame, celebrity.*

clāritūdo -ĭnis, f. *clearness, brilliancy.* Transf., *fame, celebrity.*

clāro -are, *to make bright or clear.* Transf., *to make plain to the mind; to make illustrious.*

clārus -a -um, *bright, clear, distinct*; poet., of the wind, *making clear, bringing fair weather.* Transf., to the understanding, *clear, evident, plain*; of reputation, *illustrious, distinguished*; in bad sense, *notorious.* Hence adj. **clārē**, *clearly, brightly, distinctly; illustriously.*

classiārius -a -um, *of the fleet*; m. pl. as subst., *marines.*

classicus -a -um. (1) *relating to the different classes of Roman citizens.* (2) *relating to the armed forces, esp. to the fleet*: m. pl. as subst., *marines*: n. sing. as subst., *the signal for battle or the trumpet giving this.*

classis -is, f. *a group as summoned, a division, class.* (1) *one of the classes into which Servius Tullius divided the Roman people.* (2) *the armed forces, esp. the fleet.* (3) in gen., *a class, group.*

clatri -orum, m. pl., *trellis, grating.*

claudeo -ēre and **claudo** -ēre, *to limp, halt, be lame.*

claudicātio -ōnis, f. *a limping.*

claudico -are, *to limp, be lame.* Transf., *to incline, be deflected; to halt, waver.*

Claudius (Clōdius) -a -um, *the name of two Roman gentes*; esp. of the emperor Claudius (10 B.C.-A.D. 54). Adj. **Claudiānus** -a -um, **Claudiālis** -e.

¹**claudo** claudĕre clausi clausum (and **clūdo**) *to close, shut up, make inaccessible*; of military positions, *to blockade, invest*; of prisoners, etc., *to shut in, confine.* Transf., *to conclude*; agmen, *to bring up the rear.* Hence partic. **clausus** -a -um, of character, *close, reserved*; n. as subst., *an enclosed place.*

²**claudo** = claudeo; q.v.

claudus -a -um, *limping, lame.* Transf., *crippled, defective*; poet. carmina alterno versu, *elegiac verse.*

claustrum -i, n., gen. plur., *a means of closing or shutting in: a bolt, bar; an enclosure, prison, den; a barricade, dam, fortress*; milit., *the key to a position.*

clausula -ae, f. *end, conclusion*: in rhetoric, *the close of a period.*

clāva -ae, f. *staff or cudgel.*

clāvārium -i, n. *an allowance to soldiers for buying shoe-nails.*

clāvicŭla -ae, f. *the tendril by which the vine clings to its prop.*

¹**clāviger** -gĕri, m. *the club-bearer*, of Hercules.

²**clāviger** -gĕri, m. *the key-bearer*, of Janus.

clāvis -is, f. *a key*: claves adimere uxori, *to separate from one's wife.* Transf., *a stick for trundling a hoop.*

clāvus -i, m. (1) *a nail, spike.* (2) *a tiller, helm, rudder.* (3) *a stripe of purple on the tunic, worn broad by senators, narrow by knights.*

clēmens -entis, *mild, kind, merciful*; adv. **clēmenter**, *gentle.*

clēmentia -ae, f. *mildness, gentleness, mercy.*

Cleōpatra -ae, f. *the queen of Egypt and mistress of Antony, defeated with him at Actium.*

clēpo clēpere clepsi cleptum, *to steal*; se, *to conceal oneself.*

clepsydra -ae, f. *a water clock*, esp. as used to measure the time allotted to orators.

cliens -entis, m. *a client, dependent on a* patronus (q.v.); in gen., *a vassal or ally.*

clienta -ae, f. *a female client.*

clientēla -ae, f. *clientship, the relation between client and patron*; hence, in gen., *dependence.* Transf. (gen. plur.) *clients.*

clīnāmen -Inis, n. *inclination, swerving aside.*

clīnātus -a -um, *inclined, leaning.*

Cliō -ūs, f. *the Muse of history.*

clipeātus -a -um, *armed with a shield*; m. pl. as subst., *soldiers with shields.*

clipeus -i, m. and **clipeum** -i, n. *a (round) shield.* Transf., *the disk of the sun; a medallion portrait.*

clitellae -arum, f. pl. *a pack-saddle, pair of panniers.*

clīvōsus -a -um, *hilly, steep.*

clīvus -i, m. *a slope, rise, gradient.*

clōāca -ae, f. *a sewer, drain.*

Clōācina -ae, f. *the cleanser, surname of Venus.*

Clōdius = Claudius; q.v.

Clōthō, f. *the spinner, one of the Parcae.*

clŭeo -ēre, *I hear myself called, am named.*

clūnis -is, m. and f. *the buttocks.*

Clūsium -i, n. *a town of Etruria*; adj. **Clūsinus** -a -um.

Clytaemnestra -ae, f. *wife of Agamemnon who killed her husband, and was killed by her son Orestes.*

Cnidus (-os), or **Gnidus (-os)** -i, f. *a town in Caria, famous for the worship of Venus*; adj. **Cnidius** -a -um.

Cnossus = Gnossus; q.v.

cŏācervātio -ōnis, f. *a heaping up.*

cŏācervo -are, *to heap up, accumulate.*

cŏācesco -ācescĕre -ācŭi, *to become sour.*

cŏacto -are, *to compel.*

cŏactor -ōris, m. *a collector of money*; coactores agminis, *the rear-guard.*

cŏactū, abl. sing. m. *by force, under compulsion.*

cŏactum -i, n. subst. from cogo; q.v

cŏaedifico -are, *to build on.*

cŏaequo -are, *to level, make even.*

cŏagmentātio -ōnis, *a connexion, binding together.*

cŏagmento -are, *to join together*; pacem, *to conclude.*

cŏagmentum -i, n. *a joining joint.*

cŏagulum -i, n. *rennet or curds.*

cŏalesco -ālescĕre -ālŭi -ālĭtum, *to grow together*; *to take root, grow*; hence *to become established or firm.*

cŏangusto -are, *to limit, confine.*

cŏarcto, etc. = coarto, etc.; q.v.

cŏarguo -uĕre -ŭi, *to show clearly,*

demonstrate fully; esp. *to prove
wrong* or *guilty.*

cŏartātĭo -ōnis, f. *a confining in a small
space.*

cŏarto -are, *to confine, draw together*;
of discourse, *to compress*; of time,
to shorten.

coccĭnātus -a -um, *clad in scarlet.*

coccĭnus -a -um, *scarlet-coloured*; n.
pl. as subst., *scarlet clothes.*

coccum -i, n. *the berry of the scarlet
oak*; hence *scarlet dye*; sometimes
scarlet cloth or *garments.*

coclěa (cochlěa) -ae, f. *a snail or
snail-shell.*

coclěāre (cochlěāre) -is, n. and
coclěārĭum -i, n. *a spoon.*

Cocles, *Roman cognomen*, esp. *of
Horatius Cocles, the Roman who
defended the bridge over the Tiber
against Porsenna.*

coctĭlis -a, *baked*; muri, *made of
burnt brick.*

Cōcȳtŏs and -us, -i. m. *a river of the
lower world.*

cōda = cauda; q.v.

cōdex (older caudex) -dĭcis, m. *the
trunk of a tree*; as a term of abuse,
dolt, blockhead. Transf., *a book
(made up of wooden tablets, covered
with wax)*; esp. *an account-book, ledger.*

cōdĭcārĭus (caudĭcārĭus) -a -um,
made of tree trunks.

cōdĭcilli -orum, m. *little trunks, logs.*
Transf., *small tablets for memoranda*;
hence *a letter, petition, codicil,
rescript.*

coel-; see cael-.

cŏēmo -ĕmĕre -ēmi -emptum, *to buy
up.*

cŏemptĭo -ōnis, f. *a form of marriage*;
a fictitious sale of an estate.

coen-; see caen-.

cŏēo -ire -ii -ivi -ĭtum, *to go* or *come
together, assemble*; of enemies, *to
engage*; of friends, etc., *to unite,
combine*; transit., societatem coire, *to
form an alliance*; of things, *to unite,
come together*; of blood, *to curdle*; of
water, *to freeze.*

cŏepĭo cŏepĕre, coepi coeptum (only
the perfect-stem tenses are class.; see
incipio), *to begin, commence.* N. of
partic. as subst. coeptum -i, *a thing
begun* or *undertaken.*

cŏepto -are, *to begin* or *undertake
(eagerly).*

cŏeptus -ūs. m. (only in plur.), *a
beginning.*

cŏerceo -cēre -cŭi -cĭtum, *to enclose,
shut in, confine, restrain*; vitem, *to
prune.*

cŏercĭtĭo -ōnis, f. *confining, restraint*;
hence *punishment.*

coerŭlĕus = caeruleus; q.v.

cŏetus (cŏĭtus) -ūs, m. *meeting
together, union, assemblage.*

cōgĭtātĭo -ōnis, f. *thinking, conception,
reflection, reasoning*: sometimes *a
particular thought, idea* or *intention.*

cōgĭto -are, *to turn over in the mind,
to think, reflect*; sometimes *to intend,
plan.*

Hence partic. cōgĭtātus -a -um,
considered, deliberate: n. pl. as
subst. *thoughts, reflections, ideas.*
Adv. cōgĭtātē, *thoughtfully.*

cognātĭo -ōnis, f. *relationship, connexion
by blood*; meton., *persons related,
kindred, family*: in gen., *connexion,
agreement, resemblance.*

cognātus -a -um, *related, connected by
blood*; m. and f. as subst. *a relation
either on the father's* or *mother's
side.* Transf., *akin, similar.*

cognĭtĭo -ōnis, f. *getting to know, study,
knowledge, acquaintance; recognition;
legal inquiry, investigation*; in plur.,
ideas, conceptions.

cognĭtor -ōris, m. *a knower*; legal, *a
witness* or *an attorney*; in gen., *a
supporter.*

cognōmĕn -ĭnis, n. *a surname, family
name.*

cognōmentum -i, n. *a surname, a
name.*

cognōmĭnātus -a -um, *of the same
meaning*; verba, *synonyms.*

cognōmĭnis -e, *having the same name.*

cognosco -gnoscĕre -gnōvi -gnĭtum,
*to become acquainted with, get to know,
learn*; in perf. tenses, *to know*; *to
know again, recognize*; of judges, *to
examine, hear, decide.*

Hence partic. cognĭtus -a -um,
known, proved.

cōgo cōgĕre cŏēgi cŏactum, *to bring,
drive,* or *draw to one point, to collect*;
to bring close together, compress: of
liquids, etc. *to thicken, curdle*;
milit., agmen cogere, *to bring up the
rear.* Transf., *to restrict, confine*;
to compel.

Hence partic., cŏactus, *constrained*:
n. as subst., *thick cloth, felt.*

cŏhaerentĭa -ae, f. *coherence.*

cŏhaerĕo -haerēre -haesi -haesum:
of a whole, *to cohere, hold together*;
of one thing (or person), *to cling,
adhere, be connected* to another.

cŏhaeresco -haerescĕre -haesi, *to hang
together.*

cŏhērēs -ēdis, m. *a coheir.*

cŏhĭbĕo -ēre -ŭi -ĭtum, *to hold in,
hold together*: hence *to confine,
restrain, hold back, repress.*

cŏhŏnesto -are, *to do honour to.*

cŏhorresco -horrescĕre -horrŭi, *to
shudder* or *shiver.*

cŏhors -tis, f. *an enclosure, yard.*
Transf., *a troop, company, throng*;
milit., *a cohort, the tenth part of a
legion*; praetoria cohors, *the retinue
of the governor of a province.*

cŏhortātĭo -ōnis, f. *exhortation,
encouragement.*

cŏhortor -ari, dep. *to encourage, incite,
exhort.*

cŏĭtĭo -ōnis, f. *a coming together,
meeting*; *a faction, coalition, conspiracy.*

cŏĭtus -us, see coetus.

cōlăphus -i, m. *a cuff, box on the ear.*

Colchis -ĭdis, f. *Colchis, a country on
the Black Sea*; adj. Colchĭcus and

Colchus -a -um; f. adj. **Colchis** -ĭdis.

cōlĕus -i; see culeus.

cōlĭphĭa (**cōlўphĭa**) -orum, n. *a food used by athletes.*

cōlis = caulis; q.v.

coll-; see also conl-.

Collātĭa -ae, f. *a town in Latium;* adj. **Collatīnus** -a -um.

collīnus -a -um, *hilly, relating to a hill:* porta Collina, *a gate of Rome near the Quirinal Hill.*

collis -is, m. *hill, high ground.*

collum -i, n. (**collus** -i, m.) *neck.*

collўbus -i, m. *exchange of money, or rate of exchange.*

collўrĭum -i, n. *eye-salve.*

cŏlo cŏlĕre cŏlŭi cultum, *to cultivate, till, tend; to dwell in, inhabit* a place; in gen., *to take care of, attend to foster, honour, worship, court.*
    Hence partic. **cultus** -a -um, *cultivated, tilled, planted;* n. pl. as subst., *cultivated land.* Transf., physically, *tidy, well-dressed, smart;* mentally, *refined.* Adv. **cultē,** *elegantly.*

cŏlŏcāsĭa -orum, n. pl. *the Egyptian bean.*

cŏlōna -ae, f. *a country-woman.*

cŏlōnĭa -ae, f. *a farm, estate; a colony;* meton., *colonists.*

cŏlōnĭcus -a -um, *relating to agriculture* or *to a colony.*

cŏlōnus -i, m. *a farmer, sometimes a tenant farmer; a colonist, inhabitant of a colony.*

cŏlor (**cŏlos**) -ōris, m. *colour, tint, hue;* esp. *complexion; sometimes beautiful complexion, beauty.* Transf., *outward show, external appearance; cast, character, tone; an artful excuse.*

cŏlōro -are, *to colour;* partic. **cŏlōrātus** -a -um, *coloured:* of complexion, *tanned, dark.*

cŏlossēus and **cŏlossĭcus** -a -um, *colossal, gigantic.*

cŏlossus -i, m. *a colossus, statue larger than life;* esp. *that of Apollo at Rhodes.*

cŏlŭber -bri, m. *serpent, snake.*

cŏlubra -ae, f. *female serpent.*

cŏlŭbrĭfer -fĕra -fĕrum, *snake-bearing, snaky-haired* (of Medusa).

cōlum -i, n. *colander, sieve, strainer.*

cŏlumba -ae, f. *a pigeon, dove.*

cŏlumbīnus -a -um, *belonging to a pigeon.*

cŏlumbus -i, m. *a male dove or pigeon.*

cŏlŭmella -ae, f. *a little column.*

cŏlŭmen -ĭnis, n. *a height, summit, ridge;* of buildings, *roof, gable.* Transf., *chief, summit, crown; support, pillar.*

cŏlumna -ae, f. *a pillar, column;* columnae, *pillars as signs of booksellers' shops in Rome;* columnae Herculis, *the pillars of Hercules.* Transf., *a support, pillar of the state; a water-spout.*

cŏlumnārĭum -i, n. *a tax on pillars.*

cŏlumnārĭus -i, m. *a rascal, thief.*

cŏlurnus -a -um, *of hazel-wood.*

cŏlus -i and -ūs, f. or m., *a distaff.*

cōma -ae, f. *the hair of the head.* Transf., *leaves; rays of light.*

cōmans -antis, *hairy; galea, crested; stella, a comet.*

cōmātus -a -um, *hairy;* Gallia Comata, *a name for Transalpine Gaul:* comata silva, *in full leaf.*

[1]**combĭbo** -bĭbĕre -bĭbi, *to drink in, suck up.*

[2]**combĭbo** -ōnis, m. *a comrade in drinking.*

combūro -ūrĕre -ussi -ustum, *to burn up;* hence *to ruin or consume.*

cŏmĕdo -esse -ēdi -ēsum or -estum, *to eat up, consume;* of property, *to waste, squander.*

cŏmēs -ĭtis, c. *a fellow-traveller;* hence *a companion, comrade;* sometimes *attendant;* in plur., comites, *retinue.*

cŏmētēs -ae, m. *a comet.*

cōmĭcus -a -um, *of comedy, comic;* esp. *represented in comedy.* M. as subst. *an actor in comedy or writer of comedy.* Adv. **cōmĭcē,** *in the manner of comedy.*

cŏminus=comminus; q.v.

cōmis -e, *courteous, kind, friendly, obliging;* adv. **cōmĭter.**

cōmissābundus -a -um, *revelling, rioting.*

cōmissātĭo -ōnis, f. *a revel, riotous procession.*

cōmissātor -ōris, m. *a reveller.*

cōmissor -ari, dep. *to revel.*

cōmĭtās -ātis, f. *courtesy, friendliness, civility.*

cōmĭtātus -ūs, m. *train, retinue, following.*

cōmĭter, adv. from comis; q.v.

cōmĭtĭa; see comitium.

cōmĭtĭālis -e, *relating to the* comitia.

cōmĭtĭātus -ūs, m. *the assembly of the people in the* comitia.

cōmĭtĭum -i, n. *a place of assembly,* esp. *one in the forum at Rome;* plur. **cōmĭtĭa,** *the assembly of the Roman people for the election of magistrates,* etc.; hence *elections.*

cōmĭto -are, *to accompany:* esp. as partic. **cōmĭtātus** -a -um, *accompanied.*

cōmĭtor -ari, dep. *to attend, accompany, follow.*

commăcŭlo -are, *to pollute.*

commănĭpŭlāris -is, m. *a soldier belonging to the same company.*

commĕātus -ūs, m., *free passage, going and coming;* milit., *leave of absence, furlough;* also (often plur.) *supply of provisions, food, forage.*

commēdĭtor -ari, dep. *to practise, represent.*

commĕmĭni -isse, *to remember fully.*

commĕmŏrābĭlis -e, *worthy of mention, memorable.*

commĕmŏrātĭo -ōnis, f. *reminding, mention.*

commĕmŏro -are, *to call to mind, recollect; to remind another, so to mention, relate, recount.*

commendābĭlis -e, *commendable, praiseworthy.*

commendāticius -a -um, *giving recommendation.*

commendātio -ōnis, f. *recommendation; that which recommends, excellence.*

commendātor -ōris, m. and **commendātrix** -īcis, f., *one that commends.*

commendo -are, *to commit to the care or protection of anyone.* Hence, in gen., *to commit; to recommend; to set off, render agreeable.*

commensus, partic. of commetior; q.v.

commentāriŏlum -i, n. *a short treatise.*

commentārius -i, m. and **commentārium** -i, n. *a memorandum, note-book;* as the title of a book, *a memoir* (usually plur.); legal, *a brief.*

commentātio -ōnis, f. *reflection, careful consideration; practice.*

commenticius -a -um, *invented, fictitious.*

¹commentor -ari, dep. *to consider thoroughly; to practise, prepare; to invent, compose, write.*

²commentor -ōris, m. *an inventor.*

commĕo -are, *to go up and down, come and go.*

commercium -i, n. *trade, commerce;* meton. *the right to trade, or an article of traffic, merchandise, or a place of trade, depot.* Hence in gen., *intercourse, communication.*

commercor -ari, dep. *to buy up.*

commĕrĕo -ēre (also **commereor,** dep.) *to deserve fully; to commit a fault.*

commētior -mētiri -mensus, dep. *to measure:* sometimes *to measure one thing against another, compare.*

commĕto -are, *to go frequently.*

commigro -are, *to move in a body, migrate.*

commilitium -i, n. *companionship in war* or *military service;* in gen., *fellowship.*

commilito -ōnis, m. *a fellow-soldier.*

comminātio -ōnis, f. *threatening, threat.*

commingo -mingĕre -minxi -mictum, *to make water on, defile.*

comminiscor -minisci -mentus, dep. *to think out, contrive, invent.* Perf. partic. in passive sense, **commentus** -a -um, *feigned, invented;* n. as subst. **commentum** -i, n. *a fiction, invention, contrivance.*

comminor -ari, dep. *to threaten.*

comminŭo -ŭĕre -ŭi -ūtum, *to make small, break up, diminish, weaken.*

comminus, *hand to hand, esp. in close combat;* in gen., *close up, close at hand.*

commiscĕo -miscēre -miscŭi -mixtum, *to mix together, mix up.*

commisĕrātio -ōnis, f. *pity;* rhet. *the exciting of pity.*

commisĕresco -ĕre, *to pity.*

commisĕror -ari, dep. *to pity, bewail;* of a speaker, *to excite pity.*

commissio -ōnis, f. *a setting together:* hence *the start of games, contests,* etc.

commissūra -ae, f. *a joining together, connexion, joint*

committo -mittĕre -misi -um.miss (1) *to unite, connect, combine;* esp. *to bring together in a contest, to match:* hence *to compare.* (2) *to begin, set on foot, initiate:* with ut and the subj., *to bring it about that;* esp. of crimes, etc., *to commit, perpetrate,* and of penalties *to incur.* (3) *to entrust, commit,* esp. with reflex. N. of partic. as subst. **commissum** -i. *an undertaking; a crime, fault; a trust, secret.*

commŏdĭtās -ātis, f. *proportion, fitness;* hence *a fit occasion, also convenience, advantage;* of persons, *kindness.*

commŏdo -are, *to make fit, adapt;* hence *to adapt oneself to a person, to please, oblige, serve;* with acc. *to furnish, lend, give.*

commŏdus -a -um, *to measure, in full, complete;* hence *proper, fit, appropriate;* of persons, character, etc., *friendly, obliging, pleasant.* N. as subst. **commŏdum** -i, *suitable time, opportunity, convenience; use, advantage, interest; remuneration; loan.* N. acc. as adv. **commŏdum,** *at the right time, opportunely; just then.* Adv. **commŏdē,** *rightly, properly, fitly; pleasantly, comfortably, kindly*

commōlior -iri, dep. *to set in motion.*

commŏnĕfăcio -făcĕre -fēci -factum, *to remind, warn* a person, or *to call to* mind a thing.

commŏnĕo -ēre, *to remind, warn* a person, or *to call to* mind a thing.

commonstro -are, *to show fully.*

commŏrātio -ōnis, f. *delaying, lingering.*

commŏror -ari, dep. *to linger, stay;* transit. *to delay.*

commōtio -ōnis. *violent movement excitement.*

commŏvĕo -mŏvēre -mōvi -mōtum, *to move violently, shake, disturb, carry about or away; nummum, to employ in commerce;* esp. *of the mind or passions, to excite, influence, upset;* of abstract things, *to start up, produce cause.*

Hence partic. **commōtus** -a -um, *insecure, unsteady; excited, upset.*

commūnĭcātio -ōnis, f. *communicating, imparting.*

commūnĭco -are (1) *to share out, give a share in;* hence *to communicate, impart a matter;* without object, *to take counsel, confer with a person.* (2) *to join, unite.* (3) *to take a share. participate.*

¹commūnio -ire, *to fortify thoroughly.*

²commūnio -ōnis, f. *sharing, mutual participation.*

commūnis -e, *shared, common, universal, public;* loca, *public places;* loci, *commonplaces;* of persons, *approachable, affable.* N. as subst. **commūnĕ,** *common property,* esp. in plur.; *state, commonwealth;* **in commūne,** *for the common good, also in general.* Adv. **commūnĭter,** *jointly, generally.*

commūnĭtās -ātis, f. *community, fellowship; sense of fellowship, affability.*

commurmŭror -ari, dep. *to mutter, murmur.*

commūtābilis -e, *changeable.*

commūtātus -ūs, m. *change, alteration.*

commŭto -are, *to change, alter; to exchange, barter, interchange.*

cōmo cōmĕre compsi comptum, *to put together, make tidy, arrange, adorn;* esp. of the hair. Hence partic. **comptus** -a -um, *formed, framed; adorned, neat.*

cŏmoedia -ae, f. *comedy.*

cŏmoedus, *comic;* m. as subst., *a comic actor.*

cŏmōsus -a -um, *hairy;* of plants, *leafy.*

compactio -ōnis, f. *joining together.*

compactum or **compectum** -i, n. *an agreement.*

compāgēs -is, f. *a joining together, connexion:* hence either *something that joins, a joint, seam,* or *something joined together, a structure.*

compāgo -ĭnis, f. *a joining together.*

compār -păris: as subst., *an equal, companion mate;* as adj. *like, similar.*

compărābilis -e, *capable of comparison, comparable.*

¹**compărātio** -onis, f. *preparing, providing.*

²**compărātio** -onis, f. *a putting together;* hence, *comparison.*

compărātīvus -a -um, *relating to comparison, comparative.*

comparco (comperco) -parcĕre -parsi or -persi, *to scrape together, save up.*

compărĕo -pārēre -pāruī *to appear, be visible; to be present, be in existence.*

¹**compăro** -are, *to prepare, get ready, provide;* hence *to arrange, settle.*

²**compăro** -are, *to couple together, esp. for a contest, to match.* Transf., *to liken, compare.*

compasco -pascĕre -pastum, *to feed (cattle) together.*

compascŭus -a -um, *of common pasturage.*

compellātio -ōnis, f. *accosting, rebuking.*

¹**compello** -pellĕre -pŭli -pulsum, *to drive together, collect; to force, compel.*

²**compello** -are, *to address, accost;* esp. *to reproach, rebuke;* legal, *to accuse before a court.*

compendiārĭus -a -um *short;* f. and n. as subst., *a short cut.*

compendĭum -i, n. *saving, profit, advantage; shortening, abbreviation;* compendi facere, *to make short;* in plur. *short ways, short cuts.*

compensātio -ōnis, f. *balancing, compensation.*

compenso -are, *to weight together, balance.*

comperco = comparco; q.v.

compĕrendĭnātio -ōnis, f. and **compĕrendĭnātus** -ūs, m. *a putting off to the next day but one.*

compĕrendino -are, *to remand to the next day but one.*

complector -plecti -plexus, dep. *to embrace, surround, encompass.* Transf., *to hold fast, master; to attach oneself to, esteem;* of the mind, *to embrace,* grasp, comprehend; *to unite in oneself, to include.*

complementum -i, n. *a complement.*

compleo -plēre -plēvi -plētum, *to fill up;* milit., *to man,* or *to bring up to strength;* of a sum, *to make up;* of fate, etc., *to fulfil;* of a task, *to finish.* Hence partic. **complētus** -a -um, *perfect, complete.*

complexio -ōnis, f. *connexion, combination;* in rhetoric, *a summary* or *a period;* in logic, *the statement of a syllogism* or *a dilemma.*

complexus -ūs, m. of persons, *embrace, grasp,* either in love or in combat; of things, *compass* or *connexion.*

complīco -are *to fold together;* complicata notio, *confused, intricate.*

complōrātio -ōnis, f. and **complōrātus** -ūs, m. *lamentation.*

complōro -are, *to bewail, lament.*

complūres, -ĭum, *several.*

complŭvĭum -i, n. *roofless space in the centre of a Roman house.*

compōno -pōnĕre -pŏsŭi -pŏsĭtum. (1) *to put together;* esp. of unlike persons or things, either *to match as opponents,* or *to compare.* (2) *to make up a whole, compose.* (3) *to put in place, arrange, settle;* of enemies, *to reconcile.* Hence partic. **compŏsĭtus** -a -um. *constructed, put together; arranged in order, settled;* hence *adapted to a purpose.* Adv. **compŏsĭtē,** *in an orderly way.*

comporto -are, *to bring together, collect.*

compōs -pŏtis, *having control of, possessed of, sharing in.*

compŏsĭtio -ōnis, f. *putting together;* of opponents, *matching; composing, compounding; orderly arrangement, settlement.*

compŏsĭtor -ōris, m. *an arranger, adjuster.*

compŏsĭtūra -ae, f. *connexion, joining.*

compŏsĭtus -a -um, partic. from compono; q.v.

compōtātio -ōnis, f. *drinking party.*

compōtor -ōris, m. and **compōtrix** -īcis, f. *a drinking-companion.*

compransor -ōris, m. *a dinner companion.*

comprĕcātio -ōnis, f. *(common) supplication.*

comprĕcor -ari, dep. *to pray to* or *for, supplicate.*

comprĕhendo -prĕhendere -prĕhendi -prĕhensum and **comprendo** -prendĕre -prendi -prensum, *to grasp; to take together, unite;* hence *to embrace, include; to take firmly, seize;* ignem, *to catch fire;* often of persons, *to capture, arrest;* of criminals, *to catch red-handed.* Transf., *to comprehend, perceive.*

comprĕhensĭbilis -e, *comprehensible.*

comprĕhensio -ōnis, f. (1) *a taking together, uniting;* rhet., *a period.* (2) *seizing, arrest.* Transf., *comprehending, comprehension.*

comprendo = comprehendo; q.v.

compressĭo -ōnis, f. *an embrace; compression of style, conciseness.*

compressŭ, abl. sing. m. *by pressing together; by embracing.*

comprĭmo -prĭmĕre -pressi -pressum, *to press together; to press tight'y; hence to embrace; to check, restrain, suppress.* Hence compar. adv. com-pressius, *more (or rather) concisely.*

comprŏbātĭo -ōnis, f. *approval.*

comprŏbātor -ōris, m. *one who approves.*

comprŏbo -are (1) *to approve fully.* (2) *to confirm, prove, establish.*

comprōmissum -i, n. *reference to arbitrator.*

comprōmitto -mittĕre -mīsi -missum, *to agree to refer a cause to arbitration.*

¹comptus -a -um, partic. from como; q.v.

²comptus -ūs, m. *a head-dress; a band, tie.*

compungo -pungĕre -punxi -punctum, *to prick, puncture; hence to tattoo.*

compŭto -are, *to reckon together, calculate, compute.*

computresco -ĕre, *to rot, putrefy.*

Cōmum -i, n. *a lake-side town in Cisalpine Gaul (now Como).*

cōnāmen -mĭnis, n. *effort, endeavour; concr., a support.*

cōnātum -i, n. *an undertaking.*

cōnātus -ūs, m. *an exertion, effort; sometimes impulse, inclination; an undertaking.*

concaedēs -ium, f. pl. *a barricade of trees.*

concălĕfăcĭo -făcĕre -fēci -factum (pass. concălĕfīo) *to warm thoroughly.*

concălesco -călescĕre -călŭi, *to become thoroughly warm.*

concallesco -callescĕre -callŭi, *to become thoroughly hard; hence to become practised or callous.*

concăvo -are, *to hollow out, make concave.*

concăvus -a -um, *hollow, vaulted, arched, concave; aqua, swelling.*

concēdo -cēdĕre -cessi -cessum: intransit., *to retire, withdraw;* concedere vita, *to die; hence to yield, submit, give way to,* with dat.; concedere naturae, *to die a natural death;* transit., *to yield, grant, give up;* of faults, *to pardon, overlook;* of actions, *to permit, allow.*

concĕlebro -are. *to visit often, or in large companies; to pursue an occupation eagerly; to celebrate a festivity; also to praise, extol a person or thing.*

concēnātĭo -ōnis, f. *supping together.*

concentĭo -ōnis, f. *singing together, harmony.*

concentus -ūs, m. *singing together, harmony; hence agreement, unity, concord.*

conceptĭo -ōnis, f. *conception, becoming pregnant; drawing up of legal formulae.*

conceptus -ūs, m. *conceiving, pregnancy; collecting, or a collection.*

concerpo -cerpĕre -cerpsi -cerptum, *to tear in pieces.* Transf., *to abuse.*

concertātĭo -ōnis, f. *contest, strife, dispute.*

concertātor -ōris, m. *a rival.*

concertātōrĭus -a -um, *relating to a contest.*

concerto -are, *to strive eagerly.*

concessĭo -ōnis, f. *yielding, granting.*

concessŭ, abl. sing. m. *by permission, with leave.*

concha -ae, f. *a sea-shell; hence a shell-fish, esp. mussel or pearl-oyster or the fish yielding purple dye;* poet., *a pearl or purple dye.* Transf., *a vessel like a shell, e.g. a salt-cellar or trumpet.*

conchȳlĭātus -a -um, *dyed with purple or dressed in purple.*

conchȳlĭum -i, n. *a shell-fish esp. a mussel or oyster, or the shell-fish which yielded the purple dye:* meton.. *purple dye or a purple garment.*

¹concīdo -cīdĕre -cĭdi, *to fall down.* Transf., *to sink, perish;* of winds, *to subside;* of persons, *to be ruined, to fail, esp. at law.*

²concīdo -cidere -cidi, -cisum, *to cut up, cut down, destroy.* Transf., *to ruin, strike down.*

Hence partic. concīsus -a -um, *cut up small, brief, concise.* Adv. concīsē.

concĭĕo -cĭēre -cīvi -cītum and concĭo -īre. (1) *to collect, bring together.* (2) *to move violently, excite, arouse, stir up.*

concĭlĭābŭlum -i, n. *a place of assembly.*

concĭlĭātĭo -ōnis, f. *a bringing together, uniting, conciliating, causing of good-will; sometimes inclination.*

concĭlĭātor -ōris, m. *one who brings about a result.*

concĭlĭātrix -īcis, f. *she who unites; hence a match-maker.*

concĭlĭātŭ, abl. sing. m., *by union, ty connexion.*

concĭlĭo -are, *to bring together, unite, reconcile, win over; hence of results, to bring about, cause.*

Hence partic. concĭlĭātus -a -um, *won over, inclined, favourable.*

concĭlĭum -i, n. *bringing together, connexion, assembling, union; esp. an assembly for deliberation, a council.*

concinnĭtās -ātis, and concinnĭtūdo ĭnis, f. *elegance, harmony, esp. of style.*

concinno -are, *to put together carefully, to arrange: hence to produce, cause.*

concinnus -a -um, *well put together; hence pleasing, elegant, neat, esp. of style.* Adv. concinnē, *elegantly.*

concĭno -cĭnĕre -cĭnŭi: intransit., *to sing in chorus, play together; hence to agree in saying and in gen. to agree;* transit., of songs, *to sing together;* of festivals, *to celebrate;* of the future, *to prophesy.*

¹concĭo = concieo; q.v.

²concĭo -ōnis = contio; q.v.

concĭpĭo -cĭpĕre -cēpi -ceptum. (1) *to take together, contain, hold;* of ideas, *to express in a certain form of*

words. (2) *to take completely in, absorb; of fluids, to suck in; of fire, to catch; of air, to draw in; often also to conceive. Transf., to take in, grasp by senses or intellect; to conceive, imagine; of passions, to begin to feel; of action, to devise, esp. in bad sense.*

concīsio -ōnis. f. *the breaking up of a clause into divisions.*

concīsus -a -um, partic. from *concido; q.v.*

concĭtātĭo -ōnis, f. *violent movement.* Hence *tumult, sedition;* also *disturbance of mind, passion.*

concĭtātor -ōris, m. *one who stirs up.*

concĭto -are, *to move violently, stir up, excite;* equum calcaribus, *to spur to a gallop;* aciem, *to move forward the army.* Hence in gen., *to stir up, incite;* of results, *to cause, produce.* Hence partic. **concĭtātus** -a -um, *quick, rapid; excited, violent, passionate.* Adv. **concĭtātē,** *excitedly.*

concĭtor -ōris, m. *one who stirs up.*

conclāmātĭo -ōnis, f. *loud or combined shouting.*

conclāmo -are. (1) *to shout together or loudly;* with ut, *to demand loudly that;* with acc. of a dead person, *to bewail.* (2) *to call together.*

conclāve -is, n. *a room, chamber.*

conclūdo -clūdĕre -clūsi -clūsum *to shut up, enclose, confine.* Hence *to include, comprise; to bring to an end;* in logic, *to argue, infer.* Adv. from partic., **conclūsē,** *with well-turned periods.*

conclūsĭo -ōnis, f. *a shutting, closing;* milit. *a blockade.* Transf., *a close, conclusion;* rhet., *the conclusion of a speech, peroration, or a period;* in logic, *a conclusion, consequence.*

conclūsĭuncŭla -ae, f. *a foolish inference.*

concŏlor -ōris, *similar in colour.*

concŏquo -cŏquĕre -coxi -coctum. *to boil or cook thoroughly;* hence *to digest.* Transf., *to bear, endure, stomach; to consider well, deliberate upon.*

concordĭa -ae, f. *agreement, union, harmony.*

concordĭter, adv. from concors; q.v.

concordo -are, *to agree, be in harmony.*

concors -dis, *of one mind or opinion, agreeing, harmonious.* Adv. **concordĭter.**

concrēbresco -brescĕre -brŭi *to increase.*

concrēdo -crēdĕre -crēdĭdi -crēdĭtum, *to entrust, commit.*

concrĕmo -are, *to burn down, burn entirely.*

concrĕpo -are -ŭi -ĭtum: intransit., *to rattle, creak, clash;* digitis concrepare, *to snap the fingers;* transit., *to rattle, strike upon.*

concresco -crescĕre -crēvi -crētum. *to grow, collect, be formed; to become stiff, congeal, harden.* Hence perf. partic. **concrētus** -a -um, *compounded; congealed, stiff.*

concrētĭo -ōnis, f. *a growing together, congealing; matter.*

concrŭcĭo -are, *to torture violently.*

concŭbīna -ae, f. *a concubine.*

concŭbīnus -i. m. *a man living with a concubine.*

concŭbĭtus -ūs, m. *lying or reclining together;* hence *copulation.*

concŭbĭus -a -um, in the phrase concubia nocte, *at the time of first sleep, at dead of night.*

concŭlco -are, *to tread down, trample under foot.*

concumbo -cumbĕre -cŭbŭi -cŭbĭtum, *to lie or recline together* (at table); *to lie with, have intercourse with.*

concŭpisco -piscere -pīvi or -pĭi -pĭtum, *to desire eagerly, covet, aim at.*

concurro -currĕre -curri (or -cŭcurri) -cursum, *to assemble hurriedly, flock to one spot; to rush together, clash,* esp. *to meet in conflict, engage.*

concursātĭo -ōnis, f. *running together, concourse;* hence *coincidence;* in gen., *running about;* milit. *skirmishing.*

concursātor -ōris, m. *a skirmisher.*

concursĭo -ōnis, f. *running together, concourse;* rhet., *frequent repetition of a word.*

concurso -are, *to run about, rush to and fro;* milit., *to skirmish.*

concursus -ūs, m. *running together, concourse, union; a rushing together, clashing; a hostile encounter.*

concussū, abl. sing. m. *by shaking, by concussion.*

concŭtĭo -cŭtĕre -cussi -cussum *to shake together, agitate, disturb.* Hence, physically, *to shatter, impair;* of persons, *to shake the clothes of,* and so *to examine;* mentally, *to alarm, trouble, excite.*

condĕcŏro -are, *to adorn carefully.*

condemnātor -ōris, m. *one who causes condemnation, an accuser.*

condemno -are, *to condemn;* of an accuser, *to urge or effect the condemnation of a person;* in gen.. *to blame, disapprove.*

condenso -are and **condensĕo** -ēre, *to make thick, press close together.*

condensus -a -um, *dense, thick.*

condĭcĭo -ōnis, f. *an arrangement, agreement.* Hence (1) *a condition, stipulation, provision;* esp. *conditions of marriage, marriage contract.* (2) *state, condition, place, circumstances.*

condīco -dīcĕre -dixi -dictum, *to make arrangement, agree, fix, settle;* esp. *to agree to dine with a person.*

condignus -a -um, *very worthy;* adv. **condignē.**

condīmentum -i. n. *spice. seasoning, sauce, condiment.*

condĭo -ire; of fruits, etc., *to pickle, preserve;* of corpses, *to embalm;* in gen., *to season, temper.* Hence partic. **condītus** -a -um, *seasoned, savoury.*

condiscĭpŭlus -i, m. and **condiscĭpŭla** -ae, f. *a schoolfellow.*

condisco -discĕre -dĭdĭci, *to learn thoroughly.*

¹conditio = condicio; q.v.

²condītio -ōnis, f. *pickling or seasoning.*

conditor -ōris, m. *a founder;* hence, in gen., *contriver, composer, author.*

condītōrium -i, n. *the place in which a corpse or its ashes are preserved.*

condo -dĕre -dĭdi -dĭtum. (1) *to build, found; form, establish;* of literary work, *to compose, write* a poem, etc., and also *to write of* a subject. (2) *to put up, put away safely, store, to hide, withdraw;* of corpses, *to bury;* of time, *to pass, dispose of.*

condŏcĕfăcio -făcĕre -fēci -factum, *to train, instruct, teach.*

condŏlesco -dŏlescĕre -dŏlŭi, *to suffer severely, feel much pain.*

condōnātio -ōnis, f. *a giving away.*

condōno -are, *to give away, present, give up, sacrifice;* of debts, *to excuse;* of faults, *to overlook, forgive;* sometimes *to forgive an injury for the sake of a third party* (dat.).

condūco -dūcĕre -duxi -ductum: transit., *to bring or lead together, collect, unite, connect;* as commercial term, *to hire,* also *to contract for, farm;* intransit. (3rd person only), *to be of use, to profit, serve,* wíth dat.

conductīcius -a -um, *hired.*

conductio -ōnis, f. *a bringing together, uniting;* commerc., *hiring, farming.*

conductor -ōris, m. *one who hires; a contractor.*

condŭplico -are, *to double.*

condūro -are, *to harden.*

cōnecto -nectĕre -nexŭi -nexum, *to fasten, tie together, connect, join, unite.* Hence partic. **cōnexus** -a -um, *joined, connected;* n. as subst. *logical connexion.*

cōnexio -ōnis, f. *binding together; logical sequence.*

cōnexus -ūs, m. *connexion, union.*

confābŭlor -ari, dep. *to talk, converse.*

confarrĕātio -ōnis, f. *a Roman form of marriage.*

confarrĕo -are, *to marry by the ceremony of* confarreatio.

confātālis -e, *determined by the same fate.*

confectio -ōnis, f. (1) *production, completion;* tributi, *complete exaction.* (2) *consumption.*

confector -ōris, m. *one who produces or completes; a destroyer, consumer.*

confercio -fercire -fertum, *to press close together, compress, cram together;* usually in perf. partic. **confertus** -a -um, *compressed, dense;* of troops, *in close formation;* with abl., *stuffed with, full of;* adv. **confertim,** *compactly.*

confĕro -ferre -tŭli -lātum. (1) *to bring or put together, collect, concentrate;* of money, etc. *to contribute;* milit., *to bring into contact or collision;* pedem (cum pede), *to fight foot to foot;* signa conferre, *to engage;* of speech and ideas, *to interchange,*

discuss; of diverse things, *to compare.* (2) *to bring to* a particular place, sphere, task, etc.; se conferre, *to betake oneself, or to devote oneself;* in time, *to put off, postpone;* of responsibility, *to impute, attribute.*

confertus; see confercio.

confervēfăcio -făcĕre, *to make very hot, melt.*

confervesco -fervescĕre -ferbŭi, *to begin to boil or glow.*

confessio -ōnis, f., *a confession, acknowledgment.*

confessus -a -um, partic. from confiteor; q.v.

confestim, *immediately, without delay.*

conficio -ficĕre -fēci -fectum. (1) *to finish, make ready, bring about, accomplish;* of arrangements, *to conclude, settle;* of time or space, *to complete, pass through;* of results, *to produce, cause.* (2) *to get together, obtain, win over.* (3) *to use up, exhause, consume:* of food, *to chew, eat* and also *to digest;* of property, *to waste;* of living creatures, *to destroy, kill;* in gen., *to weaken, wear out,* esp. *of persons.* Hence partic. **conficiens** -entis *productive, efficient.*

confictio -ōnis, f. *a fabrication, invention.*

confidens, confidenter; see confido.

confidentia -ae, f. *confidence;* in bad sense, *impudence, boldness.*

confido -fidĕre -fisus sum, *to have complete trust in, be assured.* Hence partic. **confidens** -entis, *confident, self-reliant;* in bad sense *bold, self-assured;* adv. **confidenter.**

configo -figĕre -fixi -fixum, *to fasten together; to pierce through, transfix, pin down.*

confingo -fingĕre -finxi -fictum, *construct, fashion, fabricate.*

confinis -e, *having the same boundary, adjacent;* m. as subst. *a neighbour.* Transf., *closely allied, similar.*

confinium -i, n. *a confine, boundary border.*

confirmātio -ōnis, f. *a thorough strengthening;* of an institution, *a securing, making firm;* of a person, *consolation, encouragement, support;* of a fact or statement, *confirmation, verification.*

confirmātor -ōris, m. *one who confirms.*

confirmo -are, *to make firm, strengthen, support;* se confirmare, *to recover strength;* polit. *to ratify;* of persons, *to strengthen in mind, encourage;* of assertions, either *to corroborate, establish* or *to affirm, state positively.* Hence partic. **confirmātus** -a -um *encouraged, emboldened;* of things, *certain.*

confisco -are, *to lay up, preserve in a chest; to appropriate to the imperial treasury, to confiscate.*

confisio -ōnis, f. *confidence, assurance.*

confitĕor -fitēri -fessus sum, dep. *to confess, admit, acknowledge; to reveal, make known.*

Hence partic. **confessus** -a -um: in act. sense, *having confessed;* pass., *undoubted, acknowledged, certain.*

conflagro -are, *to blaze up, be well alight.*

conflictio -ōnis, f. *collision, conflict.*

conflicto -are, pass. or intransit., *to collide, contend;* transit., *to harass;* pass. *to be harassed* or *tormented.*

conflictū, abl. sing. m. *by striking together.*

confligo -flīgĕre -flixi, flictum: transit., *to strike* or *throw together; to bring together in order to compare;* intransit., *to collide, clash, come into conflict.*

conflo -are, *to blow up; blow into flame;* of metals, *to melt* or *forge;* of money, *to coin.* Transf., *to excite; to forge, fabricate, put together.*

confluo -flŭĕre -fluxi, *to flow, stream* or *flock together.* Partic. **confluens** -entis, *flowing together;* m. sing. or pl. as subst. *the confluence of two rivers;* as a place-name **Confluentes**, f. pl. *Coblenz.*

confodio -fŏdĕre -fōdi -fossum, *to dig thoroughly; to stab, pierce through.*

conformātio -ōnis, f. *form, shape;* vocis, *expression;* verborum, *arrangement;* philosoph., *an idea;* rhet., *a figure of speech.*

conformo -are, *to form, to put together, to adapt one thing to another.*

confrāgōsus -a -um, *rugged, uneven;* n. pl. as subst., *uneven places.*

confragus -a -um = confragosus; q.v.

confrĕmo -frĕmĕre -frĕmŭi, *to murmur, make a noise.*

confrico -fricare -frĭcŭi -fricatum, *to rub hard.*

confringo -fringĕre -frēgi -fractum, *to break in pieces; to destroy.*

confŭgio -fŭgĕre -fūgi, *to fly, take refuge; to have recourse to.*

confŭgium -i, n. *a place of refuge.*

confulcio -fulcire -fultus, *to prop up.*

confundo -fundĕre -fūdi -fūsum, *to pour; to pour together, mingle, mix, join;* hence *to confuse, throw into disorder, trouble, disturb, upset.* Hence partic. **confūsus** -a -um, *disorderly, confused; mentally, embarrassed, troubled.* Adv. **confūsē**.

confūsio -ōnis, f. *blending, union; confusion, disorder.*

confūto -are, *to check, repress;* by speech, *to put down, silence.*

congĕlo -are: transit., *to freeze, harden, thicken;* intransit., *to freeze up, become inert.*

congĕmĭno -are, *to redouble.*

congĕmo -gĕmĕre -gĕmŭi: intransit., *to sigh* or *groan loudly;* transit., *to bewail, lament.*

conger -gri, m. *a sea* or *conger eel.*

congĕriēs -ēi, f. *a heap, mass,* esp. of wood; rhet., *accumulation.*

congĕro -gĕrĕre -gessi -gestum, *to bring together, collect, pile up, accumulate;* esp. *to build up;* in discourse, *to bring together, comprise;* of benefits, abuse, etc., *to heap upon a person.*

congesticius -a -um, *heaped up.*

congestus -ūs, m. *a heaping together;* of birds, *the building of nests.* Transf., *a heap, mass.*

conglārium -i, n. *a donation* (originally of wine, oil, etc.).

congius -i, m. *a Roman liquid measure* (= *six sextarii*).

conglacio -are; intransit., *to freeze, be inert;* transit. *to turn to ice.*

conglōbātio -ōnis, f. *a heaping* or *crowding together.*

conglōbo -are, *to form into a ball, press tightly together.*

conglōmĕro -are, *to roll, twist, entangle.*

conglūtinātio -ōnis, f. *cementing together, connexion.*

conglūtino -are, *to cement together, connect, bind closely.*

congrātŭlor -ari, dep. *to wish joy to, congratulate.*

congrĕdior -grĕdi -gressus, dep. *to meet,* esp. in conflict; in words, *to dispute, argue.*

congrĕgābilis -e, *sociable, inclined to collect.*

congrĕgātio -ōnis, f. *an assembling, society, union.*

congrĕgo -are, *to collect into a flock* or *swarm;* of men, *to gather together;* with reflex., or in pass., *to swarm, assemble.*

congressio -ōnis, f. *meeting, intercourse, association.*

congressus -ūs, m. *a meeting;* either *a friendly meeting, social intercourse,* or *a hostile encounter, combat.*

congrŭentia -ae, f. *agreement, symmetry, proportion.*

congrŭo -ŭĕre, -ŭi, *to run together, come together, meet;* in time, *to coincide;* in gen., *to be suited to, correspond with, agree.* Hence partic. **congrŭens** -entis, *agreeing, fit, appropriate, suitable;* concentus, *harmonious;* uniform; clamor, *unanimous.* Adv. **congrŭentĕr**, *agreeably, suitably.*

congrŭus -a -um, *agreeing, fit, suitable.*

conicio -icĕre -iēci -ectum, *to throw together; to cast lots;* mentally, *to put two and two together, conjecture, guess; to interpret dreams,* etc.; in gen., *to throw, hurl;* se conicere, *to betake oneself, flee;* of abstract things, *to bring up, bring in;* of money, *to throw away.*

coniectio -ōnis, f. *hurling, throwing; conjectural interpretation.*

coniecto -are, *to throw together;* hence *to put two and two together; conclude, infer, guess.*

coniector -ōris, m. *an interpreter.*

coniectūra -ae, f. *a guess, conjecture, inference; interpretation of dreams and omens, divination.*

coniectūrālis -e, *conjectural.*

coniectus -ūs, m. *a throwing* or *throwing together.*

cōnĭfĕr -fĕra -fĕrum and **cōnĭgĕr**, *cone-bearing.*

cōnitor -niti -nisus or -nixus, dep. *to lean* or *press hard; to make a great* effort, *physical* or *mental*; transit., *of offspring, to bring forth with difficulty.*

coniŭgālis -e, *of marriage, conjugal.*

coniŭgātio -ōnis, f. *etymological connexion of words.*

coniŭgātor -ōris, m., *one who connects.*

coniŭgiālis -e, *of marriage, conjugal.*

coniŭgium -i, n., *a close connexion, union;* esp. *marriage, wedlock;* meton. *a husband* or *wife.*

coniŭgo -are, *to bind together, connect.*

coniunctio -ōnis, f. *uniting, joining together, connexion;* grammat., *a connecting particle, conjunction;* of persons, *union, association, connexion* (esp. by blood or marriage).

coniungo -iungĕre -iunxi -iunctum, *to join together, connect, unite;* amicitias, *to form;* esp. *to unite persons by marriage, friendship, alliance,* etc. Hence partic. **coniunctus** -a -um, *connected, joined, agreeing, allied;* of place, with dat. *bordering on, near;* of time, *contemporary;* of persons, *connected by blood or marriage* or *friendship.* N. as subst., *an inherent property* or *quality;* rhet. *connexion.* Adv. **coniunctē**, *conjointly, in connexion; intimately, on friendly terms;* **coniunctim**, *conjointly, in common.*

coniunx (coniux) -iŭgis, c. *a husband* or *wife;* poet. *a betrothed virgin, bride.*

coniūrātio -ōnis, f. *a union confirmed by an oath;* in bad sense, *conspiracy, plot;* meton., *conspirators.*

coniūro -are, *to take an oath together;* in bad sense, *to plot, conspire;* perf. partic. (in act. sense) **coniūrātus** -a -um, *sworn, united by oath;* m. pl. as subst. *conspirators.*

coniux = coniunx; q.v.

cōnivĕo -nivēre -nivi or -nixi, *to close the eyes, wink, blink.* Transf. *to wink at, let pass.*

conlăbĕfacto -are, *to cause to totter, to soften up.*

conlăbĕfio -fiĕri -factus, *to be made to totter, to be softened or broken.*

conlābor -lābi -lapsus, dep. *to fall or sink down, collapse; to fall down in a swoon or death.*

conlăcĕrātus -a -um, *much lacerated or torn.*

conlăcrĭmātio -ōnis, f. *a weeping together.*

conlăcrĭmo -are, *to weep together* or *weep much;* transit., *to weep for.*

conlactĕus -i, m., and -a -ae, f., *a foster-brother* or *sister.*

conlātio -ōnis, f. *a bringing together;* signorum, *a battle;* of money, *a contribution, collection.* Transf., *a comparison, simile, analogy.*

conlātus -a -um, partic. from confero; q.v.

conlaudātio -ōnis, f. *strong praise.*

conlaudo -are, *to praise very much.*

conlaxo -are, *to widen, extend.*

conlecta -ae, f. *a contribution in money*

conlecticius -a -um, *gathered together;* exercitus, *quickly levied.*

conlectio -ōnis, f. *a gathering together,*

collection; rhet. *a brief recapitulation* in logic, *a conclusion, inference.*

conlēga -ae, m. *a colleague, partner i office;* in gen., *an associate.*

conlēgium -i, n.; abstr., *colleagueship* concr., *persons united as colleagues, body, guild, corporation, college.*

conlībertus -i, m. *a fellow-freedman.*

conlĭbet or **conlŭbet** -bēre -būit o -bĭtum est, impers., *it pleases, i agreeable.*

conlīdo lidĕre -lisi -līsum, *to strike o dash together, to bring into hostile collision.*

conligātio -ōnis, f. *a binding together connexion.*

[1]**conlĭgo** -ligĕre -lēgi -lectum, *to gathe* or *bring together, collect;* poet., *t gather into a smaller space, contract;* conligere se, or animum, or mentem, *to compose onesel , gain courage;* in the mind, *to put together, hence to infer conclude.*

[2]**conlĭgo** -are, *to bind, tie, fasten together, connect;* sometimes *to detain, hinder, tie down.*

conlīnĕo are, *to direct in a straight line.*

conlĭno -linĕre -lēvi -lĭtum, *to besmear, daub.*

conlĭquĕfactus -a -um, *liquefied melted.*

conlŏcātio -ōnis, f. *a placing, arrangment;* esp. *a giving in marriage.*

conlŏco -are, *to place, lay, set, arrange;* of time, money, etc. *to lay out, employ, spend;* of persons, *to settle, place;* of troops, *to billet, quarter;* of women, *to settle in marriage.*

conlŏcŭplēto -are, *to enrich.*

conlŏcŭtio -ōnis, f. *conversation.*

conlŏquium -i, n., *talk, conversation, conference.*

conlŏquor -lŏqui -lŏcūtus, dep. *tŏ speak to, converse with, to treat* or *negotiate with.*

conlūcĕo -ēre, *to shine on all sides, be completely illuminated.*

conlūdo -lūdĕre -lūsi -lūsum, *to play with; to have a secret understanding with, to act in collusion.*

conlŭo -lŭĕre -lŭi -lūtum, *to wash thoroughly, rinse.*

conlūsio -ōnis, f. *secret understanding.*

conlūsor -ōris, m. *a play-fellow; a fellow-gambler.*

conlustro -are, *to illuminate on all sides; to survey, look at on all sides.*

conlŭvio -ōnis and **conlŭviēs** -ēi *collection of impurities, filth;* of people, *scum, rabble.*

conm-; see comm-.

conn-; see conn-.

cōnōpēum or **cōnōpium** -i, n. *a mosquito net.*

cōnor -ari, dep. *to undertake. try, strive.*

conp-; see comp-.

conquassātio -ōnis, f., *a violent shaking.*

conquasso -are, *to shake thoroughly, shatter.*

conquĕror -quĕri -questus, dep. *to complain loudly (of).*

conquestio -ōnis, f. *a loud complaint.*

conquestŭ, abl. sing. m. *by loud complaint.*

conquiesco -quiescĕre -quiēvi -quiētum, *to take rest, repose, be still, stop.*

conquīro -quirĕre -quisivi -quisītum, *to seek out, get together.*
Hence partic. conquisītus -a -um, *carefully sought out, chosen, costly.*

conquisītio -ōnis, f. *search, collection;* of soldiers, *levying, conscription.*

conquisītor -ōris, m., *a recruiting officer.*

conr-: see corr-.

consaepio -saepire -saepsi -saeptum, *to fence round, hedge in;* n. of partic. as subst. consaeptum -i, *an enclosure.*

consālūtātio -ōnis, f., *mutual salutation.*

consālūto -are, *to greet (mutually), hail, salute.*

consānesco -sānescĕre -sānŭi, *to become healthy, get well.*

consanguīnĕus -a -um, *related by blood, brotherly, sisterly;* m. as subst., *brother;* f., *sister;* m. plur., *relations.*

consanguinĭtās -ātis, f., *relationship by blood, consanguinity.*

conscĕlĕro -are, *to defile with crime;* partic. conscĕlĕrātus -a -um, *villainous, depraved.*

conscendo -scendĕre -scendi -scensum, *to ascend, mount, go up;* equum, *to mount on horseback;* naut. (with or without navem, etc.), *to go on board ship, embark.*

conscensio -ōnis, f. *embarkation.*

conscientĭa -ae, f., *knowledge shared with others, "being in the know," joint knowledge; knowledge shared with oneself, i.e. consciousness, esp. of right or wrong, a good or a bad conscience.*

conscindo -scindĕre -scĭdi -scissum, *to tear in pieces.*

conscĭo -ire, *to be conscious of guilt.*

conscisco -sciscĕre -scīvi and -scĭi -scītum, *to agree on, resolve, decree; to inflict upon oneself* (with or without sibi).

conscĭus -a -um. *sharing knowledge with others, privy to a thing, cognizant of;* m. or f. as subst., *an accomplice, fellow-conspirator; sharing knowledge with oneself, i.e. conscious, esp. of right or wrong.*

conscrībo -scrībĕre -scripsi -scriptum, *to enter on a list, enroll;* of troops, *to levy;* patres conscripti (patres et conscripti), *senators; to write, compose;* of physicians, *to prescribe; to write all over an object.*

conscriptio -ōnis, f. *writing, composition.*

consĕco -sĕcare -sĕcŭi -sectum, *to cut up, dismember.*

consĕcrātio -ōnis, f. *dedication, consecration;* of dead emperors, *apotheosis.*

consĕcro -are, *to consecrate;* sometimes *to dedicate to the gods below, to curse;* of persons, *to deify;* in gen., *to make holy or immortal.*

consectārĭus -a -um, *following logically,*

consequent; n. pl. as subst., *logical conclusions, inferences.*

consectātio -ōnis, f. *eager pursuit, striving after.*

consectātrix -īcis, f., *an eager pursuer, devoted friend.*

consectĭo -ōnis, f., *cutting to pieces.*

consector -ari, dep. *to follow, pursue eagerly; to make for, try to join, imitate, attain;* in hostile sense, *to chase, hunt.*

consĕcūtĭo -ōnis, f.: philosoph., *an effect, consequence;* rhet., *order, connexion, arrangement.*

consēnesco -sēnescĕre -sēnŭi, *to become old, lose one's strength, decay.*

consensĭo -ōnis, f., *agreement, harmony, consent;* in bad sense, *plot, conspiracy.*

consensus -ūs m. *agreement, concord;* abl. consensu, *unanimously;* in bad sense, *secret agreement, conspiracy.*

consentānĕus -a -um, *agreeing, fit, suitable;* consentaneum est, *it is reasonable or suitable.*

consentĭo -sentire -sensi -sensum; of physical sensation, *to feel together;* of thought or sentiment, *to agree, assent, resolve unanimously;* with acc., bellum, *to resolve upon war;* in bad sense, *to plot, conspire;* of things, *to agree, harmonize.*
Hence partic. consentĭens -entis, *harmonious.*

consĕpĭo = consaepio; q.v.

consĕquentĭa -ae, f., *a consequence, succession.*

consĕquĭa -ae. f. = consequentia; q.v.

consĕquor -sĕqui -sĕcūtus, dep. (1) *to follow, go after;* in hostile sense, *to pursue; to follow in time, follow logically, result.* (2) *to follow right up, reach, obtain, catch, get;* of states and events, *to befall, happen to a person;* in speech or thought, *to understand, grasp.*
Hence partic. consĕquens -entis, *appropriate, consequent;* n. as subst. *a logical consequence.*

¹consĕro -sĕrĕre -sēvi -sĭtum, *to sow, plant.* Transf., *to cover.*

²consĕro -sĕrĕre -sĕrŭi -sertum, *to connect, join, twine together;* milit., *to join in conflict,* esp. manum (or manus) conserere, *to engage.*
Hence, from partic., adv. consertē, *connectedly.*

conserva -ae, f. *fellow slave.*

conservātio -ōnis, f. *preservation, keeping, laying up.*

conservātor -ōris, m., *preserver.*

conservo -are, *to keep, preserve, maintain.* Pres. partic. as adj. conservans antis, *preserving.*

conservus -i, m. *fellow slave.*

consessor -ōris m., *one who sits near, a neighbour;* in court, *an assessor.*

consessus -ūs, m. *assembly.*

consīdĕrātio -ōnis, f., *consideration, contemplation.*

consīdĕro -are, *to look at, regard carefully, contemplate;* mentally, *to consider, reflect upon.*

Hence partic. **consĭdĕrātus** -a -um; pass., *well weighed, deliberate;* act., *of persons, cautious, circumspect.* Adv. **consĭdĕrātē,** *thoughtfully, carefully.*

consīdo -sīdĕre -sēdi -sessum, *to sit down, to settle;* esp. *to sit down in an assembly or court;* milit., *to take up one's position or encamp.* Transf.: *of things, to settle, sink, subside;* *to be overcome or neglected;* *of ideas, to sink in;* *of feelings, to subside.*

consigno -are, *to seal; to vouch for, authenticate; to record.*

consĭlĭārĭus -a -um, *deliberating;* m. as subst. *an adviser, assessor, interpreter.*

consĭlĭātor -ōris, m., *counsellor, adviser.*

consĭlĭor -ari, dep. *to consult, take counsel; to give counsel, advise.*

consĭlĭum -i, n. (1) *deliberation, consultation;* meton., *persons in consultation, an assembly, council;* as a quality, *judgment, understanding.* (2) *a resolution, plan;* abl., consilio, *intentionally, designedly.* (3) *advice, suggestion.*

consĭmĭlis -e, *exactly similar.*

consĭpĭo -sĭpĕre, *to be in one's right mind.*

consisto -sistĕre -stĭti -stĭtum, *to take one's stand, place oneself; to stand still, stop; to be posted or to halt.* Transf., *of things, to fall to, come upon, rest on; to stop, stay; to stand firm;* with abl. etc., *to consist, be formed of.*

consĭtĭo -ōnis, and **consĭtūra** -ae, f., *sowing, planting.*

consĭtor -ōris, m., *sower, planter.*

consŏbrīnus -i, m. and **consŏbrīna** -ae, f., *cousin (on the mother's side).*

consŏcĭātĭo -ōnis, f., *union, connexion.*

consŏcĭo -are, *to unite, connect, share, make common.*

Hence partic. **consŏcĭātus** -a -um, *united, harmonious.*

consōlābĭlis -e, *consolable.*

consōlātĭo -ōnis, f., *consolation, encouragement, alleviation;* *consoling words.*

consōlātor -ōris, m., *consoler.*

consōlātōrĭus -a -um, *consolatory.*

consōlor -ari, dep.: *of persons, to console, comfort, encourage;* *of things, to alleviate, lighten.*

consŏno -sŏnare -sŏnŭi. (1) *to sound together;* hence *to harmonize, agree.* (2) *to resound, echo.*

consŏnus -a -um, *sounding together, harmonious, accordant, suitable.*

consōpĭo -ire, *to lull to sleep, stupefy.*

consors -sortis: act., *sharing in, partaking of;* as subst., *brother or sister;* as adj., *brotherly, sisterly;* pass., *shared.*

consortĭo -ōnis, f., *companionship, partnership.*

consortĭum -i, n., *partnership, participation.*

¹**conspectus** -a -um, partic. from conspicio; q.v.

²**conspectus** -ūs m.: act., *seeing, look,* *sight, view;* hence *mental view, survey;* pass., *appearance.*

conspergo -spergĕre -spersi -spersum, *to sprinkle or moisten by sprinkling.*

conspĭcĭo -spĭcĕre -spexi -spectum, *to catch sight of, behold, perceive; to look at with attention, watch;* pass., conspici, *to attract notice, be gazed at.* Transf., *to see mentally, understand.*

Hence partic. **conspectus** -a -um, *visible; striking, remarkable, conspicuous.* Gerundive **conspĭcĭendus** -a -um, *worth looking at, notable.*

conspĭcor -ari, dep. *to catch sight of, perceive.*

conspĭcŭus -a -um, *visible; remarkable, striking, conspicuous.*

conspīrātĭo -ōnis, f., *blowing or breathing together; harmony, agreement, union;* in bad sense, *conspiracy, plot.*

conspīro -are, *to blow or breathe together;* *of instruments, to blow together, sound together.* Transf., *to agree, harmonize in opinion and feeling;* in bad sense, *to conspire.*

Hence partic. **conspīrātus** -a -um, *sworn together, united by oath;* m. as subst., *a conspirator.*

conspōnsor -ōris, m. *a joint surety.*

conspŭo -spŭĕre, *to spit upon.*

conspurco -are, *to cover with dirt, defile.*

conspūto -are, *to spit upon.*

constans -antis, partic. from consto; q.v.

constantĭa -ae, f., *steadiness, firmness.*

consternātĭo -ōnis, f., *fear, alarm, dismay, confusion; mutiny, tumult.*

¹**consterno** -sternĕre -strāvi -strātum, *to strew, scatter, cover by strewing.*

Hence partic. **constrātus** -a -um; esp. constrata navis, *a decked ship;* n. as subst., *flooring, deck.*

²**consterno** -are, *to throw into confusion, alarm, frighten; to stampede.*

constĭpo -are, *to press, crowd together.*

constĭtŭo -stĭtŭĕre -stĭtŭi -stĭtūtum, *to cause to stand, set up, place, establish, settle;* milit., *to post, station, arrange, bring to a halt; to settle people in homes or quarters; to found, set up buildings, etc.* Transf., *to appoint a person to an office; to settle, fix upon an amount, time, etc.; to decide about a fact, decide that; to decide on a course of action, decide to.*

Hence partic. **constĭtūtus** -a -um, *arranged, settled;* n. as subst., *anything arranged, settled or agreed upon.*

constĭtūtĭo -ōnis, f., *the act of settling; settled condition, disposition; a regulation, order, ordinance;* rhet., *the issue, point in dispute.*

consto -stare -stĭti -stātum. (1) *to stand together;* hence *to be composed, consist; to depend upon, rest upon; to correspond, be consistent (with dat.);* with abl., *to cost.* (2) *to stand firm, stand still; to remain the same, be unaltered; of resolves, to be fixed, firm; of evidence, facts, etc., to be*

established, sure, well-known; impers.
constat, *it is agreed;* in gen., *to exist.*
Hence partic. **constans** -antis,
*steady, firm, unchanging, constant,
consistent, resolute;* adv. **constantĕr,**
steadily, firmly.

constringo -stringĕre -strinxi -strictum,
*to bind together, bind fast, confine,
restrain;* in speech, *to compress,
abbreviate.*

constructio -ōnis, f., *putting together,
building, construction.*

constrŭo -strŭĕre -struxi -structum, *to
heap up together; to construct, build
up; to arrange.*

constŭprātor -ōris, m. *ravisher, de-
baucher.*

constŭpro -are *to debauch, ravish,
corrupt.*

consŭasor -ōris, m. *an adviser.*

consŭēfăcio -făcĕre -fēci -factum, *to
accustom, habituate.*

consuesco -suescĕre -suēvi -suētum:
transit., *to accustom, habituate;* intransit., *to accustom oneself;* in perf.,
consuevi, *I am accustomed;* cum
homine, *to cohabit with a person.*
Hence partic. **consuetus** -a -um:
of persons, *accustomed to;* of things,
accustomed, usual.

consuētŭdo -ĭnis, f., *custom, usage,
habit;* of relations with persons,
intimacy, familiar acquaintance; of
lovers, *intrigue.*

consuētus -a -um, partic. from consuesco; q.v.

consul -sŭlis, m., *a consul;* plur.,
consules, *the consuls, the two chief
magistrates at Rome under the Republic;* consul designatus, *consul
elect;* pro consule, *an officer in the
place of the consul, a proconsul, e.g. a
governor of a province.*

consŭlāris -e. (1) *relating to a consul,
consular.* (2) *having been a consul;*
m. as subst., *an ex-consul,* or *provincial governor of consular rank.*
Adv. **consŭlārĭtĕr,** *in a manner
worthy of a consul.*

consŭlātus -ūs, m. *the office of consul,
consulship.*

consŭlo -sŭlĕre -sŭlŭi -sultum. (1) *to
reflect, consult, consider;* with dat.,
to look to the interests of; as a result of
deliberation, *to come to a conclusion,
to take meosures;* boni (or optimi)
consulere, *to take in good part.* (2) *to
ask the advice of, consult.*
Hence partic. **consultus** -a -um:
of things, *well considered, deliberated
upon;* of persons, *experienced* (with
genit). N. as subst. **consultum** -i:
the act of deliberation, *reflection,
consideration;* the result of deliberation, *a resolution, plan, decision;* esp.
a decree of the senate at Rome.
Abl. as adv. **consulto,** *deliberately,
designedly.* Adv. **consultē,** *advisedly,
after consideration.*

consultātĭo -ōnis, f., *a full consideration, deliberation; an asking for
advice, inquiry.*

consulto -are. (1) *to consider maturely,*

weigh, ponder; with dat., *to look to
the interests of.* (2) *to consult, ask
advice of.*

consultor -ōris, m. (1) *an adviser.*
(2) *one who asks advice,* esp. *legal
advice; a client.*

consummātĭo -ōnis, f. *a summing up,
adding up; a finishing, completion.*

consummo -are, *to add together, sum
up; to form a whole, complete,
perfect.*
Hence partic. **consummātus** -a
-um, *complete, perfect.*

consūmo -sūmĕre -sumpsi -sumptum,
to spend, employ on a purpose; in
gen., *to use up, finish, waste away,
destroy.*

consŭo -sŭĕre -sŭi -sūtum, *to stitch* or
put together; to form.

consurgo -surgĕre -surrexi -surrectum,
to rise up, stand up, esp. *to speak,* or
as a mark of respect. Transf.: of
persons, *to be roused to action;* of
things, *to arise, break out.*

consurrectĭo -ōnis, f., *a general
standing up.*

contăbesco -tābescĕre -tābŭi, *to waste
away gradually.*

contăbŭlātĭo -ōnis, f., *planking, floor,
storey.*

contăbŭlo -are, *to cover with boards,
equip with floors or storeys.*

contactus -ūs, m., *contact, touching;
contagion.*

contăgēs -is, f., *touch, contact.*

contăgĭo -ōnis, f., and **contăgĭum** -i,
n., *touching, contact;* hence *contagion,
infection.*

contāmĭno -are, *to pollute, infect;* of
authors, *to blend* (and so *spoil*) *Greek
plays.*

contĕgo -tĕgĕre -texi -tectum, *to
cover, shield.*

contemno ‧ temnĕre -tempsi -temptum,
to think meanly of, despise, contemn.
Hence partic. **contemptus** -a -um,
despised; despicable, contemptible.

contemplātĭo -ōnis, f., *surveying,
contemplation.*

contemplor -ari, dep., *to mark out;*
hence *to look at attentively, survey,
regard; to consider carefully.*

contemptim, *contemptuously.*

contemptĭo -ōnis, f., *contempt, scorn,
disdain.*

contemptor -ōris, m., **contemptrix**
-ricis, f., adj. and subst., *a despiser,
contemptuous.*

1contemptus -a -um, partic. from
contemno; q.v.

2contemptus -ūs, m., *contempt, disdain.*

contendo -tendĕre -tendi -tentum, *to
strain, stretch, exert;* of missiles, *to
shoot, cast;* intransit., *to strive,
strain, exert oneself, hasten;* of statements, *to assert with confidencc,
maintain.* In relation to another:
transit., *to compare, contrast;* intransit., *to compete.*
Hence partic. **contentus** -a -um,
*strained, stretched, tense; eager,
zealous.* Adv. **contentē,** *eagerly,
earnestiy.*

¹**contentĕ**, adv. from contendo; q.v.

²**contentĕ**, adv. from contineo; q.v.

contentio -ōnis, f., *exertion, effort, straining, striving.* In relation to another, *contrast, comparison;* or *combat, contest, strife.*

¹**contentus** -a -um, partic. from contendo; q.v.

²**contentus** -a -um, *contented,* partic. from contineo; q.v.

contermĭnus -a -um, *bordering upon, adjacent, near.*

contĕro -tĕrĕre -trīvi -trītum, *to rub away, grind, pound;* in gen., *to wear away, destroy, obliterate;* of time, *to consume, spend.*

conterrĕo -ēre, *to terrify, frighten much.*

contestor -ari, dep. *to call to witness; litem, to start an action by calling witnesses;* partic. **contestātus** -a -um, iŋ pass. sense, *witnessed to, approved.*

contexo -texĕre -texŭi -textum, *to weave* or *twine together, connect, unite, construct, form.*

Hence partic. **contextus** -a -um, *interwoven, connected, united.* adv. **contextĕ**, *in close connexion.*

¹**contextus** -a -um, partic. from contexo; q.v.

²**contextus** -ūs, m., *uniting, connexion.*

conticesco (**conticisco**) -tīcescĕre -tīcŭi, *to become silent, be stilled, abate.*

contignātio -ōnis, f., *floor of planks.*

contigno -are, *to floor with planks.*

contĭgŭus -a -um, *touching, contiguous, near;* with dat., *within reach of.*

contĭnens -entis, partic. from contineo; q.v.

contĭnentĭa -ae, f., *self-control, moderation, temperance.*

contĭnĕo -tĭnēre -tĭnŭi -tentum. (1) *to hold together, keep together;* hence *to connect, join.* (2) *to keep in, surround, contain, confine;* hence *to include, comprise.* (3) *to hold back, restrain.* Hence pres. partic. **continens** -entis. (1) *lying near, adjacent.* (2) *hanging together, unbroken, continuous;* f. as subst., *a continent;* n. as subst., rhet., *a main point.* (3) *self-controlled, temperate, continent.* Adv. **continenter**, *without break, continuously; continently, temperately.* Partic. **contentus** -a -um, *contented, satisfied* (with abl.).

contingo -tingĕre -tĭgi -tactum: transit., *to touch, reach, grasp; to touch with something, smear* or *sprinkle with;* hence *to affect, infect* (esp. in perf. partic.); geograph. *to border on;* intransit., *to happen, befall,* usually of good luck (with dat.).

continŭātio -ōnis, f., *unbroken continuance* or *succession;* rhet., *a period.*

continŭĭtās -ātis, f., *continuity, unbroken succession.*

¹**continŭō**, adv. from continuus; q.v.

²**continŭo** -are, *to connect up, unite, make continuous, form into a series;* verba, *to make into a sentence;* magistratum, *to prolong.*

continŭus -a -um, *connected up, hanging together, continuous, uninterrupted.* N. abl. as adv. **continŭō**, *immediately, at once;* in argument, *necessarily, as an immediate consequence.*

contio -ōnis, f., *an assembly, public meeting.* Transf. *a speech made in such an assembly,* or *the speaker's platform.*

contiōnābundus -a -um, *haranguing, speaking in public.*

contiōnālis -e and **contiōnārĭus** -a -um, *relating to a public assembly.*

contiōnātor -ōris, m., *a popular orator, demagogue.*

contiōnor -ari, dep., *to attend an assembly;* esp. *to speak in public before an assembly.*

contiuncŭla -ae, f., *a short harangue.*

contorquĕo -torquēre -torsi -tortum *to twist, whirl, turn violently, contort; to whirl a spear,* etc., in throwing, and so *to hurl.*

Hence partic. **contortus** -a -um. (1) *intricate, confused, complicated.* (2) *whirling;* so *powerful, vigorous.* Adv. **contortĕ**, *intricately.*

contortio -ōnis, f., *whirling, twisting, intricacy.*

contra. Adv., *opposite, over against. on the opposite side;* of equivalence, *in return, back;* of difference, *otherwise;* of opposition, *against.* Prep., with acc., *opposite to, over against; against, in opposition to.*

contractio -ōnis, f., *drawing together, contraction;* orationis, *abbreviation;* animi, *anxiety, depression.*

contractus -a -um, partic. from contraho; q.v.

contrādīco -dicĕre -dixi -dictum, *to gainsay, contradict.*

contrādictio -ōnis, f., *a speaking against, contradiction.*

contrăho -trăhĕre -traxi -tractum. (1) *to draw together, collect, unite; to conclude* or *complete* any arrangement; in gen., *to cause, bring on, bring about;* aes alienum, *to contract debt.* (2) *to shorten, narrow, contract, reduce;* frontem, *to frown;* vela, *to furl one's sails;* of the spirits, *to depress.*

Hence partic. **contractus** -a -um, *contracted, narrow, straitened;* of persons, *retired, quiet.*

contrārĭus -a -um, *opposite, opposed, contrary;* vulnera, *wounds in front;* with genit. or dat., *opposed to;* in gen., *hostile, injurious.* N. as subst. **contrārĭum** -i, *the opposite;* ex contrario, *on the other side.* Adv. **contrārĭē**, *in an opposite direction* or *manner.*

contrectātio -ōnis, f., *touching, handling.*

contrecto -are, *to touch, feel, handle;* of familiar handling, *to violate;* mentally, *to consider.*

contrĕmisco -trĕmiscĕre -trĕmŭi: intransit., *to tremble, quake;* transit, *to tremble before, be afraid of.*

contrĕmo -ĕre, *to tremble, quake.*

contrĭbŭo -trĭbŭĕre -trĭbŭi -trĭbūtum, *to brigade with, incorporate, unite;* of contributions, *to bring in.*

contristo -are, *to make sad or gloomy.*

contrītus -a -um, partic. from contero; q.v.

contrŏversĭa -ae, f., *a dispute* (esp. at law); sine controversia, *indisputably.*

contrŏversĭōsus -a -um, *strongly disputed.*

contrŏversus -a -um, *disputed, controverted.*

contrūcīdo -are, *to cut in pieces, hew down, slay.*

contrūdo -trūdĕre -trūsi -trūsum, *to thrust, push together.*

contrunco -are, *to cut in pieces.*

contŭbernālis -is, c. (1) *a messmate, comrade.* (2) *a young staff-officer.*

contŭbernĭum -i, n. Concrete, *a soldiers' tent; the common dwelling of a male and female slave.* Abstract, *comradeship, companionship, intimacy; concubinage; junior staff duties.*

contŭĕor -tŭēri -tŭītus, dep. *to see, survey, look at attentively;* mentally, *to consider, reflect upon.*

contŭĭtū (contūtū), abl. sing. m., *by surveying.*

contŭmācĭa -ae, f., *firmness, stubbornness, obstinacy.*

contŭmax -ācis, *firm, stubborn, obstinate;* adv. contŭmācĭtĕr.

contŭmēlĭa -ae, f. *outrage, physical violence;* of speech, *insult, affront.*

contŭmēlĭōsus -a -um, adj. *outrageous, insulting, abusive;* adv. contŭmēlĭōsē.

contŭmŭlo -are, *to bury, inter.*

contundo -tundĕre -tŭdi -tūsum, *to bruise, crush, pound, beat up, break up, demolish.*

contŭor -i = contueor; q.v.

conturbātĭo -ōnis f., *disorder, confusion.*

conturbo -are, *to throw into disorder, disturb, distress; to ruin, make bankrupt.*

contus -i, m. *a pole used in boating; a long spear or pike.*

cōnus -i, m., *a cone; the apex of a helmet.*

convālesco -vălescĕre -vălŭi, *to become strong, establish oneself;* esp. *to recover from a disease, get well.*

convallis -is, f., *an enclosed valley.*

convāso -are, *to pack up baggage.*

convecto -are, *to bring together, collect.*

convector -ōris, m. *a fellow-traveller.*

convĕho -vĕhĕre -vexi -vectum, *to bring together, carry into one place.*

convello -vellĕre -velli -vulsum, *to pluck up, pull away, wrench off;* milit., convellere signa, *to decamp;* in gen., *to weaken, overthrow, destroy.*

convĕna -ae, c.: adj., *coming together;* as subst., in plur., *a concourse, assembled multitude.*

convĕnĭentĭa -ae, f., *agreement, harmony, conformity.*

convĕnĭo -vĕnīre -vēni -ventum. (1) *to meet:* intransit., *to come to-*

gether, *assemble;* legal, convenire in manum, of the wife, *to come into the power of her husband;* transit., *to visit, meet, call upon.* (2) *to fit, be suitable, be congenial;* impers. convenit, *it is fitting.* (3) *to agree;* usually in pass. sense, *to be agreed upon;* impers., convenit, *it is agreed.*

Hence partic. convĕnĭens -entis, *agreeing, unanimous, concordant; fit, appropriate, suitable;* adv. convĕnĭenter, *agreeably, suitably.* N. of perf. partic. as subst., conventum -i, *an agreement, compact.*

conventĭcŭlum -i, n., *a coming together, assembly, association; a place of meeting.*

conventĭo -ōnis, f. *assembly; agreement, compact.*

conventum; see convenio.

conventus -ūs, m. *coming together, assembly, union, congress;* conventus agere, *to hold assizes;* in gen., *agreement.*

converro -verrĕre -verri -versum, *to sweep together, brush up; to beat thoroughly; to scrape together.*

conversātĭo -ōnis, f., *frequent use;* esp. *frequent sojourn in a place,* or *regular dealings with persons.*

conversĭo -ōnis, f. *a turning round, alteration, or periodical return;* rhet. *rounding off of a period,* or *repetition of word at the end of a clause.*

converso -are, *to turn round often;* pass. in middle sense, *to live, consort, have dealings.*

converto -vertĕre -verti -versum. (1) to *turn round, whirl round;* se convertere, *to revolve, to turn back;* milit., signa convertere, *to wheel round;* terga, or se, convertere, *to flee.* Transf., *to change, alter;* of books, *to translate.* (2) *to turn in any direction, direct;* conversus ad *facing.* Transf., *to direct, devote* (esp. with reflex.; rarely intransit.); pecuniam publicam domum, *to embezzle.*

convestĭo -ire, *to clothe; to cover, surround.*

convexus -a -um. (1) *vaulted, arched, convex;* n. as subst., *arch.* (2) *sloping downwards.*

convīcĭātor -ōris, m., *a railer, reviler.*

convīcĭor -ari, dep., *to rail, revile.*

convīcĭum n. *a loud cry, shout, clamour;* esp. *abuse, reproach, insult;* hence, in gen., *censure, reproof*

convictĭo -ōnis, f. *intercourse, familiarity;* meton., *familiar friends.*

convictor -ōris, m., *a constant associate.*

convictus -ūs, m. *living together, intercourse; entertainment, feast.*

convinco -vincĕre -vīci -victum, *to convict of a crime; to prove mistaken;* of things, esp. *crimes or mistakes, to prove conclusively, demonstrate.*

convīso -ere, *to examine carefully;* poet. *to beam upon.*

convīva -ae, m. *guest.*

convīvālis -e, *of a feast.*

convīvātor -ōris, m. *a host.*

convivium -i, n. *a feast, entertainment, banquet*; meton., *the company assembled, guests.*

convivo -vivĕre -vixi -victum, *to live with, to feast with.*

convivor -ari, dep. *to feast* (as a guest).

convŏcātĭo -ōnis, f. *calling together.*

convŏco -are, *to call together, assemble, convoke.*

convŏlo -are, *to fly together, run together.*

convolvo -volvĕre -volvi -vŏlūtum, *to roll together or roll round; to intertwine.*

convŏmo -ere, *to vomit all over.*

convulsus -a -um, partic. of convello; q.v.

cŏŏpĕrĭo -ŏpĕrīre -ŏpĕrŭi -ŏpertum, *to cover up, envelop, overwhelm*; lapidibus *to stone to death.*

cŏoptātĭo -ōnis, f., *election of a colleague, co-optation*; censoria, *filling up of the senate by the censors.*

cŏopto -are, *to choose, elect, co-opt.*

cŏŏrĭor -ŏriri -ortus, dep., *to arise, come forth together; of things, to appear, to break out; of people, to rise for insurrection or fight.*

cŏortus -ūs, m., *arising, breaking forth.*

Cŏos (Cŏus) = Cos; q.v.

cōphĭnus -i, m., *basket, hamper.*

cōpĭa -ae, f., *plenty, abundance* (of persons or things); milit., *supplies, provisions*; also *troops, forces* (esp. plur.). Transf., *means, opportunity*; with genit. of person, *access to.*

cōpĭōsus -a -um, *richly provided, wealthy; plentiful, abundant*; of speech, *copious, eloquent.* Adv. cōpĭōsē, *abundantly, plentifully, copiously.*

cōpo, cōpōna = caupo, caupona; q.v.

cōpŭla -ae, f., *a link, bond, tie, connexion; a rope, a leash*; plur. grapnels.

cōpŭlātĭo -ōnis, f., *union, connexion.*

cōpŭlo -are, *to join together, connect, unite.*

Hence partic. cōpŭlātus -a -um, *connected, united, coupled.*

cŏquo cŏquĕre coxi coctum, *to cook, prepare food; to burn, ripen; to digest*; mentally: *to think of, meditate, contrive a thing; to harass a person.*

cŏquus (cŏcus) -i m. and cŏqua -ae, f., *a cook.*

cŏr, cordis, n., *the heart*; often as seat of emotions or thought, *heart, mind, judgment*; meton., *a person.*

cōram. Adv., *personally, openly, face to face.* Prep., with abl. *in presence of.*

corbis -is, m. and f. *a wicker basket.*

corbīta -ae, f., *a slow-sailing merchant vessel.*

corcŭlum -i, n., *little heart.*

Corcŷra -ae, f., *Corcyra, an island in the Ionian Sea.*

cordātus -a -um, *prudent, wise*; adv. cordātē.

Cordŭba -ae, f. *a town in Hispania Baetica* (now *Cordova*).

Cŏrinthus -i, f. *Corinth, a city of Greece.*

Cŏrĭŏli -orum, m. pl. *a town of the Volsci in Latium*; adj. Cŏrĭŏlānus -a -um.

cŏrĭum -i, n. *hide, skin, leather; a leathern thong, strap.*

Cornēlĭus -a -um, *name of a Roman gens, including the Scipios.* Adj. Cornēllānus -a -um.

cornĕŏlus -a -um, *horny.*

¹cornĕus -a -um, *horny, made of horn; like horn, hard.*

²cornĕus -a -um, *of cornel-tree*; or *cornel-wood.*

cornĭcĕn -cĭnis, m., *a horn-blower.*

cornĭcŭlum -i, n. *a little horn; a horn-shaped decoration for soldiers.*

cornĭger -gĕra -gĕrum, *horned.*

cornĭpēs -pĕdis, *horn-footed, hoofed.*

cornix -icis, f. *crow.*

cornū -ūs, n. *a horn*; fig., *strength, courage; anything made of horn*, esp. *a bow, trumpet, lantern; anything resembling a horn, esp. a hoof, beak, tip of a helmet, end of a stick or spar, end of a promontory, wing of an army.*

Cornūcōpĭa -ae, *the horn of Amalthea, symbol of plenty.*

cornum -i, n. *the cornel-cherry*; meton. *a spear of cornel-wood.*

cornus -i (and -ūs), f. *the cornel-tree*; hence *the wood of the cornel-tree, a spear of cornel-wood.*

cornūtus -a -um, *horned.*

cŏrolla -ae, f. *a little crown.*

cŏrollārĭum -i, n. *a garland of flowers; a present, gratuity.*

cŏrōna -ae, f. *garland, chaplet, crown*; sub corona vendere, *to sell into slavery prisoners of war* (wearing chaplets). Transf., *anything resembling a crown; a constellation; a circle of people, audience*; milit. *besiegers* (or *defenders*) *of a city.*

cŏrōnārĭus -a -um, *of a garland.*

cŏrōno -are, *to wreath, crown with a garland; to surround, enclose in a circle.*

corpŏrĕus -a -um, *of the body, bodily of flesh.*

corpŭlentus -a -um, *fat, stout.*

corpus -pŏris, n. *body, substance, matter*; esp. *the body of men and animals; flesh, the trunk*; sometimes *a corpse.* Transf., *a person, "a body"; the "body politic"*; in gen., *the main mass of a thing.*

corpuscŭlum -i, n. *a little particle, atom; a small body.*

corrādo -rādĕre -rāsi -rāsum, *to scrape or rake together.*

correctĭo -ōnis, f., *straightening out, improvement, amendment.*

corrector -ōris. m. *improver, amender. corrector.*

correpo -rēpere -repsi -reptum, *to creep, slink, crawl.*

correptĭus, compar. adv. from corripio; q.v.

corrigĭa -ae, f. *a shoe-string, boot-lace.*

corrigo -rĭgĕre -rexi -rectum, *to put straight, set right, reform, amend.*

corrĭpĭo -rĭpĕre -rĭpŭi -reptum, *to seize, snatch up*; pecuniam, *to steal*;

viam, *to hasten on a journey*; se, *to hurry off.* Transf., of disease, etc., *to attack*; of the passions, *to overcome*; of persons, *to blame, rebuke, accuse, bring to trial*; in time, *to shorten*; hence, from partic., compar. adv. **correptius,** *more shortly.*

corrōbŏro -are, *to strengthen, invigorate.*

corrōdo -rōdere -rōsi, -rōsum, *to gnaw away.*

corrōgo -are, *to get together, collect by begging.*

corrūgo -are, *to wrinkle up.*

corrumpo -rumpĕre -rūpi -ruptum. (1) *to break up, destroy, annihilate.* (2) *to spoil, make worse, weaken*; of documents, *to falsify*; of characters, *to corrupt*; corrumpere pecuniā, *to bribe.*
Hence partic. **corruptus** -a -um, *spoilt, damaged, corrupt*; adv. **corruptē,** *corruptly, incorrectly.*

corrŭo -rŭere -rŭi: intransit. *to fall to the ground, sink down, be ruined*; transit., *to throw down, overthrow.*

corruptēla -ae, f., *corruption, bribery, seduction*; meton., *a corrupter.*

corruptio -ōnis, f. *corrupting; a corrupt state.*

corruptor -ōris, m. *corrupter, seducer, briber.*

corruptus -a -um, partic. from corrumpo; q.v.

cors = cohors; q.v.

Corsica -ae, f. *the island of Corsica*; adj. **Corsus** and **Corsicus** -a -um.

cortex -ticis, m. and f. *bark, rind, shell*; esp. *the bark of the cork tree, cork.*

cortina -ae, f. *a round kettle or cauldron*; esp. *the cauldron-shaped Delphic tripod*: cortina Phoebi, *the oracle of Apollo.*

cŏrŭlus = corylus; q.v.

cŏrus = caurus; q.v.

cŏrusco -are: transit., *to move quickly, swing, shake*; intransit., *to tremble, flutter*; of light, *to twinkle, flash.*

cŏruscus -a -um, *shaking, trembling*: of light, *twinkling, flashing.*

corvus -i, m. *a raven*; perhaps also *a rook.*

Cŏrŷbantes -ium, m. pl. *the priests of Cybele.*

cŏrŷcus -i, m. *a sand-bag, a punch-ball.*

cŏrŷlētum -i, n. *a hazel copse.*

cŏrŷlus -i, f. *a hazel tree.*

cŏrymbus -i, m. *a bunch of flowers or fruit, esp. a cluster of ivy berries.*

cŏrŷphaeus -i, m. *a leader, chief.*

cŏrŷtus or **cŏrŷtos** -i, m. *a quiver.*

¹**cōs** cōtis, f. *any hard, flinty stone*; esp. *a whetstone, grindstone.*

²**Cōs** or **Cŏus (Cōos)** Coi, f. *a small island in the Aegean Sea*; adj. **Cōus** -a -um; n. sing. as subst., *Coan wine*; n. plur., *Coan garments.*

cosmēta -ae, m. *a woman's valet.*

cosmicos -a -um, *of the world*; m. as subst. *a citizen of the world.*

costa -ae, f. *a rib or side.*

costum -i, n. *an eastern aromatic plant.*

cōthurnātus -a -um, *in buskins*; hence *tragic, elevated.*

cōthurnus -i, m. *a large hunting boot*; *a boot* or *buskin worn by tragic actors*; hence *tragedy, elevated style.*

cotid. = cottid.; q.v.

cottāna (cotōna, coctōna, coctăna) -orum, n. *a kind of small fig.*

cōturnix -icis, f. *a quail.*

cŏvinnārius -i, m. *a soldier in a war chariot.*

cŏvinnus -i, m. *a war-chariot; a travelling-chariot.*

coxa -ae, f. *the hip-bone.*

coxendix -icis, f. *the hip.*

crabro -ōnis, m. *a hornet.*

crambē -ēs, f. *cabbage.*

crāpŭla -ae, f. *drunkenness*; its *after-effects, " hangover ".*

crās, *tomorrow.*

crassitūdo -inis, f. *thickness, density.*

¹**crassus** -a -um, *thick, dense, solid*; aer, *misty, heavy*; of intellect, *dull or uneducated.* Adv. **crassē,** *roughly, rudely.*

²**Crassus** -i, m. *name of a family in the gens Licinia*; q.v.

crastinus -a -um, *of tomorrow*; n. as subst. *the morrow.*

crātēra -ae, f. and **crātēr** -ēris, m. *a bowl, esp. for mixing wine with water; the crater of a volcano; a constellation, the Bowl.*

crātis -is, *a wicker frame, hurdle, a harrow*; milit. *fascines*; favorum, *honeycomb*; spinae, *the joints of the backbone.*

creātio -ōnis, f., *choice, election.*

creātor -ōris, m. and **creātrix** -icis, f. *maker, founder; parent.*

crēber -bra -brum; of space, *thick, crowded together, close, numerous*; with abl., *crowded with, full of*; of time, *repeated, numerous, frequent*; of persons, to signify *repeated action*, e.g. creber pulsat, *he beats repeatedly.* Adv. **crēbrō,** *repeatedly, often.*

crēbresco (crēbesco) -escĕre -ŭi, *to become frequent, increase, gather strength.*

crēbritās -ātis, f. *frequency.*

crēbrō, adv. from creber; q.v.

crēdibilis -e, *credible, worthy of belief*; adv. **crēdibiliter,** *credibly.*

crēditor -ōris, m., *a creditor.*

crēdo -dĕre -didi -ditum, *to trust*: with acc. and dat., *to entrust, commit*, esp. of secrets and money; n. of perf. partic. as subst., creditum, *a loan*; with dat., *to trust in, rely upon*; also with dat., *to believe, give credence to*; with acc., *to believe as a fact, to accept as true*; in gen., *to believe, think, be of opinion.*

crēdŭlitās -ātis, f., *credulity.*

crēdŭlus -a -um, *believing easily, credulous, confiding.*

crĕmo -are, *to burn, consume with fire.*

crĕmor -ōris, m. *juice, pulp, cream.*

crĕo -are, *to make, create, produce; to elect to an office*; of parents, *to beget, bear.*

crĕpida -ae, f. *sandal.*

crĕpidātus -a -um, *wearing sandals.*

crĕpīdo -ĭnis, f., *a base, foundation, pedestal; a quay, pier, dam.*

crĕpĭtācŭlum and **crĕpĭtācillum** -i, n. *a rattle.*

crĕpĭto -are, *to rattle, creak, crackle rustle.*

crĕpĭtus -ūs, m. *rattling, creaking, rustling, clattering*: digitorum, *snapping of the fingers.*

crĕpo -are -ŭi -ĭtum: intransit., *to creak, rattle, rustle, crackle*; digiti crepantis signa, *a snapping of the fingers*; transit., *to make resound; to chatter about.*

crĕpundĭa -orum, n. pl. *a child's plaything; a rattle or amulet.*

crĕpuscŭlum -i, n. *twilight.*

cresco crescĕre crēvi crētum. (1) *to come into existence, spring forth, arise; past partic. cretus, sprung (from).* (2) *of what exists, to grow, grow up, increase in size, height,* etc.; luna crescens, *waxing*; fig., *to increase in fame, power,* etc.

¹Crēta -ae, f. and **Crētē** -ēs, f. *Crete.* Hence m. adj. and subst. **Crēs** -ētis; f. adj. and subst. **Cressa** -ae; adj. **Crētensis** -e, and **Crēticus** -a -um, *Cretan.*

²crēta -ae, f. *chalk, or fuller's earth.*

crētātus -a -um, *chalked; hence in white.*

crētĭo -ōnis, f. *a declaration by an heir accepting an inheritance.*

crētōsus -a -um, *abounding in chalk.*

crētŭla -ae, f. *white clay for sealing.*

Crĕūsa -ae, f. *wife of Aeneas.*

cribrum -i, n. *a sieve.*

crīmen -ĭnis, n. (1) *an accusation, charge*: esse in crimine, *to be accused*; meton., *an object of reproach.* (2) *fault, guilt, crime*; meton., *cause of crime.*

crīmĭnātĭo -ōnis, f. *accusation, calumny, charge.*

crīmĭnātor -ōris, m. *accuser, calumniator.*

crīmĭnor -ari, dep: with acc. of person, *to accuse, charge*; esp. *to calumniate*; with acc. of offence, *to complain of, bring up.*

crīmĭnōsus -a -um, *reproachful, calumnious, slanderous*; adv. **crīmĭnōsē**, *by way of accusation, reproachfully.*

crīnālis -e, *of or for the hair*; n. as subst. *a hair-band.*

crīnis -is, m. *hair*; esp. in pl.; *of a comet, the tail.*

crīnītus -a -um, *hairy, with long hair*; stella crinita, *a comet*; galea, *crested.*

crispĭsulcans -antis, *forked, wavy.*

crispo -are, *to curl; to move rapidly, brandish*; intransit. partic. **crispans** -antis, *curled, wavy.*

crispŭlus -a -um, *curly-haired, curly.*

crispus -a -um, *curly, curly-headed; trembling, quivering.*

crista -ae, f., *the crest, plume*; of a cock, *the comb.*

cristātus -a -um, *with a crest, plume or comb.*

crŏcĕus -a -um, *of saffron; saffron-coloured, golden, yellow.*

crŏcĭnus -a -um, *of saffron, saffron-coloured, yellow*; n. as subst. *saffron oil.*

crŏcŏdīlus -i, m. *crocodile.*

crŏcŏtŭla -ae, f., *a saffron-coloured robe.*

crŏcus -i, m. and **crŏcum** -i n. *the crocus; saffron, prepared from crocus*; hence *the colour of saffron, yellow.*

Croesus -i, m., *a king of Lydia, famous for his wealth.*

crŏtălĭa -orum, n. *ear-rings.*

crŏtălistrĭa -ae, f. *a castanet-dancer*

crŏtălum -i, n. *a castanet.*

Crŏtōn -ōnis, c. *a Greek town near the " toe " of Italy.*

crŭcĭāmentum -i, n. *torture.*

crŭcĭātus -ūs, m., *torture, torment.*

crŭcĭo -are, *to torture, torment.*

crūdēlis -e, adj. *unfeeling, cruel*; adv. **crūdēlĭter.**

crūdēlĭtās -ātis, f., *cruelty, inhumanity.*

crūdesco -escĕre -ŭi, *to become hard or violent.*

crūdĭtās -ātis, f., *overloading of the stomach, indigestion.*

crūdus -a -um, adj. (1) *bleeding.* (2) *uncooked, raw*; of material, *fresh, not prepared*; of fruit, *unripe*, in gen. *green, fresh, immature, untimely*; of food, *undigested*; of persons, *stuffed, dyspeptic*; of feeling, etc., *hard, cruel*; of the voice, *harsh.*

crŭento -are, *to make bloody, stain with blood.*

crŭentus -a -um, *bloody, bloodthirsty; blood-red.*

crŭmēna -ae, f. *a pouch, purse; store of money, funds.*

crŭor -ōris, m. *blood shed, gore; murder, slaughter.*

crūs crūris, n. *the shin, shin-bone, leg*; of a bridge, *pier, support.*

crusta -ae, f. (1) *crust, rind, shell, bark.* (2) *inlaid work, bas-relief, embossing.*

crustŭlum -i, n. *a little cake.*

crustum -i, n. *bread, cake.*

crux crŭcis, f. *a cross*; hence *torment, trouble*; as a term of abuse, *gallows bird.*

crypta -ae, f. *covered gallery, vault. grotto.*

crystallīnus -a -um, *of crystal*; pl. as subst., *crystal vases.*

crystallus -i, f. and **crystallum** -i, n. *crystal; a crystal drinking vessel; a precious stone looking like crystal.*

cŭbĭcŭlāris -e, *of a bedchamber.*

cŭbĭcŭlārĭus -a -um, *of a bedchamber*; m. as subst. *a chamber-servant.*

cŭbĭcŭlum -i, n. *bedroom.*

cŭbīle -is, n. *bed*; esp. *marriage-bed*; of animals, *lair, den, nest*; of bees, *hives*; in. gen., *seat, resting-place.*

cŭbĭtal -tālis, n., *an elbow cushion.*

cŭbĭtālis -e, *one cubit long.*

cŭbĭto -are, *to lie down often.*

cŭbĭtum -i, n. *the elbow; a cubit.*

cŭbĭtus -ūs, m. *lying down.*

cŭbo -are -ŭi -ĭtum, *to lie down, recline*; esp. *at table or in bed; to be ill in bed*; cubitum ire, *to go to bed*; of things, *to lie*; partic. **cubans**, *sloping.*

cŭcullus -i, m. *a hood, cowl.*

cŭcŭlus -i, m. *cuckoo.*

cŭcŭmis -mĕris, m. *cucumber.*

cŭcurbĭta -ae, f. *a gourd; a cupping-glass.*

cūdo -ĕre, *to beat, pound, thresh;* of metals, *to forge, stamp, coin.*

cūĭās -ātis, *of what country?*

cuicuimŏdī *of whatever kind.*

cūĭus (quoĭus) -a -um: interrog., *whose?;* relat., *whose;* quoĭa causa, *wherefore.*

cūĭuscĕmŏdī, *of whatever kind.*

cūĭusdammŏdī, *of a certain kind.*

cūĭusmŏdī, *of what kind?*

cūĭusquĕmŏdī, *of every kind.*

culcĭta -ae, f. *bolster, pillow.*

cūlĕus = culleus; q.v.

cūlex -ĭcis, m. *gnat, midge.*

cūlĭna -ae, f. *kitchen;* meton., *food, fare.*

cullĕus (cūlĕus) -i, m. *a leather sack.*

culmen -ĭnis, n. *top, summit; the ridge of a roof; a stalk.*

culmus -i, m. *stalk, haulm, thatch.*

culpa -ae, f. *fault, blame;* esp. the *fault of unchastity;* meton., *a cause of error or sin.*

culpo -are, *to blame, find fault with, disapprove.*

cultellus -i, m. *a little knife.*

culter -tri, m. *a knife; a ploughshare, coulter.*

cultĭo -ōnis, f. *cultivation, agriculture.*

cultor -ōris, m., *a cultivator, planter, husbandman;* with genit., *an inhabitant, occupier of a place; a friend, supporter of a person; a worshipper of gods.*

cultrix -īcis f. *she who tends or takes care; an inhabitant.*

cultūra -ae, f. *tilling, culture, cultivation, husbandry;* animi, *mental culture, cultivation;* potentis amici, *courting of.*

¹cultus -a -um, partic. from colo; q.v.

²cultus -ūs, m. *tilling, cultivation, tending;* in gen., *care, careful treatment;* deorum, *reverence,* animi, *training, education;* hence *refinement, culture, civilization.*

cŭlullus -i, m. *a drinking-vessel.*

¹cum (older form quom) conj., *when; whenever; since; although;* cum . . . tum . . ., *both . . . and. . . .*

²cum, prep., with abl., *with, together with; at the same time as;* cum eo quod, ut, or ne, *on condition that.*

Cūmae -arum, f. *a city of Campania;* adj. Cūmānus and Cūmaeus -a -um.

cumba (cymba) -ae, f. *small boat, skiff.*

cŭmēra -ae, f. *a corn-bin.*

cŭmĭnum -i, n. *a herb, cummin.*

cumprimis, see primus.

cumque (cunque, quomque), adverb, usually found added to a relative, with the force of *-ever, -soever.*

cŭmŭlo -are, *to heap up, pile up, increase, heighten; to fill up, overload;* cumulatus laude, *loaded with praise;* also *to crown, bring to perfection.*

Hence partic. cŭmŭlātus -a -um: *heaped up, increased, enlarged; crowned*

perfected. Adv. cŭmŭlātē, *abundantly, fully.*

cŭmŭlus -i, m. *heap, pile, mass; addition, increase, finishing touch.*

cūnābŭla -orum, n. pl. *cradle.*

cūnae -arum, f. pl., *cradle,* of young birds, *nest.*

cunctābundus -a -um, *loitering, dilatory.*

cunctātĭo -ōnis, f. *delay, lingering hesitation.*

cunctātor -ōris, m. *one who delays.*

cunctor -ari, dep. *to delay, linger, hesitate;* of things, *to move slowly.*

Hence partic. cunctans -antis, *lingering, slow;* adv. cunctanter.

cunctus -a -um, *all, all collectively, the whole.*

cŭnĕātim, *in wedge formation.*

cŭnĕo -are, *to secure with wedges; to shape like a wedge.*

Hence partic. cŭnĕātŭs -a -um, *pointed like a wedge.*

cŭnĕus -i, m. *a wedge; troops in wedge formation; any triangular figure;* often *of the wedge-shaped compartments into which the seats of a theatre were divided.*

cŭnĭcŭlōsus -a -um, *full of rabbits (or of caverns).*

cŭnĭcŭlus -i, m. (1) *a rabbit, cony.* (2) *an underground passage;* milit. *a mine.*

cūpa -ae, f. *cask, butt.*

cŭpĭdĭtās -ātis, f. *eager desire, passionate longing.* Esp. *ambition; avarice, factiousness, party spirit.*

cŭpīdo -ĭnis, f. and poet. m., *longing, desire.* Esp. *desire for power, ambition; avarice; physical desire, love.* Personified, Cŭpīdo -ĭnis, m. *Cupid,* god of love; plur. Cŭpīdĭnes, *Cupids;* adj. Cŭpīdĭnĕus -a -um.

cŭpĭdus -a -um, *desirous, eager, keen.* Esp. *eager for power, ambitious; avaricious; physically, desirous, passionate; towards persons, attached, partial.* Adv. cŭpĭdē, *eagerly, passionately.*

cŭpĭo cŭpĕre cŭpīvi or -ii -ītum, *to desire, long for, wish for.*

Hence partic. cŭpĭens -entis *longing, eager;* as adj., with genit.; adv. cŭpĭenter.

cŭpĭtor -ōris, m. *one who desires.*

¹cuppēdĭa -ae, f. *taste for delicacies.*

²cuppēdĭa -orum, n. pl. *delicacies, tit-bits.*

cuppēdīnārĭus -i, m. *a confectioner.*

cuppēdo = cupido; q.v.

cupressētum -i, n. *a cypress wood.*

cupressĕus -a -um, *made of cypress wood.*

cupressĭfer -fĕra -fĕrum, *cypress-bearing.*

cupressus -i (-ūs), f. *the cypress; a casket of cypress wood.*

cūr (quor) *why? wherefore?*

cūra -ae, f. *care:* (1) *care taken, carefulness, pains, attention, minding of things or persons;* of *business, management, administration;* meton., *an object of care, or a guardian, care-*

taker, (2) *care felt, anxiety, worry, disquiet.*

cŭrālĭum -i, n. *coral, esp. red coral.*

cŭrātĭo -ōnis, f. *care, attention*; esp. *medical attention, healing, curing*; of business *management, administration*; frumenti, *commission to buy corn*; agraria, *commission to divide land.*

cŭrātŏr -ōris, m. *guardian, overseer.*

cŭrātŭs, partic. from curo; q.v.

curcŭlĭo -onis, m. *a weevil, corn-worm.*

Cŭrēs -ium, f. *a town of the Sabines*; adj. Cŭrensis -e.

Cŭrētes -um, m. *ancient inhabitants of Crete*; adj. Cŭrētis -ĭdis = *Cretan.*

cŭrĭa -ae, f. (1) *a curia, a division of the Roman patricians*; meton., *the meeting-place of a curia.* (2) *the meeting-place of the senate, senate-house*; at Athens, *the Areopagus.*

cŭrĭālis -e, *belonging to the same curia.*

cŭrĭātim, *by curiae.*

cŭrĭātus -a -um, *relating to curiae*; comitia curiata, *the original assembly of the Roman people.*

cŭrĭo -ōnis, m. *the priest of a curia; a herald, crier.*

cŭrĭōsĭtās -atis, *inquisitiveness.*

cŭrĭōsus -a -um. (1) *careful, attentive.* (2) *inquisitive.* (3) *wasted by cares.* Adv. cŭrĭōsē, *carefully; inquisitively.*

cŭris or quĭris, f. *a spear.*

cūro -are, *to care for, pay attention to, trouble about*; with gerundive *to see to a thing being done*; of business, *to manage, administer*; physically, *to minister to, cure, rest*; in business *to provide or procure money*; curare Romae, *to be in charge at Rome.* Hence partic. cŭrātŭs -a -um, *cared for; showing care.* Compar. adv. cŭrātĭus, *more carefully.*

curricŭlum -i, n. *running; a contest in running, race; raceground, course lap; a racing chariot.*

curro currĕre cŭcurri cursum, *to run, hasten*; esp. *to run in a race*; at sea, *to sail*; of time, *to pass.*

currus -ūs, m. *a chariot, car*; esp. one used in racing, or war, or at a triumph; meton., *a triumph.* Transf., *a plough with wheels; a ship.*

cursim, *hastily, quickly.*

cursĭto -are, *to run up and down.*

curso -are, *to run hither and thither.*

cursor -ōris, m. *a runner; a courier, messenger; a running footman.*

cursus -ūs, m. *running, rapid motion; course, direction, movement, journey.*

curto -are, *to shorten, abbreviate.*

curtus -a -um, *shortened, mutilated, defective*; esp. *gelded.*

cŭrūlis -e, *relating to a chariot*; equi, *horses provided for the Circus*; (sella) curulis, *the curule chair, official seat of consuls, praetors, and curule aediles.*

curvāmen -ĭnis, n. and curvātūra -ae, f. *curving, arching.*

curvo -are, *to bend, arch, curve*; to *influence.*

curvus -a -um, *bent, bowed, arched, curved, winding*; morally, *crooked.*

cuspis -ĭdis, f. *point, esp. of a spear*; hence *a spear, lance; a trident; a spit.*

custōdĭa -ae, f. *watching, guarding, custody, care*; milit., *keeping guard, watch*; of prisoners, *custody, safe-keeping*; custodia libera, *house-arrest.* Transf., *persons guarding guards, sentinels; the station of the guard, post, prison; persons guarded, prisoners.*

custōdĭo -ire, *to guard, watch, keep, take care of*; *to keep in sight, observe; to keep in prison, hold captive.*

custōs -ōdis, c. *guardian, watchman, keeper, attendant; a gaoler, sentinel guard, spy.*

cŭtĭcŭla -ae, f. *skin, cuticle.*

cŭtis -is, f. *skin, hide, leather.*

cўāthus -i, m. *a ladle for filling goblets with wine*; as *measure of capacity = one-twelfth of a sextarius.*

cўbaea -ae, f. (with or without navis), *a merchantman.*

Cўbĕlē or Cўbēbē -ēs, f. *a Phrygian goddess, worshipped at Rome.*

²cyclas -ădis, f., *a female robe of state.*

¹Cyclas -ădis, f., gen. plur., Cyclădes, *a group of islands in the Aegean Sea.*

cyclĭcus -a -um, *cyclic.*

Cyclops -clōpis, m. *a Cyclops*, gen. plur., Cyclōpes, *the Cyclopes, a gigantic one-eyed race*; adj. Cyclōpĭus -a -um.

cycnēus or cygnēus -a -um, *belonging to the swan.*

cycnus or cygnus -i, m. *the swan.*

cўlindrus -dri, m. *a cylinder; a roller.*

Cyllēnē -ēs and -ae, f. *a mountain in Arcadia, where Mercury was born.* Adj. Cyllēnēus and Cyllēnĭus -a -um.

cymba -ae, f. = cumba; q.v.

cymbălum -i, n. *a cymbal.*

cymbĭum -i, n., *a small drinking-vessel.*

Cўnĭcus -a -um *Cynic, of the Cynic school.*

cўnŏcĕphălus -i. m. *the dog-faced baboon.*

Cўnŏsūra -ae, f., *the constellation Ursa Minor.*

Cynthus -i, m. *a mountain in Delos, birth-place of Apollo and Diana*; hence adj. as subst., m. Cynthĭus -i, *Apollo.* f. Cynthĭa -ae, *Diana.*

Cўpărissus, f. = cupressus; q.v.

Cyprus or Cypros -i, f., *the island of Cyprus*; adj. Cyprĭus -a -um, *Cyprian*; f. as subst. *Venus.*

Cўrēne -es and Cўrēnae -arum, f. *a city of north-eastern Africa*; adj. Cyrēnaeus and Cўrēnăĭcus -a -um, *Cyrenaic*; m. pl. as subst., *the Cyrenaic philosophers.*

Cўthēra -orum, n., *the island Cythera, sacred to Venus*; adj. Cўthērēus and Cўthērĭus -a -um, *Cytherean*; f. as subst. = *Venus.*

cўtĭsus -i, c. *clover or lucerne.*

D

D, d the fourth letter of the Latin alphabet.

Dăci -orum, m. *the Dacians, a warlike people on the Lower Danube.* **Dăcĭa** -ae, f. *their country.*

dactylicus -a -um, *dactylic.*

dactyllŏthēca -ae, f. *a casket for rings.*

dactylus -i, m. *a metrical foot, a dactyl* (— ◡ ◡).

daedălus -a -um : act., *skilful;* (natura) daedala rerum, *quaint artificer;* pass., *curiously wrought, variegated.*

¹Daedălus -i, m., *mythical Athenian, builder of the Cretan labyrinth;* adj. **Daedălĕus** and **Daedălĭus** -a -um.

Dalmătae (Delmătae) -arum, m. pl., *the Dalmatians, inhabitants of Dalmatia.*

Dămascus -i, f. *Damascus, capital of Syria;* adj. **Dămascēnus** -a -um. *Damascene;* pruna, *damsons.*

damma (older **dāma**) -ae, f. or m. *a fallow-deer, chamois, antelope:* as meat *venison.*

damnātĭo -ōnis, f. *condemnation.*

damnātōrĭus -a -um, *condemnatory.*

damno -are, *to cause loss or injury to;* at law, *to condemn, sentence, punish* (offence usually genit., *punishment* genit. or abl.); damnari inter sicarios, *to be condemned as an assassin;* in gen., *to condemn, disapprove of;* of deities, damnare voti or voto, *to grant a person's wish, and compel him to discharge his vow;* also *to assign, devote, make over.*

damnōsus -a -um: act., *causing loss or damage, detrimental;* pass., *damaged, injured;* middle sense, *self-injuring.* Adv. **damnōsē**, *ruinously.*

damnum -i, n. *loss, damage, injury;* at law, *a fine.*

Dănăē -ēs, f. *mother of Perseus.*

Dănăus -i, m. *son of Belus, who left Egypt for Argos;* adj. **Dănăus** -a -um, *Argive, Greek;* m. pl. **Dănăi** -orum, *the Greeks;* **Dănăĭdes** -um, f. *the fifty daughters of Danaus.*

dănista -ae, m. *money-lender.*

dăno = old form of do; q.v.

Dănŭvĭus -i, m. *the Danube.*

Daphnē -ēs, f. *daughter of Peneus, changed into a laurel-tree.*

daphnōn -ōnis, m. *a grove of laurels.*

daps, **dăpis**, f. *a sacrificial feast, religious banquet;* in gen., *meal, feast, banquet.*

dapsĭlis -e, *sumptuous, plentiful.*

Dardăni -orum, m. pl. *a warlike Illyrian people.*

Dardănus -i, m. *son of Jupiter, mythical ancestor of the royal family of Troy;* adj. **Dardănus** and **Dardănĭus** -a -um, *Trojan;* subst. **Dardănĭa** -ae, f. = *Troy;* **Dardănĭdes** -ae, m. *a male descendant of Dardanus;* **Dardănĭs** -ĭdis, *a Trojan woman.*

Dārēus -i, m. *name of several Persian kings.*

dătĭo -ōnis, f. *a giving;* legal, *right of alienation.*

dătīvus -a -um, *to do with giving;* (casus) dativus, *the dative case.*

dăto -are, *to give away.*

dător -ōris, m. *giver.*

Daunus -i, m. *a mythical king of Apulia, ancestor of Turnus;* adj. **Daunĭus** -a -um, *Daunian;* f. subst., **Daunĭas** -ădis, *Apulia.*

dē, prep., with abl. (1) in space, *down from, away from.* Transf., *coming from an origin; taken from a* class or stock, *made from a material, changed from a previous state;* of information, *from a source.* (2) of time; *following from, after; in the course of, during.* (3) *about a subject; on account of* a cause; *according to a* standard.

dĕa -ae, f. *goddess.*

dĕalbo -are, *to whitewash, plaster.*

dĕambŭlo -are, *to take a walk.*

dĕarmo -are, *to disarm.*

dēbacchor -ari, dep. *to rave, revel furiously.*

dēbellātor -ōris, m., *a conqueror.*

dēbello -are: intransit., *to fight to the end, finish a war;* transit. *to fight out a fight; to conquer an enemy.*

dēbĕo -ēre -ŭi -ĭtum, *to owe.* Lit. of money, etc.; n. of perf. partic. pass. as subst., debitum -i, *a debt.* Transf., *to be indebted to somebody for anything;* with infin., *to be due to do a* thing, *be morally bound to or be bound by logic or necessity or law to; to have to pay because of fate, to be destined to give.*

dēbĭlis -e, *feeble, weak.*

dēbĭlĭtās -ātis, f. *weakness, feebleness.*

dēbĭlĭtātĭo -ōnis, f. *weakening, disabling.*

dēbĭlĭto -are. *to weaken, enfeeble, disable; to enervate, break down.*

dēbĭtĭo -ōnis, f. *owing, debt.*

dēbĭtor -ōris, m. *one who owes, a debtor.*

dēbĭtum -i, subst. from debeo; q.v.

dēcanto -are: transit., *to sing or say repeatedly;* intransit., *to leave off singing.*

dēcēdo -cēdere -cessi -cessum. (1) *to move away, withdraw, retire;* milit. *to march away.* Transf., *to retire, give* up; with dat., *to yield to, retire in favour of,* esp. *to depart from life, to die.* (2) of things, *to retire, abate, cease;* sol decedens, *setting.* (3) *to go astray, deviate.*

dĕcem, indecl. *ten.*

Dĕcember -bris, adj. *of December* (originally the tenth Roman month); December (mensis), *December.*

dĕcempĕda -ae, f. *a ten-foot rule.*

dĕcempĕdātor -ōris, m. *a land-surveyor.*

dĕcemprimi -orum, m. pl. *the ten chief men in the senate of a municipium* or *colonia.*

dĕcemvir -i, m.; usually plur., *a board of ten commissioners at Rome* for various purposes.

dĕcemvirālis -e *relating to the decemvirs.*

dĕcemvirātus -ūs, m. *the office of decemvir.*

děcennis -e, *of ten years.*

děcens -entis, partic. from decet; q.v.

děcentia -ae, f., *propriety, comeliness*

děcerno -cernĕre -crēvi -crētum, *to decide, determine; to settle that a thing is so;* and *of action, to decide to do* or *to give a thing; of a body, to decide, decree;* as a member of a body, *to move, propose; of combatants, to settle by fighting.*

    Hence partic. **děcrētus** -a -um; n. as subst. **děcrētum** -i, *a resolve, decree;* philosoph. *doctrine, principle.*

děcerpo -cerpĕre -cerpsi -cerptum, *to pluck off, pluck away.* Transf., *to gather; to derive; to take away.*

děcertātio -onis, f. *contest.*

děcerto -are, *to contend, fight to a finish.*

děcessio -ōnis, f., *a withdrawing, departure;* esp. *of a governor retiring from his province.* Transf., *deduction, diminution.*

děcessor -ōris, m., *one who retires from an office, a predecessor.*

děcessus -ūs, m. *withdrawal, departure.* Esp. *the retirement of an official; death;* of water, *ebb.*

děcet -ēre -ūit, *it is proper, it is fitting* (physically or morally).

    Hence partic. **děcens** -entis, *proper, fit;* adv. **děcenter.**

¹**děcido** -cidĕre -cidi, *to fall down, to fall dead, die;* in gen., *to sink, fall.*

²**děcido** -cidĕre -cidi -cisum, *to cut down, cut off; to cut short, to settle, to arrange.*

děciens and **děciēs,** *ten times.*

decim-; see also **decum-.**

děcimus (older **děcumus**) -a -um, *tenth;* decimum, *for the tenth time.*

děcipio -cipĕre -cēpi -ceptum, *to catch;* hence *to cheat, deceive, beguile* (esp. of time).

děcisio -onis, f. *a settlement, decision.*

Děcius -a -um, *name of a Roman gens;* adj. **Děciānus** -a -um.

děclāmātio -ōnis, f., *loud, violent speaking, declamation; practice in oratory,* or *a theme for such practice.*

děclāmātor -ōris, m. *a declaimer.*

děclāmātōrius -a -um, *of declamation, rhetorical.*

děclāmito -are, *to speak loudly, declaim;* esp. *to practise public speaking;* causas, *to plead for practice.*

děclāmo -are, *to speak loudly;* esp. *to practise speaking in public;* with object, *to declaim.*

děclārātio -ōnis, f. *making clear, open expression.*

děclāro -are, *to make clear, explain, reveal, declare;* of appointments, *to proclaim a person as chosen.*

děclinātio -ōnis, f. *bending away, turning aside.* Transf., *an avoiding, declining;* rhet. *a digression;* grammat. *inflexion, declension.*

děclino -are: transit., *to bend aside, turn away, deflect.* Transf., *to avoid, to shun;* intransit., *to deviate, swerve, digress.*

děclivis -e, *inclined downwards, sloping;*

n. as subst. **děclīvĕ** -is, *a slope, declivity.*

děclīvitās -ātis, f., *a declivity.*

děcocta -ae, f. subst. from decoquo; q.v.

děcoctor -ōris, m., *spendthrift, bankrupt.*

děcollo -are, *to behead.*

děcōlo -are, *to trickle away.*

děcōlor -ōris, *off-colour, pale.*

děcōlōrātio -ōnis, f. *discolouring.*

děcōlōro -are, *to discolour.*

děcŏquo -cŏquĕre -coxi -coctum, *to boil thoroughly; to boil down, boil away;* of metals, *to melt away;* of property, *to waste;* commerc., *to ruin oneself, become bankrupt.*

    Hence partic. **děcoctus** -a -um, *boiled down;* of style, *insipid;* f. as subst. *a cold drink.*

děcor -ōris, m. *grace, comeliness beauty.*

děcŏro -are, *to embellish, beautify, adorn.*

děcōrus -a -um, physically, *graceful, beautiful comely;* morally, *proper, fit, becoming.* N. as subst. **děcōrum** -i, *propriety, grace.* Adv. **děcōrē,** *fitly, becomingly.*

děcrĕpitus -a -um, *infirm, decrepit.*

děcresco -crescĕre -crēvi -crētum, *to grow down, become smaller, decrease.*

děcrētum -i, subst. from decerno; q.v.

děcūma (**děcīma**) -ae, f. *a tenth part* tithe (as an offering, tax or largess).

děcūmānus (**děcīmānus**) -a -um, *of the tenth.* (1) *relating to the provincial tax of a tenth;* m. as subst. *the farmer of such a tax.* (2) *belonging to the tenth legion;* m. pl. as subst. *its members.* (3) *belonging to the tenth cohort.*

děcūmātes -ium, pl. adj. *relating to tithes.*

děcumbo -cumbĕre -cūbui, *to lie down, fall, fall down.*

děcūmo (**děcīmo**) -are, *to take a tithe;* milit. *to decimate troops.*

děcūria -ae, f. *a body of ten men; a class, division,* esp. *of jurors; a party, club.*

děcūriātio -ōnis, f. and **děcūriātus** -ūs, m., *a dividing into decuriae.*

¹**děcŭrio** -are, *to divide into bodies of ten,* or *into classes in gen.*

²**děcŭrio** -ōnis, m., *head of a body of ten;* milit. *company-commander in the cavalry;* polit., *a senator of a municipium* or *colonia.*

děcurro -currĕre -cŭcurri or -curri -cursum., *to run down, hasten down;* milit. *to move down* or *to manoeuvre.* Transf., *to run in a race;* transit. to *run through, traverse a set course; to have recourse to, take refuge in;* of ships *to sail downstream* or *to land;* of water, *to run down.*

děcursio -ōnis, f., milit., *a manoeuvre* or *charge.*

děcursus -ūs, m. *a running down;* milit., *a manoeuvre, a charge, attack.* Transf., *the completion of a course;* rhet., *rhythmical movement.*

dĕcurtātus -a -um., *mutilated* (of style).

dĕcŭs -ŏris, n. *distinction, honour, glory, grace*; moral *dignity, virtue*; of persons, *pride, glory*; plur., decora, *distinguished acts*.

dĕcŭtĭo -cŭtĕre -cussi -cussum. *to shake down, shake off, knock off*.

dēdĕcet -dĕcēre -dĕcŭit, *it is unbecoming, unsuitable, unfitting*.

dēdĕcŏro -are, *to dishonour bring shame upon*.

dēdĕcŏrus -a -um, *shameful, dishonourable*.

dēdĕcŭs -ŏris, n. *shame, dishonour, disgrace; a dishonourable action, crime, vice*.

dēdĭcātĭo -ōnis, f., *consecration*.

dēdĭco -are, *to dedicate, consecrate; to specify, indicate*.

dēdignor -ari, dep. *to think unworthy, scorn, reject*.

dēdisco -discĕre -dĭdĭci. *to unlearn, forget*.

dēdĭtīcĭus -a -um, *relating to surrender*; m. plur., dediticii, *subjects of Rome without rights*.

dēdĭtĭo -ōnis, *unconditional surrender, capitulation*.

dēdo dēdĕre -dĭdi -dĭtum, *to give up, surrender*; esp. of the conquered, *to give up, surrender*. Transf., *to give up to, dedicate, devote*.
     Hence partic. **dēdĭtus** -a -um, *devoted to, addicted to*; dĕdĭtă opĕrā, *intentionally*.

dēdŏceo -ēre, *to cause to unlearn, to unteach; teach not to*.

dēdŏlĕo -dŏlēre -dŏlŭi, *to make an end of grieving*.

dēdūco -dūcĕre -duxi -ductum, *to lead or bring down*; in time, from the past, *to trace downwards to the present*; in amount, *to reduce*, or, from an amount, *to subtract*; in gen., *to lead or draw away; to lead forth colonists, to found a colony; to escort a person to a place*; of persons and things, *to bring out of one state, opinion, etc. into another*; in weaving, *to draw threads*; hence, *to draw out, spin out in speech or writing*.

dēductĭo -ōnis, f. *a leading down; a reduction; a leading away of colonists, etc*.

deerro -are, *to wander from the right path, go astray*.

dēfătĭgātĭo -ōnis, f. *exhaustion, fatigue*.

dēfătĭgo -are, *to weary, fatigue*.

dēfătiscor = defetiscor; q.v.

dēfectĭo -ōnis, f. *failure*. Hence *defection, rebellion; weakening, failing, vanishing*. Partic. **dēfectus** -a -um, *failing, deficient*.

dēfector -ōris, m. *rebel, deserter*.

¹dēfectus -a -um, partic. of deficio; q.v.

²dēfectus -ūs, m., *a failing, disappearing*; esp. *a failing of light, eclipse*.

dēfendo -fendĕre -fendi -fensum. (1) *to repel, repulse, ward off, drive away*. (2) *to defend, protect*; esp. *to defend in court*; in argument, *to maintain a proposition or statement; to sustain a part*.

dēfensĭo -ōnis, f. (1) *a warding off*. (2) *defence*.

dēfensĭto -are, *to defend frequently*.

dēfenso -are, *to defend vigorously*.

dēfensor -ōris, m. (1) *one who wards off or averts*. (2) *a defender, protector*, esp. in court.

dēfĕro -ferre -tŭli -lātum, *to bring down, carry down*; in gen., *to bring or carry away*, esp. *to a particular place*; deferre rationes, *to hand in accounts*; fig., *to offer, hand over, refer*; of news. *to communicate, report*, esp. *to authority*; legal, deferre nomen *to inform against a person*, indict: deferre crimen, *to bring a charge*.

dēfervesco -fervescĕre -fervi or ferbŭi, *to cease boiling*; of passion, *to cease to rage*.

dēfĕtiscor (**dēfătiscor**) -fĕtisci -fessus, dep. *to become tired, grow weary*: esp. in perf. partic. **dēfessus** -a -um. *weary, tired*.

dēfĭcĭo -fĭcĕre -fēci -fectum: intransit. *to do less than one might, to fail*; hence, *to desert, rebel, revolt*; of things, *to fail, run short*; of sun or moon, *to become eclipsed*; of fire, *to go out*; of water, *to ebb*; of strength, etc., *to fail, become weak*; animo deficere, *to lose heart*; transit., *to abandon, leave, fail*; rarely pass. deficī, *to be failed*.
     Hence partic. **dēfectus** -a -um, *feeble*, esp. *because of age*.

dēfīgo -fīgĕre -fixi, -fixum, *to fasten down, fix in*; in gen., *to secure, plant firmly*; of sight or thought, *to concentrate, fix upon*; of persons, *to fix, make motionless*, with astonishment, etc.; partic. defixus, *astounded*; of enchantment, *to bind by a spell*.

dēfingo -fingere -finxi, *to form, mould*.

dēfīnĭo -ire, *to limit, bound, mark out; to set limits to a thing, confine; to set as a limit, appoint, assign; to interpret ideas or words in terms of each other, to understand one thing by another*; in logic, *to define*.
     Hence partic. **dēfīnītus** -a -um, *definite, distinct*; adv. **dēfīnītē**.

dēfīnītĭo -ōnis, f., *limiting, prescribing*; in logic, *a definition*.

dēfīnītīvus -a -um, *definitive, explanatory*.

dēfīt (as from defio), *fails*.

dēflagrātĭo -ōnis, f. *burning, destruction by fire*.

dēflagro -are, *to be burnt down, destroyed by fire*; in gen., *to be destroyed*; of passions, *to cease burning, abate, cool*. Partic. in pass. sense, **dēflagrātus** -a -um, *burnt down, destroyed*.

dēflecto -flectĕre -flexi -flexum: transit., *to bend down or aside*: intransit., *to turn aside, turn away*; in speech, *to digress*.

dēflĕo -flēre -flēvi -flētum, *to bewail, weep for*.

dēfloccātus -a -um, *bald.*

dēflōresco -flōrescĕre -flōrŭi, *to shed blossom, fade, wither.*

dēflŭo -flŭĕre -fluxi. (1) *to flow down, slip down, descend;* abstr., *to come down,* esp. *of the gifts of heaven.* (2) *to flow away, disappear, be lost.*

dēfŏdio -fŏdĕre fōdi -fossum, *to dig down into;* to *form by digging, excavate; to dig in, cover, bury, conceal.*

dēformātio -ōnis, f. *deforming, disfiguring; degradation.*

dēformis -e. (1) *deformed, misshapen, ugly, disgusting.* Transf., *foul, shameful.* (2) *formless, shapeless.* Adv. **dēformĭter,** *in an ugly fashion.*

dēformĭtās -ātis, f. *deformity, ugliness; disgrace, dishonour.*

dēformo -are. (1) *to form, fashion; to delineate.* (2) *to put out of shape, disfigure; to disgrace, dishonour.*

dēfraudo (**dēfrudo**) -are, *to deceive, cheat;* genium suum, *to deprive oneself of pleasure.*

dēfrēnātus -a -um, *unbridled, unrestrained.*

dēfrico -frĭcare -frĭcŭi -frictum, *to rub down;* fig. *to satirize, lash.*

dēfringo -fringĕre -frēgi -fractum, *to break down, break off.*

dēfrūtum -i, n. *new wine boiled down.*

dēfŭgio -fŭgĕre -fūgi: intransit., *to flee away;* transit., *to fly from, avoid.*

dēfundo -fundĕre -fūdi -fūsum, *to pour down, pour out.*

dēfungor -fungi -functus, dep. *to perform, discharge, have done with;* (vita) defungi, *to die.*

dēgĕner -ĕris, *fallen away from one's origin, unworthy of one's race, degenerate, unworthy, ignoble.*

dēgĕnĕro -are: intransit., *to become unlike one's kind, to fall off, degenerate;* transit., *to cause to degenerate, or disgrace by degeneracy.*

dēgĕro -ĕre, *to carry off.*

dēgo dēgĕre dēgi, *to pass time;* absol., *to live.*

dēgrandĭnat, impers., *it hails violently,* or (perhaps) *it ceases to hail.*

dēgrăvo -are, *to weigh down, bring down, lower.*

dēgrĕdĭor -grĕdi -gressus, dep., *to step down, march down.*

dēgusto -are, *to take a taste from, taste;* of fire, *to lick;* of a weapon, *to graze;* in gen., *to try, make a trial of, sound.*

dēhinc, *from here, hence; from this time, henceforth,* immediately *after that time, thereupon.*

dēhisco -ĕre, *to gape, open, split down.*

dēhŏnestāmentum -i, n. *blemish, deformity disgrace.*

dēhŏnoro -are, *to dishonour, disgrace.*

dēhortor -ari, dep. *to discourage, dissuade.*

dēĭcio -icĕre -iēci -iectum, *to throw, cast, hurl down;* with reflex., *to rush down;* of upright things, *to throw to the ground, fell;* of persons, *to kill, bring down.* In gen., *to fling away or*

aside; naut., deici, *to be thrown off course;* milit. *to dislodge; to eject, dispossess; to shift a person from an opinion, attitude; to disappoint.*
Hence partic. **dēiectus** -a -um *low-lying; dispirited, dejected.*

dēiectio -ōnis, f. *throwing down; eviction from property.*

¹**dēiectus** -a -um, partic. from deicio; q.v.

²**dēiectus** -ūs, m. *a throwing down; a declivity, steep slope.*

dēiero -are, *to swear.*

dein; see deinde.

dēinceps, *one after another, successively.*

dēinde, and abbrev. **dein:** of space, *from that place;* of time, *thereafter, thereupon, then, afterwards;* in enumerations, *next, and then.*

Dēiŏtărus -i, m. *a king of Galatia, defended by Cicero.*

dēiungo -ĕre, *to disconnect.*

dēlābor -labi -lapsus, dep. *to glide down, fall down, sink;* of liquids, *to flow down.* Transf., *to sink to, come down to circumstances, etc.; to proceed from, be derived from an origin; to fall unawares among people.*

dēlăcĕro -are, *to tear to pieces.*

dēlāmentor -ari, dep. *to bewail, lament.*

dēlasso -are, *to weary, tire out.*

dēlātio -ōnis, f. *reporting, giving information against, denunciation.*

dēlātor -ōris, m.. *an informer, denouncer.*

dēlectābĭlis -e, *delightful, pleasant.*

dēlectāmentum -i, n. *delight, amusement.*

dēlectātio -ōnis, f. *delight, pleasure.*

dēlecto -are, *to divert, attract, delight;* in pass., with abl. *to take delight in:* in pass. with infin., *to delight to.*

dēlectus -ūs, m. *choosing, choice.*

dēlēgātio -ōnis, f. *assignment of a debt.*

dēlēgo -are, *to transfer, commit, assign; to impute, attribute, ascribe.*

dēlēnimentum -i, n. *what soothes or charms.*

dēlēnio (**dēlīnio**) -ire. *to soften down; to soothe or charm.*

dēlēnitor -ōris, m. *one who soothes or cajoles.*

dēlĕo -lēre -lēvi -lētum, *to blot out, efface;* in gen., *to destroy, annihilate.*

dēlībĕrābundus -a -um, *carefully considering, deliberating.*

dēlībĕrātio -ōnis, f. *consideration, consultation.*

dēlībĕrātivus -a -um, *relating to deliberation.*

dēlībĕrātor -ōris, m., *one who deliberates.*

dēlībĕro -are, *to weigh carefully, consider, consult about; to ask advice,* esp. *of an oracle; as a result of deliberation, to resolve.*
Hence partic. **dēlībĕrātus** -a -um. *resolved, determined.*

dēlībo -are, *to take a little from, to taste;* in gen., *to extract, derive; to take from so as to enjoy; to take from so as to lessen or spoil.*

dēlĭbro -are, *to peel the bark off.*

dēlĭbūtus -a -um, *steeped.*

dēlĭcātus -a -um, *soft, tender*; in bad sense, *luxurious* of things, *spoilt, effeminate* of persons; of tastes, *fastidious, dainty, nice.* Adv. **dēlĭcātē**, *luxuriously.*

dēlĭcĭae -arum, f. pl. *allurements, charms, delights, fancies*; esse in deliciis, *to be a favourite*; concr., *darling, sweetheart.*

dēlĭcĭŏlae -arum, f. pl. *a darling.*

dēlictum -i, n. *a fault, crime.*

¹dēlĭgo -lĭgĕre -lēgi -lectum *to pick, pluck; to choose, select.*

²dēlĭgo -are, *to fasten, bind up.*

dēlĭngo -ere, *to lick off, lick up.*

dēlinquo -linquĕre -lĭqui -lictum, *to fail, be wanting,* esp. *to fail in duty, commit a crime.*

dēlĭquesco -liquescĕre -lĭcŭi, *to melt, dissolve; to vanish, disappear.*

dēlĭquo and **dēlĭco** -are, *to clarify; to explain.*

dēlīrātĭo -ōnis, f. *folly. silliness, dotage.*

dēlīro -are, " *to go off the rails* " act *crazily, rave.*

dēlīrus -a -um, *silly, crazy doting.*

dēlĭtesco -litescĕre -lĭtŭi, *to conceal oneself, lie hid, take refuge.*

dēlītigo -are, *to scold furiously.*

Dēlos -i, f., *a small island in the Aegean Sea, birth-place of Apollo and Diana*; adj. **Dēlĭācus** and **Dēlĭus** -a -um, *of Delos*; as subst. **Dēlĭus** -i, m. = *Apollo*; **Dēlĭa** -ae, f. = *Diana.*

Delphi -orum, m. *a town in Phocis, famous for its oracle of Apollo*; adj. **Delphĭcus** -a -um.

delphĭnus -i and **delphin** -ĭnis, m. *dolphin.*

dēlūbrum -i, n. *a shrine, temple.*

dēluctor -ari, dep. and **dēlucto** -are, *to wrestle.*

dēlūdo -lūdĕre -lūsi -lūsum, *to mock, cheat.*

dēlumbo -are, *to lame, enervate, weaken.*

dēmādesco -mădescĕre -mădŭi, *to become wet through.*

dēmando -are, *to entrust, commit.*

dēmens -mentis, *out of one's mind, insane, senseless*; adv. **dēmenter.**

dēmentĭa -ae, f., *senselessness, insanity*; in plur., *mad actions.*

dēmentĭo -ire, *to be mad, rave.*

dēmērĕo -ēre and **dēmērĕor** -ēri, dep. *to earn thoroughly; to deserve well of a person, to oblige.*

dēmergo -mergĕre -mersi -mersum, *to sink, plunge into, dip under*; aere alieno demersus, *over head and ears in debt.*

dēmētĭor -mētīri -mensus, dep. *to measure out*; partic. **dēmensus** -a -um, in pass. sense, with n. as subst., *an allowance.*

dēmēto -mētĕre -messŭi -messum, *to mow, reap, cut down or off.*

dēmigro -are, *to emigrate, depart.* Transf., *to die.*

dēmĭnŭo -mĭnŭĕre -mĭnŭi -mĭnūtum, *to take away from, diminish, lessen*; capite se deminuere, *to suffer a loss of civil rights.*

dēmĭnūtĭo -ōnis, f. *lessening, diminution*; sui, *loss of prestige*; capitis, *loss of civil rights; right of alienation.*

dēmīror -ari, dep. *to wonder (at).*

dēmissĭo -ōnis, f., *sinking, lowering*; animi, *dejection.*

dēmītĭgo -ari, *to make mild, soften.*

dēmitto -mittĕre -misi -missum, *to send down, lower, put down*; tunica demissa, *hanging loosely*; demissi capilli, *growing long*; milit., *to lead down*; naut., *to lower gear or bring a vessel downstream or to land.* Transf., *to sink, bury, plunge*; of spirits, *to lower.*
Hence partic. **dēmissus** -a -um, *hanging down*; of dress and hair, *long, loose*; of places, *low-lying.* Transf., *feeble, weak; unassuming, modest; down-cast, dispirited.* Adv. **dēmissē**, *low, near the ground.* Transf., *modestly, humbly meanly.*

dēmo **dēmĕre** dempsi demptum, *to take away, subtract.*

Dēmocrĭtus -i, m. *a philosopher of Abdera (c. 460-370 B.C.).* Hence adj. **Dēmocrĭticus** -a -um.

dēmōlĭor -iri, dep. *to throw down, demolish.*

dēmōlĭtĭo -ōnis, f. *throwing down, demolition.*

dēmonstrātĭo -ōnis, f. *pointing out, indication, explanation, description*; rhet., *oratory concerned with praise and censure.*

dēmonstrātīvus -a -um, *demonstrative*; rhet., of oratory, *concerned with praise and censure.*

dēmonstrātor -ōris, m., *one who points out or indicates.*

dēmonstro -are *to indicate, explain, describe.*

dēmōrĭor -mŏri -mortŭus, dep. *to die, die off*; with acc. of person, *to die for love of.*

dēmŏror -ari, dep.: intransit., *to delay, loiter*; transit., *to stop, delay, retard.*

Dēmosthĕnēs -is (also -i), *the Athenian orator (384-322 B.C.).*

dēmŏvĕo -mŏvēre -mōvi -mōtum, *to move away, remove*; hominem de sententia, *to make a person change his opinion.*

dēmūgĭtus -a -um, *filled with the noise of lowing.*

dēmulcĕo -mulcēre -mulsi, *to stroke down, caress by stroking.*

dēmum, of time, *at length, at last*; in enumerations, *finally, in short*; id demum, *that and that alone.*

dēmurmŭro -are, *to murmur or mutter over.*

dēmūtātĭo -ōnis, f., *change, alteration,* esp. for the worse.

dēmūto -are: transit., *to change, alter* a thing, esp. for the worse; intransit. *to change one's mind or become different.*

dēnārius -a -um, *containing ten*; denarius nummus, or denarius alone, *a Roman silver coin.*

dēnarro -are, *to narrate, tell, relate.*

dēnăto -are, *to swim down.*

dēnēgo -are, *to deny, say no; to deny, refuse, reject a request.*

dēni -ae, -a, *ten by ten, ten at a time, by tens.*

dēnĭcălis -e, *releasing from death*; feriae, *a funeral ceremony.*

dēniquĕ: in time, *at last, finally*; in enumerations, *again, further or finally; in short, in fine.*

dēnōmino -are, *to name.*

dēnormo -are, *to make crooked.*

dēnŏto -are, *to mark out for another, designate precisely; to take note of.*

dens dentis, m. *a tooth.* Transf., of things resembling a tooth, e.g., a *mattock or sickle*; abstr., of anything *sharp, biting, destructive.*

denso -are, and **densĕo** -ēre, *to make thick, condense, press together.*

densus -a -um, *thick close, dense*; in time, *frequent*; in degree, *intense, vehement*; in style, of work or author, *condensed.* Adv. **densē**, *densely*; of time, *frequently.*

dentālĭa -ĭum, n. pl. *the share-beam of a plough.*

dentātus -a -um, *provided with teeth, toothed; polished by teeth.*

dentio -ire, *to cut teeth*; of teeth, *to grow.*

dēnūbo -nūbĕre -nupsi -nuptum, *to be married off, to marry (of the woman), esp. beneath her.*

dēnūdo -are, *to lay bare, uncover, reveal.* Transf., *to rob, plunder.*

dēnuntĭātĭo -ōnis, f. *announcement, declaration, threat.*

dēnuntio -are, *to announce, give notice, declare, threaten*; bellum denuntiare, *to declare war*; legal, *to give notice, serve a summons.*

dēnŭŏ, *anew, again; a second time.*

deŏnĕro -are, *to unload, disburden.*

dĕorsum or **dĕorsus**, *downwards*; sursum deorsum, *up and down, backwards and forwards.*

dēpăciscor = depeciscor; q.v.

dēpactus -a -um, *fastened down, firmly fixed.*

dēpasco -pascĕre -pāvi -pastum and **dēpascor** -pasci, dep. *to feed off*; in gen., *to eat up, consume, reduce.*

dēpĕciscor -pēcisci -pectus, dep. *to make a bargain for or about; to settle for, accept a condition.*

dēpecto -pectĕre -pexum, *to comb down*; in comedy, *to beat soundly.*

dēpĕcūlātor -ōris, m. *plunderer embezzler.*

dēpĕcūlor -ari, dep. *to rob, plunder.*

dēpello -pellĕre -pŭli -pulsum, *to drive down, or away, expel, remove*; milit. *to dislodge*; naut., *to drive off course*; in gen., *to drive away, avert*; of persons, *to dissuade.*

dēpendĕo -ēre, *to hang down; to depend upon; to be derived from.*

dēpendo -pendĕre -pendi -pensum, *to weigh out and pay over.*

dēperdo -perdĕre -perdĭdi -perdĭtum, *to lose, waste, destroy*; esp. of the effects of love.

dēpĕrĕo -pĕrire -pĕrĭi, *to perish or be ruined utterly; to be desperately in love.*

dēpilo -are, *to strip of hair or feathers.*

dēpingo -pingĕre -pinxi -pictum, *to paint, depict, portray.*

dēplango -plangĕre -planxi, *to bewail, lament.*

dēplexus -a -um, *clasping.*

dēplōro -are: intransit., *to weep bitterly, lament*; transit., *to lament, bewail; to regard as lost, give up.*

dēplŭit -plŭĕre, *rains down.*

dēpōno -pōnĕre -pŏsŭi -pŏsĭtum. (1) *to lay down, put down*; esp. *to lay as wager or prize.* (2) *for safe-keeping, to put down, deposit; to commit, entrust.* (3) *to lay aside, have done with.*

Hence partic. **dēpŏsĭtus** -a -um. (1) *laid out; dying, despaired of, dead* (2) *entrusted*; n. as subst. *a deposit.*

dēpŏpŭlātĭo -ōnis, f. *laying waste ravaging.*

dēpŏpŭlātor -ōris, m. *a ravager.*

dēpŏpŭlor -ari, dep.; also **dēpŏpŭlo** -are, *to lay waste, ravage, destroy.*

dēporto -are, *to carry down, carry off, take away; to bring home; to banish for life* (with loss of rights and property).

dēposco -poscĕre -pŏposci, *to demand, usually for a purpose, esp. for punishment.*

dēprāvātĭo -ōnis, f. *perverting, distorting*; animi depravity.

dēprāvo -are, *to make crooked, pervert, disfigure*; verbally, *to distort, misrepresent*; morally, *to spoil, corrupt.* Adv. from partic., **dēprāvātē**, *perversely.*

dēprĕcābundus -a -um, *earnestly entreating.*

dēprĕcātĭo -ōnis, f. (1) *an attempt to avert by entreaty, deprecating.* (2) *an entreaty against a person, for his punishment.*

dēprĕcātor -ōris, m. (1) *one that begs off, an intercessor.* (2) *one that pleads for.*

dēprĕcor -ari, dep. (1) *to try to avert by entreaty, to deprecate; to allege in excuse* (so as to avoid punishment). (2) *to entreat against a person, to curse.* (3) *to entreat for, beg for, intercede.*

dēprĕhendo and **dēprendo** -endĕre -endi -ensum, *to seize upon, catch hold of*; esp. *to surprise, catch, detect a person in a crime or fault; to discover, detect, observe a thing.*

dēprĕhensĭo -ōnis, f. *detection.*

dēprimo -primĕre -pressi -pressum, *to press down, depress*; esp. *to plant deep in the ground, dig deep*; of ships, *to sink.*

Hence partic. **depressus** -a -um, *low-lying.*

dēproelǐans -antis, *struggling violently.*

dēprōmo -prōmĕre -prompsi -promptum, *to take down produce, fetch out.*

dēprŏpĕro: intransit, *to hasten;* transit., *to hasten over, produce in haste.*

dēpŭdet -pŭdĕre -pŭdŭit, *ceases to be ashamed, loses all sense of shame.*

dēpugno -are, *to fight hard, fight it out.*

dēpulsǐo -ōnis, f. *driving away;* rhet. *defence.*

dēpulsor -ōris, m. *an averter.*

dēpŭto -are. (1) *to prune, cut off.* (2) *to count, estimate.*

deque; see susque deque.

dērēlinquo -linquĕre -līqui -lictum, *to forsake, desert, abandon.*

dērēpentĕ, *suddenly.*

dērēpo -rēpĕre -repsi, *to creep, crawl down.*

dērīdĕo -ridēre -risi -risum, *to laugh at, mock, deride.*

dērīdǐcŭlus -a -um, *very laughable;* n. as subst. *ridicule;* esse deridiculo, *to be an object of ridicule.*

dērīgo -rigĕre -rexi -rectum, *to set straight, direct;* of placing (also in form dirigo), *to order, dispose;* milit. *to draw up.* Transf., *to direct, aim, guide* abstr. *things.*

dērīgǔi, perf., *grew quite stiff.*

dērīpǐo -rīpĕre -rīpŭi -reptum, *to tear down, snatch away.*

dērīsor -ōris, m. *a mocker.*

dērīsus -ūs, m. *mockery, derision.*

dērīvātǐo -ōnis, f. *turning away or diversion of water.*

dērīvo -are, *to turn into another channel, to divert.*

dērōgo -are, *to modify a law;* in gen., *to diminish, detract from.*

dērōsus -a -um, *gnawed away.*

dēruncǐno -are, *to cheat, fleece.*

dērŭo -rŭĕre -rŭi -rŭtum, *to cast down, make to fall.*

dēruptus -a -um, *broken off;* hence *precipitous,* ·*steep;* n. pl. as subst., *precipices.*

dēsaevǐo -ire -ii -itum, *to rage violently.*

dēscendo -scendĕre -scendi -scensum, *to climb down, come down, descend;* milit., *to march down;* of things, *to sink, pierce, penetrate;* of mountains, *to slope down;* of the voice, *to sink.* Transf., of persons, *to lower oneself, stoop;* of things, *to sink in, penetrate.*

dēscensǐo -ōnis, f. *going down, descent;* Tiberina, *voyage down the Tiber.*

dēscensus -ūs, m. *going down, descent; way down.*

dēscisco -sciscĕre -scivi or -scǐi -scitum, *to break away, revolt, withdraw, diverge.*

dēscrībo -scrībĕre -scripsi -scriptum. (1) *to transcribe, copy.* (2) *to describe, delineate, represent, portray.*

dēscriptǐo -ōnis, f. (1) *a copy.* (2) *a representation, figure, description.*

dēsĕco -sĕcare -sĕcŭi -sectum, *to hew off, cut off.*

dēsĕro -sĕrĕre -sĕrŭi -sertum, *to forsake, abandon, leave; to neglect,· disregard.*

Hence partic. **dēsertus** -a -um, *forsaken, abandoned;* n. pl. as subst., *deserts, wildernesses.*

dēsertor -ōris, m. *one who forsakes,* milit., *deserter.*

dēservǐo -ire, *to serve zealously, be a slave to.*

dēsĕs -sǐdis, m. (nom. sing. not found), *idle, lazy, inactive.*

dēsǐdĕo -sǐdēre -sēdi -sessum, *to sit idle, be slothful.*

dēsǐdĕrābilis -e, *desirable.*

dēsǐdĕrātǐo -ōnis, f. *desire, longing.*

dēsǐdĕrǐum -i, n. *desire or longing, grief for the absence or loss of a person or thing;* in gen., *a desire or request.*

dēsǐdĕro -are, *to long for what is absent or lost, to wish for; to miss, find a lack of;* milit., *to lose.*

dēsǐdǐa -ae, f. *idleness, inactivity, apathy.*

dēsǐdǐōsus -a -um, *slothful, idle, lazy;* adv. **dēsǐdǐōsē.**

dēsīdo -sīdĕre -sēdi, *to sink down, subside, settle.* Transf., *to deteriorate.*

dēsignātǐo -ōnis, f. *marking out, designation: appointment to an office.*

dēsignātor -ōris, m. = dissignator; q.v.

dēsignātor -ōris, m. = dissignator; q.v.

dēsigno -are, *to mark out, trace, plan;* in gen., *to point out, indicate, signify; to portray, delineate;* polit., *to nominate, elect;* partic. **dēsignātus,** *elected, designate.*

dēsilǐo -silire -silǔi -sultum, *to leap down;* ad pedes, *dismount.*

dēsino -sǐnĕre -sǐi -sǐtum: transit., *to cease, desist from;* intransit., *to cease, stop, end;* with in and acc., *to end in.*

dēsǐpientǐa -ae, f. *foolishness.*

dēsǐpǐo -sǐpĕre, *to be foolish, act foolishly.*

dēsisto -sistĕre -stǐti -stitum, *to stand away:* from a person, *to withdraw;* from action, etc., *to desist, leave off, cease.*

dēsōlo -are, *to leave solitary, forsake.*

dēspecto -are, *to regard from above, look down upon; to despise.*

¹**dēspectus** -a -um, partic. from despicio; q.v.

²**dēspectus** -ūs, m. *a looking down, downward view; an object of contempt.*

dēspērātǐo -ōnis, f. *hopelessness, despair.*

dēspēro -are: intransit., *to be without hope, despair;* transit., *to despair of, give up.* Adv. from pres. partic., **dēspēranter,** *despairingly, hopelessly.* Perf. partic. **dēspērātus** -a -um; in pass. sense, *despaired of;* in middle sense, *desperate.*

dēspǐcātǐo -ōnis, f. and **dēspǐcātus** -ūs, m. *contempt.*

dēspǐcǐentǐa -ae, f., *looking down upon; contempt.*

dēspǐcǐo -spǐcĕre -spexi -spectum, *to look down, regard from above; to look down upon, despise.* Pres. partic. act. **dēspǐcǐens,** *contemptuous.* Perf. partic. pass. **dēspectus** -a -um, *despised, contemptible.*

dēspĭcor -ari, *to look down upon, despise.* Perf. partic. in pass. sense despĭcātus -a -um, *despised, contemptible.*

dēspŏlĭo -are, *to plunder, despoil.*

dēspondĕo -spondēre -spondi -sponsum, *to pledge, to promise,* esp. *to promise in marriage, betroth;* in gen., *to pledge, devote;* with animum or animos, *to lose heart, despair.*

dēspūmo -are. (1) *to skim off.* Transf., *to digest.* (2) *to drop foam.*

dēspŭo -spŭere, *to spit down, spit on the ground.* Transf., *to reject.*

dēsquāmo -are, *to take off the scales, to scale.*

dēsterto -stertĕre -stertŭi, *to finish snoring or dreaming.*

dēstillo -are, *to drip down, distil.*

dēstĭnātĭo -ōnis, f. *fixing, determining, appointment.*

dēstĭno -are, *to make fast, fix down;* to *fix, determine, settle, appoint;* with infin., *to resolve to do;* of persons, *to appoint to an office;* of things *to fix upon, intend to buy.*
  Hence partic. dēstĭnātus -a -um, *fixed, determined;* n. as subst., *an objective or intention;* (ex) destinato, *intentionally.*

dēstĭtŭo -stĭtŭere -stĭtŭi -stĭtūtum, *to set down, place;* esp. *to leave in the lurch, forsake, desert.*

dēstĭtūtĭo -ōnis. f. *forsaking, abandoning.*

dēstringo -stringĕre -strinxi -strictum. (1) *to strip;* esp. *to draw or bare a* sword. Transf., *to satirize, censure.* (2) *to touch lightly, graze.*
  Hence partic. dēstrictus -a -um, *severe.*

dēstrŭo -strŭere -struxi -structum, *to pull down, dismantle, destroy, ruin.*

dēsŭbĭtō (or dē sŭbĭtō), *suddenly.*

dēsūdo -are, *to sweat violently, exert oneself hard.*

dēsŭēfĭo -fĭeri -factus sum, pass., *to be made unaccustomed.*

dēsŭesco -suescĕre -suēvi -suētum, *to become unaccustomed;* esp. partic. dēsŭētus -a -um: in pass. sense, *disused;* in middle sense, *unaccustomed, unused to.*

dēsŭētūdo -ĭnis, f. *disuse.*

dēsultor -ōris, m. *a leaper, acrobat.* Transf., *an inconstant person.*

dēsultōrĭus -a -um, *relating to a* desultor.

dēsum -esse -fŭi, *to be down, fall short, fail, be missing or remiss.*

dēsūmo -sūmĕre -sumpsi -sumptum, *to take out, choose, select.*

dēsŭpĕr, *from above.*

dēsurgo -surgĕre -surrexi -surrectum, *to rise and go down or out.*

dētĕgo -tĕgĕre -texi -tectum, *to uncover, lay bare, disclose.*

dētendo -tendĕre -tensum, *to unstretch;* tabernacula, *to strike tents.*

dētergĕo -tergēre -tersi -tersum. (1) *to wipe off, clear away, brush off.* (2) *to cleanse by wiping.*

dētĕrĭor -ĭus, genit. -ōris, compar. (superl. deterrimus), *lower, inferior, poorer, worse.* Adv. dētĕrĭus, *worse.*

dētermĭnātĭo -ōnis, f., *boundary, end.*

dētermĭno -are, *to bound, fix the limits of, determine.*

dētĕro -tĕrĕre trĭvi -trĭtum, *to rub away, wear out; to detract from, weaken.*

dēterrĕo -terrēre -terrŭi -terrĭtum, *to frighten away, deter, discourage.*

dētestābĭlis -e, *abominable, horrible.*

dētestātĭo -ōnis, f. (1) *a cursing, execration.* (2) *a warding off, averting.*

dētestor -ari, dep. (1) *to pray against: to pray for deliverance from a person or thing, or to curse, execrate.* (2) *of the gods' action, to avert, remove.*

dētexo -texĕre -texŭi -textum, *to make by plaiting; to finish, complete.*

dētĭnĕo -tinēre -tinŭi -tentum, *to hold back, detain; to prevent; to engage, occupy exclusively.*

dētondĕo -tondēre -tŏtondi and -tondi -tonsum, *to shear, clip.*

dētŏno -tŏnare -tŏnŭi *to cease to thunder or rage.*

dētorquĕo -torquēre -torsi -tortum. (1) *to turn away, bend aside.* (2) *to twist out of shape, distort.*

dētractĭo -ōnis, f. *drawing off, withdrawal, taking away;* rhet., *ellipsis.*

dētracto = detrecto; q.v.

dētractor -ōris, m., *detractor, disparager.*

dētrăho -trăhere -traxi -tractum. (1) *to draw down, drag down; to lower, humiliate.* (2) *to draw off, drag away, remove;* numerically, *to subtract;* in speech, *to detract from a* person, *disparage, slander.*

dētrectātĭo -ōnis, f. *refusal.*

dētrectātor -ōris, m. *disparager, detractor.*

dētrecto -are. (1) *to decline, refuse, shirk.* (2) *to disparage, detract from, depreciate.*

dētrĭmentōsus -a -um, *detrimental, hurtful.*

dētrĭmentum -i, n. *loss, damage, injury;* milit., *loss, defeat.*

dētrītus -a -um, partic. from detero; q.v.

dētrūdo -trūdĕre -trūsi -trūsum, *to push down, thrust down;* milit., *to dislodge;* legal, *to dispossess, eject.* Transf., of persons, *to force, compel;* of functions, *to put off, postpone.*

dētrunco -are, *to lop or cut off; to mutilate.*

dēturbo -are, *to force away, dash down;* milit., *to dislodge;* legal, *to eject dispossess.*

Deucălĭōn -ōnis, m. *son of Prometheus, saved in an ark from a great flood, with his wife Pyrrha.*

deunx -uncis, m. *eleven-twelfths of a unit.*

deūro -ūrĕre -ussi -ustum, *to burn down;* of cold, *to destroy, nip.*

dĕus -i, m. *a god, a deity;* di meliora (ferant), *God forbid.*

dēvasto -are, *to lay waste, devastate.*

dĕvĕho -vĕhĕre -vexi -vectum, to carry away or down; pass. devehi (sc. navi), to sail.

dĕvello -vellere -velli -vulsum, to pluck, tear away.

dĕvēlo -are, to unveil, uncover.

dĕvĕnĕror -ari, dep. (1) to worship, revere. (2) to avert by prayers.

dĕvĕnĭo -vĕnire -vēni -ventum, to come to, arrive at, reach.

dĕverbĕro -are, to thrash soundly.

¹dĕversor -ari, dep., to lodge as a guest.

²dĕversor -ōris, m., a guest.

dĕversōrĭŏlum -i, n. a small lodging.

dĕversōrius -a -um, fit to lodge in; n. as subst. an inn, lodging, refuge.

dĕvertĭcŭlum (dēvort-) -i, n. (1) a by-way, by-path; hence digression. (2) an inn, lodging, refuge, resort.

dĕverto (dēvorto) -vertĕre -verti -versum; to turn aside; esp. to turn aside to a lodging, to put up at, stay with. Transf., to digress.

dĕvexus -a -um, moving downwards, descending, sinking; of position, sloping down, shelving, steep; of tendency, inclining to.

dĕvincio -vincire -vinxi -vinctum, to bind, tie fast, attach, connect.
     Hence partic. dĕvinctus -a -um, attached, devoted.

dĕvinco -vincĕre -vici -victum, to conquer thoroughly, subjugate, overcome.

dĕvītātio -ōnis, f. avoiding.

dĕvīto -are, to avoid.

dĕvĭus -a -um, off the beaten track, out of the way, solitary, retired; in mind, erroneous, unreasonable.

dĕvŏco -are, to call down or away; devocare in dubium, to bring into danger.

dĕvŏlo -are, to fly down, hasten down.

dĕvolvo -volvĕre -volvi -vŏlūtum, to roll down; pass., to roll down, fall headlong, sink back.

dĕvŏro -are, to swallow, devour, seize upon; of words, to articulate badly, mispronounce; of property, to consume, waste; of disagreeable things, to swallow, accept, put up with.

dĕvortĭcŭlum; see deverticulum.

dĕvortĭum -i, n., a by-way, by-path.

dĕvōtĭo -ōnis, f. (1) consecrating, devoting. (2) cursing. (3) enchantment, incantation.

dĕvōto -are, to consecrate or devote to death.

dĕvŏvĕo -vŏvēre -vōvi -vōtum, to consecrate, devote, esp. to a god, or to death; to curse, execrate; to bewitch, enchant; in gen., to devote, give up.
     Hence partic. dĕvōtus -a -um, devoted; accursed; attached to a person; m. pl. as subst. faithful followers.

dextella -ae, f., a little right hand.

dextĕr -tĕra -tĕrum, or -tra -trum; compar. dextĕrĭor -ĭus, superl. dextĭmus -a -um; right, on the right hand, on the right side. Transf., dexterous, skilful; propitious, favourable, opportune. F. as subst., dextĕra

or dextra -ae, the right hand; (a) dextra, on the right; esp. the right hand as pledge of faith; sometimes, in gen. the hand. Adv. dextĕrē or dextrē; compar. dexterius; dexterously, skilfully.

dextĕrĭtās -ātis, f., skilfulness, readiness.

dextrorsum and dextrorsus, on the right, towards the right.

Dĭa -ae, f. mother of Mercury.

dĭădēma -ătis, n., a royal headband, diadem.

dĭaeta -ae, f. (1) a way of living prescribed by a physician, regimen, diet. (2) a living-room.

dĭălecticus -a -um, of discussion, dialectical; m. as subst., dĭălecticus -i, a dialectician, logician; f. dĭălectica -ae, and dĭălecticē -es, the art of dialectic, logic; n. pl. dĭălectĭca -orum, dialectical discussion; adv. dĭălectĭcē, dialectically.

dĭālis -e, relating to Jupiter; (flamen) dialis, the priest of Jupiter.

dĭălŏgus -i, m., a philosophical conversation.

Dĭāna (older Dīāna) -ae, f. the virgin goddess of the moon and of hunting; adj. Dĭānĭus -a -um, belonging to Diana.

dĭārĭa -orum, n. pl. a day's allowance of food or pay.

dĭbăphus (-a) -um, double-dyed; as f. subst. dĭbăphus -i, the purple-striped robe of the higher magistrates in Rome.

dĭca -ae, f., law-suit, action in a Greek court.

dĭcācĭtās -ātis, f. wit, satire, raillery.

dĭcātĭo -ōnis, f. settling as a citizen.

dĭcax -ācis, ready of speech; witty, satirical, sarcastic.

dĭchŏrēus -i, m. a double trochee.

dĭcĭō -ōnis, f. power, sovereignty, authority.

dĭcis (genit.); dicis causa, dicis gratia, for form's sake, for the sake of appearances.

¹dĭco -are, to consecrate, dedicate, devote to the gods; to deify, place among the gods; to inaugurate. Transf., to devote, give up, set apart; se civitati, or in civitatem, to become a citizen.

²dĭco -dicĕre dixi dictum, to indicate; to appoint; most commonly, to say, speak, tell, mention; in pass. with infin., to be said to; impersonally, dicitur, it is said that; of ideas, to express, put into words; ius, to administer law, give rulings; of persons or things, to mention, speak of, tell of, relate; to name, call; to mean, refer to. N. of partic. as subst. dictum -i, a word, saying, speech; a witty saying, a bon-mot; a prediction; an order, command.

dĭcrŏtum -i, n. a vessel with two banks of oars.

dictamnus -i, f. dittany, a plant.

dictātor -ōris, m. a dictator; in Rome, an extraordinary magistrate, elected *in emergency and granted absolute power*; elsewhere, *a chief magistrate.*

dictātōrius -a -um, *belonging to a dictator, dictatorial.*

dictātūra -ae, f., *the office of dictator, dictatorship.*

dictĭo -ōnis, f. *saying, speaking, talk, oratory.*

dictĭto -are, *to say often, reiterate, assert repeatedly*; dictitare causas, *to plead frequently.*

dicto -are, *to say often; to say over, dictate a thing to be written*; hence *to get written down.*

dictum -i, n. subst. from ²dico; q.v.

¹Dīdō -ūs, f., *the founder of Carthage*, also called Elisa or Elissa.

²dīdo dīdēre dīdīdī dīdĭtum, *to divide, distribute, spread round.*

dīdūco -dūcĕre -duxi -ductum, *to draw apart, separate*; milit., *to divide, distribute, also to scatter, disperse.*

dĭēcŭla -ae, f. *a little day, a short time.*

dĭērectus -a -um, an abusive expression, like *go and be hanged!*

dĭēs -ēi, m. or f., *daytime, day; a day, period of twenty-four hours*; diem ex die, *from day to day*; in dies, *daily*, esp. of a continuing process of change; in diem vivere, *to live for the day*; meton., *the business or events of the day*; in gen., *time.* Esp. *a particular day, fixed date; a historic day; day of death; anniversary*, esp. *birthday.*

Dĭespiter -tris, m. *a name for Jupiter.*

diffāmo -are, *to spread evil reports about, to defame.*

diffĕrentĭa -ae, f., *difference, distinction.*

diffĕrĭtās -ātis, f. *difference.*

diffĕro differre distŭli dīlātum. Transit., *to carry in different directions, spread abroad, scatter; to spread news; to harass, disturb, discredit* a person; in time, *to delay, postpone business, to put off* persons. Intransit., *to differ, be different*; nihil differt, *there is no difference.*

differtus -a -um, *stuffed full, crammed.*

difficĭlis -e, *difficult*; of character, *hard to deal with, morose, obstinate.* Adv. **difficĭlĭtĕr** and **difficultĕr**, *with difficulty.*

difficultās -ātis, f., *difficulty, need, trouble, distress*; of character, *obstinacy, moroseness.*

diffīdentĭa -ae, f., *want of confidence, distrust, despair.*

diffīdo -fīdĕre -fīsus sum, *to have no confidence, mistrust, despair*; partic. **diffīdens** -entis, *distrustful, diffident*; adv. **diffīdentĕr.**

diffindo -findĕre -fīdi -fissum, *to split, cleave, open*; legal, diem, *to postpone business.*

diffingo -ĕre, *to form again, forge anew*; fig., *to change.*

diffĭtĕor -ēri, dep. *to deny, disavow.*

difflo -are, *to blow apart.*

difflŭo -flŭĕre -fluxi -fluxum. *to flow*

in different directions, to dissolve, melt away.

diffringo -fringĕre -fractum, *to shatter.*

diffŭgĭo -fŭgĕre -fŭgi -fŭgĭtum, *to fly in different directions, to disperse.*

diffŭgĭum -i, n. *dispersion.*

diffundĭto -are, *to scatter.*

diffundo -fundĕre -fūdi -fūsum, *to pour in different directions, to spread out, diffuse, extend*; esp. *to make relax, brighten up, gladden.* Hence partic. **diffūsus** -a -um, *spread out, extensive, wide*; adv. **diffūsē**, *copiously, diffusely.*

diffūsĭlis -e, *capable of spreading, elastic.*

dīgĕro -gĕrĕre -gessi -gestum, *to carry in different directions, to separate, spread*; esp. *in orderly fashion, to arrange.*

dīgestĭo -ōnis, f. *arrangement, distribution.*

dīgestus -a -um, partic. from digero; q.v.

dĭgĭtŭlus -i, m. *a little finger; the touch of a finger.*

dĭgĭtus -i, m. (1) *a finger*; digitus pollex, *the thumb*; index, *the forefinger*; as a measure, *a finger's breadth, an inch.* (2) *a toe.*

dīglădĭor -ari, dep. *to flourish the sword; to fight, struggle fiercely*; in words, *to dispute.*

dignātĭo -ōnis, f. *esteem; dignity, reputation, honour.*

dignĭtās -ātis, f. *worth, worthiness, merit.* Transf., *dignified appearance or style; dignified position, esteem, honour*; esp. *official rank*; plur. dignitates, *persons of rank.*

digno -are, and **dignor** -ari, dep. *to consider worthy*; with infin., *to deign to.*

dignosco (**dīnosco**) -noscĕre -nōvi, *to recognize as different, to distinguish.*

dignus -a -um. (1) *worthy, deserving*; esp. of persons, usually with abl. or genit. (2) of things, *worth having, deserved, suitable, fittings*; dignum est. foll. by infin., *it is proper.* Adv. **dignē.**

dīgrĕdĭor -grĕdi -gressus, dep. *to go apart, depart, deviate*; in speech, *to digress.*

dīgressĭo -ōnis, f. and **dīgressus** -ūs, m. *separation, departure*; in speech, *digression.*

dĭiūdĭcātĭo -ōnis, f. *judging, decision.*

dĭiūdĭco -are. (1) *to judge between parties, to decide, determine.* (2) *to distinguish, find a difference between.*

dĭiun-; see disiun-.

dīlābor -lābi -lapsus, dep., *to glide apart*: of solids, *to fall to pieces, fall down, melt, dissolve*; of liquids, gases, etc., *to flow apart, run away*; of persons in groups, *to break up, slip away*; in gen., *to break up, vanish* of time, *to go by.*

dīlăcĕro -are, *to tear in pieces.*

dīlāmĭno -are, *to split in two.*

dīlănĭo -are, *to tear in pieces.*

dīlăpĭdo -are, *to demolish.*

dilargior -iri, dep. *to hand round, give liberally.*

dilātio -ōnis, f. *putting off, postponing.*

dilāto -are, *to spread out, extend;* litteras, *to pronounce broadly.*

dilātor -ōris, m., *a dilatory person, loiterer.*

dilātus, partic. from differo; q.v.

dilaudo -are, *to praise highly.*

¹dilectus -a -um, partic. from diligo; q.v.

²dilectus -ūs, m.: in gen., *choosing, choice, selection;* milit., *a levy, recruiting of troops, conscription;* meton., *troops so raised.*

diligens -entis partic. from diligo; q.v.

diligentia -ae, f., *carefulness, attentiveness, accuracy;* esp. *care in management, economy.*

diligo -ligĕre -lexi -lectum, *to choose out; to prize, love, esteem highly.* Hence pres. partic. **diligens** -entis, *attentive, careful;* esp. *careful in housekeeping, economical, saving;* adv. **diligentĕr,** *attentively, carefully.*

dilōrico -are, *to tear open.*

dilūceo -ēre, *to be clear, evident.*

dilūcesco -lūcescĕre -luxi, *to grow light, become day; to become clear.*

dilūcidus -a -um, *clear, lucid, plain;* adv. **dilūcidē.**

dilūcŭlum -i, n., *the break of day, dawn.*

dilūdium -i, n., *an interval, breathing-space.*

dilŭo -lŭĕre -lŭi -lūtum. (1) *to wash apart, separate, dissolve;* of troubles, *to remove, resolve;* of puzzles, *to clear up.* (2) *to dilute, temper; to weaken, lessen, impair.*

dilŭviēs -ēi, f. *washing away, inundation.*

dilŭvio -are, *to flood, inundate.*

dilŭvium -i, n. *flood, deluge, inundation.*

dimāno -are, *to flow in different directions, spread abroad.*

dimensio -ōnis, f. *measuring.*

dimētior -mētiri -mensus, dep. *to measure out.*

dimēto -are and dep. **dimētor** -ari, *to measure out.*

dimicātio -ōnis, f., *a fight, struggle, battle.*

dimico -are, -avi, *to brandish weapons; hence to fight, contend, struggle.*

dimidiātus -a -um, *halved, divided, half.*

dimidius -a -um, *halved, divided in half;* dimidia pars, *half.* N. as subst. **dimidium** -i, *half:* dimidio minus, *less by half.*

diminūtio -ōnis; see deminutio.

dimissio -ōnis, f. (1) *a sending out.* (2) *a dismissing, discharging.*

dimitto -mittĕre -misi -missum. (1) *to send forth, send in different directions; without object, to send (word) round.* (2) *to send away, let go, let fall;* milit. *to disband or to detach;* of a gathering, *to break up, dismiss;* of places, *to*

give up, leave; of abstr. things, *to give up, renounce, abandon.*

dimminŭo -ĕre, *to dash to pieces.*

dimŏvĕo -mŏvēre -mōvi -mōtum. (1) *to move asunder, part, divide.* (2) *to separate, remove, take away.*

dinosco = dignosco; q.v.

dinŭmĕrātio -ōnis, f. *enumeration.*

dinŭmĕro -are, *to count, esp. to count money, to pay.*

diœcēsis -ĕos and -is, f., *a district under a governor.*

diœcētes -ae, m., *a revenue official or treasurer.*

Diŏmēdēs -is, m. (1) *a hero of the Trojan War, son of Tydeus.* (2) *king of the Bistones in Thrace.*

Diŏnē -ēs, f. and **Diōna** -ae, f. (1) *the mother of Venus.* (2) *Venus.* Adj. **Diōnaeus** -a -um.

Diŏnȳsus (-os) -i, m., *the Greek name of Bacchus.* Hence **Diōnȳsia** -orum, n. pl. *the feast of Dionysus.*

diōta -ae, f. *a two-handled wine-jar.*

diplōma -ātis, n. (1) *a letter of introduction given to travellers.* (2) *a government document conferring privileges.*

diremptus -ūs, m. *a separation.*

direptio -ōnis, f. *plundering, pillaging.*

direptor -ōris, m., *plunderer, pillager.*

diribĕo -ēre -itum, *to sort tablets when taken out of the ballot-box.*

diribitio -ōnis, f. *sorting of voting tablets.*

diribitor -ōris, m., *the officer who sorted voting tablets.*

dirigo -rigĕre -rexi -rectum, *to arrange, direct.* Hence partic. **directus** -a -um, *straight, direct; straightforward, plain, simple.* Abl. as adv. **directō** and adv. **directē,** *straight, directly.* See also derigo.

dirimo -imĕre -ēmi -emptum, *to part, separate, divide.* Transf., *to break off, interrupt, stop temporarily or permanently.*

diripio -ripĕre -ripŭi -reptum, *to snatch apart, tear to pieces;* of spoil, *to divide,* hence, milit., *to pillage, lay waste; to tear away.*

dirĭtās -ātis, f. *misfortune, disaster; cruelty, fierceness.*

dirumpo -rumpĕre -rūpi -ruptum, *to break apart or to pieces, shatter;* of friendship, etc., *to sever, break up;* in pass., dirumpi, *to burst with envy, grief, anger.*

dirŭo -rŭĕre -ŭi -ŭtum, *to pull apart, demolish, destroy, break up;* financially, *to ruin.*

dirus -a -um, *fearful, horrible, frightful, cruel.* N. pl. **dira** -orum, and f. pl. **Dirae** -arum, as subst., *unlucky omens, curses;* **Dirae** -arum, as name for the *Furies.*

¹Dis, Ditis, m. *a name of Pluto, god of the Lower World.*

²dis, ditis (contracted from dives), *rich; having or containing or bringing wealth.*

discēdo -cēdĕre -cessi -cessum. (1) *to*

go asunder, part, separate. (2) to
depart, go away; milit., to march
away; discedere ab signis, to break
the ranks; ab armis, to lay down
arms; to come out of a contest, to come
off; in gen., to depart, pass away;
to deviate, swerve, digress; polit., of
the senate, in sententiam discedere,
to support a resolution.

disceptātio -ōnis, f. debate, discussion,
controversy.

disceptātor -ōris, m. and disceptātrix
-tricis, f. an arbitrator.

discepto -are. (1) to decide, settle,
determine. (2) to dispute, debate,
discuss.

discerno -cernĕre -crēvi -crētum, to
sever, separate, set apart. Transf.,
to distinguish, discern.

discerpo -cerpĕre -cerpsi -cerptum,
to pluck to pieces, dismember.

discessio -ōnis, f. (1) going separate
ways, separation; polit., voting, a
division in the senate. (2) a going
away, departure.

discessus -ūs, m. (1) parting, separation. (2) departure, going away;
milit., marching off; banishment.

discĭdium -i, n. tearing apart; separation, division; separation in feelings,
disagreement.

discīdo -ĕre, to cut in pieces.

discindo -ĕre -scĭdi -scissum, to cleave
asunder, split.

discingo -cingĕre -cinxi -cinctum, to
take off the girdle, ungird. Partic.
discinctus -a -um, ungirt; at ease,
careless, dissolute.

disciplīna -ae, f., instruction, teaching;
training, education; esp. military
training. Transf., results of training,
discipline, ordered way of life; that
which is taught, learning, body of
knowledge, science; a rhetorical or
philosophical school or system.

discĭpŭla -ae, f., a female pupil.

discĭpŭlus -i, m. a pupil, apprentice.

disclūdo -clūdĕre -clūsi -clūsum, to
shut away, separate, divide.

disco discĕre dĭdici, to learn, get to
know; discere fidibus, to learn to
play on the lyre; in gen., to receive
information, find out; to become
acquainted with, learn to recognize.

discŏlor -ōris, of different colours; in
gen., different.

disconvĕnio -ire, to disagree, not to
harmonize.

discordābilis -e, disagreeing.

discordia -ae, f. dissension, disagreement; milit., mutiny, sedition.

discordiōsus -a -um, full of discord,
mutinous.

discordo -are, to be at discord, disagree,
be opposed; milit., to be mutinous.

discors -cordis, disagreeing, inharmonious, opposed, different.

discrĕpantia -ae, f. disagreement,
difference.

discrĕpātio -ōnis, f. disagreement,
disunion.

discrĕpito -are, to be quite unlike.

discrĕpo -are -ŭi, to differ in sound, be
discordant; to disagree, be different.
Res discrepat, or impers., discrepat,
people are not agreed; with acc. and
infin., it is inconsistent that.

discrībo -scrībĕre -scripsi -scriptum,
to mark out, arrange, classify, define;
to allot, fix, appoint.
Hence partic. discriptus -a -um,
classified, arranged; adv. discriptē.

discrīmen -inis, n. (1) dividing line,
distinction, difference, interval.
(2) turning-point, critical moment;
crisis, hazard, danger.

discrīmino -are, to separate, sunder,
divide.

discriptio -ōnis, f. an arrangement
definition, distribution.

discrŭcio -are, to torture, torment,
esp. mentally.

discumbo -cumbĕre -cūbŭi -cūbitum.
(1) to recline at table. (2) to go to bed.

discŭpio -cupĕre (colloq.), to long.

discurro -currĕre -cŭcurri and -curri
-cursum, to run about, run to and fro.

discursus -ūs, m. a running about,
running to and fro.

discus -i, m., a quoit.

discŭtio -cŭtĕre -cussi -cussum, to
shatter. Transf., to disperse, scatter,
break up.

disertus -a -um, eloquent, expressive;
adv. disertē and disertim.

disĭcio disĭcĕre disĭēci disiectum, to
throw in different directions, cast
asunder; of buildings, etc., to throw
down; of military formations, to
break up, disperse; of abstr. things,
to break up, frustrate.

disiecto -are, to toss about.

¹disiectus -a -um, partic. from disicio,
q.v.

²disiectus -us, m., scattering, dispersing.

disiunctio -ōnis, f. separation, estrangement; in logic, a disjunctive proposition.

disiungo (diiungo) -iungĕre -iunxi
-iunctum, to unbind, loosen, separate,
remove, distinguish.
Hence partic. disiunctus -a -um,
separated, apart, distant, remote; of
speech, disconnected; in logic, disjunctive. Compar. adv. disiunctius,
rather in disjunctive fashion.

dispando -pandĕre -pandi -pansum, or
-pessum, to expand, stretch out.

dispār -pāris, unlike, dissimilar, unequal.

dispărilis -e, unlike, dissimilar, unequal.

dispăro -are, to separate, part, divide;
n. of partic. as subst. dispărātum -i,
rhet., the contradictory proposition.

dispartio = dispertio; q.v.

dispello -pellĕre -pŭli -pulsum, to
drive in different directions, to scatter.

dispendium -i, n. expenditure, expense
loss.

dispenno = dispando; q.v.

dispensātio -ōnis, f., weighing out;
management, administration; the office
of a treasurer.

dispensātor -ōris, m. steward, bailiff
treasurer.

dispenso -are, to weigh out or pay out;
in gen., to distribute, to arrange.

disperdo -děre -dĭdi -dĭtum, *to squander, ruin, spoil.*

dispĕrĕo -ire -ii, *to perish utterly, be squandered, ruined.*

dispergo -spergěre -spersi -spersum, *to scatter, disperse.* Adv. from perf. partic. **dispersě**, *dispersedly, here and there.*

dispertio -ire, and dep. **dispertior** -iri, *to separate, divide, distribute.*

dispĭcio -spĭcěre -spexi -spectum, *to see clearly,* esp. by an effort; *to make out, discern, perceive; to reflect upon, consider.*

displĭcĕo -ēre, *to displease;* displicere sibi, *to be dissatisfied with oneself, be out of spirits.*

displōdo -plōděre -plōsi -plōsum, *to burst noisily.*

dispōno -pōněre -pŏsŭi -pŏsitum, *to put in different places, to distribute, put in order;* milit., *to station at intervals.*

Hence partic. **dispŏsitus** -a -um, *arranged, orderly;* adv. **dispŏsitě,** *in order, methodically.*

dispŏsitĭo -ōnis, f. *regular arrangement or order in a speech.*

dispŏsitū abl. sing. m., *in or by arranging.*

dispŏsitūra -ae, f., *arrangement, order.*

dispŭdet -ēre -ŭit, *it is a great shame.*

dispŭtatĭo -ōnis, f. *arguing, debate.*

dispŭtator -ōris, m. *debater, disputant.*

dispŭto -are, *to reckon up; to debate, discuss, argue.*

disquiro -ěre, *to inquire into, investigate.*

disquisitĭo -ōnis, f. *inquiry, investigation.*

dissaepio -saepire -saepsi -saeptum, *to hedge off, separate, divide;* n. of perf. partic. as subst. **dissaeptum** -i, *barrier, partition.*

disséco -sěcare -sěcŭi -sectum, *to cut up.*

dissēmĭno -are, *to spread abroad, disseminate.*

dissensĭo -ōnis, f. *difference in feeling or opinion; disagreement, variance, conflict, opposition.*

dissensus -ūs, m. *disunion, disagreement.*

dissentānĕus -a -um, *disagreeing, different.*

dissentio -sentire -sensi -sensum, *to be of different feeling or opinion, to be opposed, not to agree.*

dissěrěnat -are, impers., *it is clearing up all round, of the weather.*

¹**dissěro** -sěrěre -sēvi -situm, *to scatter seed, sow; to spread.*

²**dissěro** -sěrěre -sěrŭi -sertum, *to set in order;* hence *to examine, treat of, discuss.*

disserpo -ere, *to creep about, spread.*

dissertĭo -ōnis, f. *a severance.*

disserto -are, *to treat of, discuss, argue.*

dissĭdĕo -sidēre -sēdi -sessum, *to sit apart, be distant, disagree, be opposed;* of clothes, *to sit unevenly.*

dissīdo -sideēre -sēdi, *to fall apart, disagree.*

dissignatĭo -ōnis, f. *arrangement.*

dissignātor -ōris, m. *one that arranges, a supervisor.*

dissigno -are, *to arrange, regulate, manage.*

dissĭlio -sĭlire -sĭlŭi, *to eap apart, break asunder.*

dissĭmilis -e, *unlike, dissimilar;* adv. **dissimĭlĭtěr,** *differently.*

dissĭmĭlĭtūdo -ĭnis, f. *unlikeness, difference.*

dissĭmŭlatĭo -ōnis, f. *a concealing, dissembling,* esp. *of irony.*

dissĭmŭlator -ōris, m. *dissembler, concealer.*

dissĭmŭlo -are. (1) *to dissemble, disguise, keep secret;* pass. with middle force, dissimulata deam, *concealing her divinity.* (2) *to ignore, leave unnoticed.* Adv. from pres. partic. **dissĭmŭlantěr,** *in a dissembling manner.*

dissĭpābĭlis -e, *that can be scattered.*

dissipātĭo -ōnis, f. *scattering.*

dissĭpo or **dissŭpo** -are, *to scatter, disperse;* milit. *to break up, rout; to break up, destroy, squander.*

Hence partic. **dissĭpātus** -a -um, *disconnected.*

dissĭtus, partic. from dissero; q.v.

dissŏcĭābĭlis -e: act., *separating;* pass. *unable to be united.*

dissŏcĭātĭo -ōnis, f. *separation, parting.*

dissŏcĭo -are, *to separate, sever, divide;* in feeling, *to estrange.*

dissŏlūbĭlis -e, *dissoluble, separable.*

dissŏlūtĭo -ōnis, f. *breaking up, dissolution, destruction;* naturae, *death;* navigii, *shipwreck;* criminum, *refutation;* rhet., *want of connexion.*

dissolvo -solvěre -solvi -sŏlūtum, *to loosen, break up, undo, destroy;* glaciem, *to melt;* animam, *to die;* criminationem, *to refute;* of debts, *to pay, discharge; to release a person from difficulties, to unravel, explain a difficulty.*

Hence partic. **dissŏlūtus** -a -um, *loose;* navigium, *leaky;* of style, *disconnected;* of character, *wanting in energy, lax; profligate, dissolute.* Adv. **dissŏlūtě,** *disconnectedly, loosely; carelessly, negligently; without energy.*

dissŏnus -a -um, *discordant, different, disagreeing.*

dissors -sortis, *having a different lot or fate.*

dissuā́dĕo suādēre -suāsi -suāsum, *to advise against, oppose by argument.*

dissuāsĭo -ōnis, f. *advising to the contrary, speaking against.*

dissuāsor -ōris, m. *one who advises to the contrary, one who speaks against.*

dissulto -are, *to leap apart, burst asunder.*

dissŭo -sŭěre -sŭi -sūtum, *to unstitch, undo.*

distaedet -ēre, *causes boredom or disgust.*

distantĭa -ae, f. *distance, difference, diversity.*

distendo (distenno) -tenděre -tendi -tentum, *to stretch apart, expand,* esp.

to *fill full*, distend. Transf., *to distract, perplex*.

Hence partic. **distentus** -a -um, *distended, full*.

distermino -are, *to separate by a boundary, divide*.

distichon distichi, n., *a poem of two lines, distich*.

distinctio -ōnis, f. *a distinction, difference; the finding of a difference, the act of distinguishing, discriminating*; rhet., *a division in a speech; a pause, stop*.

¹**distinctus** -a -um, partic. from distinguo; q.v.

²**distinctus** -ūs, m. *difference, distinction*.

distineo -tĭnēre -tĭnŭi -tentum, *to hold asunder, keep apart, separate*. Transf., *to divide in feeling; to distract; to keep away, prevent a thing from happening*.

Hence partic. **distentus** -a -um, *distracted, occupied*.

distinguo -stinguĕre -stinxi -stinctum, *to mark off, distinguish, divide*. Transf., *to separate, distinguish*; gram., *to punctuate; to set off, decorate, adorn*.

Hence partic. **distinctus** -a -um, *separate, distinct; set off, diversified, adorned*. Adv. **distinctē**, *clearly, distinctly*.

disto -are, *to be apart, be distant; to differ, be distinct*; impers., distat, *there is a difference*.

distorqueo torquēre -torsi -tortum, *to twist apart, distort; to torture*.

Hence partic. **distortus** -a -um, *distorted, deformed; of speech, perverse*.

distortio -ōnis, f. *distortion*.

distractio -ōnis, f. *pulling apart, separation, disunion*.

distraho -trahĕre -traxi -tractum, *to pull apart or pull to pieces; of associations, to break up, dissolve; of persons, to draw away, estrange, also to distract; of property, to sell up;* gram., *to leave a hiatus in a verse*.

distribuo -uĕre -ŭi -ūtum, *to distribute, divide*. Adv. from partic. **distribūtē**, *methodically, with logical arrangement*.

distributio -ōnis, f. *division, distribution*.

distringo -stringĕre -strinxi -strictum, *to draw apart, stretch out; to engage at different points, divert, occupy*.

Hence partic. **districtus** -a -um, *busy, occupied, engaged*.

disturbatio -onis, f. *destruction*.

disturbo -are, *to drive apart in confusion; to destroy, raze to the ground; to bring to naught, frustrate, ruin*.

ditesco -ere, *to become rich*.

dithyrambicus -a -um, *dithyrambic*.

dithyrambus -i, m. *a dithyrambic poem* (originally in honour of Bacchus).

ditio, better dicio; q.v.

ditior, ditissimus; see dis.

dito -are, *to enrich, make wealthy*.

diu, adv. (1) *by day*. (2) *for a long time*. (3) *a long time ago*. Compar. **diutius**, *longer; too long*. Superl. **diutissimē**.

diurnus -a -um, *belonging to a day or lasting for a day*; n. as subst. *a journal, account-book or a daily allowance*.

dius -a -um, *divine, god-like*; hence *fine, noble*; also (apparently) *out of doors, in the open air*.

diutinus -a -um, *lasting a long time, long*; adv. **diutinē**.

diutius, diutissimē; see diu.

diuturnitas -ātis, f. *long duration*.

diuturnus -a -um, adj., *lasting a long time, of long duration*.

divarico -are, *to stretch apart, spread out*.

divello -vellĕre -velli -vulsum (-volsum), *to pluck apart, tear asunder, break up, destroy, interrupt; to distract, pull away, remove, separate*.

divendo -vendĕre -venditum, *to sell in separate lots*.

diverbero -are, *to strike apart, cleave, divide*.

diverbium -i, n. *dialogue on the stage*.

diversitas -ātis, f. *contrariety, contradiction: difference, diversity*.

diversorium; see deversorium.

diverto (**divorto**) -vertĕre -verti -versum, *to turn different ways; hence to differ*.

Hence partic. **diversus** -a -um, *turned away, turned in different directions; of places, out of the way, remote; of character, fluctuating, irresolute; in gen., different, unlike, opposed, hostile*. Adv. **diversē**, *differently, diversely*.

dives -vitis, *rich, wealthy*; with abl. or genit., *rich in*.

divexo -are, *to tear asunder; hence to destroy, plunder, to distract*.

dividia -ae, f. *division, trouble*.

divido -vidĕre -visi -visum. (1) *to divide up, separate into parts; esp. to divide among persons, distribute, allot*; polit., sententiam, *to divide a resolution into parts so that each part can be voted on*; in music, *to accompany*. (2) *to separate from one another; to distinguish; to set off, to adorn*.

Hence partic. **divisus** -a -um, *separate*.

dividuus -a -um, *divisible; divided, parted*; fig., *distracted*.

divinatio -ōnis, f. *the gift of prophecy, divination*; legal, *the selection of a prosecutor*.

divinitas -ātis, f. *divine nature, divinity; the power of prophecy or divination; excellence, surpassing merit*.

divinitus, *divinely, by divine influence; by inspiration, by means of divination; admirably, nobly*.

divino -are, *to foretell, prophesy, forebode*.

divinus -a -um. (1) *belonging or relating to a deity, divine*; res divina, *the service of the gods*; n. as subst. *a sacrifice*, in plur. *divine things* or *attributes*. (2) *divinely inspired, prophetic*; vates, *a poet*; m. as subst., *a seer*. (3) *noble, admirable*. Adv. **divinē**, *divinely, by divine* *power; by divine inspiration, prophetically; admirably, excellently.*

divisio -ōnis, f. *division, distribution.*

divisor -ōris, m. *a divider; a distributor,* esp. of lands; *a hired bribery agent.*

divisŭi, dat. sing. m., *for division.*

divitiae -arum, f. pl. *riches, wealth; ornaments, rich offerings;* of soil, *richness.*

divortium -i, n. *divergence, separation;* of things, *a boundary, parting of the ways;* of persons, *separation, divorce.*

divorto; see diverto.

divulgo -are, *to make common, publish, spread abroad.*

Hence partic. **divulgātus** -a -um, *spread abroad, made common.*

divus -a -um: as adj., *divine or deified;* as subst., m. *a god* and f. *a goddess* (often as epithet of dead and deified emperors); *sub divo* (neuter), *in the open air.*

do dăre dĕdi dătum. (1) *to offer, give, grant, lend, bestow; to hand over, commit, devote;* of letters, *to give for dispatch;* vela dare ventis, *to sail;* poenas, *to pay a penalty;* verba, *to give words only,* i.e., *to cheat;* of news, *to tell, communicate.* (2) *to cause, bring about, put.*

dŏcĕo -dōcēre dŏcŭi doctum, *to teach, instruct* (with acc. of person and/or of thing); with clause, *to inform that or how;* docere fabulam *to teach a play to the actors, to bring out, exhibit.*

Hence partic. **doctus** -a -um, *taught; learned, instructed, well-informed; experienced, clever, shrewd.* Adv. **doctē**, *learnedly, skilfully; cleverly, shrewdly.*

dochmius -i, m. *a metrical foot, the dochmiac.*

dŏcĭlis -e, *teachable, docile.*

dŏcĭlĭtās -ātis, f. *teachableness, docility.*

doctor -ōris, m. *a teacher.*

doctrīna -ae, f. *teaching, instruction; knowledge, learning.*

doctus -a -um, partic. from doceo; q.v.

dŏcŭmen -inis, n. and **dŏcŭmentum** -i, n., *example, pattern, warning, proof.*

dodrans -antis, m. *three fourths;* as a measure of length, *nine inches.*

dogma -ātis, n. *a philosophical doctrine.*

Dolabella -ae, m. *a Roman family name* in the gens Cornelia.

dŏlabra -ae, f. *a pick-axe.*

dŏlĕo dŏlēre dŏlŭi, *to suffer pain,* physical or mental, *to be pained, to grieve;* of things, *to cause pain.*

Hence partic. **dŏlens**, *painful;* adv. **dŏlentĕr**, *painfully, sorrowfully.*

dŏlium -i, n. *a wine-jar, cask.*

¹**dŏlo** -are, *to hew with an axe, to work roughly;* caput fuste, *to cudgel.*

²**dŏlo** or **dōlon** -ōnis, m. (1) *a pike, sword-stick.* (2) *a small foresail.*

dŏlor -ōris, m., *pain,* physical or mental; esp. *disappointment, resentment.* Transf., *cause of sorrow;* rhet., *pathos.*

dŏlōsus -a -um, *crafty, deceitful, cunning;* adv. **dŏlōse.**

dŏlus -i, m. *a device, artifice; fraud, deceit, guile; a trap.*

dŏmābĭlis -e, *tameable.*

dŏmesticus -a -um. (1) *belonging to house* or *family, domestic;* m. as subst., esp. plur., *members of one's family.* (2) *native;* crudelitas, *towards citizens;* bellum, *civil war.*

dŏmicilium -i, n. *place of residence, dwelling.*

dŏmina -ae, f. *mistress of a household; wife, mistress, lady;* of abstr. things, *ruler, controller.*

dŏmĭnātĭo -ōnis, f. *mastery, control, irresponsible power, despotism.*

dŏmĭnātor -ōris, m. *ruler, governor.*

dŏmĭnātrix -īcis, f. *a female ruler, mistress.*

dŏmĭnātus -ūs, m. *mastery, absolute power.*

dŏmĭnium -i, n. (1) *rule, power, ownership.* (2) *a feast, banquet.*

dŏminor -ari, dep., *to rule, be supreme, domineer.*

dŏminus -i, m. *master of a house, lord, master.* Transf. *husband* or *lover; a master, owner, possessor; employer; ruler, lord, controller.*

dŏmiporta -ae, f. *one with her house on her back, the snail.*

Dŏmĭtĭānus -i, m. *son of Vespasian, brother of Titus, Emperor from* 81 *to* 96 A.D.

Dŏmĭtĭus -a -um, *name of a plebeian gens in Rome.*

dŏmĭto -are, *to tame, subdue, break in.*

dŏmĭtor -ōris, m, *tamer, conqueror, victor.*

dŏmĭtrix -īcis, f. *she who tames.*

dŏmĭtus -ūs, m. *taming.*

dŏmo dŏmāre dŏmŭi dŏmĭtum, *to tame, break in, conquer, subdue.*

dŏmus -ūs, f. *a house, home;* locative domi, *at home, in the house;* domi habere, *to have at home, to possess;* domum, *home, homewards;* domo, *from home.* Transf., *dwelling, abode; native country; household; philosophical school or sect.*

dōnārium -i, n. (1) *a temple, shrine, altar.* (2) *a votive offering.*

dōnātĭo -ōnis, f. *giving, donation.*

dōnātīvum -i, n. *an imperial largess.*

dōnĕc (older **donicum**). (1) *up to the time when, until.* (2) *so long as, while.*

dōno -arc. (1) rem homini, *to give as a present, to present, grant, bestow, give up;* esp. *to remit a debt or obligation; to forgive, pardon.* (2) hominem re, *to present with.*

dōnum -i, n. *a gift, present;* dono dare, *to give as a present;* esp. *a votive offering.*

dorcas -ādis, f. *gazelle, antelope.*

Dōres -um, m., *the Dorians, one of the Hellenic tribes;* adj. **Dōricus** and **Dōrius** -a -um, *Dorian, Greek.* F. **Dōris** -ĭdis: as adj., *Dorian;* as subst., *the country of the Dorians; the wife of Nereus;* meton., *the sea.*

dormio -ire, *to sleep; to rest, be inactive.*

dormíto -are, *to be sleepy, begin to sleep, nod; to dream, be lazy*; of a lamp, iam dormitante lucerna, *just going out.*

dormítōrius -a -um, *for sleeping.*

dorsum -i, n. *the back,* of men, animals or things; immane dorsum mari summo, *a reef; a mountain ridge,* ' *hog's back* '.

dōs dōtis, f., *a dowry, marriage portion; a gift, quality, endowment.*

dōtālis -e, *belonging to or forming a dowry.*

dōto -are, *to provide with a dowry, endow*; partic. dōtātus -a -um, *richly endowed.*

drachma (drachŭma) -ae, f., *a drachma, a small Greek coin.*

drăco -ōnis, m., *a kind of snake, dragon.*

drăcōnĭgĕna -ae, c. *dragon-born.*

drāpēta -ae, m. *a runaway slave.*

Drĕpănum -i, n. and Drĕpăna -orum, plur., *a town on the west coast of Sicily.*

drŏmas -ādis, m. *a dromedary.*

Drŭentia -ae, f. *a river in Gaul (now Durance).*

Drŭĭdēs -um and Drŭĭdae -arum, m. *the Druids.*

Drūsus -i, m. *a cognomen of the gens Livia*; hence adj. Drūsiănus and Drūsīnus -a -um, *of Drusus*: subst. Drūsilla -a, f. *name of several females of the gens Livia.*

Drўăs -ādis, f. *a wood nymph, Dryad.*

dŭbĭtābĭlis -e, *doubtful, uncertain.*

dŭbĭtātio -ōnis, f., *doubt, uncertainty; hesitation, irresolution.*

dŭbĭto -are. (1) *to doubt, waver in opinion, be uncertain.* (2) *to waver as to action, be irresolute, hesitate.* Adv. from partic., dŭbĭtantĕr, *doubtingly, hesitatingly.*

dŭbius -a -um, *doubtful.* (1) act., *wavering*: in opinion, *doubting; uncertain*; as to action, *hesitating, irresolute.* (2) pass., *uncertain, doubted, doubtful*; n. as subst.; in dubium vocare, *to call in question*; procul dubio, *without doubt.* (3) fig., *doubtful, dangerous, critical.* Adv. dŭbĭē, *doubtfully*; haud dubie, *certainly.*

dūcēni -ae, -a, *a group of two hundred, or two hundred each.*

dūcentēsima -ae, f. *the two hundredth part, one-half per cent.*

dūcenti -ae, -a, *two hundred.*

dūcentie(n)s, *two hundred times.*

dūco dūcĕre duxi ductum. (1) *to draw; to draw along or away*; hence *to shape anything long, to construct*; carmina, *to make verses*; of time, either *to spend or to delay, protract.* Transf., *to charm, influence, mislead; to derive.* (2) *to draw in*; aera spiritu, *to inhale*; pocula, *to quaff.* (3) *to lead*; in marriage, *to marry a wife*; milit., *either to lead on the march,* or *to command.* (4) *to calculate, count, reckon; to esteem, consider.*

ductim, *by drawing; in a stream.*

ductíto and ducto -are, *to lead, esp.*

to lead home a wife. Transf., *to cheat.*

ductor -ōris, m. *a leader, commander; a guide.*

ductus -ūs, m. (1) *drawing, drawing off.* (2) *shaping, shape*; oris, *the lineaments of the face*; muri, *line of a wall.* (3) *leading, command, leadership.*

dūdum, *some time ago; a little while ago, not long since; a long while ago or for a long time.*

dŭellum, dŭellĭcus, dŭellātor = bellum, bellicus, bellator; q.v.

Dūillus -a -um, *name of a Roman gens.*

dulcēdo -inis, f., *sweetness, pleasantness, charm.*

dulcesco -ĕre, *to become sweet.*

dulcĭcŭlus -a -um, *somewhat sweet.*

dulcis -e, *sweet*; unda, *fresh water*; in gen., *pleasant, delightful, agreeable*; of persons, *friendly, dear.* N. acc. dulcĕ and adv. dulcĭtĕr, *sweetly.*

dulcĭtūdo -inis, f. *sweetness.*

dum. (1) adv., joined as an enclitic with other words; nondum, *not yet*; vixdum, *scarcely yet*; nedum, *not to say*; age dum, *come now.* (2) conj.: *while, during the time that; while, throughout the time that; so long as, provided that; until.*

dūmētum -i, n. *a thorn brake, thicket.*

dummŏdo, *provided that, so long as.*

dūmōsus -a -um, *covered with thorn bushes, bushy.*

dumtaxat. (1) *at least, not less than.* (2) *at most, not more than.*

dūmus -i, m. *a thorn bush, bramble.*

dŭŏ -ae, -ŏ, *two.*

dŭŏdēcie(n)s, *twelve times.*

dŭŏdĕcim, *twelve.*

dŭŏdĕcimus -a -um, *twelfth.*

dŭŏdēni -ae, -a, *twelve at a time* or *twelve each.*

dŭŏdēquādrāgēsĭmus, *thirty-eighth.*

dŭŏdēquādrāginta, *thirty-eight.*

dŭŏdēquinquāgēsĭmus -a -um, *forty-eighth.*

dŭŏdētricie(n)s, *twenty-eight times.*

dŭŏdētrīginta, *twenty-eight.*

dŭŏdēvicēni -ae -a, *eighteen each.*

dŭŏdēvīginti, *eighteen.*

dŭŏetvicēsĭmāni -orum, m. *soldiers of the 22nd legion.*

dŭŏetvicēsĭmus -a -um, *twenty-second.*

duplex -plĭcis, *double, doubled, two-fold.* Transf. (1) plur., *both.* (2) *two-faced, deceitful, equivocal.* Adv. dŭplĭcĭtĕr, *doubly.*

duplĭcārius -a -um: miles, *a soldier who gets double pay.*

duplĭco -are, *to double*; of words, *to repeat*; also *to form compound words.* Transf., *to bend double*; in gen., *to lengthen, increase.*

duplus -a -um, *twice as much, double*; n. as subst. *double, esp. a double penalty.*

dŭpondĭus -i, m., *a coin of two asses.*

dūrābĭlis -e, *lasting, durable.*

dūrāmen -inis, n. *hardness.*

dūrătĕus -a -um, *wooden.*

duresco dūrescĕre dūrŭi, *to grow hard; of water, to freeze.*

dūrĭtās -ātis, f., *harshness, unfriendliness.*

dūritia -ae, and **dūritiēs** -ēi, f., *hardness;* fig., *austerity, harshness, severity.*

dūro -are: transit., *to make hard or hardy, to inure;* intransit., *to become hard or dry; to be hard or callous; to endure, hold out; to last, remain, continue.*

dūrus -a -um, *hard, harsh; tough, strong, enduring;* in demeanour or tastes, *rough, rude, uncouth;* in character, *hard, austere,* sometimes *brazen, shameless;* of things, *hard, awkward, difficult, adverse.* Adv. **dūrē** and **dūrĭtĕr**, *hardly, hardily; roughly, rudely; harshly, unpleasantly, severely.*

dŭumvir and **dŭŏvir** -vĭri, m. usually pl., *a pair of magistrates, a commission of two.*

dux dŭcis, c. (1) *a guide, conductor.* (2) *a leader, ruler, commander.*

dynastēs -is, m. *ruler, prince.*

Dyrrhăchium -i, n. *a port in Illyria.*

E

E, e, the fifth letter of the Latin alphabet.

e, prep. = ex; q.v.

ĕă, adv. = abl. of is; q.v.

ĕādem, *by the same way, likewise.*

ĕătĕnus, *so far.*

ĕbĕnus -i, m. = hebenus; q.v.

ĕbĭbo -bĭbĕre -bĭbi, *to drink up.*

ēblandĭor -iri, dep. *to obtain by flattery.*

ēbrĭĕtās -atis, f. *drunkenness.*

ēbrĭŏlus -a -um, *tipsy.*

ēbrĭōsĭtās -ātis, f. *love of drink, drunkenness.*

ēbrĭōsus -a -um, *drink-loving.*

ēbrĭus -a -um, *drunk, intoxicated.*

ēbullĭo -ire, *to boil up; to boast of.*

ĕbŭlum -i, n. (or -us -i, m.), *the dwarf elder.*

ĕbur -ŏris, n. *ivory.* Transf. (1) of things made of ivory. (2) *the elephant.*

ĕburnĕŏlus -a -um, *made of ivory.*

ĕburnĕus or **ĕburnus** -a -um, *made of ivory, white as ivory.*

ĕcastor; see Castor.

eccĕ, *behold! lo! see!*

eccĕrĕ, *there you are!*

ecclēsia -ae, f., *an assembly of the (Greek) people.*

ecdĭcus -i, m. *a solicitor for a community.*

Ēcĕtra -ae, f. *capital of the Volsci.*

ecf-; see eff-.

ĕchĕnēis -ĭdis, f., *a sucking fish, the remora.*

ĕchīnus -i, m. (1) *an edible sea-urchin.* (2) *a copper dish.*

ĕchō -ūs, f. *an echo;* personif., Echo, *a wood-nymph.*

eclŏgārĭi -orum, m. pl. *select passages or extracts.*

ecquando, adv., *ever? at any time?*

ecqui, ecquae or **ecqua, ecquod,** interrog. adj., *is there any . . . that? does any . . .?*

ecquis, ecquid, interrog. pron., *is there any that? does anyone?* Hence **ecquid** or **ecqui,** *at all?* or *whether?* **ecquō,** *whither?*

ĕcŭlĕus i, m. *a little horse, colt; a rack, instrument of torture.*

ēdācĭtās -ātis, f. *greediness, gluttony.*

ĕdax -ācis, f. *greedy, gluttonous; destructive, consuming.*

ĕdĕpol; see Pollux.

ēdīco -dīcĕre -dixi -dictum, *to announce, declare;* esp. of a magistrate, *to decree, ordain by proclamation.* Hence n. of partic. as subst. **ēdictum** -i, *a decree, edict.*

ēdictĭo -ōnis, f. *an edict.*

ēdicto -are, *to proclaim.*

ēdisco -discĕre -dĭdĭci, *to learn thoroughly.*

ēdissĕro -sĕrĕre -sĕrŭi -sertum, *to explain, set forth, relate fully.*

ēdisserto -are, *to explain exactly.*

ēdĭtĭcĭus -a -um, *announced, proposed:* iudices, *jurors chosen by a plaintiff.*

ēdĭtĭo -ōnis, f. *the publishing of a book; a statement;* editio tribuum, *a proposal by a plaintiff for the choice of a jury.*

¹ĕdo ĕdĕre or esse ĕdi ĕsum, *to eat, devour, consume, waste.*

²ēdo -dĕre -dĭdi -dĭtum, *to put forth, give out;* animam, *to breathe one's last, die;* clamorem, *to utter.* Esp. (1) *to bring into the world, to bring forth, give birth to;* of things, *to produce.* (2) *to make known:* of writings, *to publish;* of ideas and information, *to divulge, spread;* officially, *to proclaim;* as legal t. t., *to fix, determine, nominate.* (3) *to bring about, cause, produce;* of magistrates, *to provide games for the people.*

Hence partic. **ēditus** -a -um, *raised, high, lofty;* n. as subst. *a high place, eminence.*

ēdŏcĕo -dŏcēre -dŏcŭi -doctum, *to instruct thoroughly, inform fully.*

ēdŏmo -dŏmare -dŏmŭi -dŏmĭtum, *to tame thoroughly, entirely subdue.*

Ēdŏni -orum, *a Thracian people, famed for the worship of Bacchus;* adj. **Ēdŏnus** -a -um, and **Ēdōnis** -nĭdis, f. *Thracian.*

ēdormĭo -ire, *to have one's sleep out;* transit., *to sleep off.*

ēdormisco -ĕre, *to sleep off.*

ēdŭcātĭo -ōnis, f. *bringing up, training, education.*

ēdŭcātor -ōris, m. *one who brings up; a foster-father* or *a tutor.*

ēdŭcātrix -īcis, f. *a foster-mother, nurse.*

¹ēdŭco -are, *to bring up, raise, rear, educate.*

²ēdūco -dūcĕre -duxi -ductum. (1) *to draw out, lead out;* of time, *to spend;* milit., *to march troops out;* legal, *to bring before a court of law;* naut., *to take a ship out of port.* (2) *to raise up* (of persons and buildings); in astra, *to praise sky-high.* (3) *to bring up, rear.*

ĕdūlis -e, *eatable.*

ĕdūro -are, *to last, endure.*

ĕdūrus -a -um, *very hard.*

effarcio = effercio; q.v.

efflātum -i, n. from partic. of effor; q.v.

effectio -ōnis, f. *practising.* Transf., *an efficient cause.*

effector -ōris, m. *one who produces, causes, originates.*

effectrix -tricis, f. *she that causes or produces.*

¹effectus -a -um, partic. of efficio; q.v.

²effectus -ūs, m. *doing, execution, performance; effect, result.*

effēmino -are, *to make into a woman;* in character, *to make effeminate.*

Hence partic. **effēminātus** -a -um, *effeminate,womanish;* adv. **effēminātē**.

effercio or **effarcio** -fercire, -fertum, *to stuff full;* partic. **effertus**, *stuffed.*

effĕritās -ātis, f., *wildness, savagery.*

¹effĕro -are, *to make wild, make savage;* partic. **effĕrātus** -a -um, *wild, savage.*

²effĕro (**ecfĕro**) efferre extŭli ēlātum. (1) *to carry out, bring out;* efferre signa, *to march out.* Esp. *to carry to the grave, bury;* pass., efferri, *to be borne out, buried;* of the earth, *to bring forth, bear; to utter, express, publish* words or ideas. (2) *to carry off or away;* pass., efferri *to be carried away by feelings.* (3) *to raise up, lift up; to praise, extol;* efferri or se efferre, *to pride oneself, be puffed up.* (4) *to endure to the end.*

Hence partic. **ēlātus** -a -um, *elevated, exalted;* adv. **ēlātē**, *loftily.*

effertus -a -um, partic. from effercio; q.v.

effĕrus -a -um, *wild, savage.*

effervesco -fervescĕre -fervi, *to boil up, effervesce;* of an orator, *to be passionate.*

effervo -ĕre, *to boil up* or *over; to swarm forth.*

effētus -a -um, *weakened* (by giving birth); *effete.*

efficācĭtās -ātis, f. *efficacy.*

efficax -ācis, *effective, efficient, efficacious;* adv. **efficācĭter**.

efficiens -entis, partic. from efficio; q.v.

efficientia -ae, f. *efficiency.*

efficio -ficĕre -fēci -fectum, *to do, produce, effect, make;* of results, *to bring about, cause* (esp. with ut and subj.); of numbers, *to make up, amount to;* philosoph. *to prove, show;* of appointments and changes, *to make.*

Hence partic. **efficiens** -entis, *effective:* causa, *efficient cause;* adv. **efficientĕr**, *efficiently, powerfully.*

effigiēs -ēi, or **effigia** -ae, f. *an image, likeness, effigy; a shade, ghost; an ideal.*

effingo -fingĕre -finxi -fictum. (1) *to wipe.* (2) *to mould, form, fashion;* esp. *to form one thing like another,* and so

to copy, represent, express in words, *conceive* in thought.

effĭo (**ecf-**) -fĭĕri, old pass. of efficio; q.v.

efflāgĭtātĭo -ōnis, f., *an urgent demand.*

efflāgĭtātū abl. sing. m., at *an urgent request.*

efflāgĭto -are, *to ask earnestly, demand, entreat.*

efflīgo -ĕre -flixi -flictum, *to destroy.*

efflo -are, *to blow out, breathe out;* animam, *to die.*

efflōresco -flōrescĕre -flōrŭi, *to blossom, break into bloom.*

efflŭo (**ecflŭo**) -flŭĕre -fluxi, *to flow out.* Transf. (1) *to vanish, drop off.* (2) *to pass out of mind, be forgotten.* (3) *to come to light, become known.*

efflŭvĭum -i, n., *flowing out, outlet.*

effŏdĭo -fodĕre -fōdi -fossum. (1) *to dig out, gouge out.* (2) *to make by digging, to excavate.* (3) *to gut, to rummage.*

effor (**ecfor**) -fari -fatus, dep. *to speak out, express, speak:* in logic, *to state a proposition;* in religion, *formally to dedicate* a place.

Hence partic. (in pass. sense) **effātus** -a -um, *pronounced; dedicated.*

effrēnātĭo -ōnis, f. *unbridled impetuosity.*

effrēno -are, *to unbridle, let loose;* partic. **effrēnātus** -a -um, *unbridled, unrestrained, violent;* adv. **effrēnātē**.

effrēnus -a -um, *unbridled, unrestrained.*

effringo -fringĕre -frēgi -fractum, *to break open.*

effŭgĭo -fŭgĕre -fūgi -fūgitum: intransit., *to flee, fly away, escape, get off;* transit., *to escape from, avoid, shun.*

effŭgĭum -i, n. *a flying away, flight; means* or *opportunity of flight.*

effulgĕo -fulgĕre -fulsi, *to shine out, glitter; to be distinguished, conspicuous.*

effultus -a -um, *resting upon, supported by.*

effundo (**ecf-**) -fundĕre -fūdi -fūsum, *to pour out, pour forth, shed;* of solids, *to fling out, empty out;* with violence, *to throw off, fling down;* esp. of horses, *to throw their riders;* of weapons, *to discharge;* spiritum extremum, *to die;* se effundere, and effundi, *to stream forth, pour forth,* also *to give oneself up to, indulge in:* of sounds, *to utter;* with ideas of generosity, waste, etc. *to pour out freely, squander;* habenas, *to slacken.*

Hence partic. **effūsus** -a -um, *poured out;* hence *widespread, extensive; extravagant, wasteful; unrestrained;* adv. **effūsē**.

effūsĭo -ōnis, f. *a pouring forth; violent movement; extravagance, prodigality; exuberance of spirits.*

effūsus, partic. from effundo; q.v.

effūtĭo -ire, *to blab out, chatter.*

ēgĕlĭdus -a -um, *with the chill off; lukewarm, tepid.*

ĕgens -entis, partic. from egeo; q.v.

ēgēnus -a -um, *needy, destitute*; with genit. or abl., *in need of.*

ēgēo -ēre -ŭi, *to want, be in need*; with genit., or abl. *to be in want of, to be without, not to have*; also *to desire, wish for, want.*
Hence partic. **ēgens** -entis, *needy, destitute*; with genit., *in need of.*

Egērïa -ae, f. *a nymph, instructress of Numa Pompilius.*

ēgēro -gērēre -gessi -gestum, *carry out* or *off.*

ēgestās -ātis, f. *poverty, indigence, need*; with genit., *want of.*

ēgestĭo -ōnis, f. *wasting.*

ēgō, I; plur. nos. *we* (often used for sing.); alter ego, *my second self*; ad me, *to my house*; apud me, *at my house*, also *in my senses.*

ēgrēdĭor -grēdi -gressus, dep.: intransit., *to go out, pass out*; milit., *to march out*; naut., egredi (ex) navi, *to disembark*; in speech, *to digress*; sometimes *to go up, ascend*; transit., *to go out of, pass beyond, overstep, pass.*

ēgrēgĭus -a -um, *not of the common herd*; *excellent, extraordinary, distinguished*; adv. **ēgrēgĭē.**

ēgressus -ūs, m. *going out, departure*; esp. *landing from a ship, disembarkation.* Transf., *a passage out*; *the mouth of a river*; in speech, *digression.*

ēhem, *oho!*

ēheu, *alas! woe!*

ēhŏ, *hi!*

ei (hei), *ah! woe!*

ēĭā and heĭä: expressing joy or surprise, *well!*; in exhortation, *come on!*

ēĭācŭlor -ari, dep. *to throw out, hurl out.*

ēĭcĭo -ĭcēre -ĭēci -iectum, *to throw out, cast out, eject*; vocem, *to utter*; armum, *to dislocate*; se eicere, *to rush out*; naut., *to bring to shore*; pass., *to be cast ashore, stranded*; eiectus, *a shipwrecked person.* Transf., *to drive out, expel, dispossess*; domo, *to divorce*; ex patria, *to banish*; of feelings *to cast out, put aside.*

ēĭectāmentum -i, n. *that which is thrown up.*

ēĭectĭo -ōnis, f. *banishment, exile.*

ēĭecto -are, *to hurl out, eject.*

ēĭectus -ūs, m. *casting out.*

ēĭŭlātĭo -ōnis, f., and **ēĭŭlātus** -ūs, m. *wailing, lamenting.*

ēĭŭlo are, *to wail, lament.*

ēĭūro and ēĭēro -are, *to refuse or deny on oath*; bonam copiam, *to swear that one is insolvent*; forum sibi iniquum, *to declare that a court is partial*; magistratum, imperium, *to resign, abdicate*; in gen., *to give up, disown.*

ēĭusdemmŏdi, *of the same kind.*

ēĭusmŏdi, *of this kind, such, so.*

ēlābor -lābi -lapsus, dep. *to glide out, slip away, escape, disappear.*

ēlăbōro -are; intransit., *to labour hard, strive, take pains*; transit., *to labour on, work out, elaborate,* esp. in partic.

ēlăbōrātus, -a -um, *elaborate, artificial.*

ēlāmentābilis -e, *very lamentable.*

ēlanguesco -guescĕre -gŭi, *to become weak, be relaxed.*

ēlātĭo -onis, f. *a lifting up*; fig., *exaltation.*

ēlātro -are, *to bark out, cry out.*

ēlātus -a -um, partic. from effero; q.v.

Ēlĕa or Vēlĭa -ae, f. *town in Lucania, birth-place of Parmenides and Zeno, the founders of the Eleatic school of philosophy*; subst. **Ēlĕātes** -ae, m. *Zeno*; adj. **Ēlĕātĭcus** -a -um, *Eleatic.*

ēlectĭo -ōnis, f. *choice, selection.*

ēlectrum -i, n. *amber*; plur. *amber balls*; *an alloy of gold and silver, resembling amber.*

¹ēlectus -a -um, partic. from eligo; q.v.

²ēlectus -ūs, m. *choosing, choice.*

ēlĕgans -antis, *choice, fine, neat, tasteful*; in bad sense, *fastidious, fussy*; adv. **ēlĕgantĕr.**

ēlĕgantĭa -ae, f. *taste, refinement, grace*; in bad sense, *fastidiousness.*

ēlĕgi -orum, m. pl. *elegiac verses.*

ēlĕgĭa and ēlĕgēa -ae, f. *an elegy.*

ēlēmentum -i, n. *an element, first principle*; in plur., *physical elements*; *letters of the alphabet, beginnings, the elements of any science* or *art.*

ēlenchus -i, m. *a pearl pendant worn as an ear-ring.*

ēlĕphantus -i, c. *an elephant; ivory.*

ēlĕphās (-ans) -phantis, m. *an elephant*; *the disease elephantiasis.*

ēlĕvo -are, *to lift up, raise, elevate*; *to weaken, impair, disparage*; *to alleviate, lighten.*

ēlĭcĭo -lĭcēre -lĭcŭi -licitum, *to lure out, entice, call forth*; inferorum animas, *to conjure up.*

ēlīdo -līdere -līsi -līsum. (1) *to strike, knock, thrust out, expel.* (2) *to dash to pieces, shatter.*

ēlĭgo -lĭgēre -lēgi -lectum, *to pick out, choose, select*; fig., *to root out.*
Hence partic. **ēlectus** -a -um, *chosen, select*; adv. **ēlectē**, *choicely.*

ēlīmĭno -are, *to carry out of doors*; dicta, *to blab.*

ēlīmo -are, *to file off, polish, elaborate, perfect.*

ēlinguis -e, *speechless* or *without eloquence.*

Ēlissa (Ēlisa) -ae, f. *another name of Dido.*

ēlixus -a -um, *boiled, sodden.*

ellĕbŏrus (hell-) -i, m. and **ellĕbŏrum (hell-)** -i, n. *hellebore, a plant considered a remedy for madness.*

ēlŏco -are, *to let, hire out.*

ēlŏcūtĭo -ōnis, f. *oratorical delivery, elocution.*

ēlŏgĭum -i, n. *a short saying, maxim; an inscription*; esp. *on a gravestone, epitaph; a clause in a will, codicil; a record of a case.*

ēlŏquentĭa -ae, f. and **ēlŏquĭum** -i, n. *eloquence.*

ēlŏquor -lŏqui -lŏcūtus, dep. *to speak out, express;* esp. *to speak eloquently;* partic. ēlŏquens -entis, *eloquent;* adv. ēlŏquentĕr.

ēlūcĕo -lūcēre -luxi, *to beam forth, shine out, glitter.*

ēluctor -ari, dep: intransit., *to struggle out;* transit., *to struggle out of, surmount a difficulty.*

ēlūcubro -are, and ēlūcubror -ari, dep. *to compose by lamplight.*

ēlūdo -lūdēre -lūsi -lūsum: intransit., *to finish playing,* esp. of the waves of the sea; transit., *to parry a blow; to ward off, evade; to beat an opponent in play; to delude, mock.*

ēlūgĕo -lūgēre -luxi, *to mourn for the prescribed period.*

ēlumbis -e, *weak, feeble.*

ēlŭo -lŭēre -lŭi -lūtum, *to wash out, wash clean, rinse, cleanse.* Transf., *to squander; to wash away, efface, remove.*

Hence partic. ēlūtus -a -um, *washed out, watery, insipid.*

ēlŭvĭēs -ēi, f. *a flowing out, discharge; a flowing over, flood.*

ēlŭvĭo -ōnis, f., *an inundation.*

Ēlȳsĭum -i, n., *Elysium, the abode of the blessed;* adj. Ēlȳsĭus -a -um; m. plur. as subst. *the Elysian fields.*

¹em = hem; q.v.

²em, interj. *here! hi!*

ēmācĭtās -ātis, f. *fondness for buying.*

ēmancĭpātĭo -ōnis, f. *emancipation or transfer.*

ēmancĭpo (-cŭpo) -are, *to release or emancipate a son from the* patria potestas; *to transfer or make over property; to give up persons.*

ēmāno -are, *to flow out; to arise, spring, emanate, spread abroad.*

Ēmāthĭa -ae, f. *a district of Macedonia;* adj. Ēmāthĭus -a -um, and f. Ēmāthĭs -ĭdis, *Macedonian;* Emathides, *the Muses.*

ēmātūresco -tūrescēre -tūrŭi, *to become mature, to ripen; to become mild, be softened.*

ēmax -ācis, *fond of buying.*

emblēma -ătis, n. *inlaid or mosaic work.*

embŏlĭum -i, n. *a dramatic interlude.*

ēmendābĭlis -e, *that may be amended.*

ēmendātĭo -ōnis, f. *improvement, emendation, amendment.*

ēmendātor -ōris, m. and ēmendātrix -icis, f. *amender, corrector.*

ēmendo -are, *to free from errors, correct, improve;* partic. ēmendātus -a -um,' *free from mistakes, correct, faultless;* adv. ēmendātē.

ēmentior -iri -itus, dep. *to devise falsely, feign, counterfeit;* absol., *to make false statements.*

ēmercor -ari, dep. *to buy up.*

ēmĕrĕo -ēre -ŭi -itum and ēmĕrĕor -ēri -itus, dep. *to obtain by service, earn completely; to deserve well of a person;* milit., *to earn pay, to serve, finish one's time.*

Hence partic. ēmĕrĭtus -a -um:

m. as subst., *a soldier that has served his time, a veteran;* as adj. *worn out, finished with.*

ēmergo -mergēre -mersi -mersum: transit., *to cause to rise up;* emergere se *or* emergi, *to rise up, emerge, free oneself;* intransit., *to come forth, come up, emerge, free oneself, get clear;* also *to rise, come to the top; to come to light, appear.*

ēmĕrĭtus -a -um, partic. from emereo; q.v.

ēmētior -iri -mensus, dep., *to measure out.* Transf., *to pass over, traverse a distance;* partic. emensus -a -um in pass. sense, *traversed; to pass through, live through a period of time.*

ēmēto -ere, *to reap away.*

ēmĭco -micare -micŭi -micatum. (1) *to spring out, leap forth.* (2) *to gleam, shine forth, be conspicuous.*

ēmĭgro -are, *to move from a place, migrate;* e vita, *to die.*

ēmĭnentĭa -ae, f. *standing out, prominence; the lights of a picture.*

ēmĭnĕo -minēre -minŭi, *to project, stand out, be conspicuous, be remarkable.*

Hence partic. ēmĭnens -entis, *outstanding, projecting; distinguished, eminent.*

ēmĭnor -ari, *to threaten.*

ēmĭnus, *at a distance, from a distance.*

ēmĭror -ari, dep. *to wonder exceedingly, be astonished at.*

ēmissārĭum -i, n. *an outlet for water.*

ēmissārĭus -i, m. *an emissary, spy.*

ēmissĭo -ōnis, f. *sending forth, letting loose.*

ēmissus -ūs, m. *sending forth.*

ēmitto -mittēre -misi -missum, *to send forth, send out.* Hence (1) *to dispatch, send on a chosen course;* of books, *to publish.* (2) *to let go, let loose, free, let slip.*

ēmo ēmēre ēmi emptum, *to buy, purchase;* male *or* magno, *dear;* bene *or* parvo *cheap.* Transf., *to bribe, buy.*

ēmŏdĕror -ari, dep., *to moderate.*

ēmŏdŭlor -ari, dep., *to put to music.*

ēmŏlĭor -iri, dep., *to achieve by effort.*

ēmollĭo -ire -ivi -itum, *to soften, make mild or effeminate.*

ēmŏlo -ēre, *to grind away.*

ēmŏlŭmentum -i, n. *result of effort; gain, advantage.*

ēmŏnĕo -ēre, *to warn, admonish.*

ēmŏrĭor -mŏri -mortuus, dep. *to die off, perish.*

ēmŏvĕo -mŏvēre -mŏvi -mōtum, *to move out or away, remove.*

Empĕdŏcles -is, m. *a poet and philosopher of Agrigentum, of the fifth century* B.C.; adj. Empĕdŏclēus -a -um; n. pl. as subst. *the doctrines of Empedocles.*

empīrĭcus -i, m. *an unscientific physician, empiric.*

empŏrĭum -i, n. *a place of trade, market.*

emptĭo -ōnis, f. *buying, purchasing; a purchase.*

emptĭto -are, *to buy up.*

emptor -ōris, m. *buyer, purchaser.*

ēmūgĭo -ire, *to bellow.*

ēmulgĕo -mulgēre -mulsum, *to drain out, exhaust.*

ēmungo -mungĕre -munxi -munctum, *to clean a nose; with reflex. or in pass., to wipe one's nose. Transf. to cheat a person.*
    Hence partic. ēmunctus -a -um: emunctae naris, *with a clean nose, i.e. shrewd, discerning.*

ēmūnĭo -ire, *to fortify, make safe; to build up;* paludes, *to clear up.*

ēn (sometimes ēm) *lo! behold! see!* Interrog., *look, say;* with imperat., *come!*

ēnarrābĭlis -e, *that can be narrated or told.*

ēnarrātĭo -onis, f. *exposition; scansion.*

ēnarro -are, *to narrate or explain.*

ēnascor -nasci -nātus, dep. *to grow out, spring forth, arise.*

ēnāto -are, *to swim away, escape by swimming, to extricate oneself.*

ēnāvĭgo -are, *to sail away;* undam, *over the waves.*

endo; archaic = *in.*

endrŏmis -ĭdis, f. *a rough cloak worn after exercise.*

Endymĭōn -ōnis, m. *a beautiful young man, beloved by the Moon.*

ēnĕco (ēnĭco) -nĕcare -nĕcŭi -nectum, *to kill off; to wear out, exhaust, torture.*

ēnervis -e, *powerless, weak.*

ēnervo -are, *to remove the sinews from; to weaken.*
    Hence partic. ēnervātus -a -um, *weakened, powerless.*

ēnĭco = eneco; q.v.

ēnim, conj. *for; namely, for instance; indeed, truly, certainly;* at enim, *but you may object . . . ;* sed enim, *but indeed.*

ēnimvēro, *to be sure, certainly.*

ēnĭtĕo -ēre -ŭi, *to shine out, shine forth, be conspicuous.*

ēnĭtesco -ĕre, *to gleam, shine forth.*

ēnĭtor -nīti -nisus or -nixus, dep. *to work one's way up, struggle up, ascend;* with acc., *to climb;* in gen., *to strive, struggle, make an effort;* also transit. *to bring forth, bear.*
    Hence partic. ēnixus -a -um, *strenuous, eager;* adv. ēnixē.

Enna = Henna; q.v.

Ennĭus -i, m., Q. (239-169 B.C.), *the 'father of Roman poetry'.*

ēno -are, *to swim out, escape by swimming, flee.*

ēnōdātĭo -ōnis, f. *untying;* hence *explanation.*

ēnōdis -e, *without knots; clear, plain.*

ēnōdo -are, *to free from knots; to make clear, explain;* adv. from partic., ēnōdātē, *clearly, plainly.*

ēnormis -e, *irregular, unusual; very large, immense, enormous.*

ēnormĭtās -ātis, f. *irregular shape.*

ēnōtesco -nōtescĕre -nōtŭi, *to become known, be made public.*

ensĭfĕr -fĕra -fĕrum and ensĭgĕr -gĕra -gĕrum, *sword-bearing.*

ensis -is, m. *sword.*

enthymēma -ătis, n., *a thought, line of thought, argument;* esp. *a kind of syllogism.*

ēnūbo -nūbĕre -nupsi -nuptum, *of a woman, to marry out of her rank.*

ēnuclĕo -are, *to take out the kernel; hence to explain in detail;* partic. ēnuclĕātus -a -um, *straightforward, simple, clear;* adv. ēnuclĕātē.

ēnŭmĕrātĭo -ōnis, f. *counting up, enumeration; recapitulation.*

ēnŭmĕro -are, *to reckon, count up, enumerate;* esp. *to pay out; also to recount, recapitulate.*

ēnuntĭātĭo -ōnis, f. *an enunciation, proposition.*

ēnuntĭo -are, *to tell, divulge, announce, express in words;* in logic, *to state a proposition;* also *to pronounce clearly.* N. of partic. as subst., ēnuntĭātum -i, *a proposition.*

ēnuptĭo -ōnis, f.: gentis, *a woman's marrying out of her gens.*

ēnūtrĭo -ire, *to nourish, rear, bring up.*

¹ĕo ire ivi and ĭi ĭtum, *to go;* cubitum ire, *to go to bed;* milit., ire ad arma, *to fly to arms;* polit. (pedibus) ire in sententiam, *to support a motion.* Transf., *to pass, proceed;* in exclamations, i, *go to;* melius ire, *to go better;* ire in, with acc., *to be changed to.*

²ĕō. (1) old dat., *thither, to that point;* of degree, *so far, to such a pitch.* (2) locative, *there;* esp. with loci (partitive genit.). (3) abl., *for that, on that account.*

ĕōdem. (1) old dat., *to the same place; to the same point or person.* (2) locative, *in the same place; in the same condition.*

Ēōs, f. *dawn;* adj. Ēōus and Ēŏus -a -um, *belonging to the morning, or eastern.*

ēpastus -a -um, *eaten up.*

ēphēbus -i, m. *a young man between eighteen and twenty.*

ēphēmĕris -ĭdis, f. *a journal, diary.*

ēphippĭātus -a -um, *provided with a saddle.*

ēphippĭum -i, n., *a horse-cloth, saddle.*

ēphŏrus -i, m., *an ephor, a Spartan magistrate.*

ēpĭcōpus -a -um, *provided with oars.*

ēpĭcrŏcus -a -um, *transparent, fine.*

Epicūrus -i, m. *an Athenian philosopher, founder of the Epicurean school (342-270 B.C.):* adj. and subst. Epicūrĕus -a -um, *Epicurean, an Epicurean.*

ēpicus -a -um, *epic.*

ēpĭdīctĭcus -a -um, *for display.*

ēpĭdīpnis -ĭdis, f., *dessert.*

ēpigramma -ătis, n. *an inscription; an epigram.*

ēpĭlŏgus -i, m. *a conclusion, peroration, epilogue.*

ēpĭmēnĭa -orum, n. pl. *a month's rations.*

ēpĭrēdĭum -i, n., *the strap by which a horse was fastened to a vehicle; a trace.*

Ēpīrus -i, f., *a region in north-west Greece*; adj. **Ēpīrensis** -e, *of Epirus*; subst. **Ēpīrōtes** -ae, m., *an Epirote*.

ēpistŏlĭum -i, n. *a little letter, note*.

ēpistŭla (or **ēpistŏla**) -ae, f., *a written communication, letter, epistle*; ab epistulis, *to do with correspondence, of secretaries*. Transf., *sending of letters, post*.

ēpĭtăphĭum -i, m. *a funeral oration*.

ēpĭthălămĭum -i, n. *a nuptial song*.

ēpĭthēca -ae, f. *addition*.

ēpĭtŏma -ae and **ēpĭtŏmē** -ēs, f. *abridgment, epitome*.

ēpops -opis, m. *the hoopoe*.

ēpos, n. *an epic poem*.

ēpōtus -a -um, *drunk up, drained*. Transf. (1) *spent on drink.* (2) *swallowed up*.

ĕpŭlae -arum, f. *food, dishes, a banquet, feast*.

ĕpŭlāris -e, *belonging to a banquet*.

ĕpŭlo -ōnis, m. *feaster*; Tresviri (later Septemviri) epulones, *a college of priests who had charge of sacrificial feasts*.

ĕpŭlor -ari, dep. *to feast, feast on*.

ĕpŭlum -i, n. *a banquet, feast*, esp. on public occasions.

ĕqua -ae, f. *a mare*.

ĕquĕs -ĭtis, m. *a horseman, rider, cavalryman*; polit., equites, *the knights, order between senate and plebs*; also collectively in sing.

ĕquester -stris -stre, *relating to horsemen, equestrian; relating to cavalry*; polit., *relating to the knights*.

ĕquĭdem *indeed, truly, for my part*; concessive, *of course, certainly, admittedly*.

ĕquīnus -a -um, *relating to horses*.

ĕquĭtātus -ūs, m. *cavalry*.

ĕquĭto -are, *to ride on horseback*; of winds, *to rush*.

ĕquŭlĕus = eculeus; q.v.

ĕquus -i, m. (older forms **ĕquos** and **ĕcus**) *a horse*; equus bellator, *a war-horse*; equis virisque, *with horse and foot, with all one's might*; ad equum rescribere, *to make a person a knight*.

ēra -ae, f. *mistress, lady*.

ērādīco -are, *to root out*.

ērādo -rādĕre -rāsi -rāsum, *to scratch out; to destroy, get rid of*.

Ērătō, f. *the Muse of lyric and love-poetry*.

ercisco **erctum** = hercisco, herctum; q.v.

Ērĕbus -i, m. *a god of the lower world*; hence *the lower world*. Adj. **Ērĕbēus** -a -um.

Ērechtheus -ĕi, m. *a mythical king of Athens*; adj. **Ērechthēus** -a -um, m. *Athenian*; subst. **Ērechthīdae** -arum, m. pl. *the Athenians*.

ērectus, partic. from erigo; q.v.

ērēpo -rēpĕre -repsi -reptum, *to creep out; to creep up or over*.

ēreptĭo -ōnis, f. *taking by force, seizure*.

ēreptor -ōris, m., *one who takes by force, a robber*.

ergā, prep. with acc., *towards*, esp. of personal relations; more generally, *about*.

ergastŭlum -i, n. *a workhouse for debtors* or *slaves*; in plur., *the inmates of an ergastulum*.

ērgŏ: prep., preceded by genit., *because of, on account of*; adv., *therefore, accordingly, then*.

Ērichthŏnĭus -i, m. *a mythical king of Athens*; also *a mythical king of Troy*; adj. **Ērichthŏnĭus** -a -um, *Athenian* or *Trojan*.

ērĭcĭus -i, m. *hedgehog*; milit. *chevaux de frise*.

ērĭgo -rĭgĕre -rexi -rectum, *to set up, place upright, erect, raise*; milit., *to march a body of soldiers up a height*. Transf., *to arouse, excite; encourage, cheer*.

Hence partic. **ērectus** -a -um, *raised, upright, erect; high, elevated, proud; alert, anxious, intent, with minds on the stretch; resolute, cheerful*.

ērīlis -e, *of a master or mistress*.

Ērĭnȳs -ȳos, f., *one of the Furies*; plur. Erinyes, *the Furies*. Transf., *scourge, curse*.

ērĭpĭo -rĭpĕre -rĭpŭi -reptum, *to snatch away, tear out*; in good sense, *to free, rescue*.

Hence partic. **ēreptus** -a -um, *snatched away or rescued*.

ērŏgātĭo -ōnis, f., *payment, expenditure*.

ērŏgo -are, *to ask for and obtain*; used in the sense *to pay out* money, esp. *from public funds*.

errābundus -a -um, *wandering*.

errātĭcus -a -um, *wandering, erratic*.

errātĭo -ōnis, f. and **errātus** -ūs m. *wandering, straying*.

¹**erro** -are, *to wander, stray, rove*; transit., *to wander over*. Transf., *to waver; to err, be mistaken*. N. of partic. as subst. **errātum** -i, *a fault, error, technically or morally*.

²**erro** -ōnis, m. *a wanderer, vagabond*.

error -ōris, m. *wandering about*. Transf., *wavering, uncertainty, error, mistake; source of error, deception*.

ērŭbesco -rŭbescĕre -rŭbŭi, *to grow red, blush*; with infin., *to blush to*; with acc., *to blush for, to respect*; gerundive **ērŭbescendus** -a -um, *of which one should be ashamed*.

ērūca -ae, f. *a colewort*.

ēructo -are, *to belch forth, throw up, vomit*. Transf. (1) *to talk drunkenly about*. (2) *to cast out, eject*.

ērŭdĭo -ire, *to free from roughness; to instruct, teach, educate*.

Hence partic. **ērŭdĭtus** -a -um, *instructed, educated*; adv. **ērŭdĭtē**, *learnedly*.

ērŭdĭtĭo -ōnis, f. *teaching, instruction; knowledge, learning*.

ērumpo -rumpĕre -rūpi -ruptum: transit., *to break open, cause to burst forth; to vent, discharge*; intransit., *to break out, burst forth*; milit., *to rush forth*.

ērŭo -rŭĕre -rŭi -rūtum, *to tear out, dig up*; of buildings, *to raze, demolish*.

ēruptĭo -ōnis, f. *a bursting* or *breaking forth*; milit., *sally, attack*.

ĕrus -i, m. *master, owner, lord.*

ervum -i, n. *bitter vetch.*

Ēryx -rȳcis or Ērȳcus -i, m., *a mountain and city on the west coast of Sicily, with a famous temple of Venus.* Adj. Ērȳcīnus -a -um; f. as subst. *Venus.*

esca -ae, f. *food, victuals, esp. as bait.*

escārĭus -a -um, *relating to food* or *bait.*

ēscendo -scendĕre -scendi -scensum: intransit., *to climb up, ascend; to go up from the sea-coast inland;* transit., *to ascend.*

ēscensĭo -ōnis, f., *a movement inland,* esp. *hostile.*

escŭlentus -a -um, *edible, esculent.*

escŭletum, escŭlus; see aesc-.

ēsĭto -are, *to keep eating.*

Esquĭlĭae -arum, f. *one of the seven hills of Rome, the Esquiline.* Hence adj. Esquĭlĭus and Esquĭlīnus -a -um, *Esquiline;* f. as subst. Esquĭlīna -ae, *the Esquiline gate.*

essĕdārĭus -i, m. *a fighter in a British* or *Gallic war-chariot.*

essĕdum -i, n. *a war-chariot used by Gauls and Britons.*

ēsŭ, abl. sing. m., *in the eating.*

ēsŭrĭo -ire, *to be hungry, desire food:* in gen., *to long for.*

ēsŭrītĭo -ōnis, f. *hunger.*

et; as adv., *also, even;* as conj., *and; and indeed;* in narrative, *and then;* occasionally adversative, *and yet;* after alius, idem, par, *as* or *than;* repeated et . . . et . . . , *both . . . and* . . .; so -que . . . et . . .; nec (neque) . . . et, *not only not . . . but.*

ĕtĕnim, *for indeed.*

ētēsĭae -arum, m. pl. *winds which blow about the dogdays, Etesian winds.*

ēthŏlŏgus i, m. *a mimic.*

ĕtĭam, (1) as yet, still; etiam atque etiam, *again and again.* (2) *also, besides, even;* non solum (or modo) . . . sed (or verum) etiam, *not only* . . . *but also;* with comparatives, *still.* (3) in answers, *yes, certainly.* (4) in questions, expressing incredulity, *actually? really?*

ĕtĭamnum and ĕtĭamnunc, *yet, still, till now.*

ĕtĭam-si, *even if, although.*

ĕtĭam-tum and ĕtĭam-tunc, *even then, till that time, till then.*

Etrūrĭa -ae, f. *a district in north-west Italy;* hence adj. and subst. Etruscus -a -um, *Etruscan,* an *Etruscan.*

et-si, *even if, although;* elliptically, *and yet, notwithstanding.*

ĕtȳmŏlŏgĭa -ae, f., *etymology.*

eu, *good! well done!*

Euan or Euhan, m. *a name of Bacchus.*

euans or euhans -antis, *shouting Euan,* of Bacchanals.

euge and eugĕpae, *well done!*

Euĭas or Euhĭas -adis, f., *a Bacchante.*

Euĭus or Euhĭus -i, m., *a name of Bacchus.*

Eumĕnĭdes -um, f., *Eumenides, the gracious ones,* euphem. for the Furies.

eunūchus -i, m., *a eunuch.*

euoe, euhoe, interj., *shout of the Bacchantes.*

Eurīpĭdes -is, m., *the Athenian tragic poet* (c. 485-406 B.C.); adj. Eurīpĭdēus -a -um.

Eurīpus -i, m. *a channel, strait,* esp. *the strait between Euboea and Boeotia; a canal* or *water-course.*

Eurōpa -ae, f. and Eurōpē -ēs, f.: myth., *daughter of Agenor, whom Jupiter, in the form of a bull, carried off to Crete;* geograph., *the continent of Europe.* Adj. Eurōpaeus -a -um, *belonging to Europa* or *to Europe.*

Eurus -i, m., *the south-east* or *east wind;* adj. Eurŏus -a -um, *eastern.*

Euterpē -ēs, f. *Muse of harmony.*

Euxīnus -a -um, *an epithet of the Black Sea.*

ēvādo -vādĕre -vāsi -vāsum. Intransit., *to go out, go forth;* esp. *to climb up* or *out; to escape, get off.* Transf., *to turn out, result.* Transit., *to go out through, pass over; to climb up; to escape.*

ēvăgor -ari, dep.: intransit., *to wander out, stray away;* milit. *to wheel right and left, manoeuvre;* transit., *to overstep.*

ēvălesco -vălĕscĕre -vălŭi, *to grow strong, prevail, come into vogue;* in perf., *to have power, be able.*

ēvănesco -vānĕscĕre -vānŭi, *to vanish, disappear, pass away.*

ēvănĭdus -a -um, *vanishing, passing away.*

ēvasto -are, *to devastate, lay waste utterly.*

ēvĕho -vĕhĕre -vexi -vectum, *to carry out* or *up;* with reflex., or pass., of ships, *to sail away;* of riders, *to ride away.*

ēvello -vellĕre -velli -vulsum, *to tear out, pluck out.*

ēvĕnĭo -vĕnīre -vēni -ventum, *to come out.* Transf., *to turn out, result; to befall, happen, occur.* Hence n. of partic. as subst. ēventum -i, *issue, consequence, result; event, occurrence, experience.*

ēventus -ūs, m. *consequence, issue, result; event, occurrence, experience.*

ēverbĕro -are, *to strike violently.*

ēverrĭcŭlum -i, n., *a fishing-net, drag-net;* fig., *a clean sweep.*

ēverro -verrĕre -verri -versum, *to sweep out; to plunder.*

ēversĭo -ōnis, f. *overturning, destruction, ruin.*

ēversor -ōris, m. *overturner, destroyer.*

ēverto -vertĕre -verti -versum, *to turn out, dislodge, eject; to turn up stir; to overturn, throw down, demolish, destroy, ruin.*

ēvestīgātus -a -um, *tracked out, discovered.*

ēvĭdens -entis, *visible, clear, plain, evident*; adv. **ēvĭdentēr.**

ēvĭdentĭa -ae, f., *distinctness of language.*

ēvĭgĭlo -are: intransit. *to wake up; to be awake, be vigilant*; transit., *to watch through, pass in watching; to work hard at, to elaborate.*

ēvĭlesco -vĭlescĕre -vĭlŭi, *to become, contemptible.*

ēvincĭo -vincire -vinxi -vinctum, *to bind, bind round.*

ēvinco -vincĕre -vīci -victum, *to conquer entirely, utterly subdue*; in gen., *to prevail over, get through, get over*; of results *to bring about*; of conclusions, *to prove irresistibly.*

ēviscĕro -are, *to disembowel, tear in pieces.*

ēvĭtābĭlis -e, *that can be avoided.*

ēvĭto -are, *to avoid, shun.*

ēvŏcātor -ōris, m., *one who calls to arms.*

ēvŏco -are, *to call out*; esp. *to summon the spirits of the dead, or a deity*; milit. and polit. *to call out, call up, summon.* Transf., *to draw out, draw on; to call forth, produce.* M. pl. of partic. as subst. **ēvŏcāti** -orum, *veteran soldiers recalled to the colours.*

ēvoe; see euoe.

ēvŏlo -are, *to fly out, fly away; to come out quickly, rush forth, escape.*

ēvŏlūtĭo -ōnis, f., *the unrolling and reading of a book.*

ēvolvo -volvĕre -volvi -vŏlūtum. (1) *to roll out, roll forth*; of news, evolvi, *to spread.* (2) *to unroll, roll open*; esp. *to unroll a book to read it.* Transf., *to extricate, disentangle, detach; to unravel, disclose, explain.*

ēvŏmo -ĕre -ŭi -ĭtum, *to vomit forth, disgorge.*

ēvulgo -are, *to publish, make known.*

ēvulsĭo -ōnis, f. *pulling out.*

ex or **ē**, prep. with abl. (1) in space: *from* or *out of*; ex equo pugnare, *to fight on horseback* (operating *from* it); ex adverso *opposite.* (2) in time, *since*, esp. ex quo, *from which time, since*; also *immediately after*; aliud ex alio, *one thing after another.* (3) in other relations: to denote origin, *from, away from, out of, of*; ex animo, *heartily*; ex industria, *on purpose*; unus ex, *one of*; pocula ex auro, *gold cups*; to denote cause or occasion, *from, on account of, by reason of*; e vulnere mori, *to die of a wound*; to denote correspondence, *in accordance with*; ex re et ex tempore, *according to time and circumstance*; to denote advantage, e.g. e republica, *for the benefit of the state*; in gen., *in regard to, with respect to*; ex parte, *in part.*

exăcerbo -are, *to provoke, exasperate, embitter.*

exactĭo -ōnis, f. *driving out, expulsion; demanding, exacting*, esp. *collecting of debts, tribute*, etc.; in gen., *management, direction.*

exactor -ōris, m. *one who drives out; one who demands* or *exacts*, esp. *a*

collector of taxes; in gen., *superintendent, overseer.*

exactus -a -um, partic. from **exigo**; q.v.

exăcŭo -ŭĕre -ŭi -ūtum, *to sharpen to a point, make sharp, intensify, stimulate.*

exadversum or **exadversus**, *opposite.*

exaedĭfĭcātĭo -ōnis, f. *building up.*

exaedĭfĭco -are *to build up, erect, finish.*

exaequātĭo -ōnis, f. *making equal, equality.*

exaequo -are. (1) *to make level* or *equal, level up, relate.* (2) *to equal, be like.*

exaestŭo -are, *to be hot, boil up, foam up.*

exaggĕrātĭo -ōnis, f., *heaping up*; hence *elevation, exaltation.*

exaggĕro -are, *to heap up; to enlarge, increase; to heighten, exalt, magnify.*

exăgĭtātor -ōris, m. *a censurer.*

exăgĭto -are, *to chase about; to harass, disquiet, disturb; to scold, blame, censure, criticize; to excite, irritate.*

exalbesco -bescĕre -bŭi, *to grow white, turn pale.*

exāmen -ĭnis, n. (1) *a swarm; a throng, crowd, shoal.* (2) *the tongue of a balance; testing, consideration.*

exāmĭno -are, *to weigh; to consider.*

exāmussim, *according to rule, exactly.*

exanclo -are, *to drain, exhaust; to bear to the end, endure.*

exănĭmālis -e, *dead; deadly.*

exănĭmātĭo -ōnis, f. *want of breath*, esp. *from fright.*

exănĭmis -e and **exănĭmus** -a -um, *lifeless, dead*; also (exanimis only), *breathless*, esp. *from fright.*

exănĭmo -are. (1) *to take away the breath of, to wind, stun, weaken.* (2) *to deprive of life, to kill.*

exantlo = exanclo; q.v.

exardesco -ardescĕre -arsi -arsum, *to blaze up, to become hot, or inflamed*; of disturbances, *to break out.*

exāresco -ārescĕre -ārŭi, *to dry, become dry* or *exhausted.*

exarmo -are, *to disarm, deprive of arms.*

exăro -are, *to plough up, dig up; to produce by ploughing*; hence *to write on waxen tablets.*

exaspĕro -are, *to make rough, to irritate.*

exauctōro -are, *to dismiss from military service, discharge, cashier.*

exaudĭo -ire, *to hear plainly; to hear favourably, listen to.*

exaugĕo -ēre, *to increase much.*

exaugŭrātĭo -ōnis, f. *profanation, desecration.*

exaugŭro -are, *to desecrate, profane.*

exauspĭco -are, *to take an augury from.*

excaeco -are, *to make quite blind; to stop up a channel.*

excalcĕo -are, *to take the shoes from*; in drama, *to take the tragic cothurnus from* an actor.

excandescentĭa -ae, f., *heat, irascibility.*

excandesco -descĕre -dŭi, *to become hot, to glow.*

excanto -are, *to charm out, bring forth by incantations.*

excarnifico -are, *to tear to pieces.*

excăvo -are, *to hollow out.*

excēdo -cēdĕre -cessi -cessum: intransit., *to go out, go away, pass out;* e vita, *to die; to go beyond a point or limit; to attain to, result in;* transit., *to leave, pass beyond, exceed.*

excellentia -ae, f. *eminence, distinction.*

excello -ĕre, *to stand out, excel, be distinguished;* partic. excellens, *high, lofty, eminent, remarkable;* adv. excellenter, *eminently.*

excelsĭtās -ātis, f., *height, elevation.*

excelsus -a -um, adj., *lofty, high, elevated, eminent.* N. as subst. excelsum -i, *a height, eminence.* Adv. excelsē, *loftily.*

exceptio -ōnis, f. *exception, restriction, limitation;* esp. *an exception by the defendant to the plaintiff's statement of a case.*

excepto -are. (1) *to take up, catch;* auras, *to snuff up.* (2) *to take in succession.*

excerno -cernĕre -crēvi -crētum, *to separate, sift, sort.*

excerpo -cerpĕre -cerpsi -cerptum, *to pick out; to gather out, choose; to put on one side, separate.* N. of partic. as subst. excerptum -i, *an extract.*

excessus -ūs, m. *departure; from life,* i.e. *death; from subject,* i.e. *digression.*

excetra -ae, f. *a snake, viper.*

excidium -i, n. *overthrow, destruction.*

¹excido -cidĕre -cidi, *to fall out, fall away, be lost; of words, to slip out unawares, escape; of ideas, to pass from memory or thought, be forgotten.*

²excido -cidĕre -cidi -cisum, *to cut out; lapides e terra, to quarry.* Transf. (1) *to destroy, demolish;* portas, *to force open.* (2) *to root out, banish.*

excieo and excio -cire -civi and -cii -citum and cĭtum, *to call out, arouse;* esp. *to awaken from sleep or to summon to help;* in gen., of persons, *to excite, arouse;* of feelings, *to call forth, excite, produce;* of material things, *to stir, shake.*

excipio -cipĕre -cēpi -ceptum. (1) *to take out; hence to rescue; to except.* (2) *to take up, catch; to greet, welcome* a person; *to pick up news or ideas by listening;* of events, *to take* people, *come upon them.* (3) passively, *to receive; to take over from, follow, succeed, come later.*

excisio -ōnis, *destruction.*

excito -are, *to arouse, rouse up;* of things, *to provoke, call forth, cause;* of persons, *to console, cheer, inspire;* of buildings, *to raise, erect;* of fire, *to kindle, inflame.*

Hence partic. excitātus -a -um, *lively, vigorous, loud.*

exclāmātio -ōnis, f. *exclamation.*

exclāmo -are, *to shout, cry aloud; to exclaim; to call* somebody *by name.*

exclūdo -clūdĕre -clūsi -clūsum, *to shut out, exclude, keep away;* of things, *to knock out;* of birds, *to hatch.*

exclūsio -ōnis, f. *shutting out, exclusion.*

excōgĭtātio -ōnis, f. *contriving, devising.*

excōgĭto -are, *to think out, devise, contrive, invent.*

excŏlo -cŏlĕre -cŏlŭi -cultum, *to tend or cultivate carefully; to adorn, polish, refine; to serve, honour a deity or person.*

excŏquo -cŏquĕre -coxi -coctum, *to boil down, boil away; to cook, bake, make hard;* fig., *to cook up.*

excors -cordis, *foolish, silly, without intelligence.*

excrēmentum -i, n. *excrement;* oris, *spittle.*

excresco -crescĕre -crēvi -crētum, *to grow up, spring up.*

excrētus -a -um, partic. of excerno, or of excresco.

excrŭcio -are, *to torture, torment.*

excŭbiae -arum, f. pl. *lying out;* milit., *keeping watch, keeping guard.* Transf., *watchfires; watchmen, guard.*

excŭbĭtor -ōris, m. *sentinel, watchman, guard.*

excŭbo -bare -bŭi -bĭtum, *to lie or sleep out of doors;* milit., *to keep watch; to be watchful, vigilant.*

excūdo -cūdĕre -cūdi -cūsum, *to strike out, beat out;* esp. *to hammer, forge;* of birds, *to hatch.* Transf., of bees, *to mould;* of writers, *to compose.*

exculco -are, *to trample firm, tread hard.*

excūrātus -a -um, *carefully seen to.*

excurro -currĕre -cŭcurri and -curri -cursum *to run out, hasten forth;* milit., *to attack, make a sortie;* with acc., *to run over;* fig., *to run out, move freely;* of places, *to run out, to project.*

excursio -ōnis, f. *running out; movement forwards;* fig., *outset of a* speech; milit., *attack, assault, sally.*

excursor -ōris, m. *scout, skirmisher.*

excursus -ūs, m. *running out;* rhet., *digression;* milit., *attack, sally, assault.*

excūsābĭlis -e, *excusable.*

excūsātio -ōnis, *an excuse, plea, defence.*

excūso -are, *to exempt from blame or accusation; to excuse a person, to make excuses for a thing; to allege in excuse, to plead.*

Hence partic. excūsātus -a -um, *free from blame;* adv. excūsātē, *excusably.*

excŭtio -cŭtĕre -cussi -cussum. (1) *to shake out;* esp. *to shake out clothes to find anything hidden; hence to search, examine a person;* fig., *to investigate.* (2) *to strike off, throw out, knock away, shake off.*

exec-; see exsec-.

exēdo -esse -ēdi -ēsum, *to eat up, devour, consume; to wear down, exhaust, destroy.*

exedra -ae, f. *a hall for conversation or debate.*

exemplāris -e, *serving as a copy;* n. as subst. exemplar -āris, *a copy, transcript; a likeness; a pattern, ideal.*

exemplum -i, n. (1) *a sample, example;* exempli causa (or gratia), *for instance; general character, manner, fashion* (as shown by examples); *an example to be followed, model; a precedent; an example of what may happen, warning, object-lesson;* hence *a punishment intended to deter.* (2) *a copy, transcript.*

exemptus -a -um, partic. of eximo; q.v.

exentēro -are, *to torture, exhaust.*

exēo -ire -ii (-ivi) -itum: intransit., *to go out, go away, go forth; to pass from state to state; to get out, to become known;* of time, *to come to an end, pass away;* transit., *to pass over;* also *to ward off.*

exeq-; see exseq-.

exerceo -ēre -ūi -itum, *to keep at work, exercise, train, cultivate;* of abstr. things, *to employ, exploit;* of feelings, arts, and processes, *to practise, exercise;* of the mind, *to train;* hence *to overwork, harass, trouble.*

   Hence partic. exercitātus -a -um, *trained, schooled; harassed; severe, vexatious.*

exercitātio -ōnis, f. *practice, exercise; experience.*

exercitium -i, n. *practice, exercise.*

exercito -are, *to train hard, keep at work.*

   Hence partic. exercitatus -a -um, *trained, practised, exercised; troubled, harassed.*

¹exercĭtus -a -um, partic. of exerceo; q.v.

²exercitus -ūs, m. *training; a trained body of soldiers, army;* esp. *the infantry;* poet. in gen., *crowd, swarm.*

exēsor -ōris, m. *one who gnaws or eats away.*

exhālātio -ōnis, f. *exhalation, vapour.*

exhālo -are: transit., *to exhale, breathe out;* intransit., of things, *to steam;* of persons, *to expire.*

exhaurio -haurire -hausi -haustum. (1) *to draw out;* in gen., *to remove, take out, take away.* (2) *to drain dry, empty out, impoverish; to finish, bring to an end; to endure, suffer.*

exhērēdo -are, *to disinherit.*

exhērēs -ēdis, *disinherited.*

exhĭbĕo -hĭbēre -hĭbŭi -hĭbitum, *to produce, show, display, exhibit, present; to offer, allow; to produce* by making, *to cause.*

exhĭlāro -are, *to make cheerful.*

exhorresco -horrescēre -horrŭi, *to shudder exceedingly, be terrified;* transit., *to tremble at, to dread.*

exhortātio -ōnis, f. *exhortation, encouragement.*

exhortātīvus -a -um, *of exhortation.*

exhortor -ari, dep. *to exhort, encourage.*

exigo -igĕre -ēgi -actum. (1) *to drive out or away; to force out, exact demand; to sell.* (2) *to drive through* hence *to complete, finish; to determine settle, adjust, regulate; to ascertain decide.*

   Hence partic. exactus -a -um, *accurate, precise, exact.*

exigŭitās -ātis, f. *littleness, smallness.*

exigŭus -a -um, *small, little, scanty* of quantity, in size, *small;* in numbe *scanty;* in time, *short;* of quality *meagre.* N. as subst. exigŭum - *small extent.* Adv. exigŭē, *sparingly scantily, scarcely.*

exīlis -e, *thin, slender, meagre;* in possessions, *poor;* with genit., *with out;* of style, *dry, dreary.* Adv exilitĕr, *thinly, poorly, meagrely.*

exilitās -ātis, f. *thinness, meagreness wearness.*

eximĭus -a -um, *excepted;* hence *selected; exceptional, distinguished* Adv. eximĭē, *uncommonly, exceptionally.*

eximo -imēre -ēmi -emptum, *to take out, take away,* esp. *off a list or out of a group; to free, release; to take away, remove* an abstr. thing; of time, *to waste.*

exin = exinde; q.v.

exinānio -ire, *to empty;* gentes. *to plunder.*

exinde (exin, exim): in space *thence, next;* in time, *thereupon after that, then;* in logic, *consequently, accordingly.*

existĭmātio -ōnis, f. *the opinion that a man has, judgement; the opinion that others have of a man,* esp. morally, *reputation, good name, honour, character;* in finance, *credit.*

existĭmātor -ōris, m., *one who forms or gives an opinion, a critic.*

existĭmo (-ŭmo) -are, *to judge a thing according to its value;* in gen., *to judge, consider, regard.*

exitiābĭlis -e, *deadly, destructive.*

exitiālis -e, *destructive, fatal, deadly.*

exitio -ōnis, f. *going out.*

exitiōsus -a -um, *destructive, fatal deadly.*

exitĭum -i, n. *going out or away;* hence *destruction, ruin;* also *a cause of destruction.*

exitus -ūs, m. *going out, going forth; a means of going out, exit; end, finish; issue, result.*

exlex -lēgis, *bound by no law, lawless, reckless.*

exmŏvĕo = emoveo; q.v.

exobsecro -are, *to entreat earnestly.*

exŏcŭlo -are, *to deprive of eyes.*

exōdĭum -i, n., *a comic afterpiece.*

exōlesco -ōlescēre -ōlēvi -ōlētum, *to grow old and weak, decay, fade out;* partic. exōlētus -a -um, *worn out;* m. as subst. *a dissolute person.*

exŏnĕro -are, *to unload, disburden;* in gen., *to free, release, relieve.*

exopto -are, *to desire eagerly, long for;*

partic. **exoptātus** -a -um, *desired, longed for.*

exōrābĭlis -e, *able to be entreated, placable.*

exōrātor -ōris, m., *one who entreats successfully.*

exordĭor -ordiri -orsus, dep. *to begin to weave;* in gen., *to begin.* Partic. in pass. sense **exorsus** -a -um, *begun.*

exordĭum -i, n., *the warp of a web;* in gen., *a beginning;* esp. *the beginning of a speech.*

exŏrĭor -ōriri -ortus, dep. *to rise, spring up, issue, appear, come forward.*

exornātĭo -ōnis, f., *adorning, ornament.*

exornātor -ōris, m., *one who adorns, an embellisher.*

exorno -are, *to furnish, provide plentifully;* also *to ornament, adorn.*

exōro -are, *to entreat successfully, obtain* a thing *by entreaty, prevail upon* a person.

¹exorsus -a -um, partic. of exordior; q.v.

²exorsus -ūs, m., *a beginning.*

exortus -ūs, m., *a rising; the East.*

exōs -ossis, *without bones.*

exoscŭlor -ari, dep. *to kiss.*

exosso -are, *to bone, take out the bones.*

exostra -ae, f. *a theatrical machine, revealing the inside of a house to the spectators.*

exōsus -a -um, *hating exceedingly.*

exōtĭcus -a -um, *foreign, outlandish, exotic.*

expallesco -pallescĕre -pallŭi, *to become very pale;* with acc., *to dread.*

expalpo -are, *to coax out.*

expando -ĕre, *to stretch out, expand, spread out.* Transf., *to explain.*

expāvesco -pāvescĕre -pavi, *to grow very frightened;* with acc. *to dread exceedingly.*

expĕdĭo -ire -ivi and -ii -itum, *to free from a snare, disengage, disentangle, set free; to get things ready for action;* fig., *to release, clear, set free, set straight;* in speech, *to clear up* a point, *explain;* res expedit, or impers. expedit, *it is expedient, useful, advantageous.*

Hence partic. **expĕdĭtus** -a -um, *unshackled, unimpeded;* milit., *lightly equipped;* in gen., *free, ready;* n. as subst. *clear ground;* of abstr. things, *clear, settled, ready.* Adv. **expĕdītē**, *freely, easily.*

expĕdĭtĭo -ōnis, f., *a military operation, expedition.*

expello -pellĕre -pŭli -pulsum, *to drive out, expel, thrust away.*

expendo -pendĕre -pendi -pensum, *to weigh out;* esp. *to weigh out in payment, pay out, put down;* sometimes *to pay* a penalty. Transf., *to value, rate;* in gen., *to weigh up, consider.*

Hence partic. **expensus** -a -um, *weighed out,* hence *paid out;* ferre homini expensum, *to note* a thing *as paid* to a person, *charge* to. N. as subst. **expensum** -i, *payment.*

expergēfăcĭo -făcĕre -fēci -factum, *to awaken, rouse, excite.*

expergiscor -pergisci -perrectus, dep. *to wake up, arouse oneself.*

expergo -pergĕre -pergi -pergĭtum, *to awaken.*

expĕrĭentĭa -ae, f., *trial, testing, attempt; knowledge gained by experience.*

expĕrĭmentum -i, n. *experience; proof from experience.*

expĕrĭor -pĕriri -pertus, dep. *to try, test, prove, put to the test;* experiri ius, *to go to law;* in perf., *to know by having tried, know by experience; to try to do* a thing. Pres. partic. **expĕrĭens** -entis, *enterprising, venturesome.* Perf. partic. **expertus** -a -um: pass., *tested, tried, approved;* act., with *experience, experienced.*

experrectus -a -um, partic. of expergiscor; q.v.

expers -pertis, *having no part in, not sharing in; wanting in, destitute of.*

expertus -a -um, partic. from experior q.v.

expĕtesso -ere, *to desire, wish for.*

expĕto -ĕre -ii and -ivi -itum: transit., *to desire, strive after, make for;* of things due, *to demand, require;* with infin., *to seek to do;* intransit. *to fall upon.*

expĭātĭo -onis, f. *atonement, expiation.*

expĭlātĭo -ōnis, f. *plundering, robbing.*

expĭlator -ōris, m., *plunderer, robber.*

expĭlo -are, *to plunder, rob.*

expingo -pingĕre -pinxi -pictum, *to paint over;* fig., *to describe, depict in writing.*

expĭo -are, *to propitiate, appease* an offended or threatening power; *to purify* what is defiled; *to atone for* an offence.

expiscor -ari, dep. *to fish out; to search out, find out.*

explānātĭo -ōnis, f. *making clear, explanation;* rhet., *illustration,* also *clear articulation.*

explānātor -ōris, m., *one who explains; an interpreter.*

explāno -are, *to make level, smooth out;* hence *to explain, make clear: to set out clearly,* or *articulate clearly.*

explaudo = explodo; q.v.

explēmentum -i, n., *filling, stuffing.*

explĕo -plēre -plēvi -plētum, *to fill, fill up; to complete* a required amount; *to make good* losses, etc.; in quality, *to complete, perfect;* of time, *to complete, finish;* of duties, *to fulfil, discharge;* of wants, *to satisfy, quench, appease.*

Hence partic. **explētus** -a -um, *perfect, complete.*

explētĭo -ōnis, f., *satisfying.*

explĭcātĭo -ōnis, f. *unfolding, uncoiling.* Transf., *explanation, interpretation.*

explĭcātor -ōris, m. and **explĭcātrix** -icis, f. *interpreter, explainer.*

¹explĭcātus -a -um, partic. from explico; q.v.

²explĭcātus -ūs, m. *explanation, exposition.*

explĭco -are -avi -atum and -ŭi -itum, *to unfold, unroll, disentangle;* in gen.

to spread out, extend, expand; milit., *to extend ranks, deploy*. Transf., *to disentangle, put in order*; of a debt, *to pay off; to explain, expound, interpret; to set free.*

Hence partic. **explicātus** -a -um, *ordered, arranged; made plain, clear*; also **explicitus** -a -um, *straightforward, easy*; adv. **explicātē,** *plainly.*

explōdo (-plaudo) -plōdĕre -plōsi -plōsum, *to hiss an actor off the stage*; in gen., *to scare off, reject.*

explōrātio -ōnis, f. *investigation.*

explōrātor -ōris, m. *explorer, scout, spy.*

explōro -are, *to search out, investigate, explore*; milit., *to spy out, reconnoitre; to test, try, put to proof.*

Hence partic. **explōrātus** -a -um, *established, confirmed, certain*; exploratum habeo, *I am sure*; adv. **explōrātē,** *certainly, surely, definitely.*

expōlio -ire -ii and -ivi -itum, *to smooth, polish, refine*; partic. **expōlitus** -a -um, *smooth, polished.*

expōlītio -ōnis, f. *smoothing, polishing.*

expōno -pōnĕre -pōsŭi, pōsĭtum. (1) *to put outside, cast out*; *to expose* a child; naut. *to land, disembark*. (2) *to put on view, display, show*; in words, *to set forth, exhibit, explain.*

Hence partic. **expōsĭtus (expostus)** -a -um, *exposed, open, accessible*; of persons, *affable*; in bad sense, *vulgar.*

expōrrigo -rĭgĕre -rexi -rectum, *to stretch out, expand, smooth out.*

expōrtātio -ōnis, f., *exportation.*

exporto -are, *to carry out*; esp. *to export.*

exposco -poscĕre -pōposci, *to implore, entreat earnestly*; esp. *to demand the surrender of a person.*

expōsĭtio -ōnis, f. *putting out*; hence *statement, exposition, narration.*

expostŭlātio -ōnis, f. *complaint, expostulation.*

expostŭlo -are. (1) *to demand earnestly,* esp. *to demand the surrender of a person.* (2) *to make a claim or complaint, to expostulate.*

expōtus = epotus; q.v.

exprĭmo -prĭmĕre -pressi -pressum. (1) *to press out, force out; to extort.* (2) *to mould or form* one thing in imitation of another; hence *to copy, express, portray, represent*; esp. *to express in words, describe; to translate;* (3) *to raise up.*

Hence partic. **expressus** -a -um, *made clear, prominent, distinct.*

exprobrātio -ōnis, f. *reproach, upbraiding.*

exprobro -are, *to reproach; to bring up* a thing *against* a person.

exprōmo -prōmĕre -prompsi -promptum, *to bring forth, produce, exhibit, display; to disclose, set forth, state, utter.*

expugnābilis -e, *that may be taken by storm.*

expugnātio -ōnis, f., *the taking of a place by storm.*

expugnātor -ōris, m. *taker, capturer*; pudicitiae, *violator.*

expugno -are, *to take by storm, capture*; hence *to overcome, subdue; to gain forcibly, extort*: with ut and the subj., *bring it about that.*

expulsio -ōnis, f., *driving out, expulsion.*

expulsor -ōris, m. and **expultrix** -tricis, f. *one who drives out.*

expungo -pungĕre -punxi -punctum, *to prick out;* hence *to cancel, expunge.*

expurgātio -ōnis, f. *vindication, justification.*

expurgo -are, *to cleanse, purify.* Hence *to cure; to purify; to justify, defend.*

expūtesco -ĕre, *to rot away.*

expūto -are, *to lop away;* hence *to consider; to comprehend.*

exquiro (-quaero) -quirĕre -quisivi -quisitum. (1) *to search for, look for, ask for.* (2) *to search through, examine.*

Hence partic. **exquīsītus** -a -um, *carefully sought or worked out, choice, exquisite, artificial.* Adv. **exquīsītē,** *accurately, carefully.*

exsaevio -ire, *to rage to an end, cease to rage.*

exsanguis -e, *bloodless, without blood; deathly pale*; act., *making pale.*

exsarcio -sarcire -sartum, *to patch up, make good, repair.*

exsātio -are, *to satisfy thoroughly, satiate.*

exsătŭrābilis -e, *that can be satiated.*

exsătŭro -are, *to satisfy, satiate.*

exscen-; see escen-.

exscindo -scindĕre -scidi -scissum, *to tear out; to destroy utterly.*

exscrĕo -are, *to cough out.*

exscrībo -scribĕre -scripsi -scriptum, *to write out; to copy; to note down, register.*

exsculpo -sculpĕre -sculpsi -sculptum, *to scratch out, erase; to carve or scoop out.*

exsĕco -sĕcare -sĕcŭi -sectum, *to cut out, cut away.*

exsĕcrābilis -e, *cursing, execrating.*

exsĕcrātio -ōnis, f. *curse, execration; an oath containing an imprecation.*

exsĕcror -ari, dep. *to curse, execrate; to swear with an imprecation*; partic. in pass. sense, **exsĕcrātus** -a -um, *cursed, execrated.*

exsectio -ōnis, f. *cutting out.*

exsĕcūtio -ōnis, f. *performance, accomplishment;* executio Syriae, *administration;* of speech, *a discussion.*

exsĕquiae -arum, f. pl. *a funeral procession.*

exsĕquiālis -e, *belonging to a funeral procession.*

exsĕquor -sĕqui -sĕcūtus, dep. *to follow to the grave;* in gen., *to follow to the end; to maintain, keep up, to carry out, accomplish, execute; to avenge, punish; to relate, describe, explain a matter; to suffer, endure.*

exsĕro -sĕrĕre -sĕrŭi -sertum, *to stretch out, thrust out;* hence *to put* *forth, assert.* Perf. partic. **exsertus** -a -um, *bared, protruding.*

exꞩerto -are, *to stretch out.*

exsībīlo -are, *to hiss out;* esp. *to hiss* an actor *off the stage.*

exsicco -are, *to dry thoroughly;* to *drain dry, to empty* by drinking. Hence partic. **exsiccātus** -a -um, of style, *dry, jejune.*

exsigno -are, *to mark out.*

exsīlio -sīlire -sīlŭi, *to leap out or up.*

exsīlium -i, n. *banishment, exile.* Transf., *place of exile;* plur. = *exsules, exiles.*

exsisto (existo) -sistĕre -stiti -stĭtum, *to stand forth, appear; to spring forth, arise, come into existence.*

exsolvo -solvĕre -solvi -sŏlūtum. (1) *to loosen, untie, unbind, open;* glaciem, *to dissolve;* of persons, *to disentangle, free;* of things, *to explain.* (2) *to pay off; to discharge any* obligation, *perform* anything due.

exsomnis -e, *sleepless, wakeful.*

exsorbēo -ēre, *to suck up, suck dry.*

exsors -sortis, *without lot; for which no lot has been cast, specially chosen; having no share in, deprived of,* with genit.

exspătior -ari, dep. *to deviate from the course;* fig., *to digress.*

exspectābilis -e, *that is to be expected, probable.*

exspectātio -ōnis, f. *waiting, looking for, expectation* (with objective genit.).

exspecto -are, *to look out for, wait for, await, wait to see;* esp. *with longing, fear, desire,* etc., *to hope for, dread.* Hence partic. (with compar. and superl.) **exspectātus** -a -um, *awaited, wished for, welcome.*

exspergo -spergĕre -spersum. *to sprinkle, scatter.*

exspēs, *without hope, hopeless.*

exspīrātio -ōnis, f. *exhalation.*

exspiro -are: transit., *to breathe out, exhale, emit;* intransit., *to blow forth, rush forth; to give up the ghost, to die.*

exspŏlio -are, *to plunder, rob, despoil.*

exspŭo -spŭere -spŭi -spūtum, *to spit out; to get rid of, cast away.*

externo -āre, *to frighten, terrify.*

exstillo -are, *to drop moisture, drip, trickle.*

exstĭmŭlātor -ōris, m. *inciter, instigator.*

exstĭmŭlo -are, *to goad, excite, instigate.*

exstinctio -ōnis, f. *annihilation, extinction.*

exstinctor -ōris, m. *one who extinguishes, destroys, annihilates.*

exstinguo -stinguĕre -stinxi -stinctum, *to put out, extinguish;* of persons, *to kill;* in gen., *to abolish, destroy, annihilate.*

exstirpo -are, *to root out, extirpate*

exsto (exto) -are, *to stand out, project; to be visible, show itself, appear; to be still in existence, be extant.*

exstructio -ōnis, f. *building up, erection.*

exstrŭo -strŭĕre -struxi -structum, *to heap up, pile up, build up.*

exsuctus -a -um, partic. of exsugo; q.v.

exsūdo -are; intransit., *to come out in sweat, exude;* transit., *to sweat out, sweat through, perform with great labour.*

exsūgo -sūgĕre -suxi -suctum, *to suck out, suck dry.*

exsul -sŭlis, c., *a banished person, an exile.*

exsŭlo (exŭlo) -are, *to be banished, live in exile.*

exsultātio -ōnis, f. *leaping up; exultation, excessive rejoicing.*

exsultim, adv. *friskingly.*

exsulto (exulto) -are, *to leap up frequently* or *violently.* Transf., *to rejoice exceedingly, exult, triumph;* of orators, etc., *to run riot, range freely.*

exsŭpĕrābilis -e, *that can be overcome.*

exsŭpĕrantia -ae, f., *superiority, pre-eminence.*

exsŭpĕro -are: intransit., *to mount up, appear above; to be prominent, excel;* transit., *to surmount; to surpass, exceed, overcome.*

exsurdo -are, *to deafen;* of taste, *to make dull* or *blunt.*

exsurgo -surgĕre -surrexi, *to rise up, lift oneself up, stand up; to regain strength.*

exsuscito -are, *to awaken from sleep;* of fire, *to kindle* or *fan;* mentally, *to excite, arouse;* se exsuscitare, *to make an effort.*

exta -orum, n. pl. *entrails of animals,* esp. *the heart, lungs, liver,* used by Romans for divination.

extābesco -tābescĕre -tābŭi, *to waste away entirely; to vanish, disappear.*

extāris -e, *used for cooking.*

extemplo (-tempŭlo), *immediately, forthwith.*

extempŏrālis -e, *extemporary, unrehearsed.*

extendo -tendĕre -tendi -tensum and -tentum, *to stretch out, expand, extend;* milit., *to extend in order of battle;* in gen., *to increase, extend;* in time, *to extend, prolong; to strain, exert.* Hence partic. **extentus** -a -um, *wide, extensive.*

extento -are, *to stretch out, strain.*

extĕnŭātio -ōnis, f. *thinning;* as a figure of speech, *diminution, lessening.*

extĕnŭo -are, *to make thin* or *small, to reduce, diminish;* milit., *to extend;* in gen., *to lessen, weaken, diminish;* in speech, *to disparage, depreciate.* Hence partic. **extĕnŭātus** -a -um, *weak, poor, slight.*

exter and **extĕrus** -a -um, *outward, foreign, strange;* compar. **extĕrior** -ius, genit. -ōris, *outer;* superl. **extrēmus** -a -um, *outermost;* n. as subst. *outer edge, extreme;* in time, *last;* n. as subst. *an end;* extremum, acc., *for the last time;* ad extremum, *to the end* or *at the end;* in degree or quality, *extreme;* esp. *lowest, worst;* extremum bonorum, malorum, *the* *highest good, evil;* superl. **extĭmus** -a -um, *outermost.*

exiěrebro -are, *to bore out, extract by boring.*

extergĕo -tergēre -tersi -tersum, *to wipe off, wipe clean; to strip clean, plunder.*

extěrĭor, exterius; see exter.

extermĭno -are, *to drive out, expel, banish; to put aside, remove.*

externus -a -um, *outside, external, foreign, strange;* m. as subst. *a foreigner, stranger;* n. pl. as subst. *outward or foreign things.*

extěro -tĕrĕre -trivi -tritum, *to rub out; to wear away.*

exterrĕo -terrēre -terrŭi -territum, *to frighten badly, scare, terrify.*

extěrus; see exter.

extexo -ĕre, *to unweave; to cheat.*

extimesco -timescĕre -tĭmŭi: intransit. *to be terrified;* transit., *to be greatly afraid of, to dread.*

extĭmus; see exter.

extispex -spĭcis, m., *a soothsayer predicting from the entrails of victims.*

extollo -ĕre, *to lift up, raise up;* of buildings, *to raise, erect;* of spirits, etc., *to elevate, exalt;* in words, *to praise or exaggerate;* sometimes *to adorn; to defer, postpone.*

extorquĕo -torquēre -torsi -tortum, *to twist out, wrest away, wrench out, dislocate.* Transf., *to obtain by force, extort.*

extorris -e, *driven from the country, exiled, banished.*

extrā: adv. *outside;* extra quam, extra quam si, *except, unless;* prep., with acc., *beyond, outside of, without; except for;* extra iocum, *joking apart.*

extrăho -trăhĕre -traxi -tractum, *to draw out, drag out, extract, remove, extricate;* sometimes *to bring forward;* in time, *to draw out, prolong, protract.*

extrānĕus -a -um, *outside, extraneous; foreign, strange;* m. as subst. *a foreigner, stranger.*

extrāordĭnārĭus -a -um, *extraordinary, anomalous, irregular, unnatural;* milit. equites, cohortes, *picked troops of the auxiliary forces.*

extrārĭus -a -um, *outward, external, extrinsic; strange, unrelated, foreign.*

extrēmĭtās -ātis, f. *end, farthest portion, extremity.*

extrēmus -a -um; see exter.

extrīco -are, *to disentangle, extricate; to clear up, unravel.*

extrinsĕcus, *from without, from the outside; on the outside, outwardly.*

extrūdo -trūdĕre -trūsi -trūsum, *to push out, thrust forth;* merces *to get sold.*

extundo -tundĕre -tŭdi -tūsum. (1) *to form by beating with a hammer; to invent, devise.* (2) *to beat out violently, drive away.* (3) *to extort.*

exturbo -are, *to drive away, thrust out;* mentem, *to agitate.*

exūbĕro -are, *to grow thickly, abound.*

exul; see exsul.

exulcĕro -are, *to make worse, aggravate; to irritate, embitter.*

exŭlŭlo -are, *to howl out, howl loudly;* partic. **exŭlŭlātus** -a -um, *invoked with howlings.*

exundo -are, *to overflow, to flow out or over, to abound.*

exŭo -ŭĕre -ŭi -ŭtum. (1) *to lay aside, put off, put away.* (2) *to strip, deprive of a thing.*

exūro -ūrĕre -ussi -ustum, *to burn out, burn up, consume;* also *to dry up, warm, heat.*

exustĭo -ōnis, f. *burning up, conflagration.*

exŭvĭae -arum, f. pl. *that which is taken off;* of men *dress; spoils taken from the enemy, arms,* etc.; *the skin, slough,* or *hide of* animals.

F

F, f, the sixth letter of the Latin Alphabet.

făba -ae, f. *the broad bean.*

făbālis -e, *of beans.*

făbella -ae, f. *a little story, fable or drama.*

făber -bra -brum, *ingenious, skilful.* M. as subst. **făber** -bri, *a worker, craftsman;* faber tignarius, *a carpenter;* ferrarius, *a blacksmith;* milit. fabri, *the engineers;* also *a fish,* perhaps dory. Adv. **fabrē,** *skilfully.*

Făbĭus -a -um, *name of a Roman gens.*

fabrēfăcĭo -făcĕre -fēci -factum, *to make or fashion skilfully.*

fabrĭca -ae, f. *the art of a faber; a device, trick, a workshop.*

fabrĭcātĭo -ōnis, f., *making, framing, construction.*

fabrĭcātor -ōris, m. *maker, artificer.*

Fabrĭcĭus -a, -um, *name of a Roman gens.*

fabrĭco -are, and **fabrĭcor** -ari, dep., *to form, make, forge.*

fabrīlis -e, *relating to an artificer;* n.pl. as subst., *tools.*

făbŭla -e, f. (1) *talk, conversation:* fabulam fieri, *to get talked about.* (2) *a tale, story, fable, drama, myth;* fabulae! *nonsense!*

făbŭlor -ari, dep. (1) *to talk, converse, chatter.* (2) *to tell an untruth.*

făbŭlōsus -a -um, *renowned in story, fabled.*

făcesso -făcessĕre -făcessi -făcessĭtum:* transit., *to do eagerly, perform, fulfil, accomplish;* homini negotium, *to give trouble to;* intransit., *to make off, go away, depart.*

făcētĭa -ae, f.; *sing., wit;* plur., *wit, drollery, humour.*

făcētus -a -um, *fine, elegant; witty, facetious.* Adv. **făcētē,** *elegantly; wittily, humorously.*

făcĭēs -ēi, *shape, form, figure, outward appearance;* esp. *face, countenance.* Transf., *character, nature; seeming, pretence.*

făcĭlis -e, *easy to do; easy to manage,*

convenient, favourable; of movements, *easy, mobile*; of persons, *facile, dexterous, clever*; of character, *affable, easy, good-natured.* N. acc. as adv. **făcĭlĕ**, *easily, without difficulty; indisputably, certainly*; haud facile, *not easily, hardly*; facile pati, *to bear willingly.*

făcĭlĭtās -ātis, f. *easiness, ease*; of character, *willingness, friendliness, affability, good-nature.*

făcĭnŏrōsus -a -um, *wicked, criminal.*

făcĭnus -ŏris, n., *a deed, action*; esp. *a bad deed, crime, villainy*; hence *instrument of crime*; in plur., *criminals.*

făcĭo făcĕre fēci factum (the pass. is fio; q.v.). Transit., *to make, form, do, perform*; of feelings and circumstances, *to cause, bring about*; esp. copiam or potestatem, *to give a chance, grant permission*; with clause as object, esp. with subj., e.g. fac sciam, *let me know*; facere non possum quin, *I cannot but*; of troubles, *to experience, suffer*; with double acc., *to make, appoint, change into*; with genit., *to make something the property of a person or thing, to bring into the power of*, or mentally *to put into a category, to regard, to esteem, value*; with acc. and infin., *to take it, assume* or *to make out, represent* that a thing is so. Intransit., *to act*; with adverbs, *to behave*; facere cum, or ab, homine, *to act on the side of, support*; *to sacrifice*; *to be serviceable, to suit, help, be of service*; used instead of repeating another verb, *to do so.*

Hence partic. **factus** -a -um, *done, wrought*; of compar., factius, *nearer to achievement*; n. of positive as subst. **factum** -i, *a deed, act, exploit.*

factĭo -ōnis, f. (1) *a making, doing*; also *the right of making or doing.* (2) *a party, group*; esp. *a political party, faction, side.*

factĭōsus -a -um, *busy; factious, associated with a faction.*

factĭto -are. (1) *to practise, be accustomed to make or do.* (2) *to appoint openly.*

factus -a -um, partic. from facio; q.v.

făcŭla -ae, f., *a little torch.*

făcultās -ātis, f. *feasibility, opportunity, power, means; capacity, ability; resources, stock, abundance.*

fācundĭa -ae, f., *eloquence, readiness of speech.*

fācundus -a -um, *eloquent, fluent, ready of speech*; adv. **fācundē.**

faecŭla -ae, f. *lees of wine.*

faenebris -e, *relating to interest.*

faenĕrātĭo -ōnis, f. *lending at interest, usury.*

faenĕrātor -ōris, m. *money-lender, usurer.*

faenĕror -ari, dep. and **faenĕro** (**fenĕro**) -are, *to lend at interest*; provincias, *to despoil by usury*; beneficium *to trade in benefits.*

faenĕus -a -um, *of hay*; homines, *men of straw.*

faenīlĭa -ĭum, n. pl. *hay-loft.*

faenĭsĕca -ae, m., *a mower; a countryman.*

faenum (**fēnum**) -i, n. *hay.*

faenus (**fēnus**) -ōris, n. *interest on money*; pecuniam dare faenore, *to lend at interest*; accipere faenore, *to borrow.* Transf., *debt, indebtedness; capital, usury.*

Faesŭlae -arum, f. *town in Etruria*, (now *Fiesole*); adj. **Faesŭlanus** -a -um.

faex faecis, f. *the dregs or lees of liquid*, esp. *of wine*; fig. socially, *the dregs, the lower orders.*

fāgĭnĕus and **fāgĭnus** -a -um, *of beech.*

fāgus -i, f. *beech-tree.*

fāla (**phăla**) -ae, f. *a wooden tower or pillar.*

fālārĭca (**phălārĭca**) -ae, f. *a missile covered with tow and pitch.*

falcārĭus -i, m., *a sickle-maker.*

falcātus -a -um, *furnished with sickles; sickle-shaped.*

falcĭfer -fĕra -fĕrum, *carrying a scythe* or *sickle.*

Fălernus ăger, *the Falernian country, in Campania*; n. of adj. as subst. **Fălernum** -i, *Falernian wine.*

fallācĭa -ae, f. *deceit, trick, fraud.*

fallax -ācis, *deceitful, treacherous, false*; adv. **fallācĭter.**

fallo fallĕre fĕfelli falsum, *to deceive, lead astray, cause to be mistaken*; nisi fallor, *unless I am mistaken*; of abstr. things, *to disappoint, fail in*; poet., *to beguile, wile away*; *to escape the notice of, be concealed from*; impers. non fallit me, *I am not unaware.*

Hence partic. **falsus** -a -um. (1) *wrong, mistaken, misled*; n. as subst., *a mistake*; abl. as adv., falso, *falsely, mistakenly.* (2) *false, untrue, spurious*; (3) *deceitful, lying*; n. as subst. *a lie*; abl. as adv., falso, *falsely, fraudulently.* Adv. **falsē.**

falsĭdĭcus -a -um, and **falsĭlŏquus** -a -um, *lying.*

falsus -a -um, partic. from fallo; q.v.

falx falcis, f. *a sickle, bill-hook, pruning-hook; a sickle-shaped implement of war.*

fāma -ae, f. *talk, report, rumour, tradition*; fama est, *there is a rumour; public opinion; standing in public opinion, repute*, good or bad.

fămēlĭcus -a -um, *hungry, famished.*

fămes -is, f. *hunger, famine; insatiable desire; poverty of expression.*

fāmĭgĕrātor -ōris, m. *rumour-monger.*

fămĭlĭa -ae, *a household (of slaves), establishment*; pater familias or paterfamilias, *the head of the household*; materfamilias, *a married woman* or *an unmarried woman whose father was dead*; filiusfamilias, *a son still under his father's power.* Transf., *a family estate; a family*, as a subdivision of a gens; any *fraternity, group, sect.*

fămĭlĭāris -e. (1) *belonging to the*

slaves of a house; as subst. **fămĭllārĭs** -is, m. a servant, slave. (2) belonging to a family or household; known in the house or family, intimate, friendly; m. and f. as subst. a familiar friend. (3) in augury, fissum familiare, or pars familiaris, the part of the entrails relating to the persons sacrificing. Adv. **fămĭllārĭter**, familiarly, intimately.

fămĭllārĭtās -ātis, f. confidential friendship, intimacy; meton., familiar friends.

fămōsus -a -um: pass., much spoken of, renowned; in bad sense, infamous, notorious; act., libellous, defamatory.

fămul, fămŭla; see famulus.

fămŭlārĭs -e, relating to servants or slaves.

fămŭlātus -ūs, m. servitude, slavery, service; meton., an establishment of slaves.

fămŭlor -ari, dep. to be a servant, to serve.

fămŭlus -a -um, serving, servile; as subst. m. **fămŭlus (fămul)** -i, a servant, slave, attendant; f. **fămŭla** -ae, a female slave, handmaid.

fānātĭcus -a -um, inspired; enthusiastic; frenzied.

fānum -i, n. a temple with the land round it, a holy place.

făr farris, n. spelt, grain, meal.

farcio farcire farsi fartum, to fill full, stuff full.

fărīna -ae, f., meal, flour.

farrāgo -ĭnis, f. mixed fodder for cattle, mash; a medley, mixture.

farrātus -a -um, provided with grain; made of corn.

farrĕus -a -um, made of spelt or corn.

fartim (fartem), acc. sing., stuffing, minced meat.

fartor -ōris, m. a fattener of fowls.

fās, n. indecl. divine command or law; sometimes fate, destiny; in gen. right, that which is allowed, lawful; fas est, it is allowed, it is lawful.

fascia -ae, f. a bandage, band, girdle, girth.

fascĭcŭlus -i, m., a little bundle or packet; florum, a nosegay.

fascĭno -are, to bewitch; to envy.

fascĭŏla -ae, f., a little bandage.

fascis -is, m. a bundle, packet; plur., fasces, bundles of sticks with an axe projecting, carried by lictors before the chief Roman magistrates; hence high office, esp. the consulate.

fasti -orum, m.; see fastus -a -um.

fastīdĭo -ire, to loathe, feel distaste for, dislike.

fastīdĭōsus -a -um, squeamish, nice, dainty, fastidious; with genit., sick of, disgusted with, impatient of; in act. sense, disgusting, loathsome. Adv. **fastīdĭōsē**, fastidiously, with disgust.

fastīdĭum -i, n. loathing, squeamishness, disgust, dislike; hence scorn, haughtiness, disdain.

fastīgātus -a -um, pointed or sloping down; adv. **fastīgātē**, slantingly.

fastīgĭum -i, n. the gable end, pediment of a roof; hence a slope, either up or down; of measurements looking up height; looking down, depth; abstract high rank, dignity; principal point in a subject.

¹**fastus** -ūs, m. pride, haughtiness, arrogance.

²**fastus** -a -um: dies fastus, plur. dies fasti, or simply fasti, days on which the praetor could administer justice, court-days. Transf., a list of these days, with festivals, etc., the Roman calendar; a register, record; a list of magistrates.

fātālis -c, relating to destiny or fate, fated, destined by fate; in bad sense, deadly, fatal. Adv. **fātālĭter**, according to fate.

fătĕor fătēri fassus, dep., to confess, admit, allow; to reveal, make known.

fātĭcănus and -cīnus -a -um, prophetic.

fātĭdĭcus -a -um, announcing fate, prophetic; m. as subst. a prophet.

fātĭfer -fēra -fērum, deadly, fatal.

fătĭgātĭo -ōnis, f. weariness, fatigue.

fătĭgo -are, to weary, fatigue; to vex, harass; to tease, importune, worry.

fātĭlŏqua -ae, f. a prophetess.

fātisco -ere and **fătiscor** -i, dep., to gape, crack, open; to become weak, droop.

fătŭĭtās -ātis, f. foolishness, silliness.

fātum -i, n., an utterance, esp. a divine utterance; hence destiny, fate; the will of a god; personif. Fata, the Parcae or Fates; doom, fate, natural death, misfortune, ruin, calamity.

fătŭus -a -um, foolish, idiotic, silly.

Faunus -i, m. a mythic deity of the forests.

faustĭtās -ātis, f., prosperity.

faustus -a -um, favourable, lucky, auspicious; adv. **faustē**.

fautor -ōris, m. patron, promoter, partisan.

fautrix -trīcis, f., a patroness.

faux, f.; usually plur. **fauces** -ium, gullet, throat, jaws. Transf., a chasm, gorge, defile; an isthmus, neck of land; straits.

făvĕo făvēre făvi fautum, to favour, be favourable to, help, support, with dat.; with infin., to be inclined to do. Esp. as religious t. t., to speak no words of bad omen; hence to be silent.

făvilla -ae, f. glowing ashes, esp. of the dead; a spark.

făvĭtor -ōris, m. = fautor; q.v.

Făvōnĭus -i, m. = Zephyrus, the west wind.

făvor -ōris, m., favour, good-will, support, inclinaton; esp. applause at the theatre, acclamation.

făvōrābĭlis -e, in favour, popular.

făvus -i, m. honeycomb.

fax făcis, f. (1) a torch, esp. as carried at weddings and funerals. (2) a fire-brand; of persons, instigator; of things, stimulus. (3) light, flame, esp. of heavenly bodies; fig., brilliance or passion.

febrĭcŭla -ae, f., *a slight fever, feverish-ness.*

febris -is, f. *fever.*

Februārius -i, m. or Februărius Mensis, *the cleansing month, February;* Kalendae Februariae, *the 1st of February.*

februum -i, n. *religious purification;* Februa -orum, pl. *the Roman feast of purification on the 15th of February.*

fēciālis = fetialis; q.v.

fēcundĭtās -ātis, f. *fruitfulness, fecundity.*

fēcundo -are, *to fructify, fertilize.*

fēcundus -a -um, *fruitful, prolific; abundant, full, plentiful;* with genit., *rich in, abounding in;* act., *making fruitful.*

fel fellis, n. *the gall-bladder, gall, bile; poison, venom; bitterness.*

fēles -is, f. *a cat;* hence *a thief.*

fēlīcĭtās -ātis, f. *happiness, good fortune, success;* personif., *Good Fortune as a goddess.*

felix -icis, *fruitful, fertile.* Transf., *of good omen, favourable, bringing good luck; fortunate, lucky, successful;* Felix, *the Lucky One, surname of Sulla.* Adv. fēlīcĭter, *fruitfully; auspiciously, favourably; luckily, successfully.*

fēmella -ae, f. *young woman, girl.*

fēmen = femur; q.v.

fēmĭna -ae, f. *a female, woman;* of animals, *the female.*

fēmĭnĕus -a -um, *female, feminine; womanish, effeminate.*

fēmur -ŏris or -ĭnis, n. *the thigh.*

fēnestra -ae, f. *a window; a breach, loophole.*

fēra -ae, f.; see ferus.

fērālis -e, *relating to the dead, funereal; deadly, fatal; mournful;* n. pl. as subst. *the festival of the dead, in February.*

fērax -ācis, *fruitful, fertile, prolific;* compar. adv. fērācius, *more fruit-fully.*

fercŭlum -i, n. *a frame, litter, bier, tray;* of food, *a course or dish.*

fērē. (1) *almost, nearly;* with negatives, *scarcely, hardly.* (2) *just, exactly.* (3) *as a rule, generally, usually.*

fĕrentārius -i, m. *a light-armed soldier.*

fĕretrum -i, n., *a bier for carrying a corpse.*

fēriae -arum, f. pl. *festivals, holidays.*

fēriātus -a -um, *keeping holiday, idle, at leisure.*

fērinus -a -um, *relating to a wild beast, wild;* f. as subst. *flesh of wild animals, game.*

fĕrio -ire, *to strike, knock, smite, hit;* esp. *to strike dead, slay, kill;* colloq., *to cheat.*

fĕrĭtās -ātis, f. *wildness, savageness.*

fermē. (1) *almost, nearly;* with negatives, *hardly, scarcely.* (2) *usually.*

fermentum -i, n. *leaven, yeast; a kind of beer.* Transf., *anger, passion.*

fĕro ferre, with perf. tŭli, supine latum.
(1) *to bear, bring, carry;* prae se ferre,

to display, make public; often *to endure, submit to;* esp. with adv.; ferre aegre, *to take ill, be vexed at.* (2) *to bring orth, produce.* (3) *to bring to a place or person, fetch, offer;* suffragium, sententiam, *to vote;* legem, *to propose a law;* ferre ut, *to propose that;* commercial, expensum ferre, *to set down in an account-book as paid; to cause, bring about; to report to others, spread abroad, speak of;* fama fert, *the story goes;* esp. *to publish a person's praises.* (4) *to bear away, carry off;* ferre et agere, *to plunder.* Transf., *to win, get;* centuriam, tribus, *to gain the votes of.* (5) *to bear along, move forward, put in motion;* milit., signa ferre, *to march.* Transf., *to move, impel, carry away;* without object, *to lead, tend.*

fĕrōcĭa -ae, f. *high spirit, courage;* in bad sense, *arrogance, ferocity.*

fĕrōcĭtās -ātis, f. *courage, untamed spirit;* in bad sense, *arrogance.*

fĕrox -ōcis, *courageous, high-spirited, warlike;* in bad sense, *wild, unbridled, arrogant;* adv. fĕrōcĭter.

ferrāmenta -orum, n. pl. *tools made of, or shod with, iron.*

ferrārius -a -um, *of iron;* m. as subst. *a blacksmith;* f. pl. as subst., *iron-mines.*

ferrātĭlis -e, *in irons;* of slaves.

ferrātus -a -um, *furnished or covered with iron;* servi, *in irons;* m. pl. as subst. *soldiers in armour.*

ferrĕus -a -um, *of iron; made of iron or like iron; hard, unfeeling, cruel; immovable, firm.*

ferritĕrĭum -i. n. = ergastulum; q.v.

ferrūgĭnĕus and ferrūgĭnus -a -um, *rust-coloured, dusky.*

ferrūgo -ĭnis, f. *iron rust; the colour of rust.*

ferrum -i, n. *iron;* hence *any iron instrument; plough, axe, scissors, and* esp. *sword.*

fertĭlis -e, *fruitful, fertile, productive; fertilizing, making fruitful.*

fertĭlĭtās -ātis, f. *fruitfulness, fertility*

fertum (ferctum) -i, n. *a sacrificial cake.*

fĕrŭla -ae, f. (1) *the herb fennel.* (2) *a stick, cane,* esp. *to punish slaves and children.*

fĕrus -a -um, *wild, uncultivated, uncivilized, rough, cruel;* m. and f. as subst., *a wild animal.*

fervēfăcĭo -făcĕre -fēci -factum *to make hot, boil, melt.*

fervĕo fervēre ferbŭi (and fervo fervĕre fervi) *to be boiling hot, to boil, seethe, glow.* Transf., *to be in quick movement, to seethe; to be excited by passion, rage.*

Hence partic. fervens -entis, *glowing, hot, heated;* of character or feeling, *heated, fiery.* Adv. ferventer, *hotly, warmly.*

fervesco -ĕre, *to become hot, begin to glow or boil.*

fervĭdus -a -um, *boiling, seething*

foaming; of character or feelings, *fiery, passionate, excited.*

servo = ferveo; q.v.

fervor -ōris, m. *boiling heat, seething, foaming; ardour, passion.*

Fescennia -ae, f. *a town in Etruria famous for verse dialogues.* Adj. **Fescenninus** -a -um.

fessus -a -um, *weary, tired, exhausted;* fessa aetas, *old age;* res fessae, *distress.*

festinātio -ōnis, f. *haste, speed, hurry.*

festino -are: intransit., *to hasten, hurry;* transit., *to hasten, accelerate.* Hence adv. **festinanter** and **festinātō,** *hastily.*

festinus -a -um, *hastening, hasty.*

festivitās -ātis, f. *gaiety, jollity:* of speech or writing, *cheerfulness, humour.*

festivus -a -um, *of a holiday, festive; merry, good-humoured, cheerful;* adv. **festivē.**

festūca -ae, f. *a stalk, straw, stem.* Transf., *a rod used in the manumission of slaves.*

festus -a -um, *of a holiday, festive:* of people, *keeping holiday;* n. as subst. *a feast.*

fetiālis -s, m. *one of a college of priests responsible for formally making peace or declaring war;* as adj. = *belonging to the fetiales.*

fētūra -ae, f. *the bringing forth of young, breeding;* meton. *brood, offspring.*

¹fētus -a -um. (1) *pregnant; fruitful, fertile: teeming with, full of.* (2) *that has brought forth, newly delivered.*

²fētus -ūs, m. *the bringing forth or hatching of young;* of the soil, *bearing, producing.* Transf., *that which is brought forth: offspring, brood;* of plants *fruit, produce, shoot.*

fibra -ae, f. *a fibre, filament; the entrails of an animal.*

fibula -ae, f. *a buckle, brooch, clasp; an iron clamp.*

ficēdula -ae, f. *a small bird, the becafico.*

fictilis -e, *shaped;* hence *earthen, made of clay;* n. as subst., esp. pl., *earthenware, earthen vessels.*

fictio -ōnis, f. *forming, feigning; assumption.*

fictor -ōris, m. *an image-maker, a moulder;* in gen., *maker, contriver.*

fictrix -īcis, f. *she that forms or fashions.*

fictūra -ae, f. *forming, fashioning.*

fictus, partic. from fingo; q.v.

ficulnus and **ficulnĕus** -a -um, *of the fig-tree.*

ficus -i, and -ūs, f. *a fig-tree; a fig.*

fidēïcommissum -i, n. legal, *a trust.*

fidēlia -ae, f. *an earthenware pot or vase.*

fidēlis -e, *trusty, steadfast, faithful;* m. as subst., esp. pl., *confidants, faithful friends.* Adv. **fidēliter,** *faithfully; securely, without danger.*

fidēlitās -ātis, f., *faithfulness, trust, fidelity.*

Fidēnae -arum, and **Fidēna** -ae, f. *a town in Latium;* adj. **Fidēnas** -ātis.

fidens -entis, partic. from fido; q.v.

fidentia -ae, f. *confidence, boldness.*

¹fides -ei, f., *trust, confidence, reliance, belief, faith;* fidem facere, *to create confidence, cause belief;* as mercantile t. t., *credit.* Transf., *that which produces confidence; faithfulness, conscientiousness;* fidem praestare, *to be loyal;* (ex) bona fide, *in good faith, sincerely;* of things, *credibility, actuality, fulfilment; a promise, assurance, word of honour, engagement;* fidem fallere, *to break a promise;* servare, *to keep a promise;* fide mea, *on my word of honour;* fides (or fides publica) *a promise of protection, safe-conduct;* hence, in gen., *faithful protection, constant help.*

²fides -is, f., usually plur. *a gut-string for a musical instrument;* hence *a lyre, lute, harp.*

fidicen -cinis, m., *a player on the harp, lyre, lute;* poet., *a lyric poet.*

fidicina -ae, f. *a female player on the lute or harp.*

fidicinus -a -um, *of lute-playing.*

fidicula -ae, f., usually plur. *a little lyre or lute; an instrument for torturing slaves.*

Fidius -i, m., *a surname of Jupiter;* esp. in phrase. medius fidius! *So help me God!*

fido fidēre fisus sum, *to trust, believe, confide in;* with dat. or abl.

Hence partic. **fidens** -entis, *without fear, confident, courageous;* adv. **fidenter.**

fidūcia -ae, f. (1) *confidence, trust, assurance;* with sui, or absol., *self-confidence, self-reliance, courage.* (2) *fidelity.*

fidūciārius -a -um, *entrusted, committed.*

fidus -a -um, *trusty, true, faithful, sure;* superl. adv. **fidissimē.**

figo figere fixi fixum. (1) *to fix, fasten, make fast, attach, affix;* esp. with oculos, *to fix the gaze.* (2) *to thrust home a weapon,* etc. so as *to stick fast.* (3) *to transfix.*

Hence partic. **fixus** -a -um, *fixed, firm, immovable.*

figulāris -e, *of a potter.*

figulus -i, m., *a worker in clay, potter.*

figūra -ae, f. *form, shape, figure, size; an atom; shade of a dead person;* the abstr., *kind, nature, species;* rhet., *a figure of speech.*

figūro -are, *to form, mould, shape;* rhet., *to adorn with figures.*

fīlātim, *thread by thread.*

fīlia -ae, f. *daughter.*

fīlicātus -a -um, *adorned with ferns; embossed with fern leaves.*

fīliŏla -ae, f. *little daughter.*

fīliŏlus -i, m. *little son.*

fīlius -i, m. *son.*

filix -icis, f. *fern.*

fīlum -i, n. *a thread,* pendere filo (tenui), *to hang by a thread; a woollen fillet.* Transf., *form, shape;* of speech or writing, *texture, thread.*

fimbriae -arum, f. pl., *fringe, border edge.*

fimbrĭātus -a -um, *fringed.*

fĭmus -i, m. and **fĭmum** -i, n. *dung, dirt.*

findo findĕre fĭdi fissum, *to split, cleave, divide, halve.*

Hence partic. **fissus** -a -um, *split, cloven;* n. as subst., *a split, cleft;* in augury, *a divided liver.*

fingo fingĕre finxi fictum, *to shape, fashion, form, mould;* also *to arrange, put in order; to represent, imagine, conceive; to feign, fabricate, devise;* fingere vultum, *to put on an artificial expression.*

Hence partic. **fictus** -a -um, *feigned, false;* n. as subst. *a falsehood.*

fĭnĭo -ire, *to bound, limit, enclose, restrain; to define, determine, appoint; to put an end to, conclude, finish;* esp. *to finish speaking,* or *to die;* pass., *to end, cease.* Perf. partic. **fĭnitus** -a -um; *of a phrase, well-rounded;* adv. **fīnītē,** *moderately, within bounds.*

fĭnis -is, m. (sometimes f.) *boundary, limit, border; summit, end; object, aim;* in pl. *enclosed area, territory.*

fĭnĭtĭmus and **fĭnĭtŭmus** -a -um, *neighbouring, adjacent; related to, resembling, similar.* M. pl. as subst. *neighbours.*

fĭnĭtor -ōris, m., *one who determines boundaries, a land surveyor.* Transf., *the horizon.*

fīo fĭĕri factus sum, used as pass. of facio. (1) *of persons and things, to be made, come into existence;* with predicate, *to become, be appointed;* with genit., *to be valued at.* (2) *of actions, to be done; of events, to happen;* with abl., quid illo fiet? *what will happen to him?* fieri ut, *to come about that;* fieri non potest quin, *it must be that.*

firmāmen -inis, n. *support, prop.*

firmāmentum -i, n., *a means of support, prop; the main point in an argument.*

firmātor -ōris, m., *one who makes firm or establishes.*

firmĭtās -ātis and **firmĭtūdo** -dĭnis, f., *firmness, stability; strength of mind, constancy.*

firmo -are, *to make firm, strengthen; to make durable, make secure;* of spirits, *to encourage, cheer, animate;* of ideas, *to prove establish,* also *to assert, maintain.*

firmus -a -um, *firm, strong, stout; lasting, valid; morally strong.* Adv. **firmē** and **firmĭter,** *firmly strongly, steadfastly.*

fiscella and **fiscina** -ae, f., *a small basket.*

fiscus -i, m. *a basket; hence a money-bag, purse; the state treasury;* under the empire, *the emperor's privy purse* (opp. aerarium, *the state treasury*).

fissĭlis -e, *that can be split;* also *split.*

fissĭo -ōnis, f. *splitting, cleaving, dividing.*

fistūca -ae, f. *a rammer, mallet.*

fistŭla -ae, f. *a water-pipe; a reed-pipe;*

shepherd's pipe; eburneola, *a pitch-pipe of ivory.*

fistŭlātor -ōris, m., *one who plays the reed-pipe.*

fixus -a -um, partic. from figo; q.v.

flābellum -i, n. *a small fan.*

flābĭlis -e, *airy.*

flābra -orum, n. pl. *blasts of wind, breezes.*

flaccĕo -ēre, *to be flabby; to fail or flag.*

flaccesco flaccescĕre flaccŭi, *to begin to flag, become flabby.*

flaccĭdus -a -um, *flabby; weak, languid.*

flaccus -a -um, *flabby;* of men, *flap-eared.*

Flaccus; see Horatius, and Valerius.

flăgello -are, *to whip, scourge, beat.*

flăgellum -i, n. *a whip, scourge; the thong of a javelin; a young sprout vine-shoot;* plur. *the arms of a polypus;* fig., *the sting of conscience.*

flăgĭtātĭo -ōnis, f., *an earnest demand or entreaty.*

flăgĭtātor -ōris, m., *one who earnestly demands or entreats.*

flăgĭtĭōsus -a -um, *shameful, disgraceful, infamous;* adv. **flăgĭtĭōsē.**

flăgĭtĭum -i, n. *a disgraceful action, shameful crime; shame, disgrace;* meton., *scoundrel, rascal.*

flăgĭto -are, *to entreat, ask, demand earnestly; to demand to know; to summon before a court of justice.*

flagrantĭa -ae, f. *burning, blazing, glittering.*

flagrĭtrība -ae, m., *one that wears out whips, whipping-boy.*

flagro -are, *to blaze, burn, glow, flame,* also *to glitter.* Transf., *to glow or burn with passion; to suffer from,* with abl.

Hence partic. **flagrans** -antis, *blazing, burning, glittering.* Transf., *passionate, ardent.* Adv. **flagranter.**

flagrum -i, n. *scourge, whip.*

¹**flāmen** -inis, m. *the priest of some particular god.*

²**flāmen** -inis, n. *a blowing, blast.*

flāmĭnĭca -ae, f. *the wife of a flamen.*

Flāmĭnīnus, *a surname in the patrician Gens Quinctia;* see Quinctius.

flāmĭnĭum -i, n., *the office of a flamen.*

Flāmĭnĭus -a -um, *name of a Roman gens.*

flamma -ae, f., *a flame, blazing fire.* Transf., *a source of light, torch, star, lightning; lustre, glitter; the fire or glow of passion; devouring flame, destruction.*

flammĕŏlum -i, n., *a small bridal veil.*

flammesco -ĕre, *to become inflamed.*

flammĕus -a -um, *fiery, flaming; flashing, fiery-red;* n. as subst. **flammĕum** -i, *a (flame-coloured) bridal veil.*

flammĭfer -fĕra -fĕrum, *flaming, fiery.*

flammo -are: intransit., *to flame, blaze, burn;* transit., *to set on fire, inflame.*

flammŭla -ae, f. *little flame.*

flātus -ūs, m. *blowing, blast, breathing.*

Transf., *haughtiness. arrogance*, gen. plur.

flăvens -entis, *yellow or gold-coloured.*

flăvesco -ĕre, *to become yellow or gold-coloured.*

Flāvius -a -um, *name of a Roman gens to which the emperors Vespasian, Titus, and Domitian belonged.*

flāvus -a -um, *gold-coloured, yellow.*

flēbilis -e: pass., *lamentable, wretched, deserving tears;* act., *tearful, doleful.* Adv. **flēbiliter.**

flecto flectĕre flexi flexum, *to bend.* (1) *to alter the shape of, to bow, twist, curve.* Transf., *to change, alter, influence.* (2) *to alter the direction of, to turn, wheel;* vocem, *to modulate.*

flĕo fiēre flēvi flētum: intransit., *to weep; to drip, trickle;* transit., *to weep for, lament, bewail;* fiendus, *to be lamented.*

¹flētus -a -um, partic. of fleo; q.v.

²flētus -ūs, m. *weeping, bewailing.*

flexibilis -e, *that can be bent, flexible;* of speech or the voice, *adaptable;* in bad sense, *fickle, changeable.*

flexilis -e, *flexible, pliant, supple.*

flexilŏquus -a -um, *equivocal, ambiguous.*

flexio -ōnis, f. *bending;* vocis, or modorum, *modulation of the voice;* deverticula flexionesque, *twists and turns.*

flexipēs -pĕdis, *crooked-footed, twining.*

flexŭōsus -a -um, *full of windings and turnings, crooked.*

flexūra -ae, f. *bending.*

¹flexus -a -um, partic. of flecto; q.v.

²flexus -ūs, m. *bending, turning;* of the voice, *modulation.* Transf., *change, alteration.*

flictus -ūs, m. *striking together, dashing against.*

flīgo -ere, *to beat or dash down.*

flo flare flavi flatum, *to blow;* intransit., of winds, persons and instruments; transit., *to blow, blow forth; to blow on an instrument; to cast metals, to coin.*

floccus -i, m. *a flock of wool;* flocci non facere, *to think nothing of.*

Flōra -ae, f., *the goddess of flowers, ånd Spring;* adj. **Flōrālis** -e, *belonging to Flora;* n. pl. as subst. *the festival of Flora.*

Flōrentĭa -ae, f. *a town in Etruria (now Florence);* adj. **Flōrentīnus** -a -um.

florĕo -ēre -ŭi, *to bloom, flower.* Transf., *to be in one's prime, to prosper, flourish, be in repute;* with abl., *to abound in, swarm with.* Hence partic. **flōrens** -entis, *blooming, flourishing.*

flōresco -ĕre, *to begin to blossom or flourish.*

florĕus -a -um, *made of flowers; rich in flowers, flowery.*

flōridus -a -um, *flowery, blossoming; made of or rich in flowers;* of age, *fresh, blooming;* of speech. *flowery, florid.*

flōrifer -fĕra fĕrum, *flower-bearing.*

flōrilĕgus -a -um, *culling flowers.*

flōs flōris, m. *a flower, blossom.* Transf., *the prime, flower of anything, the best,*

the pride; on the face, *first beard, down;* vini bouquet; of speech, *ornament.*

floscŭlus -i, m., *a little flower.* Transf., *best part, pride;* of speech, *ornament.*

fluctifrăgus -a -um *wave-breaking.*

fluctŭātĭo -ōnis, f. *moving backwards and forwards, fluctuation; indecision.*

fluctŭo -are, *to be wave-like, move up and down;* sometimes of a glittering *effect;* of persons and passions, *to be tossed about, to waver.*

fluctŭor -ari -atus, dep. *to toss about, waver.*

fluctŭōsus -a -um, *full of waves, stormy.*

fluctus -ūs, m. *a streaming, flowing.* Transf., *commotion, disturbance.*

flŭentum -i, n., *running water, a stream.*

flŭĭdus -a -um, *flowing, fluid.* Transf., *lax, languid; relaxing.*

flŭĭto -are, *to flow hither and thither, to float, swim, sail, move up and down, be tossed about.* Transf. *to flutter; to waver. vacillate.*

flūmen -ĭnis, n. *flowing;* hence *a river, stream;* flumine secundo, *downstream;* flumine adverso, *upstream;* fig., *a stream of blood, tears, words, etc.*

flūmĭnĕus -a -um, *of a river.*

flŭo flŭere fluxi fluxum: of fluids, *to flow;* of a solid object, *to flow, drip with any liquid.* Transf., in gen., *to flow, stream, pour;* of abstr. things, *to proceed, issue, spread;* of circumstances, *to tend;* of language, *to flow; to sink, droop.* Hence pres. partic. **flŭens** -entis, *flowing;* hence *lax;* of speech, *fluent or diffuse;* adv. **flŭenter,** *in a flowing manner.* Past partic. **fluxus** -a -um, *flowing;* hence *leaky;* of solid objects, *waving, fluttering, loose;* of character, *lax, loose, weak;* of abstr. things, *fleeting, unstable.*

flŭto -are, *to flow, float, swim.*

flŭvĭālis and **flŭvĭātilis** -e, *of a river.*

flŭvĭdus -a -um, *flowing, fluid.*

flŭvĭus -ĭi, m., *flowing water; a stream, river.*

fluxus -a -um, partic. from flŭo; q.v.

focāle -is, n. *a wrapper for the neck.*

focillo -are, *to warm up, refresh by warmth.*

focŭla -orum, n pl. *stoves.*

focŭlus -i, m. *a brazier.*

focus -i, m. *a fireplace, hearth;* meton., *house, family, home;* sometimes *altar-fire or funeral pyre.*

fŏdĭco -are, *to dig, jog;* latus, *to dig in the ribs.*

fŏdĭo fŏdĕre fōdi fossum, *to dig;* also *to dig out; to excavate.* Transf., *to prick, prod, jog.*

foecundus, foecundo = fecundus, fecundo; q.v.

foedĕrātus -a -um, *confederate, allied.*

foedifrăgus -a -um, *treaty-breaking.*

foedĭtās -ātis, f. *foulness, filthiness.*

foedo -are, *to make foul, make filthy, defile, disfigure;* morally, *to dishonour, disgrace.*

¹foedus -a -um, *foul, filthy, horrible, disgusting;* adv. **foedē.**

²foedus -ĕris, n. *a league* between states; *a compact, covenant, agreement.* Transf., *a law.*

foen-; see faen-.

foetĕo -ēre, *to have a bad smell.*

foetĭdus -a -um, *having a bad smell, stinking.*

foetor -ōris, m. *a bad smell, stink.*

foetus; see fetus.

fŏlĭātus -a -um, *leafy*; n. as subst. *a salve* or *oil of spikenard leaves.*

fŏlĭum -i, n. *a leaf.*

follĭcŭlus -i, m. *a little sack or bag.*

follis -is, m. *a leather bag; a pair of bellows; a purse; a puffed-out cheek.*

fōmentum -i, n. *poultice, fomentation.* Transf., *alleviation.*

fōmĕs -ĭtis, m. *touchwood, tinder.*

fons fontis, m. *a spring, fountain; fresh* or *spring water.* Transf., *spring, origin, source.*

fontānus -a -um, *of a spring or fountain.*

Fontēius -a -um, *name of a Roman gens.*

fontĭcŭlus -i, m. *a little fountain* or *spring.*

for fāri fātus, dep. *to speak, say;* also *to speak of.*

fŏrābĭlis -e, *that can be bored through, penetrable.*

fŏrāmen -ĭnis, n. *hole, opening, aperture.*

fŏras, *out of doors, forth, out*; (scripta) foras dare, *to publish.*

forceps -cĭpis, m. and f. *a pair of tongs, pincers.*

forda -ae, *a cow in calf.*

fŏre, fŏrem, used as fut. infin. and imperf. subj. of sum; q.v.

fŏrensis -e, *relating to the market* or *forum;* hence *of the business of the Roman forum, esp. legal.*

forfex -fĭcis, f. *a pair of shears or scissors.*

¹fŏris -is, f. *a door*; plur. fores, *folding-doors.* Transf., *any opening, entrance.*

²fŏris, adv. (1) (situated) *out of doors, outside, without;* sometimes, *abroad, outside Rome.* (2) *from without, from abroad.*

forma -ae, f. *form, figure, shape; beautiful shape, beauty; image, likeness; a shape serving as model,* e.g. *a shoemaker's last; a mould, stamp;* abstr., *form, manner, type;* in logic, *species; outline, general notion.*

formālis -e, *formal, having a set form.*

formāmentum -i, n. *conformation.*

formātor -ōris, m. *a fashioner.*

formātūra -ae, f. *forming, shaping.*

Formiae -arum, f. *town on the coast of Latium;* adj. Formĭānus -a -um.

formīca -ae, f. *an ant.*

formīdābĭlis -e, *fearful, formidable.*

¹formīdo -are, *to be terrified, to dread.*

²formīdo -ĭnis, f. *dread, terror;* meton., *source of fear, dreadfulness, awfulness; a scarecrow.*

formīdŏlōsus -a -um: act., *causing dread, terrible, fearful;* pass. *fearful, timid.* Adv., formīdŏlōsē, *dreadfully, terribly.*

formo -are, *to form, shape, fashion; to arrange, order, regulate, dispose.*

formōsĭtās -ātis, f. *beauty.*

formōsus -a -um, *beautifully formed, beautiful*; adv. formōsē.

formŭla -ae, f. *physical beauty; legal, set form, formula; esp. the form of an alliance;* in gen., *rule, principle.*

fornācālis -e, *of an oven.*

fornācŭla -ae, f., *a little oven.*

fornax -ācis, f. *oven, furnace, kiln;* Aetnae, *the crater.*

fornĭcātus -a -um, *arched, vaulted.*

fornix -ĭcis, m. *arch, vault; arcade;* milit. *an arched sallyport.*

fornus = furnus; q.v.

fŏro -are, *to bore, pierce.*

fors, *chance, luck;* in nom. fors, also forsit (fors sit), forsăn (fors an), and forsĭtăn (fors sit an), *perhaps, perchance;* abl. fortĕ, *by chance, accidentally, as it happened.*

fortassĕ (fortassis), *perhaps.*

fortĕ; see fors.

fortĭcŭlus -a -um, *fairly bold.*

fortis -e, physically, *strong, powerful, robust;* morally, *brave, courageous, steadfast;* fortes fortuna adiuvat, *fortune favours the brave;* in bad sense, *bold, audacious.* Adv. fortĭter, *strongly, bravely.*

fortĭtūdo -ĭnis, f. *physical strength, moral bravery, courage;* plur., *deeds of bravery.*

fortŭĭtus -a -um, *accidental, casual, fortuitous, unpremeditated;* n. pl. as subst. *chance occurrences.* Abl. sing. as adv. fortŭĭto, *by chance, fortuitously.*

fortūna -ae, f. *chance, fate, lot, luck, fortune;* fortuna prospera, secunda, *good fortune;* adversa, *misfortune.* Transf., *lot, condition, state, mode of life; property, possessions.*

fortūno -are, *to make happy, bless, prosper.*

Hence partic. fortūnātus -a -um, *blessed, lucky, fortunate; well off, wealthy, rich.* Adv. fortūnātē, *happily, fortunately.*

fŏrŭli -orum, m., *a bookcase.*

fŏrum -i, n. *an open square, market-place;* forum bovarium, or boarium, *the cattle-market;* forum holitorium, *vegetable-market;* forum piscarium, or piscatorium, *fish-market;* in gen., *a place of public business,* commercial, political and judicial esp. in Rome. Transf., *of the business transacted in a forum;* forum agere, *to hold an assize;* forum attingere, *to apply oneself to public business.*

fŏrus -i, m. *the gangway of a ship; a block of seats in the theatre;* plur., *tiers of cells in a beehive.*

fossa -ae, f. *ditch, trench, channel.*

fossĭo -ōnis, f. *digging, excavation.*

fossor -ōris, m. *a digger, delver; a boor, clown.*

fossūra -ae, f. *digging.*

fōtus, partic. of foveo; q.v.

fŏvĕa -ae, f. *a pit, esp. as a trap for game, a pitfall.*

fŏvĕo fŏvēre fŏvi fōtum, *to warm,*

keep warm, caress: fig., *to stay constantly in a place*; in gen., *to foster, cherish, support, encourage.*

fractus -a -um, partic. from frango; q.v.

frāga -orum, n. pl. *strawberries.*

frăgilis -e, *crackling; easily broken, fragile.* Transf., *fleeting, transitory; weak, feeble.*

frăgilitās -ātis, f., *frailty, weakness.*

fragmen -minis, n. *a breaking*; hence, usually plur., *fragments, remains, ruins.*

fragmentum -i, n. *a piece broken off, fragment.*

frăgor -ōris, m., *a breaking; a noise of breaking, crack, crash.*

frăgōsus -a -um, *crashing, roaring; fragile; broken, rough.*

fragro -are, *to emit a smell, esp. a sweet smell*; pres. partic. **fragrans** -antis *sweet-smelling, fragrant.*

frāgum; see fraga.

frango frangĕre frēgi fractum, *to break, break in pieces, shatter*; gulam laqueo, *to strangle*; fruges saxo, *to grind*; diem morantem mero, *to shorten*; of persons, passions, etc., *to master, subdue, humble*; frangi animo, *to be discouraged.*
  Hence partic. **fractus** -a -um, *broken, humbled, enfeebled.*

frāter -tris, m. *a brother*; frater germanus, *own brother*; fratres, *brothers and sisters*; also *a cousin* or *a brother-in-law.* Transf., *a comrade, compatriot, ally.*

frāterculus -i, m. *little brother.*

frāternitās -ātis, f. *brotherhood, fraternity.*

frāternus -a -um, *of a brother, brotherly, fraternal*; sometimes *of a cousin.* Transf., *of a related person; of some thing related to another.* Adv. **frāternē**, *in a brotherly manner, like a brother.*

frātrĭcīda -ae, m. *one who kills a brother, a fratricide.*

fraudātio -ōnis, f. *deceit, fraud, swindling.*

fraudātor -ōris, m. *deceiver, swindler.*

fraudo -are, *to cheat, defraud, swindle; to steal, embezzle.*

fraudŭlentia -ae, f. *deceitfulness.*

fraudŭlentus -a -um, *deceitful, fraudulent.*

fraus, fraudis, f.: act., *deceit, fraud,* sine fraude, *honourably*; in gen., *a crime, offence; delusion, error; damage, harm*; sine fraude, *without harm.*

fraxĭnĕus and **fraxĭnus** -a -um, *of ashwood, ashen.*

fraxĭnus -i, f. *an ash-tree*; meton., *a spear* or *javelin, with a shaft of ash-wood.*

Frĕgellae -arum, f. *town of Volsci, in Latium.*

frĕmĕbundus -a -um, *roaring, murmuring.*

frĕmĭtus -ūs, m. *roaring, murmuring, growling.*

frĕmo -ēre -ŭi -ĭtum, *to roar, murmur, growl*; with acc. *to murmur out something, grumble, complain.*

frĕmor -ōris, m. *roaring, murmuring.*

frendo -ĕre: intransit., *to gnash the teeth*; transit., *to crush, bruise, grind.*

frēni -orum, m.; see frenum.

frēno -are. *to bridle, curb, restrain, check.*

frēnum -i, n., usually plur. **frēna** -orum, n.; also **frēni** -orum, m. *bridle, reins, bit, curb.* Transf., *restraint.*

frĕquens -entis, *crowded, numerous, full*; of places, *full, frequented, populous*; of time, *repeated, frequent, constant*; of persons, *often doing a thing*; of things, *often done* or *used.* Adv. **frĕquenter**, *in large numbers; frequently, often.*

frĕquentātio -ōnis, f., *frequency, crowding.*

frĕquentia -ae, f.: of persons, *a large concourse, numerous assembly, population*; of things, *a large number, abundance.*

frĕquento -are, of number *to crowd*; of number *to collect in large numbers; to fill a place with people* or *things; to do a thing in crowds* or *with a crowd*; of time, *to do* or *use a thing frequently*; domum, *to visit often*; Hymenaee! frequentant, *they repeat.*

frĕtum -i; n. *a strait, sound, estuary firth, channel*; fretum Siciliae, fretum Siciliense, or fretum, *the Straits of Messina; the sea in gen.*, usually plur.: fig., *disturbance, turmoil.*

¹frētus -a -um, *relying on, confiding in,* with abl.

²frētus -ūs, m. *a strait; an interval, difference.*

frico fricare fricŭi frictum and frĭcātum, *to rub, rub down.*

frīgĕo -ēre, *to be cold; to be inactive, lifeless, dull*; colloq., *to be coldly received, fall flat.*

frigesco -ĕre, *to become cold* or *dull.*

frīgĭdŭlus -a -um, *somewhat cold* or *faint.*

frīgĭdus -a -um, *cold, cool, chilly*; f. sing. as subst. *cold water.* Transf., in act. sense, *chilling, causing cold*; fig., *cold, dull, lifeless*; of speech, *flat.* Adv. **frīgĭdē**, *coldly; languidly, feebly.*

frigo frigĕre frixi frictum, *to roast, parch.*

frigus -ōris n. *cold, coolness; the cold of winter; a cold place; the cold of death* or *fright.* Transf., *coldness in action, dullness, indolence; a cold reception, coolness, disfavour.*

frĭguttio -ire, *to stammer.*

frio -are, *to rub, crumble.*

frĭtillus -i, m. *a dice-box.*

frīvŏlus -a -um, *trifling, worthless*; n. pl. as subst. *sticks of furniture.*

frondātor -ōris, m. *a pruner of trees.*

frondĕo -ēre, *to be in leaf, be leafy.*

frondesco ĕre, *to come into leaf, put forth leaves.*

frondĕus -a -um, *leafy.*

frondĭfer -fĕra -fĕrum, *leaf-bearing, leafy.*

frondōsus -a -um, *full of leaves, leafy.*

¹**frons** frondis, f. *a leaf, foliage;* meton., *a chaplet* or *crown of leaves.*

²**frons** frontis, f. *the forehead, brow;* frontem contrahere, *to frown.* Transf., in gen., *the front, forepart;* milit., *the van; the outside end of a book roll; frontage* (in measuring land).

frontālia -ium, n. pl. *the frontlet of a horse.*

fronto -ōnis, m., *a man with a broad forehead.*

fructuārius -a -um, *fruit-bearing, fruitful.*

fructuōsus -a -um, *fruitful, fertile.*

fructus -ūs, m.: abstr., *enjoyment, enjoying;* concr., *proceeds, profit, produce, income;* esp. *the fruits of the earth.*

frūgālis -e, *frugal, economical, honest;* adv. **frūgālĭter.**

frūgālĭtās -ātis, f., *frugality, economy, honesty;* of style, *restraint.*

frūgi; see frux.

frūgĭfer -fĕra -fĕrum, *fruitful, fertile; profitable, advantageous.*

frūgĭfĕrens -entis, *fruitful, fertile.*

frūgĭlĕgus -a -um, *collecting grain.*

frūgĭpărus -a -um, *fruitful, prolific.*

frūmentārius -a -um, *of grain* or *corn;* res, *the supply of corn;* m. as subst. *a corn-merchant.*

frūmentātio -ōnis, f. *a foraging; a distribution of corn.*

frūmentātor -ōris, m. *a forager* or *a provider of corn.*

frūmentor -ari, dep., *to forage, fetch corn.*

frūmentum -i, n., *corn, grain.*

frŭor frŭi fructus and frŭĭtus, dep., *to have the benefit of, to enjoy,* usually with abl.: votis, *to obtain one's wishes;* as legal t. t., *to have the use and enjoyment of.*

frustillātim, *bit by bit.*

frustrā, *in error:* frustra esse, *to be deceived, mistaken.* Transf., *in vain, without effect; wantonly, without reason.*

frustrāmen -ĭnis, n. *deception.*

frustrātio -ōnis, f. *deception, disappointment, frustration.*

frustro -are, and **frustror** -ari, dep. *to disappoint, deceive, trick.*

frustum -i, n. *a bit, piece, morsel.*

frŭtex -tĭcis, m. *a shrub, bush;* as a term of reproach, *blockhead.*

frŭtĭcētum -i, n., *a thicket.*

frŭtĭco -are and **frŭtĭcor** -ari, dep. *to shoot out, become bushy.*

frŭtĭcōsus -a -um, *bushy* or *full of bushes.*

frux frūgis, f., usually plur. **frūges** -um, *fruits of the earth;* in gen., *fruits, success;* ad bonam frugem se recipere, *to improve oneself.* Dat. sing. **frūgi,** used as adj. *useful, honest, discreet, moderate.*

fūco -are, *to colour, paint, dye;* fig., *to colour, embellish.*
Hence partic. **fūcātus** -a -um, *painted; counterfeited, simulated.*

fūcōsus -a -um, *painted; simulated, counterfeited.*

¹**fūcus** -i, m., *red* or *purple dye; red* or *purple colour; rouge;* in gen., *paint, dye* of any colour; *bee-glue.* Transf., *deceit, pretence.*

²**fūcus** -i, m. *a drone bee.*

Fūfius -a -um, *name of a Roman gens.*

fŭga -ae, f. *flight, running away;* esp. *flight from one's country, exile, banishment.* Transf., *swift course, speed; avoiding,* with genit.

fŭgax -ācis, *ready to flee, flying; speeding, fleeting, transitory;* with genit., *avoiding.* Hence compar. adv. **fŭgācius.**

fŭgio fŭgĕre fūgi fŭgitum, *to flee.* Intransit., *to take to flight, run away; to pass away, disappear.* Transit., *to flee from, run away from, avoid;* with infin., fuge - quaerere, *do not seek;* of things, *to escape the notice of a person.*
Hence partic., **fŭgiens** -entis, *fleeing; avoiding,* with genit.; *fleeting, deteriorating.*

fŭgitivus -a -um, *flying, fugitive;* m. as subst., *a fugitive,* esp. *a runaway slave.*

fŭgito -are, *to flee;* transit., *to fly from, avoid, shun.*
Hence partic., **fŭgitans** -antis, *fleeing;* with genit., *avoiding.*

fŭgo -are, *to put to flight, chase away; to drive into exile, to dismiss, avert.*

fulcĭmen -inis, n., *a prop, support, pillar.*

fulcio fulcire fulsi fultum, *to prop up, support; to strengthen, secure;* morally *to support, stay, uphold.*

fulcrum -i, n., *the post* or *foot of a couch.*

fulgĕo fulgēre fulsi, *to flash, to lighten;* in gen., *to shine, gleam, glitter;* fig., *to be distinguished, to shine.*

fulgĭdus -a -um, *shining, gleaming, glittering.*

fulgo -ĕre = fulgeo; q.v.

fulgor -ōris, m., *lightning;* in gen., *glitter, brightness;* fig., *brightness, glory.*

fulgur -ŭris, n. *a flash* or *stroke of lightning;* sometimes *an object struck by lightning;* in gen., *brightness.*

fulgŭrālis -e, *relating to lightning.*

fulgŭrātor -ōris, m., *a priest who interpreted omens from lightning.*

fulgŭrītus -a -um, *struck by lightning.*

fulgŭro -are, *to lighten; to shine, be brilliant.*

fŭlica -ae, f. *a coot.*

fūligo -inis, f. *soot; powder for darkening the eyebrows.*

fullo -ōnis, m. *a cloth-fuller.*

fullōnica -ae, f. *the art of fulling.*

fulmen -inis, n. *a stroke of lightning, a thunderbolt.* Transf. *a crushing calamity; mighty* or *irresistible power.*

fulmĭnĕus -a -um, *of lightning; like lightning, rapid* or *destructive.*

fulmĭno -are, *to lighten.*

fultūra -ae, f. *support, prop, stay.*

Fulvius -a -um, *name of a Roman gens.*

fulvus -a -um, *tawny, yellowish brown,*

fūmĕus and **fumĭdus** -a -um, *smoky, full of smoke.*

fūmĭfer -fĕra -fĕrum, *smoky.*

fūmĭfĭcus -a -um, *causing smoke.*

fūmo -are, *to smoke, steam, reek.*

fūmōsus -a -um, *smoked.*

fūmus -i, m. *smoke, steam, vapour.*

fūnālis -e, *attached to a rope.* N. as subst. **fūnāle** -is, *the thong of a sling; a wax-torch.*

fūnambŭlus -i, m. *a rope-dancer.*

functĭo -ōnis, f. *performance, execution.*

funda -ae, *a sling; a sling-stone; a casting-net.*

fundāmen -inis, n. and **fundāmentum** -i, n. usually plur., *a foundation, basis.*

fundātor -ōris, m. *founder.*

fundĭto -are, *to sling.*

fundĭtor -ōris, m. *a soldier with a sling, a slinger.*

fundĭtus, *from the bottom; completely, entirely; at the bottom, below.*

¹**fundo** -are, *to lay the foundation of, to found; also to make firm, to strengthen.* Hence partic. **fundātus** -a -um, *founded, firm.*

²**fundo** fundĕre fūdi fūsum: of liquids, *to pour, pour out;* of metals, *to melt, cast.* Transf., *to pour out, shower, give abundantly; to squander;* se fundere, *to rush, stream;* of sounds, *to utter;* with emphasis on distribution, *to spread, extend, scatter;* milit. *to rout, defeat, scatter, put to flight.* Hence partic. **fūsus** -a -um, *spread out, extended;* crines, *flowing free;* of speech, *diffuse;* adv. **fūsē**, *widely, copiously.*

fundus -i, m. *ground; the bottom or base of anything; a farm, estate.*

fūnebris -e, *of a funeral funereal; deadly, destructive.*

fūnĕrĕus -a -um, *of a funeral, funereal; fatal, ill-omened.*

fūnĕro -are, *to bury solemnly, inter with funeral rites;* partic. **fūnĕrātus** -a -um, *done to death.*

fūnesto -are, *to defile or pollute with death.*

fūnestus -a -um: pass., *filled with mourning, defiled by death;* act., *fatal, disastrous, deadly.*

fungĭnus -a -um, *of a mushroom.*

fungor fungi functus, dep. *to occupy oneself with anything, to perform, execute, undergo,* usually with abl.; absol. in special sense, *to be affected, suffer.*

fungus -i, m. *a mushroom, fungus; a dull, stupid fellow; a 'thief' in the wick of a candle, a candlesnuff.*

fūnĭcŭlus -i, m. *thin rope, cord, string.*

fūnis -is, m. *rope, cord, line.*

fūnus -ĕris, n. *a funeral, burial.* Transf., *the corpse; death; destruction, ruin; a cause of ruin.*

fūo fūi fūtūrus, etc.; see sum.

fūr fūris, c. *a thief.*

fūrax -ācis, *inclined to steal, thievish.* Hence superl. adv. **fūrācissĭmē**, *most thievishly.*

furca -ae, f., *a (two-pronged) fork, a pitch-fork; a fork-shaped prop or pole; an instrument of punishment, with two prongs to which the arms were tied;* geograph., *a narrow pass.*

furcĭfer -fĕra -fĕrum, *carrying the furca as a punishment;* applied to slaves, *gallows-bird.*

furcilla -ae, f., *a little fork.*

furcillo -are, *to support.*

furcŭla -ae, f. *a little fork; a fork-shaped prop;* geograph., *a narrow pass,* esp. of *the Caudine forks.*

furfur -ŭris, m. *bran; scales, scurf on the skin.*

fūria -ae, f., usually plur. *rage, frenzy, madness, passion;* personif., of *the mythological Furies, avenging deities;* fig., *of persons.*

fūriālis -e, *furious, raging, frenzied; belonging to the Furies;* adv. **fūriālĭter**, *furiously, madly.*

fūrĭbundus -a -um, *raging, furious; inspired.*

fūrĭo -are, *to make furious, madden;* partic., fūriātus -a -um, *raging.*

fūrĭōsus -a -um, *raging, raving, mad, furious;* adv. **fūrĭōsē**.

Fūrĭus -a -um, *name of a Roman gens.*

furnus -i, m. *an oven, bakehouse.*

fūro -ĕre, *to rage, rave, be mad;* often of impassioned persons, *to rave, be frantic;* furere aliquā, *to be madly in love with.* Adv. from partic., **fūrenter**, *furiously.*

¹**fūror** -ari, dep. *to steal, pilfer;* fig., *to steal away, withdraw; to counterfeit, personate.*

²**fūror** -ōris, m. *madness, raving, insanity; furious anger, martial rage; passionate love; inspiration, poetic or prophetic frenzy;* meton., *an object of passion.*

furtĭficus -a -um, *thievish.*

furtim, adv. *by stealth, stealthily.*

furtīvus -a -um, *stolen; secret, concealed, furtive.* Adv. **furtīvē**.

furtum -i, n. *theft, robbery;* in plur. *stolen property;* fig., *underhand methods, trick, deceit,* esp. *secret or stolen love.*

fūruncŭlus -i, m. *a sneak thief, pilferer.*

furvus -a -um, *dark-coloured, black.*

fuscina -ae, f. *a three-pronged fork, trident.*

fusco -are, *to darken, blacken.*

fuscus -a -um, *dark-coloured;* of the voice, *indistinct.*

fūsĭlis -e, *molten, liquid, soft.*

fūsĭo -ōnis, f. *pouring-out, out-pouring.*

fustis -is, m. *a stick, cudgel, club.*

fustuārium -i, n. *cudgelling to death.*

¹**fūsus** -a -um, partic. from fundo; q.v.

²**fūsus** -i, m. *a spindle.*

fūtātim, *abundantly.*

futtĭlis and **fūtĭlis** -e, *brittle; vain, worthless, good for nothing.*

futtĭlĭtās and **fūtĭlĭtās** -ātis, f. *worthlessness, folly, silliness.*

fūtūrus -a -um used as future partic. of sum; q.v.

G

G, g, the seventh letter of the Latin alphabet, originally represented by C.

Gábii -orum, m. *an ancient city of Latium;* adj. **Gábinus** -a -um.

Gábinius -a -um, *name of a Roman gens.*

Gádēs -ium, f. *a town in Hispania Baetica* (now *Cadiz*); adj. **Gáditānus** -a -um.

gaesum -i, n. *a long heavy javelin.*

Gaetūli -orum, m. pl. *a people in north-west Africa.*

Gáius, abbrev. C., *a Roman praenomen;* fem. **Gáia.**

Gálátae -arum, m. *a Celtic people settled in Asia Minor, the Galatians.*

Galba -ae, m. *a cognomen of the Sulpician gens;* esp. of Ser. Sulpicius, Roman emperor A.D. 68-69.

galbánēus -a -um, *of galbanum;* q.v.

galbánum -i, n., *the resinous sap of a Syrian plant.*

galbinus -a -um, *greenish-yellow.*

gálěa -ae, f. *helmet.*

gálěo -are, *to cover with a helmet;* partic., **gálěātus** -a -um, *helmeted.*

gálěrīcŭlum -i, n. *skull-cap; wig.*

gálěrĭtus -a -um, *wearing a hood or skull-cap.*

gálěrum -i, n. and **gálěrus** -i, m. *skull-cap; wig.*

galla -ae, f. *oakapple.*

Galli -orum, m. pl. *the Gauls, a Celtic people, to the west of the Rhine and in the north of Italy;* **Gallia** -ae, f. *Gaul, the land of the Gauls;* Cisalpina = Northern Italy; Transalpina = France; adj. **Gallicānus** and **Gallicus** -a -um, *Gaulish;* f. as subst., gallica, *a slipper.*

galliambus -i, m. *a song of the priests of Cybele.*

gallica; see Galli.

gallina -ae, f. *hen.*

gallināceus -a -um, *of poultry;* gallus, *a poultry-cock.*

gallinārius -a -um, *of poultry;* m. as subst., *poultry-farmer.*

¹gallus -i, m. *cock.*

²Gallus, *a Gaul;* see Galli.

³Gallus -i, m. usually plur. **Galli** -orum, m. *a priest of Cybele.*

gánéa -ae, f. and **gánéum** -i, n. *a brothel or a low eating-house.*

gánéo -ōnis, m. *a debauchee.*

Gangēs -is, m., *the river Ganges in India.* Adj. **Gangēticus** -a -um; f. adj. **Gangētis** -idis = *Indian.*

gannio -ire, *to yelp, snarl, growl.*

gannitus -ūs, m. *yelping, snarling.*

Gánýmēdēs -is, m. *the cup-bearer of Jove.*

garrio -ire, *to chatter, prate, babble.*

garrǔlĭtās -ātis, f. *chattering.*

garrǔlus -a -um, *talkative, chattering, babbling, noisy.*

gárum -i, n. *fish-sauce.*

Gárumna -ae, f. *a river in Gaul* (now *Garonne*). **Gárumni** -orum, m.pl. *a people living on the Garonne.*

gaudĕo gaudēre gāvisus sum, *to rejoice, be glad;* with abl. of cause, *to delight in;* in sinu gaudere, *to rejoice in secret.*

gaudīum -i, n. *joy, gladness, delight; a source of delight.*

gausápē -is, and **gausápum** -i, n. *woollen cloth with a long nap, frieze.*

gāza -ae, f. *the royal treasure of Persia;* in gen., *treasure, riches, wealth.*

gélásinus -i, m. *dimple.*

gélidus -a -um, *cold, frosty, icy;* in act. sense, *chilling;* f. as subst. **gélida** -ae, *cold water.* Adv. **gélidē,** *coldly, feebly.*

gélo -are, transit., *to cause to freeze;* intransit., *to freeze.*

gélu -ūs, n. (earlier **gélus** -ūs, m. and **gélum** -i, n.), *frost, chill.*

gémébundus -a -um, *groaning, sighing.*

gémellĭpǎra -ae, f. adj. *twin-bearing.*

gémellus -a -um, *twin, paired, double;* m. as subst., *a twin.*

gémĭnātio -ōnis, f. *doubling.*

gémĭno -are: transit., *to double; to join together, strike together, repeat;* partic. **gémĭnātus** -a -um, *doubled;* intransit., *to be double.*

gémĭnus -a -um, *twin, double; paired or half-and-half; similar, like;* m. pl. as subst. **gémĭni** -orum, *twins,* esp. *Castor and Pollux.*

gémĭtus -ūs, m., *a sigh, groan;* of things, *groaning, roaring.*

gemma -ae, f. *a bud or eye of a plant.* Transf., *a jewel, gem, precious stone; a jewelled goblet; a seal-ring, seal; a literary gem.*

gemmātus -a -um, *set or adorned with jewels.*

gemmĕus -a -um, *made of or set with jewels; bright.*

gemmĭfer -fĕra -fĕrum, *bearing or producing jewels.*

gemmo -are, *to bud;* pres. partic. **gemmans** -antis, *set with jewels, glittering like jewels.*

gémo gémēre gémŭi gémĭtum: intransit., *to sigh, groan;* of lions, *to roar;* of doves, *to coo;* of things, *to creak;* transit., *to sigh over, lament, bemoan.*

gēna -ae, f. usually plur., *cheek, cheeks and chin.* Transf., *eye-socket, eye.*

Genāva -ae, f. *a town of the Allobroges* (now *Geneva*).

gĕnĕálŏgus -i, m. *a genealogist.*

gĕner -eri, m. *a son-in-law; a grand-daughter's husband; a brother-in-law.*

gĕnĕrālis -e. (1) *belonging to a kind, generic.* (2) *universal, general.* Adv. **gĕnĕrālĭter,** *in general, generally.*

gĕnĕrasco -ĕre, *to be produced, come to birth.*

gĕnĕrātim. (1) *according to kinds or classes.* (2) *in general, generally.*

gĕnĕrātor -ōris, m. *begetter, producer.*

gĕnĕro -are, *to beget, produce, bring to life.*

gĕnĕrōsus -a -um, *of noble birth, noble, well-bred; of a place, producing well.* Transf., *of character, noble, magnanimous.* Adv. **gĕnĕrōsē,** *nobly.*

gĕnĕsis -is, f. *the constellation which presides over one's birth.*

gĕnĕtīvus -a -um, *inborn, innate; nomina, family names; casus, the genitive case.*

gĕnetrix -trīcis f. *one who brings forth, a mother.*

gĕniālis -e. (1) *relating to marriage.* (2) *relating to enjoyment; joyful, gay.* Adv. **gĕniāliter,** *jovially, gaily.*

gĕnicŭlātus -a -um, *knotty, full of knots.*

gĕnista (gĕnesta) -ae, f. *the plant broom.*

gĕnĭtābilis -e, *fruitful, productive.*

gĕnĭtālis -e, *creative, fruitful; dies, birthday; of Diana, presiding over births.* Adv. **gĕnĭtāliter,** *in a fruitful manner.*

gĕnĭtīvus; see genetivus.

gĕnĭtor -ōris, m. *a begetter, father, producer.*

gĕnĭtūra -ae, f. *begetting, engendering; in astrology, nativity.*

gĕnĭus -i, m. *the guardian spirit of a man or place, a genius; esp. as a spirit of enjoyment, one's taste, inclination; genium curare, to enjoy oneself.* Transf., *talent, genius.*

gĕno = gigno; q.v.

gens gentis, f. *a clan, stock, people, tribe, nation.* Transf., *an offspring, descendant; a district, country; esp. in partitive genit.: ubi gentium? where in the world?; plur., gentes, foreigners.*

genticus -a -um, *a nation, national.*

gentilicius -a -um, *of a particular gens.*

gentilis -e, *of a gens; of a country, national.*

gentilĭtās -ātis, f. *the relationship between the members of a gens.*

gĕnu -ūs, n. *the knee.*

Gĕnŭa -ae, f. *coast-town in Liguria (now Genoa).*

gĕnŭālia -ium, n. pl. *garters.*

¹gĕnŭīnus -a -um, *natural, innate.*

²gĕnŭīnus -a -um, *belonging to the cheek or jaw: dentes, the jaw-teeth; m. as subst. a jaw-tooth.*

¹gĕnus -ĕris, n. *birth, descent, origin; race, stock, family, house; hence offspring, descendant(s); sex; in gen., class, kind, variety, sort; in logic, genus; of action, etc., fashion, manner, way.*

²gĕnus -ūs = genu; q.v.

gĕŏgrăphia -ae, f. *geography.*

gĕōmetres -ae, m. *a geometer.*

gĕōmetria -ae, f. *geometry.*

gĕōmetrĭcus -a -um, *geometrical; m. as subst., gĕōmetrĭcus -i, a geometer; n. pl. gĕōmetrĭca, geometry.*

gĕorgĭcus -a -um, *agricultural; n. pl. as subst. Gĕorgĭca -orum, the Georgics of Vergil.*

Germāni -orum, m. pl., *the Germans;* adj. **Germānus** -a -um, *German;* f. subst. **Germānĭa** -ae, *Germany;* adj. **Germānĭcus** -a -um, *German;* m. as subst. **Germānĭcus** -i, a

surname assumed after victories in Germany.

germānĭtās -ātis, *the relationship between brothers or sisters; brotherhood, sisterhood.*

¹germānus -a -um, *having the same parents; m. or f. as subst. own brother, own sister.* Transf., *brotherly, sisterly; genuine, real, true.* Adv. **germāne,** *faithfully, honestly.*

²Germānus -a -um; see Germani.

germen -ĭnis, n. *an embryo; a bud, shoot or graft; fig., germ.*

germĭno -are, *to sprout forth.*

¹gĕro gĕrĕre gessi gestum. Lit. (1) *to carry, bear; esp. to wear.* (2) *to bear, give birth to.* Transf., *to carry about, display an appearance; personam gerere, to act a part; se gerere, to conduct oneself (with adv.); to carry about, entertain a feeling; to carry on conduct, manage business; res gestae, exploits, esp. warlike exploits.*

²gĕro -ōnis, m., *a carrier.*

gerrae -arum, f. pl. *wattled twigs.* Transf., *trifles, nonsense.*

gerro -ōnis, m. *a trifler, idler.*

gĕrŭlus -i, m. *porter, carrier.*

Gēryōn -ŏnis, and **Gēryōnēs** -ae, m. myth., *a king in Spain with three bodies, killed by Hercules.*

gestāmen -ĭnis, n. *that which is carried; that by which anything is carried, a carriage or litter.*

gesticŭlātio -ōnis, f. *pantomime, gesticulation.*

gesticŭlor -ari, dep. *gesticulate.*

gestio -ōnis, f., *management, performance.*

gestĭto -are, *to carry often, wear often.*

gesto -are, *to carry, bear about; pass. to ride about.*

gestor -ōris, m. *a tale-bearer, gossip.*

gestus -ūs, m. *carriage of the body, posture; esp. the gestures of an actor or orator.*

Gĕtae -arum, m. pl. *a people of Thrace living near the Danube.* Adj. **Gĕtĭcus** -a -um, *Thracian;* adv. **Gĕtĭce,** *after the Getic fashion.*

Gĕtŭlus, etc. = Gaetulus, etc.; q.v.

gibba -ae, f. *hump, hunch.*

gibber -ĕra, -ĕrum, *hump-backed.*

gibbus -i, m. *hump, hunch.*

Gĭgas -gantis, m. *a giant;* adj. **Gĭgantēus** -a -um.

gigno gignĕre gĕnŭi gĕnĭtum, *to beget, bear, bring forth; to cause.*

gilvus -a -um, *pale yellow.*

gingīva -ae, f. *gum (of the mouth).*

glăber -bra -brum, *bald; m. as subst., a page.*

glăcĭālis -e, *icy.*

glăcĭes -ēi, f. *ice.* Transf., *hardness.*

glăcĭo -are, *to freeze.*

glădĭātor -ōris, m. *one hired to fight at public shows, a gladiator; hence bandit, brigand; gladiatoribus, at a show of gladiators.*

glădĭātōrĭus -a -um, *of gladiators, gladiatorial; n. as subst., gladiators' pay.*

glădĭātūra -ae, f. *the profession of gladiator.*

glădĭus -i, *sword.*

glaeba = gleba; q.v.

glaesum (glesum) -i, n. *amber.*

glandĭfer -fĕra -fĕrum, *acorn-bearing.*

glandĭum -i, n. *a delicate glandule in meat.*

glans glandis, f. *mast; an acorn, chestnut, etc.* Transf., *a bullet.*

glārĕa -ae, f. *gravel.*

glārĕōsus -a -um, *gravelly full of gravel.*

glaucōma -atis, n. (also -ae, f.) *a disease of the eye, cataract.*

glaucus -a -um *bluish- or greenish-grey.*

glēba (glaeba) -ae, f. *a lump or clod of earth; hence land, soil; a piece, lump of anything.*

glēbŭla -ae, f., *a little clod or lump; a little farm or estate.*

glēsum = glaesum; q.v.

glis gliris, m. *dormouse.*

glisco -ĕre, *to grow up, swell up, blaze up.*

glŏbo -are, *to form into a ball or mass.*

glŏbōsus -a -um, *spherical.*

glŏbus -i, m. *a ball, globe, sphere; a troop, crowd, mass of people.*

glŏmĕrāmen -ĭnis, n. *a round mass, globe.*

glŏmĕro -are, *to form into a sphere, or rounded heap;* in gen., *to gather together collect, amass.*

glŏmus -ĕris, n. *clue, skein, ball of thread.*

glōrĭa -ae, f. *fame, renown, glory.* Transf., *of a member of a group, the pride, the glory; desire of glory, ambition, boastfulness;* plur., *glorious deeds.*

glōrĭātĭo -ōnis, f. *glorying, boasting.*

glōrĭŏla -ae, f. *a little glory.*

glōrĭor -ari, dep. *to glory, boast, pride oneself.*

glōrĭōsus -a -um, *famous, glorious; ambitious, pretentious, boastful.* Adv. glōrĭōsē, *gloriously; vauntingly, boastingly.*

glūbo -ĕre, *to peel.* Transf., *to rob.*

glūtĕn -tinis, n. *glue.*

glūtĭnātor -ōris, m., *one who glues books, a bookbinder.*

glūtĭo (gluttĭo) -ire, *to swallow, gulp down.*

glūto (glutto) -onis, m. *glutton.*

Gnaeus -i, m. *a Roman praenomen,* shortened Cn.

gnārĭtās -ātis, f. *knowledge.*

gnārus -a -um; act., *knowing, acquainted with, expert;* pass., *known.*

Gnătho -ōnis, m. *a parasite in the Eunuchus of Terence;* in gen. *parasite.*

Gnātĭa = Egnatia; q.v.

gnātus, gnāvus = natus, navus; q.v.

Gnīdus = Cnidus; q.v.

Gnossus (Gnōsus) -i, f., *an ancient city of Crete, the residence of Minos;* adj. Gnōsĭus and Gnōsĭăcus -a -um, *Gnosian; Cretan;* f. adj. Gnōsĭas -ădis, and Gnōsis -idis, *Cretan* and, as subst., *Ariadne.*

gōbĭus (cōbĭus) -i, and gōbĭo -ōnis, m. *a gudgeon.*

gonger; see conger.

Gorgō -gŏnis, f. *also called* Medusa, *slain by Perseus;* adj. Gorgŏnĕus -a -um.

Gortȳna -ae, f. *an ancient city in Crete.*

grăbātus -i, m. *a low couch, camp-bed.*

Gracchus -i, m. *a cognomen in the Gens Sempronia, esp. of Tiberius and Gaius, the 'Gracchi'.* Adj. Gracchānus -a -um.

grăcĭlis -e, *slender, thin, slim;* of style. etc., *simple, without ornament.*

grăcĭlĭtās -ātis, f. *thinness, slenderness.*

grăcŭlus -i, m. *jackdaw.*

grădārĭus -a -um, *going step by step.*

grădātim, adv. *step by step, by degrees.*

grădātĭo -ōnis, f., *in rhetoric, climax.*

grădĭor grădi gressus, dep. *to step, walk.*

Grădīvus -i, m. *a surname of Mars.*

grădus -ūs, m. *a step.* (1) *a step as made, a pace;* suspenso gradu, *on tiptoe;* gradum facere, *to step;* gradum inferre, *to advance;* hence in gen., *an approach.* (2) *a step as climbed, a stair;* hence any *tier, gradation; a braid of hair;* abstr., *degree, stage; rank, position;* milit. *station, post.*

Graeci -orum, m. *the Greeks;* sing. Graecus -i, m. *a Greek;* as adj. Graecus -a -um, *Greek;* adv. Graecē, *in the Greek language;* f. subst. Graecĭa -ae, f. *Greece;* Magna Graecia, *the Greek colonies in the south of Italy;* dim. Graecŭlus -i, m. *a little Greek.*

graecisso -are, and graecor -ari, dep. *to imitate the Greeks.*

Grāii -orum, m. = Graeci, *the Greeks;* adj. Grāĭus -a -um, *Greek.*

Grāĭŭgĕna -ae, m. *a Greek by birth.*

grallātor -ōris, m. *one that walks on stilts.*

grāmen -ĭnis, n. *grass, turf;* any *plant or herb.*

grāmĭnĕus -a -um, *grassy, of grass; also of cane or bamboo.*

grammătĭcus -a -um, *literary, grammatical;* as subst., m. *a philologist, grammarian;* f. sing. and n. pl. *grammar, philology.*

grammătista -ae, f. *a teacher of grammar or languages.*

grānārĭum -i, n. *granary.*

grandaevus -a -um, *very old.*

grandesco -ĕre, *to become great, grow.*

grandĭcŭlus -a -um, *rather large.*

grandĭfer -fĕra -fĕrum, *producing great profits.*

grandĭlŏquus -a -um, *speaking grandly; boastful.*

grandĭnat -are, impers. *it hails.*

grandĭo -ire, *to increase.*

grandis -e, *full-grown, great, large;* in stature, *tall;* in years, *old.* Transf., *great, important;* of style, *lofty, grand, sublime.*

grandĭtās -ātis, f. of style, *loftiness, sublimity.*

grando -ĭnis, f. *hail, hail-storm.*

grānĭfer -fĕra -fĕrum, *grain-carrying.*

grānum -i, n. *grain, seed.*

grăphicus -a -um, *concerned with painting;* hence *masterly, skilful;* adv. **grăphicē.**

grăphium -i, n. *a stilus, a pointed instrument for writing on wax.*

grassātor -ōris, m. *an idler; a footpad.*

grassor -ari, dep. *to walk about, to loiter; to go about an undertaking; to proceed against somebody.*

grātes, f. pl. *thanks;* grates agere, *to express thanks;* habere, *to feel gratitude.*

grātia -ae, f. (1) *charm, attraction, pleasantness;* personif., *of the three Graces* (Euphrosyne, Aglaia, Thalia). (2) *favour with others; esteem, regard, popularity.* (3) *a favour done, service, kindness;* abl. gratiā, *on account of;* meā gratiā, *for my sake.* (4) *thankfulness, thanks;* in sing. and plur.: gratias agere, with dat., *to express thanks;* gratias habere, *to feel grateful;* abl. plur. **grātiis** or **grātis,** *without recompense, for nothing, gratis.*

grātificātio -ōnis, f. *complaisance, obligingness.*

grātificor -ari, dep. *to oblige, gratify, do a favour to.*

grātiōsus -a -um, *favoured, beloved; showing favour, complaisant.*

grātis; see gratia.

grātor -ari, dep. *to wish joy, to congratulate; to give thanks.*

grātuītus -a -um, *not paid for or not provoked, gratuitous, spontaneous;* abl. sing. n. as adv. **grātuīto,** *gratuitously.*

grātūlābundus -a -um, *congratulating.*

grātūlātio -ōnis, f. *wishing joy, congratulation; a thanksgiving festival.*

grātūlor -ari, dep. *to wish a person joy, congratulate* (with dat.); *to give solemn thanks,* esp. to the gods.

grātus -a -um, adj. (1) *pleasing, welcome, agreeable;* gratum facere, *to do a favour.* (2) *thankful, grateful.* Adv. **grātē,** *willingly, with pleasure; thankfully.*

grăvanter and **grăvātē;** from gravo.

grăvātim, *reluctantly.*

grăvēdinōsus -a -um, *subject to colds.*

grăvēdo -inis, f. *cold in the head, catarrh.*

grăvĕolens -lentis, *strong-smelling, rank.*

grăvesco -ĕre, *to become heavy; to grow worse.*

grăviditās -ātis, f. *pregnancy.*

grăvido -are, *to load, burden; to impregnate.*

grăvidus -a -um, *heavy; laden, filled, full; pregnant.*

grăvis -e. (1) *heavy;* of sound, *low, deep;* fig., *weighty, important;* of character, *dignified, serious;* of style, *elevated, dignified.* (2) *burdened, laden, weighed down;* esp. *pregnant.* (3) *burdensome, oppressive; grievous, painful, unpleasant.* Adv. **grăviter,** *heavily, weightily, reluctantly; grievously, painfully.*

grăvitās -ātis, f. (1) *weight;* fig., *consequence, importance;* of character,

dignity, authority, seriousness. (2) *heaviness; pregnancy; dullness, faintness.* (3) *pressure;* fig., *unpleasantness.*

grăvo -are, *to load, burden; to heighten, exaggerate, increase; to oppress, burden, trouble;* pass., *to feel burdened or troubled by a thing, or to make heavy weather of doing it.* Adv. **grăvanter,** and **grăvātē,** *reluctantly.*

grĕgālis -e, *of a herd or flock; common, ordinary;* m. pl. as subst. *companions, associates, accomplices.*

grĕgārius -a -um, *of a herd or flock; miles, a private soldier.*

grĕgātim, *in troops or crowds.*

grĕmium -i, n. *lap, bosom; womb.*

gressus -ūs, m. *a step;* of a ship, *course.*

grex grĕgis, m. *a herd, flock, drove;* of people, *a troop, band,* esp. *a philosophical sect or troop of soldiers;* grege facto, *in close order.*

grunnio (grundio) -ire, *to grunt like a pig.*

grunnītus -ūs, m., *the grunting of a pig.*

grus grūis, m. and f. *a crane.*

grȳ, n. indecl. *scrap, crumb.*

gryilus -i, m. *cricket, grasshopper.*

gryps, grȳpis, m. *griffin.*

gŭbernāculum (-āclum) -i, n. *rudder, helm;* hence *direction, management, government.*

gŭbernātio -ōnis, f. *steering; direction, government.*

gŭbernātor -ōris, m. *helmsman, steersman, pilot; director, governor.*

gŭbernātrix -icis, f. *she that directs.*

gŭberno -are, *to steer a ship, be at the helm;* in gen., *to steer, direct, govern.*

gŭbernum -i, n. = gubernaculum; q.v.

gŭla -ae, f. *gullet, throat;* hence *greediness, gluttony.*

gŭlōsus -a -um, *gluttonous.*

gurges -itis, m. *whirlpool, eddy;* in gen., *troubled water, a stream, flood, sea;* fig., *abyss, depth.*

¹**gurgŭlio** -ōnis, f. *windpipe.*

²**gurgŭlio** -ōnis, m.; see curculio.

gurgustium -i, n. *hut, hovel.*

gustātus -ūs, m. *taste; appetite, flavour.*

gusto -are, *to taste, take a little of; to partake of, enjoy.*

gustus -ūs, m. *tasting; taste, flavour, a whet or relish.*

gutta -ae, f. *a drop; a spot or mark.*

guttātim, *drop by drop.*

guttŭla -ae, f. *a little drop.*

guttur -ūris, n. *the windpipe, throat; gluttony.*

guttus -i, m. *a jug.*

Gȳăros -i, f. and **Gȳăra** -orum, n. *a barren island in the Aegean, used as a place of exile under the empire.*

Gȳgēs -is and -ae, m. *a king of Lydia, famous for his ring;* adj. **Gȳgaeus** -a -um.

gymnāsiarchus -i, m. *the master of a gymnasium.*

gymnāsium -i, n. *school of gymnastics, gymnasium;* also *a place for philosophical discussion.*

gymnastĭcus and gymnĭcus -a -um, *gymnastic.*

gўnaecēum (and -īum) -i, n. *the women's apartments in a Greek house.*

gypso -are, *to cover with gypsum;* partic. **gypsātus** -a -um, *covered with gypsum, whitened.*

gypsum -i, n. *gypsum;* meton. *a plaster figure.*

gўrus -i, m *a circle, ring;* esp. *a course for training horses;* in gen., *orbit, circuit.*

H

H, h, the eighth letter of the Latin Alphabet.

ha! hahae! hahahae! exclamations of joy or amusement.

hăbēna -ae, f. *a strap; a bridle, reins* (esp. in plur.); **habenas dare,** *to loosen the rein;* **adducere,** *to tighten it.*

hăbĕo -ēre -ŭi -ĭtum, *to have, hold; to have about one, carry, wear; to contain;* more generally, *to possess, have power over;* absol., *to possess property, be wealthy;* of places, *to own, inhabit,* or *rule over;* of persons, *to keep,* esp. in a certain state, or relation. Transf., **habere in animo,** *to have in mind, intend;* **habes consilia nostra,** *you know of;* **habeo dicere,** *I have it in my power to say;* **bonum animum habere,** *to be of good courage;* **odium,** *to cherish hatred;* **invidiam,** *to experience ill-will;* **misericordiam,** *to involve* or *cause pity;* **concilium,** *to hold a council;* **orationem,** *to make a speech;* with reflex., *to keep oneself, be,* in a condition; **graviter se habere,** *to be ill;* **ut nunc res se habet,** *as things now are;* intransit., **bene habet,** *all right;* with adv., rarely, *to use, manage, treat;* with double acc., or dat., or pro and abl., *to hold, consider, regard* in a certain light. Perf. partic. **hăbĭtus** -a -um, *disposed; in a certain condition* (physical or mental).

hăbĭlis -e, *easily managed, handy; suitable, fit, convenient.*

hăbĭlĭtās -ātis, f. *aptitude, suitability.*

hăbĭtābĭlis -e, *habitable.*

hăbĭtātĭo -ōnis, f. *dwelling, habitation.*

hăbĭtātŏr -ōris, m. *inhabitant.*

hăbĭto -are: transit., *to inhabit;* intransit., *to dwell.*

hăbĭtūdo -ĭnis, f. *condition.*

¹hăbĭtus -a -um, partic. from habeo; q.v.

²hăbĭtus -ūs, m. *condition, habit, bearing;* of dress, *style;* of places, *lie of the land;* abstr., *nature, character, disposition, attitude.*

hăc, adv. from hic; q.v.

hactēnus, *as far as this, so far (and no farther); hitherto; up to this point.*

Hadrĭa -ae; f. *a town in the north of Italy;* m. *the Adriatic Sea.* Adj. **Hadrĭācus and Hadrĭātĭcus** -a -um, *Adriatic.*

Hadrĭānus -i, m., P. Aelius, Roman emperor from A.D. 117 to 138.

haedīlia -ae, f. and **haedillus** -i, m., *a little kid.*

haedĭnus -a -um *of a kid.*

haedŭlus -i, m. *a little kid.*

haedus -i, m. *a kid, young goat.*

Haemŏnĭa -ae, f. *an old name of Thessaly;* adj. **Haemŏnĭus** -a -um, *Thessalian;* f. subst. **Haemŏnis** -nĭdis, *a Thessalian woman.*

haerĕo haerēre haesi haesum. (1) *to stick, cleave, adhere, hang on to a person* or *thing.* (2) *to come to a standstill, get stuck; be embarrassed.*

haeresco -ēre, *to adhere, stick.*

haesĭtantĭa -ae, f. *faltering;* **linguae,** *stammering.*

haesĭtātĭo -ōnis, f.: in speech, *hesitation, stammering;* mentally, *hesitation, indecision.*

haesĭto -are, *to stick fast, to hesitate;* in speech, *to stammer;* mentally, *to be undecided, be at a loss.*

hālec; see alec.

hālĭaeĕtos -i, m. *sea-eagle, osprey.*

hālĭtus -ūs, m., *breath, vapour.*

hallex -ĭcis, m. *thumb* or *big toe.*

hālo -are, *to breathe out, exhale.*

hālūc-; see aluc-.

hāma (ăma) -ae, f. *bucket,* esp. *fireman's bucket.*

Hămādrўas -ădis, f., *a wood-nymph, hamadryad.*

hāmātus -a -um, *provided with hooks, hooked; curved like a hook, crooked.*

Hămĭlcăr -căris, m. *father of Hannibal.*

hāmĭōta -ae, m., *an angler.*

Hammon; see Ammon.

hāmus -i, m. *a hook,* esp. *a fish-hook; a talon; a thorn.*

Hannĭbăl -bălis, m. *leader of the Carthaginians in the second Punic war.*

hāra -ae, f. *a pen* or *coop; a pig-sty.*

hărĭŏlor -ari, dep. *to utter prophecies.* Transf., *to talk nonsense.*

hărĭŏlus -i, m. and **hărĭŏla** -ae f. *a soothsayer, prophet.*

harmŏnĭa -ae, f. *melody, concord, harmony.*

harpăgo -ōnis, m., *a large hook, drag, grappling-iron.*

harpē -es, f. *a curved sword, scimitar.*

Harpўiae (trisyll.) -arum, f. pl., *the Harpies, mythical monsters.*

hăruspex -spĭcis, m. *soothsayer; a seer, prophet.*

hăruspĭcĭnus -a -um, *concerned with divination;* f. as subst. *divination.*

hăruspĭcĭum -i, n. *inspection of entrails, divination.*

Hasdrŭbăl (Asdrŭbăl) -bălis, m. *the brother of Hannibal.*

hasta -ae, f. *a spear, pike, javelin;* milit., and in ceremonial use, at public auctions and weddings.

hastātus -a -um, *armed with a spear* m pl. as subst. **hastāti** -orum, *the front rank of a Roman army when drawn up for battle.*

hastīle -is, n., *the shaft of a spear; a spear; a prop for vines,* etc.

hau, oh!

haud (haut), *not, not at all, by no means.*

hauddum, *not yet.*

haudquāquam, *by no means, not at all.*

haurĭo haurire hausi haustum, *to draw up, draw out or in; to drink up, absorb, swallow; to shed* blood; *to drain, empty* a receptacle; in gen., *to derive, take in; also to exhaust, weaken, waste.*

haustrum -i, n. *a pump.*

haustus -ūs, m. *drawing of water;* legal, *the right to draw water;* of air, *inhaling;* of drink, *drinking, a draught;* of solids, *a handful.*

haut = haud; q.v.

hăvĕo; see aveo.

hebdŏmas -ădis, f. *seventh day of a disease* (supposed critical).

Hēbē -ēs, f. *the cup-bearer of the gods.*

hĕbĕnus -i, f. *the ebon-tree; ebony.*

hĕbĕo -ēre, *to be blunt, dull, heavy, inactive.*

hĕbĕs -ĕtis, *blunt, dull; faint, sluggish, weak;* mentally, *dull, heavy, stupid.*

hĕbesco -ēre, *to become dull, blunt, dim.*

hĕbĕto -are, *to make blunt or dull, to deaden, dim.*

Hebraeus -a -um, *Hebrew, Jewish.*

Hebrus -i, m., *the chief river of Thrace.*

Hēcătē -ēs, f. *goddess of magic and enchantment;* adj. Hēcătēius -a -um and f. Hēcătēĭs -ĭdis, *Hecatean, magical.*

hĕcătombē -ēs, f. *a hecatomb.*

Hector -tŏris, m. *son of Priam, husband of Andromache;* adj. Hectŏrēus -a -um.

Hēcŭba -ae, and Hēcŭbē -ēs, f. *wife of Priam.*

hēdĕra -ae, f. *ivy.*

hēdychrum -i, n. *a fragrant ointment.*

hei, interj. = ei; q.v.

Hēlĕna -ae, and Hĕlĕnē -ēs, f. *wife o Menelaus, carried off by Paris to Troy.*

Hĕlĭce -ēs, f. *a constellation, the Great Bear.*

Hĕlĭcon -ōnis, m., *a hill in Boeotia, sacred to Apollo and the Muses;* adj. Hĕlĭcōnĭus -a -um; subst. Hĕlĭcōnĭădes and Hĕlĭcōnĭdes -um, f. *the Muses.*

Hellē -ēs, f. *a girl drowned in the Hellespont, so named after her.*

hellĕborus; see elleborus.

Hellespontus -i, m., *the Hellespont, Dardanelles.*

hellŭo (hēlŭo) -ōnis, *glutton, squanderer.*

hellŭor (hēlŭor) -ari, dep. *to guzzle, gormandize.*

hĕlops (ĕlops, ellops) -ŏpis, m. *a fish, perhaps sturgeon.*

helvella -ae, f. *a small pot-herb.*

Helvētĭi -orum, m. *the Helvetii, a people in what is now Switzerland.*

hem, interj. *well! just look!*

hēmĕrodrŏmus -i, m. *a special courier, express.*

hēmĭcillus -i, m. *mule.*

hēmĭcyclĭum -i, n. *a semi-circle* (of seats).

hēmĭna -ae, f. *a measure of capacity, about half a pint.*

hendĕcăsyllăbi -orum, m. pl. *verses of eleven syllables, hendecasyllables.*

Henna (Enna) -ae, f. *city of Sicily, with a temple of Ceres;* adj. Hennensis -e and Hennaeus -a -um.

heptĕris -is, f. *a galley with seven banks of oars.*

hēra = ēra; q.v.

Hēra -ae, f., *the Greek goddess identified with the Roman Juno;* Hēraea -orum, n. pl., *her festival.*

herba -ae, f. *vegetation; a green plant; a blade or stalk, esp. of corn or grass.*

herbesco ēre, *to grow into blades or stalks.*

herbĭdus -a -um, and herbĭfer -fĕra -fĕrum, *grassy.*

herbōsus -a -um, *grassy.*

herbŭla -ae, f. *a little herb.*

hercisco (ercisco) -ēre, *to divide an inheritance.*

Hercle; see Hercules.

herctum -i, n. *an inheritance;* herctum ciere, *to divide an inheritance.*

Hercŭlānĕum -i, n. *town in Campania destroyed by an eruption of Vesuvius.*

Hercŭlēs -is and -i, m. *the son of Jupiter and Alcmena;* voc. Hercŭlēs or Hercŭle or Hercle, *used as an oath, by Hercules;* so also Mēhercŭlēs, Mēhercŭle, Mēhercle; adj. Hercŭlēus and Hercŭlānĕus -a -um.

Hercўnĭa silva -ae, f. *the Hercynian forest, in central Germany.*

hērĕ = heri; q.v.

hērēdĭtārĭus -a -um, *of an inheritance; inherited, hereditary.*

hērēdĭtās -ātis, f. *inheritance.*

hērēdĭum -i, n. *patrimony.*

hērēs (haerēs) -ēdis, c. *an heir, heiress, successor; an owner.*

hĕrī (hĕrē), *yesterday.*

hĕrīfŭga = erifuga; q.v.

hĕrīlis -e = erilis; q.v.

hermaphrŏdītus -i, m. *hermaphrodite.*

Hermes or Herma -ae, m. *the god Hermes, identified with the Roman Mercury.*

Hērō -ūs, f., *a priestess at Sestos, loved by Leander.*

Hērōdes -is, m. *Herod;* esp. *Herod the Great.*

Hērŏdŏtus -i, m. *the Greek historian, born 484 B.C.*

hērōĭcus -a -um, *relating to the heroes, heroic.*

hērōĭna -ae and hērōĭs -ĭdis, f. *a demigoddess, heroine.*

hērōs -ōis, m. *a demigod, hero.*

hērōus -a -um, *a hero, heroic;* m. as subst. *a hexameter.*

hērus = ērus; q.v.

Hēsĭŏdus -i, m. *an early Greek poet of Boeotia.*

Hespĕrus or -os -i, m. *the Evening Star;* adj. Hespĕrĭus -a -um, *western;* f. as subst. Hespĕrĭa -ae, *the western land; Italy or Spain;* f. adj. Hespĕris -idis, *western;* f. subst. Hespĕrĭdes -um, *daughters of Hesperus, living in the extreme west.*

hesternus -a -um, *of yesterday.*

hĕtairīa -ae, f. *a secret society.*

heu! *oh! alas!*

heus! *hallo! ho, there! hark!*

hexămĕter -tri, m.: adj., *with six feet (of metre);* as subst., *a hexameter.*

hexēris -is, f. *a galley with six banks of oars.*

hiātus -ūs, m. *a cleft, opening; the opening of the mouth, open jaws;* hence *gaping after, desire for;* gram. *hiatus.*

Hībēr -ēris, m. *an Iberian, Spaniard;* plur. Hībēres -ērum, and Hībēri -orum, m. *Spaniards;* Hībĕrus -i, m. *the river Ebro;* Hībēria -ae, *Spain;* adj. Hībēricus -a -um and Hibērus -a -um, *Spanish.*

hīberna -orum, n.; see hibernus.

hībernācŭlum -i, n.: in pl., *tents or huts for winter quarters.*

Hibernia -ae, f. *Ireland.*

hīberno -are, *to winter, spend the winter.*

hībernus -a -um, *wintry, of winter; like winter, cold* or *stormy, wintering, for the winter;* n. pl. as subst. *winter quarters.*

hibiscum -i, n. *marsh-mallow.*

hibrīda (hybrīda) -ae, *a hybrid.*

¹hīc, haec, hōc, *this, this one; this present;* in court, *my client;* strengthened form hice, haece, hōce; interrog. hicine, haecine, hōcine.

²hīc (and heic) *here; in this place, in this matter; hereupon;* strengthened hice and interrog. hicine.

hiĕmālis -e, *of winter; wintry, stormy.*

hiĕmo -are. (1) *to winter, spend the winter.* (2) *to be stormy.*

hiems (hiemps) -ĕmis, f. *winter; the cold of winter; stormy weather, storm.*

Hiĕrŏsŏlyma -orum, n. pl. *Jerusalem.*

hĭlāris -e and hĭlārus -a -um, *cheerful, merry, gay;* n. acc. sing. as adv. hĭlārĕ, *cheerfully.*

hĭlārĭtās -ātis, f. *cheerfulness, gaiety.*

hĭlāro -are, *to make joyful, to cheer up.*

hĭlārŭlus -a -um, *gay, cheerful.*

hillae -arum, f. pl. *intestines of animals; a kind of sausage.*

Hilōtae and Ilōtae -arum, m. pl., *the Helots, slaves of the Spartans.*

hilum -i, n. *a trifle;* with neg. *not a whit, not in the least.*

hinc, adv., *from here, hence;* hinc atque illinc, *on this side and on that;* of causation, *hence, from this cause;* of time, *henceforth,* or *thereupon.*

hinnio -ire, *to neigh, whinny.*

hinnītus -ūs, m. *neighing.*

hinnŭlĕus -i, m. *a young roebuck, fawn.*

hinnus -i, m. *a mule.*

hio -are, *to open, stand open; to gape,* esp. in astonishment or longing; of speech, *to hang together badly;* with acc. object, *to pour forth.*

hippăgōgi -orum, f. pl. *transports for cavalry.*

Hippias -ae, m. *son of Pisistratus, tyrant of Athens.*

hippŏcentaurus -i, m. *a centaur.*

Hippocrătēs -is, m. *a physician of Cos (flourishing about 430 B.C.).*

Hippocrēnē -ēs, f. *a fountain on Mount Helicon.*

hippodrŏmos -i, m., *a hippodrome racecourse.*

Hippŏlytus -i, m. *son of Theseus.*

hippŏtoxŏta -ae, m. *a mounted archer.*

hippūrus -i, m. *a fish,* perhaps *goldfish.*

hircīnus and hircōsus -a -um, *of a goat; goatlike.*

hircus -i, m. *a he-goat.*

hirnĕa -ae, f. *a can* or *jug.*

hirsūtus -a -um, *hairy, shaggy, rough; unadorned.*

Hirtius -a -um, *name of a Roman gens.*

hirtus -a -um, *hairy, shaggy, rough, uncultivated.*

hirūdo -inis, f. *leech.*

hirundo -inis, f. *swallow.*

hisco -ĕre, *to open, split open, gape; to open the mouth.*

Hispāni -orum, m. pl. *the Spaniards;* Hispānia -ae, f. *the whole of the Spanish peninsula;* adj. Hispāniensis -e and Hispānus -a -um.

hispĭdus -a -um, *rough, hairy, bristly.*

¹hister = histrio; q.v.

²Hister (Ister) -tri, m. *name of the lower part of the Danube.*

histōria -ae, f. *inquiry; the results of inquiry; learning; historical narrative, history;* in gen., *narrative, a story.*

histŏricus -a -um, *of history, historical;* m. as subst., *a historian.*

histricus -a -um, *of actors.*

histrio -ōnis, m. *an actor.*

histriōnālis -e, *of actors.*

hiulco -are, *to cause to gape, to split.*

hiulcus -a -um, *gaping, cleft, open; gaping with desire, longing;* of speech, *badly put together;* adv. hiulcĕ, *with hiatus.*

hŏdĭē, *today; at present, still, even now; at once.*

hŏdiernus -a -um, *of today.*

hŏlĭtor -ōris, m. *a kitchen-gardener.*

hŏlĭtōrius -a -um, *of herbs;* forum, *vegetable-market.*

hŏlus (ŏlus) -ĕris, n. *vegetable, pot-herb.*

Hŏmērus -i, m. *Homer, the Greek epic poet;* adj. Hŏmēricus -a -um.

hŏmĭcīda -ae, c. *a murderer, murderess, homicide.*

hŏmĭcīdium -i, n. *murder, homicide.*

hŏmo -inis, *a human being, man, mortal;* in pl., *men, people, the world;* used like a pronoun, *he, him;* milit. in pl., *infantry.*

hŏmullus -i, and hŏmuncio -ōnis, and hŏmuncŭlus -i, m. *a little man, manikin.*

hŏnestās -ātis, f. (1) *honour, repute, respectability;* in pl., *notabilities.* (2) *worth, virtue, probity.* (3) *beauty.*

hŏnesto -are, *to honour, adorn, dignify.*

hŏnestus -a -um. (1) *honoured, in good repute, respectable.* (2) *honourable, proper, virtuous;* n. as subst., *morality, virtue.* (3) *fine, beautiful.* Adv. hŏnestĕ, *respectably; honourably; properly.*

hŏnor = honos; q.v.

hŏnōrābilis -e, *respectful*

hŏnŏrārīus -a -um, *done or given as an honour.*

hŏnŏrīfīcus -a -um, *causing honour, honouring;* adv. hŏnŏrīfīcē.

hŏnŏro -are, *to honour, show honour to, adorn, dignify;* partic. hŏnŏrātus -a -um, *honoured, distinguished, respected,* or in act. sense, *conferring honour;* adv. hŏnŏrātē.

hŏnōrus -a -um, *honourable.*

hŏnōs and hŏnŏr -ōris, m. *honour, a mark of honour or respect, distinction;* honoris causa, *with due respect,* or *to honour,* or *for the sake of;* personif., *Honour;* frequently, *an office of dignity, a public office;* also *an offering to the gods, sacrifice;* poet., *beauty, grace.*

hoplŏmăchus -i, *a gladiator.*

hōra -ae, f. *an hour, the twelfth part of a day or night;* hora quota est? *what's o'clock?* in horam vivere, *to live for the moment;* in gen., *time, season;* in plur. *a clock, diâl;* personif. *the Hours, goddesses who presided over the seasons.*

Hōrātīus -a -um, *name of a Roman gens.*

hordēum -i, n. *barley.*

hōrīa -ae, f. *a small fishing-boat.*

hornōtīnus and hornus -a -um, *of this year, this year's;* adv. hornō, *this year.*

hōrŏlŏgium -i, n. *a clock; a sundial or water-clock.*

horrĕo -ēre, *to bristle, be rough;* of the hair, *to stand on end;* of persons, *to shudder, dread.* Gerundive as adj. horrendus -a -um, *horrible, dreadful; awful, worthy of reverence.*

horresco horrescĕre horrŭi, *to stand on end, bristle, be rough;* of persons, *to tremble, shudder, begin to dread.*

horrĕum -i, n. *a barn, granary, store-house.*

horrĭbĭlis -e, *horrible, frightful, dreadful;* colloq., *astonishing, wonderful.*

horrĭdŭlus -a -um, *somewhat rough, unadorned.*

horrĭdus -a -um *rough, shaggy, bristly; shivering with cold.* Transf., *wild, savage; unpolished, uncouth; frightful, horrible.* Adv. horrĭdē, *roughly.*

horrĭfĕr -fĕra -fĕrum, *causing shudders of cold or fear.*

horrĭfĭco -are, *to make rough; to terrify.*

horrĭfĭcus -a -um, *causing terror, dreadful;* adv. horrĭfĭcē.

horrĭsŏnus -a -um, *sounding dreadfully.*

horror -ōris, m. *bristling, shuddering; roughness of speech; dread, fright,* esp. *religious dread, awe;* meton., *object of dread, a terror.*

horsum, *in this direction.*

hortāmen -ĭnis, n. and hortāmentum -i, n. and hortātĭo -ōnis, f. *exhortation, encouragement, incitement.*

hortātīvus -a -um, *of encouragement.*

hortātor -ōris, m. *an inciter, encourager.*

hortātus -ūs, m. *incitement, encouragement.*

Hortensĭus -a -um, *name of a Roman gens.*

hortor -ari, dep. *to exhort, incite, encourage;* esp *to harangue troops.*

hortŭlus -i, m. *a little garden;* plur. *grounds, a small park.*

hortus -i, m. *a garden;* in plur. *grounds, park.*

hospēs -pĭtis, m. and hospĭta -ae, f. (1) *a host, hostess.* (2) *a guest.* (3) *a guest-friend, friend.* (4) *a stranger;* used also like adj. *foreign.*

hospĭtālis -e, *of a guest or host; friendly, hospitable;* adv. hospĭtālĭter.

hospĭtālĭtās -ātis, f. *hospitality.*

hospĭtĭum -i, n. *hospitality;* meton., *a guest-chamber, inn, quarters.*

hostĭa -ae, f. *an animal slain in sacrifice, victim.*

hostĭcus -a -um, *foreign;* but usually *of the enemy, hostile;* n, as subst. *enemy territory.*

hostīlis -e, *of, by or for the enemy; like an enemy, unfriendly, hostile;* adv. hostīlĭter.

Hostīlĭus -a -um, *name of a Roman gens.*

hostīmentum -i, n. *compensation, requital.*

hostĭo -ire, *to requite, recompense.*

hostis -is, c. *a stranger;* but esp. *an enemy, foe, opponent.*

hūc, *hither, to this place;* huc (atque) illuc, *hither and thither.* Transf., *in addition to this; to this pitch, or degree;* interrog. hūcĭnĕ?

hŭi, *exclamation of surprise, eh! hallo!*

hŭiusmŏdi or hŭiuscĕmŏdi, *of this kind.*

hum-; see also um-.

hūmānĭtās -ātis, f. *humanity, human nature, human feeling; kindness; refinement, education, culture.*

hūmānĭtūs, *after the manner of men;* also *kindly.*

hūmānus -a -um, *human, of human beings;* m. as subst. *a human being; of good qualities, humane, kind, educated, civilized, refined.* Adv. hūmānē and hūmānĭtĕr, *humanly, politely, courteously, kindly.*

hŭmātĭo -ōnis, f. *burying, interment.*

hŭmĭlis -e, *on or near the ground, low, shallow.* Transf., *of rank,* etc., *humble, poor, insignificant;* of character, *abject or submissive;* of language, *mean, without elevation.* Adv. hŭmĭlĭtĕr, *humbly, meanly, abjectly.*

hŭmĭlĭtās -ātis, f. *nearness to the ground; lowness; shallowness.* Transf., *insignificance, obscurity; submissiveness, abjectness.*

hŭmo -are, *to cover with earth, bury; to perform any funeral rites over a corpse.*

hŭmus -i, f. *ground, earth, soil;* humi, *on the ground;* meton., *land, country.*

'Hyācinthus (-os) -i, m., *a beautiful youth, accidentally killed by Apollo.*

'hy̆ăcinthus -i, m. *a flower*, perhaps *the martagon lily.*

Hy̆ădes -um, f. *the Hyades, seven stars in the constellation Taurus.*

hy̆aena -ae, f. *hyena.*

hy̆ălus -i, m. *glass*; colour *glassgreen.*

Hydra -e, f. *many-headed water-snake, slain by Hercules*; also *a constellation.*

hydraulus -i, m. *a water organ.*

hydria -ae, f. *an urn, jug.*

hydrŏpĭcus -a -um, *dropsical.*

hydrops -ōpis, m. *the dropsy.*

hydrus -i, m. *a water-snake.*

Hy̆lās -ae, m. *companion of Hercules.*

Hy̆mĕn -ēnis and **Hy̆mĕnaeos** or -us -i, m. *Hymen, the god of marriage; the marriage song; a wedding* (esp. in plur).

hy̆perbăton -i, n. *transposition of words.*

hy̆perbŏlē -ēs, f. *exaggeration.*

Hy̆perbŏrĕi -ōrum, m. pl. *a people in the extreme north*; adj. **Hy̆perbŏrĕus** -a -um = *northern.*

hy̆pŏdidascălus -i, m. *an under-teacher.*

hy̆pomnēma -mătis, n. *a memorandum, note.*

I

i, the ninth letter of the Latin alphabet, used both as a vowel and as a consonant, formerly written j.

Iacchus -i, m. *name of Bacchus*; meton., *wine.*

iăcĕo iacēre iacŭi, *to lie, be situated; to lie low, be flat; to lie sick or over-thrown or killed;* of hair or clothes, *to hang loosely*; fig., *to be neglected, or despised; to be overthrown; to be cast down, dejected.*

iăcĭo iăcĕre iēci iactum. (1) *to lay.* (2) *to throw, cast, hurl; to fling away, shed; to scatter, diffuse; to let fall in speaking, utter.*

iactantĭa -ae, f. *boasting, bragging.*

iactātĭo -ōnis, f. *a tossing, shaking.* Transf., *violent emotion; boasting, ostentation.*

iactātor -ōris, m. *boaster, braggart.*

iactātus -ūs, m. *shaking, quick movement.*

iactĭto -are, *to toss about; to bandy.*

iacto -are, *to throw, cast, toss, fling away or about; to diffuse, spread, scatter; to harass, disturb* a person; *to broadcast* words; *to bring up, discuss* a subject; *to keep bringing up, to boast of.* With reflex, or in pass., *to gesticulate*; also *to "throw one's weight about", make oneself conspicuous.* Pres. partic. **iactans** -antis, *boastful*; adv. **iactanter.**

iactūra -ae, f. *throwing away; loss, sacrifice.*

iactus -ūs, m. *cast, throw*; intra iactum, *within range.*

iăcŭlābĭlis -e, *able to be thrown.*

iăcŭlātor -ōris, m. *a thrower*; esp. *a javelin-man, light-armed soldier.*

iăcŭlātrix -icis, f. *the huntress (Diana).*

iăcŭlor -ari, dep. *to throw a javelin; to shoot at a target; to throw, cast, hurl* a missile. Transf., *to make a verbal attack; to aim at, strive after; to utter.*

iăcŭlum -i, n. (1) *a dart, javelin.* (2) *a casting-net.*

iăcŭlus -a -um, *thrown, darting.*

iam, adv. *now, by now, already*; of future time, *immediately, presently, soon; henceforth; further, moreover; just, indeed;* iam diu, iam dudum, iam pridem, *now for a long time.*

iambēus -a -um, *iambic.*

iambus -i, m. *an iambus, a metrical foot (˘ ‾); an iambic poem.*

iamdūdum, iampridem; see iam.

lānĭcŭlum -i, n. *a hill west of Rome.*

iānĭtor -ōris, m. *door-keeper, porter.*

iānĭtrix -icis, f. *portress.*

iānthinus -a um, *violet-coloured.*

iānŭa ae, f. *door; entrance, approach.*

iānus -i, m. *a covered passage, arcade*; personif., **Iānus**, *Janus, an old Italian deity with two faces*; adj. **Iānālis** and **Iānŭālis** -e; hence also adj. **Iānŭārius** -a -um, *of Janus* or *of January*; Ianuarius (mensis), *January.*

Iāpyx -pygis, m. *a west-north-west wind.*

Iāsōn -ōnis, m. *leader of the Argonauts*; adj. **Iāsŏnius** -a -um.

iaspis -idis, f. *jasper.*

ibēr-; see hiber-.

ibī, adv. *there, at that place; then, thereupon; therein, in that matter or person.*

ibĭdem, adv. *in the same place; at that moment; in that matter.*

ibis, genit. ibis and ibĭdis, f. *the ibis.*

ibiscum = hibiscum; q.v.

Icărus -i, m. *son of Daedalus, drowned whilst flying with wings made by his father*; adj. **Icărĭus** -a -um, *of Icarus.*

iccirco = idcirco; q.v.

Icēni -orum, m. *a British people in East Anglia.*

ichneumon -ōnis, m. *the ichneumon.*

icio or **ico** ici ictum, *to strike, hit, smite*; esp., *to strike* a bargain.

ictĕrĭcus -a -um, *jaundiced.*

ictus -ūs, m. *a blow, stroke*; in music, *beat.*

Ida -ae and **Idē** -ēs, f. *name of two mountains, one in Crete, one in Phrygia, near Troy*; adj. **Idaeus** -a -um.

idcirco (iccirco), *on that account; for that reason or purpose.*

idem, ĕădem, ĭdem, *the same*; with dat., or ac, et, etc., *the same as*; by way of addition, *also*; of contrast, *yet*; alter idem, *a second self.*

Identĭdem, *repeatedly, again and again.*

idĕo, adv. *on that account, therefore; for that reason or purpose.*

idiōta -ae, m. *an ignorant, uneducated man.*

idōlon -i, n. *a spectre.*

idōnĕus -a -um, *fit, appropriate, suitable*; adv. **idōnĕē.**

Idŭmaea -ae, f. *a district in Palestine.*

Idūs -ŭum, f. pl. *the Ides, a day in the Roman month; the fifteenth day in March, May, July, October; the thirteenth in other months.*

iĕcur, iĕcŏris *and* iŏcinĕris, n. *the liver; supposed seat of the passions.*

iĕcuscŭlum -i, n. *a little liver.*

iĕiūnĭtās -ātis, f. *hungriness, emptiness; of style, etc., poverty, meagreness.*

iĕiūnĭum -i, n. *fast, abstinence, hunger; hence, leanness.*

iĕiūnus -a -um, *fasting, hungry, thirsty; of objects, poor, scanty; of spirit, poor, mean: of style, meagre, weak.* Adv. **iĕiūnē,** *of style, meagrely.*

ientācŭlum -i, n. *breakfast.*

iento -are, *to breakfast.*

igĭtur, *therefore, then; so, as I was saying;* to emphasize, *I say.*

ignārus -a -um: act., *ignorant, inexperienced in* (with genit.); pass., *unknown.*

ignāvĭa -ae, f. *idleness, listlessness; cowardice.*

ignāvus -a -um. (1) *idle, listless, inactive, inert, sluggish.* (2) *cowardly;* m. as subst. *a coward.* Adv. **ignāvē** and **ignāvĭtēr,** *lazily, without spirit.*

ignesco -ĕre, *to kindle, catch fire; to glow with passion.*

ignĕus -a -um, *fiery, burning, glowing, ardent.*

ignĭcŭlus -i, m. *a little fire, flame, spark.*

ignĭfĕr -fĕra -fĕrum, *fire-bearing, fiery.*

ignĭgēna -ae, m. *born of fire.*

ignĭpēs -pĕdis, *fiery-footed.*

ignĭpŏtens -entis, *ruler of fire.*

ignis is, m. *fire, conflagration; a watch-fire, beacon; a firebrand; lightning;* in gen., *glow, glitter.* Transf., *a fire-brand* (of war); *glow of passion; the beloved.*

ignōbĭlis -e, *unknown, obscure; of humble birth.*

ignōbĭlĭtās -ātis, f. *obscurity; humble birth.*

ignōmĭnĭa -ae, f. *degradation, disgrace, dishonour.*

ignōmĭnĭōsus -a -um: *of persons, disgraced;* of things, *ignominious, disgraceful.*

ignōrābĭlis -e, *unknown.*

ignōrantĭa -ae, and **ignōrātĭo** -ōnis, f. *ignorance.*

ignōro -are, *to be ignorant of, not to know;* rarely, *to neglect, ignore.*

ignosco -noscĕre -nōvi -nōtum, *to overlook, forgive, pardon.*

ignōtus -a -um: pass., *unknown; ignoble, obscure;* act., *ignorant.*

ilĕ -is, n., plur. **īlĭa** -ium, *intestines, guts; loin, flank;* **ilia ducere,** *to become broken-winded.*

Ilerda -ae, f. *a town in Spain (now Lerida).*

ilex -īcis, f. *holm-oak.*

Ilĭa -ae, f. *mother of Romulus and Remus.*

Ilĭăcus; see Ilion.

ilicet. (1) *a formula, it is all over.* (2) *immediately, forthwith.*

ilicētum -i, n. *ilex-grove.*

īlĭco (illĭco), *on the spot; immediately.*

ilignus -a -um, *of ilex or holm-oak.*

Ilĭŏn or **Ilĭum** -i, n. and **Ilĭŏs** -i, f. *Troy;* adj. **Ilĭus** and **Ilĭăcus** -a -um, *Trojan;* **Ilĭensēs** -ium, m. pl., *Trojans;* **Ilĭădēs** -ae, *a son of Troy;* **Ilĭăs** -adis, f. *a Trojan woman, or the Iliad of Homer.*

ill-, for words compounded from in/l . . ., see in-.

illā, *by that way.*

illāc, *by that way, there;* **illac facere,** *to belong to that party.*

illĕ, illa, illŭd (older forms olle and ollus), pron., *that, that yonder, that one;* emphatically, *that well-known;* in contrast with hic, *the former* (sometimes *the latter*); **ille qui, he who, the one who.**

¹**illic, illaec, illūc,** *that one;* interrog. *illicine?*

²**illīc** or **illī,** *there, at that place; therein, in that matter.*

illim, *from that place or person.*

illinc, *from that place; on that side.*

illō, *thither, to that place; to that matter or point.*

illūc, *thither, to that place; to that matter or person.*

Illўrii -ōrum, m. pl. *a people on the Adriatic.*

imāgĭnārĭus -a -um *imaginary.*

imāgĭnātĭo -ōnis, f. *imagination, fancy.*

imāgĭnor -ari, *to imagine, conceive, picture to oneself.*

imāgo -inis, f. *an image, copy, likeness; any representation, portrait, statue;* in plur. *waxen figures, portraits of ancestors; the shade or ghost of the dead; an echo; a mental picture, idea, conception;* rhet., *metaphor, simile, image;* abstr., *mere form, appearance, pretence.*

imbēcillĭtās -ātis, f. *weakness, feebleness.*

imbēcillus -a -um, *weak, feeble.* Compar. adv. **imbēcillĭus,** *somewhat weakly.*

imbellis -e, *unwarlike, not fighting, indisposed or unable to fight;* hence *feeble, peaceful, quiet.*

imber -bris, m. *a shower or storm of rain, pelting rain; a rain-cloud; water or any fluid; a shower of missiles.*

imberbis -e and **imberbus** -a -um *beardless.*

imbĭbo -bībĕre -bĭbi, *to drink in; mentally, to conceive; to resolve, determine.*

imbrex -icis, c. *a hollow tile used in roofing.*

imbrĭfĕr -fĕra -fĕrum, *rain-bringing.*

imbŭo -ŭĕre -ŭi -ūtum, *to wet, steep, saturate;* fig., *to stain, taint;* mentally, *to accustom, initiate, instruct.*

imĭtābĭlis -e, *that can be imitated.*

imĭtāmĕn -inis, n. *an imitation;* plur., *an image.*

imĭtāmentum -i, n. *imitating, imitation.*

imĭtātĭo -ōnis, f. *imitation; pretence.*

imĭtātŏr -ōris, m. and **imĭtātrix** -īcis, f. *an imitator.*

imĭtor -ari, dep. *to imitate, copy; to depict; to be like, act like.*

immădŭi, infin. -isse, *to have become moist.*

immānis -e, *enormous, immense, monstrous;* of character, *savage, horrible, inhuman.*

immānĭtās -ātis, f. *savagery, frightfulness.*

immansuĕtus -a -um, *untamed, wild.*

immātūrĭtās -ātis, f. *immaturity; untimely haste.*

immātūrus -a -um, *unripe, immature; untimely.*

immĕdĭcābilis -e, *incurable.*

immĕmŏr -mŏris, *unmindful, forgetful, heedless.*

immĕmŏrābilis -e, *indescribable; unworthy of mention; silent, uncommunicative.*

immĕmŏrāta -orum, n. pl. *things not related.*

immensĭtās -ātis, f. *immensity.*

immensus -a -um, *immense, vast boundless;* n. as subst., *immense size, immensity.*

immĕrens -entis, *not deserving, innocent.*

immergo -mergĕre -mersi -mersum, *to dip in, plunge in, immerse.*

immĕrĭtus -a -um: act., *not deserving (punishment), innocent;* pass., *undeserved;* adv. **immĕrĭtō,** *undeservedly.*

immersābilis -e, *that cannot be sunk.*

immētātus -a -um, *unmeasured.*

immigro -are, *to move away into*

immĭnĕo -ēre, *to project, overhang;* in time, *to be imminent, hang over; to threaten; to be on the watch or look out.*

immĭnŭo -ŭĕre -ŭi -ūtum, *to lessen, diminish; to weaken, infringe.*

immĭnūtĭo -ōnis, f. *diminishing, weakening;* rhet. *meiosis.*

immiscĕo -miscĕre -miscŭi mixtum, *to mix in, intermingle; to join with, unite.*

immĭsĕrābilis -e, *unpitied.*

immĭsĕrĭcors -cordis, *unmerciful;* adv. **immĭsĕrĭcordĭtēr.**

immissĭo -ōnis, n. *letting grow.*

immītis -e, *unripe, sour; harsh, cruel, stern.*

immitto -mittĕre -mīsi -missum. (1) *to send in, put in, work in; to engraft.* (2) *to let loose;* esp. *to let grow.* (3) *to let go against, launch against;* se in hostes, *to attack;* of feelings, *to instil.*

immixtus, partic. from immisceo; q.v.

immo, *on the contrary; yes indeed, no indeed; say rather.*

immōbilis -e, *immovable* or *hard to move; inexorable.*

immōdĕrātĭo -ōnis, f. *excess.*

immōdĕrātus -a -um, *immeasurable, endless; immoderate, unrestrained;* adv. **immōdĕrātē.**

immŏdestĭa -ae, f. *want of restraint.*

immŏdestus -a -um, *unrestrained, extravagant;* adv. **immŏdestē.**

immŏdĭcus -a -um, *immoderate,*

excessive; unrestrained, unbridled; adv. **immŏdĭcē.**

immŏdŭlātus -a -um, *inharmonious.*

immoenis; see immunis.

immōlātĭo -ōnis, f. *sacrificer.*

immōlātŏr -ōris, m. *a sacrifice.*

immōlĭtus -a -um, *built up, erected.*

immōlo -are, *to sacrifice; to devote to death, to slay.*

immŏrior -mŏri -mortuus, *to die in* or *over.*

immŏror -ari, *to remain in; to dwell on a subject.*

immorsus -a -um, *bitten; stimulated.*

immortālis -e, *deathless, immortal, imperishable.* Adv. **immortālĭter,** *infinitely.*

immortālĭtās -ātis, f., *immortality; everlasting renown; extreme happiness.*

immōtus -a -um, *unmoved, motionless; undisturbed, calm; firm, steadfast.*

immūgĭo -ire, *to bellow in* or *on.*

immulgĕo -ēre, *to milk into.*

immundus -a -um, *impure, foul.*

immūnĭo -ire, *to fortify.*

immūnis -e, *without duty free, exempt;* in gen., *not working* or *not contributing; not sharing in, devoid of; stainless.*

immūnĭtās -ātis, f. *exemption from offices* or *burdens; immunity.*

immūnītus -a -um, *unfortified; unpaved.*

immurmŭro -are, *to murmur at.*

immūtābilis, -e *unchangeable.*

immūtābilĭtās -ātis, f., *immutability.*

immūtātĭo -ōnis, f. *change, alteration,* rhet., *metonymy.*

¹**immūtātus** -a -um, *unchanged.*

²**immutatus** -a -um, partic. from immuto; q.v.

immūto -are, *to change, alter;* immutata oratio, *allegory.*

impācātus -a um, *restless.*

impallesco -pallescĕre -pallŭi, *to turn pale.*

impār -pāris, *unequal, uneven; unlike, discordant; ill-matched;* of numbers, *odd;* modi impares, *hexameter and pentameter.* Adv. **impārĭtēr,** *unevenly, unequally.*

impărātus -a -um *unprepared, unprovided.*

impart-; see impert-.

impastus -a -um, *unfed, hungry.*

impătibilis = impetibilis; q.v.

impătiens -entis *unable to endure, impatient;* adv. **impătienter.**

impătientia -ae, f. *impatience, inability to endure.*

impăvidus -a -um, *fearless undaunted;* adv. **impăvidē.**

impĕdīmentum -i, n. *hindrance, impediment;* in plur., *the baggage of an army* or *traveller.*

impĕdĭo -ire, *to entangle, ensnare, obstruct, surround; to embarrass, hinder, prevent.*

Hence partic. **impĕdītus** -a -um, *entangled, hindered;* milit., *hindered by baggage;* of places, *impassable, blocked;* in gen., *embarrassed. obstructed; awkward, complicated.*

impēdītio -ōnis, f. *hindrance.*

impello -pellēre -pūli -pulsum. (1) *to drive against, strike upon.* (2) *to set in motion; to incite, urge on, impel*; esp. *to push over one already slipping.*

impendĕo -ēre, *to hang over, overhang; to threaten, be close at hand.*

impendium -i, n. *expenditure, outlay, cost; interest on money.* Abl. as adv. **impendĭō**, colloq., *by much, very much.*

impendo -pendēre -pendi -pensum, *to weigh out;* hence *to expand, lay out*; partic. **impensus** -a -um, of price, *considerable, great*; in gen., *strong, vehement.* Adv. **impensē**, *at great cost; urgently, eagerly.*

impĕnĕtrābilis -e, *impenetrable.*

impensa -ae, f. *expense, outlay.*

impĕrātor -ōris, m. *commander, leader;* milit., *the commander-in-chief;* also of the Roman emperors.

impĕrātōrius -a -um, *of a general; imperial.*

impĕrātrix -īcis, f. *a female commander.*

imperceptus -a -um *unperceived, unknown.*

impercussus -a -um, *not struck.*

imperdītus -a -um, *not lain, undestroyed.*

imperfectus -a -um, *incomplete, unfinished.*

imperfossus -a -um *unstabbed, unpierced.*

impĕriōsus -a -um, *commanding;* sibi, *master of oneself;* in bad sense, *imperious, tyrannical.*

impĕrītia -ae, f. *inexperience, ignorance.*

impĕrīto -are, *to command, be in command, give an order.*

impĕrītus -a -um, *unskilled, inexperienced, ignorant;* adv. **impĕrītē.**

impĕrium -i, n. *an order, a command; the right to order, power, mastery, command;* esp. *political power, authority, sovereignty;* in imperio esse, *to hold office;* meton. *empire,* and in plur., *persons in authority.*

imperiūrātus -a -um, *by which no one swears falsely.*

impermissus -a -un, *forbidden.*

impĕro -are, *to impose;* hence *to requisition, order a thing; to order an action to be done, give orders to a person; to rule over, govern, command.*

imperterritus -um, *undaunted, fearless.*

impertio -ire, *to give a person a share in; to share a thing with a person, to impart, bestow.*

imperturbātus -a -um, *undisturbed, calm.*

impervius -a -um, *impassable.*

impĕtibilis -e, *insufferable.*

impĕto -ēre, *to make for, attack.*

impetrābilis -e: pass., *obtainable;* act., *successful.*

impetrātio -ōnis, f *obtaining by request.*

impetrio -ire, *to seek by favourable omens.*

impetro -are, *to get, accomplish, effect;* esp. *to obtain by asking.*

impĕtus -ūs, m. *an attack, onset;* any *rapid motion; mental impulse, passion, force.*

impexus -a -um *uncombed; rude uncouth.*

impiĕtās -ātis, f. *undutifulness; impiety unfilial conduct, disloyalty.*

impigĕr -gra -grum, *diligent, active,* adv. **impigrē.**

impigritās -ātis, f. *activity.*

impingo -pingēre -pēgi -pactum, *to thrust, dash, drive against;* fig., *to press upon, bring upon* a person.

impĭus -a -um, *undutiful, disloyal; godless, unfilial, unpatriotic;* adv. **impiē.**

implācābilis -e, *implacable;* compar. adv. **implācābilius.**

implācātus -a -um, *unappeased, unsatisfied.*

implĕo -plēre -plēvi -plētum, *to fill in, fill up, complete; to satisfy, content* a person; *to fulfil, perform; to contaminate.*

implexus -a -um *involved, entwined.*

implicātio -ōnis, f. *entwining, interweaving; embarrassment.*

implico -are, -āvi -ātum and -ŭi -ītum, *to enfold, entwine, entangle, involve; to associate, unite;* partic. **implicātus** -a -um, *confused, entangled;* adv. **implicĭtē,** *confusedly.*

implōrātio -ōnis, f. *an imploring for help.*

implōro -are, *to call upon with tears, to beseech, implore; to call for, beg for.*

implūmis -e, *unfledged.*

implŭo -plŭĕre -plŭi, *to rain upon.*

implŭvium -i, n. *an opening in the roof of a Roman house,* or *the basin for rain-water below it.*

impŏlītus -a -um, *rough, unpolished;* adv. **impŏlītē.**

impollūtus -a -um, *undefiled.*

impōno -pōnēre -pŏsŭi -pŏsĭtum, *to put, lay, place in* or *upon;* naut. *to put on board ship, to embark;* fig., *to lay* or *put upon, impose; to put over as master; to impose upon, cheat, deceive* (with dat.).

importo -are, *to bring in, import. introduce; to bring upon, cause.*

importūnĭtās -ātis, f. *self-assertion, inconsiderateness, insolence.*

importūnus -a -um, *unsuitable, ill-adapted, unfavourable; troublesome, tiresome;* of character, *assertive, inconsiderate.*

importŭōsus -a -um, *without harbours.*

impōs -pŏtis, *having no power over.*

impŏsĭtus -a -um, partic. from **impono**; q.v.

impŏtens -entis, *feeble, powerless;* with genit., *not master of;* esp. *unable to command oneself, violent, unrestrained.* Adv. **impŏtentĕr,** *weakly; intemperately, passionately.*

impŏtentia -ae, f. *poverty; lack of self-restraint, violent passion.*

impraesentiārum, *in present circumstances, for the present.*

impransus -a -um, *without breakfast, fasting.*

imprĕcor -ari, dep. *to invoke harm upon, to call down upon.*

impressio -ōnis, f. *physical pressure an attack, assault;* rhet., *distinct expression, emphasis;* philos., *sense-data, the impressions of the senses.*

im.primis, *especially, first of all.*

imprimo -primĕre -pressi -pressum, *to press upon or into; to seal, chase, emboss; to make by pressing, imprint.*

improbatio -ōnis, f. *disapproval, blame.*

improbĭtās -ātis, f. *badness, depravity.*

improbo -are, *to disapprove, blame, reject.*

improbŭlus -a -um, *somewhat wicked.*

improbus -a -um, *inferior, bad; morally bad, perverse, wilful; bold, persistent, mischievous;* m.pl. as subst., *the unpatriotic.* Adv. **improbē,** *badly, wickedly; impudently, boldly.*

improcerus -a -um, *small, low of stature.*

improdictus -a -um, *not postponed.*

impromptus -a -um, *not ready.*

improperātus -a -um, *unhurried, slow.*

improsper -ēra -ērum, *unfortunate;* adv. **improsperē.**

improvidus -a -um, *without forethought, improvident;* adv. **improvidē.**

improvisus -a -um, *unforeseen, un-expected;* (ex) improviso, *unexpectedly.*

imprudens -entis, *not foreseeing, not expecting; not knowing, unaware; unwise, rash, imprudent.* Adv. **imprudenter,** *without forethought; unawares; unwisely.*

imprudentia -ae, f., *lack of foresight or knowledge; ignorance; lack of wisdom, imprudence.*

impubēs -bĕris and -bis. (1) *youthful;* genae, *beardless;* plur. as subst. *boys.* (2) *unmarried.*

impudens -entis, *shameless, impudent;* adv. **impudenter.**

impudentia -ae, f. *shamelessness, impudence.*

impudicitia -ae, f. *incontinence, un-chastity.*

impudicus -a -um *shameless;* esp. *unchaste.*

impugnātio -ōnis, f. *assault, attack.*

impugno -are, *to attack, assail.*

impulsio -ōnis, f. *pressure;* fig., *impulse, instigation.*

impulsor -ōris, m. *instigator.*

impulsus -ūs, m. *pressure, impulse; incitement, instigation.*

impūnē, *with impunity, unpunished, safely.*

impūnĭtās -ātis, f. *impunity, exemption from punishment.*

impūnītus -a -um, *unpunished, exempt from punishment; unrestrained;* adv. **impūnītē.**

impūrātus -a -um, *vile, infamous.*

impūrĭtās -ātis, f. *moral impurity.*

impūrus -a -um, *unclean, foul; morally, impure, vile, infamous.* Adv. **impūrē.**

¹impŭtātus -a -um, *unpruned, untrimmed.*

²impŭtātus -a -um, partic. from imputo; q.v.

impŭto -are, *to lay to a charge, enter*

in an account; to reckon as a merit or fault in someone, to impute to; to reckon as a service done or gift given to someone.

imus -a -um, superl. from inferus; q.v.

¹in, prep. (1) with acc., *into, on to, towards, against;* of time, *until;* in omne tempus, *for ever;* in diem vivere, *to live for the moment;* of tendency or purpose, *for;* in adverbial phrases, indicating manner or extent: in universum, *in general;* in vicem, *in vices, in turn.* (2) with abl., *in, on, among;* of time, *in, at, within; in relation to* a person, *in the case of.*

²in-, inseparable particle, *without, not.*

inaccessus -a -um, *inaccessible.*

inacesco -ăcescĕre -ăcŭi, *to become sour.*

Ināchus (Ināchŏs) -i, m. *mythical king of Argos, father of Io, after whom the river Inachus in Argolis was named.*

inadfectātus -a -um, *natural, un-affected.*

inadsuētus -a -um, *unaccustomed.*

inadustus -a -um, *unsinged.*

inaedifĭco -are *to build in or upon; to build up, block up, barricade.*

inaequābĭlis -e, *uneven, unequal;* adv. **inaequābĭlĭter.**

inaequālis -e. *uneven, unequal, various; making unequal, disturbing.* Adv. **inaequālĭter,** *unevenly.*

inaequālĭtās -ātis, f. *unevenness.*

inaequo -are, *to make even, level up.*

inaestimābĭlis -e, *that cannot be estimated; hence priceless, inestim-able;* also *having no value.*

inaestŭo -are, *to boil, rage* (in).

inaffectātus, see inadf-.

ināmābĭlis -e, *unlovely, hateful.*

ināmaresco -ĕre, *to become bitter.*

inambĭtiōsus -a -um, *unpretentious.*

inambŭlātio -ōnis, f. *walking up and down.*

inambŭlo -are, *to walk up and down.*

inamoenus -a -um, *unlovely, dismal.*

inănĭmus -a -um, *lifeless, inanimate.*

inănio -ire, *to empty, make void.*

inānis -e, *empty, void;* equus, *riderless;* navis, *unloaded;* corpus, *soulless;* with genit. or abl., *empty of;* of persons, *empty-handed, poor;* fig., *vain, hollow, idle.* N. as subst., *empty space, emptiness, vanity.* Adv. **inānĭter,** *vainly, uselessly.*

inānĭtās -ātis, f. *emptiness, empty space; uselessness.*

inărātus -a -um, *unploughed, fallow.*

inardesco -ardescĕre -arsi, *to catch fire, burn, glow.*

ināresco -ārescĕre -ārŭi, *to become dry.*

inassuētus; see inadsuetus.

inattĕnŭātus, *undiminished, unimpaired.*

inaudax -ācis, *timid, fearful.*

inaudio -ire, *to hear;* esp. *to hear as a secret.*

inaudītus -a -um, *unheard* (esp. *of accused persons); unheard of, un-usual.*

inaugŭro -are: intransit., *to take the auguries;* transit., *to consecrate,* install, inaugurate; **inaugŭrātŏ**, after taking the auguries.

ĭnaures -ĭum, f. pl. earrings.

ĭnauro -are, to cover with gold, gild, enrich.

ĭnauspĭcātus -a -um, without auspices; **ĭnauspĭcātŏ**, without consulting the auspices.

ĭnausus -a -um, not dared, not attempted.

incaedŭus -a -um, not cut, unfelled.

incālesco -cālescĕre -călŭi, to glow, become warm or passionate.

incalfăcio -făcĕre, to heat, warm.

incallĭdus -a -um, ingenuous, unskilful; adv. **incallĭdē**.

incandesco -candescĕre -candŭi, to begin to whiten, esp. with heat.

incānesco -cānescĕre -cānŭi, to become grey.

incanto -are, to enchant.

incānus -a -um, quite grey.

incassum, in vain.

incastĭgātus -a -um, unchastised.

incautus -a -um, adj. incautious, careless, unwary; unguarded; not guarded against, unforeseen. Adv. **incautē**.

incēdo -cēdĕre -cessi -cessum, to walk, step, march; to proceed, come on; of feelings, with dat., to come over.

incĕlĕbrātus -a -um, not spread abroad.

incēnātus -a -um, without dinner.

incendiārĭus -a -um, fire-raising, incendiary.

incendĭum -i, n. a conflagration, fire; a torch, firebrand; of passion, fire, glow, heat; in gen., destruction, ruin.

incendo -cendĕre -cendi -censum, to kindle, set fire to, burn; to make bright, illumine; to fire with passion, excite, incense.

incensio -ōnis, f. burning.

incensus -a -um, not enrolled by the censor, unassessed.

incensus, partic. from incendo; q.v.

inceptio -ōnis, f. a beginning; an enterprise.

incepto -are, to begin; to attempt, undertake.

inceptor -ōris, m. a beginner.

inceptum -i, n. of partic. of incipio; q.v.

incerno -cernĕre -crēvi -crētum, to sift.

incēro -are, to cover with wax.

incertus -a -um, uncertain, doubtful, not sure. (1) as to fact: act., of persons, not knowing, doubting; pass., of things, not known, obscure; n. as subst. uncertainty. (2) as to action, hesitating, irresolute, undecided; incertam securim, not surely aimed.

incesso -cessĕre -cessivi, to attack, assail.

incessus -ūs, m. march, walk; manner of walking, gait; attack, assault; entrance, approach.

incesto -are, to defile, pollute, dishonour.

¹**incestus** -a -um, impure, defiled; sinful, unchaste; n. as subst. unchastity, incest. Adv. **incestē**.

²**incestus** -ūs, m. unchastity, incest.

inchŏo; see incoho.

¹**incĭdo** -cĭdĕre -cĭdi -casum, to fall in or upon; to fall in with; in hostem, to attack; in aes alienum, to run into debt; in mentionem, to happen to mention; of abstr. things, to occur, happen, " crop up."

²**incido** -cĭdĕre -cĭdi cīsum, to cut into, cut open; to inscribe, engrave an inscription; to make by cutting; to cut through; fig., to cut short, bring to an end, break off.

Hence, from partic., n. subst. **incīsum** -i, = incisio, q.v.; adv. **incīsē**, = incisim, q.v.

incīlĕ -is, n. a ditch, trench.

incīlo -are, to blame, scold.

incingo -cingĕre -cinxi -cinctum, to surround.

incĭno -ĕre, to sing.

incĭpĭo -cĭpĕre -cēpi -ceptum (cf. coepi), to take in hand, begin, commence; sometimes, to begin to speak. N. of partic. as subst. **inceptum** -i, a beginning; an attempt, enterprise.

incĭsim, in short clauses.

incĭsio -ōnis, f. a clause of a sentence.

incĭtāmentum -i, n. inducement, incentive.

incĭtātĭo -ōnis, f.: act., inciting, instigating; pass., violent motion, excitement, vehemence.

incĭto -are, to put into rapid motion, urge on, hasten; in pass., or with reflex., to quicken one's pace, hasten. Transf., to excite, spur, inspire; to incite against, stir up; to increase.

Hence partic. **incĭtātus** -a -um, rapid, vehement; equo incitato, at full gallop; compar. adv. **incĭtātĭus**, more violently.

¹**incĭtus** -a -um, in rapid motion.

²**incĭtus** -a -um, unmoved.

inclāmo -are, to call upon loudly; esp., to scold.

inclāresco -clārescĕre -clārŭi, to become famous.

inclēmens -entis, unmerciful, harsh, rough; adv. **inclēmentĕr**.

inclēmentĭa -ae, f. unmercifulness, harshness.

inclīnātĭo -ōnis, f. leaning, bending, inclination; in gen., movement, tendency, change; good-will, liking.

inclīno -are: transit., to bend, incline, turn, change, sometimes for the worse; in pass., to fall back, waver; intransit., to take a turn, verge, incline, change; milit., to waver, yield.

Hence partic. **inclīnātus** -a -um, inclined, prone; sinking; of the voice, low, deep.

inclūdo -clūdĕre -clūsi -clūsum, to shut in, enclose; esp. to block, obstruct, confine.

inclūsĭo -ōnis, f. shutting up, confinement.

inclŭtus, inclĭtus -a -um, celebrated, famous, renowned.

¹**incoctus** -a -um, uncooked, raw.

²**incoctus** -a -um, partic. from incoquo; q.v.

incōgĭtābĭlis -e, and **incōgĭtans** -antis, inconsiderate, thoughtless.

incōgitantia -ae, f. *thoughtlessness.*

incōgitātus -a -um: pass., *unstudied;* act., *inconsiderate.*

incōgito -are, *to contrive, plan.*

incognitus -a -um, *unexamined, unknown; unrecognized,* so *unclaimed.*

incŏho -are, *to take in hand, begin.* Hence partic. incŏhātus -a -um, *only begun, not finished.*

incŏla -ae, c. *an inhabitant, native;* sometimes *a foreign resident.*

incŏlo -cŏlĕre -cŏlŭi, *to inhabit, dwell* (in).

incŏlŭmis -e, *uninjured, safe and sound.*

incŏlŭmitās -ātis, f., *safety, preservation.*

incŏmĭtātus -a -um, *unaccompanied, without retinue.*

incommendātus -a -um, *not entrusted;* hence *without protector.*

incommŏdĭtās -atis, f. *inconvenience, disadvantage, unseasonableness.*

incommŏdo -are, *to be unpleasant or troublesome.*

incommŏdus -a -um, *inconvenient, troublesome, disagreeable, annoying;* n. as subst., *inconvenience, disadvantage;* incommodo tuo, *to your disadvantage;* adv. incommŏdē, *inconveniently.*

incommūtābilis -e, *unchangeable.*

incompărābilis -e, *incomparable.*

incompertus -a -um, *unknown.*

incompŏsĭtus -a -um, *not in order, irregular;* adv. incompŏsĭtē.

incomprěhensĭbilis -e, *impossible to catch; incomprehensible.*

incomptus -a -um, *unkempt, untrimmed; rude, rough.*

inconcessus -a -um, *not allowed, forbidden.*

inconcinnus -a -um, *awkward, inelegant, absurd.*

inconcussus -a -um, *unshaken, firm.*

inconditus -a -um, *not arranged, disorderly, confused;* adv. inconditē.

incongrŭens -entis, *not agreeing, inconsistent.*

inconsĭdērātus -a -um, *thoughtless, inconsiderate;* pass. *unadvised, reckless.* Adv. inconsĭdērātē, *without consideration.*

inconsōlābilis -e, *inconsolable; incurable.*

inconstans -stantis, *changeable, inconsistent;* adv. inconstantěr.

inconstantia -ae, f. *changeableness, inconsistency.*

inconsultus -a -um: pass., *not consulted;* act., *without asking advice, unadvised;* hence *inconsiderate, imprudent.* Adv. inconsultē, *indiscreetly.*

inconsumptus -a -um, *unconsumed, undiminished.*

incontāmĭnātus -a -um, *unpolluted.*

incontentus -a -um, *not stretched;* fides, *untuned.*

incontĭnens -entis, *incontinent;* adv. incontĭnenter.

incontĭnentia -ae, f. *incontinence.*

inconvĕnĭens -entis, *not suiting, dissimilar.*

incŏquo -cŏquĕre -coxi -coctum, *to boil in* or *with; to dye.*

incorrectus -a -um, *unamended, unimproved.*

incorruptus -a -um, *not corrupted, untainted, unspoilt, unimpaired;* adv. incorruptē.

incrēbresco -ĕre -crebrŭi and incrēbesco -ĕre -crebŭi, *to become strong* or *frequent; to increase, prevail.*

incrēdĭbilis -e, *not to be believed, incredible;* adv. incrēdĭbilĭtĕr.

incrēdŭlus -a -um, *incredulous.*

incrēmentum -i, n. *growth, increase;* meton, *the makings of anything,* also *offspring.*

increpito -are, *to call loudly to; to reproach, chide.*

incrĕpo -are -ŭi (-āvi) -ĭtum (ātum), *to rustle, make a noise; to be noised abroad;* transit., *to cause to sound.* Of persons, *to chide, rebuke.*

incresco -crescĕre -crēvi, *to grow* (in or on).

incrētus -a -um, partic. from incerno; q.v.

incrŭentātus and incrŭentus -a -um, *bloodless.*

incrusto -are, *to cover with rind, encrust.*

incŭbo -are -ŭi -ĭtum, *to lie in* or *on* or *over; to watch over; to hang over, lie heavily upon; to dwell in.*

inculco -are, *to trample in, press in, force upon, impress upon.*

inculpātus -a -um, *unblamed, blameless.*

¹incultus -a -um, *uncultivated, untilled;* n. pl. as subst. *wastes, deserts;* of dress, etc., *neglected, untidy;* in gen., *unpolished, rude.* Adv. incultē.

²incultus -ūs, m. *neglect, want of cultivation.*

incumbo -cumbĕre -cŭbŭi -cŭbĭtum, *to lie upon, put weight on, lean over, overhang; to apply oneself to, concentrate upon* a thing; *to incline to favour, further* a cause or movement.

incūnābŭla -orum, n. pl. *swaddling-clothes;* hence *infancy; birthplace;* in gen., *source, origin.*

incūrātus -a -um, *uncared-for, unhealed.*

incūrĭa -ae, f. *carelessness, neglect.*

incūriōsus -a -um: act., *careless, negligent;* pass., *neglected.* Adv. incūriōsē, *carelessly.*

incurro -currĕre -curri (cŭcurri) -cursum, *to run into;* milit., *to assail, attack, make a raid into.* Transf., *to attack with words, inveigh against; to come upon, fall in with;* in space, *to extend into;* in time, *to coincide with.*

incursio -ōnis, f. *a clash, onset; collision;* milit., *attack, raid, invasion.*

incurso -are, *to run against, strike against, attack.*

incursus -ūs, m. *an attack, assault;* of the mind, *efforts, impulses.*

incurvo -are, *to bend, curve, make crooked.*

incurvus -a -um, bent, curved, crooked.
incūs -cūdis, f. anvil.
incūsātio -ōnis, f. blame, reproach, accusations.
incūso -are, to accuse, blame, find fault with.
incussū, abl. sing. m., by a clash.
incustōdītus -a -um: pass., unwatched, unguarded; act., incautious, imprudent.
incūsus -a -um, forged, fabricated.
incūtio -cūtĕre -cussi -cussum, to dash, beat against; to strike into the mind, inspire with.
indāgātio -ōnis, f. investigation.
indāgātor -ōris, m. and indāgātrix -tricis, f. investigator, explorer.
¹indāgo -are, to track down, as hounds hunting; to explore, investigate.
²indāgo -īnis, f. surrounding and driving of game.
indĕ, thence, from there; hinc . . . inde, on this side . . . on that; from that cause, for that reason; from that time, thereafter; thereupon, then.
indēbitus -a -um, not owed, not due.
indēcens -centis, unbecoming, unseemly, unsightly; adv. indēcenter.
indēclinātus -a -um, unchanged, firm.
indēcor -ris or indēcōris -e, unbecoming, shameful,
indēcōro -are, to disgrace, dishonour.
indēcōrus -a -um, unbecoming; unseemly, unsightly; disgraceful. Adv. indēcōrē,
indēfensus -a -um, undefended, unprotected.
indēfessus -a -um, unwearied, indefatigable.
indēflētus -a -um, unwept.
indēlectus -a -um, not thrown down.
indēlēbilis -e, imperishable.
indēlibātus -a -um, uninjured, undiminished.
indemnātus -a -um, uncondemned.
indēplōrātus -a -um, unwept, unlamented.
indēprensus -a -um, undiscovered.
indēsertus -a -um, not forsaken.
indēstrictus -a -um, untouched, unhurt.
indētonsus -a -um, unshorn.
indēvītātus -a -um, unavoided.
index -dīcis, m. an informer; a sign, token; the forefinger; a title; a touchstone.
Indi -orum, m. pl. the Indians; sing. Indus -i, m. an Indian, or Ethiopian; an elephant-driver, mahout. Adj. Indus and Indicus -a -um, Indian; subst. India -ae, f. India.
indīcentē, abl. sing., not saying me indicente, without my saying a word.
indicium -i, n. (1) information, evidence; leave to give evidence; a reward for giving evidence. (2) any mark, sign, token.
¹indico -are, to make known, show, indicate; esp. to inform against, give evidence about; to put a price on, value.
²indico -dīcĕre -dixi -dictum, to make publicly known, proclaim; bellum, to declare war.

¹indictus -a -um, not said, unsaid: indictā causā, without a hearing.
²indictus -a -um, partic. from ¹indico, q.v.
indidem, from the same place or matter.
indifferens -entis, indifferent; neither good nor bad; unconcerned. Adv. indifferenter.
indigēna -ae, native.
indigentia -ae, f. want, need; desire.
indigeo -ēre -ŭi, to want, need, require; also to long for. Hence partic. indigens -entis, in need.
indiges -gĕtis, m. native, indigenous.
indigestus -a -um, disordered, confused, unarranged.
indignābundus -a -um, filled with indignation.
indignātio -ōnis, f. indignation; matter for indignation; rhet., the exciting of indignation.
indignitās -ātis, f. unworthiness, vileness; unworthy behaviour or treatment of others, indignity; indignation at unworthy treatment.
indignor -ari, dep. to consider unworthy, take as an indignity, be offended. Hence partic. indignans -antis, offended.
indignus -a -um: of persons, unworthy, not deserving (with abl. or genit.); of things, unworthy; hence disgraceful, shameful. Adj. indignē, unworthily, dishonourably; impatiently, indignantly.
indigus -a -um, needing, in want of.
indīligens -entis, negligent; adv. indīligenter.
indīligentia -ae, f. carelessness, negligence.
indipiscor -dipisci -deptus, dep., and indipisco -ĕre, to reach, obtain; to attain, get.
indireptus -a -um, unpillaged.
indiscrētus -a -um, unsevered, undivided; undistinguished; indistinguishable.
indisertus -a -um, not eloquent; adv. indisertē.
indispōsitus -a -um, disorderly, confused.
indissŏlūbilis -e, indissoluble.
indissŏlūtus -a -um, undissolved.
indistinctus -a -um, not separated; indistinct, obscure; unpretentious.
indivīdŭus -a -um, indivisible, inseparable; n. as subst. an atom.
indo -dĕre -dīdi -ditum, to put in or on; of names, to give, confer; of abstr. things, to introduce, cause, occasion.
indŏcilis -e, unteachable, untaught; ignorant, rude, artless; of subjects, unable to be learned.
indoctus -a -um, untaught, untrained, unskilled; adv. indoctē.
indŏlentia -ae, f. freedom from pain.
indŏlēs -is, f. native constitution or quality; nature, disposition, character, talents.
indŏlesco -dŏlescĕre -dŏlŭi, to be pained or grieved (at).
indŏmĭtus -a -um, untamed, wild.

indormio -ire -ivi -itum, *to sleep on or over; to be negligent about*, with dat. or in.

indōtātus -a -um, *without dowry; corpora, without funeral honours*; ars, *unadorned, poor*.

indŭ, archaic form of in; q.v.

indŭbĭtātus -a -um, *undoubted, certain*.

indŭbĭto -are, *to feel doubt of*, with dat.

indŭbius -a -um, *not doubtful, certain*.

indūciae = indutiae; q.v.

indūco -dūcĕre -duxi -ductum. (1) *to draw over, spread over* so as *to cover; also to cover* one thing *with another; to put on* clothing or arms; *to erase* writing, and hence *to revoke, make invalid*. (2) *to lead* or *bring in, to introduce; to enter in an account-book; to lead on, induce, persuade;* with animum, or in animum, *to decide* to do, or *decide that* a thing is so.

inductio -ōnis, f. *leading* or *bringing in, introduction;* animi, *resolve, intention;* erroris, *misleading;* in logic, *induction*.

inductū, abl. sing. m., *by instigation*.

indulgentia -ae, f. *tenderness, indulgence*.

indulgĕo -dulgēre -dulsi: intransit., *to be forbearing, patient, indulgent;* fig., *to give oneself up to, indulge in;* transit. *to grant, allow, concede*.
Hence partic. **indulgens** -entis. *kind, tender, indulgent;* adv. **indulgentēr**.

induo -dŭĕre -dŭi -dūtum, *to put on,* esp. of dress. Transf., *to clothe, surround, cover; to put on, assume, take up, engage in;* se, with dat. or in, *to fall into, fall on; to entangle*.

indūresco -dūrescĕre -dūrŭi, *to become hard* or *firm*.

indūro -are, *to make hard* or *firm*.

industrĭa -ae, f. *industry, diligence;* de (or ex) industria, *on purpose, intentionally*.

industrĭus -a -um, *diligent, painstaking, industrious;* adv. **industriē**.

indūtiae -arum, f. pl. *truce, armistice, suspension of hostilities*.

indūtus -ūs, m. *a putting on, clothing*.

inēbrio -are, *to intoxicate; to saturate*.

inēdia -ae, f. *fasting, abstinence from food*.

inēdĭtus -a -um, *not published, unknown*.

inēlēgans -antis, *not choice, tasteless;* adv. **inēlēgantēr**.

inēluctābilis -e, *from which one cannot struggle free*.

inēmŏrior -emori, dep. *to die in* or *at*.

inemptus -a -um, *unbought*.

inēnarrābilis -e, *indescribable, inexpressible;* adv. **inēnarrābilĭtēr**.

inēnōdābilis -e, *inextricable; inexplicable*.

inĕo -ire -ĭi -ĭtum: intransit., *to go* or *come in, to enter;* of time, *to begin, commence;* transit., *to go* or *come into; to enter upon, start, begin;* consilium, *to form a plan;* numerum, or rationem, *to go into figures, make a calculation*.

ineptĭa -ae, f. *foolish behaviour, silliness, absurdity*.

ineptĭo -ire, *to talk foolishly*.

ineptus -a -um, *unsuitable, tasteless, silly;* adv. **ineptē**.

inermis -e and **inermus** -a -um, *unarmed, defenceless, helpless*.

inerrans -antis, *not wandering, fixed*.

inerro -are, *to rove about in*.

iners -ertis, *untrained, unskilful; inactive, lazy, idle, calm; cowardly; ineffective, dull, insipid*.

inertĭa -ae, f. *unskilfulness; idleness*.

inērŭdītus -a -um, *illiterate, ignorant*.

inesco -are, *to allure, entice, deceive*.

inēvītābilis -e, *unavoidable*.

inexcĭtus -a -um, *unmoved, quiet*.

inexcūsābilis -e, *without excuse; inexcusable*.

inexercĭtātus -a -um, *untrained, unpractised*.

inexhaustus -a -um, *unexhausted*.

inexōrābilis -e, *not to be moved by entreaty, stern, severe*.

inexperrectus -a -um, *not awakened*.

inexpertus -a -um: act., *inexperienced in, unacquainted with;* pass., *untried, untested, unattempted*.

inexpiābilis -e, *inexpiable; implacable irreconcilable*.

inexplēbilis -e, *insatiable*.

inexplētus -a -um, *unfilled, insatiate*.

inexplicābilis -e, *that cannot be untied; intricate, difficult; inexplicable, beyond explanation; inconclusive, without result*.

inexplōrātus -a -um, *unexplored, uninvestigated;* abl., **inexplōrātō**, *without reconnoitring*.

inexpugnābilis -e, *unconquerable, impregnable*.

inexspectātus -a -um, *unlooked-for, unexpected*.

inexstinctus -a -um, *unextinguished, inextinguishable*.

inexsŭpĕrābilis -e, *insurmountable*.

inextrīcābilis -e, *that cannot be disentangled* or *unravelled*.

infabrē, *unskilfully*.

infabrĭcātus -a -um, *unwrought, unfashioned*.

infăcētiae (**infĭc-**) -arum, f. pl. *crudity*.

infăcētus and **infĭcētus** -a -um, *dull, crude, without humour* or *wit;* adv. **infăcētē** (**infĭc-**).

infācundus -a -um, *not eloquent*.

infāmĭa -ae, f. *dishonour, disgrace;* also *a cause of disgrace*.

infāmis -e, *disgraced, disreputable*.

infāmo -are, *to put to shame, disgrace*.

infandus -a -um, *unutterable, abominable*.

infans -fantis, *speechless, unable to speak;* esp. of children; as subst., *a little child*. Transf., *tongue-tied, embarrassed; youthful, fresh; childish, silly*.

infantĭa -ae, f. *inability to speak; slowness of speech; infancy*.

infarcio (**infercio**) -ire, *to stuff in, cram in*.

infătŭo -are *to make a fool of*.

infaustus -a -um, *unlucky, unfortunate,*

infector -ōris, m. *a dyer.*

iinfectus -a -um, *unworked, umwrought; not done, unfinished, incomplete; reddere infectum, to make void, revoke; impracticable, impossible.*

¹**infectus**, partic. from inficio; q.v.

infēcundĭtās -ātis, f. *barrenness, sterility.*

infēcundus -a -um, *barren, sterile.*

infēlīcĭtās -ātis, f. *ill-luck, misfortune.*

infēlix -icis, *unfruitful, barren; arbor, the gallows. Transf., unhappy, unlucky; act. sense, causing unhappiness.* Adv. **infēlīcĭtĕr,** *unluckily.*

infenso -are, *to attack, ravage.*

infensus -a -um, *hostile, aggressive; of weapons, aimed, ready; in spirit, embittered, dangerous.* Adv. **infensē.**

infĕr -a -um, **infĕri** -orum; see inferus.

infĕrĭae -arum, f. *offerings in honour of the dead.*

infercio; see infarcio.

infĕrĭor, infĕrĭus; see infra and inferus.

infernē, *on the lower side, beneath.*

infernus -a -um, *below, coming from below; of the lower world, infernal.* As subst., m. pl. **infĕri,** *the shades;* n. pl. **infernă,** *the lower world.*

infĕro inferre intŭli inlātum, *to carry in, to put or place on;* templis ignes inferre, *to set fire to;* milit., signa in hostem, *to attack, charge;* bellum, with dat., *to make war on;* se inferre, and pass. inferri, *to betake oneself, to go;* of abstract things, *to bring on, introduce, occasion;* in accounts, *to enter;* in logic, *to infer, conclude.*

infĕrus -a -um, *below, lower, southern; o the lower world.* M. pl. as subst., **infĕri** -orum, *the dead, the lower world.* Compar. **infĕrĭor** -ius, *lower,* ex inferiore loco dicere *to speak from the body of the court; of time, later, junior;* of number, rank, etc. *lower, inferior.* Superl. (1) **infĭmus** (**infŭmus**) -a -um *lowest;* ab infima ara, *from the bottom of the altar; of rank, etc., lowest, meanest.* Superl. (2) **imus** -a -um, *lowest;* n. as subst., *the bottom; of tone, deepest, lowest; of time, last;* n. as subst., *the end.*

infervesco -fervescĕre -ferbŭi *to begin to boil, grow hot.*

infesto -are, *to attack, disquiet.*

infestus -a -um; act., *aggressive, hostile, dangerous;* pass., *infested, beset, unsafe.* Adv. **infestē,** *in a hostile manner.*

infĭcētus, infĭcētē = infacetus, infacete; q.v.

inficio -ficĕre -fēci -fectum. (1) *to tinge, dye, stain; to steep, imbue.* (2) *to poison, taint, corrupt.*

infĭdēlis -e, *untrue, disloyal, faithless;* adv. **infĭdēlĭtĕr.**

infĭdēlĭtās -ātis, f. *disloyalty.*

infĭdus -a -um, *untrue, disloyal.*

infīgo -fīgĕre -fixi -fixum, *to fix, fasten or thrust in; to imprint, impress.*

infĭmus -a -um, superl. of inferus. q.v.

infindo -findĕre -fīdi -fissum, *to cut into.*

infīnĭtās -ātis, f. *infinity, endlessness.*

infīnĭtĭo -ōnis, *infinity.*

infīnĭtus -a -um, *infinite, unbounded, immense;* n. as subst., *infinite space; of time, endless, unceasing; of number, countless;* also *indefinite, general.* Adv. **infīnĭtē,** *infinitely, endlessly.*

infirmātĭo -ōnis, f. *weakening; refuting, invalidating.*

infirmĭtās -ātis, f. *weakness, feebleness; instability, fickleness.*

infirmo -are, *to weaken, impair, shake; to refute; to annul.*

infirmus -a -um, *weak, feeble; timorous.* Adv. **infirmē,** *weakly, faintly.*

infit, defective, *he (or she) begins;* esp *begins to speak.*

infĭtĭālis -e, *negative, containing a denial.*

infĭtĭās ĭre, *to deny.*

infĭtĭātĭo -ōnis, f. *denying.*

infĭtĭātor -ōris, m. *a denier;* esp. *one who denies a debt or deposit.*

infĭtĭor -ari, *to deny;* esp. *to deny a debt, refuse to restore a deposit.*

inflammātĭo -ōnis f. *setting fire; animorum, inspiration.*

inflammo -are, *to kindle, set fire to; to inflame, excite.*

inflātĭo -ōnis, f. *inflation, flatulence.*

inflātus -ūs, m. *a blowing into, blast; inspiration.*

inflecto -flectĕre -flexi -flexum, *to bend, bow, curve. Transf., to warp, change; to sway, affect; to modulate the voice.*

inflētus -a -um, *unwept, unlamented.*

inflexĭo -ōnis, f. *bending, swaying.*

inflexus -ūs, m. *bending, curving.*

infligo -flīgĕre -flixi -flictum, *to strike, knock, dash against; to inflict a blow cause damage.*

inflo -are, *to blow into; to play on wind instruments; to give a blast; to blow out, puff out.* Transf., *to inspire; to puff up, elate.*

Hence partic., **inflātus** -a -um, *inflated, swollen; puffed up, pompous; of style, turgid.* Compar. adv. **inflātĭus,** *too pompously; on a grander scale.*

influo -flŭĕre -fluxi -fluxum, *to flow in. Transf., to steal in to stream in, rush in.*

infŏdĭo -fŏdĕre -fōdi -fossum, *to dig in, bury.*

informātĭo -ōnis, f. *conception, idea.*

informis -e, *formless, shapeless; deformed, hideous.*

informo -are, *to give form to, to shape, fashion;* mentally, *to form, dispose; to form an idea or conception of.*

infortūnātus -a -um, *unfortunate, miserable.*

infortūnĭum -i, n *misfortune, ill luck; punishment.*

infrā. Prep., with acc., *below, under,* in position, size, rank; in time, *later than.* Adv., *below, underneath; in the lower world; to the south;* in rank, *lower.* Compar., **infĕrĭus,** *lower down.*

infractĭo -ōnis, f. *breaking*; animi, *dejection.*

infrăgĭlis -e, *unbreakable, strong.*

infrĕmo -frĕmĕre -frĕmŭi, *to growl.*

infrēnātus -a -um, *without bridle*, see also infreno.

infrendĕo -ĕre, *to gnash with the teeth.*

infrēnis -e and **infrēnus** -a -um, *without bridle, unbridled.*

infrēno -are, *to bridle, rein in, to restrain, check.*

infrĕquens -entis, *scanty, thin, not crowded*; of places, *not full, scantily populated*; of time, *infrequent*; of persons, *not doing a thing often.*

infrĕquentĭa -ae, f. *fewness, scantiness thinness*; of places, *emptiness, loneliness.*

infringo -fringĕre -frēgi -fractum, *to break; to weaken, impair, discourage.* Hence partic. **infractus** -a -um, *broken, weakened, impaired.*

infrons -frondis, *leafless.*

infructŭōsus -a -um, *unfruitful, unproductive.*

infūcātus -a -um, *coloured.*

infŭla -ae, f. *a band bandage;* esp. *a fillet, a headband worn by priests, suppliants,* etc.

infundo -fundĕre -fūdi -fūsum, *to pour in or on;* with dat., *to pour out for,* hence *to administer;* se infundere, or pass. infundi, *to pour over.*

infusco -are, *to make dark, blacken; to disfigure, stain.*

ingĕmĭno -are: transit., *to redouble, repeat;* intransit., *to be redoubled, to increase.*

ingĕmisco -gĕmiscĕre (-escĕre) -gĕmŭi, *to sigh or groan over.*

ingĕmo -ĕre, *to sigh, groan over* (with dat.).

ingĕnĕro -are, *to implant, generate.*

ingĕnĭōsus -a -um, *talented, able,* of things, *requiring talent* or *naturally fit, adapted.* Adv. **ingĕnĭōsē,** *cleverly.*

ingĕnĭum -i, n. *nature, natural quality, constitution, character,* esp. *mental power, ability, genius;* meton., *a man of genius,* or *a clever invention.*

ingens -entis, *monstrous, vast, enormous.*

ingĕnŭĭtās -ātis, f. *free birth; noble-mindedness, uprightness, frankness.*

ingĕnŭus -a -um, *native, natural, innate; free-born, of free birth, worthy of a free man, noble, honourable, frank.* Adv. **ingĕnŭē.**

ingĕro -gĕrĕre -gessi gestum, *to carry or put in or upon; to press upon, force upon;* of abuse, *to heap on a person.*

ingigno only in perf. indic. **ingĕnŭi,** *I implanted,* and perf. partic. **ingĕnĭtus** -a -um, *implanted.*

inglōrĭus -a -um, *without fame, inglorious, undistinguished.*

inglŭvĭēs -ēi, f. *crop, maw;* meton., *gluttony.*

ingrātĭis or **ingrātīs,** *unwillingly.*

ingrātus -a -um. (1) *unpleasant,* *unpleasing.* (2) *unthankful, unrewarding.* Adv. **ingrātē,** *unwillingly; ungratefully.*

ingrăvesco -ĕre, *to become heavy; to become a burden,* or *become weary;* poet., *to become pregnant.*

ingrăvo -are, *to weigh down; to aggravate.*

ingrĕdĭor -grĕdi -gressus, dep. *to step in, enter, go in; to walk.* Transf., *to enter upon, begin on;* with infin., *to begin to.*

ingressĭo -ōnis, f. *an entering, going in; walking, gait, pace.* Transf., *beginning.*

ingressus -ūs, m. *going in, entering, entry;* milit., *an inroad; walking, stepping, movement.* Transf., *beginning.*

ingrŭo -ŭĕre -ŭi, *to fall upon, assail, attack.*

inguĕn -guĭnis, n. *the groin.*

ingurgĭto -are, with reflex., *to plunge oneself,* or *to glut, gorge oneself, gormandize.*

ingustātus -a -um, *untasted.*

inhăbĭlis -e, *unmanageable; unfit, ill-adapted.*

inhăbĭtābĭlis -e, *uninhabitable.*

inhăbĭto -are, *to inhabit.*

inhaerĕo -haerĕre -haesi -haesum, *to stick in, cling to, cleave to.*

inhaeresco -haerescĕre -haesi -haesum, *to adhere to, begin to cling to.*

inhālo -are, *to breathe upon.*

inhĭbĕo -ĕre -ŭi -ĭtum. (1) *to hold in, check, restrain;* naut., inhibere remis, navem retro inhibere, *to back water.* (2) *to practise, use, employ.*

inhĭbĭtĭo -ōnis, f. *restraining;* remigum, *backing water.*

inhĭo -are, *to gape;* hence *to covet, desire, long for.*

inhŏnesto -are, *to disgrace.*

inhŏnestus -a -um: morally, *degraded, dishonoured;* of things, *dishonourable, shameful;* physically, *ugly, unsightly.* Adv. **inhŏnestē,** *dishonourably.*

inhŏnōrātus -a -um, *not honoured; unrewarded.*

inhŏnōrus -a -um, *dishonoured.*

inhorrĕo -ĕre, *to bristle.*

inhorresco -horrescĕre -horrŭi, *to begin to bristle, to bristle up; to shudder, quiver,* esp. *from fright.*

inhospĭtālis -e, *inhospitable.*

inhospĭtālĭtās -ātis, f. *want of hospitality.*

inhospĭtus -a -um, *inhospitable.*

inhūmānĭtās -ātis, f. *cruelty, inhumanity; incivility, discourtesy; stinginess, niggardliness.*

inhūmānus -a -um, *cruel, barbarous, inhuman; rude, uncivil; uncivilized.* Adv. **inhūmānē,** *inhumanly;* **inhūmānĭtĕr,** *uncivilly.*

inhŭmātus -a -um, *unburied.*

ĭnĭbi, adv., *therein, in that place;* of time, *near at hand.*

inĭcĭo -Icĕre -iĕci -iectum. (1) *to throw in, put in or into.* Transf., *to cause, inspire, occasion;* in conversation, *to throw in.* (2) *to throw on or over;*

manum inicere, *to lay hands on, appropriate, take possession of.* Transf., *to impose, lay on.*

iniectio -ōnis, f. *laying on.*

iniectus -ūs, m. *throwing on or over.*

inimicitia -ae, f. *enmity.*

inimico -are, *to make hostile, set at variance.*

inimīcus -a -um, *unfriendly, adverse, hostile; of things, hurtful, prejudicial;* m. or f. as subst., *enemy, foe.* Adv. inimīcē, *in an unfriendly manner.*

iniquitās -ātis, f. *unevenness; unfavourableness, difficulty; unfairness, injustice, unreasonableness.*

iniquus -a -um, *uneven, unequal.* Transf., *of things, excessive, unbalanced, adverse, disadvantageous; of contests, ill-matched; of terms, unfair; of persons, etc. unfair, unfavourable; perverse, disgruntled;* animo iniquo ferre, *to take badly;* m. pl. as subst. *enemies.* Adv. inīque, *unequally; unfairly, adversely.*

initio -are, *to initiate.*

initium -i, n. *a beginning;* ab initio, *from the start;* initio, *at the start.* Transf., in plur. *elements, first principles; auspices; the beginning of a reign; a secret worship, mysteries.*

initus -ūs, m. *an entrance; a beginning.*

iniūcunditās -ātis, f. *unpleasantness.*

iniūcundus -a -um, *unpleasant.* Compar. adv. iniūcundius.

iniūdicātus -a -um, *undecided.*

iniungo -iungĕre -iunxi -iunctum, *to join, attach, fasten to; to inflict upon, bring upon.*

iniūrātus -a -um, *unsworn.*

iniūria -ae, f. *injury, injustice, wrong;* iniuriā, *wrongly.* Transf., *a possession wrongfully obtained; revenge for an affront.*

iniūriōsus -a -um, *doing wrong, unjust; harmful.* Adv. iniūriōsē, *wrongfully.*

iniūrius -a -um, *wrongful, unjust.*

iniussū, abl. sing. m. *without orders.*

iniussus -a -um, *unbidden, spontaneous.*

iniustitia -ae, f. *injustice; severity.*

iniustus -a -um, *unfair, unjust; harsh, oppressive;* n. as subst. *injustice.* Adv. iniustē.

inlābĕfactus -a -um, *unshaken, firm.*

inlābor -lābi -lapsus, dep. *to glide into, fall into or upon.*

inlābōro -are, *to labour at.*

inlăcessītus -a -um, *unattacked, unprovoked.*

inlacrīmābilis -e, *unwept; not to be moved by tears, pitiless.*

inlacrīmo -are, and inlacrīmor -ari, dep. *to weep over, bewail.*

inlaesus -a -um, *unhurt, uninjured.*

inlaetābilis -e, *gloomy, cheerless.*

inlăquĕo -are, *to entrap, ensnare.*

inlaudātus -a -um, *unpraised, obscure; not to be praised, bad.*

inlautus =; q.v.

inlĕcebra -ae, f. *allurement, attraction, charm; a decoy bird.*

inlĕcebrōsus -a -um, *attractive, enticing;* adv. inlĕcebrōsē.

inlectus -a -um, *unread.*

inlectus -ūs, m. *enticement.*

inlectus -a -um, partic. of inlicio; q.v.

inlĕpĭdus -a -um, *inelegant, rude unmannerly;* adv. inlĕpĭdē.

inlex -lĭcis, c. *a decoy, lure.*

inlex -lēgis, *lawless.*

inlībātus -a -um, *undiminished, unimpaired.*

inlībĕrālis -e, *unworthy of a free man, ungenerous, sordid, mean;* adv. inlībĕrālĭtĕr.

inlībĕrālĭtās -ātis, f. *stinginess, meanness.*

inlicio -līcĕre -lexi -lectum, *to entice, allure, decoy.*

inlĭcĭtātor -ōris, m. *a sham bidder at an auction, puffer.*

inlĭcĭtus -a -um, *not allowed, illegal.*

inlīdo -līdĕre -lisi -lisum, *to strike beat, dash against.*

inlĭgo -are, *to bind, tie, fasten, attach connect; to entangle, impede.*

inlĭmis -e, *free from mud, clean.*

inlĭno -lĭnĕre -lēvi -lĭtum, *to smear, daub; to spread something on a surface or to spread a surface with something.*

inlĭquĕfactus -a -um, *molten, liquefied.*

inlittĕrātus -a -um, *ignorant, illiterate.*

inlōtus (-lautus, -lūtus) -a -um, *unwashed, unclean.*

inlūcesco (-isco) -lūcescĕre -luxi, *to become light, begin to shine;* inlucescit, *it grows light, ts daylight.*

inlūdo -lūdĕre -lūsi -lūsum, *to play with, sport with; to mock, laugh at, ridicule; to maltreat.*

inlūmĭno -are, *to light up, illuminate; to make clear, set off, adorn.* Adv. from perf. partic. inlūmĭnātē, *luminously, clearly.*

inlūsio -ōnis, f. *irony.*

inlustris -e, *light, bright, brilliant; clear, plain, evident; distinguished, famous.* Compar. adv. inlustrius, *more clearly, more distinctly.*

inlustro -are, *to light up, make bright; to bring to light, make clear; to make illustrious, do honour to.*

inlŭvĭēs -ēi, f. *inundation, flood; mud, dirt.*

inm-; see imm-.

innābilis -e, *that cannot be swum in.*

innascor -nasci -nātus, dep. *to be born in, arise in or upon.* Hence partic. innātus -a -um, *innate, inborn.*

innāto -are, *to swim into; to swim or float in or upon.*

innecto -nectĕre -nexŭi -nexum, *to tie in, fasten, weave together;* fig., *to put together, connect, entangle, implicate.*

innītor -niti -nixus dep., *to lean upon support oneself by.*

inno -nare, *to swim in or on; to flow over; to sail over, navigate.*

innŏcens -entis, *harmless, inoffensive, blameless;* adv. innŏcentĕr.

innŏcentia -ae f. *harmlessness, innocence, integrity.*

innŏcŭus -a -um: act., *innocuous, harmless, blameless*; pass., *unhurt, unharmed.* Adv. **innŏcŭē**, *harmlessly.*

innōtesco -nōtescĕre -nōtŭi *to become known* or *noted.*

innŏvo -are, *to renew.*

innoxĭus -a -um: act., *harmless, innocent*; pass.. *unhurt, unharmed.*

innŭba -ae, *unmarried, without a husband.*

innūbĭlus -a -um, *unclouded, clear.*

innūbo -nūbĕre -nupsi -nuptum, *to marry into.*

innŭmĕrābĭlis -e, *countless, innumerable*; adv. **innŭmĕrābĭlĭtĕr.**

innŭmĕrābĭlĭtās -ātis, f. *an infinite number.*

innŭmĕrālis -e, and **innŭmĕrus** -a -um, *countless, innumerable.*

innŭo -nŭĕre -nŭi -nūtum, *to give a nod to, make a sign to.*

innupta -ae, *unmarried*; as subst., *a maiden.*

innūtrĭo -ire, *to bring up in* or *among.*

inoblītus -a -um. *mindful.*

inobrūtus -a, -um, *not overwhelmed.*

inobservābĭlis -e, *imperceptible.*

inobservantĭa -ae, f. *negligence, carelessness.*

inobservātus -ā -um, *unperceived.*

inoccĭdŭus -a -um, *never setting.*

inoffensus -a -im, *not struck, not stumbling; unhindered, unobstructed.*

inofficĭōsus -a -um, *undutiful, disobliging.*

inŏlens -entis, *without smell.*

inŏlesco -ŏlescĕre -ŏlĕvi, *to grow in* or *on.*

inōmĭnātus -a -um, *inauspicious, unlucky.*

inŏpĭa -ae, f. *want of means, need, poverty; helplessness.*

inŏpīnans -antis, *not expecting, unawares*; adv. **inŏpīnantĕr.**

inŏpīnātus -a -um; pass., *unexpected, unlooked for; (ex) inopinato, unexpectedly*; act., *not expecting.*

inŏpīnus -a -um, *unexpected, unlooked for.*

inops -ŏpis, *poor, helpless, in need; of language, weak, poor.*

inōrātus -a -um, *not brought forward and heard.*

inordĭnātus -a -um, *disorderly, in confusion:* n. as subst. *disorder.*

inornātus -a -um, *unadorned, plain; unpraised, uncelebrated.*

inp-; see **imp-.**

inquam, inquis, inquit, etc.; perf., inquii; *say.*

inquĭēs -ētis, *unquiet, restless.*

inquĭēto -are, *to disturb.*

inquĭētus -a -um, *unquiet, restless.*

inquĭlīnus -i, m. *tenant, lodger.*

inquĭno -are, *to befoul, pollute, stain, corrupt.* Hence partic. **inquĭnātus** -a -um, *dirty, foul, polluted;* adv. **inquĭnātē.**

inquīro -quīrĕre -quīsivi -quīsītum, *to search for; to investigate, inquire into;* legal, *to search for evidence against anyone.*

inquīsītĭo -ōnis, f. *looking for, search;* esp. *search for evidence against; a looking into, investigation, inquiry.*

inquīsītor -ōris, m. *an inquirer; investigator;* legal, *one who searches for evidence to support an accusation.*

inrāsus -a -um, *unshaved.*

inraucescō -raucescĕre -rausi, *to become hoarse.*

inrēlĭgātus -a -um, *unbound.*

inrēlĭgĭōsus -a -um, *irreligious, impious;* adv. **inrēlĭgĭōsē.**

inrĕmĕābĭlis -e, *from which there is no return.*

inrĕpărābĭlis -e, *that cannot be restored, irrecoverable.*

inrĕpertus -a -um, *not discovered.*

inrēpo -rēpĕre -repsi -reptum, *to creep, crawl in; to insinuate oneself.*

inreprĕhensus -a -um, *unblamed, blameless.*

inrēquĭētus -a -um, *restless, troubled.*

inrĕsectus -a -um, *uncut.*

inrĕsŏlūtus -a -um, *not loosed, not slackened.*

inrētĭo -ire, *to catch in a net, entangle.*

inrĕtortus -a -um, *not turned* or *twisted back.*

inrĕvĕrens -entis, *disrespectful;* adv. **inrĕvĕrentĕr.**

inrĕvĕrentĭa -ae, f. *want of respect, irreverence.*

inrĕvŏcābĭlis -e, *that cannot be called back, irrevocable; unalterable, implacable.*

inrĕvŏcātus -a -um, *not called back.*

inrīdĕo -rīdēre -risi -risum, *to laugh at, mock, ridicule.*

inrīdĭcŭlē, *without wit* or *humour.*

inrīdĭcŭlo, predicative dat., *for a laughing-stock.*

inrĭgātĭo -ōnis, f. *watering, irrigation.*

inrĭgo -are, *to conduct any liquid, to diffuse; to water, irrigate, inundate, flood over.*

inrĭgŭus -a -um: act., *watering, irrigating; refreshing;* pass., *watered, soaked.*

inrīsĭo -ōnis, f. *laughing at, mocking, derision.*

inrīsor -ōris, m. *a laugher, mocker, derider.*

inrīsus -ūs, m. *laughter, mockery, derision;* dat. inrisui, *for a laughing-stock.*

inrītābĭlis -e, *irritable, easily roused.*

inrītāmen -ĭnis, n. *incitement, inducement.*

inrītāmentum -i, m. *incitement, incentive.*

inrītātĭo -ōnis, f. *stirring up, provoking, incitement.*

inrīto -are, *to stir up, stimulate, incite, excite.*

inrĭtus -a -um, *void, invalid; vain, ineffectual, useless.*

inrŏgātĭo -ōnis, f. *the imposing of fine or penalty.*

inrŏgo -are, *to propose a measure against anyone; to inflict, impose.*

inrŏro -are, *to moisten (with dew); to trickle down upon.*

inrumpo -rumpĕre -rūpi -ruptum, *to break in, burst in, rush in.*

inrŭo -rŭĕre -rŭi: transit., *to fling in*; intransit., *to rush in.*

inruptio -ōnis, f. *bursting in irruption.*

inruptus -a -um, *unbroken, unsevered.*

insălūbris -e, *unhealthy.*

insălūtātus -a -um, *ungreeted.*

insănābilis -e, *incurable.*

insānia -ae, f. *madness, frenzy, senseless excess, extravagance; poetical rapture or inspiration.*

insănio -ire. *to be made, rage, rave; to be inspired.*

insānĭtās -ātis, f. *disease, unsoundness.*

insānus -a -um, *of unsound mind, mad, raving, senseless; of poets, inspired; of things, raging stormy.* Adv. **insānē**, *madly.*

insătiābilis -e: pass., *insatiable*: act., *that does not satiate, uncloying.* Adv. **insătĭābĭlĭtĕr**, *insatiably.*

insătŭrābĭlis -e, *insatiable*: adv. **insătŭrābĭlĭtĕr.**

inscendo -scendĕre -scendi -scensum, *to climb on, ascend, mount.*

insciens -entis, *not knowing fact, unaware; in gen., ignorant.* Adv. **inscientĕr.**

inscientia -ae f. *ignorance, inexperience.*

inscītia -ae, f. *inexperience, want of skill, ignorance.*

inscītus -a -um, *ignorant unskilful, stupid;* adv. **inscītē.**

inscius -a -um, *ignorant, not knowing.*

inscrībo -scrībere -scripsi -scriptum, *to write in or on, inscribe; to mark, impress; to entitle, mark as something; to ascribe, mark as belonging to.*

inscriptio -ōnis, f. *writing in or upon.*

¹**inscriptus** -a -um, *unwritten.*

²**inscriptus** -a -um, partic. from inscribo; q.v.

insculpo -sculpĕre -sculpsi -sculptum, *to cut or carve in engrave.* Transf., *to impress.*

insĕco -sĕcare -sĕcŭi -sectum, *to cut into, notch.*

insectātĭo -ōnis, f. *close following, hot pursuit.* Transf., *abuse.*

insectātor -oris, m. *pursuer, persecutor.*

insecto -are and **insector** -ari, dep. *to follow closely, pursue, harry; to harry with abuse, rail at, reproach.*

insĕdābĭlĭtĕr, *incessantly.*

insĕnesco -sĕnescĕre -sĕnŭi, *to grow old at or among.*

insensilis -e, *without sensation.*

insĕpultus -a -um, *unburied.*

insĕquor -sĕqui -sĕcūtus, dep., *to follow after, follow on; in time, to succeed; to pursue a subject; to pursue a person, to censure, reproach; in gen., to attack, assail.*

¹**insĕro** -sĕrĕre -sēvi -situm, *to graft in, implant.* Hence partic. **insĭtus** -a -um, *implanted, innate; incorporated.*

²**insĕro** -sĕrĕre -sĕrŭi -sertum, *to let in, introduce, insert; in gen., to connect, put in or among.*

inserto -are, *to insert, put into.*

inservio -ire, *to be a slave, to serve; to be devoted to.*

insĭbĭlo -are. *to hiss, whistle in.*

insĭdĕo -ēre, *to sit in or on; to dwell, remain.*

insidiae -arum, f. pl. *an ambush; a trap, plot.*

insĭdĭātor -oris, m. *a man in ambush; a spy, waylayer.*

insĭdĭor -ari, dep.. *to lie in ambush, lie in wait; to plot against, watch for.*

insĭdĭōsus -a -um, *deceitful treacherous*; adv. **insĭdĭōsē.**

insīdo -sīdĕre -sēdi -sessum, *to sit, settle, perch upon*; milit., *to occupy, beset*; of ideas, etc., *to sink in.*

insigne -is, n. *a distinguishing mark, token; badge, decoration, medal*; pl. as abstr., *distinctions, beauties.*

insignĭo -ire, *to mark, distinguish.* Hence partic. **insignītus** -a -um, *marked; conspicuous, clear*; adv. **insignītē,** *remarkably.*

insignis -e, *distinguished, remarkable, extraordinary*; adv. **insignĭtĕr.**

insĭlĭa n. pl. *the treadles of a loom, or perhaps leash-rods.*

insĭlĭo -sĭlire -sĭlŭi, *to leap, spring, jump in or on.*

insĭmŭlātĭo -ōnis, f. *accusation, charge.*

insĭmŭlo -are, *to charge, accuse, esp. falsely.*

insincērus -a -um, *tainted.*

insĭnŭātĭo -ōnis, f., rhet. t. t., *gaining the favour of the audience.*

insĭnŭo -are, *to introduce by turning, to insinuate;* with (and occasionally without) reflex., *to penetrate, work one's way in.*

insĭpĭens -entis, *foolish*; adv. **insĭpĭentĕr.**

insĭpĭentĭa -ae, f. *foolishness.*

insisto -sistĕre -stĭti. (1) *to set foot on, tread on;* to *enter on a journey, road, etc., to set about a task;* with dat., *to follow hard upon, pursue.* (2) *to stand still in or on;* to *halt, stop, pause; to hesitate, doubt; to dwell upon a subject; to persist in a course.*

insĭtĭo -ōnis, f. *grafting.*

insĭtīvus -a -um, *grafted; spurious.*

insĭtor -oris, m. *a grafter.*

insĭtus -a -um, partic. from insero; q.v.

insōcĭābĭlis -e, *unable to combine.*

insōlābĭlĭtĕr, *inconsolably.*

insōlens -entis, *contrary to custom.* Hence (1) *unaccustomed, unused.* (2) *unusual, excessive, extravagant; arrogant, insolent.* Adv. **insōlentĕr,** *unusually, contrary to custom; excessively, extravagantly; haughtily, arrogantly.*

insōlentĭa -ae, f. (1) *inexperience.* (2) *unusual character, novelty, extravagance, excess; pride, arrogance.*

insōlesco -escĕre, *to become haughty or insolent.*

insōlĭdus -a -um, *soft, tender.*

insōlĭtus -a -um. (1) *unaccustomed.* (2) *unusual, strange, uncommon.*

insomnĭa -ae, f. *sleeplessness, loss of sleep.*

insomnis -e, *sleepless.*

insomnĭum -i, n. *a bad dream.*

insŏno -sŏnare -sŏnŭi, *to make a noise in or with; to sound, resound.*

insons -sontis, *innocent, guiltless, harmless.*

insŏpitus -a -um, *unsleeping, watchful.*

inspectio -ŏnis, f. *scrutiny, consideration.*

inspecto -are, *to look at, observe.*

inspĕrans -antis, *not hoping, not expecting.*

inspĕrātus -a -um, *unhoped-for, unexpected.*

inspergo spergĕre -spersi -spersum, *to sprinkle in or on.*

inspĭcio -spicĕre -spexi -spectum. (1) *to look into, see into.* (2) *to view, examine, inspect; to consider.*

inspĭco -are, *to sharpen to a point.*

inspīro -are, *to breathe upon, blow upon, inspire.*

inspŏliātus -a -um, *not plundered.*

instăbilis -e. (1) *unstable, unsteady, inconstant.* (2) *not supporting, insecure.*

instans -antis, and **instantĕr**; from insto; q.v.

instantĭa -ae, f. *presence; perseverance.*

instăr, n. (only nom. and acc. sing.), *an image, likeness;* usually with genit., in the sense *corresponding to, like.*

instaurātĭo -ŏnis, f. *repetition, renewal.*

instaurātivus -a -um, *renewed, repeated.*

instauro -are. (1) *to set up, establish.* (2) *to renew, restore;* hence *to repay, requite.*

insterno -sternĕre -strāvi -strātum, *to spread over, cover over;* equus instratus, *saddled.*

instīgātor -oris, m. and **instīgātrix** -tricis, f. *an instigator.*

instīgo -are, *to goad, incite, stimulate.*

instillo -are, *to drop in, pour in by drops, instil.*

instĭmŭlātor -ōris m. *an instigator*

instĭmŭlo -are, *to incite.*

instinctor -ōris, m. *an instigator.*

instinctū, abl. sing. m. *by instigation.*

instinctus -a -um, *instigated, incited, impelled.*

instĭta -ae, f. *border or flounce on a robe.*

instĭtĭo -ōnis, f. *standing still.*

instĭtor -ōris, m. *a hawker, pedlar.*

instĭtŭo -ŭĕre -ŭi -ūtum, *to put in place, set in order; to set up, make ready, build, construct;* abstr. *to establish, introduce, arrange; to settle on a course, to undertake, resolve, determine; to appoint a person; to instruct educate, train.*

instĭtūtĭo -ŏnis, f. *arrangement; regular method; education, instruction.*

instĭtūtum -i, n. *an undertaking, purpose; an arrangement, institution, plan; an instruction, precept.*

insto -stare -stĭti. (1) *to stand in or on.* (2) *to be close to, follow closely, pursue eagerly; to devote oneself, persist, persevere; to insist, ask pressingly;* of time or events, *to approach, impend.*

     Hence partic. **instans** -antis,

present; pressing, urgent; adv. **instanter**, *urgently.*

instrēnŭus -a -um, *inactive, lazy.*

instrĕpo -ere -ŭi -ĭtum, *to rattle, clatter, creak.*

instructĭo -ōnis, f. *drawing up in order.*

instructor -ōris, m. *a preparer.*

instructus -ūs, m. *provision; matter* (in a speech).

instrŭmentum -i, n. *equipment, tool, implement; dress; store, stock: any means to an end.*

instrŭo -strŭĕre -struxi -structum, *to build in or into; to set up, construct; furnish,* hence *to train a person; to prepare, provide;* milit., *to draw up in order of battle.*

     Hence partic. **instructus** -a -um, *equipped, supplied;* of persons, *trained, instructed.*

insuāvis -e, *unpleasant, disagreeable.*

Insubres -ium, *the Insubrians, a people in Cisalpine Gaul;* as adj. **Insŭbĕr** -bris -bre, *Insubrian.*

insūdo -are, *to sweat in or at.*

insuēfactus -a -um, *accustomed to.*

insuesco -suescĕre -suēvi -suētum; intransit., *to become used to;* transit., *to accustom, habituate anyone to.*

¹**insuētus** -a -um: of persons, *unaccustomed, unused to;* of things, *unaccustomed, unusual.*

²**insuētus** -a -um, partic. from insuesco; q.v.

insŭla -ae, f. *an island.* Transf., *a detached house or block of flats.*

insŭlānus -i, m. *an islander.*

insulsĭtās -ātis, f. *tastelessness, absurdity.*

insulsus -a -um, *unsalted, insipid; tasteless, foolish;* adv. **insulsē.**

insulto -are, *to leap, prance in or on; to triumph over, insult.*

insum -esse -fŭi, *to be in or on; to be contained in, belong to.*

insūmo -sūmĕre -sumpsi -sumptum, *to take for a purpose, to expend.*

insŭo -sŭĕre -sutum, *to sew in, sew up.*

insŭpĕr: adv. *above, overhead; over and above, in addition, besides;* prep., with abl., *besides.*

insŭpĕrābilis -e, *insurmountable, impassable; unconquerable.*

insurgo -surgĕre -surrexi -surrectum, *to rise up, raise oneself up; to increase in power or force;* with dat., *to rise up against.*

insŭsurro -are, *to whisper, whisper in the ear.*

intābesco -tābescĕre -tābŭi, *to melt or wither away gradually.*

intactilis -e, *that cannot be touched.*

¹**intactus** -a -um, *untouched; untried unspoilt, unhurt, virgin.*

²**intactus** -ūs, m. *intangibility.*

intāmĭnātus -a -um, *unstained.*

¹**intectus** -a -um, *uncovered, unclothed; open, frank.*

²**intectus** -a -um, partic. from intego; q.v.

intĕgellus -a -um, *more or less pure, undamaged.*

intĕger -gra -grum. (1) *complete,*

whole, entire, intact; fresh, sound, unexhausted; in integrum restituere, to restore to its former condition. (2) in quality, unspoilt, pure, fresh; morally, innocent, uncorrupted: in thought or feeling, balanced, unbiased, impartial; of matters for discussion or action, unprejudiced, undecided; integrum est mihi, I am at liberty. (3) renewed, begun afresh. Hence adv. **integrē** wholly; honestly, uprightly, impartially; of style, purely, correctly.

intěgo -tēgěre -texi -tectum, to cover, protect.

integrasco -ěre, to break out afresh.

integrātio -ōnis, f. renewing.

integritās -ātis, f. unimpaired condition, soundness, health; uprightness, integrity; of style, purity, correctness.

integro -are, to make whole, heal, refresh; to renew, begin afresh.

intěgůmentum -i, n. a covering, cloak, disguise.

intellectus -ūs, m. understanding, comprehension.

intellěgentia -ae, f. perception; understanding, knowledge, taste; capacity for understanding, intelligence.

intellěgo -lěgěre -lexi -lectum, to discern, perceive; to understand, grasp; to understand character, judge, appreciate; to understand by a term, take as its meaning.
    Hence partic. **intellěgens** -entis, intelligent, understanding; having good sense or taste. Adv. **intellěgentěr**.

intěměrātus -a -um, unspotted, undefiled.

intempěrans -antis, extravagant, unrestrained, intemperate; adv. **intempěrantěr**.

intempěrantia -ae, f. want of restraint, extravagance, excess.

intempěrātus -a -um, intemperate, immoderate; adv. **intempěrātē**.

intempěriēs -ēi, f. wildness, lack of restraint, excess.

intempestīvus -a -um, unseasonable, untimely; immoderate. Adv. **intempestīvē**, unseasonably.

intempestus -a -um, unwholesome, unhealthy: intempesta nox, the dead of night.

intemptātus -a -um, untried.

intendo -tenděre -tendi -tentum. (1) to stretch, strain; abstr., to maintain, try to prove. (2) to extend, aim, direct; esp. to direct one's course; to apply the mind, direct the thoughts; to intend, aim at.
    Hence partic. **intentus** -a -um, stretched, tense, taut; of thought or feeling, anxious, intent; of speech, earnest; in gen, thorough, strict, rigorous. Adv. **intentē**, earnestly, attentively.

¹**intentātus** -a -um; = intemptatus; q.v.

²**intentatus** -a -um, partic., from intento; q.v.

intentio -ōnis, f. stretching, straining; of the mind, effort, exertion, attention; an attack, accusation.

intento -are, to stretch towards or against, esp. threateningly.

¹**intentus** -ūs, m. stretching out.

²**intentus** -a -um, partic. from intendo; q.v.

intěpesco -těpescěre -těpui, to become lukewarm.

inter, prep. with acc. between, among, amid; during, in the course of a period; with pronouns, inter se, inter nos, etc., between one another, mutually.

intěrāmenta -orum, n. pl. woodwork of a ship.

intěrāresco -ěre, to become dry, decay.

intercǎlāris -e and **intercǎlārius** -a -um, inserted, intercalary.

intercǎlo -are, to insert; esp. to intercalate a day or month in the calendar.

intercǎpēdo -inis, f. interval, pause, respite.

intercēdo -cēděre -cessi -cessum, to go between, come between, intervene; legal, to interpose, stand surety; to step between, withstand, protest against.

interceptio -ōnis, f. taking away.

interceptor -ōris, m. one who takes away, an embezzler.

intercessio -ōnis, f. legal, becoming surety, going bail; polit., an exercise by the tribunes of their veto.

intercessor -ōris, m. legal, surety, bail; polit., one who opposes, an obstructor.

¹**intercido** -ciděre -cidi -cisum, to cut asunder, to demolish. Hence adv. **intercisē**, piecemeal.

²**intercido** -ciděre -cidi. (1) to fall between, intervene. (2) to drop out be lost, be forgotten, perish.

intercino -ere, to sing between.

intercipio -cipěre -cēpi -ceptum, to take by the way, intercept; to embezzle, appropriate; through death, to cut off, carry off prematurely; of roads, to block.

interclūdo -clūděre -clūsi -clūsum, to shut off, block, hinder; to enclose, shut in.

interclūsio -ōnis, f. stopping or blocking up; parenthesis.

intercolumnium -i, n. the space between two columns.

intercurro -currěre -cūcurri -cursum, to run between, to run through; to intercede; to be among, mingle with; to hasten in the meanwhile.

intercurso -are, to run between, run among.

intercursū, abl. sing. m. by running between, by the interposition.

intercǔs -cǔtis, under the skin: aqua, the dropsy.

interdīco -dīcěre -dixi -dictum. (1) to stop by interposition, forbid, prohibit; interdicěre aqua et igni, with dat., to outlaw. (2) to make an injunction to order.

interdictio -ōnis, f. forbidding, prohibition: aquae et ignis, outlawing.

interdictum -i, n. a prohibition; a praetor's interdict or provisional order.

interdĭū (interdĭus), *in the daytime, by day.*

interdo -dăre -dătum, *to put between or among, distribute.*

interductus -ū, m. *interpunctuation.*

interdum, *sometimes, now and then.*

interdŭo = interdo; q.v.

intĕrĕā, *meanwhile*; sometimes *nevertheless, notwithstanding.*

intĕremptor -ōris, m. *a murderer.*

intĕrĕo -ire -ĭi -ĭtum, *to be lost, to perish.*

intĕrĕquĭto -are, *to ride between.*

interfātĭo -onis f. *speaking between, interruption.*

interfātur -fāri -fātus, dep. forms, *to speak between, interrupt.*

interfectĭo -ōnis, f. *slaying.*

interfector -ōris, m. *murderer.*

interfectrix -trīcis, f. *murderess.*

interfĭcĭo -fĭcĕre -fēci -fectum, *to do away with, destroy, put an end to, kill.*

interfĭo -fĭĕri, *to perish.*

interflŭo -flŭĕre -fluxi -fluxum, *to flow between.*

interfŏdĭo -fŏdĕre -fŏdi -fossum, *to dig into, pierce.*

interfor; see interfatur.

interfŭgĭo -fŭgĕre, *to flee between.*

interfulgens -entis, *shining or gleaming among.*

interfūsus -a -um, *poured between, flowing between*; maculis interfusa, *stained here and there.*

interiăcĕo -ēre, *to lie between or among.*

interiăcĭo = intericio; q.v.

intĕrĭbi, *meanwhile.*

intericĭo -icere -ieci -iectum, *to throw, cast, put, among or between*; anno interiecto, *after an interval of a year.*

interiectĭo -ōnis, f. *interjection or parenthesis.*

interiectus -ūs, m. *throwing between*; of time, *an interval.*

intĕrim, *meanwhile*; sometimes *however.*

intĕrĭmo -ĭmĕre -ēmi -emptum, *to take away, destroy, make an end of; to put out of the way, kill.*

intĕrĭor -ius, genit. -ōris, *inner, interior*; *remote from the sea, inland, nearer*; in racing, *on the inside.* Transf., *more secret, more intimate.* Superl. **intĭmus** -a -um; q.v. Adv. **interĭus**, *more inwardly*; *short, not far enough.*

intĕrĭtĭo -ōnis, f. *destruction, ruin.*

intĕrĭtus -ūs, m. *destruction, ruin.*

interiungo -iungĕre -iunxi -iunctum, *to join together, connect*; also *to unyoke.*

intĕrĭus; see interior.

interlābor -lābi -lapsus, dep. *to glide, flow between.*

interlĕgo -ĕre, *to pluck here and there.*

interlĭno -lĭnĕre -lēvi -litum, *to daub between*; *to erase, falsify by erasure.*

interlŏquor -lŏqui -lŏcūtus, dep. *to interrupt a person speaking.*

interlūcĕo -lūcēre -luxi, *to shine or gleam between*; *to be transparent, let light through gaps.*

interlūnĭum -i, n. *change of moon, time of new moon.*

interlŭo -lŭĕre, *to wash between.*

intermenstrŭus -a -um, *between two months*; n. as subst. *the time of the new moon.*

[1]**interminātus** -a -um, *unbounded, boundless.*

[2]**interminātus** -a -um, partic. from interminor; q.v.

interminor -ari, dep. *to threaten, forbid with threats*; perf. partic. in pass. sense, *forbidden with threats.*

intermiscĕo -miscēre, -miscŭi -mixtum, *to mix with, intermix.*

intermissĭo -ōnis, f. *leaving off, interruption.*

intermitto -mittĕre -mĭsi -missum: transit., *to leave a space between, leave free*; in space, *to separate, break off*; in time, *to let pass*; in gen., *to discontinue, interrupt*; vento intermisso, *the wind having dropped*; intransit., *to cease, leave off.*

intermŏrĭor -mŏri -mortuus, dep. *to die off, perish suddenly*; partic. **intermortuus** -a -um, *swooning, half-dead*; fig., *lifeless.*

intermundĭa -ōrum, n. pl. *spaces between the worlds.*

intermūrālis -e, *between walls.*

internascor -nasci -natus, dep. *to grow between or among.*

internĕcĭo -ōnis, f. *extermination, massacre.*

internĕcīvus (-nĕcīnus) -a -um, *murderous, deadly.*

internĕco -are, *to exterminate.*

internecto -ĕre, *to bind together, bind up.*

internōdĭum -i, n. *the space between two knots or joints.*

internosco -noscĕre -nōvi -nōtum, *to distinguish between.*

internuntĭa -ae, f. *a female messenger or go-between.*

internuntĭo -are, *to send messengers between parties.*

internuntĭus -i, m. *a messenger, mediator, go-between.*

internus -a, -im., *inward, internal; domestic, civil.*

interpellātĭo -ōnis, f. *interruption.*

interpellātor -ōris, m. *interrupter, disturber.*

interpello -are, *to interrupt, disturb, impede, obstruct.*

interpōlo -are, *to furbish, vamp up; to falsify.*

interpōno -pōnĕre -pŏsŭi -pŏsĭtum, *to place between or among, interpose*; spatio interposito, *after an interval*; fidem, *to pledge one's word*; rarely, *to falsify*; with reflex., *to engage in, interfere with.*

interpŏsĭtĭo -ōnis, f. *putting in, insertion, introduction*; rhet. *parenthesis.*

interpŏsĭtū, abl. sing. m. *by putting between, by interposition.*

interprĕs -prĕtis, c. (1) *a negotiator, mediator, messenger.* (2) *an expounder, explainer; prophet, prophetess; interpreter; translator.*

interprĕtātĭo -ōnis, f., *explanation, interpretation; translation.* Transf., *meaning, signification.*

interprĕtor -ari, dep. (1) *to put an interpretation upon, understand in a certain sense.* (2) *to translate.*

interpunctio -ōnis, f. *punctuation.*

interpungo -pungĕre -punxi -punctum, *to punctuate;* partic. **interpunctus** -a -um, *well-divided.*

interquiesco -quiēscĕre -quiēvi -quiētum, *to pause between.*

interregnum -i, n. *a period between two reigns, interregnum.*

interrex -rēgis m. *a regent, temporary king or chief magistrate.*

interritus -a -um, *undaunted.*

interrŏgātio -ōnis, f. *questioning, interrogation:* esp. legal, *examination of witnesses;* in logic, *an argument, syllogism;* gram., *interrogation.*

interrŏgo -are, *to ask, question, interrogate;* esp. *to examine a witness, or to accuse, bring an action against.*

interrumpo -rumpĕre -rūpi -ruptum, *to break in the middle, sever, interrupt, disturb.* Adv. from partic. **interruptē**, *interruptedly, disconnectedly.*

intersaepio -saepire -saepsi -s:eptum, *to enclose, hem in, block up.*

interscindo -scindĕre -scidi -scissum, *to cut open, cut off, tear apart.*

interscribo -ĕre, *to write between.*

¹**intersĕro** -sĕrĕre -sēvi -situm, *to sow or plant between.*

²**intersĕro** -sĕrĕre -sĕrŭi, *to put or place between.*

interspīrātio -ōnis, f. *breathing between, taking breath.*

interstinctus -a -um, *spotted, speckled.*

interstinguo -ĕre, *to extinguish.*

interstringo -ĕre, *to squeeze tight.*

intersum -esse -fŭi, *to be between; to be among, be present at, take part in* (with dat.); in time, *to intervene;* abstr., *to be between as a difference; rarely to differ, be different.* Hence impers. **intĕrest**, *it makes a difference, it concerns;* magni (or multum) meâ interest, *it makes a great difference to me.*

intertextus -a -um, *interwoven.*

intertrīmentum -i, n. *loss, damage.*

interturbātio -ōnis, f. *disturbance, disquiet.*

intervallum -i, n. *distance between, interval* (of time or space); *difference, unlikeness.*

intervĕnio -vĕnire -vēni -ventum, *to come between, intervene; to interrupt* (with dat.) *to delay* (with acc.).

interventor -ōris, m. *an interrupting visitor.*

interventus -ūs, m. *intervention, interference.*

interverto (**-vorto**) -vertĕre -verti -versum, *to intercept; to embezzle, purloin; to cheat, rob.*

interviso -visĕre -visi -visum, *to look in at, visit from time to time.*

intestābilis -e, *disqualified, dishonoured, infamous.*

intestātus -a -um, *having made no will, intestate;* n. abl. as adv. intestato, *intestate.*

intestīnus -a -um, *inward, internal;*

n. as subst., sing. and plur. *the intestines.*

intexo -texĕre -texŭi -textu: *to weave in, plait in, interweave; to weave around, wind around.*

intībum -i, n. *endive, succory.*

intimus (**intŭmus**) -a -um, superl. (compar. interior; q.v.), *innermost, inmost; most profound, most secret intimate;* m. as subst., *an intimate friend.* Adv. **intimē**, *intimately; cordially, strongly.*

intingo (**-tinguo**) -tingĕre -tinxi -tinctum, *to dip in.*

intŏlĕrābilis -e, *unbearable, intolerable.*

intŏlĕrandus -a -um, *unbearable, unendurable.*

intŏlĕrans -antis: act. *impatient unable to bear;* pass., *unbearable, intolerable.* Adv. **intŏlĕrantĕr**, *immoderately, impatiently.*

intŏlĕrantia -ae, f. *insufferable conduct, insolence.*

intŏno -tŏnare -tŏnŭi, *to thunder, thunder forth* (esp. of speakers).

intonsus -a -um, *unshorn, with long hair or beard;* hence of persons *rude, rough;* of country, *wooded, not cleared.*

intorquĕo -torquĕre -torsi -tortum, *to twist or turn round;* of weapons, *to hurl;* partic. **intortus** -a -um, *twisted, tangled.*

intrā: adv. *inside;* prep., with acc. *inside, within, less than, short of.*

intrābilis -e, *that can be entered, accessible.*

intractābilis -e, *unmanageable, intractable.*

intractātus -a -um, *not handled; unattempted.*

intrĕmisco -trĕmiscĕre -trĕmŭi, *to begin to tremble.*

intrĕmo -ere, *to tremble, quake.*

intrĕpidus -a -um, *unconfused, calm:* adv. **intrĕpidĕ**, *calmly.*

intrico -are, *to confuse, entangle.*

intrinsĕcus, *inside, inwardly, inwards.*

¹**intritus** -a -um, *not worn away, unexhausted.*

²**intritus** -a -um, partic. from intero; q.v.

¹**intrō**, *inwards, within.*

²**intro** -are, *to go into, enter.*

intrŏdūco -dūcĕre -duxi -ductum, *to introduce, bring in, bring forward, present, suggest.*

intrŏductio -onis, f. *bringing in, introduction.*

intrŏĕo -ire -ii -itum, *to go into, enter.*

intrŏfĕro -ferre -tŭli -lātum, *to carry in.*

intrŏgrĕdior -grĕdi -gressus, dep. *to enter.*

intrŏitus -ūs, m. *an entrance; means of entrance; passage;* in gen., *beginning, introduction.*

intrŏmitto -mittĕre -mīsi -missum, *to send in, allow to enter.*

introrsus (**-orsum**), *inwards, inwardly internally.*

intrŏrumpo -rumpĕre -rūpi -ruptum, *to break into, enter by force.*

introspicio -spicĕre -spexi -spectum,

to look into, look inside, observe, examine.

intŭbum -i, n., see intibum.

intŭĕor -tŭēri -tŭĭtus, dep. to look at attentively, gaze at; to consider, contemplate, look to.

intŭmesco -tŭmescĕre -tŭmŭi, to swell, swell up; to increase; to swell with anger.

intŭmŭlātus -a -um, unburied.

intŭor -i, dep. = intueor; q.v.

inturbĭdus -a -um, undisturbed, quiet.

intŭs, adv. within, inside; to or from the inside; inwardly.

intŭtus -a -um, (1) unprotected. (2) unsafe, dangerous.

ĭnŭla -ae, f. the plant elecampane.

ĭnultus -a -um, (1) unavenged. (2) unpunished.

ĭnumbro -are, to shade, overshadow.

ĭnundātĭo -ōnis, f. inundation, flood.

ĭnundo -are: transit., to overflow, inundate, stream over; intransit., to overflow with.

ĭnungo -ungĕre -unxi -unctum, to anoint.

ĭnurbānus -a -um, rude, unpolished; adv. **ĭnurbānē.**

ĭnurgĕo -urgēre -ursi, to push, thrust against.

ĭnūro -ūrĕre -ussi -ustum, to burn in or on, brand, imprint; to inflict; to crimp, curl, adorn.

ĭnūsĭtātus -a -um, unusual, strange, uncommon; adv. **ĭnūsĭtātē.**

ĭnūtĭlis -e, useless, unserviceable, unprofitable; injurious, harmful. Adv. **ĭnūtĭlĭtĕr.**

ĭnūtĭlĭtās -ātis, f. uselessness, unprofitableness; harmfulness.

invādo -vādĕre -vāsi -vāsum. (1) to go in, enter, get in; to undertake. (2) to attack, fall upon, assail, usurp, seize.

invălesco -vălescĕre -vălŭi, to gather strength, become strong.

invălĭdus -a -um, weak, powerless.

invectĭo -ōnis, f. (1) importation. (2) invective.

invĕho -vĕhĕre -vexi -vectum, to carry in, introduce; pass., or with reflex., to drive, ride or travel, esp. to advance against, attack; of verbal attack, to inveigh.

invĕnĭo -vĕnīre -vēni -ventum, to come upon, find, meet with, discover; to invent, devise; to procure, get, earn; pass., or with reflex., to show oneself.

Hence partic., **inventus** -a -um, discovered; n. as subst. an invention, discovery.

inventĭo -ōnis, f. inventing, invention; the inventive faculty.

inventor -ōris, m. and **inventrix** -trīcis, f. inventor.

invĕnustus -a -um, not charming, unattractive; unhappy in love.

invĕrēcundus -a -um, shameless, impudent.

invergo -ĕre, to tip or pour upon.

inversĭo -ōnis, f. irony; transposition; allegory.

inverto -vertĕre -verti -versum to

turn over, turn about; to transpose, alter, pervert. Hence partic. **inversus** -a -um, overturned, upside down.

invespĕrascit -ĕre, impers. it grows dark.

investĭgātĭo -ōnis, f. inquiry, investigation.

investĭgātor -ōris, m. inquirer, investigator.

investĭgo -are, to search out, track out.

invĕtĕrasco -ascĕre -avi, to become old; to become obsolete; to become established, fixed, rooted.

invĕtĕrātĭo -ōnis, f. inveterateness, permanence.

invĕtĕrātus -a -um, of long standing, established.

invĭcem, in turn, alternately; mutually, reciprocally.

invictus -a -um, unconquered, unsubdued; unconquerable, invincible.

invĭdentĭa -ae, f. envying, envy.

invĭdĕo -vĭdēre -vĭdi -vīsum, to envy, grudge, be envious of.

Hence partic. **invīsus** -a -um: pass., hated; act., hostile.

invĭdĭa -ae, f.: act., envy, jealously, ill-will; pass., odium, unpopularity. Transf., a source of ill-will.

invĭdĭōsus -a -um, envious; causing envy, envied; hateful. Adv. **invĭdĭōsē,** jealously, bitterly.

invĭdus -a -um, envious, grudging.

invĭgĭlo -are, to watch over (with dat.).

invĭŏlābĭlis -e, unassailable.

invĭŏlātus -a -um, uninjured, unhurt; inviolable. Adv. **invĭŏlātē,** inviolately.

invīsĭtātus -a -um, not seen; unusual, strange.

invīso -vīsĕre -vīsi -vīsum, to go to see, visit; to inspect, look at.

¹**invīsus** -a -um, unseen, secret.

²**invīsus** -a -um, partic. from invideo; q.v.

invītāmentum -i, n. invitation, attraction.

invītātĭo -ōnis, f. invitation, inducement.

invītātū, abl. sing. m. by invitation.

invīto -are, to invite, summon; to receive, entertain; to induce, allure; with reflex., to treat oneself.

invītus -a -um, unwilling, against one's will; abl. absol. me invito, against my will. Adv. **invītē,** unwillingly, against one's will.

invĭus -a -um, impassable, impenetrable; n. pl. as subst., trackless places.

invŏcātĭo -ōnis, f. calling upon, invocation.

¹**invŏcātus** -a -um, uncalled, uninvited.

²**invŏcātus** -a -um, partic. from invoco; q.v.

invŏco -are, to call in, call upon for help, invoke.

invŏlātū, abl. sing. m., by the flight.

invŏlĭto -are, to float or wave over.

invŏlo -are, to fly at, seize or pounce upon.

invŏlūcrum -i, n. a wrap, cover.

involvo -volvĕre -volvi -vŏlūtum, to roll in or on; to envelop, wrap up, cover. Hence partic. **invŏlūtus** -a -um, rolled up; involved.

invulgo -are, *to give information.*

invulnĕrātus -a -um, *unwounded.*

¹Iŏ, interj., *hurrah! hi!*

²Iō (Iŏn) -ūs (-ŏnis), f. *an Argive girl, loved by Jupiter and changed into a cow;* adj. Iŏnius -a -um, *Ionian, of the sea between Italy and Greece, across which Io swam.*

iŏcātio -ōnis, f. *joke, jest.*

iŏco -are and iŏcor -ari. dep. *to joke, jest.*

iŏcōsus -a -um, *humorous, merry, facetious;* adv. iŏcōsē.

iŏcŭlāris -e, *jocular, laughable;* adv. iŏcŭlārĭtĕr.

iŏcŭlārĭus -a -um, *laughable, droll.*

iŏcŭlātor -ōris, m. *joker.*

iŏcŭlor -ari, dep. *to joke, jest.*

iŏcus -i, m. (plur. iŏci and iŏca), *a joke, jest.*

Iōnes -um, m. *the Ionians;* Iōnĭa -ae, f. *their country in Asia Minor;* adj. Iōnĭācus and Iōnĭcus -a -um, *Ionian.*

Iphĭgēnĭa -ae, f. *daughter of Agamemnon.*

ipse -a -um, *self;* ego ipse, *I myself; the very, actual;* with numbers, etc., *just, exactly;* of action, *by oneself, of one's own accord.*

ira -ae, f. *wrath, anger, rage;* meton., *cause of anger.*

īrācundĭa -ae, f. (1) *angry disposition, irascibility.* (2) *state of anger, fury, wrath.*

īrācundus -a -um, *inclined to anger, irascible;* adv. īrācundē, *wrathfully.*

īrascor -i, dep. *to grow angry* (with dat.); partic. īrātus -a -um, *angry.*

Iris -ridis, f. *messenger of the gods, and goddess of the rainbow.*

īrōnĭa -ae, f. *irony.*

irr-; see in-.

is, ĕa, id, *he, she, it; this* or *that (person* or *thing);* with qui (or ut), *one (of those) who, such . . . as;* with et, -que, etc., *and that too, and what is more;* n. sing. id, *on that account;* id temporis, *at that time;* in eo est, *the position is such,* or, *it depends on this;* id est, *that is,* in explanation.

Isis -is and -idis, f., *the Egyptian goddess Isis.*

istāc, *by that way.*

iste ista istud, demonstr. pron. or adj. *that of yours, that beside you;* in speeches, referring to parties opposed to the speaker (opp. to hic, *my client);* often contemptuous.

Ister = Hister; q.v.

Isthmus (-os) -i, m., *the Isthmus of Corinth.*

¹istic istaec istōc or istūc, *that of yours.*

²istic, adv. *over there, there by you; therein, in that.*

istinc, *from over there, thence.*

istiusmŏdī or istius mŏdī or istimŏdī, *of that kind, such.*

istō, adv., *thither, to that place or thing.*

istōc and istūc, *thither.*

Istri; see Histri.

Ita, *so, thus;* interrog., itane? *really?*

in answers, *certainly;* in narration *and so;* with adj. or adv., *so, so very;* ita . . . ut, with subjunc., *in such a way that,* or *only to the extent that, only on condition that.*

Ităli -orum and -um, m. *the Italians;* Itălĭa -ae, f. *Italy;* adj. Itălĭcus and Itălĭus -a -um, *Italian;* f. adj. Itălĭs -idis.

ităquĕ, *and so; therefore, for that reason.*

item, *also, likewise.*

itĕr, ĭtĭnĕris, n. *going, way, direction; journey, march; right of way, permission to march;* concr., *way, road;* fig., *way, course, method.*

itĕrātio -ōnis, f. *repetition, iteration.*

itĕro -are, *to do a second time, repeat, renew.*

ĭtĕrum, *again, a second time;* iterum atque interum, *again and again.*

Ithăca -ae and Ithăcē -ēs, f., *an island in the Ionian Sea, home of Ulysses.*

itĭdem, *likewise.*

ītĭo -ōnis, f. *going, travelling.*

ito -are, *to go.*

itus -ūs, m. *movement, going, departure.*

¹iŭba -ae, f. *mane, crest.*

²Iŭba -ae, m. *name of two Numidian kings.*

iŭbăr -āris, n. *beaming light, radiance; a heavenly body,* esp. *the sun.*

iŭbātus -a -um, *having a mane, crested.*

iŭbĕo iŭbēre iussi iussum, *to order, command, bid;* salvere iubere, *to greet;* polit. *to ratify* an order. Hence, from perf. partic. iussum -i, n., *an order, command.*

iūcundĭtās -ātis, f., *pleasantness, delightfulness, pleasure.*

iūcundus -a -um, *pleasant, agreeable, delightful;* adv. iūcundē.

Iūdaea -ae, f. *Judea* or *Palestine;* adj. and subst. Iūdaeus -a -um, *Jewish* or *a Jew.*

iūdex -icis, m. *a judge;* in plur., *a panel of jurors.*

iūdĭcātĭo -onis, f. *judicial investigation; judgment, opinion.*

iūdĭcātus -ūs, m., *the office* or *business of a judge.*

iūdĭcĭālis -e and iūdĭcĭārĭus -a -um, *of a court of justice, judicial.*

iūdĭcĭum -i, n., *a trial, legal investigation; a law-court; jurisdiction; judgment, considered opinion, decision; power of judging, discernment, understanding, good judgment.*

iūdĭco -are, *to be a judge, judge, decide, declare;* perf. partic. iūdĭcātus -a -um, of persons, *condemned;* of things, *decided.*

iŭgālis -e, *yoked together;* m. pl. as subst. *a team of horses.* Transf., *matrimonial, nuptial.*

iŭgātĭo -ōnis, f. *the training of vines on a trellis.*

iŭgĕrum -i, n. *a measure of land,* about two-thirds of an English acre.

iŭgis -e, *perpetual, continuous,* esp. of water.

iŭglans -glandis, f., *a walnut* or *walnut-tree.*

iŭgo -are, *to bind together, connect, couple.*

iŭgōsus -a -um, *mountainous.*

iŭgŭlo -are, *to cut the throat of, to butcher; to ruin, destroy.*

iŭgŭlum -i, n. *and* iŭgŭlus -i, m. *the throat.*

iŭgum -i, n. (1) *a yoke or collar.* Transf., *a team of oxen or horses; a pair, couple; a chariot; any bond, union; the bond of love, marriage-tie; the yoke of slavery.* (2) *a cross-bar;* esp. *the yoke under which the vanquished were sent; the beam of a pair of scales; a ridge between mountains;* ... poet., *mountain heights.*

Iŭgurtha -ae, m. *a king of Numidia;* adj. Iŭgurthinus -a -um.

Iūlĭus -a -um, *name of a Roman gens;* including the family of the Caesars; mensis Iulius *or* Iulius, *the month of July.*

Iūlus -i, m., *son of Aeneas.*

iūmentum -i n. *a beast of burden.*

iuncĕus -a -um, *made of rushes; like a rush.*

iuncōsus -a -um, *full of rushes, rushy.*

iunctĭo -ōnis, f. *joining, connexion.*

iunctūra -ae, f., *a joining, joint; relationship; combination; putting together.*

iuncus -i, m. *a rush.*

iungo iungĕre iunxi iunctum, *to join, unite, connect; to yoke, harness; to mate; amicitiam, to form.* Hence partic. iunctus -a -um, *connected, united, associated.*

iūnĭor; see iuvenis.

iūnĭpĕrus -i, f. *the juniper-tree.*

Iūnĭus -a -um, *the name of a Roman gens;* mensis Iunius *or* Iunius, *the month of June.*

Iŭnō -ōnis, f. *the goddess Juno, Greek Hera, sister and wife of Jupiter;* adj. Iŭnōnius -a -um, *Junonian.*

Iuppĭter, Iŏvis, m. *Jupiter, the Roman supreme god;* sub Iove, *in the open air.*

iūrātor -ōris, m. *a sworn assessor.*

iūrēiŭro -are, *to swear an oath.*

iūrĕpĕritus = iurisperitus; q.v.

iurgĭum -i, n., *altercation, quarrel, brawl.*

iurgo -are: intransit., *to quarrel, brawl;* transit., *to scold.*

iūrĭdĭcĭālis -e, *relating to right or justice.*

iūrisconsultus -i, m. *one learned in law, a lawyer.*

iūrisdictĭo -onis, f. *the administration of justice; judicial authority.*

iūrisperītus *or* iūrĕpĕrītus -i, m. *skilled or experienced in the law.*

iūro -are, *to swear, take an oath,* in verba, *to swear after a prescribed formula;* perf. partic. in act. sense iūrātus -a -um, *having sworn, under oath; also having been sworn.*

¹iŭs iŭris, n. *broth, soup.*

²iŭs iŭris, n. *right, law; a court of justice; jurisdiction; right as conferred by law;* iure, *rightly.*

iusiūrandum iūrisiūrandi (or in two words), n. *an oath.*

iussū, abl. sing m., *by order, by command.*

iussum -i, n. subst. from iubeo; q.v.

iustĭtĭa -ae, f. *justice, airness, equity.*

iustĭtĭum -i, n. *a suspension of legal business;* in gen., *pause, cessation.*

iustus -a -um, *just, equitable, fair; lawful, justified, proper; regular, perfect, complete, suitable.* N. as subst., sing. iustum -i, *justice, what is right;* plur. iusta -orum, *due forms and observances,* esp. *funeral rites.* Adv. iustē, *justly, rightly.*

¹iŭvĕnālis -e, *youthful.*

²Iŭvĕnālis -is, m., D. Iunius, *a Roman writer of satires.*

iŭvencus -a -um, *young;* m. as subst., iŭvencus -i, *a young man, or young bullock;* f. iŭvenca -ae, *a young woman, or young cow, heifer.*

iŭvĕnesco iŭvĕnescĕre iŭvĕnŭi, *to come (or come back) to the prime of life.*

iŭvĕnīlis -e, *youthful;* adv. iŭvĕnīlĭter, *youthfully.*

iŭvĕnis -is, adj., *young, youthful;* as subst. *a young man, young woman.*

iŭvĕnor -ari, dep. *to act like a youth, be impetuous.*

iŭventa -ae, f. *youth.*

iŭventās -ātis, f. *youth.*

iŭventūs -ūtis, f. *youth, the prime of life* (between the ages of 20 and 45); meton., *young men.*

iŭvo -are iūvi iūtum. (1) *to help, assist, aid.* (2) *to delight, please, gratify.*

iuxtā: adv. *close by, near; in like manner, equally;* prep., with acc., *close to, near to;* in time, *just before;* in gen., *near to, just short of.*

iuxtim, *near, close by; equally.*

Ixīōn -ōnis, m. *king of the Lapithae in Thessaly, bound to a perpetually revolving wheel in Tartarus.*

J

Unknown in classical Latin; invented by Italian humanists to represent the consonantal i, but now rarely used in classical texts.

K

The letter K, k, corresponding to Greek kappa (κ) belonged to the Latin Alphabet, but in some words was replaced by C.

Kălendae (Călendae) -arum, f. *the first day of a Roman month.*

Karthāgo = Carthāgo; q.v.

L

L, l, the eleventh letter of the Latin Alphabet.

lābasco -ĕre, *to totter; to give way.*

lābēcŭla -ae, f.. *a little stain, slight disgrace.*

lăbĕfăcĭo -făcĕre -fēci -factum, pass.
lăbĕfīo -fīĕri -factus sum, to shake,
loosen, impair.

lăbĕfacto -are, to shake violently,
weaken, disturb.

¹lābellum -i, n., a little lip.

²lābellum -i, n. a small washing-vessel.

lābēs -is, f. a stain, blemish; infamy,
disgrace.

lābĭa -ae, f., and lābĭum -i, n., a lip.

Lābĭēnus -i, m., T. an officer of Julius
Caesar, who went over to Pompey.

lābĭōsus -a -um, with large lips.

lābĭum -i, n. = labia; q.v.

lābo -are, to totter, waver, be about to
fall, begin to sink.

¹lābor lābi lapsus, dep. to glide, slide,
flow; to slip, fall down, fall away,
decline; to make a mistake.

²lăbor (lăbos) -ōris, m. (1) work, toil,
effort, industry, capacity for work;
feat, work, result of labour. (2) hardship, fatigue, distress; labores solis,
eclipse of the sun.

lăbōrĭfer -fĕra -fĕrum, bearing toil.

lăbōrĭōsus -a -um: of things, toilsome, laborious; of persons, industrious,
toiling. Adv. lăbōrĭōsē, laboriously,
with toil.

lăbōro -are: intransit., to work, toil,
strive: to be troubled or anxious, to
care; to suffer, be distressed or
afflicted; luna laborat, is eclipsed;
transit., to work out, elaborate, prepare,
form.

lăbos -ōris, m. = labor; q.v.

¹labrum -i, n. lip; edge, rim.

²labrum -i, n. basin, tub; a bathing-
place.

lābrusca -ae, f. the wild vine.

lābruscum -i, n. the wild grape.

lăbȳrinthus -i, m. a labyrinth.

lăc lactis, n. milk; milky sap; milk-white
colour.

Lăcaena -ae, f. adj. (female) Spartan.

Lăcĕdaemon -ŏnis, f. the city Lace-
daemon or Sparta; adj. Lăcĕdae-
mŏnĭus -a -um, Lacedaemonian.

lăcer -cĕra -cĕrum, torn, mangled; act.,
tearing to pieces.

lăcĕrātĭo -ōnis, f. tearing, mangling.

lăcerna -ae, f. a mantle worn over the
toga.

lăcĕro -are, to tear to pieces, maim,
mangle; to squander money; to
slander, pull to pieces a character.

lăcerta -ae, f. a lizard; also a sea-fish.

lăcertōsus -a -um, muscular, powerful.

¹lăcertus -i, m., the upper arm with its
muscles; in gen., vigour.

²lăcertus -i, m. = lacerta; q.v.

lăcesso -ĕre -īvi and -ĭi -ītum, to
provoke, exasperate, excite, induce.

Lăchĕsis -is, f., one of the three Parcae
or Fates.

lăcinĭa -ae, f. the flap of a garment.

Lăco (Lăcōn) -ōnis, m., a Spartan,
Lacedaemonian; adj. Lăcōnĭcus -a
-um and f. adj. Lăcōnis -ĭdis,
Spartan.

lăcrĭma (lăcrŭma) -ae, f. a tear;
exudation from certain plants; Helia-
dum, amber.

lacrĭmābĭlis -e, deplorable, woeful.

lacrĭmābundus -a -um, breaking into
tears, weeping.

lacrĭmo (lacrŭmo) -are, to weep, shed
tears; to exude, to drip.

lacrĭmōsus -a -um: tearful, shedding
tears: causing tears, mournful, piteous.

lacrĭmŭla -ae, f., a little tear.

lacrŭma, etc.; see lacrima, etc.

lactans -antis, giving milk.

lactātĭo -ōnis, f. enticement.

lactens -entis. (1) sucking milk; plur.
as subst., sucklings, unweaned animals.
(2) milky, juicy, full of sap.

lactesco -ĕre, to be changed into milk.

lactĕus -a -um, milky, of milk; milk-
white.

lacto -are, to allure, wheedle.

lactūca -ae, f. lettuce.

lăcūna -ae, f. a cavity, hollow, dip;
esp. a pool, pond. Transf., gap,
deficiency, loss.

lăcūnăr -āris, n. a panelled ceiling.

lăcūno -are, to work in panels, to panel.

lăcūnōsus -a -um, full of hollows or
gaps.

lăcus -ūs, m. a hollow; hence a lake,
pool, trough, tank, tub.

laedo laedĕre laesi laesum, to strike,
knock; hence to hurt, injure, damage;
to offend, annoy; to violate, outrage.

laena -ae, f. cloak.

Lāertēs -ae, m. father of Ulysses.

laesio -ōnis, f. an oratorical attack.

laetābĭlis -e, joyful, glad.

laetātĭo -ōnis, f. rejoicing, joy.

laetĭfĭco -are, to fertilize; to cheer
gladden, delight.

laetĭfĭcus -a -um, gladdening, joyous.

laetĭtĭa -ae, f. (1) fertility; hence
richness, grace. (2) joy, delight.

laetor -ari, dep. to rejoice, be joyful.

laetus -a -um, fat, rich, fertile; glad,
joyful, happy; of style, rich, copious,
fluent. Adv. laetē.

laevus -a -um, left; f. as subst., the
left hand, the left; n. as subst., the
left side. Transf., left-handed, foolish,
silly; unlucky, unpropitious; but in
augury, favourable. Adv. laevē,
on the left hand; awkwardly.

lăgănum -i, n., a cake.

lăgēos -ei, f., a Greek kind of vine.

lăgoena a large earthen jar with handles.

lăgōis -idis, f. a bird, perhaps heathcock
or grouse.

lăguncŭla -ae, f. a little bottle.

Lāïus -i, m. father of Oedipus.

lambo lambĕre lambi, to lick; of rivers,
to wash.

lāmenta -orum, n. pl. wailing, weeping.

lāmentābĭlis = lamentable, deplorable;
expressing sorrow, mournful.

lāmentātĭo -ōnis, f. weeping, wailing.

lāmentor -ari, dep. to weep, wail,
lament; transit., to bewail.

lămĭa -ae, f. a witch, vampire.

lāmĭna, lammĭna, and lamna -ae,
f. a plate or thin piece of metal,
marble, etc.; knife-blade; coin; nutshell.

lampās -pădis, f. *a torch*; hence *brightness*, esp. of the sun; also *a meteor*.

lāna -ae, f., *wool*; also *the down on leaves, fruit,* etc.

lānātus -a -um, *wool-bearing, woolly.*

lancĕa -ae, f. *a light spear or lance.*

lancīno -are, *to tear to pieces; to squander.*

lānĕus -a -um, *of wool, woollen; soft as wool.*

languĕfăcio -făcĕre, *to make weak or faint.*

languĕo -ēre, *to be faint, weak, weary; to droop, flag*; partic. **languens** -entis, *faint, languid.*

languesco languescĕre langŭi, *to become faint, soft or listless.*

languidŭlus -a -um, *somewhat faint, limp.*

languidus -a -um, *faint, weak, limp*; of wine, *mild, mellow*; adv. **languĭdē.**

languor -ōris, m. *faintness, weariness, inactivity.*

lănĭātus -ūs, m. *mangling, tearing.*

lănĭĕna -ae, f. *a butcher's shop.*

lānĭfĭcus -a -um, *working in wool.*

lānĭger -gĕra -gĕrum, *wool-bearing; woollen*; m. as subst. *a ram*; f., *a sheep.*

lănĭo -are, *to tear to pieces, mangle, lacerate.*

lănista -ae, m. *a trainer of gladiators; an instigator to violence, inciter.*

lānĭtĭum -i, n. *wool.*

lānĭus -i, m. *butcher.*

lanterna -ae, f. *lantern, lamp.*

lanternārĭus -i, m. *lantern-bearer.*

lānūgo -ĭnis, f. *down, of plants or on the cheeks.*

Lānŭvĭum -i, n. *a town in Latium.*

lanx lancis, f. *a plate, platter; the scale of a balance.*

Lāŏcŏōn -ontis, m. *a Trojan priest.*

Lāŏmĕdōn -ontis, m. *a king of Troy, father of Priam.*

lăpāthum -i, n. and **lăpāthus** -i, f. *sorrel.*

lăpĭcīdīnae -arum, f. *stone quarries.*

lăpĭdātĭo -ōnis, f. *throwing of stones.*

lăpĭdātor -ōris, m. *thrower of stones.*

lăpĭdĕus -a -um, *of stone.*

lăpĭdo -are, *to throw stones at*; impers. lapidat, *it rains stones.*

lăpĭdōsus -a -um, *full of stones, stony.*

lăpillus -i, m. *a little stone, pebble; a precious stone, gem.*

lăpis -ĭdis, m. *a stone.*

Lăpĭthae -arum, m. pl. *the Lapithae, a mountain race in Thessaly, famous for their fight with the Centaurs.*

lappa -ae, f. *a burr.*

lapsĭo -ōnis, f. *gliding; inclination, tendency.*

lapso -are, *to slip, stumble.*

lapsus -ūs, m. *gradual movement; gliding, sliding, fall; a fault, error.*

lăquĕārĕ -is, n., esp. plur., *a panelled ceiling.*

lăquĕātus -a -um, *with a panelled ceiling.*

lăquĕus -i, m. *a noose, halter, snare, trap.*

Lār Lāris, m., usually plur. **Lāres,** *Roman tutelary deities,* esp. *household*

deities; meton., *hearth, dwelling, home.*

lardum (lārĭdum) -i, n. *bacon fat, lard.*

Lārentĭa -ae, f., or **Acca Lārentĭa,** *the wife of Faustulus, who brought up Romulus and Remus.*

Lāres; see Lar.

largĭfĭcus -a -um, *bountiful, liberal.*

largĭflŭus -a -um, *flowing freely.*

largĭor -iri, dep. *to give abundantly, lavish, bestow, grant; to condone.*

largĭtās -ātis, f. *liberality.*

largĭtĭo -ōnis, f. *free giving or spending, lavishing; granting, bestowing.*

largĭtor -ōris, m. *a liberal giver or spender; a briber; a waster.*

largus -a -um, *of things, abundant, plentiful, numerous*; with genit., *rich in*; of persons, *liberal, bountiful.* Adv. **largē,** *plentifully, liberally*; **largĭtĕr,** *abundantly, much.*

lārĭdum -i, n. = lardum; q.v.

larva (lărŭa) -ae, f. *a ghost, spectre; a mask.*

lascīvĭa -ae, f. *playfulness, sportiveness, wantonness, licentiousness, insolence.*

lascīvĭo -ire, *to sport, play; to wanton, run riot.*

lascīvus -a -um, *playful, wanton, licentious, insolent.* Adv. **lascīvē.**

lăserpīcĭum -i, n. *a plant from which asafoetida was obtained.*

lassĭtūdo -ĭnis, f., *weariness, exhaustion.*

lasso -are, *to make weary, exhaust.*

lassŭlus -a -um, *rather tired.*

lassus -a -um, *weary, tired, exhausted.*

lătĕbra -ae, f. *a hiding-place, retreat; a subterfuge, loophole.*

lătĕbrōsus -a -um, *full of hiding-places, secret*; pumex, *porous.* Adv. **lătĕbrōsē,** *secretly.*

lătĕo -ēre, *to lie hid, be concealed; to live in obscurity or safety; to be unknown.*
   Hence partic. **lătens** -entis, *concealed, hidden*; adv. **lătentĕr,** *secretly.*

lăter -tĕris, m. *a brick, tile.*

lătĕrāmen -inis, n. *pottery.*

lătercŭlus -i m. *a small brick or tile; a biscuit.*

lătērīcĭus -a -um, *built of brick.*

lāterna; see lanterna.

lătesco -ĕre, *to hide oneself.*

lătex -tĭcis, m. *fluid, liquid.*

lătĭbŭlum -i, n., *a hiding-place.*

lātĭclāvĭus -a -um, *having a broad purple stripe (as a distinction).*

lātĭfundĭum -i, n. *a large landed estate.*

Lătīnĭtās -ātis, f. *pure Latin style; Latin rights.*

¹**Lătīnus** -a -um; see Latium.

²**Lătīnus** -i, m. *king of the Laurentians, host of Aeneas.*

lātĭo -ōnis, f. *bringing*; legis, *proposing, bringing forward.*

lătĭto -are, *to lie hid, be concealed.*

lātĭtūdo -ĭnis, f. *breadth, extent*; verborum, *broad pronunciation, brogue.*

Lătĭum -i, n. *a district of Italy, in which Rome was situated*; adj. **Lătĭus** and **Lătīnus** -a -um, *Latin*; adv. **Lătīnē,** *in Latin.*

Lātō -ūs, f. and **Lātōna** -ae, f. *the mother of Apollo and Diana.*

lātor -ōris, m. *the proposer of a law.*

lātrātor -ōris, m. *a barker.*

lātrātus -ūs, m. *barking.*

¹lātro -are, *to bark, bay; to rant, rumble, roar;* transit., *to bark at* or *for.*

²latro -ōnis, m. *a hired servant* or *mercenary soldier; a robber, bandit, brigand; a hunter; a piece on a draught-board.*

latrōcinium -i, n. *mercenary service; highway robbery, brigandage, villainy, roguery;* meton., *a band of robbers.*

latrōcinor -ari, dep. *to serve as a mercenary; to practise robbery.*

latrunculus -i, m. *a highwayman, bandit; a piece on a draught-board.*

¹lātus -a -um, partic. from fero; q.v.

²lātus -a -um, *broad, wide, extensive;* of style, *diffuse, full, rich.* Hence adv. **lātē,** *broadly, widely, extensively;* longe lateque, *far and wide.*

³lātus -ĕris, n. *the side, flank;* of persons, in pl., *the lungs;* milit., *a latere, on the flank.*

lātusculum -i, n. *a little side.*

laudābilis -e, *praiseworthy, laudable;* adv. **laudābilĭtĕr.**

laudātĭo -ōnis, f. *praise, commendation; a testimonial; a funeral oration.*

laudātor -ōris, m. *a praiser; esp. one who delivers a testimonial* or *funeral oration.*

laudātrix -īcis, f. *a (female) praiser.*

laudo -are, *to praise, extol, commend; to name, mention, cite, quote;* partic. **laudātus** -a -um, *praiseworthy, esteemed.*

laureātus -a -um, *crowned with laurel;* litterae, *bringing news of victory.*

laureŏla -ae, f. *a laurel branch, laurel crown;* meton., *a triumph, victory.*

laureus -a -um, *of laurel;* f. as subst., **laurea,** *laurel tree* or *laurel crown.*

lauricŏmus -a -um, *covered with laurel-trees.*

laurifer -fĕra -fĕrum, and **lauriger** -gĕra -gĕrum, *crowned with laurels.*

laurus -i, f. *the laurel* or *bay-tree;* meton., *triumph, victory.*

laus laudis, f. *praise, fame, glory, commendation.* Transf., *a praiseworthy action* or *quality.*

lautia -orum, n. pl., *entertainment given to foreign ambassadors at Rome.*

lautitia -ae, f. *splendour, elegance, sumptuous living.*

lautŭmiae (lātŏmiae) -arum, f. *a stone-quarry.*

lautus -a -um, partic. from lavo; q.v.

lāvabrum -i, n. *a bath.*

lăvātĭo -ōnis, f. *washing, bathing; bathing apparatus.*

Lāvīnĭa -ae, f. *daughter of Latinus, wife of Aeneas.*

lăvo lăvare *or* lăvĕre lāvi lautum *or* lōtum *or* lăvatum, *to wash, bathe; to moisten, wet; to wash away.* Hence partic. **lautus** -a -um, *washed;* hence *fine, elegant, sumptuous, refined;* adv. **lautē.**

laxāmentum -i, n. *widening, extending; relaxing, mitigation, respite.*

laxĭtās -ātis, f. *wideness, roominess.*

laxo -are, *to widen, loosen, extend, enlarge; to undo, slacken, relax, relieve; to release, set free.*

laxus -a -um, *wide, loose, spacious;* of time, *later, postponed; loose, lax, relaxed.* Adv. **laxē,** *widely, loosely, without restraint.*

lĕa -ae, and **lĕaena** -ae, f. *a lioness.*

Lĕander -dri, m. *a youth who swam nightly across the Hellespont to visit Hero, till drowned in a storm.*

lĕbēs -ētis, m. *a bronze pan, cauldron,* or *basin.*

lectĭca -ae, f. *a litter; a bier.*

lectĭcārĭus -i, m. *litter-bearer.*

lectĭcŭla -ae, f. *a small litter* or *bier; a settee.*

lectĭo -ōnis, f. *a picking out, selection, reading, perusal;* lectio senatus, *a calling over of the names of the senators.*

lectisternĭum -i, n. *a feast offered to the gods.*

lectĭto -are, *to read often* or *eagerly.*

lector -ōris, m. *a reader.*

lectŭlus -i, m. *a small bed, couch.*

¹lectus -a -um, partic. from lego; q.v.

²lectus -i, m. *a bed, couch.*

Lēda -ae, and **Lēdē** -es, f. *mother of Castor, Pollux, Helen, and Clytemnestra.*

lēgātārĭus -i, m. *a legatee.*

lēgātĭo -ōnis, f. *delegated authority;* polit., *the office of an ambassador, an embassy, legation;* milit., *the post of subordinate commander; esp. the command of a legion.*

lēgātor -ōris, m. *testator.*

lēgātum -i, n. and **lēgātus** -i, m., from lego; q.v.

lēgĭfer -fĕra -fĕrum, *law-giving.*

lĕgĭo -ōnis, f. *a choosing; a chosen body; esp. a legion, a division of the Roman army.*

lĕgĭōnārĭus -a -um, *belonging to a legion.*

lēgĭtĭmus (lēgĭtŭmus) -a -um, *lawful, legitimate; right, proper, appropriate.* Adv. **lēgĭtĭmē,** *lawfully, properly.*

lĕgĭuncŭla -ae, f. *a small legion.*

¹lēgo -are, *to ordain, appoint;* of persons, *to make a deputy, delegate authority to;* of property, *to bequeath, leave as a legacy.* M. of partic. as subst. **lēgātus** -i, *a deputy;* polit., *an ambassador, envoy,* or *the deputy of a magistrate;* milit., *a subordinate commander; esp. commander of a legion.* N. **lēgātum** -i, *a legacy, bequest.*

²lĕgo lĕgĕre lēgi lectum, *to collect, gather, pick, pick up;* fila, *to wind up, spin;* vela, *to furl;* of places, *to pass through, traverse, coast along;* with the eyes, *to survey, scan, read, peruse;* out of a number, *to pick out, choose, select.* Hence partic. **lectus** -a -um, *chosen, selected; choice, excellent.*

lēgŭlēius -i, m. *a pettifogging lawyer.*

lĕgūmen -inis, n. *pulse; the bean.*

Lēmannus -i, m. *the Lake of Geneva.*

lembus -i, m. *a boat, cutter, pinnace.*

lemma -ătis, n. *theme, title; an epigram.*

lemniscātus -a -um, *ribboned.*

lemniscus -i, m. *a ribbon.*

Lemnos (-us) -i, f. *the island of Lemnos in the Aegean Sea;* adj. **Lemnius** -a -um, *Lemnian.*

lĕmŭrēs -um, m. pl. *ghosts, spectres;* **Lĕmŭria** -orum, n. pl. *a festival held in May to expel ghosts.*

lēna -ae, f. *a procuress, bawd.*

Lēnaeus -a -um, *Bacchic.*

lēnīmen -inis, n. *means of alleviation.*

lēnīmentum -i, n. *mitigation, alleviation.*

lēnio -ire, *to make mild, mitigate, relieve.*

lēnis -e, *smooth, mild, gentle;* vinum, *mellow;* n. acc. as adv. **lēnĕ,** *gently;* adv. **lēnĭtĕr** *smoothly, gently, mildly.*

lēnĭtās -ātis, f. and **lēnĭtūdo** -inis, f. *gentleness, mildness, smoothness.*

lēno -ōnis, m. *a procurer, a go-between.*

lēnōcĭnĭum -i, n. *the trade of a procurer; enticement, allurement;* of dress, *finery;* of style, ' *purple patch* '.

lēnōcĭnor -ari, dep. *to work as a procurer; to make up to, to flatter; to advance, promote.*

lens lentis, f. *lentil.*

lentesco -ĕre, *to become pliant, soft, sticky; to weaken, slacken.*

lentiscus -i, f. and **lentiscum** -i, n. *the mastic-tree.*

lentĭtūdo inis, f. *slowness, sluggishness, apathy.*

lento -are, *to bend.*

¹lentŭlus -a -um, *somewhat slow.*

²Lentŭlus -i, m. *the name of a family in the patrician gens Cornelia.*

lentus -a -um, *tough, resistant, inert; sticky, tenacious; supple, pliant; inactive, apathetic; slow, lingering;* in dicendo, *drawling.* Adv. **lentē,** *slowly, calmly, coolly, deliberately.*

¹lēnuncŭlus -i, m. *a little procurer.*

²lēnuncŭlus -i, m. *a small boat or skiff.*

lĕo -ōnis, m. *lion.*

lĕōnīnus -a -um, *of a lion, leonine.*

Lĕontīni -orum, m. *a town on the east coast of Sicily.*

lĕpās -ădis, f. *a limpet.*

¹lĕpĭdus -a -um, *pleasant, charming, elegant, witty;* adv. **lĕpĭdē.**

²Lĕpĭdus -i, m. *name of a family in the patrician gens Aemilia.*

lĕpor and **lĕpos** -ōris, m. *pleasantness, charm, wit.*

lĕpus -ŏris, m. *hare.*

lĕpuscŭlus -i, m. *a young hare.*

Lesbos (-us) -i, f. *an island in the Aegean Sea, birth-place of Alcaeus and Sappho.*

lētālis -e, *deadly, mortal.*

lēthargĭcus -i, m. *a drowsy, lethargic.*

lēthargus -i, m. *drowsiness, lethargy, coma.*

Lēthē -ēs, f. *the river of forgetfulness in the underworld.*

lētĭfer -fĕra -fĕrum, *deadly.*

lēto -are, *to kill, slay.*

lētum -i, n. *death; ruin, annihilation.*

leucaspis -idis, f. *having white shields.*

lĕvāmen -īnis, n. and **lĕvāmentum** -i, n. *alleviation, mitigation, solace.*

lĕvātio -ōnis, f. *alleviation, mitigation; diminution.*

lĕvĭcŭlus -a -um, *rather vain, light-headed.*

lĕvĭdensis -e, *thin, slight, poor.*

¹lĕvis -e, *light;* milit., *light-armed;* in movement, *rapid, swift;* in value, *light, trifling, unimportant;* in character, *fickle, capricious, unstable.* Adv. **lĕvĭtĕr,** *lightly, softly, slightly.*

²lēvis -e, *smooth, polished, slippery; beardless, bald.*

lēvĭsomnus -a -um, *lightly sleeping.*

¹lĕvĭtās -ātis, f. *lightness; levity, fickleness, inconstancy; groundlessness.*

²lēvĭtās -ātis, f. *smoothness, polish.*

¹lĕvo -are, *to raise, lift up; to make light, relieve, ease; to diminish, weaken, impair.*

²lēvo -are, *to make smooth, polish.*

lēvor -ōris, m. *smoothness.*

lex lēgis, f. *a set form of words, contract, covenant, agreement;* leges pacis, *conditions of peace;* esp. *a law, proposed by a magistrate as a bill, or passed and statutory;* legem ferre, rogare, *to propose a bill;* legem iubere, *to accept or pass a bill;* in gen., *a precept, rule.*

lībāmen -īnis, n. *a libation, offering to the gods; a sample, specimen.*

lībāmentum -i, n. *a libation, offering to the gods.*

lībātio -ōnis, f. *a libation.*

lībella -ae, f. (1) *a small coin, a tenth of a denarius; a farthing, mite.* (2) *a carpenter's level, plummet-line.*

libellus -i, m. *a little book, note-book, diary; a memorial, petition; programme, placard; letter.*

libens and **lŭbens** -entis, partic. from libet; q.v.

¹līber -ĕra -ĕrum, *free, independent, unrestrained; free from, exempt.* Adv. **lībĕrē,** *freely, without restraint, frankly, openly, boldly.*

²līber -bri, m. *the inner bark of a tree;* from the use of this in writing, *a book, volume, catalogue, letter.*

³Līber -ĕri, m. *an Italian deity, identified with Bacchus.*

lībĕrālis -e, *of freedom; worthy of a free man, gentlemanlike, courteous, generous;* adv. **lībĕrālĭtĕr.**

lībĕrālĭtās -ātis, f. *courtesy, kindness, generosity.* Transf. *a grant.*

lībĕrātio -ōnis, f. *setting free, release, acquittal.*

lībĕrātor -ōris, m. *a liberator.*

lībĕri -ērōrum and -ērum, m. pl. *children.*

lībĕro -are, *to set free, liberate, release, exempt;* of obstacles, *to lift, raise.*

liberta -ae, f.; see libertus.

lībertās -ātis, f. *freedom, liberty, independence; freedom of speech, frankness, candour.*

lībertīnus -a -um, *of the class of freed-man*; as subst. m. **libertinus** *a freedman*, f. **libertīna**, *a freedwoman*.

libertus -i, m. *a freedman*; **liberta** -ae, f. *a freedwoman*.

libet (**lŭbet**) -bēre -bŭit or -bitum est impers., *it pleases, is agreeable* (with dat. of person).
Hence partic. **lĭbens** (**lŭbens**) -entis, *willing, with pleasure, pleased*; me libente, *with my good-will*; adv. **lībenter** (**lŭbenter**), *willingly, with pleasure*.

lĭbīdĭnōsus -a -um, *wilful, arbitrary, capricious; passionate, lustful*. Adv. **libīdĭnōsē,** *wilfully, arbitrarily*.

lĭbīdo (**lŭbīdo**) -inis, f. *violent desire, longing*; esp. irrational *whim, caprice*; or immoderate *passion, lust*.

Lĭbītīna -ae, f. *goddess of the dead*.

lĭbo -are, *to take away from, remove, derive; to taste, touch, impair, diminish; to give a taste of, offer to the gods*.

lībra -ae, f. (1) *a balance, pair of scales*; aes et libra, *a fictitious form of sale*. (2) *the Roman pound of 12 oz*.

lībrāmentum -i, n. (1) *weight as a source of power or for balancing*. (2) *a horizontal plane*.

lībrārĭa -ae, f *a female who weighed out wool to slaves*.

lībrārĭus -a -um, *of books*; m. as subst., *a transcriber of books, a copyist,* or *a bookseller*; n. as subst., *a bookcase*.

lībrĭlis -e, *of a pound weight*.

lībrĭtor -ōris, m. *an artilleryman*.

lībro -are, *to balance, hold up, poise*; of weapons, *to swing, level, brandish*; hence, *to hurl*.

lĭbum -i, n. *a cake, offered to the gods*.

Lĭburni -orum, m. *the Liburnians, a people of Illyria*; f. of adj. as subst. **Lĭburna** -ae, *a light vessel, galley*.

Lĭbya -ae and **Lĭbyē** -ēs, f. *Libya*

lĭcens -centis, and **lĭcentĕr** from licet; q.v.

lĭcentĭa -ae, f. *freedom, leave, liberty; licentiousness*.

lĭcĕo -ēre -ŭi -ĭtum, *to be on sale, be valued at*.

lĭcĕor -ēri, dep. *to bid* or *bid for, offer a price*.

lĭcet lĭcēre lĭcŭit or lĭcĭtum est, impers., *it is allowed, one can* or *may*; as conjunction, *granted that, although*. Hence pres. partic. **lĭcens** -entis, *free, unrestrained, unbridled*; adv. **lĭcentĕr**; perf. partic. **lĭcĭtus** -a -um, *allowed, permitted*.

Lĭcĭnĭus -a -um, *name of a Roman gens*.

lĭcĭtātĭo -onis, f. *bidding at a sale* or *auction*.

lĭcĭtus -a -um, partic. from licet; q.v.

lĭcĭum -i, n.: in weaving, *the thrum* or perhaps *a leash*; in gen., *a thread*.

lictor -ōris, m. *a lictor, attending the chief Roman magistrates*.

lĭgāmen -inis, n. *string, tie, bandage*.

lĭgāmentum -i, n. *bandage*.

Lĭgĕr -gĕris, m. *a river* (now the *Loire*).

lignārĭus -i, m. *a carpenter*.

lignātĭo -ōnis, f. *wood-cutting*.

lignātor -ōris, m. *wood-cutter*.

lignĕŏlus -a -um, *wooden*.

lignĕus -a -um, *made of wood, wooden*.

lignor -ari, dep. *to cut* or *get wood*.

lignum -i, n. *wood, timber*; esp. *fire-wood*.

¹lĭgo -are, *to bind, bandage, harness; to bind together, connect, unite*.

²lĭgo -ōnis, m. *a mattock*.

lĭgŭla (**lingŭla**) ac, f. *a tongue of land, promontory; a shoe-strap*.

Lĭgŭrēs -um, m. pl. *the Ligurians, a people on the north-west coast of Italy*.

lĭgūrĭo (**lĭgurrĭo**) -ire, *to lick lick up; to gloat over; long for*.

lĭgūrītĭo (**lĭgurr**-) -ōnis, f. *daintiness*

lĭgustrum -i, n. *privet*.

lĭlĭum -i, n. *a lily*; milit. *a fortification consisting of pits and stakes*.

Lĭlȳbaeon (**-baeum**) -i, n. *a promontory and town at the western end of Sicily*.

līma -ae, f. *a file; polishing, revision of a composition*.

līmātŭlus -a -um *rather polished refined*.

limbus -i, m. *a border, hem, fringe*.

līmen -inis, n. *threshold, doorway, entrance; home, house, dwelling; any entrance* or *border* or *beginning*; esp. *the starting-point in a race-course*.

līmes -itis, m. *a by-way, path; a course, track*; esp. *a boundary-path, a boundary-line; a distinction, difference*.

līmo -are, *to file, polish, finish off; to investigate accurately; to file down, pare down, to diminish*. Partic. **līmātus** -a -um, *refined elegant*; compar. adv. **līmātĭus**.

līmōsus -a -um, *slimy, miry, muddy*.

limpĭdus -a -um, *clear, limpid*.

¹līmus -a -um, *of the eyes, sidelong, looking sideways*.

²līmus -i, m. *slime, mud, mire*.

³līmus -i, m. *a priest's apron*.

līnĕa -ae, f. *a linen thread, string; a fishing-line, plumb-line*; ad lineam, *perpendicularly*. Transf., *a geometrical line; a boundary-line, goal*.

līnĕāmentum -i, n. *a line drawn with pen* or *pencil*; plur., *drawing, sketch, outline*; in gen., *a feature, lineament*.

līnĕo -are, *to make straight*.

līnĕus -a -um, *of flax* or *linen*.

lingo lingĕre linxi linctum, *to lick*.

lingua -ae, f. *a tongue; speech, language: a tongue of land, promontory*.

lingŭlāca -ae, f. *a chatterbox*.

līnĭger -gēra -gĕrum, *clothed in linen*.

līno linĕre livi (and lēvi) lĭtum, *to smear one thing upon another*; or *to besmear one thing with another*; *to rub out* writing; *to befoul, dirty*.

linquo linquĕre liqui, *to leave, abandon, forsake*; pass., linqui, *to faint*.

lintĕātus -a -um, *clothed in linen*.

lintĕo -ōnis, m. *a linen-weaver*.

linter -tris, f. *a boat, skiff; a trough, tub, vat*.

lintĕus -a -um, *of linen*; n. as subst. *linen cloth, linen*, esp. *a sail*.

līnum -i, n. *flax, linen; a thread, line; a rope, cable.*

lippio -ire, *to have sore eyes, be bleareyed.*

lippĭtūdo -inis, f. *inflammation of the eyes.*

lippus -a -um, *blear-eyed; half-blind.*

liquĕfăcio -făcĕre -fēci -factum, pass. liquĕfĭo -fiĕri -factus sum, *to melt, dissolve; to decompose; to make weak, enervate.*

liquesco -ĕre -licŭi, *to become fluid, melt, melt away, to putrefy; to become effeminate.*

liquĭdus -a -um. (1) *fluid, flowing, liquid*; n. as subst. *a liquid.* (2) *clear, bright, serene, calm, pure, evident, certain*; n. as subst. *certainty*; abl. sing. liquĭdō and adv. liquĭdē, *clearly, plainly.*

liquo -are, *to make liquid, melt; to strain, clarify.*

¹liquor -i, dep. *to be fluid, flow, melt; to melt away*; partic. liquens -entis, *flowing.*

²liquor -ōris, m. *fluidity; a liquid, fluid.*

lis, litis, f. *a legal controversy, action, suit; in gen., contention strife, quarrel.*

lītātio -onis, f. *successful sacrifice.*

lītĭgātor -ōris, m. *a party in a law-suit, litigant.*

lītĭgiōsus -a -um, *of persons, fond of dispute, litigious; of things, full of dispute, contested at law.*

lītĭgo -are, *to go to law; in gen., to quarrel, dispute.*

līto -are: intransit., *to bring an acceptable offering, and so to obtain favourable omens*; transit., *to sacrifice successfully.*

lītōrālis -e, and lītŏrĕus -a -um *of the shore.*

littĕra (lītĕra) ae, f. *a letter of the alphabet; a letter, dispatch, epistle*; plur., *written records, documents, deeds; literature, letters, scholarship.*

littĕrārius -a -um, *of reading and writing.*

littĕrātor -ōris, m. *a philologist, grammarian, critic.*

littĕrātūra -ae, f. *the alphabet, grammar.*

littĕrātus -a -um, *lettered, inscribed with letters; learned, liberally educated.* Adv. littĕrātē, *in clear letters, legibly; literally, word for word; learnedly.*

littĕrŭla -ae, f. *a letter (of the alphabet) written small*; plur., *a little letter, a note, a smattering of literature.*

littus, etc.; see litus, etc.

litūra -ae, f. *an erasure, correction, a passage erased; a blot.*

lītus -ōris, n. *sea-shore, beach, strand, coast; the shore of a lake or river.*

lĭtŭus -i, m. *an augur's curved staff; a curved cavalry trumpet, clarion.*

līveo -ēre, *to be bluish in colour; to be envious, envy*; partic. livens -entis, *bluish, livid; envious.*

līvesco -ēre, *to become bluish.*

līvĭdŭlus -a -um, *rather envious*

līvĭdus -a -um, *bluish, livid, black and blue; envious, spiteful.*

Līvius -a -um, *name of a Roman gens.*

līvor -ōris, m. *bluish colour, a livid spot; envy, spite.*

lixa -ae, m. *a sutler, camp-follower.*

lŏcātio -ōnis, f. *placing; hence a leasing, contract, lease.*

lŏcātŏrius -a -um, *concerned with leases.*

lŏco -are, *to place, put, set; esp. to give in marriage; commerc., to let out on hire, farm out, lease, invest; to contract for work to be done.* N. of partic. as subst. lŏcātum -i, *a lease, contract.*

lŏcŭlus -i, m. *a little place*; plur., *loculi, a money-box; a school satchel.*

lŏcŭplēs -plētis, *with landed property, wealthy, rich; also trusty, sufficient, satisfactory.*

lŏcŭplēto -are, *to enrich.*

lŏcus -i, m. (plur., loci, *single places*; loca, *region), a place; milit., position, ground, post; in time, a period, or moment; position, situation, rank; occasion, cause; passage in a book.*

¹lŏcusta -ae, f. *a locust; a kind of lobster.*

²Lŏcusta -ae, f. *a notorious poisoner, accomplice of Nero.*

lŏcūtio -ōnis, f. *speech; pronunciation.*

lōdix -dicis, f. *blanket, rug.*

lŏgĭcus -a -um, *logical*; n. pl. as subst. *logic.*

lŏgŏs (-us) -i, m. *a word; a joke, jest, bon mot.*

lōlium -i, n. *darnel.*

lolligo -iginis, f. *cuttle-fish.*

lōmentum -i, n. *face-cream.*

Londīnium -i, n. *London.*

longaevus -a -um, *aged, old.*

longinquĭtās -ātis, f. *length, distance, remoteness; of time, duration.*

longinquus -a -um, *long, distant, far, remote, foreign; of time, long, distant.*

longĭtūdo -inis, f. *length.*

longŭius -a -um, *rather long*; adv. longŭlē, *rather far, at a little distance.*

longŭrius -i, m. *a pole, rod, rail.*

longus -a -um, *long; navis, a man-of-war; poet., spacious; of time, long, of long duration: esp. too long, tedious; of persons, prolix, tedious.* Adv. longē, *a long way off, far, at a distance; by far; in time, long, at length; adv. longĭtĕr, far.*

lŏquācĭtās -ātis, f. *talkativeness.*

lŏquācŭlus -a -um, *rather talkative.*

lŏquax -quācis, *talkative, garrulous, babbling, noisy*; adv. lŏquācĭtĕr.

lŏquella (lŏquēla) -ae, f. *speech, language.*

lŏquor lŏqui lŏcūtus, dep. *to speak (in conversation); to tell, say, talk of.*

lōrātus -a -um, *bound with thongs.*

lōrīca -ae, f. *cuirass, corselet, breast plate; breastwork, parapet.*

lōrīcātus -a -um, *wearing a cuirass.*

lōrĭpēs -pĕdis, *bandy-legged.*

lōrum -i, n. *a strap or thong of leather*; plur., *reins, bridle; scourge, whip.*

lōtŏs (-us) -i, f. *the name of several plants; esp. of an African tree and its fruit.*

¹lōtus -a -um, partic. from lavo; q.v.

²lōtus -i, f. = lotos; q.v.

lŭbet, lŭbīdo, etc. = libet, libido, etc.; q.v.

lūbrĭco -are, *to make slippery.*

lūbrĭcus -a -um, *slippery, smooth; quickly moving, uncertain, insecure, perilous, deceitful.*

Lūcāni -orum, m. pl. *a people in Southern Italy.*

Lūcānus -i, m., M. Annaeus, *author of the poem* Pharsalia.

lūcar -āris, n. *a forest-tax, used for paying actors.*

lūcellum -i, n. *little profit, small gain.*

lūcĕo lūcēre luxi, *to be bright, shine, glitter; to be clear, evident;* impers., lucet, *it is light, it is day.*

Lucĕrēs -um, m. *one of the three patrician tribes.*

lŭcerna -ae, f. *lamp.*

lūcesco (lūcisco) lūcescēre luxi, *to begin to shine;* impers., lucescit, *it grows light, day is breaking.*

lūcĭdus -a -um, *shining, bright; clear, lucid;* adv. lūcĭdē.

lūcĭfer -fĕra -fĕrum, *light-bearing, light-bringing;* m. as subst., *the morning star.*

lūcĭfŭgus -a -um, *shunning the light.*

Lūcīlius -a -um, *name of a Roman gens.*

Lūcīna -ae, f. *the goddess of births.*

lūcisco = lucesco; q.v.

Lūcĭus -i, m. Roman praenomen (abbreviated to L.).

Lucrētĭus -a -um, *name of a Roman gens.*

lucrĭfācĭo -fācĕre *to gain, receive as profit.*

Lucrīnus -i, m. *a lake on the coast of Campania, near Baiae, famous for oysters.*

lucror -ari, dep. *to gain, profit, win.*

lucrōsus -a -um, *gainful, profitable.*

lucrum -i, n. *gain, profit, advantage; love of gain, avarice.*

luctāmen -ĭnis, n. *effort, toil.*

luctātĭo -ōnis, f. *wrestling; a struggle contest.*

luctātor -ōris, m. *wrestler.*

luctĭfĭcus -a -um, *causing grief, baleful.*

luctĭsŏnus -a -um, *sad-sounding.*

luctor -ari, dep (and lucto -are), *to wrestle, struggle, strive, contend.*

luctŭōsus -a -um, (1) *causing sorrow, doleful.* (2) *feeling or showing sorrow, mourning.* Compar. adv. luctŭōsius.

luctus -ūs, m. *sorrow expressed, lamentation, mourning; mourning clothes.*

lūcubrātĭo -ōnis, f. *work done by night or lamp-light, nocturnal study.*

lūcubro -are, *to work by night;* in perf. partic. lūcubrātus -a -um, *done at night or spent in work.*

lūcŭlentus -a -um, *shining, bright, brilliant, splendid;* adv. lūcŭlentē and lūcŭlentĕr, *splendidly.*

Lūcullus -i, m. *name of a family in the gens* Licinia.

Lŭcūmo (Lŭcŏmo, Lucmo) -ōnis, m. *title given to Etruscan princes and priests.*

lūcus -i, m. *a (sacred) grove or wood.*

lūdĭa -ae, f. *an actress or female gladiator.*

lūdĭbrĭum -i, n. *derision, mockery; an object of derision, laughing-stock, plaything.*

lūdĭbundus -a -um, *playful, sportive.*

lūdĭcer -cra -crum, *sportive, done for sport; esp. of the stage.* N. as subst. lūdĭcrum -i, *a trifle, plaything; a theatrical performance.*

lūdĭfĭcātĭo -ōnis, f. *deriding, deceiving.*

lūdĭfĭco -are and lūdĭfĭcor -ari, dep. *to make game of, deride, delude, cheat, frustrate.*

lūdĭo -ōnis, m. and lūdĭus -i, m. *an actor.*

lūdo lūdĕre lūsi lūsum, *to play, sport; to play at or with; to imitate, banter, deceive, delude.*

lūdus -i, m. *play, game, sport, pastime;* plur., ludi, *public games or spectacles.* Transf., *a trifle, jest, joke;* ludum dare, *to give free play to; a training establishment, school.*

lūella -ae, f. *expiation.*

lūēs -is, f. *plague, pestilence, calamity.*

Lugdūnum -i, n. *a city in Gaul (now* Lyons). Adj. Lugdūnensis -e.

lūgĕo lūgēre luxi: intransit., *to mourn, be in mourning;* transit., *to bewail, lament, wear mourning for.*

lūgubris -e, *of mourning, mournful; plaintive; grievous.* N. pl. as subst. *mourning clothes.*

lumbus -i, m. *loin.*

lūmen -ĭnis, n. *light; a light, lamp; the light of day, day; the light of life; the light of the eye, the eye; an opening, a light in a building;* fig., *clearness, insight; a shining light, glory, ornament.*

lūmĭnārĕ -āris, n. *a window-shutter window.*

lūmĭnōsus -a -um, *bright.*

lūna -ae, f. *the moon; night, a month; a crescent-shaped ornament.*

lūnāris -e, *of the moon, lunar.*

lūno -are, *to bend into a crescent;* perf. partic. lūnātus -a -um, *crescent-shaped.*

lŭpa -ae, f. *a she-wolf; a prostitute.*

lŭpātus -a -um, *provided with iron spikes;* m. or n. pl. as subst., *a curb with jagged spikes.*

Lŭpercus -i, m. *an Italian pastoral deity, or one of his priests;* subst. Lŭpercal -cālis, n. *a grotto, sacred to* Lupercus: Lŭpercālĭa -ĭum and -ĭorum, n. pl., *the festival of Lupercus, celebrated in February.*

¹lŭpīnus -a -um, *of a wolf, wolfish.*

²lŭpīnus -i, m. and lŭpīnum -i, n., *the lupin.*

lŭpus -i, m. *a wolf; a voracious fish,*

the pike; a horse's bit with jagged points; a hook.

lūridus -a -um, *pale yellow, lurid, ghastly.*

lūror -ōris, m. *ghastliness, paleness.*

luscīnia -ae, f. *nightingale.*

luscīōsus and **luscitiōsus** -a -um, *purblind, dim-sighted.*

luscus -a -um, *one-eyed.*

lūsio -ōnis, f. *play, game.*

Lūsĭtānĭa -ae, f. *the modern Portugal, with part of Spain.*

lūsor -ōris, m. *a player; a playful writer; a mocker.*

lustrālis -e, *relating to expiation or to a period of five years.*

lustrātĭo -ōnis, f. *purification by sacrifice; a going round, traversing.*

¹**lustro** -are, *to brighten, illumine.*

²**lustro** -are, *to purify, cleanse by sacrifices; to go round, go over, traverse; to review, observe, examine.*

¹**lustrum** -i, n., usually plur., *the den of a wild beast, woodlands; brothels, debauchery.*

²**lustrum** -i, n. *an expiatory sacrifice; a period of five years.*

lūsus -ūs, m. *playing, game, sport; dalliance.*

lūtĕŏlus -a -um, *yellow.*

Lūtētĭa -ae, f. *a town in Gallia (now Paris).*

¹**lūtĕus** -a -um, *saffron-yellow.*

²**lūtĕus** -a -um, *of mud or clay; dirty.*

lūto -are, *to smear with mud.*

lūtŭlentus -a -um, *muddy, dirty, filthy, impure.*

¹**lŭtum** -i, n. *a plant used for dyeing yellow; yellow colour.*

²**lŭtum** -i, n. *mud, mire, dirt; clay.*

lux, lūcis, f. *light; esp. daylight, day; a day; the light of life or of day; the eye, eyesight; illustration, elucidation; hope, encouragement; ornament.*

luxŭrĭa -ae and **luxŭrĭēs** -ēi, f. *rankness, exuberant growth; excess, dissipation, extravagance.*

luxŭrĭo -are and **luxŭrĭor** -ari, dep., *to be luxuriant, rank, grow fast; to frisk, sport, run riot.*

luxŭrĭōsus -a -um, *luxuriant, rank; immoderate, excessive; luxurious, dissolute, extravagant.* Adv. **luxŭrĭōsē**, *luxuriously.*

luxus -ūs, m. *luxury, excess, extravagance.*

Lȳaeus -i, m. *surname of Bacchus; wine.*

lychnūchus -i, m. *lamp-stand, candelabrum.*

lychnus -i, m. *lamp.*

Lȳcĭa -ae, f. *a country of Asia Minor.*

Lȳdĭa -ae, f. *a country of Asia Minor;* ad. **Lȳdius** and **Lȳdus** -a -um, *Lydian.*

lympha -ae, f. *water, esp. clear spring or river water.*

lymphātĭcus and **lymphātus** -a -um, *raving, mad, frantic.*

lynx -cis, c. *lynx.*

lȳra -ae, f. *the lyre or lute, a stringed instrument; lyric poetry, song.*

lȳrĭcus -a -um, *of the lyre, lyric.*

M

M, m. the twelfth letter of the Latin Alphabet.

Măcĕdŏ (-ōn) -ŏnis, m. *a Macedonian;* subst. **Măcĕdŏnĭa** -ae, f.; adj. **Măcĕdŏnĭcus, Măcĕdŏnĭus** -a -um.

măcellum -i, n. *a provision-market.*

măcer -cra -crum, *lean; thin, poor.*

măcĕrĭa -ae, f. *a wall, esp. garden-wall.*

măcĕro -are, *to soften; to make weak, reduce; to torment, tease, vex.*

măchaera -ae, f. *a sword.*

măchĭna -ae, f. *a machine, contrivance; a crane, windlass, catapult, ballista.* Transf., *fabric; a device, trick, stratagem.*

măchĭnāmentum -i, n. *machine, instrument.*

măchĭnātĭo -ōnis, f. *contrivance, machinery, mechanism; device, machination.*

măchĭnātor -ōris, m. *a maker of machines, engineer; a deviser, contriver.*

măchĭnor -ari, dep. *to contrive, invent, devise.*

măciēs -ēi, f. *leanness, thinness, poverty, barrenness.*

macresco -ĕre, *to grow lean, become thin.*

macrŏcollum -i, n. *paper of the largest size.*

mactābĭlis -e, *deadly.*

mactātū, abl. sing. m. *by a sacrificial stroke.*

macte; see ¹**mactus**.

¹**macto** -are, *to magnify, honour, glorify.*

²**macto** -are, *to slay, smite; to afflict, punish.*

¹**mactus** -a -um, *glorified, honoured;* used only in voc. m. **mactĕ**, *well done! bravo! good luck!*

²**mactus** -a -um, *smitten.*

măcŭla -ae, f. *a spot, mark, stain; sometimes the mesh of a net; a moral stain, blemish, fault.*

măcŭlo -are, *to spot, stain, defile, pollute.*

măcŭlōsus -a -um, *spotted, speckled, stained, polluted.*

mădēfăcio -făcĕre -fēci -factum, and pass. **mădēfīo** -fĭĕri, *to mak wet, moisten, soak.*

mădĕo -ēre, *to be wet, to stream; to be drunk; to be boiled.* Transf., *to be steeped in, abound in.*

mădesco mădescĕre mădŭi, *to become wet.*

mădĭdus -a -um, *moist, wet; drunk; boiled soft; dyed, steeped.* Adv. **mădĭdē**, *drunkenly.*

mădor -ōris, m. *moisture, wetness.*

Maeandĕr and **Maeandrōs** (-us) -dri, m. *a river of Asia Minor, proverbial for its winding course; a winding.*

Maecēnās -ātis, m. C. Cilnius, *the patron of Horace and Vergil.*

maena (**mena**) -ae, f. *a small sea-fish.*

Maenăs -ādis, f. *a bacchante; a prophetess.*

maerĕo -ēre: intransit., *to grieve,*

mourn, lament; transit., *to lament, bewail.*

maeror -ōris, m. *mourning, grief, sorrow.*

maestitia -ae, f. *sadness, dejection, gloom.*

maestus -a -um, *sad, dejected, gloomy*; adv. **maestitēr.**

măgālia -ium, n. pl. *huts.*

măgē; see magis.

măgicus -a -um, *magical.*

măgis (or **măgĕ**), *more, to a greater extent; rather, for preference*; non magis . . . quam, *no more . . . than, just as much . . . as*; quo magis . . . eo magis, *the more . . . the more.* Superl. **maximē** (**maxŭmē**), *in the highest degree, most of all, especially, very much so*; quam maxime, *as much as possible*; with tum, cum, just, *precisely.*

măgister -tri, m. *master, chief, head, director*; populi, *dictator*; equitum, *master of the horse, the dictator's lieutenant*; magister (ludi), *a schoolmaster, teacher*; societatis, *director of a company*; elephanti, *driver*; navis, *master or helmsman.* Transf., *instigator, adviser, guide.*

măgistĕrium -i, n. *directorship, magistracy; direction, guidance.*

măgistra -ae, f. *a mistress, directress.*

măgistrātus -ūs, m. *a magistracy, official dignity, office.* Transf., *a magistrate, state official.*

magnănĭmĭtās -ātis, f. *greatness of soul, magnanimity.*

magnănĭmus -a -um, *high-minded, magnanimous.*

magnĭfĭcentia -ae, f. *loftiness of thought and action; grandeur, magnificence, splendour*; in bad sense, *boasting, pomposity.*

magnĭfĭco -are, *to prize highly, esteem.*

magnĭfĭcus -a -um; compar. **magnĭfĭcentior**; superl. **magnĭfĭcentissĭmus**; *grand, splendid, fine*; in bad sense, *boastful, pompous.* Adv. **magnĭfĭcē.**

magnĭlŏquentia -ae, f. *lofty or elevated language; pompous, boastful language.*

magnĭlŏquus -a -um, *lofty or elevated in language; pompous or boastful.*

magnĭtūdō -ĭnis, f. *greatness*; animi, *magnanimity.*

magnŏpĕrĕ and separately **magnŏ ŏpĕrĕ**, *greatly, very much.*

magnus -a -um; compar. **māior**, maius; superl. **maximus** (**maxŭmus**) -a -um; *great, large*; of sound, *loud*; of price or value, *high*; magno, and magni, *at a high price, dear, highly.* Transf., of time, *long, old*; of standing, *great, mighty, powerful, important*; m. pl. of compar. as subst. **māiōres**, *ancestors*; in maius, *to a higher degree*; **magnŏ ŏpĕrĕ**, see magnopere; for **maximē**, see magis.

Māgō (-ōn) -ōnis, m. *brother of Hannibal.*

¹**măgus** -i, m. *a learned Persian; a magician.*

²**măgus** -a -um, *magical.*

Māia -ae, f. *the daughter of Atlas, mother of Mercury*, adj. **Māius** -a -um, *of Maia*: (mensis) Maius, *the month of May.*

māiestās -ātis, f. *greatness, grandeur, dignity, majesty*; crimen maiestatis, *treason.*

māior, māiōres; see magnus.

Māius -a -um, adj. from Maia; q.v.

māiusculus -a -um, *somewhat greater or older.*

māla -ae, f. *cheek-bone, jaw-bone; jaw, cheek.*

mălăcia -ae, f. *a calm at sea.*

mălăcus -a -um, *soft, pliable; effeminate, delicate.*

mălēdĭco -dĭcĕre -dixi -dictum (sometimes separately, male dico), *to speak ill, abuse*; pres. partic., **mălēdĭcens** -entis, *abusive*; n. of perf. partic. as subst. **mălēdictum** -i, *cursing, abusive language.*

mălēdictio -ōnis, f. *reviling, abuse.*

mălēdĭcus -a -um, *abusive, scurrilous*; adv. **mălēdĭcē.**

mălēfăcio -făcĕre -fēci -factum (sometimes separately, male facio), *to injure*; n. of perf. partic. as subst. **mălēfactum** -i, *an ill deed, injury.*

mălēfactor -ōris, m. *an evil-doer.*

mălēfĭcium -i, n. *wrongdoing; mischief.*

mălēfĭcus -a -um, *evil-doing, mischievous*; adv. **mălēfĭcē.**

mălēsuādus -a -um, *ill-advising, seductive.*

mălēvŏlens -entis, *spiteful, ill-disposed.*

mălēvŏlentia -ae, f. *ill-will, spite, malice.*

mălēvŏlus -a -um, *ill-disposed, spiteful, malicious.*

mālĭfer -fĕra -fĕrum, *apple-bearing.*

mălignĭtās -ātis, f. *ill-nature, malignity, spite; stinginess.*

mălignus -a -um, *ill-disposed, wicked*; esp. *stingy, niggardly; barren, unfruitful; stinted, scanty.* Adv. **mălignē.**

mălĭtia -ae, f. *badness, wickedness, vice*; esp. *craft, cunning, malice.*

mălĭtĭōsus -a -um, *wicked; crafty, roguish, knavish*; adv. **mălĭtĭōsē.**

mallĕŏlus -i, m. *a little hammer; a kind of fire-dart.*

mallĕus -i m. *a hammer, mallet, pole-axe.*

mālo malle mālŭi, *to wish rather, prefer*; with dative of person, *to be more favourable to.*

mālŏbăthrum -i, n. *a plant, from which ointment was prepared.*

¹**mălum** -i, n.; see ¹malus.

²**mălum** -i, n. *an apple, or other similar fruit.*

¹**mălus** -a -um; comp. **pĕior** -us; superl. **pessĭmus** -a -um; *bad, evil* (physically or morally); *unfavourable, unsuccessful, ugly.* N. as subst. **mălum** -i, *an evil; harm, disaster; punishment*; as a term of abuse, *scoundrel.* Adv. **mălē**, compar. **pĕius**; superl. **pessĭmē**, *badly, ill*; male audire, *to be ill spoken of*; *unsuccessfully, unfortunately*; with

words bad in sense, *bitterly, excessively*; with words of favourable sense, with negative force, e.g., male gratus, *unthankful*.

²**mālus** -i, f. *an apple-tree*.

³**mālus** -i, m. *the mast of a ship; an upright, pole*.

malva -ae, f. *the mallow*.

Māmers -mertis, m. *the Oscan name of Mars*; hence **Māmertini** -orum, m. *the name assumed by certain mercenary troops*.

mămilla -ae, f. *breast, teat*.

mamma -ae, f. *breast*.

mānābilis -e, *flowing, penetrating*.

manceps -cĭpis, m. *a purchaser, farmer, contractor*.

mancĭpĭum (mancŭpĭum) -i, n. *a formal purchase of anything*. Transf., *a slave acquired by mancipium*.

mancĭpo (mancŭpo) -are, *to sell formally; to give up*.

mancus -a -um, *maimed, crippled, imperfect, defective*.

mandātū abl. sing. m. *by order*.

mandātum -i, n. subst. from mando; q.v.

¹**mando** -are, *to commit, entrust*; of actions, *to order, command, commission*. N. of partic. as subst., **mandātum** -i, *a commission charge, order*.

²**mando** mandĕre mandi mansum, *to chew, masticate, champ; to eat, consume*.

mandra -ae, f. *a stall, cattle-pen; a herd of cattle; a draughtboard*.

mānĕ, indecl. n.: as subst., *morning*; adv., *in the morning, early*.

mănĕo mănēre mansi mansum: intransit., *to remain, stay; to stay the night; to endure, last; promissis to abide by*; transit., in gen., *to wait for, await*.

mānēs -ium, m. pl. *the shades of the departed, spirits of the dead*; poet., *the lower world, infernal regions; corpse, ashes, remains*.

mango -ōnis, m. *a salesman* esp., *slave dealer*.

mănica -ae, f. *a sleeve, serving as a glove; handcuffs, manacles*.

mănicātus -a -um, *having long sleeves*.

mănicŭla -ae, f. *a little hand*.

mănifesto -are, *to show clearly, reveal*.

mănifestus -a -um, *palpable, clear, visible, evident; caught out, detected*. Abl. sing. n. as adv. **mănifestō**, *clearly*; compar. **mănifestius**.

Mānilius -a -um, *name of a Roman gens*.

mănĭpŭlāris (mănĭplāris) *belonging to a maniple*; m. as subst. *a private soldier; a fellow-soldier*.

mănĭpŭlātim, *in bundles; in maniples*.

mănĭpŭlus (poet, mănĭplus) -i, m. *a handful, bundle*; milit. *a company of infantry, a division of the Roman army*.

Manlius -a -um, *name of a Roman gens*.

mannŭlus -i, m. *a pony*.

mannus -i, m. *a pony, cob*.

māno -are, *to flow, drip, spread*; with abl., *to drip with*; with acc., *to exude*.

mansĭo -ōnis, f. *stay, sojourn; station, stage*.

mansĭto -are, *to abide, stay*.

mansuēfăcĭo -făcĕre -fēci -factum, pass. **mansuēfīo** -fĭĕri -factus sum, *to tame; to soften, pacify, civilize*.

mansuēs -is or -ētis, *tame*.

mansuesco -suescĕre -suēvi -suētum: transit., *to tame*; intransit., *to grow tame or soft*. Hence partic. **mansuētus** -a -um, *tame, mild, soft*; adv. **mansuētē**.

mansuētūdo -ĭnis, f. *tameness: mildness, gentleness*.

mantēlē -is, n. *towel, napkin*.

mantēlum -i, n. *covering, cloak*.

mantĭca -ae, f. *wallet, knapsack*.

manto -are, *to remain, wait, wait for*.

Mantŭa -ae, f. *a town in north Italy*.

mānŭālis -e, *fitted to the hand*.

mănūbĭae -arum, f. *money from the sale of booty*, esp. *the general's share; spoils, profits*.

mănubrium -i, n. *haft, handle*.

mănūf-; see manif-.

mănŭlĕus -i, m. and **mănŭlĕa** -ae, f. *a long sleeve*.

mănūmissio -ōnis, f. *the emancipation of a slave*.

mănūmitto -mittĕre -misi -missum (or as two words, manu mitto), *to manumit, emancipate a slave*.

mănuprĕtium (mănipr-) -i, n. *wages, hire, reward*.

mănus -ūs, f. *hand*; manus dare, *to surrender*; in manibus, *on hand, in preparation*; servus ad manum, *a secretary*; abl. manu, *by hand, artificially*. Transf., *the strong arm, fist, force, effort; power, jurisdiction; the hand or touch of artist or craftsman; a band or body of men; an elephant's trunk*; manus ferrea, *grappling-iron*.

māpālia -ium, n. *huts, hovels*.

mappa -ae, f. *a table-napkin*.

Marcellus -i, m. *the cognomen of a family of the gens Claudia*.

marcĕo -ēre, *to wither, droop, be feeble*.

marcesco -ĕre, *to begin to droop, grow feeble*.

marcidus -a -um, *withering, drooping, enfeebled*.

marcor -ōris, m. *rottenness, decay*.

marcŭlus -i, m. *a small hammer*.

Marcus -i, *a Roman praenomen*, abbreviated M.

mărĕ -is, n. *the sea*; mare nostrum, *the Mediterranean*; superum, *the Adriatic*; inferum, *the Tyrrhenian Sea*.

margărita -ae f. and **margăritum** -i n. *a pearl*.

margino -are, *to border*.

margo -ĭnis, m. and f. *a border, edge, boundary*.

mārinus -a -um, *of the sea, marine*: ros, *rosemary*.

măritālis -e, *conjugal, matrimonial*.

măritimus (măritŭmus) -a -um, *of*

or *on the sea, marine*; praedo, *a pirate*; n. pl. as subst. *the sea-coast.*

mărĭto -are, *to marry, give in marriage*; of vines, *to bind to a tree, to train.*

mărĭtus -a -um, *matrimonial, nuptial*; of plants, *tied or trained together*; As subst. **mărĭtus** -i, m. *husband, lover, suitor*; **mărĭta** -ae, f. *wife.*

Mārĭus -a -um, *the name of a Roman gens.*

marmor -ŏris, n. *marble statue; stone; the white foamy surface of the sea.*

marmŏrĕus -a -um, *of marble, like marble.*

Măro -ŏnis, m. *the cognomen of the poet P. Vergilius.*

marra -ae, f. *a hoe.*

Mars Martis, m. (old form, Māvors), *Mars, god of agriculture and of war.* Transf., *war, battle, fight.* Adj. **Martĭus** and poet. **Māvortĭus** -a -um, *of Mars*; Martius (mensis), *the month of March; warlike.* Adj. **Martĭālis** -e, *of Mars*; m. as subst. *a priest of Mars or soldier of the Legio Martia.*

Marsi -ŏrum, m. *an ancient people of Latium*; adj. **Marsĭcus** and **Marsus** -a -um; Marsicum bellum, *the Social War.*

marsuppĭum -i, n. *purse, pouch.*

[1]**Martĭālis** -e, adj. from Mars; q.v.

[2]**Martĭālis** -is, m. M. Valerius, *Martial, the writer of epigrams.*

Martĭgēna -ae, m. *offspring of Mars.*

Martĭus -a -um, adj. from Mars; q.v.

mas măris, m. *the male; manly, vigorous.*

mascŭlus -a -um, *male; manly, bold.*

Măsĭnissa -ae, m. *king of Numidia.*

massa -ae, f. *a lump, mass.*

massĭcum -i, n. *Massic wine.*

Massĭlĭa -ae, f. *a town in Gallia Narbonensis* (now *Marseilles*); adj. **Massĭliensis** -e.

mastīgia -ae, m. *a scoundrel.*

mastrūca -ae, f. *a sheepskin.*

matāra -ae, and **matāris** -is, f. *a pike, lance.*

mătellio -ŏnis, m. *a small pot, vessel.*

māter, mātris, f. *mother; source, origin.*

mātercŭla -ae, f. *little mother.*

mātĕrĭa -ae, and **mātĕrĭēs** -ēi, f. *matter, material, stuff; timber.* Transf., *subject-matter; occasion, cause; natural disposition.*

mātĕrĭo -are, *to construct of wood.*

mātĕrĭor -ari, dep. *to fell wood.*

mātĕris = matara; q.v.

māternus -a -um, *of a mother, maternal.*

mātertĕra -ae, f. *maternal aunt.*

māthēmătĭcus -a -um, *mathematical*; m. as subst. *a mathematician or astrologer*; f. **māthēmătĭca** -ae, *mathematics or astrology.*

mātrĭcīda -ae, c. *a matricide.*

mātrĭcīdĭum -i, n. *slaying of a mother, matricide.*

mātrĭmōnĭum -i, n. *marriage.*

mātrĭmus -a -um, *having a mother still living.*

[1]**mātrōna** -ae, f. *a married woman, matron.*

[2]**Mātrōna** -ae, m. *a river in Gaul* (now *the Marne*).

mātrōnālis -e, *of a married woman, matronly*; n. pl. as subst. **Mātrōnālĭa** -ium, *a festival held by Roman matrons.*

matta -ae, f. *a mat of rushes.*

mattĕa (mattya) -ae, f. *a dainty dish.*

mātūresco mātūrescĕre mātūrŭi, *to ripen, become ripe.*

mātūrĭtās -ātis, f. *ripeness, maturity; the right moment, fullness of time.*

mātūro -are: transit., *to make ripe, ripen; to quicken, hasten, accelerate; to anticipate, do too soon*; intransit., *to hasten, make haste.*

mātūrus -a -um, *ripe, mature, grown-up, developed, perfect; timely, quick, speedy, early.* Adv. **mātūrē** *at the right time, seasonably, opportunely; in good time, betimes, early; too soon, prematurely.*

mātūtĭnus -a -um, *early in the morning, of morning.*

Mauri -orum, m. *the Moors*; adj. **Maurus** -a -um; subst. **Maurītānĭa** -ae, f. *Mauritania.*

māvŏlo = malo; q.v.

Māvors -vortis, m. archaic and poet. for Mars; adj. **Māvortĭus** -a -um.

maxilla -ae, f. *jaw-bone, jaw.*

maxĭmĭtās -ātis, f. *greatness, size.*

maxĭmus, superl. of magnus; q.v.

măzŏnŏmus -i, m. or **măzŏnŏmon** -i, n. *a charger, large dish.*

mĕātus -ūs, m. *a going, motion; a way, path.*

Mēcastor; see Castor.

meddix -ĭcis, m. *an Oscan magistrate.*

Mēdēa -ae, f. *an enchantress, who helped Jason to obtain the golden fleece.*

mĕdĕor -ēri, dep. *to heal, to cure, assist, alleviate*; pres. partic. as subst. **mĕdens** -entis, m. *a physician.*

Mēdi -orum, m. *the Medes*; poet. = *the Persians.*

mĕdĭastīnus -i, m. *a drudge.*

mĕdĭca -ae, f. *lucerne, clover.*

mĕdĭcābĭlis -e, *curable.*

mĕdĭcāmen -ĭnis, n. *a drug, medicine, remedy; poison; dye, rouge.*

mĕdĭcāmentum -i, n. *a drug, medicine, remedy; a magic potion; poison; embellishment.*

mĕdĭcātus -ūs, m. *means of enchantment, charm.*

mĕdĭcīnus -a -um, *of the art of healing*; f. as subst. **mĕdĭcīna** -ae, *the art of healing; medicine; cure.*

mĕdĭco -are, *to drug; to dye*; partic. **mĕdĭcātus** -a -um, *steeped, drugged.*

mĕdĭcor -ari, dep., *to heal, cure.*

mĕdĭcus -a -um, *healing, medicinal*; m. as subst. **mĕdĭcus** -i, *a doctor, physician.*

mĕdimnum -i, n. and **mĕdimnus** -i, m. *a Greek measure of capacity.*

mĕdĭocris -e, *moderate, middling, ordinary*; adv. **mĕdĭocrĭter** *moderately, tolerably; with moderation.*

mĕdĭocrĭtās -ātis, f. *moderation,*

medium, the mean; mediocrity, in-significance.

Mēdiōlānum and **-lānium** -i, n. *a town in Cisalpine Gaul (now Milan).*

mēditāmentum -i, n. *preparation, practice.*

mēditātio -ōnis. f. (1) *a thinking over, contemplation.* (2) *practice, exercise, preparation.*

mēditerrānēus -a -um, *inland:* n. pl. as subst., *inland country.*

mēditor -ari, dep. (1) *to think over, consider;* esp. *to think about doing, to meditate, intend.* (2) *to practise.* Perf. partic. in pass. sense **mēditātus** -a -um, *meditated, considered, prepared;* adv. **mēditātē**, *thoughtfully, thoroughly.*

mēdius -a -um, *middle, midmost, mid; intervening, central, neutral, intermediate.* N. as subst. **mēdium** -i, *the middle; the public eye, everyday life; the community, common good.* Adv. **mēdiē**, *moderately.*

mēdius fidius; see fidius.

mēdulla -ae, f. *the marrow of the bones.*

Mēdus; see Medi.

Mēdūsa -ae, f. *one of the Gorgons, slain by Perseus.*

Mēgăra -ae, f. (and -orum, n. pl.). (1) *a town in Greece.* (2) *a town in Sicily.*

mĕgistānes -um, m. *grandees, magnates.*

mēhercŭle, mēhercle; see Hercules.

mēl mellis, n. *honey; sweetness, pleasantness.*

mēlanchŏlicus -a -um, *having black bile, melancholy.*

mēlānūrus -i, m. *small edible sea-fish.*

mēlicus -a -um, *musical; lyrical, lyric.*

mēlilōtŏs -i, f. *a species of clover.*

mēlimēla -orum, n. pl. *honey-apples.*

mēlior -us, compar. of bonus; q.v.

mēlisphyllum and **mēlissŏphyllŏn** -i, n. *balm.*

Mēlĭta -ae, f. *the island of Malta;* adj. **Mēlĭtensis** -e, *of Malta.*

mēliuscŭlus -a -um, *somewhat better;* adv. **mēliuscŭlē**, *somewhat better, pretty well (in health).*

mellifer -fēra -fērum, *producing honey.*

mellitus -a -um, *honeyed; sweet as honey.*

¹**mělōs**, n. *a tune, song.*

²**Mēlŏs** -i, f. *an island in the Aegean Sea.*

Melpŏmēnē -ēs, f. *the Muse of tragic poetry.*

membrāna -ae, f. *a thin skin, film, membrane; prepared skin, parchment.*

membrātim, *limb by limb; piecemeal, singly; in short sentences.*

membrum -i, n. *a limb, member, part (of the body); a clause in a sentence.*

mĕmĭni -nisse, perf. with sense of present, *to remember, recollect.* Transf. *to make mention of, to mention.*

mĕmor -ōris, *mindful, remembering; with a good memory; grateful, thoughtful, prudent; reminiscent, reminding.*

mĕmŏrābilis -e, *remarkable, worthy of mention, memorable.*

mĕmŏrandus -a -um, gerundive from memoro; q.v.

mĕmŏrātor -ōris, m. *a narrator.*

mĕmŏrātus -ūs, m. *mention.*

mĕmŏria -ae, *memory, the capacity for remembering, remembrance; record of the past, tradition, history.*

mĕmŏriŏla -ae, f. *memory.*

mĕmŏriter, *by heart, from memory.*

mĕmŏro -are, *to mention, call to mind, relate;* gerundive **mĕmŏrandus** -a -um, *notable, memorable.*

Memphis -is and -idos, f. *a city of Egypt.*

Mĕnander -dri, m. *a Greek comic poet.*

menda -ae, f.; see mendum.

mendācium -i, n. *lie, falsehood.*

mendax -ācis, *lying, mendacious, false.*

mendicitās -atis, f. *beggary.*

mendīco -are and **mendīcor** -ari, dep. *to beg, go begging; beg for.*

mendīcus -a -um, adj. *poor as a beggar, beggarly; paltry, pitiful;* m. as subst. *mendicus* -i, *a beggar.*

mendōsus -a -um, *full of faults, inaccurate, making mistakes;* adv. **mendōsē**, *faultily.*

mendum -i, n. and **menda** -ae, f. *a fault, defect, blemish, mistake.*

Mĕnēlāus -i, m. *brother of Agamemnon, husband of Helen.*

mens mentis, f. *mind, understanding, intellect, judgment; feelings, disposition; courage; opinion, thoughts; intention, resolve.*

mensa -ae, f. *a table, counter, altar; a course at a meal.*

mensārius -i, m. *a financial commissioner.*

mensio -ōnis, f. *measuring.*

mensis -is, m., *a month.*

mensor -ōris, m., *a measurer, surveyor; an architect.*

menstrūus -a -um, *monthly; lasting a month;* n. as subst. *rations for a month, a month in office.*

mensūra -ae, f. *measuring; measure, standard, capacity; amount, proportion.*

menta (mentha) -ae, f. *the herb mint.*

mentio -ōnis, f. *mention.*

mentior -iri, dep. *to lie; to deceive, mislead, disappoint; to say falsely, invent; fabricate; to counterfeit, put on, assume.* Hence pres. partic. **mentiens** -entis, *lying;* m. as subst. *a fallacy, sophism;* perf. partic. **mentitus** -a -um, *lying, fictitious.*

mentum -i, n. *the chin.*

mēo mēare, *to go, pass.*

mēphitis -is, f. *a noxious exhalation, malaria; personif., the goddess who protects against malaria.*

mērācus -a -um, *pure, unmixed.*

mercābilis -e, *that can be bought.*

mercātor -ōris, m. *a merchant, wholesale trader.*

mercātōrius -a -um, *relating to trade.*

mercātūra -ae, f. *trade, traffic; merchandise.*

mercātus -ūs, m. *trade, traffic, business; a market, fair, place of business.*

mercēdŭla -ae, f. *low wages or rent.*

mercennārius (mercēnārius) -a -um, *hired, paid*; m. as subst. *a hired servant.*

mercēs -ēdis, *hire, pay, wages; a bribe; cost, punishment; interest, rent, income.*

mercimōnium -i, n. *goods, merchandise.*

mercor -ari, dep. *to carry on trade, to traffic; to buy.*

Mercŭrius -a -m. *Mercury, messenger of the gods*; adj. **Mercūriālis** -e, *of Mercury*; m. pl. as subst. *a corporation of traders at Rome.*

merda -ae, f. *excrement.*

mĕrenda -ae, f. *a luncheon.*

mĕrĕo -ēre -ŭi, itum, and **mereor** -ēri -itus, dep. *to deserve, earn, obtain*; esp., *to earn pay as a soldier, serve as a soldier.* Hence perf. partic. **mĕritus** -a -um, *deserving*; in pass. sense, *deserved.* N. as subst. **mĕritum** -i, *desert, merit; a good action, benefit, service; blame, fault, grounds, reason.* Abl. as adv. **mĕritō**, *deservedly, rightly.*

mĕretrĭcius -a -um, *of a harlot*; adv. **mĕretrĭcie.**

mĕretrĭcŭla -ae, f. *a little harlot.*

mĕretrix -icis, f. *a harlot.*

mergae -arum, f. *a two-pronged fork.*

mergēs -gitis, f. *a sheaf of corn.*

mergo mergĕre mersi mersum, *to dip, plunge into liquid, immerse, sink, overwhelm.*

mergus -i, m. *a sea-bird,* esp. *a gull.*

mērĭdĭānus -a -um, *of midday, meridian; southern.*

mĕrĭdĭātĭo -ōnis, f. *midday sleep, siesta.*

mĕrĭdĭēs -ēi, m., *midday noon; the south.*

mĕrĭdĭo -are, *to take a siesta.*

¹mĕrĭto -are, *to earn regularly.*

²mĕrĭto, adv. from mereo; q.v.

mĕrĭtōrius -a -um, *hired*; n. pl. as subst., *lodgings.*

mĕrĭtum -i, n., subst. from mereo; q.v.

mĕrops -ōpis, f., *a bird, the bee-eater.*

merso -are, *to dip in, immerse.*

mērŭla -ae, f. *a blackbird; a fish, the sea-carp.*

mērus -a -um, *pure, unmixed; complete, sheer*; esp. *of wine, undiluted*; n. as subst. **mērum** -i *wine unmixed with water.*

merx (mers) mercis, f. *merchandise, goods, wares.*

Mĕsŏpŏtāmia -ae, f. *the country between the Euphrates and the Tigris.*

Messāna -ae, f. *a town in Sicily on the straits between Italy and Sicily.*

messis -is, f. *harvest, crop; time of harvest, harvest-tide.*

messor -ōris, m. *a reaper, mower.*

messōrius -a -um, *of a reaper.*

mēta -ae, f. *a pyramidal column used as a turning-post or winning-post; any turning-point; a goal, end, boundary.*

mĕtallum -i, n. *a metal; a mine, quarry* (esp. plur.).

mĕtămorphōsis -is, f. *transformation;*

plur. **Mĕtămorphōsēs** -ēōn, *the title of a poem by Ovid.*

mĕtăphŏra -ae, f. *metaphor.*

mĕtātor -ōris, m. *a measurer, one who marks out.*

Mĕtaurus -i, m. *a river in Umbria.*

mētior mētiri mensus, dep., *to measure; to traverse, pass over; to estimate, judge.*

mĕto mĕtĕre messŭi messum, *to reap, mow, gather harvest; to mow down, cut off.*

mētor -ari, dep. (and **mēto** -are) *to measure off, lay out.*

mĕtrēta -ae, f. *a Greek liquid measure.*

metrum -i, n. *a measure; metre.*

mĕtŭcŭlōsus -a -um, *timid; frightful.*

mĕtŭo -ŭĕre -ŭi -ŭtum *to fear, be afraid.*

mĕtus -ūs m. *fear, dread; reverence, awe.*

mĕus -a -um, *my, mine*; Nero meus, *my friend Nero.*

mica -ae, f. *a crumb, morsel, grain.*

mico -are -ŭi, *to move rapidly to and fro, vibrate, flicker; to shine, glitter, sparkle.*

Midās (Mida) -ae, m. *a king of Phrygia, who turned to gold everything that he touched.*

migrātĭo -ōnis, f. *removal, change of home.*

migrātū, abl. sing. m., *in transport.*

migro -are: intransit., *to migrate, depart; to change;* transit., *to move, transport; to transgress.*

mīlēs -itis, c. *a soldier; a private soldier, infantryman;* coll. *soldiery.*

mīlĭtāris -e, *of a soldier, military*; m. as subst. *a soldier*; adv. **mīlĭtārĭtĕr**, *in a soldierly manner.*

mīlĭtia -ae, f. *military service, warfare*; domi militiaeque, *at home and abroad, at peace and in war*; meton., *the military, soldiery.*

mīlĭto -are, *to serve as a soldier, be a soldier.*

mīlĭum -i, n. *millet.*

mīllĕ, *a thousand*; plur. **mīlia (millĭa)** -ĭum, *thousands*; mille passuum, *a thousand paces, a Roman mile.*

mīlle(n)sĭmus -a -um, *thousandth.*

mīllĭārĭum (mīliārium) -i, n. *a mile-stone.*

mīllĭārĭus (mīliārĭus) -a -um, *containing a thousand.*

mīllĭe(n)s, *a thousand times.*

mīlŭīnus (milvīnus) -a -um, *of a kite; kite-like.*

mīlŭus (milvus) -i, m. *a kite; a fish, the gurnard.*

mīma -ae, f. *an actress.*

mīmĭcus -a -um, *farcical*; adv. **mīmĭcē.**

mīmŭla -ae, f., *a little actress.*

mīmus -i, m. *a mimic actor; a mime, farce.*

¹mĭna f. *smooth, hairless.*

²mĭna -ae, f. *a Greek weight;* also *a Greek coin.*

mĭnae -arum, f. *battlements, parapets.* Transf., *threats, menaces.*

mĭnātĭo -ōnis, f. *threatening, menace.*

mĭnax -ācis, f. *projecting, overhanging.* Transf., *threatening.* Adv. **mĭnācĭtĕr**, *threateningly.*

mĭnĕo -ēre, *to project, overhang.*

Mĭnerva -ae, f. *goddess of wisdom and patroness of arts and sciences.* Transf., *wit, skill, art;* esp. *working in wool.*

mĭnĭātus -a -um, *coloured with red lead, painted vermilion.*

mĭnĭmē; see **minim-**.

mĭnĭmus; see **parvus**.

mĭnister -tri, m. and **mĭnistra** -ae, f. *servant, attendant, assistant.*

mĭnistĕrĭum -i, n. *service, attendance, employment;* in plur., *attendants, retinue.*

mĭnistra -ae, f.; see **minister**.

mĭnistrātor -ōris, m., **mĭnistrātrix** -icis, f. *a servant, attendant, assistant.*

mĭnistro -are, *to serve, wait,* esp. *at table; to attend to, take care of, direct; to serve, supply, provide.*

mĭnĭtābundus -a -um, *threatening.*

mĭnĭto -are and **mĭnĭtor** -ari dep. *to threaten.*

mĭnĭum -i, n. *native cinnabar; red-lead, vermilion.*

¹mĭnor -ari, dep. *to jut out, project.* Transf., *to threaten, menace* (with dat.). Adv. from partic. **mĭnantĕr**, *threateningly.*

²mĭnor -ōris, compar. of **parvus**; q.v.

Mĭnōs -ōis and -ōnis, *king of Crete; after his death, a judge in Tartarus.*

Mĭnōtaurus -i, m. *a monster, half-bull, half-man slain by Theseus.*

mĭnūmē and **mĭnūmus;** see **minim-**.

mĭnŭo -ŭĕre -ŭi -ūtum, *to make smaller, lessen, diminish; to cut to pieces.* Hence partic. **mĭnūtus** -a -um, *small, petty, insignificant;* adv. **mĭnūtē.**

mĭnus; see **parvus**.

mĭnuscŭlus -a -um, *rather small.*

mĭnūtal -ālis, n. *a dish of minced meat.*

mĭnūtātim, *bit by bit, gradually.*

mĭnūtĭa -ae, f. *smallness.*

mĭnūtus -a -um, partic. from minuo; q.v.

mīrābĭlis -e *wonderful, extraordinary, unusual;* adv. **mīrābĭlĭtĕr.**

mīrābundus -a -um, *wondering.*

mīrācŭlum -i, n. *a wonderful thing, prodigy, miracle; wonder, surprise.*

mīrātĭo -ōnis, f. *wonder, astonishment.*

mīrātor -ōris, m. *an admirer.*

mīrātrix -icis, f. adj. *wondering.*

mīrĭfĭcus -a -um *causing wonder, wonderful, astonishing;* adv. **mīrĭfĭcē.**

mirmĭllo (murm-) -ōnis, m. *a kind of gladiator.*

mīror -ari, dep. *to wonder, be astonished (at); to admire, look on with admiration;* gerundive **mīrandus** -a -um, *wonderful.*

mīrus -a -um, *wonderful, astonishing, extraordinary;* adv. **mīrē.**

miscellānĕa -ōrum, n. pl., *a hash, hotchpotch.*

miscĕo miscēre miscŭi mixtum, *to mix, mingle; to combine, unite; to prepare by mixing; to confuse, confound.*

mĭsellus -a -um, *miserable, wretched, little.*

Mĭsēnus -i, m. *the trumpeter of Aeneas;* **Mĭsēnum** -i, n. *a promontory and town in Campania.*

mĭser -ĕra -ĕrum, *wretched, unhappy, sad;* adv. **mĭsĕrē.**

mĭsĕrābĭlis -e, *sad, wretched, mournful, plaintive;* adv. **mĭsĕrābĭlĭtĕr.**

mĭsĕrātĭo -ōnis, f. *pity, compassion; a pathetic speech* or *tone.*

mĭsĕrĕo -ēre and **mĭsĕrĕor** -ēri, dep. *to pity* (with genit.); impers. **mĭsĕret** and dep. **mĭsĕrētur,** *it excites pity, one pities.*

mĭsĕresco -ĕre, *to pity, have compassion on* (with genit.).

mĭsĕrĭa -ae, f. *wretchedness, unhappiness, distress.*

mĭsĕricordĭa -ae, f. *pity, compassion, mercy; an appeal to pity.*

mĭsĕrĭcors -cordis, *pitiful, compassionate.*

mĭsĕror -ari, dep. *to bewail, deplore; to pity, have compassion on;* gerundive **mĭsĕrandus** -a -um, *pitiable, lamentable.*

missĭcĭus -a -um, *discharged from military service.*

missĭlis -e, *that can be thrown;* n. as subst., *a missile.*

missĭo -ōnis, f. *a sending off, letting go, releasing, discharge; cessation, termination.*

missĭto -are, *to send repeatedly.*

¹missus -ūs, m. *a letting go, sending, throwing; a shot, the distance shot;* in races, *a course, heat.*

²missus -a -um, partic. from mitto; q.v.

mītesco -ĕre, *to become mild, soft,* or *ripe; to be allayed, to subside.*

Mĭthrĭdātes -is, m. *name of several kings of Pontus.*

mītĭgātĭo -ōnis, f. *assuaging, appeasing.*

mītĭgo -are, *to make mild,* or *ripe; to soothe, appease, pacify.*

mītĭs -e, *mild, soft, ripe; gentle;* of style, *mellow;* compar. adv. **mītĭus;** superl. **mītissĭmē.**

mitra -ae, f. *a head-dress, turban.*

mĭtrātus -a -um, *wearing the mitra.*

mitto mittĕre misi missum, *to send, dispatch; to send as a gift; to fling; to shed; to utter; to let go, release, give up; to dismiss, discharge; to pass over a subject.*

mĭtŭlus (mȳtŭlus, mŭtŭlus) -i, m. *an edible mussel.*

mixtūra -ae, f. *a mixing, mixture.*

mna = **²mina**; q.v.

Mnēmŏnĭdes -um, f. pl. *the Muses.*

Mnēmŏsȳnē -ēs, f. *Mnemosyne, mother of the Muses.*

mnēmŏsȳnum -i, n. *a souvenir, memorial.*

mōbĭlis -e, *movable, easy to move; pliable, flexible; active, rapid; changeable, inconstant.* Adv. **mōbĭlĭtĕr,** *quickly, easily.*

mōbĭlĭtās -ātis f. *mobility; inconstancy, changeableness.*

mōbĭlĭto -are, *to set in motion.*

mŏdĕrābĭlis -e, *moderate, restrained.*

mŏdĕrāmen -ĭnis, n. *means of guiding*; rerum, *management, government.*

mŏdĕrātim, *moderately, gradually.*

mŏdĕrātĭo -ōnis, f. *moderating, restraining; moderation, restraint.*

mŏdĕrātor -ōris, m. *a governor, controller, manager*; equorum, *a driver.*

mŏdĕrātrix -ĭcis, f. *she that governs or controls.*

mŏdĕror -ari, dep. (and **mŏdĕro** -are), *to keep within bounds; to regulate, restrain; to control, govern, direct.* Hence, from pres. partic. adv. **mŏdĕrantĕr**, *with controlling force*; perf. partic. **mŏdĕrātus** -a -um, *restrained, controlled*; adv. **mŏdĕrātē**, *with restraint.*

mŏdestĭa -ae, f. *moderation; restraint, propriety, orderliness; respect, obedience to authority.*

mŏdestus -a -um, *moderate, within bounds; orderly, restrained*; adv. **mŏdestē**.

mŏdĭcus -a -um, *moderate, within bounds, limited; temperate; ordinary, undistinguished.* Adv. **mŏdĭcē**, *moderately; to a limited extent; temperately, with restraint.*

mŏdĭfĭcātus -a -um, *measured.*

mŏdĭus -i, m. *a Roman corn-measure*; pleno modio, *in full measure, abundantly.*

mŏdŏ, *by measure; hence only, merely, but, just*; si modo, modo si, or modo alone with subj., *provided that, if only*; modo ne, *provided that . . . not*; modo non, *all but, nearly*; non modo . . . sed etiam, *not only . . . but also.* Of time, *just, lately*; modo . . . modo . . ., *at one time . . . at another. . . .*

mŏdŭlātĭo -ōnis, f. *rhythmical measure.*

mŏdŭlātor -ōris, m. *a musician.*

mŏdŭlor -ari, dep. *to measure*; in music, *to modulate, to sing to the accompaniment of* an instrument; *to play* an instrument. Adv. from partic. **mŏdŭlātē**, *in time* (of music).

mŏdŭlus -i, m. *a little measure.*

mŏdus -i, m. *a measure, standard of measurement*; in music, *rhythm, measure, time*; in plur., *strains, numbers.* Transf., *limit, boundary; rule; manner, mode, way, method*; servorum modo, *after the manner of slaves*; eius modi, *in that manner, of that kind.*

moecha -ae, f. *an adulteress.*

moechor -ari, dep. *to commit adultery.*

moechus -i, m. *an adulterer.*

moenĕra=munera; *see* munus.

moenia -ium, n. pl. *the walls or fortifications of a city, ramparts, bulwarks*; poet., *castle, dwelling.*

Moesi -ōrum, m. pl. *a people between Thrace and the Danube*; **Moesia** -ae f., *their country.*

mŏla -ae, f. *a mill-stone*; plur., *a mill.* Transf., *grits, coarse meal* or *flour.*

mŏlāris -e, *of a mill, to do with grinding*; m. as subst. *a millstone; a molar tooth, grinder.*

mōlēs -is, f. *a shapeless mass, e.g. of rock; a massive construction, e.g. dam, mole, large building*; moles belli, *large military machines.* Transf., *a mass of men; greatness, might, power; trouble, difficulty.*

mŏlestĭa -ae, f. *annoyance, troublesomeness*; of style, *affectation, stiffness.*

mŏlestus -a -um, *burdensome, troublesome, irksome*; of style, *affected, laboured.* Adv. **mŏlestē**, *with annoyance*; moleste fero, *I take it badly, am annoyed*; of style, *affectedly.*

mōlīmen -ĭnis, n. and **mōlīmentum** -i, n. *great effort, exertion, endeavour.*

mōlĭor -iri,' dep.: transit., *to stir, displace, work at; to construct laboriously, build, erect, contrive; to strive after; to destroy laboriously, undermine*; intransit., *to toil, struggle, exert oneself.*

mōlĭtĭo -ōnis, f. *effort, laborious undertaking; demolition.*

mōlītor -ōris, m. *a builder, contriver.*

mollesco -ĕre, *to become soft* or *gentle.*

mollĭcŭlus -a -um, *soft, tender; effeminate.*

mollĭo -ire, *to make soft, pliable, supple; to make gentle* or *effeminate; to alleviate trouble; to ease* a gradient.

mollĭpēs -pĕdis, *soft-footed.*

mollis -e, *soft, tender, pliant, supple*; of weather, *mild*; of gradients, *easy*; of character, *tender, gentle, sensitive,* or *effeminate*; of circumstances, *easy, mild, pleasant*; of speech, *tender, moving.* Adv. **mollĭtĕr**, *softly, easily, gently, mildly; effeminately.*

mollītĭa -ae, and **mollĭtĭes** -ei, f. *softness, flexibility; tenderness, mildness, sensibility; effeminacy.*

mollĭtūdo -ĭnis, f. *softness, pliability; tenderness, sensibility.*

mŏlo -ĕre -ŭi -ĭtum, *to grind in a mill.*

Mŏlossi -orum, m. *a people in Epirus.* Adj. **Mŏlossus** -a -um, pes, *a metrical foot, consisting of three long syllables*; m. as subst. *a Molossian hound.*

mŏly -yos, n. *the herb moly.*

mōmen -ĭnis, n. *movement; a moving mass; momentum, impulse.*

mōmentum -i, n. *movement, motion; change, alteration; a cause of motion, impulse; mental impulse, influence; weight, importance;* of time, *a turning-point, minute, moment.*

Mŏna -ae, f. *the Isle of Man*; also *the Isle of Anglesey.*

mŏnēdŭla -ae, f. *jackdaw.*

mŏnĕo -ēre, *to remind, admonish, warn, advise, instruct.* N. pl. of partic. as subst. **mŏnĭta** -ōrum, *warnings; prophecies.*

mŏnēris -is, f. *a vessel with one bank of oars.*

Mŏnēta -ae, f. (1) *the mother of the Muses.* (2) *a surname of Juno.* (3) *the mint; money.*

mŏnētālis -e, *of the mint.*

mŏnīle -is, n. *necklace, collar.*

mŏnĭmentum = monumentum; q.v.

mŏnĭtĭo -ōnis, f. *reminding, warning.*

mŏnĭtor -ōris, m. *one who reminds or prompts; an adviser, instructor*.

mŏnĭtus -ūs, m. *warning, admonition*.

mŏnŏgrammos or -us -i, m. adj. *sketched, shadowy*.

mŏnŏpŏdĭum -i, n. *a table with one foot*.

mons, montis, m. *a mountain; a mass; a great rock*.

monstrātor -ōris m. *a pointer-out; an inventor*.

monstro -are, *to show, point out; to ordain, appoint; to inform against, denounce*.

monstrum -i, n. *a wonder, portent*.

monstrŭōsus (monstrōsus) -a -um, *strange, wonderful*; adv. monstrŭōsē.

montānus -a -um, *of a mountain, or mountainous*; m. as subst. *a mountaineer*; n. pl. as subst. *mountainous country*.

montĭcŏla -ae, c. *a highlander*.

montĭvăgus -a -um, *wandering over mountains*.

montŭōsus (montōsus) -a -um, *mountainous*.

mŏnŭmentum (mŏnĭmentum) -i, n. *a memorial, monument; a commemorative building; written memorials, annals, memoirs*.

¹mŏra -ae, f. *delay, hindrance; any space of time*.

²mŏra -ae, f. *a division of the Spartan army*.

mŏrālis -e, *moral, ethical*.

mŏrātor -ōris, m. *a delayer, retarder; an advocate who talks against time*.

¹mŏrātus, partic. from moror; q.v.

²mŏrātus -a -um, *having certain manners or morals; adapted to a character, in character, characteristic*.

morbĭdus -a -um, *sickly, diseased, unwholesome*.

morbus -i, m. *disease, sickness*.

mordax -ācis, *biting, snappish; stinging, pungent; satirical*. Compar. adv. mordācĭus, *more bitingly*.

mordĕo mordēre mŏmordi morsum, *to bite; to cut into; to nip, sting; to vex, hurt, pain*.

mordĭcus, *with the teeth, by biting*.

mŏrētum -i, n. *a salad*.

mŏrĭbundus -a -um, *dying, expiring; subject to death, mortal; causing death, deadly*.

mŏrĭgĕror -ari, dep. (and mŏrĭgĕro -are) *to comply with, gratify*.

mŏrĭgĕrus -a -um, *compliant, accommodating*.

mŏrĭor mŏri mortŭus mŏrĭtūrus, dep. *to die; to die away, wither away, decay*. Hence partic. mortŭus -a -um, *dead; decayed, extinct; half-dead*; m. as subst. *a corpse*.

mŏrŏlŏgus -a -um, *talking like a fool*.

¹mŏror -ari, dep. *to delay*: intransit., *to linger, loiter, stay*; transit., *to retard, detain, hinder*; nihil (nil) morari, *to care nothing for*.

²mŏror -ari, dep. *to be foolish*.

mŏrōsĭtās -ātis, f. *peevishness, fretfulness*.

mŏrōsus -a -um, *peevish, captious, fretful*; adv. mŏrōsē.

Morphēus -ĕos, m. *god of dreams*.

mors mortis, f. *death; a corpse; a cause of death or destruction*.

morsus -ūs, m. *a bite, biting; pungency; a verbal attack*; in gen. *pain, vexation*.

mortālis -e, *subject to death, mortal; transitory, perishable; human, earthly*; m. as subst. *a mortal man*.

mortālĭtās -ātis, f. *liability to death*.

mortĭfer or mortĭfĕrus -fĕra -fĕrum, *causing death, fatal, deadly*; adv. mortĭfĕrē.

mortŭālĭa -ium, n. *funeral songs, dirges*.

mortŭus -a -um, partic. from morior; q.v.

mōrum -i, n. *a mulberry; a blackberry*.

¹mōrus -i, f. *a mulberry tree*.

²mōrus -a -um, *silly, foolish*.

mōs, mōris, f. *the will, inclination*; morem homini gerere, *to humour a person; custom, usage, wont, rule*; in plur., *ways, conduct, character, morals*.

Mōsa -ae, f. *a river in Gaul* (now Meuse).

Mŏsella -ae, f. *a river in Gaul* (now Moselle).

mōtĭo -ōnis, f. *movement*.

mōto -are, *to move about*.

¹mōtus -a -um, partic. from moveo; q.v.

²mōtus -ūs, m. *motion, movement*; terrae, *an earthquake; mental activity, emotion; political movement, rebellion, rising, riot*.

mŏvĕo mŏvēre mōvi mōtum, *to move, set in motion, stir; to remove, dispossess, dislodge*; se movere, and in middle sense, moveri, *to move* (one-self): milit., movere signa, movere castra, *to march away; to move mentally, influence, affect, excite; to cause a result; to change, shake; politically, to arouse, disturb*.

mox, *soon, presently; then, thereupon*.

mūcĭdus -a -um, *snivelling; mouldy, musty*.

Mūcĭus -a -um, *name of a Roman gens*; adj. Mūcĭānus -a -um.

mucro -ōnis, m. *a sharp point or edge; a sword*.

mūcus -i, m. *mucous matter*.

mūgil (mūgĭlis) -is, m. *a fish*, perhaps *mullet*.

mūgĭnor -ari, dep. *to loiter, dally*.

mūgĭo -ire, *to bellow, low, roar, rumble, groan*.

mūgītus -ūs, m. *lowing, bellowing, rumbling, groaning*.

mūla -ae, f. *a female mule*.

mulcĕo mulcēre mulsi mulsum, *to stroke; to soothe, appease, charm*.

Mulcĭber -ēris and -ĕri, m. *surname of Vulcan*; meton., *fire*.

mulco -are, *to thrash; to handle roughly*.

mulctra -ae, f., mulctrārĭum -i, n., and mulctrum -i, n. *milk-pail*.

mulgĕo mulgēre mulsi, *to milk*.

mŭlĭĕbris -e, *of a woman, feminine; effeminate*; adv. mŭlĭĕbrĭtĕr.

mŭlĭer -ĕris, f. *a woman; a wife, matron.*

mŭlĭĕrārĭus -a -um, *womanish.*

mŭlĭercŭla -ae, f. *a little woman.*

mŭlĭĕrŏsĭtās -ātis, f. *love of women.*

mŭlĭĕrōsus -a -um, *fond of women.*

mŭlīnus -a -um, *of a mule, mulish.*

mūlĭo -ōnis, m. *a mule-keeper, mule-driver.*

mūlĭōnĭus -a -um, *of a muleteer.*

mullus -i, m. *the red mullet.*

mulsus -a -um, *honeyed; as sweet as honey*; n. as subst. *wine sweetened with honey, mead.*

multa -ae, f. *a fine, mulct.*

multangŭlus -a -um, *many-cornered.*

multātĭcĭus -a -um, *relating to a fine.*

multātĭo -ōnis, f. *fining.*

multēsĭmus -a -um, *very small.*

multĭcāvus -a -um, *porous.*

multĭcĭa -orum, n. pl. *finely woven garments.*

multĭfārĭam, *on many sides, in many places.*

multĭfĭdus -a -um, *cloven into many parts.*

multĭformis -e, *having many shapes.*

multĭfŏrus -a -um, *pierced with many holes.*

multĭgĕnĕris -e and **multĭgĕnus** -a -um, *of many kinds.*

multĭiŭgus -a -um, and **multĭiŭgis** -e, *yoked many together; manifold, of many sorts.*

multĭlŏquax -ācis, *talkative.*

multĭmŏdis, *in many ways, variously.*

multĭplex -plĭcis, *having many folds, winds or turnings; having many parts, manifold, many-sided, versatile; many times as large.*

multĭplĭco -are, *to increase many times, multiply.*

multĭtūdo -ĭnis, f. *a large number, multitude crowd; common people, mob.*

multo -are, *to punish.*

multus -a -um: sing., *much, great*; plur., *many, numerous*; multi, *the common herd*; ne multa, *briefly, in brief*; ad multum diem, *till late in the day*; in re multus, *prolix on a subject, busy in a matter*; occ., in sing., many a; n. acc. sing. as adv. **multum**, *much, greatly*; abl. **multo**, *by much, by far* Compar. **plus**: in sing. n. only, *more*; genit. of value **plūris**, at *a higher price, of more value*; in plur. **plūres**, **plūra**, *more numerous, several, many.* Superl. **plūrimus**, *most, very many*: in sing., *of a large number, like the English full many a*; of energy, etc., *strong*; genit. of value **plūrimi**, *at the highest price or value.*

mūlus -i, m. *a mule.*

Mulvĭus pons, *a bridge across the Tiber.*

Mummĭus -a -um, *name of a Roman gens.*

Munda -ae, f. *town in Hispania Baetica.*

mundānus -i, m. *a citizen of the world.*

mundĭtĭa -ae, and **mundĭtĭēs** -ēi, f. *cleanness, neatness, spruceness, elegance.*

¹mundus -a -um, *clean, neat, elegant.*

²mundus -i, m. (1) *toilet-things, adornment.* (2) *the universe, world; mankind.*

mūnĕro -are and **mūnĕror** -ari, dep. *to give, present.*

mūnĭa -ĭōrum, n. pl., *duties, functions*; esp. *official.*

mūnĭceps -cĭpis, c. *the citizen of a municipium; a fellow-citizen, fellow-countryman.*

mūnĭcĭpālis -e, *belonging to a municipium, municipal.*

mūnĭcĭpĭum -i, n. *a borough, free town, municipal town.*

mūnĭfĭcentĭa -ae, f. *generosity.*

mūnĭfĭco -are, *to present generously.*

mūnĭfĭcus -a -um, *generous, liberal*; of wealth, *splendid*; adv. **mūnĭfĭcē.**

mūnĭmen -ĭnis, n. *a protection defence.*

mūnĭmentum -i n. *a fortification, defence, protection.*

mūnĭo (moenĭo) -ire, *to build, esp. to build a wall; also to surround with a wall; to fortify; to secure, defend, protect.* Hence partic. **mūnĭtus** -a -um, *fortified, secured.*

mūnītĭo -ōnis, f. *fortifying, building up paving, bridging*; concr., *a fortification.*

mūnīto -are, *to pave, make passable.*

mūnĭtor -ōris, m. *a builder of fortifications, sapper, engineer.*

mūnus (moenus) -ĕris, n. *an office, function, duty; a charge, tax; a service, favour, gift, present; a public show*, esp. *of gladiators: a public building.*

mūnuscŭlum -i, n. *a small gift.*

mūrālis -e, *of a wall, mural*; corona, *the crown given to the first man over the wall of a besieged city.*

¹mūrēna (muraena) -ae, f. *a sea-fish, the murry or lamprey.*

²Mūrēna -ae, m. *a cognomen in the gens Licinia.*

mūrex -ĭcis, m. *the purple-fish; purple dye; a sharp stone, projecting rock.*

mūrĭa -ae, f. *brine, pickle.*

murmillo = mirmillo; q.v.

murmur -ŭris, n. *a murmur, humming, roaring, rumbling, crashing.*

murmŭro -are, *to murmur, roar, crash.*

¹murra (myrrha) -ae, f. *the myrrh-tree; myrrh.*

²murra (myrrha) -ae, f. *a mineral, perhaps fluorspar.*

¹murrĕus (myrrhĕus) -a -um, *perfumed with myrrh; myrrh-coloured.*

²murrĕus (myrrhĕus) -a -um, *made of fluorspar.*

mūrus -i, m. *a wall, bank or dyke*; fig., *protection, defence.*

mūs, mūris, c. *a mouse or rat.*

Mūsa -ae, f. *a muse: a goddess of music literature and the arts.*

mūsaeus -a -um, *poetical, musical.*

musca -ae, f. *a fly.*

muscārĭum -i, n. *a fly-trap.*

muscĭpŭla -ae, f. and **muscĭpŭlum** -i, n. *a mouse-trap.*

muscōsus -a -um, *mossy*

muscŭlus -i, m. *a little mouse; a sea-mussel;* milit., *a shed, mantelet.*

muscus -i, m. *moss.*

mūsēus -a -um = musaeus; q.v.

mūsĭcus -a -um, *belonging to poetry or music, musical;* m. as subst. *a mutician;* f. sing. mūsĭca -ae and mūsĭcē -ēs, *music, poetry, learned studies;* adv. mūsĭcē.

mussĭto -are: intransit., *to grumble, mutter;* transit., *to keep quiet about a thing.*

musso -are, *to murmur, mutter, whisper; to keep quiet about* a thing; *to be at a loss.*

mustācĕum -i, n. and mustācĕus -i, m., *a must-cake, a sort of wedding-cake.*

mustēla (mustella) -ae, f. *a weasel.*

mustus -a -um, *young, new, fresh;* n. as subst. *new wine, must.*

mūtābĭlis -e, *changeable, variable, inconstant.*

mūtābĭlĭtās -ātis, f. *changeableness.*

mūtātĭo -ōnis, *changing, change, alteration; mutual change, exchange.*

mūtĭlo -are, *to maim, mutilate, cut off; to curtail, diminish.*

mūtĭlus -a -um, *maimed, mutilated.*

Mŭtĭna -ae, f. *town in Cisalpine Gaul* (now *Modena*).

mūtĭo (muttio) -ire, *to mutter mumble.*

mūto -are: transit., *to move, shift; to change, alter; to exchange, barter;* with abl., *to give or to get* one thing *in exchange* for another; intransit., *to change, alter.*

mūtŭātĭo -ōnis, f. *borrowing.*

mūtŭor -ari dep. *to borrow.*

mūtus -a -um, *inarticulate, dumb, mute, silent, still, quiet.*

mūtŭus -a -um. (1) *interchanged, mutual, reciprocal;* n. as subst. *reciprocity, equal return;* abl. as adv. mūtŭō, *mutually, reciprocally.* (2) *borrowed, lent:* pecuniam dare mutuam, *to lend;* n. as subst., *a loan.*

mўōpăro -ōnis, m. *a small piratical gulley.*

mўrīcē -ēs, f. and mўrīca -ae, f. *the tamarisk.*

myrtētum (murtētum) -i n. *a grove of myrtle-trees.*

myrtĕus (murtĕus) -a -um, *of myrtle; adorned with myrtle.*

myrtum -i, n. *myrtle-berry.*

myrtus -i and -ūs, f. *the myrtle-tree;* also *a myrtle shaft.*

mystăgōgus -i, m. *a priest who showed sacred places to strangers.*

mystēria -orum, n. pl. *mysteries, secrets,* esp. of worship.

mystēs or mysta -ae, m. *a priest at the mysteries.*

mystĭcus -a -um, *secret, mystic.*

N

N, n, the thirteenth letter of the Latin Alphabet.

nablĭum -i, n. *a kind of harp or lyre.*

nae = ¹nē; q.v.

naenĭa = nenia; q.v.

Naevĭus -a -um, *name of a Roman gens;* esp. of Cn. Naevius, *a poet of the third century B.C.*

naevus -i, m. *a mole on the body.*

Nāĭăs -ădis and Nāĭs -ĭdis (-ĭdos); f. *a water-nymph, Naiad;* adj. Nāĭcus -a -um.

nam and namquĕ, conj., *for.*

nanciscor nancisci nactus *and* nanctus, dep. *to light upon, obtain, meet.*

nānus -i, m. *a dwarf.*

Narbo -ōnis, m. *town in southern Gaul* (now *Narbonne*); adj. Narbōnensis -e.

Narcissus -i, m. *Narcissus, a beautiful young man changed into the flower of the same name.*

nardus -i, f. and nardum -i, n. *nard.*

nāris -is, f. usually plur. nārēs -ĭum, *the nostrils, nose.*

narrābĭlis -e, *able to be told.*

narrātĭo -ōnis, f. *telling, relating; a narrative.*

narrātĭuncŭla -ae, f. *a short narrative.*

narrātor -ōris, m. *a relater, narrator.*

narrātus -ūs, m. *narration, narrative.*

narro -are, *to make known; to say speak.*

narthēcĭum -i. n. *a box for perfumes and medicines.*

nārus = gnarus; q.v.

nascor -i, natus (and gnatus), dep. *to be born; to come into existence, arise, be produced.*

    Hence partic. nātus -a -um, *born, naturally fitted or constituted;* pro re nata, *under present circumstances;* annos prope xc natus, *almost ninety years old.* As subst., m. *a son;* f. *a daughter.*

Nāsĭca -ae, m. *name of a family of the Scipios.*

Nāso -ōnis. m. *cognomen of the poet P. Ovidius.*

nassa -ae, f. *a basket for catching fish; a trap, snare.*

nasturcĭum -i, n. *a kind of cress.*

nāsus -i, m. *the nose;* naso suspendere adunco, *to turn up the nose at ridicule, mock.*

nāsūtus -a -um, *having a large nose; acute, sagacious, satirical.*

nātālĭcĭus -a -um, *relating to birth;* n. pl. as subst. *a birthday party.*

nātālĭs -e, *relating to birth, natal;* m. as subst., *a birthday;* plur. *birth, origin.*

nātātĭo -ōnis, f. *swimming.*

nātātor -ōris. m. *swimmer.*

nātĭo -ōnis, f. *being born, birth; a tribe, race, people,* esp. *uncivilized; a species, stock, class.*

nătĭs -is, f., usually plur. nătēs -ĭum, *the rump, buttocks.*

nātīvus -a -um, *born; native, natural; inborn, innate.*

năto -are, *to swim, float; to stream, flow; to swim with, be full of* (with abl.); f. pl. of partic. as subst. natantes, *fishes.*

nātrix -īcis, f. *a water-snake.*

nātū, abl. sing. m. *by birth; maior natu, older.*

nātūra -ae, f. *birth; nature, natura qualities or disposition, character; an element, substance, essence;* rerum natura, *nature, the world or universe.*

nātūrālis -e, *natural, relating to nature;* adv. **nātūrālitĕr,** *naturally, by nature.*

nātus -a -um, partic. from nascor; q.v

nauarchus -i, m. *captain of a ship.*

nauclērus -i, m. *the master of a ship.*

naucum -i, n. *a trifle;* in genit. non nauci habere, *to think nothing of.*

naufrăgium -i, n. *shipwreck; wreckage; ruin, loss;* naufragium facere, *to suffer shipwreck.*

naufrăgus -a -um, pass., *shipwrecked;* act., *causing shipwreck.*

naulum -i, n. *fare, passage-money.*

naumăchia, ae, f. *a naval battle performed as a show.*

nausĕa -ae, f. *sea-sickness, nausea.*

nausĕo -are, *to be sea-sick; to cause disgust, nauseate.*

nausĕŏla -ae, f. *squeamishness.*

nauta and **nāvīta** -ae, m. *sailor, mariner.*

nauticus -a -um, *of a sailor, nautical;* m. pl. as subst. *sailors.*

nāvālis -e, *of ships, naval, nautical;* n. as subst. **nāvălĕ** -is, *a station for ships;* plur. *a dockyard, or materials for ship-building.*

nāvĭcŭla -ae, f. *a little ship, boat.*

nāvĭcŭlārius -a -um, *of (small) ships;* f. as subst. *the business of a ship-owner;* m. as subst. *a ship-owner.*

nāvĭfrăgus -a -um, *causing shipwreck.*

nāvĭgābilis -e, *navigable.*

nāvĭgātĭo -ōnis, f. *sailing, voyage.*

nāvĭger -gĕra -gĕrum, *ship-bearing, navigable.*

nāvĭgĭum -i, n. *a vessel, ship.*

nāvĭgo -are: intransit., *to sail, voyage, go by sea; to swim;* transit., *to sail over, sail through, navigate.*

nāvis -is, f. *a ship, vessel;* navis longa, *a man-of-war;* oneraria, *a transport;* praetoria, *flag-ship.*

nāvĭta = nauta; q.v.

nāvĭtās (gnāvĭtās) -atis, f. *energy zeal.*

nāvo -are, *to do energetically.*

nāvus (gnāvus) -a -um, *zealous, energetic.* Adv. **nāvĭtĕr (gnāvĭtĕr),** *energetically; completely.*

¹**nē (nae),** used before pronouns, *indeed, truly.*

²**nē,** *not, that not, lest;* ne . . . quidem, *not even, not . . . either.*

³**-nē** (sometimes **n'**) interrog., enclitic particle.

Nĕāpŏlis -polis, f. (1) *part of Syracuse.* (2) *a sea-port (now Naples).*

nĕbŭla -ae, f. *vapour, fog, mist, cloud.*

nĕbŭlo -ōnis, m. *a good-for-nothing fellow.*

nĕbŭlōsus -a -um, *misty, foggy.*

nĕc and **nĕquĕ,** *not; and not, nor;* rarely *not even;* neque enim, *for . . . not;* nec non, *and also;* nec tamen, *and yet . . . not;* nec . . . nec, neque . . . neque, *neither . . . nor.*

necdum (nĕquĕ dum), *and not yet.*

nĕcessārĭus -a -um, *necessary, unavoidable, inevitable; pressing, urgent; closely connected;* as subst. *an intimate friend or relative;* n. abl. **nĕcessārĭō,** and adv. **nĕcessārĭē,** *necessarily, unavoidably.*

nĕcessĕ, indecl. adj. n., used with esse and habere; *necessary, unavoidable inevitable, indispensable.*

nĕcessĭtās -ātis, f. *inevitability, necessity, urgency;* plur. *requirements, necessary expenses.* Transf., *intimate connexion, friendship, relationship.*

nĕcessĭtūdo -inis, f. *necessity, inevitableness; need, want.* Transf., *close connexion, intimate friendship;* plur., *intimate friends, near relations.*

nĕcessum =necesse; q.v.

necnĕ, *or not.*

necnōn (nĕquĕ nōn); see nec.

nĕco -are, *to kill, slay, put to death.*

nĕcŏpinans -antis, *not expecting unaware.*

nĕcŏpinātus (nĕc ŏpinātus) -a -um *unexpected;* adv. **nĕcŏpinātō.**

nĕcŏpinus -a -um; pass., *unexpected;* act., *not expecting.*

nectar -āris, n. *nectar, the drink of the gods; honey, milk, wine.*

nectărĕus -a -um, *of nectar.*

necto nectĕre nexŭi *and* nexi nexum, *to tie, bind, fasten; to fetter, enslave; to affix, attach; to put together, devise.*

nĕcŭbi, *lest anywhere, that nowhere.*

nĕcundĕ, *lest from any quarter, that from no direction.*

nēdum, *not to say; after* (implied) negative, *much less, still less; after* affirmative, *much more.*

nĕfandus -a -um, *not to be spoken of; abominable.*

nĕfārius -a -um, *impious, abominable;* adv. **nĕfārĭē.**

nĕfās, n. indecl., *what is contrary to divine command; sin, crime, abomination;* per fas et nefas, *by fair means or foul;* as interj. *monstrous! dreadful!*

nĕfastus -a -um, *forbidden, unholy; unlucky; sinful;* dies nefasti, *days on which no public business could be transacted.*

nĕgātĭo -ōnis, f. *denying.*

nĕgĭto -are *to persist in denying.*

neglectĭo -ōnis, f. *neglect.*

neglectus -ūs, m. *neglect, disregard.*

neglĕgentĭa -ae, f. *carelessness, negligence.*

neglĕgo -lĕgĕre -lexi -lectum, *to neglect, disregard; to make light of, overlook, omit.*

Hence partic. **neglĕgens** -entis, *careless;* adv. **neglĕgentĕr.**

nĕgo -are, *to say no; to deny, say that . . . not; to deny a request, refuse to give or do.*

nĕgōtĭālis -e, *relating to business.*

nĕgōtĭātĭo -ōnis, f. *bankers' business.*

nĕgōtĭātor -ōris, m. *a business-man;* esp. *banker.*

nĕgōtĭŏlum -i, n. *a little business.*

nĕgōtĭor -ari, dep. *to carry on business;*

esp. as *a banker*; m. of partic. as subst.
nĕgŏtians -antis, *a businessman*.

nĕgŏtĭōsus -a -um, *full of business, busy*.

nĕgŏtĭum -i, n. *business, occupation, employment, task; pains, trouble, difficulty; a matter, piece of business*.

Nĕmĕa -ae, and **Nĕmĕē** -ēs, f. *a valley in Argolis*; adj. **Nĕmĕaeus** -a -um, subst. **Nĕmĕa** -orum, n. pl., *the Nemean games*.

nēmo -inis, c., *no one, nobody*: nemo non, *everyone*; non nemo, *some or many*.

nĕmōrālis -e and **nĕmōrensis** -e, *of woods or groves; sylvan*.

nĕmōrōsus -a -um, *full of groves; thickly leaved, full of foliage*.

nempĕ, *truly, certainly, to be sure*.

nĕmus -ŏris, n. *a wood, grove*.

nēnia -ae, f. *a funeral song, dirge; an incantation; nursery ditty, lullaby*.

nĕo nēre nēvi nētum, *to spin; to interweave*.

nĕpa -ae, f. *a scorpion; a crab*.

¹nĕpōs -ōtis, m. *a grandson, a nephew; a descendant; a spendthrift*.

²Nĕpos -pōtis, m., C. Cornelius. *a Roman historian, friend of Cicero*.

neptis -is, f. *a grand-daughter*.

Neptūnus -i, m. *Neptune, god of the sea*; adj. **Neptūnius** -a -um.

nēquam, indecl.; compar. **nēquior**, superl. **nēquissimus**; *worthless, good for nothing, bad*; adv. **nēquĭtĕr**.

nēquāquam, *by no means, not at all*.

nēquĕ = nec; q.v.

nēquĕdum = necdum; q.v.

nēquĕo -ire. ivi and -ii -itum, *to be unable*.

nēquicquam (nēquicquam), *in vain to no purpose; without good reason*.

nēquitia -ae, and **nēquitiēs** -ēi, f. *worthlessness, badness*; esp. *extravagance*.

Nērĕus -ĕos and -ĕi, m. *a sea-god*.

Nēro -ōnis, m. *a cognomen in the gens Claudia*; esp. C. Claudius Nero, *fifth Roman emperor* (54–68).

nervōsus -a -um *sinewy, nervous, strong, vigorous*; adv. **nervōsē**.

nervŭlus -i, m., *nerve, strength*.

nervus -i, m. (usually plur.), *sinew, tendon*; fig. *strength, vigour, energy; a string*, esp. *of an instrument; a strap, thong, fetter*.

nescio -ire -ivi and -ii -itum, *not to know, to be ignorant; to fail to recognise*; with infin. *to be unable to do*; nescio quis, quid, etc., *I know not who or what, somebody, something*.

nescius -a -um: act., *not knowing, ignorant, unaware; not knowing how, unable*, with infin.; pass., *unknown*.

Nestŏr -ŏris, m. *the most experienced of the Greek heroes at Troy*.

neu = neve; q.v.

neuter -tra -trum, *neither*. Transf., *of neither sex, neuter*. Adv. **neutrō**, *in neither direction, towards neither side*.

neutĭquam (ne ŭtĭquam), *by no means, not at all*.

nēvĕ or **neu**, *and not, or not, nor* (esp. following ut or ne).

nēvis, nēvult = nonvis, nonvult; see nolo.

nex, nĕcis, f. *death*; usually *violent death, murder*.

nexilis -e, *tied together, plainted*.

nexum -i, n. *an arrangement by which a debtor pledged his liberty as security for debt*.

nexus -ūs, m. *a tying together, connecting, restraining*; also in the sense of nexum, q.v.

nī (nei) and **nīvĕ**, *if not, unless*; also in the sense of ne, q.v.; quid ni? *why not?*

nīcētērĭum -i, n. *reward of victory, prize*.

nicto -are, *to wink*.

nidor -ōris, m. *vapour, reek*.

nīdūlus -i, m. *a little nest*.

nīdus -i, m. *a nest*.

niger -gra -grum, *black, dark-coloured; blackening; bad, unlucky*; n. as subst. *a black sport*.

nigresco nigrescĕre nigrŭi, *to become black, grow dark*.

nigro -are, *to be black*; partic. **nigrans** -antis, *black, dark*.

nigror -ōris, m. *blackness*.

nihil and contr. **nīl**, *nothing*; nihil non, *everything*; non nihil, *something*; nihil, as internal acc., or **adv.**, *not at all*.

nihildum, *nothing as yet*.

nihilum (nilum), *nothing*; as adv., *not at all*; nihilominus, *nevertheless*.

nīl = nihil; q.v.

Nilus -i, m. *the river Nile*; adj. **Niliācus** -a -um.

nimbifer -fĕra -fĕrum, *stormy*.

nimbōsus -a -um, *rainy, stormy*.

nimbus -i, m. *cloud, mist*; esp. *a black rain-cloud; a storm, shower*.

nimirum, *undoubtedly, certainly, of course* (often ironical).

nimis, *very much; too much, excessively*.

nimius -a -um, *very great; too great, excessive; intemperate, immoderate*. N. as subst. *a great deal, much*; also *excess, too much*.

ningo (ninguo) ningĕre ninxi, *to snow*; impers., ningit, *it snows*.

ninguēs -ium, f. pl. *snow*.

Nĭōbē -es, f and **Nĭōba** -ae, f. *daughter of Tantalus, wife of Amphion*.

nisi, *if not, unless*; after negatives and questions, *except*; nisi quod, *except that*.

¹nīsus (nixus) -ūs, m. *pressing, straining, effort*.

²nīsus -a -um, partic. from nitor; q.v.

nītēdŭla -ae, f. *dormouse*.

nĭtĕo -ēre, *to shine, glitter, be bright; to glow, be sleek, flourish*.
  Hence partic. **nitens** -entis, *shining, bright, sleek, blooming*.

nĭtesco -ĕre, *to begin to shine; to grow sleek*.

nĭtĭdus -a -um, *bright, shining; sleek, fat; flourishing, blooming*. Transf.,

spruce, elegant; refined, polished.
Adv. **nitĭdē.**

¹nitor niti nisus or nixus, dep. (1) *to rest, lean, support oneself (on); to trust (in), depend (on).* (2) *to strive, exert oneself, make an effort;* of movement, *to press on, climb up.*

²nitor -ōris, m. *brilliance, brightness, splendour, glow, elegance.*

nivālis -e, *of snow, snowy.*

nivĕ = ni, q.v., or neve, q.v.

nivĕus -a -um, *of snow, snowy.*

nivōsus -a -um, *snowy.*

nix, nĭvis, f. *snow.*

nixor -ari, dep. *to lean upon; to strive, strain.*

¹nixus = ¹nisus; q.v.

²nixus; see ¹nitor.

no nāre nāvi, *to swim.* Transf., *to sail, flow, fly.*

nōbilis -e, *known; celebrated, renowned, infamous, notorious; of noble birth, highly bred;* of things, *fine.*

nōbilĭtās -ātis, f. *fame, celebrity; noble birth, nobility;* meton., *the aristocrats, the nobility;* in gen., *excellence, worth.*

nōbilĭto -are, *to make known, make famous or notorious.*

nŏcĕo -ēre, *to hurt, injure, harm* (with dat.); partic. **nŏcens** -entis, *hurtful, injurious, guilty, wicked;* as subst., *a guilty person.*

noctĭlūca -ae, f. *the moon.*

noctĭvăgus -a -um, *wandering by night.*

noctū, abl. from nox; q.v.

noctŭa -ae, f. *owl.*

noctŭābundus -a -um, *travelling by night.*

nocturnus -a -um, *by night, nightly, nocturnal.*

nŏcŭus -a -um, *hurtful, injurious.*

nōdo -are, *to knot, tie in a knot.*

nōdōsus -a -um, *full of knots, knotty.*

nōdus -i, m. *a knot; a girdle; any tie, bond, connexion, obligation; a knotty point, difficulty.*

nōlo nolle nōlŭi, *to be unwilling, wish not to, refuse.*

nŏmăs -ădis, c. *a nomad,* esp. *a Numidian.*

nōmen -inis, n. *a name;* nomen dare, *to go for a soldier, enlist;* nomen (hominis) deferre, *to give information against, accuse;* nomina solvere, *to pay debts;* nomen Romanum, *the Roman power;* nomine meo, *in my name, on my behalf.*

nōmenclātor -ōris, m. *a slave who reminded his master of names.*

nōminātim, *by name, expressly.*

nōminātio -ōnis, f. *nomination to a public office.*

nōminĭto -are, *to call regularly by name.*

nōmino -are, *to name, give a name to, call; to mention, speak about; to make famous; to appoint, nominate to an office; to denounce, give information against.*
   Hence partic. **nōminātus** -a -um, *well-known, celebrated.*

nōmisma -mătis, n. *a coin.*

nōn (old forms **noenum, noenu**), *not;* non nihil, *something;* nihil non,

everything; non quod, non quo, *not that, not because;* non ita, *very, not particularly;* in questions nonne? q.v.; in commands = ne; answers, *no.*

nōnae -arum, f. *the nones; the fifth d. in all months, except March, Ma July and October, when it was t seventh.*

nōnāgēsimus (-ensimus) -a -ur *ninetieth.*

nōnāgiēs (-iens), *ninety times.*

nōnāgintā, *ninety.*

nōnānus -a -um, *belonging to the nin legion.*

nondum, *not yet.*

nongenti -ae -a, *nine hundred.*

nonnĕ, interrog. adv., *asks a questic to which an affirmative answer expected.*

nonnēmo, nonnihil; see nemo, nihil

nonnullus (nōn nullus) -a -um, *som in* plur., *several.*

nonnumquam (nōn numquam *sometimes.*

nōnus -a -um, *ninth;* f. as subst., *t ninth hour* (roughly 3 p.m.).

nōnusdĕcimus -a -um, *nineteenth.*

Nōricum -i, n. *Noricum, a countr between the Alps and the Danub* adj. **Nōricus** -a -um.

norma -ae, f. *a rule, standard.*

nōs, plur. of ego; q.v.

nosco noscĕre nōvi nōtum, *to becom acquainted with, get to know;* hence in perfect tenses, *to be acquainted wit know.* Transf., *to inquire into, investi gate; to recognize; to approve acknowledge.*
   Hence partic. **nōtus** -a -um *known; famous; notorious, familia customary;* m. pl. as subst. *friends acquaintances.*

noster -tra -trum, *our, ours; of us to us, for us;* m. pl. nostri, *our people* **nostrās** -ātis, adj. *of our country, native*

nŏta -ae, f. *a mark, token, note, sign in writing, a letter, character; distinguishing mark, brand;* hence *sort, quality;* also *mark of disgrace stigma* (esp. *as imposed by th censor).*

nŏtābilis -e, *remarkable, striking* adv. **nŏtābilĭter.**

nŏtārius -i, m. *secretary or shorthand writer.*

nŏtātio -ōnis, f. *marking, noting. choice. the stigma of the censor.*

nōtesco nōtescĕre nōtŭi, *to become known.*

nŏthus -a -um, *illegitimate, bastard; hybrid, mongrel;* in gen., *spurious.*

nōtio -ōnis, f. *an examination, investiga tion; an idea, notion, conception.*

nōtĭtĭa -ae, and **nōtĭtĭēs** -ēi, f.: pass., *being known, fame, celebrity;* act., *knowledge, acquaintance;* hence *idea, notion, conception.*

nŏto -are, *to mark, mark out, distinguish, denote; to observe; to write; to stigmatize* (esp. of the censor).

¹nŏtus -a -um, partic. from nosco; q.v.

²nŏtus (-ŏs) -i, m. *the south wind.*

nŏvācŭla -ae, f. *a sharp knife or razor.*

nŏvālis -is, f. and nŏvālĕ -is, n. *fallow land; a cultivated field; crops.*

nŏvātrix -icis, f. *she that renews.*

nŏvellus -a -um, *new, young; fresh, unfamiliar.*

nŏvem, *nine.*

Nŏvember and Nŏvembris -bris, m. *of the ninth month of the Roman year, of November;* m. as subst., *November.*

nŏvendĕcim, nŏvemdĕcim, *nineteen.*

nŏvendiālis -e, *of nine days; happening on the ninth day; lasting nine days.*

nŏvēni -ae -a, *nine each, nine at a time;* poet., *nine.*

Nŏvensiles divi, *gods whose worship had been introduced from foreign countries.*

nŏverca -ae, f. *step-mother.*

nŏvercālis -e, *of or like a step-mother.*

nŏvīcius -a -um. *new, fresh;* esp. *of persons new to slavery.*

nŏviēs (-iens), *nine times.*

nŏvĭtās -ātis, f. *newness, novelty, strangeness; the condition of a* nŏvus homo (see novus), *newness of nobility;* in pl. *new acquaintances.*

nŏvo -are, *to make new, renew, revive; to change, alter; to invent;* novare res, *to make a revolution.*

nŏvus -a -um, *new, fresh, young; fresh, inexperienced; revived, refreshed; novel, unusual, extraordinary;* novus homo, *the first of a family to hold curule office;* novae res, *political changes, a revolution;* novae tabulae, *new account-books (i.e. a cancellation of debts).* N. as subst., *a new thing, news, a novelty.* Adv. nŏvē, *in a new or unusual way.* Superl., nŏvissimus -a -um. *latest, last, extreme;* agmen, *the rear;* adv. nŏvissimē, *lately, lastly, in the last place.*

nox noctis, f. *night;* meton., *sleep, darkness, gloom, death.* Abl. form as adv. noctū, *by night.*

noxa -ae, f. *harm, injury, damage; a fault, offence; punishment.*

noxia -ae, f. *fault, offence, crime.*

noxius -a -um, *hurtful, injurious; culpable, guilty.*

nūbēcŭla -ae, f. *a little cloud; a troubled expression.*

nūbes -is, f. *a cloud;* fig., *any dense mass; gloom; veil, concealment.*

nūbĭfer -fĕra -fĕrum, *cloud-bearing.*

nūbĭgĕna -ae, c. *born of a cloud.*

nūbĭlis -e, *marriageable.*

nūbĭlus -a -um, *cloudy, overcast; dark, gloomy;* n. sing. as subst. *cloudy weather;* n. pl., *clouds.*

nūbo nūbĕre nupsi nuptum, *to cover, veil; of a bride, to be married to, to marry* (with dat.); f. of partic. nupta, *married,* or, as subst., *a bride.*

nŭclĕus -i, m. *the kernel of a nut, the stone of fruits.*

nūdĭus, *it is now the . . . day since* (always with ordinal numerals); nudius tertius, *the day before yesterday.*

nūdo -are, *to make bare, strip, uncover;* milit. *to leave undefended; to strip, spoil, divest, deprive.*

nūdus -a -um, *naked, bare, uncovered; defenceless, deprived; unadorned, plain; bare, mere, alone, only.*

nūgae -arum, f. pl., *trifles, nonsense, stuff.*

nūgātor -ōris, m. *a trifler, humbug.*

nūgātōrius -a -um, *trifling, frivolous, futile.*

nūgax -ācis, *trifling, frivolous.*

nūgor -ari, dep. *to trifle, talk nonsense; to trick, cheat.*

nullus -a -um, *no, none, not any; non-existent, ruined;* nullo modo, nullo pacto, *by no means;* as a strong negative, *not at all;* as subst., esp. genit. and abl., *no one.*

num, interrog. particle, introducing a direct question, to which a negative answer is expected, or an indirect question, in the sense *whether.*

Nūma -ae, m., Pompilius, *the second king of Rome.*

Nūmantia -ae, f. *a town in Spain.*

nūmen -inis, n. *nodding, a nod; as an expression of will, command, consent; of a deity, divine will, divine command;* hence, in gen., *divine majesty, divinity, deity.*

nŭmĕrābĭlis -e, *able to be counted.*

nŭmĕro -are *to count;* esp. *to count out money, to pay; to count over possessions, i.e. to own; to reckon, consider.*

Hence partic. nŭmĕrātus -a -um, *counted out; in hard cash, in ready money;* n. as subst. *hard cash, money down.*

nŭmĕrōsus -a -um. (1) *numerous.* (2) *rhythmical, metrical, melodious.* Adv. nŭmĕrōsē.

nŭmĕrus -i, m. (1) *a number, reckoning, total; a mass; a mere number, cypher; a category, band, class; rank, position, regard, consideration.* (2) *measure, part, respect;* in music, *metre, number, time.* Abl. sing. as adv. nŭmĕrō, *exactly, at the right time; too quickly, too soon.*

Nūmĭda -ae, m. *a Numidian.*

Nūmĭtor -ōris, m. *king of Alba, grandfather of Romulus and Remus.*

nummārius -a -um, *belonging to money; bribed with money, venal.*

nummātus -a -um, *provided with money, rich.*

nummŭlārius -i, m. *a money-changer.*

nummŭlus -i, m. *a little piece or sum of money.*

nummus -i, m. *a piece of money, coin;* esp. *the sesterce, a coin of small value.*

numquam = nunquam; q.v.

nunc, *now, at present; as things are;* of past or future time, *then, already.*

nuncŭpātio -ōnis, f. *naming, pronouncement.*

nuncŭpo -are, *to name, call by name to pronounce solemnly.*

nundĭnae -arum, f. pl. *market-day; the market-place; traffic, trade, business.*

nundĭnātĭo -ōnis, f. *the holding of a market, trade, business.*

nundĭnor -ari, dep. *to transact business, trade, traffic; to buy,* esp. *corruptly; to be present in great numbers.*

nundĭnum -i, n. *market-time.*

nunquam (numquam), *never*; numquam non, *always*; non numquam, *sometimes.*

nuntĭātĭo -ōnis, f. *a declaration made by the augur.*

nuntĭo -are, *to announce, give notice.*

nuntĭus -a -um, *announcing, bringing news.* M. as subst. **nuntĭus** -i: (1) *a messenger.* (2) *a message, news;* esp. *an official notice.*

nūper, *lately, not long ago.*

nupta -ae, f. subst. from nubo; q.v.

nuptĭae -arum, f. pl. *marriage, a wedding.*

nuptĭālis -e, *of marriage.*

nŭrus -us, f. *a daughter-in-law; any young married woman.*

nusquam, *nowhere, at* (or to) *no place; in nothing, on no occasion; to or for nothing;* nusquam esse, *not to exist.*

nūto -are, *to nod, keep nodding; to sway, waver.*

nūtrīcĭus -i, m. *a tutor, guardian.*

nūtrīco -are and **nūtrīcor** -ari, dep. *to suckle, nourish; to support, sustain.*

nūtrĭcŭla -ae, f. *nurse, nanny.*

nūtrīmen -ĭnis, n. *nourishment.*

nūtrīmentum -i, n. *nourishment; support, training.*

nūtrĭo -ire and **nūtrĭor** -iri, dep. *to suckle, nourish, bring up; to make good, support, sustain.*

nūtrix -icis, f. *a nurse, foster-mother.*

nūtus -ūs, m. *a nod; command, will; gravitation, downward movement.*

nux nŭcis, f. *a nut; a nut-tree.*

nympha -ae and **nymphē** -es, f. *a bride;* Nymphae, *the Nymphs.*

O

O, o, the fourteenth letter of the Latin Alphabet.

o! interj. *oh!*

ob, prep. with acc., *in front of, before; in return for; because of, on account of;* ob rem, *to the purpose, with advantage.*

ŏbaerātus -a -um, *in debt;* as subst., *a debtor.*

ŏbambŭlo -are, *to walk up and down, walk about near.*

ŏbarmo -are, *to arm.*

ŏbăro -are, *to plough up.*

obbrūtesco -ĕre, *to become stupid or dull.*

obc-; see occ-.

obdo -dĕre -dĭdi -dĭtum, *to place before, put against;* fores, *to shut the door.*

obdormisco -dormiscĕre -dormīvi, *to go to sleep.*

obdūco -dūcĕre -duxi -ductum. (1) *to draw over, draw in front;* of persons, *to bring forward.* (2) *to cover, close over;* venenum, *to swallow;* frontem, *to wrinkle;* of time, *to pass, spend.*

obductĭo -ōnis, f. *covering, veiling.*

obdūresco -ĕre, *to become hard, harden.*

obdūro -are, *to be hard (against); to stand out, hold out, persist.*

ŏbēdĭo = oboedio; q.v.

ŏbĕo -ire -īvi and -ii -ĭtum. Intransit., *to go to, go to meet, go against;* of heavenly bodies, *to set;* of the living, *to die.* Transit., *to go to, go over, traverse; to go over, encompass,* by looking or speaking; *to enter upon, engage in, perform, execute* a task; with diem or mortem, *to die.*

ŏbĕquĭto -are, *to ride up to.*

ŏberro -are, *to wander about, go astray.*

ŏbēsus -a -um, *fat, plump; swollen; coarse.*

ŏbex -ĭcis, m. and f. *bolt, bar, barrier, barricade.*

obf-; see off-.

obg-; see ogg-.

ŏbhaeresco -haerescĕre -haesi -haesum, *to stick fast, adhere to.*

obĭăcĕo -ēre, *to lie at, lie against.*

obĭcĭo -icĕre -ĭēci -iectum, *to throw in the way, to expose; to inspire, cause, produce; to put before, hold before, as protection or obstacle; to bring up* anything as a reproach, *to throw in a person's teeth.*

Hence partic. **obĭectus** -a -um, *lying near, opposite to; exposed to; brought up against* a person; n. pl. as subst., *charges.*

obĭectātĭo -ōnis, f. *a reproach.*

obĭecto -are, *to throw in the way, expose; to set against; to bring up* anything as a reproach, *to throw in a person's teeth.*

¹obĭectus -a -um, partic. from obicio; q.v.

²obĭectus -ūs, m. *placing against, putting opposite.*

ŏbīrascor -irasci -īrātus, dep. *to grow angry at.*

ŏbĭter, *on the way, by the way, in passing.*

ŏbĭtus -ūs, m. *an approach;* of heavenly bodies, *setting;* of the living, *death, downfall, destruction.*

obĭurgātĭo -ōnis, f. *scolding, reproving.*

obĭurgātor -ōris, m. *a scolder, reprover.*

obĭurgātōrĭus -a -um, *reproachful, scolding.*

obĭurgo -are, *to scold, reprove, blame, chastise.*

oblanguesco -languescĕre -languĭ, *to become weary.*

oblatro -are, *to bark at; to scold.*

oblectāmen -ĭnis, n. *delight, pleasure.*

oblectāmentum -i, n. *delight, amusement, pastime.*

oblectātĭo -ōnis, f. *delighting, amusing.*

oblecto -are, *to please, amuse; to pass time pleasantly, while away time.*

oblīdo -lidĕre -lisi -lisum, *to crush.*

oblĭgātĭo -ōnis, f. *a bond, tie.*

oblĭgo -are, *to tie, bind up, bandage.* Transf., *to bind, make liable, oblige; to make liable to punishment, make guilty.* Hence partic. **oblĭgātus** -a -um, *bound, under an obligation.*

oblīmo -are, *to cover with slime or mud.*

oblĭno -lĭnĕre -lēvi -litum, *to smear, daub, besmear; to stain, defile;* perf. partic. **oblĭtus** -a -um, *overloaded.*

oblīquo -are, *to turn sideways, turn aside.*

oblīquus -a -um, *slanting, sideways, on one side; of speech, indirect, covert; looking askance, envious.* Adv. **oblīquē,** *sideways, aslant; indirectly, by implication.*

oblītesco -lĭtescĕre -lĭtŭi, *to conceal oneself.*

oblittĕro -are, *to cancel, blot out.*

oblīvio -ōnis, f. *forgetfulness, oblivion.*

oblīvĭōsus -a -um, *oblivious, forgetful; causing forgetfulness.*

oblīviscor oblīvisci oblĭtus, dep. *to forget.*

oblīvĭum -i, n., usually plur., *oblivion, forgetfulness.*

oblongus -a -um, *oblong.*

oblŏquor -lŏqui -lŏcūtus, dep. *to speak against, answer back, contradict, abuse, interrupt; in music, to accompany.*

obluctor -ari, dep. *to struggle against.*

obmōlior -iri, dep. *to build against (as barrier or defence).*

obmurmŭro -are, *to roar against.*

obmūtesco -mūtescĕre -mūtŭi, *to become dumb; to cease.*

obnātus -a -um, *growing on.*

obnītor -nīti -nixus, dep. *to press against, strive against; to take up a stand, maintain a firm position; adv. from partic.,* **obnixē,** *firmly, vigorously.*

obnoxĭōsus -a -um, *submissive, compliant.*

obnoxius -a -um, with dat., *liable, addicted to, guilty of; indebted, obliged, dependent on; subject to, exposed to.*

obnūbo -nūbĕre -nupsi -nuptum, *to cover.*

obnuntĭātĭo -ōnis, f. *the announcement of an unfavourable omen.*

obnuntĭo -are, *to report an unfavourable omen.*

ŏboedĭentĭa -ae, f. *obedience, compliance.*

ŏboedĭo -ire, *to obey, comply with, listen to* (with dat.); partic. **ŏboedĭens** -entis, *obedient, compliant;* adv. **ŏboedĭentĕr.**

ŏbŏrĭor -ŏrīri -ortus, dep. *to arise, appear.*

obrēpo -rēpĕre -repsi -reptum, *to creep up to; to steal upon, come on by surprise.*

obrētĭo -ire, *to catch in a net.*

obrĭgesco -rīgescĕre -rīgŭi, *to become stiff, esp. to freeze.*

obrŏgo -are, *to amend or repeal a law by introducing another.*

obrŭo -rŭĕre -rŭi -rŭtum; fut. partic. -rŭtūrus. Intransit., *to fall, collapse.* Transit., *to cover, bury, swamp, drown; to overwhelm, destroy, obliterate.*

obrussa -ae, f. *assay; test.*

obsaepio -saepire -saepsi -saeptum, *to fence in, block up, render inaccessible.*

obsātūro -are, *to stuff, choke.*

obscēnĭtās (obscaen-) -ātis, f. *impurity, indecency.*

obscēnus (obscaenus) -a -um, *foul, filthy; morally, impure, indecent; ill-omened.* Adv. **obscēnē.**

obscūrātĭo -ōnis, f. *darkening; disappearance.*

obscūrĭtās -ātis, f. *darkness; of language, obscurity; of condition, obscurity, low birth.*

obscūro -are, *to cover, darken, obscure; to veil, conceal, suppress.*

obscūrus -a -um, *covered, dark, obscure; n. as subst., darkness; of language, obscure, unintelligible; of origin, etc., unknown, obscure; of character, secret, reserved, close.* Hence adv. **obscūrē,** *darkly; unintelligibly; secretly.*

obsecrātĭo -ōnis, f. *earnest entreaty, supplication; public prayer to the gods.*

obsecro -are, *to beseech, implore, entreat.*

obsĕcundo -are, *to comply with.*

obsēpĭo = obsaepio; q.v.

obsĕquella -ae, f. *compliance.*

obsĕquens -entis, partic. from obsequor; q.v.

obsĕquentĭa -ae, f. *complaisance.*

obsĕquĭum -i, n. *compliance, submission; indulgence, pliancy.*

obsĕquor -sĕqui -sĕcūtus, dep. *to comply with, yield to, obey;* partic. **obsĕquens** -entis, *compliant, obedient; favourable;* adv. **obsĕquentĕr.**

¹**obsĕro** -are, *to bolt, bar.*

²**obsĕro** -sĕrĕre -sēvi -sĭtum, *to sow thickly, cover with seeds, etc.;* partic. **obsĭtus** -a -um, *full of, covered with, beset by* (with abl.).

observantĭa -ae, f. *respect, attention.*

observātĭo -ōnis, f. *observing, watching; care, accuracy, circumspection.*

observātor -ōris, m. *observer, watcher.*

observĭto -are, *to watch carefully.*

observo -are, *to watch, regard, attend to; of rules, to keep, regard; of persons, to respect.* Hence partic. **observans** -antis, *attentive, respectful.*

obses -sĭdis, c. *a hostage; a surety, security, pledge.*

obsessĭo -ōnis, f. *blockade.*

obsessor -ōris, m. *one who besets, haunts, or besieges.*

obsĭdĕo -sĭdēre -sēdi -sessum: intransit., *to sit down near;* transit., *to beset, haunt, frequent; esp. to blockade, besiege; to watch over, be on the look-out for.*

obsĭdĭo -ōnis, f. *blockade, siege.*

¹**obsĭdĭum** -i, n. *blockade, siege.*

²**obsĭdĭum** -i, n. *the condition of a hostage.*

obsĭdo -sĭdĕre -sēdi -sessum, *to blockade, besiege, invest.*

obsignātor -ōris, m. *one who seals; a witness to a will.*

obsigno -are, *to seal; of a witness, to sign and seal; to stamp, impress.*

obsisto -sistĕre -stĭti -stĭtum, *to place oneself before or in the way of; to oppose, withstand, resist.*

obsĭtus -a -um, partic. from ²obsero; q.v.

obsŏlēfīo -fĭĕri -factus, *to become worn out; to be degraded.*

obsŏlesco -escĕre -ēvi, -ētum, *to go out of use, decay, wear out*; partic. obsŏlētus -a -um, *worn out, decayed; obsolete; threadbare, poor;* compar. adv. obsŏlētius, *more shabbily.*

obsōnātor -ōris, m. *a caterer.*

obsōnium -i, n. *what is eaten with bread;* e.g., *vegetables, fruit, fish.*

¹obsōno -are and obsōnor -ari, dep., *to buy food, cater, provide a meal.*

²obsōno -are, *to interrupt by noise.*

obsorbĕo -ēre -ŭi, *to swallow, gulp down.*

obstetrix -icis, f. *midwife.*

obstinātio -onis, f. *persistence, firmness, obstinacy.*

obstĭno -are, *to persist, be resolved.* Hence partic. obstinātus -a -um, *persistent, firm, obstinate;* adv. obstinātē.

obstĭpesco = obstupesco; q.v.

obstĭpus -a -um, *leaning to one side; bent back or down.*

obstō -stare -stĭti -stātūrus, *to stand before or in the way; to oppose, resist, obstruct* (with dat.); n. pl. of partic. as subst. obstantia, *hindrances, obstacles, impediments.*

obstrĕpo -strĕpĕre -strĕpŭi -strĕpĭtum, *to make a noise, clamour at, disturb, interrupt* (with dat.); in pass., *to be drowned by noise or filled with noise.*

obstringo -stringĕre -strinxi -strictum, *to bind up, tie fast; to entangle, involve, put under an obligation.*

obstructio -ōnis, f. *hindrance, obstruction.*

obstrūdo = obtrudo; q.v.

obstrŭo -strŭĕre -struxi -structum, *to build against; to block up, close, stop.*

obstŭpĕfăcio -făcĕre -fēci -factum, *to astound, stupefy, render senseless;* pass. obstŭpĕfio -fĭĕri -factus.

obstŭpesco (obstĭp-) -stŭpescĕre -stŭpŭi, *to become senseless, be astounded.*

obsum ŏbesse obfŭi, *to be in the way, be prejudicial to* (with dat.).

obsŭo -sŭĕre -sŭi -sūtum, *to sew on; to sew up, close up.*

obsurdesco -descĕre -dŭi, *to become deaf; to turn a deaf ear.*

obtĕgo -tĕgĕre, -texi -tectum, *to cover up; to protect; to conceal;* partic. obtĕgens -entis, *concealing.*

obtempĕrātio -ōnis, f. *compliance, obedience.*

obtempĕro -are, *to comply with, submit to* (with dat.).

obtendo -tendĕre -tendi -tentum. (1) *to stretch before, spread before.* Transf., *to put forward as an excuse, plead, allege.* (2) *to cover, conceal.*

¹obtentus -ūs, m. *stretching* or *spreading before.* Transf., *pretext, pretence, excuse.*

²obtentus -a -um, partic. from obtineo; q.v.

³obtentus -a -um, partic. from obtendo; q.v.

obtĕro -tĕrĕre -trivi -tritum, *to trample, crush, destroy.*

obtestātio -ōnis, f. *a calling of gods to*

witness; *an entreaty in the name of the gods.*

obtestor -ari, dep. *to call as witness; to adjure, implore, entreat in the name of the gods.*

obtexo -texĕre -texŭi, *to cover.*

obtĭcĕo -ēre, *to be silent.*

obtĭcesco -tĭcescĕre -tĭcŭi, *to become silent.*

obtĭnĕo -tĭnēre -tĭnŭi -tentum: transit., *to hold, possess, keep, maintain;* esp. *to maintain an assertion;* also *to take hold of, grasp;* intransit., *to hold, obtain, continue.*

obtingo -tingĕre -tĭgi, *to happen, befall.*

obtorpesco -torpescĕre -torpŭi, *to become stiff, numb, insensible.*

obtorquĕo -torquēre -torsi -tortum, *to wrench, twist round.*

obtrectātio -ōnis, f. *disparagement, detraction.*

obtrectātor -ōris, m. *detractor, disparager.*

obtrecto -are, *to disparage, detract from.*

obtrūdo (obstrūdo) -trūdĕre -trūsi -trūsum. (1) *to gulp down, swallow down.* (2) *to force, obtrude.*

obtrunco -are, *to cut down.*

obtundo -tundĕre -tŭdi -tūsum and tunsum, *to beat upon, thump; to make blunt, dull, weaken, weary.* Partic. obtūsus and obtunsus -a -um, *dull, blunt, blurred, insensible.*

obturbo -are, *to disturb, confuse, distract, harass.*

obturgesco -cĕre, *to swell up.*

obturo -are, *to stop up.*

obtūsus -a -um, partic. from obtundo; q.v.

obtūtus -ūs, m. *gaze, contemplation.*

ŏbumbro -are, *to overshadow, obscure; to conceal, protect, cover.*

ŏbuncus -a -um, *bent inwards, hooked.*

ŏbustus -a -um, *burnt, hardened in the fire.*

obvallo -are, *to surround with a wall, wall round.*

obvĕnio -vĕnire -vēni -ventum, *to come in the way of, to meet; to occur, happen, fall to a person's lot.*

obversor -ari, dep. *to move before, appear before.*

obverto (-vorto) -vertĕre -verti -versum, *to turn towards, direct against.* Partic. obversus -a -um, *turned towards;* m. pl. as subst., *opponents.*

obviam, *in the way, on the way;* hence, with dat., *towards, against, to meet;* obviam ire, with dat., *to go to meet, to oppose;* also *to help, remedy.*

obvius -a -um, *in the way, meeting* (with dat.); *exposed; ready at hand; affable, easy of access.*

obvolvo -volvĕre -volvi -vŏlūtum, *to wrap up, cover all round.*

occaeco -are, *to make blind, to blind, to darken; to conceal, make invisible, to make dull or numb.*

occallesco -callescĕre -callŭi, *to become thick-skinned, hard* or *unfeeling.*

occāno -cănĕre -cănŭi, *to sound.*

occāsĭo -ōnis, f. *a favourable moment, opportunity.*

occāsus -ūs, m. *the setting of heavenly bodies;* hence, *the west;* in gen., *fall, destruction.*

occātĭo -onis, f. *harrowing.*

occēdo -cēdĕre -cessi -cessum, *to go towards, meet.*

occento -are, *to sing a serenade to; to sing a lampoon against.*

occepto -are, *to begin.*

occĭdens -entis, m.; subst. from ²occido; q.v.

occīdĭo -ōnis, f. *slaughter, destruction, extermination.*

¹occīdo -cīdĕre -cīdi -cīsum, *to strike down, beat to the ground; to kill, slay; to plague to death, torment.*

²occĭdo -cīdĕre -cīdi -cāsum, *to fall, fall down;* of heavenly bodies, *to set;* of the living, *to die, perish, be ruined.* Hence pres. partic. occĭdens -entis, setting; m. as subst. (sc. sol), *the setting sun, the west.*

occĭdŭus -a -um, *setting, sinking;* hence, *western, westerly.*

occĭno -cĭnĕre -cĕcini and -cĭnŭi, *to sing inauspiciously.*

occĭpĭo -cĭpĕre -cēpi -ceptum, *to begin.*

occĭpĭtĭum -i, n. and occĭput -itis, n. *the back of the head, occiput.*

occĭsĭo -ōnis, f. *killing, slaughter.*

occĭsor -ōris, m. *slayer, murderer.*

occlūdo -clūdĕre -clūsi -clūsum. *to shut up, close up.*

occo -are, *to harrow.*

occŭbo -are, *to lie down,* esp. *to rest in the grave.*

occulco -are, *to trample, tread down.*

occŭlo -cŭlĕre -cŭlŭi -cultum. *to cover, hide.* Hence partic. occultus -a -um, *hidden, concealed, private;* of persons, *close, reserved.* N. as subst., *concealment, secrecy, a secret.* Adv. occultē, *secretly, obscurely.*

occultātĭo -ōnis, f. *hiding, concealment.*

occultātor -ōris, m. *hider, concealer.*

occulto -are, *to hide, conceal.*

occultus -a -um, partic. from occulo; q.v.

occumbo -cumbĕre -cŭbŭi -cŭbĭtum, *to fall down, sink down;* esp. *to fall down dead.*

occŭpātĭo -ōnis, f. *seizing, taking possession; anticipation; business, employment, occupation.*

occŭpo -are, *to take possession of, seize, occupy, master; to fall upon, attack; to take up, employ; to invest money; to anticipate, get a start on a person, be first to do a thing.* Hence partic. occŭpātus -a -um, *busy, engaged, occupied.*

occurro -currĕre -curri -cursum, *to run to meet; to fall upon, attack; to work against, oppose, counteract;* of things, *to crop up, occur, come to mind.*

occursātĭo -ōnis, f. *attention, officiousness.*

occurso -are, *to run to meet; to oppose;* of things, *to occur, come to mind.*

occursus -ūs, m. *meeting, falling in.*

Ōcĕănus -i, m. *the ocean, the sea which encompasses the earth;* personif., *the father of the Nymphs.*

ŏcellus -i, m. *a (little) eye; a darling.*

ōcĭor, ōcĭus, compar. adj., *swifter, quicker;* adv. ōcĭus, *more swiftly;* serius, ocius, *sooner or later;* sometimes = *swiftly only.*

ocrĕa -ae, f. *a greave.*

ocrĕātus -a -um, *wearing greaves.*

Octāvĭus -a -um, *name of a Roman gens;* esp. of *C. Octavius,* the *Emperor Augustus;* adj. Octāvĭānus -a -um.

octāvus -a -um, *eighth;* octavum, *for the eighth time;* f. as subst. octāva -ae, *the eighth hour.*

octāvusdĕcĭmus -a -um, *eighteenth.*

octĭēs (-ĭens), *eight times.*

octingentēsĭmus -a -um, *eight hundredth.*

octingenti -ae -a, *eight hundred.*

octĭpēs -pēdis, *having eight feet.*

octō, *eight.*

Octōber -bris, *belonging to the eighth month of the Roman year,* reckoning from March; *of October;* m. as subst., *October.*

octōdĕcĭm, *eighteen.*

octōgēnārĭus -a -um, *consisting of eighty.*

octōgēni -ae -a, *eighty each, eighty at a time.*

octōgēsĭmus -a -um, *eightieth.*

octōgĭēs (-ĭens), *eighty times.*

octōgintā, *eighty.*

octōĭŭgis -e, *yoked eight together.*

octōnārĭus -a -um, *consisting of eight together.*

octōni -ae -a, *eight each, eight at a time, eight together.*

octŏphŏros -on, *borne by eight;* n. as subst. octŏphŏron -i, *a litter carried by eight bearers.*

octŭplĭcātus -a -um, *increased eightfold.*

octŭplus -a -um, *eight-fold;* n. as subst. *an eight-fold penalty.*

octussis -is, m. *a sum of eight asses.*

ŏcŭlātus -a -um, *having eyes; catching the eye, conspicuous.*

ŏcŭlus -i, m. *the eye;* esse in oculis, *to be visible; an ornament, treasure; a bud or eye of a plant.*

ōdi odisse; fut. partic. ōsūrus, *to hate, detest, dislike.*

ōdĭōsus -a -um, *hateful, troublesome, annoying;* adv. ōdĭōsē.

ōdĭum -i, n. *hatred; an object of hatred;* esse odio, with dat., *to be hated by.*

ŏdor (older ŏdōs) -ōris, m. *a smell, odour, scent; a scent, suspicion, inkling, presentiment;* in plur., *perfumery, spices.*

ŏdōrātĭo -ōnis, f. *smelling, smell.*

¹ŏdōrātus -ūs, m. *smelling; the sense of smell.*

²ŏdōrātus -a -um, partic. from odoro; q.v.

ŏdōrĭfer, -fĕra -fĕrum, *having a pleasant smell; producing perfumes.*

ŏdōro -are, *to make odorous;* partic. ŏdōrātus -a -um, *sweet-smelling.*

ŏdŏror -ari, dep. to smell; to smell out, snuff at; hence to aim at, aspire to; to search into, investigate; to get an inkling or smattering of.

ŏdōrus -a -um. (1) sweet-smelling. (2) keen-scented, tracking by smell.

ŏdōs = odor; q.v.

Odyssēa -ae, f. the Odyssey.

oecŏnŏmĭa -ae, f. arrangement, division.

oecŏnŏmĭcus -a -um, relating to domestic economy; orderly, methodical.

Oedĭpūs -pŏdis and -i, m. king of Thebes, son of Laius and Jocasta, fated to kill his father and marry his mother.

Oenōnē -ēs, f. a Phrygian nymph, loved and deserted by Paris.

oenŏphŏrum -i, n. a basket for wine.

oenus = unus; q.v.

oestrus -i, m. the gad-fly, horse-fly; inspiration, frenzy.

oesus = usus; q.v.

oesypum -i, n. a cosmetic.

ŏfella -ae, f. a bit, morsel.

offa -ae, f. a pellet, mass, lump; a swelling.

offendo -fendĕre -fendi -fensum: transit., to strike against, knock; to hit upon, fall in with; to shock, offend, displease; intransit., to knock, strike; to run aground; to stumble, make a mistake, to give offence (with dat.); also to take offence.
Hence partic. offensus -a -um, injured, hurt; offensive.

offensa -ae, f. a striking, knocking against; injury; displeasure, offence.

offensio -ōnis, f. a striking, knocking, hitting against; pedis, a stumbling. Transf., a misfortune, setback, indisposition; displeasure, disfavour, aversion, offence.

offensiuncŭla -ae, f. a slight displeasure or check.

offenso -are, to strike, knock, stumble.

¹offensus -a -um, partic. from offensus; q.v.

²offensus -ūs, m. shock, collision; offence, dislike.

offĕro offerre obtŭli oblātum, to bring forward, place before, present, offer, expose; to inflict, occasion trouble; se offerre, and pass., offerri, to present oneself, appear.

officīna -ae, f. a workshop, factory.

officio -ficĕre -fēci -fectum, to act against; to get in the way of, impede, hinder, injure (with dat.).

officiōsus -a -um, obliging, courteous, attentive; dutiful; adv. officiōsē.

officium -i, n. dutiful or respectful action; attendance, service, duty; sense of duty, respect, courtesy; submission, allegiance.

offigo -ĕre, to fix in, fasten.

offirmo -are, to make firm, to fasten; with reflex. or intransit., to be determined, persevere; partic. offirmātus -a -um, firm, resolute.

offŭcia -ae, f. paint, rouge; deceit.

offulgĕo -fulgēre -fulsi, to shine upon.

offundo -fundĕre -fūdi -fūsum, to pour over, spread round; to overspread, cover, conceal; to overwhelm; to bring trouble, etc., upon a person.

ogganniō -ire, to growl at.

oh, interj. oh! ah!

ŏhē, interj. ho! hi!

oi, interj. oh!

ŏlĕa -ae, f. olive, olive-tree.

ŏlĕāgĭnus -a -um, of the olive-tree.

ŏlĕārĭus -a -um, of or for oil.

ŏlĕaster -tri, m. the wild olive-tree.

ŏlĕo -ēre, to emit an odour; to smell of; partic. ŏlens -entis smelling; fragrant or stinking.

ŏlĕum -i, n. olive-oil, oil.

olfăcio -făcĕre -fēci -factum, to smell to scent out, detect.

ŏlĭdus -a -um, smelling.

ŏlim, at that time; of the past, formerly once; of the future, hereafter, one day with a present, for a long time now at times, often.

ŏlit-; see holit-.

ŏlīva -ae, f. olive; olive-tree; olive wreath; staff of olive-wood.

ŏlīvētum -i, n. an olive-grove.

ŏlīvĭfer -fĕra -fĕrum, olive-bearing.

ŏlīvum -i, n. olive-oil, oil.

olla -ae, f. jar, pot.

ollus, olle, obsolete form of ille; q.v.

ŏio = oleo; q.v.

ŏlor -ōris, m. swan.

ŏlōrīnus -a -um, of a swan.

ŏlus; see holus.

Olympĭa -ae, f. a city in Elis, where th Olympic games were held.

Olympus -i, m. a mountain range between Macedonia and Thessaly supposed to be the abode of the gods.

ŏmāsum -i, n. bullocks' tripe.

ōmen -inis, n. an omen, sign, prognostication.

ōmentum -i, n. fat; entrails, bowels.

ōmĭnor -ari, dep. to presage prophesy predict.

ōmĭnōsus -a -um, foreboding, ominous.

ōmitto -mittĕre -misi -missum, to let go, let fall; to give up, lay aside; to disregard; in speaking, to leave out omit; with infin., to cease. Hence partic. ōmissus -a -um, negligent, remiss.

omnĭfer -fĕra -fĕrum, bearing everything.

omnĭgĕnus -a -um, of all kinds.

omnĭmŏdis, in every way, entirely.

omninō, altogether, entirely, wholly; in general, in all; certainly, admittedly.

omnĭpărens -entis, all-producing.

omnĭpŏtens -entis, almighty.

omnĭs -e, all, every, whole; of all kinds; in sing., each, or the whole of one person or thing.

omnĭtŭens -entis, all-seeing.

omnĭvăgus -a -um, wandering everywhere.

ŏnăger and ŏnagrus -i, m. wild ass.

ŏnĕrārĭus -a -um, of burden, freight; iumenta, beasts of burden; (navis) oneraria, a merchant or transport ship.

ŏnĕro -are, to load, burden; to fill, weigh down; to oppress, overwhelm; to make worse, aggravate.

ŏnĕrōsus -a -um, *heavy, burdensome; troublesome.*

ŏnus -ĕris, n. *a load, burden, weight; a trouble, charge; a public burden, tax.*

ŏnustus -a -um, *laden, loaded; full.*

ŏnyx -ўchis, m. and f. *onyx; a casket of onyx.*

ŏpācĭtās -ātis, f. *shadiness.*

ŏpāco -are, *to shade, overshadow.*

ŏpācus -a -um, *shaded, shady; dark, shadowy, obscure.*

ŏpella -ae, f. *a little labour or trouble.*

ŏpĕra -ae, f. *trouble, pains, exertion;* operam dare, with dat., *to work hard at;* est operae pretium, *it is worth while;* opera mea, *thanks to me.* Transf., *time for work; work done;* in pl., *labourers, workmen,* also *mobsmen, gangsters.*

ŏpĕrārius -a -um, *relating to work;* m. ŏpĕrārius -i, *a labourer, workman.*

ŏpercŭlum -i, n. *a lid, cover.*

ŏpĕrimentum -i, n. *a cover, covering.*

ŏpĕrio -pĕrīre -ĕrŭi -pertum, *to cover, bury, conceal; to close, shut up; to overwhelm;* n. of partic. as subst. ŏpertum -i, *a secret place, or secret.*

ŏpĕror -ari, dep. *to work, labour, be busy;* esp. in perf. partic. ŏpĕrātus -a -um, *engaged, busy (*esp. *engaged in worship).*

ŏpĕrōsus -a -um: act., *laborious, painstaking, industrious;* pass., *toilsome, difficult.* Adv. ŏpĕrōsē, *laboriously.*

ŏpertum -i, subst. from operio; q.v.

ŏpes; see ops.

Ŏpicus -a -um, Oscan. Transf., *stupid, philistine.*

ŏpĭfer -fĕra -fĕrum, *helpful.*

ŏpĭfex -ficis, c. *a maker, framer; a workman, artisan.*

ŏpĭfĭcina = officina; q.v.

ŏpilio and ūpilio -ōnis, m. *shepherd.*

ŏpīmus -a -um, *rich, fruitful, fertile; lucrative; wealthy; sumptuous, abundant, copious;* of speech, *overloaded;* spolia opima, *spoils taken by a general from the enemy's general in single combat.*

ŏpīnābĭlis -e, *conjectural.*

ŏpīnātĭo -ōnis, f. *supposition, conjecture.*

ŏpīnātor -ōris, m. *one who supposes or conjectures.*

¹ŏpīnātus -a -um, partic. from opinor; q.v.

²ŏpīnātus -ūs, m. *conjecture, supposition.*

ŏpīnĭo -ōnis, f. *opinion, conjecture, supposition; repute, rumour, report.*

ŏpīnĭōsus -a -um, *set in opinion.*

ŏpīnor -ari, dep. and ŏpīno -are, *to be of opinion, suppose, conjecture.* Partic. ŏpīnātus -a -um, in pass. sense, *supposed, fancied.*

ŏpĭpărus -a -um, *splendid, rich, sumptuous;* adv. ŏpĭpărē.

ŏpĭtŭlor -ari, dep. *to help, aid* (with dat.).

ŏportet -tēre -tŭit, impers. *it is proper, one should, one ought.*

oppĕto -ĕre -ivi and -ĭi -ītum, *to go to meet, encounter;* esp. *to encounter death, to die.*

oppĭdānus -a -um, *of a town;* sometimes *provincial, 'small-town';* m. pl. as subst., *the inhabitants of a town.*

oppĭdo, *quite, very much;* in answers, *certainly.*

oppĭdŭlum -i, n. *a little town.*

oppĭdum -i, n. *a town;* in Britain, *a fortified wood.*

oppignĕro -are, *to pledge, pawn, give in pledge.*

oppīlo -are, *to stop up, block up.*

opplĕo -plēre -plēvi -plētum, *to fill up, block.*

oppōno -pōnĕre -pŏsŭi -pŏsĭtum, *to put opposite or before; to pledge against, mortgage for; to set against, oppose, interpose; to allege as an objection; to contrast.* Hence partic. oppŏsĭtus -a -um, *standing against, opposite.*

opportūnĭtās -ātis, f. *convenience, fitness; a fit time, opportunity; advantage.*

opportūnus -a -um, *opportune, fit, suitable, convenient;* of time, *favourable;* with dat., *sometimes, exposed, liable to.* Adv. opportūnē, *seasonably, conveniently.*

oppŏsĭtĭo -ōnis, f. *opposing, opposition.*

¹oppŏsĭtus -a -um, partic. from oppono; q.v.

²oppŏsĭtus -ūs, m. *placing against, opposing, interposition.*

oppressĭo -ōnis, f. *pressing down, oppression; suppression; seizure.*

¹oppressus -ūs, m. *pressing down, pressure.*

²oppressus -a -um, partic. from opprimo; q.v.

opprĭmo -prĭmĕre -pressi -pressum. (1) *to press upon, press down; to crush, smother, stamp out.* (2) *to catch, take by surprise, occupy forcibly.*

opprŏbrium -i, n. *reproach, scandal, disgrace; a verbal reproach, taunt; a cause of disgrace.*

opprŏbro -are, *to taunt, reproach.*

oppugnātĭo -ōnis, f. *an assault on a town;* in gen., *an attack.*

oppugnātor -ōris, m. *an assailant, attacker.*

oppugno -are, *to attack, assault.*

Ops ŏpis, f.: in nom. sing., *the goddess of abundance;* other cases ŏpem, ŏpis, ŏpe, *might, power,* esp. *power to aid; help, support;* plur. ŏpēs, *resources, means, wealth.*

ops-; see obs-.

optābĭlis -e, *desirable, to be wished for.*

optātĭo -ōnis, f. *a wish.*

optĭmās -ātis, *one of the best, aristocratic;* m. pl. as subst. optĭmātēs, *the aristocratic party, the aristocrats.*

optĭmus (optŭmus) -a -um, superl. of bonus; q.v.

¹optĭo -ōnis, f. *choice, option.*

²optĭo -ōnis, m. *a helper, assistant.*

optīvus -a -um, *chosen.*

opto -are, *to choose, select; to wish for, desire.* Hence partic. optātus -a

-um, *wished for, desired, welcome*; n. as
subst. optātum, *a wish*; abl. optātō,
according to one's wish.

ŏpŭlens, -entis; see opulentus.

ŏpŭlentĭa -ae, f. *wealth, riches, opulence;
the power, greatness of a state*.

ŏpŭlento -are, *to make wealthy, enrich*.

ŏpŭlentus -a -um, also ŏpŭlens -entis,
adj. *rich, wealthy: powerful, mighty;
splendid, sumptuous; lucrative*. Adv.
ŏpŭlentē and ŏpŭlentēr, *richly,
splendidly*.

ŏpus -ēris. n. *work, labour; work done,
a finished work; a building; a literary
work or a work of art*; plur. milit.
works, lines, siege-engines.

ŏpus est (or sunt), *there is work, there
is need; one needs, it is necessary* (with
nom., abl., or genit. of what is needed).

ŏpuscŭlum -i, n. *a little work*.

ōra -ae, f. *edge, rim, boundary*; esp.
coast-line, coast; in gen., *region,
clime, country; the people of a district;
a hawser, cable reaching to shore*.

ōrācŭlum (ōrāclum) -i, n. *a solemn
utterance, oracle, divine response,
prophecy; also the place where an
oracle is given*.

ōrātĭo -ōnis, f. *speaking, speech: language, style*; esp. *a set speech;
eloquence; prose; an imperial message*.

ōrātĭuncŭla -ae, f. *a little speech, short
oration*.

ōrātor -ōris, m. *speaker; spokesman,
envoy; orator*.

ōrātōrĭus -a -um, *of an orator, oratorical*;
f. as subst. *oratory*; adv. ōrātōrĭē.

ōrātrix -icis, f. *a female suppliant*.

ōrātū, abl. sing. m. *by request*.

orbātor -ōris, m. *one who deprives
another of children or parents*.

orbis -is. m. *a circle, ring, disk; orbit,
coil*; orbis signifer, *the Zodiac*; orbis
lacteus, *the Milky Way*; orbis terrae,
terrarum, *the world*. Transf., *rotation, round*; of style, *roundness*.

orbĭta -ae, f. *a wheel-rut*.

orbĭtās -ātis, f. *bereavement, loss of
children or parents*.

orbo -are, *to bereave, deprive of parents
or children*.

orbus -a -um, *deprived of parents or
children*; as subst. *an orphan*; in
gen., *deprived, destitute*.

orca -ae, f. *a pot or jar with a large belly*.

orchās -ādis, f. *a species of olive*.

orchestra -ae, f. *the part of a Roman
theatre reserved for senators*; meton.,
the senate.

Orcus i-. m. *Orcus, the infernal regions*.
Transf., *the god of the lower world;
death*.

ordĕum = hordeum; q.v.

ordĭa prima = primordia; q.v.

ordĭnārĭus -a -um, *according to order,
regular, ordinary*.

ordĭnātim, *in good order, regularly,
properly*.

ordĭnātĭo -ōnis. f. *setting in order,
arrangement*.

ordĭno -are, *to set in order, settle,
arrange, appoint; to govern a country*.

Hence partic. ordĭnātus -a -um,
arranged, orderly.

ordĭor ōrdīri orsus, dep. *to begin*; esp.
to begin speaking. N. pl. of partic. as
subst. orsa -orum, *beginnings; undertaking*; esp. *words uttered, speech*.

ordo -inis, m. *a series, line, row, order;
milit., a line, rank, file*; ordinem
ducere, *to be a centurion*; polit. and
socially, *an order, rank, class*; in gen.,
order, arrangement; ordine, *in turn,
in due order, regularly*; extra ordinem,
in an unusual, irregular manner.

Ŏrēās -ādis, f. *a mountain-nymph*.

Ŏrestes -ae and -is, m. *son of Agamemnon and Clytemnestra, who killed
his mother to avenge his father*.

ŏrexis -is, f. *desire, appetite*.

orgănĭcus -i, m. *a musician*.

orgănum -i, n. *an instrument*; esp., *a
musical instrument*.

orgĭa -orum, n. pl. *a secret festival;
mysteries; orgies*.

ŏrĭchalcum -i, n. *yellow copper ore;
brass*.

ŏrĭcŭla = auricula; q.v.

ŏrĭens -entis, m. partic. from orior; q.v.

ŏrĭgo -inis, f. *origin, source, beginning;
an ancestor*.

Ŏrĭōn -ōnis, m. *the constellation Orion*.

ŏrĭor ŏrīri ortus, dep. *to rise: to spring
up, be born, proceed from a source or
cause*. Hence partic. ŏrĭens -entis,
rising. M. as subst. *the rising sun; the
east; the morning*.

ŏrĭundus -a -um, *arising from, springing
from*.

ornāmentum -i, n. *equipment, trappings, furniture; ornament, decoration;
honour, distinction*.

ornātrix -icis, f. *a female hairdresser,
tire-woman*.

¹ornātus -ūs, m. *dress, attire, equipment;
embellishment, ornament*.

²ornātus -a -um, partic. from orno; q.v.

orno -are, *to equip, furnish, fit out; also
to adorn, decorate, embellish; to honour,
distinguish*.

Hence partic. ornātus -a -um,
*furnished, equipped, provided; adorned,
decorated, embellished*. Adv. ornātē,
splendidly, elegantly.

ornus -i, f. *the mountain-ash*.

ōro -are, *to speak*; esp. *to speak as an
orator*; with acc., *to treat, argue,
plead; to beg, pray, entreat, beseech*.

Ŏrontēs -is and -ae, m. *chief river of
Syria*.

Orphēus -ĕi and -ĕos, *a mythical
minstrel, husband of Eurydice*.

orsa -orum, from ordior; q.v.

orsus -ūs, m. *a beginning, undertaking*.

¹ortus -ūs, m.: *of heavenly bodies,
rising; of persons, origin, birth*; in
gen., *origin, source*.

²ortus -a -um. partic. from orior; q.v.

ōryx -ȳgis, m. *a wild goat or gazelle*.

ōrȳza -ae, f. *rice*.

¹ōs ōris, n. (1) *the mouth; hence voice,
talk; uno ore, unanimously*; in gen.,
mouth, opening, source. (2) *the face,
countenance; presence, sight; ex-*

pression; boldness of expression, impudence; a mask.
ˀōs ossis, n. *a bone.*

oscen -ĭnis, m. *a bird from whose note auguries were taken* (e.g., raven, owl, crow).

Osci -orum, *an ancient people of Italy.*

oscillum -i, n. *a little mask.*

oscītātĭo -ōnis, f. *gaping, yawning.*

oscĭto -are, *to gape, yawn;* partic. **oscĭtans** -antis, *yawning, sleepy, listless;* adv. **oscĭtantēr.**

oscŭlātĭo -ōnis, f. *kissing.*

oscŭlor -ari, dep. *to kiss; to caress, make much of.*

oscŭlum -i, n. *a little mouth; a kiss.*

ōsor -ōris, m. *a hater.*

Ossa -ae, m. and f. *a mountain range in Thessaly.*

ossĕus -a -um, *bony.*

ossĭfrăgus -i, m. and **ossĭfrăga** -ae, f. *the sea-eagle, osprey.*

ostendo -tendĕre -tendi -tentum and -tensum, *to hold out, show, reveal, present;* in speech, *to make plain, declare.* N. of partic. as subst. **ostentum** -i, *a prodigy, portent.*

ostentātĭo -ōnis, f. *showing, revealing; showing off, display; deceitful show, pretence.*

ostentātor -ōris. m. *one who shows;* esp., *a boaster.*

ostento -are, *to hold out, present, offer; to show, reveal; to show off, display;* in speech, *to declare, make known.*

ostentŭi, dat. sing. m. *for a show; merely for show; as a sign or proof.*

ostentum -i, n., subst. from ostendo; q.v.

Ostĭa -ae, f. and **Ostĭa** -orum, n. *the harbour and port of Rome, at the mouth of the Tiber;* adj. **Ostiensis** -e.

ostĭārĭum -i, n. *a door-tax.*

ostĭātim, *from door to door.*

ostĭum -i, n. *door;* in gen., *entrance;* fluminis, *mouth.*

ostrĕa -ae, f. and **ostrĕum** -i. n. *an oyster.*

ostrĭfer -fĕra -fĕrum, *producing oysters.*

ostrīnus -a -um, *purple.*

ostrum -i, n. *purple dye prepared from a shell-fish; a purple dress.*

Otho -ōnis, m. *a Roman cognomen.*

ōtĭor -ari, dep. *to be at leisure.*

ōtĭōsus -a -um, *at leisure,* esp. *free from public duties; calm, quiet, undisturbed, neutral.* Adv. **ōtĭōsē,** *at leisure; quietly, easily.*

ōtĭum -i, n. *free time leisure, ease; peace, repose.*

ŏvans -antis, partic. *rejoicing, exulting;* esp. *celebrating the minor triumph* (the ovatio).

ŏvātĭo -ōnis, f. *an ovation, a kind of lesser triumph.*

Ŏvĭdĭus -a, *name of a Roman gens;* esp. *of the poet P. Ovidius Naso* (43 B.C.–17 A.D.).

ŏvīle -is, n. *a sheepfold, an enclosure.*

ŏvillus -a -um, *of sheep.*

ŏvis -is, f. *a sheep.*

ŏvum -i, n. *an egg.*

P

P, p, *the fifteenth letter of the Latin Alphabet.*

pābŭlātĭo -ōnis, f. *procuring fodder, foraging.*

pābŭlātor -ōris, m. *a forager.*

pābŭlor -ari, dep. *to forage, seek fodder.*

pābŭlum -i, n. *food, nourishment, fodder.*

pācālis -e, *peaceful.*

pācĭfer -fĕra -fĕrum, *peace-bringing.*

pācĭfĭcātĭo -ōnis, f. *making of peace, pacification.*

pācĭfĭcātor -ōris, m. *a peacemaker.*

pācĭfĭcātōrĭus -a -um, *peacemaking, pacific.*

pācĭfĭco -are. *to make peace; to appease, pacify.*

pācĭfĭcus -a -um, *peacemaking, pacific.*

pāciscor pācisci pactus, dep. *to make a bargain or agreement, to covenant, contract; transit., to stipulate for, bargain for; also to give in exchange.* Perf. partic. in pass. sense, **pactus** -a -um, *agreed upon, stipulated; betrothed.* N. as subst. **pactum** -i, *an agreement, treaty, pact;* quo pacto? *how?* alio pacto, *in another way.*

pāco -are, *to pacify, make peaceful;* poet., *to make fruitful.*
 Hence partic. **pācātus** -a -um, *peaceful, quiet;* n. as subst. *a peaceful country.*

pactĭo -ōnis, f. *a bargain, contract, agreement, treaty.*

pactor -ōris, m. *one who makes a contract or treaty, negotiator.*

pactum -i, n., and **pactus** -a -um, from paciscor; q.v.

Pācŭvĭus -i, m. *a Roman tragic poet.*

Pādus -i, m. *the river Po.*

paeān -ānis, m. (1) *the Healer, a surname of Apollo.* (2) *a hymn, paean.*

paedăgōgus -i, m. *a slave who accompanied children to and from school.*

paedor -ōris, m. *dirt, filth.*

paelex (pellex) -licis, f. *a mistress, concubine.*

paelicātus -ūs, m. *concubinage.*

Paeligni -orum, m. pl. *an Italian tribe.*

paenĕ, *nearly, almost.*

paeninsŭla -ae, f. *a peninsula.*

paenĭtentĭa -ae, f. *repentance, regret.*

paenĭtĕo -ēre, *to repent, regret, be sorry;* impers. **paenitet** hominem, *a person feels regret, is sorry;* gerundive **paenĭtendus** -a -um, *regrettable, unsatisfactory.*

paenŭla -ae, f. *a travelling-cloak, greatcoat.*

paenŭlātus -a -um, *wearing the paenula;* q.v.

paeōn -ōnis, m. *a metrical foot, consisting of three short syllables and one long.*

Paestum -i, n. *a town in Lucania famous for roses.*

paetŭlus -a -um, *with a slight cast in the eye.*

paetus -a -um, *with a cast in the eyes, squinting.*

pāgānus -a -um, *belonging to a village,*

rural; rustic; m. as subst. *a villager, countryman.*

păgătim, *in villages, by villages.*

păgella -ae, f. *a little page.*

păgina -ae, f. *a page of a letter, book,* etc.

păgĭnŭla -ae, f. *a little page.*

păgus -i, m. *a village or country district; a canton.*

pāla -ae, f. *a spade; the bezel of a ring.*

Pălaestina -ae, and **Pălaestinē** -ēs, f. *Palestine.*

pălaestra -ae, f. *a gymnasium or wrestling school; wrestling.* Transf., *training in rhetoric.*

pălaestrĭcus -a -um, *of the palaestra, gymnastic;* adv. **pălaestricē.**

pălaestrita -ae, m. *the superintendent of a palaestra* (q.v.).

pălam: adv. *openly, publicly*; prep., with abl., *in the presence of.*

Pălătĭum -i, n. *the Palatine Hill in Rome:* in plur., *a palace*; adj. **Pălātīnus** -a -um.

pălātum -i, n. and **pălātus** -i, m. *the roof of the mouth, palate; taste; critical judgment.*

pălĕa -ae, f. *chaff.*

pălĕar -āris, n. *the dewlap of an ox.*

Pălēs -is, f. *tutelary goddess of herds and shepherds*; adj. **Pălīlis** -e; n. pl. as subst. **Pălīlia** -ium, *the feast of Pales on the 21st of April.*

pălimpsestus -i, m. *a palimpsest.*

Pălĭnūrus -i, m. *the pilot of Aeneas; a promontory on the coast of Lucania.*

pălĭūrus -i, m. *a plant, Christ's thorn.*

palla -ae, f. *a long outer garment, esp. as worn by women and actors.*

Pallas -ādis and -ādos, f. *Athene, the Greek goddess of wisdom, identified with Minerva*; adj. **Pallădius** -a -um; n. as subst. **Pallădium** -i *an image of Pallas.*

pallĕo -ēre, *to be pale or yellow*; partic. **pallens** -entis, *pale, wan, yellow, pale green; causing paleness; drooping, weak.*

pallesco pallescĕre pallui, *to grow pale or yellow*; with acc., *to turn pale at.*

palliātus -a -um, *clad in a pallium, i.e. as a Greek* (opp. togatus).

pallĭdŭlus -a -um, *somewhat pale.*

pallĭdus -a -um, *pale, wan; causing paleness.*

pallĭŏlum -i, n. *a little Greek cloak; a hood.*

pallĭum -i, n. *a coverlet; a Greek mantle.*

pallor -ōris, m. *paleness; fading.*

palma -ae, f. (1) *the palm of the hand; a hand; the blade of an oar.* (2) *the palm-tree; a date; a palm broom; a palm-branch* as token of victory; hence, *victory, honour, glory.*

palmāris -e, *deserving the palm or prize, excellent.*

palmārĭum -i, n. *a masterpiece.*

palmātus -a -um, *embroidered with palm-branches.*

palmĕs -ĭtis, m. *a young branch esp. of a vine.*

palmētum -i, n. *a palm-grove.*

palmĭfer -fĕra -fĕrum, *abounding in palm-trees.*

palmōsus -a -um, *full of palms.*

palmŭla -ae, f. *the blade of an oar.*

pālor -ari, dep. *to wander, stray.*

palpebra -ae, f. *eyelid.*

palpĭto -are, *to move quickly, tremble, throb.*

palpo -are and **palpor** -ari, dep. *to stroke; to coax, flatter, wheedle.*

pălūdāmentum -i, n. *the military cloak.*

pălūdātus -a -um, *clad in the military cloak.*

pălūdōsus -a -um, *marshy, boggy.*

pălumbes -is, m. and f. *a wood-pigeon, ring-dove.*

¹**pālus** -i, m. *a pale, stake.*

²**pălūs** -ūdis, f. *a swamp, marsh, bog.*

păluster -tris -tre, *marshy, boggy.*

pampĭnĕus -a -um, *attached to or consisting of vine-tendrils.*

pampĭnus -i, m. and f. *a vine-tendril or vine-leaf.*

Pān Pānos, m. *the god of flocks, woods, and shepherds.*

pănăcĕa -ae, f. and **pănăcēs** -is, n. *a plant, supposed to heal all diseases; panacea, heal-all.*

pānārĭum -i, n. *a bread-basket.*

panchrestus (panchristus) -a -um, *good for everything.*

pancrătĭum (-ŏn) -i, n. *a gymnastic contest.*

pando pandĕre pandi pansum and passum. (1) *to stretch out, spread out, extend*; crines passi, *dishevelled hair.* (2) *to throw open, lay open, reveal, disclose.*

Hence partic. **passus** -a -um, *spread out, esp. spread out to dry*; n. as subst. *raisin-wine.*

pandus -a -um, *bent, curved, crooked.*

pango pangĕre panxi, *to fasten, fix, drive in.* Transf., *to compose, write.* In perf. **pĕpĭgi** and supine **pactum,** *to fix, settle, agree upon* (cf. paciscor).

pănĭcum -i, n. *a kind of wild millet.*

pānis -is, m. *bread*; in plur., *loaves.*

pannĭcŭlus -i, m. *a little garment.*

Pannŏnia -ae, f. *Pannonia, a district on the middle Danube.*

pannōsus -a -um, *ragged, tattered.*

pannūcĕus (-ius) -a -um, *ragged; wrinkled, shrivelled.*

pannus -i, m. *a piece of cloth; garment; rag.*

Pănormus -i, f. and **Pănormum** -i, n. *a town in Sicily* (modern Palermo).

pansa -ae, *splay-footed.*

panthēra -ae, f. *a panther or leopard.*

pantŏmīmus -i, m. and **pantŏmīma** -ae, f. *a dancer, mime.*

păpae, interj. *wonderful! indeed!*

păpās -ae and -ātis, m. *a tutor.*

păpāver -ĕris, n. *poppy.*

păpāvĕrĕus -a -um, *of the poppy.*

păpĭlio -ōnis, m. *butterfly.*

păpilla -ae, f. *nipple, teat, breast.*

Păpīrius -a -um, *name of a Roman gens.*

pappo -are, *to eat.*

pappus -i, m. *the woolly seed of certain plants.*

păpŭla -ae, f. *a pimple.*

păpȳrĭfer -fĕra -fĕrum, *producing papyrus.*

păpȳrus -i, m. and f. and **păpȳrum** -i, n. *the plant papyrus; clothing or paper made from papyrus.*

păr păris, *equal, like, a match*; m. and f. as subst., *a companion*; n. as subst., *the like, the equivalent,* or *a pair*; par impar ludere, *to play at odd and even*; par est, *it is appropriate.* Hence adv. **părĭtĕr**, *equally, alike; together, at the same time.*

părăbĭlis -e, *easily procured.*

părăbŏla -ae and **părăbŏlē** -ēs f. *a comparison.*

părăsītus -i, m. and **părăsīta** -ae, f. *a guest*; in bad sense, *a toady, parasite.*

părātĭo -ōnis, f. *preparing, preparation.*

¹**părātus** -a -um, partic. from paro; q.v.

²**părātus** -ūs, m. *preparation, fitting out, equipment.*

Parca -ae, f. *a goddess of fate*; pl. Parcae, *the three Fates.*

parco parcĕre pĕperci (and parci) parsum, *to be sparing, economize; to spare, refrain from injuring* (with dat.); *to refrain from, keep oneself from*; with infin., *to forbear to.*

parcus -a -um, *sparing, thrifty, economical; moderate, sparing*; of things, *scanty, small, meagre.* Adv. **parcē,** *sparingly, economically, moderately.*

pardus -i, m. *a panther or leopard.*

¹**părens** -entis, partic. from pareo; q.v.

²**părens** -entis, c. *a parent*; sometimes *grandfather or ancestor; author, cause, origin.*

părentālis -e, *parental, of parents* (or *ancestors*); n. pl. as subst. **părentālĭa** -ĭum, *a festival in honour of the dead.*

părento -are, *to celebrate the* parentalia. Transf., *to avenge the dead.*

părĕo -ere, *to appear, become evident.* Transf., *to obey, give way to; to be subject to, serve* (with dat.); partic. **părens** -entis, *obedient.*

părĭēs -ĕtis, m. *a wall, properly the wall of a house.*

părĭĕtĭnae -arum, f. pl. *old walls, ruins.*

Părĭlia = Palilia; see Pales.

părĭlis -e, *similar, like, equal.*

părĭo părĕre pĕperi partum; fut. partic. părĭtūrus; *to bring forth, bear, produce.* Transf., *to occasion, create, make, get.*

Păris -ĭdis, m. *a Trojan prince who carried off Helen.*

parma -ae, f. *a small round shield, a buckler.*

parmātus -a -um, *armed with the* parma.

parmŭla -ae, f. *a small round shield, buckler.*

Parnāsus (-ŏs) -i, m. *a mountain in Phocis, sacred to Apollo and the Muses*; f. adj. **Parnāsis** -ĭdis, and adj. **Parnāsĭus** -a -um.

păro -are, *to set, put; to prepare, provide, furnish, obtain; to buy.* Hence partic. **părātus** -a -um, *prepared, ready; provided, equipped*;

of persons, *skilled.* Adv. **părātē,** *with preparation, readily.*

părŏcha -ae, f. *a supplying of necessaries.*

părŏchus -i, m. *an officer who looked after travelling ambassadors and magistrates.* Transf., *a host.*

părŏpsis -ĭdis, f. *a dessert-dish.*

Părus (-ŏs) -i, f. *an island in the Aegean Sea, famous for marble*; adj. **Părĭus** -a -um.

parra -ae, f. *a bird of ill omen,* perhaps *owl.*

parrĭcīda -ae, f. *a parricide, one who murders a parent or near relative*; polit., *an assassin, traitor.*

parrĭcīdĭum -i, n. *the murder of a parent or any near relative*; polit., *assassination, treason.*

pars partis, *a part, piece, share; a direction, region; a side, party; an actor's role*; in gen., usually plur., *office, function, duty*; pars . . . pars, *some . . . others*; pro (sua) parte, pro virile parte, *to the best of one's ability*; magna ex parte, *to a great extent*; multis partibus, *many times, much.* Adv. **partim,** *partly*; used like a noun, *some.*

parsĭmōnĭa -ae, f. *thrift, economy.*

Parthi -orum, m. pl. *the Parthians*; adj. **Parthĭcus** and **Parthus** -a -um; subst. **Parthĭa** -ae, *Parthia.*

particeps -cipis, *sharing, participating in* (with genit.); as subst., *partner, comrade.*

participo -are, *to share with a person; to cause a person to share.*

particŭla -ae, f. *a small part, particle.*

partim, adv. from pars; q.v.

partĭo -ire and **partĭor** -iri, dep. *to share out, distribute, divide*; perf. partic. in pass. sense partitus -a -um, *divided*; adv. **partītē,** *with proper divisions.*

partītĭo -ōnis, f. *division, sharing, distribution.*

partŭrĭo -ire, *to desire to bring forth, have the pains of labour; to teem with anything, be full of.*

¹**partus** -a -um, partic. from pario; q.v.

²**partus** -ūs, m. *bearing, bringing forth, birth.* Transf., *young, offspring.*

părum, *too little, not enough* (as adv. or subst.); parum habere, *to think too little, be dissatisfied with.* Compar. **mĭnus,** *less*; sometimes = *not, not at all*; sin minus, *but if not.* Superl. **mĭnĭmē (mĭnŭmē),** *in the least degree, very little, least of all*; sometimes *not at all, by no means.*

părumper, *for a little while.*

Părus = Paros; q.v.

parvĭtās -ātis, f. *littleness, smallness.*

parvŭlus -a -um, *very small*; of age, *young, little.*

parvus -a -um, *little, small; slight, weak*; of time, *short*; of age, *young*; of value, *poor, insignificant*; n. as subst. *a little.* Compar. **mĭnor,** *smaller, less*; of time, *shorter*; of age, *minor* (natu), *younger*; of value, *inferior.* Superl. **mĭnĭmus,** *smallest; least*;

n. as adv., minimum, *very little*.
Rare superl. **parvissimus** -a -um.

pasco pascĕre păvi pastum. (1)
transit., *to feed, lead to pasture; to
keep, support; to nourish;* also *to give
as pasture.* Transf., *to feast, gratify.*
Pass. as middle, *to graze on;* also *to
feast upon, delight in.* (2) intransit.,
of animals, *to graze, browse.*

pascŭus -a -um, *for pasture or grazing;*
n. as subst. *a pasture.*

Păsĭthĕa -ae and **Păsĭthĕē** -ēs, f. *one
of the three Graces.*

passer -ēris, m. *a sparrow or other
small bird; a sea-fish, a plaice or
flounder.*

passercŭlus -i, m. *a little sparrow.*

passim, *here and there, far and wide;
indiscriminately.*

passum -i, n., subst. from pando; q.v.

¹passus -a -um, partic. from pando; q.v.

²passus -a -um, partic. from patior; q.v.

³passus -ūs, m. *a step, stride, pace;*
esp. as a measure of length = five
Roman feet. Transf., *footstep, track.*

pastillus -i, m. *a lozenge.*

pastio -ōnis, f. *pasture, pasturing.*

pastor -ōris, m. *a herd;* esp. *a shepherd.*

pastōrālis -e, **pastōrĭcius** -a -um and
pastōrĭus -a -um, *of shepherds,
pastoral.*

¹pastus -a -um, partic. from pasco; q.v.

²pastus -ūs, m. *pasture, feeding; food,
sustenance.*

Pătăvĭum -i, n. *a town in North Italy,
birthplace of Livy* (now *Padua*);
adj. **Pătăvĭnus** -a -um.

pătĕfăcĭo -făcĕre -fēci -factum; pass.
pătĕfīo -fīĕri -factus sum; *to open,
throw open, open up, make accessible;
to bring to light, disclose, reveal.*

pătĕfactĭo -ōnis, f. *throwing open,
disclosing.*

pătella -ae, f. *a dish, platter, plate.*

pătĕo -ēre, *to be open, stand open, be
accessible or exposed; to be revealed,
disclosed, clear; to stretch out, extend.*
Hence partic. **pătens** -entis, *open,
unobstructed, accessible, exposed;* also
evident. Compar. adv. **pătentius,**
more openly.

păter -tris, m. *father, sire; founder,
head;* pater familias, *or* familiae,
head of a household; plur., patres,
forefathers; also as a title of the
senators, patres, *or* patres conscripti;
pater patriae, *father of his country, a
national hero.*

pătĕra -ae, f. *a shallow dish, saucer.*

păternus -a -um, *of a father; paternal;
native.*

pătesco pătescĕre pătŭi, *to be opened,
lie open; to be revealed; to spread out.*

pătĭbĭlis -e: pass. *endurable, bearable;*
act., *sensitive.*

pătĭbŭlum -i, n. *a yoke as an instrument
of punishment, a pillory.*

pătĭentia -ae, f. *endurance, resignation;*
in bad sense, *want of spirit.*

pătina -ae, f. *a dish.*

pătĭor păti passus, dep. *to suffer,
undergo, experience; to permit, allow.*
Hence partic. **pătiens** -entis,

enduring, capable of enduring, with
genit.; *patient;* in bad sense, *stubborn.*
Adv. **pătientĕr.**

patrātor -oris, m. *accomplisher, achiever.*

patria -ae, f. *fatherland;* see patrius.

patricĭus -a -um. *of the patres,
patrician, noble;* m. as subst., *a
patrician.*

patrĭmōnĭum -i, n. *property inherited
from a father, patrimony.*

patrĭmus -a -um, *having a father still
living.*

patrītus -a -um, *inherited from one's
father.*

patrĭus -a -um, *of a father, fatherly,
paternal; hereditary; ancestral;
native.* F. as subst. **patria** -ae, f.
(sc. terra), *fatherland, native land.*

patro -are, *to accomplish, execute,
achieve.*

patrōcĭnĭum -i, n. *the services of a
patron;* esp. *defence in a court of
law;* in gen., *defence, protection;*
plur., **patrōcĭnĭa,** *clients.*

patrōcĭnor -ari, dep. *to protect, defend.*

patrōna -ae, f. *a protectress, patroness.*

patrōnus -i, m. *a protector, defender,
patron;* esp. *an advocate in a court of
law.*

patruēlis -e. *descended from a father's
brother;* as subst., *a cousin.*

¹patrŭus -i, m. *a father's brother,
paternal uncle.*

²patrŭus -a -um, adj. *of an uncle.*

pătŭlus -a -um, *open, standing open,
spreading, extended.*

paucĭtās -ātis, f. *fewness, scarcity.*

paucŭlus -a -um, *very small;* plur.
very few.

paucus -a -um, oftener plur. **pauci** -ae
-a, *few, little;* as subst., m. pl. **pauci,**
a few, the select few, the oligarchs; n.
pl. **pauca,** *a few words.*

paulātim (paullātim), *gradually, little
by little.*

paulispĕr (paullispĕr), *for a little
while.*

paulŭlus (paullŭlus) -a -um, *very
little;* n. as subst. **paulŭlum** -i, *a very
little;* acc. and abl., as adv., *a little.*

¹paulus (paullus) -a -um, *little, small;*
as subst., **paulum,** *a little;* acc., and
abl. **paulo,** like adv., *a little.*

²Paulus (Paullus) -i, m. *the name of a
family of the gens Aemilia.*

pauper -ēris, *poor;* of things, *scanty,
meagre.*

paupercŭlus -a -um, *poor.*

paupĕrĭēs -ēi, f. *poverty.*

paupĕro -are, *to make poor, to deprive.*

paupertās -ātis, f. *poverty.*

pausa -ae, f. *cessation, end.*

pausĭa -ae, f. *a species of olive.*

pauxillŭlus -a -um, *very little, very
small.*

pauxillus -a -um, *small, little;* n. as
subst. *a little.*

păvĕfactus -a -um, *frightened, terrified.*

păvĕo păvēre păvi: intransit., *to quake
with fear, panic;* transit., *to quake at.*

păvesco -ĕre: intransit., *to begin to
quake, take fright;* transit., *to be
alarmed by.*

păvĭdus -a -um, *trembling, quaking, fearful; causing fear.* Adv. **păvĭdē,** *fearfully.*

păvīmento -are, *to pave.*

păvīmentum -i, n. *a pavement of tiles, brick, stone, etc.*

păvĭo -ire, *to beat.*

păvĭto -are: intransit., *to shiver, tremble, quake with fear;* transit., *to quake at.*

păvo -ōnis, m. *peacock.*

păvor -ōris, m. *trembling, quaking; fear, panic.*

pax pācis, f. *peace; calm, quiet;* of the gods, *grace, favour;* pace tua, *with your good leave.*

pecco -are, *to make a mistake, go wrong, err* or *sin;* n. of partic. as subst. **peccātum** -i, *an error, fault, sin.*

pĕcōrōsus -a -um, *rich in cattle.*

pecten -ĭnis, m. *a comb; a weaver's comb; a rake; clasped hands; a quill,* for striking the strings of the lyre; *a shell-fish, the scallop.*

pecto pectĕre pexi pexum, *to comb; to card; to thrash;* partic. **pexus** -a -um, *with the nap on, woolly.*

pectus -ōris, n. *breast; heart, soul; mind.*

pĕcu, n. plur. **pĕcŭa,** *sheep, flocks;* also *pastures.*

pĕcŭārius -a -um *of sheep* or *cattle;* as subst., m. *a breeder of cattle, grazier;* n. pl. *herds of sheep* or *cattle.*

pĕcūlātor -ōris, m. *one who embezzles public money.*

pĕcūlātus -ūs, m. *embezzlement of public money.*

pĕcūlĭāris -e, *of one's private property; one's own, special, peculiar;* adv. **pĕcūlĭārĭtĕr,** *specially.*

pĕcūlĭum -i, n. *small property, savings;* esp. *the savings of slaves or sons.*

pĕcūnĭa -ae, f. *property, wealth;* esp. *money, cash.*

pĕcūnĭārĭus -a -um, *of money, pecuniary.*

pĕcūnĭōsus -a -um, *wealthy, rich; lucrative.*

'**pĕcus** -ōris, n. *cattle, a herd, flock,* esp. *of sheep.*

'**pĕcus** -ŭdis, f. *a single head of cattle; a beast, animal;* esp. *a sheep.*

pĕdālis -e, *a foot long* (or *wide*).

pĕdārius -a -um, *of a foot;* (senatores) pedarii, *senators of inferior rank.*

pĕdēs -itis, m.: adj., *going on foot;* subst., *a foot soldier;* coll., *infantry.*

pĕdester -tris -tre, *on foot, pedestrian;* copiae, *infantry;* sometimes, *on land.* Transf., *simple, ordinary, prosaic;* of style, *written in prose.*

pĕdētemptim, *feeling one's way; gradually, cautiously.*

pĕdĭca -ae, f. *a fetter; a trap, snare.*

pĕdĭcŭlōsus -a -um, *lousy.*

pĕdis, -is, c. *a louse.*

pĕdĭsĕquus -i, m. and **pĕdĭsĕqua** -ae, f. *a follower, attendant, lackey.*

pĕdĭtātus -ūs, m. *infantry.*

pĕdum -i, n. *a shepherd's crook.*

Pēgăsus (-os) -i, m. *the winged horse which produced the fountain Hippo-*

crene; adj. **Pēgăsēĭus** and **Pēgăsēus** -a -um; **Pēgăsĭdes,** *the Muses.*

pegma -ătis, n. *a bookcase; a stage, scaffolding.*

pĕiĕro and **periūro** -are, *to commit perjury, forswear oneself;* with acc., *to swear falsely by.*

pēior, compar. of malus; q.v.

pĕlăgus -i, n., Greek plur. pelage, *the open sea, the main.*

pēlămys -ȳdis, f. *the young tunnyfish.*

Pĕlasgi -orum, m. pl. *the Greeks.*

Pēlēus -ĕi and -ĕos, m. *king of Thessaly, husband of Thetis, father of Achilles;* **Pēlīdēs** -ae, m. *son* or *grandson of Peleus.*

Pēlĭon -i, n. *mountain range in Thessaly;* adj. **Pēliăcus** and **Pēlĭus** -a -um.

pellācia -ae, f. *enticing, allurement.*

pellax -ācis, *deceitful, seductive.*

pellĕgo = perlego; q.v.

pellex = paelex; q.v.

pellicio -licĕre -lexi -lectum, *to entice, decoy, seduce.*

pellĭcŭla -ae, f. *a little skin* or *hide.*

pellĭo -ōnis, m. *a furrier.*

pellis -is, f. *a hide, skin; dressed hide, leather, felt;* milit., *a hut covered with skins.*

pellītus -a -um, *clothed in skins.*

pello pellĕre pĕpŭli pulsum, *to strike, knock, beat; to impel, propel, move, affect; to drive away, dislodge, banish.*

pellūcĕo = perluceo; q.v.

Pēlŏponnēsus -i, f. *the Peloponnese.*

Pĕlops -ŏpis, m. *the father of Atreus and Thyestes.*

pēlōris -īdis, f. *an edible shell-fish, a clam.*

pelta -ae, f. *a small shield.*

peltastes or -a -ae, m. *a soldier armed with the pelta.*

peltātus -a -um, *armed with the pelta.*

pelvis -is, f. *a basin.*

pēnārius -a -um, *of* or *for provisions.*

Pĕnātes -ĭum, m. pl., *the Penates, Latin deities of the household and family.* Transf., *home, dwelling.*

pĕnātiger -gĕra -gĕrum, *carrying the Penates.*

pendĕo pendēre pĕpendi, *to hang; to hang upon, depend on; to hang loose, hover; to be suspended, discontinued; to be in suspense, uncertain, undecided.*

pendo pendēre pĕpendi pensum: transit., *to cause to hang down; to weigh; to pay out money; to weigh, consider, judge, value, esteem;* poenas, supplicia, *to pay a penalty, suffer punishment;* intransit., *to weigh.* Hence partic. **pensus** -a -um, *weighed; esteemed, valued, prized;* nihil pensi habere, *to put no value upon, be indifferent about.* N. as subst. **pensum** -i, *wool weighed out to a spinner;* hence, *a day's work, task, duty.*

pendŭlus -a -um, *hanging; in suspense, undecided.*

Pēnĕlŏpa -ae, and **Pēnĕlŏpē** -ēs, f. *the wife of Ulysses.*

pĕnēs, prep. with acc. *in the possession*

of, in the power of, belonging to; **penes se esse**, *to be in one's senses.*

pĕnĕtrābĭlis -e: pass., *that can be passed through, penetrable*; act., *penetrating, piercing.*

pĕnĕtrālis -e. (1) *passing through, penetrating.* (2) *inward, internal.* N. as subst. *inner chambers, interior, esp. of a temple.*

pĕnĕtro -are: transit., *to put into; to pass through* or *into, to penetrate*; intransit., *to make one's way in, to penetrate.*

pĕnĭcillus -i, m. *a painter's brush* or *pencil; style.*

pĕnĭcŭlus -i, m. *a brush; a sponge.*

pēnis -is, m. *a tail.*

pēnĭtus -a -um, adj. *inward, internal.*

pēnĭtus, adv. *internally, inwardly, inside; deeply, through and through; widely.*

penna -ae, f. *a feather; a wing.*

pennātus -a -um, *feathered, winged.*

pennĭger -gĕra -gĕrum, *feathered, winged.*

pennĭpēs -pĕdis, *wing-footed.*

pennĭpŏtens -entis, *able to fly, winged*; plur. as subst., *birds.*

pennŭla -ae, f. *a little wing.*

pensĭlis -e, *hanging, pendent.*

pensĭo -ōnis, f. *a weighing out*; hence *paying, payment, day of payment; rent.*

pensĭto -are, *to weigh carefully, weigh out*; hence, *to pay; to ponder, consider.*

penso -are, *to weigh carefully; to estimate, ponder, consider; to counter-balance, requite; to pay for, purchase one thing with another.*

pensum -i, n. subst., from pendo; q.v.

Penthēūs -ēi and -ĕos, *a king of Thebes.*

pēnūrĭa -ae, f. *lack, want, penury.*

pĕnus -ūs and -i, c., **pĕnum** -i, n., **pĕnus** -ŏris, *provisions, victuals.*

peplum -i, n. and **peplus** -i, m. *a robe of state.*

per, prep. with acc.: of space, *through, along, over*; sometimes *before, in the presence of*; of time, *throughout, during; in the course of, in a time of*; of means or instrument, *through, by, by means of, with, by way of*; of cause, *because of, on account of*; **per me licet**, *you may as far as I am concerned*; in entreaties, oaths, etc., *in the name of.*

pēra -ae, f. *bag, wallet.*

pĕrabsurdus -a -um, *excessively absurd.*

pĕraccommŏdātus -a -um, *very convenient.*

pĕrācer -cris -cre, *very sharp.*

pĕrācerbus -a -um, *very sour, very harsh.*

pĕractĭo -ōnis, f. *finishing, completion.*

pĕrācūtus -a -um, *very sharp; very shrill; very sharp-witted.* Adv. **pĕrācūtē.**

pĕrădūlescens -entis. *very young.*

pĕraequē, *quite equally.*

pĕrăgĭto -are, *to drive about violently, harass.*

pĕrăgo -ăgĕre -ēgi -actum. (1) *to pass through*; in words, *to go over,*

mention. (2) *to drive about, harass, disturb.* (3) *to carry through, complete, accomplish*; legal, *to prosecute till conviction.*

pĕragrātĭo -ōnis, f. *wandering through.*

pĕragro -are, *to wander through, travel through.*

pĕrāmans -antis, *very loving*; adv. **pĕrămantēr.**

pĕrambŭlo -are, *to walk through, pass through.*

pĕrāmoenus -a -um, *very pleasant.*

pĕramplus -a -um, *very large.*

pĕrangustus -a -um, *very narrow*; adv. **pĕrangustē.**

pĕrantīquus -a -um, *very old.*

pĕrappŏsĭtus -a -um, *very suitable.*

pĕrardŭus -a -um, *very difficult.*

pĕrargūtus -a -um, *very witty.*

pĕrāro -are, *to plough through; to furrow the brow; to scratch letters, to write, write on.*

pĕrattentus -a -um, *very attentive*; adv. **pĕrattentē.**

perbacchor -ari, dep. *to revel through-out.*

perbĕātus -a -um, *very happy.*

perbellē, *very prettily.*

perbĕnē, *very well.*

perbĕnĕvŏlus -a -um, *very well disposed.*

perbĕnignē, *very kindly.*

perbĭbo -bĭbĕre -bĭbi, *to drink up, absorb*; mentally, *to imbibe, take in.*

perblandus -a -um, *very charming.*

perbŏnus -a -um, *very good.*

perbrĕvis -e, *very short*; perbrevi, *in a very short time*; adv. **perbrĕvĭtĕr.**

perca -ae, f. *a fish, the perch.*

percălĕfactus -a -um, *thoroughly heated.*

percălesco -călescĕre -călŭi, *to become very warm.*

percallesco -callescĕre -callŭi: in-transit., *to lose sensibility, become callous*; transit., *to get a good know-ledge of.*

percārus -a -um. (1) *very dear, very costly.* (2) *very dear, much loved.*

percautus -a -um, *very cautious.*

percĕlĕbro -are, *to speak of commonly*; pass., *to be much mentioned.*

percĕlĕr -is -e, *very swiftly*; adv. **percĕlĕrĭtĕr.**

percello -cellĕre -cŭli -culsum, *to strike, push; to beat down, overturn, shatter, ruin*; mentally, *to daunt, unnerve.*

percensĕo -censēre -censŭi, *to count over, reckon; to survey, review; to travel through.*

perceptĭo -ōnis, f. *a receiving, grasping, gathering together.*

perceptus -a -um, partic. from percipio; q.v.

percĭo -cire -cīvi -cītum and **percĭĕo** -cĭēre, *to stir up, set in motion*; partic. **percĭtus** -a -um, *aroused, excited*; of character, *excitable.*

percĭpĭo -cĭpĕre -cēpi -ceptum, *to lay hold of, seize; to collect, gather, harvest, gain; with the senses, to feel, take in*; mentally, *to learn,* *grasp, understand.* N. pl. of pàrtic. as subst. **percepta** -orum, *principles, rules.*

percītus -a -um, partic. from percio; q.v.

¹percŏlo -are, *to strain, as through a sieve.*

²percŏlo -cŏlĕre -cŏlŭi -cultum, *to adorn, decorate; to honour a* person, *revere greatly; to complete.*

percŏmis -e, *very friendly.*

percommŏdus -a -um, *very fit;* adv. **percommŏdē.**

percontātĭo (percunct-) -ōnis, f. *inquiry, interrogation.*

percontātŏr (percunct-) -ōris, m. *an inquirer, asker of questions.*

percontor (percunctor) -ari, dep. *to sound; hence to inquire, interrogate, investigate.*

percŏquo -cŏquĕre -coxi -coctum, *to cook or heat thoroughly; to ripen; to scorch, blacken.*

percrēbresco -brescĕre -brŭi and **percrēbesco** -bescĕre -bŭi, *to become prevalent, get well known.*

percrĕpo -crĕpare -crĕpŭi -crĕpĭtum, *to resound, ring.*

percunct-; see **percont-.**

percŭpĭdus -a -um, *very fond.*

percŭpĭo -cŭpĕre, *to desire exceedingly.*

percūrĭōsus -a -um, *very inquisitive.*

percūro -are, *to cure, heal thoroughly.*

percurro -currĕre -cŭcurri or -curri -cursum, *to run through, hasten through, travel through; in words, to run over, mention in passing; to run over in the mind* or *with the eye; to pass through stages.*

percursātĭo -ōnis, f. *travelling through.*

percursĭo -ōnis, f. *running through; rapid consideration.*

percurso -are, *to ramble over, rove about.*

percussĭo -ōnis, f. *striking, beating;* esp. *beating time;* hence *time, rhythm.*

percussŏr -ōris, m. *a striker;* esp. *a murderer, assassin.*

percussus -ūs, m. *beating, knocking, striking.*

percŭtĭo -cŭtĕre -cussi -cussum, *to strike hard; to strike through, pierce, transfix; to strike down, cut down;* mentally, *to strike, shock;* colloq., *to deceive.*

perdĕcŏrus -a -um, *very comely.*

perdēlirus -a -um, *senseless.*

perdifficĭlis -e, *very difficult;* adv. **perdifficĭlĭtĕr.**

perdignus -a -um, *very worthy.*

perdĭlĭgens -entis, *very diligent;* adv. **perdĭlĭgentĕr.**

perdisco -discĕre -dĭdĭci, *to learn thoroughly.*

perdisertē, *very eloquently.*

perdĭtor -ōris, m. *destroyer.*

perdĭtus -a -um, partic. from perdo; q.v.

perdĭū, *for a very long time.*

perdĭūturnus -a -um, *lasting a very long time.*

perdīvĕs -vĭtis, *very rich.*

perdix -dĭcis, c. *partridge.*

perdo -dĕre -dĭdi -dĭtum (in pass., usually pereo, perire), *to destroy, do away with, ruin; to lose; to waste, squander.* /

Hence partic. **perdĭtus** -a -um, *miserable, ruined; morally lost, abandoned, profligate.* Adv. **perdĭtē,** *desperately, immoderately; in an abandoned manner.*

perdŏcĕo -dŏcēre -dŏcŭi -doctum, *to teach* or *instruct thoroughly;* partic. **perdoctus** -a -um, *very learned, very skilful;* adv. **perdoctē.**

perdŏmo -dŏmare -dŏmŭi -dŏmĭtum, *to tame or subdue thoroughly.*

perdūco -dūcĕre -duxi -ductum, *to lead through, bring along; conduct; to carry or construct buildings, from one point to another; to bring over to an opinion, to induce; in time, to continue, prolong; to smear over with* a substance.

perductor -ōris, m. *a guide; a pimp, pander.*

perdūdum, *a long time ago.*

perduellĭo -ōnis, f. *treason.*

perduellis -is, m. *a public enemy.*

perduim -is -it, alternative pres. subj. of perdo; q.v.

perdūro -are, *to last long, endure.*

pĕrēdo -esse -ēdi -ēsum, *to eat up, devour; to consume, destroy.*

pĕregrē, adv. *in,* to or *from a foreign country; abroad, from abroad.*

pĕregrīnābundus -a -um, *travelling about.*

pĕregrīnātĭo -ōnis, f. *travelling* or *staying in foreign countries; roaming.*

pĕregrīnātŏr -ōris, m. *one who travels about.*

pĕregrīnĭtās -ātis, f. *the condition of a foreigner or alien; foreign manners.*

pĕregrīnor -ari, dep. *to stay* or to *travel in foreign countries; to roam, wander, ramble; to be strange, foreign.*

pĕregrīnus -a -um, *foreign, of a foreigner, strange;* m. and f. as subst., *a foreigner, stranger,* esp. *a foreigner resident in Rome.* Transf., *inexperienced.*

pĕrēlĕgans -antis *very elegant;* adv. **pĕrēlĕgantĕr.**

pĕrēlŏquens -entis, *very eloquent.*

pĕremnĭa, n. pl. *the auspices taken on crossing any running water.*

pĕrendĭē, *the day after tomorrow.*

pĕrendĭnus -a -um, *relating to the day after tomorrow.*

pĕrennis -e, *lasting throughout the year; durable, perennial.*

pĕrennĭtās -ātis, f. *duration, perpetuity.*

pĕrenno -are, *to last many years.*

pĕrĕo -ire -ĭi and -ĭvi -itum, (often as pass. of perdo), *to go to waste, be ruined or lost, pass away, perish, die.*

pĕrĕquĭto -are, *to ride through, ride round.*

pĕrerro -are, *to wander through, ramble over; to look over, scan.*

pĕrērūdĭtus -a -um, *very learned.*

pĕrexĭgŭus -a -um, *very small, very scanty;* of time, *very short.* Adv.

pĕrexĭgŭĕ, *very scantily very sparingly*.

perfăcētus -a -um, *very witty, brilliant*; adv. perfăcētē.

perfăcĭlis -e, *very easy; very courteous*. N. acc. as adv. perfăcĭle, *very easily; very readily*.

perfămĭlĭāris -e *very familiar, intimate*; m. as subst. *a very great friend*.

perfectĭo -ōnis f. *completion; perfection*.

perfector -ōris, m. *a perfecter, finisher*.

perfectus -a -um, partic. from perficio; q.v.

perfĕro -ferre -tŭli -lātum, *to carry through, bear to the end; se perferre, to betake oneself; of news, etc., to deliver, convey; of tasks, to bring to an end; of trouble, to bear, suffer, endure*.

Hence partic. perfĕrens -entis, *enduring, patient*.

perfĭca -ae, f. adj *accomplishing, perfecting*.

perfĭcĭo -ficĕre -fēci -fectum, *to bring to an end, complete, finish, achieve; of time, to live through; of a pupil, to make perfect*.

Hence partic. perfectus -a -um, *perfect, complete, finished*; adv. perfectē.

perfĭdēlis -e, *very faithful*.

perfĭdĭa -ae, f. *faithlessness, treachery, falsehood*.

perfĭdĭōsus -a -um, *faithless, treacherous*; adv. perfĭdĭōsē.

perfĭdus -a -um, *faithless, treacherous, false*.

perfīgo -fīgĕre -fixi -fixum *to pierce through, stab*.

perflābĭlis -e, *able to be blown through*.

perflāgĭtĭōsus -a -um, *very shameful*.

perflo -are, *to blow through, blow over*.

perfluctŭo -are, *to surge over*.

perflŭo -flŭere -fluxi -fluxum, *to stream through, run away*.

perfŏdĭo -fŏdĕre -fōdi -fossum, *to dig through, pierce through; to excavate, make by digging*.

perfŏro -are, *to pierce through; to form by boring*.

perfrĕquens -entis, *much visited*.

perfrĭco -fricare -frĭcŭi -fricatum and -frictum, *to rub over; os, frontem, etc., to put on a bold face*.

perfrĭgesco -frigescĕre -frixi, *to catch a chill*.

perfrĭgĭdus -a -um, *very cold*.

perfringo -fringĕre -frēgi -fractum, *to break through; to break in pieces, shatter*.

perfrŭor -frŭi -fructus, dep. *to enjoy to the full; to execute completely*.

perfŭga -ae, m. *a deserter*.

perfŭgĭo -fŭgĕre -fūgi -fŭgitum, *to flee away, take refuge; esp. to desert to the enemy*.

perfŭgĭum -i, n. *a place of refuge, shelter*.

perfunctĭo -ōnis, f. *performing, discharging*.

perfundo -fundĕre -fūdi -fūsum, *to*

pour over; *to steep in a fluid, to dye; in gen., to steep in, fill with*.

perfungor -fungi -functus, dep. *to perform fully, execute, discharge; to go through, endure*.

perfŭro -ere, *to rage furiously*.

Pergămum -i, n. and Pergămus -i, f., also plur. Pergăma -orum, n. *the citadel of Troy; Troy*.

pergaudĕo -ēre, *to rejoice exceedingly*.

pergo pergĕre perrexi perrectum. *to continue, proceed, go on with*.

pergrandis -e, *very large, very great*.

pergrātus -a -um, *very pleasant*.

pergrăvis -e, *very weighty, very important*; adv. pergrăvitĕr.

pergŭla -ae, f., *a balcony, outhouse; a shop, workshop; a school*.

pĕrhĭbĕo -ēre -ŭi -itum, *to bring forward, cite; to maintain, assert, hold, say*.

pĕrhĭlum, *a very little*.

pĕrhŏnōrĭfĭcus -a -um, *very honourable; very respectful*; adv. pĕrhŏnōrĭfĭcē, *very respectfully*.

pĕrhorresco -horrescĕre -horrŭi, *to begin to shudder or tremble, esp. with fear; transit., to shudder at*.

pĕrhorrĭdus -a -um, *very dreadful*.

pĕrhūmānus -a -um, *very friendly, very civil*; adv. pĕrhūmānĭtĕr.

Pĕrĭclēs -is, m. *Athenian statesman*.

pĕrĭclĭtātĭo -ōnis, f. *trial, experiment*.

pĕrĭclĭtor -ari, dep.: intransit., *to try, make a trial, venture; to take a risk, be in danger*; transit., *to try, test, prove; to endanger, risk*.

pĕrĭcŭlōsus -a -um, *dangerous, perilous*; adv. pĕrĭcŭlōsē.

pĕrĭcŭlum (pĕrĭclum) -i, n. *a trial, proof, test, attempt; danger, peril, hazard; at law, a trial, action, suit; hence, a legal record or register*.

pĕrĭdōnĕus -a -um, *very suitable*.

pĕrillustris -e *very evident; very distinguished*.

pĕrimbēcillus -a -um, *very weak*.

pĕrĭmo (pĕrĕmo) -ĭmĕre -ēmi -emptum, *to do away with, destroy, kill, annihilate*. Transf., *to thwart, frustrate*.

pĕrincommŏdus -a -um, *very inconvenient*; adv. pĕrincommŏdē.

pĕrindĕ, adv. *in like manner; perinde ac, ut, or quam, just as; perinde ac si, just as if*.

pĕrindulgens -entis, *very indulgent, very tender*.

pĕrinfirmus -a -um, *very weak*.

pĕringĕnĭōsus -a -um, *very clever*.

pĕrinīquus -a -um, *very unfair; very discontented or unwilling*.

pĕrinsignis -e, *very remarkable*.

pĕrinvītus -a -um, *very unwilling*.

pĕrĭŏdus -i, m. *a sentence, period*.

Pĕrĭpătētĭcus -a -um, *belonging to the Peripatetic or Aristotelian school of philosophy*.

pĕrĭpĕtasma -ătis, n. *curtain, hanging*.

pĕrīrātus -a -um, *very angry*.

pĕriscĕlis -ĭdis, f. *garter or anklet*.

pĕristrōma -ătis, n. *curtain, coverlet, carpet, hanging*.

pĕristȳlĭum -i, n. *a court with a colon-nade round it.*

pĕristȳlum -i, n. *a peristyle, a colonnade round a building.*

pĕritĭa -ae, f. *experience, skill.*

pĕrĭtus -a -um, *experienced, skilful, practised, expert;* adv. **pĕrĭtē.**

pĕriūcundus -a -um, *very pleasant;* adv. **pĕriūcundē.**

pĕriūrĭum i-, n. *false swearing, perjury.*

pĕriūro = peiero; q.v.

pĕriūrus -a -um, *perjured; lying.*

perlābor -lābi -lapsus, dep. *to glide through, glide along.*

perlaetus -a -um, *very joyful.*

perlātē, adv. *very widely.*

perlectĭo -ōnis, f. *perusal.*

perlĕgo (pellĕgo) -lĕgĕre -lĕgi -lectum, *to survey thoroughly, scan; to read through;* senatum, *to call over the roll of senators.*

perlĕvis -e, *slight;* adv. **perlĕvĭtĕr.**

perlĭbens (perlŭbens) -entis, from perlibet; q.v.

perlĭbĕrālis -e, *well-bred, very liberal;* adv. **perlĭbĕrālĭtĕr.**

perlĭbet (perlŭbet) -ere, *it is very pleasing;* partic. **perlibens (perlŭb-)** -entis, *very willing;* adv. **perlĭbentĕr (perlub-).**

perlĭcĭo = pellicio; q.v.

perlĭto -are, *to offer an auspicious sacrifice.*

perlongus -a -um, *very long, tedious;* adv. **perlongē,** *very far.*

perlŭbet, etc. = perlibet, etc.; q.v.

perlūcĕo (pellūcĕo) -lūcēre -luxi, *to shine through; to be transparent.*

perlūcĭdŭlus -a -um, *transparent.*

perlūcĭdus (pellūcĭdus) -a -um, *shining, bright; transparent.*

perluctŭōsus -a -um, *very mournful.*

perlŭo -lŭĕre -lŭi -lūtum, *to wash, bathe.*

perlustro -are, *to traverse, pass through; to survey, examine.*

permagnus -a -um, *very great very large.*

permănĕo -mānēre -mansi -mansum, *to remain, stay, last, continue.*

permāno -are, *to flow through, trickle through; to penetrate, extend.* Adv. from partic. **permănantĕr,** *by flowing through.*

permansĭo -ōnis, f. *a remaining, abiding.*

permārīnus -a -um, *going over the sea.*

permātūresco -mātūrescĕre -mātūrŭi, *to become thoroughly ripe.*

permĕdĭocris -e, *very moderate.*

permĕo -are, *to go through, traverse.*

permētĭor -mētiri -mensus, dep. *to measure out; to traverse.*

permirus -a -um, *very wonderful.*

permiscĕo -miscēre -miscŭi -mixtum, *to mix together, mingle thoroughly to confuse, throw into confusion.*

Hence partic. **permixtus** -a -um, *mixed; promiscuous;* adv. **permixtē.**

permissĭo -ōnis, f. *yielding, surrender; permission, leave.*

permissū, abl. sing. m. *by permission.*

permītĭālis -e, *destructive, annihilating.*

permītĭēs -ēi, f. *destruction, annihilation.*

permitto -mittĕre -mīsi -missum, *to let go; esp. of weapons, to hurl; to give up, yield, surrender, concede, sacrifice; to make allowance for; to allow, permit.*

permixtē, adv. from permisceo; q.v.

permixtĭo -onis, f. *mixture; confusion.*

permŏdestus -a -um, *very modest, very moderate.*

permŏlestus -a -um, *very troublesome;* adv. **permŏlestē,** *with much difficulty.*

permŏlo -ĕre, *to grind thoroughly.*

permōtĭo -onis, f. *movement, agitation.*

permŏvĕo -mŏvēre -mōvi -mōtum, *to move or stir up thoroughly; excite, agitate; to persuade, induce, influence a person.*

permulcĕo -mulcēre -mulsi -mulsum, *to stroke; to charm, soothe, soften.*

permultus -a -um, sing., *very much;* plur., *very many;* n. sing. as subst. *very much.*

permūnĭo -ire -ivi -itum, *to fortify completely, or finish fortifying.*

permūtātĭo -ōnis, f. *complete change; exchange, interchange.*

permūto -are, *to change completely; to exchange, interchange.*

perna -ae, f. *ham.*

pernĕcessārĭus -a -um, *very necessary; very intimate.*

pernĕcessē, indecl. adj. *very necessary.*

pernĕgo -are, *to deny flatly; to persist in denying or refusing.*

pernĭcĭābilis -e, *deadly, destructive.*

pernĭcĭēs -ēi, *destruction, disaster, ruin, bane.*

pernĭcĭōsus -a -um, *destructive, ruinous;* adv. **pernĭcĭōsē.**

pernīcĭtās -ātis, f. *swiftness, agility.*

pernix -nīcis, *swift, nimble, agile;* adv. **pernīcĭtĕr.**

pernōbĭlis -e, *very famous.*

pernocto -are, *to pass the night.*

pernosco -noscĕre -nōvi -nōtum, *to investigate or find out thoroughly;* in perf., *to know thoroughly.*

pernōtŭit -uisse, *it has become well known.*

pernox -noctis, adj. *all-night.*

pernŭmĕro -are, *to count out, reckon up.*

pĕro -ōnis, m. *a boot of untanned hide.*

pĕrobscūrus -a -um, *very obscure.*

pĕrŏdĭōsus -a -um, *very troublesome.*

pĕroffĭcĭōsē, *very attentively.*

pĕrŏlĕo -ēre, *to emit a strong smell.*

pĕrōnatus -a -um, *wearing leather boots.*

pĕropportūnus -a -um, *very convenient;* adv. **pĕropportūnē.**

pĕroptāto, abl. sing. n. *just as one would wish.*

pĕrōrātĭo -ōnis, f. *conclusion of a speech, peroration.*

pĕrornātus -a -um, *very ornate.*

pĕrorno -are, *to adorn greatly.*

pĕrōro -are, *to speak from beginning to end, to plead a cause throughout explain or state thoroughly; to conclude a speech, wind up, close.*

pĕrōsus -a -um, *hating, detesting.*

perpāco -are, *to pacify thoroughly.*

perparvŭlus and perparvus -a -um, *very little.*

perpaucŭli and perpauci -ae, -a, *very few.*

perpaulum (perpaullum) i, -n. *a very little.*

perpauper -ĕris, *very poor.*

perpello -pellĕre -pŭli -pulsum, *to push hard, drive along; to urge, compel, constrain.*

perpendicŭlum -i, n. *plumbline, plummet;* ad perpendiculum, *in a straight line.*

perpendo -pendĕre -pendi -pensum, *to weigh carefully; to consider, examine.*

perpĕram, *wrongly, falsely.*

perpĕs -pĕtis, *continuous, unbroken.*

perpessio -ōnis, f. *suffering, endurance.*

perpessŭ, alb. sing. m. *in the enduring.*

perpĕtior -pĕti -pessus, dep. *to bear to the end, endure.*

perpetro -are, *to complete, accomplish, perform.*

perpĕtŭĭtās -ātis, f. *uninterrupted succession, continuity;* ad perpetuitatem, *for ever.*

¹perpĕtŭō, adv. from perpetuus; q.v.

²perpĕtŭo -are, *to make continual, continue, perpetuate.*

perpĕtŭus -a -um, *continuous, uninterrupted* (in space or time). Transf., *universal, general.* Abl. as adv. perpĕtŭō, *uninterruptedly.*

perplācĕo -ēre, *to please greatly.*

perplexābĭlis -e, *intricate, obscure.*

perplexor -ari, dep. *to perplex.*

perplexus -a -um, *confused, intricate; obscure, ambiguous.* Adv. perplexē and perplexim.

perplĭcātus -a -um, *entangled, involved.*

perplŭit -ĕre, *to let the rain through; to run away* or *pour in like rain.*

perpŏlio -ire, *to polish thoroughly; perfect, complete.*

Hence partic. perpŏlitus -a -um, *polished, accomplished, refined.*

perpŏpŭlor -ari, dep. *to lay waste, devastate completely.*

perpōtātio -ōnis, f. *continued drinking, drinking-bout.*

perpōto -are, *to continue drinking; to drink up.*

perprĭmo -primĕre -pressi -pressum, *to press hard.*

perpugnax -ācis, *very pugnacious.*

perpurgo (perpūrigo) -are, *to clean thoroughly.* Transf., *to explain thoroughly, clear up.*

perpŭsillus -a -um, *very small.*

perpŭto -are, *to explain fully.*

perquam, *very much, extremely.*

perquiro -quirĕre -quisivi -quisitum, *to search for eagerly; to inquire carefully into.* Compar. adv. from perf. partic. perquisitius *more accurately.*

perrārus -a -um, *very uncommon;* abl. as adv. perrārō.

perrĕcondĭtus -a -um, *very abstruse.*

perrēpo -rēpĕre -repsi -reptum, *to crawl through, creep over.*

perrepto -are, *to crawl through, crawl about.*

perridĭcŭlus -a -um, *very laughable;* adv. perridĭcŭle.

perrŏgo -are, *to ask in succession, to ask one after another.*

perrumpo -rumpĕre -rūpi -ruptum, *to break through, burst through; to shatter, burst.*

Persae -arum, m. pl. *the Persians;* sing. Persa and Persēs -ae, m. *a Persian;* Persĭa -ae, f. *Persia;* Persis -ĭdis, f., as adj., *Persian,* as subst., *Persia;* adj. Persĭcus -a -um.

persaepe, *very often.*

persalsus -a -um, *very witty;* adv. persalsē.

persălūtātio -ōnis, f. *a general greeting.*

persălūto -are, *to greet in succession, greet all round.*

persăpĭens -entis, *very wise;* adv. persăpĭentĕr.

perscientĕr, *very discreetly.*

perscindo -scindĕre -scĭdi -scissum, *to tear to pieces.*

perscitus -a -um, *very clever.*

perscribo -scribĕre -scripsi -scriptum, *to write in full; to note down officially, enter; to make over* or *assign in writing.*

perscriptio -ōnis, f. *entry, noting down; assigning by written document.*

perscriptor -ōris, m. *one who makes an entry.*

perscrūto -are and perscrūtor -ari, dep. *to search through, look through, examine, investigate.*

persĕco -sĕcare -sĕcŭi -sectum, *to cut through, cut away, dissect.*

persector -ari, dep. *to pursue eagerly; to investigate.*

persĕcūtio -ōnis, f. *prosecution.*

persĕdĕo (persĭdĕo) -sĕdēre -sēdi -sessum, *to remain sitting.*

persegnis -e, *very languid.*

persentio -sentire -sensi -sensum, *to perceive distinctly, feel deeply.*

persentisco -ĕre, *to begin to perceive distinctly* or *feel deeply.*

Persĕphŏnē -ēs, f. *Greek name of Proserpina;* q.v.

persĕquor -sĕqui -sĕcūtus, dep. *to follow constantly, pursue to the end, hunt out, overtake; to strive after; to imitate; to proceed against an offender, punish, avenge; to accomplish an action, perform, execute; to treat a subject, expound, describe.*

¹Persēs -ae and Persēus -ĕi, m. *the last king of Macedonia, defeated by the Roman general Aemilius Paulus in 169 B.C.;* adj. Persĭcus -a -um.

²Persēs -ae, m. *a Persian;* see Persae.

Persēus -ĕi and -ĕos, m. *Perseus, who killed Medusa, and rescued Andromeda.*

persĕvĕrantĭa -ae, f. *persistence.*

persĕvĕro -are, *to persist, persevere, continue.*

Hence partic. persĕvĕrans -antis, *enduring, persistent;* adv. persĕvĕrantĕr.

persĕvĕrus -a -um, *very strict.*

Persĭa; see Persae.

Persĭcus; see Persae and Perses.

persído -sídĕre -sēdi -sessum, *to sink in, settle down.*

persigno -are, *to note down, record.*

persimillis -e, *very like.*

persimplex -ícis, *very simple.*

persisto -ĕre, *to remain constant, persist.*

Persius -i, m. A. Persius Flaccus, *a satirist in the reign of Nero.*

persolvo -solvĕre -solvi -sŏlūtum, *to unloose; hence to explain, expound; to pay, pay off, deal out.*

persōna -ae, f. *a mask, esp. as worn by actors; hence role, part, character, personality.*

persŏnātus -a -um, *masked; disguised, counterfeit.*

persŏno -sŏnare -sŏnŭi -sŏnĭtum: intransit., *to resound, sound forth; to shout; to perform upon a musical instrument;* transit., *to make, resound; to proclaim loudly.*

perspergo -ĕre, *to sprinkle, moisten.*

perspicax -ácis, *sharp-sighted.*

perspicientĭa -ae, f. *full awareness or knowledge.*

perspicĭo -spicĕre -spexi, -spectum, *to see through, look through; to look at attentively, survey, examine;* mentally, *to regard, investigate, ascertain.*
Hence partic. perspectus -a -um, *ascertained, fully known.*

perspicŭĭtās -ātis, f. *clearness, perspicuity.*

perspicŭus -a -um, *transparent, bright; clear, evident.* Adv. perspicŭē.

persterno -sternĕre -strāvi -strātum, *to pave thoroughly.*

perstimŭlo -are, *to goad on violently.*

persto -stare -stĭti -stātum, *to stand firm, remain standing; to remain unchanged, last, endure; to stand firm, persist, persevere.*

perstringo -stringĕre -strinxi -strictum. (1) *to press tight, bind tight; to deaden, dull the senses.* (2) *to graze, scratch; to touch upon a subject; to scold, blame, reproach a person.*

perstŭdĭōsus -a -um, *very eager;* adv. perstŭdĭōsē.

persuādĕo -suādĕre -suāsi -suāsum, *to persuade.* (1) *to convince of a fact; sibi persuadere, to satisfy oneself, be convinced.* (2) *to persuade, prevail upon a person to do a thing.*

persuāsĭo -ōnis, f. *persuasion; a conviction, belief.*

persuāsū, abl. sing. m. *by persuasion.*

persubtīlis -e, *very fine; very subtle.*

persulto -are, *to leap, gambol, skip about, skip over.*

pertaedet -taedĕre -taesum est, *to cause weariness or disgust;* cf. taedet.

pertempto -are, *to prove, test, try; to weigh, consider, examine; to assail.*

pertendo -tendĕre -tendi, *to push on, proceed, continue.*

pertĕnŭis -e, *very slight.*

pertĕrebro -are, *to bore through.*

pertergĕo -tergĕre -tersi -tersum *to wipe over; to brush.*

perterrĕo -ēre, *to terrify.*

perterricrĕpus -a -um, *rattling terribly.*

pertexo -texĕre -texŭi -textum, *to weave throughout; to complete, accomplish.*

pertica -ae, f. *a long pole or rod.*

pertimesco -timescĕre -tĭmŭi, *to become very much afraid.*

pertinācĭa -ae, f. *firmness, obstinacy, stubbornness.*

pertinax -ácis, adj., *tenacious; tight-fisted, mean; firm, persistent, stubborn, obstinate.* Adv. pertĭnācĭtĕr.

pertĭnĕo -tĭnēre -tĭnŭi, *to reach to, extend to; to tend towards, have as object or result; to relate to, belong to, apply to, attach to.*

pertingo -ĕre, *to stretch out, extend.*

pertŏlĕro -are, *to endure to the end.*

pertorquĕo -ēre, *to twist, distort.*

pertractātĭo -ōnis, f. *thorough handling, detailed treatment.*

pertracto -are, *to handle, feel; to treat, study, work upon.*

pertrăho -trăhĕre -traxi -tractum, *to drag, forcibly conduct; to entice, allure.*

pertrecto = pertracto; q.v.

pertristis -e, *very sorrowful or austere.*

pertŭmultŭōsē, *in an agitated manner.*

pertundo -tundĕre -tūdi -tūsum, *to bore through, perforate.*

perturbātĭo -ōnis, f. *confusion, disorder, disturbance;* philosoph. *a passion, emotion.*

perturbātrix -ícis, f. *she that disturbs.*

perturbo -are, *to disturb thoroughly, confuse, disquiet, upset.*
Hence partic. perturbātus -a -um, *confused, disturbed;* adv. perturbātē.

perturpis -e, *very disgraceful.*

pertūsus -a -um, partic. from pertundo; q.v.

pĕrungo -ungĕre -unxi -unctum, *to anoint thoroughly, besmear.*

pĕrurbānus -a -um, *very polite or witty; over-sophisticated.*

pĕruro -urĕre -ussi -ustum, *to burn up, consume, inflame; to gall, chafe; to pinch, nip with cold.*

pērutĭlis -e, *very useful.*

pervādo -vādĕre -vāsi -vāsum. (1) *to go through, pass through, pervade.* (2) *to reach, arrive at.*

pervăgor -ari, dep. *to wander through, to rove about; to be widely spread, pervade.* Hence partic. pervăgātus -a -um, *widespread, well known; common, general.*

pervăgus -a -um, *wandering everywhere.*

pervărĭē, *very variously.*

pervasto -are, *to lay waste completely.*

pervĕho -vĕhĕre -vexi -vectum, *to carry, lead, conduct, bring (to or through a place);* pass. pervehi, *to travel to or through.*

pervello -vellĕre -velli, *to pluck, pull, twitch; to stimulate; to pain, to disparage.*

pervĕnĭo -vĕnire -vēni -ventum, *to come through to, arrive at, reach, attain to, be passed to.*

perversĭtās -ātis, f. *perversity.*

perverto (pervorto) -vertĕre -verti -versum, *to turn upside down, overturn,*

overthrow; to undermine, subvert, pervert; in speech, *to trip up.*
Hence partic. **perversus** -a -um, *crooked, awry, askew; distorted, perverse.* Adv. **perversē.**

pervespērī, *very late in the evening.*

pervestīgātio -ōnis, f. *examination, investigation.*

pervestīgo -are, *to track out, investigate, search into.*

pervĕtus -ĕris, *very old.*

pervĕtustus -a -um, *very old.*

pervīcācĭa -ae, f. *firmness, persistence; stubbornness, obstinacy.*

pervīcax -ācis, *firm, persistent; stubborn, obstinate;* compar. adv. **pervīcācĭus,** *more stubbornly.*

pervĭdĕo -vĭdēre -vĭdi -vīsum, *to look over, survey; to see through, discern, distinguish.*

pervīgĕo -ēre, *to flourish, bloom continually.*

pervīgil -ĭlis, *always watchful.*

pervīgĭlātĭo -ōnis, f. and **pervīgĭlium** -i, n. *a vigil, religious watching.*

pervīgĭlo -are, *to remain awake all night.*

pervīlis -e, *very cheap.*

pervinco -vincĕre -vīci -victum, *to conquer completely; to surpass, outdo; to induce, prevail upon; to carry one's point; to achieve, effect; to prove, demonstrate.*

pervĭus -a -um, *passable, accessible;* as subst., *a passage.*

pervolgo = pervulgo; q.v.

pervŏlĭto -are, *to fly round, flit about.*

¹**pervŏlo** -are, *to fly through, fly round.*

²**pervŏlo** -velle -vŏlŭi, *to wish greatly.*

pervŏlūto -are, *to roll round;* esp. *to unroll and read a book.*

pervolvo -volvĕre -volvi -volutum, *to roll about; to unroll and read a book.*

pervorsē, etc., = perverse, etc.; q.v.

pervulgo (pervolgo) -are, *to publish, make publicly known; to make generally available; to frequent, haunt a place.* Hence partic. **pervulgātus** -a -um, *very usual or well known.*

pēs pĕdis, m. *the foot;* pedem referre, *to return;* pedibus, *on foot,* also *by land;* servus a pedibus, *an attendant, lackey;* pedibus ire in sententiam, *to support a proposal;* milit., pedibus merere, *to serve in the infantry;* pedem conferre, *to fight hand to hand.* Transf., *a foot of a table, chair, etc.; a metrical foot; a measure of length;* pes (veli), *a rope or sheet, attached to the lower edge of a sail.*

pessimus, pessime; see malus.

pessŭlus -i, m. *a bolt.*

pessum, *to the ground, to the bottom, downwards;* pessum ire, *to sink, be ruined, perish;* pessum dare, *to destroy, ruin, put an end to.*

pestĭfer -fĕra, -fĕrum, *pestilential, destructive, injurious;* adv. **pestĭfērē.**

pestĭlens -entis, *unhealthy, fatal, noxious.*

pestĭlentĭa -ae, f. *an unhealthy condition; a plague, infectious disease, pest.*

pestĭlĭtās -ātis, f. = pestilentia; q.v.

pestis -is, f. *pest, pestilence, plague; destruction, ruin; curse, bane.*

pĕtāsātus -a -um, *wearing the petasus;* hence, *equipped for a journey.*

pĕtāso -ōnis, m. *a fore-quarter of pork.*

pĕtāsus -i, m. *a broad-brimmed felt hat, used by travellers.*

pĕtaurum -i, n. *a spring-board.*

pĕtesso (pĕtisso) -ĕre, *to long for, strive after.*

pĕtītĭo -ōnis, f. *an attack, thrust, blow; a request, application; standing for office, candidature;* at law, *a suit, a right of claim, right to bring an action.*

pĕtītor -ōris, m. *a seeker;* polit., *a candidate;* legal, *a plaintiff.*

pĕtītŭrĭo -ire, *to desire to stand for election.*

pĕtītus -ūs, m. *an inclining towards.*

pĕto -ĕre -īvi and -ii -itum, *to make for, go to; to attack, assail; to seek, strive after; to ask for, beg, request, demand;* polit., *to stand for, canvas for;* legal, *to sue for;* sometimes *to fetch, derive.*

pĕtorrĭtum (petōrĭtum) -i, n. *an open four-wheeled carriage.*

Petrōnĭus -i, m. *name of a Roman gens;* esp. *of a satirist under Nero.*

pĕtŭlans -antis, *impudent, pert, wanton;* adv. **pĕtŭlantĕr.**

pĕtŭlantĭa -ae, f. *impudence, pertness, wantonness.*

pĕtulcus -a -um, *butting with the head.*

pexātus -a -um, *wearing a garment with the nap on.*

Phaedra -ae, f. *daughter of Minos, wife of Theseus.*

Phaedrus -i, m. *a freedman of Augustus, author of Latin fables.*

Phăēthōn -ontis, m. *the son of Helios, killed trying to drive the chariot of his father.*

phălangae (pălangae) -arum, f. pl. *rollers.*

phălangītae -arum, m. pl. *soldiers belonging to a phalunx.*

phălanx -angis, f. *an array of soldiers in close formation.*

Phălāris -ĭdis, m. *a tyrant of Agrigentum.*

phălĕrae -arum, f. pl. *metal bosses; military decorations; horses' trappings.*

phălĕrātus -a -um, *wearing phalerae;* q.v.

Phălērum -i, n. *the oldest port of Athens.*

phantasma -ātis, n. *an apparition.*

phăretra -ae, f. *a quiver.*

phăretrātus -a -um, *wearing a quiver.*

pharmăceutria -ae, f. *sorceress.*

pharmăcŏpōla (-es) -ae, m. *a seller of drugs; a quack.*

Pharsālus (-ŏs) -i, f. *a town in Thessaly, where Pompey was defeated by Caesar in 48 B.C.*

Phărus (-ŏs) -i, f., rarely m., *an island off Alexandria, with a lighthouse;* hence in gen. *a lighthouse.*

phăsēlus -i, m. and f. *the kidney-bean or French bean; a light bean-shaped boat.*

Phāsis -ĭdis and -ĭdos, m. *a river in Colchis, flowing into the Black Sea;*

f. adj. **Phāsis** -ĭdis, and **Phāsiānus** -a -um, *Colchian.*

phasma -ătis, n. *a ghost, spectre.*

phĭăla -ae, f. *a drinking-vessel; a bowl, saucer.*

Phīdĭās -ae, m. *an Athenian sculptor.*

Philippi -orum, m. pl. *a city in Macedonia, where Octavian and Antony defeated Brutus and Cassius.*

Philippus -i, m. *the name of several kings of Macedon;* adj. **Philippēus** and **Philippĭcus** -a -um; f. as subst. **Philippĭca** -ae, *one of the speeches of Demosthenes against Philip, or of Cicero against Antony.*

phĭlŏlŏgĭa -ae, f. *love of learning, study of literature.*

phĭlŏlŏgus -a -um, *learned, literary;* m. as subst. *a scholar.*

Phĭlŏmēla -ae, f. *the daughter of Pandion, turned into a nightingale.*

phĭlŏsŏphĭa -ae, f. *philosophy.*

phĭlŏsŏphor -ari, dep. *to philosophize, apply oneself to philosophy.*

phĭlŏsŏphus -a -um, *philosophical;* m. and f. as subst. *a philosopher.*

philtrum -i, n. *a love-potion, philtre.*

phĭlўra -ae, f. *the inner bark of the linden-tree.*

phimus -i, m. *a dice-box.*

Phlĕgĕthōn -ontis, m. *a river in the infernal regions.*

phōca -ae, f. and **phōcē** -ēs, f. *a seal.*

Phōcis -ĭdis, f. *a district in the north of Greece;* adj. **Phōcēus** -a -um.

Phoebē -ēs, f. *the sister of Phoebus, the Moon-goddess, Diana.*

Phoebĭgĕna -ae, m. *the son of Phoebus, Aesculapius.*

Phoebus -i, m. *Apollo, the Sun-god;* hence subst. **Phoebăs** -ădis, f. *a priestess of Phoebus, a prophetess;* adj. **Phoebēius** and **Phoebēus** -a -um, *of Phoebus.*

Phoenīcē -ēs, f. *Phoenicia;* m. subst. **Phoenīces** -um, *the Phoenicians;* f. subst. **Phoenissa** -ae, f. *a Phoenician woman.*

phoenīcoptĕros -i, m. *the flamingo.*

phoenix -īcis, m. *the phoenix, a fabulous bird of Arabia.*

phōnascus -i, m. *a teacher of music.*

phrĕnēsis -is, f. *madness, frenzy.*

phrĕnētĭcus -a -um, *mad, frantic.*

Phrixus -i, m. *brother of Helle.*

Phrўges -um, m. pl. *the Phrygians;* sing. **Phryx** -ўgis; **Phrўgĭa** -ae, f. *the country of Phrygia in Asia Minor;* adj. **Phrўgĭus** -a -um, *Phrygian;* poet. = *Trojan.*

phthĭsis -is, f. *consumption.*

phy, interj. *pish! tush!*

phўlarchus -i, m. *the head of a tribe, an emir.*

phўsĭca -ae, and **phўsĭcē** -ēs, f. *physics, natural science.*

phўsĭcus -a -um, *relating to physics, physical;* m. as subst. *a scientist;* n. pl. **phўsĭca** -orum, *physics;* adv. **phўsĭcē,** *in the manner of the scientists.*

phўsiognōmōn -onis, m. *a physiognomist.*

phўsĭŏlŏgĭa -ae, f. *natural science.*

pĭābĭlis -e, *able to be atoned for.*

pĭācŭlāris -e, *atoning, expiating;* n. pl. as subst. *expiatory sacrifices.*

pĭācŭlum -i, n. *a means of expiating or appeasing; sacrifice, remedy; punishment; a victim; an act needing expiation, a sin, crime.*

pĭāmen -ĭnis, m. *means of atonement or expiation.*

pĭca -ae, f. *a jay or magpie.*

pĭcārĭa -ae, f. *a place where pitch is made.*

pĭcēa -ae, f. *the spruce-fir.*

Pīcēnum -i, n. *a district in central Italy.*

pĭcĕus -a -um, *of pitch; pitch-black.*

pĭco -are, *to smear with pitch.*

pictor -ōris, m. *a painter.*

pictūra -ae, f. *the art of painting; a painting, picture;* pictura textilis, *embroidery.*

pictūrātus -a -um, *painted;* vestes, *embroidered.*

picus -i, m. *a woodpecker.*

Pĭĕris -ĭdis or -ĭdos, f. *a Muse;* plur. **Pĭĕrĭdes,** *the Muses;* adj. **Pĭĕrĭus** -a -um, *Pierian, poetic.*

pĭĕtās -ātis, f. *dutifulness, dutiful conduct; piety; patriotism; devotion; kindness.*

pĭger -gra -grum, *sluggish, unwilling, slow;* campus, *unfruitful.* Adv. **pĭgrē.**

pĭget -gēre -gŭit -gĭtum est, impers., *it causes annoyance* (or *regret* or *shame); it disgusts;* piget me, with genit., *I am disgusted with.*

pigmentārĭus -i, m. *a seller of paints and unguents.*

pigmentum -i, n. *paint, pigment;* of style, *ornament, decoration.*

pignĕrātor -ōris, m. *a mortgagee.*

pignĕro -are, *to give as a pledge, pawn, mortgage.*

pignĕror -ari, dep. *to take as a pledge; to claim.*

pignus -nŏris and -nĕris, n. *a pledge, pawn, security; a wager, bet, stake; a token, assurance, proof;* in plur., *persons as pledges of love.*

pigrĭtĭa -ae, and **pigrĭties** -ēi, f. *sluggishness, indolence.*

pigro -are and **pigror** -ari, dep. *to be sluggish.*

¹pĭla -ae, f. *a mortar.*

²pĭla -ae, f. *a pillar, pier; a bookstall.*

³pĭla -ae, f. *a ball; a game of ball.*

pĭlanus -i, m. = triarius; q.v.

pĭlātus -a -um, *armed with the pilum or javelin.*

pĭlentum -i, n. *a carriage, coach.*

pĭllĕātus (pĭlĕ-) -a -um, *wearing the felt cap.*

pĭllĕŏlus (pĭlĕ-) -i, m. *a little cap, skull-cap.*

pĭllĕus (pĭlĕus) -i, m. and **pĭllĕum** -i, n. *a felt cap, esp. as worn by manumitted slaves.*

pĭlo -are, *to deprive of hair.*

pĭlōsus -a -um, *covered with hair, hairy.*

pīlum -i, n. *the heavy javelin of the Roman infantry.*

¹pĭlus -i, m. *a single hair; a trifle.*

²pĭlus -i, m. *a division of the triarii in the Roman army;* primus pilus, *the* chief centurion of the triarii and of the legion.

Pindărus -i, m. a lyric poet of Thebes.

pīnētum -i, n. a pine-wood.

pīnĕus -a -um, made of pine-wood or deal.

pingo pingĕre pinxi pictum, to paint, to draw; to embroider; to stain, dye; to decorate, adorn; in speech or writing, to embellish, depict.

pinguesco -ĕre, to become fat, grow fertile.

pinguis -e, fat; oily; rich, fertile; n. as subst. fatness, fat. Transf., thick, dense; heavy, stupid; easy, quiet.

pinguĭtūdo -inis, f. fatness, broadness.

pīnĭfer -fĕra -fĕrum and **pīnĭgĕr** -gĕra -gĕrum, producing pines.

¹**pinna** -ae, f. a feather; a feathered arrow; a wing; a battlement along the top of a wall.

²**pinna** (pina) -ae, f. a species of mussel.

pinnātus -a -um, feathered, winged.

pinnĭger -gĕra -gĕrum, feathered, winged; piscis, having fins.

pinnĭrăpus -i, m. a crestsnatcher, i.e. a kind of gladiator.

pinnŭla -ae, f. a small feather or wing.

pinso, pinsĕre; pinsi and pinsŭi; pinsum pinsitum and pistum, to stamp, pound, crush.

pīnus -i and -ūs, f. a fir or pine; anything made of pine-wood, e.g. a torch, oar, ship.

pĭo -are, to appease, propitiate; to venerate; to make good, atone for.

pĭper pĭpĕris, n. pepper.

pīpĭlo -are, to twitter, chirp.

pīpŭlus -i, m. and **pīpŭlum** -i, n. outcry.

Pīraeĕus and **Pīraeus** -i, m. the Piraeus, the main port of Athens.

pīrāta -ae, m. pirate.

pīrātĭcus -a -um, piratical; f. as subst. piracy.

pĭrum -i, n. a pear.

pĭrus -i, f. a pear-tree.

piscātor -ōris, m. a fisherman; a fishmonger.

piscātōrĭus -a -um, of fishermen or fishing.

piscātus -ūs, m. fishes; fishing, a catch.

piscĭcŭlus -i, m. a little fish.

piscīna -ae, f. a fish-pond; a swimming-bath.

piscīnārĭus -i, m. one fond of fish-ponds.

piscis -is, m. a fish.

piscor -ari, dep. to fish.

piscōsus -a -um, abounding in fish.

pistillum -i, n. a pestle.

pistor -ōris, m. a grinder, miller; a baker.

pistrīnum -i, n. a mill; a bakery.

pistris -is, and **pistrix** -tricis, f. a sea monster; a whale, shark, saw-fish. Transf., a small fast ship.

pītŭīta -ae, f. phlegm, rheum.

pītŭītōsus -a -um, full of phlegm.

pĭus -a -um, dutiful; godly, holy; patriotic; devoted, affectionate; in gen., honest, upright, kind.

pix pĭcis, f. pitch.

plăcābĭlis -e; pass., easy to appease; act., appeasing.

plăcābĭlĭtās -ātis, f. placability.

plăcāmen -ĭnis, and **plăcāmentum** -i, n. means of appeasing.

plăcātĭo -ōnis, f. soothing, appeasing.

plăcĕo -ēre -ŭi and -itus sum, -itum, to please, be agreeable to; impers. plăcet, it seems good, it is agreed or resolved.

Hence partic. **plăcĭtus** -a -um, pleasing, agreeable; agreed upon. N. as subst. what is agreeable; plur., opinions, teaching.

plăcĭdus -a -um, quiet, still; gentle; adv. **plăcĭdē**.

plăcĭtus -a -um, partic. from placeo; q.v.

plăco -are, to soothe, calm; to reconcile, appease.

Hence partic. **plăcātus** -a -um, soothed, appeased; calm, gentle, quiet; adv. **plăcātē**.

¹**plāga** -ae, f. a blow, stroke; a wound.

²**plăga** -ae, f. a district, zone, region.

³**plăga** -ae, f. a net for hunting; a trap, snare.

plăgĭārĭus -i, m. a kidnapper; a plagiarist.

plăgōsus -a -um, fond of flogging.

plăgŭla -ae, f. a bed-curtain.

planctus -ūs, m. beating; esp. beating of the breast, lamentations.

plango plangĕre planxi planctum, to beat, strike, esp. noisily; to strike the breast, head, etc., as a sign of grief; hence plangere and pass. plangi, to bewail.

plangor -ōris, m. loud striking or beating; esp. beating of the head and breast, loud lamentations.

plānĭpēs -pēdis, m. an actor who wore no shoes.

plānĭtās -ātis, f. plainness, distinctness.

plānĭtĭa -ae, and **plānĭtĭēs** -ēi, f. a level surface, a plain.

planta -ae, f. (1) a green twig, cutting, graft; a plant. (2) the sole of the foot.

plantārĭa -ĭum, n. pl. young trees, slips.

¹**plānus** -a -um, even, flat; n. as subst. a plain, level ground; de plano, off-hand, easily. Transf., plain, clear, intelligible. Adv. **plānē**, distinctly, intelligibly; wholly, quite, thoroughly; in answers, certainly.

²**plānus** -i, m. a vagabond, a charlatan.

plătălĕa -ae, f. a water-bird, the spoonbill.

plătănus -i, f. the plane-tree.

plătĕa -ae, f. a street.

Plătō (-ōn) -ōnis, m. the Greek philosopher, disciple of Socrates.

plaudo (plōdo) plaudĕre plausi plausum, to strike, beat, clap together; to make a clapping noise, clap, applaud.

plausĭbĭlis -e, worthy of applause.

plausor -ōris, m. an applauder at the theatre.

plaustrum (plostrum) -i, n. a waggon, cart; Charles's Wain.

plausus -ūs, m. a noise of clapping; approbation, applause.

Plautus -i, m., T. Maccius, *the Roman comic poet, born about* 254 B.C. Adj. **Plautīnus** -a -um.

plēbēcŭla -ae, f. *the common people, mob, rabble.*

plēbēius -a -um, *of the plebs or people, plebeian; common, low, mean.*

plēbēs -ēi and -i, f. = plebs; q.v.

plēbĭcŏla -ae, m. *a friend of the common people.*

plēbiscitum -i, n. *a decree of the people.*

plebs plēbis, f. *the plebeians, the common people, lower orders.*

¹plecto; see plexus.

²plecto -ĕre, *to punish;* usually pass.. **plector** -i, *to be punished* (with blows).

plectrum -i, n. *a stick with which the strings of a stringed instrument were struck; a quill.* Transf., *the lyre; lyric poetry.*

Plēĭas -ădis, f. *a Pleiad;* usually plur. **Plēĭădes** -ădum, f. *the Pleiads, the Seven Stars.*

plēnus -a -um, *full, full of* (with genit. or abl.); *complete; plump, thick; pregnant; filled, satisfied; well-stocked, rich;* of age, *mature:* of the voice, *strong, loud;* of style, *full, copious.* Adv. **plēnē,** *fully, completely.*

plērusquĕ -raque -rumque and plur. **plērīquĕ** -raeque -raque, *very many, a large part, the most part;* n. sing. as subst., *the greater part;* acc. as adv. *for the most part, mostly, commonly.*

plexus -a -um, partic. as from plecto, *braided, plaited.*

Plias = Pleias; q.v.

plĭco -are, -ŭi and -avi, -atum and ĭtum, *to fold.*

Plīnius -a -um, *name of a Roman gens;* esp. of C. Plinius Secundus (Maior, *the Elder*), *author of a Natural History,* and C. Plinius Caecilius Secundus (Iunior, *the Younger*), *author of letters,* etc.

plōdo = plaudo; q.v.

plōrābĭlis -e, *deplorable.*

plōrātor -ōris, m. *a lamenter.*

plōrātus -ūs, m. *weeping, lamenting.*

plōro -are, *to lament, wail;* transit., *to weep over, deplore.*

plostellum -i, n. *a little waggon.*

plostrum = plaustrum; q.v.

plŭit plŭĕre, plŭit or plŭvit, *it rains, a shower falls.*

plūma -ae, f. *a small, soft feather; down* (esp. in pl.); meton. *bolster, featherbed; the first down on the chin.*

plūmātus -a -um, *covered with feathers.*

plumbĕus -a -um, *leaden, of lead.* Transf., *dull, stupid; heavy, oppressive; bad.*

plumbum -i, n. *lead; a bullet; a leaden pipe;* plumbum album, *tin.*

plūmĕus -a -um, *downy, of fine feathers.*

plūmōsus -a -um, *feathered, downy.*

plŭo; see pluit.

plūrĭmus and **plūs;** see multus.

pluscŭlus -a -um, *somewhat more, rather more.*

plŭtĕus -i, m. and **plŭtĕum** -i, n. *a shelter;* milit., *penthouse, shed, mantlet; breastwork, battlement.* Transf., *a board, couch, bookshelf.*

Plŭtō (-ōn) -ōnis, m. *the king of the lower world;* adj. **Plŭtōnĭus** -a -um.

plŭviālis -e, *of or from rain; bringing rain.*

plŭvĭus -a -um, *of or from rain, bringing rain;* as subst. **plŭvĭa** -ae, *rain.*

pōcillum -i, n. *a little cup.*

pōcŭlum -i, n. *a drinking-cup, goblet; a drink, draught.*

pōdagra -ae, f. *gout in the feet.*

pōdex -icis, m. *fundament, anus.*

pōdĭum -i, n. *a balcony,* esp. *in the amphitheatre.*

pŏēma -ătis, n. *a poem.*

poena -ae, f. *money paid as atonement, a fine;* in gen., *punishment, penalty; loss, hardship;* poenas dare, *to be punished.*

Poenī -orum, m. pl. *the Carthaginians;* sing. **Poenus** -i, m. adj. **Poenus, Pūnĭcus, Poenĭcĕus** -a -um, *Punic, Carthaginian.*

poenĭo = punio; q.v.

poenitet; see paenitet.

pŏēsis -is, acc. -in, f. *poetry.*

pŏēta -ae, m. *a maker;* esp. *a poet.*

pŏētĭcus -a -um, *poetical;* f. as subst. **pŏētĭca** -ae and **pŏētĭcē** -ēs, *the art of poetry;* adv. **pŏētĭcē.**

pŏētria -ae, f. *a poetess.*

pōl! interj. *by Pollux! truly! really!*

pŏlenta -ae, f. *pearl-barley, barley-groats.*

pōlĭo -ire, *to polish, file, make smooth;* esp. *to cover with white, whiten; to adorn, to finish off.*
    Hence partic. **pŏlītus** -a -um, *polished, refined, accomplished;* adv. **pŏlītē.**

pōlītīa -ae, acc. -an. f. *the Republic* (Plato's work).

pŏlītĭcus -a -um *of the state, political.*

pŏlītus -a -um, partic. from polio; q.v.

pollen -ĭnis, n. and **pollis** -ĭnis, c. *fine flour, meal.*

pollentĭa -ae, f. *power, might.*

pollĕo -ēre, *to be strong, powerful, able;* partic. **pollens** -entis, *powerful, mighty.*

pollex -ĭcis, m. *the thumb;* also *the big toe.*

pollicĕor -cēri -cītus, dep. *to offer, promise;* perf. partic. in pass. sense, **pollicĭtus** -a -um, *promised.* N. as subst. *a promise.*

pollicĭtātĭo -ōnis, f. *an offer, promise.*

pollicĭtor -ari, dep. *to keep promising.*

pollinctor -ōris, m. *an undertaker.*

pollūcĕo -lūcēre -luxi -luctum, *to offer, serve up.*

pollŭo -ŭĕre -ŭi -ūtum, *to defile, pollute, dishonour;* partic. **pollūtus** -a -um, *defiled, polluted; unchaste.*

Pollux -ūcis, m. *the twin-brother of Castor.*

pōlus -i, m. *the end of an axis, a pole; the sky, heaven.*

Pŏlÿhymnĭa -ae, f. *one of the Muses.*

pŏlÿpus -i, m. *polypus.*

pŏmārĭus -a -um, *of fruit;* m. *as subst.,
a fruiterer;* n. *as subst., a fruit-
garden, orchard.*

pŏmērĭdĭānus = postmeridianus; q.v.

pŏmērĭum or pŏmoerĭum -i, n. *a
clear space beside the walls of a town.*

pōmĭfer -fĕra -fĕrum, *fruit-bearing.*

pōmōsus -a -um, *abounding in fruit.*

pompa -ae, f. *a solemn procession; a
suite, retinue; display, parade, ostentation.*

Pompēii -orum, m. pl. *a town in
Campania, destroyed by an eruption of
Vesuvius;* adj. Pompēiānus -a -um.

Pompēius (trisyl.) or Pompēĭus -a
-um, *name of a Roman gens;* esp. of
Cn. Pompeius, *Pompey the Great*
(106-48 B.C.); adj. Pompēiānus -a
-um, *belonging to Pompey.*

Pompilius -a -um, *name of a Roman
gens;* esp. *of* Numa Pompilius,
second king of Rome.

pompilus -i, m. *the pilot-fish.*

Pomptīnus -a -um, *Pomptine* or
Pontine: palus or paludes, *a marshy
district in Latium.*

pōmum -i, n. *any kind of fruit; a
fruit-tree.*

pōmus -i, f. *a fruit-tree.*

pondĕro -are, *to weigh, consider, ponder.*

pondĕrōsus -a -um, *heavy, weighty;
significant.*

pondo (abl.) *in weight;* as indecl. subst.
a pound, pounds.

pondus -ĕris, n. *weight; a weight,
burden, mass; balance; authority,
influence.*

pŏne: adv. *behind, at the back;* prep.
with acc., *behind.*

pōno pōnĕre pŏsŭi (pŏsīvi) pŏsĭtum
(postum), *to lay, put, place, set; to
put in place, settle; to put aside, lay
down, discard; to lay to rest, lay out
for burial;* milit., *to post, station;
of money, etc., to store, deposit,
invest; to stake, wager; of food, to
put on table, to serve;* of buildings,
to found, set up; of laws, etc. *to
establish, ordain;* of persons, *to
appoint;* of an artist, *to represent,
picture; to reckon, count, regard; to
lay down, assert, cite.*

Hence partic. pŏsĭtus -a -um, *in
place;* nix, *fallen snow;* of places,
situated.

pons pontis, m. *a bridge, gangway;
the deck of a ship.*

ponticŭlus -i, m. *a little bridge.*

pontifex -ficis, m. *a pontiff, member of a
Roman guild of priests.*

pontĭfĭcālis -e, *pontifical.*

pontĭfĭcātus -ūs, m. *the office of pontiff.*

pontĭfĭcus -a -um, *pontifical.*

Pontius -a -um, *name of a Roman*
(originally Samnite) gens.

ponto -ōnis, m. *a flat-bottomed boat,
punt.*

¹pontus -i, n. *the sea.*

²Pontus -i, m. *the Black Sea;* also *the
country on the shores of the Black Sea;*
adj. Ponticus -a -um.

pōpa -ae, m. *a junior priest or temple-
servant.*

pŏpānum -i, n. *a sacrificial cake.*

pŏpellus -i, m. *common people, rabble.*

pŏpīna -ae, f. *a cook-shop, eating-house;
the food sold there.*

pŏpīno -ōnis, m. *a glutton.*

poplĕs -ĭtis, m. *the ham, hough; the
knee.*

pōpŭlābĭlis -e, *that can be laid waste,
destructible.*

pōpŭlābundus -a -um, *laying waste,
devastating.*

pōpŭlāris -e. (1) *belonging to the same
people or country, native;* as subst.
fellow-countryman, adherent, partner.
(2) *of the people or state; popular;
democratic;* m. pl. as subst. *the
popular party, the democrats.*
Adv. pŏpŭlārĭter, *after the manner of
the people, vulgarly; in a popular
manner, like a demagogue.*

pŏpŭlārĭtās -ātis, f. *fellow-citizenship;
an attempt to please the people.*

pōpŭlātĭo -ōnis, f. *laying waste,
devastating, plundering.*

pōpŭlātor -ōris, m. *a devastator,
plunderer.*

pōpŭlĕus -a -um, *of the poplar.*

pōpŭlĭfer -fĕra -fĕrum, *producing
poplars.*

pōpŭlo -are and pōpŭlor -ari, dep. *to
lay waste, devastate, plunder; to ruin,
spoil, rob.*

¹pŏpŭlus -i, m. *a people, political community, nation;* as a section of the
community, *the people;* in gen., *the
people, the public;* hence *any crowd,
host, multitude.*

²pōpŭlus -i, f. *a poplar-tree.*

porca -ae, f. *a sow.*

porcīnus -a -um, *of a swine or hog.*

Porcĭus -a -um, *name of a Roman gens.*

porcus -i, m. *a pig, hog.*

porgo = porrigo; q.v.

porrectĭo -ōnis, f. *stretching out,
extension.*

porricĭo -rĭcĕre -rectum, *to offer as a
sacrifice.*

¹porrĭgo -rĭgĕre -rexi -rectum, *to
stretch out, extend; to offer, grant;*
pass., porrigi, *to lie stretched out;*
partic. porrectus -a -um, *stretched
out, extended, long.*

²porrĭgo -ginis, f. *scurf, dandruff.*

porro, *forward, further; next, again, in
turn; in time, far back, long ago, or
in future.*

porrus -i, m. and porrum -i, n. *a leek.*

porta -ae, f. *a gate.*

portātĭo -ōnis, f. *carrying, conveying.*

portendo -tendĕre -tendi -tentum, *to
indicate, predict, presage.*

portentĭfĭcus -a -um, *marvellous,
miraculous.*

portentōsus -a -um, *extraordinary,
monstrous, unnatural.*

portentum -i, n. subst. from portendo;
q.v.

porthmĕus, acc. -ĕă, m. *ferryman.*

portĭcŭla -ae, f. *a little gallery or
portico.*

portĭcus -ūs, f. *a portico, colonnade,
arcade, gallery.* Transf., *the Stoic
school of philosophers.*

portĭo -ōnis, f. *a part, section;* pro portione, *in proportion.*

¹portĭtor -ōris, m. *a customs-officer.*

²portĭtor -ōris, m. *a carrier;* usually *a boatman, ferryman.*

porto -are, *to bear, carry, convey, bring.*

portōrĭum i, n. *customs, harbour-dues;* any *toll, tax.*

portŭla -ae, f. *a little gate, postern.*

portŭōsus -a -um, *having many harbours.*

portus -ūs, m. *harbour, port; haven, refuge.*

posco poscĕre pŏposci, *to ask earnestly, request, call upon;* poscimur, *we are asked to sing;* esp. *to demand for punishment,* or *challenge to fight;* of things, *to demand, require.*

pŏsĭtĭo -ōnis, f. *placing, putting posture;* caeli, *situation, climate.*

pŏsĭtor -ōris, m. *founder, builder.*

pŏsĭtūra -ae, f. *placing; situation, posture; ordering, formation.*

pŏsĭtus -ūs, m. *position, place, arrangement.*

possessĭo -ōnis, f. *a getting possession* or *possessing; occupation, enjoyment.* Transf., *a thing possessed, possession, property.*

possessĭuncŭla -ae, f. *a small property.*

possessor -ōris, m. *a possessor, occupier.*

possĭdĕo -sĭdēre -sēdi -sessum, *to possess, have, hold.*

possĭdo -sĭdēre -sēdi sessum, *to take possession of, occupy.*

possum posse pŏtŭi, *to be able; one may, one can; to avail, have influence.*
Hence partic. **pŏtens** -entis, *able, powerful, capable; influential, efficacious;* with genit., *master of.* Adv. **pŏtentĕr**, *strongly, efficaciously; according to one's power.*

post (older **postĕ**). Adv. *behind, in the rear;* of time, *afterwards;* multo post, *much later.* Prep., with acc., *behind;* of time, *after;* in rank, etc., *next after.*

posteă, *thereafter, afterwards, next.*

posteăquam, conj. *after.*

postĕrĭtas -ātis, f. *future generations, posterity.*

postĕrus (**postĕr**) -a -um, *subsequent, following, next, future;* in posterum, *for the next day* or *for the future;* m. pl. as subst. *posterity.* Compar. **postĕrĭor** -us, *next, later; inferior, worse;* n. acc. as adv., posterius, *later.* Superl. **postrēmus** -a -um, *hindmost, last; lowest, worst.* N. abl. as adv., postremo, *at last;* n. acc. postremum, *for the last time;* ad postremum, *at last.* Superl. **postŭmus** -a -um, *the last, last-born* (esp. of children born after the father's will or death).

postfĕro -ferre, *to consider of less account.*

postgĕnĭti -ōrum, m. pl. *posterity, descendants.*

posthăbĕo -ēre -ŭi -ĭtum, *to consider of less account, put after.*

posthāc, *hereafter, in future, afterwards.*

posthinc, *next.*

posthōc, *afterwards.*

postĭcus -a -um, *hinder, back;* n. as subst. **postĭcum** -i, *a back-door.*

postilēna -ae, f. *a crupper.*

postillā, *afterwards.*

postis -is, m. *a door-post;* plur., *a door, doorway.*

postlimĭnĭum -i, n. *the right to return home.*

postmĕrĭdĭānus -a -um, *of the afternoon.*

postmŏdŏ and **postmŏdum**, *presently, soon.*

postpartor -ōris, m. *heir.*

postpōno -pōnĕre -pōsŭi -pōsĭtum, *to consider of less account, put after.*

postquam (or **post quam**), conj. *after, when.*

postrēmo, etc.; see posterus.

postrīdĭē, *the day after, on the next day.*

postcaenĭum -i, n. *the theatre behind the scenes.*

postscrībo -scrībĕre -scripsi -scriptum, *to write after.*

postŭlātĭo -ōnis, f. *a claim, demand, application; a complaint.*

postŭlātum -i, n. subst. from postulo; q.v.

postŭlātus -ūs, m. *a legal complaint, accusation, suit.*

postŭlo -are, *to claim, demand, request; legal to demand a writ,* or *to impeach, accuse a person;* of things, *to demand, require.* N. of partic. as subst. **postŭlātum** -i, *a demand.*

postŭmus -a -um, superl. of posterus; q.v.

pōtātĭo -ōnis, f. *a drinking-bout.*

pŏtĕ; see potis.

pŏtens -entis, partic. from possum; q.v.

pŏtentātus -ūs, m. *political power, supremacy.*

pŏtentĭa -ae, f. *power, might, ability; efficacy, potency;* esp. (*unofficial*) *political power.*

pŏtestās -ātis, f. *power, ability, control.* Esp. *political supremacy, dominion; the authority of a magistrate, office command;* concr., *an officer, magistrate.* Transf., *opportunity, possibility, occasion;* facere potestatem, *to give opportunity* or *permission;* potestas est, *it is possible.*

¹pōtĭo -ōnis, f. *drinking; a drink, a draught;* esp. *a love-draught, philtre.*

²pōtĭo -ire, *to put in the power of.*

¹pŏtĭor -iri, dep., *to get possession of, to obtain; to possess, be master of.*

²pŏtĭor; see potis.

pŏtis, pŏtĕ; *able, capable;* potis (or pote) est, *can, is able* (or *possible*). Compar. **pŏtĭor** -us, *preferable, better;* n. acc. as adv. **pŏtĭus**, *rather, preferably.* Superl. **pŏtissĭmus** -a -um, *best of all, chief, principal;* n. as adv. **pŏtissĭmum**, *chiefly, above all.*

pōto pōtāre pōtāvi pōtātum and pōtum, *to drink;* esp. *to drink heavily;* of things, *to absorb.*
Hence partic. **pōtus** -a -um: pass., *drunk, drained,* act., *having drunk, drunken.*

pŏtor -ōris m. *a drinker*; esp. *a tippler, drunkard.*

pŏtŭlentus (pōcŭlentus) -a -um, *drinkable; drunk, intoxicated.*

¹pōtus, partic. from poto; q.v.

²pōtus -ūs, m. *a drinking, draught.*

prae. Adv. *before, in front*; prae quam, *in comparison with.* Prep. with abl., *before*; prae se ferre, *to show, exhibit; in comparison with; on account of, because of.*

praeăcūtus -a -um, *sharpened to a point, pointed.*

praealtus -a -um, *very high or deep.*

praebĕo -bēre -bŭi -bĭtum, *to offer, hold out; to provide, supply, allow*; with reflex., *to present or show oneself in a certain character, behave as.*

praebĭbo -bĭbĕre -bĭbi, *to drink before, drink to.*

praebĭtor -ōris, m. *a furnisher, supplier.*

praecălĭdus -a -um, *very hot.*

praecantrix -īcis, f. *a witch.*

praecānus -a -um, *prematurely grey.*

praecăvĕo -căvēre -cāvi -cautum: intransit., *to take precautions, be on one's guard*; transit., *to beware of, guard against beforehand.*

praecēdo -cēdĕre -cessi -cessum, *to go before, precede*, in space or time; in rank, etc., *to surpass, excel.*

praecello -ĕre, *to surpass, excel*; genti, *to rule over*; partic. **praecellens** -entis, *excellent, distinguished, surpassing.*

praecelsus -a -um, *very high.*

praecentio -ōnis, f. *a musical prelude.*

praeceps -cĭpĭtis: of motion, *headlong, fast-falling, quick*; of character, *hasty, rash, blind*; of places, *steep, precipitous*; hence *dangerous.* N. as subst., *a steep place, precipice; danger*; as adv., *headlong.*

praeceptio -ōnis, f. *a pre-conception; a precept; the right to receive in advance.*

praeceptor -ōris, m. and **praeceptrix** -trīcis, f. *a teacher, instructor.*

praeceptum -i, n. subst. from praecipio; q.v.

praecerpo -cerpĕre -cerpsi -cerptum, *to pluck prematurely; to intercept.*

praecīdo -cīdĕre -cīdi -cīsum, *to cut short, lop, mutilate*; ancoras, *to cut the cables*; of speech, brevi praecidam, *I will put it briefly.*

Hence partic. **praecīsus** -a -um, *broken off*; of places, *steep, precipitous*; of speech, *brief.* Adv. **praecīsē,** *briefly, in few words; absolutely, decidedly.*

praecingo -cingĕre -cinxi -cinctum, *to gird in front, surround with a girdle.*

praecĭno -cinĕre -cinŭi -centum: intransit. *to sing or play before; to sing an incantation*; transit. *to prophesy, predict.*

praecipes -is = praeceps; q.v.

praecĭpio -cĭpĕre -cēpi -ceptum, *to take before, receive in advance*; iter, *to get the start*; mentally, *to anticipate; to instruct, advise, warn.* N. of partic. as subst. **praeceptum** -i, *a command, rule, injunction.*

praecĭpito -are: transit. *to cast headlong down; to hurry along*; intransit. *to fall headlong, rush down,* Adv. from pres. partic., **praecĭpĭtantĕr,** *headlong.*

praecĭpŭus -a -um, *peculiar, special; excellent, distinguished, extraordinary*, as legal term *received beforehand.* N. as subst. **praecĭpŭum** -i, *pre-eminence, superiority.* Adv. **praecĭpŭē,** *especially, chiefly, particularly.*

praecīsus -a -um partic. from praecido; q.v.

praeclārus -a -um, *very bright, very clear; striking, beautiful; remarkable, excellent, famous*; in bad sense, *notorious.* Adv. **praeclārē,** *very clearly; admirably, excellently.*

praeclūdo -clūdĕre -clūsi -clūsum, *to close in front, shut up, make inaccessible.*

praeco -ōnis, m. *a public crier, herald.*

praecōgĭto -are, *to consider carefully beforehand.*

praecognosco -cognoscĕre -cognĭtum, *to learn beforehand.*

praecŏlo -cŏlĕre -cultum, *to cultivate before*; partic. **praecultus** -a -um, *cultivated, adorned.*

praecompŏsĭtus -a -um, *composed beforehand, studied.*

praecōnĭus -a -um, *belonging to a praeco or crier.* N. as subst. **praecōnĭum** -i, *the office of a crier*; hence, *publishing, making known; a public commendation.*

praeconsūmo -sūmĕre -sumptum, *to use up beforehand.*

praecontrecto -are, *to handle beforehand.*

praecordĭa -ōrum, n. pl. *the midriff, diaphragm; the stomach; the breast, heart* (as seat of passions).

praecorrumpo -rumpĕre -ruptum, *to bribe beforehand.*

praecox -cócis and **praecŏquis** -e, *ripe before the time, premature.*

praecultus -a -um, partic. from praecolo; q.v.

praecurro -currĕre -cŭcurri and -curri -cursum, *to run before, go on ahead*; in time, *to precede*; in quality, *to surpass.* N. pl. of partic. as subst. **praecurrentia** -ium, *antecedents.*

praecursio -ōnis, f. *going before, running ahead*; rhet., *preparation of the hearer.*

praecursor -ōris, m. *a forerunner*; milit., *vanguard, advance-guard; spy, scout.*

praecursōrĭus -a -um, *sent in advance.*

praecŭtio -cŭtĕre -cussi -cussum, *to shake before, brandish before.*

praeda -ae, f. *spoils of war, plunder, booty*; of animals, *prey*; in gen., *plunder, gain.*

praedābundus -a -um, *plundering.*

praedamno -are, *to condemn before*; spem, *to give up hope.*

praedātĭo -ōnis, f. *plundering, pillaging.*

praedātor -ōris, m. *plunderer, robber; poet, hunter.*

praedātōrius -a -um, *plundering, predatory.*

praedēlasso -are, *to weary beforehand.*

praedestīno -are, *to appoint beforehand.*

praediātor -ōris, m. *a buyer of landed estates.*

praediātōrius -a -um, *relating to the sale of land.*

praedicābilis -e, *praiseworthy.*

praedicātio -ōnis, f. *making publicly known, proclamation; praising, commending.*

praedicātor -ōris, m. *a praiser, commender, public eulogist.*

¹**praedico** -are, *to make publicly known, publish, proclaim, declare; to praise, commend; to boast.*

²**praedico** -dīcĕre -dixi -dictum, *to say or name beforehand; to predict, foretell, prophesy; to warn, admonish, instruct.* Hence n. of partic. as subst. **praedictum** -i, *a prophecy, prediction; an order, command; a previous agreement.*

praedictio -ōnis, f. *prophesying, predicting;* rhet. *premising.*

praedictum -i, n. subst. from praedico; q.v.

praediŏlum -i, n. *a small estate, little farm.*

praedisco -ĕre, *to learn before.*

praedispŏsitus -a -um, *arranged at intervals beforehand.*

praedītus -a -um, *endowed, furnished, provided.*

praedium -i, n. *a farm, landed estate.*

praedīvēs -ĭtis, *very rich.*

praedo -ōnis, m. *robber, plunderer.*

praedŏcĕo -dŏcēre -doctum *to teach before.*

praedor -ari. dep. *to plunder, rob; to carry off.*

praedūco -dūcĕre -duxi -ductum *to lead forward, bring in front.*

praedulcis -e, *very sweet.*

praedūrus -a -um, *very hard, very strong.*

praeēminĕo -ēre, *to project; to excel.*

praeĕo -ire -ivi and -ii -itum, *to go before, precede; hence to go over beforehand verbally, say in advance, dictate; to order, command.*

praefātio -ōnis, f. *saying beforehand; a religious or legal form of words, formula; a preface, introduction.*

praefectūra -ae, f. *the office of superintendent;* esp. *a subordinate provincial command.* Transf., *a town or district governed by a praefectus.*

praefectus -a -um, partic. from praeficio; q.v.

praefĕro -ferre -tūli -lātum. (1) *carry in front; to show, display; to prefer; to anticipate.* (2) *to carry by;* praeferri, *to ride by.*

praefĕrox -ōcis, *very bold, impetuous.*

praeferrātus -a -um, *tipped with iron.*

praefervidus -a -um, *burning hot, very hot.*

praefestīno -are, *to hasten prematurely; to hasten by.*

praeficio -ficĕre -fēci -fectum, *to set over, appoint as superintendent.* M. of

partic. as subst. **praefectus** -i, *an overseer, superintendent, civil* or *military officer;* praefectus urbis, *governor of the city* (Rome).

praefīdens -entis, *over-confident.*

praefīgo -figĕre -fixi -fixum, *to fix in front, fasten before; to tip, point with; to pierce through, transfix.*

praefīnio -ire, *to fix, prescribe, appoint beforehand.*

praeflōro -are, *to deprive of blossom;* fig., *to diminish, lessen.*

praeflŭo -flŭĕre, *to flow past.*

praefōco -are, *to choke, suffocate.*

praefŏdio -fŏdĕre -fōdi -fossum, *to dig in front of; to bury previously.*

praefor -fāri -fātus, dep. *to speak before, to say beforehand, esp.* of prayers; divos, *to invoke.*

praefrigidus -a -um, *very cold.*

praefringo -fringĕre -frēgi -fractum, *to break off in front;* partic. **praefractus** -a -um, *of style, abrupt, disconnected;* of character, *stern, harsh;* adv. **praefractē.**

praefulcio -fulcire -fulsi -fultum, *to support, prop up; to use as a prop.*

praefulgĕo -fulgēre -fulsi, *to gleam, shine forth;* with dat., *to outshine.*

praegĕlidus -a -um, *very cold.*

praegestio -ire, *to desire exceedingly.*

praegnans -antis, *pregnant; full.*

praegrācilis -e, *very slim, lank.*

praegrăvis -e, *very heavy; unwieldy, wearisome; stupefied.*

praegrăvo -are, *to press heavily upon, to weigh down, oppress; to outweigh.*

praegrĕdior -grĕdi -gressus, dep. *to go before, precede; to outstrip; to pass by, march by.*

praegressio -ōnis, f. *going before, precedence.*

praegustātor -ōris, m. *one who tastes before, a taster.*

praegusto -are, *to taste before.*

praeiăcĕo -ēre, *to lie before.*

praeiūdicium -i, n. *a previous judgment, preliminary decision or examination; a premature decision; an example, precedent.*

praeiūdico -are, *to decide beforehand, give a preliminary judgment.* Hence partic. **praeiūdicātus** -a -um, *previously decided;* opinio praeiudicata, *a prejudice.*

praeiŭvo -iŭvāre -iŭvi, *to assist before.*

praelābor -lābi -lapsus, dep. *to glide past before or along.*

praelambo -ĕre, *to lick before, taste before.*

praelĕgo -legĕre -lēgi -lectum. (1) *to read out as a teacher, to lecture upon.* (2) *to sail past, coast along.*

praeligo -are, *to bind in front; to bind up.*

praelongus -a -um, *very long.*

praelŏquor -lŏqui -lŏcūtus, dep. *to speak beforehand or first.*

praelūcĕo -lūcēre -luxi, *to shine or carry a light before;* with dat., *to outshine, surpass.*

praelūsio -ōnis, f. *prelude.*

praelustris -e, *very fine.*

praemando -are, *to order beforehand;* n. pl. of partic. as subst. **praeman-dāta** -orum, *a warrant of arrest.*

praemātūrus -a -um, *too early, premature.*

praemĕdĭcātus -a -um, *protected by medicine or charms.*

praemĕdĭtātĭo -ōnis, f. *considering beforehand.*

praemĕdĭtor -ari, dep. *to practise or consider beforehand;* perf. partic., in pass. sense, **praemĕdĭtātus** -a -um, *considered beforehand.*

praemĕtŭo -ĕre, *to fear beforehand, be apprehensive;* adv. from partic. **praemĕtŭentĕr,** *apprehensively, anxiously.*

praemitto -mittĕre -mĭsi -missum, *to send before, send on ahead.*

praemĭum -i, n. *that which is taken first, the pick; a gift, award, reward, recompense;* poet., *notable exploit.*

praemōlestia -ae, f. *trouble beforehand.*

praemōlĭor -iri, dep. *to prepare beforehand.*

praemŏnĕo -ēre, *to warn, advise beforehand; to foretell, presage.*

praemŏnĭtus -ūs, m. *prediction, warning.*

praemonstro -are, *to point out the way; to prophesy, predict.*

praemordĕo -mordēre -mordi -morsum, *to bite off; to pilfer.*

praemŏrĭor -mŏri -mortŭus, dep. *to die prematurely.*

praemūnĭo -ire, *to fortify in front; to secure, make safe.*

praemūnĭtĭo -ōnis, f. *fortifying beforehand;* rhet., *preparation of one's hearers.*

praenăto -are, *to swim before or past.*

praenĭtĕo -ēre, *to outshine.*

praenōmen -inis, n. *the first name, usually standing before the gentile name* (e.g., Marcus, in M. T. Cicero).

praenosco -ĕre, *to get to know beforehand.*

praenōtĭo -ōnis, f. *a preconception, innate idea.*

praenūbĭlus -a -um, *very cloudy or dark.*

praenuntĭo -are, *to announce beforehand, foretell.*

praenuntĭus -a -um, *foretelling;* as subst. *a harbinger, token, omen.*

praeoccŭpo -are, *to seize beforehand, to preoccupy; to anticipate, prevent.*

praeopto -are, *to choose before, to prefer.*

praepando -ĕre, *to open wide in front, extend before.*

praepărātĭo -ōnis, f. *preparation.*

praepăro -are, *to make ready, prepare;* ex praeparato, *by arrangement.*

praepĕdĭo -ire, *to entangle, shackle, fetter; to hinder, impede, obstruct.*

praependĕo -ēre, intransit., *to hang before; hang in front.*

praepĕs -pĕtis, *rapidly flying, swift;* m. and f. as subst., *a bird,* esp. *a bird of good omen.*

praepĭlātus -a -um, *having a button in front* (of foils, etc.).

praepinguis -e, *very fat or rich.*

praepollĕo -ēre, *to be very or mor. powerful.*

praepondĕro -are, *to outweigh, to turi the scale.*

praepōno -pōnĕre -pŏsŭi -pŏsĭtum *to put before; to put over, set over a: commander,* etc.; *to prefer.* Henc: m. of partic., as subst. **praepŏsĭtus** -i *a commander.*

praeporto -are, *to carry before.*

praepŏsĭtĭo -ōnis, f. *placing before, preferring, preference;* gram., *a pre: position.*

praepossum -posse -pŏtŭi, *to have th: chief power.*

praepostĕrus -a -um, *having the las: first, inverted, perverse;* adv. **prae: postĕrē.**

praepŏtens -entis, *very powerful.*

praeprŏpĕrantĕr, *very hastily.*

praeprŏpĕrus -a -um, *over-hasty precipitate;* adv. **praeprŏpĕrē.**

praequam; see prae.

praequĕror -quĕri -questus, dep. tc *complain beforehand.*

praerādĭo -are, *to outshine.*

praerăpĭdus -a -um, *very rapid.*

praerĭgesco -rīgescĕre -rīgŭi, *to grou: very stiff.*

praerĭpĭo -rĭpĕre -rĭpŭi -reptum, *to snatch before somebody else; to carry off before the time; to anticipate, forestall.*

praerōdo -rōdĕre -rōdi -rōsum, *to gnaw off, bite through.*

praerŏgātīvus -a -um, *asked before others* (for vote, opinion, etc.); f. as subst. **praerŏgātīva** -ae, f. *the tribe or century voting first in the* comitia; hence *the first century's vote;* in gen., *a previous choice; a sure sign, indica-tion.*

praerumpo -rumpĕre -rūpi -ruptum *to break off in front.*

Hence partic. **praeruptus** -a -um, *broken off;* of places, *steep, pre-cipitous;* of character, *headstrong, hasty.*

[1]**praes** praedis, m. *a surety, security, one who stands bail.*

[2]**praes,** adv. *at hand.*

praesaepes (praesaepis) -is, f. **prae-saepe** -is, n. and **praesaepium** -i, n. *an enclosure; a crib, manger, stall; a hive; a haunt, lodging, tavern.*

praesaepio, *to block up in front.*

praesăgĭo -ire, *to presage, forebode, have a presentiment of.*

praesăgĭtĭo -ōnis, f. *foreboding, pre-sentiment.*

praesăgĭum -i, n. *presage, presentiment, foreboding; prediction.*

praesăgus -a -um, *foreboding; pre-dicting.*

praescisco -ĕre, *to find out beforehand.*

praescĭus -a -um, *knowing beforehand, prescient.*

praescrībo -scrībĕre -scripsi -scriptum, *to write before, set out in writing; to put forward or use as a pretext; to outline; dictate; to prescribe, ordain, direct beforehand.* Hence n. partic. as subst. **praescriptum** -i, *a prescribed limit, regulation, rule.*

praescriptio -ōnis, f. *a title, inscription, introduction; a precept, rule; a pretext; legal, an objection, demurrer.*

praeséco -sĕcare -sĕcŭi -sectum, *to cut in front, cut short.*

praesens -entis, partic. from praesum; q.v.

praesensio -ōnis, f. *a presentiment, foreboding; preconception.*

praesentia -ae, f. *presence;* animi, *presence of mind;* in praesentia, *for the present;* sometimes *power, effect.*

praesentio -sentire -sensi -sensum, *to feel beforehand, have a presentiment of.*

praesertim, *especially, chiefly.*

praesēs -sĭdis, *sitting before, protecting.* As subst. *a protector;* also *a chief, ruler, president.*

praesĭdĕo -sĭdēre -sēdi -sessum, *to sit before; to watch over, protect, guard; to preside over, manage, direct.* M. of partic. as subst. **praesĭdens** -entis, *a president, ruler.*

praesĭdĭārius -a -um, *on guard.*

praesĭdĭum -i, n. *sitting before; protection, help, support.* Milit., *guard, escort; a garrison; a post.*

praesignĭfico -are, *to indicate beforehand.*

praesignis -e, *distinguished, remarkable.*

praesŏno -sŏnare -sŏnŭi, *to sound forth.*

praespargo -ĕre, *to scatter in front.*

praestăbilis -e, *distinguished, pre-eminent;* in compar., *preferable.*

praestans -antis, partic. from praesto; q.v.

praestantia -ae, f. *superiority, excellence.*

praestēs -stĭtis, *protecting.*

praestigiae -ārum, f. pl. *deception, illusion, juggling.*

praestĭtŭo -stĭtŭĕre -stĭtŭi -stĭtūtum, *to prescribe, appoint beforehand.*

'praestō, adv. *present, at hand ready;* with esse, *to be at hand, be ready to help.*

'praesto -stare -stĭti -stĭtum. (1) *to stand before; to be outstanding, surpass, excel;* impers., praestat, *it is better, preferable.* (2) transit., *to become surety for, answer for, be responsible for.* Transf., *to perform, execute, fulfil; to show, manifest, exhibit; to offer, present;* with se and acc. *to show oneself, behave as.*
Hence partic. **praestans** -antis, *excellent, distinguished eminent.*

praestŏlor -ari, dep., *to wait for, expect.*

praestringo -stringĕre -strinxi -strictum, *to bind up, in front.* Transf., *to make blunt or dull.*

praestrŭo -strŭĕre -struxi -structum. (1) *to build in front; to block up, make impassable.* (2) *to build beforehand; to prepare.*

praesŭl -sŭlis, c. and **praesultător** -ōris, m. *a dancer.*

praesulto -are, *to leap or dance before.*

praesum -esse -fŭi, *to be before; to be over, preside over; to take the lead.*
Hence partic. (with compar.) **praesens** -entis, *present, at hand, in* space or time; in praesens (tempus), *for the present time;* esp. *immediate, ready; effective, powerful, helpful, resolute, determined.*

praesūmo -sūmĕre -sumpsi -sumptum, *to take beforehand; to anticipate; to take for granted.*
Hence partic. **praesumptus** -a -um, *taken for granted, presumed.*

praesŭtus -a -um, *sewn over in front.*

praetempto -are, *to try, test beforehand.*

praetendo -tendĕre -tendi -tentum, *to stretch or hold out;* pass., praetendi, *of places, to lie before or in front.* Transf., *to hold out as a pretext, allege in excuse.*

praetento = praetempto; q.v.

praetĕpesco -tĕpescĕre -tĕpŭi, *to glow beforehand.*

praeter. Adv., *except.* Prep. with acc., *beyond, past; beside, contrary to, beside; more than; except;* in addition to.

praetĕrăgo -ĕre, *to drive past, drive by.*

praetĕrĕā, *besides, further; after this, hereafter.*

praetĕrĕo -ire -ivi and oftener -ii -itum, *to go by, pass by.* Transf., *to escape the notice of a person; to pass by, pass over, omit; to surpass, outstrip; to transgress.*
Hence partic. **praetĕritus** -a -um, *past, gone by.*

praetĕrĕquito -are, *to ride past, ride by.*

praeterfĕro -ferre -tŭli -lātum, *to carry past.*

praeterflŭo -flŭĕre, *to flow past, flow by.*

praetergrĕdior -grĕdi -gressus, dep. *to pass by, go beyond.*

praetĕritus -a -um, partic. from praetereo; q.v.

praeterlābor -lābi -lapsus, dep. *to glide by, flow by, slip away.*

praetermĕo -are, *to pass by.*

praetermissio -ōnis, f. *leaving out, omission; passing over, neglecting.*

praetermitto -mittĕre -misi -missum, *to let pass, let go by; to neglect, omit; to pass over, overlook.*

praeterquam or **praeter quam**, *more than, beyond;* after neg., *except;* with quod, *apart from the fact that.*

praetervectio -ōnis, f. *a passing place.*

praetervĕhor -vĕhi -vectus sum, *to ride by, be carried past, march past, pass by.*

praetervŏlo -are, *to fly past; to slip by, escape.*

praetexo -texĕre -texŭi -textum, *to weave in front, form a border; to adorn; to cover, conceal; to put forward as a pretext.*
Hence partic. **praetextus** -a -um, *bordered,* esp. of the toga. F. as subst. **praetexta** -ae, f. *a toga bordered with purple, worn by magistrates and boys;* also praetexta (fabula), *a tragedy with Roman characters.* N. as subst. **praetextum** -i, *a pretence, pretext.*

praetextātus -a -um, *wearing the toga praetexta; veiled; licentious.*

praetextŭ, abl. sing. m. *in outward appearance; under a pretext.*

praetinctus -a -um, *moistened beforehand.*

praetor -ōris, m. *leader, chief; a magistrate,* esp. *one who helped the consuls by administering justice, commanding armies,* etc.

praetōriānus -a -um, *belonging to the imperial body-guard, praetorian.*

praetōrius -a -um. (1) *relating to the praetor, praetorian.* (2) *relating to any general* or *commander*; *praetoria navis, flagship*; *cohors, the general's body-guard.* As subst.: m. **praetōrius** -i, *an ex-praetor* or *man of praetorian rank*; n. **praetōrium** -i, *the official residence of the praetor* or *propraetor; a palace;* also *the headquarters in a Roman camp.*

praetrĕpido -are, *to be hasty* or *impatient.*

praetūra -ae, f. *the office of praetor.*

praeumbro -are, *to overshadow; to obscure.*

praeustus -a -um, *burnt at the end* or *tip; frost-bitten.*

praevălĕo -vălēre -vălŭi, *to be very strong; to prevail, get the upper hand.*

praevălĭdus -a -um, *very strong; terra, too productive.*

praevārĭcātĭo -ōnis, f. *collusion.*

praevārĭcātor -ōris, m. *an advocate guilty of collusion.*

praevārĭcor -ari, dep. of an advocate, *to have a secret understanding with the other side, to be guilty of collusion.*

praevĕhor -vĕhi -vectus sum, *to ride* (or *run*) *before* or *past.*

praevĕnĭo -vĕnire -vēni -ventum, *to come before, anticipate, get the start of.*

praeverro -ĕre, *to sweep before.*

praeverto (praevorto) -vertĕre -verti -versum, and **praevertor** -verti -versus sum; of preference, *to put first, take first, turn first to*; of early action, *to anticipate, outstrip, forestall; to surprise, preoccupy.*

praevĭdĕo -vĭdēre -vīdi -visum, *to see before, foresee.*

praevĭtĭo -are, *to corrupt beforehand.*

praevĭus -a -um, *going before, preceding.*

praevŏlo -are, *to fly before.*

pragmătĭcus -a -um, *skilled in business;* m. as subst. *a person who supplied speakers with material.*

prandĕo prandēre prandi pransum, *to take lunch; to lunch upon;* perf. partic. in act. sense **pransus** -a -um, *having lunched; well-fed.*

prandĭum -i, n. *a late breakfast* or *lunch.*

pransus -a -um, partic. from prandeo; q.v.

prăsĭnus -a -um, *leek-green.*

prātensis -e, *of a meadow.*

prātŭlum -i, n. *a little meadow.*

prātum -i, n. *a meadow; meadow-grass.*

prāvĭtās -ātis, f. *crookedness, deformity; perversity, depravity.*

prāvus -a -um, adj. *crooked, deformed; perverse; depraved.* Adv. **prăvē.**

Praxĭtĕlēs -is and -i, m. *a sculptor of Athens.*

prĕcārĭus -a -um, *begged for,* or *got by entreaty; uncertain, precarious.* N. abl. as adv. **prĕcārĭo,** *by entreaty.*

prĕcātĭo -ōnis, f. *begging, request prayer.*

prĕces; see prex.

prĕcĭae -arum, f. *a kind of vine.*

prĕcor -ari, dep. *to beg, entreat, pray, invoke.*

prĕhendo prĕhendĕre prĕhendi prehensum and prendo prendĕre prendi prensum, *to lay hold of, seize, grasp; to catch, detain, arrest; to take in,* mentally or by the senses.

prĕhenso and **prenso** -are, *to lay hold of, clutch at.* Transf., *to canvass for votes.*

prēlum -i, n. *a wine* or *olive-press.*

prĕmo prĕmĕre pressi pressum, *to press; to step on, lie on; to hug, keep close to; to press hard, squeeze; to pursue closely, press upon; to press down, strike down; to disparage, slander; to press together, close; to check, curb.* Hence partic. **pressus** -a -um, *subdued, measured;* of style, *compressed, concise.* Adv. **pressē,** *accurately, precisely, distinctly;* of style, *briefly, concisely.*

prendo = prehendo; q.v.

prensātĭo -ōnis, f. *canvassing for office.*

prenso = prehenso; q.v.

pressĭo -ōnis, f. *leverage* or *means of leverage.*

presso -are, *to press.*

¹pressus -a -um, partic. from premo; q.v.

²pressus -ūs, m. *pressing, pressure.*

prestĕr -ēris, m. *a fiery whirlwind* or *a waterspout.*

prĕtĭōsus -a -um, *costly, precious, dear;* of persons, *extravagant.* Adv. **prĕtĭōsē.**

prĕtĭum -i, n. *worth, value, price;* esse in pretio, *to be prized;* operae pretium, *worth while.* Transf., *prize, reward; a ransom; a bribe; punishment.*

prex prĕcis (usually plur.) f. *request entreaty;* esp. *prayer to a god;* sometimes *a curse, execration.*

Prĭāmus -i, m. *the last king of Troy;* adj. **Prĭămēïus** -a -um.

Prĭāpus -i, m. *the god of gardens and vineyards.*

prīdem, *long ago, long since.*

prīdĭē, *on the day before.*

prīmaevus -a -um, *young, youthful.*

prīmāni -orum, m. pl. *soldiers of the first legion.*

prīmārĭus -a -um, *in the first rank, distinguished.*

prīmĭgĕnus -a -um, *original, primitive.*

prīmĭpīlārĭs -is, m. *the centurion of the first maniple of the triarii, the chief centurion of a legion.*

prīmĭpīlus; see pilus.

prīmĭtĭae -arum, f. *first-fruits.*

prīmĭtŭs, *first, for the first time.*

prīmordĭum -i, n. *first beginning, origin;* plur. often = *atoms.*

prīmōris -e, *first, foremost; at the tip;* primoribus labris, *superficially;* of rank, *first, most distinguished.*

prīmus; see prior.

princeps -cĭpis, adj. *first, foremost.* As subst., *leader;* polit., often as a title of the Roman emperor; milit., plur., principes, *the second line in a Roman army, between* hastati *and* triarii.

principālis -e. (1) *first, in time or rank.* (2) *of a prince.* (3) *of the* principia *in a Roman camp.*

principātus -ūs, m. (1) *first place, pre-eminence; rule, dominion.* (2) *beginning, origin.*

principĭālis -e, *original.*

princĭpium -i, n. *beginning, origin; groundwork, foundation;* in plur., *elements, first principles;* polit., *the tribe or curia which voted first;* milit., in plur., *the front ranks or the head-quarters in a camp.*

prior prius, genit. -ōris, compar. adj., *fore, former,* of place or time; *higher in importance;* m. pl. as subst., *ancestors.* N. acc. as adv. **prius,** *before, previously; formerly; sooner, rather;* prius quam, *or* priusquam, conj., *before.* Superl. **primus** -a -um, *first, foremost,* of place or time; *of rank,* etc., *first, most distinguished;* (partes) primae, *the leading part;* in primis, *especially.* N. acc. as adv. **primum,** *at first or for the first time.* N. abl. **primo,** *at first.*

priscus -a -um, *ancient, antique; of the old school, venerable; former, previous.* Adv. **priscē,** *in the old-fashioned way.*

pristĭnus -a -um, *former, previous, earlier.*

prius; see prior.

prīvātim, *privately, as a private person, in private life; at home.*

prīvātio -ōnis, f. *freeing, release.*

prīvigna -ae, f. *stepdaughter.*

prīvignus -i, m. *stepson.*

prīvilēgium i, n. *a special law, private law.*

prīvo -are, *to strip, deprive; to free, release.*

Hence partic. **prīvātus** -a -um, as adj., *private, unofficial;* in privato, *in private;* (vir) privatus, *a private person.*

prīvus -a -um, *single, every;* distributively, *one each; particular, special, one's own;* with genit., *deprived of.*

¹prō, prep., with abl., *before, in front of; for, on behalf of, in favour of; in place of; like, as good as;* se pro cive gerere, *to behave as a citizen; as a reward for; in proportion to, according to, by virtue of;* pro virili parte, *to the best of one's abilities;* pro eo quantum, *in proportion as.*

²pro! (proh!), interj. *oh! ah!*

prōăvia -ae, f. *a great-grandmother.*

prōăvītus -a -um, *ancestral.*

prōăvus -i, m. *a great-grandfather; an ancestor, forefather.*

prŏbābilis -e, (1) *probable, credible.* (2) *acceptable, good.* Adv. **prŏbābilitĕr,** *probably, credibly.*

prŏbābilitās -ātis, f. *probability, credibility.*

prŏbātio -ōnis, f. *proving, trial, examination; approval, proof, demonstration.*

prŏbātor -ōris, m. *one who approves, an approver.*

prŏbitās -ātis, f. *honesty, uprightness.*

prŏbo -are, *to make or find good; to approve, pronounce good;* with dat., *to recommend to;* with abl., *to judge by a standard;* in gen., *to show, prove, demonstrate.*

Hence partic. **prŏbātus** -a -um, *found good, approved; acceptable.*

prŏbrōsus -a -um, *shameful, disgraceful, infamous.*

probrum -i, n. *abuse, reproach; ground for reproach, disgrace; infamous conduct, esp. unchastity.*

prŏbus -a -um, *good, excellent, fine; morally good, upright, virtuous.* Adv. **prŏbē,** *well, rightly, properly.*

prŏcācitās -ātis f. *shamelessness, impudence.*

prŏcax -cācis, *shameless, bold, impudent;* adv. **prŏcācĭtĕr.**

prōcēdo -cēdĕre -cessi -cessum, *to go ahead, proceed, advance, continue; to come out, go out;* of actions, etc., *to turn out, result;* sometimes *to turn out well, prosper.*

prōcella -ae, f. *a storm, tempest, gale;* in fighting, *charge, onset, wave.*

prōcellōsus -a -um, *stormy, tempestuous.*

prōcer -ēris, m. *a chief noble, prince.*

prōcērĭtās -ātis, f. *height, length.*

prōcērus -a -um, *tall, long;* compar. adv. **prōcērius,** *farther forward.*

prōcessio -ōnis, f. *a (military) advance*

prōcessus -ūs, m. *advance, progress.*

prōcido -cidĕre -cĭdi, *to fall forwards.*

prōcinctū, abl. sing. m. *being girded or equipped; readiness for battle.*

proclāmātor -ōris, m. *a bawler.*

proclāmo -are, *to call out, cry out.*

prōclīno -are. *to bend over, incline forwards.*

prōclivis -e *and* **prōclīvus** -a -um, *inclined forwards, sloping downwards; proclive,* or *pro proclive, downwards.* Transf., *inclined, ready, prone; easy to do.*

prōclīvĭtās -ātis, f. *a slope.* Transf., *inclination, tendency.*

prōclīvus = proclivis; q.v.

Procnē (Prognē) -ēs, f. *wife of Tereus, changed into a swallow.*

prŏco -are *and* **prŏcor** -ari, dep. *to ask, demand.*

prōconsul -sŭlis, m. (also **prō consŭlĕ),** *a proconsul, one who serves as a consul,* in command of any army, or as governor of a province.

prōconsŭlāris -e, *proconsular.*

prōconsŭlātus -ūs, m. *the office of proconsul.*

prōcrastinātio -ōnis. f. *procrastination.*

prōcrastĭno -are, *to put off till tomorrow, defer.*

prōcrĕātĭo -ōnis, f. *begetting, procreation.*

prōcrĕātor -ōris, m. *begetter, creator.*

prōcrĕātrix -icis, f. *mother.*

prōcrĕo -are, *to beget; to produce, cause make*

prōcresco -ĕre, *to come forth, arise; to increase.*

Procrustēs -ae, m. *a robber killed by Theseus.*

prōcŭbo -are, *to lie stretched out.*

prōcūdo -cūdĕre -cūdi -cūsum, *to hammer out, forge; to form, produce.*

prŏcŭl, *far; at, to, or from a distance.*

prōculco -are, *to tread on, trample down.*

prōcumbo -cumbĕre -cŭbŭi -cŭbĭtum, *to lean or bend forward; to fall down, sink down, be laid low.*

prōcūrātĭo -ōnis, f. *taking care, management, administration.* Esp. (1) *the office of imperial procurator.* (2) *an attempt to propitiate a deity.*

prōcūrātor -ōris, m. *a manager, bailiff, agent, factor; regni, a viceroy; under the empire, a financial agent or under-governor.*

prōcūrātrix -tricis, f. *she that governs.*

prōcūro -are, *to take care of, look after; to manage, administer; to be a procurator; to sacrifice in order to avert evil.*

prōcurro -currĕre -curri and -cŭcurri -cursum, *to run forward; of places, to project, jut out.*

prōcursātĭo -ōnis, f. *running forward, skirmishing.*

prōcursātor -ōris, m. *a skirmisher.*

prōcurso -are, *to run forward;* milit. *to skirmish.*

prōcursus -ūs, m. *running forward;* milit., *advance, charge.*

prōcurvus -a -um, *bent forward.*

¹prŏcus -i, m. = procer, q.v.

²prŏcus -i, m. *a wooer, suitor; a canvasser.*

prōdĕo -ire -ii -itum, *to advance, go forward; to project; to come out, appear.*

prōdĭco -dicĕre -dixi -dictum, *to put off.*

prōdictātor -ōris, m. *one who acts as dictator.*

prōdĭgentĭa -ae, f. *profusion, prodigality.*

prōdĭgĭālis -e, *dealing in wonders;* adv. prōdĭgĭālĭtĕr, *wonderfully.*

prōdĭgĭōsus -a -um, *unnatural, wonderful.*

prōdĭgĭum -i, n. *a prodigy, portent; an enormity, an unnatural thing; a monster.*

prōdĭgo -ĭgĕre -ēgi -actum, *to drive forth; to spend, waste.*

prōdĭgus -a -um, *profuse, extravagant; rich, abound in.* Adv. prōdĭgē.

prōdĭtĭo -ōnis, f. *betrayal, treason.*

prōdĭtor -ōris, m. *a betrayer, traitor.*

prōdo -dĕre -dĭdi -dĭtum. (1) *to put forth, bring forth; to show, publish; to appoint.* (2) *to forsake, betray.* (3) *to hand over, deliver, transmit.*

prōdŏcĕo -ēre, *to teach, inculcate.*

prōdrŏmus -i, m. *forerunner.*

prōdūco -dūcĕre -duxi -ductum, *to bring forward, bring out, extend; to produce, bring up, advance, promote; to divulge, bring to light;* in pronunciation, *to lengthen out, make long;* in time, *to prolong, continue;* also *to put off, postpone.*

Hence partic. prōductus -a -um, *extended, lengthened, prolonged;* of syllables, *pronounced long;* n. pl. as subst. *preferable things* (in the Stoic philosophy). Adv. prōductē, *long* (of pronunciation).

prōductĭo -ōnis, f. *extending, lengthening, prolonging.*

proelĭātor -ōris, m. *warrior.*

proelĭor -ari, dep. *to give battle, fight, strive.*

proelĭum -i, n. *battle, fight, strife.*

prŏfāno -are, *to profane, desecrate.*

prŏfānus -a -um, *not sacred; uninitiated; ordinary, common, profane; impious.*

prŏfectĭo -ōnis, f. *departure; source, origin.*

prŏfecto, *truly, really, indeed.*

prōfĕro -ferre -tŭli -lātum. (1) *to bring forth, bring forward, offer to publish, bring to light, reveal; to produce, cite, mention.* (2) *to advance, bring forward, impel.* (3) *to enlarge, extend;* in time, *to lengthen;* also *to put off, postpone.*

prŏfessĭo -ōnis, f. *declaration, profession.* Transf., *a register of persons and property; an occupation, art, profession.*

prŏfessor -ōris, m. *an authority, expert.*

prŏfessōrĭus -a -um, *authoritative.*

prŏfestus -a -um, *not kept as a festival, common.*

prōfĭcĭo -fĭcĕre -fēci -fectum: of persons, *to make progress, advance;* of things, *to be of use, assist, help.*

prŏfĭciscor -fĭcisci -fectus, dep. *to start forward, set out, depart; to arise or spring from an origin.*

prŏfĭtĕor -fĭtēri -fessus, dep. *to acknowledge, confess; to profess or declare oneself anything; to profess a science, art, etc.; to make any public statement; to offer, promise.*

prōflĭgātor -ōris, m. *a spendthrift.*

prōflĭgo -are, *to overthrow, overcome, ruin; to lower, debase; to bring almost to an end, nearly finish.*

Hence partic. prōflĭgātus -a -um, *ruined, degraded.*

prōflo -are, *to blow forth, breathe forth.*

prōflŭentĭa -ae, f. *fluency.*

prōflŭo -flŭĕre -fluxi fluxum, *to flow forth; to proceed.*

Hence partic. prōflŭens -entis, *flowing;* f. as subst. (sc. aqua), *running water;* of style, *flowing, fluent.* Adv. prōflŭentĕr.

prōflŭvĭum -i, n. *flowing forth.*

prōfor -fari -fatus, dep. *to say, speak, declare.*

prōfŭgĭo -fŭgĕre -fūgi: intransit., *to flee away, escape;* transit., *to flee away from.*

prŏfŭgus -a -um, *fleeing, fugitive; banished; migratory.*

prŏfundo -fundĕre -fūdi -fūsum, *to pour forth, shed, cause to flow;* pass., *profundi, to stream forth.* Transf., *to stretch at full length; to release, discharge; to utter; to spend, sacrifice, give up; to lavish, squander.* Hence partic. **prŏfūsus** -a -um, *lavish, extravagant.* Adv. **prŏfūsē,** *in disorder; lavishly, extravagantly.*

prŏfundus -a -um, *deep, profound; high; thick, dense; boundless.* N. as subst. **prŏfundum** -i, *depth, abyss;* poet., *the sea.*

prŏfūsus -a -um, partic. from profundo; q.v.

prŏgĕner -i, *a grand-daughter's husband.*

prŏgĕnĕro -are, *to engender, produce.*

prŏgĕnĭes -ēi, f. *descent, lineage; progeny, offspring, descendants.*

prŏgĕnĭtor -ōris, m. *founder of a family, ancestor.*

prōgigno -gignĕre -gēnŭi -gĕnĭtum, *to engender, bring forth.*

prŏgnātus -a -um, *born, sprung from;* m. as subst., *a son.*

Prognē = Procne; q.v.

prŏgrĕdĭor -grĕdi -gressus, dep., *to go forth, go out; to go forwards, advance, proceed.*

prŏgressĭo -ōnis, f. *advance, progress; increase;* rhet., *climax.*

prŏgressus -ūs, m. *going forwards, advance, progress; increase.*

proh! = pro!; q.v.

prŏhĭbĕo -ēre, *to hold back, restrain, hinder; to forbid, prohibit; to preserve, defend, protect.*

prŏhĭbĭtĭo -ōnis, f. *hindering, prohibition.*

prōĭcĭo -icĕre -iēci -iectum, *to throw forth; to fling forward; to put forward, cause to project* (pass., *to project); to fling out, throw away, abandon; to defer, put off.* Hence partic. **prōiectus** -a -um, *jutting forward, prominent; stretched out, prostrate;* hence *abject, contemptible, downcast;* with ad, *addicted to.*

prōĭectĭo -ōnis, f., *throwing forward, stretching out.*

prōĭectū, abl. sing. m. *by jutting out.*

prŏinde and **prŏin** (o and i sometimes scanned as one syllable), *consequently, therefore;* foll. by ut or quam, *just as;* foll. by quasi, ac, ac si, *just as if.*

prōlābor -lābi -lapsus dep. (1) *to glide forward, slip along or out.* (2) *to fall forward, fall down.*

prōlapsĭo -ōnis, f. *slipping, sliding.*

prōlātĭo -ōnis, f. *bringing forward, mentioning; an extension; putting off, deferring.*

prōlāto -are, *to extend, enlarge, lengthen; to put off, defer.*

prōlecto -are, *to entice, allure.*

prōlēs -is, f. *offspring, descendants; posterity; the young men of a race; of plants, fruit.*

prōlētārĭus -i, m. *a citizen of the lowest class, serving the state only by begetting children.*

prōlĭcĭo -licĕre -lixi, *to lure forth, entice.*

prōlixus -a -um, *wide, broad, long.* Transf., *willing, obliging; favourable.* Adv. **prōlixē,** *freely; willingly.*

prŏlŏgus -i, m. *prologue.*

prōlŏquor -lŏqui -lŏcūtus, dep. *to speak out, say openly.*

prōlūdo -lūdĕre -lūsi -lūsum, *to play beforehand, to prelude.*

prōlŭo -lŭĕre -lŭi -lūtum, *to wash away or off; to wash clean.*

prōlūsĭo -ōnis, f. *a prelude, preliminary exercise.*

prōlŭvĭēs -ēi, f. *an inundation; scourings, discharge.*

prōmĕrĕo -ēre -ŭi -ĭtum and **prōmĕrĕor** -ēri -ĭtus, dep. *to deserve;* n. of partic. as subst. **prōmĕrĭtum** -i, *deserts, merit.*

Prōmēthĕus -ĕi and -ĕos, m. *Prometheus, punished for stealing fire from heaven and giving it to mankind;* adj. **Prōmēthĕus** -a -um.

prōmĭnĕo -ēre -ŭi, *to stand out, jut out, project, extend;* partic. **prōmĭnens** -entis, *jutting out, projecting;* n. as subst. *a projection.*

prōmiscus and **prōmiscŭus** -a -um, *mixed, indiscriminate, promiscuous; commonplace, usual.* Adv. **prōmiscē** and **prōmiscŭē.**

prōmissĭo -ōnis, f. *a promise.*

prōmissor -ōris, m. *a promiser.*

prōmitto -mittĕre -misi -missum, *to let go forward, send forth; to let grow; to promise, undertake.* Hence partic. **prōmissus** -a -um, *let grow, long, hanging down.* N. of partic. as subst. **prōmissum** -i, *a promise.*

prōmo prōmĕre prompsi promptum, *to bring out, produce; to bring forward, disclose, express.* Hence partic. **promptus** -a -um, *ready, at hand; easy; visible, apparent;* of persons, *prepared, resolute, prompt.* Adv. **promptē.**

prōmontŏrĭum -i, n. *a mountain ridge; a promontory.*

prōmŏvĕo -mŏvēre -mōvi -mōtum, *to move forwards, push onwards, make to advance; to extend; to postpone.*

promptū, abl. sing. m.: in promptu esse, *to be ready, easy,* or *manifest;* in promptu ponere, *to make manifest;* in promptu habere, *to have ready or have on show.*

promptus -a -um, partic. from promo; q.v.

prōmulgātĭo -ōnis, f. *publication, promulgation* (of a proposed law).

prōmulgo -are, *to publish, promulgate* (esp. a proposed law).

prōmulsis -idis, f. *hors d'oeuvres.*

prōmuntŭrĭum = promontorium; q.v.

prōmus -i, m. *a steward, butler.*

prōmūtŭus -a -um, *advanced, paid beforehand.*

prōnĕpōs -pōtis, m. *great-grandson.*

prōneptis -is, f. *great-granddaughter.*

prōnoea -ae, f. *providence.*

prōnŭba -ae, f. (1) *a matron attending a bride.* (2) *epithet of Juno, as the goddess presiding over marriage.*

prōnuntiātĭo -ōnis, f. *public declaration; the decision of a judge, a judgment;* in logic, *a proposition;* in rhetoric, *delivery.*

prōnuntiātor -ōris, m. *a relater.*

prōnuntĭo -are, *to make publicly known, declare;* in the senate, *to announce a resolution;* at a sale, *to make a statement as to defects;* rhet. *to declaim, recite, deliver.* N. of partic. as subst. **prōnuntiātum** -i, in logic, *a proposition.*

prōnŭrus -us, f. *a grandson's wife.*

prōnus -a -um, *inclined forward, stooping forward; rushing down or past; precipitous, steep.* Transf., *inclined, well-disposed, favourable; easy.* Adv. **prōnē,** *on a slope.*

prŏoemĭum -i, n. *preface, introduction, prelude.*

prōpāgātĭo -ōnis, f. *spreading, propagation; extension, enlargement.*

prōpāgātor -ōris, m. *an extender, enlarger.*

¹**prōpāgo** -are, *to spread propagate plants; to extend, enlarge, prolong.*

²**prōpāgo** -ĭnis, f. *a layer, slip or shoot* (esp. *of the vine*); *of men and animals, offspring, race, posterity.*

prōpălam, *publicly, in public.*

prōpătŭlus -a -um, *open, uncovered;* n. as subst. *an open place, unroofed space;* in propatulo, *publicly.*

prŏpē, adv. and prep; compar. **prŏpius;** superl. **prŏximē.** Adv. *near,* in space or time; *nearly;* propius, *more nearly, more closely;* proxime, of time, *just now.* Prep. with acc. *near to,* in space or time; in gen., *approximating to, not far from.*

prŏpēdĭem, *at an early date, very soon.*

prōpello -pellĕre -pŭli -pulsum, *to drive before one, drive forth or away.*

prōpĕmŏdō and **prōpĕmŏdum,** *almost, nearly.*

prōpendĕo -pendēre -pendi -pensum *to hang down; to preponderate; to incline, be favourable.*

Hence partic. **prōpensus** -a -um, *weighty; tending, inclined, disposed;* esp. *favourably disposed.* Adv. **prōpensē,** *readily, willingly.*

prōpensĭo -ōnis, f. *inclination, propensity.*

prŏpĕrantĕr, adv. from propero; q.v.

prŏpĕrantĭa -ae, f. *haste, rapidity.*

prŏpĕrātĭo -ōnis, f. *haste.*

prŏpĕro -are: intransit., *to hasten;* transit., *to hasten something, to accelerate, complete quickly.* Adv. from pres. partic. **prŏpĕrantĕr,** *hastily.* Past. partic. **prŏpĕrātus** -a -um, *hasty;* n. as subst. **prŏpĕrātum** -i, *haste;* abl. **prŏpĕrātō,** *in haste.*

Prŏpertĭus -i, m., Sex. Aurelius *a poet of the Augustan age.*

prōpĕrus -a -um, *quick, rapid, hasty* adv. **prōpĕrē**

prōpexus -a -um, *combed forward hanging down.*

prōpīno -are, *to drink to anyone.*

prōpinquĭtās -ātis, f. *nearness, prox imity; friendship or relationship.*

prōpinquo -are: intransit., *to com near, draw near, approach;* transit. *to bring near, hasten on.*

prōpinquus -a -um, *near, close neighbouring; similar; nearly relatea closely connected;* as subst., *a kinsman* Adv. **prōpinquē.**

prōpĭor -us, genit. -ōris, *nearer,* in spac or time (cf. prope); *more like; mor closely connected; more suitable* Superl. **proximus (proxŭmus)** -i -um, *very near, nearest;* in time *next, following,* or *most recent; ir rank,* etc., *next, next best; most like most nearly connected;* m. pl. as subst *near relations* or *close friends.*

prōpitĭo -are, *to soothe, appease.*

prōpitĭus -a -um, *favourable, gracious.*

prōpĭus, compar. of prope; q.v.

prōpōla -ae, m. *a retailer, huckster.*

prōpollŭo -ŭĕre, *to pollute worse.*

prōpōno -pōnĕre -pŏsŭi -pŏsĭtum, t put on view, expose, display; to publish, relate, tell; to propose promise, offer as a reward* or *hold ovei as a threat; to imagine, put before the mind; to propose to oneself purpose, intend.* N. of partic. as subst. **prōpŏsĭtum** -i, *a design, purpose; the subject* or *theme of a discourse; the first premiss of a syllogism.*

prōporrō, adv. *further, moreover, oi altogether.*

prōportĭo -ōnis, f. *proportion, analogy similarity.*

prōpŏsĭtĭo -ōnis, f. *a purpose; the subject of a discourse;* in logic, *the first proposition of a syllogism.*

prōpŏsĭtum -i, n. subst. from propono; q.v.

prōpraetor -ōris, m. (and **prō praetōre)** *a praetor's deputy; an ex-praetor,* sent as governor to a province or given a military command.

prōprĭĕtās -ātis, f. *a property, peculiarity; ownership.*

prōprĭtim, *peculiarly, specially.*

prōprĭus -a -um, *one's own, special, peculiar characteristic; lasting, permanent.* Hence adv. **prōprĭē,** *exclusively, peculiarly, characteristically; in a proper sense.*

propter, adv., *near, close by.* Prep. with acc. *near; on account of, because of.*

proptĕrĕā, adv. *on that account, therefore.*

prōpŭdĭum -i, n. *a shameful action; a wretch, villain.*

prōpugnācŭlum -i, n. *a fortification rampart, defence.*

prōpugnātĭo -ōnis, f. *defence.*

prōpugnātor -ōris, m. *a defender.*

prōpugno -are, *to skirmish in front; fight in defence, defend.*

prōpulso -are, *to drive back, repel, ward off.*

prō-quaestŏre, *an ex-quaestor who helped to govern a province.*

prōquam (or **prō quam**), *in proportion as, according as.*

prōra -ae, f. *the prow, bow of a ship;* poet., *a ship.*

prōrēpo -rēpĕre -repsi, *to creep forward, crawl forth.*

prōrēta -ae, and **prōrēus** -i, m. *a look-out man.*

prōrĭpĭo -rĭpĕre -rĭpŭi -reptum, *to snatch, tear, drag forth;* se proripere, *to rush forward.*

prērŏgātĭo -ōnis, f. *prolongation of a term of office; deferring.*

prōrŏgo -are, *to prolong; to defer, put off.*

prorsum and **prorsūs**, *forwards, straight ahead.* Transf., *utterly, wholly; in a word, to sum up.*

prorsus (**prōsus**) -a -um, *straight-forward; of style, in prose.*

prōrumpo -rumpĕre -rūpi -ruptum: transit., *to cause to break out, to thrust out;* prorupta audacia, *unbridled;* intransit., *to burst forth, break out.*

prōrŭo -rŭĕre -rŭi -rŭtum: intransit., *to rush forth, to fall down;* transit., *to fling forward or down, overthrow, destroy.*

prōsāpĭa -ae, f. *family, race, stock.*

proscaenĭum -i, n. *the stage of a theatre.*

proscindo -scindĕre -scĭdi -scissum, *to tear up; to break up fallow land, plough up.* Transf., *to censure, defame, satirize.*

proscrībo -scrībĕre -scripsi -scriptum, *to make publicly known, publish; to offer publicly for sale or hire, advertise; to confiscate; to proscribe, outlaw.*

proscriptĭo -ōnis, f. *an advertisement of sale; a proscription, outlawry.*

proscriptūrĭo -ire, *to desire a proscription.*

prōsĕco -sĕcare -sĕcŭi -sectum, *to cut off; to plough up.* N. of partic. as subst. **prōsectum** -i, *part of a victim cut out to be offered to a god; the entrails.*

prōsēda -ae, f. *a prostitute.*

prōsēmĭno -are, *to sow or scatter as seed; to disseminate.*

prōsĕquor -sĕqui -sĕcūtus, dep. *to follow or accompany out, to ' see off'; in hostile sense, to attack, pursue;* in gen., *to attend; to go on with, continue; to imitate.*

Prōserpĭna -ae, f. *the daughter of Ceres, carried off by Pluto to the lower world.*

prōseucha -ae, f. *a (Jewish) house of prayer, a conventicle.*

prōsĭlĭo -ire -ŭi (-īvi or -ĭi), *to spring up, leap forth.*

prōsŏcer -ĕri, m. *a wife's grandfather.*

prospecto -are, *to look forward, look out upon, survey; to look forward to, expect.*

prospectus -ūs, m. *outlook, view, prospect; sight, gaze.*

prospĕcŭlor -ari, dep. intransit., *to explore, reconnoitre;* transit., *to look out for, wait for.*

prosper (**prospĕrus**) -a -um, *fortunate, favourable, lucky, prosperous;* n. pl. as subst. *prosperity, good fortune.* Adv. **prospĕrē.**

prospĕrĭtās -ātis, f. *prosperity, good fortune.*

prospĕro -are, *to make fortunate, cause to succeed.*

prospĕrus = prosper; q.v.

prospĭcĭentĭa -ae, f. *foresight, precaution.*

prospĭcĭo -spĭcĕre -spexi -spectum: intransit., *to look forward, look out; to take care, exercise foresight;* transit., *to see ahead, make out in the distance; to look towards; to foresee; to look out for, provide, procure.*

prosterno -sternĕre -strāvi -strātum, *to cast down; to debase; to overthrow, destroy, ruin.*

prostĭtŭo -stĭtŭĕre -stĭtŭi -stĭtūtum, *to prostitute.*

prosto -stare -stĭti, *to stand out, project; to be exposed for sale; to prostitute oneself.*

prōsŭbĭgo -ĕre, *to dig up, root up.*

prōsum prōdesse prōfŭi, *to be useful, do good, benefit* (with dat.).

prōtĕgo -tĕgĕre -texi -tectum, *to cover in front; to cover over, protect; to furnish with a roof.*

prōtēlum -i, n. *a team of oxen; a series, succession.*

prōtendo -tendĕre -tendi -tentum, *to stretch forward, stretch out.*

prōtĕnŭs = protinus; q.v.

prōtĕro -tĕrĕre -trīvi -tritum, *to trample under foot, tread down; to overthrow, rout, defeat; to drive away, push aside.*

prōterrĕo -ĕre, *to scare away.*

prōtervĭtās -ātis, f. *boldness, impudence; pertness.*

prōtervus -a -um, *bold, impudent; in milder sense, pert; of things, violent.* Adv. **prōtervē.**

Prōtĕūs -ĕi and -ĕos, m. *a god of the sea, with the power of changing himself into different shapes.*

prōtĭnam, *immediately, at once.*

prōtĭnŭs (**prōtĕnŭs**), adv. *forward, further on; of time, continuously or immediately.*

prōtollo -ĕre, *to put forward; to lengthen, prolong.*

prōtrăho -trăhĕre -traxi -tractum, *to draw, forward, drag out; to bring to light, reveal, make known; to compel, force; to protract, defer.*

prōtrūdo -trūdĕre -trūsi -trūsum, *to push forward, thrust out; to put off, defer.*

prōturbo -are, *to drive forward, drive away; to throw down, overcome.*

prŏŭt, *just as, according as.*

prōvĕho -vĕhĕre -vexi -vectum, *to carry forward; to carry on; to advance, promote;* pass., provehi, *to ride forward, drive, sail,* and fig. *to be carried away.*

Hence partic. **prōvectus** -a -um, *advanced, esp. in age.*

prōvěnĭo -věnire -věni -ventum, to come on, appear; of corn, to come up, grow; of events, to result, come about; esp. to turn out well, succeed.

prōventus -ūs, m. coming forth, growing; product, crop; result, issue, success.

prōverbĭum -i, n. a proverb.

prōvĭdentĭa -ae, f. foresight, foreknowledge; forethought, providence.

prōvĭděo -vidēre -vidi -visum, to look forward to, see at a distance; to see beforehand, foresee; to take precautions for or against, provide for, make preparation for.
Hence partic. prōvĭdens -entis, provident, prudent; adv. prōvĭděntěr. N. abl. of perf. partic. prōvīso, with forethought.

prōvĭdus -a -um, foreseeing; providing, taking measures for; in gen., cautious, prudent.

prōvincĭa -ae, f. employment, sphere of duty, office, esp. that of a magistrate. Transf., a country governed by a Roman magistrate, a province.

prōvincĭālis -e, of a province; m. as subst., esp. plur., inhabitants of provinces, provincials.

prōvīsĭo -ōnis, f. foresight: hence provision, planning.

prōvīso -ěre, to look out for, go to see.

prōvīsor -ōris, m. one who provides for or against. ·

prōvīsū, abl. sing. m. by foreseeing; by providing for or against.

prōvixisse, perf. infin. to have lived on.

prōvŏcātĭo -ōnis, f. a challenge; esp. an appeal to a higher court.

prōvŏcātor -ōris, m. a challenger; a kind of gladiator.

prōvŏco -are, to call out; to excite, rouse, provoke; to challenge to a contest; legal, to appeal to a higher court.

prōvŏlo -are, to fly forth, to rush out.

prōvolvo -volvěre -volvi -vŏlūtum, to roll forward, roll over and over; provolvere se, and provolvi, to throw oneself down, hence to abase oneself.

prōvŏmo -ěre, to vomit forth.

prōxĭmĭtās -atis, f. nearness, close connexion; similarity.

proxĭmus -a -um, superl.; see propior.

prūdens -entis, foreseeing, aware; skilled, experienced, practised; prudent, discreet, judicious. Adv. prūděntěr.

prūdentĭa -ae, f. foresight; knowledge; sagacity, discretion.

prŭīna -ae, f. hoar-frost, rime.

prŭīnōsus -a -um, frosty.

prūna -ae, f. a live coal.

prūnĭtĭus -a -um, of plum-tree wood.

prūnum -i, n. a plum.

prūnus -i, f. plum-tree.

prūrīgo -inis, f. the itch.

prūrĭo -ire, to itch.

prȳtănēum -i, n. the town-hall in a Greek city.

prȳtănis -is, acc. -in, m. chief magistrate in a Greek state.

psallo psallěre psalli, to play on or sing to a stringed instrument.

psaltērĭum -i, n. a stringed instrument.

psaltrĭa -ae, f. a female player on the cithara.

psēcăs -ădis, f. an anointer of hair.

pseudŏthȳrum -i, n. a secret door.

psĭthĭa (vitis) -ae, f. a kind of Greek vine.

psittăcus -i, m. parrot.

psȳchŏmantĭum or -ēum -i n. a place of necromancy

-ptĕ, suffix, self, own.

ptĭsănārĭum -i, n. a decoction of crushed barley or rice.

pūbens -entis, of plants, in full growth, luxuriant.

pūběr -běris = pubes; q.v.

pūbertās -ātis, f. puberty, the age of maturity; signs of puberty, growth of hair, etc.

[1]pūbēs -is, f. the signs of puberty, growth of hair, etc.; the youth, adult male population.

[2]pūbēs and pūběr -ěris, arrived at the age of puberty, adult, ripe; m. pl. as subst. pūběres -um, the men, the adult male population.

pūbesco -bescěre -bŭi, to grow up, arrive at maturity.

publĭcānus -a -um, of the farming of the public taxes; m. as subst. a farmer of the Roman taxes.

publĭcātĭo -ōnis, f. confiscation.

publĭcĭtŭs, at the public expense, in the public service; publicly.

publĭco -are, to confiscate; to make public, throw open, publish.

publĭcus -a -um, belonging to the people, public; res publica, or respublica, the state. Transf., universal, general; common, ordinary. M. as subst. publĭcus -i, a state official; N. publĭcum -i, public territory; the public revenue, the treasury; an open place, the open street. Adv. publĭcē, for the people, publicly, at the public expense; all together.

Publĭus -i, m. a Roman praenomen, abbrev. P.

pŭděo -ēre, to be ashamed; usually 3rd person, to cause shame, fill with shame; often impers., pŭdet; te huius templi pudet, you are ashamed of. Hence gerundive pŭdendus -a -um, shameful, disgraceful. Partic. pŭdens -entis, modest, shamefaced; adv. pŭděntěr, modestly, bashfully.

pŭdĭbundus -a -um, modest, bashful.

pŭdĭcĭtĭa -ae, f. modesty, chastity, virtue.

pŭdĭcus -a -um, modest, chaste, virtuous; adv. pŭdĭcē.

pŭdor -ōris, m. feeling of shame, bashfulness, decency, honour; chastity, purity; that which causes shame, a disgrace.

pŭella -ae, f. a girl, maiden; a young woman, young wife, or sweetheart.

pŭellāris -e, girlish, maidenly. Adv. pŭellārĭtěr.

pŭellŭla -ae, f. a little girl.

pŭellus -i, m. a little boy.

pŭer -i, m. *a child*; in plur., *children*; esp. *a boy, lad*; a puero, a pueris, *from boyhood.* Transf., *a serving-lad, page, slave.*

pŭĕrilis -e, *youthful, boyish; puerile, silly, childish.* Adv. pŭĕrilĭtĕr, *boyishly; childishly.*

pŭĕrĭtĭa -ae, f. *boyhood.*

pŭerpĕrĭum -i, n. *childbirth, labour.*

pŭerpĕrus -a -um, *of childbirth;* f. as subst. *a woman in labour.*

pŭertĭa = pueritia; q.v.

pŭĕrŭlus -i, m. *a little boy, young slave.*

pūga (pȳga) -ae, f. *the rump, buttocks.*

pŭgil -ilis, m. *a boxer, fighter with the caestus.*

pŭgĭlātĭo -ōnis, f. *fighting with the caestus; boxing.*

pŭgillāris -e, *that can be grasped with the fist;* m. pl. as subst. pŭgillāres -ĭum (sc. libelli), *writing-tablets.*

pūgĭo -ōnis, m. *a dagger, dirk, poniard.*

pūgĭuncŭlus -i, m. *a little dagger.*

pugna -ae, f. *a fight, battle; battle-line, array;* in gen., *contest.*

pugnācĭtās -ātis, f. *desire to fight, pugnacity.*

pugnācŭlum -i, n. *a fortress.*

pugnātor -ōris, m. *a fighter, combatant.*

pŭgnax -ācis, *fond of fighting, combative; obstinate, contentious.* Adv. pugnācĭtĕr.

pugno -are, *to fight, give battle; to struggle, contend, fight, to strive, exert oneself.*

pugnus -i m. *the fist.*

pulchellus -a -um, *pretty.*

pulcher -chra -chrum and pulcer -cra -crum, *beautiful, lovely; morally excellent, fine.* Adv. pulchrē (pulcrē), *beautifully, finely;* as exclamation, *bravo! well done!*

pulchrĭtūdo -ĭnis, f. *beauty, excellence.*

pūlēĭum (pūlēgĭum) -i, n *fleabane, penny-royal.*

pūlex -icis, m. *a flea.*

pullārĭus -i, m. *feeder of sacred chickens.*

pullātus -a -um, *clad in dirty or black garments.*

pullŭlo -are, *to shoot up, sprout, burgeon, luxuriate.*

'pullus -i, m. *a young animal;* esp. *a chicken, chick.*

²pullus -a -um, *dark-coloured, blackish;* poet., *sad, gloomy.* N. as subst. *a dark garment.*

pulmentārĭum -i, n. *a relish.*

pulmentum -i, n. *a relish;* in gen., *food, victuals.*

pulmo -ōnis, m. *the lung* (usually plur.).

pulpa -ae, f. *flesh.*

pulpāmentum -i, n. *flesh, esp. tit-bits.*

pulpĭtum -i, n. *a platform or stage.*

puls pultis, f. *porridge, pulse.*

pulsātĭo -ōnis, f. *knocking, beating.*

pulso -are, *to strike, beat, knock; to stir, move, affect.*

pulsus -ūs, m. *beating, blow, push; influence, impulse.*

pulto -are, *to knock; strike.*

pulvĕrĕus -a -um, *full of dust, dusty.*

pulvĕrŭlentus -a -um, *full of dust, dusty.*

pulvillus -i, m. *a little pillow.*

pulvīnar -aris, n. *a couch,* esp. *one carrying images of the gods at the* Lectisternium (q.v.).

pulvīnārĭum -i, n. *anchorage.*

pulvīnus -i, m. *pillow, cushion; a seat of honour.*

pulvis -ĕris, m. (rarely f.) *dust, powder.* Transf., *arena, scene of action;* sine pulvere palmae, *prize without effort.*

pūmex -icis, m. *pumice-stone; any soft, porous stone.*

pūmĭcĕus -a -um, *made of pumice-stone.*

pūmĭco -are, *to polish with pumice-stone.*

pūmĭlĭo -ōnis, c. and pūmĭlus -i, m. *a dwarf.*

punctim, *by stabbing, by thrusting* (opp. caesim).

pungo pungĕre pŭpŭgi punctum, *to prick, puncture, stab; to touch, move, penetrate; to sting, vex, annoy.* N. of partic. as subst. punctum -i, *a prick, a little hole, small puncture; a point, spot.* Hence *a vote; a moment of time;* in speech, etc., *a short clause, section.*

pūnĭcĕus -a -um, *purple, red.*

Pūnĭcus; see Poeni.

pūnĭo (poenĭo) -ire and pūnĭor -iri dep. *to punish; to avenge.*

pūnĭtor -ōris, m. *punisher, avenger.*

pūpa -ae, f. *a little girl; a doll.*

pūpilla -ae, f. (1) *an orphan girl, ward, minor.* (2) *the pupil of the eye.*

pūpillāris -e, *of an orphan or ward.*

pūpillus -i, m. *an orphan or ward.*

puppis -is, f. *the poop or stern of a vessel;* poet., *the whole ship.*

pūpŭla -ae, f. *the pupil of the eye.*

purgāmen -ĭnis, n. (1) *sweepings, filth.* (2) *a means of purgation.*

purgāmentum -i, n. *sweepings, rubbish, filth.*

purgātĭo -ōnis, f. *cleaning out, cleansing; excusing, justification.*

purgo -are. (1) *to clean, cleanse, purify.* Hence *to excuse, defend, justify; to allege in defence.* (2) *to clear away, wash off.*

purpŭra -ae, f. *the purple-fish.* Transf., *purple dye; purple cloth;* ' *the purple* ', = *high rank,* etc.

purpŭrātus -a -um, *clad in purple.* M. as subst., *a man of high rank, a courtier.*

purpŭrĕus -a -um, *purple-coloured; dark-red, dark-brown.* Transf., *clad in purple;* in gen., *gleaming, bright, beautiful.*

pūrus -a -um, *clean, pure, cleared.* Transf., *without addition, simple, plain; morally, upright, pure;* of style, *pure, faultless;* legally, *without conditions, absolute.* N. as subst. *the clear sky.* Adv pūrē and poet. pūrĭtĕr, *purely, cleanly;* of style *faultlessly.*

pūs pūris, n. *corrupt matter; bitterness.*

pŭsillus -a -um, *tiny; puny; petty, mean.*

pūsĭo -onis, m. *little boy.*

pŭtāmen -ĭnis, n. *cutting, paring, shell*

pŭtātor -ōris, m. *pruner.*

pŭtĕal -ālis, n. *stone curb round the mouth of a well or sacred place.*

pŭtĕālis -e, *of a well.*

pŭtĕo -ēre, *to stink.*

pŭter -tris -tre and **putris** -e, *rotten, putrid; loose, crumbling, friable, flabby.*

pūtesco pūtescĕre, *to decay.*

pŭtĕus -i, m. *a well, pit.*

pūtĭdus -a -um, *rotten, stinking, foul; of style, affected, in bad taste; adv.* **pūtĭdē,** *affectedly.*

pŭto -are, *to cleanse, clear; of trees, io lop.* Transf., *to clear up, settle, esp. of accounts; hence to weigh up, ponder, reckon, estimate; to consider, believe, think;* parenthetically, puto or ut puto, *I suppose.*

putrĕfăcĭo -făcĕre -fēci -factum *to make rotten or soft.*

putresco -ĕre, *to become rotten.*

putrĭdus -a -um, *rotten, decayed.*

pūtus -a -um, *pure, unmixed, unadulterated.*

pȳga = puga; q.v.

Pygmaei -orum, m. *the Pygmies, a race of dwarfs in Africa.*

pȳra -ae f. *funeral pyre.*

pȳrămis -ĭdis, f. *pyramid;* hence *a cone.*

pȳrōpus -i, m. *bronze.*

Pyrrhus -i, m. (1) *son of Achilles.* (2) *a king of Epirus, enemy of the Romans.*

Pȳthăgŏras -ae, m. *Greek philosopher of Samos* (about 540 B.C.).

Pȳtho -ūs, f. *the old name of Delphi;* adj. **Pȳthĭcus, Pȳthĭus** -a -um, *Delphic, relating to Apollo;* f. as subst., *the priestess of Apollo;* n. pl., *the Pythian games, celebrated every fourth year in honour of Apollo.*

pyxis -ĭdis, f. *a little box, casket.*

Q

Q, q, the sixteenth letter of the Latin Alphabet, only used before u and another vowel.

quā, abl. f. of qui, as adv.: relat., *by which way, where;* also *whereby,* or *as far as;* qua . . . qua, *partly . . . partly;* interrog., *by what way? how?;* indef., *in any way, at all.*

quācumque (-cunque), *wherever; by whatever way.*

quādamtĕnŭs, *to a certain point.*

quadra -ae, f. *a square;* used of any square object or square piece.

quadrāgēni -ae -a, *forty at a time, forty each.*

quadrāgēsĭmus (-ensĭmus) -a -um, *fortieth;* f. as subst. *the fortieth part, esp. as a tax.*

quadrāgiēs (-iens), *forty times.*

quadrāgintā, *forty.*

quadrans -antis, m. *a fourth part, quarter;* as a coin, *the fourth part of an as.*

quadrantārius -a -um, *of a quarter; of price, costing a quarter of an as.*

quadrīdŭum (quatrīdŭum) -i, n. *a space of four days.*

quadrĭennĭum -i, n. *a period of four years.*

quadrĭfārĭam, *in four parts.*

quadrĭfĭdus -a -um, *split into four.*

quadrīgae -arum, f. *a team of four horses abreast, esp. drawing a chariot.*

quadrīgārĭus -a -um, *of a racing charioteer.*

quadrīgātus -a -um, *stamped with the figure of a four-horse chariot.*

quadrīgŭlae -arum, f. *a little team of four horses.*

quadriiŭgĭs -e, *in a team of four.*

quadriiŭgus -a -um, *in or with a team of four.*

quadrimus -a -um, *four years old.*

quadringēnārĭus -a -um, *of four hundred each.*

quadringēni -ae -a, *four hundred at a time, four hundred each.*

quadringentēsĭmus (-ensĭmus) -a -um, *four hundredth.*

quadringenti -ae -a, *four hundred.*

quadringentiens (-iēs), *four hundred times.*

quadripertītus -a -um, *divided into four parts, fourfold.*

quadrirēmis -e, *with four banks of oars;* f. as subst., *a quadrireme.*

quadrivĭum -i, n. *a crossroads, place where four roads meet.*

quadro -are: transit., *to make square; to join properly together;* intransit., *to be square; to fit exactly, to suit;* esp. of accounts, *to agree.* Partic. **quadrātus** -a -um, *squared, square;* n. as subst., *a square.*

quadrum -i, n. *a square.*

quadrŭpēdans -antis, *going on four feet, galloping;* plur. as subst., *horses.*

quadrŭpēs -pēdis, *four-footed, on four feet;* as subst., *a quadruped.*

quadrŭplātor -ōris, m. *a multiplier by four; an exaggerator; an informer.*

quadrŭplex -plicis, *fourfold, quadruple.*

quadrŭplor -ari, dep. *to be an informer.*

quadrŭplus -a -um, *fourfold;* n. as subst., *four times the amount.*

quaerĭto -are, *to seek or enquire about eagerly.*

quaero quaerĕre quaesii or quaesivi quaesītum, *to seek, search for;* sometimes *to obtain, get; to miss, want; to seek to know, ask, enquire into a matter.* Partic. **quaesītus** -a -um, *sought out; unusual, select;* in bad sense, *far-fetched, affected;* n. as subst., *a question or a gain.*

quaesītĭo -ōnis, f. *an interrogation.*

quaesītor -ōris, m. *investigator, inquirer,* esp. *judicial.*

quaeso -ĕre, *to seek for, ask for;* first person, quaeso, *I beg.*

quaestĭo -ōnis, f. *seeking, searching; inquiry, investigation;* esp. *judicial inquiry;* quaestiones perpetuae, *standing courts of justice.*

quaestĭuncŭla -ae, f. *a little question.*

quaestor -ōris, m. *one of the quaestors, magistrates in Rome, occupied with matters of law and finance.*

quaestōrĭus -a -um, *belonging to a quaestor.* N. as subst., *the quaestor's tent in camp, or residence in a province.* M. as subst., *an ex-quaestor.*

quaestŭōsus -a -um, *profitable; fond of gain; having gained much, rich.*

quaestūra -ae, f. *the office of quaestor, quaestorship.*

quaestus -ūs, m. *gaining, getting, profit; a source of profit, occupation, business.*

quālĭbet (quālŭbĕt) *wherever you like; in any way you please.*

quālis -e: interrog., *of what kind?*; relat. (with or without antecedent talis), *of the kind that, such as;* indef., *having some quality or other.* Adv. **quālĭtĕr**, *as, just as.*

quāliscumque (-cunque) quālecumque: relat., *of whatever kind;* indef., *any whatever.*

quālislĭbĕt, quālēlĭbĕt, *of what sort you will.*

quālĭtās -ātis, f. *quality, property.*

quālus -i, m. and **quālum** -i. n. *wicker-basket.*

quam, adv. *how, in what way:* interrog., *how much? how?*; exclam., *how!;* relat., *of correspondence as* (often with tam); with superl. adj. or adv., *as . . . as possible* (with or without possum); quam primum, *as soon as possible;* of comparison, *than, as.*

quamlĭbĕt (quamlŭbĕt), *as much as you please.*

quamobrem (quam ob rem): interrog., *wherefore? why?;* relat., *for which reason, wherefore.*

quamquam (quanquam), *although, though;* at the beginning of a sentence, *nevertheless, and yet.*

quamvīs, *as much as you please, ever so much;* as conj., *however much, although.*

quānam, *by what way?*

quandō, *when:* interrog., *when?*; indef., *at any time, ever;* relat., *at the time when;* sometimes causal, *since, because.*

quandōcumque (-cunque): relat., *whenever, as often as;* indef., *at some time or other.*

quandōquĕ: relat., *whenever, as often as;* indef., *at some time or other.*

quandŏquĭdem, *since, because.*

quantŏpĕrĕ (quantō ŏpĕrĕ), *with what great trouble; how much.*

quantŭlus -a -um, *how little, how small.*

quantŭluscumque -ācumque -um-cumque, *however small.*

quantus -a -um; interrog., *how great?*; exclam., *how great!*; relat. (with or without tantus), *(as great) as;* quantus quantus, *however great.* N. as subst. **quantum:** interrog., *how much?*; exclam., *how much!*; relat., *as much as;* quantum in me est, *as far as in me lies.* Neuter in genit. (or locative) of price, **quantī,** *for how much, at what price;* in abl., **quantō,** *(by) how much,* with compar. adj. or adv.

quantuscumque -acumque -um-cumque, *however great.*

quantuslĭbĕt -tālĭbĕt -tumlĭbĕt, *as great as you will, however great.*

quantusvĭs -āvĭs -umvĭs, *as great as you please, however great.*

quāpropter, *wherefore.*

quārĕ (quā rĕ), *wherefore.*

quartădĕcŭmāni -orum, m. *soldiers of the fourteenth legion.*

quartānus -a -um, *of the fourth;* f. as subst. (sc. febris) *a quartan fever;* m. pl. as subst., *the soldiers of the fourth legion.*

quartārĭus -i, m. *the fourth part of a sextarius.*

quartus -a -um, *the fourth;* f. as subst., *the fourth hour;* n. acc. or abl. **quartum, quartō,** *for the fourth time.*

quartusdĕcĭmus -a -um, *fourteenth.*

quăsĭ, *as if, just as,* esp. in hypothetical comparisons; also with descriptions, *as it were, a sort of;* with numerals, *about.*

quăsillus -i, m. and **quăsillum** -i, n. *little basket.*

quassātĭo -ōnis, f. *a shaking.*

quasso -are: transit., *to shake violently; to shatter, break in pieces;* intransit., *to shake.*

quătĕfăcĭo -făcĕre -fēci, *to shake, weaken.*

quătĕnŭs, *how far, to what extent; in so far as, since.*

quătĕr, *four times;* hence *again and again.*

quăterni -ae -a, *four at a time, four each.*

quătĭo quătĕre quassi quassum, *to shake, brandish, agitate;* sometimes *to shatter.*

quattŭor, *four.*

quattŭordĕcim, *fourteen.*

quattŭorvĭrātus -ūs, m. *the office of the quattuorviri.*

quattŭorvĭri -ōrum, m. *a board of four magistrates.*

-quĕ, enclitic conj., *and;* repeated, *-que . . . -que, both . . . and . . .*

queis = quibus; *see* qui.

quēmadmŏdum (quem ad mŏdum), *in what manner, how* (interrog. or relat.); esp. corresponding with sic, ita, item, etc., *as, just as.*

quĕo quīre quivi and quii quitum, *to be able.*

quercētum -i, n. *an oak-wood.*

quercĕus -a -um, *oaken.*

quercus -ūs, f. *the oak;* sometimes *a crown of oak leaves.*

quĕrēla (quĕrella) -ae, f. *a complaint, complaining.*

quĕrĭbundus -a -um, *complaining, plaintive.*

quĕrĭmōnĭa -ae, f. *a complaining, complaint.*

quĕrĭtor -ari, dep., *to complain excessively.*

quernus -a -um, *of oak, oaken.*

quĕror quĕri questus, dep. *to complain, lament, bewail;* of animals, *to make a plaintive sound.*

querquĕtŭlānus -a -um, *of an oak-wood.*

quĕrŭlus -a -um, *complaining, plaintive.*

questus -ūs, m. *complaint, lament.*

¹quī quae quod: interrog. adj., *which? what? what kind of?*; exclam., *what!*; indef., (with f. quae or qua) *any, some*; relat., *who, which, what, that.* Acc. n. sing., **quod,** as adv.: quod sciam, *as far as I know.* Abl. quō, with comparatives: quo celerius, eo melius, *the faster the better.*

²quī (old abl. of ¹qui): interrog., *in what manner? how?*; relat., *wherewith, wherefrom*; indef., *somehow.*

quiā, *because.*

quiǎnam, quiǎnĕ, *why?*

quīcum, *with whom, with which.*

quīcumque (-cunque) quaecumque quodcumque: relat., *whoever, whichever, whatever*; indef., *any available.*

quīdam quaedam quoddam (subst. quiddam), *a certain person or thing* (known but not necessarily named). Transf., *a kind of.*

quidem, *indeed*; ne . . . quidem *not, even . .*

quidnī? *why not?*

quiēs -ētis, f. *rest, quiet; peace; sleep; a dream; a resting-place.*

quiēsco -escěre -ēvi -ētum, *to rest; to be at peace; to sleep; to cease from action.*

quiētus -a -um, *resting; sleeping; at peace, undisturbed, neutral*; of character, *quiet, calm.* Adv. **quiētē.**

quīlǐbět quaelĭbet quodlĭbet (subst. quidlibet), *any you will, anyone, anything.*

quīn: in questions, *why not?*; in commands, *to encourage, but come now*; in statements, *rather, but indeed*; in subordinate clauses, with subjunctive, *but that, without, that not, who not.*

quīnam quaenam quodnam, *which, what?*

quīncunx -cuncis, *five-twelfths.*

quīnděcǐens (-iēs), *fifteen times.*

quīnděcim, *fifteen.*

quīnděcimprīmi -orum, m. *the fifteen chief senators of a municipium.*

quīnděcimvir -i, m. *one of a board of fifteen magistrates.*

quīnděcimvirālis -e, *of the quindecimviri.*

quīndēni or **quīni děni** -ae -a, *fifteen at a time, fifteen each.*

quīngēni -ae -a, *five hundred at a time, five hundred each.*

quīngentēsimus (-ēnsimus) -a -um, *five hundredth.*

quīngenti -ae -a, *five hundred.*

quīngentiēns (-iēs), *five hundred times.*

quīni -ae -a, *five at a time, five each.*

quīnīvīcēni -ae -a, *twenty-five each.*

quīnquāgēni -ae -a, *fifty at a time, fifty each.*

quīnquāgēsimus (-ēnsimus) -a -um, *fiftieth*; f. as subst. (*a tax of*) *a fiftieth part.*

quīnquāgintā, *fifty.*

quīnquātrūs -ūum, f. pl., and **quīnquātria** -ōrum and -ium, n. pl. *a festival of Minerva.*

quīnquě, *five.*

quīnquennālis -e, *happening every five years, or lasting for five years.*

quīnquennis -e, *of five years; five years old.*

quīnquennium -i, n. *a period of five years.*

quīnquěpertītus -a -um, *in five portions, fivefold.*

quīnquěprīmi -orum, m. *the five chief senators in a municipium.*

quīnquěrēmis -e, *having five banks of oars*; f. as subst., *a quinquereme.*

quīnquěvir -i, m., *one of a board of five.*

quīnquěvirātus -ūs, m. *the office of quinquevir.*

quīnquiēs (-iens), *five times.*

quīnquiplico -are, *to multiply by five.*

quīntǎděcǐmāni -ōrum, m. *soldiers of the fifteenth legion.*

quīntānus -a -um, *of the fifth*; f. as subst. (sc. via), *a road in a Roman camp*; m. pl., *soldiers of the fifth legion.*

Quīntǐliānus (Quinct-) -i, m. M. Fabius Quintilianus, *head of a school of rhetoric at Rome.*

Quīntǐlis (Quinctilis) -is, m. (with or without mensis), *the fifth month afterwards called Iulius.*

¹quīntus -a -um, *fifth*; quintum, quinto, *for the fifth time.*

²Quīntus (abbrev. Q.) and f. **Quīnta.** *a Roman praenomen.*

quīntusděcǐmus -a -um, *fifteenth.*

quippě, *certainly, indeed, to be sure of course.*

quippinī, *why not?*

Quirīnus -i, m. *the name of Romulus after his apotheosis*; adj. **Quirīnus** -a -um, and **Quirīnālis** -e, *of Romulus*: collis, *the Quirinal Hill* at Rome; n. pl. **Quirīnālia** -ium, *a festival in honour of Romulus.*

¹Quirīs -itis and pl. **Quirītēs** -ium and -um, m. *the inhabitants of the Sabine town Cures*; also used *of the citizens of Rome* in their civil capacity.

²quiris or **cūris,** f. *a spear.*

quirītātio -ōnis, f. *a shriek, scream.*

quirīto -are, *to shriek, scream, cry out.*

¹quis quid, pron.: interrog., *who? what? which?*; indef., *anyone, anybody, anything.* N. nom. and acc. **quid?** *what?*; with genit., *how much? how many?* sometimes *why?*; quid ita? *why so?*

²quis = quibus; see qui.

quisnam quaenam quidnam, pron. *who? what?*

quispǐam quaepǐam quodpǐam (subst. quidpiam, quippiam), *anyone, anything; someone, something*; n. acc. as adv. *at all.*

quisquam quaequam quidquam (quicquam), *anybody, anyone, anything,* esp. in negative sentences and questions.

quisque quaeque quidque (adj. quodque), *each, every, everyone, everything.*

quisquiliae -arum, f. pl. *rubbish, sweepings, refuse.*

quisquis quaequae quidquid (quicquid), and adj. quodquod: relat., *whoever, whatever, whichever;* indef., *anyone, anything.*

quīvis quaevis quidvis (adj. quodvis), *whoever or whatever you will, anyone, anything.*

quīviscumque quaeviscumque quodviscumque, *whosoever, whatsoever.*

¹quō: interrog., *where? to what place? whither? how far? to what extent? to what end?;* indef., *to any place, anywhither;* relat., *to the end that, in order that.*

²quō, *because, whereby;* see also quominus.

quoad, *how far; as far as, as long as;* also *until.*

quōcircā, *wherefore, on which account.*

quōcumque, *whithersoever*

quod, conj.; *the fact that, the point that; as to the fact that, whereas; because, on the ground that; why, on which account;* with temporal clause, *since; as far as, to the extent that;* introducing a fresh sentence, *and, but, now,* esp. foll. by si.

quōdammodo, *in a certain way in a certain measure.*

quōiās = cuias; q.v.

quōlibet, *whithersoever you please.*

quōminus, *by which the less, so that not.*

quōmodo, *in what manner, how.*

quōmodocumque, *in whatever way; somehow.*

quōmōdonam, *how then?*

quōnam, *whither then?*

quondam, *in the past, formerly, once; in the future, sometime;* in gen., *at times, sometimes.*

quōniam, *since, whereas, because.*

quōpiam, and **quōquam,** *to any place at all.*

quōque, placed after the word which it emphasizes, *also, too.*

quōquō or **quō quō,** *whithersoever, to whatever place.*

quōquōversūs (-versum, -vorsum), *in every direction.*

quorsum (quorsus), *whither? to what place? to what purpose?*

quŏt, indecl., *how many* (interrog. and exclam.); relat. (often with tot) *as many;* quot annis, *every year.*

quŏtannis = quot annis; *see* quot.

quotcumquĕ, *as many as, however many.*

quŏtēni -ae -a, *how many each.*

quŏtīdiānus (cottīdiānus, cŏtīd-), *daily, of every day; everyday, common, ordinary.*

quŏtīdiē (cottīdiē, cŏtīd-), *daily, every day.*

quŏtiēs (quŏtiens), *how often* (interrog. and exclam.); relat. (often with toties), *as often as.*

quŏtiēscumquĕ (-cunquĕ), *however often.*

quotquŏt, indecl., *however many.*

quŏtus -a -um, *which in number? quota pars, how small a fraction? quotus quisque, one in how many? how rare?*

quŏtuscumquĕ (-cunquĕ) -ācumquĕ -umcumquĕ, *whatever in number;* pars quotacumque, *however small a fraction.*

quŏtusquisquĕ; see quotus.

quŏtusquē (quŏ usquē), *how long? how far?*

quōvis, *to whatever place you will.*

quum = ²cum; q.v.

R

R, r, seventeenth letter of the Latin Alphabet.

răbidus -a -um, *raging, mad, savage;* adv. **răbidē.**

răbiēs -ēi, f. *madness, rage, fury, frenzy.*

răbiōsŭlus -a -um, *rather furious.*

răbiōsus -a -um, *raging, mad, savage;* adv. **răbiōsē.**

Răbirius -a -um, *name of a Roman gens.*

răbŭla -ae, m. *a bawling advocate.*

răcēmifer -fēra -fērum, *bearing clusters.*

răcēmus -i, m. *a cluster,* esp. *of grapes.*

rădiātus -a -um, *provided with spokes or rays.*

rădīcĭtŭs, *with or by the root; utterly.*

rădīcŭla -ae, f. *a little root.*

rădĭo -are and **rădĭor** -ari, dep. *to gleam, radiate.*

rădĭus -i, m. *a staff, rod; the spoke of a wheel; the radius of a circle;* in weaving, *a shuttle;* in botany, *a kind of long olive.* Transf., *a ray, beam of light.*

rădix -ĭcis, f. *a root; the foot of a mountain;* in gen., *foundation, basis, origin.*

rādo -ĕre rāsi rāsum, *to scrape, shave graze; to erase; to hurt, offend.*

raeda -ae, f. *a travelling carriage.*

raedārius -i, m. *coachman.*

rāmālĕ -is, n. usually plur., *sticks, brushwood.*

rāmentum -i, n., usually plur., *shavings, splinters, chips.*

rāmĕus -a -um, *of branches.*

rāmex -ĭcis, m. *a rupture;* plur., *the lungs.*

Ramnes and **Ramnenses** -ĭum, m. pl. *one of the three tribes into which the early Roman citizens were divided.*

rāmōsus -a -um, *full of boughs, branching.*

rāmŭlus -i, m. *a little branch, twig.*

rāmus -i, m. *a bough, branch, twig.*

rāna -ae, f. *a frog.*

rancens -entis, *stinking, putrid.*

rancĭdŭlus -a -um, *rather putrid.*

rancĭdus -a -um, *stinking, rank, offensive.*

rānunculus -i, m. *a little frog, tadpole.*

răpācĭtās -ātis, f. *greediness.*

răpax -ācis, *snatching, grasping, greedy.*

răpĭdĭtās -ātis, f. *rapid flow, rapidity.*

răpĭdus -a -um, *rushing, swift, violent;* adv. **răpĭdē.**

răpīna -ae, f. *robbery, pillage; booty, plunder.*

răpĭo răpĕre răpŭi raptum, *to seize, snatch, tear away; to plunder a place; to hurry along a person or thing;* se rapere, *to rush off.* Transf., *to pervert, lead astray.* N. of partic. as subst. **raptum** -i, *plunder.*

raptim, *violently, hastily, hurriedly.*

raptio -ōnis, f. *carrying off, abduction.*

rapto -are, *to seize and carry off, to hurry away; to rob, plunder* a place

raptor -ōris, m. *a robber, plunderer.*

raptus -ūs, m. *tearing off, rending away; carrying off, abduction, rape; plundering.*

răpŭlum -i, n. *a little turnip.*

rārēfăcĭo -făcĕre -fēci -factum *to make thin, rarefy.*

rāresco -ĕre, *to become thin, to lose density; to widen out; to grow less.*

rārĭtās -ātis, f. *thinness, looseness of texture; fewness, rarity.*

rārus -a -um, *loose, thin; scattered, scanty, far apart;* milit.; *in loose order;* in gen., *rare, infrequent;* sometimes *extraordinary, distinguished.* Adv. **rārō, rārē,** *seldom, rarely*

rāsilis -e, *scraped, smooth.*

rastrum -i, n. plur. gen. rastri -orum, *a hoe, rake, mattock.*

rătĭo -ōnis, f. *a reckoning, account, consideration, calculation;* rationem ducere, *to compute; any transaction, affair, business; a reason, motive, ground; a plan, scheme, system; reasonableness, method, order; a theory, doctrine, science; the reasoning faculty.*

rătĭōcĭnātĭo -ōnis, f. *reasoning;* esp. *a form of argument, syllogism.*

rătĭōcĭnātīvus -a -um, *argumentative; syllogistic.*

rătĭōcĭnātŏr -ōris, m. *a calculator, accountant.*

rătĭōcĭnor -ari, dep. *to compute calculate; to argue, infer, conclude.*

rătĭōnālis -e, *reasonable, rational.*

rătĭōnārĭum -i, n. *a statistical account*

rătis -is, f. *a raft;* poet., *a ship, boat.*

rătĭuncŭla -ae, f. *a little reckoning, account; a poor reason; a petty syllogism.*

rătus -a -um, partic. from reor; q.v.

raucĭsŏnus -a -um, *hoarsely sounding.*

raucus -a -um, *hoarse, harsh-sounding.*

raudus (rōdus, rūdus) -ĕris, n. *a rough mass, lump,* esp. of copper money.

rauduscŭlum -i, n. *a small sum of money.*

Răvenna -ae, f. *a town in Gallia Cispadana, near the Adriatic.*

răvus -a -um, *tawny or greyish.*

rĕa; *see* reus.

rĕapsĕ, *in truth, really.*

rĕbellātĭo = rebellio; q.v.

rĕbellātrix -īcis, f. *renewing war, rebellious.*

rĕbellĭo -ōnis, f. *a renewal of war,* esp. by the conquered; *a revolt.*

rĕbellis -e, *renewing war, insurgent.*

rĕbellĭum = rebellio; q.v.

rĕbello -are, *to renew war, revolt, fight back.*

rĕbŏo -are, *to echo, resound; to make to resound.*

rĕcalcĭtro -are, *to kick back;* fig., *to deny access.*

rĕcălĕo -ēre, *to be warm again.*

rĕcălesco -ĕre, *to become warm again.*

rĕcalfăcĭo -făcĕre -fēci -factum, *to make warm again.*

rĕcandesco -candescĕre -candŭi, *to grow white; to become hot, begin to glow.*

rĕcanto -are: intransit., *to resound echo;* transit., *to recall, recant; to charm away.*

rĕcēdo -cēdĕre -cessi -cessum, *to go back, retreat, retire; to disappear.*

rĕcello -ere, *to spring back, fly back.*

rĕcens -entis, *new, fresh, young, recent; vigorous.* As adv. **rĕcens,** *lately recently.*

rĕcensĕo -censēre -censŭi -censum, *to review, muster, examine; to recount.*

rĕcensĭo -ōnis, f. *reviewing, mustering.*

rĕceptăcŭlum -i, n. *a reservoir, receptacle; a place of refuge, shelter, retreat.*

rĕcepto -are, *to draw back, receive back take in; to receive frequently, harbour.*

rĕceptor -ōris, m. and **receptrix** -tricis, f. *a receiver, harbourer.*

rĕceptus -ūs, m. *drawing back; withdrawal, recantation; retiring, retreat, return;* poet., *a place of retreat.*

rĕcessim, *backwards.*

rĕcessus -ūs, m. *going back, retreat, withdrawal; a place of retreat, quiet place.*

rĕcīdīvus -a -um, *returning, repeated.*

¹rĕcĭdo -cĭdĕre -ccĭdi -cāsūrus, *to fall back; to relapse, recoil, descend, sink, fall.*

²rĕcīdo -cīdĕre -cĭdi -cīsum, *to cu! back, lop away.*

rĕcingo -cingĕre -cinxi -cinctum, *to ungird, loosen.*

rĕcĭno -ĕre, *to resound, echo;* transit., *to cause to resound.*

rĕcĭpĭo -cĭpĕre -cēpi -ceptum, *to hold back, retain; to take back, fetch back;* se recipere, *to withdraw, retreat; to regain, recover; to receive, accept, take to oneself; to receive hospitably. Transf., to accept, admit, allow; to accept an obligation; hence to guarantee, promise, be responsible for.* N. of partic. as subst., receptum -i. *an engagement, guarantee.*

rĕcĭprōco -are, *to move backwards and forwards;* animam, *to breathe.*

rĕcĭprŏcus -a -um, *going backwards and forwards; mare, ebbing.*

rĕcĭtātĭo -ōnis, f. *a reading aloud.*

rĕcĭtātŏr -ōris, m. *a reader aloud.*

rĕcĭto -are, *to read aloud, read out, recite.*

reclāmātĭo -ōnis, f. *loud disapprobation.*

reclāmĭto -are, *to cry out against.*

reclāmo -are, *to cry out against, contradict loudly;* poet., *to re-echo, resound.*

reclinis -e, *leaning backwards.*

reclino -are, *to bend back, cause to lean back.*

reclūdo -clūdĕre -clūsi -clūsum, *to open; to reveal;* fata, *to relax.*

rĕcōgĭto -are, *to think again, reconsider.*

rĕcognĭtĭo -ōnis, f. *inspection, examination.*

rĕcognosco -noscĕre -nōvi -nĭtum,
to recognize, know again, recall; to
review, inspect, investigate.

rĕcŏlo -cŏlĕre -cŏlŭi -cultum, to
cultivate or work again; to resume;
to set up again, rehabilitate; to reflect
upon, to recall.

rĕcompŏno -pōnĕre -pŏsĭtum, to
readjust.

rĕconcĭliātĭo -ōnis, f. winning back,
restoration.

rĕconcĭliātŏr -ōris, m. a restorer.

rĕconcĭlĭo -are, to restore, repair; of
persons, to reunite, reconcile.

rĕconcinno -are, to restore, renovate,
repair.

rĕcondo -dĕre -dĭdi -dĭtum to put
away, put back, store, hide.
Hence partic. **rĕcondĭtus** -a -um,
put away, concealed; abstruse, profound; of character, reserved,
mysterious.

rĕconflo -are, to rekindle.

rĕconlĭgo -lĭgĕre -lēgi -lectum, to
collect again, recover.

rĕcŏquo -cŏquĕre -coxi -coctum, to boil
again, heat up again, remould.

rĕcordātĭo -ōnis, f. recollection, remembrance.

rĕcordor -ari, dep. to remember,
recollect; to think of, ponder over.

rĕcrĕo -are, to restore, refresh, invigorate, revive.

rĕcrĕpo -are, to echo, resound.

rĕcresco -crescĕre -crēvi -crētum, to
grow again.

rĕcrūdesco -crūdescĕre -crūdŭi, to
become raw again, break out afresh.

rectĭo -ōnis, f. ruling, direction.

rector -ōris, m. ruler, governor, director,
guia; navis, steersman; of animals,
driver or rider.

rectus; see rego.

rĕcŭbo -are, to lie back, recline.

rĕcumbo -cumbĕre -cŭbŭi, to lie back,
recline (esp. at table); in gen., to sink
down, fall down.

rĕcŭpĕrātĭo -ōnis, f. recovery.

rĕcŭpĕrātŏr (**rĕcĭpĕrātŏr**) -ōris, m. a
recoverer; pl., recuperatores, a board
of arbiters appointed by the praetor.

rĕcŭpĕrātōrĭus -a -um, of the recuperatores (q.v.).

rĕcŭpĕro (**rĕcĭpĕro**) -are, to regain,
recover.

rĕcŭro -are, to restore, refresh.

rĕcurro -currĕre -curri -cursum, to run
back; to revert, return.

rĕcurso -are, to run back, return.

rĕcursus -ūs, m. return, retreat.

rĕcurvo -are, to bend or curve backwards.

rĕcurvus -a -um, bent or curved backwards; winding.

rĕcūsātĭo -ōnis, f. refusal; legal, a
protest, counter-plea.

rĕcūso -are, to object to, protest against,
refuse; legal, to take exception, plead
in defence.

rĕcŭtĭo -cŭtĕre -cussi -cussum, to
strike back, cause to rebound.

rēda -ae, f. = raeda; q.v.

rĕdămo -are, to love in return.

rĕdargŭo -gŭĕre -gŭi, to refute, disprove, contradict.

reddo -dĕre -dĭdi -dĭtum. (1) to give
back, restore; reddi, or se reddere,
to return; in words, to repeat, recite;
to reproduce by imitation, to represent,
reflect. (2) to give in return; hence
to answer; to translate, render
interpret; to make, render, cause to be.
(3) to give as due; to pay up, deliver;
fulfil; reddere ius, to administer
justice.

rĕdemptĭo -ōnis, f. a buying up,
bribing; farming of taxes; buying
back, ransoming, redemption.

rĕdempto -are, to ransom, redeem.

rĕdemptŏr -ōris, m. buyer, contractor,
farmer (of taxes).

rĕdemptūra -ae, f. contracting, farming
(of taxes, etc.).

rĕdĕo -ire -ii (-ĭvi) -ĭtum. (1) to go
back, come back, return; ad se, to
come to one's senses; redit, the matter
comes up again. (2) of revenue,
income, etc., to come in. (3) to fall
back upon, be reduced or brought to.

rĕdhālo -are, to breathe out again.

rĕdhĭbĕo -ēre -ŭi -ĭtum, to take back.

rĕdĭgo -ĭgĕre -ēgi -actum, to drive
back, bring back; of money, etc., to
draw in, call in; in gen., to bring or
reduce to a condition; to reduce in
number, value, etc.; to lessen, bring
down.

rĕdĭmĭcŭlum -i, n. a fillet, chaplet.

rĕdĭmĭo -ire -ĭi -ĭtum, to bind round,
wreathe, crown.

rĕdĭmo -imĕre -ēmi -emptum, to buy
back, redeem; to ransom, redeem;
in gen., to buy up, contract for, farm,
hire, procure.

rĕdintegro -are, to restore, renew,
repair.

rĕdĭpiscor -i, dep. to get back.

rĕdĭtĭo -ōnis, f. going back, return.

rĕdĭtus -ūs, m. going back, return; in
gratiam, reconciliation; of money,
etc., returns, income, revenue.

rĕdĭvia = reduvia; q.v.

rĕdĭvīvus -a -um, renewed, renovated;
n. as subst., old building materials
used again.

rĕdŏlĕo -ēre -ŭi, to emit an odour,
smell of.

rĕdŏmĭtus -a -um, tamed again.

rĕdōno -are, to give back; to give up.

rĕdūco -dūcĕre -duxi -ductum, to draw
backwards, bring back, lead home;
also to bring to a state or condition.
Hence partic. **rĕductus** -a -um,
drawn back; withdrawn, retired,
remote, sequestered.

rĕductĭo -ōnis, f. bringing back,
restoration.

rĕductŏr -ōris, one who brings back.

rĕduncus -a -um, bent back, curved.

rĕdundantĭa -ae, f. overflowing; redundancy.

rĕdundo -are, to overflow, stream over;
to be in excess, be copious, diffuse, to
abound in (with abl.); to be left over,
overflow, spread.

rĕdŭvĭa (rĕdīvĭa) -ae, f. *a hangnail, whitlow.*

rĕdux -dŭcis, adj.: act., *bringing back restoring*; pass., *brought back returned.*

rĕfectĭo -ōnis, f. *repairing, restoring.*

rĕfello -fellĕre -felli, *to refute, disprove.*

rĕfercĭo -fercire -fersi -fertum, *to stuff, to cram*; partic. **rĕfertus** -a -um, *stuffed, crammed, filled.*

rĕfērĭo -ire, *to strike back, strike again.* Transf., *to reflect.*

rĕfĕro rĕferre rettŭli rĕlātum. (1) *to carry back, bring back*; referre pedem, *or se, or* pass., referri, *to return, go back.* (2) *to bring again, restore, repeat; to echo; to reproduce, recall.* (3) *to say back, answer.* (4) *to bring as expected, pay up, deliver; to bring back a message, report; to refer a matter to authority; to enter in a record,* etc., *register, put down, enter; to assign to a cause.*

rĕfert rĕferre rĕtŭlit, impers., *it matters, it concerns, it makes a difference*; meā, illorum refert, *it matters to me, to them.*

rĕfertus -a -um, partic. from refercio; q.v.

rĕfervĕo -ēre, *to boil over.*

rĕfervesco -ĕre, *to boil up, bubble up.*

rĕficĭo -ficĕre -fēci -fectum. (1) *to make again, restore, repair, re-establish, refresh, revive.* (2) *to get back, receive, get.*

rĕfigo -figĕre -fixi -fixum, *to unfasten, demolish, remove;* of laws, *to repeal, abrogate.*

rĕfingo -ĕre, *to form anew.*

rĕflāgĭto -are, *to ask back, demand again.*

rĕflātū, abl. sing. m. *by a contrary wind.*

rĕflecto -flectĕre -flexi -flexum, *to bend back, turn back, divert*; intransit., *to yield, retreat.*

rĕflo -are: intransit., *to blow back, blow contrary;* transit., *to blow out.*

rĕflŭo -flŭĕre -fluxi -fluxum, *to flow back; to overflow.*

rĕflŭus -a -um, *flowing back.*

rĕformātŏr -ōris, m. *a reviver.*

rĕformīdātĭo -ōnis, f. *dread, terror.*

rĕformīdo -are, *to dread, fear, shun, avoid.*

rĕformo -are, *to form again, mould anew.*

rĕfŏvĕo -fŏvēre -fōvi -fōtum, *to warm again, revive, restore, refresh.*

refractārĭŏlus -a -um, *somewhat contentious, stubborn.*

refrāgor -ari, dep. *to oppose, withstand, thwart.*

refrēno -are, *to rein back, hold in, restrain, curb.*

refrĭco -fricare -fricŭi -fricatum, *to rub again; to excite again, renew.*

refrīgĕrātĭo -ōnis, f. *cooling, coolness.*

refrīgĕro -are, *to cool off;* pass., refrigerari, *to cool oneself, grow cool, grow languid.*

refrĭgesco -frīgescĕre -frixi, *to grow cold, cool down; to flag, fail, grow stale.*

refringo -fringĕre -frēgi -fractum, *to break up, break open; to curb check.*

rĕfŭgĭo -fŭgĕre -fūgi: intransit., *to flee back, run away; to shrink;* of places, *to recede;* transit., *to fly from, avoid.*

rĕfŭgĭum -i, n. *refuge.*

rĕfŭgus -a -um, *fugitive, receding, recoiling.*

rĕfulgĕo -fulgēre -fulsi, *to gleam back, shine brightly, glitter.*

rĕfundo -fundĕre -fūdi -fūsum, *to pour back, to make overflow.*

rĕfūtātĭo -ōnis, f. *refutation.*

rĕfūtātū, abl. sing. m. *by refutation.*

rĕfūto -are, *to drive back, check, repress, to refute, disprove.*

rēgālis -e, *of a king, royal, regal*; adv. **rēgālĭtĕr**, *regally, tyrannically.*

rēgĕlo -are, *to thaw, warm.*

rēgĕro -gĕrĕre -gessi -gestum, *to carry back, throw back.*

rēgĭa; see regius.

rēgĭficus -a -um, *princely, splendid.*

rēgĭgno -ĕre, *to bring forth again.*

Rēgillus -i, m. *a lake in Latium, scene of a victory of the Romans over the Latins,* 496 B.C.

rēgĭmen -inis, n. *control, guidance, rule, direction, government; a ruler, governor;* poet., *rudder.*

rēgīna -ae, f. *queen; princess; lady, mistress, sovereign.*

rēgĭo -ōnis, f. (1) *a direction, line;* esp. *a boundary line, boundary;* e regione, *in a straight line,* also *opposite, over against* (with genit. or dat.). (2) *a region, district, province.* Transf., *sphere, department.*

rēgĭōnātim, *according to districts.*

Rēgĭum (Rhēgĭum) -i, n. (1) *a town in Gallia Cispadana.* (2) *a town in Calabria.*

rēgĭus -a -um, *of a king, royal, regal; splendid, magnificent.* F. as subst. **rēgĭa** -ae, *palace, court, the royal family; capital city.* Adv. **rēgĭē**, *royally; tyrannically.*

regnātŏr -ōris, m. *ruler, king.*

regnātrix -tricis, f. adj., *ruling.*

regno -are: intransit., *to be a king, reign; to be master, be a tyrant; to prevail;* transit., in pass., regnari, *to be ruled by a king.*

regnum -i, n. (1) *royal power, monarchy, supremacy; tyranny.* (2) *a realm, kingdom, estate.*

rēgo rĕgĕre rexi rectum, *to guide, direct, to rule, govern, administer.* Hence partic. **rectus** -a -um, *ruled;* as adj. *straight; upright.* Transf., *right, correct, proper; honest, upright; natural, plain, straightforward;* n. as subst., *right.* Adv. **rectē**, *in a straight line; rightly properly;* recte est, *all is well.*

regrĕdĭor -grĕdi -gressus, dep. *to step back, go back;* milit., *to retire, retreat.*

regressus -ūs, m. *a going back, return; retreat; refuge, recourse.*

rēgŭla -ae, f. *a ruler, a plank.* Transf., *a rule, pattern, model.*

rēgŭlus -i, m. *a petty king,* or *king's son, prince.*

¹**Rĕgŭlus,** *a surname in the gens Atilia.*

rĕgusto -are, *to taste again or repeatedly.*

rĕicio -icĕre -iĕci -iectum, *to throw back, throw behind, throw away; to drive off; of a storm, to drive back, cast up.* Transf., *to throw off, reject; to refer; in time, to put off; legal, to challenge a juror.*

rĕiectĭo -ōnis, f. *throwing back, rejection; legal, the challenging of a juror.*

rĕiecto -are, *to throw back.*

rĕlābor -lābi -lapsus, dep. *to glide back, fall back.*

rĕlanguesco -languescĕre -langŭi, *to become faint; to slacken.*

rĕlātĭo -ōnis, f. *carrying back, bringing back; polit., a report; gram., repetition.*

rĕlātor -ōris, m. *one who makes a report.*

rĕlātus -ūs, m. *a narrative; a report.*

rĕlaxātĭo -ōnis, f. *relaxation, easing.*

rĕlaxo -are, *to loosen, enlarge; to ease, lighten, relax.*

rĕlēgātĭo -ōnis, f. *banishment.*

¹**rĕlēgo** -are, *to send away; to put aside reject; to banish.*

²**rĕlēgo** -lĕgĕre -lēgi -lectum, *to gather up again; of places, to pass again; of topics, to go over again.*

rĕlentesco -ĕre *to become languid again.*

rĕlĕvo -are, *to lift again; to lighten; to relieve, alleviate.*

rĕlictĭo -ōnis, f. *leaving, deserting.*

rĕlicŭos and **rĕlicus** = reliquus; q.v.

rĕligātĭo -ōnis, f. *tying up.*

rĕligĭo (rellĭgĭo) -ōnis, f. *of persons, scrupulousness, conscientious exactness; esp. religious scruple, awe, superstition, strict observance; in gen., moral scruples, conscientiousness; of gods, etc., sanctity; an object of worship, holy thing or place.*

rĕligĭōsus (rellĭgĭōsus) -a -um, *of persons, scrupulous, conscientious; holy, strict, superstitious; of actions, either required or forbidden by religion; of gods, etc., holy, sacred.* Adv. **rĕligĭōsē,** *conscientiously, scrupulously; religiously.*

rĕligo -are, *to tie on, fasten behind.*

rĕlino -linĕre -lēvi -litum, *to unseal.*

rĕlinquo -linquĕre -lĭqui -lictum, *to leave behind; at death, to bequeath; to leave unchanged; pass., to remain; to omit, leave out, pass over; to desert, abandon, forsake.*

rĕlĭquĭae (rellĭquĭae) -ārum, f. pl. *remains, relics, remnant.*

rĕlĭquus (rĕlĭcus) -a -um, *left behind, remaining, other; of a debt, outstanding; of time, remaining, future.* N. as subst., sing. and plur., *the rest; the remainder; in reliquum, for the future.*

relli-; see reli-.

rĕlūcĕo -lūcēre -luxi, *to glitter.*

rĕlūcesco -lūcescĕre -luxi, *to become bright again.*

rĕluctor -ari, dep. *to struggle against, resist.*

rĕmănĕo -mănēre -mansi -mansum, *to remain behind, stay, continue.*

rĕmāno -are, *to flow back.*

rĕmansĭo -ōnis, f. *remaining in a place.*

rĕmĕdĭum -i, n. *means of healing, cure, remedy, medicine.*

rĕmĕo -are, *to go back, return.*

rĕmētĭor -mētĭri -mensus, dep. *to measure again, go back over;* perf. partic. sometimes pass. in meaning.

rēmex -mĭgis, m. *a rower.*

rēmĭgātĭo -ōnis, f. *rowing.*

rēmĭgĭum -i, n. *rowing.* Transf. *oars; crew.*

rēmĭgo -are, *to row.*

rĕmĭgro -are, *to wander back, come back, return.*

rĕmĭniscor -i, dep. *to call to mind, recollect, remember.*

rĕmiscĕo -miscēre -mixtum, *to mix up, mingle.*

rĕmissĭo -ōnis, f. *letting go back, letting fall, lowering; breaking off, interrupting; remitting; animi relaxation, quiet.*

rĕmitto -mittĕre -mīsi -missum. (1) *to send back, send again; throw back; echo.* (2) *to let go back, relax, loosen; to relieve, abate;* with infin., *to give up doing;* intransit., *to ease off.* (3) *to give up, yield; abandon, sacrifice; to forgive an offence, remit punishment.* Hence partic. **rĕmissus** -a -um, *relaxed, mild, gentle;* in bad sense *negligent, remiss.* Adv. **rĕmissē.**

rĕmōlĭor -iri, dep. *to push back.*

rĕmollesco -ĕre, *to become soft again.*

rĕmollĭo -ire, *to make soft again, to weaken.*

rĕmŏra -ae, f. *delay, hindrance.*

rĕmŏrāmen -ĭnis, n. *delay.*

rĕmordĕo -mordēre -morsum. *to worry, harass.*

rĕmŏror -ari, dep.: intransit., *to remain behind, linger, loiter;* transit., *to obstruct, hinder.*

rĕmōtĭo -ōnis, f. *putting away, removing.*

rĕmŏvĕo -mŏvēre -mōvi -mōtum *to move back, withdraw.* Hence partic. **rĕmōtus** -a -um, *removed, withdrawn, distant, far off, remote;* adv. **rĕmōtē,** *far off, at a distance.*

rĕmūgĭo -ire, *to bellow again, bellow back.*

rĕmulcĕo -mulcēre -mulsi *to stroke back.*

rĕmulcum -i, n. *a tow-rope.*

rĕmūnĕrātĭo -ōnis, f. *a recompense, return.*

rĕmūnĕror -ari, dep. *to repay, reward.*

rĕmurmŭro -are, *to murmur back.*

¹**rēmus** -i, m. *an oar.*

²**Rēmus** -i, m. *twin brother of Romulus.*

rĕnarro -are, *to relate again.*

rĕnascor -nasci -nātus, dep. *to be born again, grow again.*

rĕnāvĭgo -are, *to sail back.*

rĕnĕo -nēre, *to unravel.*

rēnes -um, m. pl. *the kidneys.*

rĕnĭdĕo -ēre, *to shine back, glitter; to beam with joy, laugh, smile.*

rĕnītor -i, dep. *to oppose, withstand, resist.*

¹**rĕno** -nare, *to swim back.*

'rēno (rhēno) -onis, m. *a garment made of fur.*

rēnōdo -are, *to tie back.*

rĕnŏvāmen -ĭnis, n. *renewal.*

rĕnŏvātĭo -ōnis, f. *renewal, renovation;* renovatio singulorum annorum, *compound interest.*

rĕnŏvo -are, *to renew, restore, repair; to repeat.*

rĕnŭmĕro -are. *to count over again; to pay back.*

rĕnuntiātĭo -ōnis, f. *a formal report, public announcement.*

rĕnuntio -are. (1) *to bring back word, report, announce.* (2) *to disclaim, refuse, renounce.*

rĕnŭo -nŭĕre -nŭi, *to deny, refuse, reject.*

rĕnūto -are, *to refuse, decline.*

rĕor rēri rātus, dep. *to think suppose, judge;* partic., in pass. sense, rātus -a -um, *determined, settled;* ratum facere, *to ratify, confirm, make valid;* pro rata, *in proportion.*

rĕpāgŭla -orum, n. pl. *bars or bolts; restraints, limits.*

rĕpandus -a -um, *bent backwards, turned up.*

rĕpārābĭlis -e, *that can be restored.*

rĕparco = reperco; q.v.

rĕpāro -are, *to restore, renew, make good; to get in exchange, purchase.*

rĕpastĭnātĭo -ōnis, f. *digging up again.*

rĕpecto -pectĕre -pexum, *to comb back.*

rĕpello rĕpellĕre reppŭli, rĕpulsum, *to drive back, drive away; to banish, repel;* a spe, *to disappoint;* criminationes, *to refute.*

rĕpendo -pendĕre -pendi -pensum, *to weigh back again; to ransom; to repay, requite.*

rĕpens -entis, *sudden, unexpected; fresh, recent.* Adv. rĕpentĕ, *suddenly, unexpectedly.*

rĕpentīnus -a -um, *sudden, unexpected;* n. abl. as adv. rĕpentīnō, *suddenly.*

rĕperco (rĕparco) -percĕre -persi or -pĕperci, *to spare, be sparing, abstain.*

rĕpercussus -ūs, m. *reverberation; echo, reflection.*

rĕpercŭtĭo -cŭtĕre -cussi -cussum, *to strike back, make rebound;* perf. partic. rĕpercussus -a -um, *rebounding, reflected.*

rĕpĕrĭo rĕpĕrīre reppĕri rĕpertum, *to get again; to find, discover, ascertain, invent.*

rĕpertor -ōris, m. *discoverer, inventor.*

rĕpĕtentĭa -ae. f. *recollection, remembrance.*

rĕpĕtītĭo -ōnis, f. *repetition.*

rĕpĕtītor -ōris, m. *one who demands back.*

rĕpĕto -ĕre -īvi and -ĭi -ītum, *to seek again, go back for or to; to ask back;* res repetere, *to demand satisfaction;* (pecuniae) repetundae, *money claimed back, as having been extorted; to return to, renew, begin again; to trace back, deduce; to recollect, recall.*

rĕpĕtundae; see repeto.

replĕo -plēre -plēvi -plētum, *to fill again, fill up; to make full, fill, satisfy.* Hence partic. replētus -a -um, *filled, full.*

replĭcātĭo -ōnis, f. *rolling again, folding round.*

replĭco -are, *to unroll; to turn over, review.*

rēpo rēpĕre repsi reptum, *to creep, crawl.*

rĕpōno -pōnĕre -pōsŭi -pōsĭtum, *to lay back; to put aside, lay up, deposit, store; mentally, to reckon, place; to replace, restore; to replace by a substitute; to requite.*

rĕporto -are, *to bring back, carry back;* of reports, *to deliver.*

rĕposco -ĕre, *to ask back again; to demand as a right, claim.*

rĕpostor -ōris, m. *a restorer.*

rĕpōtĭa -ōrum, n. *an after-party, second entertainment.*

repraesentātĭo -ōnis, f. (1) *vivid presentation, lively description.* (2) *payment in cash.*

repraesento -are, *to bring back, reproduce; to perform immediately, hasten on;* pecuniam, *to pay cash.*

reprĕhendo -prĕhendĕre -prĕhendi -prĕhensum, and reprendo -prendĕre -prendi -prensum, *to catch, hold fast, detain, check; tn blame, reprove; to refute.*

reprĕhensĭo -ōnis, f. *stopping, check; blame, censure; refutation.*

reprĕhenso -are, *to hold back, hold fast.*

reprĕhensor -ōris, m. *a censurer reprover; an improver, reformer.*

repressor -ōris, m. *a restrainer.*

reprimo -primĕre -pressi -pressum, *to hold back, restrain, hinder, repress.*

reprōmissĭo -ōnis, f. *a counterpromise.*

reprōmitto -mittĕre -misi -missum, *to promise in return.*

repto -are, *to creep, crawl along.*

rĕpŭdĭātĭo -ōnis, f. *refusal, rejection.*

rĕpŭdĭo -are, *to refuse, reject, disdain; to divorce.*

rĕpŭdĭum -i, n. *divorce.*

rĕpŭĕrasco -ĕre, *to become a boy again, to frolic.*

rĕpugnantĭa -ae, f. *incompatibility.*

rĕpugno -are *to fight against, oppose, resist; to be opposed, repugnant, inconsistent, incompatible.* Hence partic. rĕpugnans, *contrary opposed;* n. pl. as subst. *contradictions,* adv. rĕpugnantĕr, *unwillingly.*

rĕpulsa -ae, f. *repulse, rejection; denial refusal.*

rĕpulsans -antis, partic., *beating back;* colles verba repulsantes, *echoing.*

rĕpulsū, abl. sing. m. *by striking back, by reflection, by echoing.*

rĕpungo -ĕre, *to prick again.*

rĕpurgo -are. *to clean again; to purge away.*

rĕpŭtātĭo -ōnis, f. *re-appraisal.*

rĕpŭto -are. (1) *to reckon back, count, compute.* (2) *to think over, reconsider.*

rĕquĭēs -ētis, f. *rest, repose.*

rĕquĭesco -quĭescĕre -quĭēvi -quĭētum, *to rest, repose;* pass. partic. **rĕquĭētus** -a -um, *rested, refreshed;* ager, *fallow.*

rĕquīro -quīrĕre -quīsĭi *and* -quīsĭvi -quisītum, *to ask for, look for, enquire after; to demand, desire; to miss, feel the want of.*

rēs rĕi, f. *a thing, object, matter, affair, circumstance;* natura rerum, *the world, the universe, nature;* pro re, *according to circumstance;* esp. *the real thing, fact, truth, reality;* rē verā, *in truth; possessions, property, wealth; interest, advantage, benefit;* in rem, *to one's advantage; cause, ground, reason;* qua re, quam ob rem, *wherefore; a matter of business; a law-suit, action;* res publica *or* respublica, *the republic, state, commonwealth;* e republicā, *in the public interest.*

rĕsacro = resecro; q.v.

rĕsaevĭo -ire, *to rage again.*

rĕsălūto -are, *to salute back, greet in return.*

rĕsānesco -sānescĕre -sānŭi, *to become sound again.*

rĕsarcĭo -sarcire -sartum, *to patch up, mend, repair, restore.*

rescindo -scindĕre -scĭdi -scissum, *to tear back, cut away, break open; vulnus, to reopen; of laws, etc., to rescind, repeal.*

rescisco -scĭscĕre -scĭvi *and* -scĭi -scĭtum, *to find out, ascertain.*

rescrībo -scrībĕre -scripsi -scriptum, *to write again, rewrite; to enrol again, transfer; to write back, answer in writing;* in book-keeping, *to pay, repay.*

rĕsĕco -sĕcare -sĕcŭi -sectum, *to cut back, cut short.*

rĕsēmĭno -are, *to produce again.*

rĕsĕquor -sĕqui -sĕcūtus, dep. *to follow again;* dictis, *to answer.*

rĕsĕro -are, *to unbolt, open up, disclose, reveal.*

rĕservo -are, *to lay up, keep back, reserve; to save, preserve, keep.*

rĕsĕs -sĭdis, *sitting; inactive, calm, quiet.*

rĕsīdĕo -sīdĕre -sēdi -sessum, *to remain sitting, stay, rest.*

rĕsīdo -sīdĕre -sēdi, *to sit down, settle, sink, subside, abate.*

rĕsĭdŭus -a -um, *remaining, outstanding;* pecuniae, *arrears.*

rĕsigno -are, *to unseal, open, reveal; to cancel, annul; to transfer, give back, resign.*

rĕsĭlĭo -sīlire -sīlŭi -sultum, *to leap back, rebound; to shrink, contract.*

rĕsīmus -a -um, *bent backwards, turned up.*

rēsīna -ae, f. *resin.*

rĕsĭpĭo -sipere, *to have a flavour of anything.*

rĕsĭpisco -sĭpiscĕre -sĭpĭi, *also* -sīpĭvi, *to recover one's senses; to become rational again.*

rĕsisto -sistĕre -stĭti. (1) *to stay, still, stop, continue; to recover one's footing.* (2) *to resist, oppose, withstand;* usually with dat.

rĕsolvo -solvĕre -solvi -sŏlūtum, *to untie, loosen, open; to melt; to dissipate; to dispel; to release; to reveal; to weaken.*

rĕsŏnābĭlis -e, *resounding.*

rĕsŏno -are; intransit., *to resound, echo;* transit., *to make resound.*

rĕsŏnus -a -um, *resounding, echoing.*

rĕsorbĕo -ēre, *to swallow again, suck back.*

respecto -are, *to look eagerly back (at); to have a regard for, give thought to.*

respectus -ūs, m. *looking back;* hence *care, regard, consideration; looking around one;* meton., *refuge, retreat.*

respergo -spergĕre -spersi -spersum *to sprinkle, splash.*

respersĭo -ōnis, f. *sprinkling.*

respĭcĭo -spĭcĕre -spexi -spectum, *to look behind, look back (at); to look back upon; to look to, provide for; to look to, depend upon; to have a regard for, care for, consider.*

respīrāmen -ĭnis, n. *windpipe.*

respīrātĭo -ōnis, f. *taking breath, respiration; exhalation.*

respīrātus -ū, m. *taking breath.*

respīro -are. (1) *to breathe back, blow in a contrary direction.* (2) *to breathe again, to take breath; to recover from fear, etc.;* of things, *to abate, decline.*

resplendĕo -ēre, *to glitter back, gleam again.*

respondĕo -spondēre -spondi -sponsum: intransit., *to match, correspond to, answer to; to resemble;* legal, *to answer to one's name, appear, be present;* transit., *to give an answer to person or thing, to answer, reply.* N. of partic. as subst. **responsum** -i, *an answer, reply;* a lawyer's *opinion.*

responsĭo -ōnis, f. *a reply, answer.*

responsĭto -are, *to keep giving an answer* or *opinion.*

responso -are, *to keep answering; to re-echo;* with dat., *to defy, withstand.*

responsum -i, n. subst. from respondeo; q.v.

respublica; see res.

respŭo -spŭĕre -spŭi, *to spit out, reject, refuse, repel.*

restagno -are, *to overflow, be swamped.*

restauro -are, *to restore, rebuild.*

restĭcŭla -ae, f. *a thin rope.*

restinctĭo -ōnis, f. *slaking, quenching.*

restinguo -stinguĕre -stinxi -stinctum, *to put out again, extinguish, quench, slake, destroy.*

restĭo -ōnis, m. *a rope-maker.*

restĭpŭlātĭo -ōnis, f. *a counter-engagement.*

restĭpŭlor -ari, dep. *to obtain a promise in return.*

restis -is, f. *a rope, cord.*

restĭto -are, *to remain behind, linger.*

restĭtŭo -ŭĕre -ŭi -ūtum, *to put back, replace, restore; to reinstate, re-establish; to repair, make good.*

restĭtūtĭo -ōnis, f. *restoration, reinstatement.*

restĭtūtor -ōris, m. *restorer.*

resto -stare -stĭti. (1) *to make a stand, resist, oppose.* (2) *to stand still, stay behind; to be left over, survive; to remain available* or *possible; of the future, to await, be in store.*

restringo -stringĕre -strinxi -strictum, *to bind back, draw back; to confine, restrict, restrain.*

Hence partic. **restrictus** -a -um, *close, tight; stingy; strict, severe.* Adv. **restrictē,** *sparingly; strictly.*

resulto -are *to spring back, rebound; to echo, resound; of style, to go jerkily.*

resūmo -sūmĕre -sumpsi -sumptum, *to take again, resume; to renew, repeat.*

resŭpino -are, *to throw down, prostrate.*

resŭpinus -a -um, *bent backwards, on one's back; also with head thrown back.*

resurgo -surgĕre -surrexi -surrectum, *to rise up again, appear again.*

resuscĭto -are, *to revive, resuscitate.*

rĕtardātĭo -ōnis, f. *hindering.*

rĕtardo -are, *to slow down, retard, impede.*

rētē -is, n. *a net.*

rĕtĕgo -tĕgĕre -texi -tectum, *to uncover, reveal, open, disclose.*

rĕtempto -are, *to attempt again.*

rĕtendo -tendĕre -tendi -tensum *and* -tentum, *to slacken, unbend.*

rĕtentĭo -ōnis, f. *keeping back; withholding.*

[1]**rĕtento** -are, *to hold firmly; to preserve, maintain.*

[2]**rĕtento** = retempto; q.v.

rĕtentus -a -um, partic. from retendo or from retineo; q.v.

rĕtexo -texĕre -texŭi -textum, *to unravel, undo, reverse; to cancel, annul; to retract; to revise.*

rētĭārĭus -i, m. *a gladiator using a net.*

rĕticentia -ae, f. *keeping silent.*

rĕticĕo -ēre: intransit., *to keep silence, say nothing;* transit., *to keep silent about.*

rētĭcŭlum -i, n. *a little net; a net-bag; a hair-net.*

rētĭnācŭla -ōrum, n. pl. *a rope, cable.*

rĕtinentĭa -ae, f. *recollection.*

rĕtĭnĕo -tĭnēre -tĭnŭi -tentum, *to hold back, detain; to restrain; to keep, reserve, maintain.*

Hence partic. **rĕtinens** -entis, *tenacious.*

rĕtinnĭo -ire, *to resound, ring again.*

rĕtōno -are, *to thunder back, resound.*

rĕtorquĕo -torquēre -torsi -tortum, *to twist back, bend back.*

rĕtractātĭo -ōnis, f. (1) *refusal, denial.* (2) *reconsideration.*

rĕtracto (**retrecto**) -are. (1) *to handle again, undertake anew, reconsider.* (2) *to draw back, refuse, be reluctant; dicta, to withdraw.*

rĕtrăho -trăhĕre -traxi -tractum, *to draw back; to hold back, withdraw; to draw on again, induce.*

Hence partic. **retractus** -a -um, *withdrawn; distant, remote.*

rĕtrĭbŭo -trĭbŭĕre -trĭbŭi -trĭbūtum, *to give again* or *give as due.*

retrō, *backwards, back, behind.*

retrōăgo -ăgĕre -ēgi -actum, *to drive back, reverse.*

retrorsum, *backwards, behind, in return, in reversed order.*

retrūdo -trūdĕre -trūsum, *to push back;* perf. partic. **retrūsus,** *remote, obscure.*

rĕtundo rĕtundĕre rĕtūdi (rettūdi) rĕtūsum (rĕtunsum), *to hammer back, blunt, dull; to check* or *weaken;* partic. **rĕtūsus** (**rĕtunsus**) -a -um, *dull, blunt.*

rĕus -i, m. and **rĕa** -ae, f. *a party in a law-suit, whether plaintiff* or *defendant;* esp. *a defendant, accused person;* in gen., *one bound* or *answerable.*

rĕvălesco -vălescĕre -vălŭi, *to become well again, be restored, recover.*

rĕvĕho -vĕhĕre -vexi -vectum, *to carry back;* pass., *to drive back, ride back, sail back.*

rĕvello -vellĕre -velli -vulsum, *to tear back, pull away; to remove, banish.*

rĕvēlo -are, *to unveil, lay bare.*

rĕvĕnĭo -vĕnire -vēni -ventum, *to come back, return.*

rĕvērā, adv. from res; q.v.

rĕvĕrĕor -vĕrēri -vĕritus, dep. *to revere, respect, fear;* partic. **rĕvĕrens** -entis, *respectful, reverent;* adv. **rĕvĕrenter;** gerundive, **rĕvĕrendus** -a -um, *awesome, venerable.*

rĕversĭo (**rĕvorsĭo**) -ōnis f. *turning back, return, recurrence.*

rĕverto (**rĕvorto**) -vertĕre -verti, and pass. **rĕvertor** (**rĕvortor**) *to return come back, revert.*

rĕvincĭo -vincire -vinxi -vinctum, *to tie back, bind fast.*

rĕvinco -vincĕre -vici -victum, *to beat back, subdue; to refute.*

rĕviresco -virescĕre -virŭi, *to grow green* or *strong again; to revive.*

rĕviso -ĕre: intransit., *to pay a fresh visit, return;* transit., *to come to see again, revisit.*

rĕvivisco -viviscĕre -vixi, *to come to life again, revive.*

rĕvŏcābĭlis -e, *able to be called back.*

rĕvŏcāmen -inis, n. *calling back, recall.*

rĕvŏcātĭo -ōnis, f. *calling back; withdrawing, revocation.*

rĕvŏco -are, *to call again* or *back; to recall; to bring* or *get back, recover; to refer; to revoke.*

rĕvŏlo -are, *to fly back.*

rĕvŏlūbĭlis -e, *able to be rolled back.*

rĕvolvo -volvĕre -volvi -vŏlūtum, *to roll backwards; esp. to unroll* or *open a book; hence to go over again;* pass., *to roll back, come round again in due course.*

rĕvŏmo -vŏmĕre -vŏmŭi, *to vomit up, disgorge.*

rĕvor-; see rever-.

rex, rēgis, m. *ruler, king, prince, chief; monarch, tyrant.*

Rhădămanthus -i, m. *brother of Minos, a judge in the lower world.*

¹**Rhĕa (Rēa) Silvĭa,** *mother of Romulus and Remus.*

²**Rhĕa** -ae, f. *old name of Cybele.*

rhēda = raeda; q.v.

Rhēnus -i, m. *the Rhine.*

rhētor -ŏris, m. *a teacher of rhetoric, a rhetorician.*

rhētŏrĭcus -a -um, *rhetorical;* subst., f. **rhētŏrĭca** -ae and **rhētŏrĭcē** -ēs, *the art of oratory;* m. pl. **rhētŏrĭci** -ōrum, *teachers of rhetoric;* adv. **rhētŏrĭcē,** *rhetorically.*

rhīnŏcĕrōs -ōtis, m. *a rhinoceros.*

rhō, n. indecl. *the Greek name of the letter R.*

Rhŏdánus -i, m. *the Rhone.*

Rhŏdus (-ŏs) -i, f. *Rhodes;* adj. **Rhŏdĭus** -a -um, and **Rhŏdĭensis** -e.

rhombus (-ŏs) -i, m. (1) *a magician's circle.* (2) *the turbot.*

rhomphaea (rumpĭa) -ae, f. *a long javelin.*

rhythmĭcus -i, m. *one who teaches rhythm.*

rhythmus (-ŏs) -i, m. *rhythm, time, harmony.*

rhўtĭum -i, n. *a drinking-horn*

rīca -ae, f. *a veil.*

rīcĭnum -i, n. *a small veil.*

rictus -ūs, m. and **rictum** -i, n. *the open mouth.*

rīdĕo rīdēre rīsi rīsum: intransit., *to laugh, smile, look cheerful;* with dat., *to please;* transit., *to laugh at.*

rīdĭcŭlārĭus and **rīdĭcŭlōsus** -a -um, *laughable, droll.*

rīdĭcŭlus, *exciting laughter; droll, humorous; absurd, ridiculous;* m. as subst., *a joker, jester;* n., *a joke, jest.* Adv. **rīdĭcŭlē,** *humorously; absurdly.*

rĭgĕo -ēre, *to be stiff* (esp. with cold); of hair, *to stand on end;* partic. **rĭgens** -entis, *stiff.*

rĭgesco rĭgescēre rĭgŭi, *to grow stiff;* of hair, *to stand on end.*

rĭgĭdus -a -um, *stiff, unbending, hard; stern, inflexible.* Adv. **rĭgĭdē.**

rĭgo -are, *to lead or conduct water; to wet, moisten, bedew.*

rĭgor -ōris, m. *stiffness, hardness,* esp. from cold. Transf., *sternness.*

rĭgŭus -a -um; act., *watering;* pass., *well-watered, irrigated.*

rīma -ae, f. *a crack, fissure, leak.*

rīmor -ari, dep. *to cleave; to probe, pry into, examine.*

rīmōsus -a -um, *full of cracks, leaky.*

ringor -i, dep. *to show the teeth; to snarl, be angry.*

rīpa -ae, f. *bank, shore.*

rīpŭla -ae, f. *a little bank.*

riscus -i, m. *a box, trunk.*

rīsĭo -ōnis, f. *laughter.*

rīsor -ōris, m. *a laugher, mocker.*

rīsus -ūs, m. *laughing, laughter; ridicule; an object of laughter.*

rītē, *in due form, with proper ceremonies, properly, fitly, rightly.*

rītus -ūs, m. *usage, ceremony, rite;* abl. **ritu,** with genit., *after the manner of.*

rīvālis -is, m. *a rival in love.*

rīvālĭtās -ātis, f. *rivalry* (in love).

rīvŭlus -i, m. *small brook, rivulet.*

rivus -i, m. *stream.*

rixa -ae, f. *quarrel, brawl, contention.*

rixor -ari, dep. *to quarrel, brawl, contend.*

rōbĭgĭnōsus -a -um, *rusty.*

rōbigo (rūbīgo) -īnis, f. *rust; blight, mildew; inaction, mental rust.* Personif. **Rōbīgo (Rūb-)** -īnis, f. or **Rōbīgus (Rūb-)** -i, m. *a deity invoked to preserve grain from mildew;* **Rōbĭgālĭa** -ium, n. *the festival of Robigo.*

rōbŏrĕus -a -um, *oaken.*

rōbŏro -are, *to strengthen, make firm.*

rōbur -ŏris, n. *hard wood;* esp., *oak, oak-wood; a dungeon at Rome,* also called the Tullianum; as a quality, *hardness, strength;* in gen., *the pick, flower, of anything.*

rōbustus -a -um, *of hard wood;* esp. *of oak, oaken; strong, powerful, firm.*

rōdo rōdēre rōsi rōsum, *to gnaw, nibble at; to corrode, consume; to disparage, backbite, slander.*

rŏgālis -e *of the funeral pile.*

rŏgātĭo -ōnis, f. *asking; a question; a request; a proposed law, a bill.*

rŏgātĭuncŭla -ae, f. *a minor question or bill.*

rŏgātor -ōris, m. *one who asks; the proposer of a bill; a polling-clerk.*

rŏgātū, abl. sing. m. *at the request.*

rŏgĭto -are, *to ask eagerly.*

rŏgo -are, *to ask, inquire; to ask for, request;* polit., rogare aliquem sententiam, *to ask a person his opinion;* rogare populum or legem, *to propose a law, introduce a bill;* rogare magistratum, *to offer a person for election.*

rŏgus -i, m. *funeral pile.*

Rōma -ae, f. *Rome;* adj. **Rōmānus** -a -um.

Rōmŭlus -i, m. *son of Mars, founder and first king of Rome;* adj. **Rōmŭlĕus** and **Rōmŭlus** -a -um.

rōrārii -ōrum, m. pl. *light-armed troops, skirmishers.*

rōrĭdus -a-um, *bedewed.*

rōrĭfer -fēra -fērum, *dew-bringing.*

rōro -are: intransit., *to drop dew, drip, be moist;* transit., *to bedew, moisten, water; to drip, let fall in drops.*

rōs rōris, m. *dew, moisture;* ros marinus, rosmarinus, *rosemary.*

rŏsa -ae, f. *a rose; a garland of roses; a rose-tree.*

rŏsārĭus -a -um, *of roses;* n. as subst. *a rose-garden.*

rōscĭdus -a -um, *bedewed, dewy; dripping like dew; moistened.*

Roscĭus -a -um, *name of a Roman gens.*

rŏsētum -i, n. *a garden of roses.*

rŏsĕus -a -um, *of roses; rose-coloured, rosy.*

rosmărīnus; see ros.

rostrātus -a -um, *having a beak, beaked, curved;* columna rostrata, *a pillar in the forum, adorned with ships' prows.*

rostrum -i, n. *beak, snout; a ship's prow;* plur. **rostra** -ōrum, *the speaker's platform in the Forum* (ornamented with prows of ships).

rŏta -ae, f. *a wheel;* poet., *a chariot.*

rŏto -are, *to whirl round, swing, brandish;* pass. rotari, *to revolve, to roll round.*

rŏtundo -are, *to round, make round.*

rŏtundus -a -um, *round circular;* sometimes *spherical; rounded, complete, self-contained.* Adv. rŏtundē, of style, *elegantly, smoothly.*

rŭbĕfacio -făcĕre -fēci -factum, *to redden, make red.*

rŭbellus -a -um, *reddish.*

rŭbĕo -ēre, *to be red; to blush;* partic. rŭbens -entis, *red, blushing.*

rŭber -bra -brum, *red, ruddy.*

rŭbesco -bescĕre -bŭi, *to become red.*

¹rŭbēta -ae, f. *a species of toad.*

²rŭbēta -ōrum, n. pl. *bramble-thickets.*

rŭbĕus -a -um, *of bramble.*

Rŭbico -ōnis, m. *a river, once the boundary between Italia and Gallia Cisalpina.*

rŭbĭcundus -a -um, *red, ruddy.*

rŭbigo = robigo; q.v.

rŭbor -ōris, m. *redness; a blush; modesty; shame, disgrace.*

rubrica -ae, f. *red earth; red ochre; a law with its title written in red.*

rŭbus -i, m. *a bramble-bush; a blackberry.*

ructo -are, and ructor -ari, dep. *to belch.*

ructus -ūs, m. *belching.*

rūdens -entis, m. *a rope, halyard.*

rūdīmentum -i, n. *a trial, attempt, essay.*

¹rŭdis -e, *rough, raw, uncultivated; unrefined, unskilled, awkward.*

²rŭdis -is, f. *a small stick; a foil (given to gladiators on their discharge).*

rūdo rūdĕre rūdivi rūditum, *to bellow, roar.*

¹rūdus (rōdus) -ĕris, n. *broken fragments of stone.*

²rūdus = raudus; q.v.

rūfus -a -um, *red, ruddy.*

rūga -ae, f. *a wrinkle.*

rūgōsus -a -um, *wrinkled.*

rŭina -ae, f. *falling down, collapse, ruin, destruction; the ruins of a building, debris.*

rŭinōsus -a -um, *going to ruin.*

rūmex -ĭcis, f. *sorrel.*

Rūmĭna -ae, f. *a Roman goddess;* Rūmĭnālis ficus, m. *a fig-tree under which the she-wolf had suckled Romulus and Remus.*

rūmĭnātĭo -ōnis, f. *chewing the cud; ruminating.*

rūmĭno -are, *to chew the cud, ruminate.*

rūmor -ōris, m. *report, rumour, common talk, hearsay; general opinion, popular judgment.*

rumpo rumpĕre rūpi ruptum, *to break, shatter, burst open; to cause to break forth; to destroy, violate, annul; to break off, interrupt.*

rūmuscŭlus -i, m. *trifling rumour, idle talk, gossip.*

rŭna -ae, f. *a dart.*

runco -are, *to weed, thin out.*

rŭo rŭĕre rŭi rŭtum; fut. partic. rŭĭtūrus; intransit., *to rush down, fall,* collapse, *be ruined; to rush along; to be precipitate;* transit., *to hurl down; also to cast up.*

rūpēs -is, f. *rock, cliff.*

ruptor -ōris, m. *breaker, violator.*

rūrĭcŏla -ae, *inhabiting* or *cultivating the country.*

rūrĭgĕna -ae, m. *one born in the country, a rustic.*

rūro -are and rūror -ari, dep. *to live in the country.*

rursus and rursum, *backward, back; on the other hand, in return; again, afresh.*

rūs rūris, n. *the country, a country-seat, farm, estate;* acc., rus, *to the country;* locative, ruri (or rure), *in the country.*

russus -a -um, *red, russet.*

rustĭcānus -a -um, *of the country, rustic.*

rustĭcātĭo -ōnis, f. *living in the country.*

rustĭcĭtās -ātis, f. *rustic manners, rusticity.*

rustĭcor -ari, dep. *to live in the country.*

rustĭcŭlus -a -um, *countrified;* m. as subst., *a rustic.*

rustĭcus -a -um, *of the country, rural, rustic; plain, simple; awkward, boorish;* m. as subst. *a countryman, a boor.* Adv. rustĭcē.

rūta -ae, *the herb* rue; *bitterness, unpleasantness.*

rūtĭlo -are: intransit., *to shine reddish;* transit., *to make red.*

rūtĭlus -a -um, *red, golden, auburn.*

rutrum -i, n. *a spade, shovel.*

rŭtŭla -ae, f. *a little bit of rue.*

Rŭtŭli -ōrum, m. pl. *an ancient people of Latium.*

S

S, s, *the eighteenth letter of the Latin alphabet.*

Săba -ae, f. *a town in Arabia, famous for perfumes.*

sabbăta -ōrum, n. pl. *the Sabbath, the Jewish day of rest.*

Săbelli -ōrum, m. *poetic name of the Sabines.*

Săbīni -orum, m. pl. *an ancient people of Italy, northerly neighbours of the Latins.*

săbŭlum -i, n. *gravel, sand.*

săburra -ae, f. *sand used as ballast.*

sacco -are, *to strain or filter.*

saccŭlus -i, m. *a small bag.*

saccus -i, m. *a sack, bag;* esp. *a purse.*

săcellum -i, n. *a small shrine, chapel.*

săcer -cra -crum, *sacred, holy, consecrated;* in bad sense, *accursed, devoted to destruction, horrible.* N. sing. as subst. sacrum -i, *a holy thing* or *place; a sacrifice* or *victim;* n. pl. *sacred rites, worship.*

săcerdōs -dōtis, c. *a priest, priestess.*

săcerdōtālis -e, *priestly.*

săcerdōtĭum -i, n. *priesthood.*

sacrāmentum -i, n.: legal, *money deposited by the parties in a suit;* hence *a civil suit, legal process;* milit., *oath of allegiance;* hence *an oath* or *solemn promise.*

sacrārĭum -i, n. (1) *a place where sacred things are kept, sacristy.* (2) *a place of worship, chapel, shrine.*

sacrĭcŏla -ae, c. *a sacrificing priest or priestess.*

sacrĭfer -fĕra -fĕrum, *carrying sacred things.*

sacrĭfĭcālis -e, *of sacrifices.*

sacrĭfĭcātĭo -ōnis, f. *sacrificing.*

sacrĭfĭcĭum -i, n. *sacrifice.*

sacrĭfĭco -are, *to sacrifice.*

sacrĭfĭcŭlus -i, m. *a sacrificing priest.*

sacrĭfĭcus -a -um, *sacrificial, sacrificing.*

sacrĭlĕgĭum -i, n. *stealing of sacred things, sacrilege, profanation.*

sacrĭlĕgus -a -um, *stealing sacred things, sacrilegious, impious.*

sacro -are. (1) *to dedicate to a god, consecrate; to devote, allot; to doom, curse.* (2) *to make holy, make inviolable; to immortalize.*
  Hence partic. **sacrātus** -a -um, *holy, consecrated.*

sacrōsanctus -a -um, *consecrated, holy, sacred, inviolable.*

sacrum; see sacer.

saecŭlāris -e, *relating to a saeculum or age;* ludi, *secular games* (celebrated at intervals of about 100 years).

saecŭlum (poet. **saeclum**) -i, n. *a generation; the spirit of the age, the times; a hundred years, a century, an age.*

saepe, *often, frequently;* **saepĕnŭmĕrō,** *repeatedly, again and again.*

saepes (**sēpes**) -is, f. *hedge, fence.*

saepīmentum -i, n. *hedge, enclosure.*

saepĭo saepire saepsi saeptum, *to hedge in, enclose, surround, confine;* n. of partic. as subst. **saeptum** -i, *barrier, wall, enclosure;* in plur., *the enclosure where the Romans voted at the comitia.*

saeta -ae, f. *a bristle, stiff hair; part of an angler's line.*

saetĭger -gĕra -gĕrum, *having bristles, bristly;* m. as subst. *a boar.*

saetōsus -a -um, *bristly.*

saevĭdĭcus -a -um, *angrily spoken.*

saevĭo -ire -ĭi -ītum, *to rage, be furious, take violent action.*

saevĭtĭa -ae, f. *rage, ferocity.*

saevus -a -um, *raging, fierce, furious, violent, savage, cruel;* adv. **saevē** and **saevĭtĕr.**

sāga -ae, f., *a prophetess, fortune-teller.*

săgācĭtās -ātis, f. *keenness, acuteness, shrewdness.*

săgātus -a -um, *clothed in a* sagum; q.v.

săgax -ācis, *keen, acute;* esp. *keen-scented; mentally acute, shrewd, clever.* Adv. **săgācĭtĕr.**

săgīna -ae, f. *fattening, cramming; food, nourishment.*

săgīno -are, *to fatten, cram.*

săgitta -ae, f. *arrow.*

săgittārĭus -a -um, *of an arrow;* m. as subst. *an archer.*

săgittĭfer -fĕra -fĕrum, *carrying arrows.*

săgitto -are, *to shoot arrows.*

sagmen -ĭnis, n. *a bunch of sacred herbs.*

săgŭlum -i, n. *a small military cloak.*

săgum -i, n. *a cloak of coarse wool, as* worn by servants, and esp. by soldiers, saga sumere, *to take up arms, prepare for war.*

Săguntum -i, n. and **Săguntus** (-ŏs) -i, f. *a town on the coast of Spain.*

săl, sălis, m. *salt; brine, sea-water;* fig., sing. and plur., *wit.*

sălăco -ōnis, m. *a swaggerer, braggart.*

Sălămis -mīnis, f. (1) *an island in the Saronic Gulf.* (2) *a town in Cyprus.*

sălăpūtĭum -i, n. *a little man, manikin.*

sălārĭus -a -um, *of salt;* n. as subst. *salt money, an allowance, pay.*

sălax -ācis, *lustful, lecherous.*

sălebra -ae, f. *jolting; a rough patch of road;* of style, *ruggedness.*

sălebrōsus -a -um, *rugged, rough.*

Sălĭātus -ūs, m. *the office of a priest of Mars;* see Salii.

sălictum -i, n. *a plantation of willows.*

sălignus -a -um, *of willow-wood.*

Sălii -ōrum, m. *a college of 12 priests of Mars Gradivus;* adj. **Sălĭāris** -e, *relating to the Salii; splendid, magnificent.*

sălillum -i, n. *a little salt-cellar.*

sălīnae -arum, f. *salt-works, brine-pits.*

sălīnum -i, n. *a salt-cellar.*

sălĭo sălire sălŭi saltum, *to spring, leap, bound;* f. pl. of partic. as subst. **sălĭentēs** -ium, *fountains.*

sălĭunca -ae, f. *wild nard.*

sălīva -ae, f. *spittle, saliva; appetite, taste.*

sălix -ĭcis, f. *a willow.*

Sallustĭus -i, m.: C. Sallustius Crispus, *the Roman historian Sallust, contemporary of Cicero.*

salpa -ae, f. *a kind of stock-fish.*

salsāmentum -i, n. *fish-pickle, brine; salted or pickled fish.*

salsūra -ae, f. *salting, pickling.*

salsus -a, -um, *salted, salty;* hence *sharp, biting, witty;* adv. **salsē.**

saltātĭo -ōnis, f. *a dancing, dance.*

saltātŏr -ōris, m. *a dancer.*

saltātōrĭus -a -um, *of dancing.*

saltātrix -tricis, f. *a dancing-girl.*

saltātus -ūs, m. *a dancing, dance.*

saltem, *at least, at all events.*

salto -are, *to dance, esp. with gesticulation;* with acc., *to represent in pantomime, to sing with gestures.*

saltŭōsus -a -um, *wooded.*

¹saltus -ūs, m. *a spring, leap, bound.*

²saltus -ūs, m. *a forest or mountain pasture; a pass, dale, ravine, glade.*

sălūbris and **sălūber** -bris -bre, *healthful, healthy, wholesome; sound, useful; healthy, vigorous.* Adv. **sălūbrĭtĕr,** *wholesomely, advantageously.*

sălūbrĭtās -ātis, f. *wholesomeness; soundness, health.*

sălum -i, n. *the open sea.*

sălūs -ūtis, f. *health, soundness; safety, welfare, well-being, salvation; a wish for a person's welfare, salutation, greeting.*

sălūtāris -e, *healthful, wholesome, advantageous;* n. pl. as subst. *remedies, medicines.* Adv. **sălūtārĭtĕr.**

sălūtătĭo -ōnis, f. *greeting, salutation; a call, ceremonial visit;* concr., *visitors.*

sălūtātor -ōris, m. *a visitor, caller.*

sălūtātrix -tricis, f. adj. *greeting, paying a visit.*

sălūtĭfer -fēra -fĕrum, *health-bringing.*

sălūto -are, *to wish well, greet, call upon, pay respect to, reverence.*

salvĕo -ēre, *to be well, be in good health;* salve, salvete, as a greeting, *Good day! Good morning!,* used also in bidding farewell.

salvus -a -um, *safe, unhurt, well, all right;* salvo iure, *without infraction of law.* Adv. **salvĕ.**

sambūca -ae, f. *a species of harp.*

sambūcistria -ae, f. *a female harpist.*

Samnĭum -i, n. *a region of central Italy;* adj. and subst. **Samnīs** -itis, *Samnite,* a *Samnite.*

Sămŏs (-ŭs) -i, f. *an island in the Aegean Sea;* adj. **Sămĭus** -a -um.

Sămŏthrācē, -ēs, **Sămŏthrāca** -ae, and **Sămothrācĭa** -ae, f. *Samothrace, an island in the northern Aegean.*

sănābĭlis -e, *curable.*

sānātĭo -ōnis, f. *healing, curing.*

sancĭo sancire sanxi sanctum (sancĭtum), *to consecrate, hallow, make inviolable, confirm, ratify, decree;* also *to forbid on pain of punishment, provide against.* Hence partic. **sanctus** -a -um. *consecrated, holy, sacred; pure, virtuous.* Adv. **sanctē,** *solemnly, conscientiously.*

sanctĭmōnĭa -ae, f. *sanctity, sacredness; purity, chastity, virtue.*

sanctĭo -ōnis, f. *a clause in a law defining a penalty.*

sanctĭtās -ātis, f. *inviolability, sanctity; purity, chastity.*

sanctĭtūdo -ĭnis, f., *sanctity.*

sanctor -ōris, m., *an enacter.*

sanctus -a -um, partic. from sancio; q.v.

sandālĭum -i, n. *a slipper, sandal.*

sandăpĭla -ae, f. *a bier used for poor people.*

sandyx -dȳcis, f. *vermilion.*

sanguĭnans -antis, *bloodthirsty.*

sanguĭnārĭus -a -um, *of blood; blood-thirsty, savage.*

sanguĭnĕus -a -um, *of blood, bloody; blood-red.*

sanguĭnŏlentus -a -um, *stained with blood, bloody; wounding, injuring; blood-red.*

sanguis -ĭnis, m. (and **sanguen,** n.) *blood.* Transf. *blood-relationship, race, family, progeny; life-blood, strength, vigour.*

săniēs -ēi, f. *corrupted blood, matter; slaver, venom, poison.*

sānĭtās -ātis, f. *health, soundness; good sense, sanity;* of style, *correctness, purity.*

sanna -ae,f . *a mocking grimace.*

sannĭo -ōnis, m. *a buffoon.*

sāno -are, *to heal, cure, restore, repair.*

sānus -a, -um, *sound, healthy, uninjured; of sound mind, rational, sane;* of style, *correct.* Hence adv. **sānē,** *rationally, sensibly.* Transf., *really, indeed, to be sure;* with imperatives, *then, if you will;* sane quam, *exceedingly, extremely.*

săpa -ae, f. *must* or *new wine.*

săpientĭa -ae, f. *wisdom, good sense, discernment;* esp. *proficiency in philosophy, science,* etc.

săpĭo săpĕre săpĭvi or săplī. (1) *to taste;* with acc., *to taste of* or *smell of.* (2) *to have taste, be able to taste.* (3) mentally, *to discern, be sensible, be wise, think.* Hence partic. **săpĭens** -entis. *wise, sensible, judicious;* as subst., *a sensible, judicious person;* also *wise man, philosopher, sage.* Adv. **săpĭentĕr.**

săpor -ōris, m. *taste, flavour, flavouring; sense of taste; taste in style* or *conduct.*

Sapphō -ūs, f. *a lyric poetess of Mytilene in Lesbos.*

sarcĭna -ae, f. *a bundle, pack, burden, load.*

sarcĭnārĭus -a -um, *of burdens* or *baggage.*

sarcĭnātor -ōris, m. *cobbler.*

sarcĭnŭla -ae, f. *a little bundle.*

sarcĭo sarcire sarsi sartum, *to mend, patch, repair, make good.* Hence partic. **sartus** -a -um; sartus (et) tectus, *in good condition, well-preserved.*

sarcŏphăgus -i, m. *coffin, grave.*

sarcŭlum -i, n. *a light hoe.*

Sardēs (Sardīs) -ium, f. pl. *Sardis, the old capital of Lydia;* adj. **Sardĭā-nus** -a -um.

Sardi -ōrum, m. *the Sardinians;* adj. **Sardus, Sardōnĭus, Sardōus** -a -um, *Sardinian;* subst. **Sardinĭa** ae, f. *Sardinia.*

sardōnyx -nȳchis, m. and f. *a precious stone, sardonyx.*

sargus -i, m. *a salt-water fish, the sargue.*

sărisa -ae, f. *the long Macedonian pike.*

sărĭsŏphŏrus -i, m. *a Macedonian pikeman.*

Sarmăta -ae, m. *a Sarmatian;* subst. **Sarmătĭa** -ae, f. *Sarmatia;* adj. **Sarmătĭcus** -a -um, *Sarmatic;* adv. **Sarmătĭcē;** f. adj. **Sarmătis** -ĭdis.

sarmentum -i, n. *twigs, brushwood.*

sarrācum -i, n. = serracum; q.v.

sarrĭo (sărĭo) -ire -ŭi and -ivi, *to hoe, weed.*

sartāgo -ĭnis, f. *frying-pan.*

sartus -a -um, partic. from sarcio; q.v.

săt, sătăgĭto, sătăgo; see satis.

sătellĕs -ĭtis, c. *a guard, attendant; an accomplice;* plur., *escort, suite, train.*

sătĭās -ātis, f. *sufficiency, abundance; satiety.*

sătĭĕtās -ātis, f. *sufficiency, abundance; satiety.*

sătĭnĕ, sătĭn = satisne; see satis.

¹sătĭo -are, *to satisfy, fill;* to cloy, *satiate.*

²sătĭo -ōnis, f. *a sowing* or *planting;* in plur. *sown fields.*

sătĭra; see satur.

sătis or săt, *enough, sufficient; as adv.,
enough, sufficiently, fairly, quite;*
compar. **sătius,** *better, more advantageous;* **sătinĕ, sătin** = satisne,
introducing questions; **sătis** (or **săt**)
ăgo or **sătăgo** -ăgĕre, *to satisfy or
pay a creditor; to have enough to do,
have one's hands full;* **sătis do** dare,
to give bail or security; **sătis accipĭo**
accipĕre, *to take bail or security;*
sătis făcĭo or **sătisfăcĭo** -făcĕre, *to give
satisfaction, satisfy, pay up, make
amends; also to prove sufficiently.*

sătisdătĭo -ōnis, f. *a giving bail or
security.*

sătisfactĭo -ōnis, f. *amends, reparation,
apology.*

sătius, compar. of satis; q.v.

sător -ōris, m. *a sower, planter, begetter,
father, producer.*

satrăpes -is; plur. satrapae -arum; m.,
*the governor of a Persian province,
viceroy.*

sătur -ŭra -ŭrum, *full, sated, rich,
copious.* F. as subst. **sătŭra** -ae,
*a dish of various ingredients, a medley;
per saturam, indiscriminately;* **sătŭra**
(or **sătira**), ' *satire* ', *as a literary form.*

sătŭrēia -ae, f., plur. sătŭrēia -ōrum,
n.; *the herb savory.*

sătŭrĭtās -ātis, f. *satiety, abundance.*

Sāturnālia, etc.; see Saturnus.

Sāturnus -i, m. (1) *the planet Saturn.*
(2) *a mythical king of Latium.* Hence
adj. **Sāturnĭus** -a -um, and **Sāturn-
ālis** -e; n. pl. as subst. **Sāturnālia**
-ium and -iorum, *a festival of Saturn
beginning on the 17th of December.*

sătŭro -are, *to satisfy, fill.*

¹sătus -a -um, partic. from sero; q.v.

²sătus -ūs, m. *sowing, planting; begetting, origin.*

sătўrus -i m. *a satyr.* Transf.,
Greek Satyric drama.

sauciātĭo -onis, f. *wounding.*

saucĭo -are, *to wound, hurt.*

saucĭus -a -um, *wounded, hurt, stricken,
distressed.*

sāvĭor -ari, dep. *to kiss.*

sāvĭum (suāvĭum) -i, n. *a kiss.*

saxĕtum -i, n. *a rocky place.*

saxĕus -a -um, *of rock, stony.*

saxĭfĭcus -a -um, *petrifying.*

saxōsus -a -um, *full of rocks, rocky.*

saxŭlum -i, n. *a little rock.*

saxum -i, n. *a rock, stone;* esp. *the
Tarpeian rock.*

scăbellum (scăbillum) -i, n. *footstool; a musical instrument played with
the foot.*

scăber -bra -brum, *scabby; rough.*

scăbĭes -ēi, f. *scab, mange, itch;
roughness; itching desire.*

scăbĭōsus -a -um, *scabby; rough.*

scăbo scăbĕre scăbi, *to scratch.*

scaena (scēna) -ae, f. *stage, scene,
theatre; natural background; publicity, the public eye.*

scaenālis -e, *theatrical.*

scaenĭcus -a -um, *of the stage, theatrical;*
m. as subst. *a stage-hero, an actor.*

Scaevŏla -ae, m. *the left-handed, a surname of the gens Mucia.*

scaevus -a -um, *left, on the left.*
Transf., *awkward.*

scālae -arum, f. pl. *a flight of stairs,
ladder;* milit., *scaling-ladders.*

scalmus -i, m. *a thole-pin, rowlock.*

scalpellum -i, n. *a lancet, scalpel.*

scalpo scalpĕre scalpsi scalptum, *to
carve, scrape, scratch.*

scalprum -i, n. *a chisel; a penknife.*

scammōnĕa (-mōnia) -ae, f. *the plant
scammony.*

scamnum -i, n. *a bench, stool.*

scando scandĕre scandi scansum, *to
climb, mount, rise.*

scăpha -ae, f. *a small boat, skiff.*

scăphĭum -i, n. *a pot, bowl, drinking-
vessel.*

scăpŭlae -ārum, f. pl. *the shoulder-
blades; the shoulders, back.*

scăpus -i, m. *a weaver's beam, or
perhaps leash-rod.*

scărus -i, m. *a salt-water fish; perhaps
parrot-fish.*

scătebra -ae, f. *a spouting up, bubbling
up.*

scătĕo -ēre and scăto -ĕre, *to gush,
spout up; to teem, abound.*

scătŭrrĭgo -gĭnis, f. *a bubbling spring.*

scătŭrrĭo -ire, *to gush, bubble over.*

scaurus -a -um, *with swollen ankles.*

scazŏn -ontis, m. *an iambic trimeter
with a spondee or trochee in the last
foot.*

scĕlĕro -are, *to pollute with guilt.*
Partic. **scĕlĕrātus** -a -um, *polluted
with guilt; impious, wicked; tiresome, noxious;* adv. **scĕlĕrātē,**
impiously, wickedly.

scĕlĕrōsus -a -um, *guilty, wicked.*

scĕlestus -a -um, *guilty, wicked,
accursed;* adv. **scĕlestē.**

scĕlus -ĕris, n. *a crime.* Transf.,
misfortune, calamity. As a term of
abuse, scoundrel, rascal.

scēn-; see scaen-.

sceptrĭfer -fĕra -fĕrum, *sceptre-bearing.*

sceptrum -i, n. *a sceptre;* poet.,
dominion, kingdom.

sceptūchus -i, m. *wand-bearer, a court
official.*

schĕda and scida -ae, f. *a strip of
papyrus bark; a leaf of paper.*

schēma -ae, f. and -ătis, n. *shape,
figure, form.*

schoenŏbătēs -ae, m. *a rope-walker.*

schŏla -ae, f. *learned leisure; conversation, debate; a lecture, dissertation; a
school; a sect.*

schŏlastĭcus -a -um, *of a school;* esp.
rhetorical; m. as subst. *a student or
teacher of rhetoric.*

scĭda = schida; q.v.

scĭentĭa -ae, f. *knowing, knowledge,
acquaintance, skill.*

scĭlĭcĕt, *evidently, certainly, of course;*
ironically, *no doubt;* in answers,
certainly; explanatory, *namely.*

scilla (squilla) -ae, f. *a sea-leek,
squill; a crayfish or prawn.*

scīn = scisne; see scio.

scindo scindĕre scĭdi scissum, *to cut, rend, split; to divide, separate.* Partic. **scissus** -a -um, *torn, rent;* of the voice, *harsh.*

scintilla -ae, f. *a spark; a glimmer.*

scintillo -are, *to sparkle, glitter.*

scintillŭla -ae, f. *a little spark.*

scio scire scivi or scii scitum, *to know, understand;* with infin., *to know how to;* with adv., scire Graece, *to understand Greek.*
Hence partic. **sciens** -entis, *knowing, aware; understanding; versed in, acquainted with* (with genit.); adv. **scientĕr;** for **scitus** -a -um, see scisco.

¹scĭpio -ōnis, m. *a staff, wand.*

²Scĭpio -ōnis, m. *a family of the gens Cornelia;* **Scĭpĭădēs** -ae, *one of the family of the Scipios, a Scipio.*

scirpĕus (**sirpĕus**) -a -um, *of rushes:* f. as subst. *basket-work.*

scirpĭcŭlus (**sirpĭcŭlus**) -a -um, *of rushes;* m. and f. as subst. *a rush-basket.*

scirpus (**sirpus**) -i, m. *a rush, bulrush.*

sciscĭtor -ari, dep. and **sciscito** -are, *to inquire, examine, interrogate.*

scisco scire scivi scitum, *to investigate, inquire;* polit. *to vote, ordain, resolve.*
Hence partic. **scitus** -a -um, *knowing, shrewd, judicious; pretty, fine;* adv. **scitē,** *skilfully;* n. of partic. as subst., *a decree, statute;* plebis scitum, *a decree of the people of Rome.*

scissus -a -um, partic. from scindo; q.v.

scitor -ari, dep., *to seek to know, inquire, ask.*

scitū, abl. sing. m. *by a decree.*

scitus -a -um, partic. from scisco; q.v.

sciŭrus -i, m. *a squirrel.*

scŏbis -is, f. *filings, chips, shavings, sawdust.*

scomber -bri, m. *a mackerel.*

scōpae -ārum, f. pl. *a besom, broom.*

scōpŭlōsus -a -um, *rocky, craggy.*

scōpŭlus -i, m. *a rock, crag, cliff, danger, ruin.*

scorpio -ōnis, and **scorpius** (-ŏs) -i, m. *a scorpion;* milit., *an engine for throwing missiles;* a *salt-water fish,* perhaps *the sculpin.*

scortĕus -a -um, *leathern, made of leather;* f. as subst. *a leathern garment.*

scortor -ari, dep. *to whore, go with harlots.*

scortum -i, n. *a harlot, prostitute.*

scrĕo -are, *to clear the throat, hawk, hem.*

scriba -ae, m. *a clerk, secretary, notary.*

scriblīta -ae, f. *a kind of pastry.*

scribo scribĕre scripsi scriptum, *to engrave, draw lines, write, write on, write about;* polit., *to draw up laws,* etc.; legal, dicam scribere, *to bring an action;* with double acc., *to appoint in writing;* milit., *to enrol.* N. of partic.

as subst. **scriptum** -i *a mark or line; a composition, piece of writing;* esp. *a decree, law.*

scrinium -i, n. *a case for books or papers.*

scriptio -ōnis, f. *the act of writing; authorship, composition; wording.*

scriptĭto -are, *to write often.*

scriptor -ōris, m. *a scribe, clerk, secretary; a writer, author, composer.*

scriptŭla -ōrum, n. *the lines on a draught-board.*

scriptum -i, n. subst. from scribo; q.v.

scriptūra -ae, f. *a piece of writing, composition; a testamentary disposition; a rent paid on public pastures.*

scrĭpŭlum (**scrŭpŭlum, scriptŭlum**) -i, m. *a small weight or measure.*

scrŏbis -is, c. *a ditch; a grave.*

scrōfa -ae, f. *a breeding sow.*

scrŭpĕus and **scrŭpōsus** -a -um, *of sharp stones, rugged, rough.*

scrŭpŭlōsus -a -um, *full of stones, rough, rugged.* Transf., *exact, scrupulous, precise.*

scrŭpŭlum = scripulum; q.v.

scrŭpŭlus -i, m. *a small stone.* Transf. *an anxiety, doubt, scruple.*

scrŭpus -i, m. *a sharp stone.* Transf., *a worry, anxiety.*

scrūta -ōrum, n. pl. *frippery, trash.*

scrūtor -ari, dep. *to search through, investigate, examine.*

sculpo sculpĕre sculpsi sculptum, *to carve, cut, chisel.*

sculptilis -e, *carved.*

sculptor -ōris, m. *sculptor.*

scurra -ae, m. *a dandy, man-about-town; a jester, buffoon.*

scurrīlis -e, *like a buffoon; mocking, jeering.*

scurrīlitās -ātis, f. *buffoonery.*

scurror -ari, dep. *to play the buffoon.*

scŭtāle -is, n. *the thong of a sling.*

scŭtātus -a -um, *armed with a shield.*

scŭtella -ae, f. *a flat dish, saucer.*

scŭtĭca -ae, f. *a whip.*

¹scŭtŭla -ae, f. *a little square-shaped dish.*

²scŭtŭla -ae, f. *a roller, cylinder.*

scŭtŭlāta -ōrum, n. pl. *checked cloths, checks.*

scŭtŭlum -i, n. *a little shield.*

scŭtum -i, n. *a large quadrangular shield.*

Scylla -ae, f. *a rock at the straits between Sicily and Italy,* opposite to Charybdis; adj. **Scyllaeus** -a -um.

scymnus -i, m. *cub, whelp.*

scўphus -i, m. *a drinking-cup, goblet.*

scўtăla -ae and **scўtălē** ēs, f. = scutula; q.v.

Scўthēs (**Scўthă**) -ae, m. *a Scythian;* **Scўthia** -ae, f. *Scythia.*

sē or **sēsē,** acc. sing. and plur.; **sŭi,** genit.; **sĭbi,** dat.; se or **sēsē,** abl.; strengthened forms, **sēpse, sēmet;** reflexive pronoun of third person, *himself, herself, itself, themselves;* sibi velle, *to mean;* secum = cum se; inter se, *reciprocally.*

sēbum -i, n. *tallow, fat.*

sēcēdo -cēdĕre -cessi -cessum, *to go apart, withdraw.*

sēcerno -cernĕre -crēvi -crētum, *to separate, part, sunder; to distinguish; to set aside, reject.*
  Hence partic. **sēcrētus** -a -um, *separate, alone, special; retired, solitary; hidden, secret;* with abl., *deprived of.* N. as subst. **sēcrētum** -i, *retirement, solitude; a secret, mystery.* Abl. as adv. **sēcrētō**, *apart, separately.*

sēcessio -ōnis, f. *a going apart, withdrawal, secession.*

sēcessus -ūs, m. *a going apart, withdrawal, retirement; a retreat, recess.*

sēcius; see secus.

sēclūdo -clūdĕre -clūsi -clūsum, *to shut off; to confine, to separate from others.*

sĕco sĕcāre sĕcŭi sectum, *to cut, amputate, to wound, hurt; to divide, part;* hence *to settle* disputes; *to cut out, make by cutting.*

sēcretus -a -um, partic. from secerno; q.v.

secta -ae, f. *a way, mode of life, procedure; a school of thought.*

sēctātor -ōris, m. *a follower, hanger-on;* plur., *train, retinue.*

sectilis -e, *cut; able to be cut.*

sectio -ōnis, f. *cutting.* Transf., *the buying up of state property;* concr., *auctioned property, a lot.*

¹sector -ōris, m. *a cutter.* Transf., *a buyer of state property.*

²sector -ari, dep. *to follow eagerly; to accompany, attend;* of enemies, *to run after, chase;* in gen., *to strive after, try to get or find.*

sectūra -ae, f. *cutting;* aerariae secturae, *copper-mines.*

sēcŭbitus -ūs, m. *lying alone.*

sēcŭbo -are, -ui, *to sleep alone.*

sēcŭl-; see saecul-.

sēcum = cum se; see se.

sēcundāni -ōrum, m. pl. *soldiers of the second legion.*

sēcundārius -a -um, *second-rate.*

sēcundo -are, *to favour, assist.*

sēcundum: adv., *after, behind;* prep., with acc., *following, after, along beside; during; in addition to; next after, next to; according to; in favour of.*

sēcundus -a -um. (1) *going after, second, following; inferior, second-rate.* (2) *going the same way, attending, favouring;* secundo flumine, *downstream;* res secundae, *prosperity, success.* As subst.: n. abl. sing. **sēcundō**, *secondly;* f. pl. **sēcundae** -ārum, *the second role, second fiddle;* n. pl. **sēcundă** -ōrum, *prosperity, success.*

sēcūrifer -fĕra -fĕrum, and **sēcūriger** -gĕra -gĕrum, *carrying an axe.*

sēcūris -is, f. *an axe, hatchet;* esp. *the headsman's axe;* hence *supreme power, Roman supremacy.*

sēcūritās -ātis, f. *freedom from care; peace of mind, composure; careless-*
ness, *false confidence.* Transf., *freedom from danger, security.*

sēcūrus -a -um, *free from care, unconcerned, fearless, tranquil; careless;* objectively, *safe, secure.* Adv. **sēcūrē**.

¹sĕcus, n. indecl., *sex.*

²sĕcŭs, adv. *otherwise, not so;* foll. by atque (ac), or quam, *otherwise than, differently from;* non secus, haud secus, *just so.* Transf., *not as one would wish,* i.e. *wrongly, badly.* Compar. **sēquĭŭs** or **sētĭŭs**, *otherwise, not so; less; rather badly.*

sēcūtor -ōris, m. *a gladiator armed with sword and shield.*

sĕd (**sĕt**), *but, however;* sed enim, *but in fact;* confirming, *and indeed, and what is more.*

sēdātio -ōnis, f. *allaying, soothing.*

sēdĕcim, *sixteen.*

sēdēcŭla -ae, f. *a low seat, stool.*

sēdĕo sēdēre sēdi sessum, *to sit; to sit in council or judgment; to sit about, be inactive;* milit. *to remain encamped;* of things, *to be settled, stay fixed;* of resolves, *to be firmly determined.*

sēdēs -is, f. *a seat; a chair, throne; an abode, home;* of things, *place, seat, base, foundation.*

sēdile -is, n. *a seat, bench.*

sēditio -ōnis, f. *insurrection, rising, mutiny; dissension, quarrel.*

sēditiōsus -a -um, *quarrelsome, turbulent, restless;* adv. **sēditiōsē**.

sēdo -are, *to settle, soothe, calm, allay;* partic. **sēdātus** -a -um, *calm, composed;* adv. **sēdātē**.

sēdūco -dūcĕre -duxi -ductum, *to lead apart, turn aside, separate;* partic. **sēductus** -a -um, *remote, distant.*

sēductio -ōnis, f. *leading aside.*

sēdūlĭtās -ātis, f. *zeal, application.*

sēdŭlus -a -um, *busy, diligent;* in bad sense, *officious.* N. abl. as adv. **sēdŭlō**, *busily; purposely, designedly.*

sĕgĕs -ĕtis, f. *a cornfield; standing corn, a crop;* in gen., *field, ground, soil; source, origin; profit.*

segmentātus -a -um *adorned with borders or patches.*

segmentum -i, n. *a cutting, shred;* plur., *borders or patches of purple or gold.*

sēgnipēs -pĕdis, *slow-footed.*

sēgnis -e, *slow, tardy, sluggish, lingering.* N. acc. as adv. **segnĕ**, and adv. **segnĭtĕr**, *slowly, sluggishly.*

sēgnĭtia -ae, and **sēgnĭtiēs** -ēi, f. *sluggishness, slowness.*

sēgrĕgo -are, *to segregate, separate, remove.*

sēiūgātus -a -um, *separated.*

sēiŭgis -is, m. *a chariot drawn by six horses.*

sēiunctim, *separately.*

sēiunctio -ōnis, f. *separation.*

sēiungo -iungĕre -iunxi -iunctum, *to separate, sever, disjoin.*

sēlectio -ōnis, f. *choosing out, selection.*

Sēleucus -i, m. *name of several kings of Syria.*

sēlibra -ae, f. *half a pound.*

sēligo -līgĕre -lēgi -lectum, *to choose, select.*

sella -ae, f. *a seat, chair, stool;* sella (curulis), *a magistrate's seat;* sella (gestatoria), *a sedan-chair.*

sellisternia -ōrum, n. pl. *religious banquets in honour of goddesses.*

sellŭla -ae, f. *a little chair.*

sellŭlārius -i, m. *a sedentary worker.*

sēmĕl, *once, a single time; for the first time; once for all;* indef., *once, ever, at any time.*

Sĕmĕla -ae, *and* Sĕmĕlē -ēs, f. *mother of Bacchus.*

sēmen -ĭnis, n. *seed; a seedling, scion, shoot; a stock, race; an element; a cause, origin; an author, instigator.*

sēmentĭfer -fĕra -fĕrum, *seed-bearing, fruitful.*

sēmentis -is, *a sowing or planting;* plur., sementes, *young growing corn.*

sēmentīvus -a -um, *of seed-time.*

sēmestris (sēmenstris) -e, *of six months, lasting six months.*

sēmēsus -a -um, *half-eaten.*

sēmiădăpertus -a -um, *half-open.*

sēmiănīmis -e *and* sēmiănīmus -a -um, *half-alive, half-dead.*

sēmiăpertus -a -um, *half-open.*

sēmibŏs -bŏvis, m. *half-ox.*

sēmicāper -pri, m. *half-goat.*

sēmicrĕmātus *and* sēmicrĕmus -a -um, *half-burnt.*

sēmicŭbĭtālis -e, *half a cubit long.*

sēmidĕus -a -um, *half-divine;* as subst., *a demigod.*

sēmidoctus -a -um, *half-taught.*

sēmiermis (sēmermis) -e *and* sēmiermus (sēmermus) -a -um, *half-armed, half-equipped.*

sēmiēsus = semesus; q.v.

sēmifactus -a -um, *half-done, half-finished.*

sēmifer -fĕra -fĕrum, *half-animal; half-savage.*

sēmigermānus -a -um, *half-German.*

sēmigrăvis -e, *half-overcome.*

sēmigro -are, *to go away, depart.*

sēmihians -antis, *half-open.*

sēmihŏmo -hŏmĭnis, m. *half-man; half-wild.*

sēmihora -ae, f. *half an hour.*

sēmilācer -cĕra -cĕrum, *half-mangled.*

sēmilīber -bĕra -bĕrum, *half-free.*

sēmilixa -ae, m. *half a sutler.*

sēmimărīnus -a -um, *half in the sea.*

sēmimas -măris, m. *half-male, hermaphrodite; castrated.*

sēmĭnārium -i, n. *a plantation, nursery.*

sēmĭnātor -oris, m. *begetter, author.*

sēmĭnex -nĕcis, *half-dead.*

sēmĭnium -i, n. *a begetting; a race or breed.*

sēmĭno -are, *to sow, plant; to beget, produce.*

sēmĭnŭdus -a -um, *half-naked; ill-protected.*

sēmĭplēnus -a -um, *half-full, half-manned.*

sēmĭpŭtātus -a -um, *half-pruned.*

sēmirĕductus -a -um, *half bent back.*

sēmirĕfectus -a -um, *half-repaired.*

sēmirŭtus -a -um, *half-ruined, half pulled down.*

sēmis -issis, m. *the half of anything,* e.g. *of an as or* iuger; *as a rate of* interest = 6 *per cent per annum.*

sēmisĕpultus -a -um, *half-buried.*

sēmisomnus -a -um *and* sēmisomnis -e, *half-asleep, drowsy.*

sēmisŭpinus -a -um, *half on the back.*

sēmĭta -ae, f. *a narrow way, footpath.*

sēmītālis -e, *and* sēmītārius -a -um *of the footpaths.*

sēmiustŭlātus = semustulatus; q.v.

sēmiustus (sēmustus) -a -um, *half-burnt.*

sēmivir -viri, m. adj., *half-man half-animal; hermaphrodite; castrated effeminate.*

sēmivīvus -a -um, *half-dead, very faint.*

sēmŏdius -i, m. *half a modius.*

sēmŏvĕo -mŏvēre -mōvi -mōtum, *to move away, set aside, separate;* partic. sēmōtus -a -um, *remote distant.*

semper, *always, at all times.*

sempĭternus -a -um, *continual, everlasting.*

Semprōnius -a -um, *name of a Roman gens.*

sēmuncia -ae, f. *half an uncia.*

sēmunciārius -a- um, *of the fraction* 1/24: faenus, 1/24 *per cent monthly,* i.e. ½ *per cent per annum.*

sēmustŭlātus (sēmiustŭlātus) -a -um *half-burnt.*

sēnācŭlum -i, n. *an open space in the Forum, used by the Senate.*

sēnāriŏlus -i, m. *a trifling senarius.*

sēnārius -a -um, *composed of six in a group;* senarius (versus), m. *a senarius, a verse of six feet.*

sēnātor -ōris, m. *a member of the senate, a senator.*

sēnātōrius -a -um, *of a senator, senatorial.*

sēnātus -ūs, (or -i), m *a council of elders, the Senate;* senatus (senati) consultum, *a formal resolution of the senate.*

Sĕnĕca -ae, m. M. Annaeus Seneca, *a rhetorician from Corduba in Spain;* L. Annaeus Seneca, *his son, a Stoic philosopher, tutor of Nero.*

¹sĕnectus -a -um, *old, aged;* f. as subst. sĕnecta -ae, *old age.*

²sĕnectūs -ūtis, f. *old age;* concr., *old men.*

sĕnĕo -ēre, *to be old.*

sĕnesco senescĕre sĕnŭi, *to grow old; to flag, wane.*

sĕnex sĕnis; compar. sĕnior: adj., *old, aged;* subst., *an old person.*

sēni -ae -a, *six at a time, or six each.*

sĕnīlis -e, *of an old man, senile;* adv. sĕnīlĭter.

sĕnio -ōnis, m. *the number six upon dice.*

sĕnior, compar. of senex; q.v.

sĕnium -i, n. *old age; decline, decay; gloom, grief.*

sensicŭlus -i, m. *a little sentence.*

sensifer -fĕra -fĕrum, *producing sensation.*

sensilis -e, *having sensation, sensitive.*

sensim, *just perceptibly, gradually, by degrees.*

sensus -ūs, m. *sense, sensation; feeling, attitude; judgment, perception, understanding; sense, meaning of words, etc.; a sentence.*

sententia -ae, f. *a way of thinking, opinion, thought, meaning, purpose; a decision, vote; meaning, sense of words, etc.; a sentence, period; esp., a maxim, aphorism.*

sententiŏla -ae, f. *a short sentence, maxim, aphorism.*

sententiōsus -a -um, *pithy, sententious;* adv. **sententiōsē.**

senticētum -i, n. *a thorn-brake.*

sentina -ae, f. *bilge-water; rabble, dregs of the population.*

sentio sentire sensi sensum, *to feel, perceive; to experience, feel the force of a thing; to realize a truth; to hold an opinion, judge, suppose; legal, to decide, to vote.* N. pl. of partic. as subst. **sensa** -ōrum, *thoughts, sentiments.*

sentis -is, c. *a thorn-bush, briar.*

sentisco -ĕre, *to begin to perceive*

sentus -a -um, *neglected, rough.*

sĕorsum, sorsum, sorsus, *apart, separately.*

sēpărātim, *apart, separately, differently.*

sēpărātio -ōnis, f. *separation, severance.*

sēpăro -are, *to sever, separate; to consider or treat separately.*
Hence partic. **sēpărātus** -a -um, *separate, distinct;* compar. adv. **sēpărātiŭs,** *less closely.*

sēpĕlio -pĕlire -pĕlivi and -pĕlii -pultum, *to bury; to ruin, destroy;* partic. **sēpultus,** *buried, sunk, immersed.*

sēp-; see also **saep-.**

sēpia -ae, f. *cuttle-fish.*

sēpōno -pōnĕre -pōsŭi -pŏsĭtum, *to put on one side, place apart, reserve; to put out of the way, banish; to distinguish, divide.* Partic. **sēpŏsitus** -a -um, *distant, remote; choice, select.*

sepse = *se ipse;* see **ipse.**

septem, *seven.*

September -bris, *of September;* (mensis) *September, the seventh month of the Roman year, September.*

septemdĕcim, *seventeen.*

septemflŭus -a -um, *with seven mouths.*

septemgĕmĭnus -a -um, *sevenfold.*

septemplex -plĭcis, *sevenfold.*

septemtriōnālis -e, *northern.*

septemtriōnēs (septen-) -um, m. pl. *the seven stars of either the Great Bear or the Little Bear; in gen., the north; the north wind.*

septemvir -vĭri, m. *one of the septemviri, a college or guild of seven persons;* adj. **septemvirālis** -e, *of septemviri;* subst. **septemvirātus** -ūs, m. *the office of a septemvir.*

septēnārius -a -um, *containing seven;* m. pl. as subst. **septēnārii,** *verses containing seven feet, heptameters.*

septendĕcim = septemdecim; q.v.

septēni -ae, -a, *seven at a time or seven each.*

septentrio = septemtrio; q.v.

septies (-iens), *seven times.*

septimānus -a -um, *of the seventh;* m. pl. as subst. *soldiers of the seventh legion.*

septimus (septŭmus) -a -um, *seventh;* **septimum,** *for the seventh time.*

septimus dĕcimus -a -um, *seventeenth.*

septingentēsimus (-ensimus) -a -um, *seven hundredth.*

septingenti -ae -a, *seven hundred.*

septŭāgēsimus (-ensimus) -a -um, *seventieth.*

septŭāgintā, *seventy.*

septŭennis -e, *of seven years.*

septum = saeptum; q.v.

septunx -uncis, m. *seven-twelfths.*

sĕpulcrālis -e, *of a tomb, sepulchral.*

sĕpulcrētum -i, n. *a burial-place, cemetery.*

sĕpulcrum -i n., *a place of burial, grave, tomb.*

sĕpultūra -ae, f. *burial, interment; also the burning of a dead body.*

Sēquāna -ae, m. *a river of Gaul (now the Seine).*

sĕquax -ācis, *following, attending, pursuing.*

sĕquester -tri or -tris, m. *a depositary; a go-between, agent, mediator.*

sĕquestra -ae, f. *a mediator.*

sĕquĭus = secius, compar. of secus; q.v.

sĕquor sĕqui sĕcūtus, dep. *to follow, accompany, attend; to pursue, chase; in time, to follow, ensue; to follow logically, follow as a consequence; of property, to go to, fall to; to conform to; to strive after, aim at.*

sēra -ae, f. *a bar or bolt.*

sĕrēnĭtās -ātis, f. *clear weather.*

sĕrēno -are, *to make clear, make bright.*

sĕrēnus -a -um, *clear, bright, fair;* n. as subst. *fair weather.*

Sērēs -um, m. *the Chinese famous for their silks;* adj. **Sēricus** -a -um, *Chinese; silken.*

sēresco -ere, *to become dry.*

sēria -ae, f. *a large jar.*

sēries, acc. -em, abl. -e, f. *a row, chain, series; a line of descent, lineage.*

sērius -a -um, *serious, earnest;* n. as subst. *earnest, seriousness;* abl. as adv. **sēriō,** *in earnest, seriously.*

sermo -ōnis, m. *talk, conversation; discussion; common talk, report, rumour; a subject of conversation; a conversational style, or prose; any manner of speaking, style, expression, diction, language, dialect.*

sermōcinor -āri, dep. *to converse, talk, discuss.*

sermuncŭlus -i, m. *rumour, tittle-tattle.*

[1]**sĕro** sĕrĕre sĕvi sătum, *to sow, set, plant;* n. pl. of partic. as subst., **sāta** -ōrum, *standing corn, crops; to beget, engender, bring forth;* partic. **sātus** -a -um, *sprung, born; in gen., to produce, give rise to.*

¹sĕro sĕrĕre sĕrŭi sertum, *to join together, put in a row, connect*, partic. sertus -a -um, *linked, connected*; n. as subst. sertum -i, and plur. serta -orum, *a garland, wreath*; also f. serta -ae.

serpens -entis, c. *a snake, serpent*.

serpentīgĕna -ae, m. *sprung from a serpent*.

serpentĭpēs -pēdis, *snake-footed*.

serpĕrastra -orum. n. *bandages or knee-splints*.

serpo serpĕre serpsi serptum, *to creep, crawl, advance slowly*.

serpyllum (-pillum, -pullum) -i, n. *wild thyme*.

serra -ae, f. *a saw*.

serrācum (sarr-) -i, n. *a kind of waggon*.

serrātus -a -um, *toothed like a saw, serrated*; m. pl. as subst. (sc. nummi), *milled coins*.

serrŭla -ae, f. *a little saw*.

sertum; see sero.

sĕrum -i, n. *whey*.

sĕrus -a -um, *late, too late*; n. as subst. serum -i, *a late hour*; n. abl. sing. as adv. sērō, *late, too late*.

serva -ae, f. see servus.

servābilis -e, *able to be saved*.

servātor -ōris, m. and servātrix -icis, f., *a preserver, saviour; a watcher*.

servilis -e, *of a slave, servile*; adv. servilitĕr.

Servīlius -a -um, *name of Roman gens*.

servio -ire, (with dat.), *to be a slave, to serve, help, gratify; legal, of buildings, etc., to be subject to certain rights, e.g. to be mortgaged*.

servītium -i, n. *slavery, servitude, subjection*; concr., *slaves, servants, a household*.

servitūdo -inis, f. *slavery, servitude*.

servitūs -ūtis, f. *slavery, servitude*; in gen., *subjection, obedience; legal, of houses, etc., liability to certain burdens, e.g. a right of way*; concr., *slaves*.

servo -are, *to watch over, observe; to keep, protect, save; to lay up, reserve; to keep, retain a promise, etc.; to keep to, stay in a place*. Partic., in superl., servantissimus -i, *most careful, most observant*.

servŭlus (servŏlus) -i, m. and servŭla (servŏla) -ae, f. *a young slave*.

servus, -a -um, adj., *serving, servile, subject; legal, of lands, etc., subject to other rights*; m. and f. as subst., *a slave, servant*.

sescēnāris -e, *a year and a half old*.

sescēnārius -a -um, *consisting of six hundred*.

sescēni -ae -a, *six hundred at a time or six hundred each*.

sescentēsĭmus (-ensĭmus) -a -um, *six hundredth*.

sescenti -ae -a, *six hundred*; in gen., *countless*.

sescentiēs (-iens), *six hundred times*.

sĕsĕlis -is, f. *a plant, hartwort*.

sesqui, *one half more, half as much again*.

sesquĭalter -altĕra -altĕrum, *one and a half*.

sesquihŏra -ae, f. *an hour and a half*.

sesquĭmŏdius -i, m. *a modius and a half*.

sesquĭoctāvus -a -um, *containing 9/8 of a thing*.

sesquĭpĕdālis -e, *a foot and a half long*.

sesquĭpēs -pĕdis, m. *a foot and a half long, wide, etc*.

sesquĭplāga -ae, f. *a blow and a half*.

sesquĭplex -plicis, *one and a half times as much*.

sesquĭtertius -a -um, *containing 4/3 of anything*.

sessĭbŭlum -i, n. *a seat, stool, chair*.

sessilis -e, *fit for sitting*; of plants, *low, dwarf*.

sessĭo -ōnis, f. *the act of sitting; loitering, idling; a session; a place for sitting, seat*.

sessĭto -are, *to sit much, sit often*.

sessiuncŭla -ae, f. *a little company or assembly*.

sessor -ōris, m. *a sitter; an inhabitant*.

sestertius -a -um, *consisting of two and a half*; m. as subst. sestertius -i. *a sesterce, a silver coin*, = ¼ denarius, = 2½ asses.

Sestius -a -um, *name of a Roman gens*.

sēt = sed; q.v.

sēta = saeta; q.v.

seu; see sive.

sĕvēritās -ātis, and sĕvērĭtūdo -inis f. *gravity, sternness*.

sĕvērus -a -um, *grave, serious, strict, stern, hard*; adv. sĕvērē.

sēvŏco -are, *to call aside, withdraw, separate*.

sēvum = sebum; q.v.

sex, *six*.

sexāgēnārius -a -um, *containing sixty; sixty years old*.

sexāgēni -ae -a, *sixty at a time*, or *sixty each*.

sexāgēsĭmus (-ensĭmus) -a -um, *sixtieth*.

sexāgiēs (-iens), *sixty times*.

sexāgintā, *sixty*.

sexangŭlus -a -um, *hexagonal*.

sexcen-; see sescen-.

sexdĕcim = sedecim; q.v.

sexennis -e, *six years old*.

sexennium -i, n. *a period of six years*.

sexiēs (-iens), *six times*.

sexprĭmi -ōrum, m. *a board of six magistrates in a provincial town*.

sextādĕcĭmāni -orum, m. pl. *soldiers of the 16th legion*.

sextans -antis, m. *one sixth*.

sextārius -i, m. *one sixth, esp. of a congius (about a pint)*.

Sextilis -e, *of the sixth month of the old Roman year*; sextilis (mensis), *the sixth month, afterwards called Augustus*.

sextŭla -ae, f. 1/72.

sextus -a -um, *sixth*; sextum, *for the sixth time*.

sextusdĕcĭmus -a -um, *sixteenth*.

sexus -ūs, m. *sex*.

si, *if, supposing that*; quod si, *and if, but if*; si modo, *if only*; si quis, *if anybody*; si non, si minus, nisi, *if not, unless*.

sibila -ōrum, n. pl.: as adj., *hissing*; as subst., = plur. of sibilus (q.v.).

sibilo -are,: intransit., *to hiss, whistle*; transit., *to hiss at*.

sibilus -i, m. (poet. plur. sibila; q.v.), *a hissing, whistling*.

Sibylla -ae, f. *a prophetess of Apollo, a Sibyl*; adj. **Sibyllinus** -a -um, *of the Sibyl, Sibylline*.

sic, *so, thus, in this way; like this, as follows; in that case, with this limitation*; leading up to consecutive clause, *so much, to such a degree*; interrog. **sicine**, *is it thus that?*

sica -ae, f. *dagger, dirk, poniard*.

Sicāni -ōrum, m. pl. *an ancient people of Sicily*; adj. **Sicānus** and **Sicānius** -a -um, *Sicanian*; subst. **Sicānia** -ae, f. *Sicania = Sicily*.

sicārius -i, m. *an assassin, murderer*.

siccitās -ātis, f. *dryness, drought; sound health*; of style *plainness, simplicity*.

sicco -are, *to make dry, to dry; to stanch; to drain*.

siccus -a -um, *dry; thirsting, thirsty*; of health, *sound; sober, temperate*; of style *plain, simple*; adv. **siccē**.

Sicilia -ae, f.; see Siculi.

sicine; see sic.

sicūbi, *if anywhere*.

Siculi -ōrum, m. pl., *the Sicilians*; adj. **Siculus** -a -um, *Sicilian*; subst. **Sicilia** -ae, f. *Sicily*.

sicunde, *if from anywhere*.

sicut and **sicuti**, *as, just as; as for example; as it were*; with verb in subj., *just as if*.

Sicyōn -ōnis, f. *a city in the Peloponnese*; adj. **Sicyōnius** -a -um, *Sicyonian*; n. pl. as subst. *a kind of soft shoes from Sicyon*.

sidēreus -a -um, *of the stars starry; gleaming*.

sido sidere sidi and sēdi sessum, *to sit or sink down, settle, alight; to remain lying or fixed*; naut. *to stick fast, be stranded*; of feelings, *to subside*.

Sidōn -ōnis, f. *a city of Phoenicia*; adj. **Sidōnius** -a -um; f. adj. **Sidōnis** -idis.

sidus -ēris, n. *a constellation, or a single star; any luminary, heavenly body; time of year, season, weather*; in astrology, *star, destiny*; plur., *the heavens*. Transf., *pride, glory*.

sigilla -ōrum, n. pl. *small figures, images; a seal*.

sigillātus -a -um, *adorned with small figures*.

sigma -ātis, n. *the Greek letter sigma; a semicircular dining-couch*.

signātor -ōris, m. *one who seals; a witness*.

signifer -fēra -fērum, *bearing signs or figures; covered with constellations*. M. as subst. **signifer** -fēri *a standard-bearer; a leader*.

significātio -ōnis, f. *indication, sign, token; sign of assent, approbation; emphasis; meaning, signification*.

significo -are, *to indicate, show; to foreshow; to mean, signify*; partic. **significans** -antis, *distinct, clear*; adv. **significanter**.

signo -are, *to mark, inscribe; to seal, seal up; to coin, stamp* money. Transf., *to impress, indicate; to observe, notice*.

signum -i, n. *a sign, mark, token; a warning, symptom*; milit., *a standard, banner, ensign, or a signal, order, command, or a watchword, password; a figure, image, statute; a seal, signet; a group of stars, constellation*.

silānus -i, m. *a fountain*.

silentium -i, n. *silence, stillness, quiet; repose; obscurity*.

sileo -ēre -ūi, *to be still, silent*; with acc., *to be silent about; to be still, rest, be inactive*; partic. **silens** -entis, *silent, still*; pl. as subst. *the dead*.

siler -ēris, n. *the brook-willow*.

silesco -ere, *to become silent, grow still*.

silex -icis, m. (rarely f.), *any hard stone, such as flint; crag, rock, cliff*.

silicernium -i, n. *a funeral feast*.

siligo -inis, f. *wheat; wheaten flour*.

siliqua -ae, f. *a husk, pod, shell*; in plur., *pulse*.

Silius -a -um, *name of Roman gens*.

Silūres -um, pl. *a British people*.

silus -a -um, *snub-nosed, pug-nosed*.

silva, *a wood, forest; bush; a plantation, grove; a mass, plenty, abundance*.

Silvānus -i, m. *god of woods and forests*.

silvesco -ēre, of a vine, *to run wild, run to wood*.

silvestris -e, *of woods; wooded; wild, rural*.

silvicola -ae, m. and f. and **silvicultrix** -tricis, f. *inhabiting woods*.

silvifragus -a -um, *shattering the woods*.

silvōsus -a -um *well wooded*.

simia -ae, f. *ape, monkey*.

similis -e; compar. similior, superl. simillimus; *like, resembling, similar* (with genit. or dat.); veri similis, *probable*; n. as subst. *a resemblance or comparison*; adv. **similiter**, *similarly*.

similitūdo -inis, f. *likeness, resemblance*; veri similitudo, *probability; intended likeness, imitation; a metaphor, simile; uniformity, monotony*.

similo = simulo; q.v.

simiolus -i, m. *little ape*.

simitū, *together*.

simius -i, m. *ape, monkey*.

simplex -plicis; *simple, single; unmixed, pure, plain, absolute; morally simple, straightforward*. Adv. **simpliciter**, *simply, plainly; artlessly, frankly*.

simplicitās -ātis, f. *simplicity; straightforwardness, honesty, candour*.

simplum -i, m. *the simple sum or number* (opp. double, etc.).

simpulum -i, n. *a ladle*.

simpuvium -i, n. *a sacrificial bowl*.

sĭmul, *at once, at the same time, together*; simul atque (ac), *as soon as.*

sĭmŭlācrum -i, n. *an image, likeness, portrait; effigy; a shade, ghost, imitation, phantom, appearance.*

sĭmŭlāmen -ĭnis, n. *an imitation.*

sĭmŭlātĭo -ōnis, f. *assumed appearance, pretence, feint.*

sĭmŭlātor -ōris, m. *an imitator; a pretender, feigner.*

sĭmŭlo -are, *to make like, cause to resemble; to make a copy of, to represent; to play the part of; to pretend a thing is so, simulate, feign*; partic. **sĭmŭlans** -antis, *imitating, imitative;* adv. from perf. partic. **sĭmŭlātē,** *feignedly.*

sĭmultās -ātis, f. *a clash, rivalry, feud.*

sĭmŭlus -a -um, *rather snub-nosed.*

sīmus -a -um, *snub-nosed.*

sin, conj. *but if, if however.*

sĭnāpī -is, n. and **sĭnāpis** -is, f. *mustard.*

sincērĭtās -ātis, f. *purity, soundness, integrity.*

sincērus -a -um, *pure, whole, sound, genuine, uncorrupt;* adv. **sincērē,** *honestly, frankly.*

sinciput -pitis, n. *half a head; the smoked chap of a pig.*

sindōn -ōnis, f. *fine cotton cloth, muslin.*

sĭnĕ, prep. with abl., *without.*

singillātim, *singly, one by one.*

singŭlāris -e, *alone, single individual, singular; unique, extraordinary.* Adv. **singŭlārĭtĕr,** *singly; in the singular number; particularly, extraordinarily.*

singŭli; see singulus.

singultim, *with sobs.*

singulto -are: intransit., *to gasp, sob;* transit., *to sob out, gasp out.*

singultus -ūs, m. *a sobbing, gasping.*

singŭlus -a -um, more freq. plur. **singŭli** -ae, -a, *single, separate, one at a time; distributive, one each.*

sĭnister -tra -trum, *left, on the left hand; wrong, perverse; unfavourable, adverse;* sometimes, in augury, *favourable.* F. as subst. **sĭnistra** -ae, *the left hand;* also *the left side.* Adv. **sĭnistrē,** *wrongly, unfavourably.*

sĭnistrorsus (-orsum), *to the left.*

sĭno sĭnĕre sivi sĭtum, *to let alone, leave; to let, allow, permit;* partic. **sĭtus** -a -um, *placed, laid down; lying, situated.*

Sĭnōpa -ae, and **Sĭnōpē** -ēs, f. *a town on the Black Sea.*

sinum; see ¹sinus.

sĭnŭo -are, *to bend, curve.*

sĭnŭōsus -a -um, *winding, sinuous.* Transf., *roundabout, diffuse.*

¹sĭnus -i, m. and **sinum** -i, n. *a large bowl.*

²sĭnus -ūs, m. *a curve, fold, winding; of dress, a fold, pocket, lap; in a coastline, a bay, gulf.* Transf., *heart, secret feelings.*

sĭpārĭum -i, n. *a curtain; a drop-scene at a theatre.*

sĭpho (sīfo) -ōnis, m. *a siphon; a fire-engine.*

sĭquando, *if ever.*

sĭquĭdem, *if indeed;* sometimes *since, because.*

Sīrēn -ēnis, f., usually plur. **Sīrēnes** -um, *the Sirens, nymphs who by their song lured mariners to destruction.*

Sīrius -i, m. *the Dog-Star Sirius.*

sīs = (1) si vis; see volo. (2) second sing. of pres. subj. of sum; q.v. (3) dat. or abl. plur. of suus; q.v.

sisto sistĕre stiti stātum: transit., *to cause to stand, set, place;* legal, *to cause to appear in court;* vadimonium sistere, *to appear on the appointed day; to stop, check; to establish firmly;* intransit., *to place oneself, stand;* legal, *to present oneself in court; to stand still to halt; to stand firm.*
    Hence partic. **stătus** -a -um, *fixed, determined, regular.*

sistrum -i, n. *a sort of rattle used in the worship of Isis.*

sĭsymbrĭum -i, n. *an aromatic herb, perhaps mint.*

Sĭsyphus -i, m. *a robber, condemned in the lower world to roll a stone uphill for ever.*

sĭtella -ae, f. *an urn for drawing lots.*

sĭtĭcŭlōsus -a -um, *very dry, parched.*

sĭtĭo -ire: intransit., *to thirst, to be thirsty, dry, parched;* transit., *to thirst for, thirst after;* partic. **sĭtĭens** -entis, *thirsty, dry, parched; eager, desirous;* adv. **sĭtĭentĕr.**

sĭtis -is, f. *thirst; dryness, drought; eager desire.*

sĭtĭtor -ōris, m. *a thirster.*

sittўbus -i, m. *a strip of parchment showing the title of a book.*

sĭtŭla -ae, f. *a jar.*

¹sĭtus -a -um, partic. from sino; q v.

²sĭtus -ūs, m. (1) *layout, site, position, situation.* (2) *being left; neglect, dirt, decay; mental rusting, dullness.*

sīvĕ and **sĕu,** *or if;* sive (seu) . . . sive (seu), *whether . . . or.*

smăragdus -i, m. and f. *emerald.*

sŏbŏles, sŏbŏlesco = suboles, subolesco; q.v.

sōbrīnus -i, m. and **sōbrīna** -ae, f. *a cousin on the mother's side.*

sōbrĭus -a -um, *sober; without wine; moderate, frugal; sober-minded, reasonable, sensible.* Adv. **sōbrĭē.**

soccŭlus -i, m. *a little soccus: q.v.*

soccus -i, m. *a light shoe or slipper, esp. as worn by comic actors.*

sŏcer -ĕri, m. *father-in-law;* plur., soceri, *father- and mother-in-law.*

sŏcĕïa -ae, f., see socius.

sŏcĭābĭlis -e, *easily united, compatible.*

sŏcĭālis -e, *of partners or allies; conjugal; sociable.* Adv. **sŏcĭālĭtĕr,** *sociably.*

sŏcĭĕtās -ātis, f. *partnership, fellowship, association, alliance.*

sŏcĭo -are, *to unite, combine, associate.*

sŏcĭus -a -um, *sharing, associated, allied.* M. and f. as subst. *a partner, comrade, associate, ally.*

sŏcordĭa (sēcordĭa) -ae, f. *folly, stupidity; negligence, indolence.*

sŏcors -cordis, *weak-minded, stupid; negligent, slothful, careless*; compar. adv. **sŏcordĭus,** *too feebly.*

Sŏcrătēs -is, m. *the Athenian philosopher, put to death in* 399 B.C. Adj. **Sŏcrătĭcus** -a -um, *Socratic*; m. pl. *as subst., followers of Socrates.*

socrus -ūs, f. *mother-in-law.*

sŏdālĭcĭum -i, n. *an association*; esp. *a secret society*; in gen., *comradeship.*

sŏdālĭcĭus -a -um, *of companionship.*

sŏdālĭs -is, c. *member of an association,* esp. *of a priesthood or a secret society*; in gen., *a comrade*; of things, *companion, attendant on.*

sŏdālĭtās -ātis, f. *an association; comradeship, intimacy.*

sŏdēs, *if you please, with your leave.*

sōl **sōlis,** m. *the sun*; poet., *a day*; personif., *the Sun-god.*

sōlācĭŏlum -i, n. *a small consolation.*

sōlācĭum -i, n. *consolation, comfort, relief.*

sōlāmen -ĭnis, n. *consolation comfort.*

sōlāris -e, *of the sun, solar.*

sōlārĭum -i, n. *a sundial; a terrace exposed to the sun.*

sōlātor ōris, m. *a consoler, comforter.*

soldūrĭi -ōrum, m. pl. *retainers, vassals.*

soldus = solidus; q.v.

sŏlěa -ae, f. *a sandal; a kind of fetter; a shoe for an animal; a fish, the sole.*

sŏlěātus -a -um, *wearing sandals.*

sŏlennis = sollemnis; q.v.

sŏlěo **sŏlēre** **sŏlĭtus sum,** *to be accustomed*; ut solet, *as usual*; partic. **sŏlĭtus** -a -um, *accustomed, habitual, usual*; n. as subst. *that which is usual.*

sōlers = sollers; q.v.

sōlĭdĭtās -ātis, f. *solidity.*

sōlĭdo -are, *to make firm or solid.*

sōlĭdus (soldus) -a -um, *dense, solid; whole, complete, entire; firm, enduring, real*; n. as subst., *firm ground, solid substance, entirety.* Adv. **sōlĭdē,** *firmly*; scire, *to know for certain.*

sōlĭferrěum -i, n. *a javelin entirely of iron.*

sōlistĭmus -a -um; *see* tripudium.

sōlĭtārĭus -a -um, *alone, lonely.*

sōlĭtūdo -ĭnis, f. *solitude, loneliness; desertion, deprivation, want.*

sōlĭtus -a -um, partic. from soleo; q.v.

sōlĭum -i, n. (1) *a chair of state, throne;* hence *dominion, regal power.* (2) *a bath-tub.*

sōlĭvăgus -a -um, *wandering alone; solitary, lonely.*

sollemnis -e, *yearly, annual, recurring; solemn, festive, religious; usual, customary.* N. as subst. **sollemne** -is. *a solemn feast, religious rite; a custom.* Adv. **sollemnĭtěr.**

sollers -ertis, *clever, skilful*; adv. **sollertěr.**

sollertĭa -ae, f. *cleverness, skill.*

sollĭcĭtātĭo -ōnis, f. *inciting, instigation.*

sollĭcĭto -are, *to move violently, disturb, agitate; to rouse, vex, disquiet; to incite, instigate, tamper with.*

sollĭcĭtūdo -ĭnis, f. *uneasiness, disquiet, anxiety.*

sollĭcĭtus -a -um, *disturbed, agitated, restless; anxious, uneasy, worried*; of animals, *watchful*; in act. sense, *disquieting.* Adv. **sollĭcĭtē,** *anxiously, carefully.*

sōlo -are, *to make solitary.*

sŏloecismus -i, m. *a grammatical error.*

Sŏlōn -ōnis, m. *a famous Athenian legislator, active about* 600 B.C.

sōlor -ari, dep. *to comfort, console; to assuage, relieve troubles,* etc.

solstĭtĭālis -e, *of the summer solstice; of summer; of the sun.*

solstĭtĭum -i, n. *solstice,* esp. *the summer solstice; summer.*

sŏlum -i, n. *bottom, floor, foundation; the sole of the foot, or shoe; soil, ground, earth, land, country.*

sōlus -a -um, *alone, only, sole*; of places, *solitary, uninhabited.* N. acc. as adv. **sōlum,** *alone, only.*

sŏlūtĭo -ōnis, f. *a loosening; a paying, payment; a solution, explanation.*

solvo **solvěre** **solvi** **sŏlūtum,** *to loosen; to untie, release, free; to dissolve, break up; to exempt; to break up, weaken, bring to an end; to pay off, discharge a debt*; solvendo non esse, *to be insolvent; to meet engagements, perform duties; to break down a restraining influence; to solve a problem, explain a difficulty.*
Hence partic. **sŏlūtus** -a -um, *loosened, unbound, free, unencumbered, independent*; in bad sense, *unrestrained, unbridled; lax, lazy, negligent*: of style, *fluent or in prose.* Adv. **sŏlūtē,** *loosely, freely; carelessly.*

somnĭcŭlōsus -a -um, *sleepy, drowsy*; adv. **somnĭcŭlōsē.**

somnĭfer -fěra -ferum, *sleep-bringing; narcotic, deadly.*

somnĭo -are, *to dream*; with acc., *to dream of; to imagine foolishly.*

somnĭum -i, n. *a dream; a fancy, day-dream; foolishness, nonsense.*

somnus -i, m. *sleep, slumber; drowsiness, laziness, inactivity; night.*

sŏnābĭlis -e, *resounding.*

sŏnĭpēs -pědis, *sounding with the feet*; m. as subst., *a horse.*

sŏnĭtus -ūs, m. *a sound, noise.*

sŏnĭvĭus -a -um, *sounding*; sonivium tripudium, *the noise of the food falling from the beaks of the sacred chickens.*

sŏno **sŏnare** **sŏnŭi** **sŏnĭtum,** *to sound, resound, make a noise; to sing of, to celebrate*; of words, *to mean.*

sŏnor -ōris, m. *sound, noise, din.*

sŏnōrus -a -um, *sounding, resonant, loud.*

sons sontis, *guilty.*

sontĭcus -a -um, *important, serious.*

sŏnus -i, m. *noise, sound; tone, character, style.*

sŏphĭa -ae, f. *wisdom.*

sŏphistēs -ae, m. *a sophist.*

Sŏphŏclēs -is and -i, m. *the Greek tragic poet*; adj. **Sŏphŏclěus** -a -um.

¹sŏphŏs (-ŭs) -i, m. *wise*; as subst., *a wise man.*

²sŏphŏs, adv. *bravo! well done!*

sŏpĭo -ire, *to put to sleep, lull to sleep, quieten; to stun, render senseless.*

sŏpor -ōris, m. *deep sleep; laziness; a sleeping draught.*

sŏpōrātus -a -um, *full of sleep.*

sŏpōrĭfer -fĕra -fĕrum, *causing deep sleep.*

sŏpōrus -a -um, *sleep-bringing.*

Sōractē -is, n. *a mountain in Etruria.*

sorbĕo -ēre, *to suck in, drink, swallow.*

sorbĭlo, *by sipping; drop by drop.*

sorbum -i, n. *a service-berry.*

sordĕo -ēre, *to be dirty; to appear vile.*

sordēs -is, f. often plur. sordēs -ĭum, *dirt, filth; shabby or dirty garments; low rank; sordid conduct, meanness.*

sordesco sordescĕre sordŭi, *to become dirty.*

sordĭdātus -a -um, *wearing shabby or dirty clothes.*

sordĭdŭlus -a -um *somewhat dirty or mean.*

sordĭdus -a -um, *dirty, filthy, shabby; low, base in rank; mean in conduct.* Adv. sordĭdē, *meanly; stingily.*

sōrex -ĭcis, m. *a shrew-mouse.*

sŏror -ōris, f. *a sister.*

sŏrōrĭcīda -ae, m. *one who murders a sister.*

sŏrōrĭus -a -um, *of a sister, sisterly.*

sors sortis, f. *a lot; a casting of lots; an oracular response, prophecy; official duty as allotted; with genit., share, part; fate, fortune, destiny; money, capital out at interest.*

sortĭlĕgus -a -um, *prophetic, oracular; m. as subst., a soothsayer, fortune-teller.*

sortĭor -iri, dep., and sortĭo -ire: instransit., *to cast lots;* transit., *to allot, cast lots for; share out;* also *to obtain by lot; to choose.* Hence partic. sortītus -a -um; dep., *having obtained* (by lots) *or cast lots for;* pass. *gained by lot;* n. abl. as adv., sortītō, *by lot, by fate.*

sortītio -ōnis, f. *casting lots, deciding by lot.*

¹sortītus -ūs, m. *casting lots, deciding by lot.*

²sortītus -a -um, partic. from sortior; q.v.

sospĕs -ĭtis, *safe, unhurt, uninjured; lucky, favourable.*

Sospĭta -ae, f. *the Saviour;* epithet of Juno.

sospĭto -are, *to keep safe, preserve.*

sōtēr -ēris; acc. -ēra; m. *a saviour.*

sōtērĭa -ōrum, n. pl. *presents given on recovery from sickness.*

spādix -dĭcis, *chestnut-coloured*

spādo -ōnis, m. *a eunuch.*

spargo spargĕre sparsi sparsum, *to scatter, sprinkle, throw about; to spread, circulate, distribute; to disperse, dissipate;* with abl. *to besprinkle with.* Hence partic. sparsus -a -um, *spread out, scattered; speckled, spotted.*

sparsĭo -ōnis, f. *a sprinkling.*

Sparta -ae, and Spartē -es, f. *Sparta, the capital of Laconia;* adj. Spartānus -a -um, *Spartan.*

spartum -i, n. *Spanish broom.*

spărŭlus -i, m. *a fish, sea-bream.*

spărus -i, m. *a spear with a curved blade.*

spătha -ae, f. *a broad two-edged sword.*

spătĭor -ari, dep. *to walk about, take a walk;* of things, *to spread out, expand.*

spătĭōsus -a -um, *ample, wide;* of time, *long;* adv. spătĭōsē.

spătĭum -i, n. *space, extent, room; distance, interval; dimensions, size; a tract, course, esp. in a race; an open space, a walk.* Transf., *a space of time, period; leisure, opportunity; metrical time, measure, quantity.*

spĕcĭālis -e, *individual, particular, special.*

spĕcĭes -ēi, f.: act., *a seeing, view;* pass., *sight, look; shape, form, outward appearance; beauty; a vision, phantom; a representation, image, statue.* Transf., *pretext, pretence; notion, idea; kind, species.*

spĕcillum -i, n. *a surgeon's probe.*

spĕcĭmen -ĭnis, n. *a visible mark, example, model; a pattern, ideal.*

spĕcĭo (spĭcĭo) spĕcĕre spexi, *to look at, see.*

spĕcĭōsus -a -um, *beautiful, handsome, imposing;* in bad sense, *plausible, specious.* Adv. spĕcĭōsē.

spectābĭlis -e, *visible; worth seeing, notable.*

spectācŭlum -i, n. *sight, show, spectacle; the seats in the theatre or circus.*

spectātĭo -ōnis, f. *looking, watching, viewing; inspection of money.*

spectātor -ōris, m. and spectātrix -trīcĭs, f. *a watcher, spectator, observer; an examiner, critic.*

spectĭo -ōnis, f. *the right to observe auspices.*

specto -are, *to look at, contemplate, watch; to test, examine;* of places, *to look towards, face.* Transf., *to consider, contemplate, look for; to bear in mind, have in view;* of things, *to tend, incline.* Hence partic. spectatus -a -um, *tried, approved; hence esteemed, respected.*

spectrum -i, n. *a spectre, apparition.*

¹spĕcŭla -ae, f. *a look out, watch-tower.*

²spĕcŭla -ae, f. *a little hope, ray of hope.*

spĕcŭlābundus -a -um, *watching, on the watch.*

spĕcŭlāris -e, *like a mirror; transparent;* n. pl. spĕcŭlārĭa -ōrum, *window-panes.*

spĕcŭlātor -ōris, m.: milit., *scout, spy;* in gen., *observer, investigator.*

spĕcŭlātōrĭus -a -um, *of a scout;* f. as subst. *a spy-boat.*

spĕcŭlātrix -ĭcis, f. *a (female) observer, watcher.*

spĕcŭlor -ari, dep. *to look out, spy, watch.*

spĕcŭlum -i, n. *a mirror;* fig., *image, copy.*

spĕcus -ūs, m., f., and n. *a cave, hole, hollow.*

spēlaeum -i, n. *a cave, den.*

spēlunca -ae, f. *a cave, den.*

sperno spernĕre sprēvi sprētum, *to remove; to reject, scorn, spurn.*

spēro -are, *to look for, expect;* of good things, *to hope, hope for;* of bad, *to anticipate, forebode.*

spēs -ĕi, f. *expectation*; of good things, *hope;* of bad, *anticipation, foreboding.*

sphaera -ae, f. *a globe, sphere.*

sphaeristērium -i, n. *a place for playing ball.*

Sphinx Sphingis, f. *the Sphinx, a mythical monster at Thebes.*

spīca -ae, f. *a spike; an ear of corn; a tuft.*

spīcĕus -a -um, *of ears of corn.*

spīcĭfer -fĕra -fĕrum, *carrying ears of corn.*

spīcŭlum -i, n. *sharp point; sting; spear, dart.*

spīna -ae, f. *a thorn, prickle; a thorn-bush;* in pl., *anxieties, difficulties, perplexities.*

spīnētum -i, n. *thorn-hedge, thorn-brake.*

spīnĕus -a -um, *of thorns, thorny.*

spīnōsus -a -um, *of thorns, thorny, prickly;* of style, *crabbed, obscure;* of feeling, *anxious.*

spīnus -i, m. *blackthorn.*

spīra -ae, f. *a coil, twist.*

spīrābilis -e, *that may be breathed.*

spīrācŭlum -i, n. *an air-hole.*

spīrāmen -ĭnis, n. *an air-hole; a breath, puff.*

spīrāmentum -i, n. *an air-hole; a breathing-space, pause, interval.*

spīrĭtŭs -ūs, m. *breathing, breath, exhalation; a sigh, the breath of life, life; inspiration; spirit, disposition; a high spirit, pride.*

spīro -are: intransit., *to breathe, blow, draw breath; to be alive; to have inspiration, be inspired;* transit., *to breathe out, exhale.*

spisseso -ĕre, *to become thick.*

spisso -are, *to make thick, thickness.*

spissus -a -um, *close, dense, thick, crowded; slow, tardy, difficult;* adv. **spissē.**

splendĕo -ēre, *to shine, glitter, be bright.*

splendesco -ĕre, *to become bright.*

splendĭdus -a -um, *shining, bright, brilliant; distinguished, outstanding; showy, specious;* of sound, *clear.* Hence adv. **splendĭdē**, *splendidly, finely, nobly.*

splendor -ōris, m. *brilliance, brightness, lustre, distinction;* of sound, *clarity.*

splēnĭum -i, n. *an adhesive plaster.*

spŏlĭātĭo -ōnis, f. *plundering, stripping.*

spŏlĭātor -ōris, m. and **spŏlĭātrix** -trīcis, f. *plunderer.*

spŏlĭo -are, *to strip, despoil, plunder, rob.*

spŏlĭum -i, n. usually plur., *skin or hide stripped from an animal; arms, clothing, etc., taken from an enemy;* in gen., *spoils, plunder, booty.*

sponda -ae, f. *a bedstead, bed, sofa, bier.*

spondālĭum -i, n. *a sacrificial hymn.*

spondĕo spondēre spŏpondi sponsum, *to pledge oneself to, promise solemnly, vow; to be a security, go bail for a person.* Partic. as subst.: **sponsus** -i, m. *a betrothed man, bridegroom;* **sponsa** -ae, f. *a betrothed woman, bride;* **sponsum** -i, n. *a covenant.*

spondēus -i, m. *a spondee* (— —).

spondȳlus -i, m. *a kind of mussel.*

spongia (-ĕa) -ae, f. *a sponge; an open-worked cuirass.*

sponsa -ae, f. subst. from spondeo; q.v.

sponsālis -e, *of betrothal;* n. pl. as subst. **sponsālia** -ĭum or -ĭōrum, *a betrothal, betrothal feast.*

sponsĭo -ōnis, f. *a solemn promise, engagement, guarantee; a wager.*

sponsor -ōris, m. *a surety, bail.*

sponsŭ, abl. sing. m. *by an engagement.*

sponsus -i, m. and **sponsum** -i, n. subst. from spondeo; q.v.

spontĕ, abl. f.: of persons, *willingly, of one's own accord; unaided;* of things, *by itself, automatically; in itself, alone.*

sporta -ae, f. *a basket, hamper.*

sportella -ae, f. *a little basket.*

sportŭla -ae, f. *a little basket; a dole, given by the great to their clients.*

sprētĭo -ōnis, f. *contempt, disdain.*

sprētor -ōris, m. *a despiser.*

spūma -ae, f. *foam, froth.*

spūmesco -ĕre, *to begin to foam.*

spūmĕus -a -um, *foaming, frothy.*

spūmĭfer -fĕra -fĕrum, and **spūmĭger** -gĕra -gĕrum, *foaming.*

spūmo -are, *to foam, froth.*

spūmōsus -a -um, *foaming, frothy.*

spŭo spŭĕre spŭi spūtum, *to spit out;* n. of partic. as subst. **spūtum** -i, *spittle.*

spurcĭtĭa -ae, f. and **spurcĭtĭēs** -ēi, f. *filthiness, dirt.*

spurco -are, *to make dirty, defile;* partic. **spurcātus** -a -um, *foul.*

spurcus -a -um, *dirty, filthy, unclean;* adv. **spurcē.**

spūto -are, *to spit, spit out.*

spūtum -i, n. subst. from spuo; q.v.

squālĕo -ēre, *to be rough, stiff; to be overgrown or dirty from neglect; to wear mourning.*

squālĭdus -a -um, *rough, stiff, scaly; squalid, dirty; in mourning;* of style, *rough;* adv. **squālĭdē.**

squālor -ōris, m. *roughness, stiffness; dirt caused by neglect; mourning;* of style, *roughness.*

squālus -i, m. *a kind of fish.*

squāma -ae, f. *a scale; scale armour; a fish.*

squāmĕus -a -um, *scaly.*

squāmĭger -gĕra -gĕrum, *scale-bearing, scaly;* m.pl. as subst. *fishes.*

squāmōsus -a -um, *covered with scales, scaly.*

st! *hush! hist!*

stăbĭlīmentum -i, n. *a stay, support.*

stăbĭlĭo -īre, *to make firm; to establish.*

stăbĭlis -e, *firm, steady, stable*; adv. stăbĭlĭtĕr.

stăbĭlĭtās -ātis, f. *firmness, stability; durability.*

stăbŭlo -are: transit., *to stable cattle*; intransit., *to have a stall.*

stăbŭlum -i, n. *standing-room; quarters, habitation; a pothouse, brothel.*

stacta -ae, and stactē -ēs, f. *oil of myrrh.*

stădĭum -i, n. *a stade, a Greek measure of length; a race-course.*

stagno -are: intransit. *to be stagnant, stagnate; of places, to lie under water*; transit., *to overflow, inundate.*

stagnum -i, n. *standing water; a pond, marsh, swamp; a lake, strait.*

stāmen -ĭnis, n. *the warp on a loom; the thread hanging from a distaff; stamina ducere, to spin; any thread or woven cloth.*

stāmĭnĕus -a -um, *full of threads.*

stannum -i, n. *an alloy of silver and lead.*

stătārĭus -a -um, *steady, stable, stationary*; f. as subst. stătārĭa -ae, *a quiet kind of comedy*; m. pl. stătārĭi -ōrum, *the actors in this.*

stătēra -ae, f. *a steelyard, a balance.*

stătim, *firmly, steadfastly; on the spot, at once.*

stătĭo -ōnis, f. *a standing still; a place of abode*; milit., *post, station, or picket*; naut., *roadstead, anchorage.*

Stătĭus -m.: Caecilius Statius, *a comic poet, born 168 B.C.*: P. Papinius Statius, *a poet of Domitian's time.*

stătīvus -a -um, *standing still, fixed*; n. pl. as subst. *a permanent camp.*

¹stător -ōris, m. *a magistrate's attendant.*

²Stător -ōris, m. *stayer of flight, a surname of Jupiter.*

stătŭa -ae, f. *a statue, image.*

stătŭārĭus -a -um, *of statues*; f. as subst. *the art of sculpture*; m. *a statuary.*

stătūmen -ĭnis, n. *stay, support*; in pl., *the ribs of a ship.*

stătŭo -ŭĕre -ŭi -ūtum *to cause to stand, place, set up; to establish, settle a point; to give a ruling, make arrangements; to decide (on a course of action or matter of fact).*

stătūra -ae, f. *stature, height.*

¹stătŭs, partic. from sisto; q.v.

²stătŭs -ūs, m. *a standing posture, position, condition, state*; rhet. *the answer to an action.*

stella -ae, f. *a star*; stella comans, *a comet.*

stellans -antis, *starry, set with stars, bright.*

stellātus -a -um, *set with stars, starry, bright.*

stellĭfer -fĕra -fĕrum and stellĭger -gĕra -gĕrum, *star-bearing, starry.*

stellĭo (stēlĭo) -ōnis, m. *a spotted lizard.*

stemma -ătis, n. *a garland, chaplet; a genealogical tree.*

stercŏro -are, *to dung, manure.*

stercus -ŏris, n. *dung, manure.*

stĕrĭlis -e *barren; bare, empty; fruitless, vain.*

stĕrĭlĭtās -ātis, f. *barrenness.*

sternax -ācis, *throwing to the ground.*

sterno sternĕre strāvi strātum, *to stretch out, spread; se sternere, to lie down; to strike down, lay down, overthrow; to make smooth; to calm, allay; to strew, spread a thing (with something else); lectum, to make, make up; equos, to saddle; viam, to pave. N. of partic. as subst. strātum -i, a coverlet blanket; a bed; a saddle-cloth, saddle; a pavement.*

sternūmentum -i, n. *a sneeze.*

sternŭo -ŭĕre -ŭi, *to sneeze*; of a light, *to sputter.*

sterquilinium -i, n. *a dung-heap.*

sterto -ĕre, *to snore.*

stĭbădĭum -i, n. *a semicircular seat.*

stigma -ătis, n. *a brand put upon slaves; in gen., infamy, stigma.*

stigmătĭas -ae, m. *a branded slave.*

stilla -ae, f. *a drop.*

stillĭcĭdĭum -i, n. *dripping moisture; rain-water falling from the eaves of houses.*

stillo -are: intransit., *to drip, drop*; transit., *to drop, let drop; to instil feelings or ideas.*

stĭlus, *a stake, pale; the pointed instrument with which the Romans wrote on waxen tablets; hence writing, composition; mode of writing, style.*

stĭmŭlātĭo -ōnis, f. *spurring on, stimulating.*

stĭmŭlo -are *to goad, prick; to vex, annoy; to incite, stir up.*

stĭmŭlus -i, m. *a goad; a sting, torment; spur, incentive*; milit., *a pointed stake.*

stinguo -ĕre, *to extinguish, annihilate.*

stĭpātĭo -ōnis, f. *a crowd of attendants, retinue.*

stĭpātor -ōris, m. *an attendant, follower*; in plur., *train, retinue.*

stĭpendĭārĭus -a -um. (1) *liable to taxes, tributary*; m. pl. as subst. *tributaries.* (2) of soldiers, *serving for pay.*

stĭpendĭum -i, n. (1) *a tax, tribute, contribution.* Transf., *punishment.* (2) *the pay of a soldier; military service; a year's service, campaign.*

stĭpes -ĭtis, m. *a log, stump, tree-trunk; a branch, post, club; a blockhead.*

stĭpo -are, *to press closely, compress; to crowd a place; to press round a person, accompany, attend.*

stips stĭpis, f. *a small coin, gift, ee.*

stĭpŭla -ae, f. *stalk, haulm, stubble; a reed-pipe.*

stĭpŭlātĭo -ōnis, f. *agreement, covenant, stipulation.*

stĭpŭlor -ari, dep. *to make demands, bargain, stipulate.*

stīria -ae, f. *icicle.*

stirpĭtŭs, *root and branch, thoroughly.*

stirps (stirpes, stirpis), stirpis, f. rarely m., *the stock or stem of a plant; a young shoot; of men, stock, source, origin; of things, root, foundation.*

stīva -ae, f. *a plough-handle.*

stīlātārius -a -um, *brought by sea;* hence *costly.*

stlis, archaic, = lis; q.v.

sto stare stĕti stătum, *to stand, stand still, remain standing; to stand up stiffly;* milit., *to be stationed, or to stand firm;* naut., *to lie at anchor;* of abstr. things, *to remain, be fixed, stand firm, persist; to be resolved;* with ab, cum, pro, *to stand by, support, favour;* with abl. of price, *to cost;* per hominem stare, *to happen through a person's fault, be due to a person.*

Stōïcus -a -um, *Stoic;* m. as subst., *a Stoic;* n. pl. *the Stoic philosophy;* adv. Stōïcē, *like a Stoic, stoically.*

stŏla -ae, f. *a long outer garment, worn by Roman matrons and musicians.*

stŏlĭdus -a -um, *stupid, dull, obtuse;* adv. stŏlĭdē.

stŏmăchor -ari, dep. *to be angry.*

stŏmăchōsus -a -um, *angry, peevish, cross;* compar. adv. stŏmăchōsius.

stŏmăchus -i, m. *the gullet, oesophagus; the stomach;* stomachus bonus, *a good digestion,* hence *good humour, taste, liking; distaste, chagrin, anger.*

stŏrĕa (stōrĭa) -ae, f. *a rush mat.*

strābo -ōnis, m. *a squinter.*

strāgēs -is, f. *an overthrow; debris; slaughter, massacre, carnage.*

strāgŭlus -a -um, *covering, serving as a cover;* n. as subst. strāgŭlum -i, *a covering, carpet, mattress.*

strāmen -ĭnis, n. *straw, litter.*

strāmentum -i, n. *straw, litter; a saddle, housing* (for mules).

strāmĭnĕus -a -um, *made of straw.*

strangŭlo -are, *to choke, strangle, throttle.*

strangūria -ae, f. *strangury.*

strătēgēma -ătis, n. *a piece of generalship, a stratagem.*

strātum -i, n. subst. from sterno; q.v.

strēna -ae, f. *a favourable omen; a new year's gift.*

strēnŭĭtās -ātis, f. *briskness.*

strēnŭus -a -um, *brisk, active, vigorous;* in bad sense, *turbulent, restless;* adv. strēnŭē.

strēpito -are, *to rustle, rattle, clatter.*

strēpĭtus -ūs, m. *clattering, crashing, creaking, rumbling.*

strēpo -ĕre -ŭi -ĭtum, *to clatter, creak, clash, rumble;* of persons *to cry out;* of places, *to resound.*

strictim, *so as to graze; superficially, slightly, summarily.*

strictūra -ae, f. *a mass of iron.*

strictus -a -um, partic. from stringo; q.v.

strīdĕo strīdēre stridi and strīdo strīdēre, *to make a harsh noise; to creak, grate, hiss.*

strīdor -ōris, m. *a creaking, grating or hissing noise.*

strīdŭlus -a -um, *creaking, hissing, grating.*

strĭgĭlis -is, f. *a scraper used at the baths.*

strĭgo -are, *to halt, stop.*

strĭgōsus -a -um, *lean, thin;* of style, *dry, meagre.*

stringo stringĕre strinxi strictum. (1) *to draw tight together, to bind, tie.* (2) *to strip off, pluck, prune;* esp. *to draw a weapon from its sheath.* (3) *to graze, touch lightly; to affect, injure;* in speech, *to touch upon.*

Hence partic. strictus -a -um, *close, tight; strict;* of style, *brief, concise.*

stringor -ōris, m. *a shock, a twinge.*

strix strigis, f. *a screech-owl.*

strōpha -ae, f. *a trick, artifice.*

strōphium -i, n. *a breast-band; a head-band, chaplet.*

structĭlis -e, *used in building.*

structor -ōris, m. (1) *a builder, mason, carpenter.* (2) *a waiter, carver.*

structūra -ae, f. *the act of building;* concr. *a building;* of style, *arrangement, putting together.*

strŭēs -is, f. *a heap.*

strūma -ae, f. *a scrofulous tumour.*

strūmōsus -a -um, *scrofulous.*

strŭo strŭĕre struxi structum, *to put together, arrange; to pile up; to build, erect, construct; to devise, contrive.*

stŭdĕo -ēre -ŭi, *to be eager, take pains, strive after* (usually with dat.); *to side with, support, favour a person; to study a subject.*

stŭdĭōsus -a -um, *eager, zealous, keen; favouring a person or side, partial, devoted;* esp. *devoted to learning, studious.* Adv. stŭdĭōsē, *eagerly.*

stŭdĭum -i, n. *zeal, eagerness, application, enthusiasm; devotion to, goodwill towards a person or cause; application to learning, study.*

stultĭtĭa -ae, f. *foolishness, silliness.*

stultus -a -um, *foolish, silly;* m. as subst., *a simpleton, fool;* adv. stultē.

stūpa = stuppa; q.v.

stūpĕfăcĭo -făcĕre -fēci -factum, pass. stūpĕfīo -fīĕri, *to make senseless, benumb, stun.*

stŭpĕo -ēre -ŭi, *to be stunned, astounded, amazed;* of inanimate things, *to stand still, halt, cease.*

stŭpesco stŭpescĕre stŭpŭi, *to become amazed, astounded.*

stŭpĭdĭtās -ātis, f. *dullness, senselessness.*

stŭpĭdus -a -um, *senseless, stunned; stupid, dull.*

stŭpor -ōris, m. *senselessness, insensibility; astonishment; dullness, stupidity.*

stuppa (stūpa) -ae, f. *tow, oakum.*

stuppĕus -a -um, *of tow.*

stŭpro -are, *to ravish, defile, pollute.*

stŭprum -i, n. *disgrace, defilement;* esp. *ravishing, violation.*

sturnus -i, m. *a starling.*

Stӯgĭālis, Stӯgĭus; see Styx.

stӯlus; see stilus.

Styx, Stӯgis and Stӯgos; acc. Stӯgem and Stӯga; f. *a river in Arcadia;* also *a river in the infernal regions;* adj. Stӯgĭālis -e, and Stӯgĭus -a -um, *Stygian, infernal.*

suādēla -ae, f. *persuasion.*

suădĕo suădĕre suăsi suăsum, *to recommend, advise* (a course of action to a person).

suădus -a -um, *persuasive*; f. as subst., *persuasion*.

suāsio -ōnis, f. *advice, recommendation; persuasive eloquence*.

suāsor -ōris, m. *an adviser, recommender; one who advocates a law.*

suāsōrius -a -um, *of persuasion*; as subst. *persuasive discourse*.

suāsus -ūs, m. *persuasion.*

suāvĕŏlens -entis, *sweet-smelling.*

suāvidĭcus -a -um, *sweetly speaking.*

suāvĭlŏquens -entis, *sweetly speaking.*

suāvĭlŏquentia -ae, f. *sweetness of speech.*

suāvĭŏlum, suāvĭor; see sav-.

suāvis -e, *sweet, pleasant*; adv. suāvĭtĕr.

suāvĭtās -ātis, f. *sweetness, pleasantness.*

suāvĭum = savium; q.v.

sŭb, prep. (1) with abl.: *underneath, under; close under, at the foot of; in time, at, near to; in the power of, under; under cover of.* (2) with acc., *to (or along) the underside of; up under, down under, along under; close up to; in time, towards, just before; also immediately after; into the power of.*

sŭbabsurdus -a -um, *somewhat absurd*; adv. sŭbabsurdē.

sŭbaccūso -are, *to accuse a little.*

sŭbactio -ōnis, f. *preparation, discipline.*

sŭbadrŏganter, *somewhat arrogantly.*

sŭbagrestis -e, *somewhat rustic or boorish.*

sŭbămārus -a -um, *somewhat bitter.*

sŭbausculto -are, *to listen secretly.*

subc-; see succ-.

subdifficilis -e, *somewhat difficult.*

subdiffido -ĕre, *to be somewhat distrustful.*

subdĭtīcĭus and subdĭtīvus -a -um, *supposititious, substituted, counterfeit.*

subdo -dĕre -dĭdi dĭtum, *to put, place or lay under; to subject, subdue; to put in the place of another substitute; to counterfeit.*

subdŏcĕo -ĕre, *to teach as an assistant, help in teaching.*

subdŏlus -a -um, *with secret guile; sly, crafty*; adv. subdŏlē.

subdŭbĭto -are, *to doubt or hesitate a little.*

subdūco -dūcĕre -duxi -ductum, *to draw up from under, pull up, raise, remove; to take away stealthily, steal;* naut., *to draw a ship up on shore;* milit., *to withdraw;* of accounts, *to balance, cast up.*

subductio -ōnis, f. *the drawing up of a ship on dry land; a reckoning, computing.*

sŭbĕdo -esse -ēdi, *to eat from under, wear away.*

sŭbĕo -ire -ii or -īvi -ĭtum. (1) *to go under, pass under;* of a bearer, *to come to and support; to undergo, submit to, take upon oneself.* (2) *to come from under, approach, advance, mount, climb;* of thoughts, etc., *to*

come into, or *come over, the mind.* (3) *to come on after, to follow;* sometimes *to come and support.*

Hence partic. **sŭbĭtus** -a -um, as adj., *sudden; coming suddenly, taking by surprise;* pass., *suddenly done, hastily contrived, improvised.* N. as subst. *a sudden occurrence, emergency.* N. abl. as adv. **sŭbĭtō,** *suddenly.*

sūber -ĕris, n. *cork-tree; cork.*

subf-; see suff-.

subg-; see sugg-.

sŭbhorrĭdus -a -um, *somewhat rough.*

sŭbiăcĕo -ŭi, *to lie under; to be subject to, be connected with.*

sŭbicio -icĕre -iēci -iectum. (1) *to throw* or *place under; to submit, subject;* in speech or writing, *to append, reply.* (2) *to throw up from below, raise, lift; to put into a mind, suggest.* (3) *to substitute, insert by guile, counterfeit.*

Hence partic. **subiectus** -a -um, *subjected;* of places, *lying near, adjacent;* superl adv. **subiectissimē,** *most submissively.*

subiectio -ōnis, f. *a laying under, placing under; a counterfeiting, forging.*

subiecto -are, *to put under;* also *to throw up from below.*

subiector -ōris, m. *forger, counterfeiter.*

sŭbĭgo -igĕre -ēgi -actum, *to drive under; to subject, constrain, subdue, compel; to drive up from below, to propel; to work the soil;* in gen., *to work at; to train, discipline.*

sŭbimpŭdens -entis, *somewhat impudent.*

sŭbĭnānis -e, *somewhat vain.*

sŭbindĕ, *immediately afterwards; repeatedly.*

sŭbinsulsus -a -um, *somewhat insipid.*

sŭbinvĭdĕo -ere, *to envy somewhat;* partic. sŭbinvīsus -a -um, *somewhat hated.*

sŭbinvīto -are, *to invite mildly.*

sŭbīrascor -irasci -īrātus, dep. *to get a little angry.*

sŭbĭtārius -a -um, *hastily contrived, improvised.*

sŭbĭto, sŭbĭtus; from subeo; q.v.

subiungo -iungĕre -iunxi -iunctum, *to yoke beneath; to join on, attach; to subdue, subjugate.*

sublābor -lābi -lapsus, dep. *to glide up; to glide from beneath, slip away.*

sublatio -ōnis, f. *lifting up, elevation.*

sublātus -a -um, partic. from tollo; q.v.

sublēgo -lēgĕre -lēgi -lectum, *to gather from below, pick up; to carry off secretly; to choose in the place of another.*

sublĕvātio -ōnis, f. *a relieving, lightening.*

sublĕvo -are, *to raise, lift, support; to encourage a person; to alleviate troubles.*

sublica -ae, f. *a pile, stake.*

sublicius -a -um, *resting upon piles.*

sublĭgācŭlum -i, and sublĭgar -āris, n. *a loincloth, kilt.*

subligo -are, *to bind below, bind on.*

sublimis -e (archaic **sublimus** -a -um), *high, raised, lofty; elevated, sublime.* N. acc. sing. as adv. **sublimĕ**, *on high, aloft.*

sublimitās -ātis, f. *loftiness height, sublimity.*

sublimus; see sublimis.

sublūcĕo -ēre, *to gleam faintly, glimmer.*

sublŭo -lŭĕre -lūtum, *to wash below; of rivers, to flow beneath.*

sublustris -e, *gleaming faintly, glimmering.*

subm -; see summ-.

subnascor -nasci -nātus, dep. *to grow up out of* or *after.*

subnecto -nectĕre -nexŭi -nexum, *to tie on, bind on beneath.*

subnĕgo -are, *to deny a little, partly refuse.*

subnixus (subnisus) -a -um, *propped up, supported.*

subnŏto -are, *to mark beneath, write underneath; to notice secretly.*

subnŭba -ae, f. *a rival.*

subnūbilus -a -um, *somewhat cloudy.*

sŭbo -are, *to be in heat.*

sŭbobscēnus -a -um, *somewhat obscene.*

sŭbobscūrus -a -um, *somewhat obscure.*

sŭbŏdiōsus -a -um, *rather unpleasant.*

sŭboffendo -ĕre, *to give some offence.*

sŭbŏlĕo -ēre (only in 3 pers.), *to emit a smell; hence to make itself felt.*

sŭbŏlēs -is, f. *a sprout, shoot, offspring, progeny.*

sŭbŏlesco -ĕre, *to grow up.*

sŭborior -ŏriri, dep. *to arise after or in succession.*

sŭborno -are. (1) *to furnish, equip, provide.* (2) *to instigate secretly, suborn.*

sŭbortus -us, m. *an arising after or in succession.*

subp -; see supp-.

subrancĭdus -a -um, *somewhat putrid.*

subrauous -a -um, *somewhat hoarse.*

subrectus (surr-), partic. from subrigo; q.v.

subremigo (surr-) -are, *to row underneath.*

subrēpo (surr-) -rēpĕre -repsi, *to creep* or *crawl up to from below.*

subrepticius = surrepticius; q.v.

subrīdĕo (surr-) -ridēre -risi -risum, *to smile.*

subrīdĭcŭlē, *somewhat laughably.*

subrigo (surr-) -rigere -rexi -rectum, *to raise, lift up.*

subringor -i, dep. *to make a wry face.*

subripio = surripio; q.v.

subrŏgo (surr-) -are, *to suggest that a person be chosen as substitute for another.*

subrostrāni -ōrum, m. *loungers about the rostra, idlers.*

subrŭbĕo -ēre, *to blush slightly, be rather red.*

subrŭo -rŭĕre -rŭi -rŭtum, *to undermine, overthrow, destroy.*

subrusticus -a -um, *somewhat clownish.*

subscrībo -scrībĕre -scripsi -scriptum, *to write under, write beneath; to sign a document; to complete an indict-*

ment, hence to prosecute, accuse; with dat., to support, assent to; to note down, make a note of.

subscriptio -ōnis, f. *a writing beneath, signature; the completion of an indictment; a record, register.*

subscriptor -ōris, m. *the signer of an indictment; an accuser.*

subsĕcivus = subsicivus; q.v.

subsĕco -sĕcare -sĕcŭi -sectum, *to cut away below.*

subsellium -i, n. *a bench, seat, esp. in the courts.*

subsentio -sentire -sensi, *to notice secretly.*

subsĕquor -sĕqui -sĕcūtus, dep. *to follow after; to support a cause, etc.*

subservio -ire, *to be subject to, comply with.*

subsicivus (subsec-) -a -um, *left over; extra, superfluous, spare.*

subsidiārius -a -um, *in reserve.*

subsidium -i, n.: milit., *reserve troops, auxiliary forces;* in gen., *support, help, assistance.*

subsīdo -sīdĕre -sēdi -sessum, *to crouch down, settle, sink, subside; to stay, remain; to lie in wait, lurk in ambush.*

subsignānus -a -um, *serving beneath the standard;* milites, *reserve legionaries.*

subsigno -are, *to write under, endorse; to enter on a list, to register.*

subsilio -silire -silŭi, *to leap up, spring up.*

subsisto -sistĕre -stĭti, *to stand; to make a stand, to withstand; to come to a stand, stop, halt, cease; to stay, remain.*

subsortior -iri, dep. *to choose by lot as a substitute.*

subsortitio -ōnis, f. *the choice of a substitute by lot.*

substantia -ae, f. *substance, essence; property, means of subsistence.*

substerno -sternĕre -strāvi -strātum, *to spread beneath, lay under; to set out, provide.*

substĭtŭo -ŭĕre -ŭi -ūtum, *to put next; to put under, to put in the place of another, to substitute.*

substo -stare, *to stand firm.*

substringo -stringĕre -strinxi -strictum, *to draw together, bind up;* partic. **substrictus** -a -um, *narrow, contracted, small.*

substructio -ōnis, f. *a base, foundation.*

substrŭo -strŭĕre -struxi -structum, *to build beneath, lay a foundation.*

subsulto -are, *to spring up, leap up.*

subsum -esse -fŭi, *to be near, be close at hand; to be under; to be subject; to be there, to exist.*

subsūtus -a -um, *fringed, edged below.*

subtēmen -inis, n. *the weft or woof in weaving.*

subter (supter), adv. and prep., *beneath, below, underneath.*

subterfūgio -fŭgĕre -fūgi, *to escape.*

subterlābor -lābi -lapsus, dep. *to glide under, flow under; to slip away, escape.*

subtĕro -tĕrĕre -trivi -tritum, *to wear away underneath.*

subterrānĕus -a -um. *underground, subterranean.*

subtexo -texĕre -texŭi -textum, *to weave beneath; to connect, join on; to cover, darken.*

subtilis -e, *finely woven, slender, fine; of senses, etc., discriminating, nice; of style, plain, simple, unadorned.* Hence adv. subtilĭtĕr, *by fine links or passages; of judgment, with discrimination; of style, plainly, simply.*

subtilĭtās -ātis, f. *fineness, minuteness; of judgment, discrimination; of style, plainness, simplicity.*

subtĭmĕo -ĕre, *to be a little afraid.*

subtrăho -trăhĕre -traxi -tractum, *to draw up from beneath; to draw away secretly, remove, steal away.*

subturpĭcŭlus -a -um, *rather on the disgraceful side.*

subturpis -e, *rather disgraceful.*

subtūs, adv. *beneath, below, underneath.*

subtūsus -a -um, *somewhat bruised.*

sŭbūcŭla -ae, f. *a shirt.*

sŭbŭla -ae, f. *a shoemaker's awl.*

sŭbulcus -i, m. *a swineherd.*

Sŭbūra -ae, f. *a part of Rome, north-east of the Forum.*

sŭburbānĭtās -ātis, f. *nearness to the city.*

sŭburbānus -a -um. *near the city (Rome), suburban; n. as subst. an estate near Rome.*

sŭburbĭum -i, n. *a suburb.*

sŭburgŭĕo -ĕre, *to drive close.*

subvectĭo -ōnis, f. *carrying up, conveyance, transport.*

subvecto -are *to carry up, convey, transport.*

subvectus -ūs, m. *a carrying up.*

subvĕho -vĕhĕre -vexi -vectum, *carry up, convey, transport.*

subvĕnĭo -vĕnire -vēni -ventum, *to come up to aid, to succour, relieve.*

subvĕrĕor -ĕri, dep. *to be rather anxious.*

subversor -ōris, m. *overthrower.*

subverto (-vorto) -vertĕre -verti -versum, *to overthrow, overturn, destroy.*

subvexus -a -um, *sloping upwards.*

subvŏlo -are, *to fly up.*

subvolvo -ĕre, *to roll up.*

succăvus -a -um, *hollow underneath.*

succēdo -cēdĕre -cessi -cessum, (1) *to go under; to submit to.* (2) *to go from under, ascend, mount.* (3) *to come after; to succeed, relieve, follow; of things, to turn out well, prosper, succeed.*

succendo -cendĕre -cendi -censum, *to set on fire from below; to kindle, inflame.*

succensĕo = suscenseo; q.v.

¹succentŭrĭo -are, *to put in the place of another, to substitute.*

²succentŭrĭo -ōnis, m. *an under-centurion.*

successĭo -ōnis, f. *succeeding, succession.*

successor -ōris, m. *a successor, follower, heir.*

successus -ūs, m. (1) *an advance uphill, approach.* (2) *success.*

succidĭa -ae, f. *a flitch of bacon.*

¹succĭdo -cĭdĕre -cĭdi, *to fall under; to sink, flag, fail.*

²succīdo -cīdĕre -cīdi -cisum. *to cut from under, cut down.*

succĭdŭus -a -um, *sinking, failing.*

succingo -cingĕre -cinxi -cinctum. *to gird below, gird up; to equip, arm, provide, surround;* partic. succinctus -a -um, as adj., *concise, succinct.*

succingŭlum -i, n. *a girdle.*

succĭno -ĕre, *to sing to, accompany; in speech, to chime in.*

succlāmatĭo -ōnis, f. *shouting in reply.*

succlāmo -are, *to shout back.*

succontŭmēlĭōsē, *somewhat insolently.*

succresco -crescĕre -crēvi, *to grow up, increase; to grow up to, match.*

succrispus = subcrispus; q.v.

succumbo -cumbĕre -cŭbŭi -cŭbĭtum, *to lie down under, sink down, give way, succumb, surrender.*

succurro -currĕre -curri -cursum. (1) *to run beneath, go under; to undergo;* of ideas, *to come into the mind.* (2) *to come to aid, succour, help, assist.*

succŭtĭo -cŭtĕre -cussi -cussum, *to shake from beneath, fling aloft.*

sūcĭdus -a -um, *juicy, full of sap.*

sūcĭnus -a -um, *of amber.*

sūco -ōnis, m. *a sucker.*

sūcus (succus) -i, m. *juice, sap; a draught; flavour, taste; sap, vigour, energy.*

sūdārĭum -i, n. *handkerchief, towel.*

sūdātōrĭus -a -um, *of sweating;* n. as subst. *a sweating-room.*

sūdātrix -tricis, f. *causing perspiration.*

sūdis -is, f. *a stake, pile; a spike, point.*

sūdo -are: intransit., *to sweat, perspire; to make a great effort; to drip with moisture; to drip from, distil;* transit. *to sweat out, to exude; to soak with sweat.*

sūdor -ōris, m. *sweat, perspiration; great exertion; any moisture.*

sūdus -a -um, *dry;* of weather, *bright cloudless;* n. as subst. *fine weather.*

Suēbi (Suēvi) -orum, m. *a Germanic tribe.*

suemus, 1 plur. as from sueo, *we are accustomed.*

suesco -suescĕre suēvi suētum: intransit., *to become accustomed;* transit., *to accustom.* Hence partic. suētus -a -um *accustomed; customary, usual.*

Suētōnĭus -i, m. C. Suetonius Tranquillus, *author of the Lives of the Caesars.*

suētus -a -um, partic. from suesco; q.v.

Suēvi = Suebi; q.v.

sūfes (suffes) -fĕtis, m. *the chief magistrate at Carthage.*

suffarcĭno -are, *to stuff, cram.*

suffĕro sufferre, *to hold up, support, to endure, suffer.*

suffĭcĭo -fĭcĕre -fēci -fectum: transit.,
to put under; hence, *to stain, steep,
suffuse; to provide, supply; to put
in place of another, to substitute,
choose as a substitute*; intransit., *to
be adequate, suffice*; with infin., *to be
able.*

suffīgo -fīgĕre -fixi -fixum, *to fix up,
fasten.*

suffīmen -ĭnis and **suffīmentum** -i,
n. *incense.*

sufflo -ire, *to fumigate, perfume; to
warm.*

sufflāmen -ĭnis, n. *a brake, drag,
hindrance.*

sufflo -are: intransit., *to blow*; transit.,
to blow up, inflate.

suffōco -are, *to strangle, choke, suffocate.*

suffōdĭo -fŏdĕre -fŏdi -fossum, *to
pierce underneath, excavate, undermine.*

suffrāgātĭo -ōnis. f. *voting in favour,
support.*

suffrāgātor -ōris, m. *a voter in favour;
a (political) supporter.*

suffrāgātōrĭus -a -um, *relating to the
support of a candidate.*

suffrāgĭum -i, n. *a voting tablet, a vote;
the right to vote, franchise*; in gen.,
judgment; approval, support.

suffrāgor -ari, dep. *to vote for; to
favour, approve, support.*

suffringo -ĕre, *to break underneath.*

suffŭgĭo -fŭgĕre -fūgi, *to flee, escape.*

suffŭgĭum -i, n. *a shelter, place of
refuge.*

suffulcĭo -fulcire -fulsi -fultum, *to
support beneath, undergo, underprop.*

suffundo -fundĕre -fūdi -fūsum, *to pour
over, spread through, suffuse; to steep,
stain, cover.*

suffuscus -a -um, *brownish, dark.*

Sŭgambri (**Sўg-**, **Sĭg-**) -ōrum, m. pl. *a
Germanic tribe.*

suggĕro -gĕrĕre -gessi -gestum, *to
bring up, supply, provide; to add,
attach; to place next.*

suggestum -i, n. and **suggestus** -ūs,
m. *a raised place, height, elevation*;
esp., *a platform.*

suggrandis -e, *somewhat large.*

suggrĕdĭor -grĕdi -gressus, dep. *to go
up to, approach, attack.*

sŭgillātĭo -ōnis, f. *a bruise; mockery,
insult.*

sŭgillo -are, *to beat, to insult.*

sūgo sūgĕre suxi suctum, *to suck.*

sŭillus -a -um, *of swine.*

sulcātor -ōris, m. *a plougher.*

sulco -are, *to furrow, plough; to
wrinkle.*

sulcus -i, m. *a furrow; ploughing; a
trench or ditch; a track, path.*

sulfur (**sulpur**) -ŭris, n. *sulphur;
lightning.*

sulfŭrātus -a -um, *containing sulphur.*

sulfŭrĕus -a -um, *sulphurous.*

Sulla (**Sylla**) -ae, m. *a name of a family
in the gens Cornelia*; adj. **Sullānus**
-a -um; verb **sullātŭrĭo** -ire, *to
wish to imitate Sulla.*

Sulmo -ōnis, m. *birth-place of Ovid*;
adj. **Sulmōnensis** -e.

sulpur = *sulfur; q.v.*

sultis = *si vultus; see volo.*

sum, esse, fŭi, *to be, to exist, be there,
be so*; with dat., *to be in one's
possession*; copulative, *to be so and
so*, with complement; fut. partic.
fŭtūrus -a -um, *future, about to be*;
n. as subst. *the future.*

sūmen -ĭnis, n. *the udder of a sow;
a sow.*

summa -ae; see summus.

summātim, adv. *summarily, briefly.*

summātus -ūs, m. *supremacy, chief
authority.*

summergo -mergĕre -mersi -mersum,
to plunge under, to sink.

summĭnistro -are, *to help by supplying.*

summissĭo (subm-) -ōnis, f. *a letting
down, lowering.*

summitto (subm-) -mittĕre -misi
-missum, (1) *to let down, send
under, lower; subject, subordinate*;
with animum, or se, *to condescend,
submit.* (2) *to send up from below,
to raise, rear, make to grow.* (3) *to
send as help.* (4) *to send secretly.*
Hence partic. **summissus** (subm-)
-a -um, *let down, lowered; mild,
gentle, humble*; in bad sense, *mean,
abject.* Adv. **summissē**, *softly, calmly;
modestly, humbly.*

summŏlestus (subm-) -a -um, *somewhat troublesome*; adv. **summŏlestē**,
with some vexation.

summŏnĕo (subm-) -ēre, *to remind
secretly.*

summŏpĕrĕ (summō ŏpĕrĕ), *very
much, exceedingly.*

summŏrosus (subm-) -a -um, *somewhat peevish.*

summŏvĕo (subm-) mŏvēre -mōvi
-mōtum, *to move up from below; to
move away, drive off, expel*; esp. of
the lictor *to clear a way* for a
magistrate, *to keep back the crowd*;
*to force away from, compel, to give
up*; pass. partic. **summōtus**, *lying
out of the way, remote.*

summŭto (subm-) -are, *to exchange.*

sūmo sūmĕre sumpsi sumptum, *to take,
choose, obtain, buy*; of clothes, etc.,
to put on; to exact a *punishment*;
*to take upon oneself, claim; to take
for granted, assume.*

sumptĭo -ōnis f. *the premiss of a
syllogism.*

sumptŭārĭus -a -um, *relating to
expense, sumptuary.*

sumptŭōsus -a -um: of things, *costly,
expensive*; of persons, *lavish, extravagant*; adv. **sumptŭōsē**, *expensively,
sumptuously.*

sumptus -ūs, m. *cost, expense.*

sŭo sŭĕre sŭi sūtum, *to sew, stitch
together, join together.*

sŭŏmet and **sŭŏpte**; see suus.

sŭŏvĕtaurĭlĭa -ĭum, n. pl., *a sacrifice
of a pig, sheep and bull.*

sŭpellex -lectĭlis, f. *household furniture.*

¹sŭper -a -um; see superus.

'**sŭper.** Adv., *over, above; besides, beyond, moreover; remaining, over and above.* Prep.: with abl., of place *over, above;* of time, *at;* concerning, *about; besides, beyond;* with acc., of place, *over, above, upon; besides, beyond;* of time, *during;* of superiority, *above, more than.*

sŭpĕrā; see supra.

sŭpĕrābĭlis -e, *that can be surmounted; conquerable.*

sŭpĕraddo -addĕre -addĭtum, *to add as well, put on besides.*

sŭpĕrātor -ōris, m. *a conqueror.*

sŭperbĭa -ae, f. *pride; haughtiness, arrogance.*

sŭperbĭo -ire: of persons, *to be proud, pride oneself;* of things, *to be splendid, superb.*

sŭperbus -a -um, *haughty, exalted, proud; arrogant, overbearing; brilliant, splendid.* Adv. **sŭperbē,** *haughtily, proudly.*

sŭpercĭlĭum -i, n. *an eyebrow; the eyebrows; a nod* (as expression of will); *arrogance, censoriousness; ridge, summit.*

sŭpĕrēmĭneo -ēre, *to overtop.*

sŭperfĭcĭēs -ēi, f. *top, surface.*

sŭperfĭo -fĭĕri, *to be left over.*

sŭperfixus -a -um, *fixed on the top.*

sŭperflŭo -flŭĕre, *to flow over, overflow, be superfluous.*

sŭperfundo -fundĕre -fūdi -fūsum, *to pour over, pour upon;* pass., *to overflow;* in gen., *to spread about, spread over.*

sŭpergrĕdĭor -grĕdi -gressus, dep. *to step beyond, overstep; to exceed, surpass.*

sŭperiăcio -iăcĕre -iĕci -iectum or -iactum, *to throw over, throw upon; to overtop, exceed, go beyond.*

sŭperimmĭneo -ēre, *to overhang.*

sŭperimpendens -entis, *overhanging.*

sŭperimpŏsĭtus -a -um, *laid over, placed upon.*

sŭperincĭdens -entis, *falling on top.*

sŭperincŭbans -antis, *lying over or upon.*

sŭperincumbo -cumbĕre -cŭbŭi *to lie on, lie over.*

sŭperinĭcĭo -inĭcĕre -inĭĕci -iniectum, *to throw upon.*

sŭperinsterno -sternĕre -strāvi, *to spread over, lay over.*

sŭpĕrĭor -ōris, compar. of superus, q.v.

sŭperlātĭo -ōnis, f. *exaggeration, hyperbole.*

sŭperlātus -a -um, *exaggerated, hyperbolical.*

sŭpernus -a -um, *above, upper, high;* adv. **sŭpernē,** *above or from above.*

sŭpĕro -are: intransit., *to go above, overtop, project; to prevail, conquer; to abound; to remain, be over;* esp. *to remain alive, survive; to be too much, to exceed;* transit., *to rise above, surmount, overtop, pass; to surpass, excel, exceed; to overcome, conquer.* Compar. of pres. partic. **sŭperantĭor** -ōris, *more dominant.*

sŭperobrŭo -ŭĕre, *to overwhelm.*

sŭperpendens -entis, *overhanging.*

sŭperpōno -pōnĕre -pŏsŭi -pŏsĭtum, *to place over, or upon; to put in authority.*

sŭperscando -ĕre, *to climb over.*

sŭpersĕdĕo -sĕdĕre -sēdi -sessum, *to sit above, sit out;* hence *to forbear, refrain.*

sŭperstagno -are, *to spread out into a lake.*

sŭpersterno -sternĕre -strāvi -strātum, *to spread over or upon.*

sŭperstĕs -stĭtis, *standing over or near; present, witnessing; surviving, living on.*

sŭperstĭtĭo -ōnis, f. *superstition, fanaticism.*

sŭperstĭtĭōsus -a -um, *superstitious;* adv. **sŭperstĭtĭōsē.**

sŭpersto -are, *to stand over or upon.*

sŭperstrŭo -strŭĕre -struxi -structum, *to build upon.*

sŭpersum -esse -fŭi -fŭtūrus, *to be over and above; to be left, remain, survive; to be plentiful, to abound; to be superfluous, be redundant.*

sŭperurgĕo -ēre, *to press from above.*

sŭperus (rarely sŭper) -a -um, *situated above; upper, higher;* m. pl. as subst. *the gods above;* also *men on earth;* n. pl. *heights or heavenly bodies.* Compar. **sŭperĭor** -īus, *higher, upper;* of time, *earlier, former, past;* of rank, etc., *higher, greater.* Superl. **suprēmus** -a -um, of place, *highest, uppermost;* in time, *last, final;* of degree, *highest, greatest;* of rank, *highest;* n. sing. as subst., *the end;* n. pl., **suprēma** -ōrum, *death, funeral rites, last will and testament.* Used as another superl. **summus** -a -um, *highest, uppermost, at the top;* summa urbs, *the highest part of the city;* of the voice, *highest, loudest;* of time, *last;* of rank, etc., *greatest, highest, most distinguished.* F. as subst. **summa** -ae *the highest place, the main thing, most important point; a summary, the gist, the sum total of an amount.* N. as subst. **summum** -i, *surface, top;* acc. as adv., *at most.* Adv. **summē,** *in the highest degree, extremely.*

sŭpervăcănĕus and **sŭpervăcŭus** -a -um, *superfluous, unnecessary, extra.*

sŭpervado -ĕre, *to go over, surmount.*

sŭpervĕhor -vĕhi -vectus sum, *to ride or sail past.*

sŭpervĕnĭo -vĕnire -vēni -ventum, *to come upon, rise above; to arrive, come up,* esp. *unexpectedly.*

sŭperventus -ūs, m. *coming up, (unexpected) arrival.*

sŭpervīvo -ĕre, *to survive.*

sŭpervŏlĭto -are, and **sŭpervŏlo** -are, *to fly over, fly above.*

sŭpĭno -are, *to put face upwards, throw on the back.*

sŭpĭnus -a -um, *lying on the back, face-upwards;* manus, *with palm upwards;* of streams, *flowing up, returning;* of ground, *sloping upwards;* of character, *negligent, lazy.*

suppaenĭtet -ēre, to cause slight regret.

suppār -păris, almost equal.

suppēdĭtātĭo -ōnis, f. abundant provision.

suppēdĭto -are: intransit., to be at hand, be ready, suffice; transit., to provide, supply, give.

suppernātus -a -um, lamed in the hip.

suppĕtĭae -ārum, f. pl. help, aid.

suppĕtĭor -ari, dep. to help, assist.

suppĕto -ēre, -īvi and -ĭi, -ĭtum, to be in store, be at hand; to suffice, be enough.

supplanto -are, to trip up.

supplēmentum -i, n. filling up, completion; milit., a body of recruits, reinforcements.

supplĕo -plēre -plēvi -plētum, to fill up, make complete.

supplex -plicis, kneeling; entreating, suppliant; adv. supplĭcĭtĕr.

supplĭcātĭo -ōnis, f. solemn public prayer or thanksgiving; a religious festival or fast.

supplĭcĭum -i, n. (1) a humble entreaty, supplication, prayer. (2) punishment; esp. capital punishment.

▸upplĭco -are, to kneel, beseech, entreat; esp. to pray to the gods.

supplōdo -plōdĕre -plōsi, to stamp.

supplōsĭo -ōnis, f. a stamping.

suppōno -pōnĕre -pŏsŭi -pŏsĭtum. (1) to put under; to subject. (2) to put next to, to add. (3) to put in the place of; to substitute, counterfeit, forge.

supporto -are, to carry up.

suppŏsĭtīcĭus -a -um, substituted, spurious.

suppressĭo -ōnis, f. embezzlement.

supprĭmo -prĭmĕre -pressi -pressum, to press under; to hold down, check, restrain; to keep back, suppress, conceal; pecuniam, nummos, to embezzle. Partic. suppresssus -a -um, checked, restrained; of the voice, low, subdued.

suppŭdet -ēre, to cause some shame.

suppus -a -um, head-downwards.

suppŭto -are, to count up, compute.

suprā. Adv. over, on the top; of time, before, previously; in writing, above; of amount, etc., over, more, beyond; supra quam, more than. Prep., with acc., above, over; of time, before; of amount, more than, above, beyond.

suprascando -ēre, to climb over, surmount.

suprēmus, etc.; see superus.

sūra -ae, f. the calf of the leg.

surcŭlus -i, m. a young shoot, sprout, twig; a slip, sucker.

surdaster -tra -trum, somewhat deaf.

surdĭtās -ātis, f. deafness.

surdus -a -um, deaf; unwilling to hear, insensible; not heard, still, silent; of sounds, etc., indistinct, faint.

surēna -ae, m. a Parthian grand vizier.

surgo surgĕre surrexi surrectum, to rise, get up; to spring up, arise.

surpŭit, etc., forms from surripio; q.v.

surr-; see also subr-.

surreptīcĭus (subr-) -a -um, stolen, secret, surreptitious.

surrĭpĭo -rĭpĕre -rĭpŭi -reptum, to take away secretly; to steal, filch.

sursum (sursus), upwards, on high; sursum deorsum, up and down, backwards, and forwards.

sus sŭis, c. a sow, swine, pig, hog; a kind of fish.

suscensĕo -ēre -ŭi, to be angry, bear a grudge.

susceptĭo -ōnis, f. undertaking.

suscĭpĭo -cĭpĕre -cēpi -ceptum, to take up, catch up; to support, raise; to accept, receive, esp. to acknowledge a child as one's own; to take upon oneself, undertake, begin; to maintain a point, be ready to prove.

suscĭto -are, to stir up, arouse, excite.

suspecto -are, to keep looking at, gaze upon; to look upon with suspicion, suspect.

¹suspectus -a -um, partic. from suspicio; q.v.

²suspectus -ūs, m. looking upwards; respect, esteem.

suspendĭum -i, n. a hanging of oneself.

suspendo -pendĕre -pendi -pensum, to hang up; to prop up, support; to keep in suspense, leave undecided; to check, break off.

Hence partic. suspensus -a -um, hovering, hanging, suspended; dependent; ambiguous, doubtful, in suspense.

suspĭcax -ācis: act., suspicious, suspecting; pass., suspicious, suspected.

¹suspĭcĭo -spĭcĕre -spexi -spectum, to look from below, look upwards; to look up to, esteem, respect; to look askance at, suspect.

Hence partic. suspectus -a -um, suspected.

²suspĭcĭo -ōnis, f. mistrust, suspicion; a faint idea, imperfect conception.

suspĭcĭōsus -a -um, feeling suspicion, suspecting; exciting suspicion, suspicious; adv. suspĭcĭōsē, in a suspicious manner, suspiciously.

suspĭcor -ari, dep. to suspect; to conjecture, suppose, surmise.

suspīrātus -ūs, and suspīrĭtus -ūs, and suspīrĭum -i, n. a deep breath, a sigh.

suspīro -are: intransit., to draw a deep breath, to sigh; transit., to sigh for, long for.

susquĕ dequĕ, up and down.

sustentācŭlum -i, n. a prop, support.

sustentātĭo -ōnis, f. forbearance.

sustento -are, to hold up, support, sustain; to maintain; to put off, hinder, delay.

sustĭnĕo -tĭnēre -tĭnŭi -tentum, to hold up, support, sustain; with infin., to endure to, have the heart to; to maintain; to put off, delay; to hold back, check, restrain.

sustollo -ēre, to lift up, raise; to take away, remove, destroy.

sŭsurrātor -ōris, m. a mutterer.

sŭsurro -are, to murmur, mutter, whisper; of bees, to hum.

¹sŭsurrus -i, m. a murmur, muttering, whisper, hum, buzz.

²sŭsurrus -a -um, whispering, muttering.

sūtĭlis -e, stitched together, fastened together.

sūtor -ōris, m. a shoemaker, cobbler.

sūtōrĭus and **sūtrīnus** -a -um, *of a shoemaker.*

sūtūra -ae, f. *a seam, suture.*

sŭus -a -um, reflexive possessive pronoun of 3rd person, *his, her, its, their (own)*; often strengthened by -pte or -met; sometimes *proper, due, suitable, favourable; independent.* As subst., *one's own people, property,* etc.

Sўbăris -ris, f. *a town in Lucania, famous for luxury.*

sўcŏphanta -ae, f. *an informer, trickster.*

Sylla = Sulla; q.v.

syllăba -ae, f. *a syllable;* in plur., *verses, poems.*

syllăbātim, *syllable by syllable.*

syllŏgismus (or -ŏs) -i, m. *a syllogism.*

symbŏla -ae, f. *a contribution towards a common feast.*

symphōnĭa -ae, f. *a concert, musical performance.*

symphōnĭăcus -a -um, *of or for a concert.*

sўnedrus -i, m. *a Macedonian councillor.*

syngrăpha -ae, f. *a bond, agreement to pay.*

sўnŏdūs -ontis, m. *a fish, perhaps bream.*

synthĕsis -is, f. *a dinner-service; a suit of clothes; a dressing-gown.*

Sўrācūsae -ārum, f. pl. *the chief town of Sicily.*

Sўria -ae, f. *Syria;* adj. **Sўrĭus, Sўrus, Sўrĭăcus** -a -um, *Syrian;* subst. **Sўri** -orum, *the Syrians.*

syrma -mātis, n. *a long robe, worn by tragic actors.*

syrtis -is, f. *a sandbank, quicksand; esp. one on the coast of Northern Africa.*

T

T, t, the nineteenth letter of the Latin Alphabet.

tăbella -ae, f. *a small flat board or tablet; a writing-tablet; a document, letter, record; a votive tablet; a voting-ticket, ballot; a picture.*

tăbellārĭus -a -um, *of letters* or *of voting.* M. as subst. *a letter-carrier.*

tābĕo -ere, *to waste away; to drip, run.*

tăberna -ae, f. *a booth, hut; a cottage, hovel; a stall, shop; an inn, tavern; a block of seats in the Circus.*

tăbernăcŭlum -i, n. *a hut, tent.*

tăbernārĭus -i, m. *a shopkeeper.*

tābēs -is, f. *wasting away, decay, melting; disease, pestilence; demoralization; decayed matter, corruption.*

tābesco tābescĕre tābŭi, *to melt, waste away; to pine, be spoiled.*

tābĭdŭlus -a -um, *wasting, consuming.*

tābĭdus -a -um: pass., *melting, wasting, dissolving;* act., *consuming.*

tābĭfĭcus -a -um, *consuming.*

tăbŭla -ae, f. *a board, plank; a draught-board; a painted board, a painting; a votive tablet; a map; a writing-tablet; a document;* in plur., *record, register; a catalogue; an auction.*

tăbŭlārĭum -i, n. *archives, records.*

tăbŭlātĭo -ōnis, f. *flooring, planking; a storey.*

tăbŭlātus -a -um, *floored, boarded;* n. as subst., *a floor, storey; a row* or *layers of vines.*

tābum -i, n. *corrupt moisture, matter; a plague, pestilence.*

tăcĕo -ēre -ŭi -ĭtum, *to be silent, say nothing; to be still, quiet;* transit., *to be silent about, pass over in silence.*
  Hence partic. **tăcĭtus** -a -um: pass., *passed over in silence, unmentioned; implied, tacit; secret, concealed;* act., *silent, mute, still, quiet.* Adv. **tăcĭtē.**

tăcĭturnĭtās -ātis, f., *silence, taciturnity.*

tăcĭturnus -a -um, *silent, still, quiet.*

tăcĭtus -a -um, partic. from taceo; q.v.

Tăcĭtus -i, m., Cornelius, *the historian of the early Empire.*

tactĭlis -e, *able to be touched.*

tactĭo -ōnis, f. *touching, sense of touch.*

tactus -ūs, m. *touch, touching; influence, operation; the sense of touch.*

taeda -ae, f. *pine-wood; a board, a torch,* esp. as used at weddings.

taedet taedēre taedŭit, and taesum est. impers., *it causes weariness or boredom.*

taedĭfer -fĕra -fĕrum, *torch-bearing.*

taedĭum -i, n. *disgust, weariness, boredom.*

taenĭa -ae, f. *a fillet, head-band.*

taeter -tra -trum, *foul, hideous, offensive; disgraceful, abominable;* adv. **taetrē.**

tăgax -ācis, *thievish, given to pilfering.*

tălāris -e, *of or stretching to the ankles;* n. pl. as subst. *wings on the ankles, winged sandals,* or *a robe reaching to the ankles.*

tălārĭus -a -um, *of dice.*

tālĕa -ae, f. *a cutting, slip; a short stake or bar.*

tălentum -i, n. *a (Greek) weight;* also *a sum of money.*

tālĭo -ōnis, f. *retaliation.*

tālis -e, *of such a kind, such.*

talpa -ae, f. *or* m. *a mole.*

tālus -i, m. *the ankle, ankle-bone; the heel; a die* (made originally of ankle-bones of animals).

tam, *so, so far, to such a degree.*

tămărix -icis, f. *the tamarisk.*

tamdĭū, *so long.*

tămen, *however, yet, nevertheless.*

Tămĕsis -is, m. and **Tămĕsa** -ae, *the Thames.*

tămetsi, *even if, although.*

tamquam (tanquam), *as, just as, like as; just as if.*

tandem, *at length, at last;* in questions. *after all, may I ask?*

tango tangĕre tĕtĭgi tactum, *to touch, strike, push, hit; to border on, to reach; to steal; to defile; to taste; to affect the feelings; to touch upon a subject.*

Tantălus i-, m. *a son of Jupiter, who offended the gods and was "tantalised" in Hades.*

tantillus -a -um, *so little, so small.*

tantispĕr, *just so long.*

tantŏpĕrĕ, *so greatly, so much.*

tantŭlus -a -um, *so small, so little;* n. as subst. *such a trifle.*

tantum; see tantus.

tantummŏdo, *only just.*

tantus -a -um, *of such a size, so great.* N. as subst. **tantum** -i, *so much;* acc. as adv., *so far,* or *only;* tantum non, *all but;* genit. **tanti,** *for so much, worth so much;* abl. **tanto,** *by so much.*

tantusdem tantādem tantundem, *just so much, just so great.*

tăpēta -ae, m. **tăpēta** -ōrum, n. pl., and **tăpētia** -ium, n. pl., *drapery, tapestry.*

tardesco -ĕre, *to become slow.*

tardipēs -pēdis, *slow-footed, limping.*

tardĭtās -ātis, f. *slowness, tardiness; dullness, stupidity.*

tardo +are: intransit., *to loiter, be slow;* transit., *to slow down, hinder, delay.*

tardus -a -um, adj. *slow, tardy; dull, stupid;* poet., *making slow;* of speech, *measured, deliberate.* Adv. **tardē,** *slowly.*

Tărentum -i, n. *a coastal town of southern Italy* (now Taranto); adj. **Tărentīnus** -a -um.

Tarpēius -a -um, *name of a Roman family;* mons Tarpeius, *the Tarpeian rock, from which criminals were thrown.*

Tarquinii -orum, m. pl. *an old town in Etruria, whence came the Tarquin family, including two kings of Rome.*

Tarrāco -ōnis, f. *a town in Spain.*

Tartărus (-ŏs) -i, m.; plur. **Tartără** -ōrum, n. *the infernal regions;* adj. **Tartărĕus** -a -um.

taurĕus -a -um, *of a bull;* f. as subst. *a whip of bull's hide.*

taurĭformis -e, *shaped like a bull.*

taurīnus -a -um, *of* or *like a bull.*

taurus -i, m. *a bull.*

Taurus -i, m *a mountain range in Asia Minor.*

taxātĭo -onis, f. *rating, valuing, appraising.*

taxillus -i, m. *a small die.*

taxus -i, f. *yew-tree.*

[1]tē; see tu.

[2]-tĕ, suffix added to tu, etc.

techna -ae, f. *a cunning trick, artifice.*

tector -ōris, m. *a plasterer.*

tectōrĭŏlum -i, n. *plaster* or *stucco work.*

tectōrĭus -a -um, *used for covering,* of or *for plastering;* n. as subst. *plaster, stucco, fresco painting, cosmetic.*

tectus -a -um, partic. from tego; q.v.

tĕgēs -ētis, f. *a mat, rug, covering.*

tĕgĭmen, tĕgŭmen, tegmĕn -inis, n. *a cover, covering.*

tĕgĭmentum, tĕgŭmentum, tegmentum -i, n. *a covering.*

tĕgo tĕgĕre texi tectum, *to cover; to bury; to conceal; to shield, protect.* Hence partic. as adj. **tectus** -a -um, *covered, concealed; close, reserved, cautious.* N. as subst. **tectum** -i, *a roof* or *ceiling; a shelter, dwelling.* Adv. **tectē,** *covertly.*

tegu-; see also tegi-.

tĕgŭla -ae, f. *a roof-tile.*

tela -ae, f. *a web in weaving; a warp; a spider's web; a loom; a design.*

Tělěmăchus -i, m. *son of Penelope and Ulysses.*

tellūs -ōris, f. *earth, soil, land; a country; the world.*

tēlum -i, n. *a missile; a dart, javelin, spear; any weapon; a beam of light.*

tĕmĕrārius -a -um, *accidental; inconsiderate, thoughtless, rash.*

tĕmĕrē, adv. *blindly, by chance, casually, heedlessly;* non temere, *not for nothing, not lightly, not easily.*

tĕmĕrĭtās -ātis, f. *chance, accident; rashness.*

tĕmĕro -are, *to darken; to defile, dishonour.*

tēmētum -i, n. *intoxicating drink; wine, etc.*

temno temnĕre tempsi temptum, *to despise.*

tēmo -ōnis, m. *a pole; the pole of a waggon; a waggon; Charles's Wain.*

Tempē, n. pl., indecl. *a valley in Thessaly.*

tempěrāmentum -i, n. *a right proportion, middle way, mean, moderation.*

temperantĭa -ae, f. *temperance moderation, self-control.*

tempěrātĭo -ōnis, f. *moderation, just proportion; an organizing principle.*

tempěrātor -ōris, m. *one who arranges* or *governs.*

tempĕri; see tempus.

tempěrĭēs -ēi, f. *a proper mixture, tempering;* of climate, *mildness.*

tempěro -are: intransit., *to be moderate, control oneself;* with dat. *to control, use with moderation,* or *to spare;* with ab, or with abl., *to keep from, refrain from;* transit., *to mix properly, temper, mitigate, regulate.* Hence partic. as adj. **tempěrans** -antis, *moderate, temperate, restrained;* adv. **tempěranter;** perf. partic. **tempěrātus** -a -um, *tempered, ordered, moderate;* adv. **tempěrātē.**

tempestās -ātis, f. *a period of time, a season; weather;* esp. *bad weather, storm, tempest;* fig., *attack, fury.*

tempestīvĭtās -ātis, f. *fit time, proper season.*

tempestīvus -a -um, *opportune, fit, appropriate; early; ripe, mature.* Adv. **tempestīvē,** *seasonably.*

templum -i, n. *a section, a part cut off; a space marked out by the augur for auspices; consecrated ground;* esp. *a sanctuary, asylum; a place dedicated to a deity, a shrine, temple; any open space, quarter, region; a rafter, cross-beam*

tempŏrālis -e, *temporary, lasting for a time.*

tempŏrārius -a -um *temporary; seasonable.*

tempŏri; see tempus.

temptăbundus -a -um, *trying, attempting.*

temptāmĕn -inis, and **temptāmentum** -i, n. *a trial, attempt, essay.*

temptātĭo -ōnis, f. *a trial, test; an attack.*

temptātor -ōris, m. *an assailant.*

tempto -are, *to prove, try, test, attempt; to test by attack, to assail; to work upon, tamper with, excite, disturb.*

tempus -ŏris, n. *a division, section;* of the temples of the head; *of time, a space, period, moment; time,* in gen.; *a fit time, occasion, opportunity; the state, condition of things* (esp. bad); *time in pronouncing a syllable, quantity; time in grammar, tense.* As adv. **tempŏrĕ, tempŏri,** and **tempĕri,** *at the right time,* or *for the occasion;* **in tempŏrĕ,** *at the right moment;* **ex tempŏrĕ,** *on the spur of the moment.*

tēmŭlentus -a -um, *drunken, tipsy.*

tēnācitās -ātis, f. *tenacity; stinginess.*

tēnax -ācis, *holding fast, clinging, tenacious; sparing, frugal, stingy; firm, steady; obstinate.* Adv. **tēnācitĕr,** *firmly, steadily.*

tendīcŭla -ae, f. *a snare, trap.*

tendo tendĕre tĕtendi tentum and tensum: transit., *to stretch, extend, spread; to direct, present, give;* barbiton, *to string;* praetorium, *to pitch;* intransit., *to direct one's course, tend, make towards; to be inclined, aim at, strive after;* with infin., *to try, attempt;* milit., *to pitch one's tent, encamp.*

tĕnebrae -arum, f. pl. *darkness; night; blindness; obscurity.*

tĕnebricōsus -a -um, *dark, gloomy, obscure.*

tĕnebrōsus -a -um, *dark, gloomy.*

tĕnĕo tĕnēre tĕnŭi tentum, *to hold; to possess, keep, preserve, maintain; to understand, grasp, know, remember; to contain, comprise;* milit. *to occupy, garrison; to master, restrain, keep back; to charm, amuse;* intransit., *to keep on, persevere, persist, endure.*

tĕner -ēra -ērum, *tender, delicate, soft; young;* adv. **tĕnĕrĕ.**

tĕnĕrasco -ĕre, *to grow tender.*

tĕnĕritās -ātis, f. *tenderness, softness.*

tĕnor -ōris, m. *course, continued movement; duration, career.*

tensa -ae, f. *a car on which images of the gods were carried.*

tento, etc.; see **tempto,** etc.

tentīgo -inis, f. *lecherousness.*

tentōrium -i, n. *a tent.*

tentus -a -um, partic. from **tendo** and **teneo;** q.v.

tĕnŭīcŭlus -a -um, *very mean, slight.*

tĕnŭis -e, *thin, slight, slender; refined, subtle; little, trivial, feeble; mean, low.* Adv. **tĕnŭitĕr,** *thinly; subtly; slightly, poorly.*

tĕnŭitās -ātis, f. *thinness; refinement, subtlety; slightness, poverty.*

tĕnŭo -are, *to make thin, attenuate; to weaken, diminish.*

tĕnŭs, prep. after noun or pronoun in abl. or genit., *up to, down to, as far as.*

tĕpĕfăcio -făcĕre -fēci -factum, *to make warm.*

tĕpĕo -ēre, *to be warm,* or *lukewarm.*

tĕpesco tĕpescĕre tĕpŭi, *to grow warm* or *lukewarm.*

tĕpĭdus -a -um, *warm, lukewarm, tepid;* compar. adv. **tĕpĭdius.**

tĕpor -ōris, m. *lukewarmness, moderate heat.*

tĕr, *three times, thrice.*

terdĕcĭēs (-ĭens) *thirteen times.*

tĕrēbinthus -i, f. *the terebinth-tree.*

tĕrebro -are, *to bore through, pierce, perforate.*

tĕrēdo -ĭnis, f. *a worm that gnaws wood.*

Tĕrentius -a -um, *the name of a Roman gens;* esp. of M. Terentius Afer, *the comic dramatist.*

tĕrĕs -rĕtis, *rounded, polished, well-turned, smooth; refined, elegant.*

tergĕmĭnus = **trigeminus;** q.v.

tergĕo -ēre and **tergo** -ĕre, tersi tersum, *to wipe, scour, clean;* partic. **tersus** -a -um, *clean, neat, correct.*

tergiversātio -ōnis, f. *backwardness, reluctance, evasion.*

tergiversor -ari, dep. *to be backward and reluctant, shuffle, find excuses, evade.*

tergo = **tergeo;** q.v.

tergum -i, n. *the back;* terga dare, *to flee;* a tergo, *in the rear; a hide, skin;* meton., *a thing made out of hide.*

tergus -ŏris, n. *the back; skin, hide, leather.*

termĕs -itis, m. *a branch,* esp. of olive.

Terminālia -ĭum and -ĭōrum, n. *the Festival of Terminus (god of boundaries).*

termĭnātio -ōnis, f. *limiting, determining, termination.*

termĭno -are, *to limit, set bounds to, restrict, define, close.*

termĭnus -i, m. *a boundary-mark, limit, end;* personif., *the god of boundaries.*

terni -ae -a, *three at a time,* or *three each.*

tĕro tĕrĕre trivi tritum, *to rub; to whet, smooth; to grind, thresh; to wear out, use up, spend.*

Hence partic. as adj. **tritus** -a -um, *worn; frequented; practised;* of words, etc., *trite, well-known.*

Terpsichŏrē -ēs, f. *the Muse of dancing;* in gen., *poetry.*

terra -ae, f. *earth, land, ground, soil; a country, land, region;* orbis terrarum, *the whole world.*

terrēnus -a -um, *belonging to the earth, terrestrial; made of earth, earthen;* n. as subst. *land, ground.*

terrĕo terrēre, *to frighten, terrify; scare away; to deter.*

terrestris -e, *of the earth, terrestrial.*

terrĕus -a -um, *of earth, earthly.*

terrĭbĭlis -e, *terrible, dreadful.*

terrĭcŭla -ōrum, n. pl. *a bogey.*

terrĭfico -āre, *to frighten, terrify.*

terrĭfĭcus -a -um, *frightful, terrible.*

terrĭgĕna -ae, m. and f. *earth-born.*

terrĭlŏquus -a -um, *terror-speaking.*

territo -are, *to frighten, intimidate, scare.*

territōrium -i, n. *land belonging to a town, district, territory.*

terror -ōris, m. *fright, fear, terror; a frightening object.*

tersus -a-um. partic. from tergeo; q.v.

tertiădĕcĭmāni -ōrum, m. pl. *soldiers of the thirteenth legion.*

tertĭānus -a -um. (1) *of the third day;* f. as subst., *a tertian fever.* (2) *belonging to the third legion;* m. pl. as subst., *soldiers of the third legion.*

tertĭus -a -um, *third;* acc. n. sing. tertĭum, *for the third time;* abl. tertĭō, *for the third time,* or *thirdly.*

tertĭusdĕcĭmus -a -um, *thirteenth.*

tĕruncĭus -i, m. *one quarter;* ne teruncius quidem, *not a farthing.*

tesqua (tesca) -ōrum, n. pl. *wastes, deserts.*

tessella -ae, f. *a small cube of stone.*

tessĕra -ae, f. *a cube; a piece of mosaic paving; a die* (with numbers on all six sides); *a token; a watchword.*

tessĕrārĭus -i, m. *the officer who received the watchword.*

testa -ae, f. *an earthen vessel, pot, jug, urn,* etc.; *a potsherd; a brick or tile; the shell of shell-fish;* any *shell, covering.*

testāmentārĭus -a -um, *relating to a will;* m. as subst., *a forger of wills.*

testāmentum -i, n. *a last will, testament.*

testātĭo -onis, f. *calling to witness,* or *bearing witness.*

testĭfĭcātĭo -onis, f. *bearing witness, testifying; evidence, proof.*

testĭfĭcor -ari, dep. *to bear witness to, give evidence of; to show, bring to light; to call to witness.*

testĭmōnĭum -i, n. *witness, evidence; proof, indication.*

¹testis -is, c. *one who gives evidence, a witness; an eye-witness, spectator.*

²testis -is, m. *a testicle.*

testor -ari, dep. (1) *to bear witness to, give evidence of; to make known, publish, declare;* as pass., *to be attested, declared.* (2) *to make a will.* (3) *to call to witness.*

testūdĭnĕus -a -um, *of a tortoise; of tortoise-shell.*

testūdo -inis, f. *a tortoise; tortoise-shell; a lyre, cithara,* etc.; *an arch or vault;* milit., *a shed, to protect soldiers while attacking fortifications, also a formation with shields held over the soldiers' heads and interlocking.*

testŭla -ae, f. *a potsherd.*

testum -i, n. with abl. testo and testu, *an earthen pot.*

teter; see taeter.

Tēthys -thȳos; acc. -thyn; f. *a marine goddess.*

tetrachmum or tetradrachmum -i, n. *a Greek coin of four drachmae.*

tetrarchēs -ae, m. *ruler over one-fourth of a country, tetrarch.*

tetrarchĭa -ae, f. *a tetrarchy.*

tetrĭcus -a -um, *harsh, gloomy, severe.*

Teucer -cri, and Teucrus -i, m. (1) *son of Telamon, and brother of Ajax.* (2) *first king of Troy;* hence adj. Teucrus -a -um, *Trojan;* m. pl. as subst. *the Trojans;* Teucrĭa -ae, f. *Troy.*

Teutŏni -ōrum, and Teutŏnes -um, m. pl. *the Teutons, a Germanic people.*

texo texĕre texŭi textum, *to weave; to twine together, plait; to put together, construct, build;* of speech or writing, *to compose.* N. of partic. as subst. textum -i, *woven cloth, a web, fabric; of composition, style.*

textĭlis -e. *woven, textile, plaited.* N. as subst. *a woven fabric, piece of cloth.*

textor -ōris, m. and textrix -tricis, f. *a weaver.*

textrīnum -i, n. *weaving.*

textum -i, n. subst. from texo; q.v.

textūra -ae, f. *a web, texture; putting together, construction.*

textus -ūs, m. *a web; texture, structure; of speech or writing, connexion.*

thălămus -i, m. *a room, esp. a woman's bedroom; a marriage-bed; any abode, dwelling.*

thălassĭnus -a -um, *sea-green.*

Thălĭa -ae, f. *the Muse of comic poetry.*

thallus -i, m. *a green branch.*

Thapsus (-ŏs) -i, f. *a town in Africa, where Caesar conquered the Pompeians.*

thĕātrālis -e, *of a theatre, theatrical.*

thĕātrum -i, n. *a theatre.*

Thēbae -arum, f. pl. *Thebes.* (1) *a city of Upper Egypt.* (2) *the chief city of Boeotia.* Adj. Thēbānus -a -um, *belonging to Thebes in Boeotia.*

thēca -ae, f. *a case, envelope, covering.*

thēma -ătis, n. *a topic, subject.*

thĕōlŏgus -i, m. *a theologian.*

thermae -arum, f. pl. *warm springs, warm baths.*

thēsaurus -i, m. *a treasure, store, hoard; a treasury, store-house.*

Thēsēus -ĕi and -ĕos. m. *a king of Athens, conqueror of the Minotaur;* adj. Thēsēus and Thēsēĭus -a -um. *of Theseus.*

thĕsis -is, f. *a proposition, thesis.*

Thessălĭa -ae, f. *Thessaly, a region in the north of Greece;* adj. Thessălĭcus and Thessălus -a -um, *Thessalian;* f. adj. Thessălis -idis, *Thessalian.*

Thĕtis -idis or -idos, f. *a sea-nymph, mother of Achilles;* poet., *the sea.*

thĭāsus -i, m. *a Bacchic rout, band of revellers.*

Thisbē -ēs, f. *a Babylonian maiden, loved by Pyramus.*

thŏlus -i, m. *a cupola, dome.*

thōrax -ācis, m. *a breastplate, cuirass.*

Thrācĭa -ae; also Thrāca -ae and Thrācē -ēs; f. *the country of Thrace;* adj. Thrācĭus and Thrēĭcĭus -a -um, *Thracian;* Thrax -ācis and Thrēx -ĕcis, m. *Thracian, a Thracian.*

Thūcȳdĭdēs -is, m. *the Athenian historian of the Peloponnesian war.*

Thūlē (Thȳlē) -ēs, f. *an island in the extreme north of Europe.*

thunnus (thynnus) -i, m. *a tunny-fish.*

thūs, thūrārĭus, etc. = tus, turarius, etc.; q.v.

Thȳestēs -ae and -is, m. *son of Pelops, brother of Atreus.*

Thȳĭas and Thȳas -ădis, f. *a Bacchante.*

Thȳlē = Thule; q.v.

thymbra -ae, f. *the herb savory.*

thȳmum -i, n. *the herb thyme.*

thynnus = thunnus; q.v.

thyrsus -i, m. *the stalk of a plant; a wand, as carried by Bacchus and his attendants.*

tiăra -ae, f. and **tiărus** -ae, m. *a turban.*

Tibĕris -bĕris, m.; also poet. **Tibris** or **Thibris** -bridis, m. *the river Tiber;* adj. **Tibĕrīnus** -a -um, *of the river Tiber;* m. as subst. *the river-god of the Tiber.*

Tibĕrius -i, m. *a Roman praenomen,* abbreviated Ti.

tibĭa -ae, f. *the shin-bone, tibia; a pipe, flute* (originally made of a hollow bone).

tibĭcĕn -ĭnis, m. *a flute-player, piper; a pillar, prop.*

tibĭcĭna -ae, f. *a female flute-player.*

tibĭcĭnium -i, *playing on the flute.*

Tibris = Tiberis; q.v.

Tibullus -i, m.; Albius, *a Roman elegiac poet.*

Tibŭr -bŭris, n. *an old town in Latium;* adj. **Tibŭrs** -burtis, **Tiburtīnus** and **Tiburnus** -a -um.

tigillum -i, n. *a small beam.*

tignārius -a -um, *of beams;* faber. *a carpenter.*

tignum -i, n. *a beam.*

Tigrānēs -is, m. *a king of Armenia.*

tigris -īdis or -is, c. *a tiger.*

tilĭa -ae, f. *linden or lime-tree.*

timĕfactus -a -um, *frightened, alarmed.*

timĕo -ēre, *to be afraid, fear, dread;* partic. **timens** -entis, *fearing, fearful.*

timĭdĭtās -ātis, f. *fearfulness, timidity.*

timĭdus -a -um, *fearful, timid;* adv. **timĭdē.**

timor -ōris, m. *fear, dread; an object exciting fear.*

tinctĭlis -e, *in which something is dipped.*

tinĕa -ae, f. *a grub, larva, worm.*

tingo tingĕre tinxi tinctum, *to wet, moisten; to dye, colour, imbue.*

tinnĭo -ire, *to ring, tinkle; to talk shrilly; to make to chink;* hence *to pay money.*

tinnītus -ūs, m. *ringing, tinkle, jingle.*

tinnŭlus -a -um, *ringing, tinkling, jingling.*

tintinnābŭlum -i, n. *a bell.*

tintinno (**tintino**) -are, *to ring, tinkle.*

tīnus -i, f. *a shrub, the laurustinus.*

Tirĭdātēs -dātis, m. *name of several kings of Armenia.*

tīro -ōnis, m. *a young soldier; a recruit, beginner, learner.*

tīrōcinium -i, n. *the state of a recruit, rawness, inexperience; beginning, apprenticeship;* concr. *a body of recruits.*

tīruncŭlus -i, m. *a young beginner.*

Tīryns -nthis or -nthos, f. *an Argive town where Hercules was brought up;* adj. **Tīrynthius** -a -um.

Tīsĭphŏnē -ēs, f. *one of the Furies.*

Tītān -tānis, and **Tītānus** -i, m.; usually plur. **Tītānes** -um and **Tītāni** -ōrum, *the Titans, who warred against Jupiter and were by him cast into Hades.*

Tīthōnus -i, m. *husband of Aurora.*

Titĭes -ium and **Titĭenses** -ium, m. pl., *one of the three original tribes at Rome.*

tĭtillātĭo -ōnis, f. *a tickling.*

tĭtillo -are, *to tickle.*

tĭtŭbātĭo -ōnis, f. *a staggering, reeling; uncertainty.*

tĭtŭbo -are, *to totter, stagger; to stammer; to falter, waver, hesitate;* adv. from partic. **tĭtŭbantĕr,** *hesitatingly, uncertainly.*

tĭtŭlus -i, m. *an inscription, label, notice; a title, honour; pretence, pretext.*

Titus -i, m. *a Roman praenomen,* abbreviated T.

tŏcŭlĭo -ōnis, m. *a usurer.*

tŏfus (**tŏphus**) -i, m. *tufa.*

tŏga -ae, f. *the white woollen upper garment worn by Roman citizens.*

tŏgātŭlus -i, m. *a little client.*

tŏgātus -a -um, *wearing the toga;* m. as subst. *a Roman citizen;* f. as subst. *the national drama of the Romans.*

tŏgŭla -ae, f. *a little toga.*

tŏlĕrābĭlis -e; pass., *bearable;* act., *tolerant, patient;* compar. adv. **tŏlĕrābĭlius,** *rather patiently.*

tŏlĕrantia -ae and **tŏlĕrātĭo** -onis, f. *bearing, endurance.*

tŏlĕro -are, *to carry, bear, endure, sustain; to sustain; to support, keep up, maintain.* Hence pres. partic. **tŏlĕrans** -antis, *enduring, patient;* adv. **tŏlĕrantĕr;** perf. partic. **tŏlĕrātus** -a -um, *endurable.*

tollēno -ōnis, m. *a machine for raising weights, a crane.*

tollo tollĕre sustŭli sublātum. (1) *to lift up, raise, elevate;* in crucem, *to crucify;* tollere ancoras, *to weigh anchor;* laudibus, *to extol;* of children, *to acknowledge as one's own, to bring up.* (2) *to take away, remove, carry off, steal; to destroy, abolish.*

tŏmācŭlum (**-aclum**) -i, n. *a kind of sausage.*

tōmentum -i, n. *the stuffing of a pillow, mattress, etc.*

Tŏmi -ōrum, m. pl. and **Tŏmis** -is, f. *a town on the Black Sea, Ovid's place of exile.*

tŏmus -i, m. *a cutting, chip, shred.*

tondĕo tondēre tŏtondi tonsum, *to shave, shear, clip; to mow, reap, prune; to browse on, crop; to fleece a person.*

tŏnitrus -ūs, m. and **tŏnitruum** -i, n. *thunder.*

tŏno -are -ŭi -itum, *to thunder.* Transf.: instransit., *to make a loud noise;* transit., *to thunder forth.*

tonsa -ae, f. *an oar.*

tonsĭlis -e, *shorn, clipped, cut.*

tonsillae -arum, f. *the tonsils.*

tonsor -ōris, m. *a hair-cutter, barber.*

tonsōrius -a -um, *of or for clipping.*

tonstrīcŭla -ae, f. *a little female barber.*

tonstrīna -ae, f. *a barber's shop.*

tonstrix -icis, f. *a female barber.*

tonsūra -ae, f. *clipping, shearing, shaving.*

tophus, etc. = tofus, etc.; q.v.

tŏpīārīus -a -um, *of ornamental gardening*; m. as subst. *a landscape gardener*; f. as subst. *the art of landscape gardening.*

tŏrāl -ālis, n. *the valance of a couch.*

tŏreuma -ătis, n. *carved or embossed work.*

tormentum -i, n. *an instrument for twisting or pressing; a windlass; the rack; any instrument of torture*; hence *suasion, pressure; torture, torment*; milit., *a piece of artillery, or a missile.*

tormīna -um, n. pl. *the colic, gripes.*

tormīnōsus -a -um, *suffering from colic.*

torno -are, *to turn in a lathe; to round, make round.*

tornus -i, m. *a lathe.*

tŏrōsus -a -um, *muscular, brawny.*

torpēdo -īnis, f. (1) *lethargy, sluggishness.* (2) *a fish, the electric ray.*

torpĕo -ēre, *to be sluggish, numb, inert, inactive.*

torpesco -pescĕre -pŭi, *to become sluggish or numb.*

torpīdus -a -um, *numb, sluggish.*

torpor -ōris, m. *numbness, sluggishness, dullness, inactivity.*

torquātus -a -um, *wearing a twisted collar or necklace.*

torquĕo torquēre torsi tortum, *to twist, wind, curl, wrench; to distort; to hurl violently, whirl; to rack, torture, torment, plague, try, test.*
  Hence partic. **tortus** -a -um, *twisted, crooked, intricate*; adv. **tortē.**

torquis (**torquēs**) -is, m. and f. *a twisted collar or necklace; a ring, wreath, chaplet.*

torrĕo torrēre torrŭi tostum, *to burn, parch, dry up.*
  Hence partic. as adj. **torrens** -entis, *burning, hot, parched; rushing, seething.* M. as subst. *a torrent.*

torresco -ĕre, *to become parched.*

torrīdus -a -um, *parched, burnt, dry.* Transf., *pinched, nipped with cold.*

torris, is, m. *a firebrand.*

tortīlis -e, *twisted, twined.*

torto -are, *to torture, torment.*

tortor -ōris, m. *a torturer, tormentor; a wielder.*

tortŭōsus -a -um, *tortuous, intricate, involved.*

¹**tortus** -a -um, partic. from torqueo; q.v.

²**tortus** -ūs, m. *a twisting, curve.*

tŏrus -i, m. *any round protuberance; a muscle; a bed, sofa; a marriage couch; a bier; a mound*; fig., *an ornament.*

torvĭtās -ātis, f. *savageness, wildness.*

torvus -a -um, *savage, grim, fierce.*

tŏt, indecl. *so many.*

tŏtīdem, indecl. *just as many.*

tŏtiēs (**-iens**), *so often, so many times.*

tŏtus -a -um, genit. **tōtīus**, dat. **tōtī**; *whole, complete, entire; whole-hearted, absorbed.* N. as subst. **tōtum** -i, *the whole*; ex toto, in toto, *on the whole.*

toxĭcum -i, n. *poison (for arrows).*

trābālis -e, *of beams of wood; like a beam.*

trăbĕa -ae, f. *a white robe with scarlet stripes and a purple seam, worn by kings and knights.*

trăbĕātus -a -um, *clad in the trabea*; q.v.

trabs trābis, f. *a beam of wood; a tree-trunk; a ship; a roof; a table.*

tractābĭlis -e, *that can be handled, manageable; yielding, compliant.*

tractātĭo -ōnis, f. *handling, management.*

tractātor -ōris, m. *a masseur.*

tractātrix -īcis, f. *a masseuse.*

tractātus -ūs, m. *handling, management, treatment.*

tractim, *gradually, by degrees.*

tracto -are, *to drag along, haul, pull about; to handle, manage, treat; to behave towards a person.*

¹**tractus** -a -um, partic. from traho; q.v.

²**tractus** -ūs, m. *a dragging process; verborum, drawling; belli, extension; concr., a track, trail; extent, position; a tract, district.*

tradĭtĭo -ōnis, f. *giving up, surrender; instruction, relation.*

trādĭtor -ōris, m. *traitor.*

trādo (**transdo**) -dĕre -dĭdi -dĭtum, *to hand over, give up, surrender, betray; to hand down to posterity; esp. to hand down an account of an event, to report, relate, teach*; with reflex., *to commit, surrender, devote oneself.*

trādūco (**transdūco**) -dūcĕre -duxi -ductum, *to lead over, bring over or across; to lead past in front of others; to transpose, transfer; of time, to pass, spend, lead; to show, display; to expose to ridicule, " show up ".*

trāductĭo -ōnis, f. *transferring*; rhet., *metonymy; temporis, passage or lapse of time.*

trāductor -ōris, m. *a transferrer.*

trādux -ūcis, m. *vine-layer.*

trăgĭcus -a -um, *tragic; lofty, sublime; awful, fearful.* M. as subst. *a tragic poet.* Adv. **trăgĭcē**, *tragically.*

trăgoedĭa -ae, f. *tragedy; a dramatic scene.*

trăgoedus -i, m. *tragic actor, tragedian.*

trăgŭla -ae, f. *a species of javelin.*

trăhĕa -ae, f. *sledge, drag.*

trăho trăhĕre traxi tractum, *to trail, pull along; to drag, pull violently; to draw in, take up; of air, to breathe; to draw out, hence to lengthen; to draw together, contract.* Transf., *to draw, attract; to take in or on, assume, derive; to prolong, spin out; to ascribe, refer, interpret.*
  Hence partic. **tractus** -a -um, of speech, *fluent, flowing.* N. as subst., *a flock of wool.*

trāĭcĭo (**transĭcĭo**) -ĭcĕre -ĭēci -ĭectum. (1) *to throw a thing (or person) across something; to convey over, transport.* (2) *to pass through or across a thing (or person); to cross, penetrate, pierce.*

trāĭectĭo -ōnis, f. *a passing over, crossing over; transferring, transposition; hyperbole.*

trāĭectus -ūs, m. *crossing over, passage.*

tralat- = translat-; q.v.

trālūcěo = transluceo; q.v.

trāma -ae, f. *the woof in weaving.*

trāměo = transmeo; q.v.

trāmēs -itis, m. *by-way, foot-path.*

trāmigro = transmigro; q.v.

trāmitto = transmitto; q.v.

trānāto (transnāto) -are, *to swim across, pass through.*

tranquillitās -ātis, f. *quiet, calm.*

tranquillo -are, *to calm.*

tranquillus -a -um, *quiet, calm.* N. as subst. *a calm, quietness.* Adv. tranquillē.

trans, prep. with acc., *over, across, on or to the other side of.*

transāběo -ire -ĭi, *to go through or past.*

transactor -ōris, m. *manager, accomplisher.*

transădīgo -ĭgěre -ěgi -actum, *to drive a thing through something else; also to pierce, penetrate.*

Transalpīnus -a -um, *beyond the Alps, transalpine.*

transcendo (transscendo) -scenděre -scendi -scensum, *to climb over, pass over; to step over, transgress.*

transcrībo (transscribo) -scrīběre -scripsi -scriptum, *to copy, transcribe.* Transf., *to transfer, convey, assign.*

transcurro -currěre -cŭcurri and -curri -cursum, *to run across or over, hasten past.*

transcursus -ūs, m. *a running past, hastening through.*

transdo = trado; q.v.

transdūco = traduco; q.v.

transenna -ae, f. *lattice-work, grating.*

transěo -ire -ĭi -ĭtum, *to go over, cross, pass over, go past.* Transf., *to be changed; to pass time; to pass beyond, transgress; to pass over, ignore, or touch lightly on.*

transfěro transferre transtŭli translātum and trālātum, *to carry over or across; to transfer, transport, convey.* Transf., *to put off, defer; to change; in writing, to copy; to translate into another language; to use a word figuratively or metaphorically.*

transfīgo -fīgěre -fixi -fixum, *to pierce through, or thrust through.*

transfŏdio -fŏděre -fōdi -fossum, *to stab through, transfix.*

transformis -e, *changed, transformed.*

transformo -are, *to change, transform.*

transfŭga -ae, *deserter.*

transfŭgio -fŭgěre -fūgi -fūgĭtum, *to desert to the enemy.*

transfŭgium -i, n. *desertion.*

transfundo -funděre -fūdi -fūsum, *to pour from one vessel into another, to transfer.*

transfūsio -ōnis, f. *a pouring out, pouring off.*

transgrědĭor -grědi -gressus, dep. *to go across, pass over.*

transgressio -ōnis, f. *going over, passage; transposition of words.*

transgressus -ūs, m. *going over, passage.*

transĭgo -ĭgěre -ēgi -actum, *to stab, pierce through; of time, to pass, spend;* of business, *to finish, complete, accomplish, transact;* of a difference or dispute, *to settle.*

transĭlio (transsĭlio) -sĭlire -sĭlŭi, *to spring over, leap across; to pass over a thing, or to pass beyond, transgress.*

transĭtio -ōnis, f. *going across, passing over; communication, infection, contagion;* concr., *a passage.*

transĭtus -ūs, m. *passing over or across, transit; changing over, transition.*

translātīcius (trālātīcius) -a -um, *customary, prescriptive; common, usual.*

translātĭo (trālātĭo) -ōnis, f. *transferring, handing over;* of plants, *grafting; a translation; a metaphor, trope.*

translātīvus -a -um, *transferable.*

translātor -ōris, m. *transferrer.*

translūcěo (trālūcěo) -ēre, *to shine through or across.*

transmărīnus -a -um, *from beyond the sea, foreign.*

transměo (trāměo) -měare, *to go over or through.*

transmigro -are, *to migrate.*

transmissio -ōnis, f. and transmissus -ūs, m. *passage.*

transmitto (trāmitto) -mittěre -mīsi -missum, (1) *to send across, send over, transmit; to convey, make over, entrust;* of time, *to let pass.* (2) *to go across, pass through or over; to leave unnoticed.*

transmontāni -ōrum, m. pl. *dwellers beyond the mountains.*

transmŏvěo -mŏvěre -mōvi -mōtum, *to remove, transfer.*

transmūto -are, *to change, transmute.*

transnāto = tranato; q.v.

transpădānus -a -um, *beyond (i.e. north of) the Po, transpadane.*

transpectus -ūs, m. *a looking through, seeing through.*

transpĭcio (transspĭcio) -spĭcěre, *to look through, see through.*

transpōno -pōněre -pŏsŭi -pŏsĭtum, *to put over, remove, transfer.*

transporto -are, *to convey across, transport.*

transrhēnānus -a -um, *beyond the Rhine.*

transtĭběrīnus -a -um, *beyond the Tiber.*

transtrum -i, n. *cross-beam; thwart.*

transulto (transsulto) -are, *to spring across.*

transŭo (transsŭo) -sŭěre, *to sew through; hence to pierce through.*

transvectio (trāvectio) -ōnis, f. *a carrying across or past; esp. the riding of a Roman knight past the censor at the periodical muster.*

transvěho (trāvěho) -věhěre -vexi -vectum, *to carry over or past;* pass., *to ride, sail, etc., across;* of a knight, *to ride past the censor at a muster;* of time, *to pass by.*

transverběro -are, *to pierce through, transfix.*

transversārius -a, -um, *lying across, transverse.*

transversus, tráversus and trans-
vorsus -a -um, *transverse, oblique,*
athwart; transverso itinere, *obliquely;*
transversum digitum, *a finger's*
breadth; de transverso, *unexpectedly.*

transvŏlito -are, *to fly across.*

transvŏlo (trăvŏlo) -are, *to fly over*
or across; to hasten through or past.

trăpētus -i, m. **trăpētum** -i, n. and
plur. **trăpētes** -um, m. *an oil-press.*

Trăsŭmĕnus (also Trasy- and Trasi-;
also with double n) -i, m. *the Trasi-*
mene lake, where Hannibal conquered
the Romans under Flaminius (217
B.C.).

trav- = transv-; q.v.

trĕcēni -ae, -a, *three hundred at a time*
or each.

trĕcentēsĭmus -a -um, *three-hundredth.*

trĕcenti -ae -a, *three hundred.*

trĕcentiēs (-iens) *three hundred times.*

trĕchĕdĭpnum -i, n. *a light garment*
worn at table.

trĕdĕcim, *thirteen.*

trĕmĕbundus -a -um, *trembling.*

trĕmĕfăcĭo -făcĕre -fēci -factum, *to*
cause to tremble.

trĕmesco (-isco) -ĕre, *to tremble,*
quake; with acc., *to tremble at.*

tremi-; see treme-.

trĕmo -ĕre -ŭi, *to tremble, quake;* with
acc. *to tremble at;* gerundive as adj.
trĕmendus -a -um, *fearful, terrible.*

trĕmor -ōris, m. *a trembling, quaking.*

trĕmŭlus -a -um, *trembling, quaking;*
poet., *that causes trembling.*

trĕpĭdātĭo -ōnis, f. *agitation, anxiety.*

trĕpĭdo -are, *to be agitated, be busy,*
bustle about; with acc., *to be anxious*
about; with infin., *to be in a hurry to*
do a thing; of flame, *to flicker.* Adv.
from partic. **trĕpĭdantĕr,** *anxiously,*
hurriedly.

trĕpĭdus -a -um, *agitated, restless,*
disturbed, in an emergency; adv.
trĕpĭdē.

trēs tria, *three.*

tresvĭri = triumviri; q.v.

Trĕvĕri (Trēvĭri) -ōrum, m. pl. *a*
Germanic people.

trĭangŭlus -a -um, *three-cornered,*
triangular. N. as subst. *a triangle.*

trĭarii -ōrum, m. pl. *experienced Roman*
soldiers, drawn up in the third rank,
behind the others.

trĭbŭārĭus -a -um, *relating to a tribe.*

trĭbūlis -is, m. *a fellow-tribesman.*

trĭbŭlum -i, n. *threshing machine.*

trĭbŭlus -i, m. *a thorny plant, the*
caltrop.

trĭbūnăl -ālis, n. *the tribunal, a raised*
platform used by magistrates and
generals.

trĭbūnātus -ūs, m. *tribuneship.*

trĭbūnĭcĭus -a -um, *of a tribune, tri-*
bunicial; m. as subst. *an ex-tribune.*

trĭbūnus -i, m. *a tribune:* tribuni
aerarii, *paymasters who assisted the*
quaestors; tribuni militum, or mili-
tares, *military officers, of whom there*
were six to every legion; tribuni
plebis, *tribunes of the people, magis-*
trates who protected the plebeians.

trĭbŭo -ŭĕre -ŭi -ūtum, *to divide out,*
allot, assign; to grant, give, allow,
yield, ascribe, attribute.

trĭbus -ūs, f. *a tribe, a division of the*
Roman people.

trĭbūtărĭus -e -um, *relating to tribute.*

trĭbūtim, *tribe by tribe.*

trĭbūtĭo -ōnis, f. *a distribution.*

trĭbūtum -i, n. *tax, tribute.* Transf., *a*
gift, present.

trĭbūtus -a -um, *arranged according to*
tribes.

trīcae -ārum, f. pl. *trifles, nonsense;*
vexations, troubles.

trĭcēni -ae -a, *thirty at a time* or *each.*

trĭceps -cĭpĭtis, *three-headed.*

trĭcēsĭm:us (-ensĭmus) *thirtieth.*

trĭchĭla -ae, f. *summer-house, arbour.*

trĭcĭēs (-iens), *thirty times.*

trĭclīnĭum -i, n. *dining-couch;* hence
dining-room.

trĭcor -ari, dep. *to make difficulties,*
shuffle, trifle.

trĭcorpŏr -pŏris, *having three bodies.*

trĭcuspis -ĭdis, *having three points.*

trĭdens -entis, *having three teeth* or
prongs. M. as subst. *a trident, a*
three-pronged spear.

trĭdentĭfer and trĭdentĭger -ĕri, m.
the trident-bearer (of Neptune).

trĭdŭum -i, n. *a space of three days.*

triennia -ĭum, n. pl. *a festival cele-*
brated every three years.

triennĭum -i, n. *a space of three years.*

triens -entis, m. *a third part, one-third.*

trientābŭlum -i, n. *the equivalent in*
land for the third part of a sum of
money.

triērarchus -i, m. *the commander of a*
trireme.

triētĕrĭcus -a -um, *recurring every*
three years, triennial.

triētēris -ĭdis, f. *a space of three years*
or *a triennial festival.*

trĭfārĭam, *in three places, on three sides.*

trĭfaux -faucis, *having three throats.*

trĭfĭdus -a -um, *split in three parts, three-*
forked.

trĭformis -e, *having three forms.*

trĭgĕminus (tergĕminus) -a -um,
threefold, triple.

trĭgintā, *thirty.*

trĭgon -ōnis, m. *a ball for playing.*

trĭlĭbris -e, *of three pounds' weight.*

trĭlinguis -e, *having three tongues.*

trĭlix -icis, *having three threads.*

trĭmetrōs (-us) -a -um, *containing*
three double feet. M. as subst., *a*
trimeter.

trĭmus -a -um, *three years old.*

Trĭnacrĭa -ae, f. *the triangular land,*
i.e. Sicily; adj. **Trĭnacrĭus** -a -um,
and f. **Trĭnacris** -ĭdis, *Sicilian.*

trĭni -ae, -a; *three at a time, three*
together.

Trĭnobantes -um, m. *a people in east*
Britain.

trĭnōdis -e, *having three knots.*

trĭōnēs -um, m. pl. *the ploughing oxen;*
the constellations Great Bear and Little
Bear.

trĭpart-; see tripert-.

trĭpectŏrus -a -um, *having three breasts.*

trĭpĕdālis -e, *of three feet in measure.*

trĭpertītus (-partītus) -a -um, *three-fold, triple.* N. abl. sing. trĭpertītō (-partītō), *in three parts.*

trĭpēs -pĕdis, *having three feet.*

trĭplex -lĭcis, *threefold, triple.* M. pl. as subst. *a writing tablet with three leaves.*

trĭplus -a -um, *threefold, triple.*

trĭpŭdio -are, *to beat the ground with the feet, to dance,* esp. as a religious rite.

trĭpŭdĭum -i, n. (1) *a religious dance.* (2) *a favourable omen, when the sacred chickens ate fast.*

trĭpūs -pŏdis, m. *three-legged seat, tripod,* esp. *that at Delphi.*

trĭquetrus -a -um, *three-cornered, triangular.*

trĭrēmis -e, *having three banks of oars;* f. as subst., *a trireme.*

triscurria -ōrum, n. pl. *gross buffooneries.*

tristĭcŭlus -a -um, *somewhat sorrowful.*

tristis -e, *sad, gloomy, dismal, forbidding, harsh;* of taste or smell, *harsh, bitter.* N. acc. tristĕ used like adv. *harshly.*

tristĭtia -ae and tristĭtĭēs -ēi, f. *sadness, gloom, harshness.*

trĭsulcus -a -um, *three-pointed, three-pronged.*

trītĭcĕus -a -um, *wheaten.*

trīticum -i, n. *wheat.*

Trītōn -ōnis or -ōnos, m. (1) *Triton, son of Neptune, a god of the sea.* (2) *a lake in Africa, supposed birth-place of Minerva;* adj. Trītōnĭācus, Trītōnĭus -a -um, and f. Trītōnis -ĭdis or -ĭdos, esp. *in connexion with Minerva.*

trītūra -ae, f. *threshing.*

trĭumphālis -e, *triumphal.* N. pl. as subst. *the distinctions of a triumphing general.*

trĭumpho -are, *to triumph, to have a triumph;* hence, fig., *to exult;* pass., *to be triumphed over, be completely conquered.*

triumphus (old form trĭumpus) -i, m., *triumphal procession, triumph.*

triumvir -viri, m. *a triumvir;* usually plur. triumvĭri (also trēsvĭri), *a board or commission of three.*

triumvĭrālis -e, *of a triumvir.*

triumvĭrātus -ūs, m. *the office of a triumvir.*

trĭvĭālis -e, *ordinary, trivial.*

trĭvĭum -i, n. *a place where three roads meet, crossroads, public place.*

trivius -a -um, *of three ways, of crossroads;* esp. *of deities worshipped at crossroads;* f. as subst. Trivia -ae, *Diana or Hecate.*

Trōās -ādis; see Tros.

trŏchaeus -i, m. *a trochee, a metrical foot* (— ⏑).

trochlĕa -ae, f. *a set of blocks and pulleys for raising weights.*

trŏchus -i, m. *child's hoop.*

Trōes; see Tros.

Trōĭa, Trōĭādes, Trōĭcus; see Tros.

Trōĭŭgĕna -ae, *born in Troy, Trojan.*

trŏpaeum, -i, n. *a trophy, monument of victory.* Transf., *any memorial.*

Trōs Trōis, m. *a king of Phrygia, after whom Troy was named;* Trōĭa or Trōĭā -ae, f. *the town of Troy, besieged and finally captured by the Greeks;* adj. Trōus, Trōĭus, Trōĭcus, Trōĭānus -a -um, *Trojan;* subst. Trōs Trōis, m. *a Trojan;* f. adj. and subst. Trōās -ādos, *Trojan, a Trojan woman.*

trŭcīdātĭo -onis, f. *slaughtering, massacre.*

trŭcīdo -are, *to slaughter, massacre;* *to demolish, destroy.*

trŭcŭlentia -ae, f. *roughness, ferocity.*

trŭcŭlentus -a -um, *rough, ferocious, cruel, wild;* compar. adv. trŭcŭlentius.

trŭdis -is, f. *pointed staff, stake.*

trūdo trūdĕre trūsi trūsum, *to push, thrust; to press, urge on, force.*

trulla -ae, f. *ladle, pan or basin.*

trunco -are, *to shorten, maim, mutilate.*

truncus -a -um, *maimed, mutilated, cut short.* M. as subst. truncus -i, *a lopped tree, the trunk of a tree; the trunk of the human body.* Transf., *dolt, blockhead.*

trŭtĭna -ae, f. *a balance, pair of scales.*

trux trŭcis, *savage, fierce, grim.*

tū; pron. of the 2nd person; strengthened forms in -te, -met, temet; *thou, you;* plur. vos, etc. *ye, you.*

tŭba -ae, f. *the straight war-trumpet of the Romans.*

[1]tŭber -ĕris, n. *swelling, hump.* Transf., *truffle.*

[2]tŭber -ĕris; m. *a kind of apple-tree;* f. *the fruit of this tree.*

tŭbĭcĕn -ĭnis, m. *a trumpeter.*

tŭbĭlustrĭum -i, n. *a feast of trumpets.*

tŭdĭto -are, *to strike of tem.*

tŭĕor (or tŭŏr) tŭēri tŭĭtus and tūtus, dep., and tŭĕo -ēre, *to look at, regard;* esp. *to look after, watch over, guard.* Perf. partic. as pass. adj. tūtus -a -um, *watched over;* hence *safe, secure, out of danger; watchful, cautious.* N. as subst. tūtum -i, *a safe place, safety.* N. abl. tūtō and adv. tūtē, *safely.*

tŭgŭrĭum -i, n. *peasant's hut, cottage.*

tŭĭtĭo -ōnis, f. *a protecting, preservation.*

Tullĭus -a -um, *the name of a Roman gens;* esp. *of Servius Tullius, sixth king of Rome,* and of M. Tullius Cicero, *the Roman orator and statesman.* Hence adj. Tullĭānus -a -um, *Tullian;* n. as subst. Tullĭānum, -i, *part of a Roman state prison.*

tum, *then, at that time; next, thereupon, afterwards;* cum . . . tum, *both . . . and especially,* or *not only . . . but also.*

tŭmĕfăcio -făcĕre -fēci -factum, *to cause to swell; to puff up with pride.*

tŭmĕo -ēre, *to swell, be swollen, be puffed up; to swell with pride, anger* or *excitement;* of style, *to be pompous, tumid.*

tŭmesco tŭmescĕre tŭmŭi, *to begin to swell; to swell with anger or excitement.*

tŭmĭdus -a -um, adj. *swollen, puffed up; swollen with pride, anger or excitement;* of style, *pompous, tumid, bombastic.*

tŭmor -ōris, m. *swelling, protuberance; excitement of the mind,* esp. *in pride or anger;* in gen., *ferment, commotion;* of style, *turgidity, bombast.*

tŭmŭlo -are, *to bury.*

tŭmŭlōsus -a -um, *full of mounds, hilly.*

tŭmultŭārius -a -um; of troops, *hastily brought together, suddenly levied;* in gen., *sudden, hasty, improvised.*

tŭmultŭātio -ōnis, f. *confusion, bustle.*

tŭmultŭor -ari, dep. and tŭmultŭo -are, *to be confused, be in an uproar.*

tŭmultŭōsus -a -um, adj. *alarmed, disturbed, confused; disquieting, turbulent;* adv. tŭmultŭōsē, *confusedly, tumultuously.*

tŭmultus -ūs, m. *confusion, uproar, bustle;* esp. *of political commotion, insurrection, rebellion.* Transf., *mental disturbance, excitement.*

tŭmŭlus -i, m. *mound of earth, hillock, hill;* esp. *a sepulchral mound.*

tunc, *then, at that time; next.*

tundo tundĕre tŭtŭdi tunsum and tūsum, *to thump, pound, strike repeatedly; to deafen, importune.*

tŭnĭca -ae, f. *a sleeved garment, tunic; a jacket, coat, covering.*

tŭnĭcātus -a -um, *clothed in a tunic.*

tŭor = tueor; q.v.

turba -ae, f. *tumult, disturbance;* hence *a mob, throng, crowd.*

turbāmentum -i, n. *means of disturbance.*

turbātĭo -ōnis, f. *disturbance, confusion.*

turbātor -ōris, m. *disturber, troubler.*

turbēn -ĭnis, n. = ¹turbo; q.v.

turbĭdus -a -um, *confused, disordered, wild;* adv. turbĭdē.

turbĭnĕus -a -um, *shaped like a top.*

¹turbo -are, *to disturb, throw into disorder* or *confusion; to upset;* esp. *to cause political disturbance, to unsettle.*

Hence partic. as adj. turbātus -a -um, *disturbed, disordered, restless, troubled;* sometimes *angered, exasperated;* adv. turbātē.

²turbo -ĭnis, m. *an eddy, whirling round; a mental* or *political disturbance; a child's top; a reel; a spindle.*

turbŭlentus -a -um: pass., *confused, restless, stormy, boisterous;* act., *turbulent, causing disturbance;* adv. turbŭlentē and turbŭlentĕr, in *confusion, tumultuously.*

turdus -i, m. and turda -ae, f. *a thrush.*

tūrĕus -a -um, *of incense.*

turgĕo turgēre tursi, *to swell up, be swollen;* of style, *to be pompous, turgid.*

turgesco -ĕre, *to begin to swell, swell up; to swell with passion;* of style, *to be pompous.*

turgĭdus -a -um, *swollen;* of style, *turgid, bombastic.*

tūrĭbŭlum -i, n. *a censer for burning incense.*

tūricrĕmus -a -um, *burning incense.*

tūriĭer -fĕra -fĕrum, *producing incense.*

tūrĭlĕgus -a -um, *collecting incense.*

turma -ae, f. *a troop of cavalry, a squadron; any troop, throng.*

turmālis -e, *of a troop* or *squadron.*

turmātim, *troop by troop, in troops.*

Turnus -i, m. *a king of the Rutuli, killed by Aeneas.*

turpĭcŭlus -a -um, *somewhat ugly* or *deformed.*

turpĭfĭcātus -a -um, *corrupted.*

turpis -e, *ugly, foul; morally foul, disgraceful;* n. as subst. turpĕ, *a disgrace;* adv. turpĭtĕr, *foully, disgracefully.*

turpĭtūdo -ĭnis, f. *ugliness; moral baseness, disgrace.*

turpo -are, *to make ugly, befoul; to disgrace, dishonour.*

turriger -gĕra -gĕrum, *tower-bearing.*

turris -is, f. *tower;* esp. *as used in military operations;* sometimes *howdah.* Transf., *dove-cote.*

turrītus -a -um, *turreted, furnished with towers; towering.*

turtur -ŭris, m. *turtle-dove.*

tūs (thūs) tūris, n. *incense, frankincense.*

Tusci -ōrum, m. *the Tuscans, Etruscans, inhabitants of Etruria;* adj. Tuscus -a -um, *Etruscan.*

tussio -ire, *to have a cough, to cough.*

tussis -is, f. *a cough.*

tūtāmen -ĭnis, and tūtāmentum -i, n. *a defence, protection.*

tūtēla -ae, f. *protection, guard, charge,* esp. *of wards,* etc., *guardianship, tutelage;* concr., act. *protector, guardian;* pass., *the person* or *thing protected.*

¹tūtor -ōris, m. *a watcher, protector;* esp. *the guardian of a woman, minor,* or *imbecile.*

²tūtor -ari dep.: also tūto -are; *to protect, watch, keep.* Transf., *to guard against.*

tūtus -a -um, partic. from tueo; q.v.

tŭus -a -um, possess. pron. of the 2nd pers. sing., *thy, thine, your.*

Tўdēus -ĕi and -ĕos, m. *the son of Oeneus;* hence Tўdīdes -ae, m. *son of Tydeus,* i.e. *Diomedes.*

tympănum (tўpánum) -i, n. *a tambourine, kettle-drum; a drum* or *wheel for raising weights.*

Tyndărēus -ĕi, and Tyndărus -i, m. *king of Sparta, father of Castor and Pollux, Helen and Clytemnestra;* adj. Tyndărius -a -um; subst. m. Tyndărĭdēs -ae, *a male descendant,* and f. Tyndăris -ĭdis, *a female descendant of Tyndareus.*

tўpus -i, m. *a figure on a wall.*

tўrannĭcīda -ae, m. *the slayer of a tyrant.*

tўrannĭcus -a -um, *tyrannical;* adv. tўrannĭcē.

tўrannis -ĭdis, f. *despotism, tyranny.*

tўrannoctŏnus -i, m. *the slayer of a tyrant.*

tўrannus -i, m. *an absolute ruler, prince, lord; a usurper, despot, tyrant.*

Tўrius, see Tyrus.

tўrōtărĭchŏs -ı, m. *a dish of cheese and salt-fish.*

Tyrrhēni -ōrum, m. pl. *a Pelasgian people;* subst. **Tyrrhēnĭa** -ae, f. *their country, Etruria;* adj. **Tyrrhēnus** -a -um, *Etruscan.*

Tўrus (-ŏs) -i, f. *Tyre, a city of Phoenicia, famous for its purple;* adj. **Tўrĭus** -a -um.

U

U, u, originally written V, v, the 20th letter of the Latin Alphabet.

¹**ūber** -ĕris, n. *an udder, teat, breast; richness, abundance, fertility.*

²**ūber** -eris, adj., *rich, fertile, fruitful, copious;* adv. in compar. **ūbĕrĭus** and superl. **ūberrĭmē,** *more and most abundantly.*

ūbertās -ātis, f. *fruitfulness, abundance.*

ūbertim, *abundantly, copiously.*

ŭbi, *where* (interrog. and relat.); *of time, when, as soon as;* of other relations, *wherein, whereby, with whom.*

ŭbĭcumquĕ (-cunquĕ): relat., *wherever;* indef., *anywhere, everywhere.*

Ubii -ōrum, m. *a Germanic people.*

ŭbĭquĕ, *everywhere.*

ŭbĭvīs, *wherever you will, anywhere.*

ūdus -a -um, *wet, moist.*

ulcĕro -are, *to make sore, ulcerate, wound.*

ulcĕrōsus -a -um, *full of sores, ulcerous, wounded.*

ulciscor ulcisci ultus, dep. (1) *to take vengeance for, to avenge.* (2) *to take vengeance on, to punish.*

ulcus -ĕris, n. *a sore, ulcer, wound.*

ūlĭgo -ĭnis, f. *moisture, damp.*

Ūlixēs -is or ei, m. *Latin name for Ulysses or Odysseus, husband of Penelope, king of Ithaca.*

ullus -a -um; genit. ullius, dat. ulli; *any;* as subst., *anyone, anything.*

ulmĕus -a -um, *of elm-wood.*

ulmus -i, f. *elm.*

ulna -ae, f. *elbow, arm; an ell.*

ultĕrĭor -ius, compar. as from ulter, *farther, more distant, more advanced, more remote.* Superl. **ultĭmus** -a -um, *most distant, farthest, extreme;* in time or succession, either *original* or *last, final;* ad ultimum, *to the last;* ultimum, *for the last time;* in rank, etc., *either highest, greatest,* or *meanest, lowest.*

ultĭo -ōnis, f. *avenging, punishment, revenge.*

ultor -ōris, m. *avenger, punisher.*

ultrā, adv. and prep. *beyond, on the far side* (of), *farther* (than), *more* (than).

ultrix -ĭcis, f. *avenging.*

ultrō, adv. *to the far side, beyond;* ultro et citro, *up and d wn.* Transf.,

besides, moreover; of one's own accord, spontaneously, gratuitously.

ŭlŭla, ae, f. *an owl.*

ŭlŭlātus -ūs, m. *howling, wailing, yelling.*

ŭlŭlo -are, *to howl, yell;* transit., *to howl to;* of places, *to resound with howling.*

ulva -ae, f. *sedge.*

umbella -ae, f. *a parasol.*

umbĭlicus -i, m. *the navel; middle, centre; the end of the roller of a scroll; a kind of sea-snail.*

umbo -ōnis, m. *a boss, round projection;* esp. *the centre of a shield; a shield; the elbow.*

umbra -ae, f. *a shade, shadow; a shady place; protection; idleness, pleasant rest; a phantom, ghost, shade, semblance; an uninvited guest; a fish,* perhaps *grayling.*

umbrācŭlum -i, n. *a shady place, arbour; quiet, retirement; a parasol.*

umbrātĭlis -e, *retired, contemplative.*

Umbri -ōrum, m. pl. *a people of central Italy;* **Umbrĭa** -ae, f. *Umbria.*

umbrĭfer -fĕra -fĕrum, *shady.*

umbro -are, *to shade, over-shadow.*

umbrōsus -a -um, *shady.*

ūmecto (hū-) -are, *to wet, moisten.*

ūmectus (hū-) -a -um, *moist.*

ūmĕo (hū-) -ēre, *to be moist;* partic. **ūmens** -entis, *moist.*

ūmĕrus (hū-) -i, m. *the upper arm or shoulder.*

ūmesco (hū-) -ĕre, *to become moist.*

ūmĭdŭlus (hū-), -a -um, *moist.*

ūmĭdus (hū-) -a -um, *wet, moist, damp;* ligna, *unseasoned;* n. as subst. *a wet place.*

ūmor (hū-) -ōris, m. *moisture, fluid.*

umquam (unquam), *at any time, ever.*

ūnā, adv. *from unus;* q.v.

ūnănĭmĭtās -ātis, f. *concord, unanimity.*

ūnănĭmus -a -um, *of one mind, agreeing, unanimous.*

uncĭa -ae, f. *a twelfth; an ounce.*

uncĭārĭus -a -um, *of a twelfth part;* faenus, 8⅓%.

uncĭātim, *little by little.*

uncĭnātus -a -um, *hooked.*

uncĭŏla -ae, f. *a mere twelfth.*

unctĭo -ōnis, f. *anointing.*

unctĭto -are, *to anoint, besmear.*

unctor -ōris, m. *an anointer.*

unctūra -ae, f. *anointing of the dead.*

unctus -a -um, partic. from ungo; q.v.

¹**uncus** -i, m. *a hook.*

²**uncus** -a -um, *hooked, curved.*

unda -ae, f. *water, fluid, esp. as a wave;* fig. *a stream of people, etc.*

undĕ, *whence, from where* (interrog. and relat.). Transf., *how, from whom.*

undēcĭēs (-ĭens) *eleven times.*

undĕcim, *eleven.*

undĕcĭmus -a -um, *eleventh.*

undĕcumquĕ (-cunquĕ), *from whatever place.*

undēni -ae -a, *eleven at a time* or *eleven each.*

undēnōnāgintā, *eighty-nine.*

undēoctōgintā, *seventy-nine.*

undēquadrāgintā, *thirty-nine.*

undēquīnquāgēsĭmus -a -um, *forty-ninth.*

undēquīnquāgīntā, *forty-nine.*

undēsexāgīntā, *fifty-nine.*

undētrīcēsĭmus -a -um, *twenty-ninth.*

undēvīcēsĭmus, *nineteenth.*

undēvīgīntī, *nineteen.*

undĭquĕ, *from* or *on all sides, from everywhere, everywhere; altogether, in every respect.*

undĭsŏnus -a -um, *resounding with waves.*

undo -are: intransit., *to surge, wave, undulate;* transit., *to flood.*

undōsus -a -um, *surging, billowy.*

ūnĕtvīcēsĭmānĭ -ōrum, m. pl. *soldiers of the twenty-first legion.*

ūnĕtvīcēsĭmus -a -um, *twenty-first.*

ungo (unguo) ungĕre unxi unctum, *to anoint, besmear;* partic. **unctus** -a -um, *besmeared, anointed, greasy; rich, copious;* n. as subst. *a sumptuous repast.*

unguĕn -ĭnis, n. *fatty substance, ointment.*

unguentārĭus -a -um, *of ointment;* m. as subst. *a dealer in unguents.*

unguentātus -a -um, *anointed.*

unguentum -i, n. *salve, ointment, perfume.*

ungŭĭcŭlus -i, m. *a finger* or *toe-nail.*

unguis -is, m. *a finger-* or *toe-nail;* of animals, *claw, hoof;* de tenero ungui, *from childhood;* ad (or in) unguem, *to a hair, nicely, perfectly.*

ungŭla -ae, f. *a hoof, claw, talon.*

unguo = ungo; q.v.

ūnĭcŏlor -oris, *of one colour.*

ūnĭcus -a -um, *one, only, sole; singular, unique;* adv. **ūnĭcĕ,** *singly, especially.*

ūnĭformis -e, *having one form, simple.*

ūnĭgĕna -ae, *of the same race; only-begotten, unique.*

ūnĭmănus -a -um, *having but one hand.*

ūnĭo -ōnis, m. *a large pearl.*

ūnĭtās -ātis, f. *unity, oneness.*

ūnĭter, *in one, together.*

ūnĭversālis -e, *general, universal.*

ūnĭversĭtās -atis, f. *the whole, total; the universe, the world.*

ūnĭversus (archaic **ūnĭvorsus**) -a -um, *combined in one, whole, entire;* plur. **ūnĭversi** -ae -a, *all together;* n. as subst. **ūnĭversum** -i, *the whole; the world, the universe;* phrase, in universum, and adv. **ūnĭversē,** *generally, in general.*

ūnus -a -um, genit. **ūnīus,** dat. **ūni,** *one; only one; one and the same; any one;* ad unum omnes, *all to a man;* in unum, *into one place;* uno tempore, *at the same time.* Adv. **ūnā,** *in one, together.*

ūpĭlĭo (ōpĭlĭo) -ōnis, m. *a shepherd.*

Ūrănĭa -ae and **Ūrănĭē** -ēs, f. *the Muse of Astronomy.*

urbānĭtās -ātis, f. *city life,* esp. *life in Rome.* Hence *politeness, urbanity, refinement; wit, pleasantry.*

urbānus -a -um, *of a city* (esp. Rome); *urban;* hence *refined; elegant; witty, pleasant;* m. pl. as subst. *the inhabitants of a city, the townsfolk.* Adv.

urbānē, *politely, courteously; wittily, elegantly.*

urbs -bis, f. *a walled town* or *city;* esp. *the city of Rome.*

urcĕŏlus -i, m. *a small jug* or *pitcher.*

urcĕus -i, m. *a jug, pitcher.*

ūrēdo -ĭnis, f. *a blight on plants.*

urgĕo urgēre ursi, *to push, press, drive, urge; to beset, oppress; to stress;* of work, *to press on with, ply hard, follow up.*

ūrīna -ae, f. *urine.*

ūrīnātor -ōris, m. *a diver.*

ūrīno -are and **ūrīnor** -ari, dep. *to dive.*

urna -ae, f. *a jug, pitcher, jar, pot.*

ūro ūrĕre ussi ustum, *to burn; to dry up, parch; chafe, gall; to disturb, harass.*

ursa -ae, f. *a she-bear.*

ursus -i, m. *a bear.*

urtīca -ae, f. *a nettle.* Transf., *desire.*

ūrus -i, m. *a kind of wild ox.*

ūsĭtātus -a -um, *customary, usual;* adv. **ūsĭtātē.**

uspĭam, *anywhere.*

usquam, *anywhere; at all, in any way; in any direction.*

usquĕ, *through and through, all the way, continuously; always;* usque Romam, *as far as Rome;* usque a Romulo, *ever since Romulus.*

usquĕquāquĕ, *always.*

ustor -ōris, m. *a burner of corpses.*

ustŭlo -are, *to burn, scorch, singe.*

[1]**ūsŭcăpĭo** -căpĕre -cēpi -captum, *to acquire ownership by long use.*

[2]**ūsŭcăpĭo** -ōnis, f. *ownership acquired by long possession* or *use.*

ūsūra -ae, f. *use, enjoyment;* esp. *use of borrowed capital; interest paid for money borrowed.*

ūsurpātĭo -ōnis, f. *using, use; under-taking.*

ūsurpo -are, *to use, bring into use; to take possession of, acquire, appropriate, usurp; to perceive, to notice; to use a word, to mention;* hence *to call, name.*

ūsus -ūs, m. *use, application, practice, exercise; social intercourse, familiarity; legal,* usus et fructus, ususfructus, *the use of others' property.* Transf., *practice, skill, experience; utility, usefulness, profit;* usui esse, ex usu esse, *to be useful, be of use;* usus est, *there is need of;* occasion for; usu venit, *it happens.*

ūsusfructus; see usus.

ŭt or **ŭtī.** (1) with indic. verb: *how* (interrog. and exclam.); relat., *as,* esp. with corresponding sic or ita; ut ut, *in whatever way;* explanatory, *as, as being* (sometimes without verb); temporal, *as when, while, since;* of place, *where.* (2) with subjunctive: in indirect questions, *how;* in wishes, *o that;* concessive, *granted that;* consecutive, *so that,* often preceded by ita, tam, etc.; explaining or defining, *namely that;* final, *in order that* (negat. ne or ut ne); in " indirect command " *that,* to; after verbs of fearing (= ne non), *that . . . not.*

utcumquĕ (-cunquĕ), in whatever manner, however; whenever.

ūtensĭlĭa -ĭum, n. pl., useful things, utensils.

¹ūter ūtris, m. the skin of an animal used as bag or bottle.

²ūtĕr utra utrum; genit. utrĭus, dat. utri; interrog., which of the two?; plur., which side? which set?; relat., that (of two) which; indef., either of the two.

ŭtercumquĕ (-cunquĕ) utrăcumquĕ utrumcumquĕ, whichever of the two.

ūterlĭbet utrălĭbet utrumlĭbet, whichever of the two you please.

ŭterquĕ utrăquĕ utrumquĕ; genit. utrĭusquĕ, dat. utrīquĕ; each of two; in plur., usually, each side, each set; sometimes of individuals, both.

ŭtĕrus -i, m. and ŭtĕrum -i, n. womb; belly.

ŭtervĭs utrāvĭs utrumvĭs; genit. utrī-usvĭs, dat. utrivĭs; whichever of the two you please.

ūti = ut; q.v.

Ūtĭca -ae, f. a town in Africa where Cato the younger killed himself; adj. Ūtĭcensis -e.

ūtĭlis -e, useful, fit, profitable; adv. ūtĭlĭter.

ūtĭlĭtās -ātis, f. usefulness profit, advantage.

ŭtĭnam, would that! oh that!

ŭtĭquĕ, at any rate, certainly, at least.

ūtor ūti ūsus, dep. to use, employ; to possess, enjoy; of persons, to associate with, or, with a predicate, to find.
  Hence partic. ūtens -entis, possess-ing.

 utpŏtĕ, seeing that, inasmuch as.

utrārĭus -i, m. a water-carrier.

utrimquĕ (-inquĕ) from or on both sides.

utrŏ, to which of two places? to which side?

utrōbĭquĕ (utrūbĭquĕ), on each of two sides; both ways.

utrōquĕ, to both sides, in both directions; at each point, both ways.

utrum, whether; used mainly in alternative questions, direct or in-direct.

ŭtŭt, however; see ut.

ūva -ae, f. a bunch of grapes; meton., vine. Transf., a cluster.

ūvesco -ĕre, to become moist.

ūvĭdŭlus -a -um, moist.

ūvĭdus -a -um, moist, damp, wet. Transf., drunken.

uxor -ōris, f. a wife; uxorem ducere, to marry a wife.

uxōrĭus -a -um. (1) of a wife. (2) too devoted to one's wife, uxorious.

V

V, v, the twenty-first letter of the Latin Alphabet.

văcātĭo -ōnis, f. freedom, immunity, exemption. Transf., money paid for exemption from military duties.

---

vacca -ae, f. a cow.

vaccīnĭum -i, n. the blueberry, whortle-berry; according to some, the hyacinth.

văcēfĭo -fĭĕri, to be made empty.

văcillātĭo -ōnis, f. rocking, reeling.

văcillo (vaccillo) -are, to totter, reel stagger.

văcīvus (vŏcīvus) -a -um, empty.

văco -are, to be empty; of property, to be vacant, to have no master; in gen., to be free from anything, be without; to be free from work, be at leisure; with dat., to have time for; impers., vacat, there is time (for).

văcŭēfăcĭo -făcĕre -fēci -factum, to make empty.

văcŭĭtās -ātis, f. freedom, exemption. immunity; a vacancy in a public office.

văcŭo -are, to make void, to empty.

văcŭus -a -um, empty, void; empty-handed; vacant; devoid, exempt, without (with abl. or ab); free, at leisure; with dat., free for; worthless, useless, vain. N. as subst. văcŭum -i, an empty place, vacuum.

vădĭmōnĭum -i. n. bail, security recognizance.

vădo -ĕre, to go, hasten, rush.

vădor -ari, dep. to bind over by bail.

vădōsus -a -um, shallow.

vădum -i, n. a shallow, shoal, ford in river or sea; in gen., water, river, sea; fig., shallows, typical either of safety or of danger.

vae, interj. alas! woe!

văfer vafra vafrum, artful, sly, crafty; adv. vafrē.

văgīna -ae, f. a scabbard, sheath, case; the husk of grain.

văgĭo -ire, to whimper as a child.

văgītus -ūs, m. whimpering, crying.

văgor -ōris, m. = vagitus; q.v.

văgor -ari, dep. to wander, ramble, rove.

văgus -a -um, wandering, roaming; fickle; diffuse, aimless. Adv. văgē, dispersedly.

vah (vaha), interj. ah! oh!

valdĕ, intensely, very much; in replies certainly, very much so.

vălēdīco -ĕre, to say good-bye.

vălĕo -ĕre, to be strong, vigorous, in good health, well; to have force, avail, prevail, be able; to be worth; of words, to mean, signify; as a farewell greeting, vale, or valeas, farewell, good-bye; valere iubere, to bid farewell, say good-bye to.
  Hence partic. vălens -entis, strong, powerful, healthy; adv. vălentĕr.

Vălĕrĭus -a -um, name of a Roman gens.

vălesco -ĕre, to grow strong.

vălētūdo -ĭnis, f. state of health; sometimes either ill-health, weakness, or good health.

vălĭdus -a -um, strong, powerful; healthy, well; mighty, influential; of medicines, efficacious. Adv. vălĭdē, strongly, powerfully; in replies, certainly to be sure.

vallāris -e, *relating to the* vallum; q.v.

vallēs (vallis) -is, f. *a vale, valley, hollow.*

vallo -are, *to fortify with a palisade; to strengthen.*

vallum -i, n. *a palisade of stakes; a fortification, defence.*

vallus -i, m. *a post, stake;* collectively, *a palisade, stockade.*

valvae -ārum, f. pl. *folding-doors.*

vānesco -ĕre, *to pass away, disappear.*

vānilŏquentia -ae, f. *idle talk, vaunting.*

vānilŏquus -a -um, *lying; boastful.*

vānĭtās -ātis, f. *emptiness; worthlessness, unreality; boasting, ostentation.*

vannus -i, f. *winnowing-fan.*

vānus -a -um, *empty, void; vain, idle, worthless, meaningless;* of persons, *ostentatious, boastful, unreliable.*

vāpĭdus -a -um, *spiritless, spoiled, flat.*

vāpor (vāpōs) -ōris, m. *vapour, steam; warm exhalation, warmth.*

vāpōrārĭum -i, n. *a steam flue.*

vāpōro -are; intransit., *to steam, reek;* transit., *to fill with vapour, heat, warm.*

vappa -ae, f. *flat wine.* Transf., *a worthless fellow.*

vāpŭlo -are, *to be flogged, beaten, knocked about;* of things, *to be wasted.*

vărĭantĭa -ae, and vărĭātĭo -ōnis, f. *difference, variation.*

vărĭco -are, *to stand with feet apart.*

vărĭcōsus -a -um, *having varicose veins.*

vārĭcus -a -um, *straddling.*

vărĭĕtās -ātis, f. *variety, difference, diversity.*

vărĭo -are: transit., *to vary, diversify, change, alter, do or say differently;* pass., variari, *to waver, be divided, vary;* intransit., *to be different, vary.*

¹vărĭus -a -um, *various, manifold, changeable, diverse;* of persons, in bad sense, *fickle, changeable;* adv. vărĭē, *diversely, variously.*

²Vărĭus -a -um, *name of a Roman gens.*

vārix -īcis, c. *a varicose vein.*

Varro -ōnis, m. *a surname in the gens* Terentia.

¹vārus -a -um, *knock-kneed;* in gen., *crooked, bent; diverse, different.*

²Vārus -i, m. *a Roman surname.*

¹vās vădis, m. *a bail, surety.*

²vās vāsis, n. *a utensil;* plur. (vāsa-ōrurn) milit., *war materials, equipment.*

vāsārĭum -i, n. *an outfit allowance.*

vāscŭlārĭus -i, m. *a maker of vessels,* esp. *in metal.*

vāscŭlum -i, n. *a small vessel.*

vastātĭo -ōnis, f. *devastating, laying waste.*

vastātor -ōris, m. *devastator, ravager.*

vastĭfĭcus -a -um, *devastating.*

vastĭtās -ātis, f. *a waste, emptiness, desolation;* concr. in plur., *devastators.*

vasto -are, *to empty; to lay waste, ravage, devastate, prey upon.*

vastus -a -um, *empty, waste, desolate; laid waste, devastated.* Transf., *vast,*

enormous; rough, rude. Adv. **vastē**, *widely, extensively; rudely, roughly.*

vātēs -is, c. *a prophet, seer; a bard,* poet.

Vātīcānus -a -um, *Vatican:* mons, collis, *the Vatican Hill on the west side of the Tiber.*

vātĭcĭnātĭo -ōnis, f. *soothsaying, prophecy.*

vātĭcĭnātor, ōris, m. *soothsayer, prophet.*

vātĭcĭnor -ari, dep. *to prophesy; to talk wildly, to rave.*

vātĭcĭnus -a -um, *soothsaying, prophetic.*

vătillum (băt-) -i, n. *a chafing-dish or shovel.*

Vătĭnĭus -a -um, *the name of a Roman gens.*

-vĕ, enclitic, *or, or perhaps.*

vēcordĭa (vae-) -ae, f. *folly, madness.*

vēcors (vae-) -cordis, *senseless, mad.*

vectīgal -gālis, n. *revenue, income;* esp. *a tax, impost, duty.*

vectīgālis -e, *relating to income or to taxes; liable to tax, tributary.*

vectĭo -ōnis, f. *carrying, conveyance.*

vectis -is, m. *a lever, crow-bar; a bar, bolt.*

vecto -are, *to carry, convey;* pass., *to ride or be driven.*

vector -ōris, m.: act., *a carrier, bearer;* pass., *a passenger, rider.*

vectōrĭus -a -um, *for carrying;* navigia, *transports.*

vectūra -ae, f. *conveying, transportation; passage-money, fare.*

vĕgĕo -ĕre, *to stir up, excite.*

vĕgĕtus -a -um, *lively, vigorous, fresh.*

vēgrandis -e, *diminutive.*

vĕhĕmens (poet. vēmens) -entis, *violent, furious, impetuous;* adv. vĕhĕmentĕr, *violently; forcibly, exceedingly.*

vĕhĭcŭlum -i, n. *vehicle, conveyance.*

vĕho vĕhĕre vexi vectum, *to carry, convey;* pass., *to sail, ride, drive,* etc.; so also pres. partic., vehens, *riding.*

Vēii -orum, m. pl. *an old town in Etruria;* adj. Vēĭens -entis.

vĕl: conj., *singly, or;* doubled, *either . . . or;* adv. *even, actually; for example.*

vēlāmen -ĭnis, n. *covering, garment.*

vēlāmentum -i, n. *a covering, veil;* in plur., *olive-branches wrapped in wool, carried by suppliants.*

vēlārĭum -i, n. *an awning in a theatre.*

vēlātī -ōrum, m. pl., milit. *the reserve, supernumary troops.*

vēlēs -ĭtis, m. usually plur., velites, *light-armed infantry, skirmishers.*

vēlĭfer -fĕra -fĕrum, *carrying sail.*

vēlĭfĭcātĭo -ōnis, f. *sailing.*

vēlĭfĭco -are and vēlĭfĭcor -āri, dep. *to sail.* Transf., *to work for an end.*

vēlĭtārĭs -e, *of light-armed troops.*

vēlĭvŏlans -antis, and vēlĭvŏlus -a -um, *flying with sails.*

vellĭco -are, *to pluck, twitch; to taunt, criticize.*

vello vellĕre velli (vulsi, volsi) vulsum (volsum), *to pull, twitch; to pluck out;* partic. vulsus -a -um, *plucked, smooth.*

vellus -ĕris, n. *a fleece; skin, hide.*

vēlo -are, *to cover, veil, hide.*

vēlōcĭtās -ātis, f. *quickness, rapidity.*

vēlox -ōcis, *quick, rapid, swift;* adv. **vēlōcĭtěr.**

vēlum -i, *a sail;* vela dare, *to sail; a covering, awning, curtain.*

vělŭt (**vělŭti**), *as, just as; even as; as for instance;* with subjunctive, velut, or velut si, *as if, just as if.*

vēmens = vehemens; q.v.

vēna -ae, f. *a blood-vessel, vein, artery; a water-course; a vein of metal; a vein of talent, disposition, natural inclination.*

vēnābŭlum -i, n. *a hunting-spear.*

Vēnăfrum -i, n. *a Samnite town in Campania.*

vēnālīcĭus -a -um, *of the sale of slaves;* m. as subst. *a slave-dealer.*

vēnālis -e, *on sale, to be sold; venal;* m. as subst. *a slave put up for sale.*

vēnātĭcus -a -um, *of or for the chase.*

vēnātĭo -ōnis, f. *the chase, hunting; game.*

vēnātor -ōris, m. *a hunter, sportsman.*

vēnātōrĭus -a -um, *of or for the chase.*

vēnātrix -īcis, f. *huntress.*

vēnātus -ūs, m. *the chase, hunting.*

vendĭbĭlis -e, *on sale, saleable; popular, acceptable.*

venditātĭo -onis, f. *a putting up for sale;* hence *boasting, vaunting.*

venditātor -ōris, m. *vaunter, boaster.*

venditĭo -ōnis, f. *selling, sale.*

vendĭto -are, *to offer for sale, try to sell; to praise, advertise.*

vendĭtor -ōris, m. *seller, vendor.*

vendo -děre -dĭdi -dĭtum (pass. usually veneo; q.v.), *to put up for sale, sell; to betray; to recommend, advertise.*

věnēfĭcĭum -i, n. *poisoning; magic, sorcery.*

věnēfĭcus -a -um, *poisonous, magical;* m. as subst., *a poisoner, sorcerer; a sorceress, witch.*

věnēnĭfer -fěra -fěrum, *poisonous.*

věnēno -are, *to poison, drug;* partic. **věnēnātus** -a -um, *poisoned, drugged, enchanted.*

věnēnum -i, n. *a drug; poison* (fig. *ruin, destruction); a love-potion; colouring matter, dye; rouge.*

věnēo věnire věnii věnum, *to go for sale, to be sold* (used as pass. of vendo).

věněrābĭlis -e, *venerable, reverend.*

věněrābundus -a -um, *reverent, respectful.*

věněrātĭo -ōnis, f. *reverence, respect.*

věněrātor -ōris, m. *a venerator, reverer.*

věněrĭus; see venus.

věněror -ari, dep. *to ask reverently; to revere, respect, worship.*

věnĭa -ae, f. *grace, indulgence, favour, permission; pardon, forgiveness.*

věnĭo věnire věni ventum, *to come;* in course of time, *to happen, come, arrive; to grow, arise.*

vēnor -ari, dep. *to hunt.*

venter -tris, m. *the belly, stomach; the womb.*

ventĭlo -are, *to wave, brandish, fan.*

ventĭto -are, *to come often, resort.*

ventōsus -a -um, *full of wind, windy; swift or light as wind; puffed up, vain; changeable, inconstant.*

ventrĭcŭlus -i, m. *the belly; a ventricle.*

ventŭlus -i, m. *a slight wind.*

ventus -i, m. *wind; rumour, favour.*

vēnūcŭla (**venn-**) -ae, f. *a kind of grape.*

vēnum and **vēno,** acc. and dat. n., *for sale.*

vēnumdo (**vēnundo**) -dăre -dēdi -dătum, *to offer for sale, to sell.*

věnus -ěris, f. *charm, loveliness; love; a loved one;* personif., **Věnus,** *goddess of love; the Venus throw, highest throw of the dice;* adj. **Věněrěus** (**-ĭus**) -a -um, *of Venus or of love.*

Věnūsĭa -ae, f. *a town on the borders of Lucania and Apulia, birthplace of Horace.*

věnustās -ātis, f. *loveliness, charm, attractiveness.*

věnustus -a -um, *charming, lovely, graceful;* adv. **věnustē.**

vēpallĭdus -a -um, *very pale.*

veprēcŭla -ae, f. *a thorn-bush.*

veprēs -is, m. *a thorn-bush, briar-bush.*

věr věris, n. *spring;* primo vere, *in the beginning of spring;* ver sacrum, *an offering of the firstlings.*

vērātrum -i, n. *hellebore.*

vērax -ācis, *speaking the truth, truthful.*

verbēna -ae, f., often in pl., *sacred boughs carried by the Fetiales.*

verber -ěris, n. *a lash; a whip, scourge, thong; a blow, stroke; whipping.*

¹verběro -are, *to beat, whip, thrash;* with words, *to assail, lash.*

²verběro -ōnis, m. *a rascal.*

verbōsus -a -um, *copious, diffuse, wordy;* adv. **verbōsē.**

verbum -i, n. *a word;* verbum facere, *to speak;* uno verbo, *in a word, briefly;* ad verbum, *word for word;* verbi causa, *for example;* grammat., *a verb; an expression, saying; mere words, mere talk;* verba dare homini, *to cheat a person.*

Vercingětōrix -rĭgis, m. *a Gallic chief.*

věrēcundĭa -ae, f. *modesty, diffidence, bashfulness;* with genit., *respect for, scruple about.*

věrēcundor -ari, dep. *to be bashful, ashamed, shy.*

věrēcundus -a -um, *bashful, modest, shy, diffident;* adv. **věrēcundē.**

věrēdus -i, *a swift horse, hunter.*

věrěor -ēri -ĭtus, dep. *to be afraid, fear; to have respect for, revere;* gerundive **věrendus** -a -um, *venerable, reverend.*

Vergĭlĭus -i, m. P. Vergilius Maro, *author of the Aeneid, Georgics, and Eclogues.*

Vergĭnĭus -a -um, *the name of a Roman gens.*

vergo vergěre versi: intransit., *to bend, be inclined, verge;* of time, *to draw to an end;* transit., *to bend, turn, incline.*

vērĭdĭcus -a -um, *truthful.*

vērĭlŏquĭum -i, n. *etymology.*

vērĭsĭmĭlis -e, *probable, likely.*

vērĭsĭmĭlĭtūdo ĭnis, f. *probability.*

vērĭtās -ātis, f. *the truth, reality; truthfulness, telling of truth;* in gen., *honesty.*

vermen -ĭnis, n. *a griping pain.*

vermĭcŭlus -i, m. *little worm, grub.*

vermis -is, m. *worm.*

verna -ae, c. *a slave born in the master's house; a native.*

vernācŭlus -a -um, *of a slave born in the house; native, domestic.*

vernīlis -e, *like a slave; mean, abject, pert, forward;* adv. **vernīlĭtĕr,** *like a slave.*

verno -are, *to flourish, grow green.*

vernŭla -ae, c. *a little slave born in the house;* as adj. *native, indigenous.*

vernus -a -um, *of spring, vernal.*

Vērōna -ae, f. *a town of northern Italy, birthplace of Catullus.*

¹**verrēs** -is, m. *a boar.*

²**Verrēs** -is, m. *C. Cornelius, praetor in Sicily, prosecuted by Cicero;* adj. **Verrĭus** and **Verrīnus** -a -um.

verrīnus -a -um, *of a boar.*

verro verrĕre verri versum, *to drag, pull, sweep, sweep up; to sweep clean, brush, scour.*

verrūca -ae, f. *a wart; blemish.*

verrunco -are, *to turn out;* bene verruncare, *to turn out well.*

versābundus -a -um, *whirling round, revolving.*

versātĭlis -e, *turning round, revolving; versatile.*

versĭcŏlor -ōris, *of various colours.*

versĭcŭlus -i, m. *a little line; a poor little verse.*

versĭfĭcātĭo -ōnis, f. *making of verses.*

versĭfĭcātor -ōris, m. *versifier.*

versĭfĭco -are, *to write verse.*

verso (vorso) -are, *to turn about, turn this way and that; to bend, ply, twist; to influence, agitate; to turn over in the mind, think of.* Pass., *to be about, hover, resort; to be engaged, take part, be employed.*

versum = versus; q.v.

versūra -ae, f. *turning; the borrowing of money to pay a debt;* hence *a loan.*

¹**versus** (vors-) and **versum** (vors-), *towards;* used esp. after an accusative or prep. and acc.; sursum versus, *upwards.*

²**versus** (vors-) -a -um, partic. from verro or verto; q.v.

³**versus** (vors-) -ūs, m. *a row, line; a line of writing,* esp. *of poetry.*

versūtĭa -ae, f. *wile, stratagem.*

versūtus -a -um, *dexterous; cunning, crafty, sly;* adv. **versūtē.**

vertex (vortex) -ĭcis, m. (1) *a whirl, eddy, whirlwind, gust.* (2) *the crown of the head;* in gen., *head, summit, elevation.* (3) *the pole of the heavens.*

vertĭcōsus (vortĭc-) -a -um, *eddying.*

vertĭgo -ĭnis, f. *whirling round, revolution; giddiness, vertigo.*

verto (vorto) vertĕre verti versum, *to turn, turn round, turn up;* intransit., *to turn oneself;* milit., vertere in fugam, *to put to flight, rout;* terga vertere, *to flee; to interpret, construe, understand in a certain way, to impute; to*

alter, change; to translate; to change for another, exchange; vertere solum, *to go into exile;* pass. or intransit., *of time, to roll round;* pass., *to move in a certain sphere, to depend on, centre in.*

Vertumnus (vor-) -i, m. *god of the changing year.*

vērū -ūs, n. *a spit; a javelin.*

vērus -a -um, *true, real, genuine; truthful, veracious; just, reasonable.* N. as subst. *truth, reality; right, duty;* veri similis, *likely, probable.* N. nom. as adv. **vērum,** *but yet, still, however;* strengthened, **vēruntāmen** (vērum-), *notwithstanding, nevertheless.* N. abl. as adv. **vērō,** *in truth, indeed, in fact;* in a climax, *even, indeed;* ironically, *to be sure;* adversative, *but indeed, but in fact.* Adv. **vērē,** *truly, really, rightly.*

vērutum -i, n. *javelin.*

vērūtus -a -um, *armed with a javelin.*

vervex -vēcis, m. *a wether; a sheep, dolt.*

vēsānĭa -ae, f. *madness, insanity.*

vēsānĭens -entis, *raging.*

vēsānus -a -um, *mad, insane;* of things, *furious, wild.*

vescor -i, dep. *to eat, feed on; to use, enjoy.*

vescus -a -um: act., *consuming;* pass., *wasted, thin.*

vēsīca -ae, f. *the bladder; a purse, a lantern of style, bombast.*

vēsīcŭla -ae, f. *a little bladder.*

vespa -ae, f. *wasp.*

Vespāsĭānus -i, m., T. Flavius, *Roman emperor,* A.D. 69-79.

vesper -ĕris or -ĕri, m. *evening; the west; the evening star;* vespere, vesperi, *in the evening.*

vespĕrasco -ĕre, *to become evening.*

vespertīnus -a -um, *of evening; western.*

vespillo -ōnis, m. *a corpse-bearer for the poor.*

Vesta -ae, f. *goddess of the hearth and domestic life;* adj. **Vestālis** -e, *Vestal;* f. as subst. *a Vestal virgin, priestess of Vesta.*

vester (voster) -tra -trum, *your, yours.*

vestĭbŭlum -i, n. *entrance-court, courtyard;* in gen., *entrance; beginning.*

vestīgĭum -i, n. *a foot-step, track; a trace, mark;* in plur., *the foot;* in vestigio, e vestigio, *at that moment.*

vestīgo -are, *to track, trace.*

vestīmentum -i, n. *clothing, a garment.*

vestĭo -ire, *to dress, clothe; to cover, adorn.*

vestis -is, f. *a covering* or *garment, clothing; a blanket, carpet, tapestry.*

vestītus -ūs, m. *clothing, clothes; a covering.*

Vēsŭvĭus -i, m. *Vesuvius, the volcano in Campania.*

vĕtĕrānus -a -um, *old;* m. pl. *old soldiers, veterans.*

vĕtĕrasco -ascĕre -āvi, *to grow old.*

vĕtĕrātor -ōris, m. *an old hand, old stager.*

vĕtĕrătōrĭus -a -um, *cunning, crafty*; adv. **vĕtĕrătōrĭē**.

vĕtĕrīnus -a -um, *of draught*; bestia, *a beast of burden*.

vĕternōsus -a -um, *lethargic, sleepy, dull*.

vĕternus -i, m. *age; lethargy, inactivity, sloth*.

vēto (vŏto) vĕtare vĕtŭi vĕtĭtum, *to forbid, prohibit*; n. of perf. partic. as subst. **vĕtĭtum** -i, *that which is forbidden; a prohibition*.

vĕtŭlus -a -um, *little old, poor little old*; as subst., *an old man or woman*.

vĕtus -ĕris; superl. vĕterrĭmus; *old, ancient, of long standing; experienced*. M. pl. as subst. *the ancients*.

vĕtustās -ātis, f. *age; antiquity, past time; long duration, length of time* (including future time).

vĕtustus -a -um, *old, ancient, of long standing; old-fashioned, antiquated*.

vexāmen -ĭnis, n. *shaking, upheaval*.

vexātĭo -ōnis, f. *shaking, jolting, shock; ill-treatment*.

vexātor -ōris, m. *one who shakes, harasses, disturbs*.

vexillārĭus -i, m. *a standard-bearer*; in plur. *a corps of veterans, a reserve*.

vexillum -i, n. *a standard, flag; a company, troop*.

vexo -are, *to shake, toss, jostle; to harass, annoy*.

vĭa -ae, f. *a way, passage; a highway, road, street; a course, march, journey; means, way, method*; abl. **vĭā**, *methodically*.

vĭātĭcus -a -um, *relating to a journey*; n. as subst., *journey money*; also *savings or prize-money*.

vĭātor -ōris, m. (1) *a traveller, wayfarer*. (2) *an apparitor, messenger*.

vibro -are: transit., *to cause to vibrate, brandish, shake; to brandish and hurl a weapon; to curl, frizzle hair*; intransit., *to shake, tremble, quiver, vibrate*.

vīburnum -i, n. *the wayfaring-tree*.

vīcānus -a -um, *dwelling in a village*; m. pl. as subst. *villagers*.

vīcārĭus -a -um, *substituted, vicarious*; m. as subst., *a substitute*; esp. *an under-servant*.

vĭcātim, *from street to street; in villages*.

vĭcē, vĭcem,; see vicis.

vĭcēni -ae -a, *twenty at a time or twenty each*.

vĭcēsĭmāni -ōrum, m. pl. *soldiers of the twentieth legion*.

vĭcēsĭmārĭus -a -um, *relating to the* vicesima.

vĭcēsĭmus (vīcens-) -a -um, *twentieth*; f. as subst. vīcēsĭma (vīcens-) -ae, *the twentieth part, as a toll or tax*.

vĭcĭa -ae, f. *vetch*.

vĭcĭēs (-iens), *twenty times*.

vĭcīnālis -e, *neighbouring, near*.

vĭcīnĭa -ae, and vīcīnĭtās -ātis, f. *neighbourhood; vicinity; likeness*; concr., *the neighbours*.

vīcīnus -a -um, *near, neighbouring*; m. and f. as subst., *a neighbour*; n. as subst., *neighbourhood, vicinity*.

vĭcis (genit. nom. not found); *change, interchange, alternation; per vices, in vices, alternately, reciprocally; recompense, retaliation; the vicissitude of fate, lot, destiny; one's place, office, duty; vicem, vice, in vicem, ad vicem, in place of, instead of, like*.

vĭcissim, *in turn*.

vĭcissĭtūdo -ĭnis, f. *change, alteration*.

victĭma -ae, f. *an animal offered in sacrifice, victim*.

victĭmārĭus -i, m. *to live on, feed on*.

victor -ōris, m. and victrix -tricis, f. *conqueror, victor*; as adj., *victorious*.

victōrĭa -ae, f. *victory, conquest*.

victōrĭātus -i, m. *a silver coin stamped with a figure of Victory*.

victōrĭŏla -ae, f. *a small statue of Victory*.

victrix -tricis, f.; see victor.

victus -ūs, m. *living; manner of life; nourishment, food*.

vīcŭlus -i, m. *a little village, hamlet*.

vīcus -i, m. *part of a town, a street; a village, hamlet; an estate, country-seat*.

vĭdēlĭcet, *it is clear*; as adv. *clearly, plainly, manifestly; namely, ironically, of course, to be sure*.

vĭdēo vĭdēre vidi vīsum, *to see; to perceive, notice, observe; to look into a matter, see to, provide for*. Pass., *to be seen; to seem, appear, be thought; also to seem good, seem right*. N. of perf. partic. as subst. **vīsum** -i, *a sight, appearance, vision*.

vĭdŭĭtās -ātis, f. *want; widowhood*.

vĭdŭo -are, *to deprive*; f. of perf. partic. vĭdŭāta -ae, *widowed*.

vĭdŭus -a -um, *deprived, bereaved, widowed*; f. as subst. vĭdŭa -ae, *a widow, or an unmarried woman*.

Vĭenna -ae, f. *town in Gallia Narbonensis* (now Vienne).

vĭĕo -ēre, *to weave together*; partic. vĭētus -a -um, *shrivelled, shrunken*.

vĭgĕo -ēre, *to be vigorous, thrive, flourish*.

vĭgesco -ĕre, *to become vigorous, begin to thrive*.

vĭgēsĭmus = vicesimus; q.v.

vĭgil -ĭlis, *wakeful, watchful*; m. as subst., *a watchman*.

vĭgĭlantĭa -ae, f. *watchfulness, vigilance*.

vĭgĭlax -ācis, *watchful, wakeful*.

vĭgĭlĭa -ae, f. *wakefulness, sleeplessness, watch; a watch of the night; the watch, sentinels*; fig. *watchfulness, vigilance, care*.

vĭgĭlo -are: intransit., *to keep awake, watch; to be vigilant, watchful, careful*; transit. in pass, *to be watched through, watched over*. Pres. partic. vĭgĭlans -antis, *watch ul, vigilant*; adv. vĭgĭlantĕr.

vĭginti, *twenty*.

vĭgintĭvīrātus -ūs, *the office of the* vigintiviri.

vĭgintĭvīri -ōrum, m. pl. *a commission of twenty*.

vīgor -ōris, m. *force, energy.*

vīlĭco -are, *to manage an estate as bailiff.*

vīlĭcus -i, m. *a bailiff, steward, overseer of an estate*; f. **vīlĭca** -ae, *a bailiff's wife.*

vīlis -e, *cheap, worth little*; adv. **vīlĭtĕr.**

vīlĭtās -ātis, f. *cheapness, low price*; in gen., *worthlessness.*

villa -ae, f. *a country-house, estate, farm.*

villĭc-; see vilic-.

villōsus -a -um, *shaggy, hairy.*

villŭla -ae, f. *a small country-house, little farm.*

villum -i, n. *a sup of wine.*

villus -i, m. *shaggy hair.*

vīmen -ĭnis, n. *an osier, twig; a basket.*

vīmentum = vimen; q.v.

Vīmĭnālis collis, *one of the seven hills of Rome.*

vīmĭnĕus -a -um, *of osiers, wicker.*

vīn = visne; see volo.

vīnācĕus -a -um, *belonging to wine or a grape.*

vīnālĭa -ĭum and -ĭōrum, n. pl. *wine festivals, one in April, one in August.*

vīnārĭus -a -um, *of wine*; as subst. m. *a vintner*; n. *a wine-jar.*

vincĭbĭlis -e, *easily gained.*

vincĭo vincīre vinxi vinctum, *to bind, tie up; to surround, encompass; to restrain, confine, secure.*

vinco vincĕre vīci victum, *to conquer, overcome, master, surpass; to prove successfully, win one's point.*

vincŭlum (vinclum) -i, n. *a band, cord, chain, fetter, tie*; plur., *imprisonment.*

Vindēlĭci -ōrum, m. pl. *a Germanic people.*

vindēmĭa -ae, f. *vintage; grapes, wine.*

vindēmĭātor -ōris, m. *a harvester of grapes.*

vindēmĭŏla -ae, f. *a little vintage; a perquisite.*

vindex -ĭcis, c. *a claimant or protector; an avenger, punisher.*

vindĭcātĭo -ōnis, f. *defending, protecting; avenging.*

vindĭcĭae -ārum, f. pl. *things or persons claimed as property; the making of a claim.* Transf., *protection.*

vindĭco -are, *to claim; to arrogate, assume; appropriate; to claim as free; hence to liberate, deliver or protect; to avenge, punish.*

vindicta -ae, f. *a rod used in manumitting slaves.* Transf., *deliverance; vengeance, punishment.*

vīnĕa -ae, f. *a vineyard*; milit. *a mantlet, penthouse.*

vīnētum -i, n. *vineyard.*

vīnĭtor -ōris, m. *a vinedresser.*

vīnŏlentĭa -ae, f. *wine-drinking, intoxication.*

vīnŏlentus -a -um, *mixed with wine; drunk, intoxicated.*

vīnōsus -a -um, *full or fond of wine.*

vīnum -i, n. *wine, wine-drinking.*

vĭŏla -ae, f. *a violet or stock; the colour violet.*

vĭŏlābĭlis -e, *able to be injured.*

vĭŏlārĭum -i, n. *a bed of violets.*

vĭŏlātĭo -ōnis, f. *injury, violation, profanation.*

vĭŏlātor -ōris, m. *injurer, violator, profaner.*

vĭŏlens -entis, *violent, furious, impetuous*; adv. **vĭŏlentĕr.**

vĭŏlentĭa -ae, f. *violence, impetuosity.*

vĭŏlentus -a -um, *violent, vehement, furious, impetuous.*

vĭŏlo -are, *to violate, outrage, injure.*

vīpĕra -ae, f. *a viper; a snake, serpent.*

vīpĕrĕus -a -um, *of a viper or snake; snaky.*

vīpĕrīnus -a -um, *of a viper or snake.*

vir, vĭri, m. *a man, male person*; esp. *a grown man; a husband; a man of character or courage, "he-man"*; milit. *a soldier*, esp. *an infantryman; a single man, individual.*

vīrāgo -ĭnis, f. *a female warrior, heroine.*

vīrectum (-ētum) -i, n. *greensward, turf.*

vīrĕo -ēre, *to be green, vigorous, healthy, fresh.*

vīres -ĭum, f. pl.; see vis.

vīresco -ĕre, *to grow green.*

vīrētum = virectum; q.v.

virga -ae, f. *a green twig, a slip; a rod; a wand; a broom; a streak, stripe*; in plur., *virgae, the lictors' rods.*

virgātus -a -um. (1) *made of twigs.* (2) *striped.*

virgētum -i, n. *an osier-bed.*

virgĕus -a -um, *of twigs or rods.*

Virgĭlĭus = Vergilius; q.v.

virgĭnālis -e, **virgĭnārĭus**, **virgĭnĕus** -a -um, *maidenly.*

virgĭnĭtās -ātis, f. *virginity.*

virgo -ĭnis, f. *a maiden, virgin, girl.*

virgŭla -ae, f. *a little bough, twig; a rod, staff.*

virgultum -i, n. (1) *a thicket, copse.* (2) *a slip for planting.*

virguncŭla -ae, f. *a little girl.*

vĭrĭdans -antis, *green*; hence verb **vĭrĭdor** -ari, *to become green.*

vĭrĭdārĭum -i, n. *a pleasure-garden.*

vĭrĭdis -e, *green.* Transf., *fresh, young, vigorous.*

vĭrĭdĭtās -ātis, f. *greenness; freshness, bloom.*

vĭrīlis -e, *manly, male, virile; of a grown man, adult; courageous, spirited; pro virili parte, to the best of one's ability.* Adv. **vĭrīlĭtĕr**, *manfully.*

vĭrīlĭtās -ātis, f. *manhood, virility.*

vĭrītim, *man by man, individually.*

vĭrōsus -a -um, *stinking, fetid.*

virtūs -ūtis, f. *manliness; excellence, worth, goodness, virtue; bravery, courage.*

vīrus -i, n. *slimy liquid, slime; poison,* esp. *of snakes, venom; any harsh taste or smell.*

vīs, acc. **vim**, abl. **vī**; plur. **vīrēs** -ĭum, f. *force, power, strength; might, influence*; in sing. also *violence; a large number, quantity; the force,* *nature, meaning* of a thing; plur., milit., *troops, forces.*

viscātus -a -um, *smeared with bird-lime.*

viscĕrātĭo -ōnis, f. *public distribution of meat.*

viscum -i, n. and **viscus** -i, m. *mistletoe; bird-lime.*

viscus -ĕris, usually plur. **viscĕra** -um, n. *flesh; also internal organs, entrails; inmost part* or *heart of anything.*

visĭo -ōnis, f. *seeing, view; appearance; notion, idea.*

visĭto -are, *to see often; to visit.*

viso visĕre vixi visum, *to look at, look into, see after; to go to see, visit, call upon*; gerundive **visendus** -a -um, *worth seeing, notable.*

visum -i, n. subst. from video; q.v.

visus -ūs, m. *seeing, sight; an appearance.*

vīta -ae, f. *life.*

vītābĭlis -e, *that can* or *should be avoided.*

vītābundus -a -um, *trying to avoid.*

vītālis -e, *of life, vital; living, surviving*; adv. **vītālĭtĕr,** *vitally.*

vītātĭo -ōnis, f. *avoiding, shunning.*

Vitellius -a -um, *the name of a Roman gens; Aulus Vitellius, the Roman emperor who succeeded Otho* (A.D. 69).

vitellus -i, m. *the yolk of an egg.*

vītĕus -a -um, *of a vine.*

vītĭcŭla -ae, f. *a little vine.*

vītĭfer -fĕra -fĕrum, *vine-bearing.*

vītĭgĕnus -a -um, *produced from the vine.*

vĭtĭo -are, *to injure, damage, corrupt; to forge, falsify.*

vĭtĭōsĭtās -ātis, f. *viciousness, corruption.*

vĭtĭōsus -a -um, *faulty, corrupt, bad, wrong*; adv. **vĭtĭōsē.**

vītis -is, f. *a vine; a centurion's staff.*

vītĭsător -ōris, m. *one who plants vines.*

vĭtĭum -i, n. *a fault, defect, blemish; crime, vice*; relig., *a defect in auguries* or *auspices.*

vīto -are, *to avoid, shun.*

vĭtrĕus -a -um, *of glass; glassy, transparent, glittering.*

vĭtrĭcus -i, m. *stepfather.*

vĭtrum -i, n. (1) *glass.* (2) *woad.*

vitta -ae, f. *a ribbon, band, fillet.*

vittātus -a -um, *bound with a fillet.*

vĭtŭla -ae, f. *calf, heifer.*

vĭtŭlīnus -a -um, *of a calf; assum, roast veal; f.* as subst. *veal.*

vĭtŭlus -i, m. *a bull-calf; also of the young of other animals.*

vĭtŭpĕrābĭlis -e, *blamable.*

vĭtŭpĕrātĭo -ōnis, f. *blaming, scolding, censure*; meton., *blameworthy conduct.*

vĭtŭpĕrātor -ōris, m. *a blamer.*

vĭtŭpĕro -are, *to blame, scold, censure.*

vīvārĭum -i, n. *a warren, preserve, fish-pond.*

vīvātus -a -um, *quickened, vivid.*

vīvax -ācis, *long-lived, lasting, enduring; brisk, lively, vigorous.*

vivesco vivescĕre vixi, *to grow lively.*

vīvĭdus -a -um, *full of life, animated, vigorous; life-like.*

vīvĭrādix -īcis, f. *a cutting with a root, a layer.*

vīvisco = vivesco; q.v.

vīvo vivĕre vixi victum, *to live, be alive; to live well, to enjoy life; to survive; to live on anything; to dwell.*

vīvus (**vīvŏs**) -a -um, *alive, living; lifelike;* flumen, *running water*; ros, *fresh*; sulfur, *natural.*

vix, *with difficulty, scarcely, only just*: vix dum, or vixdum, *hardly yet*

vŏcābŭlum -i, n. *name, appellation*; grammat. *a noun.*

vōcālis -e, *vocal; speaking, singing*; f. as subst. *a vowel.*

vŏcāmen -īnis, n. *name, appellation.*

vŏcātĭo -ōnis, f. *summons, invitation.*

vŏcātor -ōris, m. *an inviter.*

vŏcātus -ūs, m. *summons, invocation.*

vōcĭfĕrātĭo -ōnis, f. *loud calling, shouting.*

vōcĭfĕror -ari, dep. *to cry aloud, shout.*

vŏcĭto -are, *to be accustomed to name; to shout loudly or often.*

vŏco -are, *to call, summon, invoke, invite; to name, designate; to bring* or *put into any state* or *condition*; in dubium, *to call in question.*

vōcŭla -ae, f. *a low, weak voice; a low tone; a petty speech.*

vŏlaema pīra, n. pl. *a kind of large pear.*

vŏlātĭcus -a -um, *winged, flying; flighty, inconstant.*

vŏlātilis -e, *winged, flying; swift, rapid; fleeting, transitory.*

vŏlātus -ūs, m. *flying, flight.*

Volcānus (**Vulc-**) -i, m. *Vulcan, the god of fire, husband of Venus.*

volgo, volgus = vulgo, vulgus; q.v.

vŏlĭto -are, *to fly about, flit, flutter, rush around.*

volnĕro = vulnero; q.v.

¹**vŏlo** velle vŏlŭi (vīn = visne; sīs = si vis; sultis = si vultis); *to be willing, to wish, want; to will, ordain; to suppose, maintain that; sibi velle to mean, signify.*
   Hence partic. **vŏlens** -entis, *willing, favourable.*

²**vŏlo** -are, *to fly; to move rapidly, rush;* f. pl. of partic. volantes, -ium = *birds.*

vŏlōnes -um, m. pl. *volunteers (in the Second Punic War).*

Volsci -ōrum, m. pl. *a people in Latium.*

volsella -ae, f. *a pair of tweezers.*

volsus -a -um, partic. from vello; q.v.

volt-; see vult-.

vŏlūbĭlis -e, *rolling, revolving, turning round; changeable, inconstant;* of speech, *rapid, fluent*; adv. **vŏlūbĭlĭtĕr,** *fluently.*

vŏlūbĭlĭtās -ātis, f. *turning, revolution; roundness; inconstancy, flow of words, fluency.*

vŏlŭcer volucris volucre, *flying, winged; fleet, swift, fleeting.* F. as subst. *a bird* or *flying insect.*

vŏlūmen -ĭnis, n. *a scroll, book; a roll, wreath, fold.*

vŏluntārĭus -a -um, *voluntary, acting* or *done voluntarily*; m. pl. as subst. *volunteers.*

vŏluntās -ātis, f. *will, wish, inclination;* esp. *goodwill; last will, testament;* of words, etc., *meaning, sense.*

vŏlup, *agreeably, pleasantly.*

vŏluptārius -a -um, *pleasant; concerned with or devoted to pleasure.*

vŏluptās -ātis, f. *pleasure, delight, enjoyment;* in plur., *public shows.*

vŏluptŭōsus -a -um, *delightful.*

vŏlŭtābrum -i, n. *a place for pigs, a slough.*

vŏlŭtābundus -a -um, *rolling, wallowing.*

vŏlŭtātio -ōnis, f. *rolling about, wallowing; disquiet.*

vŏlŭto -are, *to roll round, tumble about;* partic. volutans, *rolling about.* Transf., *to turn over in the mind, consider;* *to busy, occupy.*

volva (vulva) -ae, f. *womb;* esp. *a sow's womb*

volvo volvĕre volvi vŏlūtum, *to wind, turn, roll, twist round;* in pass. *to roll.* Esp. *to unroll a book, to read.* Transf., of time, *to make roll by;* of persons, *to turn over in the mind, consider;* *to experience, go through.*

vŏmer (vŏmis) -ĕris, m. *ploughshare.*

vŏmĭca -ae, f. *an ulcer, sore, boil; a plague, curse.*

vŏmis -eris, m. = vomer; q.v.

vŏmĭtio -ōnis, f. *vomiting, throwing up.*

vŏmo -ere -ŭi -ĭtum, *to vomit; to vomit forth, throw up.*

vŏrāgo -ĭnis, f. *pit, chasm, abyss.*

vŏrax -ācis, *gluttonous, voracious.*

vŏro -are, *to eat greedily, swallow up, consume, devour.*

vors-; see vers-.

vort-; see vert-.

vōs, *you,* plur. of tu; q.v.

vōtīvus -a -um, *of a vow, votive, vowed.*

vōtum -i, n. *a vow, promise to the gods; a votive offering;* in gen., *prayer, wish, desire.*

vŏvĕo vŏvēre vōvi vōtum, *to vow, promise to a god; to pray for, wish.*

vox vōcis, f. *voice, cry, call; accent, language; sound, tone; a saying, utterance.*

Vulcānus = Volcanus; q.v.

vulgāris (volg-) -e, *common, ordinary, usual;* adv. **vulgārĭtĕr,** *in the ordinary way.*

vulgātus -a -um, partic. from vulgo; q.v.

vulgĭvăgus -a -um, *wandering, vagrant.*

vulgo (volgo) -are, *to make common or accessible, spread, publish, impart;* partic. **vulgātus** -a -um, *common, commonly known.*

vulgus (volgus) -i, n. (occ. m.) *the people, the public; a mass, crowd, rabble, mob.* Abl. as adv. **vulgō,** *commonly, generally, in public.*

vulnĕrātĭo (voln-) -ōnis, f. *wounding, a wound.*

vulnĕro (voln-) -are, *to wound, injure.*

vulnĭfĭcus (voln-) -a -um, *inflicting wounds.*

vulnus (volnus) -ĕris, n. *a wound, injury.*

vulpēcŭla (volp-) -ae, f. *a little fox.*

vulpēs (volpēs) -is, f. *a fox.*

vulsus -a -um, partic. from vello; q.v.

vultĭcŭlus -i, m. *look, aspect.*

vultŭōsus -a -um, *grimacing, affected.*

vultur (voltur) -ŭris, m. *a vulture.*

vultŭrīnus (volt-) -a -um, *of or like a vulture.*

vultŭrĭus (volt-) -i, m. *a vulture.* Transf., *a rapacious man.*

Vulturnus (Volt-) -i, m. *a river in Campania.*

vultus (voltus) -ūs, m. *expression of face, countenance, look, aspect.* Transf., *face.*

X

X, x, the twenty-second letter of the Latin alphabet.

xĕnĭum -i, n. *a present to a guest.*

Xĕnŏphōn -ōntis, m. *an Athenian soldier and writer.*

xĕrampēlīnae -ārum, f. pl. *dark-red garments.*

Xerxēs -is, m. *king of the Persians, defeated at Salamis.*

xiphĭas -ae, m. *sword-fish.*

xystus -i, m. and **xystum** -i, n. *an open colonnade, a walk planted with trees.*

Y

Y, y, a letter borrowed from the Greek in order to represent the Greek upsilon.

Z

Z, z, representing the Greek zeta.

Zăma -ae, f. *a town in Numidia, where Scipio defeated Hannibal* (201 B.C.).

zēlŏtўpus -a -um, *jealous.*

Zēno (-ōn) -ōnis, m. *name of several Greek philosophers.*

zĕphўrus -i, m. *a warm west wind, zephyr.*

zm-; see sm-.

zōdĭăcus -i, m. *the zodiac.*

zōna -ae, f. *a girdle, money-belt;* in pl. zonae, *terrestrial zones.*

zōnārĭus -a -um, *of a girdle;* m. as subst. *girdle-maker.*

zōthēca -ae, f. *a private room.*

CASSELL'S ENGLISH-LATIN DICTIONARY

A

A, an; often not translated; sometimes *unus*; a certain, *aliquis, quidam*.

abandon, *relinquĕre, deserĕre, destituĕre*; of things, *omittĕre*.

abandoned, *perditus, nefarius*.

abase, *frangĕre, (de)minuĕre, comprimĕre*.

abasement, *demissio, deminutio*.

abash, *percellĕre, perturbare*.

abate: = transit. *imminuĕre, remittĕre*: intransit. *cadĕre, imminui, decrescĕre*; of passion, *defervescĕre*.

abatement, *remissio, deminutio*.

abbreviate, *imminuĕre, contrahĕre*.

abbreviation, *compendium, contractio*.

abdicate, (*magistratu*) *se abdicare*; (*magistratum*) *eiurare*.

abdication, *abdicatio, eiuratio*.

abdomen, *abdomen*.

abduction, *raptus (-ūs), raptio*.

aberration, *error*.

abet, *adiuvare*.

abettor, *socius, adiutor*.

abeyance: to be in —, *in dubio esse, intermitti*; to leave in —, *rem integram relinquĕre*.

abhor, *abhorrēre ab, odisse, odio habēre*.

abhorrence, *odium*.

abhorrent, = inconsistent, *abhorrens, alienus, contrarius*; see also hateful.

abide: = linger, (*com*)*morari, manēre*; = last, *durare*; to abide by, *stare in*.

abiding, *diuturnus, stabilis, mansurus*.

ability, *potestas, vires, facultas*; = mental strength, *ingenium*; according to one's —, *pro sua parte, pro parte virili*.

abject, *abiectus, contemptus, humilis*.

abjure, *abiurare, recusare*.

ablative, (*casus*) *ablativus*.

able, *potens*; = mentally strong, *ingeniosus*; to be able, *posse, valēre*.

able-bodied, *firmus, robustus, validus*.

ablution, *lavatio, ablutio*.

abnegation, *temperantia*.

abnormal, *novus, inusitatus, singularis*.

aboard: to go —, (*navem*) *conscendĕre*; to be —, *in nave esse*.

abode: = sojourn, *habitatio*; see also house.

abolish, *abolēre, tollĕre, delēre, exstinguĕre*.

abolition, *dissolutio*; — of debts, *tabulae novae*.

abominable, *detestabilis, immanis*.

abominate, *odisse, detestari*.

aborigines, *indigenae, aborigines*.

abortive: of premature birth, *abortivus*; fig., = unsuccessful, *inritus*.

abound, *abundare, superesse*; — in, (*re*) *abundare*.

about; adv. of time or number, *fere, ferme, circiter*; prep., of place, *circa, circum*; of time, *circa*; of respect, = concerning, *de* with *abl*.

above, adv. of place, *supra*; from above, *desuper, superne*; prep., *super, supra*.

abreast, *pariter*; two horses yoked —, *equi biiugi* or *biiuges*.

abridge; see abbreviate.

abroad, adv.: = out of doors, *foras* (of motion), *foris* (of rest); = in a foreign land, *peregre*; to travel —, *peregrinari*; to spread —, = publish, *divulgare*.

abrogate, *abrogare, rescindĕre*.

abrupt: = steep, *abruptus, arduus, praeruptus*: of speech, *abruptus*; = sudden, *subitus, repentinus, improvisus*. Adv. *abrupte, praerupte*; *subito, de improviso, repente*.

abscess, *vomica*.

abscond, *delitescĕre, latēre, occultari*.

absence, *absentia*; in my —, *me absente*.

absent, adj. *absens*; to be —, *abesse*.

absent, v. to absent oneself, *se removēre, non comparēre*.

absolute, *absolutus, simplex*; absolute power, *dominatio, imperium singulare*. Adv. *plane, prorsus, omnino*; opp. to relatively, *per se, simpliciter*.

absolve, (*ab*)*solvĕre*.

absorb, (*com*)*bibĕre, absorbēre*; absorbed in a thing, *totus in re*.

abstain, (*se*) *re abstinēre*.

abstinence, *abstinentia, temperantia*. days of —, *ieiunium*.

abstinent, *abstinens, temperatus*.

abstract, subst. *epitome, epitoma*.

abstract, adj. *quod nullo sensu percipi potest*.

abstract, v. *abstrahĕre, sevocare*; see also steal.

abstracted, *omnium rerum* (or *sui*) *oblitus*.

abstraction, *oblivio*.

abstruse, *abstrusus, obscurus, reconditus*.

abstruseness, *obscuritas*.

absurd, *absurdus, ineptus, ridiculus*; adv. *absurde, inepte, ridicule*.

absurdity, *insulsitas, ineptia*.

abundance, *abundantia, ubertas, copia*.

abundant, *largus, amplus*; adv. *abunde, abundanter, large*.

abuse, subst.; = wrong use, *usus (-ūs) perversus*; = abusive language, *convicium*; a bad custom, *mos pravus*.

abuse, v.: to misuse, (*re*) *abuti*; = to speak abusively to, (*homini*) *maledicĕre*.

abusive, *maledicus, maledicens, contumeliosus*; adv. *maledice, contumeliose*.

abut, *adiacēre, attingĕre*.

abyss, *gurges, barathrum, vorago*.

academy: at Athens, *Academia*; = school, *ludus, schola*.

accede; see agree.

accelerate, *accelerare*.

accent, *vox, sonus (-ūs), tenor*.

accept, *accipĕre, recipĕre*.

acceptable, *iucundus, acceptus, gratus*.

acceptation; = significance, *significatio*.

access, *aditus (-ūs), accessus (-ūs)*.

accessary; = accomplice, *conscius, (culpae) socius*.

accessible, *facilis.*

accession; = increase, *accessio;* to the throne, *initium regni.*

accessory, = additional; use verb *accedo.*

accident, *casus (-ūs).*

accidental, *fortuitus;* adv. *forte, casu, fortuito.*

acclaim, subst., *clamor, acclamatio.*

acclaim, v. *acclamare.*

accommodate, *accommodare.*

accommodating, *obsequens, facilis.*

accommodation, *hospitium;* see also agreement.

accompaniment, *comitatus (-ūs).*

accompany, *comitari;* in a crowd, *stipare;* accompanied by, *cum* (with abl.); in music, *concinĕre.*

accomplice, *socius, sceleris conscius.*

accomplish, *conficĕre, perficĕre, absolvĕre, peragĕre, exsequi.*

accomplished, *politus, elegans, doctus, eruditus.*

accomplishment: = fulfilment, *confectio, perfectio, absolutio;* = skill, *ars.*

accord, subst.: of one's own —, *sponte (sua), ultro;* see also harmony.

accordance: in — with, *ex, de, pro,* with abl.; in — with circumstances, *ad tempus, pro re.*

according to; see accordance.

accordingly, *ergo, itaque.*

accost, *appellare, compellare, adoriri.*

account, subst. = reckoning, *ratio:* = account books, *tabulae (-arum);* to be of —, *magni habēri;* to be of no —, *nullo numero esse;* on my —, *mea de causa, meo nomine;* on — of, *propter, ob;* = narrative, *memoria, narratio.*

account, v.: = to think, *habēre, aestimare, ducĕre;* to — for, *rationem de re reddĕre.*

accountable; see responsible.

accountant, *scriba.*

accretion, *accessio, incrementum, cumulus.*

accumulate, *(co)acervare, exaggerare.*

accumulation, *cumulus, acervus.*

accuracy: = care taken, *cura, diligentia;* = truth, *veritas.*

accurate: = careful, *diligens, religiosus;* = carefully done, *accuratus;* = true, *verus.*

accusation, *accusatio, crimen.*

accusative, *accusativus (casus).*

accuse, *accusare, arguĕre, insimulare.*

accused, *reus.*

accuser: on a criminal charge, *accusator;* in a civil suit, *petitor;* = informer, *index, delator.*

accustom, *adsuefacĕre;* to grow accustomed, *adsuescĕre;* to be accustomed, *solēre.*

accustomed, *adsuetus, solitus.*

ache, subst., *dolor.*

ache, v. *dolēre.*

achieve: = to finish, *conficĕre, efficĕre, perficĕre;* = to gain, reach, *adsequi, consequi.*

achievement: = doing, *confectio;* = deed, *facinus (-oris).*

acid, adj., *acidus, acerbus, acer;* in temper, *acerbus, morosus.*

acknowledge: = to accept as one's own, *agnoscĕre;* to — a child, *suscipĕre, tollĕre;* = to admit, *fateri, confiteri;* = to give thanks, *gratias agĕre;* to — a payment, (in) *acceptum referre.*

acknowledged, *cognitus, probatus, spectatus.*

acknowledgement: = confession, *confessio;* = thanks, *gratiae (-arum).*

acme, *fastigium;* or use *summus.*

acorn, *glans.*

acquaint; see inform.

acquaintance: = knowledge; of things, *scientia;* of persons, *usus, familiaritas;* = person known, *amicus, familiaris.*

acquainted, *notus, cognitus;* — with a person, *familiaris;* — with a thing, *peritus, sciens.*

acquiesce, *acquiescĕre, rem aequo animo ferre.*

acquiescence, *adsensus (-ūs)*

acquire; see gain.

acquirement, acquisition: = thing gained, see gain; = skill or knowledge, *ars, scientia;* the process of — *comparatio, adeptio.*

acquisitive, *lucri studiosus.*

acquit, *absolvĕre.*

acquittal, *absolutio, liberatio.*

acrid, *acer, acerbus.*

acrimonious, *mordax, acerbus, amarus, aculeatus.*

acrimony, *acerbitas.*

across: adv., use compound verb with *trans-;* prep., *trans.*

act, subst.: of a play, *actus (-ūs);* of Parliament, *lex;* = thing done, *factum.*

act, v.: = to behave, *agĕre, facĕre, 'e gerĕre;* of drugs, *efficax esse;* to act on the stage, *in scena esse;* to act the chief part, *primas partes agĕre.*

action: = doing, *actio;* = deed, *factum;* := battle, *pugna, proelium;* = part of a play, *actio;* = legal proceedings, *lis, actio;* to take (legal) —, *litem* or *actionem intendĕre, diem dicĕre, lege agĕre.*

actionable, *(res) cuius actio est.*

active: = quick, *celer, acer, promptus;* = industrious, *impiger,(g)navus, strenuus;* adv. actively, *impiger, (g)naviter, strenue.*

activity; = quickness, *celeritas, agilitas;* = industry, *industria, (g)navitas.*

actor, *qui agit* or *facit, actor;* on a stage, *histrio, actor:* comic —, *comoedus;* tragic —, *tragoedus.*

actress, *mima.*

actual, *verus;* adv. *vere, re vera.*

actuate, *movēre, impellĕre.*

acumen, *ingenii acies* or *acumen.*

acute: of pain, *acer, gravis, vehemens;* of intellect, *acutus, perspicax, sagax.* Adv., of feeling, *acute;* of intellect, *acriter, subtilier.*

acuteness, *ingenii acies* or *acumen, subtilitas.*

adage, *proverbium.*

adamant, subst. *adamas (-antis),* m.

adamantine, adj. *adamantinus.*

adapt, *accommodare, aptare.*

adaptation, *accommodatio.*
adapted, *aptus, idoneus.*
add, *addĕre, adicĕre;* to — up, *computare.*
adder, *vipera.*
addict, v.; to — oneself, *se dare, dedĕre, tradĕre.*
addicted, *deditus.*
addition: = adding, *accessio;* in arithmetic, *additio.*
additional, *novus, additus, adiectus.*
address, v. = to speak to, *adloqui, adfari, appellare, compellare;* to address a letter, *(homini) epistulam inscribere.*
address, subst.: speech, *contio, oratio;* the — of a letter, *inscriptio;* = place, *locus;* = adroitness, *dexteritas, sollertia.*
adduce, *adducĕre, proferre.*
adept, *callidus, peritus.*
adequate, *aptus, idoneus;* adv. *apte, satis.*
adhere, *(in)haerēre.*
adherent, *socius, fautor, cliens.*
adhesive, *tenax.*
adieu! *vale!* plur. *valete;* to bid —, *(hominem) valēre iubēre.*
adjacent, *contiguus, vicinus, finitimus;* to be —, *adiacēre.*
adjective, *nomen adiectivum.*
adjoin; see adjacent.
adjourn, *ampliare, rem differre.*
adjournment, *dilatio.*
adjudge, *addicĕre, adiudicare.*
adjudicate; see judge.
adjunct; see addition.
adjure, = entreat, *obsecrare, obtestari.*
adjust; see arrange, adapt.
adjustment, *accommodatio.*
administer, *administrare, procurare;* to — medicine, *medicinam dare, adhibēre;* to — justice, *ius dicĕre.*
administration: the act, *administratio, procuratio;* = the government, *ei qui reipublicae praesunt.*
admirable, *(ad)mirabilis, praeclarus;* adv. *admirabiliter, mirum in modum, praeclare.*
admiral, *praefectus classis*
admiration, *admiratio.*
admire, *(ad)mirari.*
admissible, *aequus;* or use verb.
admission: = leave to enter, *aditus (-ūs), accessus (-ūs);* = confession, *confessio;* in argument, *concessio.*
admit, to let in, *admittĕre, recipĕre;* in 'argument, *concedĕre, dare;* = to confess, *fateri, confiteri;* to — of, = allow, *recipĕre, pati.*
admonish, *(ad)monēre, commonēre.*
admonition, *(ad)monitio.*
ado: with much —, *vix, aegre;* see fuss.
adolescence, *adulescentia.*
adolescent, *adulescens.*
adopt, *adoptare;* = to choose, accept, *adsumĕre, accipĕre, recipĕre;* to — a resolution, *constituĕre.*
adoption, *adoptio.*
adoptive, *adoptivus.*
adorable, *sanctus, venerandus.*
adoration, *cultus (-ūs), veneratio.*

adore, *venerari, colĕre;* = to love, *diligĕre, amare.*
adorn, *(ex)ornare, decorare.*
adornment, *ornatus (-ūs), exornatio.*
adrift, to be, *fluctibus iactari.*
adroit, *callidus, sollers, dexter;* adv. *callide, dextere.*
adroitness, *dexteritas.*
adulation, *adulatio, adsentatio.*
adult, *adultus, pubes.*
adulterate, *corrumpĕre, vitiare.*
adulterer, *adulter, moechus.*
adultery, *adulterium.*
adults, subst. *puberes* (plur. only).
adumbrate, *adumbrare.*
adumbration, *adumbratio.*
advance, v.: intransit., *progredi, procedĕre;* to become advanced in years, *aetate provehi;* transit., *promovēre, provehĕre, adiuvare, augēre.*
advance-guard, *primum agmen.*
advantage, *commodum, lucrum, fructus (-ūs), utilitas, bonum;* to be of — *expedire, prodesse, usui esse.*
advantageous, *utilis, fructuosus, opportunus;* adv. *utiliter.*
advent, *adventus (-ūs).*
adventitious, *adventicius, externus.*
adventure, subst.: = exploit, *facinus (-oris), inceptum;* = happening, *casus (-ūs).*
adventure, v. *audēre, tentare, experiri, periclitari.*
adventurous, *audax;* adv. *audacter*
adverb, *adverbium.*
adversary, *adversarius.*
adverse, *adversus, contrarius;* adv. *contra, secus.*
adversity, *res adversae, calamitas.*
advertise, = to make known, *praedicare, pronuntiare;* of goods, *proscribĕre, inscribere.*
advertisement, = notice of sale, *proscriptio.*
advice, *consilium,* by my —, *me auctore.*
advise, *suadēre, monēre;* see also inform.
advisedly, *consulte, considerate, de industria.*
adviser, *suasor, auctor.*
advocate, subst.; legal, *patronus;* in gen., *suasor, auctor.*
advocate, v. *suadēre.*
adze, *ascia.*
aerial, *aerius, aetherius.*
afar, *procul, longe.*
affability, *comitas.*
affable, *adfabilis, comis;* adv. *comiter.*
affair, *res, negotium.*
affect, v.: = to influence, *adficĕre, tangĕre, (com)movēre;* = to be fond of, *diligĕre, amare;* = to make a show of, *simulare, imitari.*
affectation, *simulatio.*
affected, *quaesitus, simulatus;* of style, *putidus, molestus;* adv. *putide, moleste.*
affection: in gen., *adfectio, adfectus (-ūs);* = friendly sentiment, *amor, caritas, studium;* dutiful —, *pietas.*
affectionate, adj. *amans;* dutifully — *pius;* adv. *amanter, pie.*

affiance, = betroth, (de)spondēre.

affidavit, testimonium per tabulas datum.

affinity, propinquitas, necessitudo; in gen., = close connexion, cognatio, coniunctio.

affirm, adfirmare, confirmare

affirmation, adfirmatio.

affirmative, use verb.

affix, adfigere, adligare, adnectēre.

afflict, adflictare, vexare.

affliction, aegritudo, dolor, molestia.

affluence, divitiae, opes, copia.

affluent, dives.

afford, = supply, praestare praebēre, sufficēre, suppeditare.

affray, rixa, pugna.

affright; see frighten.

affront, subst. contumelia.

affront, v. contumeliā adficēre.

afloat, to be —, navigare, navi vehi.

afoot, pedibus.

aforesaid, quem (quod) supra scripsi.

afraid, timidus, pavidus, trepidus; to be —, timēre, metuēre.

afresh; see again.

after. Prep.: of place or time, post, with acc.; of rank, etc., secundum, with acc.; of conformity, = according to, ad, with acc. Conj., postquam, cum, ubi.

afterwards, post, postea, dein(de), inde; = after this, posthac; some months —, paucis postea mensibus, aliquot post menses.

afternoon: in the —, post meridiem; adj. postmeridianus.

again, rursus, rursum, denuo; = a second time, iterum; again and again, identidem; = further, moreover, porro, autem.

against, contra, adversus, in, with acc.; — the stream, adverso flumine; — my will, me invito.

age: = time (esp. time of life), aetas; of the same —, aequalis; = old age, of persons, senectus, of things, vetustas.

aged, aetate provectus; an — man, senex (-is).

agency, = instrumentality, opera.

agent, procurator.

aggrandize, amplificare, augēre.

aggrandizement, amplificatio; or use verb.

aggravate: = to make worse, (ad)-gravare; = to annoy, exasperare, lacessēre.

aggregate, summa.

aggression, impetus (-ūs), incursus (-ūs), iniuria.

aggressive, hostilis, infensus.

aggressor, qui prior oppugnat qui iniuriam facit.

aggrieve; see grieve.

aghast, stupefactus, perturbatus; to stand —, stupēre, obstupescēre.

agile, agilis, velox, pernix.

agility, agilitas, pernicitas, velocitas.

agitate: = to shake, agitare, quatēre, vibrare; mentally, = to disturb, percutēre, perturbare, sollicitare; = to discuss, agitare, disputare, disserēre.

agitated, sollicitus, trepidus.

agitation: physical, agitatio, iactatio; mental, animi motus (-ūs), commotio, concitatio.

agitator, turbator.

ago, abhinc; long —, (iam) pridem, iam dudum.

agony, aegritudo, dolor.

agrarian, agrarius.

agree, concinēre, consentire; it is agreed, constat; to — upon, = settle, componēre, constituēre.

agreeable: of things, acceptus, gratus, dulcis; of persons, commodus, lepidus.

agreement; = harmony, consensus (-ūs), concordia; = arrangement, compact, pactum, pactio, conventum.

agricultural, rusticus.

agriculture, agri cultura, agri cultio.

agriculturist, agricola.

aground, to run, sidēre.

ague, febris.

ah! aha! interj. a, ah, aha.

ahead, use compound verb with prae- or pro-.

aid, subst. auxilium, adiumentum, subsidium, opem (nom. ops not used).

aid, adiuvare, subvenire, succurrēre, opem ferre.

ailing, aeger; see sick.

aim, subst. finis, propositum, consilium.

aim, v. to take aim, telum dirigēre or intendēre; to aim at, telo petēre; fig., adfectare, petēre, quaerēre, spectare.

air, subst. (1), aer, aether (upper air), aura (breeze), anima (= breath); in the open —, sub Iove, sub divo. (2), = look manner, vultus (-ūs), aspectus (-ūs), species. (3) = tune, modus, numeri.

air, v. ventilare.

airy, aerius.

akin: = related, consanguineus, propinquus, agnatus, cognatus; = similar, connected, finitimus, vicinus.

alacrity, alacritas, pernicitas.

alarm, subst.: = loud noise, clamor, strepitus (-ūs); = disturbance, turba, tumultus (-ūs); = fear, terror, trepidatio.

alas! heu! eheu! vae! ei!

alcove, zotheca.

alder, alnus; adj. alneus.

alert, vigil, alacer, promptus.

alias, nomen alienum.

alien, adj.: = foreign, peregrinus, externus; = adverse, alienus, aversus.

alien, subst. peregrinus, advena, alienigena.

alienate, (ab)alienare, avertēre.

alienation, (ab)alienatio.

alight, v. descendēre.

alike: adj. par, similis; adv. pariter, similiter, aeque.

alive, vivus; to be —, vivēre.

all: = every single, omnis; = the whole, totus; all together, cunctus, universus; in —, omnino; not at —, minime; — but, tantum non.

allay, lenire, sedare, mitigare.

allegation, adfirmatio; see also accusation.

allege: see assert.

allegiance, *fides*; to swear — to. *in verba hominis iurare.*

allegory, *allegoria.*

alleviate, (*ad*)*levare*; see also allay.

alleviation, *levatio, mitigatio, levamen.*

alley, *angiportus (-ūs).*

alliance, *societas, foedus (-eris).*

allot: by lot, *sortiri*; in gen., *distribuĕre, adsignare, adiudicare.*

allotment, *adsignatio*; of land. *ager adsignatus, possessio.*

allow. (1) ➡ permit, *sinĕre, pati; permittĕre, concedĕre*; I am —ed, *licet mihi.* (2) ➡ admit, *concedĕre, confiteri.* (3) ➡ grant; q.v.

allowable, *concessus, licitus.*

allowance: ➡ indulgence, *indulgentia*; to make — for, *ignoscĕre, condonare*; an — of food, *diaria, demensum.*

alloy: without —, *sincerus, purus.*

allude to, ➡ to refer to, *significare, designare.*

allure, *adlicĕre, inlicĕre, invitare, inescare.*

allurement, *invitamentum, blanditia, inlecebra.*

alluring, *blandus.*

allusion, *significatio, mentio*; or use verb.

ally, subst. *socius.*

ally, v.: ➡ make an alliance. *foedus facĕre (or ferire), societatem inire*; ➡ join together as allies, *sociare.*

almanack, *fasti (-orum), ephemeris.*

almighty, *omnipotens.*

almond, *amygdala.*

almost, *prope, paene.*

alms, *stips (-is,* f.: nom. not used).

aloft, *sublime, alte; sublimis,* adj.

alone: adj. *solus, unus;* adv. ➡ only; q.v.

along: adv., *porro, protinus;* prep., *secundum, praeter;* — with, *una cum.*

aloof, *procul.*

aloud, *clara* or *magna voce.*

already, *iam.*

also, *etiam, praeterea, quoque, item.*

altar, *ara, altaria* (plur.).

alter: transit., *mutare, commutare, immutare, (con)vertĕre;* intransit., use passive, e.g. *mutari.*

alterable, adj. *mutabilis.*

alteration, (*com*)*mutatio;* a sudden —, *conversio.*

altercation, *altercatio, iurgium, rixa.*

alternate, v.; transit., *alternare, variare;* intransit., *variare.*

alternate, adj. *alternus;* adv. *invicem.*

alternation, *vicissitudo.*

alternative: there is no alternative left except . . ., *nihil restat nisi ut . . . .*

although, *quamquam; etsi* (➡ even if); *quamvis* (➡ however much); *licet* (➡ granted that).

altitude, *altitudo.*

altogether, ➡ wholly, *omnino.*

always, *semper.*

amalgamate, (*com*)*miscĕre.*

amalgamation, *coniunctio, mixtura.*

amanuensis, *librarius, servus a manu.*

amass, (*co*)*acervare, aggerare. accumulare.*

amaze, *obstupefacĕre.*

amazed, (*ob*)*stupefactus, stupidus;* to be —, *stupĕre, (ob)stupescĕre.*

amazement, *stupor.*

amazing, *mirus, admirabilis;* adj. *admirabiliter, mirum in modum.*

ambassador, *legatus.*

amber, *sucinum, electrum.*

ambiguity, *ambiguitas; ambages* (plur.; ➡ riddle).

ambiguous, *anceps, ambiguus, dubius;* adv. *ambigue.*

ambition, *ambitio, gloria; laudis studium contentio honorum.*

ambitious, *gloriae* (or *laudis*) *cupidus.*

ambrosia, *ambrosia.*

ambush, *insidiae* (plur.).

ameliorate, *corrigĕre, emendare.*

amen! *fiat! esto!*

amenable, (*dicto*) *oboediens.*

amend, *emendare, corrigĕre.*

amendment, *correctio, emendatio.*

amends, *satisfactio, expiatio:* to make — for, *expiare, satisfacĕre.*

amenity, *amoenitas.*

amiability, *suavitas.*

amiable, *suavis, amabilis;* adv. *suaviter*

amicable; see friendly.

amidst, *inter,* with acc.

amiss, *male, perperam, prave:* to take —, *aegre ferre.*

ammunition, *apparatus (-ūs) belli, arma (-orum);* see also bullet.

amnesty, use *venia,* or *ignoscĕre.*

among, *inter,* with acc.; *in,* with abl.; *apud,* with acc.

amorous, *amans;* in bad sense, *libidinosus.*

amount, *summa.*

amount to, v. *efficere:* what does it — to? *quae summa est?* it —s to the same thing, *idem est, nihil interest.*

amphitheatre, *amphitheatrum.*

ample, *amplus;* adv. *ample, abunde.*

amplify, *amplificare.*

amplitude, *amplitudo.*

amputate, *praecidĕre, amputare.*

amuse, *delectare, oblectare.*

amusement, *delectatio, oblectatio, oblectamentum.*

amusing, *facetus, festivus.*

anachronism; use phrase, e.g. *tempora miscĕre.*

analogous, *similis.*

analogy, *similitudo.*

analyse, *explicare; quasi in membra discerpĕre.*

analysis, *explicatio, enodatio.*

anarchy, *licentia.*

anatomy; refer to the structure of the body, ➡ *compages* or *conformatio corporis.*

ancestor; sing. *auctor generis;* plur. *maiores.*

ancestral, *avitus, proavitus.*

ancestry, *origo, genus.*

anchor, subst. *ancora;* to cast —. *ancoram iacĕre:* to weigh —. *ancoram tollĕre.*

anchor, v. transit. (*navem*) *ad ancoras deligare.*

anchorage, *statio.*

ancient, *antiquus, vetus, vetustus, priscus;* the ancients. *veteres, antiqui.*

and, *et; -que* (enclitic); *atque, ac;* — **so,** *itaque;* — **yet,** *tamen;* — **not,** *et non, neque, nec.*

anecdote, *fabula, fabella.*

anew, *denuo, ab integro.*

anger, subst. *ira, iracundia, indignatio.*

anger, v. *lacessĕre, inritare.*

angle, *angulus.*

angle, v. *piscari.*

angler, *piscator.*

angry, adj. *iratus, iracundus;* **to be (or become) angry,** *irasci;* adv. *iracunde.*

anguish, *cruciatus (-ūs), dolor, angor.*

angular, *angulatus.*

animadvert, *animadvertĕre.*

animal, subst. *animal, animans;* — **a beast,** *bestia, pecus (-udis,* domestic), *belua* (large), *fera* (wild).

animal, adj. *animalis;* or genit. of *animal, corpus,* etc.

animate, v. *animare;* fig., *excitare, incitare.*

animate, adj. *animalis, animatus.*

animated, *animatus, animans, animalis;* — **lively,** *vegetus, alacer.*

animation, *alacritas, vigor.*

animosity, *odium, invidia.*

ankle, ankle-bone, *talus.*

annals, *annales (-ium,* plur.).

annex, v.: — **add,** *(ad)iungĕre, addĕre;* — **conquer,** *sibi subicĕre.*

annihilate, *delēre, exstinguĕre.*

annihilation, *exstinctio, excidium.*

anniversary, *festus dies anniversarius.*

annotate, *adnotare.*

annotation, *adnotatio.*

announce, *(re)nuntiare, praedicare.*

annoy, *lacessĕre, inritare, vexare.*

annoyance, *molestia, vexatio.*

annual, *annuus. anniversarius;* adv. *quotannis.*

annuity, *annua pecunia.*

annul, *tollĕre, delēre, abrogare, abolēre.*

anoint, *(in)unguĕre.*

anointing, subst. *unctio.*

anon, *brevi (tempore), mox.*

anonymous, *sine nomine.*

another, pron. and adj. *alius; alter* (= **a second**); **they fear one** —, *alius alium timet, inter se timent.*

answer, subst. *responsum;* **to a charge,** *defensio, excusatio.*

answer, v. *respondēre;* **to a charge,** *se defendĕre, excusare;* **of an oracle,** *responsum dare;* **to — for,** *(rem) praestare.*

answerable: to be — **to a person,** *homini rationem reddĕre.*

ant, *formica.*

antagonist, *adversarius.*

antagonistic, *contrarius, adversus, infensus.*

antecedent, adj. *antecedens, prior.*

antecedents, subst. *antecedentia (-ium).*

antechamber, *vestibulum, atriolum.*

antelope; see **deer.**

anterior, *antecedens, prior.*

anthem, *cantus (-ūs).*

anticipate: — **to act first, forestall,** *occupare, praevertĕre, antevertĕre;* — **to expect,** *exspectare.*

anticipation: see **anticipate;** — **expectation,** *exspectatio, spes.*

antics, *ludi, ioca.*

antidote, *remedium.*

antipathy: of things, *(rerum) discordia, repugnantia;* **of persons,** *odium.*

antiquary, antiquarian, *rerum antiquarum studiosus.*

antiquated, *obsoletus, priscus.*

antique, *antiquus.*

antiquity, *antiquitas, vetustas.*

antithesis: rhet. *contentio;* — **the opposite,** *contrarium.*

antler, *cornu.*

anvil, *incus (-udis).*

anxiety, *anxietas, cura, sollicitudo.*

anxious, *anxius, sollicitus, trepidus;* adv. *anxie, sollicite.*

any, anyone: with negative, or in questions, *ullus* (adj.) *quisquam* (substantival); after *si, nisi,* or *ne,* use *qui, qua, quod* (adj.), *quis* (subst.); — **you like,** — **you please,** *quivis, quilibet.*

anywhere, *usquam; ubivis* (= **anywhere you please);** *quoquam* (= **to any place).**

apace, *celeriter.*

apart, *seorsum;* or use compound verbs with *dis-* and *se-.*

apartment; see **room.**

apathetic, *hebes, lentus.*

apathy, *stupor, lentitudo.*

ape, *simia, simius.*

ape, v. *imitari.*

Apennines, *Apenninus.*

aperture; see **opening.**

apex, *cacumen, apex.*

aphorism, *sententia, dictum, elogium.*

apiece, use distrib. num.

apologise, *excusare.*

apology: — **defence,** *defensio;* — **excuse,** *excusatio.*

apophthegm, *elogium, sententia, dictum.*

apostrophize; see **address.**

apothecary, *medicus.*

appal, *(ex)terrēre;* see **frighten.**

apparatus, *apparatus (-ūs).*

apparel, *vestis, vestimentum.*

apparent: — **evident, manifestus,** *apertus;* **to be** —, *apparēre;* — **not real,** *fictus, simulatus;* adv. *ut videtur.*

apparition: — **appearing,** *adventus(-ūs);* — **spectre,** *simulacrum, species.*

appeal, subst.: **legal,** *appellatio, provocatio;* — **entreaty,** *obsecratio, preces.*

appeal, v.: **legal, to a magistrate,** *(hominem) appellare;* **to the people,** *ad populum provocare;* **appeal to,** — **entreat,** *obtestari, obsecrare;* **appeal to,** — **please,** *placēre.*

appealing, *supplex.*

appear: — **become visible, be evident,** *apparere, conspici;* **to appear in public,** *in publicum prodire;* —, — **be present, put in an appearance,** *comparēre, adesse;* **to** —, — **seem,** *videri.*

appearance: — **arrival,** *adventus (-ūs);* or use verb; — **looks,** *species, facies, habitus (-ūs);* — **semblance, species.**

appease, *placēre;* **of hunger** etc., *sedare.*

appeasement, *placatio.*

appellant; see **appeal.**

append, *addĕre, adiungĕre.*

appendage, *appendix, accessio.*

appetite, *appetentia, appetitio*; for food, *fames.*

applaud, *(ap)plaudĕre.*

applause, *plausus (-ūs).*

apple, *malum*; — tree, *malus, f.*

appliance, *apparatus (-ūs), instrumentum.*

application: — *reques: petitio*; of the mind, *animi intentio, diligentia.*

apply, v.: transit., — bring to bear, *adhibēre, admovēre*; to — oneself, *se conferre*; intransit., — refer, *pertinēre*; — make application, *adīre.*

appoint, *constituĕre, dicĕre, destinare*; of officials, *creare, facĕre*; to — to command, *praeponĕre, praeficĕre.*

appointment: — office, *munus (-eris), magistratus (-ūs)*; — agreement to meet, *constitutum.*

apportion, *dividĕre, distribuĕre, adsignare.*

apposite, *aptus, accommodatus.*

appraise, *aestimare.*

appreciate, *aestimare; agnoscĕre.*

apprehend, *comprehendĕre*; — to grasp mentally, *comprehendĕre, complecti (animo or mente), intellegĕre*; — fear; q.v.

apprehension: — mental grasp, *intellegentia*; — fear, *timor.*

apprehensive: see timid.

apprentice, subst. *homo (homini) addictus.*

apprentice, v. *addicĕre.*

approach, subst. *adventus (-ūs), aditus (-ūs).*

approach, v. *accedĕre, appropinquare, adventare.*

approbation; see approval.

appropriate, adj. *idoneus, aptus, accommodatus*; adv. *apte, accommodate.*

appropriate, v. *(ad)sumĕre, sibi adrogare, sibi vindicare.*

approval, *approbatio, comprobatio*; with your approval, *pace tua.*

approve, *(ap)probare, comprobare.*

approved, *probatus, spectatus.*

approximate, adj. *propinquus.*

approximate, v., see approach.

April, *Aprilis (mensis).*

apron, *subligaculum.*

apt: — appropriate; q.v.; — prone, *pronus, propensus*; adv. *apte.*

aptitude, *habilitas.*

aquatic, *aquatilis.*

aqueduct, *aquae ductus (-ūs).*

aquiline, *aduncus.*

arable; see plough.

arbiter, *arbiter, disceptator.*

arbitrarily, *libidinose.*

arbitrary: — capricious, *libidinosus*; of power, use *dominari* or *dominatio.*

arbitrate, v. *disceptare, diiudicare.*

arbitration, *arbitrium.*

arbour, *umbraculum.*

arc, *arcus (-ūs).*

arcade, *porticus (-ūs).*

arch, subst. *arcus (-ūs), fornix.*

arch, adj. *petulans, improbus, malus.*

arch, v. *arcuare*; see curve.

archaeology, *rerum antiquarum scientia.*

archaism, *verbum obsoletum.*

archer, *sagittarius.*

architect, *architectus.*

architecture, *architectura.*

archives, *tabulae publicae.*

arctic, *septentrionalis, arctous.*

ardent, *ardens, fervens, acer*; adv., *ardenter, acriter.*

ardour, *ardor, fevor, studium.*

arduous, *arduus, difficilis.*

area, *area, superficies.*

arena, *harena.*

argue: — to discuss, *disserĕre, disputare*; — conclude, seek to prove, *argumentari, conligĕre.*

argument: — dispute, *disputatio*; line of —, *argumentum.*

arid, *aridus, siccus.*

aright, *recte, bene.*

arise, *surgĕre, (ex)oriri, exsistĕre.*

aristocracy: — aristocrats, *optimates, patricii, nobiles*; as a form of government, *optimatium dominatus (-ūs).*

aristocrat, aristocratic; see aristocracy.

arithmetic, *arithmetica (-orum).*

arithmetical, *arithmeticus.*

ark, — chest, *arca.*

arm, subst. *bracchium*; upper —, *lacertus*; arms, — embrace, *complexus (-ūs), manūs* (plur.); see also arms.

arm, v. transit. *armare*; intransit., *armari, arma capĕre.*

arm-chair, *sella.*

armed, *armatus.*

armistice, *indutiae (-arum).*

armour, *arma (-orum)*; armour-bearer, *armiger.*

armourer, *faber armorum.*

armpit, *ala.*

arms, *arma (-orum), tela (-orum),* (offensive).

army, *exercitus (-ūs)*; in marching array, *agmen*; in battle array, *acies.*

aromatic, *odorus, odoratus.*

around: adv. and prep., *circa, circum.*

arouse, *excitare, suscitare.*

arraign; see accuse.

arrange, *ordinare, componĕre, disponĕre, digerĕre*; abstr., *constituĕre, componĕre.*

arrangement, *ordo, ratio, dispositio*; or use verb.

arrant, render by superl., or *summus.*

array: of battle, *acies*; — dress, *vestis.*

array, v. = dress, *vestire.*

arrears, *pecuniae residuae.*

arrest: — put under arrest, *comprehendĕre, in custodiam dare*; — stop; q.v.

arrival, *adventus (-ūs), accessus (-ūs).*

arrive, *advenire, pervenire, adventare.*

arrogance, *adrogantia, superbia.*

arrogant, *adrogans, superbus*; adv. *adroganter, superbe.*

arrogate, v. *sibi adrogare, (ad)sumĕre.*

arrow, *sagitta.*

arsenal, *armamentarium*; naval —, *navalia (-ium).*

art, *ars, artificium, peritia* (— acquired skill); the fine —s, *artes ingenuae* or *liberales.*

artful, *astutus, callidus*; adv. *astute, callide.*

artfulness *astutia, calliditas, dolus.*

article, res; = clause or. item, caput, condicio.
articulate, adj. clarus.
articulate, v. dicĕre.
artificer, artifex, opifex.
artificial, adj. artificiosus; adv. arte, manu, opere.
artillery, tormenta (-orum).
artisan, opifex, faber.
artist, artifex; or poeta, pictor, etc.
artistic, adj. artifex; adv. artificiose, summa arte.
artless, adj. simplex; adv. simpliciter, sine arte.
as, adv. and conj.: see while, because, since, though; as . . . as., tam . . . quam . . .; such . . . as . . ., talis . . . qualis . . .; as great as . . ., tantus . . . quantus; as soon as, simul ac; the same as, idem ac, atque, qui; as far as, tenus (prep.), usque (adv., = all the way); as if, as though, quasi, tamquam, velut; as regards . . ., quod ad . . . attinet.
ascend, scandĕre, ascendĕre.
ascendency, render by superior or summus.
ascent, ascensus (-ūs).
ascertain, explorare, cognoscĕre, comperire.
ascetic, render by phrase (e.g. cibo abstinĕre).
ascribe, ascribĕre, adiudicare, attribuĕre.
ash (tree), fraxinus; adj. fraxineus; mountain-ash, ornus.
ashamed, pudore adfectus; I am ashamed, pudet me.
ashes, cinis, favilla.
ashore: of rest, in litore; of motion, in litus; to put —, exponĕre.
aside, seorsum; see apart.
ask: of questions, rogare, interrogare, quaerĕre; of favours, etc., rogare, petĕre, poscĕre.
askance: to look — at, limis oculis adspicĕre.
aslant, oblique, ex transverso.
asleep, dormiens, in somno, per somnum.
asp, aspis.
aspect, aspectus (-ūs), forma, facies, species.
asperity, asperitas, acerbitas.
asperse, infamiā aspergĕre, calumniari.
aspersion, calumnia, opprobrium.
aspirate, aspiratio.
aspire, (ad rem) aspirare, contendĕre; (rem) adfectare.
aspiration, appetitio, adfectatio.
ass, asinus; a little —, asellus.
ass-driver, asinarius.
assail, oppugnare, adoriri.
assailant, qui oppugnat.
assassin, sicarius, percussor.
assassinate, insidiis interficĕre.
assassination, caedes; to accuse of —, accusare inter sicarios.
assault, impetus (-ūs), incursus (-ūs), oppugnatio; legal, vis.
assay, subst. obrussa.
assemble, v. transit., convocare; intransit., convenire, coire.
assembly, conventus (-ūs), concilium.
assent, subst. adsensio, adsensus (-ūs).

assent, v. adsentire, adnuĕre.
assert: = to state, dicĕre, adfirmare, confirmare; to — a right, ius retinĕre, obtinĕre.
assertion: = statement, adfirmatio; = maintenance, defensio, vindicatio.
assess, aestimare.
assessment, aestimatio, census (-ūs).
assessor, censor; = a judge's assistant, adsessor.
assets, bona (-orum).
assiduity, adsiduitas, sedulitas.
assiduous, adsiduus, sedulus, industrius; adv. adsidue, sedulo, industrie.
assign, adsignare, (at)tribuĕre.
assignation, constitutum.
assimilate: = to make like, (ad) aequare, similem facĕre; = to digest, concoquĕre.
assist, (ad)iuvare, auxilium ferre, auxiliari, opitulari, subvenire.
assistance, opem (nom. sing. not used), auxilium, adiumentum.
assistant, adiutor.
associate, subst. socius, sodalis.
associate, v. transit., (con)iungĕre, (con)sociare, congregare; intransit., use pass., or reflex.
association, societas, sodalitas, sodalicum.
assort, digerĕre.
assuage, mitigare, lenire, sedare, levare.
assume: = take to oneself, sibi adrogare, (ad)sumĕre, occupare; = take for granted, ponĕre, sumĕre.
assurance: = strong assertion, confirmatio; = confidence, fiducia.
assure, homini (pro certo) adfirmare, confirmare; = to secure; q.v.
assured: of things, certus, exploratus; to feel assured, credĕre, confidĕre, pro certo habĕre.
assuredly, profecto, certe.
astern, in or a puppi.
astonish, obstupefacĕre.
astonished, attonitus; to be —, obstupescĕre, stupēre.
astonishing, mirabilis, mirus; adv. mire, mirum in modum, mirabiliter.
astonishment, stupor, (ad)miratio.
astray, use adj. vagus, or verb vagari.
astrologer, astrologus, mathematicus.
astrology, astrologia.
astronomy; treat as astrology; q.v.
astute, astutus, callidus.
asunder, seorsum; see apart.
asylum; see refuge.
at: of place, ad, apud, in, or locative case; of time, in, ad, or abl. case.
atheism, deum esse negare.
athlete, athleta.
athwart; see across.
atmosphere, aer, caelum.
atmospheric, use genit. aeris or caeli.
atom, atomus, corpusculum.
atone, (ex)piare.
atonement, piaculum.
atrocious, nefandus, nefarius, atrox; adv. nefarie.
atrocity: as quality, inmanitas, atrocitas; as deed, res atrox, nefas.
attach, adfigĕre, adligare; fig., adiungĕre, applicare.

attached, *aptus;* = fond, *studiosus.*

attachment, *studium, amor, caritas.*

attack, *impetus (-ūs), oppugnatio, incursus (-ūs).*

attack, v. *oppugnare, adoriri, adgredi (ap)petĕre;* to be —ed by disease, *morbo corripi.*

attacker, *oppugnator.*

attain, *adsequi, consequi.*

attainment, *adeptio, comparatio;* = acquired skill, *ars, doctrina, eruditio.*

attempt, subst. *conatus (-ūs), inceptum.*

attempt, v. *conari, temptare.*

attend: of physical presence, *(hominem) comitari, prosequi, deducĕre;* as a servant, *(homini) famulari, ministrare;* at a gathering, *adesse, interesse, frequentare;* mentally, = to pay attention, *operam dare, curare, animadvertĕre, animum attendĕre, hᵹc agĕre;* not to attend, *aliud agĕre.*

attendance, *apparitio, adsectatio;* of large numbers, *frequentia.*

attendant: = escort, *(ad)sector, stipator;* = servant, *servus, minister, famulus.*

attention, *animus attentus, animi intentio;* = an attentive act, *officium.*

attentive, = paying attention, *attentus, intentus, erectus;* adv. *attente, intente;* = helpful, kind, *officiosus, observans.*

attenuate, v. *attenuare, extenuare.*

attest: = vouch for, *testari, testificari;* = call to witness, *testari, testem facĕre.*

attestation, *testificatio;* = evidence, *testimonium.*

attire; see dress.

attitude: physical, *(corporis) habitus (-ūs), status (-ūs);* mental, *animus.*

attract, *attrahĕre, allicĕre.*

attraction, *vis attrahendi;* = pleasant object, *oblectamentum.*

attractive, adj. *iucundus, suavis.*

attribute, subst.; use phrase with *natura* or *proprius;* gram., *attributio, attributum.*

attribute, v. *(at)tribuĕre, adsignare.*

attrition; render by verb *terĕre.*

attune; use phrase with *concinĕre* or *consonus.*

auburn, *fulvus.*

auction, *auctio;* to hold an —, *auctionari.*

auctioneer, *magister auctionis, praeco.*

audacious, *audax, protervus, confidens.*

audacity, *audacia, protervitas.*

audience: = hearing *admissio, aditus (-ūs);* = hearers, *audientes, corona;* a large —, *audientium frequentia.*

audit, v. *rationes dispungĕre.*

augment, v. *(ad)augĕre, amplificare.*

augmentation, *amplificatio.*

augur, subst. *augur.*

augur, v., = foretell, *praedicĕre, vaticinari, augurari.*

augury, *augurium, omen.*

August, *(mensis) Sextilis;* later *Augustus.*

august, adj. *augustus, inlustris, magnificus.*

aunt, *amita* (= father's sister); *matertera* (= mother's sister).

auspices, *auspicium.*

auspicious, *felix, prosper, faustus;* adv. *feliciter, prospere, fauste.*

austere, *austerus, severus, tristis;* adv. *austere, severe.*

austerity, *austeritas, severitas.*

authentic, *certus, verus;* adv. *certo auctore.*

authenticity, *fides, auctoritas.*

author: = originator, *auctor, inventor;* = writer, *scriptor.*

authoritative, *gravis.*

authority, *auctoritas, gravitas;* an — for speech or action, *auctor;* the —s, *magistratus, potestates.*

authorize, *auctor esse, potestatem facĕre, permittĕre.*

autocrat, *dominus.*

autumn, *autumnus.*

autumnal, *autumnalis.*

auxiliaries, *auxilia, (milites) auxiliares.*

auxiliary, adj. *auxiliaris, auxiliarus.*

avail, *valēre, prodesse;* to — oneself of, *uti.*

avarice, *avaritia.*

avaricious, *avarus.*

avaunt! *abi! apage!*

avenge, *vindicare, ulcisci.*

avenger, *ultor, vindex.*

avenue, *xystus.*

aver; see affirm, assert.

averse, *aversus, alienus.*

avert, *avertĕre, prohibĕre.*

aversion, *odium, animus aversus.*

avoid, *vitare, declinare, aversari.*

avow, *profitēri, confitēri.*

avowal, *confessio.*

avowed, *apertus;* adv. *aperte.*

await, *exspectare, manēre, opperiri.*

awake, adj. *vigilans;* to be —, *vigilare.*

awake, v.: transit., *(e somno) excitare;* intransit., *expergisci, excitari.*

award, subst. *arbitrium, addictio.*

award, v. *addicĕre, adiudicare;* see give.

aware, *gnarus;* to be —, *scire, novisse.*

away, *procul;* often rendered by compound verb with *ab-.*

awe, subst. *formido, reverentia, veneratio.*

awe, v. *terrēre; formidinem inicĕre.*

awe-inspiring, awful, *dirus, formidolosus, terribilis.*

awhile, *aliquamdiu, paulisper, parumper.*

awkward, *agrestis, rusticus, rudis, inscitus;* adv. *inscite, rustice.*

awkwardness, *rusticitas inscitia.*

awl, *subula.*

awning, *velum.*

awry; adj. *obliquus, perversus;* adv. *oblique, perverse.*

axe, *securis, dolabra.*

axis, axle, *axis.*

ay, aye, adv. *ita, certe, sane;* I say ay, *aio.*

azure, *caeruleus.*

B

baa, v. *balare.*

babble, v. *blaterare, garrire.*

babbler, *garrulus.*

babe, baby, *infans.*

baboon: see ape.

bachelor, *caelebs*.

back, subst. *tergum*: on one's back, *supinus* (adj.).

back, v.: transit., = move backwards, *retro movēre*; = support, *favēre*; intransit., = go back, *se recipēre*, *recedēre*.

back, backwards, *retro*, *retrorsum*; or use compound verb with *re-*.

backbite, *rodēre*, *absenti maledicēre*.

bacon, *lardum*.

bad, *malus*, *pravus* (= crooked), *turpis* (= ugly, foul); *improbus*, *perversus*, *nequam*; in = health, *aeger*; adv. *male*, *prave*, *turpiter*, *improbe*.

badge, *signum*, *insigne*, *nota*.

badger, *meles*.

badness, *pravitas*, *turpitas*, *nequitia*.

baffle, *eludēre*, *ad irritum redigēre*.

bag, *saccus*, *culeus*.

baggage, *sarcinae*, *impedimenta* (-orum), *vasa* (-orum).

bail, subst.: = security given, *vadimonium*; = person giving security, *vas*, *sponsor*.

bail, v. *spondēre*.

bailiff: on an estate, *procurator*, *vilicus*; at law courts, *apparitor*.

bait, subst. *esca*.

bait, v. = put bait on (a hook), *escam* (hamo) *imponēre*; = feed, *cibum praebēre*; = worry, *vexare*, *lacessēre*.

bake, *coquēre*, *torrēre*.

baker, *pistor*.

bakery, *pistrinum*.

balance, subst.: = scales, *trutina*, *libra*; = remainder, use adj. *reliquus*.

balance, v. *aequis ponderibus librare*; fig., *compensare*; the accounts —, *ratio constat*.

bald, *glaber*, *calvus*; of language, *incultus*.

baldness, *calvitium*.

bale, subst. *fascis*.

bale (out), v. *egerēre*, *exhaurire*.

baleful, *perniciosus*, *exitiosus*.

balk, v. *frustrari*, *eludēre*.

ball: = round object, *globus*; a — to play with, *pila*, *follis* (= football); see also bullet; —, = dance, *saltatio*.

ballad, *carmen*.

ballast, *saburra*.

ballet, *pantomimus*; — dancer, *pantomimus*.

ballot, *suffragium*, *tabella*.

balm, *balsamum*; fig., *solatium*.

balustrade, *cancelli* (-orum).

ban; see forbid.

band, subst.: for binding, *fascia*, *ligamen*; = company, *manus*, *turba*, *grex*, *caterva*.

band (together), v.; see combine.

bandage; see band and bind.

bandit, *latro*.

bandy: to — words, *altercari*.

bandy, bandy-legged, *loripes*.

bane, *venenum*, *virus*; fig., *pernicies*, *pestis*.

baneful, *perniciosus*, *exitiosus*.

bang, subst., *crepitus* (-ūs), *sonitus* (-ūs).

bang, v.; see strike.

banish, v. (*homini*) *aqua et igni interdicĕre*; (*hominem*) (*ex*)*pellĕre*, *exterminare*, *relegare*, *deportare*. Transf., *exterminare*, (*ex*)*pellĕre*, *amovēre*.

banishment, *interdictio aquae et ignis*, *relegatio*, *deportatio*, *exsilium*.

bank, subst.: of earth, *agger*; of a river, *ripa*; financial, *argentaria*, *mensa publica*.

banker, *argentarius*.

bankrupt, *decoctor*; to become —, (*rationes*) *conturbare*, *decoquĕre*.

banner, *vexillum*.

banquet, *epulae* (-arum), *convivium*, *cena*.

banter, subst. *cavillatio*, *ludibrium*.

banter, v. *cavillari*, *iocari*.

bar, subst.: = a long piece, *asser*, *later*; = bolt, *claustrum*, *obex*, *sera*; legal, *forum*; to practise at the —, *causas agĕre*, *dicĕre*, *orare*.

bar, v. = bolt, *occludĕre*, *obserare*; = hinder, *impedire*, *prohibēre*.

barbarian, *barbarus*.

barbaric, barbarous, *barbarus*; = savage, cruel, *immanis*, *saevus*, *crudelis*; adv. *barbare*, *saeve*, *crudeliter*.

barbarity, *immanitas*.

barbed, *hamatus*.

barber, n. *tonsor*: a —'s shop, *tonstrina*.

bard, *vates*.

bare, adj. *nudus*; = mere, *merus*.

bare, v. *nudare*, *aperire*.

barefaced, *impudens*.

barefoot, *pedibus nudis*.

barely, *vix*, *aegre*.

bargain, subst. *pactio*, *pactum*.

bargain, v. *pacisci*.

bark, subst.: of trees, *cortex*, *liber*; of dogs, *latratus*.

bark, v. *latrare*.

barley, *hordeum*.

barn, *horreum*.

barracks, *castra* (-orum).

barrel, *cupa*, *seria*, *dolium*, *orca*.

barren, *sterilis*, *infecundus*.

barrenness, *sterilitas*.

barricade, subst. *munimentum*.

barricade, v. *praesepire*, *obstruĕre*, *oppilare*.

barrier, *septum*, *cancelli* (-orum), *claustra* (-orum).

barrister; see advocate.

barrow, *ferculum*.

barter, subst. (*per*)*mutatio mercium*.

barter, v. *merces mutare*.

base, subst. *basis*, *fundamentum*, *radix*.

base, adj. *turpis*; — coin, *nummi adulterini*; — born, *ignobilis*, *humili loco natus*. Adv. *turpiter*.

baseness, *turpitudo*.

bashful, *pudens*, *pudicus*, *verecundus*; adv. *verecunde*.

bashfulness, *pudor*, *verecundia*.

basin, *pelvis*, *trulla*.

basis; see base.

bask, *apricari*.

basket, *corbis*, *qualus*, *sporta*, *calathus*.

bas-relief, *toreuma* (-atis, n.).

bass, (in music), *gravis*.

bastard, *nothus*.

bat: the flying creature, *vespertilio*; for games, *clava*.

batch, *numerus*.

bath, subst. *balineum, balneum, balneae (-arum,* plur.).

bath, bathe, v.: transit. *lavare, abluĕre, perfundĕre*; intransit., *lavari, perlui*.

bath-tub, *alveus*.

battalion, *cohors*.

batter, *pulsare, percutĕre, verberare*.

battering-ram, *aries*.

battery: = assault, *vis*; of artillery, *tormenta (-orum)*.

battle, *proelium, pugna*.

battle-array, *acies*.

battle-axe, *bipennis, securis*.

battle-cry, *clamor*.

battle-field, *locus pugnae*; sometimes *acies*.

battlement, *pinna*.

bawl, *vociferari, clamitare*.

bay, subst.: the tree, *laurea, laurus*; of the sea, *sinus (-ūs)*.

bay, adj. *spadix, badius*.

bay, v. *latrare*.

be, *esse; exsistĕre, exstare*.

beach, *litus*.

beacon: = lighthouse, *pharus*; = fire, *ignis*.

bead, *baca*.

beak, *rostrum*.

beaker, *poculum*.

beam, subst.: of wood, *tignum, trabs*; of light, *radius, iubar*.

beam, v. (*ad*)*fulgēre*.

bean, *faba*.

bear, subst.: the animal, *ursus, ursa*; the constellation, *arctos, septentriones*: the Great —, *ursa major*; the Little —, *ursa minor*.

bear, v.: = carry, *ferre, gestare, portare*; = endure, (*per*)*ferre, pati, sustinēre, tolerare*; = have, (feeling, etc.), *gerĕre*; = produce, bring forth, *parĕre, ferre*.

beard, subst. *barba*.

beard, v.; see defy.

bearer: = porter, *baiulus*; — of letters, *tabellarius*.

beast, *bestia* (wild); *belua; pecus (-udis,* tame); *fera* (wild); *iumentum* (— of burden).

beastliness, *spurcitia*.

beastly, *spurcus, immundus*.

beat, v.: = strike, *ferire, percutĕre, pulsare*; to be beaten, *vapulare*; to beat down, (*pro*)*sternĕre*; —, = overcome, *vincĕre, superare*; intransit., *palpitare, salire*.

beating, subst. *ictus (-ūs), verbera (-um,* plur.).

beau, *homo bellus* or *elegans*.

beautiful, *pulcher, speciosus, formosus, bellus, amoenus* (of landscapes, etc.); adv. *pulchre, belle*.

beautify, (*ex*)*ornare*.

beauty, *pulchritudo, species, forma, amoenitas* (of places).

beaver, *castor, fiber*.

becalmed, *ventis destitutus*.

because, *quod, quia, quoniam*; because of, *propter, ob*.

beck, = nod, *nutus (-ūs)*.

beckon, *digito innuĕre*.

become, v. *fieri, evadĕre*; = to suit, *decēre, convenire*.

bed: for sleeping, *lectus*: to make a —, *lectum sternĕre*; to go to —, *cubitum ire*: of a river, *alveus*.

bedaub, (*ob*)*linĕre, perungĕre*.

bed-clothes, bedding, *stragulum, lodix*.

bedew, *inrorare*.

bedizen, (*ex*)*ornare*.

bedroom, *cubiculum*.

bee, *apis*: — hive, *alvus, alveus*; a swarm of —s, *examen apium*.

beech, *fagus*; adj. *fageus, faginus*.

beef, (*caro*) *bubula*.

beetle, subst. *scarabaeus*.

befall, *accidĕre, contingĕre*.

befit, *convenire, aptum esse, decēre*.

before. Adv.: in space, *prae*; in time, *prius, ante*. Prep.: in space, =in presence of, *coram*; = in front of, *ante*; in time, *ante*. Conj., *antequam, priusquam*.

beforehand, *antea*.

befoul, *inquinare, foedare*.

befriend, *adiuvare, favēre*.

beg, *mendicare*; = to ask earnestly, *precari, orare, rogare*.

beget, *gignĕre, generare, procreare*.

beggar, *mendicus*.

beggarly, *miser, vilis*.

beggary, *egestas, paupertas, mendicitas*.

begin, *incipĕre, ordiri, inchoare*.

beginning, *initium, principium, primordium*; — of a speech, *exordium*; the —s of a science, *elementa (-orum), rudimenta (-orum)*.

beginner, = novice, *tiro*.

begone! *abi! apage te!*

begrudge, *invidēre*.

beguile, *decipĕre, fallĕre*.

behalf: on — of, *pro*.

behave, *se gerĕre*.

behaviour, *mores (-um,* plur.).

behead, *detruncare, obtruncare*; in execution, *securi ferire*.

behind: adv. *pone, post, retro, a tergo*; prep. *pone, post*.

behold, v. *adspicĕre, intueri, contemplari, spectare*.

behold! *en! ecce!*

beholden, = indebted, *obnoxius*.

behove: it behoves, *decet, convenit, oportet*.

being, *natura*; a human being, *homo*.

belated, *serus*.

beleaguer, *obsidēre*.

belie: = misrepresent, *criminari, calumniari*; = refute, *refellĕre, refutare*.

belief, *fides, opinio, persuasio*.

believe, *credĕre, fidem habēre*; = to think, *credĕre, putare, arbitari, opinari*; I firmly —, *mihi persuasum est*.

bell, *tintinnabulum*; sometimes *aes*.

bellow, subst. *mugitus (-ūs)*.

bellow, v. *mugire*.

bellows, *follis*.

belly, *venter, alvus, abdomen*.

belong, *esse*, with genit. or possess. adj.; *attinēre, pertinēre*.

below: adv., *subter, infra*; prep., *infra, subter, sub.*

belt, *cingulum, zona, balteus.*

bench, *scamnum, subsellium*; for rowers, *transtrum.*

bend: transit., *(in)flectěre, inclinare*; intransit., pass. or reflex.

bending, *flexus (-ūs), flexio, inclinatio.*

beneath; see below.

beneficence, *beneficentia, liberalitas.*

beneficent, *liberalis, beneficus.*

beneficial, *utilis, salutaris.*

benefit, subst. *beneficium.*

benefit, v.: transit., *prodesse,(ad)iuvare*; intransit., *proficěre.*

benevolence, *benevolentia.*

benevolent, *benevolus.*

benign, *benignus.*

benignity, *benignitas.*

bent, subst. *animi inclinatio, voluntas.*

bent, adj. *curvus*; bent on a thing, *rei* (genit.) *studiosus, cupidus.*

benumb; to be —ed, *obtorpescěre, torpēre.*

bequeath, *legare.*

bequest, *legatum.*

bereave, *orbare.*

bereaved, *orbus.*

bereavement, *orbitas.*

berry, *baca, bacula, acinus.*

beseech, *orare, implorare, obtestari.*

beset, *obsidēre, urgēre, preměre.*

beside, prep.: = near, *prope, iuxta*; = except, *praeter*; — the point, *nihil ad rem*; — oneself, *sui impotens.*

besides, *praeter (quam)*; as adv. = in addition, *praeterea, ultro.*

besiege, *obsidēre, circumsedēre.*

besmear, *(ob)liněre.*

bespatter, *adspergěre, conspergěre.*

bespeak, *imperare.*

best, *optimus*; see good.

bestir: to bestir oneself, *se (com)movēre, excitare.*

bestow; see give.

bet, subst. *pignus (-oris).*

betake: to betake oneself, *se conferre.*

betimes, *mature.*

betoken, *significare.*

betray, *proděre.*

betrayal, *proditio.*

betrayer, *proditor.*

betroth, *(de)spondēre.*

betrothal, *sponsalia (-ium* or *-iorum).*

better, adj. *melior, potior* (= preferable); I am getting better, *convalesco.*

better, adv. *melius.*

better, v. transit. *meliorem facěre, corrigěre, emendare.*

between, *inter*, with acc.

beverage, *potio, potus (-ūs).*

bevy, *grex.*

bewail, *deplorare, deflēre, (con)queri.*

beware, v. *cavēre.*

bewilder, *(con)turbare.*

bewitch, *fascinare*; see also charm.

beyond: adv., *ultra, supra*; prep., *trans, ultra, extra, praeter.*

bias, subst. *inclinatio animi.*

bias, v. *inclinare* (animum).

bibulous, *bibulus.*

bid, subst. (at a sale), *licitatio.*

bid, v.: = command, *iubēre, imperare*; = invite, *invitare*; at a sale, *liceri.*

bide, *manēre.*

bier, *feretrum, sandapila.*

big, *magnus, grandis, vastus.*

bile, *bilis.*

bilge-water, *sentina.*

bill: of a bird, *rostrum*; = a proposed law, *rogatio*; to bring forward a —, *rogationem ferre*; to reject a —, *antiquare*; to carry a —, *perferre.*

billet, subst., = letter, *epistula.*

billet, v.: to billet troops, *milites per domos disponěre.*

billow, *fluctus (-ūs).*

billowy, *fluctuosus.*

bind, v. *(ad)ligare, vincire*; fig., *obligare, adstringěre*: to — together, *conligare, constringěre*; to — over, *vadari.*

biographer; see historian.

biped, *bipes.*

birch, *betula.*

bird, *avis, volucris, ales*; — catcher, *auceps*; — lime, *viscum.*

birth, *ortus (-ūs)*; of noble —, *nobili genere natus.*

birthday, *dies natalis.*

bishop, *episcopus.*

bit: of a horse, *frenum*; = piece, *frustum.*

bitch, *canis* (femina).

bite, subst., *morsus (-ūs).*

bite, v. *mordēre.*

biting, *mordens, mordax, acidus.*

bitter, *amarus, acerbus, acidus*; adv. *amare, acerbe.*

bitterness, *acerbitas.*

bivouac, subst. *excubiae (-arum).*

black, *ater, niger*; dressed in —, *sordidatus, pullatus, atratus*; a black man, *Aethiops.*

blackberry, *rubus.*

blackbird, *merula.*

blacken, v.: transit., *nigrum facěre*; intransit., *nigrescěre.*

Black Sea, *Pontus Euxinus.*

blacksmith, *faber (ferrarius).*

bladder, *vesica.*

blade: of grass, *herba*; of an oar, *palma*; of a knife, *lamina.*

blame, subst. *culpa, reprehensio, vituperatio.*

blame, v. *reprehenděre, culpare, vituperare.*

blameless, *innocens, integer, sanctus.*

blamelessness, *innocentia, integritas, sanctitas.*

bland, *blandus, lenis, mitis*; adv. *blande.*

blandishment, *blanditia, blandimentum.*

blank, *vacuus.*

blanket, *lodix.*

blast, subst. *flamen, flatus (-ūs).*

blast, v. transit.; see blight.

blaze, subst. *flamma.*

blaze, v. *ardēre, (con)flagrare.*

bleach, *candidum facěre.*

bleak; see cold.

blear-eyed, *lippus*; to be —, *lippire.*

bleat, subst. *balatus (-ūs).*

bleat, v. *balare.*

bleed, v. *sanguinem dare* or *effunděre.*

blemish, subst. *vitium, mendum, macula.*

blemish, v. *(com)maculare.*

blend, (com)miscēre.
bless: in words, bonis ominibus prosequi; in gen., beare, fortunare.
blessed, beatus, fortunatus.
blessedness, felicitas.
blight, subst. robigo.
blight, v. robigine adficěre; of hopes, frustrari.
blind, adj. caecus, oculis captus; adv., = rashly, temere.
blind, v. (oc)caecare, oculis privare.
blindfold, oculis opertis.
blindness, caecitas.
blink, connivēre, nictare.
bliss, felicitas.
blister, pustula.
blithe, laetus, hilaris.
bloated, turgidus, tumidus.
block, subst. stipes, truncus, caudex.
block, v. clauděre, occluděre, opplēre, obstruěre.
blockade, subst. obsessio, obsĭdio.
blockade, v. obsĭdēre, obsidēre, circumvallare.
blockhead; see block.
blood, sanguis, cruor; = birth, race, sanguis, genus.
bloodless, exsanguis, incruentus.
blood-red, cruentus, sanguineus.
blood-relation, consanguineus.
bloodshed, caedes.
bloodshot, sanguine suffusus.
blood-stained, cruentus.
blood-thirsty, sanguinarius.
bloody, cruentus, sanguineus.
bloom, subst. flos.
bloom, v. florēre, vigēre.
blossom; see bloom.
blot, subst.; on paper, litura; in gen. macula, labes.
blot, v. (com)maculare; to — out, delēre, exstinguěre.
blow, subst. ictus (-ūs), plaga.
blow, v. flare; to — into, inflare; to — on, adflare.
blowing, subst. flatus (-ūs).
bludgeon, fustis.
blue, caeruleus.
blunder, subst. error, erratum, mendum.
blunder, v. errare.
blunt, adj. hebes; fig., = rude, agrestis, rusticus; adv., of speech, libere.
blunt, v. transit. hebetare, obtunděre.
blurt out, effutire.
blush, subst. rubor.
blush, v. erubescěre, rubēre.
bluster, subst. declamatio.
bluster, v. declamare, declamitare.
boar, verres; a wild —, aper.
board, subst.: = plank, tabula; = food, victus (-ūs), alimentum; = body of officials, conlegium.
board, v.: to — over, contabulare; to — a ship, navem conscenděre; to — with anyone, apud hominem habitare.
boast, gloriari, (se) iactare.
boaster, iactator, homo gloriosus.
boasting, subst. gloriatio, iactatio.
boastful, gloriosus; adv. gloriose.
boat, linter, scapha, navicula.
boatman, nauta.
bodily, corporeus.

body, corpus (-oris); a — of men, manus, numerus, grex.
bodyguard, stipatores, satellites.
bog, palūs (-ūdis).
boggy, uliginosus, paluster.
bogy, terrĭcula (-orum, plur.).
boil, subst. vomica.
boil, v. transit., coquěre; intransit., fervēre, (ef)fervescěre, (ex)aestuare.
boisterous, turbidus; of weather, turbulentus.
bold, audax, confidens, ferox, animosus; adv. audacter, confidenter, ferociter, animose.
boldness, audacia, confidentia.
bole, truncus, stirps.
bolster, cervical, culcita, pulvinus.
bolt, subst.: = fastening, obex, sera, pessulus; = weapon, telum.
bolt, v. clauděre, occluděre, obserare.
bombast, (verborum) tumor, inflata oratio.
bombastic, inflatus.
bond, vinculum, ligamentum, compes, catena; = legal document, chirographum, syngrapha.
bondage, servitūs (-ūtis), servitium.
bone, os (ossis).
bony, osseus.
book, liber, volumen, codex.
bookseller, bibliopola.
boon, beneficium.
boorish, agrestis, inurbanus, rusticus; adv. rustice, inurbane.
boot, calceus; an army —, caliga.
bootless, inutilis, inritus; adv. frustra.
booty, praeda.
border, margo; of a stream, ripa; of a country, finis.
border, v.; to border on, adiacere, attingěre.
bore, subst. homo importunus or odiosus.
bore, v.: = perforate, perforare, terebrare; = weary, obtundere, defatigare, vexare; I am bored, taedet me.
boredom, taedium.
born: to be —, nasci.
borrow, mutuari, mutuum suměre.
borrowed, mutuus, alienus.
bosom, sinus (-ūs), pectus (-oris), gremium.
boss, umbo, bulla.
botany, (ars) herbaria.
both, ambo; uterque (= each); both . . . and . . ., et . . . et . . ., cum . . . tum . . .
bother, subst. molestia, incommodum.
bother, v.; see annoy; = to take trouble, curare.
bottle, lagena, ampulla.
bottom, fundus, solum; the bottom of the sea, imum mare.
bough, ramus.
bounce, resilire.
bound, subst.: = limit, finis, modus, terminus; = jump, saltus (-ūs).
bound, v.: = limit, (de)finire, terminare; = jump, salire.
boundary, finis, terminus, confinium.
boundless, infinitus, immensus.
bountiful, largus, liberalis; adv. large, liberaliter.
bounty, largitas, liberalitas, munificentia.
bout, certamen; a drinking —, comissatio.

bow, subst.: the weapon, *arcus* (*-ūs*); of a ship, *prora*; = movement of the body, *corporis inclinatio.*

bow, v. *flectĕre, demittĕre, inclinare*; to bow to, *salutare*; fig., *obsequi, obtemperare.*

bowman, *sagittarius.*

bowstring, *nervus.*

bowels, *viscera* (*-um*), *alvus.*

bower, *umbraculum.*

bowl, subst. *crater, cratera, patera.*

bowl, v. *volvĕre.*

box, subst.: = receptacle, *arca, cista, pyxis*; the shrub, *buxus*; adj. *buxeus.*

box, v. intransit. *pugnis certare.*

boxer, *pugil.*

boy, *puer.*

boyhood, *aetas puerilis, pueritia.*

boyish, *puerilis*; adv. *pueriliter.*

brace, subst.: = strap, *fascia, vinculum*; = stay (rigid), *fibula*; = a pair, *par.*

brace, v. (*ad*)*ligare*; mentally, (*con*)*firmare.*

bracelet, *armilla.*

brackish, *amarus.*

brag; see boast.

braid, subst. *limbus*; of hair, *gradus.*

braid, v. *texĕre, nectĕre.*

brain, *cerebrum.*

bramble, *rubus, vepris.*

branch, subst. *ramus.*

branch, v. *dividi.*

brand, subst.: = firebrand, *torris, fax*; = a mark, *nota.*

brand, v. *notam inurĕre, notare.*

brandish, *vibrare, iactare.*

brass, *orichalcum.*

bravado, *iactatio.*

brave, *fortis, strenuus, animosus*; adv. *fortiter, strenue.*

bravery, *fortitudo.*

bravo! *euge! factum bene! macte!*

brawl, subst. *rixa, iurgium.*

brawl, v. *rixari.*

brawny, *robustus, lacertosus.*

brazen, *a*(*h*)*eneus, aereus*; fig., = shameless, *impudens*; — face, *os durum.*

breach, subst.: to make a —, *perfringĕre, discutĕre*; a — of treaty, *foedus ruptum* or *violatum.*

bread, *panis*; = subsistence, *victus* (*-ūs*).

breadth, *latitudo.*

break, subst. *intervallum*; — of day, *prima lux, diluculum.*

break, v. (1) transit. *frangĕre, confringĕre, rumpĕre*; to — open, *refringĕre*; fig., = to weaken, subdue, *domare, frangĕre, infringĕre*; to — a treaty, *foedus violare*; — a promise, *fidem fallĕre.* (2) intransit. *frangi, confringi, rumpi*; to break in, *inrumpĕre*; to — out, *erumpĕre*, fig. *exoriri, exardescĕre, gliscĕre.*

breaker, *fluctus* (*-ūs*).

breakfast, *ientaculum.*

breakwater, *moles.*

breast, *pectus, animus* (fig.).

breast-plate, *lorica, thorax.*

breastwork, *pluteus, lorica.*

breath, *spiritus* (*-ūs*), *anima*; to put out of —, *exanimare.*

breathe, *spirare*; to — again, *respirare*; to — upon, *adflare*; to — out, *exhalare.*

breathless, *exanimatus, exanimis.*

breeches, *bracae*; wearing —, *bracatus.*

breed, subst. *genus* (*-eris*, n.).

breed, v. transit. *gignĕre, generare parĕre, procreare*; intransit., *nasci.*

breeding, *cultus* (*-ūs*).

breeze, *aura.*

brevity, *brevitas.*

brew, *coquĕre*; of trouble, *imminĕre, impendĕre.*

briar; see brier.

bribe, subst. *pretium.*

bribe, v. (*pretio, pecuniā, etc.*) *corrumpĕre.*

briber, *corruptor.*

bribery, *largitio*; or use verb.

brick, *later*; adj. *latericius.*

bridal, adj. *nuptialis.*

bride, bridegroom, (*nova*) *nupta,* (*novus*) *maritus.*

bridge, *pons.*

bridle, *frenum.*

bridle, v. (*in*)*frenare.*

brief, *brevis*; in —, *ne longus sim.* Adv. *breviter, paucis* (*verbis*).

brier, briar, *vepris, dumus, frutex.*

brigade, *legio.*

brigand, *latro.*

bright, *clarus, lucidus, splendidus, fulgens*; of weather, *serenus*; to be —, *clarēre.* Adv. *clare, lucide.*

brighten, v.: transit., *inlustrare, inluminare*; intransit., *clarescĕre.*

brightness, *candor, splendor, nitor fulgor*; of weather, *serenitas.*

brilliant, *splendidus, inlustris, luculentus, praeclarus.*

brim, *ora, margo, labrum.*

Brindisi, *Brundisium.*

brine, *muria, salsamentum.*

bring: by carrying, (*ad*)*ferre,* (*ap*)*portare*; by leading, etc., (*ad*)*ducĕre*: to — back, *referre, reducĕre*; to — together, *cogĕre*; to — about, *efficĕre* (*ut*); to — forward, *in medium proferre*; to — in, yield, *reddĕre*; to — up, *educare.*

brink, *margo, ripa.*

brisk, *alacer, vegetus.*

briskness, *alacritas.*

bristle, subst. *saeta.*

bristle, v. *horrēre.*

bristly, *saetosus.*

brittle, *fragilis.*

broach, *aperire.*

broad, *latus, amplus*; adv. *late.*

broil, subst. *rixa.*

broil, v. *torrēre.*

bronze, subst. *aes.*

bronze, adj. *a*(*h*)*eneus, aereus.*

brooch, *fibula.*

brood, subst. *fetus* (*-ūs*).

brood, v. *incubare.*

brook, subst. *rivus, rivulus.*

brook, v. *ferre, tolerare.*

broom: the plant, *genista*; for sweeping, *scopae* (*-arum*, plur.).

broth, *ius* (*iuris*).

brother, *frater.*

brotherhood, = association, *societas, sodalitas.*
brotherly, *fraternus.*
brow: = eyebrow, *supercilium;* = forehead, *frons;* of a hill, *summus collis.*
brown, *fuscus, fulvus.*
bruise, v. *contundĕre.*
bruit, v. *(di)vulgare.*
brush, subst. *penicillus;* see broom.
brush, v. transit. *verrĕre, (de)tergĕre.*
brush-wood, *virgultum, sarmentum.*
brutal, *ferus, inhumanus, immanis;* adv. *inhumane, immaniter.*
brutality, *immanitas.*
brute, *pecus, belua;* see beast.
bubble, subst. *bulla.*
buccaneer, *pirata, praedo.*
bucket, *situla, hama.*
buckle, *fibula.*
buckler, *scutum, clipeus, parma.*
bud, subst. *gemma, germen.*
bud, v. *gemmare.*
budge, *loco cedĕre.*
buff, *luteus.*
buffalo, *bos.*
buffet, = blow, *alapa, colaphus.*
buffoon, *sannio, scurra.*
buffoonery, *scurrilitas.*
bug, *cimex (-icis).*
bugbear; see bogy.
bugle, *bucina.*
build, *aedificare, (ex)struĕre.*
builder, *aedificator, structor.*
building, subst.: the process, *aedificatio, exstructio;* the thing built, *aedificium.*
bulb, *bulbus.*
bulk, *magnitudo, amplitudo, moles.*
bulky, *amplus, ingens.*
bull, *taurus.*
bullock, *iuvencus.*
bullet, *glans.*
bullion, *aurum, argentum.*
bulrush, *iuncus, scirpus.*
bulwark, *propugnaculum.*
bump, subst.: = swelling, *tumor, tuber;* = bang, *ictus (-ûs).*
bump, v.: to bump into, *offendĕre.*
bumper; see cup.
bunch, of fruit, *racemus, uva;* see bundle.
bundle, *fascis, manipulus, sarcina.*
bung, *obturamentum.*
buoyant, *levis.* Transf., *hilaris.*
burden, subst. *onus (-eris):* beast of —, *iumentum.*
burden, v. *onerare, opprimĕre.*
burdensome, *gravis, molestus.*
bureau, *scrinium.*
burgess, burgher, *municeps, civis.*
burglar, *fur.*
burglary, *furtum.*
burial, *sepultura, humatio.*
burial-ground, *sepulturae locus, sepulcrum.*
burn, v. transit., = set on fire, *incendĕre;* to burn up, *comburĕre, (con)cremare;* intransit., = to blaze, *ardĕre, flagare.*
burnish, *polire.*
burrow, *cuniculus.*
burst, v. transit. *(di)rumpĕre.*
bury, *humare, sepelire.*
bush, *frutex, dumus.*
bushy, *fruticosus.*

bushel, *medimnus.*
business, *res, negotium.*
buskin, *cothurnus.*
bust, *effigies.*
bustle, subst. *festinatio, trepidatio.*
bustle, v. *festinare, trepidare.*
busy, *occupatus, negotiosus;* adv. *sedulo, industrie.*
busy-body, *ardelio.*
but: = except, *praeter;* all but, *tantum non;* = only, *modo, tantum, solum;* as adversat. conj., *sed, verum, at; atqui* (= and yet); *tamen* (= however); but if, *sin, quodsi.*
butcher, *lanius.*
butcher, v. *caedĕre;* of persons, *trucidare.*
butchery, *caedes.*
butler, *cellarius, promus.*
butt, = object of ridicule, *ludibrium.*
butt, v. *arietare, cornu petĕre.*
butterfly, *papilio.*
buttocks, *clunes (-ium), nates (-ium), pyga.*
buttress, v. *fulcire.*
buxom, *hilaris.*
buy, v. *(co)emĕre, mercari.*
buyer, *emptor.*
by: of place, *ad, apud, iuxta, prope;* to go —, *praeterire;* to stand —, *adesse;* of time, — night, *noctu, nocte;* — moonlight, *ad lunam;* of means or manner, *per* with acc.; of agency, *ab (homine);* in adjuration, *per* with acc.; of distribution, one — one, *singuli, singillatim.*
by-way, *trames (-itis), semita, deverticulum.*
by-word: to become a —, *contemptui esse.*

C

cabbage, *brassica, caulis.*
cabin, *casa, tugurium.*
cabinet: = room, *conclave;* = cupboard, desk, etc., *armarium, thesaurus, scrinium.*
cable, *ancorale, funis ancorarius.*
cackle, *strepĕre.*
cadaverous, *exsanguis.*
cadence, *numerus.*
cadet, *tiro.*
Cadiz, *Gades (-ium,* plur.).
cage, *cavea.*
cajolery, *blanditiae (-arum).*
cake, subst. *placenta.*
cake, v.: = stick together, *concrescĕre.*
calamitous, *calamitosus, luctuosus.*
calamity, *calamitas, clades.*
calculate, *computare.*
calculated, *accommodatus, aptus, idoneus.*
calculation, *ratio.*
caldron, *a(h)enum, cortina.*
calendar, *fasti (-orum).*
calf, *vitulus, vitula;* — of the leg, *sura.*
call, subst.: = cry, *vox;* = visit, *salutatio.*
call, v.: = cry out, *clamare;* = name, *vocare, nominare, appellare;* = summon, *(ad)vocare;* to — together.

convocare; to — for, = to demand, (de)*poscere, flagitare*; to — on, = visit, *salutare, visĕre.*

caller, = visitor, *salutator.*

callous, *callosus.* Transf., *durus.*

calm, subst. *quies, tranquillitas, otium, pax*; — at sea, *malacia.*

calm, adj. *quietus, tranquillus, placidus*; adv. *tranquille, placide; aequo animo.*

calm, v. *sedare, lenire, tranquillare.*

calumniate, *calumniari, criminari.*

calumniator, *obtrectator.*

calumny, *criminatio, calumnia.*

camel, *camelus.*

camp, *castra (-orum).*

campaign, *stipendium.*

can, subst.; see jug.

can, v. *posse*; see able.

canal, *fossa.*

cancel, *delēre, tollĕre.*

candid, *liber, apertus, verus, simplex*; adv. *libere, aperte.*

candidate, *candidatus.*

candour, *libertas, candor.*

candle, *candela.*

candlestick, *candelabrum.*

cane, subst. *harundo, calamus*; for walking, *baculum*; for correction, *ferula.*

cane, v. (*ferulā*) *verberare.*

canine, *caninus.*

canker, v. *corrumpĕre.*

cannon, *tormentum.*

canoe, *cymba.*

canon, = a rule, *lex, regula, norma.*

canopy, *aulaeum.*

canton, *pagus.*

canvas, in a sail, *carbasus, velum.*

canvass, *ambire.*

canvassing, *ambitio, ambitus (-ūs).*

cap, *pileus, galerus.*

capability, *facultas.*

capable, *aptus, idoneus*; often rendered by *posse.*

capacious, *capax, amplus.*

caparison, *phalerae (-arum,* plur.).

capital, subst.: = chief city, *caput*; or use *urbs* with adj.: of a pillar, *capitulum*; of money, *sors, caput.*

capital, adj., *capitalis*; see excellent, etc.

capitulate; see surrender.

caprice, *libido, levitas.*

capricious, *inconstans, levis.*

captain, *princeps, dux*; of a ship, *navarchus, magister.*

captious, *morosus, difficilis.*

captivate, *capĕre.*

captive, *captus, captivus.*

captivity, *captivitas.*

capture, *capĕre, comprehendĕre.*

car, *carrus, cisium, plaustrum, vehiculum.*

caravan, *comitatus (-ūs).*

carcase, *cadaver.*

card, subst. *charta.*

card, v. *pectĕre.*

care, subst.: = attention, caution, *cura, diligentia*; = anxiety, *cura, sollicitudo*; = management, *cura, curatio.*

care, v.; to — for, — about, *curare.*

career, *curriculum, cursus (-ūs).*

careful, *diligens, accuratus, attentus*; adv. *diligenter, accurate.*

careless, *neglegens.*

carelessness, *imprudentia, neglegentia, incuria.*

caress, subst. *complexus (-ūs)*

caress, v. *blandiri, permulcēre.*

caressing, *blandus.*

cargo, *onus (-eris).*

carnage, *caedus, strages.*

carnal, render by genit. *corporis.*

carnival, *feriae (-arum).*

carousal, *comissatio, potatio.*

carouse, v. *comissari, potare.*

carp, v.: to — at, *carpĕre, vellicare.*

carpenter, *faber (tignarius).*

carpet, *tapeta (-ae), tapeta (-orum), tapetia (-ium).*

carriage: = act of carrying, *gestura*; = bearing, *habitus*; = vehicle, *vehiculum.*

carrier, *gerulus*; letter —, *tabellarius.*

carry, *ferre, portare, vehĕre, gerĕre*; to — out (= perform), *conficĕre, exsequi.*

cart, *plaustrum.*

carve, *caelare, scalpĕre, sculpĕre*: to — meat, *scindere, secare.*

carver, *caelator, sculptor.*

carving, *caelatura, scalptura, sculptura.*

cascade, *aquae ex alto desilientes.*

case: = receptacle, *theca, involucrum*; gram., *casus (-ūs)*; judicial, *causa*; = chance, *res, casus (-ūs).*

casement, *fenestra.*

cash, subst. *pecunia praesens* or *numerata.*

cash, v. *praesenti pecunia solvĕre.*

cashier, v. = discharge, *exauctorare.*

cask, *dolium, cupa.*

casket, *arcula, capsula.*

casque, *galea, cassis.*

cast, subst., = throw, *iactus (-ūs).*

cast, v. *iacĕre, conicĕre, iactare, mittĕre*; to — in metal, *fundĕre*; to be — down, *adfligi.*

castaway, *perditus, profligatus*; by ship-wreck, *naufragus.*

castigate; see punish.

castle, *castellum.*

casual, *fortuitus, forte oblatus*; adv. *forte, casu, fortuito.*

cat, *feles (or felis).*

catalogue, *index.*

catapult, *catapulta.*

cataract, in the eye, *glaucoma*; see also cascade.

catarrh, *gravedo, pituita.*

catastrophe; see disaster.

catch, *capĕre, excipĕre, deprehendĕre, comprehendĕre*; to — up, *adsequi, consequi*; to — fire, *ignem concipĕre.*

categorical, *simplex, definitus.*

category, *genus (-eris), numerus.*

cater, *obsonare.*

caterpillar, *eruca.*

cattle, *boves*; coll., *pecus (-oris)*; a head of —, *pecus (-udis).*

cauldron; see caldron.

cause, subst. *causa; materia* (= occasion, ground); *res* (= case, affair).

cause, v. transit., *facĕre, efficĕre (ut); movēre, excitare.*

causeway, *agger.*

caustic, *mordax, acerbus.*
cauterize, *adurĕre.*
caution, = *care, cautio, cura, prudentia.*
caution, v. *monēre.*
cautious, *providus, prudens, cautus;*
  adv. *prudenter, caute.*
cavalcade, *comitatus (-ūs).*
cavalier = horseman, *eques.*
cavalierly, *adroganter, insolenter.*
cavalry, *equitatus, equites (-um, plur.).*
cave, *caverna, specus, spelunca, antrum.*
cavil; see carp.
cavity; see hole.
cease, *desinĕre, desistĕre.*
ceaseless, *perpetuus, adsiduus;* adv.
  perpetuo, adsidue.
cedar, *cedrus.*
cede, *concedĕre.*
ceiling, *tectum.*
celebrate, *celebrare.*
celebrated, *celeber, clarus, inlustris.*
celebration, *celebratio.*
celebrity, *gloria, laus;* = celebrated
  person, *vir insignis.*
celerity, *celeritas.*
celestial, *caelestis, divinus.*
ceil, *cella, cubiculum.*
cellar, *cella;* a wine — *apotheca.*
cement, subst. *gluten.*
cemetery, *sepulchra (-orum).*
censor, *censor.*
censorious, *severus.*
censure, subst. *reprehensio, vituperatio.*
censure, v. *reprehendĕre, vituperare.*
census, *census (-ūs);* to take a census,
  censēre.
centaur, *centaurus.*
centre, subst. *media pars;* or use
  medius (e.g. the — of the city, *media
  urbs*).
centurion, *centurio.*
century, *centum anni, saeculum.*
ceremonious, *sollemnis.*
ceremony, *ritus (-ūs), caerimonia.*
certain, *certus, stabilis, fidus* (= trustworthy); a — person, *quidam;* to
  know for —, *certo scire.*
certainly, *certo;* in answers, *profecto,
  sane;* = admittedly, *certe, quidem,
  sane.*
certify, *confirmare.*
cessation, *intermissio.*
chafe, v.: transit., *calefacĕre;* intransit., *stomachari, aestuare.*
chaff, *palea.*
chagrin, *aegritudo, stomachus, dolor.*
chain, subst., *catena, vinculum;* =
  series, *series.*
chain, v. *vincire.*
chair, *sella, sedile, cathedra.*
chalice, *calix.*
chalk, *creta.*
challenge, (*ad pugnam*) *provocare*
chamber, *cubiculum.*
champ, *mandĕre.*
champion, *propugnator, defensor.*
chance, *casus (-ūs), fors;* by —, *forte,
  casu.*
chance, v. *accidĕre;* see also happen,
  risk.
change, subst. (*com*)*mutatio, vicissitudo.*
change, v.: transit., (*com*)*mutare,
  convertĕre;* intransit., (*com*)*mutari.*

changeable, *mutabilis, inconstans, varius.*
changeableness, *mutabilitas, varietas.*
changeling, *puer subditus.*
channel, *fossa, canalis, fretum.*
chant, v. *canĕre, cantare.*
chaos, *chaos, confusio, perturbatio.*
chaotic, *confusus, perturbatus.*
chapel, *aedicula, sacellum.*
chapter, of a book, *caput.*
character: = symbol, letter, *littera;*
  = disposition, nature, *natura, ingenium, mores (-um);* = part played,
  persona, partes (-ium); = reputation,
  fama, existimatio.
characteristic, subst. *proprietas.*
characteristic, adj. *proprius;* adj.
  proprie, more suo.
characterize, *notare, designare.*
charcoal, *carbo.*
charge, subst.: = price, *pretium;*
  = command, *mandatum;* = care (of),
  cura, custodia; = accusation, *accusatio, crimen;* = attack, *impetus (-ūs),
  incursus (-ūs).*
charge, v. to — to a person, *homini
  imputare;* to — with a duty, (*homini*)
  committĕre, mandare.; = accuse, *accusare, insimulare;* = attack, *invadĕre,
  impetum facĕre, incurrĕre.*
charger: = dish, *lanx;* = horse, *equus.*
chariot, *currus (-ūs).*
charioteer, *auriga.*
charitable, *benignus, liberalis, beneficus;*
  adv. *benigne, liberaliter.*
charity, *benignitas;* as conduct, *beneficentia, liberalitas.*
Charles, *Carolus.*
charm, subst.: = magic formula,
  carmen; = amulet, *fascinum;* = attraction, *blandimentum, dulcedo, lepor.*
charm, v.: by magic, *fascinare;* see
  delight.
charming, *suavis, lepidus;* of country,
  amoenus.
chart, *tabula.*
chary, *parcus.*
chase, subst. *venatio, venatus (-ūs).*
chase, v. *venari;* = engrave, *caelare.*
chasm, *hiatus (-ūs), specus (-ūs).*
chaste, *castus, pudicus.*
chastise, *castigare;* see punish.
chastisement, *castigatio, animadversio.*
chastity, *castitas, pudicitia.*
chat, subst. *sermo.*
chat, v. *fabulari, garrire.*
chatter, *garrulitas.*
chattering, *garrulus, loquax.*
cheap, *vilis.*
cheat, subst.: = deception, *fraus, dolus;*
  = deceiver, *circumscriptor, fraudator.*
cheat, v. *fallĕre, decipĕre, fraudare.*
check, subst. *impedimentum, mora.*
check, v. *continēre, impedire, reprimĕre.*
cheek, *gena;* puffed out, *bucca.*
cheer, subst.: = shout, *clamor;* to be
  of good —, *bono animo esse.*
cheer, v. = shout, *clamare;* = gladden
  exhilarare, erigĕre.
cheerful, *hilaris, laetus;* adv. *hilare
  laete.*
cheering, subst. *favor.*
cheerless, *tristis, maestus.*

cheese, *caseus*.
chequered, *varius*.
cherish, *fovēre, colēre, tuēri*.
cherry, *cerasus*.
chest, *pectus (-oris)*; = receptacle, *arca, cista*.
Chester, *Deva*.
chestnut, *castanea*.
chew, *mandēre*.
chicanery, *dolus, calumnia*.
chicken, *pullus (gallinaceus)*.
chide, *obiurgare, increpare*.
chiding, *obiurgatio*.
chief, subst. *caput, princeps, dux*.
chief, adj. *primus*; adv. *praecipue*.
chieftain, *regulus*.
child: male, *filius*; female, *filia*: a small —, *infans*; children, *pueri, liberi*.
child-birth, *partus (-ūs)*.
childhood, *pueritia, aetas puerilis*.
childish, *puerilis*; adv. *pueriliter*.
childless, *(liberis) orbus*.
chill, subst. *horror, frigus (-oris)*.
chill, v. *refrigerare*.
chin, *mentum*.
china, use *murra*; adj. *murrinus*.
chink, *rima*.
chip, *assula*.
chirp, *pipilare*.
chisel, subst. *scalprum, caelum*.
chivalrous, *magnanimus*.
chivalry, as an institution, *ordo equester*; as a spirit, *magnanimitas*.
choice, subst. *delectus (-ūs), magnanimitas*.
choice, adj. *electus, eximius*.
choir, *chorus*.
choke, v. *suffocare, animam interclūdere*.
choler; see anger.
choose, v. *eligēre, diligēre*.
chop, *abscidēre, praecidēre*.
chord, *nervus*.
chorus, *chorus*.
Christ, *Christus*.
Christian, *Christianus*.
chronic, *longinquus, diuturnus*.
chronicle, subst. *annales (-ium)*.
chronicle, v. transit., *in annales referre*.
chronicler, *annalium scriptor*.
chronology, *temporum (or rerum) ordo*.
church, *ecclesia*.
churlish, *agrestis, rusticus, inurbanus*.
cinder, *cinis*.
cipher, subst.: = a secret writing, *notae*; = a nobody, *numerus*.
cipher, v. *computare*.
circle, *orbis, circulus*; of people, *corona*.
circuit, *circuitus (-ūs), orbis, circulus*.
circular, *rotundus*.
circulate, v. transit. *circumagēre, dispergēre*; of news, etc., *divulgare*.
circumlocution, *circumitio verborum*.
circumnavigate, *circumvehi (navi)*.
circumscribe, *circumscribēre, definire*.
circumspect, *cautus, providus, prudens*.
circumspection, *cautio, prudentia*.
circumstance, *res, tempus*: according to —s, *pro re (natā)*; in these —s, *quae cum ita sint*.
circumvallation, *circummunitio*.

circumvent, *circumvenire, circumscribēre*.
cistern, *cisterna, lacus, puteus*.
citadel, *arx*.
cite, v. *proferre, memorare*; before a court, *citare, in ius vocare*.
citizen, *civis*.
citizenship, *civitas*.
city, *urbs*.
civic, *civilis, civicus*.
civil: = civic, *civilis, civicus*: — war, *bellum civile, intestinum, domesticum*; = polite, *urbanus*; adv. *urbane*.
civilization, *cultus (-ūs), humanitas*.
civilize, *expolire*.
civilized, *humanus*.
clad, *vestitus*.
claim, v. *postulare, vindicare*; to — back, *repetēre*.
claimant (at law), *petitor*.
clammy, *lentus*.
clamour, subst. *vociferatio, clamor*.
clamour, v. *(con)clamare, vociferari*.
clan, *gens, tribus (-ūs)*.
clandestine, *clandestinus, furtivus*; adv. *clam, furtim*.
clang, subst. *sonus (-ūs), sonitus (-ūs)*.
clang, v. *strepēre, (re)sonare*.
clank, subst. *crepitus (-ūs), strepitus (-ūs)*.
clank, v. *crepare, crepitare*.
clap, subst.: of hands, *plausus (-ūs)*; of thunder, *tonitrus (-ūs)*.
clap, v. *(manibus) plaudēre*.
clash, subst.: = collision, *concursus (-ūs)*; = loud noise, *crepitus (-ūs), strepitus (-ūs)*.
clash, v. *concrepare*; = disagree, *inter se (re)pugnare, dissidēre, discrepare*.
clasp, subst.: = fastener, *fibula*; see also embrace, grasp.
class, *genus (-eris), classis, ordo*.
classical, from the Roman point of view, *Graecus*.
classify, *in genera describēre*.
clatter, subst. *crepitus (-ūs), strepitus (-ūs)*.
clatter, v. *crepare, strepēre*.
clause, *pars, membrum, caput*.
claw, *unguis*.
clay, *argilla*.
clean, adj. *purus, mundus*.
clean, v. *purgare*.
cleanliness, *munditia, mundities*.
clear, adj. *clarus*; of weather, *serenus, lucidus*; of style, *lucidus*; = evident, intelligible, *planus, manifestus*: it is —, *apparet, liquet*. Adv. *clare, plane, manifeste, lucide*.
clear, v. *expedire, purgare*; to — up a matter, *expedire, explicare*.
clearness, *claritas*; of weather, *serenitas*.
cleave: = split, *(dif)findēre, scindēre*; = stick, *(ad)haerēre*.
cleaver, *culter*.
cleft, *rima*.
clemency, *clementia, mansuetudo*.
clement, *clemens, mansuetus, indulgens, lenis*.
clench: to — the fist, *digitos comprimēre*.

clerk, *scriba.*

clever, *sollers, callidus, astutus*; adv. *sollerter, callide, astute.*

cleverness, *sollertia, calliditas.*

client, *cliens, consultor.*

cliff, *scopulus, cautes.*

climate, *caelum.*

climax, *gradatio.*

climb, subst. *ascensus (-ūs).*

climb, v. *scandĕre, ascendĕre, eniti.*

cling, (*ad*)*haerēre, amplecti.*

clip, *tondĕre, praecidĕre, resecare.*

cloak, subst. *amiculum, pallium*; for journeys, *lacerna*; a soldier's —, *sagum.*

cloak, v. *dissimulare, tegĕre.*

clod, *glaeba.*

clog, v. *impedire.*

cloister, *porticus (-ūs).*

close, subst., = end, *finis, exitus.*

close, adj.: = reserved, *taciturnus, tectus*; = niggardly, *parcus*; = near, *propinquus, vicinus, finitimus*; = closely packed, *densus, confertus, artus*; adv. *arte, dense.*

close, adv. *prope, iuxta.*

close, v.: transit., = shut, *claudĕre, occludĕre*; = finish, *finire*; intransit., = be shut, *claudi*; = come to an end, *finiri.*

closeness, = nearness, *propinquitas, vicinitas.*

closet, *cubiculum.*

clot, subst., of blood, *sanguis concretus.*

clot, v. *concrescĕre.*

cloth, *textum, textile.*

clothe, v. *vestire, amicire.*

clothes, clothing, *vestis, vestimenta (-orum).*

cloud, subst. *nubes, nimbus.*

cloud, v. *obscurare.*

cloudless, *serenus.*

cloudy, *nubilus.*

clownish, *rusticus, agrestis.*

cloy, *satiare, saturare.*

club, subst.: = cudgel, *clava, fustis*; = association, *circulus, sodalitas.*

clubfooted, *scaurus.*

clue, *glomus (-eris), filum*; = indication, *indicium.*

clump, *globus.*

clumsiness, *inscitia.*

clumsy, *inhabilis, ineptus, inscitus*; adv. *inepte, inscite.*

cluster, = bunch, *racemus, uva.*

clutch, *comprehendĕre, adripĕre.*

coach; see carriage.

coachman, *raedarius, auriga.*

coagulate, v. *coire, concrescĕre.*

coal, *carbo*; a live —, *pruna.*

coalesce, *coalescĕre, coire.*

coalition, *coniunctio, consociatio.*

coarse, *crassus*; of behaviour, etc., *incultus, inurbanus.* Adv. *crasse*; *inculte.*

coarseness, *crassitudo*; *mores inculti.*

coast, subst. *litus (-oris), ora*; on the —, adj., *maritimus.*

coast, v. *oram legĕre, praetervehi.*

coat, *toga, tunica*; = hide, *vellus (-eris), pellis.*

coax, *blandiri, permulcēre.*

cobble, (*re*)*sarcire.*

cobbler, *sutor.*

cock, *gallus (gallinaceus).*

code, *leges.*

coerce, *coercēre, cohibēre, cogĕre.*

coercion, *coercitio, vis.*

coffer, *cista, arca.*

coffin, *arca, capulus.*

cog, of a wheel, *dens.*

cogency, *pondus (-eris), vis.*

cogent, *firmus, validus, gravis.*

cogitate, *cogitare.*

cognizance, *cognitio.*

cognizant, *conscius.*

coheir, *coheres.*

cohere, *cohaerēre.*

coherent, *cohaerens, contextus, congruens.*

cohort, *cohors.*

coin, *nummus.*

coin, v. transit. *cudĕre, signare.*

coinage, *res nummaria.*

coincide, *congruĕre, eodem tempore fieri.*

coincidence, = chance; q.v.

Colchester, *Camulodunum.*

cold, subst. *frigus (-oris), algor*; in the head, *gravedo.*

cold, *frigidus, gelidus*: to be —, *frigēre, algēre*; adv. *frigide, gelide.*

collapse, v. *conlabi, concidĕre, corruĕre.*

collar, subst. *monile, torques.*

collate, v. transit. *conferre.*

collation: = comparison, *conlatio*; = meal, *cena.*

colleague, *conlega.*

collect, v.: transit. *conligĕre, congerĕre*; to — money, etc., *exigĕre*; intransit., *convenire, coire.*

collection, *conlatio, congeries.*

college, *conlegium, societas, sodalitas.*

collide, *confligĕre.*

collision, *concursus (-ūs), concursio.*

collocation, *conlocatio.*

colloquial; — speech, *sermo humilis.*

colloquy, *conloquium.*

collusion, *conlusio, praevaricatio.*

Cologne, *Colonia Agrippina.*

colonel, *tribunus militum, praefectus.*

colonist, *colonus.*

colonnade, *porticus (-ūs).*

colony, *colonia.*

colossal, *vastus, ingens.*

colour, subst. *color*; = paint, *pigmentum.*

colour, v. *colorare, tingĕre, inficĕre*; intransit., see blush.

colt, *eculeus.*

column: = pillar, *columna*; milit., *agmen.*

comb, *pecten*; of a cock, *crista.*

comb, v. (*de*)*pectĕre.*

combat, subst. *pugna, certamen.*

combat, v.: see fight.

combination (*con*)*iunctio, societas.*

combine, v. transit. (*con*)*iungĕre, consociare.*

come, *venire, pervenire, advenire, accedĕre*; to — about, *fieri*; to — back, *redire*; to — together, *convenire*; to — upon, *invenire.*

comedy, *comoedia.*

comeliness, *venustas, decor, pulchritudo.*

comely, *bellus, venustus, pulcher.*

comet, *cometes (-ae).*

comfort, subst.; = consolation, *sola-tium, consolatio*; —s, *commoda (-orum)*.
comfort, v. *(con)solari, adlevare*.
comfortable, *commodus*.
comforter, *consolator*.
comic, comical: = of comedy, *comicus*; = ridiculous, *ridiculus, facetus*; adv. *ridicule, facete*.
coming, subst. *adventus (-ūs)*.
command, subst.; = right to give orders, *imperium*; supreme —, *summa imperii*; = an order given, *imperium, iussum, mandatum*; a — of the senate, *decretum*.
command, v. *(hominem) iubērē, (homini) imperare*; of places, = dominate, *imminēre, despectare*.
commander, *dux, imperator, praefectus*.
commemorate, *celebrare*.
commemoration, *celebratio*.
commence, *incipēre*; see begin.
commend: = commit, entrust, *commendare, committēre, credēre*; = praise, *laudare, commendare, probare*.
commendable, *laudabilis*.
commendation, *commendatio, laus*.
commendatory, *commendaticius*.
comment, subst. *dictum*.
comment, v. *sententiam dicēre, censēre*.
commentator, *interpres, explanator*.
commerce, *commercium, negotia (-orum), mercatura*.
commiserate, *(com)miserari*; see pity.
commissariat, *res frumentaria, commeatus (-ūs)*.
commission, subst. = allotted task, *mandatum*; = position of trust, *munus (-eris)*.
commission, v. *mandare*.
commit: = entrust, *mandare, commendare, committēre, credēre*; = do, perpetrate, *facēre, committēre, patrare*; = oblige, engage, *obligare, obstringēre*.
committee, *consilium*.
commodious, *commodus, opportunus, aptus*; adv. *commode, opportune, apte*.
commodity, *res, merx*.
common, subst. *ager publicus*.
common, adj.: = belonging to several or all, *communis*; = belonging to people or state, *publicus*; = commonplace, ordinary, *vulgaris, quotidianus*; the — people, *plebs*. Adv., = usually, *fere, ferme, plerumque*.
commonplace, subst. *locus communis*.
commonwealth, *respublica, civitas*.
commotion, *tumultus (-ūs), motus (-ūs)*.
commune, *conloqui*.
communicate, *communicare*; see also share, tell.
communication, *communicatio*.
communicative, *loquax*.
communion, *commercium, societas*.
community, = state, society, *civitas, respublica*.
commute; see exchange.
compact, subst. *pactio, pactum, conventus (-ūs)*.
compact, adj. *densus, crassus, confertus*; adv. *confertim*.
companion, *comes, socius, sodalis*.
companionable, *adfabilis, facilis*.
company, *societas*; milit., *manipulus*.

comparable, *comparabilis*.
comparative, *comparativus*.
compare, *comparare, componēre, conferre*.
comparison, *comparatio, conlatio*; in — with, *prae, ad*.
compass, subst.: = extent, *ambitus (-ūs), circuitus (-ūs)*; a pair of —es, *circinus*.
compass, v.; see encompass, accomplish.
compassion, *misericordia*.
compassionate, *misericors*.
compatible, *congruens, conveniens*.
compatriot, *civis*.
compel, *cogēre, compellēre, adigēre*.
compendious, *brevis*.
compensate; to — for, *compensare, rependēre*.
compensation, *compensatio*.
compete, *contendēre, certare*.
competent: see able: to be —, *competēre*.
competition, *contentio, certamen, certatio*.
competitor, *competitor*.
compile, *componēre*.
complacent, *qui sibi placet*.
complain, *(con)queri*.
complaint, *questus (-ūs), querimonia, querela*; = illness, *morbus*.
complaisance, *obsequium, obsequentia, indulgentia*.
complaisant, *indulgens, facilis, obsequens*.
complement, *complementum*.
complete, adj. *absolutus, perfectus, iustus*; adv. *omnino, prorsus*.
complete, v. *complēre, explēre, absolvēre, conficēre*.
completion, *confectio, absolutio, finis*.
complex, *multiplex*.
complexion, *color*.
compliance, *obsequium*.
complicate, *impedire*.
complicated, *involutus, impeditus*.
complication, *implicatio*.
compliment, *laus*; to pay —s, *laudare*.
complimentary, *honorificus*.
comply, v. *obsequi, (con)cedēre, morem gerēre*.
components, *partes (-ium)*.
compose: = make up, constitute, *componēre, efficēre*; of literature, *componēre, scribēre*.
composed, = calm, *tranquillus*.
composer, *scriptor*.
composition: the act, *compositio*; literary, *scriptio, scriptura*; the product, *scriptum*.
composure, *tranquillitas, aequus animus*.
compound, adj. *compositus, multiplex*.
compound, v. *miscēre, confundēre*.
comprehend: = contain, *continēre, complecti*; = understand, *(mente) comprehendēre, complecti, intellegēre*.
comprehension, *comprehensio, intellegentia*.
comprehensive, *late patens*.
compress, *comprimēre, condensare*.
compression, of style, *compressio*.
compromise, v.: = to settle, *componēre*,

compromittĕre; = to embarrass, *impedire*.

compulsion, *vis, necessitas*; under —, *coactus -a -um*.

compunction, *paenitentia*.

compute, *computare*.

comrade, *socius, comes, sodalis*.

comradeship, *sodalitas, contubernium*.

concave, *(con)cavus*.

conceal, *celare, occulĕre, occultare, abdĕre*.

concede, *(con)cedĕre, permittĕre*.

conceit; render by *sibi placĕre*.

conceive: physically, *concipĕre*; mentally, *concipĕre, intellegĕre, comprehendĕre*.

concentrate: = bring together, *conligĕre, contrahĕre*; to — on, = attend to, *(animum) attendĕre*.

conception: physical, *conceptio, conceptus (-ūs)*; mental, *notio, opinio*.

concern, subst.: = affair, *res, negotium*; = anxiety, *cura, anxietas, sollicitudo*.

concern, v. *pertinēre, attinēre*; it —s, *interest, refert*.

concerning, = about, *de*.

conciliate, *conciliare*.

conciliation, *conciliatio*.

conciliatory, *pacificus, blandus*.

concise, *brevis, pressus, adstrictus*; adv. *adstricte, breviter*.

conciseness, *brevitas*.

conclave; see assembly.

conclude: = finish, *finire, conficĕre*; = draw a conclusion, *concludĕre, conligĕre*.

conclusion, *finis, conclusio*.

conclusive, *gravis, certus*.

concoct, *miscēre*; fig., *fingĕre, excogitare, conflare*.

concoction, *potus (-ūs)*.

concord, *concordia, consensus (-ūs)*.

concordant, *concors*.

concourse, *concursus (-ūs), concursio*.

concrete, = solid, *solidus*.

concur, *consentire, congruĕre*.

concurrence, *consensio, consensus (-ūs)*.

concurrently, *una, simul*.

condemn, *damnare, condemnare*.

condemnation, *damnatio, condemnatio*.

condense, v. transit., *densare, spissare*; intransit., *concrescĕre*.

condensed, *densus, spissus, concretus*; of style, *pressus, densus*.

condescend, *se submittĕre, descendĕre*.

condescending, *comis, facilis*.

condescension, *comitas, facilitas*.

condign, = due, *debitus, meritus*.

condiment, *condimentum*.

condition: = state, *condicio, status (-ūs)*; = stipulation, *condicio, pactum, lex*.

conditioned, adj. *adfectus*.

condole, *casum (hominis) dolēre*.

conduce, *conducĕre (ad rem)*.

conducive, *utilis*.

conduct, subst.: = behaviour, *vita, mores (-um, plur.)*; = management, *administratio*.

conduct, v.: = lead, *(de)ducĕre*; = manage, *gerĕre, administrare*.

conductor, *dux*.

conduit, *canalis*.

cone, *conus, meta*.

confederacy, f *lus (-eris, n.), societas*.

confederates, *socii, foederati*.

confer: = give, *conferre, tribuĕre*; = talk, *conloqui, consultare*.

conference, *conloquium*.

confess, *fateri, confiteri*.

confession, *confessio*.

confidant, *conscius (f. conscia)*.

confide: = entrust, *committĕre, mandare, credĕre*; to — in, *(con)fidere*.

confidence, *fides, fiducia, confidentia*.

confident, *(con)fidens*; adv. *(con)fidenter*.

confidential; see secret.

confiding, adj. *credulus*.

confine, subst. *finis, terminus, confinium*.

confine, v. *includĕre, coercēre, cohibēre*.

confined, adj. *artus*.

confinement, *inclusio*; = imprisonment, *custodia*.

confirm, *(con)firmare*; = ratify, *sancire, ratum facĕre*.

confiscate, *publicare*.

confiscation, *publicatio*.

conflagration, *incendium, ignis*.

conflict, subst. *certamen, pugna*.

conflict, v.: = fight, *pugnare, certare, contendĕre*; = differ, *dissentire, discrepare, repugnare*.

confluence, *confluens* or plur. *confluentes*.

conform, *obsequi, obtemperare*.

conformable, *accommodatus, congruens*.

conformation, *conformatio, forma, figura*.

conformity, *convenientia*; in — with, *ex, secundum*.

confound; = confuse, *confundĕre*; = astonish, *obstupefacĕre*; = frustrate, *frustrari*.

confront, v. *obviam ire, se opponĕre*.

confuse, *confundĕre, (per)miscēre, (per)turbare*.

confused, *confusus, perplexus*; adv. *confuse, perplexe*.

confusion, *confusio, perturbatio*.

confute, *refellĕre, redarguĕre, confutare*.

congeal: transit. *congelare*; intransit. *concrescĕre*.

congenial, *gratus, concors*.

congratulate, *gratulari*.

congratulation, *gratulatio*.

congregate, *congregari, convenire, confluĕre*.

congregation, *conventus (-ūs), coetus (-ūs)*.

congress, *conventus (-ūs), concilium*.

conjecture, subst. *coniectura, opinio*.

conjecture, v. *augurari, conicĕre, coniectare*.

conjugal, adj. *coniugalis*.

conjugate, gram., *declinare*.

conjugation, gram., *declinatio*.

conjure, v.: transit., = entreat, *obtestari, obsecrare*; to — up, *(mortuorum) animas elicĕre*; intransit., =perform tricks, *praestigiis uti*.

conjurer, *magus, praestigiator*.

connect, *adligare, (con)iungĕre, conectĕre*.

connexion, *coniunctio*; between persons, *societas, necessitudo*; by marriage, *adfinitas*.

connive, *connivēre*, (*rem*) *dissimulare*.

connivance, *indulgentia*.

connoisseur, *iudex, existimator*.

conquer, (*de*)*vincēre, superare*.

conqueror, *victor*.

conquest, *victoria*.

consanguinity, *consanguinitas*.

conscience, *conscientia*.

conscientious, *religiosus, sanctus*; adv. *religiose, sancte*.

conscientiousness, *religio, sanctitas, fides*.

conscious, = aware, *gnarus, conscius*; adv., render by adj. *prudens*.

consciousness, *sensus* (-*ūs*).

conscript: see recruit.

conscription, *delectus* (-*ūs*).

consecrate, *consecrare, dedicare*.

consecrated, *sacer*.

consecration, *consecratio, dedicatio*.

consecutive, *continens, continuus*; adv. *continenter*.

consent, subst. *consensus* (-*ūs*).

consent, v. *velle*.

consequence: = result, *exitus* (-*ūs*), *eventus* (-*ūs*); in — of, *ex, propter*; = importance, *momentum, auctoritas*.

consequently, *itaque, ergo, igitur*.

conserve, (*con*)*servare*; of fruit, *condire*.

conservative, polit., *qui nihil in republica immutari vult*.

consider: = think about, *considerare, expendēre, deliberare, contemplari*; = take into account, *respicēre*; to — that, *arbitrari, ducēre*; = to regard as, *ducēre, habēre, existimare*.

considerable, *magnus, gravis*; adv. *aliquantum*.

considerate, *humanus, officiosus, benignus*.

considerateness, *humanitas, benignitas*.

consideration: = thought, *consideratio, deliberatio, contemplatio*; = proper regard, *ratio, respectus* (-*ūs*).

consign, *committēre, credēre, mandare*.

consist, *consistēre, constare*.

consistent: — with, *consentaneus, congruens*; = unchanging, *constans*; adv. *constanter*.

consolation, *solatium, consolatio*.

console, (*con*)*solari*.

consoler, *consolator*.

consonant, subst., gram., *consonans*.

consonant, adj. *consentaneus, congruens*.

consort, subst. *comes, socius*; = husband or wife, *coniunx*.

consort, v.; to — with, *familiariter uti*.

conspicuous, *conspicuus, clarus, insignis*; adv. *clare*.

conspiracy, *coniuratio*.

conspirator, *coniuratus*.

conspire, *coniurare, conspirare*.

constable, *lictor*.

constancy, *constantia, fides, fidelitas*.

constant, *constans, firmus*; = incessant, *continuus, perpetuus*; = faithful, *fidelis, fidus*. Adv. *constanter*; *semper, perpetuo*.

constellation, *sidus* (-*eris*, n.); *signum*.

consternation, *pavor, terror*.

constitute, = to make up, *componēre, efficēre*; = to establish, *statuēre, constituēre, designare*; = to appoint, *creare, facēre*.

constitution, *constitutio, habitus* (-*ūs*); of a state, *civitatis status* (*ūs*).

constitutional: = natural, *innatus, insitus*; = legal, *legitimus*. Adv. *naturā*; *legitime, e republica*.

constrain, *cogēre, compellēre*.

constraint, *vis*.

construct, *facēre, fabricari*.

construction: As an act, *fabricatio, aedificatio*; = form, plan, *structura, figura, forma*; = interpretation, *interpretatio*; to put a good — on, *rem in bonam partem accipēre*.

construe, *interpretari, accipēre*.

consul, *consul*; ex-consul, *vir consularis*.

consulship, *consulatus* (-*ūs*).

consult, *consultare, deliberare*; to — a person, *hominem consulēre*.

consume, *consumēre, conficēre, absumēre*.

consummate, adj. *summus, absolutus, perfectus*; adv. *summe, absolute, perfecte*.

consummation, *absolutio, perfectio*.

contact, (*con*)*tactus* (-*ūs*).

contagion, *contagio*.

contain, *capēre, habēre, continēre*.

contaminate, *contaminare, inquinare, polluēre*.

contamination, *macula, labes*.

contemplate, *contemplari, intuēri*.

contemplation, *contemplatio*.

contemporary, *aequalis*.

contempt, *contemptus* (-*ūs*), *fastidium*.

contemptible, *contemptus, turpis*.

contend: = to struggle, *contendēre, (de)certare*; = to maintain, *contendēre, confirmare, adfirmare*.

content, subst. *animus contentus*.

content, adj. *contentus*.

content, v. *satisfacēre* (with dat.); to — oneself with saying, *satis habēre dicēre*.

contentedly, *aequo animo*; or use adj. *contentus*.

contentious, *pugnax*.

conterminous, *confinis*.

contest, subst. *certatio, certamen, contentio*.

contest, v. *contendēre*.

context, *argumentum*.

contiguity, *vicinitas, propinquitas*.

contiguous, *confinis, continens*.

continence, *continentia, temperantia*.

continent, subst. *continens*.

continent, adj. *continens, castus*; adv. *continenter, caste*.

contingency, *casus* (-*ūs*).

contingent, subst. *auxilia* (-*orum*).

contingent, adj. *fortuitus, forte oblatus*.

continual, *continuus, perpetuus, adsiduus*; adv. *continenter, adsidue, perpetuo*.

continuance, continuation, *perpetuitas, adsiduitas, diuturnitas*.

continue, v.: transit. *extendēre, producēre, continuare*; intransit., = to persevere, *pergēre, perseverare*; = to last, *durare, (per)manēre*.

continuity, *continuatio, perpetuitas*.

contort, *depravare, distorquēre*.

contortion, *distortio, depravatio*.

contour, *forma, figura*.

contract, subst. *pactum, conductio, locatio, redemptio.*

contract, v.: = draw in, *contrahĕre, adducĕre*; = incur, *contrahĕre*; to — for, *locare, conducĕre,* or *redimĕre*; intransit., = become smaller, *se contrahĕre, minui.*

contracted, *contractus, angustus, brevis.*

contraction, *contractio.*

contractor, *conductor, redemptor.*

contradict, *obloqui, contradicĕre*; fig., *repugnare, discrepare.*

contradictory, *contrarius, repugnans, diversus.*

contrary, subst.: on the —, *contra*; in answers, *immo.*

contrary, adj. *adversus, contrarius.*

contrary to, *contra, praeter,* with acc.

contrast, subst. *diversitas, dissimilitudo.*

contrast, v. transit. *comparare, conferre*; intransit. *discrepare.*

contravene, *violare, frangĕre.*

contribute, v.: = give, *contribuĕre, conferre*; = help, *prodesse, adiuvare.*

contrite, adj.; see penitent.

contrivance: = contriving, *inventio, excogitatio*; = thing contrived, *machina.*

contrive, *excogitare, invenire, fingĕre, efficĕre.*

control, subst. *potestas, imperium, dicio*; self —, *moderatio, temperantia.*

control, v. *moderari, temperare, coercĕre.*

controversial, = disputed, *controversus.*

controversy, *controversia, contentio.*

controvert, *refellĕre, refutare.*

contumacious, *contumax, pertinax*; adv. *contumaciter, pertinaciter.*

contumacy, *pertinacia, contumacia.*

contumelious, *contumeliosus, probrosus.*

contumely, *contumelia.*

convalescent, use verb *convalescĕre.*

convene, *convocare.*

convenience, *commoditas, opportunitas.*

convenient, *commodus, opportunus, accommodatus*; adv. *commode, opportune, accommodate.*

convention: = assembly, *conventus (-ūs)*; = agreement, *foedus (-eris, n.), pactio*; = custom, *mos.*

conventional, *translaticius, usu receptus.*

converge, *coire,* in unum *vergĕre.*

conversant, *versatus, exercitatus, peritus.*

conversation, *sermo, conloquium.*

converse, v. *conloqui, sermonem conferre.*

conversion, (com)*mutatio, conversio.*

convert, v. (com)*mutare, convertĕre*; — to an opinion, *ad sententiam traducĕre.*

convex, *convexus.*

convey: see carry; legal, *transcribĕre, abalienare.*

convict, v. *condemnare, convincĕre.*

conviction, *damnatio*; = belief, *opinio, sententia.*

convince, *persuadĕre.*

convivial, *hilaris.*

conviviality, *hilaritas.*

convoke, *convocare.*

convoy, subst. *praesidium.*

convoy, v. *deducĕre, comitari.*

convulse, *agitare, percutĕre,* (com)*movĕre.*

convulsion, *motus (-ūs), turba*; medical, *convulsio.*

cook, subst. *coquus.*

cook, v. *coquĕre.*

cool, subst. *frigus (-oris, n.).*

cool, adj. *frigidus*; of temper, etc., *lentus* (= phlegmatic), *impavidus* (= undismayed), *impudens* (= impudent). Adv. *frigide; lente.*

cool, v.: transit., *refrigerare*; intransit., *refrigerari, defervescĕre.*

co-operate, una *agĕre*; to — with, *adiuvare.*

co-operation, *opera, auxilium.*

cope, v. *resistĕre, certare*; able to —, *par.*

coping, *fastigium.*

copious, *copiosus, abundans, largus*; adv. *copiose, abundanter, large.*

copiousness, *copia, abundantia.*

copper, subst. *aes.*

copper, adj. *a(h)enus.*

coppice, copse, *silva.*

copy, subst. *exemplum, exemplar.*

copy, v. *imitari*; to — out, *transcribĕre, describĕre.*

cord, *restis, funis.*

cordial, *benignus, comis*; adv. *benigne, comiter.*

cordiality, *benignitas, comitas.*

core, *nucleus, granum.*

cork, subst. *cortex.*

corn, *frumentum*; the price of —, *annona*; = field, *seges.*

corner, *angulus.*

cornet, *cornu, buccina.*

corporal, subst. *decurio.*

corporal, corporeal, adj. *corporeus,* or genit. of *corpus.*

corporation, *municipium, conlegium.*

corps, *manus (-ūs).*

corpse, *cadaver.*

corpulent, *obesus, pinguis.*

correct, adj.; of conduct, *honestus, rectus*; of style, *emendatus, purus*; = true, *verus.* Adv. *recte, honeste; pure; vere.*

correct, v. *corrigĕre, emendare*; see also punish.

correction, *correctio, emendatio*; see also punishment.

correspond, v. *respondĕre, congruĕre*; letter, *litteras dare et accipĕre.*

correspondence: = agreement, *congruentia, convenientia*; = letters, *litterae, epistulae.*

corresponding, *par.*

corroborate, *confirmare, comprobare.*

corroboration, *confirmatio.*

corrode, *rodĕre.*

corrupt, adj. *corruptus, impurus, pravus*; adv. *corrupte, impure, prave.*

corrupt, v. *corrumpĕre, depravare, vitiare.*

corrupter, *corruptor.*

corruptible, = venal, *venalis.*

corruption, *corruptio, depravatio, corruptela.*

corsair, *pirata.*

corslet, *thorax, lorica.*

cortege, *comitatus (-ūs).*

cosmetic, *fucus.*

cost, subst. *pretium, sumptus* (*-ūs*); — of living, *annona.*

cost, v. (con)*stare, venire.*

costly, *carus, pretiosus.*

costume, *vestitus* (*-ūs*), *habitus* (*-ūs*).

cot, *lectulus.*

cottage, *casa, tugurium.*

cottager, *rusticus.*

couch, subst. *lectus, lectulus, cubile.*

couch, v. *cubare, latēre, delitescēre.*

cough, subst. *tussis.*

cough, v. *tussire.*

council, *concilium;* a — of war, *consilium, praetorium.*

councillor, *senator, decurio.*

counsel, = advice, *consilium, auctoritas.*

counsel, v.; see advise.

count: = to number, (e)*numerare, percensēre, computare;* = to consider, *habēre, ducēre;* to — upon, *confidēre.*

countenance, subst.: = face, *vultus* (*-ūs*), *os;* = favour, *favor.*

countenance, v.: = approve, *approbare;* = allow, *permittēre.*

counter, subst.: for counting, *calculus;* in a shop, *mensa.*

counter, adv.: — to, *contra;* to run — to, *adversari.*

counteract, *resistēre.*

counter-balance, (ex)*aequare, compensare.*

counterfeit, adj. *falsus.*

counterfeit, v. *simulare.*

counterpane, *lodix.*

countless, *innumerabilis, inumerus.*

country: opp. to town, *rus:* in the —, *ruri;* = native land, *patria;* = region, *terra, regio.*

country-house, *villa.*

countryman, (*homo*) *rusticus.*

country-town, *municipium, oppidum.*

couple, subst. *par, bini -ae -a.*

couple, v. transit. (con)*iungēre, copulare.*

courage, *fortudo, virtus, animus.*

courageous, *fortis, strenuus, animosus;* adv. *fortiter, strenue.*

courier, *nuntius, tabellarius.*

course, *cursus* (*-ūs*); — of life, *vitae curriculum;* a — of action, *ratio;* of —, *scilicet, sane;* a — at dinner, *ferculum.*

court, subst.: = enclosed space, *area;* a royal —, *aula, regia;* a — of justice, *forum, basilica.*

court, v. transit. *petēre, colēre, captare.*

courteous, *comis, urbanus;* adv. *comiter, urbane.*

courtesy, *urbanitas, comitas.*

courtier, *aulicus.*

cousin, (con)*sobrinus, patruelis.*

covenant, subst. *pactio, pactum, conventio.*

covenant, v. *pacisci.*

cover, subst.: = lid, *operimentum;* = shelter, *perfugium.*

cover, v.: to — up, (con)*tegēre, operire, velare;* = to protect, *protegēre, defendēre.*

covering, *tegmen.*

covert, subst., = thicket, *dumetum.*

covert, adj.: see secret.

covet, *adpetēre, concupiscēre.*

covetous, *avarus, avidus;* adv. *avare, avide.*

covetousness, *avaritia, aviditas.*

cow, subst. *vacca.*

cow, v. *domare.*

coward, *homo ignavus* or *timidus.*

cowardice, *ignavia, timiditas.*

cowardly, *ignavus, timidus.*

cowl, *cucullus.*

coy, *verecundus.*

crab, *cancer.*

crabbed: in temper, *acerbus, morosus;* of style, *implicatus, impeditus.*

crack, subst.: = noise, *crepitus* (*-ūs*), *fragor;* = fissure, *rima.*

crack, v.: transit., *frangēre, findēre, rumpēre;* intransit., = break open, *dissilire, dehiscēre;* = make a noise, *crepare.*

cradle, *cunae* (*-arum*), *cunabula* (*-orum*).

craft: = cunning, *dolus, astutia;* = skill, trade, *ars, artificium;* = boat, *cymba, scapha.*

craftsman, *artifex, opifex.*

crafty, *astutus, callidus, dolosus;* adv. *astute, callide, dolose.*

crag, *scopulus, rupes.*

cram, *farcire, refercire, stipare.*

cramp; see confine.

crane: the bird, *grus;* the machine, *trochlea, tolleno.*

crank, of a machine, *uncus.*

cranny, *rima.*

crash, subst. *fragor, strepitus* (*-ūs*).

crash, v. *strepēre.*

crater, *crater.*

crave; see beg, need.

craving, *desiderium.*

crawl, *repēre, serpēre.*

crazy: = decrepit, *decrepitus, imbecillus;* = deranged, *cerritus.*

creak, v. *stridēre, crepare.*

creaking, subst. *stridor, crepitus* (*-ūs*).

crease, v. *rugare.*

crease, subst. *ruga.*

create, *creare, gignēre, generare, facēre.*

creator, *creator, fabricator, auctor.*

creature, *animal.*

credibility, *fides, auctoritas.*

credible, *credibilis.*

credit, subst. *fides.*

credit, v.: = to believe, *credēre;* to — a thing (to a person), *rem acceptam* (*homini*) *referre.*

creditable, *honestus, honorificus;* adv. *honeste.*

creditor, *creditor.*

credulity, *credulitas.*

credulous, *credulus.*

creek, *sinus* (*-ūs*), *aestuarium.*

creep, see crawl.

crest, *crista, iuba.*

crested, *cristatus, iubatus.*

crestfallen, *demissus.*

crevice; see crack.

crew: on a ship, *nautae* (*-arum*); in gen., *grex.*

crib, *praesepe.*

crime, *scelus* (*-eris*), *delictum, facinus* (*-oris*).

criminal, *scelestus, sceleratus, nefarius:* adv. *nefarie.*

crimson, *coccineus.*
cringe, *adulari.*
cringing, *abiectus.*
cripple, *debilitare, frangĕre, infringĕre.*
crippled, *claudus, mancus, debilis.*
crisis, *discrimen.*
crisp: = curled, *crispus*; = brittle, *fragilis.*
criterion, *norma, obrussa.*
critic, *iudex, criticus, existimator.*
critical: = discriminating, *elegans, subtilis*; = of a crisis, *anceps, dubius.*
criticism, *iudicium.*
criticize; = to judge, *iudicare*; = to find fault with, *reprehendĕre, culpare.*
croak, v. *crocire, queri.*
crockery, *fictilia (-ium).*
crocodile, *crocodilus.*
crocus, *crocus.*
crone, *vetula, anus (-ūs), anicula.*
crook, a shepherd's, *pedum.*
crooked, *pravus*; adv. *prave.*
crookedness, *pravitas.*
crop, subst.: of corn, etc., *messis, fruges (-um)*; of birds, *ingluvies.*
crop, v.: = to browse on, *(at)tondĕre*; = to cut short, *praecidĕre, amputare.*
cross, subst. *crux.*
cross, adj.: = transverse, *transversus, obliquus*; = annoyed, *difficilis, morosus.*
cross, v.: = to go across, *transire, transgredi*; = to oppose, *obsistĕre, adversari*; to — out, *delĕre.*
cross-examine, *interrogare.*
crossing, subst. *transitus (-ūs).*
crouch, *se demittĕre.*
crow, subst. *cornix.*
crow, v. *canĕre.*
crowd, subst. *turba, vulgus, multitudo.*
crowd, v.: transit., *stipare, cogĕre*; intransit., *concurrĕre, congregari.*
crown, subst.: = garland, *corona*; a king's *diadema (-atis)*; fig., = sovereignty, *regnum*; the — of the head, *vertex.*
crown, v. *coronare, diadema (regi) imponĕre.*
crucifixion, *crucis supplicium.*
crucify, *cruci adfigĕre.*
crude: = raw, unripe, *crudus*; = rough, informis, incultus, *rudis*; adv. *inculte.*
cruel, *crudelis, saevus, atrox*; adv. *crudeliter, atrociter.*
cruelty, *crudelitas, saevitia.*
cruise, v. *(per)vagari, circumvectari, navigare.*
crumb, *mica.*
crumble: transit., *comminuĕre, conterĕre*; intransit., render by pass.
crumple, *(con)rugare.*
crush, v. *opprimĕre, contundĕre, conterĕre*; fig., *adfligĕre.*
crust, *crusta.*
crutch, *baculum.*
cry, subst. *clamor, vociferatio*; of distress, *ploratus (-ūs).*
crystal: subst. *crystallus*; adj. *crystallinus.*
cub, *catulus.*
cube, *tessera, cubus.*
cuckoo, *cuculus.*

cucumber, *cucumis.*
cud: to chew the cud, *ruminare, remandĕre.*
cudgel, subst. *baculum, fustis.*
cue, = hint, *signum, indicium.*
cuff, subst.: = blow, *alapa, colaphus*; = sleeve, *manica extrema.*
cuirass, *thorax, lorica.*
culmination, *fastigium.*
culpable, *culpandus.*
culprit; see criminal.
cultivate, *(ex)colĕre, exercĕre.*
cultivation, culture, *cultus (-ūs), cultura*; = education, etc., *humanitas, litterae (-arum).*
cultivator, *cultor.*
cumber, *impedire,(prae)gravare, onerare.*
cumbrous, *gravis, incommodus.*
cunning, subst. *calliditas, astutia, dolus.*
cunning, adj. *callidus, astutus, dolosus*; adv. *callide, astute.*
cup, *poculum, scyphus, calix.*
cup-bearer, *minister, servus.*
cupboard, *armarium.*
cupidity, *cupiditas, avaritia.*
curb, subst. *frenum.*
curb, v. *frenare, coercĕre, cohibēre.*
curdle, v.: transit., *coagulare*; intransit., *concrescĕre.*
cure, subst. *medicina, sanatio.*
cure, v. *sanare, medĕri.*
curiosity, *noscendi studium.*
curious: = inquisitive, *curiosus*; = strange, *insolitus, novus, mirus.*
curl, v. transit. *crispare.*
curling-irons, *calamister.*
curly, *crispus.*
currency, *nummi (-orum).*
current, subst.: in a river, *flumen*; at sea, *aestus (-ūs).*
current, adj.: = this, *hic*; = common, *usitatus, vulgaris*; adv. *vulgo.*
curse, subst.: of speech, *exsecratio, imprecatio*; = malign influence, *pernicies, pestis.*
curse, v. *exsecrari, detestari.*
cursory; see brief.
curt, *brevis, abruptus*; adv. *breviter, praecise.*
curtail, *(co)artare, (im)minuĕre.*
curtain, *velum, aulaeum.*
curve, subst. *flexus (-ūs), sinus (-ūs).*
curve, v. transit. *(in)curvare, (in)flectĕre.*
cushion, *pulvinus, pulvinar.*
custody, *custodia, vincula (-orum).*
custom, *consuetudo, mos, usus (-ūs).*
customary, *usitatus, quotidianus, solitus.*
custom-duty, *vectigal, portorium.*
customer, *emptor.*
cut, v. *secare, caedĕre*; to — corn, etc., *(de)metĕre*; to — down, *succidĕre*; to — off, = destroy, *absumĕre, exstinguĕre*; to — short, *praecidĕre, amputare.*
cutlery, *cultri (-orum).*
cut-throat, *sicarius.*
cutting, adj., of speech, *mordax.*
cuttlefish, *sepia, lolligo.*
cycle, *orbis, circulus.*
cylinder, *cylindrus.*
cymbal, *cymbalum.*
cynic, *cynicus.*

cynical, *mordax*.
cypress, *cupressus*.

D

dabble: to — in, *attingĕre*.
daffodil, *narcissus*.
dagger, *pugio*, *sica*.
daily: adj., *quotidianus*; adv., *quotidie*.
daintiness: = fussiness, *cuppedia*;
= elegance, *venustas*.
dainty: = particular, *fastidiosus*;   =
elegant, *elegans*, *delicatus*.
dale, *vallis*.
dalliance, *lascivia*, *ludus*.
dally: = to linger, *morari*;   = to
sport, *lascivire*, *ludĕre*.
dam, subst.:   = mother, *mater*;   =
breakwater, *moles*, *agger*.
dam, v. *obstruĕre*, *coercēre*.
damage, subst. *damnum*, *incommodum*,
noxa.
damage, v. *laedĕre*, *nocēre*.
dame, *matrona*, *domina*.
damn, *damnare*, *condemnare*.
damp, subst. *umor*.
damp, adj. *umidus*, *udus*.
damp, v. *umectare*; fig., *comprimĕre*,
restinguĕre.
damsel, *puella*, *virgo*.
dance, subst. *saltatio*, *saltatus* (-*ūs*).
dance, v. *saltare*.
dancer, *saltator* (f. *saltatrix*).
dandy, *homo elegans*.
danger, *periculum*, *discrimen*.
dangerous, *periculosus*, *infestus*, *lubricus*;
adv. *periculose*.
dangle, (*de*)*pendēre*.
dank, *umidus*.
Danube, *Danubius*.
dapper, *nitidus*.
dappled, *maculosus*.
dare, *audēre*;   = to challenge, *provocare*.
daring, subst. *audacia*.
daring, adj. *audax*.
dark, subst.; see darkness.
dark, adj. *obscurus*; in colour, *fuscus*,
pullus.   Adv. *obscure*.
darken, v. *obscurare*, *occaecare*.
darkness, *obscuritas*, *tenebrae* (-*arum*),
caligo.
darling, subst. *deliciae* (-*arum*).
darling, adj. *suavissimus*, *mellitus*.
darn, *sarcire*.
dart, subst. *telum*, *iaculum*; to throw
—s, *iaculari*.
dart, v.   = to dash, *provolare*, *se
conicĕre*.
dash, subst.,   = rush, *impetus* (-*ūs*).
dash, v.: transit., to — one thing
against another, *adfligĕre*, *offendĕre*;
to — down, *proruĕre*; intransit., see
dart.
dastardly, *ignavus*.
date, subst.:   the fruit, *palmula*;
= a particular time, *dies*, *tempus*
(-*oris*); out of —, *obsoletus*.
date, v.; to — a letter, *diem in epistula
ascribĕre*.
dative, (*casus*) *dativus*.
daub, (*ob*)*linĕre*, (*per*)*ungĕre*.

daughter, *filia*: — -in-law, *nurus* (-*ūs*).
dauntless, *impavidus*.
dawdle, *cessare*.
dawn, *diluculum*, *prima lux*, *aurora*
(poet.); it is —, *lucescit*.
day, *dies*: at break of —, *prima luce*;
good —, *salve*(*te*);   a period of two
—, *biduum*; on the — before, *pridie*;
on the — after, *postridie*.
day-break; see dawn.
dazzle, *perstringĕre*, *caecare*.
dead, *mortuus*. Transf.,   = dull, *languidus*; at — of night, *nocte intempesta*.
deaden, *hebetare*, *enervare*, *debilitare*.
deadly, *mortifer*, *exitialis*, *perniciosus*.
deaf, *surdus*, *auribus captus*.
deafen, *exsurdare*, *obtundĕre*.
deafness, *surditas*.
deal, v.: to — out, *dividĕre*, *distribuĕre*;
to — with, see treat.
dealer, *mercator*, *negotiator*; a retail —,
institor, *propola*.
dealing, *commercium*, *negotium*, *usus*
(-*ūs*).
dear: = expensive, *carus*, *pretiosus*;
= beloved, *carus*.
dearly,   = at a high price, *care*, *magno
pretio*.
dearness, *caritas*.
dearth, *inopia*, *caritas*, *penuria*.
death, *mors*, *letum*, *obitus* (-*ūs*).
debar, *excludĕre*, *prohibēre*.
debase, *corrumpĕre*, *vitiare*.
debasement, *ignominia*.
debate, subst. *disceptatio*, *disputatio*.
debate, v. *disceptare*, *disputare*.
debauch, subst. *comissatio*.
debauch,   v. *corrumpĕre*,   *depravare*,
vitiare.
debauchery, *stuprum*.
debenture, *syngrapha*.
debility, *infirmitas*, *imbecilitas*, *debilitas*.
debit, v.: to — a thing to a person,
homini rem expensam ferre.
debt, *aes alienum*.
debtor, *debitor*, *obaeratus*.
decade, *decem anni*.
decamp, *discedĕre*.
decant, *diffundĕre*.
decanter, *lagena*.
decapitate; see behead.
decay, *tabes*, *defectio virium*.
decay, v. *marcescĕre*, *senescĕre*, *tabescĕre*.
decease, *obitus* (-*ūs*).
deceit, *fallacia*, *fraus*, *dolus*.
deceitful, *fallax*, *dolosus*, *fraudulentus*;
adv. *fallaciter*, *dolose*.
deceive, *decipĕre*, *fallĕre*, *circumvenire*.
deceiver, *fraudator*.
December, (*mensis*) *December*.
decency, *honestas*, *decentia*, *decorum*.
decent, *honestus*, *decens*, *decorus*; adv.
honeste, *decenter*, *decore*.
deception, *fraus*, *dolus*, *fallacia*.
decide, *statuĕre*, *constituĕre*.
decided, *certus*; of persons, *constans*,
firmus. Adv. *firme*, *constanter*; in
answers, *vero*, *plane*, *sane*.
decimate, *decimare*.
decipher, *explanare*, *explicare*.
decision: = settlement,   *arbitrium*,

sententia; of character, *constantia, firmitas.*

deck, subst. *pons.*

deck, v.; see adorn; a decked ship, *navis constrata.*

declaim, *pronuntiare, declamare.*

declamation, *declamatio, pronuntiatio.*

declaration, *declaratio, praedicatio;* — of war, *belli denuntiatio.*

declare, *declarare, praedicare, pronuntiare;* to — war, *bellum denuntiare* or *indicĕre.*

declension, *declinatio.*

decline, subst. *deminutio.*

decline, v.: = refuse, *recusare, renuĕre;* to — battle, *pugnam detrectare;* = fail, *deficĕre, (de)minui, decrescĕre.*

declivity, *declivitas, clivus.*

decompose: transit., *(dis)solvĕre, resolvĕre;* intransit., *dissolvi, tabescĕre, putrescĕre.*

decomposition, *(dis)solutio, tabes.*

decorate, *(ex)ornare, decorare.*

decoration, *ornatus (-ūs), ornamentum.*

decorous, *decorus;* adv. *decore.*

decoy, subst. *inlex.*

decoy, v. *inlicĕre, adlicĕre, inescare.*

decrease, subst. *deminutio, imminutio.*

decrease, v.: transit., *(de)minuĕre, imminuĕre, extenuare;* intransit., *decrescĕre, (de)minui.*

decree, subst. *decretum, edictum.*

decree, v. *decernĕre, edicĕre, sancire.*

decrepit, *decrepitus.*

decry, *vituperare, obtrectare.*

dedicate, *(de)dicare, consecrare.*

deduce: = derive, *(de)ducĕre;* = infer, *conligĕre, concludĕre.*

deduct, *detrahĕre, deducĕre.*

deduction: = decrease, *deductio, deminutio;* = inference, render by verb.

deed: = action, *factum, res gesta;* = document, *tabula, syngrapha.*

deep, subst. *altum, pontus.*

deep, adj. *altus, profundus;* of sounds, *gravis;* fig., *summus, gravis.* Adv. *alte, penitus; graviter.*

deer, *cervus* (f. *cerva*).

deface, *deformare, foedare.*

defame, *calumniari, obtrectare.*

default: = error, *culpa, peccatum;* = lack, *defectio, inopia;* legal, to let judgment go by —, *vadimonium deserĕre.*

defeat, subst. *clades.*

defeat, v.: see conquer, baffle.

defect, *labes, vitium, mendum.*

defection, *defectio.*

defective, *imperfectus, mendosus, vitiosus;* adv. *imperfecte, mendose, vitiose.*

defence, *defensio, tutela, praesidium.*

defenceless, *inermis.*

defend, *defendĕre, tuĕri.*

defendant, *reus.*

defensive: — weapons, *arma (-orum).*

defer, *differre, proferre, procrastinare;* to — to, *cedĕre, obsequi.*

deference, *observantia, obsequium.*

deferential, *submissus, observans;* adv. *submisse.*

defiance, *provocatio.*

deficiency, *defectio, inopia.*

deficient; see defective.

defile, subst. *angustiae (-arum), fauces (-ium).*

defile, v. *contaminare, maculare, foedare, polluĕre.*

defilement, *macula, labes.*

define, *(de)finire, circumscribĕre.*

definite, *certus, status, definitus;* adv. *certe, certo, definite.*

definition, *(de)finitio.*

deflect, v.: transit., *deflectĕre;* intransit., *declinare, errare.*

deform, *deformare.*

deformed, *distortus, deformatus.*

deformity, *deformitas, pravitas.*

defraud, *(de)fraudare, circumvenire.*

defray, *suppeditare, solvĕre.*

defunct, *mortuus.*

defy, = challenge, *provocare.*

degenerate, adj. *degener.*

degenerate, v. *degenerare, depravari, peior fieri.*

degradation, *ignominia, dedecus (-oris, n.).*

degrade, = lower in rank, *in ordinem cogĕre* (of soldiers), *ex loco movere;* see also disgrace.

degrading, *indignus, indecorus.*

degree: = amount, *gradus (-ūs);* by —s, *gradatim, sensim;* = rank, *gradus, ordo.*

deify, *consecrare, in deorum numerum, referre.*

deign, *dignari, velle,* with infin.

deity, *deus, numen.*

dejected, *maestus, perculsus, adflictus;* adv. *maeste.*

dejection, *maestitia, tristitia, maeror.*

delay, subst. *mora, cunctatio.*

delay, v.: transit., *(re)morari, detinĕre;* intransit., *(com)morari, cunctari.*

delegate, subst. *legatus.*

delegate, v.: = to depute, *legare, adlegare;* = to entrust, *committĕre, mandare.*

deleterious, *noxius.*

deliberate, adj. *consideratus, cogitatus;* adv. *considerate, cogitate, consulto.*

deliberate, v. *deliberare, consulĕre, considerare.*

deliberation, *deliberatio, consultatio;* see also slowness.

deliberative, *deliberativus;* a — body, *consilium.*

delicacy: of taste, etc., *elegantia, subtilitas, humanitas;* of health, *suavitas.*

delicate: = tender, *tener, mollis, delicatus;* in taste, etc., *elegans, subtilis, humanus;* in health, *imbecillus, infirmus;* of tasks, *difficilis.* Adv. *molliter, delicate, eleganter, subtiliter.*

delicious, *suavis, dulcis;* adv. *suaviter.*

delight, subst. *delectatio, voluptas.*

delight, v.: transit., *delectare, oblectare;* intransit., *gaudēre, delectari, oblectari.*

delightful, *iucundus, suavis, gratus;* adv. *iucunde, suaviter, grate.*

delightfulness, *suavitas, incunditas.*

delineate, *describĕre, adumbrare.*

delineation, *adumbratio, descriptio.*

delinquency, *delictum, scelus (-eris, n.).*

delirious, *delirus.*

delirium, *delirium, furor.*

deliver: = to hand over, *prodĕre, dedĕre, tradĕre*; = to utter, *pronuntiare*; see also free.

deliverance, *liberatio, salūs (-ūtis).*

deliverer, *liberator, vindex.*

delivery, *actio, elocutio, dictio.*

dell, *vallis.*

delude, *deludĕre.*

deluge, subst. *eluvio.*

deluge, v. transit. *inundare.*

delusion, *fraus, dolus, fallacia; error.*

delusive, *falsus, fallax, vanus.*

delve, *fodĕre.*

demagogue, *plebicola, plebis dux.*

demand, subst. *postulatio, flagitatio.*

demand, v. *poscĕre, postulare, flagitare.*

demarcation: a line of —, *finis, confinium.*

demean, v.; to — oneself; = to behave, *se gerĕre*; = to stoop, *descendĕre, se demittĕre.*

demeanour, *mores (-um), habitus (-ūs).*

demerit, *culpa.*

demigod, *heros.*

demise, subst. *obitus (-ūs).*

democracy, *reipublicae forma popularis.*

democrat, *plebicola, popularium fautor.*

democratic, *popularis.*

demolish, *demoliri, evertĕre.*

demolition, *demolitio, eversio.*

demonstrate, *demonstrare, docēre, probare.*

demonstration: =proof, *demonstratio*; = display, *ostentatio.*

demoralize: = corrupt, *mores corrumpĕre*; = unnerve, *percellĕre.*

demur: legal, *exceptionem facĕre*; = to hesitate, *dubitare, haesitare.*

demure, *verecundus.*

demurrer, legal, *exceptio.*

den, *specus (-ūs), latibulum.*

denial, *negatio, repudiatio.*

denizen, *incola.*

denominate, *(de)nominare.*

denotation, *significatio.*

denote, *designare, indicare, significare.*

denounce, *increpare, vituperare;* in court, *accusare, nomen deferre.*

dense, *densus, confertus, crassus;* adv. *dense, confertim.*

dent, subst. *nota, vestigium.*

denunciation, *delatio, accusatio.*

deny: = say that . . . not, *negare, infitias ire*; = refuse to give, *negare.*

depart, *abire, discedĕre, digredi.*

department: = office, *munus (-eris, n.); provincia*; = branch, *pars, genus (-eris, n.).*

departure, *abitus (-ūs), discessus (-ūs).*

depend: = to be dependent, *pendēre (ex), positum* or *situm esse (in)*; = to rely on, *(con)fidĕre*; — upon it, *mihi crede.*

dependence, *clientela*; = reliance, *fiducia.*

dependent, subst. *cliens.*

dependent, adj. *obnoxius.*

depict, *depingĕre, describĕre.*

deplorable, *flebilis, miserabilis.*

deplore, *deplorare, deflēre.*

deploy, *explicare, dilatare.*

deport, = to remove, *deportare.*

deportment, *gestus (-ūs), habitus (-ūs), mores (-um).*

depose, *loco movēre;* as a witness, *testari, testificari.*

deposit, v., *(de)ponĕre.*

deposition: = evidence, *testimonium.*

depravation, *depravatio, corruptio.*

deprave, *depravare, corrumpĕre, vitiare.*

depravity, *pravitas, mores corrupti.*

deprecate, *deprecari.*

depreciate, = disparage, *elevare, obtrectare.*

depreciation, *obtrectatio.*

depredation, *latrocinium.*

depress, *premĕre, deprimĕre;* mentally, *animum frangĕre, infringĕre.*

depression, = low spirits, *tristitia.*

deprivation, *privatio, spoliatio.*

deprive, *privare, (de)spoliare.*

deprived, *orbus.*

depth, *altitudo.*

deputation, *legatio, legati (-orum).*

depute, *(ad)legare.*

deputy, *legatus, vicarius.*

derange, *perturbare, conturbare.*

deranged, *demens, insanus.*

derangement, *perturbatio*; =insanity, *dementia, insania.*

deride, *deridēre, inridēre.*

derision, *inrisio.*

derive, *(de)ducĕre, trahĕre.*

derogate; to — from, *derogare, detrahĕre.*

descend, *descendĕre;* of property, *pervenire (ad hominem).*

descendant, *prognatus;* plur. *posteri.*

descent: = movement, *descensus (-ūs);* = slope, *declivitas;* = origin, *origo, genus (-eris, n.).*

describe, *describĕre, depingĕre, explicare.*

description, *descriptio.*

desecrate, *profanare, polluĕre, violare.*

desecration, *violatio.*

desert, subst. *dignitas, meritum.*

desert, subst., = wilderness, *solitudo, vastitas.*

desert, adj. *desertus, solus, vastus.*

desert, v.: = abandon, *deserĕre, (de)relinquĕre, destituĕre;* = change sides, *transfugĕre.*

deserter, *desertor, transfuga.*

desertion, *(de)relictio; transitio ad hostem.*

deserve, *(com)merēre, (com)merēri; dignum esse (re).*

deservedly, *merito, pro meritis, iure.*

deserving, *(re) dignus.*

design, subst.: = outline, form, *descriptio, forma;* = purpose, consilium.

design, v. = delineate, *designare, describĕre;* = intend, *in animo habēre, cogitare.*

designate, *designare, notare, nominare.*

designedly, *consulto, de industria.*

designing, *callidus, astutus, vafer.*

desirable, *optabilis.*

desire, subst. *appetitio, cupiditas, cupido.*

desire, v. *appetĕre, cupĕre, avēre.*

desirous, *cupidus, studiosus.*

desist, *desistĕre, absistĕre.*

desk, *mensa, scrinium.*

desolate, adj. *vastus, desertus.*

desolate, v. *vastare, populari.*

despair, subst. *desperare, spem abicĕre.*

despatch, *litterae (-arum), epistula.*

despatch, v.: = send, *mittĕre*; = complete, finish, *conficĕre, perficĕre*; = hasten, haste, *maturare*; = kill, *interficĕre, interimĕre.*

desperate: = hopeless, *desperatus, exspes*; = dangerous, *periculosus.* Adv. *desperanter.*

desperation, *desperatio.*

despicable, *contemptus.*

despise, *contemnĕre, despicĕre, spernĕre.*

despite: in — of, *contra.*

despond, v. *desperare, animum demittĕre.*

despondency, *animus demissus.*

despot, *tyrannus, dominus.*

despotic, *imperiosus, superbus*; adv. *superbe, tyrannice.*

despotism, *dominatus (-ūs), tyrannis, regnum.*

dessert, *mensa secunda.*

destine, *destinare, constituĕre.*

destiny, *fatum, sors.*

destitute, *inops, egens, privatus.*

destitution, *inopia, egestas.*

destroy, *perdĕre, delĕre, exstinguĕre.*

destruction, *excidium, exstinctio, pernicies.*

destructive, *perniciosus, exitiosus*; adv. *perniciose.*

desuetude, *desuetudo*; to fall into —, *obsolescĕre.*

desultory, *inconstans, levis.*

detach, *separare, seiungĕre, disiungĕre.*

detachment, of troops, *manus (-ūs).*

details, *singula (-orum).*

detail, v. *(singula) explicare, exsequi.*

detain, *tenēre, retinēre.*

detect, *invenire, deprehendĕre.*

detention, *retentio; custodia.*

deter, *deterrēre, absterrēre.*

deteriorate: transit., *depravare, corrumpĕre*; intransit., *in peius mutari.*

deterioration, *deterior condicio.*

determination: = intention, *institutum, consilium*; of character, *constantia, firmitas animi.*

determine, *statuĕre, constituĕre.*

determined, *certus*; = resolute, *constans, firmus.*

detest, *odisse, detestari.*

detestable, *detestabilis.*

detestation, *odium.*

dethrone, *regno expellĕre.*

detract; see derogate, depreciate.

detriment, *damnum, detrimentum.*

detrimental, *perniciosus, iniquus.*

devastate, *(per)vastare, (de)populari.*

devastation, *vastatio; vastitas.*

develop, v. transit., *educare, excolĕre, alĕre*; intransit., *crescĕre, adulescĕre, augeri.*

development, *auctus (-ūs), progressus (-ūs).*

deviate, *declinare, decedĕre, aberrare.*

deviation, *declinatio, digressio.*

device: = emblem, *insigne*; = plan, *machina, dolus.*

devil, *diabolus* (eccl.); go to the —! *abi in malam crucem.*

devious, *devius, vagus.*

devise, *excogitare, fingĕre, machinari*; see also bequeath.

devoid, *vacuus, liber.*

devolve, v.: transit., *deferre, permittĕre, mandare*; intransit., *(per)venire, permitti.*

devote, *devovēre, consecrare, (de)dicare*; fig., *dedĕre, conferre.*

devoted, *deditus, studiosus*; adv. *studiose.*

devotion, = zeal, *studium*; plur., see prayers.

devour, *(de)vorare, consumĕre.*

devouring, *edax.*

devout, *pius (erga deos)*; adv. *pie, sancte.*

dew, *ros.*

dewy, *roscidus.*

dexterity, *dexteritas, sollertia.*

dexterous, *dexter, sollers*; adv. *dext(e)re sollerter.*

diadem, *diadema (-atis, n.).*

diagonal, *diagonalis.*

diagram, *descriptio, forma.*

dial, *solarium.*

dialect, *lingua.*

dialectics, *dialectica.*

dialogue, *dialogus*; in plays, *diverbium*; = conversation, *sermo, conloquium.*

diamond, *adamas.*

diaphragm, *praecordia (-ium, plur.).*

diary, *commentarii diurni.*

dice, die, *talus, tessera*; — box, *fritillus.*

dictate, *dictare*; see also order.

dictator, *dictator.*

dictatorial, *dictatorius, imperiosus*

dictatorship, *dictatura.*

diction, *dicendi* or *scribendi genus (-eris).*

die, v. *mori, (mortem) obire*; of wind, *cadĕre.*

diet, *victus (-ūs), diaeta.*

differ, *discrepare, differre.*

difference, *varietas, diversitas, dissensio.*

different, *alius, diversus, varius*; adv. *aliter, diverse, varie.*

difficult, *difficilis, arduus, impeditus.*

difficulty, *difficultas*; to be in difficulties, *laborare*; with —, *vix, aegre.*

diffidence, *verecundia, diffidentia.*

diffident, *verecundus, diffidens*; adv. *verecunde, diffidenter.*

diffuse, v.: transit., *diffundĕre*; intransit., *diffundi, permeare.*

diffuse, adj. *verbosus, fusus*; adv. *verbose, fuse.*

dig, *fodĕre*; to — up, *effodĕre.*

digest, v. *concoquĕre.*

digger, *fossor.*

dignified, *gravis, augustus.*

dignify, *honestare, honorare.*

dignity, *dignitas, amplitudo, auctoritas maiestas.*

digress, *digredi, aberrare.*

digression, *digressio.*

dike: = earthwork, *moles, agger*; = ditch, *fossa.*

dilapidated, *ruinosus.*

dilapidation, *ruina.*

dilate: = to extend, *dilatare*; in speech, *latius dicĕre.*

dilatory, *tardus, lentus.*

dilemma, in logic, *complexio.*

diligence, *diligentia, industria.*

diligent, *diligens, industrius;* adv. *diligenter, industrie.*

dilute, *aquâ miscēre, diluēre.*

dim, adj. *obscurus, hebes;* to grow —, *hebescēre.*

dim, v. transit., *obscurare, hebetare.*

diminish, v.: transit., *(im)minuēre, deminuēre;* intransit., render by passive.

din, subst. *strepitus (-ūs).*

din, v.: to — into (a person), *(hominis) aures obtundēre.*

dine, *prandēre, cenare.*

dingy, *fuscus, sordidus.*

dining-room, *triclinium.*

dinner, *prandium* (morning), *cena* (evening).

dint: by — of, *per,* or abl.

dip, v.: transit., *tingēre, mergēre;* intransit., *tingi, mergi, vergēre;* to — into a book, *librum attingēre.*

diploma, *diploma (-atis,* n.).

diplomat, *legatus.*

diplomatic, = clever, *astutus, callidus.*

dire, *dirus, atrox.*

direct, adj. *rectus.* Adv. *recte;* = immediately, *statim, confestim.*

direct, v. *regēre, dirigēre, intendēre; gubernare, administrare;* = to show the way, *viam monstrare;* to — a letter, *epistolam inscribēre.*

direction: = course, *cursus (-ūs), via, regio;* = management, *cura, regimen, administratio.*

director, *magister, curator, praefectus.*

dirge, *nenia.*

dirt, *caenum, sordes.*

dirty, adj. *spurcus, sordidus, turpis;* to be —, *sordēre.* Adv. *spurce.*

dirty, v. *inquinare, polluēre.*

disable, *enervare, debilitare.*

disadvantage, *incommodum, iniquitas.*

disadvantageous, *incommodus, iniquus;* adv. *incommode, inique.*

disaffected, *(ab)alienatus, aversus.*

disaffection, *animus alienus* or *aversus.*

disagree, *dissentire, dissidēre.*

disagreeable, *ingratus, gravis, molestus;* adv. *ingrate, graviter, moleste.*

disagreement, *discrepantia, dissensio, dissidium.*

disallow, *vetare.*

disappear, *e conspectu abire, evanescēre.*

disappoint, *frustrari, spem fallēre, spe depellēre.*

disapproval, *improbatio.*

disapprove, *improbare, condemnare.*

disarm, *armis exuēre.*

disarrange, *(per)turbare, confundēre.*

disarrangement, *perturbatio.*

disaster, *clades, calamitas.*

disastrous, *calamitosus, funestus;* adv. *calamitose, funeste.*

disavow, *infitiari, abnuēre.*

disavowal, *infitiatio.*

disband, *exauctorare, dimittēre.*

disbelieve, *non credēre.*

disburden, *exonerare liberare, expedire.*

disc, *orbis.*

discern, *(dis)cernēre, dispicēre.*

discerning, *perspicax, sagax, subtilis, prudens.*

discernment, *prudentia, iudicium, subtilitas.*

discharge, subst., *(di)missio;* = shooting, *emissio, coniectio, coniectus (-ūs).*

discharge, v.: from service, *missum facēre, dimittēre;* = to shoot, *(e)mittēre, conicēre;* = to perform, *(per)fungi.*

disciple, *discipulus, auditor.*

discipline, subst. *disciplina;* sense of —, *modestia.*

discipline, v. *instituēre, exercēre.*

disclaim, *repudiare.*

disclose, *detegēre, aperire, patefacēre.*

disclosure, *patefactio, indicium.*

discolour, *decolorare.*

discomfit, *profligare, adfligēre.*

discomfiture, *clades.*

discomfort, *incommodum.*

disconcert, *percellēre, perturbare.*

disconsolate, *maestus.*

discontent, *molestia, taedium.*

discontinue, *interrumpēre, intermittēre, omittēre.*

discord, = disagreement, *dissensio, dissidium, discordia.*

discordant: in music, *dissonus, absonus;* = disagreeing, *discors, discrepans.*

discount, subst. *deductio, decessio.*

discountenance, *improbare, condemnare.*

discourage, *animum frangēre, infringēre;* to — from, *deterrēre, dissuadēre.*

discourse, subst., = conversation, *sermo, conloquium;* = set speech, *oratio, contio.*

discourse, v.: = to converse, *confabulari, conloqui;* = to make a speech, *orationem habēre, contionari.*

discourteous, *inurbanus, inlepidus;* adv *inurbane, inlepide.*

discourtesy, *inurbanitas.*

discover, v. *invenire, reperire, cognoscēre;* see also disclose.

discoverer, *inventor.*

discovery, *inventio, investigatio;* = thing discovered, *inventum.*

discredit, subst., = disgrace, *dedecus (-oris,* n.), *ignominia.*

discreditable, *inhonestus, turpis.*

discreet, *prudens, cautus;* adv. *prudenter, caute.*

discretion, *prudentia, iudicium.*

discriminate, *diiudicare, discernēre, distinguēre.*

discrimination, *distinctio, discrimen.*

discursive, *varius, vagus.*

discuss, *disceptare, disputare, disserēre.*

discussion, *disceptatio, disputatio.*

disdain, subst. *fastidium, contemptio.*

disdain, v. *spernēre, fastidire, aspernari.*

disdainful, *fastidiosus.*

disease, *morbus.*

diseased, *aeger, aegrotus.*

disembark, v.: transit., *exponēre;* intransit., *egredi.*

disembarkation, *egressus (-ūs).*

disengage, *solvēre, liberare.*

disengaged, *otiosus, vacuus.*

disentangle, *expedire, explicare.*

disfavour, *invidia, offensa.*

disfigure, *deformare.*

disfranchise, *civitatem adimĕre, suffragio privare.*

disgrace, *dedecus (-oris, n.), infamia, ignominia.*

disgrace, v. *dedecorare, dehonestare.*

disgraceful, *turpis, inhonestus, flagitiosus;* adv. *turpiter, inhoneste, flagitiose.*

disguise, *vestis mutata, persona (= mask);* fig., *simulatio.*

disguise, v. *aliena veste occultare;* fig., *dissimulare.*

disgust, subst. *fastidium, taedium, satietas.*

disgust, v. *fastidium (o; taedium) movēre.*

disgusting, *foedus, molestus;* adv. *foede, moleste.*

dish, subst. *patina, lanx.*

dish, v.: to — up, *adponĕre.*

dishearten, *animum frangĕre.*

dishonest, *malus, improbus;* adv. *male, improbe.*

dishonesty, *improbitas, fraus.*

dishonour: see disgrace.

dishonourable, *inhonestus.*

disinclination, *declinatio, animus aversus.*

disinclined, *aversus;* to be —, *nolle.*

disinherit, *exheredare.*

disinherited, *exheres.*

disintegrate, v. transit. *dissolvĕre.*

disinter, *effodĕre, eruĕre.*

disinterested, *suae utilitatis immemor.*

disjoin, *disiungĕre, seiungĕre.*

disjointed, *incompositus;* adv. *incomposite.*

disk, *orbis.*

dislike, subst. *odium, fastidium.*

dislike, v. *fastidire, abhorrēre.*

dislocate, *extorquēre, luxare.*

dislodge, (de)pellĕre, expellĕre, deicĕre.

disloyal, *improbus, infidus, infidelis.*

disloyalty, *infidelitas.*

dismal, *maestus, miser;* adv. *maeste, misere.*

dismantle, *nudare, diruĕre.*

dismast, *malo privare.*

dismay, *consternatio, pavor, terror.*

dismay, v. *consternare, pavefacĕre, (per)terrēre.*

dismember, *discerpĕre.*

dismiss, *dimittĕre, ablegare.*

dismissal, *dimissio.*

dismount, *ex equo desilire.*

disobedience, *contumacia.*

disobey, *non parēre.*

disoblige, *offendĕre.*

disorder, subst. *confusio, turba.*

disorder, v. (per)turbare, miscĕre, confundĕre.

disordered, =sick, *aeger.*

disorderly: =confused, *confusus,* (per)turbatus, perplexus, incompositus; = insubordinate, *turbidus, turbulentus.*

disown, *repudiare, infitiari.*

disparage, *extenuare, elevare, obtrectare.*

disparagement, *obtrectatio.*

disparity, *dissimilitudo, differentia.*

dispassionate, *placidus, placatus, tranquillus.*

dispatch: see despatch.

dispel, *discutĕre, dissipare, dispellĕre.*

dispense, *distribuĕre, dividĕre;* to — with, *(di)mittĕre.*

dispersal, *dissipatio, diffugium.*

disperse, v.: transit., *dissipare, dispergĕre, dispellĕre;* intransit., *dilabi, diffugĕre.*

displace, *loco (suo) movēre.*

display, subst. *ostentatio.*

display, v. *ostentare, ostendĕre.*

displease, *displicēre, offendĕre.*

displeasure, *offensio, offensa.*

disposal, *arbitrium:* at the — of, *penes (with acc.).*

dispose: = to arrange, *ordinare, constituĕre;* = to incline, *inclinare;* see also sell, use, and rid.

disposed, *inclinatus, propensus, pronus.*

disposition: = arrangement, *conlocatio, ordinatio;* = character, *ingenium, indoles, natura.*

dispossess, *possessione depellĕre.*

disproportion, *dissimilitudo.*

disproportionate, *impar.*

disprove, *refellĕre, redarguĕre.*

dispute, subst. *controversia, altercatio, rixa.*

dispute, v. *ambigĕre, disputare;* contendĕre, rixari.

disqualify, = hinder, *impedire.*

disquieted, *inquietus, sollicitus.*

disregard, subst., *neglegentia, incuria.*

disregard, v. *neglegĕre, omittĕre.*

disreputable, *infamis.*

disrepute, *infamia.*

disrespect, *insolentia.*

disrespectful, *insolens.*

dissatisfaction, *molestia, offensa, offensio.*

dissatisfied: I am —, *paenitet me* (with genit.).

dissatisfy, *displicēre.*

dissect, *persecare.*

dissemble, *dissimulare.*

dissembler, *dissimulator.*

disseminate, *spargĕre, dispergĕre.*

dissension, *discordia.*

dissent, subst *dissensio.*

dissent, v. *dissentire, dissidēre.*

dissimilar, *dissimilis, dispar.*

dissimulation, *dissimulatio.*

dissipate, *dissipare.*

dissipated, *dissolutus, luxuriosus.*

dissipation, *luxuria, licentia.*

dissolute; see dissipated.

dissolution, *dissolutio.*

dissolve, v.: transit., *liquefacĕre, (dis)solvĕre;* intransit., *liquescĕre, (dis)solvi.*

dissonant, *dissonus, absonus.*

dissuade, *dissuadēre, dehortari, deterrēre.*

dissuasion, *dissuasio.*

distaff, *colus. f.*

distance, subst. *spatium, intervallum;* at a —, *procul, longe;* from a —, *eminus.*

distance, v. *superare.*

distant, *remotus, longinquus;* to be —, *distare, abesse.*

distaste, *fastidium.*

distasteful, *molestus, ingratus.*

distemper, *morbus.*

distend, *distendĕre.*

distil, v. *stillare*.

distinct: = separate, *separatus, disiunctus*; = clear, *distinctus, clarus, perspicuus*. Adv. *distincte, clare, perspicue*.

distinction, *discrimen, distinctio*; honourable —, *honor, dignitas*; a mark of —, *insigne*.

distinctive, *proprius*; adv. *proprie*.

distinguish, *distinguēre, secernēre, diiudicare*; see also honour.

distinguished, *insignis (prae)clarus*.

distort, *detorquēre, distorquēre*.

distorted, *pravus*.

distract; = to make inattentive, *distrahēre, distinēre*; = to agitate, (per)*turbare*.

distracted, distraught, (per)*turbatus, amens, vecors*.

distraction: see agitation, frenzy.

distrain, v. *bona vendēre*.

distress, subst. *miseria, aerumna, labor*.

distress, v. *angēre, vexare, sollicitare, adflictare*.

distressed, *sollicitus, anxius, adflictus*; to be —, *laborare*.

distressing, *gravis, acerbus*.

distribute, *distribuēre, dividēre*.

distribution, *distributio*.

district, *ager, regio, terra*.

distrust, subst. *diffidentia*.

distrust, v. *diffidēre*.

distrustful, *suspiciosus, diffidens*.

disturb, (per)*turbare, commovēre*.

disturbance, *turba, turbatio, tumultus (-ūs)*.

disturber, *turbator*.

disunion, *dissensio, dissidium, discordia*.

disunite, *seiungēre, secernēre, disiungēre*.

disused, *desuetus*.

ditch, *fossa*.

ditcher, *fossor*.

ditty, *nenia, carmen*.

diurnal, *diurnus*.

dive, *urinari, se (de)mergēre*.

diver, *urinator*.

diverge, *decedēre, discedēre*; of roads, *in diversas partes ferre*.

divergence, *declinatio*.

diverse, *alius, diversus, dissimilis*; adv. *aliter, diverse, dissimiliter*.

diversify, *variare, distinguēre*.

diversion: = turning aside, *derivatio, deductio*; = distracting, *avocatio*; = recreation, *oblectatio, oblectamentum*.

diversity, *diversitas, discrepantia*.

divert: = turn aside, *avertēre*; = amuse, *delectare, oblectare*; see also distract.

divest, *nudare, spoliare, privare*; to — oneself of a thing, *exuēre*.

divide: transit., *dividēre, partiri, distribuēre*; intransit., *dividi, discedēre*.

divination, *divinatio, vaticinatio, auguratio*.

divine, adj. *divinus, caelestis*; adv. *divine, divinitus*.

divine, v. *divinare, vaticinari, augurari, coniectare*.

diviner, *haruspex, hariolus*.

divinity, *divinitas, numen*.

divisible, *dividuus*.

   vision, *partitio, divisio*; = part, *pars*; milit., *legio*.

divorce, subst. *divortium, repudium*.

divorce, v. *divortium facēre*.

divulge, (di)*vulgare, (in medium) proferre, aperire, patefacēre*.

dizziness, *vertigo*.

dizzy, *vertiginosus*.

do, *facēre, efficēre, agēre, gerēre*: how do you —? *quid agis?* he is done for, *de eo actum est*.

docile, *docilis*.

docility, *docilitas*.

dock, subst.: for ships, *navale*; in the —, *reus*.

dock, v.; see curtail.

doctor, subst. *medicus*.

doctor, v. *curare*.

doctrine, *dogma (-atis, n.), disciplina*.

document, *litterae (-arum), instrumentum*.

dodge, v. *eludēre*.

doe, *cerva*.

doer, *actor, auctor*.

doff, *exuēre*.

dog, subst. *canis*; of a —, *caninus*.

dog, v. *indagare, investigare*.

dogged, *pervicax, pertinax*; adv. *pertinaciter*.

dogma, *dogma, placitum*.

doing; see action.

dole, subst. *stips, diaria (-orum), sportula*.

dole, v.; see distribute.

doleful, *tristis, flebilis, maestus*; adv. *flebiliter, maeste*.

dolphin, *delphinus*.

dolt, *stipes, caudex, baro*.

domain: = kingdom, *regnum*; = estate, *possessio*.

dome, *tholus*.

domestic, subst.; see servant.

domestic, adj.; = of the home, *domesticus, familiaris, privatus*; = not foreign, *intestinus, domesticus*.

domesticate; see tame.

domicile, *domicilium, domus*.

dominate, *dominari, regnare*.

domination, *dominatio, dominatus (-ūs)*.

domineer, *dominari*.

domineering, *imperiosus, superbus*.

dominion, *potestas, imperium, dicio*; of a king, *regnum*.

Don, *Tanais*.

donation, *donum*.

doom, subst. *fatum, sors*.

doom, v. *condemnare, damnare*.

door, *ostium, ianua*; back —, *posticum*; out of —s, *foras, foris*.

doorkeeper, *ianitor* (f. *ianitrix*).

doorpost, *postis*.

dormant: to lie —, *iacēre*.

dormitory, *cubiculum*.

dormouse, *glis*.

dose, subst. *potio, medicamentum*.

dose, v. *medicamentum dare*.

dot, *punctum*.

dotage, *senium*.

dotard, *senex, delirus*.

dote, v.: to — upon, *deamare, deperire*.

double, adj. *duplex* (=twofold), *duplus* (=twice as much), *geminus* (=twin).

double, v. *duplicare*; = to sail round. *flectēre, circumvehi*.

doublet, *tunica*.

double-tongued, *bilinguis*.

doubly, *bis*, *dupliciter*.

doubt, subst. *dubitatio*, *scrupulus*.

doubt, v. *dubitare*, *animi pendēre*.

doubtful, adj. *dubius*, *incertus*; adv. *dubie*, *ambigue*, *dubitanter* (= doubtingly).

doubtless, *sine dubio*.

dough, *farina*.

doughty, *fortis*, *strenuus*.

dove, *columba*.

Dover, *Portus Dubris*.

dower, **dowry**, *dos*.

down, subst.: of feathers, etc., *pluma*, *lanugo*; = hill, *collis*, *clivus*.

down: prep., — from, *de*; — stream, *secundo flumine*; adv. rendered by compound verb with *de* —; see downwards.

downcast, *demissus*, *tristis*, *maestus*.

downfall, *(oc)casus (-ūs)*, *ruina*.

downpour, *imber*.

downright, adj.: = complete, *merus*, *summus*; = straight-forward, *simplex*.

downright, adv. *prorsus*, *omnino*.

downtrodden, *adflictus*.

downwards, *desuper*, *deorsum*.

downy, *plumeus*.

doze, v. *dormitare*.

dozen, *duodecim*.

drab, *ravus*; see brown.

drag, v. *trahēre*.

dragon, *draco*, *serpens*.

drain, subst. *fossa*, *cloaca*.

drain, v. *siccare*, *(ex)haurire*.

drama, *fabula*.

dramatic, *scaenicus*.

draper, *qui pannos vendit*.

draught; of drink, *haustus (-ūs)*, *potio*; of air, *spiritus (-ūs)*, *aura*.

draw, v. (1) transit., *trahēre*, *ducēre*; of fluids, *haurire*: to — a sword, *gladium (de)stringēre*; to — tight, *adducēre*, *adstringēre*; = to portray by drawing, *describēre*, *(de)pingēre*; = to induce, *movēre*; to — up (a document), *concipēre*; to — up (troops) *instruēre*. (2) intransit.: to — near, *accedēre*, *appropinquare*; to — back, *recedēre*, *se recipēre*.

draw-bridge, *pons*, *ponticulus*.

drawer: of water, *aquarius*; chest of drawers, *armarium*.

drawing, *pictura*.

dray, *carrus*, *plaustrum*.

dread: see fear.

dream, subst. *somnium*; in a —, *in somno*.

dream, v. *somniare*; to — of, *vidēre in somnis*.

dreamy, *somniculosus*.

dreary, *tristis*, *miser*; adv. *misere*.

dregs, *faex*.

drench, *madefacēre*, *perfundēre*.

dress, subst. *vestis*, *vestitus (-ūs)*, *ornatus (-ūs)*.

dress, v. *vestire*; of food, *coquēre*; of wounds, *curare*.

dressed, *vestitus*; — in black, *sordidatus*; — in white, *albatus*.

dressing, medic., *fomentum*.

drift, subst. = aim, *consilium*, *ratio*.

drift, v. *ferri*, *fluitare*.

drill, subst.: the tool, *terebra*; of troops, *exercitatio*.

drill, v.; = to bore, *perforare*, *terebrare*; = to train, *exercēre*, *exercitare*.

drink, subst. *potio*, *potus (-ūs)*.

drink, v. *bibēre*, *potare*, *haurire* (= drink up); to — to a person, *homini propinare*.

drinker, *potor*, *potator* (habitual).

drinking-bout, *potatio*, *comissatio*.

drip, *stillare*.

drive, subst. *gestatio*.

drive, v. (1) transit., *agēre*, *pellēre*; to — out, *expellēre*, *exturbare*; = to force, *cogēre*, *compellēre*. (2) intransit.: in a carriage, etc., *(in)vehi*, *gestari*; to — at, *petēre*.

drivel: see nonsense.

driver, *raedarius*, *auriga*; of animals, *agitator*.

drizzle, v. *leniter pluēre*.

droll, *lepidus*, *ridiculus*, *facetus*; adv. *lepide*, *ridicule*, *facete*.

drone, *fucus*.

droop, v.: transit., *demittēre*; intransit., *(de)pendēre*; = wither, *languescēre*, *flaccescēre*.

drop, subst. *gutta*, *stilla*.

drop, v.: transit., *demittēre*, *deicēre*; intransit., = fall in drops, *(de)stillare*; = fall to the ground, *delabi*, *decidēre*.

dropsy, *hydrops*.

dross, = refuse; q.v.

drought, *siccitas*.

drove, *grex*, *armentum*.

drover, *pecuarius*, *armentarius*.

drown, *(in aquam) summergēre*; with noise, *obstrepēre*.

drowsy, *somniculosus*, *semisomnus*.

drudge, subst. *servus*, *mediastinus*.

drudge, v. *servire*.

drudgery, *opera servilis*.

drug, subst. *medicamentum*; poisonous —, *venenum*.

drum, *tympanum*.

drunk, *ebrius*, *temulentus*.

drunkenness, *ebrietas*; as habit, *ebriositas*, *vinolentia*.

dry, adj. *siccus*, *aridus*, *sitiens* (= thirsty). Transf., *exilis*, *ieiunus*, *aridus*. Adv., of style, *exiliter*, *ieiune*.

dry, v. transit. *siccare*; to — tears, *abstergēre lacrimas*; intransit., *siccari*, *arescēre*.

dryness, *siccitas*.

dubious; see doubtful.

duck, subst. *anas*.

duck, v. *(sub)mergēre*; to — the head, *caput demittēre*.

dudgeon, *ira*, *stomachus*.

due, subst. *ius (iuris)*, *debitum*; —s, *vectigal*; harbour —s, *portorium*.

due, adj. *debitus*; *meritus*, *iustus*, *idoneus*.

duel, *certamen*.

dulcimer, *sambuca*.

dull, adj. *hebes*, *obtusus*, *tardus*; = uninteresting, *aridus*, *frigidus*. Adv. *tarde*, *frigide*.

dull, v. *hebetare*, *obscurare*, *obtundēre*.

dulness, of mind, *(ingenii) tarditas*, *stupor*.

dumb, *mutus*; to become —, *obmutescēre*.

dumbfounder, *obstupefacĕre.*
dun, adj. *fucus, suffuscus.*
dunce, *stipes.*
dung, *stercus (-oris), fimus.*
dungeon, *carcer, robur.*
dunghill, *sterquilinium.*
dupe, subst. *homo credulus.*
duplicate; see copy.
duplicity, *allacia, fraus.*
durable, *firmus, stabilis, perpetuus;* adv. *firme, stabiliter.*
duration, *temporis spatium.*
during, *per* with acc.; *in* with abl.; *inter* with acc.
dusk, *crepusculum.*
dusky, *fuscus;* see dark.
dust, subst. *pulvis.*
dust, v. *detergēre.*
dusty, *pulverulentus.*
dutiful, *pius, officiosus;* adv. *pie, officiose.*
dutifulness, *pietas.*
duty, *officium, munus;* sense of —, *pietas, religio;* —tax, *vectigal.*
dwarf, *nanus, pumilio.*
dwarfish, *pusillus.*
dwell, *habitare, (in)colĕre.*
dweller, *incola.*
dwelling, *domicilium, sedes, domus.*
dwindle, *(de)minui, decrescĕre.*
dye, v. *tingĕre, inficĕre.*
dyer, *infector.*
dynasty; use phrase with *domus.*
dyspepsia, *cruditas.*
dyspeptic, *crudus.*

E

each: of two, *uterque;* of three or more, *unusquisque, quisque, omnis;* — other, *inter se, alius alium.*
eager, *cupidus, studiosus, acer;* adv. *cupide, studiose, acriter.*
eagerness, *cupiditas, studium, ardor.*
eagle, *aquila.*
ear, *auris;* of corn, *spica, arista.*
early, adj. *matutinus* (= in the morning), *novus* (= fresh), *maturus, tempestivus* (= in good time).
early, adv. *mane* (in the morning); *mature, tempestive.*
earn, *merēre* and *merēri.*
earnest, adj. *intentus, gravis, serius;* in —, *serio.* Adv. *intente, impense.*
earnestness, *studium, contentio.*
earnings, *quaestus (-ūs), lucrum.*
earth: = soil, *terra, solum;* = the globe, *terra, orbis (terrarum).*
earthen, *terrenus.*
earthenware; adj., *fictilis;* subst., *fictilia (-ium).*
earthly, *terrestris; humanus.*
earthquake, *terrae motus (-ūs).*
earthwork, *agger.*
ease, subst. = rest, *tranquillitas, quies, otium, pax;* to be at ease, *quiescĕre;* = readiness, *facilitas.*
ease, v. *exonerare, expedire.*
easiness, *facilitas.*
east, subst. *oriens, orientis (solis) partes.*
eastern, easterly, *orientis;* ad *orientem versus.*

easy, *facilis;* = tranquil *tranquillus, quietus, otiosus.*
eat, *edĕre, (re)vesci;* to — away, *rodĕre.*
eatable, *esculentus.*
eating-house, *popina.*
eaves-dropper, *auceps.*
ebb, subst. *aestūs decessus (-ūs).*
ebb, v. *recedĕre.*
ebony, *hebenus.*
Ebro, *Hiberus.*
ebullition: use *effervescĕre;* of passions, *impetus (-ūs), aestus (-ūs).*
eccentric, *inusitatus.*
echo, subst. *imago vocis.*
echo, v. *vocem reddĕre, resonare;* see also *imitate.*
eclipse, subst. *defectio, defectus (-ūs).*
eclipse, v. transit. *obscurare.*
economical, *frugi, parcus;* adv. *parce.*
economy: = management, in gen., *rei familiaris administratio;* = frugality, *parsimonia.*
ecstasy: = frenzy, *insania, furor;* = bliss, *elatio voluptaria.*
ecstatic, *fanaticus, furens, insanus.*
eddy, *vertex.*
edge, a cutting —, *acies;* = margin, *margo, ora.*
edible, *esculentus.*
edict, *edictum, decretum, iussum*
edify, *docēre.*
edit, (librum) *edĕre.*
educate, *instituĕre, erudire, educare.*
education, *educatio, disciplina, eruditio.*
eel, *anguilla.*
efface, *delēre, abolēre.*
effect, subst. (1), = consequence, *effectus (-ūs), eventus (-ūs), consecutio.* (2), = influence, *vis, effectus (-ūs);* without —, *frustra;* in —, *revera, reapse.* (3), —s, = property, *res, bona (-orum).*
effect, v. *facĕre, efficĕre, conficĕre.*
effective, effectual, *efficiens, efficax;* adv. *efficienter, efficaciter.*
effeminacy, *mollitia, mollities.*
effeminate, *mollis, effeminatus;* adv. *molliter, effeminate.*
effervesce, *effervescĕre.*
effete, *effetus, obsoletus.*
efficacy, *efficientia, vis.*
effigy, *effigies, imago, simulacrum.*
effort, *opera, labor, conatus (-ūs);* to make an —, *operam dare, contendĕre.*
effrontery, *impudentia, os (impudens).*
effulgence, *splendor, fulgor.*
egg, *ovum.*
egoism, egotism, *sui ostentatio, sui amor.*
egoist, egotist, *qui sibi soli studet.*
egregious, *singularis, praeclarus.*
egress, *egressus (-ūs), exitus (-ūs).*
eight, adj. *octo;* — each, *octoni;* — times, *octies.*
eighteen, *duodeviginti.*
eighteenth, *duodevicesimus.*
eighth, *octavus;* an —, *octava pars.*
eightieth, *octogesimus.*
eighty, *octoginta;* — each, *octogeni;* — times, *octogies.*
either, *alteruter, utervis, uterlibet;* either . . . or, *aut . . . aut, vel. . . . vel.*

ejaculate, *vocem emittĕre.*
ejaculation, *vox.*
eject, *expellĕre, eicĕre, deicĕre.*
ejection, *expulsio, eiectio, deiectio.*
eke, v.: to — out, *rei* (dat.) *parcĕre.*
elaborate, adj. *elaboratus, exquisitus;* adv. *exquisite.*
elaborate, v *elaborare, expolire.*
elapse, *intercedĕre, praeterire.*
elated, *elatus.*
elation, *animus elatus; gaudium.*
Elbe, *Albis.*
elbow, *cubitum.*
elder, *maior (natu).*
elderly, *aetate provectus.*
elect, adj. *designatus.*
elect, v. *creare, legĕre, eligĕre.*
election, *electio;* as an occasion, *comitia (-orum).*
electioneering, subst. *ambitio.*
elective, *suffragiis creatus.*
elector, *qui ius suffragii habet.*
elegance, *elegantia, venustas.*
elegant, *elegans, venustus, nitidus;* adv. *eleganter, venuste, nitide.*
elegy, *elegia (-orum).*
element: scientific, *elementum;* =part, *membrum, pars;* the —s of a subject, *elementa (-orum), principia (-orum).*
elementary, *primus.*
elephant, *elephantus, elephas.*
elevate, *(at)tollĕre, extollĕre.*
elevated, of places, *editus, altus;* of spirits, *elatus.*
elevation: = raising, *elatio;* of spirits, *elatio, altitudo;* = rising ground, *locus editus* or *superior.*
eleven, *undecim:* — each *undeni;* — times, *undecies.*
eleventh, *undecimus.*
elicit, *elicĕre, evocare.*
eligible, *opportunus, idoneus, dignus.*
elk, *alces.*
ell, *ulna, cubitum.*
elm, *ulnus.*
elocution, *pronuntiatio.*
elongate; see lengthen.
elope, *clam fugĕre.*
eloquence, *eloquentia, facundia.*
eloquent, *eloquens, facundus;* adv. *facunde, diserte.*
else, adj. *alius.*
else, adv.: = besides, *praeterea;* = otherwise, *aliter, alioqui(n).*
elsewhere, *alibi.*
elucidate; see explain.
elude, *(e)vitare, declinare.*
elusive, *fallax.*
Elysian, *Elysius.*
Elysium, *Elysium.*
emaciate, *attenuare, macerare.*
emaciated, *macer.*
emaciation, *macies.*
emanate, *emanare, effundi.*
emancipate, *liberare;* of slaves, *manumittĕre.*
emancipation, *liberatio;* of slaves, *manumissio.*
emancipator, *liberator.*
embalm, *condire.*
embankment, *agger, moles.*
embark, v.: transit., *imponĕre in navem;* intransit. *conscendĕre (navem).*

embarrass, *(con)turbare, impedire.*
embarrassing, *difficilis.*
embarrassment, *implicatio, conturbatio;* financial —, *angustiae (-arum).*
embassy, *legatio, legati (-orum).*
embellish, *(ex)ornare, decorare.*
embellishment, *decus (-oris, n.), ornamentum.*
embers, *cinis, favilla.*
embezzle, *avertĕre, supprimĕre.*
embezzlement, *peculatus (-ūs), suppressio.*
embezzler, *pecuniae aversor.*
embitter, *exacerbare.*
emblem, *insigne, signum.*
embody: to — troops, *milites conscribĕre;* = to include, *includĕre.*
emboss, *caelare.*
embrace, subst. *amplexus (-ūs), complexus (-ūs).*
embrace, v. *amplecti, amplexari, complecti;* = to contain, *comprehendĕre;* to — an opportunity, *occasionem capĕre;* to — an opinion, *in sententiam transire.*
embrocation, *fomentum.*
embroider, *(acu) pingĕre.*
embroil, *conturbare;* to — in a matter, *re implicare.*
emend, *emendare, corrigĕre.*
emendation, *emendatio.*
emerald, *smaragdus.*
emerge, *emergĕre, exsistĕre.*
emergency, *casus(-ūs), discrimen.*
emigrate, *(e)migrare, demigrare.*
emigration, *(e)migratio.*
eminence: = high ground, *locus editus, tumulus;* = distinction, *praestantia, fastigium.*
eminent, *insignis, (prae)clarus, egregius.* Adv. *egregie, praecipue, imprimis.*
emissary, *legatus, emissarius.*
emit, *(e)mittĕre, iacĕre.*
emolument, *emolumentum, lucrum.*
emotion, *animi motus (-ūs)* or *adfectus (-ūs).*
emperor, *imperator, princeps.*
emphasis, *vis.*
emphatic, *gravis, vehemens;* adv. *graviter, vehementer.*
empire, *imperium, principatus (-ūs).*
employ, *(re) uti; (rem) usurpare, exercĕre, adhibĕre;* of persons, to be —ed, *detineri, versari.*
employment: as an act, *usus (-ūs), usurpatio;* = business, *res, negotium.*
emptiness, *inanitas.*
empty, adj. *inanis, vacuus, vanus, cassus.*
empty, v. *vacuefacĕre, exinanire.*
emulate, *aemulari.*
emulation, *aemulatio.*
emulous, *aemulus;* adv. *certatim.*
enable, *homini rei* (genit.) *facultatem facĕre.*
enact, *(legem) sancire, iubĕre, statuĕre, constituĕre.*
enactment; see law.
enamoured; see love.
encamp, v. *castra ponĕre, considĕre.*
enchant, *(ef)fascinare.* Transf., *capĕre, delectare.*
enchantment; see charm.
enchantress, *venefica.*

encircle, *cingĕre, circumdare.*
enclose, *includĕre, saepire, continĕre.*
enclosure, *saeptum, saepimentum.*
encomium, *laus, laudatio.*
encompass; see encircle.
encounter, subst. *congressus (-ūs), concursio.*
encounter, v. *concurrĕre, congredi, obviam fieri;* = to face unwelcome things, *obire, oppetĕre.*
encourage, *(ad)hortari, confirmare, erigĕre.*
encouragement, *confirmatio, (ad)hortatio.*
encroach, v.: to — on, *occupare, invadĕre.*
encroachment, *iniuria.*
encumber, *onerare, praegravare, impedire.*
encumbrance, *onus (-eris, n.), impedimentum.*
end, subst.: = termination, *finis, exitus (-ūs);* in the —, *tandem, denique;* = aim, object, *finis, consilium, propositum.*
end, v.: transit., *finire, conficĕre, terminare;* intransit., *finem habĕre, desinĕre;* to — well, *bene evenire.*
endanger, *in periculum adducĕre, periclitari.*
endear, *devincire.*
endearments, *blanditiae (-arum, plur.).*
endeavour, subst. *conatus (-ūs), nisus (-ūs).*
endeavour, v. *conari, (e)niti.*
endless, *infinitus, aeternus, perpetuus;* adv. *sine fine, perpetuo.*
endorse; see allow, sanction.
endow: to — a daughter, *dotem filiae dare;* see also give.
endowed, *ornatus, praeditus, instructus.*
endurable, *tolerabilis, patibilis.*
endurance, *patientia, perpessio.*
endure: = to bear, *(per)ferre, sustinēre, pati, perpeti;* = to last, *(per)manēre, durare.*
enemy, *hostis* (public), *inimicus* (personal or private); *adversarius.*
energetic, *acer, strenuus, impiger;* adv. *acriter, strenue, impigre.*
energy, *vis, impetus (-ūs), contentio.*
enervate, *enervare, debilitare, (e)mollire.*
enervation, *debilitatio, languor.*
enforce, *exsequi.*
enfranchise, *in civitatem adscribĕre; civitate donare.*
enfranchisement, *civitas, civitatis donatio.*
engage: = to bind, make liable, *obligare, obstringĕre;* = to promise, undertake, *spondēre, promittĕre, recipĕre;* = to join battle, *confligĕre, congredi.*
engaged: = busy, *occupatus;* — to be married, *sponsus, pactus.*
engagement: = promise, *sponsio, pactum, pactio, promissum;* an — to marry, *pactio nuptialis;* = piece of business, *negotium;* = battle *pugna, proelium.*
engaging, *blandus, suavis.*
engender, *gignĕre, generare.*

engine, *machina, machinatio, machinamentum.*
engineer, *machinator, faber.*
England, *Anglia; Britannia* (= Britain).
English, *Anglus, Anglicus; Britannus, Britannicus.*
engrave, *incidĕre, insculpĕre, scalpĕre.*
engraver, *sculptor.*
engross, = occupy exclusively, *occupare, tenēre.*
engulf, *absorbēre, (de)vorare, (ex)haurire.*
enhance, *augēre, amplificare.*
enhancement, *amplificatio.*
enigma, *aenigma (-atis, n.), ambages (-um).*
enigmatic, *obscurus, ambiguus;* adv. *ambigue, per ambages.*
enjoin; see command.
enjoy, *(re) frui, gaudēre;* = to have, *uti, habēre.*
enjoyment, *gaudium, voluptas.*
enlarge, *amplificare, dilatare, augēre;* to — upon, *pluribus (verbis) disputare.*
enlighten, *inlustrare, inluminare.* Transf., *docēre, erudire.*
enlightenment, *humanitas.*
enlist, v.; transit., of troops, *(con)scribĕre;* in gen., = win over, *conciliare;* intransit., *nomen dare.*
enliven, *excitare, exhilarare.*
enmity, *inimicitia, odium, simultas.*
ennoble, *nobilium ordini adscribĕre; ornare, honestare.*
ennui, *taedium.*
enormity, *immanitas;* = monstrous action, *scelus (-eris, n.), flagitium.*
enormous, *ingens, immanis;* adv. *praeter modum.*
enough, *sat, satis, adfatim;* more than —, *nimis;* not —, *parum.*
enquire; see ask; to — into, *quaerĕre, inquirĕre, cognoscĕre.*
enquiry, *quaestio, inquisitio, cognitio.*
enrage, *inritare, exasperare.*
enrich, *locupletare, ditare.*
enroll, *(ad)scribĕre;* see enlist.
enshrine, *dedicare, consecrare.*
ensign: = banner, *signum, vexillum;* = banner-bearer, *signifer, aquilifer.*
enslave, *(hominem) in servitutem redigĕre.*
enslaved, *servus.* Transf., *addictus, emancipatus.*
ensnare, *capĕre, inretire, inlicĕre.*
entail, *adferre, inferre;* see cause.
entangle, *impedire, implicare.*
entanglement, *implicatio.*
enter, *intrare, introire, inire, ingredi;* to — upon an undertaking, *ingredi, inire, suscipĕre, incipĕre;* to — public life, *ad rempublicam accedĕre;* to — an alliance, *societatem facĕre.*
enterprise, *inceptum, opus (-eris, n.).*
enterprising, *promptus, acer, audax.*
entertain: = to have, *habēre;* = to amuse, *delectare, oblectare;* = to receive hospitably, *hospitio accipĕre, excipĕre.*
entertaining; see amusing.
entertainment: = hospitality, *hospitium;* = banquet, *epulae (-arum) convivium.*
enthusiasm, *studium, fervor, ardor.*

enthusiastic, *fanaticus, ardens, fervidus;* adv. *ardenter, acriter.*

entice, *adlicĕre, adlectare, inlicĕre.*

enticement, *inlecebrae, esca.*

enticing, *blandus.*

entire, *totus, integer, solidus.* Adv. *omnino, plane, prorsus, penitus.*

entitle : =to name, *appellare, nominare;* =to give a title to, *ius* or *potestatem dare.*

entrails, *intestina (-orum), viscera (-um).*

entrance, subst.: as act, *ingressio, introitus (-ūs);* = place of —, *aditus (-ūs), introitus (-ūs), ostium.*

entrap; see ensnare.

entreat, *precari, rogare, orare, obsecrare.*

entrench, *fossā (com)munire, vallare.*

entrenchment, *vallum, munitio, munimentum.*

entrust, *(con)credĕre, committĕre, mandare, commendare.*

entry; see entrance; in accounts, *nomen.*

entwine, *(in)nectĕre, implicare, redimire.*

enumerate, *(di)numerare, enumerare.*

enunciate, *edicĕre, pronuntiare, enuntiare.*

enunciation, *enuntiatio.*

envelope, subst. *involucrum.*

envelope, v. *involvĕre, obducĕre.*

envenom, *venenare, veneno imbuĕre.*

enviable, *fortunatus, beatus.*

envious, *invidus, lividus.*

environs, render by phrase with *loca* and *circum.*

envoy, *legatus.*

envy, subst. *invidia, livor.*

envy, v. *invidēre.*

ephemeral, *unius diei, caducus, brevis.*

epic, *epicus, heroicus;* an — poem, *epos.*

Epicurean, *Epicureus;* = hedonist, *voluptarius.*

epidemic, *morbus, pestilentia.*

epigram, *epigramma (-atis, n.).*

epigrammatic, *salsus.*

epilepsy, *morbus comitialis.*

epilogue, *epilogus.*

episode, *embolium, excursus (-ūs).*

epistle, *epistula, litterae (-arum).*

epitaph, *titulus, elogium.*

epitome, *epitome, summarium.*

epoch, *tempus (-oris, n.), aetas, saeculum.*

equability, *aequus animus, aequabilitas.*

equable, *aequus, aequabilis;* adv. *aequo animo, aequabiliter.*

equal, subst. *par, compar.*

equal, adj. *aequus, aequalis, par, compar;* adv. *aeque, aequaliter, pariter.*

equal, v. *(ad)aequare, aequiparare.*

equality, *aequalitas, aequabilitas.*

equalize, *(ex)aequare, adaequare.*

equanimity, *aequus animus, aequitas animi.*

equestrian, subst. *eques (-itis).*

equestrian, adj. *equester* or *equestris.*

equidistant, to be, *pari intervallo inter se distare.*

equilateral, *aequis lateribus.*

equilibrium, *aequilibrium;* to hold in —, *librare.*

equinox, *aequinoctium.*

equip, *armare, instruĕre, ornare.*

equipment, *arma (-orum), armamenta (-orum), armatura.*

equitable, adj. *aequus, iustus, meritus.*

equity, *aequitas, aequum, iustitia.*

equivalent; see equal.

equivocal, *ambiguus, anceps, dubius.*

equivocate, *tergiversari.*

equivocation, *ambiguitas.*

era, *tempus.*

eradicate, *extirpare, evellĕre, eruĕre.*

erase, *delēre, inducĕre.*

erasure, *litura.*

ere; see before.

erect, adj. *(e)rectus.*

erect, v. *erigĕre, tollĕre;* = build, *aedificare, exstruĕre.*

erection : as act, *aedificatio, exstructio;* = a building, *aedificium.*

erotic, *amatorius.*

err, *errare, vagari; falli* (= be mistaken); *peccare* or *delinquĕre* (= do wrong).

errand, *mandatum.*

erratic, *vagus, inconstans.*

erroneous, *falsus;* adv. *falso, perperam.*

error, *error, erratum; peccatum* (=sin).

erst, *quondam, olim.*

erudite, *litteratus, doctus, eruditus.*

erudition, *doctrina, eruditio.*

eruption, *eruptio.*

escape, subst. *fuga, effugium.*

escape, v. *(ef)fugĕre, elabi, evadĕre.*

escarpment, *vallum.*

eschew, *vitare;* see avoid.

escort, *comitatus (-ūs);* under a person's —, *homine comitante.*

escort, v. *comitari, deducĕre, prosequi.*

esoteric, *arcanus, occultus.*

especial, *praecipuus;* adv. *praesertim, praecipue, maxime.*

espouse; see betroth and marry.

essay, subst.: = attempt, *conatus (-ūs);* = treatise, *libellus.*

essay, v. *conari.*

essence, *natura, vis.*

essential, *verus, proprius;* adv. *reapse, vere, necessario.*

establish : = set up, *statuĕre, instituĕre;* = make strong, *confirmare, stabilire;* = prove, *probare, vincĕre.*

establishment, *constitutio, confirmatio;* = household, *familia.*

estate : = condition, *status (-ūs), habitus (-ūs), condicio, sors;* = property, *res, fundus, praedium.*

esteem, subst. *opinio, existimatio.*

esteem, v.: = think, *existimare, putare;* = respect, *diligĕre, vereri.*

estimable, *bonus, gravis, probus.*

estimate, subst. *aestimatio;* in gen., = judgment, *iudicium.*

estimate, v., = value, *aestimare, censēre.*

estimation; see esteem.

estrange, *(ab)alienare.*

estrangement, *alienatio, discidium.*

estuary, *aestuarium.*

eternal, *aeternus, sempiternus, perpetuus;* adv. *in aeternum, perpetuo.*

eternity, *aeternitas.*

ether, *aether.*

ethereal, *aetherius.*

ethical, *moralis;* or use phrase with *mores.*

ethics, *philosophia moralis*; see ethical.

etiquette, *mos, usus (-ūs).*

eulogy, *laudatio, laus.*

euphemism; render by phrase, such as *mitiorem in partem vertēre dicendo.*

euphony, *sonus dulcis.*

evacuate, *vacuefacĕre, (de)relinquĕre; loco discedĕre.*

evade, *(ef)fugĕre, subterfugĕre.*

evaporate, *in vaporem vertĕre.*

evasion, *ambages (-um), tergiversatio.*

evasive, *ambiguus*; adv. *ambigue.*

even, adj. *aequus, planus*; of numbers, *par.* Adv. *aequaliter, pariter.*

even, adv. *etiam, vel, adeo*: not —, *ne . . . quidem*; — if, *etsi, etiamsi.*

evening, subst. *vesper (-eris or -eri)*; in the —, *vesperi.*

evening, adj. *vespertinus*; the — star, *Hesperus, Vesper.*

evenness, *aequalitas*; of temper, *aequus animus.*

event: = result, *eventus (-ūs), exitus (-ūs)*; = occurrence, *factum, casus (-ūs)*: at all —s, *certe, saltem.*

eventful, *memorabilis.*

ever, adv.: = always, *semper*; = at any time, *umquam (unquam), quando* (after *num* and *si*); for —. in *aeternum, in perpetuum.*

everlasting; see eternal.

every, *quisque, omnis*: — ōne, *unusquisque*; one in — ten, *decimus quisque*; — body, *omnes (-ium), nemo non*; — day, *quotidie*; — thing, *omnia (-ium)*; — where, *ubique, passim.*

evict, *(ex)pellĕre, detrudĕre.*

evidence: legal, *testimonium, indicium*; in gen., *argumentum.*

evident, *manifestus, apertus*; it is —, *apparet, liquet.* Adv. *aperte, manifesto.*

evil, subst. *malum, incommodum.*

evil, adj. *malus, pravus, improbus.*

evil-doer, *maleficus.*

evil-speaking, *maledicus.*

evince, *ostendĕre, probare, praestare.*

evoke, *evocare, elicĕre, excitare.*

evolution: — of soldiers, *decursus (-ūs)*; in nature, *rerum progressio.*

ewe, *ovis femina*; — lamb, *agna.*

ewer, *urceus, hydria, urna.*

exact, *exactus, subtilis, diligens*; adv. *diligenter, accurate, subtiliter.*

exacting, *rapax.*

exaction, *exactio.*

exactitude, *subtilitas, diligentia.*

exaggerate, *augēre, in maius extollĕre.*

exaggeration, *superlatio, traiectio.*

exalt, *augēre, amplificare, (ex)tollĕre.*

exaltation: of feeling, *elatio*; in rank, *dignitatis accessio.*

exalted, *altus, (ex)celsus, elatus.*

examination, *investigatio, inquisitio.*

examine, *investigare, inquirĕre.*

example, *exemplum, exemplar, documentum*; for —, *verbi causa, exempli gratia, vel.*

exasperate *inritare, exasperare.*

exasperation, *ira.*

excavate, *(ex)cavare, effodĕre.*

excavation, *cavum.*

exceed, *excedĕre, egredi.*

excel, *excellĕre, praestare* (with dat).

excellence, *excellentia, praestantia.*

excellent, *excellens, praestans, egregius, optimus*; adv. *excellenter, egregie, optime.*

except, prep. *praeter, extra*; except you, *te excepto.*

except, v. *excipĕre, eximĕre.*

exception, *exceptio*; all without —, *omnes ad unum.*

exceptional, *rarus*; adv. *praeter modum.*

excess: — in quantity, *nimium*; in conduct, *intemperantia, licentia.*

excessive, *nimius, immodicus*; adv. *nimis, immodice, praeter modum.*

exchange, subst. *permutatio*; of money, *collybus.*

exchange, v. *(per)mutare.*

exchequer, *aerarium, fiscus.*

excitable, *inritabilis, fervidus.*

excite, *excitare, concitare, (com)movēre, incendĕre.*

excited, *trepidus.*

excitement, *concitatio, commotio.*

exclaim, *(ex)clamare, vociferari.*

exclamation, *exclamatio, vox.*

exclude, *excludĕre, prohibēre, arcēre.*

exclusive: of persons, *rari aditūs*; of properties, = belonging to one only, *proprius.*

excrescence, *tuber.*

excruciating, *acerbissimus.*

exculpate, *excusare, (ex)purgare.*

exculpation, *purgatio.*

excursion, *iter (-ineris).*

excuse, subst. *excusatio.*

excuse, v.: = make excuses for, *excusare, (ex)purgare*; = pardon, *ignoscĕre, veniam dare.*

execrable; see abominable.

execrate, *execrari, detestari, abominari.*

execute: = carry out, *exsequi, persequi, efficĕre*; = punish by death, *necare, securi ferire.*

execution: = carrying out, *effectio*; = capital punishment, *supplicium*; = slaughter, in gen., *strages, caedes.*

executioner, *carnifex.*

executive: use phrase with *administrare.*

exegesis, *explanatio, interpretatio.*

exemplary, adj.; see excellent.

exempt, adj. *immunis, liber, solutus.*

exempt, v. *excipĕre, eximĕre, liberare.*

exemption, *immunitas.*

exercise, subst. *exercitatio*; = literary task, *thema (-atis).*

exercise, v.: = carry on, *exercēre, facĕre, efficĕre*; = work, train, *exercēre.*

exert, v. *contendĕre, intendĕre*; to — oneself, *niti, eniti, conari.*

exertion, *contentio, conatus (-ūs).*

Exeter, *Isca (Dumnoniorum).*

exhale, *(ex)halare.*

exhalation, *exhalatio.*

exhaust, *exhaurire*; = wear out, *consumĕre, conficĕre.*

exhausted, *confectus, defessus, fatigatus.*

exhaustion; see fatigue.

exhibit, v. *proponĕre, exhibēre*; see show.

exhibition, *spectaculum*, *ludi* (*-orum*).

exhilarate, (*ex*)*hilarare*, *hilarem facĕre*.

exhilaration, *hilaritas*.

exhort, (*ad*)*hortari*.

exigence, *necessitas*, *angustiae* (*-arum*).

exile, subst.: = banishment, *exsilium*, *relegatio*; to be in —, *exsulare*; = person banished, *exsul*.

exile, v. *eicĕre*, *relegare*, (*ex*)*pellĕre*.

exist, *esse*, *existĕre*, *exstare*.

existence; use *esse*.

exit: = going out, *exitus* (*-ūs*); = way out, *exitus* (*-ūs*), *ostium*.

exonerate, (*culpa*) *liberare*.

exorbitant, *immodicus*; adv. *immodice*.

exordium, *exordium*, *prooemium*.

exotic, *peregrinus*, *externus*.

expand, v. transit. (*ex*)*pandĕre*, *extendĕre*, *laxare*.

expanse, *spatium*.

expatiate, *pluribus* (*verbis*) *disputare*.

expatriate; see banish.

expect, *exspectare*, *sperare*.

expectant, *adrectus*, *suspensus*.

expectation, *exspectatio*, *spes*.

expectorate, *exscreare*, *exspuĕre*.

expediency, *utilitas*.

expedient, subst. *ratio*, *consilium*.

expedient, adj. *commodus*, *utilis*: it is —, *expedit*.

expedite, *expedire*, *maturare*.

expedition: = speed, *celeritas*; milit., *expeditio*.

expeditious, *celer*, *promptus*; adv. *celeriter*, *prompte*.

expel, (*ex*)*pellĕre*, *eicĕre*.

expend, *expendĕre*, *impendĕre*.

expense, *impensa*, *impendium*.

expensive, *sumptuosus*, *carus*, *pretiosus*; adv. *sumptuose*, *pretiose*.

expenditure, of public money, *erogatio*; see also expense.

experience, subst. *rerum usus* (*-ūs*), *experientia*; I speak from —, *expertus dico*.

experience, v. *experiri*, *pati*.

experienced, (*rerum*) *peritus*.

experiment, *experimentum*, *periculum*.

expert, *sciens*, *callidus*, *peritus*.

expertness, **expertise**, *calliditas*, *peritia*.

expiate, *luere*, *expiare*.

expiation, *expiatio*, *poena*, *piaculum*.

expiatory, *piacularis*.

expire, *exspirare*; of time, *exire*.

explain, *exponĕre*, *explicare*, *interpretari*.

explanation, *explicatio*, *interpretatio*.

explicit, *apertus*, *definitus*; adv. *plane*, *definite*.

explode: = to discredit (a theory), *explodĕre*, *refellĕre*, *confutare*; intransit., = to burst, *dirumpi*.

export, *exportare*.

exportation, *exportatio*.

exports, *merces* (*quae exportantur*).

expose, *exponĕre*; to danger, etc., *obicĕre*, *offerre*; = to unmask, *detegĕre*.

exposition, *expositio*.

expound; see explain.

express, (in words), *significare*, *declarare*; to — oneself, *loqui*, *dicĕre*.

expression: = thing said, *verbum*, *sententia*, *dictum*, *vox*; of the features, *vultus* (*-ūs*).

expressive, *significans*; adv. *significanter*.

expressiveness, *vis*.

expulsion, *exactio*, *expulsio*.

expunge, *delēre*, *oblitterare*.

expurgate, (*ex*)*purgare*.

exquisite, *exquisitus*, *venustus*; adv. *exquisite*, *venuste*.

extant: to be —, *exstare*.

extempore, *subitus*; to speak —, *ex tempore dicĕre*.

extend, v.; transit., *extendĕre*, *augēre*, *amplificare*; intransit., *patēre*, *extendi*.

extensive, *magnus*, *amplus*, *latus*; adv. *late*.

extent, *ambitus* (*-ūs*), *spatium*; to this —, *hactenus*; to a certain —, *aliqua ex parte*.

extenuate, *levare*, *mitigare*, *minuĕre*.

extenuation, *imminutio*.

exterior, subst. *forma*, *species*.

exterior, adj.; see external.

exterminate, *ad unum interficĕre*; *eradicare*, *exstirpare*.

extermination, *internecio*, *occidio*.

external, *externus* *exter*(*us*), *exterior*; adv. *extrinsecus*.

extinct, *exstinctus*, *obsoletus*.

extinction, *exstinctio*.

extinguish, *exstinguĕre*, *restinguĕre*.

extirpate, *exstirpare*, *eradicare*, *excidĕre*.

extol, *laudibus*, (*ef*)*ferre*, (*con*)*laudare*.

extort, *exprimĕre*, *extorquēre*.

extortion, *res repetundae*.

extortionate, *rapax*, *avarus*.

extra, adv. *praeterea*.

extract, v. *extrahĕre*, *evellĕre*, *exprimĕre*; from a book, *excerpĕre*.

extraction: as act, *evulsio*; = origin, *origo*, *genus* (*-eris*, n.).

extraneous; see external.

extraordinary, *inusitatus*, *insolitus*, *novus*, *mirus*. Adv. *extra ordinem*, *praeter morem*, *mire*.

extravagance: in expenditure, *sumptus* (*-ūs*); in gen., = excess, *intemperantia*, *immoderatio*.

extravagant: = lavish, *prodigus*, *sumptuosus*; in gen., = excessive, *nimius*, *immoderatus*, *intemperans*. Adv. *prodige*, *sumptuose*; *immoderate*, *intemperanter*.

extreme, subst.; see extremity.

extreme, adj. *extremus*, *ultimus*, *summus*. Adv. *summe*; often rendered by superl.

extremity: = top, *cacumen*, *fastigium*; = farthest part, or extreme degree, render by adj. *extremus*.

extricate, *expedire*, (*ex*)*solvĕre*.

extrude, *extrudĕre*, *eicĕre*.

exuberance, *ubertas*, *luxuria*.

exuberant, *luxuriosus*, *laetus*; adv. *uberrime*.

exude, (*ex*)*sudare*, *manare*.

exult, *exsultare*, *gestire*, *laetari*.

exultant, *laetus*.

exultation, *laetatio*, *exsultatio*.

eye, subst. *oculus*, *ocellus*.

eye, v. *adspicĕre*, *contemplari*, *intueri*.

eye-ball, *pupula*.
eye-brow, *supercilium*.
eye-lid, *palpebra* (usually plur.)
eyesight, *acies*.
eye-witness, *arbiter, spectator et testis*.

F

fable, *fabula (commenticia)*.
fabled, fabulous, *fabulosus, fictus, commenticius*.
fabric: built, *aedificium*; woven, *textum, textile*; fig., *compages*.
fabricate, *fabricari, texĕre*.
fabrication: = making, *fabricatio*; = falsehood, *commentum, mendacium*.
fabricator, *auctor*.
face, subst. *facies, vultus (-ūs), us (oris)*; — to —, *coram*.
face, v.: = to be opposite, (a)*spectare*; = to encounter, *obire, obviam ire*.
facetious, *iocosus, facetus*; adv. *iocose, facete*.
facetiousness, *facetiae (-arum)*.
facilitate, *faciliorem reddĕre*.
facility, *facilitas*.
facing, *contra, adversus*.
facsimile, *descriptio imagoque*.
fact, *res, factum*; in —, *reapse, sane*.
faction, *factio, pars*.
factious, *factiosus, seditiosus*; adv. *per factionem, seditiose*.
factiousness, *factio, studium partium*.
factitious; see false.
factory, *fabrica, officina*.
faculty, *vis, facultas*.
fade, *pallescĕre*.
faded; see pale.
fading, = transient, *caducus, fluxus*.
fagot, *fascis, sarmenta (-orum, plur.)*.
fail, subst.: without —, *certo, omnino*.
fail, v.: = to give out, *deficĕre, deesse*; = not to succeed, *concidĕre, cadĕre*; transit., *deficĕre, deserĕre, destituĕre*.
failing, *peccatum, vitum*.
failure, *defectio*.
fain: I would — do, *velim facĕre, libens faciam*.
faint, adj. *languidus, defessus*.
faint, v. *conlabi, (animo) linqui*.
faint-hearted, *timidus*.
faintness, *languor*.
fair, subst. *nundinae (-arum)*.
fair, adj.: = beautiful, *pulcher, venustus, formosus*; of weather, *serenus*; = favourable, *secundus, idoneus*; morally, *aequus, iustus*; = moderately good, *mediocris*. Adv., *aeque, iuste*; *mediocriter*.
fairness: = beauty, *pulchritudo, forma, venustas*; = justice, *iustitia, aequitas*.
fairy, *nympha*.
faith: = fidelity, *fides, fidilitas, pietas*; = belief, *opinio, persuasio, fides*; to have — in, *credĕre, confidĕre*.
faithful, *fidelis, fidus*; adv. *fideliter*.
faithfulness, *fidelitas, fides, constantia*.
faithless, *perfidus*; adv. *perfide*.
faithlessness, *perfidia, infidelitas*.
fall, subst. *casus (-ūs), lapsūs (-us)*; = ruin, *ruina, excidium*; = lessening, *deminutio*.

fall, v. *cadĕre, decidĕre, ruĕre*; to — dead, *cadĕre, concidĕre, occidĕre*; of a city, *expugnari, capi*; to — back, = retreat, *pedem referre*; to — back on, *recurrĕre* or *confugĕre ad*; to — upon, = attack, *invadĕre, incurrĕre*; to — out, = happen, *evenire*; = disagree, *dissentire, dissidĕre*.
fallacious, *fallax, falsus*; adv. *fallaciter, falso*.
fallacy, *vitium, captio*.
fallible, *errori obnoxius*.
fallow: the field lies —, *ager cessat*; — ground, *novalis*.
false, *falsus; fictus, commenticius* (= made up), *subditus* (=forged), *perfidus* (=treacherous); to play —, *deesse*. Adv. *falso, perperam*.
falsehood, *mendacium, commentum*.
falsify, *vitiare, corrumpĕre*.
falter, *haesitare, haerēre, titubare*.
falteringly, *titubanter*.
fame, *laus, gloria, fama*.
familiar: = well known, *familiaris, notus*; = acquainted, *sciens, gnarus, peritus*. Adv. *familiariter*.
familiarity, *familiaritas, consuetudo*.
family, subst. *familia* (= household); *domus; gens* (= clan); *genus (-eris,* = race, stock); of good —, *nobilis*.
family, adj. *familiaris, domesticus; gentilis; privatus* (opp. to *publicus*).
famine, *fames, cibi inopia*.
famish, *fame enecare, conficĕre*.
famous, *(prae)clarus, inlustris, celeber*.
fan, subst.: for winnowing, *vannus*; for fanning oneself, *flabellum*.
fan, v. *ventilare*.
fanatical, *fanaticus*.
fancied, *opinabilis, opinatus*.
fancy, subst.: as a faculty, *inventio, cogitatio*; = idea, notion, *opinio*; = liking, preference, *libido*.
fancy, v.: = to imagine, *fingĕre*; = to think, *opinari, putare*.
fang, *dens*.
fanged, *dentatus*.
far: in space, *procul, longe*: from — off, *eminus*; farther, *longius, ultra*; as — as, *tenus* (prep.), *usque* (adv. = all the way); — and wide, *longe lateque*; in degree, — better, *longe* or *multo melior*; — from it, *minime*; so —, *hactenus*.
farce, *mimus*.
farcical, *mimicus, ridiculus*; adv. *mimice, ridicule*.
fare, subst.: = food, *cibus, victus (-ūs)*; = money for journey, *vectura, naulum*.
fare, v. *se habēre*, with adv.
farewell! *valĕ! valĕte!*; to bid — *valĕre iubēre*.
far-fetched, *longe repetitus, arcessitus*.
farm, subst. *fundus, praedium, ager*.
farm, v.: = till, *arare, colĕre*; = hire, *redimĕre, conducĕre*; — out, = let out on contract, *(e)locare*.
farmer, *agricola, colonus*; a — of revenues, *publicanus*.
farming, *agricultura, res rusticae*; = hiring, *redemptio, conductio*.
farthing, *quadrans, teruncius*; I do not care a — for, *haud flocci facio*.

fascinate, *fascinare;* see charm.

fascination, *fascinum.* Transf., *blanditia, dulcedo.*

fashion, subst.: = custom, way, *mos, consuetudo, ritus (-ūs);* = style of dress, *habitus (-ūs), ornatus (-ūs);* = what is fashionable, *saeculum;* out of —, *obsoletus.*

fashion, v. *fabricari, (ef)fingěre.*

fashionable, *elegans;* adv. *eleganter.*

fast, subst. *ieiunium.*

fast, adj.;= quick, *celer, citus, rapidus;* = fixed, firm, *firmus, stabilis;* to make —, *firmare, stabilire.*

fast, adv.: = quickly, *celeriter, rapide;* = firmly, *firme, firmiter.*

fast, v. *ieiunium servare.*

fasten, *(ad)figěre, (ad)ligare, adnectěre;* to — together, *connectěre.*

fastening, *vinculum, claustra (-orum).*

fastidious, *fastidiosus, delicatus;* adv. *fastidiose, delicate.*

fat, subst. *adeps, sebum.*

fat, adj. *pinguis, obesus.*

fatal, *perniciosus, funestus.*

fatality: = power of fate, *fatum;* = accident, *casus (-ūs).*

fate, *fatum, necessitas, sors;* the Fates, *Parcae.*

fated, *fatalis.*

father, subst. *pater, parens;* fathers= ancestors, *maiores (-um).*

father, v. *ascriběre, tribuěre.*

father-in-law, *socer.*

fatherless, *orbus.*

fatherly, *paternus.*

fathom, subst. *ulna.*

fathom, v. *explorare.*

fatigue, subst. *(de)fatigatio, lassitudo.*

fatigue, v. *(de)fatigare.*

fatigued, *(de)fatigatus, (de)fessus.*

fatten: transit., *saginare;* intransit., *pinguescěre.*

fatuity, *fatuitas, ineptia.*

fatuous, *fatuus, ineptus;* adv. *inepte.*

fault, *culpa, vitium, delictum;* to find — with, *culpare, accusare.*

faultless, *integer, innocens;* adv. *integre, innocenter.*

faulty, *mendosus, vitiosus;* adv. *mendose, vitiose.*

favour, subst.; as position, *gratia;* as disposition, goodwill, *favor, benevolentia;* an act of —, *beneficium;* to do a —, *gratificari.*

favour, v. *favēre, studēre, suffragari.*

favourable, *propitius* (of gods), *commodus, secundus;* adv. *benigne, commode.*

favourer, *fautor* (f. *fautrix).*

favourite, subst. *deliciae (-arum).*

favourite, adj. *carus, gratiosus.*

fawn, subst. *hinnuleus.*

fawn, v.: to — upon, *adulari.*

fawning, subst. *adulatio.*

fealty, *fides, fidelitas.*

fear, subst. *metus (-ūs), timor, pavor.*

fear, v. *metuěre, timēre, verēri.*

fearful: = afraid, *timidus, pavidus;* = dreadful, *dirus, terribilis.* Adv. *timide, pavide; dire.*

fearless, *impavidus, intrepidus;* adv. *sine timore, impavide.*

feasible, *quod fieri potest.*

feast, subst.: = feast-day, *dies festus;* = banquet, *convivium, epulae (-arum).*

feast, v.: transit., *pascěre;* intransit., *epulari, convivari.*

feat, *facinus (-oris,* n.), *factum.*

feather, subst. *penna (pinna).*

feature, of the face, *lineamentum;* the —s, *vultus (-ūs).*

February, (mensis) *Februarius.*

fecund, *fecundus.*

fecundity, *fecunditas, fertilitas.*

federal, *foederatus, foedere, sociatus.*

fee, subst. *merces.*

fee, v. *mercedem dare.*

feeble, *infirmus, invalidus, debilis;* adv. *infirme.*

feebleness, *debilitas, infirmitas.*

feed, v.: transit., *pascěre, alěre;* intransit., *vesci, (de)pasci.*

feel: = to touch, handle, *temptare, tangěre;* to — an emotion, *laetitiam,* etc., *capěre, percipěre, sentire.*

feeler, *crinis, corniculum.*

feeling, subst. *sensus (-ūs), tactus (-ūs);* = emotion, *animus, animi motus (-ūs)* or *adfectus (-ūs).*

feeling, adj. *humanus, misericors.*

feign, *fingěre, simulare.*

feigned, *fictus, simulatus;* adv. *ficte, simulate.*

feint, *simulatio.*

felicitate, *gratulari.*

felicitation, *gratulatio.*

felicitous, of style, *venustus.*

felicity: = happiness, *vita beata;* of style, *venustas.*

fell, adj. *dirus, saevus.*

fell, v. *caedere, exciděre;* in gen., = knock down, *(con)sternere.*

fellow: = associate, *socius, comes;* = equal, *par;* = person, *homo.*

fellow-citizen, fellow-countryman, *civis.*

fellow-heir, *coheres.*

fellow-servant, *conservus.*

fellowship, *societas;* = corporation, *conlegium.*

fellow-soldier, *commilito.*

felon: see criminal.

felt, *coactum.*

female, subst. *femina, mulier.*

female, feminine, *muliebris, femineus;* gram., *femininus.*

fen, *palus (-ūdis,* f.), *uligo.*

fence, subst. *saepes, saepimentum.*

fence, v.: = enclose, *saepire;* = fight with swords, *batuěre.*

fencer, *gladiator.*

fenny, *uliginosus, paluster.*

ferment, *fermentum.* Transf., *frevor, aestus (-ūs).*

ferment, v. *fervēre.*

fern, *filix.*

ferocious, *ferus, saevus, atrox.*

ferocity, *saevitia, atrocitas.*

ferret, subst. *viverra.*

ferry, subst. *traiectus (-ūs);* — -boat, *scapha, cymba;* — -man, *portitor.*

ferry, v. *traicěre, transmittěre.*

fertile, *fecundus, fertilis, uber.*

fertility, *fertilitas, ubertas, fecunditas.*

fervent, fervid, *fervidus, fervens, ardens*; adv. *ardenter, ferventer.*

fervour, *ardor, fervor.*

festival, *dies festus, feriae (-arum).*

festive, *hilaris, festus.*

festivity: see festival; = mirth, *festivitas, hilaritas.*

festoon, subst. *serta (-orum).*

fetch, *adferre, adducěre.*

fetid, *teter, foetidus, gravis.*

fetter, subst. *compes, catena, vinculum.*

fetter, v. *vincula inicěre.* Transf., *impedire.*

feud, *simultas; inimicitia.*

fever, *febris;* to be in a — (fig.), *trepidare, aestuare.*

feverish, *febriculosus.* Transf., *trepidus;* — excitement, *summa trepidatio.*

few, *pauci, rari.*

fib, *mendaciunculum.*

fibre, *fibra.*

fickle, *inconstans, levis.*

fickleness, *inconstantia, levitas.*

fiction, *res ficta, fabula, commentum.*

fictitious, *commenticius, fictus.*

fiddle, *fides (-ium).*

fiddler, *fidicen.*

fidelity, *fidelitas, fides.*

fidget, v. *trepidare.*

fidgety, *inquietus.*

field: = piece of land, *ager, arvum, campus* (= plain); — of battle, *acies;* fig., = sphere, *campus, locus, area.*

fiendish, *nefandus, immanis, atrox.*

fierce, *ferox, ferus, saevus;* adv. *ferociter, saeve.*

fierceness, *ferocitas, saevitia.*

fiery, *igneus, flammeus.* Transf., *ardens, fervidus, ferox.*

fife, *tibia.*

fifteen, *quindecim:* — each, *quini deni;* — times, *quindecie(n)s.*

fifteenth, *quintus decimus.*

fifth, *quintus.*

fiftieth, *quinquagesimus.*

fifty, *quinquaginta;* — each, *quinquageni.*

fig, *ficus.*

fight, subst. *pugna, certamen.*

fight, v. (de)*pugnare, dimicare, proeliari.*

fighter, *pugnator, proeliator.*

figment: see fiction.

figurative, *translatus;* adv. *per translationem.*

figure, subst.: = form, shape, *figura, forma, species;* = image, representation, *signum, figura, imago;* a — of speech, *conformatio, figura.*

figure, v. *fingěre;* see imagine.

figured, *sigillatus, caelatus.*

filament, *fibra, filum.*

file, subst.: the tool, *lima, scobina;* milit., *ordo;* rank and —, *milites.*

file, v. *limare, polire.*

filial, *pius (erga parentes);* adv. *pie.*

filings, *scobis.*

fill, v. *implēre, complēre.*

fillet, *vitta, infula* (religious).

film, *membrana.*

filter, subst. *colum.*

filter, v. (per)*colare, liquare.*

filth, *impuritas;* see dirt.

filthy, *impurus, obscenus;* adv. *impure.*

fin, *pinna.*

final, *ultimus, extremus;* adv. *ad extremum, postremo.*

finance, finances: domestic, *res familiaris;* of a state, *vectigalia (-ium), aerarium.*

find, v. *invenire, reperire;* to — out, *cognoscere, invenire.*

finder, *inventor, repertor.*

fine, subst. *multa.*

fine, adj. *praeclarus, pulcher;* the — arts, *artes liberales;* = thin, *tenuis, subtilis;* of weather, *serenus, sudus.* Adv. *praeclare; tenuiter, subtiliter.*

fine, v. *multare.*

fineness, *elegantia;* = thinness, *tenuitas, subtilitas;* of weather, *serenitas.*

finery, *munditia, apparatus (-ūs).*

finesse, *artificium.*

finger, subst. *digitus.*

finger, v. *tangěre, attrectare.*

finish, subst. *absolutio, perfectio.*

finish, v.: = complete, *conficěre, absolvěre, peragěre;* = put an end to, *finire, terminare.*

finished, *absolutus, perfectus.*

finite, *finitus, circumscriptus.*

fir, *abies, pinus.*

fire, subst. *ignis, flamma, incendium;* to be on —, *ardēre, flagrare;* to set on —, *incenděre.* Transf., = ardour, (animi) *vis, ardor, fervor;* of missiles, *telorum coniectus (-ūs).*

fire, v.: transit., *incenděre;* intransit., to — up, *exardescěre.*

fire-brand, *fax, torris.*

fire-brigade, *vigiles.*

fire-engine, *sipho(n).*

fire-place, fire-side, *caminus, focus.*

fire-wood, *lignum* (usually plur.).

firm, *firmus, stabilis, solidus;* adv. *firmiter, firme, solide.*

firmness, *firmitas, stabilitas;* of mind, *constantia.*

first, adj. *primus, prior* (of two).

first, adv. *primum, primo.*

first-born, *natu maximus* (of two, *maior*).

first-fruits, *primitiae (-arum).*

fish, subst. *piscis.*

fish, v. *piscari;* fig., to — for, *captare.*

fisherman, *piscator.*

fishhook, *hamus.*

fishing, *piscatus (-ūs);* of —, adj., *piscatorius.*

fishing-line, *linum.*

fishing-net, *rete, iaculum.*

fishing-rod, *harundo.*

fishmonger, *cetarius.*

fissure, *rima.*

fist, *pugnus.*

fisticuffs, *pugilatio.*

fit, subst. *impetus (-ūs).*

fit, fitted, adj. *aptus, idoneus, commodus;* adv. *apte, commode.*

fit, v.: transit. *aptare, accommodare;* to — out, (ex)*ornare, instruěre;* intransit. *convenire.*

fitness, *habilitas, opportunitas.*

five, *quinque;* — each, *quini;* a period of — years, *lustrum, quinquennium;* — times, *quinquie(n)s.*

fix, v. (ad)*figěre.*

fixed, *certus.*

flabby, flaccid, *marcidus, fluidus.*

flag, subst. *signum, vexillum;* — ship, *navis praetoria.*

flagon, *lagena.*

flagrant, *impudens;* adv. *impudenter.*

flail, *pertica.*

flame, subst. *flamma.*

flame, v. *ardēre, flagrare.*

flaming, *flammeus.*

flank, *latus (-eris, n.).*

flap, subst. *lacinia.*

flap, v.: to — the wings, *alis plaudēre;* in gen., *fluitare.*

flare, v. *flagrare.*

flash, subst. *fulgor.*

flash, v. *fulgēre, splendēre.*

flask, *ampulla.*

flat: = level, *planus, aequus, pronus* (= lying —); of wine, *vapidus;* of jokes, etc., *frigidus.* Adv. *plane.*

flatter, *adulari, blandiri.*

flatterer, *adsentator.*

flattering, *blandus.*

flattery, *adulatio, blandimentum.*

flaunt, *iactare, ostentare.*

flavour, subst. *sapor, sucus.*

flavour, v. *condire.*

flaw, *vitium, mendum.*

flawless, *emendatus.*

flax, *linum, carbasus.*

flaxen, *lineus;* of colour, *flavus.*

flay, *pellem detrahēre (corpori).*

flea, *pulex.*

fledged, *plumatus.*

flee, *(ef)fugēre.*

fleece, subst. *vellus (-eris, n.).*

fleece, v. *tondēre;* = rob, *expilare, spoliare.*

fleecy, *laniger.*

fleet, subst. *classis.*

fleet, adj. *velox, celer, pernix.*

fleeting, *fugax, caducus, fluxus.*

fleetness, *velocitas, pernicitas.*

flesh, *caro* (= meat), *viscera (-um), corpus (-oris, n.).*

flexible, *flexibilis, lentus, facilis.*

flicker, *trepidare, micare.*

flight: = fleeing, *effugium, fuga;* to put to —, *fugare;* = flying, *lapsus (-ūs), volatus (-ūs);* of stairs, *scalae (-arum).*

flightiness, *mobilitas, levitas.*

flighty, *mobilis, levis, inconstans.*

flimsiness, *tenuitas.*

flimsy, *tenuis.* Transf., *inanis.*

flinch, *refugēre.*

fling, *iacēre, conicēre.*

flint, *silex.*

flippancy, *petulantia.*

flippant, *petulans.*

flirt, v., perhaps *subblandiri.*

flit, *volitare.*

flitch, *succidia.*

float, *innare, fluitare;* in the air, *pendēre, volitare.*

flock, subst. *grex.*

flock, v. *adfluēre, confluēre;* to — together, *concurrēre.*

flog, *verberare;* to be flogged, *vapulare.*

flogging, *verbera (-um).*

flood, subst. *eluvio;* — tide, *aestūs accessus (-ūs).* Transf., *vis magna, flumen.*

flood, v. transit. *inundare.*

floor, *solum, pavimentum* (of stone).

floral, *floreus* (poet).

Florence, *Florentia.*

florid, *rubicundus.* Transf., *floridus.*

flounder, *fluitare.* Transf., *titubare.*

flour, *farina.*

flourish, subst., in style, *calamister.*

flourish, v.: intransit., *florēre, vigēre;* transit., *vibrare.*

flout, *ludificari, deridēre.*

flow, subst. *fluxio, lapsus (-ūs);* of words, *volubilitas, copia (verborum).*

flow, v. *fluēre, labi* (= glide), *manare* (= ooze).

flower, subst. *flos, flosculus;* = best part, *flos, robur.*

flower, v. *florēre, (ef)florescēre.*

flowery, *floreus, floridus.*

flowing, of speech, *fluens, volubilis, fusus.*

fluctuate, *fluctuare, pendēre.*

fluency, *facundia, volubilitas.*

fluent, *volubilis, disertus;* adv. *volubiliter.*

fluid, subst. *liquor, humor.*

fluid, adj. *liquidus.*

flush, subst. *rubor.*

flush, v. *rubescēre.*

fluster, *agitare, sollicitare.*

flute, *tibia, harundo.*

flute-player, *tibicen.*

fluted, *striatus.*

flutter, subst. *trepidatio.*

flutter, v. *trepidare, volitare.*

fly, subst. *musca.*

fly, v. *volare, volitare,* see also flee.

flying, *volatilis, volucer.*

foal, *eculeus, pullus equinus.*

foam, subst. *spuma.*

foam, v. *spumare, (ex)aestuare.*

foamy, *spumeus, spumosus.*

fodder, *pabulum.*

foe, *hostis* (public), *inimicus* (private).

fog, *nebula, caligo.*

foggy, *nebulosus, caliginosus.*

foible, *vitium.*

foil, subst.: a fencer's —, *rudis;* of metal, *lamina.*

foil, v. *ad inritum redigēre, eludēre.*

foist, *supponēre, subdēre.*

fold, subst.: in fabric, etc., *sinus (-ūs);* for animals, *ovile, stabulum.*

fold, v. *(com)plicare;* with -ed hands, *compressis manibus.*

folding-doors, *valvae (-arum).*

foliage, *frons,* plur. *frondes.*

folk; see people.

follow, *(con)sequi, insequi, persequi* (to the end); to — after, succeed, *succedēre.*

follower, *(ad)sectator.*

following, subst. *secta.*

following, *(in)sequens, proximus, posterus.*

folly, *stultitia, ineptia.*

foment, *fovēre.* Transf., *excitare.*

fond: = loving, *amans, studiosus;* = foolish, *stultus.* Adv. *amanter; stulte.*

fondle, *(per)mulcēre, amplexari.*

fondness: = love, *studium, amor, caritas;* = folly, *stultitia.*

food, *cibus, victus (-ūs), alimentum;* of animals, *pabulum.*

fool, subst. *homo stultus;* to play the —, *ineptire, desipēre.*

fool, v. (e)ludĕre, ludificare.

foolery, ineptiae (-arum), nugae (-arum).

foolhardy, temerarius.

foolish, stultus, ineptus, insulsus; adv. stulte, inepte, insulse.

foot, pes; on — (adj.), pedes, pedester; the — of the mountain, infimus mons; as a measure, pes; a — in size, pedalis; a metrical —, pes.

footing, ratio, status (-ūs).

footman, pedisequus, servus a pedibus.

footpad, latro.

foot-path, semita, callis.

foot-print, vestigium.

foot-soldier, pedes.

footstool, scamnum, scabillum.

for, prep.: = on behalf of, instead of, in return for, pro, with abl.; — this reason, propter hoc; — a sum of money, render by genit. or abl. of price; of time, to last for, for the purposes of, in with acc.: = during, render by acc., or per with acc.

for, conj. nam(que), etenim enim (second word in clause).

forage, subst. pabulum.

forage, v. pabulari, frumentari.

forager, pabulator, frumentator.

foraging, subst. pabulatio, frumentatio.

forbear, parcĕre, temperare, (se) abstinēre.

forbearance, abstinentia, patientia.

forbid, vetare, interdicĕre; it is forbidden, non licet.

force, subst. vis; to be in —, valēre; milit., forces, copiae (-arum).

force, v.; see compel.

forced, of language, accessitus; a — march, magnum iter.

forcible: = done by force, per vim factus; = strong, validus, gravis, vehemens. Adv. vi, per vim; valide, vehementer.

ford, subst. vadum.

ford, v. vado transire.

forearm, subst. bracchium.

forebode: = to prophesy, portendĕre; = to expect, praesagire, praesentire.

foreboding, subst. praesensio.

forecast, v. praevidēre, prospicĕre.

forefather, avus, proavus; —s, maiores (-um).

forefinger, digitus index.

forego, dimittĕre, (con)cedĕre.

forehead, frons (-ntis).

foreign, peregrinus, externus, adventicius; = incompatible, abhorrens, alienus.

foreigner, peregrinus, advena.

foremost, primus, princeps.

forenoon, dies antemeridianus.

forensic, forensis.

forerunner, praenuntius.

foresee, praevidēre, prospicĕre.

foresight, providentia.

forest, silva.

forestall, praevenire.

foretell, praedicĕre.

forethought, providentia.

forewarn, praemonēre.

forfeit, subst. poena, multa.

forfeit, v. amittĕre; multari.

forge, subst. fornax, officina.

forge, v. procudĕre, fabricari. Transf.: = make, in gen., fabricari, fingĕre; = counterfeit, subicĕre, supponĕre.

forged, of money, adulterinus.

forger, (of documents) subiector.

forgery, (of documents) subiectio.

forget, oblivisci, dediscĕre: to be forgotten, e memoria excidĕre.

forgetful, obliviosus, immemor.

forgetfulness, oblivio.

forgive, ignoscĕre; veniam dare.

forgiveness, venia.

forgiving, clemens, exorabilis.

fork, (for hay-making), furca, furcilla.

forked, bifurcus.

forlorn, relictus, destitutus.

form, subst.: = shape, figura, forma, facies; in proper —, rite; = bench, scamnum.

form, v.: = shape, make, (ef)fingĕre (con)formare, fabricari; milit., to — (up) troops, instruĕre, ordinare.

formality, ritus (-ūs).

formation, conformatio, forma.

former, prior, pristinus, superior; the — . . . the latter, ille . . . hic. Adv. antea, olim, quondam.

formidable, metuendus, terribilis, formidolosus; adv. formidolose.

formless, informis, rudis.

formula, formula, carmen, verba (-orum).

forsake, descrĕre, destituĕre.

forsooth! scilicet, sane.

forswear, = swear falsely, periurare. See also abjure.

fort, arx, castellum, castrum.

forth, of place, foras; often rendered by compound verb with e- or ex- or pro; and so —, et cetera.

forthcoming, express by future tense.

forthwith, extemplo, statim.

fortification, munitio, munimentum.

fortify, (com)munire.

fortitude, fortitudo, virtūs (-ūtis, f.).

fortuitous, fortuitus, forte oblatus; adv. forte, fortuito, casu.

fortunate, felix, fortunatus, beatus; adv. feliciter, fortunate.

fortune, fortuna, fors, casus (-ūs); = wealth, divitiae (-arum), res (familiaris), bona (-orum).

fortune-teller, sortilegus; female, saga.

forty, quadraginta; — each, quadrageni; — times, quadragie(n)s.

forward, adj., = pert, protervus.

forward, adv. porro, ante; to go —, pergĕre.

forward, v.; of letters, perferendum curare; = help, promote, adiuvare.

foster, nutrire, alĕre.

foster-child, alumnus, f. alumna.

foster-father, nutricius.

foster-mother, nutrix.

foul, foedus, turpis, immundus; adv. foede, turpiter.

foulness, foeditas.

found: of cities, etc., condĕre, fundare; = cast in metal, fundĕre.

foundation, fundamenta (-orum); from the —s, funditus.

founder, subst. conditor, auctor

founder, v. submergi, deperire

fount, fountain, *fons, caput.* Transf., *fons, principium, origo.*

four, *quattuor:* — each, *quaterni;* — times, *quater;* a period of — years, *quadriennium;* — fold, *quadruplex.*

fourteen, *quattuordecim:* — each, *quaterni deni;* — times. *quater decie(n)s.*

fourteenth, *quartus decimus.*

fourth, *quartus:* for the — time, *quartum.*

fowl, subst. *avis, volucris, ales;* = hen, *gallina.*

fowl, v. *aucupari.*

fowler, *auceps.*

fowling, *aucupium.*

fox, *vulpes;* of a —, adj. *vulpinus.*

fraction, *pars.*

fractious, *morosus, difficilis*

fracture, v. *frangĕre.*

fragile, *fragilis.*

fragility, *fragilitas.*

fragment, *fragmentum.*

fragrance, *odor suavis.*

fragrant, *suavis; suaveolens* (poet).

frail, adj. *infirmus, debilis.*

frailty, *infirmitas.*

frame, subst. *compages;* — of mind, *animus.*

frame, v. *fingĕre, fabricari;* — draw up in words, *concipĕre, componĕre.*

framework, *compages, contignatio.*

France, *Gallia.*

franchise, *civitas, iūs (iūris, n.).*

frank, *candidus, apertus;* adv. *candide, aperte.*

frankincense, *tūs (tūris, n.).*

frankness, *simplicitas, libertas.*

frantic, *insanus, amens;* adv. *insane.*

fraternal, *fraternus;* adv. *fraterne.*

fraternity, *germanitas, fraternitas;* = society, *sodalitas, sodalicium.*

fratricide: as act, *parricidium fraternum;* as person, *fratricida.*

fraud, *fraus, dolus (malus), fallacia.*

fraudulent, *fraudulentus, dolosus;* adv. *fraudulenter, dolo malo, dolose.*

fraught, *refertus, repletus.*

fray, *pugna.*

free, adj.: = unrestricted, *liber, solutus, vacuus;* to be — from, (re) *carēre;* of space, = unoccupied, *patens, apertus;* = without cost, *gratuitus;* = generous, *largus, liberalis.* Adv. *libere, solute;* = generously, *large.*

free, v. *liberare, eximĕre, solvĕre;* of slaves, *manumittĕre.*

freebooter, *latro, praedo.*

free-born, *ingenuus.*

freedman, *libertus, libertinus.*

freedom, *libertas, licentia;* — of choice, *arbitrium;* — from punishment, *impunitas.*

freehold, *praedium liberum.*

freeholder, *possessor.*

freewill, *voluntas.*

freeze, transit., *glaciare,* (con)*gelare.*

freight, *onus (oneris, n.).*

French, *Gallicus;* a — man, *Gallus.*

frenzied, *furens, insanus, amens.*

frenzy, *furor, insania, amentia.*

frequency, *frequentia, crebritas.*

frequent, adj. *frequens, creber;* adv. *frequenter, crebro, saepe.*

frequent, v. *celebrare, frequentare.*

frequented, *frequens, celeber.*

fresh: = new, *recens, novus;* = refreshed, *untired, recens, integer. vegetus;* = cold, *frigidus.*

freshen, *recreare, reficere;* intransit., of wind, *increbrescere.*

freshness, *viriditas.*

fret: transit., = chafe, *atterĕre,* = distress, *sollicitare vexare;* intransit., *dolere, macerari.*

fretful, *morosus, stomachosus;* adv. *morose, stomachose.*

fretfulness, *morositas, stomachus.*

friable, *puter* or *putris.*

friction, *tritus (-ūs).*

friend, *amicus* (f. *amica*), *sodalis.*

friendliness, *comitas, adfabilitas.*

friendly, *amicus, comis.*

friendship, *amicitia, familiaritas.*

frieze, (the cloth), *gausape* or *gausapum*

fright, *terror, pavor.*

frighten, (ex)*terrēre.*

frightful, *terribilis, formidolosus;* adv. *terribilem in modum, formidolose.*

frigid, *frigidus.*

frill, *segmenta (-orum).*

fringe, *fimbriae (-arum), limbus.*

frisk, *salire, lascivire.*

frisky, *lascivus.*

fritter, subst., *laganum.*

fritter, v. (con)*terĕre, dissipare.*

frivolity, *nugae (-arum), levitas.*

frivolous, *levis, inanis.*

fro: to and —, *huc* (et) *illuc, ultro citro(que).*

frog, *rana.*

frolic, subst. *ludus, lascivia.*

frolic, v. *ludĕre, lascivire.*

frolicsome, *lascivus, ludibundus, iocosus.*

from, *a, ab; ex* (= out of); *de* (=down from).

front, subst. *frons, pars prior;* in — of, *pro,* with abl.

front, v., = look towards, *aspectare.*

frontier, *finis, terminus, confinium.*

fronting, *adversus, oppositus.*

frost, *gelu, pruina; frigus (-oris,* n. = frosty weather).

frosty, *frigidus.*

froth, subst. *spuma.*

froth, v. *spumare.*

frothy, *spumosus, spumeus.*

froward, *contumax, pertinax;* adv. *contumaciter, pertinaciter.*

frowardness, *contumacia, pertinacia.*

frown, subst. *frontis contractio.*

frown, v. *frontem contrahĕre.*

frozen, *rigidus.*

frugal, *parcus, frugi* (indecl.); adv. *parce, frugaliter.*

frugality, *parsimonia, frugalitas.*

fruit, *fructus (-ūs), frux* and plur. *fruges* (esp. of grain), *pomum* (esp. = fruit of trees), *baca* (= berry).

fruitful, *fecundus, fertilis, uber;* adv. *fecunde.*

fruitfulness, *fecunditas, fertilitas.*

fruition, *fructus (-ūs).*

fruitless, *inutilis, cassus, inritus;* adv. *incassum, frustra, re infecta.*

fruit-tree, *pomum.*

frustrate, *ad inritum redigĕre.*

fry, v. *frigĕre.*

frying-pan, *sartago.*

fuel, *ligna (-orum).*

fugitive, subst. *fugitivus, profugus.*

fugitive, adj. *fugax, fugitivus.*

fulfil, *explēre, exsequi, conficĕre.*

fulfilment, *confectio.*

full: = filled, *plenus, repletus;* — of food, *satur;* = complete, *plenus, integer;* of a writer or speaker, *copiosus.* Adv. *plene; copiose, abundanter.*

fuller, *fullo.*

full-grown, *adultus.*

fulminate, *fulminare, intonare.*

fulsome, *putidus;* adv. *putide.*

fumble; see feel.

fume, subst. *vapor, halitus (-ūs).*

fume, v. *(ex)aestuare.*

fumigate, *suffire.*

fun, *iocus, ludus.*

function, *munus (-eris, n.), officium.*

fund, *pecunia.*

fundamental, *primus, principalis;* adv. *penitus.*

fundamentals, *elementa (-orum), principia (-orum).*

funeral, subst. *funus (-eris, n.), exsequiae (-arum).*

funeral, adj. *funebris;* — pile, *rogus, pyra.*

funereal, *funebris, lugubris.*

funnel, *infundibulum.*

funny, *ridiculus, iocularis;* adv. *ridicule.*

fur, *pellis.*

furbish, *interpolare, expolire.*

furious, *rabidus, furens;* adv. *rabide.*

furl, *(vela) contrahĕre.*

furlong, *stadium.*

furlough, *commeatus (-ūs).*

furnace, *fornax.*

furnish: = equip, *(ad)ornare, instruĕre;* = supply, give, *suppeditare, praebere.*

furnished, *instructus, praeditus.*

furniture, *supellex; apparatus (-ūs).*

furrow, subst. *sulcus.*

furrow, v. *sulcare.*

further: adj. *ulterior;* adv. *ulterius, amplius; praeterea.*

furthest, *ultimus.*

furtive, *furtivus;* adv. *furtim, furtive.*

fury, *furor, rabies.*

fuse, *liquefacĕre, fundĕre.*

fuss, subst. *trepidatio, tumultus (-ūs).*

fuss, v. *trepidare.*

fusty; see mouldy.

futile, *futilis, inanis, vanus.*

futility, *futilitas.*

future, subst. *futura (-orum);* for the —, *in futurum.*

future, adj. *futurus, posterus.*

G

gabble, *garrire, blaterare.*

gable, *fastigium.*

gadfly, *asilus, tabanus.*

gage, *pignus (-oris, n.).*

gaiety, *hilaritas, laetitia.*

gain, subst. *lucrum, quaestus (-ūs;* = profit), *commodum (= advantage).*

gain, v. *lucrari, lucri facĕre, consequi, capĕre;* to — over, *conciliare.*

gainful, *quaestuosus, lucrosus.*

gait, *incessus (-ūs).*

gala; see festival.

galaxy, *orbis lacteus.*

gale, *ventus, aura (= breeze).*

gall, subst. *fel, bilis.*

gall, v. *terĕre;* = annoy, *mordēre, urĕre.*

gallant, *amator.*

gallant, adj.: = brave, *fortis, animosus;* adv. *fortiter, animose;* = attentive to females, *officiosus.*

gallantry, *virtus (-utis, f.), fortitudo;* in love, *amores (-um).*

gallery, *porticus (-ūs).*

galley, *navis longa, triremis.*

gallon, *congius.*

gallop, subst. *gradus (-ūs) citatus:* at a —, *equo admisso.*

gallop, v. *equo admisso vehi or currĕre.*

gallows, *crux.*

gamble, v. *aleā ludĕre.*

gambler, *aleator.*

gambling, *alea.*

gambol, subst. *lusus (-ūs).*

gambol, v. *ludĕre, lascivire.*

game, susbt.: as played, *ludus;* a — of chance, *alea;* as hunted, *ferae (-arum);* on table, *(caro) ferina.*

gammon, *perna.*

gammon, interj. *gerrae!*

gander, *anser (mas or masculus).*

gang, *grex, caterva.*

gangway, *forus.*

gaol, *carcer; vincula (-orum).*

gaoler, *custos.*

gap, *lacuna, hiatus (-ūs).*

gape, *(in)hiare, (de)hiscĕre.*

garbage, *purgamentum, quisquiliae (-arum).*

garble, *corrumpĕre, vitiare.*

garden, subst. *hortus.*

garden, v. *in horto fodĕre, hortum colĕre.*

garish, *clarus, splendidus.*

garland, *corona, sertum (usually plur.).*

garlic, *alium.*

garment, *vestimentum.*

garner, subst. *horreum.*

garner, v. *condĕre.*

garnish, *(ex)ornare, instruĕre, decorare.*

garret, *cenaculum.*

garrison, subst. *praesidium.*

garrison, v. *(urbi) praesidium imponĕre.*

garrulity, *garrulitas, loquacitas.*

garrulous, *garrulus, loquax, verbosus;* adv. *loquaciter.*

gas, *spiritus (-ūs), vapor.*

gash, subst. *vulnus (-eris, n.).*

gash, v. *vulnerare.*

gasp, subst. *anhelitus (-ūs).*

gasp, v. *anhelare.*

gasping, adj. *anhelus.*

gate, *ianua, ostium;* of a city, *porta.*

gate-keeper, *ianitor.*

gate-post, *postis.*

gather, v.: transit., *legĕre, conligĕre.*

conferre; = conjecture, *conicĕre*; intransit., *convenire, congregari*.

gathering, subst.: as act, *collectio*; = assembly, *coetus (-ūs)*; = a sore, *suppuratio*.

gaudy, *fucatus, magnificus*.

gauge, v. *metiri*.

gaunt, *macer*.

gauntlets, *manicae (-arum)*.

gay: of spirits, *hilaris, laetus*; adv. *hilare, laete*; of colour, etc., *splendidus, nitidus*.

gaze, subst. *obtutus (-ūs)*.

gaze, v.: to — at, *intueri, contemplari*.

gazelle, *dorcas*.

gazette, *acta (diurna)*.

gear, *ornatus (-ūs), supellex, apparatus (-ūs)*.

gem, *gemma*.

gender, *genus (-eris, n.)*.

genealogy, render by *origo* or *stirps*.

general, subst. *dux, imperator*; a lieutenant—, *legatus*; the —'s tent, *praetorium*.

general, adj. *generalis, communis, vulgaris*; often rendered by genit. plur. *omnium*. Adv., = in —, *ad summam, in universum, generatim*; = usually, *fere, vulgo, plerumque*.

generalship, *ductus (-ūs)*; under the — of Caesar, *Caesare duce*.

generate, *gignĕre, generare, parĕre*.

generation, *saeculum, aetas*.

generosity, *benignitas, liberalitas*.

generous, *benignus, liberalis*; of birth, *generosus, nobilis*. Adv. *benigne, liberaliter, large*.

genial, *comis, benignus*; adv. *comiter*.

geniality, *comitas*.

genitive, *(casus) genitivus*.

genius, = ability, *ingenium* or *indoles*, with adj. such as *praeclarus*; a man of —, *homo ingeniosus* or *praeclaro ingenio (praeditus)*.

genteel, *elegans, urbanus*; adv. *eleganter, urbane*.

gentility, *elegantia, urbanitas*.

gentle: = well-born, *generosus, ingenuus, nobilis*; = mild, *lenis, mitis, mansuetus*; adv. *leniter, mite, mansuete*.

gentleman: by birth, see gentle; in behaviour, etc., *homo liberalis*.

gentlemanly, *liberalis, urbanus, honestus*.

gentleness, *mansuetudo, lenitas*.

gentlewoman: see lady.

gentry, *nobilitas, nobiles (-ium)*.

genuine, *sincerus, merus, germanus*; adv. *reapse, sincere, vere*.

geography, *geographia, terrarum descriptio*.

geometrical, *geometricus*.

geometrician, *geometres (-ae)*.

geometry, *geometria*.

George, *Georgius* (late Latin).

germ, *germen, semen*.

German, *Germanus, Germanicus*.

germane, *adfinis*.

Germany, *Germania*.

germinate, *germinare*.

germination, *germinatio*.

gesticulate, *se iactare, gestum facĕre*.

gesticulation, gesture, *iactatio, gestus (-ūs)*.

get, v.: transit., *capĕre, adipisci, (com)parare, consequi*; to — anything done, *rem faciendam curare*; intransit., = become, *fieri*; to — along, *procedĕre*; — at, *attingĕre*; — away, *effugĕre*; — down, *descendĕre*; — in, *introire*; — out, *egredi, exire*; — up, *surgĕre*.

ghastliness, *pallor*.

ghastly, *exsanguis, pallidus*.

ghost, *manes (-ium), lemures (-um)*; the Holy Ghost, *Spiritus Sanctus*; to give up the —, *exspirare*.

giant, *vir maior quam pro humano habitu*; myth., *gigas*.

gibe, subst. *cavillatio*.

gibe, v. *cavillari*.

giddiness, *vertigo*.

giddy, *vertiginosus*. Transf., *levis, inconstans*.

gift, *donum*.

gig, *cisium*.

gild, *inaurare*.

gills, *branchiae (-arum)*.

gimlet, *terebra*.

gingerly, *pedetemptim, sensim*.

giraffe, *camelopardalis*.

gird, *(suc)cingĕre, accingĕre*: to — on, *accingĕre*; to — oneself, *(suc)cingi* or *accingi*.

girdle, *zona, cingulum*.

girl, *puella, virgo*.

girlhood, *aetas puellaris*.

girlish, *puellaris*.

girth, *ambitus (-ūs), circuitus (-ūs)*; of a horse, *cingula*.

give, *dare, tribuĕre, donare*; to — back, *reddĕre*; to give up, = surrender, *tradĕre, dedĕre*; = cease, *desistĕre*; to — in, — way, *cedĕre*.

gizzard, *ingluvies, guttur*.

glad, *laetus, hilaris*; adv. *laete, libenter*.

gladden, *(ex)hilarare*.

glade, *silva, saltus (-ūs)*.

gladiator, *gladiator*; a trainer of —s, *lanista*.

gladiatorial, *gladiatorius*.

gladness, *laetitia, hilaritas*.

glance, subst. *aspectus (-ūs)*.

glance, v. *aspicĕre*.

glare, subst.: of light, *fulgor*; = fierce look, *oculi torvi*.

glare, v., of light, *fulgĕre*; = look fiercely, *torvis oculis intuĕri*.

glass, subst. *vitrum*; a looking- —, *speculum*.

glass, adj., or glassy, *vitreus*.

gleam, subst. *fulgor*.

gleam, v. *fulgĕre*.

gleaning, subst. *spicilegium*.

glee, *hilaritas, laetitia, gaudium*.

glen, *(con)vallis*.

glib, *loquax, volubilis*; adv. *loquaciter, volubiliter*.

glibness, *loquacitas, volubilitas*.

glide, *(pro)labi*.

glimmer, *sublucēre*.

glimmering, adj. *sublustris*.

glitter, subst. *fulgor*.

glitter, v. *fulgēre, nitēre, lucēre*.

glittering, *lucidus, nitidus*; — white, *candidus*.

gloat, aspectu se delectare.

globe, globus, sphaera; = the earth, orbis terrarum.

globular, globosus.

gloom, obscuritas, caligo, tenebrae (-arum); = sadness, tristitia, maestitia.

gloomy: = dark, obscurus; = sad, tristis, maestus; adv. maeste.

glorify, laudare, celebrare.

glorious, (prae)clarus, amplus, inlustris; adv. (prae)clare, ample.

glory, subst. gloria, honor, decus (-oris, n.).

gloss, subst.: = shine, nitor; = explanation, interpretatio.

gloss, v.: to — over, extenuare.

glossary, glossarium.

glossy, nitidus.

Gloucester, Glevum.

gloves, manicae (-arum, = long sleeves).

glow, subst. ardor, fervor.

glow, v. ardēre, flagrare.

glow-worm, cicindela.

glue, subst. gluten.

glue, v. glutinare.

glut, subst. satietas.

glut, v. satiare, explēre.

glutinous, lentus, glutinosus.

glutton, helluo.

gluttonous, edax, vorax.

gluttony, gula, edacitas.

gnarled; see knotty.

gnash; to — the teeth, (dentibus) (in)frendĕre.

gnat, culex.

gnaw, (ad)rodĕre.

gnawing, adj. mordax.

go, v. ire, vadĕre (esp. fast), gradi (= to step), proficisci (= set out) discedĕre (= depart); to — back, redire, reverti; — beyond, excedĕre; — down, descendĕre; — forward, procedĕre; — in, inire, intrare, ingredi; — off, abire; — on, = continue, pergĕre, = happen, fieri, agi; — out, exire, egredi; — up, ascendĕre; — without, carēre; to —, = to become, fieri.

goad, subst. stimulus.

goad, v. stimulare, incitare.

goal, meta, calx.

goat, m. caper, hircus; f. capra, capella.

gobble, (de)vorare.

go-between, conciliator, interpres.

goblet, poculum, scyphus.

god, deus, divus, numen (divinum); the —s, di (dii), divi, numina, caelestes, superi; —s of the household, lares, penates; so help me —, ita me deus (ad)iuvet.

goddess, dea, diva.

godhead, numen.

godless, impius.

godlike, divinus.

godliness, pietas (erga deos).

godly, pius (erga deos).

godsend, res quasi divinitus oblata.

gold, aurum.

golden, aureus.

gold-mine, aurifodina.

goldsmith, aurifex.

good, subst. bonum, salus (-utis, f.); to do —, prodesse; —s, = property,

possessions, bona (-orum); = merchandise, merx.

good, adj. bonus, probus; morally —, bonus, probus, honestus; = kind, bonus, benignus; = useful, utilis; = convenient, commodus; = wholesome, saluber, salutaris; — day! salve! good!, interj., euge! bene habet.

goodbye, vale (plur. valete).

good-for-nothing, nequam.

good-humour, comitas, facilitas.

good-humoured, comis, facilis.

good-looking, pulcher, venustus.

good-nature, facilitas, comitas, benignitas.

good-natured, facilis, comis, benignus.

goodness, bonitas; moral —, probitas, virtūs (-ūtis, f.); = kindness, benignitas, bonitas.

good-tempered, mitis, lenis.

goose, anser.

gore, subst. cruor.

gore, v. (cornibus) transfigĕre.

gorge, subst.: = throat, gula, guttur, fauces (-ium); = narrow pass, angustiae (-arum), fauces (-ium).

gorge, v. (ex)satiare.

georgeous, splendidus, magnificus; adv. splendide, magnifice.

georgeousness, splendor, magnificentia.

gory, cruentus, cruentatus.

gospel, evangelium.

gossamer, aranea.

gossip, subst.: = talk, sermo, rumor; = talker, garrulus or loquax; = friend, familiaris.

gossip, v. sermonem conferre, garrire.

gourd, cucurbita.

gout, articulorum dolor; — in the hands, chiragra; — in the feet, podagra.

gouty, adj. arthriticus.

govern: politically, gubernare, administrare, curare; in gen., = restrain, guide, moderari, temperare, regĕre.

government, administratio, gubernatio; = supreme power, imperium, regnum; = those in power, render by relative clause.

governor, gubernator, rector; with delegated powers, praefectus, legatus.

governorship, praefectura.

gown: man's, toga; woman's, stola palla.

grace, subst.: = favour, goodwill, gratia, favor; by the — of god, deo favente; = gracefulness, charm, lepos (lepor), venustas, elegantia; myth., the Graces, Gratiae (-arum).

grace, v. (ad)ornare, decorare.

graceful, venustus, elegans; adv. venuste, eleganter.

gracious, propitius; see also kind.

grade, gradus (-ūs).

gradually, paullatim, gradatim, sensim.

graft, subst. surculus.

graft, v. inserĕre.

grain: = particle, granum, mica; = corn, frumentum.

grammar, grammatica (-ae, f., or -orum, n. pl.).

grammarian, *grammaticus*.
grammatical, *grammaticus*.
granary, *horreum, granaria (-orum)*.
grand, *grandis, magnificus, amplus*.
granddaughter, *neptis*.
grandees, *nobiles, proceres*.
grandeur, *amplitudo, magnificentia*.
grandfather, *avus*.
grandiloquent, *grandiloquus*.
grandmother, *avia*.
grandson, *nepos*.
grant, subst. *domum*; = act of granting, *concessio*.
grant, v.: = bestow, *permittĕre, concedĕre*; = admit, *concedĕre, dare*; —ed that, *ut* with subj.
grape, *acinus*; bunch of grapes, *uva*.
graphic, *expressus*.
grapple, *luctari*.
grappling-iron, *ferrea manus (-ūs), harpago*.
grasp, subst.: physical, *complexus (-ūs), manūs* (plur.); mental, *captus (-ūs)*.
grasp, v.: physically, *(ap)prehendĕre, comprehendĕre, prensare*; mentally, *intellegĕre, animo comprehendĕre*; to = at, *captare, adfectare, appetĕre*.
grasping, *avarus, appetens*.
grass, *gramen, herba*.
grasshopper, *gryllus*.
grassy, *gramineus, herbidus*.
grate, subst. *focus, caminus*.
grate, v.: = rub, *(con)terĕre*; = make a grating noise, *stridĕre*.
grateful: = thankful, *gratus*; adv. *grate, grato animo*; = pleasant, *gratus, acceptus*.
gratification: as act, *expletio, delectatio*; = pleasure, *voluptas*.
gratify: see please.
grating, subst.: = bars, *cancelli (-orum), clatri (-orum)*; = harsh noise, *stridor*.
gratitude, *gratus animus*.
gratuitous, *gratuitus*; adv. *gratis, gratuito*.
gratuity; see alms, gift.
grave, subst.: = place of burial, *sepulcrum*; = place of cremation, *bustum*; = state of death, *mors*.
grave, adj. *gravis, serius, tristis*.
gravel, *glarea*.
gravity, *gravitas*.
gravy, *ius (iuris, n.), sucus*.
graze: of animals, transit. *pascĕre*, intransit. *pasci*; = to touch in passing, *radĕre, stringĕre*.
grazier, *pecuarius*.
grazing, subst. *pascua (-orum, plur.)*.
grease, subst. *adeps, lardum*.
grease, v. *ung(u)ĕre*.
greasy, *unctus, pinguis*.
great, *magnus, grandis, amplus; clarus, summus, ingens*; as plur., the great, *nobiles (-ium)*; greater, *maior*; greatest, *maximus*; how —, *quantus*; so —, *tantus*; too —, *nimius*. Adv., greatly, *magnopere*.
greaves, *ocreae*.
Greece, *Graecia*.
greed, *aviditas, cupiditas*.
greedy, *avidus. cupidus*; adv. *avide, cupide*.
Greek, adj. and subst. *Graecus*.

green, subst.: = greenness, *viriditas, color viridis*: = grassy space, *campus*.
green, adj. *viridis, virens*; to be — *virēre*; = fresh, *viridis, recens*.
greens, *holus (-eris, n.)*.
greet, *salutare, salvēre iubēre*.
greeting, *(con)salutatio*.
grey, *canus* (= hoary); *caesius* or *glaucus* (grey-blue).
greyness, *canities*.
gridiron, *craticula*.
grief, *dolor, aegritudo, maeror, luctus (-ūs; = mourning)*.
grievance, *iniuria; querimonia* (=complaint).
grieve, v.: transit., *dolore adficĕre, angĕre*: intransit., *dolēre, maerēre, lugēre*.
grievous, *acerbus, gravis*; adv. *acerbe, graviter*.
grill, v. *torrēre*.
grim, *torvus, saevus*.
grimace, subst. *os distortum*.
grimness, *saevitia, torvitas*.
grimy; see dirty.
grin, subst. *rictus (-ūs)*.
grin, v. *ridēre*.
grind, v. *molĕre*; to — the teeth, *dentibus frendĕre*.
grinder, (of teeth) *dens genuinus*.
grindstone, *cos*.
grip; see grasp.
grisly, *foedus, horrendus*.
grist, *farina*.
groan, subst. *gemitus (-ūs)*.
groan, v. *gemĕre*.
groin, *inguen*.
groom, subst. *agaso*.
groom, v. *curare*.
groove, *canalis*.
grope, *praetemptare*.
gross: = great, too great, *magnus, nimius*; = disgraceful, *turpis, foedus*. Adv. *nimium*; *turpiter, foede*.
grot, grotto, *antrum*.
grotesque, *mirus; ridiculus*.
ground, subst.: = earth, soil, *humus (f.), solum, terra*; on the —, *humi*; = place, position, *locus*; = reason, basis, *causa, ratio*: on the — that, *quod*.
ground, v. of a ship, *sidĕre*.
groundless, *vanus, falsus*; adv. *temere, falso*.
groundlessness, *vanitas*.
groundwork, *fundamentum*.
group, subst. *caterva, globus, circulus*.
group, v. *disponĕre*.
grouping, *dispositio*.
grove, *lucus, nemus (-oris, n.)*.
grovel, *humi iacēre*.
grovelling, *abiectus, humilis, submissus*.
grow: intransit., *crescĕre, augeri*; to — up, *adolescere*; = to become, *fieri*; transit., *alĕre, colĕre*.
grower, *cultor*.
growl, subst. *fremitus (-ūs)*.
growl, v. *fremĕre*.
grown, grown-up, *adultus, pubes*.
growth, *auctus(-ūs), incrementum*.
grub, subst. *vermiculus*.
grub, v.: to — up, *eruĕre*.
grudge, subst. *simultas, invidia*.

grudge, v. (*rem homini*) *invidēre*.
gruff, *asper*; adv. *aspere*.
grumble, *murmurare, fremēre*.
grunt, subst. *grunnitus (-ūs)*.
grunt, v. *grunnire*.
Guadalquivir, *Baetis*.
guarantee, subst.: as a thing, *fides, sponsio, vadimonium*; = guarantor, *vas, sponsor*.
guarantee, v. *praestare, fidem dare*.
guard, subst. *custodia, praesidium*; to mount —, *excubare, excubias or vigilias agēre*; to be on one's —, *(prae)cavēre*; off one's —, *incautus, imprudens*; = persons on guard, *custodes (-um), custodia, praesidium*.
guard, v. *custodire, tueri*.
guarded, *cautus, circumspectus*; adv. *caute*.
guardian, *custos, defensor*; of a ward, *tutor*.
guardianship, *custodia*; of a ward, *tutela*.
guess, subst. *coniectura*.
guess, v. *conicēre, divinare, augurari*.
guest, *hospes (-itis)*, f. *hospita*; at a party, *conviva*.
guidance, *ductus (-ūs), consilium*.
guide, *dux*.
guide, v. *ducēre*. Transf., *regēre, gubernare, moderari*.
guild, *conlegium*.
guile, *dolus, astutia*.
guileless, *simplex, apertus*; adv. *simpliciter*.
guilelessness, *simplicitas*.
guilt, *vitium, culpa, noxia*.
guiltless, *innocens, insons*.
guilty, *sons, sceleratus, nocens*; adv. *scelerate*.
guise, *habitus (-ūs), species*.
gulf, *sinus (-ūs,* = bay); *gurges* (= abyss).
gullet, *gula, guttur*.
gullible, *credulus*.
gully, *alveus*.
gulp, subst. *haustus (-ūs)*.
gulp, v. *haurire, obsorbēre*.
gum: of the mouth, *gingiva*; of plants, *gummi*.
gun: use *tormentum*.
gurgle, *murmurare*.
gush, v. *effundi*.
gust, *flabra (-orum,* n. plur.).
gusty, *turbidus, procellosus*.
gut, subst. *intestinum*.
gut, v. *exinanire*.
gutter, *canalis, cloaca*.
guttural, of sounds, *gravis*.
gymnasium, *gymnasium, palaestra*.
gymnastic, *gymnicus, palaestricus*.

H

ha! *ha!*
habit: = custom, *consuetudo, mos, usus (-ūs)*; = state, *habitus (-ūs)*.
habitable, *habitabilis*.
habitation, *domicilium, sedes, domus*.
habitual, *inveteratus, usitatus*; adv. *de* or *ex more*.
habituate, *adsuefacēre*.

hack, v. *caedēre*.
hackneyed, *tritus*.
haft, *manubrium*.
hag, *anus (-ūs), anicula*.
haggle, *de pretio ambigēre*.
hail, subst. *grando*.
hail, v.: it —, *grandinat*; = to greet, *salutare, appellare*.
hail, interj. *salve!* plur. *salvete!*
hair: single, *pilus, capillus, saeta* (= bristle); coll., use plur., or *crinis, comae (-arum), caesaries* (flowing).
hairdresser, *tonsor*.
hairpin, *crinale*.
hairsplitting, *disserendi spinae (-arum)*.
hairy, *pilosus, capillatus*.
halcyon, subst. *alcedo, (h)alcyon*.
halcyon, adj. *serenus*.
hale, adj. *sanus, validus, robustus*.
hale, v. *rapēre, trahēre*.
half, subst. *dimidium*.
half, adj. *dimidius, dimidiatus*.
half-asleep, *semisomnus, semisopitus*.
half-burnt, *semiustus*.
half-hour, *semihora*.
half-open, *semiapertus*.
half-pound, *selibra*.
hall, *atrium*.
halloo! *heus! ohe!*
halloo, subst. *clamor*.
halloo, v. *clamare, vociferari*.
hallow, *consecrare, dedicare*.
hallowed, *sacer, sanctus*.
hallucination, *error*.
halm, *calamus*.
halt, adj. *claudus*.
halt, v.: = limp, *claudicare*; = stop *consistēre*.
halter, *capistrum, laqueus* (= noose).
halve, *ex aequo dividēre*.
halved, *dimidiatus*.
ham, *poples*; salted, smoked, etc., *perna*.
hamlet, *vicus, viculus*.
hammer, subst. *malleus*.
hammer, v. *malleo (con)tundēre*.
hamper, subst. *corbis*.
hamper, v. *implicare, impedire*.
hamstring, v. *poplitem succidēre*.
hand, subst. *manus (-ūs, f.), palma* (= palm); right —, *(manus) dextra or dextera*; left —, *(manus) sinistra or laeva*; to give a person one's —, *homini dextram porrigēre*; = workman, *opera* (usually plur.); an old —, *veterator*; to be at —, *praesto esse, adesse*; in —, on —, *in manibus*; — to — (in fighting), *comminus*.
hand, v. *dare, tradēre, porrigēre*.
handcuffs, *manicae (-arum)*.
handful, *manipulus*.
handicraft, *artificium*.
handiwork, *opus (-eris, n.), opificium*.
handkerchief, *sudarium*.
handle, subst. *manubrium, capulus, ansa* (lit. and fig.).
handle, v. *tractare, contrectare*.
handling, *tractatio*.
handsome, *formosus, venustus, pulcher*. Transf., *liberalis*; adv. *praeclare, liberaliter*.
handwriting, *manus (-ūs, f.), chirographum*.

handy, *habilis, promptus.*

hang, v.: intransit., *pendēre;* to — over, *imminēre;* to — back, *cessare;* transit., *suspendēre;* to — the head, *caput demittĕre.*

hanger-on, *adsecla.*

hanging, subst. *suspendium.*

hangman, *carnifex.*

hanker; to — after, *desiderare.*

haphazard, adv. *temere.*

hapless, *miser, infelix.*

haply, *fortasse, forsitan.*

happen, *fieri, accidĕre, contingĕre.*

happiness, *vita beata, felicitas.*

happy, *beatus, felix, fortunatus;* of language, *aptus.* Adv. *beate, feliciter.*

harangue, *contio;* to deliver a —, *contionari.*

harass, *vexare, sollicitare.*

harbinger, *praenuntius, antecursor.*

harbour, subst. *portus (-ūs);* — -dues, *portorium;* full of —s, *portuosus.*

harbour, v. (*hospitio*) *excipĕre.*

hard, adj. *durus;* = difficult, *difficilis, arduus.*

hard, adv. *summa vi, enixe.*

harden, v.: transit., *durum facĕre;* intransit., *obdurescĕre.*

hard-hearted, *durus, ferreus.*

hardihood, *audacia.*

hardly, = scarcely, *vix, aegre.*

hardness, *duritia* (or *durities*); = severity, *iniquitas, crudelitas.*

hardship, *labor, incommodum, molestia.*

hardware, *ferramenta (-orum).*

hardy, *robustus.*

hare, *lepus (leporis, m.).*

hark! interj. *heus!*

harlequin, *sannio.*

harm, subst. *damnum, detrimentum.*

harm, v. *nocēre, laedĕre.*

harmful, *nocens, noxius.*

harmless, *innocens, innoxius.*

harmlessness, *innocentia.*

harmonious, *concors* (lit. and fig.); *congruens, conveniens.* Adv. *concorditer, congruenter, convenienter.*

harmonize, v.: transit. *concordes facĕre, componĕre, (re)conciliare;* intransit., *concinĕre, consentire.*

harmony, *concordia* (lit. and fig.); *consensus (-ūs), convenientia.*

harness, subst. *ornamenta equi.*

harness, v. (*equum*) *ornare.*

harp, subst. *lyra.*

harp, v. *psallĕre.*

harpist: m. *fidicen, psaltes (-ae);* f. *fidicina, psaltria.*

harpy, *harpyia.*

harrow, subst. (*h*)*irpex, crates.*

harrow, v. *occare;* to — the feelings, (*ex*)*cruciare.*

harrowing, *terribilis, atrox.*

harry, *vexare, cruciare.*

harsh: in sound, *raucus, asper;* in taste, *acer, asper;* in temper, *asper, morosus, durus.* Adv. *aspere.*

harshness, *asperitas.*

hart, *cervus.*

harvest, subst. *messis.*

harvester, *messor.*

haste, subst. *festinatio, celeritas;* nervous —, *trepidatio.*

haste, hasten, v.: intransit., *properare, festinare, maturare;* transit., *accelerare, maturare, properare.*

hastiness, of temper, *iracundia.*

hasty: = hurried, (*prae*)*properus, citus, praeceps:* = irritable, *iracundus, stomachosus.* Adv. *propere, properanter, raptim.*

hat, *petasus.*

hatch, v. (*ex ovis*) *excludĕre:* = to concoct, *moliri, machinari.*

hatches, *claustra (-orum).*

hatchet, *securis, ascia, dolabra.*

hate, hatred, *odium, invidia.*

hate, v. *odisse;* to be hated, *odio esse.*

hateful, *odiosus, invisus;* adv. *odiose.*

haughtiness, *superbia, insolentia, adrogantia.*

haughty, *superbus, insolens, adrogans;* adv. *superbe, insolenter, adroganter.*

haul, v. *trahĕre, ducĕre.*

haulm, v. see stalk.

haunch, *clunis.*

haunt, subst. *latebrae (-arum), latibulum, lustra (-orum).*

haunt, v. *frequentare,* (*con*)*celebrare;* of spirits, cares, etc., *agitare, sollicitare.*

have, *habēre, tenēre;* to — to do, *debēre facĕre.*

haven, *portus (-ūs).*

havoc, *vastatio, strages.*

hawk, subst. *accipiter (-tris, m.).*

hawk, v. = sell, *venditare.*

hay, *faenum.*

hay-fork, *furca.*

hazard, subst. *fors, casus (-ūs), periculum* (= risk), *alea* (= gambling).

hazard, v.: see dare or endanger.

hazardous, *periculosus;* adv. *periculose.*

haze, *nebula, caligo.*

hazel, *corylus.*

hazy, *nebulosus.*

he, *hic, ille, is;* = himself, *ipse.*

head, subst. *caput, vertex;* the back of the —, *occipitium;* = understanding or memory, *mens, animus, iudicium;* = chief, leader, *caput, princeps, dux;* to be at the —, *praeesse;* to put at the —, *praeficere;* = point, heading, *caput.*

head, adj. *primus, primarius, princeps.*

head, v. *ducĕre, praeesse.*

head-band, *infula, vita, redimiculum.*

head-dress, *mitra.*

headland, *promuntorium.*

headlong, *praeceps.*

headquarters, *praetorium, principia (-orum).*

headstrong, *pervicax, temerarius.*

head-wind, *ventus adversus.*

heady, = intoxicating, *fervidus.*

heal, v.: transit., *sanare, medēri, curare;* intransit., *consanescĕre.*

healing, subst. *sanatio.*

healing, adj. *saluber, salutaris.*

health, *sanitas, valetudo.*

healthful, *saluber, salutaris.*

healthy, *sanus, salvus, saluber* (of places); adv. *salubriter.*

heap, subst. *acervus, agger.*

heap, v. *cumulare, coacervare, congerĕre.*

hear, *audire, auscultare* (= listen to). Transf., = find out, learn, *cognoscĕre, accipĕre.*

hearer, *auditor.*

hearing, subst.: as sense, *auditus (-ūs);* as process, *auditio;* = an audience, *audientia;* a judicial —, *cognitio.*

hearken, *auscultare.*

hearsay, *rumor, auditio.*

heart: physical, *cor;* = seat of feeling, etc. *animus, mens, pectus (-oris,* n.); from the —, *ex animo;* = courage, *animus;* = memory: to know by —, *memoria tenēre;* to learn by —, *ediscĕre;* dear —, *(mea) vita.*

heart-breaking, *miserabilis, maestus, flebilis.*

heart-broken, *animo fractus* or *adflictus.*

heartfelt, *verus.*

hearth, *focus.*

heartiness, *studium, alacritas.*

heartless, *crudelis, saevus;* adv. *crudeliter, saeve.*

heartlessness, *crudelitas, saevitia.*

heart-sick, *animo aeger.*

hearty, *verus* (= true), *alacer* (= brisk), *benignus* (=kind). Adv. *summo studio.*

heat, subst. *calor, ardor, fervor, aestus (-ūs);* of passion, etc., *ardor, fervor, aestus.*

heat, v. *calefacĕre, fervefacĕre.* Transf., *accendĕre.*

heath: as plant, *erice(-es,* f.); as a place, *loca inculta.*

heathen, adj. *paganus.*

heave, v.: transit., *(at)tollĕre, extollĕre;* to — a sigh, *gemitum dare,* or *ducĕre;* intransit., *aestuare, fluctuare, tumescĕre.*

heaven: = sky, *caelum;* = gods, *di (dei), superi;* the will of —, *numen divinum;* for —'s sake! *per deos immortales!* — forbid, *di meliora.*

heavenly, *caelestis, divinus.*

heaviness, *gravitas, pondus(-eris,* n.); of atmosphere, *crassitudo;* = sadness, *tristitia, maestitia.*

heavy, *gravis, ponderosus;* of air, *crassus;* of soil, *spissus;* of rain, *magnus;* abstr., = oppressive, *gravis, molestus;* = downcast, *tristis, adflictus, maestus.* Adv. *graviter.*

heavy-armed; — troops. *gravior armatus (-ūs).*

Hebrew, adj. *Hebraeus, Hebraicus.*

hectic, *febriculosus.*

hector, *se iactare.*

hedge, subst. *saepes, saepimentum*

hedge, v. *saepire.*

hedgehog, *ericus, echinus.*

heed, subst.: to take —, *cavēre.*

heed, v. *curare, observare;* = obey, *parēre, obedire.*

heedless, *neglegens, temerarius;* adv. *neglegenter, temere.*

heedlessness, *neglegentia, temeritas.*

heel, subst. *calx.*

heel, v. *in latus labi* or *inclinari.*

heifer, *iuvenca.*

height, *altitudo, proceritas;* the — of glory, *summa gloria;* = high place, *locus editus, altitudines (-um,* plur.).

heighten; render by *altior;* = increase, *augēre, amplificare, exaggerare.*

heinous, *foedus, nefarius, atrox;* adv. *foede, nefarie, atrociter.*

heinousness, *atrocitas.*

heir, *heres;* sole —, *heres ex asse.*

heirloom, *res hereditaria.*

Helen, *Helena.*

hell, *inferi (-orum), Tartarus,* or n. plur. *Tartara.*

hellebore, *(h)elleborus, veratrum.*

Hellenic, *Graecus.*

hellish, *infernus, nefandus*

helm, *gubernaculum.*

helmet, *cassis, galea.*

helmsman, *gubernator.*

help, subst. *auxilium, subsidium.*

help, v. *(ad)iuvare, subvenire, succurrĕre;* so — me God, *ita me di ament;* I can't — saying, *facĕre non possum quin dicam.*

helper, *adiutor;* f. *adiutrix.*

helpful, *utilis.*

helpless, *inermis, inops.*

helplessness, *inopia.*

hem, subst. *limbus, instita.*

hem, v.: = sew, *suĕre;* to — in, *circumsedĕre, obsidēre.*

hemp, *cannabis.*

hen, *gallina.*

hence, *hinc;* as interj., *apage;* a few days —, *paucis diebus, post paucos dies.*

henceforth, *posthac.*

Henry, *Henricus.*

her, possessive, *eius, illius;* — own, *suus -a -um.*

herald, subst., *caduceator, fetialis, praeco;* = forerunner, *praenuntius.*

herald, v. *nuntiare.*

herb, *herba, olus (oleris,* n.).

herd, subst. *grex;* of large cattle, *armentum;* of a —, *gregalis, gregarius;* in —s, *gregatim;* of people, the common —, *vulgus (-i,* n.).

herd, v. intransit. *congregari.*

herdsman, *pastor, armentarius.*

here: = at this place, *hic;* to be —, *adesse;* = to this place, hither, *huc;* from — (hence), *hinc;* — and there *rarus* (adv. *raro).*

hereafter, *posthac, aliquando.*

hereditary, *hereditarius, paternus.*

herein, *in hac re.*

hereupon, *hic.*

heritage, *hereditas, patrimonium.*

hermit, *homo solitarius.*

hero: = demigod, *heros;* = brave man, *vir fortissimus:* in a play, *persona prima.*

heroic, *heroicus;* = brave. valiant, *fortis;* adv. *fortiter.*

heroine: = demi-goddess, *heroina, herois;* = brave woman, *femina fortissima.*

heroism, *eximia virtus (-utis). animus fortis.*

heron, *ardea.*

hers; see her.

herself, reflex., *se;* otherwise *ipsa.*

hesitate, *dubitare, cunctari, haesitare.*

hesitation, *dubitatio, haesitatio, cunctatio.*

heterogeneous, *diversus, dissimilis.*

hew, *caedĕre, dolare.*

hewn; hewn stone, *saxum quadratum.*

hexameter, *hexameter* (or *-trus).*

heyday, *flos aetatis.*

hiatus, *hiatus (-ūs).*

hibernate, *per hiemen dormire* or *quiescĕre.*

hiccough, hiccup, *singultus (-ūs).*

hidden, *occultus;* to lie —, *latĕre.*

hide, subst. *corium, pellis.*

hide, v.: transit., *abdĕre, celare;* of feelings, etc., *dissimulare;* intransit., render by reflex.

hideous, *foedus, turpis;* adv. *foede.*

hideousness, *foeditas, deformitas.*

hiding-place, *latibulum, latebra.*

higgledy-piggledy, *confuse.*

high, adj. *altus, (ex)celsus, procerus* (= tall), *sublimis* (= raised aloft); in rank, *amplus;* of prices, *magnus;* of sound, *acutus;* of meat, *rancidus.* Adv. *alte;* to value —, *magni aestimare.*

high-born, *generosus, nobili loco ortus.*

high-flown, *tumidus.*

high-handed, *superbus, imperiosus.*

highlander, *homo montanus*

highlands, *loca montuosa (-orum)*

high-minded, *magnanimus, generosus.*

high-priest, *Pontifex Maximus*

high-spirited, *ferox, animosus.*

high-tide *plurimus aestūs accessus (-ūs).*

highway, *via.*

highwayman, *latro, grassator.*

hilarity, *hilaritas, laetitia.*

hill, *collis, tumulus;* up —, *adverso colle*

hilly, *montuosus, clivosus.*

hilt, *capulus.*

him; see he.

himself, reflex., *se;* otherwise *ipse.*

hind, subst.: = female stag, *cerva;* = servant, *verna, servus;* = peasant, *rusticus, agrestis.*

hind, adj. *aversus, posterior.*

hinder, *impedire, obstare, officĕre.*

hindmost, *postremus, ultimus, novissimus.*

hindrance, *impedimentum.*

hinge, subst. *cardo.*

hint, subst. *significatio.*

hint, v. *significare.*

hip, *coxendix.*

hire, subst. *merces.*

hire, v. *conducĕre.*

hired, *conductus, mercenarius*

hireling, *mercenarius.*

hirer, *conductor.*

his, *eius, illius, huius;* — own *suus -a -um.*

hiss, subst. *sibilus* (plur. *sibila*).

hiss, v. *sibilare;* to — off the stage, *exsibilare, explodĕre.*

hist! *st!*

historian, *rerum (gestarum) scriptor.*

historic, historical, *historicus;* — writings, *libri ad historiam pertinentes.*

history, *historia, rerum gestarum memoria, annales;* ancient —, *antiquitatis memoria.*

histrionic, *scaenicus.*

hit, subst. *plaga, ictus (-ūs).*

hit, v. *ferire, tundĕre, percutĕre;* to — it off, = agree, *convenire;* to — upon, *offendĕre, incidĕre.*

hitch, subst. *impedimentum* (= hindrance), *mora* (= delay).

hitch, v. *(ad)iungĕre, adnectĕre.*

hither, adj. *citerior.*

hither, adj. *huc;* — and thither, *huc illuc.*

hitherto, *adhuc, hactenus.*

hive, *alvearium, alvus.*

ho! *heus!*

hoard, subst. *copia, acervus.*

hoard, v. *conquirĕre, coacervare.*

hoar-frost, *pruina.*

hoarse, *raucus;* adv. *rauca voce.*

hoary, *canus.*

hoax, subst. *ludificatio.*

hoax, v. *ludificari, inludĕre.*

hobble, *claudicare.*

hobby, *studium.*

hock, *poples.*

hoe, subst. *sarculum, marra*

hoe, v. *sarire.*

hog, *sus, porcus.*

hoggish, *suillus.*

hogshead, *dolium.*

hoist, *sublevare, tollĕre.*

hold, subst.: = grasp *manus (-ūs);* of a ship, *caverna.*

hold, v.: = to have, possess, *tenēre, obtinēre, possidēre, habēre;* = to contain, *capĕre, continēre;* = to conduct, *agĕre, habēre;* to — an opinion, — that, *censēre, ducĕre;* = to check, *cohibēre;* to — out (= endure), *durare, sustinēre.*

holding, subst. *possessio.*

hole, *cavum, foramen; rima* (= chink); *lacuna* (= pit).

holiday, *dies festus, feriae(-arum).*

holiness, *sanctitas, religio.*

Holland, *Batavia.*

hollow, subst.: = valley, *convallis, valles (vallis);* see also hole.

hollow, adj. *(con)cavus;* of sounds, *fuscus, raucus;* = insincere, *vanus, simulatus.*

hollow, v. *(ex)cavare.*

holm-oak, *ilex.*

holy, *sacer, sanctus;* adv. *sancte.*

homage, *cultus (-ūs), observantia.*

home, subst. *domus, domicilium;* at — *domi;* from —, *domo;* —wards *to* one's —, *domum.*

home, adj. *domesticus, familiaris.*

homeless, *domo carens.*

homeliness, *simplicitas.*

homely, *simplex, rudis.*

homewards, *domum.*

homicide; see murder.

homily, *oratio.*

homogeneous, *eiusdem generis.*

honest, *probus, sincerus, frugi.* adv. *probe, sincere.*

honesty, *probitas, sinceritas, fides.*

honey, *mel*

honeycomb, *favus.*

honeyed, honied, *mellitus, suavis. dulcis.*

honour, subst.: = official distinction, *dignitas, honos (honor);* = moral integrity, *honestas, fides;* sense of — *pudor;* an — to, = a credit to, *decus.*

honour, v. *colĕre, honorare, celebrare.*

honourable: = honoured, *honoratus, amplus;* = bring honour, *honestus, honorificus.* Adv. *honeste, honorifice.*

hood, *cucullus.*

hoodwink, *ludificari, inludĕre.*

hoof, *ungula.*
hook, subst. *hamus, uncus.*
hook, v. *hamo capĕre.*
hooked, *aduncus, hamatus.*
hoop, *circulus;* a child's —, *trochus.*
hoopoe, *upupa.*
hoot, hooting, subst.: of owls, *cantus (-ūs);* of persons, *vociferatio.*
hoot, v.: of owls, *canĕre;* of persons, *vociferari, obstrepĕre.*
hop, v. *salire.*
hope, subst. *spes;* a gleam of —, *specula;* to have no —. *desperare.*
hope, v. *sperare.*
hopeful, hopefully; render by phrase with *spes.*
hopeless: = despairing, *spe carens;* = despaired of, *desperatus.*
hopelessness, *desperatio; res desperatae.*
horde, *grex, caterva.*
horizon, *orbis finiens;* = sky, in gen., *caelum.*
horizontal, *aequus, libratus;* adv. *ad libram.*
horn, *cornu;* as a drinking-cup, *poculum.*
horned, *corniger, cornutus.*
hornet, *crabro.*
horny, *corneus.*
horoscope, *horoscopus, genesis;* to cast a —, *sidera natalicia notare.*
horrible, horrid, *horribilis, foedus, atrox;* adv. *foede.*
horrify, *(ex)terrēre, obstupefacĕre.*
horror, *horror, timor, pavor;* a —, = a monster, *monstrum.*
horse, *equus;* = cavalry, *equites (-um), equitatus (-ūs).*
horseback; to ride on —, *in equo vehi, equitare;* to fight on — *ex equo pugnare.*
horse-fly, *tabanus.*
horse-hair, *pilus equinus.*
horseman, *eques.*
horse-race, *curriculum equorum*
horse-shoe, *solea.*
horticulture, *hortorum cultus (-ūs).*
hospitable, *hospitalis;* adv. *hospitaliter, comiter.*
hospitality, *hospitium, hospitalitas.*
host, *hospes;* at a feast, *convivator;* at an inn, *caupo;* = multitude; army, *exercitus (-ūs).*
hostage, *obses.*
hostelry, *caupona.*
hostess, *hospita.*
hostile, *hostilis, inimicus, infestus.*
hostility, *animus infestus, inimicitia, odium;* hostilities, *hostilia (-ium), bellum.*
hot, *calidus, fervidus, fervens, ardens;* to be —, *calēre, fervēre, aestuare;* to make —, *calefacĕre.* Adv. *ardenter.*
hotel, *deversorium, hospitium.*
hotheaded, *fervidus, temerarius.*
hound, subst. *canis (venaticus).*
hound, v. *instigare, urgēre.*
hour, *hora;* half an —, *semihora;* what — is it? *quota hora est?*
hourly, *singulis horis, in horas.*
house, subst. *domus, aedes, aedificium, domicilium;* = race, clan, *gens, genus;* at my —, *apud me, domi meae*
house, v. = store, *condĕre.*

housebreaker, *fur.*
household, subst. *domus, familia.*
household, adj. *domesticus;* —-gods, *lares (-um), penates (-ium).*
householder, *paterfamilias.*
house-keeper, *promus.*
house-maid, *ancilla.*
house-wife. *materfamilias, hera.*
hovel, *tugurium, gurgustium.*
hover, *(circum)volitare, imminēre.*
how. (1) interrog. *quomodo? quemadmodum? qui?;* with adj. or adv., *quam?;* how great? *quantus?;* how small? *quantulus?;* how many? *quot?;* how often? *quotie(n)s?.* (2) in exclamation, *ut, quam;* also *quantus, quantulus,* etc.
howbeit, *(at)tamen.*
however: adv. *quamvis quamlibet;* — great, *quantuscunque, quantus quantus;* — many, *quotquot;* — often, *quotienscunque;* conj., *sed, autem, (at)tamen, nihilominus.*
howl, subst. *ululatus (-ūs), eiulatus (-ūs).*
howl, v. *ululare, fremĕre, eiulare.*
hubbub, *tumultus (-ūs), turba.*
huckster, *caupo, institor.*
huddled, *conferti.*
hue, *color.*
hug, subst. *complexus (-ūs).*
hug, v. *amplecti, complecti;* to — the shore, *litus premĕre* or *legĕre.*
huge, *immanis, ingens.*
hulk, *alveus navis.*
hum, subst. *fremitus (-ūs), murmur, susurrus.*
hum, v. *fremĕre, murmurare;* = sing softly, *secum canĕre.*
human, *humanus, hominum (* = of men*);* — feelings, *humanitas;* — being, *homo.* Adv. *humano modo.*
humane, *misericors, clemens;* adv. *clementer, humane.*
humanity = nature of man, *humanitas, natura humana;* = mankind, *homines (-um), gens humana;* = kindly feeling, *clementia, misericordia.*
humble, adj.: = obscure, *humilis, obscurus:* of — origin, *humili loco natus;* = modest, unassuming, *summissus, verecundus.* Adv. *summisse.*
humble, v. *infringĕre, comprimĕre;* to — oneself, *se* or *animum summittĕre.*
humid, *humidus.*
humidity, *humor.*
humiliation, *dedecus (-oris, n.).*
humility, *animus summissus.*
humorous: of situations, *ridiculus;* of persons, *iocosus, lepidus, facetus.*
humour: = fluid, *humor;* = disposition, *ingenium, natura, animus;* = fancy, caprice, *voluptas, libido;* I am in the — to do, *libet mihi facere;* = sense of fun, *festivitas, facetiae(-arum).*
humour, v. *indulgĕre, morem gerĕre* (with dat.).
hump, *gibbus, gibba.*
humpbacked, *gibber.*
hundred, adj. *centum;* a — at a time, *centeni -ae -a;* a — times, *centie(n)s*
hundred-fold, *centuplex.*
hunger, subst. *fames.*
hunger, v. *esurire.*

hungry, *esuriens, ieiunus;* adv. *avide.*

hunt, v. *venari, consectari.*

hunt, subst. *venatio, venatus (-ūs).*

hunter, huntsman, *venator.*

huntress, *venatrix.*

hurdle, *crates.*

hurl, *iacĕre, iaculari, conicĕre.*

hurling, subst. *coniectus (-ūs).*

hurrah! *io!*

hurricane, *tempestas, procella.*

hurried, *citatus, praeceps;* adv. *festinanter, propere, raptim.*

hurry, subst. *festinatio, trepidatio.*

hurry, v.: transit. *accelerare, incitare, rapĕre; maturare* (= to hurry on); instransit., *festinare, properare, maturare.*

hurt, subst. *vulnus (-eris, n.).*

hurt, adj.: physically, *saucius;* in feelings, *offensus.*

hurt, v. *laedĕre, nocĕre;* to — a person's feelings, *hominem offendĕre;* to be — at a thing, *rem aegre ferre;* it —s, *dolet.*

hurtful, *nocens, noxius molestus.*

husband, subst. *maritus, vir, coniunx.*

husband, v. *parcĕre.*

husbandman, *agricola, colonus.*

husbandry, *res rustica, agricultura.*

hush! interj. *st! tacĕ* (plur. *tacĕte*).

hush, v. *comprimĕre*

husk, *folliculus.*

hustings, *suggestus (-ūs), comitium.*

hustle, v. *offendĕre, pulsare.*

hut, *casa, tugurium.*

hutch, *cavea* (= cage).

hyacinth, *hyacinthus (hyacinthos).*

hymeneal, *nuptialis.*

hymn, subst. *carmen, hymnus* (ecclesiastical).

hymn, v. *canĕre, cantare, celebrare.*

hyperbole, *hyperbole, veritatis superlatio.*

hyperbolical, *superlatus.*

hypercritical, *nimium severus.*

hypochondria, *atra* (or *nigra*) *bilis.*

hypochondriacal, *melancholicus.*

hypocrisy, *(dis)simulatio, fraus.*

hypocrite, *(dis)simulator.*

hypocritical, *simulatus, fictus;* adv. *simulate, ficte.*

hypothesis, *opinio, sententia, coniectura.*

I

iambic, subst. *iambus.*

iambic, adj. *iambeus.*

ice, *glacies, gelu.*

icicle, *stiria.*

icy, *glacialis, gelidus, frigidus.*

idea: = notion, conception, *notio, notitia, imago;* in gen., = thought, *cogitatio, opinio, sententia;* = purpose, *consilium.*

ideal, subst., = perfect type, *exemplar, specimen.*

ideal, adj.: = perfect, *perfectus, optimus, summus;* = existing only in the mind, *commenticius.*

identical, *idem.*

identify. = recognize, *agnoscĕre.*

identify; render by *idem* (= same), or phrase like *quis sit* (= who he is).

ides, *idūs (-uum).*

idiocy, *fatuitas.*

idiom, *propria loquendi ratio.*

idiotic, *fatuus.*

idle, adj.: = inactive, lazy, *otiosus, vacuus, piger, segnis;* = useless, *inutilis, vanus, inritus.* Adv. *segniter;* = in vain, *frustra, incassum.*

idle, v. *cessare, nihil agĕre.*

idleness: = inactivity, *cessatio, otium;* = laziness, *segnitia, pigritia.*

idler, *homo deses; cessator.*

idol, *idolum* (ecclesiastical); *fictus deus.*

idolize, *(tamquam deum) colĕre.*

idyl, *bucolica (-orum, n.;* = pastoral poetry).

if, *si;* and —, *quodsi;* but —, *sin;* — only, *si modo* (or *dum modo* with subj.); even —, *etsi, etiamsi;* as —, *quasi, tamquam;* in indirect questions, if (= whether) is *num.*

igneous, *igneus.*

ignite, v.: transit., *accendĕre, incendĕre;* intransit., *exardescĕre, accendi, incendi.*

ignoble: by descent, *ignobilis, obscuro loco natus;* in character, *inliberalis, abiectus, turpis;* adv. *trupiter.*

ignominious, *turpis;* adv. *turpiter, cum ignominia.*

ignominy, *ignominia, dedecus (-oris).*

ignorance, *inscientia, ignoratio.*

ignorant, *inscius, ignarus, imperitus* (= inexperienced), *indoctus* (= untaught); to be —, *nescire, ignorare.* Adv. *inscienter, imperite;* or render by adj.

ignore, *praeterire, neglegĕre.*

ill, subst. *malum.*

ill, adj.: = sick, *aeger, aegrotus:* to be —, *aegrotare;* = evil, *malus;* —-fame, *infamia.*

ill, adv. *male, prave.*

ill-advised, *inconsultus, temerarius.*

ill-bred, *inhumanus, inurbanus.*

ill-disposed, *malevolus.*

illegally, *contra leges.*

illegitimate: of actions, *non legitimus;* of persons, *nothus.*

ill-fated, *infelix, miser.*

ill-gotten, *male partus.*

ill-health, *valetudo infirma.*

illiberal, *inliberalis, sordidus, malignus.*

illicit, *inlicitus, vetitus;* see illegally.

illiterate, *indoctus.*

ill-matched, *impar.*

ill-natured, *malevolus, malignus.*

illness, *aegrotatio, valetudo infirma.*

illogical, *absurdus.*

ill-omened, *dirus, tristis.*

ill-starred, *infelix.*

ill-tempered, *acerbitas, morositas, iracundia.*

illume, illuminate: = throw light on, *inlustrare, inluminare;* = enlighten the mind, *docĕre, erudire;* = adorn with pictures, *varie pingĕre, coloribus distinguĕre.*

illusion, *error, opinio vana.*

illusory, *vanus, falsus.*

illustrate (*librum*) *picturis ornare;* see also explain.

illustration; in a book, *pictura, tabula*; — example, *exemplum*.

illustrious, *(prae)clarus, inlustris, insignis*.

ill-will, *malevolentia*.

image, *imago, simulacrum, species*.

imaginary, *opinabilis, commenticius; fictus, falsus*.

imagination, *cogitatio*.

imagine, *animo concipĕre, (cogitatione) fingĕre, excogitare*; — to think, *putare, opinari*.

imbecile, *fatuus, stultus*.

imbecility, *imbecillitas animi, stultitia*.

imbibe, *(com)bibĕre, imbibĕre*.

imbue, *inficĕre, imbuĕre, tingĕre*.

imitable, *imitabilis*.

imitate, *imitari*; — portray, *exprimĕre, effingĕre*; — emulate, *aemulari*.

imitation, *imitatio, aemulatio*; — a copy, *effigies, imago, simulacrum*.

imitator, *imitator* (f. *imitatrix*); *aemulus, aemulator*.

immaculate, *purus, integer*; adv. *pure*.

immaterial, *sine corpore, expers corporis*; — unimportant, *nullius momenti, levis*.

immature, *immaturus, crudus*.

immeasurable, *immensus, infinitus*.

immediate: — direct, *proximus*; — without delay, *praesens*. Adv.: — directly, render by *ipse*; —before, or —after, *sub* with acc.; — at once, *statim, confestim, extemplo*.

immemorial; render by *antiquus*.

immense, *ingens, vastus, immensus* Adv. *in immensum*; — very much *maxime, valde*.

immensity, *immensitas*.

immigrate, *(im)migrare*.

immigrant, *advena*.

imminent, *praesens*; to be —, *instare, imminēre, impendēre*.

immoderate, *immodicus, nimius, intemperans*; adv. *immodice, intemperanter, praeter modum, nimis*.

immodest, *impudicus, impudens*; adv. *impudenter*.

immodesty, *impudicitia*.

immolate, *immolare*.

immolation, *immolatio*.

immoral, *pravus, inhonestus, turpis*; adv. *prave, inhoneste, turpiter*.

immorality, *mores corrupti; turpitudo*.

immortal, *immortalis, aeternus, sempiternus* (of things).

mmortality, *immortalitas, aeternitas; sempiterna gloria*.

immoveable, *immobilis, stabilis*.

immune, *immunis*; see also free.

immunity, *vacatio, immunitas*.

immure, *includĕre*.

immutability, *immutabilitas, constantia*.

immutable, *immutabilis, constans, stabilis*; adv. *constanter*.

impair, *(im)minuĕre, debilitare, infringĕre*.

impale, *(hasta or palo) transfigĕre*.

impart, *impertire, communicare, dare*.

impartial, *aequus*; to be —, *neutri favēre*.

impartiality, *aequitas*.

impassable, *invius, impeditus*.

impassioned, *ardens, vehemens*.

impassive, *lentus*.

impassivity, *lentitudo, lentus animus*.

impatience, *festinatio*.

impatient, *impatiens morae, ardens acer*; adv. *ardenter, acriter*.

impeach, *accusare*.

impeachment, *accusatio*.

impede, *impedire*.

impediment, *impedimentum*; in speech. *haesitantia linguae*.

impel, *impellĕre, urgēre*.

impend, *impendēre, imminēre*.

impenetrable, *impenetrabilis impervius, impeditus*.

impenitent, *obstinatus, offirmatus*.

imperative, gram., *imperativus* (adj.).

imperfect: gram., *imperfectus* (adj.); — unfinished, *imperfectus, rudis*; — faulty, *vitiosus, mendosus*; adv. *vitiose, mendose, male*.

imperfection, *vitium, mendum, culpa*.

imperial, render by· genit., e.g. *imperatoris, principis*.

imperil, *in discrimen adducĕre*.

imperious, *superbus, adrogans*; adv. *superbe, adroganter*.

imperishable, *immortalis, aeternus*.

impersonate; see imitate.

impertinence, *insolentia*.

impertinent: — rude, *insolens*; adv. *insolenter*; — not to the point, *nihil ad rem*.

imperturbable, *stabilis, firmus, gravis*; adv. *firme, graviter*.

impervious; see impenetrable.

impetuosity, *violentia, impetus (-ūs)*.

impetuous, *violentus, rapidus, vehemens*; adv. *violenter, vehementer*.

impetus, *impetus (-ūs), vis*.

impiety, *impietas (erga deos), nefas*.

impious, *impius (erga deos) nefarius*; adv. *impie, nefarie*.

impinge, *incidĕre, impingi*.

implacable, *implacabilis, inexorabilis*; adv. *atrociter, saeve*.

implant, *inserĕre, ingenerare*.

implement, *instrumentum*.

implicate, *implicare, admiscēre, inligare*.

implicated, *implicatus, conscius*.

implicit: — implied, *tacitus*; — complete, *totus, summus*. Adv. *tacite*; see also altogether.

implore, *implorare, rogare, orare*.

imply: — to mean, indicate, *significare*; — to involve, *(in se) habēre*; to be implied, *(in re) inesse*.

impolite, *inurbanus*; adv. *inurbane*.

impoliteness, *inhumanitas, rusticitas*.

import, subst.; in plur., — imported goods, *res quae importantur*; — meaning, *vis, significatio*.

import, v.: — bring into a country. *invehĕre, importare*; — signify, *significare, valēre*.

importance: of things, *momentum, pondus (-eris), vis*; of persons, — position, etc., *amplitudo, dignitas, auctoritas*.

important, *gravis, magnus*; to be —, *magni momenti esse, multum valēre*.

import-duty, *portorium.*
importunate, *molestus, improbus.*
importune, *fatigare; flagitare.*
importunity, *flagitatio.*
impose, *imponĕre;* see also cheat.
imposing, *speciosus, magnificus.*
imposition, = deception, *fallacia, fraus.*
impossible, *quod fieri non potest.*
impost, *vectigal, tributum.*
impostor, *fraudator.*
impotence, *imbecillitas, infirmitas.*
impotent, *invalidus, infirmus, imbecillus.*
impound, = confiscate, *publicare.*
impoverish, *in egestatem redigĕre.*
impoverishment, *egestas, inopia.*
impracticable, *quod fieri non potest.*
imprecate, *(im)precari;* see also curse.
imprecation, *preces (-um), exsecratio.*
impregnable, *inexpugnabilis.*
impress, *imprimĕre, inculcare.*
impression, *impressio;* = copy, *exemplum, imago expressa;* = footstep, *vestigium.* Transf., = effect on the mind, *animi motus (-ūs);* to make an —, *animum (com)movēre;* = thought, idea, *opinio;* to be under an —, *putare, opinari.*
impressive, *gravis;* adv. *graviter.*
impressiveness, *gravitas.*
imprint; see impress.
imprison, *in custodiam* (or *carcerem*) *conicĕre.*
imprisonment, *custodia, carcer, vincula (-orum).*
improbable, *non verisimilis.*
impromptu, *ex tempore.*
improper, *indecorus, indignus;* adv. *indecore, indigne, perperam.*
improve, v.: transit., *meliorem facĕre, emendare, corrigĕre;* intransit., *meliorem fieri, proficĕre.*
improvement, *correctio, emendatio;* or render by *melior.*
improvidence, *imprudentia.*
improvident, *improvidus, imprudens;* adv. *improvide, imprudenter.*
improvised, *subitarius, ex tempore.*
imprudence, *imprudentia, temeritas.*
imprudent, *imprudens, temerarius;* adv. *imprudenter, temere.*
impudence, *impudentia, os impudens.*
impudent, *impudens, procax, improbus;* adv. *impudenter.*
impugn, *impugnare, improbare.*
impulse, *impulsio, impulsus (-ūs);* or render by verb.
impulsive, *vehemens, acer.*
impunity, *impunitas;* with —, *impune.*
impure, *impurus, obscenus, foedus, turpis;* adv. *impure, obscene, foede, turpiter.*
impurity, *impuritas, obscenitas, turpitudo.*
imputation, = charge, *crimen, culpa, accusatio.*
impute, *adsignare, ascribĕre, attribuĕre.*
in: of place, render by locative, or *in* with abl., or plain abl.; when = into, *in* with acc.; of time, render by abl., or by *in* and abl.; in the case of, *in* with abl.; in the hands of, *penes* with acc.; in the writings of, *apud* with acc.

inability, *infirmitas, inopia;* or render by *non posse.*
inaccessible, *inaccessus;* of persons, *rari aditūs.*
inaccurate: of a person, *indiligens;* of reports, etc., *falsus.*
inaction, inactivity, *otium, quies;* = laziness, *desidia, inertia.*
inactive, *quietus, iners; segnis.*
inadequate, *impar;* adv. *parum, haud satis.*
inadmissible, *inlicitus.*
inadvertence, *imprudentia.*
inadvertent, *imprudens;* adv. *imprudenter, temere.*
inalienable, *quod abalienari non potest*
inane, *inanis.*
inanimate, *inanimus, inanimatus.*
inanition, *inanitas.*
inapplicable, to be, *non valēre.*
inapposite; see inappropriate.
inappropriate, *non idoneus.*
inaptitude, *inutilitas.*
inarticulate, *parum distinctus.*
inasmuch as, *quandoquidem.*
inattention, *neglegentia, incuria.*
inattentive, *non attentus;* to be — *aliud agĕre.*
inaugurate, *inaugurare, dedicare, consecrare.*
inauguration, *dedicatio, consecratio.*
inauspicious, *infelix, nefastus;* adv. *infeliciter, malis ominibus.*
incalculable, *immensus, ingens.*
incandescent, *candens.*
incantation, *carmen, cantio.*
incapable; render by *non posse.*
incarcerate; see imposing.
incarnate, *incarnatus* (ecclesiastical); *specie humana* (or *corpore*) *indutus.*
incautious, *incautus, inconsultus;* adv. *incaute, inconsulte, temere.*
incendiary, *incendiarius, incendiorum auctor.*
incense, subst. *tus (turis).*
incense, *accendĕre, incendĕre.*
incentive, *stimulus, incitamentum.*
inception, *initium.*
inceptive, *incipiens.*
incessant, *perpetuus, adsiduus, continuus;* adv. *perpetuo, adsidue.*
inch, *uncia.*
inchoate, *inchoatus.*
incident, *casus (-ūs), res.*
incidental, *fortuitus, forte oblatus;* adv. *casu, forte, fortuito.*
incipient, render by *initium* or *incipio.*
incisive, *mordax;* adv. *praecise.*
incite, *incitare, stimulare, impellĕre.*
incivility, *inurbanitas, inhumanitas.*
inclement: of persons, *severus, saevus;* of weather, *gravis, asper.*
inclination: physical, *inclinatio;* = slope, *fastigium, clivus;* mental, = propensity, *inclinatio, studium.*
incline, v.: transit., *inclinare;* intransit., *inclinari, (se) inclinare, propendēre.*
inclined, *inclinatus, propensus pronus.*
inclose; see enclose.
include, *comprehendĕre, complecti, adscribĕre;* to — among the accused, *in reos referre.*
including, *cum* with abl.

incognito, *alieno* or *dissimulato nomine.*

incoherent, *interruptus;* adv. *interrupte;* to speak —, *haud cohaerentia dicĕre.*

income, *vectigal, reditus (-ūs,* = returns), *pecunia, quaestus (-ūs).*

incommode, *incommodum* or *molestum esse.*

incomparable, *unicus, singularis, egregius;* adv. *unice, egregie.*

incompatibility, *repugnantia, diversitas.*

incompatible, *alienus, contrarius;* to be —, *abhorrēre, repugnare.*

incompetence, *inscitia.*

incompetent, *inscitus, inhabilis;* adv. *inscite.* Legally, render by phrase with *ius* or *potestas.*

incomplete, *imperfectus;* adv. *imperfecte.*

incomprehensible, *quod comprehendi non potest.*

inconceivable, *quod (mente) comprehendi non potest;* sometimes *incredibilis.* Adv. *incredibiliter, mirum in modum.*

inconclusive, *(argumentum) quo nihil efficitur.*

incongruity, *repugnantia.*

incongruous, *alienus, non aptus.*

inconsiderable, *levis, tenuis, exiguus.*

inconsiderate, = unthinking, *inconsideratus, inconsultus;* adv. *inconsiderate, nullo consilio, temere.*

inconsistency, *inconstantia, repugnantia.*

inconsistent, *inconstans, contrarius, repugnans;* adv. *inconstanter.*

inconsolable, *inconsolabilis; qui nullo solacio levari potest.*

inconspicuous, *obscurus.*

inconstancy, *inconstantia, levitas, varietas.*

inconstant, *inconstans, levis, varius.*

incontinence, *incontinentia, intemperantia.*

incontinent, *incontinens, intemperans;* adv. *incontinenter;* = immediately, *statim.*

incontrovertible, *quod refutari non potest.*

inconvenience, *incommodum;* to cause —, *negotium exhibēre.*

inconvenient, *inopportunus, incommodus;* adv. *incommode.*

incorrect, *falsus, mendosus;* = morally wrong, *improbus, iniustus.* Adv. *perperam, falso, mendose.*

incorrigible, *perditus; qui corrigi non potest.*

incorruptibility, *integritas, sanctitas.*

incorruptible, *incorruptus, integer, sanctus;* adv. *incorrupte, integre, sancte.*

increase, subst. *incrementum, auctus (-ūs).*

increase, v.: transit., *augēre, amplificare;* intransit., *crescĕre, augēri, gliscĕre.*

incredible, *incredibilis;* adv. *incredibiliter.*

incredulous, *incredulus.*

increment, *incrementum.*

incriminate, *suspectum reddĕre;* to — oneself, *se scelere adligare.*

inculcate, *inculcare; docēre.*

incumbent; see ought, must.

incur, *suscipĕre, contrahĕre;* to — disgrace, *dedecus in se admittĕre.*

incurable, *insanabilis.*

incursion, *incursio;* see attack.

indebted: = owing money, *obaeratus;* = obliged, *obnoxius, obligatus.*

indecency, *turpitudo, obscenitas.*

indecent, *indecorus, turpis;* adv. *indecore, turpiter.*

indecision, *dubitatio, haesitatio.*

indecisive, *dubius, anceps;* adv. (of fighting), *aequo marte.*

indecorous, *indecorus.*

indeed: emphatic, *vere, profecto, sane;* and —, *atque adeo;* then —, *tum vero,* concessive, *quidem;* interrogative, *ain tu? itane est?;* ironical, *scilicet, nimirum, videlicet.*

indefatigable, *adsiduus, impiger;* adv. *adsidue, impigre.*

indefensible, *quod defendi non potest.*

indefinable, *quod (verbis) definiri non potest.*

indefinite, *incertus, dubius, anceps, ambiguus:* for an — period, *in incertum;* gram., *infinitus, indefinitus.*

indelible, *quod deleri non potest.*

indelicate, *impudicus, impurus.*

indemnify, *damnum restituĕre.*

independence, *libertas.*

independent, *liber, solutus, sui iuris.* from taxes, etc., *immunis;* adv *libere, suo arbitrio.*

indescribable, *inenarrabilis, singularis;* adv. *inenarrabiliter, singulariter.*

indestructible, *quod everti non potest; perennis, perpetuus.*

indeterminate, *incertus.*

index, *index;* of a dial, *gnomon, horarum index.*

India, *India.*

Indian: subst. *Indus;* adj. *Indicus.*

indicate, *indicare, significare.*

indication, *indicium, significatio, signum.*

indicative: render by *indicium* or *indico;* gram., the — mood, *modus indicativus.*

indict, *accusare, nomen deferre.*

indictment; bill of —, *crimen, accusatio.*

indifference: = neglect, *neglegentia, incuria;* = calmness, *aequus animus, securitas;* = apathy, *lentitudo.*

indifferent: = negligent, *neglegens, remissus;* = calm, *securus,* or render by *aequo animo;* = apathetic, *lentus;* = mediocre, *mediocris.* Adv. *neglegenter, lente, aequo animo;* = without discrimination, *promiscue.*

indigence, *inopia, egestas.*

indigenous, *vernaculus;* applied to persons, *indigena.*

indigent, *inops, egens.*

indigestible, *gravis.*

indigestion, *cruditas.*

indignant, *indignans, (sub)iratus.*

indignation, *indignatio, stomachus, ira.*

indignity, *ignominia, contumelia.*

indirect: physically, *non rectus, devius;* of speech, *obliquus;* gram., *obliquus;* adv. *oblique.*

indirectness; in speech, *circumitio.*
indiscreet, *inconsultus.*
indiscretion, see imprudence.
indiscriminate, *promiscuus;* adv. *promiscue, sine ullo discrimine, temere.*
indispensable, *necessarius.*
indispose, *abstrahĕre, avocare.*
indisposed: = unwell, *aegrotus, infirma valetudine;* = disinclined, *aversus, alienus.*
indisputable, *certus, manifestus;* adv. *certe, haud dubie.*
indissoluble, *indissolubilis; aeternus.*
indistinct: *parum clarus, obscurus;* adv. *parum clare, obscure.*
indistinguishable, *quod discerni non potest.*
indite, *scribĕre.*
individual, subst.; see man, person.
individual, adj. *proprius, singularis; singuli -ae -a.*
individuality, *propria natura.*
individually, *singillatim, viritim; in singulos.*
indivisible, *individuus, quod dividi non potest.*
indoctrinate, *erudire, docēre, instituĕre.*
indolence, *ignavia, desidia, segnities.*
indolent, *ignavus, deses, segnis;* adv. *ignave, segniter.*
indomitable, *invictus, indomitus.*
indoor, adj. *umbratilis.*
indoors, *domi, intus.*
indorse; see endorse.
indubitable, *haud dubius, certus.*
induce, *inducĕre, impellĕre, inlicĕre, persuadēre.*
inducement, *incitamentum, inlecebra.*
induct, *inaugurare.*
induction, in logic, *inductio.*
indulge, v. *indulgēre, morem gerĕre, (in)servire.*
indulgence, *indulgentia, venia* (= pardon).
indulgent, *indulgens, benignus;* adv. *indulgenter, benigne.*
industrious, *industrius, sedulus, strenuus;* adv. *industrie, strenue.*
industry, *industria, sedulitas.*
indwelling, *insitus, innatus.*
inebriated, *ebrius, temulentus.*
inebriation, *ebrietas.*
ineffable, *inauditus, incredibilis;* adv. *incredibiliter.*
ineffective, *inritus, inutilis;* to be —, *effectu carēre;* adv. *frustra, nequicquam.*
inelegant, *invenustus, inelegans, inurbanus;* adv. *ineleganter, inurbane.*
ineligible, = unsuitable, *inopportunus.*
inept, *ineptus.*
inequality, *inaequalitas, dissimilitudo.*
inequitable, *iniquus, iniustus;* adv. *inique, iniuste.*
inert, *iners, tardus, segnis;* adv. *tarde, segniter.*
inestimable, *inaestimabilis, singularis, unicus;* adv. *singulariter, unice.*
inevitable, *necessarius, haud dubius, inevitabilis;* adv. *necessario.*
inexact, *haud accuratus* (of things), *indiligens* (of persons).
inexcusable, *quod nihil excusationis habet.*

inexhaustible, *quod exhauriri non potest; infinitus.*
inexorable, *inexorabilis, severus, durus.*
inexpediency, *inutilitas.*
inexpedient, *inutilis, inopportunus.*
inexperience, *imperitia, inscientia.*
inexperienced, *imperitus, ignarus, rudis.*
inexpiable, *inexpiabilis.*
inexplicable, *inexplicabilis.*
inexpressible, *inauditus, inenarrabilis.*
inextinguishable, *quod exstingui non potest.*
inextricable, *inexplicabilis, inextricabilis.*
infallible, *certus, haud dubius;* to be —, *omni errore carēre.* Adv. *certo.*
infamous, *infamis, turpis, flagitiosus;* adv. *turpiter, flagitiose.*
infamy, *infamia, dedecus, ignominia.*
infancy, *infantia, pueritia.*
infant: subst. *infans;* adj. *infans, puerilis.*
infantine, *puerilis.*
infantry, *pedites (-um), peditatus (-ūs).*
infatuate, *infatuare, occaecare, pellicĕre.*
infatuated, *amens, demens.*
infatuation, *amentia, dementia.*
infect, *inficĕre, contaminare.*
infection, *contagio, contactus (-ūs).*
infectious; an — disease, *pestilentia.*
infelicity, *infelicitas, malum.*
infer, *concludĕre, conligĕre.*
inference: as a process, *argumentatio, coniectura;* = conclusion, *conclusio, coniectura.*
inferior, adj. *inferior, deterior, minor.*
infernal, *infernus;* the — regions, *inferi (-orum);* = diabolical, *nefandus, nefarius.*
infertility, *sterilitas.*
infest, *infestum reddĕre.*
infested, *infestus.*
infidelity, *infidelitas, perfidia.*
infinite, *infinitus, immensus.* Adv., = very much, *incredibiliter, sane quam.*
infinitesimal, *minimus, (per)exiguus.*
infinity, *infinitas.*
infirm, *infirmus, invalidus, debilis.*
infirmity: = weakness, *infirmitas, imbecillitas, debilitas;* = a failing, *vitium.*
inflame, *inflammare, accendĕre, incendĕre.*
inflammable, *facilis ad exardescendum.*
inflammatory, *seditiosus, turbulentus.*
inflate, *inflare.*
inflated, *inflatus, tumidus, turgidus.*
inflation, *inflatio.*
inflect, gram., *declinare.*
inflection, gram., *declinatio, flexus (-ūs).*
inflexibility, *obstinatio, pertinacia.*
inflexible, *obstinatus, pertinax;* adv. *obstinate, pertinaciter.*
inflict, *(rem homini) adferre, infligĕre, imponĕre; (re hominem) adficĕre.*
infliction, = trouble, *malum, incommodum.*
influence, subst. *vis, pondus (-eris), momentum:* divine —, *adflatus (-ūs) divinus;* personal —, *auctorita* (= prestige), *potentia* (= unofficial power), *gratia* (= interest); to have — *valēre, pollēre, posse.*

influence, v. *movēre, impellēre.*

influential, *potens, gravis, gratiosus.*

influx; render by *influere.*

inform: = to form, shape, *(ef)fingĕre, (con)formare;* = to tell, *certiorem facĕre, docēre;* to — against a person, *hominis nomen deferre.*

informality, at auspices, etc., *vitium;* otherwise phrase, e.g. *res haud sollemni more facta.*

information: = news, *nuntius;* = knowledge, *scientia, doctrina;* = accusation, *delatio, indicium.*

informer, *delator, index.*

infrequency, *raritas.*

infrequent, *rarus.*

infringe, *rumpĕre, frangĕre, violare.*

infringement, *immunitio, violatio.*

infuriate, *efferare, exasperare.*

infuriated, *furens.*

infuse, *infundĕre; inicĕre, incutĕre.*

ingenious, *sollers, callidus, artificiosus;* adv. *sollerter, callide, artificiose.*

ingenuity, *ars, sollertia, subtilitas.*

ingenuous, *apertus, simplex, liber;* adv. *aperte, simpliciter, libere.*

ingenuousness, *libertas.*

inglorious, *inglorius, inhonestus;* adv. *sine gloria, inhoneste.*

ingraft, *inserĕre.*

ingrained, *insitus, inveteratus.*

ingratiate: to — oneself, *favorem sibi conciliare.*

ingratitude, *animus ingratus.*

ingredient, *pars.*

ingress, *ingressus (-ūs).*

inhabit, *incolere, habitare;* thickly —ed, *frequens.*

inhabitable, *habitabilis.*

inhabitant, *incola, habitator;* of a city, *civis.*

inhale, *spiritu ducĕre.*

inharmonious, *discors, absonus, dissonus.*

inhere, *inesse, inhaerēre.*

inherent, *insitus, innatus, proprius;* adv. *naturā, per se.*

inherit, *(rem) hereditate accipĕre;* see also heir.

inheritance, *hereditas.*

inherited, *hereditarius, patrius.*

inhibit, *interdicĕre.*

inhibition, *interdictum.*

inhospitable, *inhospitalis.*

inhospitality, *inhospitalitas.*

inhuman, *inhumanus, crudelis,* adv. *inhumane, crudeliter.*

inhumanity, *inhumanitas, crudelitas.*

inimical, *inimicus;* see also hostile.

inimitable, *haud imitabilis.*

iniquitous, *iniustus, iniquus;* adv. *iniuste, inique, improbe.*

iniquity, *iniustitia, iniquitas.*

initial, adj. *primus.*

initiate, *initiare; imbuĕre, instituĕre;* see also begin.

initiative: to take the —, *occupare.*

injudicious, *inconsultus, temerarius;* adv. *inconsulte, temere.*

injunction; see command.

injure, *laedĕre, violare, nocēre.*

injurious, *noxius, damnosus, gravis, malus;* adv. *male.*

injury, *detrimentum, incommodum, damnum, malum, iniuria.*

injustice, *iniustitia;* = unjust act, *iniuria.*

ink, *atramentum.*

inkling, *odor.*

inland, *mediterraneus.*

inlay, *inserĕre, variare, distinguĕre.*

inlet, of the sea, *aestuarium.*

inmate, *deversor, inquilinus;* see inhabitant.

inmost, *intimus;* — being, *viscera (-um), medulla.*

inn, *deversorium, hospitium, caupona.*

innate, *innatus, insitus, proprius.*

inner, *interior, intestinus, domesticus.*

innkeeper, *caupo.*

innocence, *innocentia, integritas;* = simplicity, *simplicitas.*

innocent, *innocens, insons; integer, sanctus;* adv. *integre, caste.*

innocuous, *innocuus;* adv. *sine fraude.*

innovate, *(res) novare, mutare.*

innovation: political —s, *res novae* (plur.).

innumerable, *innumerabilis.*

inoffensive, adj. *innocens.*

inopportune, *inopportunus.*

inordinate, *immodicus, nimius;* adv. *praeter modum, immodice, nimis.*

inquire: = ask questions, *quaerĕre, sciscitari, percontari, rogare;* = hold an inquiry, *quaerĕre, inquirĕre, cognoscĕre.*

inquiry, *percontatio, interrogatio;* a judicial —, *quaestio, inquisitio, cognitio.*

inquisitive, *audiendi cupidus, curiosus;* adv. *curiose.*

inquisitiveness, *studium audiendi, curiositas.*

inquisitor, *quaesitor.*

inroad, *incursio, incursus (-ūs), inruptio.*

insane, *insanus, amens (= distracted), demens (= deranged), furiosus (= raving);* adv. *insane, dementer, furiose.*

insanity, *insania, furor, amentia, dementia.*

insatiable, *insatiabilis, inexplebilis.*

inscribe, *inscribĕre, ascribĕre.*

inscription, *inscriptio, index, titulus, epigramma (-atis, n.).*

inscrutable, *obscurus, occultus, tectus.*

insect, *insectum, bestiola.*

insecure, *instabilis, incertus, lubricus,* or neg. with *tutus* or *firmus.*

insensibility, *torpor.* Transf., *lentitudo.*

insensible, *sensūs expers.* Transf., *lentus.* Adv. *sensim, paulatim.*

insert, *inserĕre, includĕre, intericĕre, addĕre, adscribĕre* (in writing).

insertion, *interpositio;* or render by verb.

inside, subst. *pars interior.*

inside, adv. *intus, intro.*

inside, prep. *in* (with abl.), *intra* (with acc.).

insidious, *fallax, dolosus;* adv. *fallaciter, dolose.*

insidiousness, *fallacia, dolus, fraus.*

insight: = knowledge, *cognitio, intellegentia, perspicientia;* = intelligence, *iudicium, consilium.*

insignia, *fasces (-ium), insignia (-ium).*

insignificance, *exiguitas.*

insignificant, *exiguus, minutus, levis, nullius momenti.*

insincere, *falsus, simulatus;* adv. *falso, simulate.*

insincerity, *fallacia, simulatio.*

insinuate: to — oneself, *se insinuare, adrepĕre;* = to suggest, hint. *significare.*

insinuating, *blandus.*

insinuation, *significatio.*

insipid, *insulsus, ineptus, frigidus;* adv. *insulse, inepte, frigide.*

insist: = state positively, *confirmare, declarare, dictitare;* = demand, *flagitare, (ex)poscĕre.*

insolence, *insolentia, impudentia, adrogantia.*

insolent, *insolens, impudens, adrogans;* adv. *insolenter, impudenter, adroganter.*

insoluble, *quod liquefieri non potest.* Transf., *inexplicabilis.*

insolvent, to be, *non esse solvendo.*

insomuch, . . . that, *sic, ita* or *adeo . . . ut.*

inspect, *inspicĕre, intuĕri, contemplari.*

inspection, *cura, custodia.*

inspector, *custos, curator.*

inspiration, = breathing in, *spiritus (-ūs);* divine —, *divinus adflatus (-ūs);* by divine —, *divinitus;* = suggestion, in gen., *monitus (-ūs), consilium.*

inspire, *inspirare;* = instil, *inicĕre, incutĕre;* = excite, *excitare, incendĕre.*

inspired, *divino spiritu inflatus.*

inspirit, *animum addĕre.*

instability, *inconstantia.*

install, *inaugurare.*

instalment, *pensio, pars, portio.*

instance, subst.: = urgent request, *preces (-um);* = example *exemplum, specimen;* for —, *verbi causa, velut, vel.*

instant, subst. *punctum* or *momentum temporis;* at the very —, *(in) tempore ipso.*

instant, adj.; = urgent, *vehemens, intentus, impensus;* = immediate, *praesens.*

instantaneous, *subitus, praesens;* adv. *momento temporis, e vestigio.*

instantly: = immediately, *statim, confestim, extemplo;* = urgently, *intente, vehementer, impense.*

instead, adv. *potius, magis.*

instead of, prep., *pro* with abl., *(in) loco* with genit.; — fighting he sleeps, *non pugnat sed dormit,* or *cum possit pugnare, dormit.*

instep, *pes superior.*

instigate, *incitare, impellĕre, stimulare.*

instigation, *stimulus;* at your —, *impulsu tuo.*

instigator, *auctor, impulsor, suasor.*

instil, *instillare;* see also inspire.

instinct, subst. *natura;* = natural appetite, *appetitus (-ūs).*

instinct, adj. *imbutus.*

instinctive, *naturalis;* adv. *naturā, naturaliter.*

institute, institution: as act, *initium;* or render by verb; = custom,

institutum, *lex, mos;* = corporation, *conlegium, sodalitas.*

institute, v. *condĕre, instituĕre, constituĕre.*

instruct: = teach, *erudire, docēre, instituĕre;* = order, *mandare, praecipĕre.*

instruction: = teaching, *institutio, eruditio, doctrina;* = direction, *praeceptum, mandatum.*

instructor, *magister, praeceptor.*

instrument, *instrumentum, machina;* steel —s, *ferramenta (-orum);* a stringed —, *fides (-ium);* legal, =deed, *instrumentum, tabula.*

instrumental, *utilis, aptus;* — music, *cantus nervorum et tibiarum.*

instrumentality, *opera, ministerium.*

insubordinate, *seditiosus, turbulentus.*

insubordination, *immodestia.*

insufferable, *intolerabilis.*

insufficient, *haud sufficiens, impar;* adv. *parum, haud satis.*

insult, subst. *contumelia, probrum.*

insult, v. *contumeliam imponĕre.*

insulting, *contumeliosus, maledicus;* adv. *contumeliose, maledice.*

insuperable, *in(ex)superabilis;* = invincible, *invictus.*

insurgent, subst. and adj., *rebellis.*

insurrection, *rebellio, seditio, motus (-ūs).*

intact, *integer, salvus, incolumis.*

intangible, *intactilis; quod tangi non potest.*

integral, *necessarius.*

integrity, *integritas, probitas.*

intellect, *mens, ingenium, intelligentia.*

intelligence: see intellect; = news *nuntius.*

intelligent, *mente praeditus, intellegens; sapiens, prudens.* Adv. *intellegenter, sapienter, prudenter.*

intelligible, *quod facile intellegi potest; planus, perspicuus;* adv. *perspicue, plane.*

intemperance, *intemperantia, impotentia;* in drink, *ebrietas.*

intemperate, *intemperans, impotens, immodicus;* — in drink, *ebriosus* Adv. *intemperanter, immodice.*

intend, *(facĕre) in animo habĕre; cogitare, destinare, intendĕre.*

intense, *acer, magnus, summus, nimius;* adv. *valde, magnopere, acriter, summe.*

intensify, *maiorem reddĕre, augĕre.*

intent, *intentus, attentus;* to be —, *animum intendĕre, incumbĕre, studĕre.*

intention, *consilium, propositum, institutum.*

intentionally, *consulto, de industria.*

inter, *sepelire, humare.*

intercalary, *intercalaris, intercalarius.*

intercede, *(de)precari.*

intercession, *deprecatio.*

intercessor, *deprecator.*

intercept, *intercipĕre, excipĕre;* in gen., = cut off, *intercludĕre.*

interchange, subst. *permutatio, vicissitudo.*

interchange, v. *(com)mutare, permutare.*

interchangeably, *invicem.*

intercourse, in gen. *usus (-ūs), commercium;* sexual, *concubitus (-ūs), consuetudo, coitus (-ūs).*

interdict; subst. *interdictum.*

interdict, v. *interdicĕre.*

interest, subst.: = attention, *studium;* = advantage, *bonum, utilitas, usus (-ūs);* it is in my —, *interest meā, refert meā, expedit mihi;* = influence, *gratia;* — on money, *faenus (-oris), usura;* compound —, *anatocismus;* simple —, *perpetuum faenus;* to lend out money on —, *faenerari.*

interest, v.: = to hold the attention, *tenēre;* sometimes *placēre;* to — oneself in, *studēre, operam dare.*

interested = attentive, *attentus, erectus; studiosus,* with genit.: = concerned, see interest, subst.

interfere, *intervenire, se interponĕre, se immiscēre;* to — with, = to hinder, *impedire.*

interim, *temporis intervallum;* an — decree, *edictum ad tempus propositum.*

interior, subst. *pars interior.*

interior, adj. *interior, internus.*

interject, *interponĕre, intericĕre.*

interjection, *interiectio.*

interlace, *implicare.*

interlude, *embolium.*

intermarriage, *connubium.*

intermediate, *medius.*

interment, *sepultura, humatio.*

interminable, *infinitus;* adv. *infinite, sine fine.*

intermingle, (inter)*miscēre.*

intermission, *intermissio.*

intermittently, *aliquando, nonnumquam, interdum.*

internal; see inner; adv. *intus, penitus.*

international: — law. *ius (iuris,* n.) *gentium.*

internecine, *internecivus.*

interpellation, *interpellatio.*

interpolate, *addĕre, inserĕre;* = to falsify, *corrumpĕre, interpolare.*

interpose, *interponĕre, intericĕre;* = to intervene, *se interponĕre.*

interposition, *interiectus (-ūs), interventus (-ūs);* = mediation, intervention, *interventus (-ūs).*

interpret, *interpretari;* to — favourably, *in bonam partem interpretari* or *accipĕre.*

interpretation, *interpretatio, explanatio.*

interpreter, *interpres.*

interregnum, *interregnum.*

interrogate, (inter)*rogare, quaerĕre, exquirĕre.*

interrogation, *percontatio, quaestio, interrogatio.*

interrogative, gram., *interrogativus.*

interrupt, *interrumpĕre, interpellare, interfari.*

interruptedly, *interrupte.*

interruption: in speaking. *interpellatio, interfatio;* in gen., = pause, *intermissio, intervallum.*

intersect, *secare, scindĕre;* so as to form the figure X, *decussare.*

intersection, = the figure X, *decussatio, decussis.*

intersperse, (in)*miscēre.*

interstice, *rima, foramen.*

interval, *intervallum, spatium;* in the —, *interim;* at —s, *aliquando, nonnumquam.*

intervene: = be between, *interiacēre, intercedĕre;* = come between, *intercedĕre, intervenire.*

intervention, *interventus (-ūs).*

interview, subst. *congressio, congressus (-ūs), conloquium.*

interweave, *intexĕre.*

intestate, *intestatus;* adv. *intestato.*

intestine, adj. *intestinus.*

intestine(s), subst. *intestina, viscera, exta* (all plur.).

intimacy, *familiaritas, consuetudo, necessitudo.*

intimate, adj. *familiaris, intimus, coniunctus;* adv. *familiariter, intime, penitus.*

intimate, v. *significare, indicare.*

intimation, *significatio, nuntius.*

intimidate, (de)*terrēre, timorem inicĕre.*

intimidation, = threats, *minae (-arum).*

into, in with acc.

intolerable, *intolerabilis;* adv. *intoleranter.*

intolerance, *superbia, adrogantia.*

intolerant, *immitis, difficilis, superbus.*

intone, *canĕre.*

intoxicate, *ebrium reddĕre.*

intoxicated, *ebrius, temulentus.*

intoxication, *ebrietas.*

intractable, *indocilis, difficilis.*

intrepid, *intrepidus, impavidus.*

intrepidity, *animus intrepidus* or *impavidus; fortitudo.*

intricacy, *contortio.*

intricate, *contortus implicatus, perplexus, impeditus.*

intrigue, subst.; = plot, *dolus, fallacia;* = amour, *adulterium.*

intrigue, v. = plot, *dolis* or *fallacia contendĕre;* see also interest.

intrinsic, *verus, in re ipsa positus;* adv. *per se, vere.*

introduce, *introducĕre, inducĕre, invehĕre;* of persons, = make one known to another, *introducĕre, commendare.*

introduction, *introductio, inductio, invectio;* an — to a book, etc., *prooemium, exordium, praefatio.*

introspection, *ipsum se inspicĕre.*

intrude, *se interponĕre* or *offerre.*

intrusion, *importunitas.*

intrusive, *molestus, importunus;* adv. *moleste.*

intuition, *cognitio, perceptio;* as a quality, *ingenii, acumen* or *acies.*

inundation, *eluvio, diluvium.*

inure, *adsuefacĕre.*

invade, *invadĕre, incurrĕre, incursionem facĕre.*

invader, *hostis.*

invalid, subst. *aeger, aegrotus.*

invalid, adj. *inritus, infirmus, vitiosus.*

invalidate, *inritum facĕre, tollĕre, rescindĕre.*

invasion, *incursio, inruptio.*

invective, *convicium, probrum.*

inveigh, *invehi, insectari, increpare.*

inveigle; see mislead.

invent, *invenire, reperire, excogitare.*

invention, *inventio, excogitatio;* = thing invented, *inventum, reperta* (*-orum,* plur.); = falsehood, *commentum, mendacium.*

inventor, *inventor, repertor, auctor.*

inventory, *tabula, index.*

inverse, *inversus, conversus.*

inversion, *conversio.*

invert, (con)*vertĕre, invertĕre.*

invest, to — with an office, *magistratum mandare, deferre;* to — with a quality, *addĕre, impertire;* to — money, *pecuniam conlocare, occupare;* = to besiege, *circumsedĕre, obsidĕre.*

investigate, *exquirĕre,* (per)*scrutari, investigare;* judicially, *quaerĕre, cognoscĕre.*

investigation, *investigatio, inquisitio;* a judicial —, *quaestio, cognitio.*

investigator, *investigator, indagator.*

inveterate, *inveteratus;* to become —, *inveterascĕre.* Adv. *penitus.*

invidious, *invidiosus;* adv. *invidiose.*

invidiousness, *invidia.*

invigorate, *corroborare,* (con)*firmare.*

invincible, *invictus, in*(ex)*superabilis.*

inviolability, *sanctitas.*

inviolable, *inviolabilis, inviolatus; sanctus, sacrosanctus;* adv. *inviolate.*

inviolate, *integer; inviolatus, intactus.*

invisible, *caecus;* to be —, *sub oculos non cadĕre.*

invitation, *invitatio;* at your —, *invitatus* (or *vocatus*) *a te.*

invite, *invitare, vocare;* = to allure, *adlectare, invitare.*

inviting, *blandus, gratus, amoenus.*

invocation: of help, *imploratio;* of witnesses, *testatio.*

invoice, *libellus.*

invoke, *invocare, implorare;* as a witness, *testari, invocare testem.*

involuntary, *invitus, coactus;* adv. *non sponte,* or render by adj. *invitus.*

involve: = to envelop, *involvĕre;* = to implicate, *implicare, adligare, admiscēre;* to be —d in debt, *aere alieno laborare;* = to imply, *comprise, continēre, habēre.*

invulnerable, *invulnerabilis.*

inward, *interior;* adv. *introrsus, intus, intrinsecus.*

inweave, *intexĕre.*

inwrought, *intextus.*

irascibility, *iracundia.*

irascible, *iracundus, in iram praeceps, stomachosus.*

ire; see **anger.**

Ireland, *Hibernia.*

irk: it —s, *piget, taedet, molestum est.*

irksome, *gravis, molestus, odiosus.*

irksomeness, *taedium, molestia.*

iron, subst. *ferrum;* of —, adj. *ferreus;* tipped with —, *ferratus;* —s, = fetters, *vincula, compedes.*

iron, adj. *ferreus;* — tools, *ferramenta* (*-orum*).

ironically, *per ironiam.*

ironmongery, *ferramenta* (*-orum,* plur.).

irony, *ironia, dissimulatio.*

irradiate, *inlustrare, conlustrare.*

irrational, *absurdus, rationis expers, stultus;* adv. *absurde.*

irreconcilable: of persons, etc. *implacabilis, inexorabilis;* of ideas, (*res*) *inter se repugnantes, contrariae.*

irrecoverable, *inreparabilis.*

irrefragable, *certus, firmus; quod refelli non potest.*

irregular, *enormis* (= shapeless), *incompositus* (= rough), *insuitatus* (= unusual); *inaequalis* (= not uniform); gram., *anomalus;* at elections, *vitiosus;* of troops, *tumultuarius.* Adv. *enormiter, incomposite, praeter morem; vitio.*

irregularity, *enormitas;* gram., *anomalia;* of conduct, *licentia;* at an election, *vitium.*

irrelevant, *alienus;* it is —, *nihil ad rem pertinet.*

irreligion, *impietas* (*erga deos*), *deorum neglegentia.*

irreligious, *impius* (*erga deos*); adv. *impie.*

irremediable; see **incurable.**

irremovable, *immobilis, immutabilis.*

irreparable, *inreparabilis.*

irreproachable; see **blameless.**

irresistible, *invictus, in*(ex)*superabilis cui nulla vi resisti potest.*

irresolute, *dubius, incertus;* to be —, *dubitare, haesitare.* Adv. *dubitanter.*

irresolution, *dubitatio, haesitantia.*

irrespective, *sine ullo discrimine.*

irreverence, *impietas* (*erga deos*).

irreverent, *inverecundus, impius* (*erga deos*); adv. *impie.*

irrevocable, *inrevocabilis.*

irrigate, *inrigare.*

irrigation, *inrigatio, inductio aquarum.*

irritable, *stomachosus, iracundus;* adv. *stomachose.*

irritate: to — a wound, *inflammare;* mentally, *inritare.*

irritation, = annoyance, *stomachus.*

irruption, *inruptio, incursio.*

island, *insula.*

islander, *insulanus, insulae incola.*

isle; see **island.**

isolate, *secernĕre, seiungĕre, separare.*

isolated, *remotus, solus.*

isolation, *solitudo.*

issue, subst.: = outcome, *exitus* (*-ūs*), *eventus* (*-ūs*); = subject, *res, causa;* = offspring, *liberi* (*-orum*), *progenies, stirps.*

issue, v.: transit., = give out, of orders, etc. *edĕre, proponĕre, pronuntiare;* of stores, etc., *dispensare, distribuĕre;* intransit., = come out, *egredi, erumpĕre;* = end up, turn out, *evadĕre, exire, evenire.*

isthmus, *isthmus* or *isthmos.*

it, *hic, haec, hoc; is, ea, id; ille, illa, illud.*

Italian, *Italicus, Italus.*

Italy, *Italia.*

itch, subst.: as disease, *scabies;* as sensation, *prurigo, pruritus* (*-ūs*).

itch, v. *prurire;* to — to do a thing, *gestire facĕre.*

item, in a list, *pars, res.*

iterate, *iterare.*

itinerant, *circumforaneus*.
itinerary, *itineris descriptio*.
ivory, subst. *ebur*.
ivory, adj. *eburneus*.
ivy, *hedera*.

J

jabber, v. *blaterare, garrire*.
jabbering, subst. *clamor, strepitus -ūs*).
jackass, *asinus*.
jackdaw, *graculus*.
jacket, *tunica*.
jade: of a horse, *caballus*; of a woman, *mulier importuna*.
jaded, *fatigatus, (de)fessus*.
jagged, *serratus*; of rocks, *asper, praeruptus*.
jail, *carcer*.
jailbird, *furcifer*.
jamb, *postis*.
James, *Iacobus*.
janitor, *tanitor, ostiarius*.
January, *Ianuarius (mensis)*.
jar, subst. *olla, cadus, urceus, urna, amphora*; on the —, of a door, *semiapertus*.
jar, v. *discrepare*.
jargon, *sermo barbarus*.
jarring, *dissonus, absonus, discors*.
jasper, subst. *iaspis*.
jaundice, *morbus regius or arquatus*.
jaundiced, *arquatus*. Transf., *lividus, invidus*.
jaunt, *iter, excursio; to take a —, excurrēre*.
javelin, *pilum, iaculum; to throw a —, iaculari*.
jaw, *mala*; the —s of death, etc., *fauces (-ium)*.
jealous, *invidus, lividus*; to be —, *aemulari, invidēre*.
jealousy, *invidia, aemulatio*.
jeer, subst. *cavillatio, ludibrium, inrisio*.
jeer, v. *cavillari, inridēre, in ludibrium vertēre*.
jejune, *ieiunus, aridus, exilis*; adv. *ieiune*.
jeopardize, *in periculum adducēre*.
jeopardy; see danger.
jerkin, *tunica*.
jerky, of style, *salebrosus*.
Jerusalem, *Hierosolyma (-orum)*.
jest, subst. *iocus, ridiculum; in —, ioco, per iocum*.
jest, v. *iocari, ioculari, cavillari*.
jester, *scurra*.
jet, *gagates*; — black, *niger*; a — of water, *aqua saliens*.
jetsam, *res naufragio eiectae*.
jetty, *moles*.
Jew, *Iudaeus*.
jewel, *gemma*.
jewelled, *gemmeus, gemmatus*.
jeweller, *aurifex*.
Jewish, *Iudaicus*.
jig; see dance.
jilt, *repudiare*.
jingle, *tinnire*.
jingling, subst. *tinnitus (-ūs)*.
job, *opus (-eris, n.)*; a put-up —, *fraus*.
jockey, *agaso (= groom)*.

jocose, **jocular**, *iocosus, ridiculus, facetus*; adv. *iocose, per iocum, facete*.
jocularity, *iocus, facetiae (-arum)*.
jog, subst. *impulsus (-ūs)*.
jog, v.: transit., *fodicare, impellēre*; intransit., to — on, — along, *lente progredi*.
John, *Ioannes*.
join, v.: transit., = connect, *(con)-iungēre, conectēre, copulare*; to — battle, *proelium or pugnam committēre*; intransit., *(con)iungi, conecti*; to — in, *interesse*.
joiner, *faber*.
joint, subst.: in a body, *commissura, articulus*; in a plant, *nodus*; in other things, *coagmentum, compages compactura*.
joint, adj. *communis*; adv. *coniuncte, coniunctim, una, communiter*.
jointed, *geniculatus*.
joint-heir, *coheres*.
joist, *tignum transversum*.
joke; see jest.
joker, *homo ridiculus*.
jollity, *hilaritas, lascivia*.
jolly, *hilaris, lascivus*.
jolt, v. *iactare, concutēre, quassare*.
jolting, subst. *iactatio, quassatio*.
jostle, *fodicare*.
jot, subst.: not a —, *nihil, minime*; not to care a — for, *non flocci facēre*.
jot, v.: to — down, *adnotare, scribēre*.
journal: = diary, *ephemeris*; = newspaper, *acta diurna (-orum)*.
journey, subst. *iter, cursus (-ūs), via*; a — abroad, *peregrinatio*; a — by sea, *navigatio*.
journey, v. *iter facēre*; to — abroad, *peregrinari*.
journeyman, *opifex*.
Jove, *Iuppiter*; by —! *mehercle!*
jovial, *hilaris, lascivus*; adv. *hilare, lascive*.
joviality, *hilaritas, lascivia*.
joy, *gaudium, laetitia*; = pleasure, *voluptas*.
joy, v. *gaudēre, laetari, exsultare*.
joyful, *laetus, hilaris*. Adv. *laete, libenter, hilare*; often rendered by adj. *laetus or libens*.
jubilant, *gaudio exsultans or triumphans*.
judge, subst.: in court, *iudex, quaesitor, praetor*; in gen., *iudex, aestimator, existimator*.
judge, v., *iudicare; existimare, censēre*: to — between *diiudicare*.
judgment: in court, *iudicium*; to pronounce —, *ius dicēre*; a — seat, *tribunal*; in gen., = considered opinion, *iudicium, sententia*; in my —, *meo iudicio, me iudice*; = discernment, *iudicium, consilium*.
judicature, *iurisdictio*.
judicial, *iudicialis, forensis*; a — decree, *edictum*; a = investigation, *iudicium*. Adv. *iure, lege*; to proceed —, *lege agēre*.
judicious, *sagax, sapiens, prudens*: adv. *sagaciter, sapienter, prudenter*.
jug, *urceus, urceolus*.
juggle, *praestigias agēre*.
juggler, *praestigiator*.

juggling, subst. *praestigiae* (*-arum*); = trickery, *dolus, fraus.*

juice, *sucus.*

July, *Quinctilis* or *Iulius* (*mensis*).

jumble, subst. *congeries, turba. farrago.*

jumble, v. (*per)miscēre.*

jump, subst. *saltus* (*-ūs*).

jump, v. *salīre*; to — for joy, *exsultare gaudio*; to — in, *insilīre*; to — over, *transilīre.*

junction, (*con)iunctio.*

juncture, *tempus, tempestas.*

June, (*mensis*) *Iunius.*

jungle, *loca virgultis obsita.*

junior, *iunior*, (*natu*) *minor.*

juniper, *iuniperus.*

jurisconsult, *iuris* or *iure peritus.*

jurisdiction, *iurisdictio.*

jurisprudence, *iuris prudentia.*

jurist; see jurisconsult.

juror, *iudex.*

jury, *iudices* (*-um*).

just, adj. *iustus, aequus, meritus* (= deserved); adv. *iuste, iure, legitime, merito.*

just, adv.: of time, *commodum*; — now, *in praesentia*; — lately, *modo. nuperrime, recens*; in gen., = exactly, *admodum*, or render by *ipse*, esp. with numerals; — as, *ita* (or *sic*) *ut, perinde ac*; in replies, — so, *ita vero, admodum*; = only, *modo, solum, tantum.*

justice, *iustitia, aequitas*; = rights, just treatment, *ius* (*iuris*, n.).

justifiable, *iustus, legitimus*; adv. *recte, iure.*

justification, *purgatio, excusatio.*

justify, *purgare, excusare.*

jut: to — out, *exstare, eminēre*; of geographical features, *excurrēre.*

juvenile, *puerilis, iuvenilis.*

K

keel, *carina.*

keen: physically, *acer*; of perception, *acutus, perspicax, sagax*; = enthusiastic, *acer, studiosus.* Adv. *acriter*; *acute, sagaciter*; *studiose, summo studio.*

keenness: = poignancy, *acerbitas*; = penetration, *sagacitas, perspicacitas*; — of vision, *acies*; = enthusiasm, *studium.*

keep, v. Transit., (*con)servare, custodire, tenēre, habēre*: of animals = to support, *alēre*; to — in, *includēre, continēre*; to — apart, *distinēre*; to — back, *retinēre, cohibēre*; to — off, *arcēre*; to — faith, *fidem servare*; to — watch, *custodias agēre*; to — a secret, *rem celare* or *occultam tenēre*: Intransit.: = to remain, (*re)manēre*: to — silent, *tacēre*; to — on doing a thing, *pergēre, perseverare.*

keeper, *custos, curator.*

keeping, subst. *custodia, tutela.*

keg, *dolium.*

ken, *conspectus* (*-ūs*).

kennel, *stabulum* (*canis*).

Kent, *Cantium.*

kerb, *crepido.*

kerchief, *sudarium.*

kernal, *nucleus.* Transf., *medulla, flos, robur.*

kettle, *cortina, lebes, a(h)enum.*

kettle-drum, *tympanum.*

key, *clavis.*

kick, subst. *pedis* or *calcis ictus* (*-ūs*).

kick, v. *calcitrare, calce petēre*; to — back, *recalcitrare.*

kid, *haedus, haedulus.*

kidnap; see steal.

kidney, *renes* (*renum*).

kidney-bean, *phaselus.*

kill, *interficēre, caedēre, occidēre, necare* (violently), *trucidare* (= butcher, massacre); to — oneself, *mortem sibi conciscēre, se interimēre*; to — time, *horas fallēre.*

kiln, *fornax.*

kin; see kindred.

kind, subst. *genus* (*-eris*, n.); *modus*; of such a —, *talis*; a — of, render by *quasi* or *quidam*; every — of, *omnis* or plur., *omnes.*

kind, adj. *benignus, beneficus* (in action), *benevolus* (in disposition), *humanus, indulgens, clemens*; a — action, *beneficium, officium.* Adv. *benigne, clementer, indulgenter, humane.*

kindle, v.: transit., *accendĕre, incendēre, inflammare*; intransit., *accendi*, (*ex)ardescēre.*

kindness, *bonitas, benignitas, benevolentia, humanitas*; an act of —, *beneficium, officium.*

kindred, subst., abstr. *consanguinitas, cognatio, necessitudo*; = relatives, *consanguinei, cognati, necessarii* (*-orum*).

king, *rēx*; a petty —, *regulus.*

kingdom, *regnum.*

kingfisher, n. (*h)alcedo*, (*h)alcyon.*

kingly, *regius, regalis.*

kingship, *regia potestas, regnum.*

kinsman; see relative.

kiss, subst. *osculum, suavium.*

kiss, v. *osculari, suaviari.*

kissing, subst. *osculatio.*

kitchen, *culina.*

knapsack, *mantica, sarcina.*

knave, *homo nequam* or *sceleratus*; colloquially, *scelestus, furcifer.*

knavery, *nequitia, fraus, dolus.*

knavish, *nequam, fraudulentus*; adv. *fraudulenter.*

knead, *depsēre, subigēre.*

knee, *genu.*

kneel, *genibus niti.*

knife, *culter*; small —, *cultellus.*

knight, *eques.*

knighthood, *ordo equester*; *dignitas equestris.*

knit, *texēre*; to — the brow, *frontem contrahēre.*

knob, *bulla, nodus* (in plants).

knobbed, knobbly, *nodosus.*

knock, v. *pulsare*; to — against, *offendēre*; to — down, *sternēre*; to — up, = arouse, *suscitare*; -ed up, = exhausted, (*de)fessus.*

knocking, subst. *pulsatio.*

knock-kneed, *varus.*

knot, subst. *nodus*; ⚊ group of people, *circulus*.

knot, v. *nodare, nectĕre*.

knotty, *nodosus*. Transf., *difficilis, spinosus*; a ⚊ point, *nodus*.

know, *scire, cognitum* or *compertum habĕre*; to get to ⚊, *(cog)noscĕre*; not to ⚊, *nescire, ignorare*; ⚊ be acquainted with, *novisse* (perf. of *noscere*); to ⚊ again, ⚊ recognize, *agnoscĕre, noscitare*.

knowing, adj. *sciens, prudens*; ⚊ clever, *callidus, astutus*. Adv. *consulto, de industria*; or render by adj. *sciens* or *prudens*.

knowledge, *scientia, notitia, cognitio*; as ⚊ imparted and acquired, *doctrina, disciplina*; without the ⚊ of a person, *clam homine*.

known, *notus*; to make ⚊, *declarare*.

knuckle, *articulus (digiti)*.

L

laborious, *laboriosus, operosus*; adv. *laboriose, operose*.

labour, subst. *labor, opus* (*-eris* n.), *opera*; in childbirth, *partus* (*-ūs*); to be in ⚊, *parturire*.

labour, v.: ⚊ work, toil, *laborare, niti, contendĕre*; ⚊ be distressed, *laborare* (with abl.); to ⚊ under a delusion, *decipi, falli*.

laboured, *adfectatus, nimis exquisitus*.

labourer, *operarius, opera*.

labyrinth, *labyrinthus*.

labyrinthine, *perplexus, impeditus*.

lacerate, *lacerare, laniare*.

laceration, *laceratio, laniatus* (*-ūs*).

lachrymose, *lacrimabundus*.

lack, subst. *inopia, penuria, egestas*.

lack, v. *carēre, egēre, indigēre*.

lackey, *pedisequus*.

lack-lustre, *decolor*.

laconic, ⚊ concise, *brevis, adstrictus*; adv. *breviter, adstricte*.

lad, *puer*.

ladder, *scalae* (*-arum*).

lade, ⚊ to load, *onerare*.

laden, *onustus, oneratus, gravis*.

lading, subst. *onus* (*-eris*, n.).

ladle, subst. *trulla, cyathus*.

ladle, v. *haurire*.

lady, in gen., *femina, mulier, matrona*; the ⚊ of the house, *domina, hera, materfamilias*.

lady-like, *liberalis; quod matronā dignum est*.

lady's-maid, *famula, ornatrix*.

lag, *cessare, morari, cunctari*.

laggard, *cessator, cunctator*.

lagoon, *lacus* (*-ūs*), *lacuna*.

lair, *latibulum, cubile*.

laird, *dominus, possessor*.

lamb, *agnus*, f. *agna*; as meat, (*caro*) *agnina*.

lame, adj. *claudus*; ⚊ feeble, *debilis*; to be ⚊, *claudicare*; a ⚊ excuse, *excusatio vana*.

lameness, *claudicatio*.

lament, **lamentation**, *lamentum*

(usually plur.), *lamentatio, ploratus* (*-ūs*).

lament, v. *lamentari, deflēre, (de)plorare*.

lamentable, *lamentabilis, flebilis*; adv. *flebiliter*.

lamented, *flebilis*.

lamp, *lucerna, lychnus*.

lamp-black, *fuligo*.

lampoon, *carmen famosum*.

lance, subst., *lancea, hasta, sarisa*.

lance, v. *incidĕre*.

lancet, *scalpellum*.

land, subst.: opp. to sea, *terra*; ⚊ as possessed, cultivated, etc., *ager, solum, terra*; ⚊ a particular country, *terra, regio, ager, fines* (*-ium*).

land, adj. *terrestris, terrenus*.

land, v.: transit., (*in terram*) *exponĕre*; intransit., (*ex nave*) *egredi*.

landed, ⚊ property, *ager, possessio* (usually plur.); a ⚊ proprietor, *agrorum possessor*.

landing, subst. *egressus* (*-ūs*).

landlord, *agrorum possessor; caupo* (⚊ innkeeper).

landmark, *lapis, terminus*.

landslide, *terrae lapsus* (*-ūs*).

lane, *angiportum*; a country ⚊ *semita*.

language, *oratio*; the ⚊ of a people, tongue, *lingua, sermo*; ⚊ diction, style, *oratio, sermo*; ⚊ things said, *verba* or *dicta* (*-orum*).

languid, *languidus*; to be ⚊, *languēre*; adv. *languide*.

languish, *languere, languescĕre; tabescĕre*.

languor, *languor*.

lank, lanky, *prolixus*.

lantern, *-lanterna*.

lap, subst. *gremium* (⚊ bosom), *sinus* (*-ūs*); ⚊ fold (of the gown); on a race-course, *spatium*.

lap, v. *lambĕre*.

lap-dog, *catellus*.

lapse, subst.: ⚊ error, *lapsus* (*-ūs*), *error, peccatum*; of time, *fuga*; after the ⚊ of a year, *interiecto anno*.

lapse, v.: ⚊ go wrong, *errare, peccare*; of property, *reverti*.

lard, *adeps, lar(i)dum*.

larder, *cella penaria, carnarium*.

large, *magnus, grandis, amplus*. Adv., ⚊ to a great extent, *magna ex parte*.

large-hearted, *magnanimus, liberalis, benignus*.

largeness, *magnitudo, amplitudo*; ⚊ of mind, *magnanimitas*.

largess, *largitio, congiarium*.

lark, *alauda*.

larynx, *guttur*.

lascivious, *impudicus*; adv. *impudice*.

lash, subst.: ⚊ whip, *flagrum, flagellum, scutica*; ⚊ blow (lit. and fig.). *verber*.

lash, v.: ⚊ whip, *flagellare, verberare*; ⚊ tie, bind, *(ad)nectĕre, (ad)ligare*.

lassitude, *lassitudo, languor*.

last, subst.: let the cobbler stick to his ⚊, *ne sutor supra crepidam*.

last, adj.: ⚊ final, *ultimus, extremus, postremus, novissimus*; ⚊ most recent, *proximus*. **At last**, *tandem, postremum*. Adv. **lastly**, *postremo, denique*.

last, v. durare, (per)manēre.
lasting, stabilis, diuturnus, perennis.
latch, pessulus (=bolt).
late, adj.: = coming —, serus; = recent, recens; the —, = the dead, demortuus; of an emperor, divus. Adv. **lately, of late,** nuper, recens, modo.
late, adv.: = too —, sero; rather —, serius; — at night, multa nocte.
lateness, render by adj.
latent, occultus, abditus.
lateral, a latere.
lathe, tornus; to work at the —, tornare.
Latin, adj. Latinus; the — tongue, lingua Latina, sermo Latinus; to translate into —, Latine reddere.
latinity, latinitas.
latitude, = freedom, libertas, licentia.
latter, posterior: the former ... the —, hic ... ille.
lattice, cancelli (-orum).
laud; see praise.
laudable, laudabilis, laude dignus; adv. laudabiliter.
laudatory, honorificus.
laugh, laughter, risus (-ūs), cachinnus (loud), cachinnatio; to be a —ing stock, ludibrio or inrisui esse; to raise a —, risum movēre.
laugh, v.: intransit., ridēre; loudly, cachinnare; to — at, transit., (de)ridēre, inridēre.
laughable, ridiculus.
laughter; see laugh.
launch, v.: transit., of ships, deducēre; intransit., to — out, in aequor efferri. Transf., exspatiari.
laurel, laurus (-i and -us), laurea; adj., of —, laureus; decked with —, laureatus.
lava, massa ardens, saxa (-orum, pl.) liquefacta.
lavish, adj. prodigus, profusus; a — giver, largitor. Adv. large, prodige, effuse.
lavishness, effusio, largitas, munificentia.
law, lex, ius (iuris, n.); fas (= divine —); norma, regula (= rule, standard); to carry a —, legem perferre; to go to —, lege agĕre.
lawful, legitimus; it is —, licet. Adv. legitime, lege, per leges.
lawgiver; see legislator.
lawless, effrenatus; adv. effrenate, licenter, contra legem.
lawlessness, (effrenata) licentia.
lawn: = fine linen, sindon; of grass, pratum, herba.
lawsuit, lis, controversia.
lawyer, iurisconsultus, iurisperitus.
lax, (dis)solutus, remissus, neglegens; adv. (dis)solute, remisse, neglegenter.
lay, subst.; see song.
lay, v. ponĕre, (con)locare; to — foundations, fundamenta iacĕre; to — an ambush, insidiari; to — siege, obsidēre; to — eggs, (ova) parĕre; to — aside, (de)ponĕre; to — before, proponĕre; to — down an office, magistratu se abdicare; to — down arms, ab armis discedĕre; to — up, condĕre, reponĕre; to — waste, vastare.

layer, of a plant, propago.
laziness, ignavia, segnitia.
lazy, piger, ignavus, segnis; adv. pigre, ignave, segniter.
lead, subst. plumbum.
lead, v.: = conduct, ducĕre; to — past, traducĕre; to — back, reducĕre; to — the way, praeire; = command, ducĕre, praeesse; = induce, adducĕre, persuadēre; = pass, spend, agĕre; of roads, to — in a certain direction, ferre, ducere.
leaden, plumbeus.
leader, dux, ductor, auctor.
leadership, ductus (-ūs); under my —, me duce.
leading, princeps, primarius, summus.
leaf: of a tree, folium, frons; of a book, scheda, pagina, charta; of metal, bractea, lamina.
leafy, frondosus, frondeus, frondifer.
league, subst. foedus (-eris, n.), pactum, societas.
leak, v.; to spring a —, rimam agĕre.
leak, v.; to — away, perfluĕre.
leaky, rimosus, rimarum plenus.
lean, adj. macer, exilis; strigosus (of horses, etc.).
lean, v. (se) inclinare; to — upon, (re) (in)niti.
leanness, macies.
leap, subst. saltus (-ūs).
leap, v. salire: to — down, desilire; — forward, prosilire; — for joy, gestire, exsultare.
leap-year, annus bisextus.
learn, discĕre, ediscĕre (by heart), perdiscĕre (thoroughly); cognoscĕre (= get to know, in gen.).
learned, doctus, eruditus; adv. docte, erudite.
learner, discipulus.
learning, doctrina, eruditio.
lease, subst. conductio.
lease, v. conducĕre (= take a — of), locare (= give a — of).
leash, lorum, copula.
least, adj. minimus.
least, adv. minime; at —, saltem, certe; not in the —, nihil omnino.
leather, corium, aluta (tanned); adj., of —, scorteus.
leave, subst.: = permission, permissio, licentia; to give —, potestatem facĕre; with your —, pace tua; I have —, mihi licet; to take — of, valēre iubēre; — of absence, commeatus (-ūs).
leave, v.: = desert, abandon, relinquĕre, deserĕre, destituĕre; to — property, relinquĕre, legare; = to depart, discedĕre, proficisci; to — off, desistĕre; to — out, omittĕre, praetermittĕre.
leaven, subst. fermentum.
leaven, v. fermentare.
leavings, reliquiae (-arum).
lecture, schola, acroasis.
lecture-room, schola, auditorium.
ledge, — of rock, dorsum.
ledger, codex (accepti et expensi).
leech, hirudo, sanguisuga.
leek, porrum, porrus.
leer, oculis limis intuēri.

leering, *limus.*

lees, *faex.*

left, = remaining, *reliquus*; to be —, *restare.*

left, (opp. right) *sinister, laevus*; the — hand, *sinistra*; on the —, *a sinistra.*

leg, *crus (cruris,* n.); — of a table, *pes.*

legacy, *legatum.*

legal, *legitimus*; adv. *legitime, lege.*

legate, *legatus, nuntius.*

legation, *legatio.*

legend: on coins, etc., *inscriptio, titulus*; = myth, fable, *fabula.*

legendary, *fictus, fabulosus.*

leggings, *ocreae (-arum).*

legible, *quod facile legi potest.*

legion, *legio.*

legionary, *legionarius.*

legislate, *leges facère* or *constituère.*

leisure, *otium*; to be at —, *vacare, otiari, cessare*; at —, *otiosus, vacuus.*

leisurely, *lentus*; adv. *otiose.*

lend, *mutuum dare, commodare*; to — at interest, *faenerari.*

length, *longitudo*; in time, *longinquitas, diuturnitas*: at —, *tandem.*

lengthen, v. *longiorem facère*; in time, *producère, prorogare.*

length-wise, *in longitudinem.*

lengthy, in words, *verbosus, longus.*

leniency, *clementia, lenitas.*

lenient, *clemens, lenis*; adv. *clementer.*

lentil, *lens.*

less: adj. *minor*; adv. *minus*; much —, *nedum.*

lessee, *conductor.*

lessen, *(de)minuère, imminuère.*

lessening, *deminutio, imminutio.*

lesson: to give —s, *docère*; = warning or example, *documentum.*

lest, conj., *ne* with subj.

let, = to allow, *sinère, pati, permittère*; — us go, *eamus*; to — alone, *omittère*; to — down, *demittère*; to — fly, *emittère*; to — go, *(di)mittère*; to — in, *admittère*; to — off, *absolvère*; to — slip, *omittère*; see also lease.

lethal, *mortifer, exitialis.*

lethargic, *torpidus*; a — person, *lethargicus.*

lethargy, *lethargus, torpor.*

letter: of the alphabet, *littera*; to the —, *ad verbum*; = epistle, *litterae (-arum), epistula.*

letter-carrier, *tabellarius.*

lettered, *litteratus.*

letters, = learning, *doctrina, litterae (-arum)*; a man of —, *homo doctus.*

lettuce, *lactuca.*

levee, *salutatio.*

level, adj. *aequus, planus*; — ground, *planities.*

level, v.: = make even, *(ex)aequare*; = bring to the ground, *solo aequare, sternère*; to — a weapon, *librare.*

lever, *vectis.*

leveret, *lepusculus.*

levity, *inconstantia, levitas*; *iocus, iocatio.*

levy, subst. *dilectus (-ūs)*; to hold a —, *dilectum habère.*

levy, v.: to — soldiers, *milites (con)-scribère*; to — tribute, *tributum imponère, vectigal exigère.*

lewd, *impudicus, impurus*; adv. *impure.*

liable, *obnoxius.*

liar, *(homo) mendax.*

libation, *libamentum*; to make a —, *libare.*

libellous, *famosus, probrosus.*

liberal, *liberalis, largus, munificus*; too —, *prodigus, profusus*; the — arts, *artes liberales* or *ingenuae.* Adv. *liberaliter, large, munifice*; to give —ly, *largiri.*

liberate, *liberare*; to — a slave, *manu-mittère.*

liberation, *liberatio*; of a slave, *manu-missio.*

liberator, *liberator.*

libertine, *homo dissolutus, ganeo.*

liberty, *libertas*; excessive —, *licentia*: at —, *liber.*

library, *bibliotheca.*

licence, subst.: = permission, *copia, potestas*; = liberty, *licentia.*

license, v. *potestatem dare.*

licentious, *dissolutus, impudicus*; adv. *dissolute, impudice.*

licentiousness, *libido, impudicitia.*

lick, *lingère, lambère*; to — up, *ligur(r)ire.*

lid, *operculum, operimentum.*

lie, subst. *mendacium.*

lie, v. = tell a lie, *mentiri.*

lie, v. = be situated, *tacère, cubare, positum esse*; to — between, *interiacère*; to — down, *procumbère*; to — hid, *latère*; to — in wait, *insidiari.*

lief; I had as —, *malim.*

lieu; in — of, *pro, loco, vice.*

lieutenant, *legatus.*

life, *vita, anima*; to come to — again, *reviviscère*; the necessaries of —, *victus (-ūs)*; time of —, *aetas*; the prime of —, *flos aetatis, aetas integra.* Transf., = liveliness, *vis, vigor, alacritas*; full of — *vividus, vegetus, alacer.*

life-guards, *(milites) praetoriani.*

lifeless, *exanimis*; of style, *frigidus, exilis, ieiunus*; adv. *frigide.*

life-time, *aetas*; in my —, *me vivo.*

lift, v. *(at)tollère, extollère, (sub)levare.*

ligament, *ligamentum, ligamen.*

light, subst. *lumen, lux*; to bring to —, *in lucem proferre, patefacère*; source of —, *lumen, lucerna* (= lamp), *candela* or *cereus* (= taper or torch); to work by lamp- —, *lucubrare.*

light, adj.: opp. to dark, *clarus, inlustris, candidus* (in colour); opp. to heavy, *levis*; — soil, *solum tenue*; —-hearted, *hilaris, curis vacuus.* Adv. *leviter*; — clad, *expeditus.*

light, v.: = set light to, *accendère*; = illuminate, *inlustrare*; to — upon, *incidère, offendère.*

lighten: = make less heavy, *exonerare*; = cause lightning, *fulgurare, fulgère.*

lighthouse, *pharus.*

lightness, *levitas.*

lightning, *fulmen, fulgur*; struck by —, *fulmine ictus, de caelo tactus.*

like, adj. *similis, par.*
like, adv. *similiter; instar, modo, ritu* (all with genit.).
like, v. *amare, diligĕre;* I — this, *hoc mihi placet* or *cordi est;* I — to do it, *iuvat me facĕre.*
likelihood, *veri similitudo, probabilitas.*
likely, *veri similis, probabilis.*
like-minded, *concors.*
liken, *comparare.*
likeness: = resemblance, *similitudo;* = portrait, *effigies, imago.*
likewise, *item, itidem.*
liking, *amor, voluptas* (= pleasure), *libido* (= caprice); to one's —, *gratus, iucundus.*
lily, *lilium.*
limb, *membrum, artus (-uum, plur.).*
lime, subst.: the mineral, *calx;* bird- —, *viscum;* the tree, *tilia.*
lime, v. (with bird- —), *visco inlinĕre.*
lime-kiln, *(fornax) calcaria.*
limit, subst. *terminus, finis, modus.*
limit, v. *finire, terminare.*
limitation, *determinatio;* = exception, *exceptio.*
limited, *parvus, angustus, brevis.*
limp, adj. *languidus.*
limp, v. *claudicare, claudum esse.*
limpet, *lepas.*
limpid, *limpidus, pellucidus.*
limpness, *languor.*
Lincoln, *Lindum.*
linden-tree, *tilia.*
line, *linea;* in a straight —, *e regione, rectā lineā, ad lineam;* a — of poetry, *versus (-ūs), versiculus;* milit., — of battle, *acies;* — of march, *agmen;* the front —, *prima acies, hastati (-orum);* second —, *principes (-um);* third —, *triarii (-orum);* in plur., lines (= entrenchments, etc.), *munitiones (-um), munimenta (-orum), vallum;* = cord, thin rope, *funis, funiculus;* a fishing —, *linea;* plumb--, *perpendiculum.*
line, v. *complēre.*
lineage, *stirps, genus (-eris, n.), origo.*
lineaments, *lineamenta (-orum).*
linen, *linum;* — cloth, *linteum;* adj., of —, *linteus.*
linger, *cessare, morari, cunctari*
lingerer, *cunctator, cessator.*
lingering, subst. *mora, cunctatio, cessatio.*
lingering, adj. *tardus, lentus.*
liniment, *unguentum.*
link, subst.: = torch, *fax, taeda, funale;* = bond, *vinculum, necessitudo;* — of a chain, *annulus.*
link, v. *connectĕre, (con)iungĕre.*
lint, *linamentum.*
lintel, *limen superum.*
lion, *leo;* adj., of a —, *leoninus.*
lioness, *leaena.*
lion-hearted, *magnanimus.*
lip, *labrum, labia.*
liquid, subst. *liquor, umor, latex.*
liquid, adj. *liquidus;* to become —, *liquescĕre, liquefieri;* to make —, *liquefacĕre.*
Lisbon, *Olisipo.*
lisp, *balbutire.*
lisping, *blaesus.*

list, *tabula, libellus, index.*
listen; see hear.
listless, *socors, deses, languidus;* adv. *languide.*
listlessness, *languor, socordia, desiaia.*
literal: the — sense *propria vis.* Adv. *ad verbum;* to translate —ly, *ad verbum transferre.*
literary, *litteratus, litterarum studiosus;* — tastes, *studia (-orum) litterarum.*
literature, *litterae (-arum), litterarum monumenta (-orum).*
lithe, *mollis, flexibilis.*
litigate, *litigare, rem lite persequi.*
litigation, *lis.*
litigious, *litigiosus.*
litter, subst.: = the vehicle, *lectica;* = brood, *fetus (-ūs), suboles;* of straw, *stramentum.*
little, a little, as subst., *paulum, nonnihil, parum* (= too little); just a —, *paululum;* a — better, *paulo melior;* a — before, sub (with acc.); a — sad, *subtristis;* — by —, *sensim, gradatim;* he said —, *pauca dixit.*
little, adj. *parvus, parvulus, exiguus;* often rendered by diminutive of subst; so —, *tantulus;* how —, *quantulus;* for a — while, *parumper, paulisper.*
little, adv. *paulum;* see also little, subst.
littleness, *parvitas, exiguitas.*
live, adj = living; q.v.
live, v. *esse, spirare, vivĕre;* to — on a thing, *re vivĕre* or *vesci;* to — in a place, *locum incolĕre* or *habitare*
livelihood, *victus (-ūs).*
liveliness, *alacritas.*
lively, *alacer, vegetus, vehemens.*
liver, *iecur.*
livid, *lividus;* — colour, *livor;* to be —, *livēre.*
living, adj. *vivus.*
lizard, *lacerta, lacertus, stellio.*
lo! *en, ecce.*
load, subst. *onus (-eris, n.).*
load, v. *onerare, onus imponĕre;* of firearms *(arma) parare, instruĕre.*
loaded, *onustus, oneratus.*
loaf, *panis.*
loam, *lutum.*
loan, *mutuum, res commodata;* of money, *pecunia mutua.*
loath, *invitus:* I am —, *piget me, nolo.*
loathe, v. *fastidire, odisse, aspernari.*
loathing, *fastidium, odium.*
loathsome, *teter, foedus.*
lobby, *vestibulum.*
lobster, *cancer* (= crab).
local, render by genitive *loci* or *regionis*
locality, *locus, loci natura.*
loch, *lacus (-ūs).*
lock, subst.: on a door, *claustra (-orum);* see also hair.
lock, v. *obserĕre, occludĕre;* to — up, *concludĕre.*
locker, *armarium.*
lock-jaw, *tetanus.*
locust, *locusta.*
lodge, v.: intransit., = stay, *deversari, devertĕre;* = stick, *haerēre;* transit., *hospitio excipĕre.*

lodger, *deversor, inquilinus.*
lodgings, *deversorium, deverticulum, meritoria (-orum).*
loft, *cenaculum.*
loftiness, *altitudo, elatio, excelsitas.*
lofty, *altus, (ex)celsus, editus, sublimis;* of speech, *grandis.* Adv. *alte, excelse.*
log, *lignum, stipes* (= tree-trunk).
logic, *logica (-orum), dialectica (-ae,* f. or *-orum,* n.); *disserendi ratio.*
logical, *logicus, dialecticus;* a — consequence, *consequens.* Adv. *dialectice;* often *ratione.*
logician, *dialecticus.*
loin, *lumbus.*
Loire, *Liger.*
loiter, *cessare.*
loll, *recumbère, recubare.*
London, *Londinium.*
lone, lonely, *solus, solitarius.*
loneliness, *solitudo.*
long, adj.: in space, *longus, procerus* (= tall): very —, *praelongus;* — hair, *capillus promissus;* six feet —, *longus pedes sex;* a — way, *longe, procul;* in time, *longus, diuturnus;* for a — time, *diu;* a — time ago, *iam pridem.*
long, adv. of time, *diu;* how —?, *quamdiu?* so —, *tam diu;* see also long, adj.
long, v. *avère, cupère, gestire.*
longer, of time, *diutius, longius, amplius;* no —, *non iam, non diutius.*
longing, *appetitus (-ūs), appetitio, cupido.*
look, subst. *aspectus (-ūs), conspectus (-ūs), obtutus (-ūs,* = gaze) = expression, *vultus (-ūs);* = appearance, in gen., *species, facies.*
look, v.: to — at, *aspicère, intuèri, contemplari, spectare;* to — about, *circumspicère;* to — back, *respicère;* to — down, *despicère;* to — up, *suspicère;* of position, to — in a certain direction, *spectare;* = to appear, seem, *vidèri.*
looking-glass, *speculum.*
loom, subst. *tela.*
loop, subst. *laqueus.*
loophole, *foramen, fenestra.*
loose, adj.: = slack, *laxus, fluxus, remissus;* of soil, *rarus;* at liberty, *liberatus, liber;* of morals, *(dis)solutus, effrenatus.* Adv. *laxe, (dis)solute.*
loose, v. *(re)laxare, remittère, (re)solvère.*
lop; to — off, *amputare, praecidère.*
lopsided; see uneven.
loquacious, *loquax, verbosus;* adv. *loquaciter.*
loquacity, *loquacitas.*
lord, *dominus.*
lordly, = proud; q.v.
lordship, *imperium, dominatus (-ūs).*
lore, *eruditio, doctrina.*
lose, *amittère, perdère* (wilfully); to — a battle, *vinci;* to — colour, *pallescère;* to — heart, *animo cadère or deficère;* to — one's way, *errare;* = to be bereft of, *privari, orbari.*
losing, subst. *amissio.*

loss, *damnum, detrimentum, iactura;* I am at a —, *dubius sum, haereo dubito.*
lost, to be, *perire;* — in thought, *in cogitation defixus.*
lot, *sors:* casting of —s, *sortitio, sortitus (-us);* to decide by —, *sortiri.*
loth; see loath.
lottery, *sors, sortitio, alea.*
loud, *clarus, magnus;* adv. *magna voce.*
lounge, v. *nihil agère, desidère.*
louse, *pediculus.*
loutish, *rusticus, agrestis.*
love, subst. *amor, caritas* (= affection), *pietas* (= devotion), *studium* (= enthusiasm); a — affair, *amor;* god of —, *Cupido, Amor;* goddess of —, *Venus;* my —! *mea voluptas! deliciae meae!*
love, v. *amare, diligère, studère* (with dat.).
loved, *carus.*
loveliness, *venustas, amoenitas.*
lovely, *venustus; amoenus* (esp. of scenery).
lover, *amator, amans,* and f. *amatrix.*
loving, adj. *amans, studiosus;* adv. *amanter.*
low, adj. *humilis, demissus;* of voice, *summissus;* of price, *vilis;* of character or standing, *humilis, ignobilis, obscurus;* of spirits, *tristis, maestus.*
low, adv. *humiliter, demisse;* to speak —, *submissa voce dicère.*
low, v., of cattle, *mugire.*
low-born, *obscuro* (or *humili) loco natus.*
lower, adj. *inferior.*
lower, v. *demittère;* to — the voice, *vocem submittère;* to — oneself = condescend, *se submittère, descendère.*
lowering; see dark, threatening.
lowest, *infimus, imus.*
lowing, of cattle, *mugitus (-ūs).*
lowlands, *loca (-orum) plana.*
lowliness, *humilitas, obscuritas;* as a virtue, *modestia.*
lowly: of rank, *humilis, obscurus;* = unassuming, *modestus.*
lowness, *humilitas* (lit. and fig.); of price, *vilitas.*
loyal, *fidelis, fidus;* adv. *fideliter.*
loyalty, *fides, fidelitas.*
lubricate, *ung(u)ère.*
lucid, *(pel)lucidus, dilucidus, perspicuus;* adv. *(di)lucide, perspicue.*
lucidity, *perspicuitas.*
luck, *fortuna, fors, casus (-ūs);* good —, *res secundae, felicitas;* good — to it! *bene vertat!*
lucky, *felix, fortunatus, faustus;* adv. *feliciter, fauste.*
lucrative, *quaestuosus, lucrosus.*
lucre, *lucrum, quaestus (-ūs).*
ludicrous, *ridiculus.*
lug, *trahère.*
luggage, *impedimenta (-orum), vasa (-orum), sarcinae (-arum,* = knapsacks).
lugubrious, *lugubris, flebilis, maestus.*
lukewarm, *tepidus;* = unenthusiastic, *languidus, frigidus.*

lull, v.: transit., *sedare*; to — to sleep, *sopire*; intransit., the wind —s, *venti vis cadit.*

lullaby, *cantus (-ūs).*

lumber, *scruta (-orum).*

luminary, = heavenly body, *sidus (-eris,* n.).

luminous, *lucidus, inlustris;* see also lucid.

lump, *massa, glaeba (gleba).*

lumpy, *crassus, glebosus.*

lunar, *lunaris.*

lunatic; see mad, madman.

lunch, subst. *prandium.*

lunch, v. *prandēre.*

lung, *pulmo;* —s, *pulmones, latera.*

lurch, see roll; to leave in the —, *deserēre, destituēre.*

lure, subst. *inlex, inlecebra.*

lure, v. *adlicēre, inlicēre, pellicēre.*

lurid, *obscurus, caliginosus.*

lurk, *latēre, latitare, delitescēre.*

luscious, *(prae)dulcis.*

lust, subst. *libido, cupiditas.*

lust, v. *concupiscēre.*

lustful, *libidinosus, impudicus.*

lustily, *valide.*

lustre, = brightness, *nitor, splendor;* = a space of five years, *lustrum.*

lusty, *validus, vegetus.*

lute, *lyra, fides (-ium), cithara* (poet.).

luxuriant, *laetus, luxuriosus.*

luxuriate, *luxuriare.*

luxurious, *luxuriosus, mollis, delicatus;* adv. *luxuriose, molliter, delicate.*

luxury, *luxus (-ūs), luxuria.*

lynx, *lynx.*

lynx-eyed, *lynceus.*

Lyons, *Lugdunum.*

lyre; see lute.

lyric, lyrical, *melicus, lyricus.*

M

Maas or **Meuse,** *Mosa.*

mace, *fasces (-ium).*

Macedonia, *Macedonia;* a —n, *Macedo;* —n, adj., *Macedonius, Macedonicus.*

macerate, *macerare.*

machination, *machina, dolus.*

machine, *machina, machinatio, machinamentum.*

mackerel, *scomber.*

mad, *insanus, furiosus, demens;* to be —, *furēre, insanire.* Adv. *insane, furiose, dementer.*

madden, *(homini) furorem incutēre, mentem alienare;* fig., *exacerbare, exasperare.*

madness, *insania, dementia, furor.*

magazine, = store, *horreum, receptaculum, armamentarium;* see also journal.

maggot, *vermis, vermiculus.*

magic, subst. *ars magica, magice.*

magic, adj. *magicus; mirabilis, mirus.*

magician, *magus.*

magistracy, *magistratus (-ūs).*

magistrate, *magistratus (-ūs).*

magnanimity, *magnanimitas, magnus animus.*

magnanimous, *magnanimus.*

magnet, *(lapis) magnes.*

magnificence, *magnificentia, splendor.*

magnificent, *magnificus, splendidus, amplus;* adv. *magnifice, splendide, ample.*

magnify, *augēre, amplificare, exaggerare.*

magniloquence, *magniloquentia.*

magniloquent, *magniloquus.*

magnitude, *magnitudo, spatium (=* extent).

magpie, *pica.*

maid: = virgin, *virgo;* = any girl, *puella;* = servant-girl, *ancilla, famula.*

maidenhood, *virginitas.*

maidenly, *virgineus, virginalis.*

mail: = armour, *arma (-orum);* = letters, *litterae (-arum).*

maim, *mutilare, truncare.*

maimed, *mancus, truncus.*

main, subst. = sea, *pelagus, altum.*

main, adj. *primus, praecipuus, princeps;* the — point, *caput, res (summa).* Adv. *praecipue, potissimum.*

mainland, *terra (continens).*

maintain: = preserve, *sustinēre, sustentare, (con)servare, retinēre;* = keep alive, *alēre;* to — in argument, *contendēre, confirmare, adfirmare.*

maintenance, *conservatio, salus;* = livelihood, *victus (-ūs).*

maize, *far.*

majestic, *augustus, sanctus, magnificus;* adv. *auguste.*

majesty, *maiestas, dignitas, amplitudo;* divine —, *numen.*

major, subst.: milit., *tribunus militum;* in law, *(homo) sui iuris.*

major, adj. *maior.*

majority, *maior pars, maior numerus, plures (=* more people), *plurimi (=* most).

make, subst. *figura, forma, conformatio.*

make: = form, create, *facēre, efficēre, fabricari, aedificare;* to — one's way, *iter facēre;* = render, cause to be, *facēre, reddēre;* to — good, *reparare, resarcire;* = to appoint, *facēre, creare, instituēre;* in valuing, to — much of a thing, *rem magni facēre;* = cause, compel, *facēre* or *efficēre* (with *ut* and subj.), *cogēre* (with infin.); in arithmetic, = form, come to, *efficēre, esse;* to — away with, *interficēre, tollēre;* to — for, *petēre;* to — up a story. *fingēre, comminisci;* to — way, *cedēre.*

maker, *fabricator;* or use verb.

makeshift, adj. *subitarius.*

maladministration, *prava rerum administratio.*

malady; see illness.

malapropos, adv. *intempestive.*

malaria, *caelum grave et pestilens.*

malcontent, *homo rerum novarum cupidus.*

male, adj. *virilis, mas, masculus;* the — sex, *virilis sexus (-ūs).*

malediction, *exsecratio, dirae (-arum).*

malefactor, *homo maleficus* or *sceleratus.*

malevolent, *malevolus.*

malice, *malignitas, invidia, malevolentia.*

malicious, *malevolus, malignus, invidus.*

malign, v.; see slander.

maligner, *obtrectator.*

malignity, *malevolentia*; of a disease, *vis (morbi).*

malleable, *lentus, mollis.*

mallet, *fistuca, malleus.*

mallow, *malva, malache.*

Malta, *Melita.*

maltreat, *male tractare, vexare.*

mammal, *animal.*

man, *homo* (= human being); *vir* (i.e. not woman or child); men, plur., *mortales, homines, genus humanum*; all to a —, *omnes ad unum*; — by —, *viritim*; no —, *nemo.* Transf., in draughts, *calculus*; in chess, *latro, latrunculus*; of ships, merchant—, *navis mercatoria*; — -of-war, *navis longa.*

man, v. = furnish with men, *complēre.*

manacle, subst. *compes, catena.*

manacle, v. *vincire.*

manage, *tractare, administrare, gerēre, (pro)curare.*

manageable, *habilis, docilis, facilis.*

management, *administratio, tractatio, cura, (pro)curatio.*

manager, *administrator, (pro)curator.*

mandate, *iussum, mandatum.*

mandible, *maxilla.*

mane, *iuba*; with a —, *iubatus.*

mange, *scabies.*

manger, *praesepe* or *praesepis.*

mangle, v. *(di)laniare, lacerare.*

mangled, *truncus, lacer.*

manhood, *aetas adulta*; to reach —, *togam virilem sumēre.*

mania, *insania.*

manifest, adj. *apertus, manifestus, perspicuus*, it is —, *patet, apparet*; adv. *aperte, manifesto.*

manifest, v. *aperire, patefacēre, manifestum facēre.*

manifestation, *demonstratio, indicium.*

manifesto, *edictum.*

manifold, *multiplex, varius.*

manipulate, *tractare.*

mankind, *homines (-um), genus humanum.*

manliness, *virtūs (-ūtis)*; *animus virilis.*

manly, *virilis, fortis.*

manner, *ratio, modus, via*; = sort, kind, *genus (-eris,* n.); — of writing, *oratio, sermo.*

manners, *mores (-um)*; a person of good —, *homo bene moratus.*

mannikin, *homuncio, homunculus, homullus.*

manoeuvre, *decursus (-ūs), decursio*; = trick, stratagem, *artificium, dolus.*

manoeuvre, v. *(in armis) decurrēre, evagari.*

manor, *fundus, praedium.*

mansion, *aedes (-ium), domus.*

manslaughter, *hominis caedes, homicidium.*

mantelet, *vinea, pluteus, testudo.*

mantel-piece, *mensa, abacus, tabula.*

mantle, *amiculum, palla* (for women),

pallium; *lacerna* or *paenula* (for travelling); *sagum* (= soldier's —).

manual, subst. *libellus.*

manual, adj., render by *manu.*

manufacture, subst. *fabrica.*

manufacture, v. *fabricari* or *fabricare.*

manufacturer, *opifex, artifex, fabricator.*

manumission, *manumissio.*

manumit, *manu mittĕre*, or *manumittĕre.*

manure, *stercus (-oris,* n.), *fimus.*

manure, v. *stercorare.*

manuscript, *chirographum.*

many, *multi*; a good —, *complures, plerique*; very —, *permulti, plurimi*; — times as great, *multiplex*; — a time, *saepe, saepenumero*; as — as, *tot . . . quot*; just as —, *totidem*; so — times, *totie(n)s.*

many-coloured, *variis coloribus distinctus.*

map, *tabula.*

map, v., to — out, *designare, describĕre.*

maple, *acer*; adj., of —, *acernus.*

mar, *foedare, deformare, corrumpĕre.*

marauder, *praedator, direptor.*

marauding, *praedatorius, praedabundus.*

marble, subst. *marmor.*

marble, adj. *marmoreus.*

March, (mensis) *Martius.*

march, subst. *iter*; a regular day's —, *iustum iter*; to make forced —es, *magnis itineribus contendĕre*; troops on the —, *agmen.*

march, v.: intransit., *iter facĕre, incedĕre*: — off, *proficisci*; — fast, *contendĕre*; — in the rear, *agmen cogĕre*; transit., *ducĕre*; to — back, *reducĕre*; to — across, *tra(ns)ducĕre.*

marches, *fines (-ium), confinium.*

mare, *equa.*

margin, *margo.*

marginal, *in margine scriptus* or *positus.*

marine, adj. *marinus, ad mare pertinens.*

mariner, *nauta.*

marines, *classiarii, classici milites.*

maritime, *maritimus.*

marjoram, *amaracus.*

mark, subst. *nota, signum, indicium*; it is the — of a wise man to do so, *est sapientis facĕre*; to make one's —, *clarum fieri.*

mark, v. *(de)signare, notare*; = take notice of, *observare, animadvertĕre*; to — out, *metiri, designare.*

marked, *inlustris, insignis.*

market: the place, *macellum, forum*; cattle —, *forum boarium*; the business, *mercatus (-ūs), nundinae (-arum).*

marketable, *venalis.*

marriage, *coniugium, matrimonium, nuptiae (-arum), conubium.*

marriageable, *nubilis, adultus.*

marriage-contract, *pactio nuptialis.*

marriage-settlement, *dos.*

marrow, *medulla.*

marry, v.: = give in marriage, *in matrimonium dare*; of a man, to — a woman, *ducĕre (in matrimonium)*; of a woman, to — a man, *nubĕre* (with dat.); to — out of her station, *enubere*; to — beneath her, *denubēre*; of a couple, to — each other, *matrimonio* or *nuptiis* (con)*iungi*.

marry! interj. *medius fidius, mehercle.*

Marseilles, *Massilia.*

marsh, *palūs,* (-*ūdis,* f.).

marshal, subst. *dux.*

marshal, v. *instruĕre, disponĕre.*

marshy, *paluster, uliginosus.*

martial, *militaris, bellicosus.*

martyr: to become a — for a cause, *pro re mortem occumbēre.*

marvel, subst. *miraculum, portentum.*

marvellous, (*per*)*mirus, mirificus,* (*ad*)*mirabilis*; adv. *mire mirifice,* (*ad*)*mirabiliter.*

masculine, *virilis, masculus.*

mask, subst., *persona, larva.* Transf., *persona, species, simulatio.*

mask, v. *tegĕre, occultare, dissimulare.*

mass, *massa, moles*; a great —, *magna copia* or *vis*; — of people, *multitudo.*

massive, *solidus, magnus gravis.*

massacre, subst. *caedes, strages, trucidatio.*

massacre, v. *caedĕre, trucidare.*

mast: on ships, *malus*; = acorns, etc., *glans.*

master, subst.: = owner, ruler, *dominus*; — of a house, *pater familias, herus*; — of property, *possessor*; to become —, *potiri*; a school- —, *magister*; one's own —, *sui potens, sui iuris*; = expert, *artifex, homo peritus.*

master, v.: = subdue, *domare, vincĕre, superare*; to — passions, *continēre, coercēre*; to — a subject, = understand, *intellegĕre,* (*per*)*discĕre, comprehendĕre.*

masterful, *superbus, imperiosus adrogans.*

masterly, *artificiosus, artifex* (of persons); or render by *ars.*

mastery, = victory, *victoria.*

masticate, *manducare, mandĕre.*

mat, subst. *storea* or *storia, teges.*

mat, v.; to — together, *implicare.*

match, subst.: = one's equal, *par* (with dat.); no — for, *impar*; = contest, *certamen*; = marriage, *condicio, nuptiae* (-*arum*).

match, v.: = equal, suit, *parem esse, aequare*; = bring together as opponents, *componĕre, conferre*; to — oneself with *congredi, certare.*

matchless, *singularis, unicus, egregius.*

match-maker, (*nuptiarum*) *conciliator* (f. -*trix*).

mate, subst. *socius* (= companion), *coniunx* (= husband or wife).

mate, v.: in chess, *ad incitas redigĕre*; = be united, *coniungi.*

material, subst. *materies* or *materia, copia rerum.*

material, adj., *corporeus*; see also important. Adv.; see much.

maternal, *maternus.*

mathematical, *mathematicus.*

mathematician, *mathematicus.*

mathematics, *mathematica.*

matricide, *matricidium* (the crime); *matricida* (the person).

matrimonial; see conjugal.

matrimony, *matrimonium*; see marriage.

matron, = married woman, *matrona.*

matronly, *matronalis.*

matter, subst. (1), = physical substance, *corpus, res corporeae.* (2) in discussion, etc.: — available, *materies* or *materia, silva, copia rerum*; subject- —, the — in hand, *res, propositum, institutum.* (3), = affair, in gen., *res, causa*; how do —s stand? *quo loco res est?*; a business —, *negotium.* (4), = trouble; what's the —? *quid* (*rei*) *est?* (5), = pus, *pus* (*puris*).

it **matters,** *interest, refert*; — to me, *meā*; — to him, *eius*; — a great deal, *magnopere* or *multum* or *magni.*

mattock, *dolabra.*

mature, *maturus, adultus.*

maturity, *maturitas.*

matutinal, *matutinus.*

maudlin; see drunken, silly.

maul; see injure.

maw, *ingluvies, venter.*

mawkish, *putidus*; adv. *putide.*

maxim, *praeceptum, regula, institutum, sententia.*

maximum, *quod maximum est.*

May, (*mensis*) *Maius.*

may, v., I may do: = I can, *possum facĕre*; = I have permission, *licet mihi facĕre*; = perhaps I will do, *fortasse faciam.*

mayor, *urbis praefectus.*

maze, *labyrinthus.*

mead, as a drink, *mulsum.*

mead, meadow, *pratum*; adj., of the —, *pratensis.*

meagre, *ieiunus, exilis, exiguus*; adv. *ieiune, exiliter.*

meagreness, *ieiunitas, exilitas.*

meal: = flour, *farina*; of food, in gen. *cibus, epulae* (-*arum,* = banquet); a morning —, *prandium*; the main — of the day, *cena.*

mean, subst. *modus, mediocritas.*

mean, adj.: = central, *medius*; = low in rank, *humilis, ignobilis, obscurus*; = morally low, *inliberalis, abiectus, sordidus.* Adv. *inliberaliter, abiecte, sordide.*

mean, v.: = intend, *in animo habēre, cogitare, velle*; = signify, indicate, *significare, sibi velle, valēre*; = refer to, allude to, *significare, dicĕre, intellegĕre.*

meaning: = signification, *significatio, vis, sententia*; see also purpose.

meanness: moral, *inliberalitas, animus abiectus, sordes* (plur.); of rank, *humilitas, obscuritas.*

means: = instrument, method, way, *via, ratio, consilium*; by all —, *omnino*; by no —, *minime, nullo modo*; by — of, render by abl. or *per*; = resources, *res familiaris, fortuna, opes* (-*um,* plur.).

meantime, in the, *interea, interim.*

measure, subst. *mensura, modus*; in full —, *pleno modio, cumulate*; according to the — of, *pro,* with abl.; beyond —, *praeter modum,*

immodice, *nimis*; in some —, *aliqua-tenus, aliqua ex parte*; = steps taken, course of action, *ratio, consilium*; in music, *modi, numeri (-orum).*

measure, v.: transit., *(di)metiri*; intransit., *esse,* with genit.

measured; see moderate.

measureless, *immensus, infinitus.*

measurement, *mensio, mensura.*

measurer, *mensor.*

measuring-rod, *decempeda.*

meat, *cibus*; = flesh, *caro.*

mechanic, *faber, opifex.*

mechanical, *mechanicus.*

mechanism, *machina, machinatio.*

medallion, *clipeus* or *clipeum.*

meddle, *se interponère, (rem) attingère.*

meddler, *ardelio, homo importunus.*

mediate, v. *se interponère*; to — a peace, *pacem conciliare.*

mediator, *deprecator, arbiter, con-ciliator.*

medical, *medicus.*

medicinal, *saluber, salutaris.*

medicine: = remedy, *medicina, medicamentum, remedium:* = medical science, *medicina, ars medendi.*

mediocre, *mediocris.*

mediocrity, *mediocritas.*

meditate, *cogitare, meditari, com-mentari.*

meditation, *cogitatio, commentatio, meditatio.*

meditative, *in cogitatione defixus.*

Mediterranean Sea, *Mare Internum, mare nostrum.*

medium; see mean and means.

medley, *farrago; conluvies, conluvio.*

meek, *demissus, verecundus*; adv. *verecunde.*

meekness, *animus demissus, vere-cundia.*

meet, adj.; see fit, proper.

meet, v.: transit., *obviam fieri, incidère, offendère*; to go to —, *obviam ire, occurrère*; to — death, *mortem obire* or *oppetère*; intransit., to — together, *(inter se) congredi, convenire, coire; confluère* (in large numbers), *convolare* (in haste).

meeting, *congressio, concursus (-ūs)*; = assembly, *conventus (-ūs), coetus (-ūs)*; a crowded —, *frequentia.*

melancholy, subst.: = hypochondria, *atra bilis*; = sorrow, *tristitia, maes-titia.*

melancholy, adj. *tristis, maestus.*

melee, *pugna, proelium.*

mellow, adj. *maturus, mitis*; of wine, *lenis, mollis.*

mellow, v.: transit., *coquère*; in-transit., *maturescère.*

melodious, *canorus, numerosus*; adv. *numerose.*

melody, *melos, cantus (-ūs).*

melt, v.: transit., *liquidum facère, liquefacère, dissolvère*; intransit., *liquescère, liquefieri, dissolvi, tabescère.*

member: of the body, *membrum*; a — of a nation, *civis*; of the senate, *senator*; of a corporation, *sodalis.*

membrane, *membrana.*

memoirs, *historiae (-arum), commen-tarii (-orum).*

memorable, *memorabilis, memoriā dignus.*

memorandum, *libellus, index.*

memorial, *monumentum.*

memory, *memoria, recordatio* (= re-collection): to keep in —, *memoriā tenēre*; from —, *ex memoria, memor-iter*; to commit to —, *ediscère*; in the — of man, *post hominum memoriam.*

menace; see threat.

mend, v.: transit., *reficère, reparare, reconcinnare, (re)sarcire*; fig., *emen-dare, corrigère*; intransit., = im-prove; q.v.

mendacious, *mendax*; adv. *falso, per mendacium.*

mendacity, *mendacium.*

mendicancy, *mendicitas, egestas.*

mendicant, *mendicus.*

menial, adj. *servilis.*

mensuration, *ars metiendi.*

mental, render by genit. *animi, ingenii, mentis.* Adv. *mente, animo, cogitatione.*

mention, subst. *mentio, commemoratio.*

mention, v. *mentionem facère, com-memorare*; above- —ed, render by *supra,* with *commemorare* or *dicère.*

mentor; see adviser.

mercenary, subst. *miles mercennarius* or *conducticius.*

mercenary, adj. *mercennarius, con-ductus; venalis* (= readily bribed).

merchandise, *merx, res (rerum) venales.*

merchant, *mercator, negotiator.*

merchant-ship, *navis mercatoria* or *oneraria.*

merciful, *misericors, clemens, mansue-tus*; adv. *clementer, mansuete.*

merciless, *immitis, inclemens, in-humanus, crudelis*; adv. *inclementer, inhumane, crudeliter.*

mercilessness, *inclementia, inhuman-itas, crudelitas.*

mercurial, *mobilis, levis.*

mercury; the god, *Mercurius*; the metal, *argentum vivum.*

mercy, *misericordia, clementia, mansue-tudo.*

mere, subst. *lacus (-ūs).*

mere, adj. *merus, solus, unus*; often *ipse.* Adv. *tantum, modo, solum.*

meretricious, *fucatus.*

merge; see dip or mingle.

meridian, adj. *meridianus.*

merit, subst. *meritum, dignitas, virtus*; according to —, *pro merito.*

merit, v.; see deserve.

merited, *meritus, debitus.*

meritorious, *laude dignus, laudabilis*; adv. *bene, optime.*

merriment, *hilaritas, festivitas.*

merry, *hilarus, hilaris, festivus*; adv. *hilariter, festive.*

mesh, *macula.*

mess, subst.: = common meal, *con-vivium*; = dirt, *squalor, conluvio*; = confusion, *turba, perturbatio rerum.*

message, *nuntius, mandatum.*

messenger, *nuntius* (f. *nuntia).*

messmate, *conviva, sodalis.*

metal, *metallum.*

metaphor, *translatio, verba (-orum) translata.*

metaphorical, *translatus;* adv. *per translationem, translatis verbis.*

metaphysics; render by *philosophia.*

mete; see measure.

meteor, *fax (caelestis).*

method, *ratio, via, modus, ars.*

methodical, render by phrase; adv., *ratione et via.*

metonymy, *immutatio.*

metre, *numerus, metrum.*

metrical, *numerosus, metricus.*

metropolis, *caput.*

mettle, *animus, audacia, ferocitas.*

mettlesome, *animosus, audax, ferox.*

Meuse; see Maas.

midday, subst. *meridies, tempus meridianum.*

midday, adj. *meridianus.*

middle, subst. *medium;* the — of the road, *media via.*

middle, adj. *medius;* the — way, *mediocritas.*

middling, *mediocris.*

midland, adj. *mediterraneus.*

midnight, subst. *media nox.*

midst, render by adj. *medius;* in the — of, *inter, in.*

midsummer, *summa aestas.*

midway, render by adj. *medius.*

midwife, *obstetrix.*

midwinter, *bruma.*

mien, *habitus (-ūs), vultus (-ūs).*

might, subst. *vis, robur, nervi (-orum, plur.);* with all one's —, *summa vi, summa ope.*

mighty, *potens, validus;* adv. *magnopere, valde, summa vi.*

migrate, *abire, discedĕre, migrare.*

migration, *profectio.*

Milan, *Mediolanum.*

mild, adj. *lenis, mitis;* to make —, *mitigare, lenire;* to grow —, *mitescĕre;* of character, etc., *mitis, clemens, mansuetus.* Adv. *leniter, clementer, mansuete.*

mildew, *robigo* or *rubigo, mucor, situs (-ūs).*

mildness, of character, *lenitas, mansuetudo, clementia.*

mile (Roman), *mille,* plur. *milia (passuum).*

milestone, *miliarium.*

military, adj. *militaris, bellicus;* — service, *militia;* — stores, *apparatus (-ūs) belli;* — skill, *rei militaris peritia.*

militate, to — against, *obstare, adversari.*

milk, subst. *lac;* new —, *lac recens;* curdled —, *lac concretum.*

milk, v. *mulgēre.*

milk-pail, *mulctra, mulctrum.*

milk-white, milky, *lacteus;* the — Way, *lacteus orbis, via lactea.*

mill, *mola, pistrinum.*

miller, *pistor.*

millet, *milium.*

million, *decies centena mil(l)ia.*

mimic, v. *imitari.*

mimicry, *imitatio.*

minaret, *turris.*

mince, v. *concidĕre, consecare.*

mince, minced meat, subst. *minutal.*

mincing, *putidus.*

mind, subst. *animus, mens, ingenium* (= intellect or character); to show presence of —, *praesenti animo uti;* to be in one's right —, *sanae mentis esse;* to be out of one's —, *insanire;* to bear in —, *meminisse;* to call to —, *recordari;* to make up one's —, *statuĕre, constituĕre.*

mind, v.: = attend to, *animum (ad rem) advertĕre, (rem) animadvertĕre, curare, agĕre;* mind you come, *cura (ut) venias;* object to, *aegre ferre.*

mindful, *memor.*

mine, subst., *metallum;* milit., *cuniculus.*

mine, possess. pron., *meus.*

mine, v. *(cf)fodĕre;* milit., *cuniculos agĕre.*

mineral, subst. *metallum.*

mingle; see mix.

minimum, *minimum, pars minima.*

minion, *minister, servus.*

minister, subst., *minister, servus;* a — of state, *principis socius et administer omnium consiliorum, ille penes quem est cura administrandae reipublicae.*

minister, *conducĕre, prodesse.*

ministry, *ministerium, administratio.*

minor, subst., *filius (f. filia) familias.*

minor, adj.; see little, small.

minority, *aetas nondum adulta;* = smaller number, *pars* or *numerus minor.*

minstrel, *citharoedus.*

mint, subst.: the plant, *ment(h)a;* where money is coined, *moneta.*

mint, v.; see coin.

minute, subst.. = moment, *punctum* or *momentum temporis.*

minute, adj.: = very small, *exiguus, pusillus, minutus;* = exact, *subtilis, accuratus;* adv. *subtiliter, accurate.*

minutes, plur. subst. *libellus, commentarii (-orum).*

miracle, *res mira, miraculum.*

miraculous, *mirus, mirificus, mirabilis;* in a — manner, *mirum in modum.*

mire, *lutum.*

mirror, *speculum.*

mirth, *hilaritas, laetitia, gaudium.*

mirthful, *hilaris (hilarus), laetus.*

miry, *luteus, lutulentus.*

misadventure, *casus (-ūs), incommodum.*

misanthrope, *qui genus humanum odit.*

misapply, *abuti, perverse uti.*

misapprehend; see misunderstand.

misbehave, *male se gerĕre.*

miscalculate, *male computare; errare, falli, decipi.*

miscalculation, *error.*

miscarriage, *abortus (-ūs), abortio;* a — of justice, *iudicium perversum.*

miscarry, *abortum facĕre;* in gen. = fail, *cadĕre, secus procedĕre.*

miscellaneous, *varius, diversus.*

miscellany, as a literary form, *satura.*

mischance; see misfortune.

mischief; = damage, *malum, incommodum, damnum*; = wrongdoing, *maleficium.*

mischief-maker, *mali auctor.*

mischievous; = harmful, *noxius, perniciosus;* = playful, *lascivus.*

misconceive, *perperam accipěre.*

misconception, *opinio falsa, error.*

misconduct, *delictum, peccatum.*

misconstrue; see misinterpret.

miscreant, *(homo) scelestus* or *sceleratus.*

misdeed, *scelus (-eris, n.), maleficium.*

misdemeanour, *delictum.*

misdirect, *(epistulam) perperam inscriběre;* = to misuse, *abuti, perperam uti.*

miser, *homo avarus.*

miserable, *miser, infelix, adflictus;* adv. *misere.*

miserliness, *avaritia, sordes (-ium).*

miserly, *avarus, tenax.*

misery, *miseria, aerumna, tristitia.*

misfortune, *fortuna adversa, res adversae, calamitas, incommodum*; he had the — to, *accidit ei ut.*

misgive; see distrust, doubt.

misgiving, *timor, sollicitudo, praesagium.*

misgovern, *male regěre* or *administrare.*

misguide, *in errorem inducěre.*

mishap; see misfortune.

misinform, *falso docěre.*

misinterpret, *male* or *perperam interpretari.*

misjudge, *male iudicare.*

mislead, *decipěre, fallěre, in errorem inducěre.*

mismanage; see misgovern.

misogynist, *qui mulieres odit.*

misplace, *(in) alieno loco conlocare;* misplaced, fig., can be rendered by *male* or *perperam*, e.g. with —d humour, *male salsus.*

misprint, *mendum.*

mispronounce, *male pronuntiare.*

misquote, render by phrase, such as *verba (auctoris) vitiose proferre.*

misrepresent, *calumniari, depravare.*

misrule; see misgovern.

miss, subst.; render by verb.

miss, v.: = feel the loss of *desiderare, requirěre;* = fail to meet or find, *(de)errare;* = out, = omit, *omittěre, praetermittěre.*

misshapen, *deformis, distortus.*

missile, subst. *telum, (telum) missile.*

missile, adj. *missilis.*

missing, to be, *desiderari, deesse.*

mission, *missio;* = delegation, *legatio.*

misspend, *perděre;* see also waste.

misstatement, *quod falsum est; mendacium.*

mist, *nebula, caligo.*

mistake, subst. *error, erratum;* to make a —, *errare, peccare;* a — in writing, *mendum.*

mistaken, to be, *errare, falli.*

mistakenly, *per errorem, perperam.*

mistress, *domina;* — of a house, *materfamilias, hera;* a school- —, *praeceptrix, magistra;* = sweetheart, *amica.*

misty, *nebulosus, caliginosus;* fig. *obscurus.*

misunderstand, *perperam intellegěre.*

misunderstanding, *error;* between persons, *offensio, dissidium.*

misuse, subst. *usus (-ūs) perversus.*

misuse, v. *abuti, male uti.*

mitigate, *lenire, mitigare.*

mitigation, *mitigatio, levatio.*

mix, v.: transit., *miscēre, admiscēre, temperare;* to — up, = confuse, *confunděre, permiscēre;* intransit., use transit. verb in pass. or with reflex.

mixed, *(per)mixtus, promiscuus.*

mixture, *mixtura, temperatio; permixtio;* a — of good and evil, *bona mixta malis.*

moan, subst. *gemitus (-ūs).*

moan, v. *geměre.*

moat, *fossa.*

mob, *turba, multitudo; vulgus, plebs.*

mobile, *mobilis.*

mobility, *mobilitas, agilitas.*

mock, adj. *simulatus, fictus, falsus.*

mock, v. *deridēre, inludēre, ludibrio habēre;* see also disappoint.

mocker, *derisor.*

mockery, *ludibrium.*

mockingly, *per ludibrium.*

mode, *ratio, modus;* — of dress, *habitus (-ūs).*

model, subst. *exemplar, exemplum.*

model, adj. *optimus.*

model, v. *fingěre, formare.*

moderate, adj.: = restrained, *moderatus, modestus, temperatus;* = middling, *modicus, mediocris.* Adv. *moderate, modeste, temperate; modice, mediocriter.*

moderate, v. *moderari, temperare, coercēre.*

moderation, *modus, modestia, temperantia.*

modern, *recens, novus; huius aetatis.*

modest, *pudens, verecundus;* = moderate, slight, *mediocris, modicus.* Adv. *pudenter, verecunde.*

modesty, *pudor, verecundia.*

modify, *(im)mutare;* see also change.

modulate, *modulari.*

modulation, *flexio, flexus (-ūs).*

moiety; see half.

moist, *humidus.*

moisten, *conspergěre* (= sprinkle), *rigare* (= water).

moisture, *humor.*

molar, subst. *dens genuinus.*

mole, = mound, *moles, agger;* the animal, *talpa;* = mark on the body, *naevus.*

molest, *sollicitare, vexare.*

mollify, *mollire, mitigare, lenire.*

molten, *liquefactus.*

moment: of time, *punctum* or *momentum temporis;* for the —, *in praesens;* at the —, *hoc tempore, in praesentia;* = importance, *momentum.*

momentary, *brevissimus.*

momentous, adj. *magni momenti.*

momentum, *momentum, vis.*

monarch, *rex, princeps, dominus.*

monarchical, *regius;* a — form of government, *genus reipublicae regium,*

monarchy, *imperium singulare, potestas regia, regnum.*

monetary, *pecuniarius, nummarius, argentarius.*

money, *pecunia, argentum;* ready —, *pecunia praesens* or *numerata;* a piece of —, *nummus.*

money-bag; see purse.

mongrel, *hibrida.*

monk, *monachus* (eccl.).

monkey, *simia.*

monotheist, *qui unum modo deum esse credit.*

monotonous, *canorus;* or render by *idem* and *semper.*

monsoon, *ventus (qui certo tempore flare consuevit).*

monster, *monstrum, portentum, belua.*

monstrous, *immanis, monstruosus;* adv. *monstruose, praeter naturam.*

month, *mensis.*

monthly: adj. *menstruus;* adv. *singulis mensibus, in singulos menses.*

monument, *monumentum.*

monumental, = important, *gravis, magni momenti.*

mood, *animus;* gram., *modus.*

moody, *morosus.*

moon, *luna;* — -light *lunae lumen;* a —light night, *nox lunā inlustris.*

moor, moorland, *loca (-orum) fruticetis obsita.*

moor, v. *religare, deligare.*

moot point; it is a —, *incertum* or *dubium est.*

mop subst. *peniculus.*

mop, v. *detergere.*

moping, *tristis, maestus.*

moral, adj.: = relating to morals, *moralis;* — teaching, *morum praecepta (-orum);* = morally correct, *honestus, probus.*

morale, *animus.*

morality, morals, *mores (-um).*

moralize, *de moribus praecipēre.*

morass, *palūs (-ūdis).*

morbid, *aeger, aegrotus.*

more, subst. = a greater amount, *plus.*

more, adj.: sing., *plus* or *amplius* with genit.; plur., *plures.*

more, adv., render by compar. of adj. or adv.; otherwise by *magis* or *potius* (= rather); no — (= no longer), *non iam;* the — . . . the — . . ., *quo* (with compar.), *eo* (with compar.).

moreover, *praeterea, ultro.*

moribund, *moribundus.*

morn, morning, subst. *tempus matutinum;* in the —, *mane, matutino tempore;* early in the —, *multo mane, prima luce;* good —! *salve!*

morning, adj. *matutinus.*

morning-star, *Lucifer.*

morose, *morosus, acerbus, difficilis;* adv. *morose, acerbe.*

moroseness, *morositas, acerbitas.*

morrow, *posterus dies; crastinus dies* (= tomorrow).

morsel, *offa, mica, pars exigua.*

mortal, adj. *mortalis;* see also fatal.

mortality *condicio mortalis, mortalitas;* see also death.

mortar: for mixing, *pila;* for binding together, *arenatum.*

mortgage, subst. *pignus (-oris, n.).*

mortgage, v. *pignori dare, obligare.*

mortification, *offensio, dolor.*

mortify, v.: intransit., *putrescēre;* transit., fig., *offendēre, vexare.*

mosaic, subst. *pavimentum* or *opus tessellatum.*

mosaic; adj. *tessellatus.*

mosquito, *culex.*

moss, *muscus.*

mossy, *muscosus, musco circumlitus.*

most, adj. *plurimus;* for the — part, *plerumque, maximam partem;* at the —, *summum.*

most, adv., render by superl. of adj. or adv.; otherwise *maxime; plurimum.*

mostly, *fere, plerumque; maximam partem.*

moth, *blatta.*

mother, *mater;* of a —, adj., *maternus.*

mother-in-law, *socrus (-ūs).*

motherly, *maternus.*

mother-tongue, *patrius sermo.*

motion, subst.: = movement, *motus (-ūs);* to be in —, *movēri;* = proposal, *sententia, rogatio.*

motion, v. = to gesture, *adnuēre, significare.*

motionless, *immotus, immobilis.*

motive, *causa, ratio.*

mottled, *maculosus.*

motto, *sententia, dictum, praeceptum.*

mould, subst.: = shape, *forma;* = soil, *terra.*

mouldy, *mucidus.*

moult, *plumas ponēre.*

mound, *tumulus, agger.*

mount, subst.: see horse.

mount, v.: intransit., see rise; transit., = ascend, *scandēre, ascendēre;* to — a horse, *conscendēre equum;* = furnish with horses, (milites) *equis imponēre:* —ed, *equo vectus.*

mountain, *mons;* of a —, *montanus.*

mountainous, *montuosus.*

mountebank, *circulator, planus.*

mourn, *maerēre, lugēre;* see also lament.

mournful, *tristis, maestus, flebilis;* adv. *maeste, flebiliter.*

mourning, subst. *maeror, maestitia luctus (-ūs); vestis lugubris;* in —, adj. *sordidatus.*

mouse, *mus (muris).*

mouse-trap, *muscipula.*

mouth, *os;* with open —, *hians.*

movable, *mobilis, agilis.*

move: transit., *(com)movēre;* to — rapidly, *agitare;* to — round *versare;* to — to action, *impellēre;* intransit., *movēri,* se *movēre, ferri.*

movement, *motus (-ūs).*

mow, *demetēre, secare.*

mower, *faenisex.*

much, subst. *multum* or *multa.*

much, adj. *multus;* sometimes *magnus* (= great); too —, adj. *nimius.*

much, adv. *multum, valde:* very —, *plurimum;* with compar. or superl., *multo;* too —, adv., *nimium, nimis;* — less, *nedum, ne dicam.*

mud, *lutum, caenum.*

muddle, subst. *turba, confusio.*

muddle, v. *confundĕre, (per)miscĕre, turbare.*

muddy, *lutulentus, luteus.*

muffle, *velare, obvolvĕre.*

muggy, *humidus* (= damp), *calidus* (= warm).

mulberry, *morum;* — -tree, *morus.*

mulct, *multare.*

mule, *mulus.*

mull: —ed wine, *vinum fervidum.*

mullet, *mullus, mugil(is).*

multifarious, *multiplex, varius.*

multiform, *multiformis.*

multiply, *multiplicare.*

multitude, *multitudo, vis, vulgus.*

multitudinous, *creber, frequens, multus.*

munch, *manducare.*

mundane, *humanus, quotidianus.*

municipality, *municipium.*

munificence, *munificentia, liberalitas.*

munificent, *munificus, liberalis.*

munition, *belli instrumenta* (-orum) or *apparatus* (-ūs).

mural *muralis.*

murder, subst. *caedes, occisio, homicidium;* — of a near relative, *parricida.*

murderous, *sanguinarius, cruentus.*

murmur, subst. *murmur, susurrus, fremitus* (-ūs); = complaint, *querela.*

murmur, v. *murmurare, fremĕre, mussare;* = complain, *fremĕre, queri.*

muscle, in anatomy, *musculus, torus;* —s, = strength, *lacerti* (-orum), *nervi* (-orum).

muscular, *lacertosus.*

muse, *Musa, Camena.*

mushroom, *fungus, boletus.*

music, (ars) *musica;* a piece of —, *modi* (-orum), *cantus* (-ūs).

musical, *musicus, symphoniacus;* = understanding music, *artis musicae peritus;* = melodious, *canorus, numerosus.*

musician, *musicus;* or *fidicen, tibicen,* etc.

muslin, *sindon.*

must, subst. *mustum.*

must, v.: I — go, *eundum est mihi, ire debeo, ire me oportet, necesse est eam.*

mustard, *sinapi.*

muster, v.: transit., *recensēre;* = assemble, *convocare;* to — up courage, *animum sumĕre;* intransit., *congregari, coire, convenire.*

musty, *mucidus.*

mutability, *mutabilitas.*

mutable, *mutabilis, inconstans, mobilis.*

mute, adj. *mutus.*

mutilate, *mutilare, truncare.*

mutilated, *mutilus, mutilatus, truncatus.*

mutinous, *seditiosus;* adv. *seditiose.*

mutiny, subst. *seditio, motus* (-ūs).

mutiny, v. *seditionem facĕre.*

mutter, *mussare, mussitare, murmurare.*

muttering, subst. *murmur.*

mutton, *caro (ovilla).*

mutual, *mutuus;* adv. *mutuo*

my, *meus,* sometimes *noster.*

myriad, *decem millia;* = an indefinitely large number, *sescenti.*

myrmidon, *satelles, adsecula.*

myrrh, *murra;* of —, *murrinus.*

myrtle, *myrtus;* of —, adj. *myrteus;* —berry, *myrtum;* — grove, *myrtetum.*

myself; see self.

mysterious, *occultus, secretus, arcanus.*

mystery: religious, *mysteria* (-orum); in gen., *res occulta.*

mystic, *mysticus;* see also secret, strange.

mystification, *ambages* (-um).

mystify, *tenebras (homini) offundĕre.*

myth, *fabula.*

mythical, *fabulosus.*

mythology, *fabulae* (-arum), *historia fabularis.*

N

nail, subst.: on finger or toe, *unguis;* for hammering, *clavus.*

nail, v. (clavis) *adfigĕre.*

naive, *simplex.*

naked, *nudus;* adv. *aperte.*

nakedness, *nudatum corpus;* of style, *ieiunitas, exilitas.*

name, subst. *nomen, vocabulum, cognomen* (= family name); in — (only) *verbo;* good — (= reputation) *nomen, fama, existimatio.*

name, v. *nominare, appellare, dicĕre;* = mention, *nominare;* = appoint q.v.

nameless, *nominis expers.*

namely; render by simple apposition, or relative clause or *dico* (= I mean).

namesake (homo) *eodem nomine appellatus.*

nap, subst.: = sleep, *somnus (brevis);* of cloth, *villi* (-orum).

nap, v.: see sleep; Homer is caught —ping, *dormitat Homerus.*

napkin, *mappa, mantele.*

Naples, *Neapolis.*

narrate, (e)narrare, referre, *memorare.*

narration, *narratio, expositio.*

narrative, subst. *narratio, historia.*

narrator, *narrator.*

narrow, adj. *angustus, artus* (= tight), *contractus* (= narrowed); to have a — escape, *aegre periculum effugĕre.* Adv.: = scarcely, *aegre, vix;* = carefully, *accurate, diligenter.*

narrowness, *angustiae* (-arum); — of mind, *animus angustus.*

narrows, *augustiaᵓ* (-arum), *fauces* (-ium).

nasal, *narium* (genit.).

nastiness: = unpleasantness, *amaritudo, gravitas;* = foulness, *foeditas.*

nasty: = disagreeable, *amarus, gravis;* = foul, *foedus, spurcus.*

natal, *natalis, natalicius.*

nation, *populus, gens* (= people), *civitas* (= body of citizens), *respublica* (= state).

national, render by genit.; in the — interest, *e republica.*

native, subst. *indigena;* a — of Rome, *homo Romae natus.*

native, adj. *indigena;* — land, *patria;* — language, *patrius sermo.*

natural, *naturalis, nativus, innatus* or *insitus* (= inborn); *simplex* or *candidus* (= unaffected); — ability or disposition, *indoles, ingenium, natura*; — death, *mors necessaria*; — science or philosophy, *physica, naturae investigatio.* Adv. *secundum naturam, naturaliter; sponte* (= without compulsion); *simpliciter* (= unaffectedly).

naturalize: to — a person, *homini civitatem dare*; to — an animal or plant, *importare.*

nature, *natura*; the realm of —, *rerum natura*; the — of a person (or thing), *natura, ingenium, indoles.*

naught, *nihil*; to set at —, *neglegēre.*

naughtiness, *improbitas, petulantia, malitia.*

naughty, *improbus, petulans, malus.*

nausea, *nausea, fastidium* (= disgust).

nauseous: see loathsome, disgusting.

nautical, naval, adj. *navalis, nauticus.*

navigable, *navigabilis, navium patiens.*

navigate, *navigare.*

navigation, *navigatio, res nauticae.*

navigator: see sailor.

navy, *classis.*

nay, = no, *non*; — rather —, *immo* (*vero*), *atque adeo.*

near, adj. *propinquus*; —er, *propior*; —est, *proximus*; *vicinus* (= neighbouring).

near, adv. *prope, iuxta, propter.*

nearly, *prope, paene, fere* or *ferme.*

nearness, *propinquitas.*

neat: = clean, tidy, *nitidus, mundus, concinnus*; = undiluted, *merus.* Adv. *nitide, concinne.*

neatness, *munditia, concinnitas.*

nebulous, *nebulosus.*

necessaries, *res necessariae.*

necessary, adj. *necessarius*: this is —, *hoc est necessarium, opus est hoc*; adv. *necessarie, necessario.*

necessitate, *cogēre*; see compel.

necessity: = what must be, *necessitas, res necessaria*; = want, *necessitas, egestas.*

neck, *collum, cervix* (often plur., *cervices*).

necklace, *monile, torques.*

need, subst. *necessitas*: there is — of, *opus est* (with nom. or abl.).

need, v. *requirēre, egēre.*

needful, *necessarius.*

needle, *acus (-ūs).*

needless: see unnecessary.

needlework, *opus acu factum.*

needy, *egens, indigens, inops.*

nefarious, *nefarius.*

negation, *negatio, infitiatio.*

neglect, negligence, *neglegentia, incuria.*

negotiate, *agēre, conloqui*; to — a peace, *pacem componēre.*

negotiation, *conloquium*; —s are in progress, *agitur (de re).*

negotiator, *legatus, orator, internuntius.*

Negro, *Aethiops.*

neigh, *hinnire.*

neighbour, *vicinus* (f. *vicina*); —s, *vicini, finitimi vicinia*; = fellow man, *alter, ceteri* (plur., = others).

neighbourhood, *vicinia, vicinitas.*

neighbouring, *vicinus, propinquus, finitimus.*

neighbourly, *ut decet vicinum.*

neighing, *hinnitus (-ūs).*

neither, pron. *neuter*; in — direction, *neutro.*

neither, conj. *nec* (or *neque*); — . . . nor, *nec . . . nec*; in commands, wishes, etc., *neve* (or *neu*).

nephew, *filius fratris* or *sororis.*

nereid, *Nereis.*

nerve, = vigour, etc., *nervi (-orum).*

nervous, = vigorous, *nervosus*; see also timid.

nervousness, *timiditas, trepidatio.*

nest, *nidus.*

nestling, *pullus.*

net, subst. *rete, plaga* (usually plur.).

nettle, *urtica.*

nettled, adj. *offensus, subiratus.*

network, *reticulum.*

neuter, gram., *neuter, neutralis.*

neutral, *medius, neutrius partis.*

never, *nunquam.*

nevertheless, *nihilominus, (at)tamen.*

new, *novus, recens, insolitus* (= unaccustomed). Adv. *nuper, modo, recens.*

new-comer, *advena.*

new-fangled, *mirus, novus.*

newness, *novitas, insolentia.*

news, *res, nuntius*; what —? *quid novi?*

newspaper, *acta (-orum) diurna* or *publica.*

newt, *lacertus, lacerta* (= lizard).

next, adj. *proximus*; the — year, *proximus* or *insequens annus*; the — day, *posterus dies*; on the — day *postero die, postridie.*

next, adv. *deinceps, deinde, postea.*

nibble, *(ad)rodēre, gustare* (= to taste).

nice: = pleasant, *suavis, dulcis*; = fastidious, *delicatus*; = discerning, *diligens, subtilis.* Adv. *bene, probe; diligenter, subtiliter.*

nicety: = fastidiousness, *fastidium*; = precision, *subtilitas.*

niche, *aedicula* (for statues).

nick; in the — of time, *in ipso articulo (temporis).*

nickname, *nomen per ludibrium datum.*

niece, *fratris* or *sororis filia.*

niggardly: see miserly.

night, *nox*; by —, *nocte, noctu*; in the dead of —, *intempesta nocte.*

nightfall; at —, *sub noctem.*

nightingale, *luscinia.*

nightly, adj. *nocturnus.*

nightmare, *insomnium.*

Nile, *Nilus.*

nimble, *agilis.*

nine, *novem*; — times, *novie(n)s*; — each, *noveni.*

nineteen, *undeviginti*; — each, *undeviceni.*

nineteenth, *undevicesimus, nonus decimus.*

ninety, *nonaginta*; — each, *nonageni.*

ninth, *nonus.*

no, adj. *nullus*; often *nihil*, with partitive genit.; by — means, *minime, haudquaquam.*

no, adv.: in answers, *non, minime (vero)*; — but, *immo (vero)*; to answer yes or —, *aut etiam aut non respondēre*; to say —, *negare*; with comparatives *non, nihilo.*

nobility: of birth, *nobilitas, genus nobile*; of character, *ingenuus.*

noble, subst. *homo nobilis*; —s, plur., *nobiles, proceres.*

noble, adj.: by birth, *nobilis, generosus*; morally, *ingenuus, honestus, liberalis*; adv. *ingenue, honeste.*

nobody, *nemo*; and —, *nec quisquam.*

nocturnal, *nocturnus.*

nod, subst. *nutus (-ūs).*

nod, v. *nutare*; to — assent, *adnuěre*; = doze, *dormitare.*

noise, subst. *sonitus (-ūs); strepitus (-ūs;* loud); *crepitus (-ūs;* = clattering, creaking); *fragor* (= — of breaking); to make a —, *strepěre, (con)crepare.*

noise, v.: see publish.

noiseless, *tacitus*; adv. *tacite, (cum) silentio.*

noisily, noisy; *tumultuosus*; adv. *cum strepitu.*

nomadic, *vagus.*

nominally, *nomine, verbo.*

nominate, *nominare, dicěre, creare.*

nomination, *nominatio.*

nominative, *casus (-ūs) nominativus.*

none, *nemo, nullus.*

nonentity, *nihil*; = obscure person, *terrae filius.*

nonsense, *ineptiae (-arum), nugae (-arum)*; as interj., nonsense! *gerrae!, fabulae!*; to talk —, *garrire.*

nonsensical, *absurdus, ineptus.*

nook, *angulus.*

noon, *meridies*; of —, adj. *meridianus.*

noose, *laqueus.*

nor, *nec* or *neque*; in commands, *neve* or *neu.*

normal; see regular.

north, subst. *septentrio* (or pl. *septentriones*).

northern, northerly, *septentrionalis, aquilonaris*; — wind, *aquilo.*

north pole, *polus glacialis, arctos.*

North Sea, *Oceanus Germanicus.*

northwards, *(ad) septentrionem versus.*

nose, *nasus, nares (-ium* = nostrils).

nostrils, *naris* (usually plur.).

not, *non, haud*; — at all, *minime, nullo modo, haudquaquam*; — enough, *parum, minus*; not even . . ., *ne . . . quidem*; and —, = nor, *nec* or *neque*; to say that . . ., *negare.*

notable; see remarkable.

notary, *scriba.*

notch, v. *inciděre.*

note, subst. *adnotatio*; in music, *sonus, vox*; = letter, *epistula.*

note, v. *adnotare*; see also write, notice.

note-book, *adversaria (-orum), commentarius.*

noted; see famous.

nothing, *nihil (nil), nulla res*; — of the kind, *nihil tale*; — new, *nihil novi*; good for —, *nequam*; — but, *nihil aliud nisi.*

notice, subst.: = act of noticing, *animadversio, notatio*; = announcement, warning, *promulgatio, denuntiatio*; as a visible object, *proscriptio, titulus.*

notice, v. *animadvertěre.*

noticeable; see remarkable.

notification, *promulgatio, denuntiatio.*

notify; see inform.

notion, *notio, suspicio.*

notoriety, *infamia.*

notorious, *notus, infamis.*

notwithstanding, as adv. *nihilominus, tamen*; as prep. see spite.

nought; see nothing.

noun, *nomen.*

nourish, *alěre, nutrire.*

nourishment, *alimentum, cibus.*

novel, subst. *fabula.*

novel, adj. *novus.*

novelty: = newness, *novitas, insolentia*; = new thing, *res nova.*

November, *(mensis) Novembris* or *November.*

novice, *tiro.*

now: as adv. of time, *nunc, iam, hoc tempore, in praesentia*; now . . . now . . ., *modo . . . modo . . .*; — and then, *interdum, nonnunquam*; as a particle of transition, *autem, vero, quidem.*

nowadays, *nunc, hodie.*

nowhere, *nusquam.*

nude, *nudus.*

nudge, *fodicare.*

nuisance, render by adj. *molestus* or *gravis.*

null, *vanus, inritus, inanis.*

nullify, *ad inritum redigěre.*

numb, adj. *torpens*; to be —, *torpēre*; to grow —, *torpescěre.*

number, subst. *numerus*; a large —, *multitudo, copia.*

number, v. *(di)numerare.*

numbering: a — of the people, *census (-ūs).*

numberless, *innumerus, innumerabilis.*

numbness, *torpor.*

numerical, render by subst. *numerus.*

numerous, plur. *multi, plurimi, frequentes, crebri.*

nuptial, *nuptialis*; a — song, *epithalamium, hymenaeus.*

nuptials, subst. *nuptiae (-arum).*

nurse, subst. *nutrix* (= children's —).

nurse, v. *nutrire, fovēre*; to — the sick, *curare (hominem), adsidēre (homini).*

nursery, for plants, *seminarium.*

nursling, *alumnus.*

nurture, *educatio.*

nut, *nux.*

nutriment, nutrition; see food.

nutshell, *putamen.*

nymph, *nympha*; water- —, *Naias*; wood- —, *Dryas, Hamadryas*; sea- —, *Nereis.*

O

O! Oh! interj. *o! pro! heu!* — that (in wishes), *utinam, o si.*

oak, *quercus (-ūs), aesculus* (= winter- —), *ilex* (= holm- —); adj., of —, *quernus;* the wood of the —, *robur;* an — -wood, *quercetum.*

oakum, *stuppa.*

oar, *remus.*

oath, *iusiurandum, sacramentum* (military).

oats, *avena.*

obdurate; see obstinate.

obedience, *oboedientia, obtemperatio.*

obedient, *obediens, dicto audiens, obtemperans;* adv. *oboedienter.*

obeisance; see bow.

obelisk, *obeliscus.*

obey, *parére, oboedire, obtemperare, obsequi.*

object, subst. *res;* to be an — of hatred, *odio esse;* = purpose, aim, *consilium, propositum, finis;* my —, *quod volo* or *sequor.*

object, v.: = feel annoyance, *gravari, moleste ferre;* = make objections, *contra dicére, recusare, repugnare.*

objection, *quod contra dicitur, contradictio.*

objective, adj. *externus, verus* (= true).

oblation; see offering.

obligation, *officium* (= duty), *religio* (= sense of —); under —, adj., *obnoxius.*

oblige: = compel, *cogére;* = to put under obligation, *obligare, obstringére;* = do a favour to, *gratum facére, commodare.*

obliging, *comis, officiosus;* adv. *comiter, officiose.*

oblique, *obliquus.* Adv., *oblique, in obliquum;* fig., *per ambages.*

obliquity, *obliquitas;* moral —, *pravitas, iniquitas.*

obliterate, *delére, abolére.*

oblivion, *oblivio, oblivium.*

oblivious, *immemor, obliviosus.*

oblong, *oblongus.*

obloquy, *odium; opprobrium,* (= abuse).

obnoxious: = subject, liable, *obnoxius;* = objectionable, *noxius, invisus.*

obscene, *obscenus, turpis;* adv. *obscene, turpiter.*

obscenity, *obscenitas, turpitudo.*

obscure, *obscurus; reconditus* (= abstruse), *ambiguus* (= uncertain); *humilis* (= undistinguished). Adv. *obscure; ambigue, per ambages.*

obscure, v. *obscurare, tenebras offundére.*

obscurity, *obscuritas; tenebrae* (= arum; = dark).

obsequies; see funeral.

obsequious, *(nimis) obsequens.*

obsequiousness, *obsequentia.*

observance, *mos, ritus (-ūs);* religious —, *cultus (-ūs) deorum.*

observant, *attentus;* — of, *diligens,* with genit.

observation, *observatio, animadversio, notatio;* = remark, *dictum.*

observe: = watch, notice, *observare, animadvertére, contemplari;* = keep up, maintain, *(ob)servare, conservare.*

observer, *spectator* (f. *spectatrix*); *speculator* (f. *speculatrix*).

obsolete, *obsoletus;* to become —, *obsolescére.*

obstacle, *impedimentum, obex* (= barrier).

obstinacy, *pertinacia, pervicacia, obstinatio.*

obstinate, *pertinax, pervicax, obstinatus;* adv. *pertinaciter, pervicaciter, obstinate.*

obstreperous, *tumultuosus.*

obstruct, *obstruére, obstare* (with dat.)

obstruction, *impedimentum, obstructio.*

obtain, v.: transit., *adipisci, consequi;* to — by asking, *impetrare, exorare* intransit., see prevail.

obtrude, *ingerére, inculcare.*

obtuse, *hebes, obtusus.*

obviate, *occurrére, obviam ire.*

obvious, *apertus, manifestus;* adv. *aperte, manifesto.*

occasion, subst.: = time, *tempus;* = suitable time, opportunity, *occasio.*

occasion, v. *auctorem esse* (with genit.) *creare, movére.*

occasionally, *raro, interdum.*

occult, *occultus.*

occupation: = taking, *occupatio;* = business, *occupatio, negotium.*

occupy: = take, *capére, occupare;* = hold, *habére, tenére, obtinére, possidére;* = engage, keep busy, *occupare, tenére, detinére.*

occur: = come to mind, *in mentem (homini) venire, subire;* = be found in books, *reperiri, legi;* = happen, *fieri, accidére.*

occurrence, *casus (-ūs), res (gesta).*

ocean, *oceanus.*

October, *(mensis) October.*

octogenarian, *homo octoginta annos natus.*

odd: = not even, *impar;* see also strange, extraordinary.

ode, *carmen.*

odious, *invisus, invidiosus.*

odium, *invidia;* causing —, *invidiosus.*

odour, *odor.*

of, render by genitive; of, = composed of, *ex,* or use special adj. (e.g. of marble, *marmoreus*); of = concerning, *de.*

off, adv. render by compound verbs in *ab- (au-), de-, ex-;* far —, *longe* or *procul.*

off, prep., *contra* (= opposite).

offence: = displeasure, *offensio, offensa;* = fault, *peccatum, delictum.*

offend: = hurt, displease, *offendére, laedére;* to be —ed, *aegre ferre;* = commit an offence, *peccare.*

offensive: = giving offence, *odiosus molestus, gravis;* opp. to defensive, render by *bellum inferre.*

offer, subst. *condicio;* or use verb.

offer, v.: transit., *offerre, praebére, porrigére* (= hold out); to — violence, *vim adferre;* intransit., = present itself, *offerri, dari, incidére.*

office: = duty, function, *munus (-eris,* n.), *officium;* = official position, *magistratus (-ūs), honor, provincia;* a good —, = a kindness, *beneficium, officium.*

officer, official, *praefectus.*

official, adj. *publicus;* adv. *publice.*

officiate, *munere* (or *officio*) *fungi.*

officious, *molestus;* adv. *moleste.*

officiousness, *nimium studium.*

offspring, *progenies, stirps, liberi* (-*orum*). = children).

oft, often, *saepe, saepenumero;* how —? *quotie(n)s?;* so —, *totie(n)s.*

ogle, *oculis limis intueri.*

ogre, *larva.*

oil, subst. *oleum;* of —, adj., *olearius.*

oil, v. *oleo ungere* or *perfundere.*

ointment, *unguentum.*

old. (1), in gen., = not new, *vetus, vetustus;* an — soldier, *veteranus.* (2), = having lived long, *grandis* (*natu*); an — man, *senex, vetulus;* an — woman, *anus, anicula, vetula;* to grow —, *senescere.* (3), = no longer existing, *antiquus, priscus, pristinus;* in the — days, *olim, quondam.*

old age, *senectus* (-*ūtis*).

older, *grandior, maior* (*natu*).

oldest, *natu maximus.*

old-fashioned, *obsoletus, antiquus, priscus.*

oligarchy, *paucorum dominatio.*

olive, (tree or fruit) *oliva, olea;* an — grove, *olivetum.*

omen, *omen, auspicium.*

ominous, render by phrase, such as *omen infaustum.*

omission, *praetermissio.*

omit, *omittere, praetermittere, praeterire.*

omnipotent, *omnipotens.*

on, adv. *porro;* or render by compound verb in *pro-:* to go —, *pergere, procedere;* — to, *in* with acc.

on, prep.: of place, *in* with abl.; sometimes *a, ab* (of sides, etc.), or abl. alone; of time when, abl. alone; = immediately after, *e* (*ex*) or abl. absol.; on, = about, concerning, *de.*

once: as numeral, *semel;* = at one time, *aliquando, olim, quondam;* at —, *simul* (= at the same time), *statim, continuo* (= immediately).

one, *unus, unicus;* — of two, *alter;* — at a time, — by —, *singuli* (-*orum*) or adv. *singillatim;* — or two, *unus vel alter;* it is all — to me, *nihil mea interest;* indef., = a person, *homo,* or render by verb in second pers. sing. (esp. subj.); — another, render by *inter,* with acc. of plur. pron.; — day, *aliquando.*

one-eyed, *luscus, altero oculo captus.*

onerous, *gravis.*

oneself, *ipse.*

one-sided, *iniquus, impar.*

onion, *caepa* or *caepe.*

only, adj. *unus, unicus, solus.*

only, adv. *solum, tantum, modo* (esp. after *si* and *dum*); not — . . . but also, *non solum . . . sed etiam.*

onset, onslaught, *impetus* (-*ūs*), *incursio.*

onward; see on, adv

ooze, subst. *uligo.*

ooze, v. *manare, sudare.*

open, adj. (*ad*)*apertus; patens* or *hians* (= wide —); to stand —, *patere;* an — space, *propatulum;* in the —

air, *sub divo, sub Iove.* Transf., = candid, *apertus, simplex, candidus;* of questions, = undecided, *integer.* Adv. *aperte, palam, manifesto.*

open, v.: transit., *aperire, patefacere;* to — a book, *librum* (*e*)*volvere;* to — one's mouth, *hiscere;* intransit., *aperiri, se aperire, patefieri, dehiscere* (= to gape —).

opening: = aperture, *foramen, fenestra;* = opportunity, *occasio, opportunitas, ansa;* = beginning, *initium, exordium.*

operate, *vim* or *effectum habere;* in war, *rem agere* or *gerere;* in surgery, *secare.*

operation, *effectio; res* (*gesta* or *gerenda*); a business —, *negotium.*

operative, adj. *efficax.*

opinion, *opinio, iudicium, sententia.*

opponent, *adversarius;* in a lawcourt, *my* —, *iste.*

opportune, *opportunus;* adv. *opportune, commode.*

opportuneness, *opportunitas, commoditas.*

opportunity, *occasio, facultas, copia.*

oppose: = to set against, *opponere, obicere;* = to resist, *adversari, resistere, obsistere, obstare.*

opposed, *adversus, adversarius, contrarius.*

opposite, adj. *adversus, oppositus, contrarius;* — to (or —), as prep., *contra, e regione* (with genit. or dat.).

opposition: = difference, *repugnantia, discrepantia;* = body of opponents, *factio adversa.*

oppress, *premere, opprimere, vexare.*

oppression, *vexatio, iniuria.*

oppressive, *gravis, iniquus* (= unjust); adv. *graviter, inique.*

oppressor, *tyrannus;* or render by verb.

opprobrious, *probrosus, turpis.*

opprobrium, *dedecus, opprobrium.*

optical, render by *oculorum* (= of eyes).

option, *optio;* see also choice.

opulence, *opulentia;* see wealth.

opulent, *opulentus;* see rich.

or, *aut;* — perhaps, — if you like, *vel, -ve;* — else, *aut, vel;* — rather, *vel* (*potius*); either . . . or, *aut . . . aut, vel . . . vel;* in conditions, whether or . . ., *sive* (or *seu*); in alternative questions, *an;* — not, direct, *an non,* indirect, *necne.*

oracle, *oraculum, sors, responsum* (*oraculi*); to give an —, or oracular response, *oraculum dare.*

oral, render by verb *dicere* or *loqui.*

oration, *oratio, contio;* to deliver an —, *orationem* (or *contionem*) *habere.*

orator, *orator.*

oratorical, *oratorius.*

oratory, *doctrina dicendi, ars oratoria.*

orb, *globus, sphaera, orbis.*

orbit, *orbis, orbita, circulus, ambitus* (-*ūs*).

orchard, *pomarium.*

orchid, *orchis.*

ordain; see decree, appoint.

ordeal; see danger, trial.

order: = methodical arrangement, *ordo;* to arrange in —, *ordinare, disponere, digerere;* in —, *ordine;*

out of —, *extra ordinem*; = class, group, *ordo*; = fraternity, *conlegium*; = a command, *iussum*; by — of the consul, *consulis iussu*; in — that, render by *ut* with subj. (neg. *ne*), or by *ad* with gerund or gerundive, etc.

order, v.: = arrange, *ordinare, digerĕre, disponĕre*; = command, *iubĕre, imperare*; = demand, *imperare* (with acc.).

orderly, adj. *compositus, dispositus*; = well-behaved, *modestus*.

ordinal, adj.: an — number, *numerus ordinalis*.

ordinance, *edictum*.

ordinary, adj. = usual, *usitatus, quotidianus, communis*; = mediocre, *mediocris, vulgaris*. Adv. *ferme, fere, plerumque*.

ore, *aes*.

organ; see instrument, means; musical, *organum*.

organic; render by *animal* or *corpus*.

organization, *descriptio, temperatio*; political —, *reipublicae forma*.

organize, *ordinare, constituĕre, describĕre, temperare*.

orgies; see revelry.

Orient, Oriental; see east, eastern.

origin, *origo, fons*.

original, subst. = pattern, *exemplum, exemplar*.

original, adj.: = primary, *primus, principalis; antiquus, pristinus*; = one's own, *proprius, (sui) ipsius, novus* (= new). Adv., = at first, *primum, primo, initio*.

originate, v., intransit., *(ex)oriri*.

originator, *auctor*.

ornament, subst. *ornamentum, decus (-oris, n.)*.

ornament, v. *(ex)ornare, decorare*.

ornate, *(per)ornatus*; adv. *ornate*.

orphan, *orbus* (subst. and adj.).

oscillate, *agitari*; mentally, *dubitare*.

oscillation, *agitatio*; mental, *dubitatio*.

osier; subst. *vimen*; adj. *vimineus*.

ostensible, *simulatus, fictus*; adv. *specie, per speciem*.

ostentation, *iactatio, ostentatio*.

ostentatious, *gloriosus iactans*; adv. *gloriose*.

ostler, *agaso*.

ostracism, at Athens, *testarum suffragia (-orum)*; or render by *expellĕre*.

ostrich, *struthiocamelus*.

other: as adj. = different, *alius, diversus*; as pron., *alius*; the — (of two), *alter*; all the —s, *ceteri, reliqui*; belonging to —s, adj., *alienus*; on the — hand, *contra, autem*.

otherwise, *aliter, alioqui(n)*.

ought, v.: I — to go, *eundum est mihi, ire debeo, ire me oportet*.

ounce, *uncia*: half- —, *semuncia*.

our, ours, *noster*; — people, *nostri (-orum)*; of — country, *nostras*.

out, adv. *foras* (of going out), *foris* (of being out), *extra*.

out of, prep.: = away from, outside, *e (ex), extra*; — one's mind, *sui* or *mentis non compos*; = arising from,

because of, *propter, per*, or rendered by participle with abl., e.g. — fear, *metu coactus*.

outbid, *licitatione vincĕre*.

outbreak, *eruptio*; = beginning, *initium, principium*; = disturbance, *seditio*.

outcast, *exsul, extorris, profugus*.

outcry, *clamor, vociferatio, convicium*.

outdo, *superare, vincĕre*.

outer, *exterior*.

outflank, *circumire, circumvenire*.

outlandish, *peregrinus, barbarus*.

outlast, *diutius durare* (with *quam* or abl.).

outlaw, subst. *proscriptus*.

outlaw, v. *proscribĕre, (homini) aqua et igni interdicĕre*.

outlawry, *proscriptio*.

outlay, *sumptus (-ūs), impensa*.

outlet, *exitus (-ūs)*; see also mouth.

outline, subst. *(extrema) lineamenta (-orum)*; in a sketch, *adumbratio*.

outline, v. *describĕre, adumbrare*.

outlive, *(homini) superesse*.

outlook: physical, render by *spectare*; = prospects, *spes*; = attitude, *animus*.

outlying, *longinquus*.

outnumber, *numero* (or *multitudine*) *superare*.

outpost, *statio*.

outrage, subst. *iniuria, indignitas*.

outrage, v. *violare, iniuriâ adficĕre*.

outrageous, *immanis, indignus*; adv. *indigne*.

outright: = at once, *statim, ilico*; = completely, *plane, prorsus, omnino*.

outrun, *cursu superare*.

outset, *initium*.

outside, *superficies* (= surface), *species*; on the —, *extrinsecus*.

outside, adj. *exter (exterus), externus*.

outside, adv. *extra, extrinsecus, foris* (of rest), *foras* (of motion).

outskirts; see suburb.

outspoken; see frank.

outspread, *patulus, passus*.

outstanding, *reliquus*; see also debt.

outstrip, *(cursu) superare*.

outvote, *suffragiis vincĕre*.

outward, adj. *exter (exterus), externus*; — show, *species*; adv. *extra, extrinsecus*.

outweigh, *praeponderare, vincĕre superare*.

outwit, *circumvenire*.

outworks, *munimenta (exteriora)*.

oval, adj. *ovatus*.

ovation, *ovatio*; fig., to receive an — *magnis clamoribus excipi*.

oven, *furnus*.

over, adv. *super, insuper, supra*; to be — (= remain), *superesse, superare*; — and done with, *confectus, peractus*; it is all — with us, *actum est de nobis*.

over, prep.: = across, *super, trans*; = above, *super, supra*; = more than, *super, amplius* (with numerals), *plus quam*.

overawe, *(de)terrēre*.

overbalance, *praeponderare*.

overbearing, *adrogans, superbus*.

overboard: to throw —, *iacturam facĕre*; with genit., to fall —, *in mare excidĕre*.

overcast, of sky, *nubilus*.

overcharge, *nimium exigĕre, nimio vendĕre*.

overcome, *(de)vincĕre, superare*.

overdone, *(nimis) elaboratus*.

overdraw: to — an account, *aes alienum contrahĕre* (= incur debt).

overdressed, *nimis splendide ornatus*.

overdue, *debitus*; see owing.

overeat, *nimis ĕdĕre, helluari*.

overfill, *supra modum implĕre*.

overflow, subst.; see flood.

overflow, v. *redundare, effundi*: to — on to, *inundare*.

overgrown, = covered with foliage, etc., *obtitus*; see also huge, enormous.

overhang, *imminēre, impendēre*.

overhasty, *praeproperus, praeceps*; adv. *praepropere*.

overhaul; see examine; also overtake.

overhead, adv. *supra, insuper*: from —, *desuper*.

overhear, *subauscultare, exaudire*.

overjoyed, *laetitiā exsultans*.

overland, adv. *terrā* (opp. *mari*).

overlap, *imminēre, impendēre*.

overlay, *inducĕre, inlinĕre*; with gold, *inaurare*.

overload, *nimis onerare*.

overlook: = watch, examine, *observare, inspicĕre, intuēri*; = pardon, *ignoscĕre, condonare*; = miss, fail to notice, *praeterire, omittĕre*.

overmuch, adv. *nimis, nimium*.

overpower, *superare, vincĕre, debellare*.

overpowering; see overwhelming.

overrate, *nimis magni facĕre*.

overreach, *circumvenire, circumscribĕre*.

overrule, *vincĕre*; of providence, *gubernare*.

overrun, *(per)vagari*.

overscrupulous, *diligentior, religiosior*.

oversee, *(pro)curare*.

overseer, *custos, (pro)curator*.

oversight: = failure to notice, *error, incuria*; = superintendence, *curatio, procuratio, cura*.

oversleep, *diutius dormire*.

overspread, *obducĕre, inducĕre*.

overstate; see exaggerate.

overt, *apertus, manifestus*.

overtake: = catch up with, *consequi*; = surprise, *opprimĕre, deprehendĕre*.

overtax, *iniquis oneribus premĕre*.

overthrow, subst. *clades, ruina, excidium*.

overthrow, v. *deicĕre, adfligĕre, evertĕre*.

overture: diplomatic, *condicio*; musical, *exordium*.

overturn, *evertĕre, subvertĕre*.

overweening, *superbus, insolens*.

overwhelm, *obruĕre, opprimĕre*.

overwork, subst. *labor nimius*.

overwrought, *nimis intentus*.

overzealous, *nimis studiosus*.

owe, v. *debēre*.

owing, to, prep. *propter, ob, per*; it was — you that . . . not, *per te stetit quominus*.

owl, *ulula, noctua, strix*.

own: one's —, *proprius*; my —, *meus*; your —, *tuus, vester*; his —, *suus, ipsius* (genit.), *ipsorum*.

own, v.: = confess, *fatēri, confitēri*; = possess, *habēre, possidēre*.

owner, *possessor, dominus*.

ownership, *dominium*.

ox, *bos*; of oxen, adj. *bubulus*; a driver of oxen, *bubulcus*.

oxherd, *armentarius*.

oyster, *ostrea*; — shell, *ostreae testa*.

P

pace, subst.: = a step, *gradus (-ūs), passus (-ūs)*; as a measure = *passus (-ūs)*; = speed, *velocitas, gradus (-ūs)*; at a quick —, *pleno* or *citato gradu*.

pace, v. *gradi, incedĕre, ambulare, spatiari*; = measure by pacing, *passibus metiri*.

pacific, *pacificus*, or *pacis* (genit.).

pacify, *placare, pacare, sedare*.

pack, subst.: = bundle, *sarcina*; = crowd, *turba, grex*.

pack, v. *stipare, co(artare)*; of luggage, etc., *conligĕre, componĕre*.

packet, *fasciculus*.

pack-horse, *equus clitellarius*.

pack-saddle, *clitellae (-arum)*.

pact, *pactio, pactum*.

paddle; see oar, row.

Padua, *Patavium*.

page, of a book, *pagina*.

pageant, *spectaculum, pompa*.

pail, *hama, situla*.

pain, subst. *dolor*; violent — *cruciatus (-ūs)*.

pain, v. transit. *dolore adficĕre, cruciare, angĕre*.

painful, *gravis, acerbus, molestus*; adv. *graviter, acerbe, dolenter*.

painless, *sine dolore, doloris expers*.

pains, = exertion, *opera, labor, studium*; to take —, *operam dare*.

painstaking, *operosus, laboriosus*.

paint, subst. *pigmentum, fucus*.

paint, v.: as an artist, *pingĕre*; = to colour, *inficĕre, fucare*.

paint-brush, *penicillus*.

painter, *pictor*.

painting, *pictura*; ars pingendi.

pair, subst. *par*; of horses or oxen, *iugum*; often *bini* (= two at a time).

pair, v.: transit., *(con)iungĕre*; intransit., *(con)iungi, coire*.

palace, *(domus) regia*.

palatable, *iucundus, suavis, dulcis*.

palate, *palatum*.

palatial, *regius*.

palaver, *nugae (-arum)*.

pale, subst.: = stake *palus, sudis*; = fence, *saepes*.

pale, adj. *pallidus, luridus*; to be —, *pallēre*.

Palermo, *Panormus*.

palfrey, *equus* or *caballus*.

palimpsest, *palimpsestus*.

palisade, *vallum, vallus*.

pall, v. or render by *taedet*.

pallet, *lectulus, grabatus*.

palliate, *excusare, extenuare*.

pallid; see pale.

pallor, *pallor.*

palm, subst. *palma*; adorned with —, *palmatus.*

palm, v.: to — off, *imponĕre, supponĕre.*

palmer; see pilgrim.

palmy, *florens, optimus.*

palpable, *tractabilis, quod tangi potest*; = obvious, *manifestus, apertus*; adv. *manifesto, aperte.*

palpitate, *palpitare, micare.*

paltry, *vilis, minutus, pusillus.*

pamper, *nimis indulgēre.*

pamphlet, *libellus.*

pan, *patina*; frying- —, *sartago.*

panacea, *panchrestum medicamentum.*

pander, subst. *leno.*

pander, v. *lenocinari*; see flatter, indulge.

panegyric, *laudatio, laudes.*

panegyrist, *laudator, praedicator.*

panel, *tympanum*; a panelled ceiling, *lacunar.*

pang, *dolor.*

panic, subst. *pavor, terror.*

panic, v. *pavēre.*

panic-stricken, *pavidus.*

pannier, *clitellae (-arum).*

panoply; see armour.

panorama; see prospect, view.

pant, v. *anhelare.*

pantheism, *deum in universa rerum natura situm esse credĕre.*

panther, *panthera.*

panting, subst. *anhelitus (-ūs).*

pantomime, *mimus.*

pantry, *cella penaria.*

paper, subst. *charta, papyrus*; a written (printed) —, *charta, scriptum, libellus*; public —s, *tabulae publicae*; a news —, *acta (diurna).*

papyrus, *papyrus* or *papyrum.*

par: on a — with, *aequus, par.*

parable, *parabola, similitudo.*

parade, subst.: = show, *ostentatio*; milit., *decursus (-ūs).*

parade, v.: = display, *ostentare*; milit., intransit., *decurrĕre.*

paradise, *sedes beatorum* or *piorum.*

paradox: render by *admirabilis* or *contra opinionem.*

paragon, *specimen.*

paragraph, *caput* (= section).

parallel, adj.: — to, *e regione*, with genit. or dat.; = similar, *par, (con)similis, congruens.*

paralyse, *debilitare, enervare, adfligĕre.*

paralysed, *pede, manu*, etc., *captus.* Transf., *debilis, torpens, torpidus*; to be —, *torpēre.*

paralysis, *nervorum remissio.* Transf., *debilitas, torpedo.*

paramount, *summus.*

paramour; see lover.

parapet, *pluteus, lorica.*

paraphernalia, *apparatus (-ūs).*

paraphrase, subst., *interpretatio, paraphrasis.*

paraphrase, v. *interpretari.*

parasite, *parasitus*; *adsecula* (=hanger-on).

parasitic, *parasiticus.*

parasol, *umbella, umbraculum.*

parcel, *fascis, fasciculus*; see part, portion.

parcel out, v. *partiri, dividĕre, distribuĕre.*

parch, *torrēre, (ex)urĕre.*

parched, *aridus, torridus.*

parchment, *membrana.*

pardon, subst. *venia.*

pardon, v., *(homini rem) ignoscĕre* or *condonare.*

pardonable, *excusabilis.*

pare, *(re)secare, subsecare.*

parent, *parens.*

parentage, *stirps, genus (-eris, n.).*

parental, *parentum* (genit.).

parenthesis, *interpositio, interclusio.*

Paris, *Lutetia.*

parity; see equality.

park, subst. *vivarium* (= preserve), *horti (-orum*, = pleasure-gardens).

parley, subst. *conloquium, sermo.*

parley, v. *conloqui, sermones conferre.*

parliament, *senatus (-ūs)*; act of — *senatūs consultum*; house of — *curia*; member of —, *senator.*

parliamentary, *senatorius.*

parody, subst. *ridicula imitatio.*

parole, *fides (data).*

paroxysm, *febris accessio.* Transf. *vis, impetus (-ūs).*

parricide: as person, *parricida*; as act, *parricidium.*

parrot, *psittacus.*

parry, v. = check, ward off, *propulsare, defendĕre, arcēre.*

parsimonious, *parcus, sordidus, tenax*; adv. *parce, sordide.*

parsimony, *parsimonia, tenacitas.*

parsley, *apium.*

part, subst., *pars, membrum*; in two, three —s, *bifariam, trifariam* or *bipartito, tripartito*; for the most —, *maximam partem, fere, plerumque*; to do one's — *officio* or *munere fungi*; to take — in, *partem capĕre* or *participem esse*; —, = side, cause, *partes (-ium)*; to take a person's —, *homini adesse, favēre*; — in a play, role, *partes (-ium), persona*; to play the chief —, *primas (partes) agĕre.*

part, v. transit., *separare, dividĕre, dissociare*; intransit., *digredi, discedĕre.*

partake, *participem esse*; of food, *gustare.*

partaker, *particeps, socius, adfinis.*

partial, = favouring, *studiosus, cupidus.*

partiality, *studium, cupiditas.*

partially, *per studium*; see also partly.

participate, *(rei*, genit.) *esse participem*; *(rei*, dat.) *interesse.*

participation, *societas.*

participator, *particeps, socius, adfinis.*

participle, *participium.*

particle, *particula, frustum* (esp. of food); gram., *particula.*

particoloured, *versicolor, varius.*

particular, adj.: = individual, *proprius, separatus*; = special, outstanding, *singularis, praecipuus*; = exacting, fussy, *elegans, delicatus.* Adv., *magnopere, praesertim, praecipue.*

particularize, *nominare* (= name), *enumerare* (= enumerate).

particulars, subst. *singula* (-*orum*).

parting, subst. *digressus* (-*ūs*), *discessus* (-*ūs*).

partisan, *fautor, homo studiosus.*

partisanship, *studium, favor.*

partition, *partitio*; = wall, barrier, *paries.*

partly, *partim, parte, (aliqua) ex parte.*

partner, *socius, consors*; in marriage *coniunx.*

partnership, *consortio, societas.*

partridge, *perdix.*

party, *partes* (-*ium*), *factio* (esp. polit.) *secta* (of philosophers, etc.); to belong to a —, *partes sequi*; —, = social gathering, *convivium.*

party-wall, *paries.*

parvenu, *novus homo.*

pass, subst. *angustiae* (-*arum*), *saltus* (-*ūs*), *fauces* (-*ium*); things have come to such a — that . . ., *eo ventum est ut . . .*

pass, v. (1) = go along, go past, *transgredi, transire, praeterire*; to — over, let —, *praeterire, transire, omittere*; to — off, *abire, decedere.* (2) of time: to — time, *agere, degere, (tra)ducere, consumere*; of time itself, to —, *transire, abire, praeterire.* (3) to — a law, get a law —ed, *legem perferre.* (4) to — down, — along, *tradere, porrigere, traicere.* (5) to — a test, be approved, (*ap*)*probari, satisfacere.*

passable = tolerable, *tolerabilis, mediocris*; adv. *tolerabiliter, mediocriter.*

passage, *transitus* (-*ūs*), *transitio, transgressio*; = way, road, *iter, via*; in a book, *locus.*

passenger, *viator*; *vector* (on horseback, etc.).

passing; in —, *praeteriens* (partic.), *obiter.*

passion: = suffering, *perpessio, toleratio*; = emotion, *animi motus* (-*ūs*) *commotio*; = uncontrolled emotion, *libido, cupiditas*; = anger, *ira, iracundia*: to fly into a —, *exardescere*; = extreme fondness, *studium.*

passionate, adj. *cupidus, concitatus, vehemens, ardens*; = hot-tempered, *iracundus, cerebrosus.* Adv. *cupide, vehementer, effuse*; *iracunde.*

passionless, *cupiditatis expers.*

passive: to remain —, *quiescere*; gram. *passivus.* Adv. *aequo animo, patienter.*

passiveness, *patientia.*

password, *tessera.*

past, subst. *praeteritum tempus.*

past, adj. *praeteritus, ante actus*; = immediately preceding, *prior, superior, proximus.*

past, adv., render by compound verbs in *praeter-* or *trans-*

past, prep., *praeter, trans.*

pastime, *ludus, oblectamentum.*

pastoral, *pastoralis, pastoricius*; *agrestis, rusticus*: = poetry, *bucolica* (-*orum*).

pastry, *crustum, crustulum.*

pasture, subst. *pascuum, ager pascuus.*

pasture, v.: transit., *pascere*; intransit., *pabulari, pasci.*

patch, subst. *pannus.*

patch, v. (*re*)*sarcire.*

patchwork, *cento.*

patent, = open, plain, *manifestus, apertus.*

paternal, *paternus, patrius.*

path, *via, iter, semita, trames.*

pathetic, *flebilis, maestus*; adv. *flebiliter, maeste.*

pathless, *invius.*

pathos, *maestitia, tristitia.*

patience, *patientia, tolerantia, perseverantia* (at work), *aequus animus* (= calmness).

patient, subst. *aeger, aegrotus.*

patient, adj. *patiens, tolerans*; adv. *patienter, toleranter, aequo animo.*

patrician, *patricius.*

patrimony, *patrimonium.*

patriot, *civis bonus.*

patriotic, *patriae* (or *reipublicae*) *amans*; adv. *pro patria.*

patriotism, *patriae amor.*

patrol, v. *circumire, lustrare.*

patron, *patronus, praeses.*

patronage, *patrocinium* (from the patron's side), *clientela* (from the client's); in gen., *praesidium.*

patroness, *patrona.*

patronize, *favēre* (with dat.).

patter, subst. *crepitus* (-*ūs*).

patter, v. *crepare, crepitare.*

pattern, *exemplum, exemplar, specimen, documentum.*

paucity, *paucitas*, or render by adj.

paunch, *abdomen, venter.*

pause, subst. *mora, intervallum, intermissio.*

pause, v. *intermittere, subsistere, morari.*

pave, (*viam*) *sternere* or *munire.*

pavement, *pavimentum, via strata.*

paving, *stratura.*

paving-stone, *saxum quadratum.*

paw, subst. *pes* (= foot), *ungula* (= claw).

paw, v. (*solum*) *pedibus ferire.*

pawn, subst. *pignus* (-*oris*, n.); at chess, *latrunculus, latro.*

pawn, v. (*op*)*pignerare, pignori dare.*

pay, subst. *stipendium, merces.*

pay, v.: transit., (*per*)*solvere, pendere, numerare*; to — a penalty *poenam dare* or *luere*; int.nsit., = be profitable, *prodesse, lucro esse.*

paymaster, *dispensator*; milit., *tribunus aerarius.*

payment, *solutio, repraesentatio* (in cash).

pea, *pisum, cicer.*

peace, subst. *pax, otium, concordia.*

peaceful, *pacatus, placidus, quietus, tranquillus*; adv. *placide, quiete, tranquille.*

peace-offering, *piaculum, placamen.*

peach, (*malum*) *persicum.*

peacock, *pavo.*

peak, *cacumen, apex*; or rendered by adj. *summus.*

peal, subst.: — of laughter, *cachinnus*; — of thunder, *tonitrus* (-*ūs*).

peal, v. *sonare.*

pear, *pirum*; — tree, *pirus*.
pearl, *margarita*.
peasant, *rusticus, agrestis*.
pebble, *calculus, lapillus*.
peccadillo, (*leve*) *delictum*.
peck, as measure, *modius*.
peck, v. *vellicare*.
peculation, *peculatus (-ūs)*.
peculiar; = of one only, *proprius, peculiaris*; = remarkable, *singularis, praecipuus, mirus*. Adv., = especially, *praecipue, praesertim*.
peculiarity, *proprietas*.
pecuniary, *pecuniarius*.
pedagogue, *paedagogus*; = schoolmaster, *magister*.
pedant, pedantic; render by (*nimis*) *diligens*.
pedestal, *basis*.
pedestrian, subst. *pedes*.
pedestrian, adj. *pedester*.
pedigree, *stemma (-atis n.)*.
pedlar, *institor*.
peel, subst. *cutis, corium*.
peel, v.: transit., *cutem detrahěre*; intransit., *cutem (de)poněre*.
peep, subst. *aspectus (-ūs), conspectus (-ūs)*.
peep, v. (*strictim*) *prospicěre, inspicěre*.
peer, subst.: = equal, *par*; = noble, *unus e patriciis or nobilibus*.
peer, v.: to — into, *rimari, scrutari*.
peerless, *unicus, singularis*.
peevish, *stomachosus, morosus, difficilis*; adv. *stomachose, morose*.
peevishness, *stomachus, morositas*.
peg, *clavus* (= nail).
pell-mell, *effuse, confuse, passim*.
pellucid; see transparent.
pelt, v.: transit., see throw; of rain, *ferri, descendere*; —ing rain, *maximus imber*.
pen, subst.: for writing, *calamus, stilus*; = fold, *saeptum*.
pen, v.: = write, *scriběre, litteris mandare*; = fold, *saeptis includěre*.
penalty, *poena, multa, supplicium*.
penance, *piaculum, poena, satisfactio*.
pence; see penny.
pencil: for drawing *penicillus*; for writing, *stilus*.
pending: adj.. the matter is still —, *adhuc sub iudice lis est*.
pending, prep.: = during *per*; = until, *dum* with subj.
pendulous, *pendulus*.
penetrable, *penetrabilis*.
penetrate, *penetrare, pervaděre*; by stealth, (*se*) *insinuare*; into a mind, *descendere*.
penetrating, adj., of cold, etc.. *acutus, acer*; mentally, *sagax, perspicax, subtilis*.
penetration, *acies, acumen*.
peninsula, *paeninsula*.
penitence, *paenitentia*.
penny, as, *nummus (sestertius)*.
pension, *annua (-orum)*.
pensive, *in cogitatione defixus*.
penthouse, milit., *vinea*.
penurious, *parcus, sordidus, avarus*; adv. *sordide*.
penury, *inopia, egestas*.

people, subst. (1), = persons, *homines, mortales*; our —, *nostri*; young —, *pueri, adulescentes*. (2), = a community, *populus*; adj., of the —, *publicus*; (3), = race, tribe, *gens, natio*. (4) common —, *plebs, vulgus, multitudo*.
people, v. *frequentare, complěre*.
pepper, *piper*.
perambulate, *perambulare, peragrare, pervagari*.
perceive, *sentire, percipěre*; *viděre* (= see), *audire* (= hear), *intellegěre* (= understand).
percentage, *pars, portio*.
perceptible, *manifestus*; *quod percipěre possis*.
perception; render by verb; = discernment, *iudicium, sagacitas*.
perch, subst., as fish, *perca*.
perch, v. *insiděre*.
percolate, *permanare*.
percussion, *ictus (-ūs)*; = blow).
perdition, *exitium, pernicies*.
peremptory, *adrogans*. Adv. *adroganter*; in refusals, *praecise*.
perennial, *perennis, iugis*.
perfect, adj. *plenus, absolutus, perfectus, integer* (= sound intact), *merus* (= sheer). Adv. *plene, absolute, perfecte*; *plane* (= wholly).
perfect, v. *perficěre, absolvěre*.
perfection, *absolutio, perfectio*.
perfidious, *perfidus, perfidiosus*; adv. *perfidiose*.
perfidy, *perfidia*.
perforate, *perforare, (per)terebrare*.
perforce, *vi, per vim, necessario*; or adj. *invitus* (= unwilling).
perform, (*per*)*fungi, exsequi, perficěre, conficěre, peragěre*; on the stage, *partes agěre*.
performance, (*per*)*functio, confectio*; on the stage, *fabula*.
performer, *actor, auctor, confector*; on the stage, *actor, histrio* (= actor), *acroama (-atis, n.*; musical).
perfume, subst. *odor, unguentum*.
perfume, v. *odorare, odore adficěre*.
perfunctory, *neglegens*.
perhaps, *fortasse, forsitan*; unless —, *nisi forte*, lest —, *ne forte*.
peril; see danger, risk.
period: of time, *tempus, spatium temporis*; = end, *finis, terminus*; rhet. or gram., *periodus*, (*verborum or orationis*) *circuitus (-ūs)*.
periodical, adj. *sollemnis*; adv. *certis* (or *statis*) *temporibus*.
perish, *perire, interire, occiděre*.
perishable, *fragilis, caducus, fluxus*.
perjure, *periurare* (or *peierare*); *periurium facěre*.
perjured, *periurus*.
perjury, *periurium*.
permanence, *perennitas, stabilitas*.
permanent, *perennis, stabilis*; adv. *perpetuo*.
permissible, *licitus*; it is —, *licet*.
permission, *facultas, potestas, copia, venia*; with your —, *pace tua*.
permit, v. (*hominem*) *siněre*; (*homini*) *permittěre, conceděre, copiam facěre*.

permutation, (*per*)*mutatio.*
pernicious, *perniciosus, exitiosus;* adv. *perniciose, exitiose, funeste.*
peroration, *peroratio, conclusio.*
perpendicular, *directus;* adv. *ad lineam, rectā lineā.*
perpetrate, *committěre, in se admittěre.*
perpetrator, *auctor; qui facinus in se admisit.*
perpetual, *sempiternus, perennis, assiduus;* adv. *adsidue, perpetuo.*
perpetuity, *perpetuitas.*
perplex, *distrahěre, sollicitare.*
perplexed, *dubius, inops consilii.*
perplexing, *difficilis, perplexus, impeditus.*
perplexity, *dubitatio.*
persecute, *insectari, vexare.*
persecution, *insectatio, vexatio.*
persecutor, *vexator, insectator.*
perseverance, *perseverantia, constantia, pertinacia.*
persevere, *perseverare, perstare, persistěre.*
persevering, *perseverans, constans, pertinax;* adv. *perseveranter, constanter.*
persist; see persevere.
person: = human being, *homo, caput;* in person, *ipse, praesens, coram;* = body, form, *corpus, species, forma;* gram. *persona.*
personal, *privatus, proprius;* to make a — appearance, *ipse adesse.*
personality, *persona, hominis natura, ingenium* (= disposition).
personate, (*hominis*) *partes agěre.*
personification, *prosopopoeia, personarum fictio.*
personify, *humana specie induěre.*
perspicacious, *perspicax, sagax, acutus;* adv. *perspicaciter.*
perspicacity, *perspicacitas, acies ingenii.*
perspicuity, *perspicuitas.*
perspicuous, (*di*)*lucidus, perspicuus, apertus;* adv. (*di*)*lucide, perspicue, aperte.*
perspiration, *sudor.*
perspire, *sudare.*
persuade, *persuadēre, adducěre;* to try to —, *suadēre.*
persuasion, *persuasio.*
persuasive; render by verb.
pert, *protervus, procax;* adv. *proterve.*
pertain, *pertiněre, attiněre.*
pertinacious, *pertinax, obstinatus;* adv. *pertinaciter, obstinate.*
pertinacity, *pertinacia, obstinatio.*
pertness, *protervitas, procacitas.*
perturbation, *perturbatio.*
Perugia, *Perusia.*
perusal, *lectio, perlectio.*
peruse, (*per*)*legěre, evolvěre.*
pervade, *permanare.*
perverse, *perversus, pravus;* adv. *perverse, perperam, prave.*
perversion, *corruptio, depravatio.*
perversity, *perversitas, pravitas.*
pervert, v. *depravare, corrumpěre, detorquěre.*
pest, *pestis, pernicies, lues.*
pester, *sollicitare, vexare.*

pestilence, *pestilentia, pestis, lues, morbus.*
pestilential, *pestilens, foedus.*
pestle, *pilum, pistillum.*
pet, subst. *deliciae (-arum), amores (-um).*
pet, v. *fověre, in deliciis habēre.*
Peter, *Petrus* (late Latin).
petition: see prayer, request; a formal —, *libellus;* to grant a —, *petenti satisfacěre.*
petition, v. *petěre, rogare, implorare.*
petrify, *in lapidem* (*con*)*vertěre.* Transf., *obstupefacěre:* to be petrified, *obstupescěre, stupěre.*
pettifogger, *leguleius, rabula.*
petty, *minutus, tenuis.*
petulance, *petulantia, protervitas.*
petulant, *petulans, protervus.*
phantom, *simulacrum, imago.*
phase, *status (-ūs), ratio;* different —s, *vices* (plur.).
pheasant, (*avis*) *Phasiana, Phasianus.*
phenomenon: = remarkable event, *prodigium, portentum, miraculum.*
phial; see bottle.
philanthropic, *hominibus amicus, humanus.*
philanthropy, *benevolentia, humanitas.*
Philip, *Philippus.*
philological, *grammaticus.*
philologist, *grammaticus, philologus.*
philology, *grammatica (-ae* or *-orum), philologia.*
philosopher, *philosophus, sapiens.*
philosophical, *philosophus;* = wise, *sapiens.* Adv. *philosophorum more, sapienter;* = calmly, *aequo animo.*
philosophize, *philosophari; ratiocinari, disputare.*
philosophy, *philosophia.*
philtre, *philtrum.*
phlegm, *pituita;* = coolness, *patientia, lentitudo.*
phlegmatic, *tardus, patiens, lentus;* adv. *patienter, lente, aequo animo.*
phrase, *locutio; verbum.*
phrase, v.; see express, say.
phraseology, *locutio, dicendi genus (-eris, n.).*
physic, subst.; see medicine.
physical: = natural, render by genit. *naturae* or *corporis;* = of physics, *physicus.* Adv. *naturā;* = in the manner of physics, *physice.*
physician; see doctor.
physics, *physica (-orum).*
physiognomy, *oris habitus (-ūs)* or *lineamenta (-orum).*
physiology, *physiologia.*
Piacenza, *Placentia.*
pick: = pluck, gather, *legěre, carpěre, conligěre;* to — up, *tollěre;* to — out, *eligěre.*
pick-axe, *dolabra.*
picked, *delectus, electus.*
picket, *statio, custodia.*
pickle, subst. *salsura, muria.*
pickle, v. *muriā condire.*
picture, subst. *tabula (picta), pictura.*
picture, v., = imagine, *cogitatione fingěre, depingěre, ante oculos proponěre.*
picturesque, *amoenus, venustus.*

pie, *crustum.*

piebald, *bicolor.*

piece, *pars, fragmentum* (broken off), *frustum* (esp. of food), *mica* (= crumb); — of cloth, *pannus*; a piece of money, *nummus*; to break into —s, *confringĕre, comminuĕre*; to tear to —s, *discerpĕre, dilacerare, dilaniare*; to fall to —s, *dilabi, (dis)solvi.*

piecemeal, *membratim, minutatim.*

piece together, v. *consuĕre, fabricari.*

pied, *maculosus, versicolor.*

pier, *pila, moles, agger.*

pierce, *pungĕre*; to — through, *perforare, perfodere, transfigĕre.*

piercing, adj. *acer, acutus.*

piety, *pietas (erga deos), religio (= religious feeling), sanctitas (= holiness).*

pig, *porcus, sus.*

pigeon, *columba, columbus, palumbes (= wood- —).*

piggish, *suillus, porcinus.*

pigment; see paint.

pigmy; see Pygmy.

pigsty, *hara.*

pike: the weapon, *hasta, sarissa*; the fish, *lupus.*

pile, subst., *strues, cumulus, acervus*; a — driven into the ground, *sublica, sudis*; a bridge built on —s, *pons sublicius.*

pile, v. *(co)acervare, cumulare, congerĕre, exstruĕre.*

pilfer, *surripĕre, furari.*

pilgrim, *viator, peregrinator.*

pilgrimage, *iter, peregrinatio (sacra).*

pill, *pilula.*

pillage, subst. *rapina, direptio, compilatio, expilatio.*

pillage, v. *diripĕre, compilare, expilare, praedari.*

pillager, *praedator, direptor, expilator.*

pillar, *columna, pila*; fig., = support, stay, *columen.*

pillow, *pulvinus, cervical.*

pilot, subst. *gubernator.*

pilot, v. *gubernare.*

pimple, *pustula.*

pin, subst. *acus (-ūs;* = needle).

pin, v. *(ad)figĕre.*

pincers, *forceps.*

pinch, subst. *aculeus (= sting), morsus (-ūs;* = bite).

pinch, v.: = nip, *urĕre*; = stint, confine, *coartare, urgēre.*

pinching, of poverty, *angustus.*

pine, subst. *pinus*; of —, adj. *pineus.*

pine, v. *tabescĕre, confici*; to — for, *desiderare.*

pining, subst. *tabes.*

pinion, subst. of a bird, *penna.*

pinion, v. *(re)vincire.*

pink, *puniceus.*

pinnace, *(navis) actuaria, lcmbus.*

pinnacle, *fastigium.*

pint, perhaps *sextarius*; half a —, *hemina.*

pioneer, *praecursor, explorator*; or render by *primus.*

pious, *pius, religiosus (= scrupulous), sanctus (= saintly).* Adv. *pie, religiose, sancte.*

pip, in fruit, *acinus, granum.*

pipe, subst.: = tube, *tubus, canalis, fistula*; = musical instrument, *fistula, tibia, calamus (= reed- —).*

pipe, v. *fistulā (or tibiā) canĕre.*

piper, *fistulator, tibicen.*

pipkin, *olla.*

piquancy, *sal, vis.*

piquant, *acer*; = stimulating, humorous, *salsus, facetus.*

pique, subst. *offensio, ira.*

pique, v. *vexare, sollicitare.*

piracy, *latrocinium (maritimum).*

pirate, *praedo (maritimus).*

piratical, *piraticus, praedatorius.*

pit, subst. *fovea, puteus, fossa (= ditch);* in the theatre, *cavea (media or summa).*

pit against, v. *opponĕre.*

pitch, subst.: the substance, *pix*; of —, adj. *piceus*; = degree, *fastigium, gradus (-ūs)*; to such a — of madness, *eo amentiae*; in music, *sonus, vox*; = slope, *fastigium.*

pitch, v.: of tents, etc., *ponĕre, constituĕre*; = throw, *iacĕre, conicĕre.*

pitcher, *urceus.*

pitchfork, *furca.*

piteous, pitiable, *miser, miserabilis*; adv. *misere, miserabiliter.*

pitfall, *fovea.*

pith, *medulla.*

pithy, *medullosus.* Transf., *sententiosus, nervosus.*

pitiful: = full of pity, *clemens, misericors*; = mean, *abiectus, humilis, vilis*; see also piteous. Adv. *clementer*; *abiecte, humiliter.*

pitifulness, *clementia, misericordia*; = meanness, *humilitas.*

pitiless, *immisericors, inexorabilis, inhumanus, crudelis*; adv. *immisericorditer, inhumane, crudeliter.*

pitilessness, *crudelitas, inhumanitas, saevitia.*

pittance, *mercedula, stips, pecunia exigua.*

pity, subst. *misericordia, miseratio.*

pity, v. *misereri, miserari,* or impers. *miseret.*

pivot, *cardo (= hinge).*

placability, *placabilitas.*

placable, *exorabilis, placabilis.*

placard, *libellus, titulus.*

place, subst. (1), = position, spot, *locus, regio*; at, to, from this —, *hic, huc, hinc*; at, to, from that —, *ibi, eo, inde.* (2), = proper position, *locus, sedes, statio*; in — of, *(in) loco* with genit., or *pro* with abl. (3), = situation, office, *munus (-eris,* n.), *officium.* (4) in the first —, *primo, primum*; in the next —, *deinceps.*

place, v. *ponĕre, (con)locare*; to — oneself, *consistĕre*; to — here and there, *disponĕre.*

placid, *placidus, quietus, tranquillus.*

plagiarism, *furtum.*

plagiarize, *furari.*

plague, subst. *pestis, pestilentia.* Transf., *pernicies, lues, malum.*

plague, v. *vexare, sollicitare, exagitare.*

plain, subst. *campus, planities;* of the —, adj. *campestris.*

plain, adj.: = clear, *clarus, perspicuus, manifestus;* = candid, *simplex, apertus, liber;* = unadorned, *simplex, inornatus;* = not beautiful, *invenustus.* Adv.: = clearly, *clare, perspicue, manifesto;* = candidly, simply, *simpliciter, aperte, libere.*

plainness: = clearness, *perspicuitas;* = candour, simplicity, *simplicitas.*

plaint; see complaint.

plaintiff, *petitor.*

plaintive, *miserabilis, flebilis, queribundus;* adv. *miserabiliter, flebiliter.*

plait, subst.: = fold, *sinus (-ūs), ruga;* = braid of hair, *gradus (-ūs).*

plait, v. *plicare, intexĕre.*

plan, subst.: as drawn, *descriptio;* = layout, scheme, *forma, figura, conformatio;* = of action, *consilium, propositum, institutum.*

plan, v.: = design, mark out, *designare, describĕre;* = form a — of action, *intendĕre, consilium capĕre* or *inire.*

plane, subst.: = flat surface, *planum, libramentum;* the tool, *runcina;* the tree, *platanus.*

planet, *stella errans* or *vaga.*

plank, *tabula, axis;* to cover with —s, *contabulare.*

plant, subst. *herba, planta.*

plant, v. *serĕre, conserĕre, obserĕre;* in gen., = put in position, *ponĕre, statuĕre, constituĕre.*

plantation, *plantarium* or *seminarium* (= nursery garden), *arbustum, locus arboribus consitus.*

planter, *sator, qui serit.*

planting, subst., as act, *satio, satus (-ūs).*

plash, subst. *murmur, sonus.*

plash, v. *murmurare.*

plaster, subst. *gypsum, tectorium;* in medicine, *emplastrum.*

plaster, v. *gypsare, gypso inlinĕre.*

plasterer, *tector.*

plate, subst.: = thin layer of metal, *lam(i)na, bractea;* = wrought metal, at table, *vasa argentea* or *aurea;* = platter, *catillus, patella.*

plate, v.: to — with silver, *argento inducĕre.*

platform, *suggestus (-ūs), tribunal.*

Platonic, *Platonicus;* the — philosophy, *Academia.*

platter, *catillus, patella.*

plaudit, *plausus (-ūs).*

plausibility, *veritsimilitudo; simulatio, species.*

plausible: = probable, *veri similis, probabilis;* in bad sense, *speciosus.* Adv. *probabiliter;* in bad sense, *in speciem, simulate.*

play, subst.: = amusement, *ludus, lusus (-ūs), lusio;* at the theatre, *fabula, ludus scaemicus;* = scope, free action, *campus, area;* = movement, *motus (-ūs), gestus (-ūs);* fair —, *aequum (et) bonum.*

play, v.: on an instrument, *modulari;* on a stringed instrument, *psallĕre;* = amuse oneself, *ludĕre;* to — a part, *partes agĕre, personam gerĕre;*

to — the fool, *ineptire, desipĕre;* to — into the hands of an opponent, *praevaricari.*

player: on strings, *fidicen (f. fidicina), psaltes, citharista;* on a wind instrument, *tibicen (f. tibicina);* see also gambler and actor.

playfellow, playmate, *conlusor.*

playful, *lascivus, iocosus;* adv. *iocose.*

playfulness, *lascivia.*

plaything, *ludibrium.*

playwriter, playwright, *fabularum scriptor.*

plea: at law, *petitio, exceptio, defensio;* in gen., = excuse, *excusatio.*

plead: at law, *causam agĕre, dicĕre, orare;* to — as an excuse, *causari, obtendĕre;* = to beg, entreat, *orare, obsecrare, implorare.*

pleader, *orator, causidicus.*

pleasant, pleasing *gratus, iucundus, suavis, dulcis;* of places, *amoenus;* of manner, *comis, urbanus.* Adv., pleasantly, *iucunde, suaviter;* = affably, *comiter, urbane.*

pleasantness, *iucunditas, dulcedo, suavitas;* of places, *amoenitas;* of manner, *comitas, urbanitas.*

pleasantry, *facetiae (-arum), iocus.*

please, v.: = to give pleasure to, *placēre, delectare,* or impers. *libet;* = to see fit, be disposed, *velle;* if you please, *si placet;* colloq., please! *sis, amabo.*

pleasing; see pleasant.

pleasure: = enjoyment, delight, *voluptas, delectatio, oblectamentum;* fond of —, *voluptarius;* = liking, inclination, *arbitrium, libido.*

plebeian, adj. *plebeius* (opp. *patricius*).

pledge, subst. *pignus (-eris* or *-oris), cautio, arrabo.*

pledge, v. *(op)pignerare, obligare;* to — one's word, *fidem interponĕre, promittĕre, recipĕre.*

plenary; see full, complete.

plenipotentiary, *legatus.*

plenteous, plentiful, *uber, abundans, copiosus;* adv. *abunde, abundanter, copiose.*

plenty, *ubertas, copia, abundantia;* sometimes *satis* with genit.

pliable, pliant, *lentus, flexibilis, mollis.*

pliancy, pliability, *mollitia.*

plight; see condition, and pledge.

plod, *repĕre, tarde progredi.*

plot, subst.: of ground, *agellus, area;* = scheme, conspiracy, *coniuratio;* of a play, etc., *argumentum (fabulae).*

plot, v.: intransit., *coniurare;* transit. *machinari.*

plotter; see conspirator.

plough, subst. *aratrum;* — -man, — -boy, *arator, bubulcus;* — -share, *vomer;* — -handle, *stiva.*

plough, v. *arare;* to — up, *exarare;* to — round, *circumarare.*

ploughing, subst. *aratio.*

pluck, subst. *animus, virtūs (-ūtis).*

pluck, v. *(e)vellĕre;* to — flowers, *flores carpĕre, decerpĕre;* to — up courage, *animum recipĕre.*

plum, *prunum.*

plumage, *plumae, pennae (pinnae)*.
plumb-line, plummet, *linea, perpendiculum*.
plume, subst. *pluma, penna (pinna)*.
plump, *pinguis*.
plum-tree, *prunus*.
plunder, subst. *praeda, rapina*.
plunder, v. *praedari, diripěre, expilare, (de)spoliare*.
plunderer, *direptor, praedator*.
plunge, v.: transit., *(sub)mergěre, immergěre*; intransit., *se mergěre*, etc.
plural, *pluralis*; in the —, *pluraliter*.
ply, v. *exercěre*.
Po, the river, *Padus*.
poacher, *fur*.
pocket, subst. *sinus (-ūs*; = fold in the toga); *sacculus* (= a small bag), *crumena* (= purse).
pocket, v. *intercipěre, avertěre*.
pocket-book, *pugillares (-ium)*.
pod, *siliqua*.
poem, *carmen, poema (-atis, n.)*.
poet, *poeta, carminum auctor, vates* (= bard).
poetess, *poetria*.
poetical, *poeticus*; adv. *poetice, poetarum more*.
poetry, *poetice or poetica, poesis*.
poignant, *acer*.
point, subst.: = sharp end, *acumen, cuspis, spiculum, mucro*; geograph., *promontorium*; = spot, *locus*; on the — of doing, render by *in eo est ut*, or fut. partic.; the — at issue, *res, caput*; to the —, *ad rem*.
point, v.: = make sharp, *(prae)acuěre*; to — out, indicate, *(digito) monstrare, indicare*.
point-blank, *directus*: to refuse —, *praecise negare*.
pointed, adj. *(prae)acutus*; = significant, *salsus, aculeatus*; adv. *salse*.
pointless, *insulsus, frigidus, ineptus*.
poise, v. *librare*.
poison, subst. *venenum, virus, toxicum*.
poison, v.: = render poisonous, *venenare, veneno imbuěre*; = attack with —, *veneno necare, venenum dare*.
poisoner, *veneficus* (f. *venefica*).
poisoning, subst. *veneficium*.
poisonous, *venenatus, veneno imbutus*.
poke, v. *(hominem) foděre*; to — the fire, *ignem excitare*; to — about, *rimari, perscrutari*.
polar, *septentrionalis* (= northern).
pole, *contus, pertica, longurius*; of the earth, *axis, cardo, polus*; south —, *axis meridianus*; north —, *axis septentrionalis*.
polecat, *feles*.
polemics, *disputationes (-um)*, controversiae *(-arum)*.
police; render by *aediles (-ium)*; —men, *vigiles (-um)*.
policy, *ratio rei publicae gerendae, consilia (-orum)*; = prudence, *prudentia, consilium*.
polish, subst., = polished state, *nitor*.
polish, v. *(per)polire, expolire*.
polished, *nitidus, mundus, (per)politus*.
polite, *urbanus, comis, humanus*; adv. *urbane, comiter, humane, humaniter*

politeness, *urbanitas, comitas, humanitas*.
politic, *prudens, circumspectus, providus*.
political, *publicus, civilis*; a — discussion, *sermo de republica habitus*; — science, *ratio civilis, reipublicae gerendae ratio*.
politician, *vir rerum civilium* (or *reipublicae) peritus*.
politics, *civilis ratio, respublica*; to take up —, *ad rempublicam acceděre*.
polity, *reipublicae forma*.
poll, subst. = voting, *suffragium, comitia (-orum)*.
pollard, *amputatus*.
polling-booth, *saeptum, ovile*.
poll-tax, *exactio capitum*.
pollute, *polluere, inquinare, contaminare*.
pollution, = filth, *conluvio, impuritas*.
polygamy, *plures uxores habēre*.
polytheism, *multorum deorum cultus (-ūs)*.
pomade, *capillare, unguentum*.
pomegranate, *malum granatum or Punicum*.
pomp, *apparatus (-ūs)*.
pompous, *magnificus, gloriosus*; of style, *tumidus*. Adv. *magnifice, gloriose*.
pomposity, *magnificentia*.
pond, *stagnum, piscina, lacus (-ūs)*.
ponder, *considerare, ponderare, secum reputare*.
ponderous, *ponderosus, gravis*.
pontiff, *pontifex*.
pony, *mannus, mannulus*.
pool; see pond.
poop, *puppis*.
poor: = not rich, *pauper*; *inops, egens, mendicus* (= destitute); = inferior, *mediocris, tenuis*; of language, or of soil, *exilis, ieiunus*; = pitiable, *miser, infelix*; = little, *misellus*. Adv. *tenuiter, mediocriter, misere*.
pop, v. *crepare*; to — out, *evaděre, exsilire*.
poplar, *pobulus*; of the —, adj. *populeus*.
poppy, n *apaver (-eris, n.)*.
populace, *multitudo, plebs*.
popular: = belonging to the people, *popularis*; the — party, *populares (-ium)*; = liked, *gratiosus, (in vulgus) gratus or acceptus*.
popularity, *gratia, populi favor*.
populate; see people, v.
population, *civium or incolarum numerus, cives (-ium), incolae (-arum)*.
populous, *frequens, celeber*.
porch, *vestibulum*.
pore, subst. *foramen*.
pore, v. *(totum) se abděre (re or in re)*.
pork, *porcina*.
porker, *porcus*.
porous, *rarus*.
porridge, *puls*.
port, = harbour, *portus (ūs)*.
portcullis, *cataracta*.
portend, *portenděre, denuntiare*.
portent, *portentum, prodigium, monstrum, omen*.
portentous, *portentosus, monstr(u)osus*; adv. *monstr(u)ose*.

porter: at a gate, *ianitor*; for luggage, *baiulus*.
portfolio, *scrinium*.
portico, *porticus (-ūs)*.
portion, *pars, portio*; a marriage —, *dos*.
portmanteau, *vidulus, mantica*.
portrait, *imago (picta)*.
portray, *depingĕre*.
position: = place, *locus, situs (-ūs), sedes*; = state, *locus, status (-ūs), condicio*.
positive; = certain, *certus*; a — statement, *adfirmatio*; adv. *adfirmate* (of assertion), *certe, certo* (of knowing).
possess: = to have, *possidēre, habēre, tenēre*; or render by *esse*, with dat. of possessor; of feelings, etc., = to overwhelm, *invadĕre, occupare*.
possession, *possessio*; to take —, *occupare, capĕre, potiri*.
possessive, *tenax (suorum)*; gram., *possessivus*.
possessor, *possessor, dominus*.
possibility: render by *posse*; see also opportunity.
possible: render *posse*; it is — for me to live, *vivĕre possum*; it is — that, *fieri potest ut*; as quickly as —, *quam celerrime*. Adv.; see perhaps.
post, subst.; = stake, *palus*; door —, *postis*; milit., *statio, praesidium*; = office, *locus, munus (-eris, n.)*; for letters, *tabellarii (-orum*; = letter-carriers).
post, v.: milit., *(dis)ponĕre*; to — a letter, *litteras tabellario dare*.
postage, *vecturae pretium*.
posterior, adj. *posterior*.
posterity, *posteritas, posteri (-orum)*.
postern, *posticum*.
posthaste, *quam celerrime*.
posthumous; *post patrem mortuum natus*.
postman, *tabellarius*.
postpone, *differre, proferre, prorogare*.
postulate, subst. *sumptio*.
posture: of body, *status (-ūs), habitus (-ūs)*; of affairs, *status (-ūs), condicio, ratio*.
pot; *olla*.
potent; see powerful, efficacious.
potentate, *res, tyrannus, princeps*.
potential; see possible.
pothouse, *caupona*.
potion, *potio*; see also philtre.
potsherd, *testa*.
potter, *figulus*; —'s workshop, *figlina*.
pottery, = pots, etc., *fictilia (-ium)*.
pouch, *sacculus, saccus*.
poultice, *emplastrum*.
pounce: to — upon, *involare*.
pound, subst.: as measure of weight, *libra*; = enclosure, *saeptum (publicum)*.
pound, v. *(con)tundĕre, (con)terĕre*.
pour, v.: transit., *fundĕre*; to — in, *infundĕre*; to — out, *effundĕre*; intransit. *fundi, fluĕre, ferri*.
pouring, adj. (of rain), *effusus*.
poverty, *paupertas*; extreme —, *egestas, inopia, mendicitas*.
powder, subst. *pulvis*.

power. (1), = force, vigour, *vis* (plur. *vires*), *robur, lacerti (-orum,* physical); military —, *opes (-um)*. (2), = authority, *imperium, potestas, ius (iuris, n.)*; unofficial —, *potentia*; in the — of, *penes (hominem)*, in manu *(hominis)*; to have great —, *multum posse* or *valēre*.
powerful, *validus, valens, potens, robustus* (physically); of speech, *gravis, nervosus*. Adv. *graviter, vehementer, valde*.
powerless, *invalidus, impotens*; to be —, *nihil posse*.
practicable; see possible.
practical, of a person, *(rerum) usu peritus*; — knowledge, *usus (-ūs)*.
practice: = experience, *usus (-ūs), tractatio*; = custom, *mos, consuetudo*; = deed, *factum*.
practise: = do, engage in, *facĕre, exercēre, tractare*; = rehearse, *meditari*.
praetor, *praetor*.
praetorship, *praetura*.
prairie, *campus*.
praise, subst. *laus, laudatio* (= laudatory oration).
praise, v. *(con)laudare, laude adficĕre, praedicare*.
praiseworthy, *laudabilis, laude dignus*.
prance, *exsilire, exsultare*.
prank, *iocus*.
prate, prattle, *garrire*.
pray, *precari, rogare, orare, supplicare*.
prayer, *preces (-um), precatio, votum*.
prayerful, *supplex*.
preach, *docēre, orationem habēre*.
preamble, *exordium*.
precarious, *incertus, dubius*.
precaution: to take —s, *providēre, praecavēre*.
precede, *anteire, antegredi, antecedĕre*.
precedence, *prior locus*; to take —, *(homini) antecedĕre*.
precedent, *exemplum*.
preceding, *prior, superior*; = immediately before, *proximus*.
precept, *praeceptum, mandatum*.
preceptor, *magister, praeceptor*.
preceptor, *magister, praeceptor*.
precincts, *termini (-orum), fines (-ium)*.
precious, *magni pretii, splendidus, egregius*; a — stone, *gemma*.
precipice, *locus praeceps*.
precipitate, adj. *temerarius, praeceps, inconsultus*. Adv. *temere*.
precipitate, v. *praecipitare, deicĕre, deturbare*.
precipitous, *praeceps, praeruptus*.
precise: of things, *definitus, accuratus*; of persons, *diligens*. Adv. *subtiliter*; see also just.
precision, *subtilitas*; of persons, *diligentia*.
preclude, *prohibēre*.
precocious, *praecox*.
preconceived, *praeiudicatus*.
preconception, *praeiudicata opinio*.
preconcerted, *ex composito factus*.
precursor, *praecursor, praenuntius*.
predatory, *praedatorius, praedabundus*.
predecessor, in an office, *decessor*.

predetermine, *praefinire, praestituĕre.*

predicament, *difficultas, angustiae (-arum).*

predicate, subst. *attributio, attributum.*

predicate, v. *praedicare, dicĕre.*

predict, *praedicĕre.*

prediction, *praedictio, praedictum.*

predilection, *studium.*

predispose, *(animum) inclinare.*

predisposed, *propensus, proclivis.*

predisposition, *(animi) proclivitas, studium.*

predominance, *potentia, principatus (-ūs).*

predominant, *potens, praepollens;* = more numerous, *plures.*

predominate, *(prae)pollēre;* = be more numerous, *plures esse.*

preeminence, *praestantia, eminentia.*

preeminent, *praestans, praecipuus, egregius;* adv. *praecipue.*

preexist, *antea exstare* or *esse.*

preface, *prooemium, praefatio.*

prefatory; to make a few — remarks, *pauca praefari.*

prefect, *praefectus.*

prefecture, *praefectura.*

prefer, *antepōnĕre, anteferre, praeferre;* with infin., *malle.*

preferable, *potior, melior;* adv. *potius.*

preferment, *honor* (= office).

prefix, v. *praepōnĕre.*

pregnant, *praegnans, gravida;* of language, *pressus;* of events, *magni momenti.*

prejudge, *praeiudicare.*

prejudice, subst.: = premature judgment, *opinio praeiudicata;* = damage, *detrimentum.*

prejudice, v.: to be —d about a matter, *rem praeiudicatam habēre;* see also harm.

preliminary, adj.: a — inquiry, *praeiudicium;* — remarks, *praefatio.*

prelude, *prooemium.* Transf., *prolusio.*

premature, *immaturus, praeproperus;* adv. *ante tempus.*

premeditate, *praemeditari, cogitare.*

premeditation, *praemeditatio.*

premise, premises: in logic, —s, *principia (-orum);* minor —, *ad-sumptio;* major —, *propositio;* —s, = building, *aedificium, domus.*

premise, v. *praefari, pōnĕre.*

premium, *praemium.*

premonition, *monitio, monitum.*

preoccupation, *animus rei* (dat.) *deditus.*

preoccupy, = seize beforehand, *(prae)-occupare;* to be preoccupied about a thing, *totum in re versari.*

preparation, *praeparatio, apparatus (-ūs), meditatio* (of a lesson, etc.); to make —s, *parare.*

prepare, *(ap)parare, praeparare, in-struĕre;* to — for war, *bellum (ap)parare;* to — a speech, lesson, etc., *meditari, commentari.*

preponderate; see predominance.

prepossess, = win over, *delenire, permulcēre.*

prepossession; see prejudice.

preposterous, *praeposterus.*

prerogative; see right.

presage, subst. *praesagium, augurium.*

presage, v.: = foreshow, *portendĕre, significare;* = forebode, *praesagire, augurari.*

prescient, *praesciens, sagax.*

prescribe, *praescribĕre.*

presence, *praesentia;* in my —, *coram me* (abl.); — of mind, *praesens animus.*

present, subst. *donum, munus.*

present, adj.: physically, *praesens;* to be —, *adesse;* of time, *praesens, hic;* at —, *nunc, hoc tempore;* for the —, *in praesentia, in praesens* (tempus); gram. *praesens.* Adv., soon, *mox, brevi.*

present, v.: = bring forward, *offerre, obicĕre, praebēre;* to — oneself, *occurrĕre, obvenire;* = give, *donare, munerari, dare;* = introduce, *introducĕre, inducĕre.*

presentiment, *praesagitio, augurium;* to have a —, *praesagire.*

preservation, *conservatio;* = safety, *salūs (-ūtis).*

preserve, v. *(con)servare, tuēri* (=watch over), *sustinēre* (= uphold).

preserver, *(con)servator* (f. *servatrix*).

preside, *praesidēre, praeesse.*

presidency, *praefectura.*

president, *praefectus;* or use verb.

press, subst. *prelum, torcular* (for wine, etc.).

press, v.: transit., *premĕre, comprimĕre;* to — out, *exprimĕre;* = urge, harry, *premĕre, urgēre, instare;* intransit., to — on, *pergĕre, contendĕre.*

pressing; see urgent.

pressure, *pressus (-ūs) vis, pondus (-eris, n.).*

prestige, *nomen, gloria, fama.*

presume, = take liberties, *sibi adrogare* or *sumĕre, audēre;* = to suppose, *sumĕre, credĕre.*

presumption: = presumptuousness, *adrogantia;* = supposition, *con-iectura, opinio.*

presumptuous, *adrogans;* adv. *adro-ganter.*

pretence, *simulatio, species;* without —, *sine fuco ac fallaciis.*

pretend, *simulare, fingĕre.*

pretender, *simulator;* to the throne, *qui regnum sibi adrogat.*

pretention: = claim, *postulatio;* = display, *ostentatio.*

preterite, gram., *praeteritum* (tempus).

preternaturally, *praeter naturam, mirabili quodam modo.*

pretext, *causa, simulatio, species;* to use as a —, *praetendĕre.*

prettiness, *concinnitas, venustas.*

pretty, adj. *bellus, pulcher, concinnus, lepidus;* adv. *belle, concinne, lepide.*

pretty, adv. *satis, admodum.*

prevail, = be prevalent, *esse, obtinēre;* = win, *vincĕre, superare;* to — upon, = persuade, *persuadēre, adducĕre.*

prevalent, *(per)vulgatus;* to become —, *increbrescĕre.*

prevaricate, *tergiversari.*

prevarication, *tergiversatio.*

prevent, *prohibēre, impedire.*

previous; see preceding.

prey, subst. *praeda:* a beast of —, *fera.*

prey, v. *praedari;* fig., to — upon, *(animum) (ex)edĕre, consumĕre.*

price, subst. *pretium;* — of corn, *annona;* at a high —, *magni (pretii);* to set a — on, *(rei,* dat.) *pretium constituĕre.*

priceless, *inaestimabilis.*

prick, v. *pungĕre, stimulare;* to — up one's ears, *aures erigĕre.*

prickle, *aculeus, spina.*

prickly, *aculeatus, spinosus.*

pride, *superbia, insolentia, adrogantia;* source of —, *decus (-oris).*

priest, *sacerdos, flamen;* high —, *pontifex maximus.*

priestess, *sacerdos.*

priesthood, *sacerdotium.*

prim, *(nimis) diligens.*

primal, primeval; see ancient, first.

primary, *primus, principalis;* = chief, *praecipuus.* Adv. *initio, primo; praecipue.*

prime, subst.: of life, *integra aetas;* to be in one's —, *vigēre, florēre;* — of anything, *flos, robur.*

prime, adj.: = first, *primus;* = excellent, *eximius, optimus.*

primitive, *priscus, antiquus.*

prince: = king's son, *filius regis, regulus;* = king, *rex.*

princess, *mulier regii generis, filia regis.*

principal, subst.: of a school, *magister;* = capital, *caput, sors.*

principal, adj., *primus, princeps, praecipuus* (= chief). Adv. *maxime, praecipue.*

principle, *principium, elementum, ratio;* of conduct, *institutum, praeceptum;* a man of —, *homo constans* or *gravis;* want of —, *levitas.*

print, v. *imprimĕre.*

prior, adj. *prior;* see also preceding.

prison, *carcer, vincula (-orum,* =chains), *custodia* (=confinement).

prisoner: a — of war, *captivus* (f. *captiva);* in gen. *(homo) captus, comprehensus;* = a person on trial, render by *reus.*

pristine, *pristinus, priscus, antiquus.*

prithee! *quaeso, cedo.*

privacy, *solitudo.*

private, *privatus, proprius, domesticus;* = secret, *arcanus, secretus;* a — soldier, *miles gregarius, manipularis.* Adv. *clam, secreto, occulte, privatim* (= in a private capacity).

privateer, *navis praedatoria.*

privation, *inopia, egestas.*

privet, *ligustrum.*

privilege, *ius (iuris,* n.), *praecipuum, beneficium.*

privy, adj.: see private; — to, *conscius rei* (genit.); — council, *consilium regis;* — purse, *fiscus.*

prize, subst.: = reward, *praemium, palma;* = prey, *praeda.*

prize, v. *magni aestimare.*

pro and con, *in utramque partem.*

probability, *veri similitudo, probabilitas.*

probable, *veri similis; probabilis* (of guesses, etc.); adv. *probabiliter.*

probe, v. *scrutari, rimari.*

probity, *probitas.*

problem, *quaestio.*

problematical, *dubius, incertus.*

proceed, *pergere, procedĕre, progredi;* = to act, *agĕre, facĕre;* to — from, *emanare, oriri;* to — against, in the courts, *litem intendĕre.*

proceeding, proceedings, in gen., *acta (-orum);* legal, *lis, actio.*

proceeds, *reditus (-ūs), fructus (-ūs).*

process, *ratio;* legal, *lis, actio.*

procession, *pompa.*

proclaim, *declarare, pronuntiare, edicĕre* (by decree).

proclamation, *pronuntiatio, declaratio, praedicatio;* = thing proclaimed, *edictum.*

proconsul, *pro consule.*

proconsular, *proconsularis.*

procrastinate, *differre, procrastinare.*

procrastination, *procrastinatio.*

procreate, *procreare.*

procreation, *procreatio.*

procure, *(com)parare;* to — in addition, *adquirĕre.*

prodigal, subst. *nepos.*

prodigal, adj. *prodigus, profusus, effusus.*

prodigality, *effusio, prodigentia.*

prodigious, *ingens, immanis.*

prodigy, *prodigium, portentum, miraculum.*

produce, subst. *fructus (-ūs).*

produce, v.: = bring forward, *proferre, exhibēre, producĕre;* = bring into existence, *(pro)creare, gignĕre, parĕre;* = cause, bring about, *facĕre, efficĕre.*

product, production, *opus (-eris* = work); an artistic —, *artificium.*

productive, *ferax, uber.*

productiveness, *ubertas.*

proem, *prooemium.*

profanation, *violatio, nefas.*

profane, adj.: = not sacred, *profanus;* = impious, *impius;* adv. *impie.*

profane, v. *violare, polluĕre.*

profanity, *impietas.*

profess, *profiteri.*

professed, *manifestus, apertus.*

profession: = declaration, *professio;* = employment, *munus (-eris,* n.), *ars.*

proffer, v. *promittĕre;* see offer.

proficiency, *scientia, peritia.*

proficient, *peritus, sciens.*

profit, subst. *lucrum, quaestus (-ūs), fructus (-ūs).*

profit, v.: = be of service, *prodesse;* = gain advantage, *proficĕre, lucrum facĕre.*

profitable, *utilis, fructuosus;* adv. *utiliter.*

profitless, *inutilis, vanus.*

profligacy, subst. *homo perditus* or *profligatus.*

profligate, adj. *perditus, flagitiosus, profligatus;* adv. *perdite.*

profound, *altus.* Adv. *penitus* (= completely).

profundity, *altitudo.*

profuse, *effusus, profusus.*

profusion, *largitas, effusio.*

progenitor, *parens.*

progeny, *progenies.*

prognostic, *signum.*

prognosticate; see forebode.

programme, *libellus.*

progress, subst.: = journey, *iter*; = advance, *progressus (-ūs)*; to make much —, *multum proficēre.*

progress, v. *progredi, proficēre.*

progression, *progressus (-ūs).*

prohibit, *vetare, interdicēre.*

prohibition, *interdictum.*

project, subst. *consilium, propositum.*

project, v. *prominēre, eminēre, exstare.*

projectile, *(telum) missile.*

proletariat *proletarii (-orum).*

prolific; see fruitful.

prolix, *longus, verbosus.*

prologue, *(pro)ducēre, prorogare, extendēre.*

prolongation, *productio, prorogatio.*

prolonged, *longus, diuturnus.*

promenade, *ambulatio.*

prominence, *eminentia*; = importance *dignitas, auctoritas.*

prominent: = projecting, *prominens,* or render by verb; = distinguished, *praestans, egregius, inlustris.*

promiscuous, *promiscuus*; adv. *promiscue, temere.*

promise, subst., *promissum, fides.*

promise, v.: = to make a —, *promittēre, pollicēri, fidem dare*; = to show —, *bonam spem ostendēre.*

promising, adj. *bonae spei* (genit.).

promissory; a — note, *chirographum.*

promontory, *promontorium*; small —, *lingua, li(n)gula.*

promote: of person, *provehēre, producēre*; of causes, etc., *(ad)iuvare, amplificare; consulēre, prodesse,* with dat.

promoter, *auctor, adiutor, fautor.*

promotion: = rise to higher position, *dignitatis accessio*; = furthering, *amplificatio.*

prompt, *promptus*; adv. *cito.*

prompt, v., = suggest, *subicēre.*

prompter, *qui rem homini subicit.*

promptitude, *celeritas.*

promulgate, *promulgare.*

promulgation, *promulgatio.*

prone: = face-down, *pronus*; =liable, inclined, *pronus, proclivis, propensus.*

proneness, *proclivitas.*

prong, *dens.*

pronoun, *pronomen.*

pronounce, *enuntiare, exprimēre, dicēre*; formally, *pronuntiare, declarare.*

pronunciation, *appellatio, locutio.*

proof, subst.: = act of proving, *probatio, demonstratio*; = means of proving, *argumentum, signum, indicium*; = trial, *experimentum*; to put to the —, *experiri, temptare.*

prop, subst. *adminiculum.*

prop, v. *fulcire;* see support.

propagate: of plants, *propagare, inserēre;* of living creatures, *gignēre, procreare;* abstr., *vulgare, serēre.*

propagation: *propagatio;* abstr., use verb.

propel, *propellēre, impellēre.*

propensity, *proclivitas, animus proclivis.*

proper: = peculiar, characteristic, *proprius*; = genuine, *verus, germanus*; = becoming, *decorus, honestus*; it is —, *decet;* = suitable, *aptus, idoneus.* Adv. *proprie, vere; apte.*

property: = characteristic, *proprietas*; = what one owns, *bona (-orum), res*; private —, *res familiaris;* inherited —, *patrimonium.*

prophecy: the act, *praedictio, vaticinatio*; = what is prophesied, *praedictum.*

prophesy, *praedicēre, praenuntiare, vaticinari.*

prophet, *vates.*

prophetic, *divinus, fatidicus, vaticinus*; adv. *divinitus.*

propinquity; see nearness.

propitiate, *placare, propitiare.*

propitiation, *placatio*; means of —, *piaculum.*

propitious, *propitius, faustus*; adv. *fauste.*

proportion: = portion, *pars, portio*; = relationship, *ratio;* in —. *pro portione, pro rata parte;* in — to, *pro,* with abl.

proposal, *condicio, sententia, consilium.*

propose: = bring forward for consideration, *ponēre;* to — a law, *legem ferre* or *rogare;* = intend, *cogitare, in animo habēre.*

proposer: of a law, *legis lator;* in gen., *auctor.*

proposition, in logic, *pronuntiatum, propositio.*

proprietor, *possessor, dominus.*

propriety, *convenientia, decorum, honestas.*

prorogation, *prorogatio.*

prorogue, *prorogare.*

prosaic, *ieiunus, frigidus.*

proscribe, *proscribēre.*

proscription, *proscriptio.*

prose, *(soluta) oratio.*

prosecute: = carry out, *exsequi, perficēre;* = bring action against, *iudicio persequi, accusare.*

prosecution: = carrying out, *exsecutio;* at law, *accusatio, actio, lis.*

prosecutor, *accusator.*

proselyte, *discipulus.*

prospect: = view, *prospectus (-ūs)*; = hope, *spes.*

prospective, *futurus;* adv. *in futurum.*

prosper: transit., *fortunare, secundare;* intransit., *florēre, vigēre.*

prosperity, *res* (plur) *secundae* or *prosperae; prosperitas.*

prosperous, *secundus, prosper(us)*; adv. *bene, prospere.*

prostitute, subst. *meretrix, scortum.*

prostrate, v. *(pro)sternēre;* to — oneself before a person, *ad pedes hominis procumbēre;* to be —d by grief, *in maerore iacēre.*

protect, *tuēri, defendēre, (pro)tegēre, custodire.*

protection, *tutela, praesidium, custodia;* to take under one's —, *in fidem recipēre.*

protector, *defensor, propugnator, custos.*

protest, subst. *recusatio.*

protest, v.: = state positively, *adseverare, adfirmare;* to — against, *recusare, intercedĕre.*

prototype, *exemplum, exemplar.*

protract, (*pro*)*ducĕre, prorogare, trahĕre.*

protrude: transit., *protrudĕre;* intransit., *protrudi, prominēre.*

protuberance, *tuber, gibber.*

proud, *superbus, adrogans, fastidiosus;* adv. *superbe, adroganter.*

prove: = show clearly, *probare ostendĕre, docēre;* to — oneself, *se praestare* or *praebēre;* intransit., = to turn out, *fieri, evadĕre, exire.*

provender, *pabulum.*

proverb, *proverbium;* according to the —, *ut aiunt.*

proverbial, proverbially, *proverbii loco* (= as a proverb).

provide: = supply, furnish, (*com*)*parare, praebēre, suppeditare;* to — for, *consulĕre* or *providēre,* with dat.; of laws, = require, order, *iubēre.*

provided that, *dum, dummodo* (with subj.).

provided with, adj. *instructus, ornatus, praeditus.*

providence, *providentia.*

provident, *providus, diligens.* Adv. *diligenter.*

providentially, *divinitus.*

province: = duty, *provincia, officium;* = district, *regio, provincia.*

provincial, *provincialis;* = countrified, *rusticus, agrestis, inurbanus.*

provision, = stipulation, *condicio, cautio.*

provision, v. (*oppidum*) *cibo instruĕre.*

provisional, render by phrase, *ad* or *in tempus.*

provisions, *cibus, cibaria* (-*orum*), *alimentum;* for an army, *commeatus* (-*ūs*).

provoke: = call forth, (*com*)*movēre, ciēre;* = make angry, *irritare, lacessĕre;* to — to action, *incitare, concitare, impellĕre.*

provoking, *molestus.*

prow, *prora.*

prowess, *virtūs* (-*ūtis*).

prowl, *vagari, peragrare.*

proximity; see nearness.

proxy, *procurator, vicarius.*

prudence, *prudentia, cautio, circumspectio.*

prudent, *prudens, cautus, circumspectus;* adv. *caute, considerate.*

prudish, *rusticus, severus, tetricus.*

prune, (*am*)*putare, recidĕre.*

pruner, of trees, *putator.*

pruning, subst. *putatio.*

pruning-hook, *falx.*

pry, *rimari, investigare, scrutari.*

pshaw! *phy!*

public, subst. *homines* (-*um*, plur.), *populus, vulgus.*

public, *publicus, communis* (= not private); to show oneself in —, *in publicum prodire;* — life, *respublica, forum;* the — interest, *respublica;* at the — expense, *sumptu publico,*

publice; in a — capacity, *publice;* — opinion, *vulgi opinio.* Adv. publicly, in —, *aperte, palam, coram omnibus.*

publican, *publicanus;* = inn-keeper, *caupo.*

publication, *praedicatio;* of a book, *editio libri;* = book, *liber.*

publicity, *celebritas, lux.*

publish, *proferre, ēdĕre.*

pudding, *placenta.*

puddle, *stagnum.*

puerile, *puerilis, ineptus.*

puff, v. *anhelare;* to — out, = inflate, *inflare.*

pugilism, *pugilatus* (-*ūs*), *pugilatio.*

pugilist, *pugil.*

pull, v.: = twitch, tweak, *vellĕre, vellicare;* = drag, *trahĕre;* to — out, (*e*)*vellĕre, eripĕre.*

pullet, *pullus* (*gallinaceus*).

pulley, *trochlea.*

pulsate, *palpitare, agitari, moveri.*

pulse: of the blood, *venarum pulsus* (-*ūs*); the vegetable, *legumen.*

pulverize, *in pulverem redigĕre.*

pumice, *pumex;* of —, adj., *pumiceus.*

pump, subst. *antlia.*

pump, v. *exhaurire.*

pun, subst. *facetiae* (-*arum*), *logos* (or -*us*).

punch, subst., the drink, *calidum;* — bowl, *cratera;* see also blow.

punch, v. *tundĕre.*

punctilious, *diligens;* in religious matters, *religiosus;* adv. *diligenter, accurate.*

punctual, *diligens;* adv. *diligenter, ad tempus.*

punctuality, *diligentia* (= care).

punctuate, *distinguĕre, interpungĕre.*

punctuation, *distinctio, interpunctio;* — mark, *interpunctum.*

puncture, subst. *punctum.*

puncture, v. (*com*)*pungĕre.*

pungent, *acer, acutus;* adv. *acriter, acute.*

punish, *punire, poenā adficĕre, ulcisci;* to be —ed, *puniri, poenas dare.*

punisher, *vindex, ultor.*

punishment, *castigatio, animadversio;* = what is inflicted, *poena, supplicium, multa.*

puny, *pusillus, exiguus.*

pupil: of the eye, *pupula;* at school, *alumnus* (f. *alumna*), *discipulus* (f. *discipula*).

puppy, *catulus, catellus.*

purchasable, *venalis.*

purchase, subst.: as act, *emptio;* = thing bought, *merx, quod emptum est.*

purchase, v. (*co*)*emĕre, mercari.*

purchaser, *emptor.*

pure: physically, *purus;* pure and simple, *merus, sincerus;* morally, *purus, integer, sanctus, castus.* Adv.: = wholly, *prorsus, plane;* morally, *pure, integre, caste.*

purgation, *purgatio, lustratio.*

purge, *purgare.*

purification, *purgatio;* ceremonial —, *lustratio.*

purify, (ex)purgare, purum facĕre; lustrare (with ceremonial).

purity: moral, integritas, sanctimonia, sanctitas; of language, integritas, sinceritas.

purloin, avertĕre, surripĕre, furari.

purple, subst. purpura, ostrum, conchylium, color purpureus.

purport; see meaning, mean.

purpose, subst. propositum, consilium, animus, voluntas; for the — of, (eo consilio) ut; on —, consulto, de industria; to no —, frustra, nequiquam; to the —, ad rem.

purpose, v. statuĕre, cogitare, in animo habēre.

purposeless, vanus, inanis, inritus.

purposely; see purpose.

purse, marsupium, zona, crumena.

pursuant to, ex (with abl.), secundum (with acc.).

pursue, (per)sequi, insequi, insectari.

pursuit: = search, consectatio; = occupation, negotium, occupatio, artificium.

push, subst. (im)pulsus (-ūs), impetus (-ūs).

push, v. (im)pellĕre, (pro)trudĕre, urgēre; intransit., to — on, contendĕre, instare, pergĕre.

pushing, adj. protervus, confidens.

pusillanimity, timiditas; animus timidus.

pusillanimous, timidus, abiectus; adv. timide, abiecte.

put, ponĕre, (con)locare; — away, abdĕre; — back, reponĕre; — down, deponĕre, demittĕre; — comprimĕre (= suppress); — on, of clothes, induĕre, sumĕre; — off, of clothes, exuĕre, (de)ponĕre; — off, — postpone, differre; — out, eicĕre, extrudĕre, expellĕre; — exstinguĕre (= quench); — together, conferre, componĕre; — up, erigĕre, statuĕre; — up with (= tolerate), ferre, tolerare.

putative, falsus; qui dicitur esse.

putrefy, putescĕre; to cause to —, putrefacĕre.

putrid, putridus, putidus.

puzzle, quaestio, aenigma, nodus.

puzzle, v. dubium facĕre, impedire; to be —d, dubitare, haerēre.

puzzling, difficilis, ambiguus.

Pygmy, pygmaeus; = any dwarf, nanus, pumilio, pumilus.

pyramid, pyramis.

pyre, rogus, pyra.

Pyrenees, Pyrenaei montes, Pyrenaeum.

Q

quadripartite, quadripartitus.

quadruped, quadrupes.

quadruple, quadruplex.

quaff, v. ducĕre, haurire.

quag(mire), palūs (-ūdis).

quail, subst. coturnix.

quail, v. animo deficĕre, pavēre.

quaint, lepidus, facetus, concinnus = odd, insolitus, novus.

quake, tremĕre, contremiscĕre.

qualification: = right, ius (iuris, n.); = limitation, exceptio, condicio.

qualified, idoneus, aptus, dignus.

qualify, v.: transit., = make fit, idoneum reddĕre, instituĕre; =modify, restrict, circumscribĕre, deminuĕre; intransit., idoneum esse (or habēri).

quality: = nature, character, natura, ingenium, indoles; of what —? qualis?; of such a —, talis; good —, virtūs (-ūtis); bad —, vitium; =kind, sort, genus (-eris, n.), nota (of wine); a lady of —, generosa femina.

qualm, fastidium (= disgust), nausea, nauseola (= squeamishness); — of conscience, conscientia (mala).

quantity, = number, numerus; a certain —, aliquot, aliquantum; a large —, multitudo, copia, vis; — in scansion, mensura, quantitas.

quarrel, subst. iurgium, altercatio, rixa.

quarrel, v. iurgare, altercari, rixari.

quarrelsome, litigiosus, pugnax.

quarry, subst.: a stone —, lapicidinae (-arum), lautumiae (-arum); = prey, praeda.

quart, (as measure) duo sextarii.

quartan, adj. quartanus.

quarter = fourth part, quarta pars, quadrans; = district, vicus, regio; = mercy, venia.

quarter, v. quadrifariam dividĕre; to — troops, milites per hospitia disponĕre.

quarterly, trimestris; adv. tertio quoque mense.

quarters, hospitium, habitatio, tectum; milit., winter — (for troops), hiberna (-orum), summer —, aestiva (-orum); at close —, comminus; to come to close —, manum conserĕre.

quash, rescindĕre, infirmare.

quaver; see tremble.

quay, margo, crepido.

queen, regina.

queer, novus, insolitus, mirus.

quell, opprimĕre, comprimĕre.

quench, exstinguĕre, restinguĕre.

querulous, queribundus, querulus.

query; see question.

quest; see seek, search.

question, subst.: = inquiry, quaestio, interrogatum; to ask —s, (inter)rogare; = doubt, dispute, controversia, dubium; there is no — that, haud dubium est quin.

question, v.: = to ask questions, (inter)rogare, percontari, quaerĕre; = to doubt, dubitare.

questionable, incertus, ambiguus, dubius.

questioning, subst. (inter)rogatio, percontatio.

quibble, subst. captio, cavillatio.

quibble, v. cavillari.

quibbling, adj. captiosus.

quick, = prompt, active, promptus, alacer, expeditus; — witted, astutus, sagax, catus. Adv., = fast, cito, celeriter.

quicken: = accelerate, accelerare, maturare; in gen., = stimulate, incitare, stimulare, incendĕre.

quicklime, *calx viva.*
quickness, *velocitas;* of intellect, *ingenii acumen, sagacitas.*
quicksand, *syrtis.*
quicksilver, *argentum vivum.*
quiet, subst. *tranquillitas, pax, otium, silentium.*
quiet, adj. *quietus, tranquillus, taciturnus* (= not talking); to be —, *quiescĕre, silēre, tacēre.* Adv. *quiete, tranquille, silentio* (= in silence).
quiet, quieten, v. *tranquillare, pacare.*
quill, *penna; spina;* for striking strings, *plectrum.*
quinquennial, *quinquennalis.*
quintessence, *flos.*
quip, *dictum.*
quit, *decedĕre (de loco).*
quite, adv.: = completely, *admodum, prorsus, omnino, funditus;* = fairly, moderately, *satis.*
quiver, subst. *pharetra.*
quiver, v. *tremĕre, micare.*
quivering, adj. *tremulus.*
quoit, *discus.*
quotation, *prolatio, commemoratio;* = passage quoted, *locus adlatus.*
quote, *adferre, proferre, (com)memorare.*
quoth he, or she, *inquit, ait.*

R

rabbit, *cuniculus.*
rabble, *multitudo, turba, plebecula.*
rabid, *rabidus;* adv. *rabide.*
race, subst.: = family, people, *genus (-eris, n.), gens;* = contest of speed, *cursus (-ūs), certamen, curriculum.*
race, v. *(cursus) certare.*
race-course, *curriculum, stadium, circus.*
race-horse, *equus, celes.*
raciness, *sucus, sapor.*
rack, subst., for torture, *eculeus, tormentum.*
rack, v. *torquēre, (ex)cruciare, vexare.*
racket, = noise, *strepitus (-ūs).*
racy, *salsus.*
radiance, *fulgor, candor, splendor.*
radiant, *clarus, candidus, splendidus.*
radiate, *fulgēre, radiare.*
radical, adj.: = innate, *insitus, innatus;* = complete, *totus;* in politics, *novarum rerum cupidus* or *studiosus.* Adv. *radicitus, funditus, prorsus, omnino.*
radish, *raphanus, radix.*
raft, *ratis.*
rafter, *tignum, trabs.*
rag, *pannus.*
rage, subst. *rabies, furor, ira* (= anger).
rage, v. *furĕre, saevire.*
raging, *furens, furibundus, saevus.*
ragged: of people, *pannosus;* of clothes, *lacer.*
rail, subst. *tignum transversum.*
rail, v.: to — off, *(con)saepire;* to — at, *maledicĕre, conviciari.*
railing, subst. *saepimentum, saepes.*
raillery, *iocus, cavillatio.*
raiment, *vestis, vestitus (-ūs).*
rain, subst. *pluvia, imber.*
rain, v.: it —s, *pluit.*

rainbow, *arcus (-ūs) pluvius.*
rain-cloud, *nimbus.*
rainy, *pluvius, pluvialis.*
raise: = lift, *(ex)tollĕre, (e)levare, erigĕre;* = increase, *augēre;* = promote, elevate, *producĕre, provehĕre;* = arouse, excitare, *erigĕre, tollĕre.*
rake, subst. *rastellus, pecten;* = prodigal *roué, ganeo, nepos, vappa.*
rake, v. *radĕre, pectine verrĕre.*
rakish, *profligatus, dissolutus.*
rally, v.: transit.; to — troops, *ordines restituĕre;* = banter, *ludĕre, irridĕre;* intransit., = recover, *se conligĕre, convalescĕre* (from illness).
ram, subst. *aries.*
ramble, subst. *ambulatio.*
ramble, v. *errare, vagari, ambulare* (= walk about).
rambling, *vagus.*
rampant, *ferox, superbus;* to be — *superbire.*
rampart, *vallum, agger; praesidium.*
rancid, *rancidus.*
rancorous, *malevolus, malignus, invidus;* adv. *maligne, infeste.*
rancour, *odium, invidia, malevolentia.*
random; at —, *temere.*
range, subst.: = row, *ordo, series;* a — of mountains, *montes perpetui;* of a missile, *(teli) coniectus (-ūs).*
rank, subst.: of soldiers, *ordo;* = degree, station, *ordo, gradus (-ūs), locus.*
rank, adj.: of plants, *luxuriosus;* of smell, *foetidus, graveolens;* = great, extreme, *maximus, summus.*
rank, v. *numerare, habēre.*
rankle, v. *mordēre, pungĕre.*
ransack: = plunder, *diripĕre, spoliare;* = search thoroughly, *rimari, (per)scrutari.*
ransom, subst.: = money paid, *pretium, pecunia;* = the arrangement, *redemptio.*
ransom, v. *redimĕre.*
rant, v. *declamare, ampullari.*
rap, subst. *pulsatio.*
rap, v. *pulsare.*
rapacious, *rapax, avidus.*
rapacity, *rapacitas, aviditas.*
rapid, subst. *vertex, gurges.*
rapid, *rapidus, citus, celer;* adv. *rapide, cito, celeriter.*
rapidity, *rapiditas, celeritas.*
rapine, *rapina.*
rapture, *(summa) voluptas, exsultatio.*
rare: = uncommon, *rarus, inusitatus;* = thin, *rarus, tenuis;* = exceptional, *singularis, eximius.* Adv. *raro.*
rarefy, *extenuare.*
rarity, = fewness, *raritas, paucitas.*
rascal, *homo scelestus, furcifer, verbero.*
rascality, *scelus (-eris, n.).*
rascally, *scelestus, nequam.*
rash, *praeceps, inconsultus, temerarius;* adv. *inconsulte, temere.*
rashness, *temeritas.*
rat, *mus.*
rate, subst.: = price, *pretium;* — of interest, *usura;* — of exchange, *collybus;* = tax, *vectigal, tributum;* at any —, *certe, utique.*

rate, v., = value, *aestimare.*

rather: = in preference, *potius, libentius, prius*; I would —, *malo*; = somewhat, *aliquantum.*

ratification, *sanctio*; or use verb.

ratify, *sancire, ratum facĕre, confirmare.*

ration, *demensum, cibaria* (-orum).

rational, *ratione praeditus*; (rationi) *consentaneus*; to act —ly, *prudenter agĕre.*

rationality; see *ratio.*

rattle, subst.: = noise, *crepitus* (-ūs), *strepitus* (-ūs); a child's —, *crepitaculum, crepitacillum.*

rattle, v. *crepare, strepĕre.*

ravage, (per)vastare, (de)populari.

ravaging, *vastatio, populatio.*

rave, *furĕre, insanire.*

raven, *corvus.*

ravening, ravenous, *rapax, vorax.*

ravine, *fauces* (-ium).

raving, *furens, furibundus, insanus.*

ravish: = carry off, *rapĕre, abducĕre*; = debauch, (con)stuprare.

ravishing; see *delightful.*

raw, *crudus*; = inexperienced, *rudis, imperitus*; of weather, *frigidus, humidus.*

ray, *radius, iubar.*

raze, *solo* (ad)aequare.

razor, *novacula.*

reach, subst.: = grasp, capacity, *captus* (-ūs).

reach, v. = touch, get to, *tangĕre, contingĕre, attingĕre*; (ad locum) (per)venire, accedĕre.

react: to — upon, = affect, *adficĕre*; to — to, (rem) *ferre* or *accipere*, with adv.

reactionary, *qui* (rempublicam) ad pristinum statum revocare vult.

read, *legĕre, evolvĕre*; to — through, *perlegĕre*; to — aloud, *recitare*; well —, of a person, *litteratus.*

reader, *legens, qui legit.*

readiness, *animus promptus* or *paratus*; — of speech, *volubilitas linguae, lingua prompta.*

reading, subst. *lectio*; a — aloud, *recitatio.*

ready, *paratus, promptus*; — money, *pecunia praesens* or *numerata*; to make —, (com)parare, instruĕre; to be —, *praesto esse.* Adv., = willingly, *prompto* or *parato animo, libenter.*

real, *verus, sincerus*; — estate, *fundus, praedium.* Adv. *revera, vere.*

realistic, to be, *veritatem imitari.*

reality, *res* (vera), *veritas.*

realization, = completion, *effectus* (-ūs).

realize: = effect, *efficĕre, perficĕre*; = understand, *intellegĕre, comprehendĕre*; of money, *pecuniam redigĕre.*

realm, *civitas, respublica, regnum.*

reap, (de)metĕre, messem facĕre; fig., *fructum capĕre, percipĕre.*

reaper, *messor.*

reaping-hook, *falx.*

reappear, *redire, rursus apparēre.*

rear, subst.; use adj. *extremus* or *novissimus*, with *agmen* or *acies*; to

form the — guard, *agmen claudĕre* or *cogĕre.*

rear, v. = bring up, *alĕre, educare.*

reason, subst.: = cause, *causa, ratio*; for this (or that) —, *ideo, idcirco*; by — of, *propter, ob*; there is no — why, *non est cur*, with subj.; for no —, *temere*; as a faculty, *ratio, mens, consilium.*

reason, v. *ratiocinari, reputare*; to — with another person, *disceptare, disputare.*

reasonable: of persons, *rationis particeps, prudens*; = fair, (rationi) *consentaneus, aequus, iustus.* Adv. *ratione*; = adequately, *satis.*

reasonableness: = rationality, *ratio*; = fairness, *aequitas, moderatio.*

reasoner, *disputator.*

reasoning, *ratio, ratiocinatio.*

reassert, *iterare* (= repeat).

reassure, (animum) confirmare, erigĕre.

rebel, subst. *homo seditiosus, hostis patriae.*

rebel, v. *seditionem* (com)movēre, deficĕre, desciscĕre.

rebellion, *seditio, defectio, motus* (-ūs).

rebellious, *seditiosus, turbulentus, novarum rerum cupidus*; adv. *seditiose, turbulente(r).*

rebound, v. *repelli, resilire.*

rebuff, subst. *repulsa.*

rebuff, v. *repellĕre, reicĕre.*

rebuild, *restituĕre, reficĕre.*

rebuke, subst. *reprehensio, vituperatio, obiurgatio.*

rebuke, v. *reprehendĕre, vituperare, obiurgare.*

rebuker, *obiurgator.*

rebut, *redarguĕre, repellĕre, refellĕre.*

recall, subst. *revocatio.*

recall, v. *revocare*; to — to mind, *recordari, in memoriam revocare.*

recant, *recantare.*

recantation, *receptus* (-ūs).

recapitulate, *enumerare, commemorare.*

recapitulation, *enumeratio.*

recapture, v. *recipĕre.*

recast, *reficĕre.*

recede, *recedĕre, retro cedĕre.*

receipt, = act of receiving, *acceptio*, or use verb; in a ledger, a —, *acceptum*; to enter as a —, *acceptum referre.*

receive, *accipĕre, excipĕre, recipĕre.*

receiver, *receptor* (f. *receptrix*).

recent, *recens, novus*; adv. *nuper, recens.*

receptacle, *recaptaculum, cella, horreum.*

reception, *acceptio, hospitium* (in a house).

receptive, *docilis.*

receptiveness, *docilitas.*

recess, *recessus* (-ūs), *latibulum.*

reciprocal, *mutuus*; adv. *mutuo, invicem.*

reciprocate, *inter se dare.*

recital, *narratio, commemoratio.*

recitation, *recitatio.*

recite, *recitare*; = narrate, (com)memorare, dicĕre, (e)narrare.

reckless, *neglegens, temerarius, imprudens;* adv. *neglegenter, temere, imprudenter.*

recklessness, *imprudentia, neglegentia, temeritas.*

reckon, = count, calculate, *computare;* see also consider.

reckoning, subst. *ratio, computatio.*

reclaim, v.: = ask back, *repetĕre; reposcĕre;* = reform, *corrigĕre, emendare.*

recline, v. *se reclinare, recumbĕre.*

recluse, *homo solitarius.*

recognizance, *sponsio, vadimonium.*

recognize: = know again, *agnoscĕre, cognoscĕre, noscitare;* = acknowledge, *noscĕre;* = approve, *(com)probare.*

recoil, *resilire, recellĕre;* to — in horror, *refugĕre.*

recollect, *(com)meminisse, reminisci, recordari.*

recollection, *memoria, recordatio.*

recommence, v.: transit., *redintegrare, renovare;* intransit., *renasci, renovari.*

recommend, *commendare, probare.*

recommendation, *commendatio, laus, laudatio.*

recommendatory, *commendaticius.*

recompense, subst. *remuneratio, praemium.*

recompense, v. *remunerari.*

reconcile, *placare, reconciliare, in gratiam reducĕre;* = make congruous, *accommodare.*

reconciliation, *reconciliatio gratiae.*

recondite, *reconditus, exquisitus.*

reconnoitre, *explorare, (pro)speculari.*

reconsider, *denuo considerare.*

record, v. *perscribĕre, in tabulas referre.*

record-office, *tabularium.*

records, *tabulae (-arum), historia; annales (-ium,* = chronicles).

recount, *referre, (e)narrare, (com)memorare.*

recourse: to have — to, *confugĕre, se conferre (ad);* = stoop to, *descendĕre (ad).*

recover, v.: transit., *recuperare, recipĕre, reparare;* intransit., *refici, convalescĕre, se colligĕre.*

recovery, *recuperatio;* in health, *salus* or *sanitas restituta.*

recreant; see coward.

recreate, *renovare, recreare.*

recreation, *requies, (animi) remissio.*

recrimination, *(mutua) accusatio.*

recruit, subst. *tiro.*

recruit, v. *recreare, reficĕre;* milit., = enrol, *conscribĕre, delectum habĕre.*

recruiting, subst. *delectus (-ūs), conquisitio.*

rectification, *correctio, emendatio.*

rectify, *corrigĕre, emendare.*

rectilinear, *(di)rectus.*

rectitude, *probitas, integritas, honestas.*

recumbent, *(re)supinus, recubans.*

red, *ruber;* of the hair, *rufus, rutilus;* to be —, *rubēre;* the — Sea, *Sinus Arabicus.*

redden, v.: transit., *rubefacĕre;* intransit., *rubescĕre.*

redeem, *redimĕre, liberare (= set free).*

redeemer, *liberator, vindex.*

redemption, *redemptio, liberatio.*

red-hot, *candens, fervens.*

redness, *rubor.*

redolent, *redolens* (with acc.).

redouble, *ingeminare.*

redound, *redundare;* it —s to my credit, *est mihi honori.*

redress, subst. *satisfactio.*

redress, v. *restituĕre, compensare, sarcire.*

reduce: = to bring, *redigĕre, revocare* — to order, *in integrum reducĕre;* to be —ed to, *redire;* = diminish *(im)minuĕre, deminuĕre;* = conquer. *vincĕre, expugnare.*

reduction, = diminution, *deminutio.*

redundancy, of style, *redundantio.*

redundant, *supervacaneus.*

re-echo, v.: transit., *referre;* intransit. *resonare.*

reed, *harundo, calamus.*

reedy, *harundineus.*

reef, = rocks, *scopuli, saxa.*

reef, v.: to — sails, *contrahĕre vela.*

reek, *fumare.*

reel, subst., = dance, *saltatio.*

reel, v. *titubare, vacillare.*

reestablish, *restituĕre.*

reestablishment, *restitutio.*

refer: to — a matter, *referre, deferre;* — to, = mention, *mentionem facĕre;* — to, = mean, be speaking of, *dicĕre, spectare.*

referee, *arbiter.*

reference, render by verbs; with — to, *quod attinet ad.*

refill, *replēre.*

refine: of liquids, *liquare;* of metals *purgare.*

refined, *(ex)politus, urbanus, humanus.*

refinement, *urbanitas, humanitas;* of language, etc., *subtilitas.*

reflect, v.: transit., of light, *repercutĕre;* in gen., = show, *ostendĕre;* this —s credit on you, *hoc tibi est honori;* intransit., = think, *considerare, reputare, cogitare.*

reflection: of light, *repercussus (-ūs);* = image reflected, *imago;* = thought, *cogitatio, consideratio;* = blame, *reprehensio, vituperatio.*

reform, v.: of troops, *restituĕre, reficĕre;* = amend, *corrigĕre, emendare;* intransit., = get better, *se corrigĕre.*

reformation, *correctio, emendatio.*

reformer, *corrector, emendator.*

refract, *infringĕre.*

refractory, *contumax.*

refrain, subst. *carmen.*

refrain, v. *(se) abstinēre, temperare.*

refresh, *recreare, reficĕre.*

refreshment: abstr., *refectio;* = food, *cibus.*

refrigerate, *refrigerare.*

refuge, *perfugium, refugium, asylum;* to seek — at, *confugĕre ad.*

refugee, *fugitivus (= runaway), exsul (= exile).*

refund, *reddĕre, dissolvĕre.*

refusal, *recusatio, repudiatio.*

refuse, subst. *purgamentum faex, quisquiliae (-arum).*

refuse, v.: to — to give, (de)negare;
to — to accept, recusare, respuĕre,
repudiare; to — battle, pugnam
detrectare; to — to do, nolle, recusare.

refutation, refutatio, dissolutio.

refute, refellĕre, redarguĕre, refutare,
convincĕre.

regain, recipĕre, reciperare.

regal; see royal.

regale; see entertain, feast.

regalia, insignia (-ium) regia.

regard, subst.: = consideration, respectus (-ūs), cura; = esteem, studium,
amor; Cicero sends his —s, Cicero
tibi salutem plurimam dicit; see also
reference.

regard, v.: = look at, observare,
intuĕri; = bear in mind, respicĕre,
spectare; = consider, ducĕre, habĕre;
= concern, relate to, attinēre or
pertinēre ad.

regardless, neglegens, incuriosus.

regency, regni administratio, interregnum.

regent, interrex.

regicide, regis caedes (= deed); regis
interfector (= person).

regiment, legio (= of cavalry, turma
(equitum).

region, regio, tractus (-ūs), locus.

register, liber, tabulae (-arum), album.

register, v. perscribĕre, in album
referre.

regret, subst. dolor, desiderium (= longing), paenitentia (= repentance).

regret, v.: = grieve, dolēre; = feel
loss of, desiderare, requirĕre; = repent
of an action, impers. paenitet;
I — having done it, paenitet me fecisse.

regular: = correct, iustus, legitimus,
rectus; — troops, milites legionarii;
= constant, even, certus, constans,
aequabilis. Adv., = correctly, ordine,
iuste, legitime, recte; = constantly,
evenly, constanter, aequabiliter.

regularity, ordo, constantia, aequabilitas.

regulate, ordinare, dirigĕre, moderari.

regulation, administratio; = an order,
iussum, praeceptum, lex.

rehabilitate, restituĕre.

reign, subst., regnum; in your —,
te regnante or rege.

reign, v. regnare (as king), imperare
(as emperor).

reimburse, (rem homini) reddĕre.

rein, subst. habena, frenum; to pull in
the —s, habenas adducĕre; to loosen
the —s, frenos dare.

rein, v. frenare.

reinforce, (con)firmare, augēre.

reinforcement, supplementum, novae
copiae (-arum), subsidium.

reinstate, restituĕre.

reiterate, iterare.

reject, reicĕre, repudiare, respuĕre;
to — a bill, legem antiquare.

rejection, reiectio, repudiatio, repulsa
(of a candidate).

rejoice, gaudēre, laetari; transit.,
laetificare, exhilarare.

rejoicing, gaudium, laetitia.

rejoin; see return or answer.

relapse, v. recidĕre, relabi.

relate, v. (e)narrare, (com)memorare,
referre; — to, = concern, spectare,
pertinere, attinere ad.

related, propinquus, cognatus, consanguineus, adfinis (by marriage).

relation, ratio; in — to, ad, pro, erga;
—s, familiaritas, necessitudo, amicitia;
see also relative and narrative.

relationship, propinquitas, cognatio,
adfinitas (by marriage).

relative, subst.; see related.

relative, adj.; render by spectare ad
(= relate to) or comparare (= compare).

relax, v.: transit. (re)laxare, remittĕre;
intransit., (re)languescĕre, relaxari.

relaxation, (animi) relaxatio, remissio.

relay, subst. equi per viam dispositi.

release, subst. liberatio, missio.

release, v. liberare, (ex)solvĕre, missum
facĕre; to — a slave, manu mittĕre.

relent, molliri, iram remittĕre.

relentless, immisericors, inexorabilis,
crudelis; adv. crudeliter.

relevant, to be, ad rem attinēre.

reliance, fides, fiducia.

relic, relics, reliquiae (-arum).

relict, vidua.

relief: = alleviation, (ad)levatio, sub-
levatio, levamen(tum); = aid, auxilium,
subsidium; in art, asperitas; to
engrave in —, caelare.

relieve: = lighten, ease, (ad)levare,
sublevare; = take another's place,
excipĕre, succedĕre (with dat.).

religion, religio, cultus (-ūs) deorum.

religious: of persons, erga deos pius,
sanctus, religiosus; — observances,
ritūs (-uum), religiones (-um). Adv.
pie, sancte, religiose.

relinquish, relinquĕre.

relish, subst., = liking, fondness,
studium.

relish, v.; see enjoy.

reluctant, invitus, coactus; to be —,
nolle.

rely, (con)fidĕre, fidem habēre, niti;
—ing upon, fretus.

remain: = stay, endure, (per)manēre,
remanēre, durare, morari (= linger);
= be left over, restare, superesse.

remainder, residuum, quod restat.

remaining, reliquus, superstes.

remains, reliquiae (-arum).

remand, subst. comperendinatio.

remand, v., remittĕre; legal, (reum)
ampliare, comperendinare.

remark, subst. dictum.

remark, v.; see observe, say.

remarkable, singularis, insignis, mirus;
adv. singulariter, insigniter, mire.

remedial, salutaris.

remedy, remedium, medicina, medica-
men(tum).

remember, meminisse, reminisci, recordari, memoriā tenēre.

remembrance, memoria, recordatio.

remind, (ad)monēre, commonēre, com-
monefacĕre.

reminiscence, recordatio; —s, written
up, commentarii (-orum).

remiss, neglegens.

remit: = send back, *remittĕre*; = let off (debts, etc.), *remittĕre, condonare*.

remittance, *pecunia*.

remnant; see remainder.

remonstrance, *reclamatio, (ad)monitio*.

remonstrate, *reclamare, reclamitare*.

remorse, *conscientia mala, paenitentia*.

remorseless; see pitiless.

remote, *remotus, disiunctus, longinquus*.

remoteness, *longinquitas*.

removal, *amotio*; to a new home, *(de)migratio*.

remove, v.: transit., *amovere, submovere, tollĕre, auferre*; = lead away, *abducĕre*; intransit., *se movere, discedĕre, abire, migrare*.

remunerate, *remunerari*.

remuneration, *remuneratio, praemium*.

rend, *(di)scindĕre, divellere*.

render: = give (back), *reddĕre, referre, tribuĕre*; to — thanks, *gratias agĕre*; = make, cause to be, *facĕre, reddĕre*.

rendezvous, perhaps *locus ad conveniendum constitutus*.

renegade, *transfuga*.

renew: = make new, *(re)novare, reficĕre*; = begin again, repeat, *renovare, redintegrare, iterare*.

renewal, *renovatio, instauratio*.

renounce, *renuntiare, repudiare, se (re) abdicare*.

renovate: see renew.

renown, *fama, gloria, laus*.

renowned, *clarus, inlustris*.

rent, subst., *reditus (-ūs), vectigal, merces (-edis)*.

renunciation, *abdicatio, repudiatio*.

reopen, *iterum aperire*.

repair, v., *reficĕre, reparare, restituĕre*; see also go.

reparation, *satisfactio*.

repast; see meal.

repay, *reddĕre, reponĕre, solvĕre*.

repayment, *solutio*; or use verb.

repeal, subst. *abrogatio*.

repeal, v. *rescindĕre, tollĕre, abrogare*.

repeat, *iterare, redintegrare*.

repeatedly, *identidem, saepenumero, etiam atque etiam*.

repel, *repellĕre, propulsare, reicĕre*.

repent, impers. *paenitet*; I — of having done that, *paenitet me id fecisse*; I — of the crime, *paenitet me sceleris*.

repentance, *paenitentia*.

repentant, *paenitens*.

repetition, *iteratio, repetitio*.

repine, *(con)queri*.

repining, *querela* (= complaint).

replace: = put back, *reponĕre, restituĕre*; to — bv another, *substituĕre*.

replenish, *replēre, supplēre*.

replete; see full.

repletion, *satietas*.

reply, subst. *responsum, responsio*.

reply, v. *respondēre*; — by letter, *rescribere*.

report, subst.: official, *relatio, renuntiatio*; = rumour, *fama, rumor*; = loud noise, *fragor, crepitus (-ūs)*.

report, v. *(re)nuntiare, referre*; it is —ed, *ferunt, traditur, dicitur*.

repose, subst. *(re)quies, otium*.

repose, v.: transit., *(re)ponĕre*; intransit., *quiescĕre*.

repository, *thesaurus, receptaculum*.

reprehend, *reprehendĕre*.

reprehensible, *culpā dignus*.

represent: = portray, *exprimĕre, (ef)fingĕre, (de)pingĕre, adumbrare* (= sketch); = state, *dicĕre, monēre*; = play a part, *personam gerĕre, partes agĕre*.

representation, = image, likeness, *imago, effigies*.

representative, subst. *vicarius, procurator*.

repress, *comprimĕre, cohibēre*.

reprieve, *supplicium differre*.

reprimand, subst. *reprehensio*.

reprimand, v. *reprehendĕre*.

reprisals, *talio*; to make —s, *par pari respondere*.

reproach, subst. *exprobratio, obiectatio*; in words, *probrum, convicium*.

reproach, v. *increpitare, obiurgare*.

reproachful, *obiurgatorius*.

reprobate, adj. *perditus, profligatus*.

reproduce, *regignĕre, denuo generare*.

reproof, *vituperatio, reprehensio, obiurgatio*.

reprove, *vituperare, reprehendĕre*.

reprover, *reprehensor, obiurgator*.

reptile, *bestia serpens*.

republic, *respublica (libera); civitas*.

republican, *vir liberae reipublicae studiosus*.

republican, adj. *popularis*; or genit. *reipublicae liberae*.

repudiate; see reject.

repudiation, *repudiatio*.

repugnance, *repugnantia, odium* (= hatred).

repugnant, *repugnans, diversus, alienus*.

repulse, subst., of a candidate, *repulsa*.

repulse, v. *repellĕre, propulsare, reicĕre*.

repulsive, *odiosus, foedus*.

reputable, *honestus*.

reputation, *fama, opinio*; good —, *existimatio, gloria*; bad —, *infamia*.

repute; to be in good —, *bene audire*.

request, subst. *preces (-um), rogatio*; at my —, *rogatu meo, me rogante*.

request, v. *precari, orare, rogare*.

require: = demand, *poscĕre, postulare, imperare*; = need, *egēre, requirĕre, desiderare*.

requirement, *postulatio*; or use verb.

requisite, adj. *necessarius*.

requisition, *postulatio*; or render by *imperare*.

requite, *compensare, rependĕre*.

rescind, *rescindĕre, abrogare, tollĕre*.

rescript, *responsum, rescriptum*.

rescue, subst. *liberatio*; or use verb.

rescue, v. *liberare, servare, eripĕre*.

research, *eruditio, investigatio*.

resemblance, *similitudo*; bearing a —, *similis*.

resemble, *similem esse* (with genit. or dat.).

resent, *aegre* or *moleste ferre*.

resentful, *iracundus*.

resentment, *ira, stomachus*.

reservation, *exceptio, condicio*.

reserve, subst.: = store, *copia*; milit., —s, *subsidia (-orum)* in —, adj. *subsidiarius*; — of manner, *taciturnitas*; without —, *aperte*.

reserve, *retinēre, reponēre*.

reserved, *taciturnus, occultus, tectus*.

reservoir, *lacus (-ūs), cisterna* (underground).

reside, v. *habitare.* Transf., *residēre, inesse*.

residence: act, *habitatio, mansio, commoratio*; place of —, *domus, domicilium, sedes*.

resident, subst. *habitator, incola*.

residue, *quod reliquum est*.

resign, (*magistratu*) *abire* or *se abdicare*; in gen., = give up, (*con*)*cedēre, deponēre*; to — oneself, *animum submittēre*.

resignation, *abdicatio*; = resigned attitude, *animus submissus* or *aequus*.

resin, *resina*.

resist, *resistēre, repugnare, adversari*.

resolute, *fortis, firmus, constans*; adv. *fortiter, firme, firmiter, constanter*.

resolution: = determination, *constantia, firmitudo*; = a purpose, *sententia, consilium, propositum*.

resolve, v.: = break down, *dissolvēre, dissipare*; = determine, *statuēre, constituēre, decernēre*; of a deliberative body, *sciscēre, iubēre*.

resolved, *certus*.

resonant, *resonans*.

resort, subst. = place, *locus*.

resort, v.: to a place, *celebrare, frequentare*; — to, = have recourse to, *confugēre, decurrēre, descendēre*.

resound, *resonare, personare*.

resource, resources, *facultates (-um), opes (-um)*; = wealth or power).

respect, subst.: = esteem, *observantia, reverentia*; to pay one's —s to, *salutare*; in all —s, *omnino*; in — of, *ad, de, ab*.

respect, v. *observare,* (*re*)*vereri, colēre*; see also concern, relate.

respectability, *honestas*.

respectable, *honestus*; adv. *honeste, bene*.

respectful, *observans, verecundus*; adv. *verecunde*.

respecting, *de* with abl.

respective, *proprius, suus* (often with *quisque*).

respiration, *respiratio, spiritus (-ūs)*.

respite; see reprieve.

resplendent, *splendidus*.

respond, response; see answer.

respondent, legal, *reus*.

responsibility, responsible; render by *rationem reddēre* (= give an account); to make oneself —, (*rem*) *praestare, in se recipēre, promittēre*.

responsive, *apertus* (= open), *facilis* (= tractable).

rest, subst.: = repose, (*re*)*quies, otium, tranquillitas*; = remainder, *reliquum, quod restat*.

rest, v., intransit., (*re*)*quiscēre, conquiescēre*; — upon, (*re*) (*in*)*niti*.

restless, *inquietus, turbidus, sollicitus* (= anxious).

restoration, *refectio*; or use verb.

restorative, subst. *medicina*.

restore: = give back, *reddēre*; = reinstate, replace, *restituēre, redintegrare, reficēre*; to — to health, *sanare*.

restrain, *coercēre, continēre, cohibēre, inhibēre*.

restraint, *moderatio, modus*; = hindrance, *impedimentum*.

restrict, *coercēre, circumscribēre,* (*de*)*finire*.

restriction, *modus, finis*; see restraint.

result, subst. *exitus (-ūs), eventus (-ūs)*; the — is that, *evenit ut*; without —, *nequiquam*.

result, v. *fieri, evenire, evadēre, oriri*.

resume, *repetēre, recolēre*.

resuscitate, *ab inferis excitare*; see also revive.

retail, *divendēre*.

retailer, *caupo*.

retain, *tenēre, retinēre,* (*con*)*servare*.

retainer = attendant, *cliens, adsectator, satelles*; = retaining fee, *arrhabo*.

retaliate, *par pari respondēre, ulcisci*.

retaliation, *ultio* (= revenge).

retard, (*re*)*morari,* (*re*)*tardare*.

retire, v. *abire,* (*re*)*cedēre, se removēre*; milit., *pedem referre, se recipēre*.

retired, adj. *secretus, remotus, solitarius*.

retirement, *solitudo, otium*.

retiring; see modest.

retort; see reply.

retrace, *repetēre*; — one's steps, *pedem referre*.

retract, *renuntiare*.

retreat, subst. *reditus (-ūs), recessus (-ūs), receptus (-ūs), fuga*; see also refuge.

retreat, v. *se recipēre, pedem referre, fugēre* (= flee).

retrench, *sumptūs minuēre*.

retribution, *poena*.

retrieve; see recover.

retrograde; render by *retro* (= backwards), or *in deteriorem partem* (= for the worse).

retrogression, *recessus (-ūs), regressus (-ūs)*.

retrospect, (*praeteritorum*) *memoria*.

retrospective, render by *retro* (= backwards) or by *praeterita (-orum;* = the past).

return, subst.: = journey back, *reditus (-ūs), regressus (-ūs)*; = giving back, *remuneratio*; = official declaration, *renuntiatio, professio*.

return, v.: transit., *reddēre, referre*; intransit., *redire, reverti* (= turn back).

returned, adj. *redux*.

reunion, *reconciliatio*; see also assembly.

reunite, *iterum coniungēre; reconciliare*.

reveal, *patefacēre, aperire, evulgare*.

revel, revelry, *comissatio, bachatio*.

revel, v. *comissari,* (*per*)*bacchari; luxuriare, exsultare*.

reveller, *comissator*.

revenge, subst. *ultio, vindicta, vindicatio*.

revenge, v. *ulcisci, vindicare*.

revengeful, *ulciscendi cupidus*.

revenue, *vectigal, reditus* (*-ūs*).

reverberate, = resound, *resonare.*

reverberation, *repercussus* (*-ūs*).

revere, *(re)verēri, venerari.*

reverence, subst. *reverentia, veneratio, verecundia;* religious —, *religio, pietas erga deos.*

reverend, *venerabilis, reverendus.*

reverent, *verecundus;* in religious sense, *religiosus, pius.* Adv. *verecunde; religiose.*

reverie, *cogitatio.*

reverse, subst.: = change, *conversio,* (*com)mutatio, vicissitudo;* = the opposite, *contrarium;* = defeat, *clades;* = hind part, *pars aversa.*

reverse, v. *invertĕre, (com)mutare, convertĕre.*

reversion, legal, *hereditas.*

revert, *redire, revolvi.*

review, subst. *recognitio;* milit., *recensio, lustratio.*

review, v. *inspicĕre, contemplari;* milit., *recensēre, lustrare.*

revile, *conviciari, insectari, maledicĕre.*

reviler, *conviciator.*

reviling, subst. *maledictio, probrum, convicium.*

revise, *retractare;* see also correct.

revision, *emendatio.*

revisit, *revisĕre.*

revive, v.: transit., *recreare, excitare;* fig. *redintegrare;* intransit., *revirescĕre, recreari;* fig. *renasci.*

revocation, *revocatio, abrogatio.*

revoke, *abrogare, rescindĕre.*

revolt, subst. *defectio, seditio;* of a conquered people, *rebellio.*

revolt, v. *deficĕre, desciscĕre;* of a conquered people, *rebellare.*

revolting, adj. *taeter, foedus, turpis.*

revolution, *conversio, orbis, ambitus* (*-ūs*); political —, *res (rerum,* plur.) *novae.*

revolutionary, adj. *seditiosus, turbulentus, novarum rerum cupidus.*

revolutionize, *novare, commutare.*

revolve, *se (re)volvĕre* or *(re)volvi, circumverti.*

revulsion, see disgust.

reward, subst. *praemium, merces.*

reward, v. *remunerari, compensare, praemium dare.*

rewrite, *iterum scribĕre.*

rhetoric, *rhetorica, ars dicendi.*

rhetorical, *rhetoricus, oratorius;* adv. *rhetorice.*

rheumatism, *dolor artuum.*

Rhine, river, *Rhenus.*

Rhone, river, *Rhodanus.*

rhythm, *numerus, modus.*

rhythmical, *numerosus;* adv. *numerose, modulate.*

rib, *costa;* of a ship, *statumen.*

ribald, *obscenus.*

ribbon, *redimiculum, taenia, vitta.*

rich, = possessing wealth, *dives, locuples, opulentus;* to grow —, *ditescĕre;* = costly, *sumptuous, opimus, pretiosus, lautus;* = copious, fertile, *copiosus, abundans, uber, ferax.* Adv. *copiose, abundanter, pretiose.*

riches, *divitiae* (*-arum,* plur.), *opes* (*-um,* plur.); *pecunia* (= money).

richness, *abundantia, ubertas.*

rid, *liberare;* to get — of, — oneself of, *deponĕre, dimittĕre.*

riddance, *liberatio.*

riddle, subst. *aenigma* (*-atis,* n.), *ambages* (*-um,* plur.).

riddled, e.g. with wounds, *confossus.*

ride, v.: on a horse, *equitare, (equo) vehi;* in a chariot, *ire curru;* at anchor, *in ancoris consistĕre.*

rider, *eques.*

ridge, *iugum, montis dorsum.*

ridicule, subst. *ridiculum.*

ridicule, v. *inridēre, deridēre, (in)ludĕre.*

ridiculous, *ridiculus;* adv. *ridicule.*

riding, *equitatio;* or use verb.

rife, to become —, *percrebescĕre.*

rifle, see plunder.

rift, *rima.*

rig, subst. *habitus* (*-ūs*).

rig, v. *armare, ornare.*

rigging, *armamenta* (*-orum*), *rudentes* (*-um*).

right, subst. *fas, ius* (*iuris,* n.).

right, adj.: opp. to left, *dexter;* — hand, (*manus*) *dextra;* at — angles *ad pares angulos;* morally —, *rectus, iustus, aequus;* = suitable, proper, *rectus, verus;* at the — time, *ad tempus;* you are —, *ita est ut dicis;* it is all —, *bene habet.* Adv. *recte, iuste, iure, merito* (= deservedly) *bene* (= well).

righteous, *probus, aequus, iustus;* adv. *probe, iuste.*

righteousness, *probitas.*

rightful, *legitimus, iustus;* adv. *legitime, iuste, iure.*

rigid, *rigidus, durus;* adv. *rigide, dure.*

rigidity, *rigor.*

rigour, *severitas, duritia.*

rill, *rivus, rivulus.*

rim, *ora.*

rime, *pruina.*

Rimini, *Ariminum.*

rind, *cortex, liber* (= inner bark).

ring, subst. *orbis, anulus;* a — of people, *corona.*

ring, v. *tinnire;* = resound, *resonare.*

ringing, subst. *tinnitus* (*-ūs*).

ringing, adj. *tinnulus, canorus.*

ringleader, *auctor, princeps, dux.*

ringlet, *cincinnus, cirrus.*

rinse, *eluĕre.*

riot, subst. *seditio, motus* (*-ūs*), *tumultus* (*-ūs*).

riot, v. *seditionem movēre;* = revel, *comissari, luxuriare.*

rioter, *homo turbulentus.*

riotous, adj. *turbulentus;* = wild, in gen., *luxuriosus;* — living, *luxuria.* Adv. *turbulente.*

rip, *scindĕre, divellĕre.*

ripe, *maturus, tempestivus.*

ripen: transit., *maturare;* intransit., *maturari, maturescĕre.*

ripeness, *maturitas.*

ripple, subst., *unda.*

rise, subst.: = origin, *ortus* (*-ūs*); to give — to, *parĕre, efficĕre;* = increase, *incrementum*; = rising ground, *clivus, collis*.

rise, v.: = get up, (*ex*)*surgĕre, se erigĕre, se levare*; of sun, stars, etc., *oriri*; = originate, start, (*co*)*oriri, surgĕre, nasci*; = increase, *increbescĕre, crescĕre*; to — in dignity, etc., *crescĕre, emergĕre, ascendĕre*; = rebel, *consurgĕre, cooriri*.

rising, subst. *ortus* (-*ūs*); see also rebellion.

rising, adj.: — ground, *clivus, collis*.

risk, subst. *periculum, discrimen*.

risk, v. *in periculum adducĕre* or *vocare*.

rite, ritual, subst. *ritus* (-*ūs*).

rival, subst. *aemulus* (f. *aemula*), *competitor* (f. *competitrix*); in love, *rivalis*.

rival, adj. *aemulus*.

rival, v. *aemulari, certare* (*cum*).

rivalry, *aemulatio, certamen*; in love, *rivalitas*.

river, subst. *flumen, fluvius, amnis*; adj. *fluviatilis, fluvialis*.

river-bed, *alveus*.

road, *via, iter*; on the — *in itinere, obiter*.

roadstead, *statio*.

roam, *palari, vagari, errare*.

roaming, *vagus, errabundus*.

roar, subst. *fremitus* (-*ūs*), *mugitus* (-*ūs*).

roar, v. *mugire, fremĕre, vociferari* (of persons).

roast, v. *torrēre, frigĕre*.

roasted, *assus*; — meat, *assum*.

rob, (*ex*)*spoliare, compilare, latrocinari*.

robber, *praedo, latro, fur*.

robbery, *latrocinium, spoliatio, rapina*.

robe, subst.: *vestis, vestimentum*; woman's —, *palla, stola*; — of state, *trabea*.

robe, v. *vestire*.

robust, *robustus, validus*.

rock, subst. *saxum, rupes, scopulus*.

rock, v.: transit., *agitare, quatĕre*; intransit., *agitari, nutare, vacillare*.

rocky, *scopulosus, saxeus*.

rod, *virga, ferula, decempeda* (for measuring).

roe: of fish, *ova* (-*orum*); = female deer, *caprea*.

roebuck, *capreolus*.

rogue, (*homo*) *nequam* or *scelestus; veterator*.

roguery, *fraus, dolus, nequitia*.

role, *partes* (-*ium*), *persona*.

roll, subst. *volumen*; = list of names, *album*.

roll, v.: transit., *volvĕre, volutare, versare*; intransit., *volvi, volutari*.

roll-call; to answer a —, *ad nomina respondēre*.

roller, *cylindrus, phalangae* (-*arum*).

rolling, adj. *volubilis*.

Roman, *Romanus*.

romance, subst. *fabula*.

romance, v. *fabulari*.

romantic, *fictus, commenticius* (= imaginary); *mirus, novus* (= strange).

Rome, *Roma*.

roof, subst. *tectum, culmen*.

roof, v. (*tecto*) *tegĕre*.

room: = space, *locus, spatium*; to make —, *locum dare*; = apartment, *conclave, cubiculum*.

roomy, *laxus, spatiosus*.

root, subst. *radix, stirps*: by the —s, *radicitus*.

root, v. to —, or become —ed, *radices agĕre, inveterascĕre*; to be —ed, *inhaerēre*; —ed, *inveteratus*; for — up, see uproot.

rope, *funis, restis*.

rose, *rosa*.

rosemary, *ros marinus*.

rosy, *roseus*.

rot, subst. *tabes*.

rot, v. *putescĕre, tabescĕre*.

rotate, *volvi, circumagi*.

rotation, *ambitus* (-*ūs*); in —, *ordine*.

rotatory, *versatilis*.

rotten, *putrefactus, putridus*.

rotundity, *figura rotunda*.

rouge, subst. *fucus*.

rouge, v. *fucare*.

rough, *asper, horridus, atrox, hirsutus* (= shaggy). Adv. *aspere*.

roughen, (*ex*)*asperare*.

roughness, *asperitas*; of style, *salebra*.

round, subst. *orbis*; in fighting, *congressus* (-*ūs*).

round, adj. *rotundus, globosus*.

round, adv. and prep., *circum, circa*.

round, v.: = make round, *rotundare, tornare*; = sail round, *flectĕre*; — off, = complete, *concludĕre, absolvĕre*.

roundabout, *devius*; a — way, *ambages* (-*um*), *circuitus* (-*ūs*).

rounded, *teres*.

roundly, *plane, praecise*.

rouse, *excitare*.

rout, subst. *fuga*; see also mob.

rout, v. *fugare, dissipare, fundĕre*.

route; see way, road, journey.

routine, *usus* (-*ūs*), *ordo*.

rove; see wander.

row, subst.: = line, *ordo, versus* (-*ūs*); in a row, (*ex*) *ordine*; see also quarrel and noise.

row, v. *remigare*; to — a boat, *lintrem remis propellĕre*; to — hard, *remis contendĕre*.

royal: = of a king, *regius*, or *regis* (genit.); = like a king, *regalis*. Adv. *regie, regaliter*.

royalty, *regnum, regia potestas*.

rub, *terĕre, conterĕre*; to — down, (*de*)*fricare*; to — out, *delēre*.

rubbish, *rudus* (-*eris*, n.), *quisquiliae* (-*arum*).

rubble, *rudus* (-*eris*, n.).

rudder, *gubernaculum, clavus*.

ruddy, *rubicundus*.

rude: = unfinished, *rudis, inconditus*; = ill-mannered, *importunus, inhumanus, insolens*. Adv. *incondite; insolenter*.

rudeness, *inhumanitas, importunitas, insolentia*.

rudimentary, *inchoatus*.

rudiments, *elementa* (-*orum*).

ruffian, *latro, sicarius*.

ruffianly, *nefarius, nequam, sceleratus*.

ruffle, v. *agitare*: to be —d, *inhorrescĕre*. Transf., see irritate.

rug, *stragulum.*

rugged, *asper, horridus, praeruptus.*

ruin, subst.: = collapse, *ruina, exitium, pernicies;* concr., —s, *parietinae (-arum), ruinae (-arum).*

ruin, v. *perdĕre, pessum dare, conficĕre.*

ruinous, *exitiosus;* = in ruins, *ruinosus.*

rule, subst.: = ruler, *regula, decempeda;* = regulation, *lex, praeceptum;* = government, *imperium, regnum.*

rule, v. *dominari, regĕre, praeesse, imperare;* to — as a king, *regnare;* to — passions, etc., *temperare,* with dat.

ruler, *rector, dominus, rex* (= king); see also rule.

rumble, subst. *murmur.*

rumble, v. *(in)sonare, murmurare.*

ruminate, *ruminare.*

rumination, *ruminatio.*

rumour, subst. *rumor, fama, sermo.*

rumour, v.: it is —ed, *fertur, fama est.*

run, subst. *cursus (-ūs) citatus.*

run, v. *currĕre, cursu ferri;* of fluids, = flow, *fluĕre;* — about, *cursare;* — into, *incurrĕre;* — through, *percurrĕre.*

runaway, *fugitivus.*

runner, *cursor.*

running, of water, *vivus.*

rupture, v. *frangĕre, confringĕre, rumpĕre.*

rural, *rusticus, rusticanus, agrestis.*

ruse, *dolus.*

rush, subst.: the plant, *iuncus, scirpus:* of —es, adj., *iunceus, scirpeus;* = dash, *impetus (-ūs).*

rush, v. *ruĕre, ferri, currĕre.*

russet, *fulvus* (poet).

rust, subst. *robigo, ferrugo* (of iron only).

rust, v. *robiginem trahĕre;* fig. *torpescĕre.*

rustic, *rusticus, agrestis.*

rustle, subst. *crepitus (-ūs), sonus.*

rustle, v. *crepare, crepitare.*

rusty, *robiginosus.*

rut, *orbita.*

S

sable, adj. *niger, ater.*

sabre, *gladius, ensis, acinaces.*

sack, subst.: = bag, *saccus, culeus;* — of a city, *direptio.*

sack, v. *diripĕre, spoliare.*

sacker, *direptor.*

sacred, *sacer, sanctus;* to declare —, *sancire.* Adv. *sancte.*

sacredness, *sanctitas, religio.*

sacrifice, subst. *sacrificium, sacra (-orum);* = victim, *victima, hostia.* Transf., = loss, *iactura.*

sacrifice, v. *sacrificare, immolare.* Transf., = give up, *iacturam facĕre,* with genit.; *dedĕre.*

sacrilege, *sacrilegium.*

sacrilegious, *sacrilegus.*

sad, *maestus, tristis;* = causing sadness, *gravis, acerbus, luctuosus.*

sadden, *dolore adficĕre.*

saddle, subst. *ephippium.*

saddle, (equum) *sternĕre.*

sadness, *maestitia, tristitia, dolor.*

safe, subst. *armarium, arca.*

safe, adj.: = protected, *tutus;* feeling —, *securus;* = and sound, *incolumis, salvus;* —, = reliable, *fidus.* Adv. *tuto.*

safe-conduct, *fides (publica).*

safeguard, *propugnaculum, munimentum.*

safety, *salūs (-ūtis), incolumitas.*

saffron, *crocus;* adj., *croceus.*

sagacious, *sagax, prudens;* adv. *sagaciter, prudenter.*

sagacity, *sagacitas, prudentia.*

sage, subst. and adj. *sapiens.*

sail, subst. *velum;* to set —, *vela dare;* to furl one's —s, *vela contrahĕre.*

sail, v. *navigare;* to — past, *praetervehi;* — out, *enavigare.*

sailing, subst. *navigatio.*

sailor, *nauta.*

saintly, *sanctus.*

sake: for the — of, *causā, gratiā* (with genit.); *pro* (with abl.); *ob* or *propter* (with acc.).

salaam, v. *corpus humi prosternĕre.*

salad, *acetaria (-orum).*

salary, *merces, salarium.*

sale, *venditio, hasta* (= auction); to offer for —, *venum dare* for —, adj., *venalis.*

salesman, *venditor.*

salient, *praecipuus.*

saline, *salsus.*

sallow, *pallidus, luridus.*

sally, *eruptio.*

sally, v. *erumpĕre, eruptionem facĕre.*

salt, subst. *sal.*

salt, adj. *salsus.*

salt, v. *sale condire.*

salt-cellar, *salinum.*

salt-mine, salt-works, *salinae (-arum).*

salubrious, *saluber* or *salubris;* adv. *salubriter.*

salutary, *salutaris, utilis.*

salutation, *salutatio.*

salute, *salutare.*

salvation, *salūs (-ūtis).*

salve, *unguentum;* for eyes, *collyrium.*

same, *idem, eadem, idem;* the — as, *idem qui, idem ac* (atque); in the — place, *ibidem;* at the — time, *simul, eodem tempore;* it is all the — to me, *meā nihil interest.*

sample, *exemplum, specimen.*

sanctify, *(con)secrare, dedicare.*

sanction, subst. *confirmatio, auctoritas;* with the — of a person, *hominis iussu.*

sanctity, *sanctitas, sanctimonia.*

sanctuary: = holy place, *templum, delubrum, fanum;* = refuge, *asylum, receptaculum.*

sand, *harena, saburra.*

sandal, *crepida, solea;* wearing —s, *crepidatus, soleatus.*

sandy, *harenosus.*

sane, *sanus, mentis compos.*

sanguinary, *cruentus, sanguineus, sanguinarius.*

sanguine; see hopeful.

sanity, *mens sana.*

sap, subst. *sucus.*

sap, v. *cuniculos agĕre.* Transf. *corrumpĕre, haurire.*

sapling, *arbor novella*.
sarcastic, *acerbus*; adv. *acerbe*.
sash, *zona*.
satchel, *loculus, pera, sacculus*.
satellite, *satelles*.
satiate, (ex)*satiare, explēre, saturare*.
satiety, *satietas, satias*.
satire, *satura* or *satira*; see also *satirical*.
satirical, *famosus, probrosus, acerbus*.
satirist, *satirarum scriptor; derisor*.
satisfaction, *satisfactio, expletio, voluptas* (= pleasure).
satisfactory, *idoneus*; adv. *bene, ex sententia*.
satisfy, *satisfacēre, placēre*; satisfied, *contentus*.
saturate; see soak.
satyr, *satyrus*.
sauce, *iūs (iūris*, n.), *condimentum*.
saucer, *patella*.
sauciness, *protervitas, procacitas*.
saucy, *protervus, procax*; adv. *proterve, procaciter*.
saunter, *ambulare, vagari, repēre*.
sausage, *tomaculum*.
savage, adj. *ferus, saevus, trux, atrox*; adv. *saeve, atrociter*.
savageness, *feritas, saevitia, atrocitas*.
save, prep. and conj.; see except.
save, v.: = preserve, (con)*servare, tuēri*; = rescue, *liberare, eripēre, servare*; to — up, *reservare, parcēre*.
saving, subst. *conservatio, compendium*.
saving, adj. *parcus*.
savings, *peculium*.
saviour, (con)*servator* (with f. *servatrix*); *liberator*.
savour, subst. *sapor*.
savour, v. *sapēre*.
savoury, adj. *conditus*.
saw: = saying, *dictum, proverbium*; the tool, *serra*.
saw, v. *serrā secare*.
sawdust, *scobis*.
say, *dicēre, loqui, narrare*; to — that not, *negare*.
saying, subst. *dictio*; = thing said, *dictum, verbum*.
scabbard, *vagina*.
scaffold; see execution.
scaffolding, *machina, pegma*.
scale, subst.: of a fish, *squama*; of a balance, *lanx*; a pair of —s, *libra, trutina*; = gradation, *gradus (-ūs)*.
scale, v. = climb, *ascendēre, conscendēre*.
scaling-ladder, *scalae (-arum)*.
scalp, *cutis capitis*.
scaly, *squameus, squamosus*.
scamp; see knave.
scamper: see hurry.
scan, = examine, *inspicēre,* (per)*scrutari, contemplari*; metrically, *metiri*.
scandal; see disgrace, slander.
scandalize, *offendēre*.
scandalous, *pessimi exempli, probrosus, turpis*.
scantiness, *exiguitas*.
scanty, *exiguus, parvus, tenuis*; adv. *exigue*.
scar, *cicatrix*.
scarce, *rarus*; adv. *vix, aegre*.

scarcity, *paucitas, raritas, inopia*.
scare, *terrēre*.
scarecrow, *formido*.
scarf, *fascia*.
scarlet: subst. *coccum*; adj. *coccineus* or *coccinus*.
scathe; see harm.
scatheless, *salvus, incolumis*.
scathing (of words), *aculeatus, acerbus*.
scatter, v.: transit., *spargēre, dispergēre*; of troops, *dissipare, fundēre*; intransit., *dilabi, diffugēre*.
scene: = stage, *scaena*; = place, *locus*; = spectacle, *prospectus (-ūs), spectaculum*.
scenery: in a theatre, *apparatus (-ūs) scaenae*; natural —, *loca (-orum)*.
scent, subst.: = sense of smell, *odoratus (-ūs)*; = odour, *odor*; = perfume, *unguentum*.
scent, v.: = detect by —, *odorari*; = perfume, *odorare, odoribus perfundēre*.
scented, adj. *odoratus*.
sceptic, sceptical; render by verb *dubitare*.
sceptre, *sceptrum*.
scheme, subst. *consilium, ratio*.
scholar: = pupil, *discipulus*; = man of learning, *vir doctus* or *litteratus*.
scholarly, *doctus, litteratus, eruditus*.
scholarship, *litterae (-arum), doctrina, eruditio*.
school, subst. *ludus* (litterarum), *schola*.
school, v. *docēre*.
school-fellow, *condiscipulus*.
school-master,   **school-mistress**, *magister, magistra*.
science, *scientia, ars, doctrina, disciplina*; natural —, *physica, rerum naturae scientia*.
scientific, *physicus*; — principles, *artis praecepta*; adv. *physice, ratione*.
scientist, *physicus*.
scimitar, *acinaces*.
scintillate, *scintillare*.
scintillation, *scintilla* (= spark).
scion, *progenies*.
scissors, *forfices (-um)*.
scoff, v.: to — at, *inridēre, ludibrio habēre*; to be —ed at, *ludibrio esse*.
scoffer, *inrisor*.
scoffing, subst. *inrisio, inrisus (-ūs)*.
scold, v. *obiurgare, increpare, conviciari*.
scolding, subst. *obiurgatio, convicium*.
scoop, v.: to — out, (ex)*cavare*.
scope, = free play, *campus, area*.
scorch, *amburēre, adurēre, torrēre*.
scorched, *torridus*.
score, subst.: = account, *ratio, nomen*; = total, *summa*; = 20, *viginti*.
score, v.: = mark, *notare, signare*; = obtain, q.v.
scorn, subst. *contemptus (-ūs), fastidium*.
scorn, v. *contemnēre, fastidire, spernēre*.
scorner, *contemptor*.
scornful, *fastidiosus*; adv. *fastidiose, contemptim*.
scorpion, *scorpio, nepa*.
scot; = -free, *immunis*.
Scotland, *Caledonia*.
Scottish, *Caledonius*.
scoundrel, *homo nefarius* or *nequam*.

scour, (*de*)*tergēre,* (*ex*)*purgare;* to — the land, *agrum pervagari, percurrēre.*

scourge, subst. *flagrum, flagellum.* Transf., *pestis.*

scourge, v. *virgis caedēre, verberare.*

scourging, subst. *verbera* (*-um*).

scout, subst. *explorator, speculator.*

scout, v. *explorare, speculari.*

scowl, v. *frontem contrahēre.*

scramble, v.; to — up, *scandēre, escendēre.*

scrap, *frustum, fragmentum.*

scrape, subst. *angustiae* (*-arum*), *difficultas.*

scrape, v. *radēre:* to — off, *abradēre;* to — together, *corradēre.*

scraper, (for flesh) *strigil, strigilis.*

scratch, v. *scabēre, radēre;* to — out, *delēre.*

scream, subst. *vociferatio, ululatus* (*-ūs*).

scream, v. *clamitare, vociferari, ululare.*

screech, v. *ululare.*

screeching, subst. *ululatus* (*-ūs*)

screen, *umbraculum.*

screen, v. (*pro*)*tegēre, tueri, defendēre.*

screw, subst. *clavus* (= nail).

scribe, *scriba, librarius.*

scroll, *volumen.*

scrub, (*de*)*tergēre.*

scruple, *religio, scrupulus.*

scruple, v. *dubitare.*

scrupulous, *religiosus;* adv. *religiose.*

scrutinize, (*per*)*scrutari.*

scrutiny, (*per*)*scrutatio.*

scuffle, *rixa, turba.*

scull, subst., = oar, *remus.*

scull, v. *remigare.*

sculptor, *sculptor.*

sculpture, subst.: the art, *ars fingendi, sculptura;* a work of —, *opus* (*-eris,* n.) or *signum* (= statue).

sculpture, v. *sculpēre.*

scum, *spuma.* Transf., *faex, sentina.*

scurrilous, *contumeliosus, probrosus, scurrilis;* adv. *contumeliose.*

scutcheon, *insigne* (or in plur.).

scythe, *falx.*

sea, subst. *mare, pelagus* (*-i,* n.), *aequor* (poet.), *pontus* (poet.), *altum* (= 'the deep'); on the —, of the —, adj. *maritimus, marinus.*

sea-gull, *gavia.*

seal, subst.: on a letter, *signum;* the animal, *phoca.*

seal, v. (*con*)*signare, obsignare.*

sealing-wax, *cera.*

seam, *sutura.*

seaman, *nauta.*

seamanship, *ars navigandi.*

sear, v. (*ad*)*urēre.*

search, subst. *investigatio, inquisitio.*

search, v.: to — a place, *investigare, explorare;* a person, *excutēre;* to — for, *quaerēre, exquirēre, petēre.*

seasickness, *nausea.*

season, subst., *tempus, tempestas, hora;* in due —, *tempore, ad tempus;* for a —, *in tempus.*

season, v.: = flavour, *condire;* = harden, *durare.*

seasonable, *tempestivus, opportunus;* adv. *tempore, tempestive, opportune.*

seasoning, *condimentum.*

seat, subst. *sedes, sella;* a row of —s, *subsellium;* = abode, dwelling, *domicilium, sedes.*

seat, v. *ponēre, conlocare.*

seaweed, *alga.*

secede, *abire, decedēre, secedēre.*

secession, *secessio.*

seclude, *secludēre, segregare, removēre.*

secluded, *secretus, seclusus.*

seclusion, *solitudo.*

second, subst., of time, *momentum* (*temporis*).

second, adj. *secundus, alter;* for the — time, *iterum.* Adv. *secundo, deinde.*

second, v., = support, *adesse, auxilio esse, suffragari* (all with dat.).

secondary, *secundarius, inferior.*

seconder, *suasor, auctor.*

second-rate, *inferior.*

secrecy, *secretum.*

secret, subst. *res occulta* or *arcana;* in —, *clam.*

secret, adj. *occultus, arcanus, secretus;* = underhand, *clandestinus, furtivus.* Adv. *clam, in occulto, occulte, furtim.*

secretary, *scriba, servus a manu.*

secrete, *celare, occultare, abdēre.*

sect, *secta, schola.*

section, *pars, portio.*

secure, = carefree, *securus;* = safe, *tutus;* adv. *tuto.*

secure, v.: = make safe, *munire, confirmare;* = arrest, *comprehendēre.*

security: = safety, *salūs* (*-ūtis,* f.); = pledge, *pignus* (*-eris,* n.), *cautio, vadimonium* (= bail).

sedan, *lectica.*

sedate, *sedatus, gravis;* adv. *sedate, graviter.*

sedentary, render by *sedēre.*

sedge, *ulva.*

sediment, *faex, sedimentum.*

sedition, *seditio, motus* (*-ūs*).

seditious, *seditiosus, turbulentus;* adv. *seditiose.*

seduce, *corrumpēre.*

seducer, *corruptor, corruptela.*

seduction, *corruptela, stuprum.*

sedulity, *sedulitas, assiduitas, diligentia.*

sedulous, *sedulus, assiduus, diligens;* adv. *sedulo, assidue, diligenter.*

see, *vidēre, cernēre conspicēre* (= catch sight of), *aspicēre* (= look at), *spectare* (= watch); to go to —, *visēre, visitare;* = to understand, *vidēre, intellegēre;* to — to, *curare, providēre.*

seed, *semen.*

seed-time, *sementis.*

seedling, *arbor novella.*

seek, *quaerēre, exquirēre,* (*ex*)*petēre;* — to do, = endeavour, *conari, tendēre.*

seem, *vidēri;* to — good, *vidēri.*

seeming, adj. *fictus, falsus;* adv. *in speciem, ut videtur.*

seemliness, *decorum.*

seemly, *decorus, honestus;* it is —, *decet, convenit.*

seer, *vates.*

seethe, v.: transit., *fervefacēre, coquēre;* intransit., *fervēre, aestuare.*

segregate, *segregare, seponĕre, seiungĕre.*

Seine, river, *Sequana.*

seize, *(ap)prehendĕre, rapĕre, corripĕre, occupare.*

seldom, *raro.*

select, adj. *(e)lectus, delectus, exquisitus.*

select, v. *legĕre, eligĕre, deligĕre.*

selection, *electio, delectus (-ūs);* = things chosen, *res selectae.*

self: emphatic, *ipse;* reflexive, render by personal pronoun with *ipse* (third person *se* or *sese);* by one—, *solus;* beside one—, *mente captus;* in it—, *per se.*

self-confidence, *fiducia sui.*

self-confident, *confidens.*

self-control, *imperium sui, continentia, temperantia.*

self-evident, *manifestus, apertus.*

self-indulgence, *intemperantia.*

self-indulgent, *impotens sui, intemperans.*

self-love, *amor sui.*

self-satisfied, to be, *sibi placēre.*

self-seeking, *cupiditas.*

self-willed, *pertinax, pervicax.*

selfish, to be, *sibi (soli) consulĕre.*

sell, *vendĕre, venum dare;* to try to —, *venditare;* to be sold, *venire.*

seller, *venditor, institor, propola.*

semblance, *species, imago.*

senate, *senatus (-ūs);* = house, *curia.*

senator, *senator.*

senatorial, *senatorius.*

send, *mittĕre;* — away, *relegare, dimittĕre;* — for, *accessĕre, accire;* — forward, *praemittĕre.*

senior, = older, *(natu) grandior* or *maior.*

sensation, *sensus (-ūs);* a — of pain, *dolor;* = excitement, *(animi) commotio;* to create a —, *admirationem movēre.*

sensational, *mirificus, mirus;* adv. *mirifice, mire.*

sense: = sensation, feeling, *sensus (-ūs);* = understanding, intelligence, *iudicium, prudentia;* out of one's —s, *mentis compos;* = meaning (of a word), *vis, significatio, sententia.*

senseless; = unconscious, *(omni) sensu carens;* = foolish, *rationis expers.*

sensible, = intelligent, *prudens;* adv. *prudenter.*

sensitive, *patibilis, sensilis;* emotionally, *mollis.*

sensual, *libidinosus.*

sensuality, *libido.*

sentence, subst. *sententia, enuntiatio;* in court, *iudicium, decretum, sententia.*

sentence, v. *damnare, condemnare.*

sentiment : = opinion, *sententia, opinio;* = feeling, *sensus (-ūs), animus.*

sentimental, *mollis, effeminatus.*

sentimentality, *mollitia (animi).*

sentinel, sentry, *excubitor, vigil;* —s, plur., *stationes, vigiliae, excubiae.*

separable, *separabilis, dividuus.*

separate, adj. *separatus, secretus, disiunctus.* Adv. *separatim, singuli* (adj., = one by one).

separate, v. *separare, seiungĕre, dividĕre.*

separation, *separatio, disiunctio.*

September, *(mensis) September.*

sepulchral, *sepulcralis, feralis.*

sepulchre, *sepulcrum.*

sequel, *eventus (-ūs), exitus (-ūs).*

sequence, *ordo, series.*

serene, *serenus, tranquillus.*

serf, *servus.*

serious: of persons, *gravis, severus;* of things, *serius, gravis, magni momenti.* Adv. *serio, graviter.*

seriousness, *gravitas. severitas, tristitia.*

serpent, *serpens, anguis.*

serried, *densus, confertus.*

servant, *servus, famulus, puer* (= boy), *ancilla* (= maid).

serve, *servire, praesto esse;* at table, *famulari, ministrare;* to — up food, *apponĕre;* as a soldier, *(stipendia) merēre, militare.*

service, *opera, ministerium;* = a helpful action, *officium;* — in the army, *militia, stipendia (-orum).*

serviceable, *utilis, opportunus, aptus.*

servile, *servilis.* Transf., *humilis, abiectus.*

servility, *adulatio.*

servitude, *servitus (-ūtis), servitium.*

session, *conventus (-ūs).*

set, subst.; see company, collection.

set, adj. *status, constitutus.*

set, v.: transit. *ponĕre, statuĕre, (con)locare;* — apart, *secernĕre, seponĕre;* — forth, *exponĕre;* — over, *praeficĕre;* — up, *statuĕre, constituĕre;* intransit., of sun, etc., *occidĕre;* to — out, *proficisci.*

setting, subst., of sun, etc., *occasus (-ūs).*

settle, v.: transit., *conlocare, constituĕre, statuĕre, componĕre;* — accounts, *rationes putare* or *conficĕre;* — a debt, *solvĕre, expedire;* intransit., *(con)sidĕre, se conlocare.*

settlement, *constitutio, compositio, pactum;* of a colony, *deductio.*

settler, *advena, colonus.*

seven, septem: — at a time, — each, *septeni;* — times, *septie(n)s.*

seven hundred, *septingenti.*

seventeen, *septemdecim (septen-);* — at a time, — each, *septeni deni;* — times, *septie(n)s decie(n)s.*

seventeenth, *septimus decimus.*

seventh, *septimus.*

seventieth, *septuagesimus.*

seventy, septuaginta: — at a time, — each, *septuageni;* — times, *septuagie(n)s.*

sever, *dividĕre, dirimĕre, disiungĕre.*

several: = some, *nonnulli, (com)plures, aliquot;* = respective, *suus, proprius;* adv. *singillatim.*

severe, *severus, austerus, gravis;* adv. *severe, austere;* —ly wounded, *graviter ictus.*

severity, *severitas, gravitas.*

Seville, *Hispalis.*

sew, *suĕre.*

sewer, *cloaca.*

sex, *sexus (-ūs).*

shabbiness, *sordes (-ium).*

shabby, *obsoletus.* Transf., *sordidus turpis.* Adv. *obsolete; sordide.*

shackle, v. *constringĕre, vincire.*

shackles, *vincula, catenae, compedes (-um).*

shade, subst. *umbra;* living in —, *umbratilis;* = disembodied spirit, *umbra, simulacrum;* in plur., *manes.*

shade, v. *opacare, (in)umbrare.*

shadow, *umbra.*

shadowy, *vanus, inanis.*

shady, *umbrosus, opacus.*

shaft: = arrow, *sagitta;* = handle, *hastile;* of a carriage, *temo;* — of a mine, *puteus.*

shake, v.: transit., *quatĕre, concutĕre, agitare, vibrare;* to — hands, *iungĕre dextras;* to — off, *excutĕre;* intransit., *agitari, tremĕre.*

shaking, subst., *quassatio* (act.), *tremor* (pass.).

shallow, subst. *vadum.*

shallow, adj. *humilis, vadosus.* Transf., *levis.*

sham, subst. *fallacia, dolus, fraus.*

sham, adj. *fictus, falsus, simulatus.*

sham, v. *simulare.*

shambles, *laniena, strages* (= massacre).

shame, subst.: = modesty, *pudor, verecundia;* = disgrace, *dedecus* (-*oris,* n.), *ignominia, infamia;* shame! *pro pudor!*

shame, v. *pudorem adferre.*

shameful, *turpis, foedus, inhonestus;* adv. *turpiter, foede, inhoneste.*

shameless, *impudens, inverecundus;* adv. *impudenter.*

shamelessness, *impudentia.*

shank, *crūs (crūris, n.).*

shape, subst. *forma, figura, species.*

shape, v. *(con)formare, figurare, fingĕre.*

shapeless, *informis.*

shapely, *formosus.*

share, subst. *pars, portio, sors;* of a plough, *vomer.*

share, v. *partiri, communicare.*

sharer, *particeps, socius, consors.*

shark, *pistrix.*

sharp, *acutus;* = bitter, *acer, acerbus;* = acute, keen, *acer, acutus, sagax.* Adv. *acriter, acute, acerbe* (= bitterly).

sharpness, *acerbitas* (= bitterness); of intellect, *(ingenii) acumen.*

shatter, *frangĕre, confringĕre.*

shave, *(caput,* etc.) *(ab)radĕre, tondĕre.*

shavings, *scobis.*

shawl; see mantle.

she, when emphatic, *illa, ea, ista, haec.*

sheaf, *merges.*

shear, *tondĕre.*

shearing, subst. *tonsura.*

shears, *forfex.*

sheath, *vagina.*

sheathe, *in vaginam recondĕre.*

shed, subst. *tugurium;* milit., *pluteus, vinea.*

shedding, subst. *effusio;* of tears, *fletus (-ūs).*

sheep, *ovis, bidens.*

sheep-fold, *ovile.*

sheepish, *insulsus.*

sheer: = steep, *abruptus, praeruptus;* = pure, *merus.*

sheet, *lodix* (= blanket); of paper,

scheda; of metal, *lamina;* of a **sail,** *pes.*

shelf, *pluteus, pegma (-atis,* n.).

shell, subst.: of fish, *testa, concha;* of nuts, *putamen, cortex.*

shell-fish, *concha, conchylium.*

shelter, subst. *perfugium, asylum, receptaculum.*

shelter, v.: transit., *(pro)tegĕre, de-fendĕre, tutari;* intransit., *latĕre.*

shelving, *declivis, proclivis.*

shepherd, *pastor, upilio;* of a —, adj., *pastoralis, pastoricius.*

shield, subst. *scutum, clipeus, parma.*

shield, v. *(scuto) defendĕre, (pro)tegĕre.*

shift, subst. = expedient, *ratio, con-silium, dolus* (= trick).

shift, v., = change, *(per)mutare.*

shifty, *versutus, varius.*

shin, *crūs (crūris,* n.), *tibia.*

shine, *lucēre, fulgēre, splendēre, nitēre.*

ship, subst. *navis, navigium* (smaller); war- —, *navis longa;* flag- —, *navis praetoria;* merchant- —, *navis oner-aria;* of a —, adj., *navalis, nauticus.*

ship, v. *in navem imponĕre.*

shipwreck, *naufragium;* —ed, adj., *naufragus.*

shirk, *dētrectare, subterfūgĕre.*

shirt, *subucula, tunica.*

shiver, v. *horrēre, tremĕre* (= tremble), *algēre* (= be cold).

shoal = shallow, *vadum.*

shock, subst.: physical, *impetus (-ūs);* mental, *stupor, offensio.*

shock, v. *perturbare, offendĕre.*

shocking, *indignus, turpis.*

shoe, *calceus, solea* (= slipper).

shoe-maker, *sutor.*

shoot, subst. *surculus, planta, virga.*

shoot, v.; transit., *iaculari, (e)mittĕre, iacĕre;* to — at, *telo petĕre;* intransit., *volare.*

shooting-star; see meteor.

shop, *taberna;* work- —, *officina.*

shopkeeper, *tabernarii* (-*orum,* plur. only).

shore, *litus (-oris,* n.), *ora.*

short, *brevis;* — of stature, *humilis;* — cut, *via compendiaria;* in —, *denique, ad summam, ne multa;* to fall — of, *non attingĕre.* Adv.: = briefly, *breviter;* = in a short time, *brevi, mox.*

shortness, *brevitas, exiguitas.*

short-sighted, *lusciosus.* Transf., *im-providus.*

shot, *(telum) missile, glans* (= bullet).

shoulder, subst. *humerus;* — -blades, *scapulae.*

shoulder, v. *in humeros tollĕre.*

shout, shouting, subst. *clamor, voci-feratio.*

shout, v. *(con)clamare, vociferari.*

shove, v. *trudĕre, impellĕre.*

shovel, subst. *pala, batillum.*

show, subst.: = exhibition, *specta-culum, ludi (-orum);* = display, *osten-tatio;* = (mere) appearance, *species.*

show, v.: = point out, *(de)monstrare;* = display, *exhibit, ostendĕre, ostentare.*

shower, subst. *imber, pluvia.*

shower, v. *effundĕre.*

showy, *speciosus, magnificus.*

shred, *frustum.*

shrew, *oblatratrix, mulier importuna.*

shrewd, *acutus, perspicax, sagax;* adv. *acute, sagaciter.*

shrewdness, (*ingenii*) *acumen* or *acies; sagacitas.*

shriek, subst. *ululatus* (-*ūs*), *clamor.*

shriek, v. *ululare, clamare.*

shrill, *acutus, argutus;* adv. *acute.*

shrine, *aedicula, delubrum, sacellum.*

shrink; transit., *contrahēre;* intransit., *se contrahēre;* to — from, *refugēre, abhorrēre.*

shrivelled, *rugosus, vietus* (=shrivelled).

shroud, v. *involvēre, velare, tegēre.*

shrub, *frutex.*

shrubbery, *arbustum.*

shudder, subst. *horror, tremor.*

shudder, v. *horrēre, tremēre.*

shuffle, *claudicare* (= limp), *tergiversari* (= be evasive).

shuffling, subst. *tergiversatio.*

shun, (*de*)*fugēre, vitare, declinare.*

shutter, *foricula, valvae* (-*arum*, plur.).

shuttle, *radius.*

shy, adj. *timidus, verecundus;* adv. *timide, verecunde.*

shy, v., of a horse, *consternari.*

shyness, *timor, verecundia, pudor.*

Sicily, *Sicilia.*

sick, *aeger, aegrotus;* to be —, *aegrotare* (= to vomit, *vomēre*); to feel —, *nauseare.* Transf., of boredom, render by *taedet.*

sickle, *falx.*

sickly, *infirmus.*

sickness; = nausea, *vomitus* (-*ūs*), *nausea;* = illness, *morbus aegrotatio.*

side, subst. *latus* (-*eris*, n.), *pars* (= part or faction); on this —, *hinc;* on this — of, *citra, cis;* on (or from) all —s, *undique;* on both —s, *utrinque.*

side, adj. *obliquus, transversus.*

side, v.: to — with, (*ab homine*) *stare;* (*homini*) *favēre* or *studēre.*

sideboard, *abacus.*

sidelong, *obliquus, transversus, limus.*

sideways, *oblique;* or use *obliquus* as adj.

siege, *oppugnatio* (= attack), *obsidio* (= blockade).

sieve, *cribrum.*

sift, *cribrare.* Transf., *investigare.*

sigh, subst. *suspirium.*

sigh, v. *suspirare, suspiria ducēre.*

sight, subst. *visus* (-*ūs*), *aspectus* (-*ūs*); to catch — of, *conspicēre, conspicari;* = view, range of —, *conspectus* (-*ūs*); = thing seen, *species, facies, spectaculum.*

sign, subst. *signum, indicium, vestigium* (= foot-mark), *insigne* (= badge); a good —, *omen faustum;* a bad —, *omen sinistrum.*

sign, v.: to — a document, (*con*)*signare, subscribēre;* see also signal.

signal, subst. *signum;* to give a —, *signum dare.*

signal, adj. *insignis, maximus, egregius;* adv. *insigniter, egregie.*

signal, v. *significare, signum dare.*

signalize, v. *insignire.*

signature, *nomen* (*subscriptum*).

signet, *signum* (= seal).

significance, *significatio, vis.*

significant: see expressive.

signify, *significare;* of words, *valēre.*

silence, subst. *silentium;* to keep —, *tacēre, silēre.*

silence, v. *in silentium redigēre, comprimēre, confutare.*

silent, *silens, tacitus, mutus;* to be —, *silēre* (= make no noise), *tacēre* (= not speak). Adv. *tacite, silentio.*

silk, *bombyx, vestis serica.*

silken, *sericus, bombycinus.*

silk-worm, *bombyx.*

sill, *limen inferum.*

silliness, *stultitia, fatuitas, infacetiae* (-*arum*).

silly, *stuitus, fatuus, infacetus.*

silt, subst. *limus.*

silver, subst. *argentum;* adorned with —, *argentatus.*

silver, silvery, adj. *argenteus;* — mine, *argenti metalla* (-*orum*).

silver, silvery, adj. *argenteus.*

silver, v. *argento inducēre.*

similar, *similis, par;* adv. *similiter, pariter.*

similarity, *similitudo.*

simile, *similitudo, translatio.*

similitude, *similitudo.*

simmer, *fervescēre, lente fervēre.*

simper, v. *subridēre, inepte ridēre.*

simple, *simplex; sincerus* (= guileless), *inconditus* (= artless), *ineptus* (= silly); adv. *simpliciter.*

simplicity, *simplicitas, natura simplex; stultitia* (= folly).

simplify, *simplicem reddēre.*

simulate, *simulare.*

simulation, *simulatio.*

simultaneously, *eodem tempore, simul, una.*

sin, subst. *peccatum, delictum, nefas.*

sin, v. *peccare, delinquēre.*

since, adv. *postea, abhinc;* long —, *iamdudum, iampridem.*

since, prep. *ex, ab, post;* — the foundation of the city, *post urbem conditam.*

since, conj.: of time, *cum, postquam, ex quo* (*tempore*); causal, *cum, quandoquidem, quia, quoniam.*

sincere, *sincerus, simplex, candidus, verus;* adv. *sincere, ex animo, simpliciter.*

sincerity, *animus sincerus, veritas, simplicitas.*

sinew, *nervus.*

sinewy, *nervosus.*

sinful, *impius, improbus, pravus, malus.*

sing, *canere, cantare, modulari.*

singe, *amburēre, adurēre.*

singer, *cantor, cantator.*

singing, subst. *cantus* (-*ūs*), *concentus* (-*ūs*).

single, adj. *unus, solus, unicus, singularis;* = unmarried, *caelebs;* not a — one, *ne unus quidem.* Adv. *singillatim, viritim;* or adj. *singuli* (= one by one).

singular: opp. to plural, *singularis;* = outstanding, *singularis, unicus,* *egregius, maximus*; = strange, *mirus, mirabilis.* Adv. *singulariter, unice, egregie, maxime, mire, mirabiliter.*

sinister, *sinister; infaustus* (= unlucky), *pravus* (= wrong).

sink, v.: transit., *(sub)mergĕre, demergĕre, deprimĕre;* intransit. *(con)-sīdĕre, desīdĕre, submergi, demeǝgi;* of prices, courage, etc., *cadĕre.*

sinuous, *sinuosus.*

sip, v. *(primis labris) degustare.*

sir, in addresses, *bone vir, vir optime.*

sire, *pater, genitor.*

sister, *soror, germana.*

sit, v.: transit., to — a horse, *in equo haerēre;* intransit., *sedēre;* to — down, *consīdĕre, adsīdĕre;* of a court, *habĕri.*

site, *situs (-ūs).*

sitting, subst. *sessio, consessus (-ūs).*

situated, *situs, positus, conlocatus.*

situation: *situs (-ūs), locus;* = state of affairs, *(rerum) status (-ūs);* = office, *munus (-eris, n.).*

six, *sex;* — at a time, — each, *seni;* — times, *sexie(n)s.*

sixteen, *sedecim;* — at a time, — each, *seni deni;* — times, *sedecie(n)s.*

sixteenth, *sextus decimus.*

sixth, *sextus;* for the — time, *sextum.*

sixtieth, *sexagesimus.*

sixty, *sexaginta;* — at a time, — each, *sexageni;* — times *sexagie(n)s.*

size: *magnitudo, amplitudo;* = glue, *gluten.*

skeleton, *ossa (-ium, n.), ossium compages.*

sketch, subst. *adumbratio, descriptio.*

sketch, v. *describĕre, designare, adum-brare.*

skiff, *scapha, cymba, navicula.*

skilful, *sollers, peritus, callidus;* adv. *sollerter, perite, callide.*

skill, *sollertia, peritia, ars, calliditas.*

skim, *despumare, spumam eximĕre;* to — over a thing, *perstringĕre, percurrĕre, transcurrĕre.*

skin, subst. *cutis, pellis, membrana* (thin).

skin, v. *pellem or corium detrahĕre.*

skip, *salire* (= leap); to — for joy, *exsultare;* = pass over, *transilire, praeterire.*

skipper, *navis magister.*

skirmish, subst. *proelium.*

skirmisher, *veles.*

skirt, v. *tangĕre;* — the coast, *oram legĕre.*

skittish, *protervus;* to be —, *lascivire;* adv. *proterve.*

skittishness, *protervitas, lascivia.*

skulk, *latēre, delitescĕre.*

skull, *caput.*

sky, *caelum;* under the open —, *sub divo.*

slack: = loose, *laxus, remissus;* = careless, *remissus, segnis, neglegens;* adv. *laxe, neglegenter.*

slacken, v.: transit., *(re)laxare. remittĕre;* intransit., *laxari, remitti.*

slackness, *remissio, neglegentia.*

slake, v., of thirst, *restinguĕre, ex-stinguĕre, explēre.*

slander, subst. *calumnia, (falsa) crimin-atio.*

slander, v. *calumniarı. criminari, obtrectare.*

slanderer, *obtrectator.*

slanderous, *maledicus, famosus;* adv. *falso, per calumniam.*

slanting, *obliquus, transversus.*

slash, v. *caedĕre, incidĕre;* see cut.

slate: for writing, *tabula;* = tile, *tegula.*

slaughter, subst. *caedes, occidio, strages.*

slaughterer, *lanius.*

slaughterhouse, *laniena.*

slave, subst. *servus, ancilla* (female), *verna* (home-born); *famulus;* fellow——, *conservus;* of a —, adj., *servilis;* to be a —, *servire.*

slave-dealer, *venalicius, mango.*

slavery, *servitūs (-ūtis), servitium.*

slavish, *servilis;* adv. *serviliter.*

slay, *interficĕre, occidĕre, necare.*

slayer, *interfector;* of a man, *homicida;* of a close relative, *parricida.*

sledge, *trahea.*

sleek, *lēvis, nitidus* (= shining); to be —, *nitēre.*

sleep, subst. *somnus, sopor;* want of —, *vigilia.*

sleep, v. *dormire.*

sleepiness, *veternus, somni cupido.*

sleepless, *insomnis, vigilans.*

sleeplessness, *insomia, vigilia.*

sleepy, *semisomnus, somniculosus, somno gravis.*

sleet, *nix grandine mixta.*

sleeves, *manicae (-arum).*

slender, *tenuis, gracilis, exilis.*

slenderness, *tenuitas, gracilitas.*

slice, v. *concīdĕre, secare.*

slide, v. *labi.*

slight, adj. *levis, tenuis, exiguus.*

slight, v. *neglegĕre, contemnĕre.*

slim, *exilis.*

slime, *limus.*

slimy, *limosus.*

sling, subst.: the weapon, *funda;* for the arm, *fascia.*

sling, v. *(fundā) mittĕre, torquēre.*

slink, v.: to — away, *sese subducĕre.*

slip, subst. *lapsus (-ūs), culpa* (= fault), *error* (= mistake); of a plant, *surculus.*

slip, v. *labi;* — away, *se subducĕre, elabi;* to let —, *amittĕre, omittĕre.*

slipper, *crepida, solea.*

slippery, *lubricus.*

slit, subst. *rima.*

slit, v. *incidĕre, findĕre, scindĕre.*

slope, subst. *clivus, fastigium;* upward. *acclivitas;* downward, *declivitas.*

slope, v. *vergĕre.*

sloping, *acclivis, declivis, pronus.*

sloth, *inertia, segnitia, desidia, ignavia.*

slothful, *iners, segnis, ignavus;* adv. *segniter, ignave.*

slough, *palūs (-ūdis);* of a snake, *vernatio, exuviae (-arum).*

slovenliness, *sordes (-ium), neglegentia.*

slovenly, *sordidus, discinctus, neglegens.*

slow, *tardus, lentus;* adv. *tarde, lente, sensim* (= gradually).

slowness, *tarditas, segnitas, pigritia.*

slug, *limax.*

sluggish, *segnis, piger, ignavus*; adv. *segniter, ignave.*

sluggishness, *pigritia, ignavia, inertia.*

sluice, *emissarium.*

slumber; see sleep

slur; see disgrace.

slur over, v. *extenuare.*

sly, *vafer, subdolus*; adv. *vafre, subdole.*

slyness, *dolus, astutia.*

smack, subst.: = flavour, *sapor, gustus (-ūs)*; = blow, *alapa*; = small ship, *lemunculus*; fishing-—, *horia.*

smack, v.; to — of, *sapĕre, (red)olēre.*

small, *parvus, parvulus, exiguus, minutus*; a — mind, *animus pusillus*; so —, *tantulus*; how —? *quantulus?*

smallness, *parvitas, exiguitas.*

smart, subst. *dolor, cruciatus (-ūs).*

smart, v. = to feel pain, *dolere, plecti.*

smart, adj.: = active, *acer, alacer*; = witty, *salsus*; = elegant, *lautus, mundus, nitidus.*

smear, v. *(in)linĕre, oblinĕre.*

smell, subst. *odor, odoratus (-ūs*; = the sense), to have a bad —, *male olēre.*

smell, v.: = perceive a —, *olfacĕre*; = give off a smell, *olēre*; to — of, *redolēre.*

smelt, *fundĕre, coquĕre.*

smile, subst. *risus (-ūs)*; with a —, *subridens.*

smile, v. *(sub)ridēre, renidēre.*

smite, v. *ferire, percutĕre.*

smith, *faber*; black—, *faber ferrarius.*

smithy, *officina, fabrica.*

smoke, subst. *fumus.*

smoke, v. *fumare.*

smoky, *fumosus.*

smooth, adj. *levis, teres*; of style, *lenis*; of manner, *blandus*; of temper, *aequus.* Adv. *leniter.*

smoothness, *levitas, aequabilitas.*

smother, *suffocare, animam intercludĕre.* Transf., *opprimĕre, comprimĕre.*

smuts, *fuligo.*

snail, *cochlea.*

snake, *anguis, serpens, vipera.*

snaky, *vipereus, anguineus.*

snap, v.: transit., = break, *frangĕre*; — the fingers, *digitis concrepare*; — up, *adripĕre, corripĕre*; intransit., *dissilire, frangi.*

snappish, *morosus, difficilis, mordax.*

snare, subst. *laqueus, plaga, insidiae (-arum).*

snare, v. *inlaqueare.*

snarl, subst. *gannitus (-ūs).*

snarl, v. *(og)gannire, (sub)ringi.*

snatch, *rapĕre, corripĕre*; — at, *captare*; — away, *eripĕre, avellĕre.*

sneak, = go stealthily, *(cor)repĕre*; — in, *inrepĕre*; — away, *(furtim) se subducĕre.*

sneer, subst., *rhonchus.*

sneer, v. *deridēre, inridēre*

sneeze, *sternuĕre.*

sneezing, *sternumentum.*

snore, *stertĕre.*

snort, v. *fremĕre.*

snout, *rostrum.*

sn.̣.̇, subst. *nix.*

snow, v.: it —s, *ningit.*

snowy, *nivosus, niveus.*

snub; see rebuke.

snub-nosed, *silus, simus.*

snuff, of a candle, *fungus.*

so: adv., = thus, *sic, ita*; = to such an extent, *sic, ita, adeo, tam*; so . . . as, *tam . . . quam*; so that (final), *ut*; so great, *tantus*; so many, *tot*; so many times, *totie(n)s*; so far as, *quantum*; so long as, *dum (modo)*, with subjunc.; as conj., so, and so, *itaque, ergo, igitur.*

soak, *madefacĕre*; — up, *bibĕre*; — through, *permanare.*

soap, *sapo.*

soar, *sublime ferri, subvolare.*

sob, subst. *singultus (-ūs)*,

sob, v. *singultare.*

sober, *sobrius, temperans, temperatus*; adv. *sobrie, temperate.*

sobriety, *sobrietas, temperantia.*

sociable, *comis, facilis, socialis*; adv. *socialiter.*

social, *communis, civilis*; — life, *vitae societas, vita communis.*

socialism, *bona communia habēre.*

society, *homines (-um), hominum conventus (-ūs)*; more limited, *societas, sodalitas, conlegium, factio* (political); the — of an individual, *convictus (-ūs), consuetudo.*

sock; see stocking.

socket, *cavum.*

sod, *caespes.*

soda, *nitrum.*

sodden, *madidus.*

sofa, *lectulus, grabatus.*

soft, *mollis, tener, lenis, effeminatus*; adv. *molliter, leniter.*

soften, v.: transit., *(e)mollire, mitigare, lenire*; intransit., *molliri, mitescĕre.*

softness, *mollitia, mollities.*

soil, subst. *solum, terra, humus.*

soil, v. *inquinare, polluĕre, maculare.*

sojourn, subst. *commoratio, mansio.*

sojourn, v. *(com)morari, manēre.*

sojourner, *hospes, peregrinus, advena.*

solace, subst. *solatium, consolatio.*

solace, v. *(con)solari.*

solar, render by genit. *solis.*

soldier, *miles*; fellow —, *commilito*; foot —, *pedes*; horse —, *eques.*

soldierly, *militaris.*

soldiery, *milites (-um)*, or coll. sing. *miles.*

sole, subst.: of the foot, *solum, planta*; the fish, *solea.*

sole, adj. *solus, unus, unicus*; adv. *solum, tantum.*

solemn, *sanctus, religiosus*; see also serious. Adv. *sancte, graviter.*

solemnization, *celebratio.*

solemnize, *celebrare.*

solicit: = ask for, *petĕre, poscĕre, captare*; = incite, *sollicitare.*

solicitation, *preces (-um).*

solicitous, *sollicitus, anxius*; adv. *sollicite, anxie.*

solicitude, *sollicitudo, cura, anxietas.*

solid, *solidus, stabilis, firmus*; adv. *firme, firmiter.*

solidity, *soliditas.*

solitary, *solus, solitarius;* of places, *desertus.*

solitude, *solitudo.*

solstice: the summer —, *solstitium;* winter —, *bruma.*

solution, *(dis)solutio;* of problems, *explicatio.*

solve, *(dis)solvĕre, expedire, explicare.*

solvent; to be —, *solvendo esse.*

some, somebody, someone, *aliquis -quid,* pron., and *aliqui -qua -quod,* adj.; *quis, quid,* pron., and *qui, qua, quod,* adj. (indef., usually after *si, nisi, ne* or *num*); *nescioquis,* pron., and *nescioqui,* adj.; *nonnullus* (esp. plur., = — few); *aliquot* (plur., indecl.); distributively, — . . . others, *alii . . . alii;* to — degree, *aliquantum;* at — time, *aliquando.*

somehow, *nescio quomodo, nescio quo pacto.*

something, *aliquid, nonnihil.*

sometimes, *aliquando, nonnunquam, interdum.*

somewhat, *aliquantum, aliquantulum.*

somewhere, *alicubi.*

son, *filius, natus;* — -in-law, *gener;* step- —, *privignus.*

song, *carmen, cantus (-ūs), canticum.*

sonorous, *canorus, clarus;* adv. *canore, clare.*

soon, *mox, brevi (tempore), cito;* too —, *ante tempus;* as — as possible, *quam primum;* as — as, *simul ac.*

sooner, *maturius;* = for preference, *potius, libentius.*

soot, *fuligo.*

soothe, *mulcēre, lenire, placare, sedare.*

soothing, *blandus.*

soothsayer, *haruspex, hariolus, auspex.*

soothsaying, subst. *haruspicina, auspicium.*

sop, *frustum, offa (panis).*

sophism, sophistry, *captio, sophisma.*

sophistical, *captiosus.*

soporific, adj. *soporifer, soporus.*

sorcerer, *veneficus.*

sorceress, *venefica, maga, saga.*

sorcery, *ars magica.*

sordid, *sordidus, abiectus;* adv. *sordide.*

sordidness, *sordes (-ium).*

sore, subst. *ulcus (-eris,* n.).

sore, *adj.,* = painful, *gravis, acerbus;* adv. *graviter.*

sorrow, subst. *dolor, maestitia, tristitia, luctus (-ūs).*

sorrow, v. *dolēre, maerēre, lugēre.*

sorrowful, *tristis, maestus, lugubris;* adv. *maeste.*

sorry; see **sorrowful;** I am —, = I regret, *me paenitet;* = I pity, *me miseret.*

sort, subst., = kind, *genus;* of what —? *qualis? cuiusmodi?* of that —, *talis, eiusmodi;* he is not the — of man to, *non is est qui,* with subjunc.

sort, v. *digerĕre.*

sortie, *excursio, eruptio;* to make a —, *erumpĕre.*

sot, *potator, homo ebriosus.*

soul, *anima, animus* (rational or emotional); not a —, *nemo, ne unus quidem.*

sound, subst. *sonus, sonitus (-ūs), strepitus (-ūs).*

sound, adj. *sanus, integer;* safe and —, *incolumis, salvus;* of sleep, *altus, artus;* of arguments, *gravis.* Adv., of sleep, *arte;* of beating, etc., *graviter.*

soundness, *sanitas, integritas;* of arguments, *gravitas.*

sour, adj. *acerbus, amarus.*

sour, v. *exacerbare.*

source, *fons, caput, origo, principium.*

sourness, *acerbitas, amaritudo.*

south, subst. *meridies, regio meridiana.*

south, southern, adj. *meridianus, australis;* — wind, *auster;* — -west wind, *Africus.*

southwards, *in* or *ad meridiem.*

sovereign, subst. *rex, dominus, princeps.*

sovereign, adj. *sui iuris;* — remedy, *remedium efficacissimum.*

sovereignty, *summa imperii, (summum) imperium, dominatio, regnum.*

sow, subst. *sus.*

sow, v. *serĕre, semen spargĕre.*

sower, *sator.*

sowing, subst. *satio, satus (-ūs).*

space, *spatium, locus.*

spacious, *amplus.*

spaciousness, *amplitudo, laxitas.*

spade, *pala.*

Spain, *Hispania.*

span, subst., as measure, *palmus;* the — of life, *vitae summa.*

span, v.; see **measure;** of bridges, *iungĕre.*

spangled, *distinctus.*

Spanish, *Hispanus, Hispanicus, Hispaniensis.*

spar, subst. *asser, longurius.*

spare, v. *parcĕre* (with dat.).

sparing, *parcus;* adv. *parce.*

spark, *scintilla, igniculus.*

sparkle, v. *scintillare, fulgēre, nitēre.*

sparrow, *passer.*

spatter, *spargĕre, aspergĕre.*

speak, *dicĕre, loqui, fari;* — out, — up, *eloqui;* — to, *adfari, appellare, adloqui;* — together, *conloqui.*

speaker, *orator, is qui dicit.*

spear, subst. *hasta.*

spear, v. *hastā transfigĕre.*

special, *praecipuus, proprius, peculiaris;* adv. *praecipue, imprimis, praesertim.*

species, *genus (-eris,* n.), *species.*

specific, adj.: = peculiar, *proprius, peculiaris;* = explicit, *disertus;* adv. *diserte.*

specify, *denotare, enumerare.*

specimen, *specimen, documentum, exemplum.*

specious, *speciosus.*

speck, *macula.*

speckled, *maculis distinctus, maculatus.*

spectacle, *spectaculum.*

spectator, *spectator, is qui spectat.*

spectre; see **ghost.**

speculate, = consider, *cogitare, quaerĕre.*

speculation: = thought, *cogitatio;* scientific —, *rerum contemplatio;* = guess, *coniectura.*

speculative, = conjectural, *coniecturalis.*

speech, oratio; a — before the people, contio; to deliver a —, orationem (or contionem) habère.

speechless; see dumb.

speed, subst. celeritas, velocitas.

speed, v.: transit., maturare; ι = make prosperous, fortunare; intransit., = hasten, properare, festinare.

speedy, citus, celer, velox; adv. cito, celeriter, velociter.

spell, subst. carmen.

spellbound, defixus, stupens, stupefactus.

spend: of money, insumère; of time, agère, degère, consumère.

spendthrift, nepos, homo prodigus.

sphere, sphaera, globus; = field of activity, provincia.

spherical, globosus.

spice, condimentum.

spicy, conditus; fig. salsus.

spider, aranea; —'s web, aranea.

spike, clavus, cuspis.

spikenard, nardus.

spill, effundère.

spin, nère; — round, transit., versare, circumagère; intransit., use pass.; to — out, = prolong, ducère.

spindle, fusus.

spine, spina.

spinster, virgo, innupta.

spiral, adj. tortuosus.

spire, turris.

spirit: = character, animus, ingenium, indoles, natura; = animation, courage, animus, spiritus (-ūs), ferocia; a disembodied —, anima, plur. manes (-ium); = intention, meaning, consilium, sententia.

spirited, animosus, ferox, acer.

spiritless, ignavus.

spiritual, render by genit., animi or ingenii.

spit, subst. veru.

spit, v. spuère; — out, respuère.

spite, subst. malignitas, malevolentia, invidia, odium.

spite, v.; see vex, annoy.

spiteful, malignus, malevolus; adv. maligne.

splash, v. transit., aspergère.

splendid, splendidus, egregius, (prae)clarus; adv. splendide, (prae)clare.

splendour, splendor; apparatus (-ūs, = pomp).

splinter, fragmentum.

split, subst. fissura, scissura, rima.

split, v.: transit., (dif)findère, scindère; intransit., (dif)findi, dissilire.

spoil, subst. praeda; —s of war, spolia (-orum, plur.).

spoil, v.: — plunder, (ex)spoliare; = to injure, mar, corrumpère, perdère, vitiare.

spoiler, spoliator.

spoiling, spoliation, spoliatio.

spoke, radius.

spondee, spondeus.

sponge, subst. spongia.

sponsor, of measures, etc., auctor.

spontaneous, voluntarius; adv. (sua) sponte, ultro.

spoon, cocleare.

sport, subst. ludus, lusus (-ūs); = hunting, venatio; = mockery, ludibrium, inrisio.

sport, v. ludère, lascivire.

sportive, adj. lascivus, iocosus, festivus; adv. per iocum, iocose.

sportiveness, lascivia, iocus.

sportsman, venator.

spot, subst.: = mark, stain, macula, nota; = place, locus.

spot, v. notare, maculare.

spotless, sine maculis, purus.

spotted, maculosus, maculis distinctus.

spouse, coniunx.

spray, subst.: liquid, aspergo; on a tree, virgula.

spread, v.: transit. (ex)pandère, explicare, extendère, spargère (= scatter), (di)vulgare (= publish); intransit., render by pass.

sprig, surculus, virgula.

sprightliness, alacritas, facetiae (-arum, = pleasantries).

sprightly, alacer; facetus (= humorous).

spring, subst. fons; fig., origo, principium; the season, ver, tempus vernum.

spring, v. = leap, salire; to — from, (ex re) nasci, (ex)oriri; to — up, of plants, crescère; of winds, surgère.

spring-tide, aestus (-ūs) maximus.

sprinkle, spargère, aspergère, conspergère.

sprite, faunus, nympha.

sprout, v. pullulare, germinare.

spruce, adj. comptus, bellus, nitidus, elegans; adv. belle, nitide, eleganter.

spur, subst. calcar.

spur, v.: to — a horse, equo calcaria subdère.

spurious, adulterinus, falsus.

spurn, fastidire, aspernari, repudiare.

spy, subst. explorator, speculator.

spy, v. explorare, speculari.

squabble, subst. rixa, altercatio, iurgium.

squabble, v. rixari.

squadron, of cavalry, (equitum) turma or ala; of ships, classis.

squalid, sordidus, spurcus; adv. sordide.

squall, subst. procella; an infant's, vagitus (-ūs).

squall, v. vagire.

squalor, sordes (-ium).

squander, profundère, perdère, dissipare.

squanderer, nepos.

square, subst. quadratum, quadra.

square, adj. quadratus.

square, v. quadrare.

squash, v. conterère, contundère.

squat, v. subsidère, considère.

squeak, subst. stridor.

squeak, v. stridère.

squeamish, fastidiosus, delicatus.

squeamishness, fastidium.

squeeze, subst. compressio.

squeeze, v. premère, comprimère; — out, exprimère.

squint, v. limis or perversis oculis esse; one who —s, strabo.

squirrel, sciurus.

stab, v. confodère.

stability, stabilitas, firmitas, constantia.

stable, subst. stabulum.

stable, adj. stabilis, firmus, constans.

stable, v. stabulare.

stack, subst. *cumulus, acervus, strues.*

stack, v. *cumulare.*

staff: = stick, *baculum, scipio*; a herald's —, *caduceus*; = assistants, military, *legati (-orum)*, civil, *adiutores.*

stag, *cervus.*

stage, *proscaenium, scaena*; of the —, *scaenicus*; = degree, *gradus (-ūs).*

stagger, v. *titubare, vacillare.*

stagnant, *stagnans, piger, lentus.*

stagnate, *stagnare.* Transf., *hebescĕre, languĕre.*

staid; see sober.

stain, subst. *macula, labes, nota.*

stain, v. *maculare, foedare, polluĕre.*

stainless, *purus, integer.*

stair, *gradus (-ūs)*; —case, *scalae (-arum).*

stake, subst.: = post, *palus, stipes, sudes*; = pledge, *pignus (-oris, n.)*; to be at —, *agi, in discrimine esse.*

stake, v. *(de)ponĕre.*

stale, subst. *culmus, caulis, calamus.*

stalk, v.; = strut, *incedĕre.*

stall, subst. *stabulum*; = shop, *taberna.*

stall, v. *stabulare.*

stammer, v. *balbutire, lingua haesitare.*

stammering, adj. *balbus.*

stamp, subst. *nota, signum, imago (impressa)*; of the foot, *pedis supplosio.*

stamp, v. *signare, notare*; with the foot, *pedem supplodĕre*: to — underfoot, *conculcare.*

stand, subst.: to come to a —, *consistĕre, subsistĕre*; to make a — against, *resistĕre* (with dat.)

stand, v. (1) = be upright, *stare, consistĕre*; to — by, *adesse*; = fast, *consistĕre, subsistĕre, restare*; — for office, *petĕre*; stand in the way, *obstare*; — out, *eminĕre, exstare*; — up, *surgĕre.* (2) = set upright, place, *statuĕre, constituĕre.* (3) = tolerate, *tolerare, perferre, sustinēre.*

standard: = flag, *vexillum, signum*; = measure, *regula, norma.*

standard-bearer, *vexillarius, signifer.*

standing, subst. *condicio, gradus (-ūs)*, *locus*; of long —, *vetus.*

standstill: to be at a —, *haerēre.*

star, *stella, astrum.* Transf., *lumen.*

stare, subst. *obtutus (-ūs).*

stare, v. *spectare, intuēri*; in astonishment, *stupēre.*

stark, *rigidus.*

starling, *sturnus.*

start, subst.: = sudden movement, *saltus (-ūs)*; = beginning, *initium, principium*; = setting out, *profectio.*

start, v.: transit., *instituĕre, aggredi, incipĕre*; intransit., = move suddenly, *expavescĕre*; to — up, *exsilire*; = begin, *incipĕre, (ex)ordiri*; = set out, *proficisci.*

startle; see frighten.

startling, *terribilis*; = strange, *mirus.*

starve, v.: transit., *fame necare*; intransit., *fame confici* or *perire.*

state, subst.: = condition, *status (-ūs)*, *condicio, locus*; polit., *respublica, civitas*; = grandeur, *apparatus (-ūs)*, *magnificentia.*

state, adj. *publicus.*

state, v. *adfirmare, adseverare, dicĕre.*

stately, *lautus, magnificus.*

statesman, *vir reipublicae peritus.*

statesmanship, *ars reipublicae regendae.*

station, subst. see position; v. see place, set.

stationary, *immobilis, immotus*; — camp. (*castra*) *stativa (-orum).*

statue, *signum, statua, effigies.*

stature, *statura.*

statute, *lex.*

staunch, adj. *firmus, certus, fidus.*

staunch, v. (*sanguinem*) *sistĕre* or *cohibēre.*

stay, subst.: = prop, *adminiculum*; = sojourn, *mansio, commoratio.*

stay, v.: transit., = prop, *fulcire*; = stop, *(de)morari, detinēre, cohibēre*; intransit., *(com)morari, manēre.*

stead: in— of, *pro*, with abl.: *loco* or *in vicem*, with genit.

steadiness, *stabilitas, firmitas, constantia.*

steady, *stabilis, firmus, constans*; adv. *firme, firmiter, constanter.*

steal, v.: transit., *furari, surripĕre*; intransit., = go stealthily, *subrepĕre*; — in, *inrepĕre*; — away, *se subducĕre.*

stealthy, *furtivus, clandestinus*; adv. *furtim, clam.*

steam, subst. (*aquae*) *vapor, nidor, fumus.*

steam, v. *vaporare.*

steed, *equus.*

steel, subst. *chalybs*; = sword, *ferrum.*

steel, v.: to — oneself, *obdurescĕre.*

steep, adj. *praeruptus, praeceps, arduus.*

steep, v. *madefacĕre, imbuĕre.*

steer, subst. *iuvencus.*

steer, v. *gubernare, regĕre.*

steering, subst. *gubernatio.*

steersman, *gubernator, rector.*

stem, subst.: of a tree, *stirps, truncus*; of a plant, *caulis, calamus*; = race, *stirps, genus (-eris, n.).*

stem, v. = check, *cohibēre, coercēre.*

step, subst.: = stair, *gradus (-ūs)*; = pace, *gradus, passus, gressus* (all -ūs); — by —, *gradatim, pedetentim*; = plan, measure, *ratio, consilium.*

step, v. *gradi*; — in, *ingredi*; — forwards, *progredi.*

step-brother, *filius vitrici*, or *novercae.*

step-daughter, *privigna.*

step-father, *vitricus.*

step-mother, *noverca.*

step-sister, *filia vitrici* or *novercae.*

step-son, *privignus.*

sterile, *sterilis.*

sterility, *sterilitas.*

sterling, *verus, bonus.*

stern, subst., *puppis.*

stern, adj. *durus, severus*; adv. *severe, dure.*

sternness, *severitas.*

steward, *procurator*; of an estate, *vilicus.*

stewardship, *cura, procuratio.*

stick, subst. *baculum, virga* (= rod), *fustis* (= cudgel).

stick, v.: transit., (ad)fīgĕre; intransit., (ad)haerēre, adhaerescĕre; = get stuck, haerēre, haesitare, dubitare.

sticky, tenax, lentus.

stiff, rigidus, durus; to be —, rigēre. Adv., rigide, dure, duriter.

stiffen, v.: transit., rigidum facĕre; intransit., rigescĕre.

stiffness, rigor.

stifle, suffocare.

stigma, nota.

stigmatize, notare, notam inurēre.

still, adj. tranquillus, quietus, placidus.

still, adv. adhuc, etiam; see also never-theless.

still, v. sedare, placare.

stilling, subst. sedatio.

stillness, silentium, tranquillitas, quies.

stimulate, stimulare, excitare, incitare.

stimulus, stimulus, incitamentum.

sting, subst. aculeus.

sting, v. pungĕre, aculeos infigĕre.

stinginess, parsimonia, tenacitas.

stinging, mordax, acerbus, aculeatus.

stingy, parcus, sodidus, tenax; adv. parce, sordide.

stink; see smell.

stint, v. parce dare, parcĕre.

stipend; see salary.

stipendiary, mercenarius, stipendiarius.

stipulate, stipulari, (de)pacisci.

stipulation, pactum, condicio.

stir, subst. motus (-ūs), tumultus (-ūs).

stir, v.: transit., (com)movēre, exagitare; intransit., se movēre, progredi.

stitch, v. (con)suĕre.

stock, subst.: of a tree, truncus, stirps; = family, genus, stirps; = store, copia.

stock, adj.; see common, trite.

stock, v. instruĕre, ornare.

stockade, vallum.

stocking, tibiale.

stoic, subst. and adj. stoicus.

stoical, ferreus, rigidus, austerus; adv. austere, stoice.

stoicism, stoicorum ratio or doctrina.

stomach, subst. stomachus.

stone, subst. lapis, saxum; of —, adj. lapideus; in fruit, nucleus; precious —, gemma.

stone, v. lapides in hominem conicĕre.

stony: = of stone, lapideus, saxeus; = full of stones, lapidosus, saxosus.

stony-hearted, durus, ferreus.

stoop, v. se inclinare or demittĕre.

stooping, adj. pronus, inclinatus.

stop, subst.: = stay, mansio; = pause, intermissio, pausa; as punctuation, interpunctum.

stop, v.: transit., sistĕre, prohibēre, comprimĕre; — up, obturare, occlu-dĕre; intransit., = halt, (con)sistĕre; = stay, manēre, (com)morari; = cease, refrain, desinĕre.

stoppage, obstructio, impedimentum.

store, subst. copia, vis.

store, v. coacervare, reponĕre, condĕre.

store-house, horreum, thesaurus, apotheca.

store-room, cella.

storey, tabulatio, tabulatum.

stork, ciconia.

storm, subst. tempestas, procella.

storm, v.: transit., expugnare, vi capĕre; intransit., furĕre, saevire.

storm-cloud, nimbus.

storming, subst. expugnatio.

stormy, turbulentus, turbidus; adv. turbulente, turbide.

story: = tale, fabula, res, narratio; to tell a —, narrare; = falsehood, mendacium; see also storey.

stout: = fat, obesus, pinguis; = thick, crassus, densus; = strong, validus, robustus; = brave, fortis. Adv. fortiter, valide, robuste.

stove, focus, caminus.

stow; see store.

straggle, vagari, deerare, palari.

straight: adj. (di)rectus, erectus; adv. recta recto itinere.

straighten, corrigĕre.

straightforward, simplex, apertus.

strain, subst.: = exertion, intentio, contentio; of music, etc., modus; = manner, modus; in this —, ita, sic.

strain, v. contendĕre; see also filter.

strained; see far-fetched.

strait, subst.: = narrow sea, fretum; = any narrow passage, or difficulty, angustiae (-arum, plur.).

strait, artus, angustus.

straiten, in angustias adducĕre.

strand, subst. litus (-oris, n.), ripa.

strand, v. navem vadis inlidĕre.

strange, adj.: = foreign, peregrinus, externus; = alien, not one's own, alienus; = unusual, insolitus, novus, mirus, mirabilis. Adv. mirum in modum, mirabiliter.

strangeness, novitas, insolentia.

stranger, hospes, advena, peregrinus.

strangle, strangulare, gulam laqueo frangĕre.

strap, subst. lorum.

strap, v. loris (con)stringĕre.

stratagem, ars, dolus.

strategy, ars belli gerendi.

straw, stramentum.

strawberry, fragum.

stray, adj. errabundus.

stray, v. (ab)errare, vagari, palari.

streak, subst. linea, nota.

streak, v. lineis distinguĕre.

stream, subst. flumen, rivus; up —, adverso flumine; down —, secundo flumine.

stream, v. fluĕre, effundi.

streamer, vexillum.

street, via, vicus.

strength, vires (-ium, plur.), robur, nervi (-orum).

strengthen, transit., (con)firmare, (con)-roborare.

strengthening, subst. confirmatio.

strenuous, strenuus, impiger, (g)navus; adv. strenue, impigre.

strenuousness, (g)navitas, studium.

stress, momentum, vis.

stretch, subst.: = effort, contentio, nisus (-ūs); at a —, uno tenore; = expanse, tractus (-ūs), spatium.

stretch, v.: transit., (ex)tendĕre, con-tendĕre; to — out, porrigĕre; in-transit., render by pass.

strew, sternĕre, spargĕre.

strict: = exact, *diligens, religiosus*; = severe, *severus, rigidus.* Adv. *accurate; severe, rigide.*

strictness: = carefulness, *accuratio, diligentia*; = severity, *severitas, rigor.*

stricture, *animadversio, reprehensio.*

stride, subst. *ingens gradus (-ūs).*

strife, *certamen, contentio, controversia.*

strike, v.: transit., *ferire, percutĕre, pulsare, caedĕre*; mentally, *percutĕre, percellĕre*; to be struck by lightning, *de caelo tangi*; to — down, *adfligĕre*; — out, *elidĕre, delĕre*; intransit., to — against, *offendĕre, incurrĕre.*

striking; see remarkable.

string, subst. *linum, linea, filum*; bow—, *nervus*; of a musical instrument *nervus, fides* (usually plur.).

string, v. *nervos aptare* (of an instrument); see also bind.

stringent; see severe.

strip, subst.; of paper, *scidula chartae*; of cloth, *lacinia.*

strip, v.: transit., *spoliare, (de)nudare, exuĕre*; intransit., *vestem exuĕre* or *deponĕre.*

stripe; see streak and stroke.

stripling, *adulescens, adulescentulus.*

strive, (e)niti, contendĕre.

striving, *nisus (-ūs), certatio, contentio.*

stroke, subst. *ictus (-ūs), verber, plaga*; of lightning, *fulmen*; — of fortune, *eventus (-ūs).*

stroke, v. (per)mulcĕre, demulcĕre.

stroll, subst. *ambulatio.*

stroll, v. *ambulare, spatiari, reptare.*

strong, adj. *validus, firmus, robustus, fortis*; of flavours, *acer*; of winds, *vehemens*; of arguments, *gravis, firmus*; to be —, *valēre, pollēre.* Adv. *valide, firmiter, fortiter, vehementer.*

stronghold, *arx.*

structure: abstract, *ratio, forma, conformatio*; material, *aedificium, moles, compages.*

struggle, subst. *certamen, luctatio.*

struggle, v. *luctari, niti, contendĕre.*

strut, (superbe) incedĕre.

stubble, *stipulae (-arum,* plur.).

stubborn, *pertinax, pervicax, obstinatus*; adv. *pertinaciter, pervicaciter, obstinate.*

stubbornness, *pertinacia, pervicacia, obstinatio.*

stud, *bulla.*

studded, *distinctus.*

student; see scholar.

studied, *meditatus, commentatus.*

studious; *litterarum studiosus*; adv. *summo studio, studiose.*

study, subst., *studium, meditatio, commentatio, cognitio* (with genit.).

study, v. *rei* (dat.) *studēre; in rem inquirĕre.*

stuff, subst. *materia, materies*; = gear, *impedimenta (-orum)*, *supellex*; = fabric, *textile, tela*; — and nonsense! *nugae! gerrae!*

stuff, v. *farcire, refercire, replēre.*

stuffing, *fartum* (in food), *tomentum* (for cushions).

stultify, *ad inritum redigĕre.*

stumble, *offendĕre*; — upon, *incidĕre.*

stumbling, subst. *offensio.*

stump, *stipes (-itis), truncus.*

stun, *sensu privare.* Transf., *(ob)stupe-facĕre.*

stupefaction, *stupor, torpor.*

stupefy; see stun.

stupendous, *ingens, immanis*; *mirus.*

stupid, *stupidus, stolidus, stultus*; adv. *stolide, stulte.*

stupidity, *stupiditas, stupor, stultitia.*

stupor, *stupor, torpor.*

sturdy; see strong, firm.

sturgeon, *acipenser.*

stutter, v. *balbutire.*

sty, *hara, suile.*

style, subst., *genus (-eris,* n.), *ratio, modus*; — of dress, *habitus (-ūs)*; of language, *dicendi* or *scribendi genus, oratio, sermo.*

style, v. *appellare.*

stylish, *speciosus, elegans*; adv. *speciose, eleganter.*

suave, *suavis, urbanus, blandus.*

suavity, *suavitas, urbanitas.*

subdivide, *iterum dividĕre.*

subdivision, *pars.*

subdue, *in imperium redigĕre, domare.*

subject, subst.: of a person, *civis*; = a matter, *res, quaestio*; gram., *subiectum.*

subject, adj. *subiectus, obnoxius.*

subject, v. *subicere, obnoxium reddĕre.*

subject-matter, *materia, res.*

subjection, *servitus (-ūtis), officium.*

subjective, render by personal pronouns or by *opinio.*

subjoin, *subiungĕre, subicĕre.*

subjugate, (per)domare, subigĕre.

subjunctive, (modus) subiunctivus.

sublime, *elatus, excelsus*; adv. *elate, excelse.*

sublimity, *elatio, excelsitas.*

submerge, *submergĕre.*

submission, *obsequium, officium.*

submissive, *oboediens, submissus.*

submit, v.: transit., *referre* (*ad senatum,* etc.); — to, = endure, *perferre.*

subordinate, subst. *minister.*

subordinate, adj. *inferior, subiectus* (with dat.).

subordinate, v. *subicĕre, posthabēre.*

subordination, *obsequium, disciplina.*

suborn, *subornare, subicĕre.*

subscribe: = write underneath, *subscribĕre*; = contribute, *conferre.*

subscription, = contribution, *conlatio, conlecta.*

subsequent, (in)sequens, posterior; adv. *postea.*

subserve, (in)servire, obtemperare, obsequi.

subservience, *obtemperatio.*

subside, *residĕre, considĕre.*

subsidiary, *subsidiarius.*

subsidy, *subsidium, vectigal, tributum.*

subsist, *esse*; — on a thing, *re vesci.*

subsistence, *victus (-ūs).*

substance, *natura, corpus (-oris,* n.), *res*; = property, *res, bona (-orum,* plur.).

substantial, *verus* (= real), *solidus* (= firm), *gravis* (= important), amplus (= large). Adv. *firmiter* (=solidly), *magna ex parte* (=largely).

substantiate; see prove, establish.

substantive, gram., *nomen.*

substitute, subst. *vicarius.*

substitute, v. transit., *substituĕre, sufficĕre* (esp. of the replacing of magistrates).

subterfuge, *tergiversatio.*

subterranean, *subterraneus.*

subtle, *subtilis; argutus, acutus.* Adv. *subtiliter, argute, acute.*

subtlety, *ingenii acumen, subtilitas, argutiae (-arum,* plur.).

subtract, *deducĕre.*

suburban, *suburbanus.*

subvert, *subvertĕre, evertĕre.*

succeed, v.: transit., = come after, *(sub)sequi, excipĕre, succedĕre* (with dat.); intransit., = do well, of persons, *rem bene gerĕre, florĕre;* of things, *succedĕre, bene evenire.*

success, *res secundae, successus (-ūs).*

successful, of things, *secundus, prosper.* Adv. *feliciter, prospere, bene.*

succession, *successio;* = series, *continuatio, series;* in —, *ex ordine.*

successive, *continuus;* adv. *(ex) ordine, deinceps.*

successor, *successor.*

succinct, *brevis;* adv. *breviter.*

succour, subst. *auxilium, subsidium.*

succour, v. *subvenire, succurrĕre,* with dat.

succumb, *succumbĕre.*

such, adj. *talis; huius modi, eius modi;* such . . . as, *talis . . . qualis;* such that, *talis ut,* with subj.; in — a way, *tali modo, ita, sic.*

suck, v. *sugĕre;* — out, *exsorbĕre.*

sucker, *surculus, planta.*

suckle, v. *mammam praebĕre.*

suckling, *(infans) lactens.*

sudden, *subitus, repentinus, inopinatus;* adv. *subito, repente.*

sue: = entreat, *rogare, orare;* at law, *(hominem) in ius vocare.*

suet, *sebum.*

suffer: = endure, *pati, (per)ferre, tolerare, subire;* = be in pain, *dolorem ferre, dolore adfici;* = be ill, *aegrotare;* = be punished, *plecti, poenas dare;* = allow, *pati, sinere.*

sufferance, *patientia;* on —, *precarius,* adj.

suffering, *dolor, miseria;* see pain.

suffice, *sufficĕre, satis esse.*

sufficient; render by adv. *satis.*

suffocate, *suffocare;* see strangle.

suffrage, *suffragium.*

suffuse, *suffundĕre.*

suggest, *(rem homini) subicĕre.*

suggestion, *admonitio, consilium.*

suicide: to commit —, *sibi mortem consciscĕre.*

suit, subst.: at law, *actio, lis, causa;* of clothes, *vestis, vestitus (-ūs).*

suit, v.: = adapt, *accommodare;* = fit, be suitable, *convenire, congruĕre.*

suitable, *idoneus, aptus, accommodatus, opportunus;* adv. *idonee, apte, accommodate, opportune.*

suitableness, *opportunitas.*

suite: = retinue, *comitatus (-ūs), comites (-um);* of rooms, *conclavia (-ium).*

suitor, = wooer, *procus.*

sulkiness, sullenness, *morositas.*

sulky, sullen, *morosus;* adv. *morose.*

sully, *maculare, inquinare.*

sulphur, *sulfur;* dipped in —, *sulfuratus.*

sulphurous, *sulpureus.*

sultry, *aestuosus.*

sum, subst. *summa;* of money, *pecunia.*

sum up, v. *breviter repetĕre.*

summary, subst. *epitoma* or *epitome.*

summary, adj.: = brief, *brevis;* = quick, *subitus, repentinus.* Adv. *breviter, summatim; statim.*

summer, *aestas;* of —, adj., *aestivus.*

summit, *cacumen, culmen;* or render by adj. *summus.*

summon, *(ad)vocare, arcessĕre, accire;* before a court, *appellare, in ius vocare;* to — up courage, *animum conligĕre.*

summons: at a person's —, *hominis accitu.*

sumptuous, *sumptuosus, lautus;* adv. *sumptuose.*

sumptuousness, *apparatus (-ūs), lautitia.*

sun, subst. *sol;* rising —, *sol oriens;* setting —, *sol occidens.*

sunburnt, *adustus.*

sunder, *separare, disiungĕre.*

sundial, *solarium.*

sundry, *diversus, varius.*

sunny, *apricus.*

sunrise, *solis ortus (-ūs).*

sunset, *solis occasus (-ūs).*

sunshine, *sol.*

sup, *cenare.*

superannuated, *emeritus, rude donatus.*

superb, *magnificus, lautus;* adv. *magnifice, laute.*

supercilious, *superbus, fastidiosus, insolens.*

superciliousness, *superbia, insolentia.*

superficial, = exterior, *externus;* = shallow, *levis;* adv. *strictim, leviter.*

superfluous, adj. *supervacaneus, supervacuus;* to be —, *superesse.* Adv. *ex supervacuo.*

superhuman, *divinus, maior quam pro homine.*

superintend, *administrare, praeesse.*

superintendent, *praefectus.*

superior, *superior, melior* (= better).

superlative, *optimus, egregius, singularis;* gram., *superlativus.*

supernatural, *divinus, caelestis;* by — agency, *divinitus.*

supernumerary, praeter *(iustum) numerum;* of soldiers, *ascriptivus;* in plur., *accensi.*

superscription, *inscriptio.*

supersede, *succedĕre* (with dat.).

superstition, *si perstitio.*

superstitious, *superstitiosus;* adv. *superstitiose.*

supervene, *supervenire;* see also follow.

supervise, *(pro)curare.*

supervision, *(pro)curatio.*

supine, subst. *supinum* (gram.).

supine, adj. *supinus*. Transf., *iners, neglegens*; adv. *neglegenter*.

supineness, *neglegentia, inertia*.

supper, *cena*.

supplant, *in alterius locum inrepěre*.

supple, *mollis, lentus*.

supplement, *supplementum, incrementum*.

suppliant, *supplex*.

supplicate, *supplicare, obsecrare, obtestari*.

supplication, *obsecratio, obtestatio*.

supply, supplies, *copia, facultas*; milit. *commeatus (-ūs)*.

supply, v. = provide, *suppeditare, ministrare*.

support, subst. *firmamentum*; = maintenance, *alimentum, victus (-ūs)*; = help, *subsidium, auxilium*.

support, v.: = hold up, *sustiněre, fulcire*; = endure, (*per*)*ferre, tolerare*; = maintain, *aleěre*; = help, *adesse, suffragari*, with dat.

supporter, *adiutor, suffragator, fautor*.

suppose: = assume, *poněre, suměre*; = believe, *creděre, putare, opinari*.

supposition, *opinio, coniectura*.

supposititious, *subditus, subditivus*.

suppress, *suppriměre, compriměre*.

supremacy, *principatus (-ūs), dominatio, imperium*.

supreme, *supremus, summus*; adv. *unice, maxime*.

sure, *certus, tutus* (= safe), *firmus* (= trustworthy); I am —, *pro certo habeo*.

surely, *certe, profecto, scilicet*; in questions, *nonne? — not? num?*

surety, *vas, sponsor* (of a person).

surface, *superficies*, or render by adj. *summus*.

surfeit, subst. *satietas*.

surfeit, v.: to — oneself, *se ingurgitare*.

surge, subst. *fluctus (-ūs)*.

surge, *fluctuare*; — forward, *proruěre*.

surgeon, *medicus, chirurgus*.

surliness, *morositas, difficultas*.

surly, *morosus, difficilis*.

surmise, subst. *coniectura*.

surmise, v. *suspicari, coniecturam facěre*.

surmount, *transcenděre, (ex)superare*.

surmountable, (*ex*)*superabilis*.

surname, *cognomen, cognomentum*.

surpass, *vincěre, (ex)superare, praestare* (with dat.).

surplus, subst. *residuum, quod superest*.

surprise, subst., (*ad*)*miratio*; or render by v. or adj.

surprise, v. *admirationem* (*homini*) *mověre*; to be —d, (*ad*)*mirari*; = take by —, *oppriměre, necopinantem adoriri*.

surprising, *mirus, mirabilis*.

surrender, subst. *deditio, traditio*.

surrender, v. *dedere, tradere, (con)cedere*; intransit., *se dedere*.

surreptitious, *furtivus, clandestinus*; adv. *furtim, clam*.

surround, *cingěre, circumdare, circumvenire*.

survey, subst. *contemplatio, conspectus (-ūs)*; of land, *mensura*.

survey, v. *spectare, contemplari*; = measure land, *agrum metiri, mensuram agěre*.

surveyor, (of land), *decempedator, metator*.

survive, *superesse, superstitem esse*.

surviving, survivor, *superstes*.

susceptible, *mollis*.

suspect, adj. *suspectus*.

suspect, v. *suspicari*; = think, fancy, *putare*.

suspend, *suspenděre*; = break off, defer, *intermittěre, differre*; from office, *loco mověre, magistratum abrogare*.

suspense, *dubitatio*: in —, adj., *suspensus*.

suspension, *dilatio* (= delay); — of hostilities, *indutiae (-arum)*.

suspicion, *suspicio*.

suspicious, *suspiciosus, suspicax*; adv. *suspiciose*.

sustain, *sustinere, sustentare*.

sustenance, *alimentum, victus (-ūs)*.

sutler, *lixa*.

swaddling-clothes, *fasciae (-arum), incunabula (-orum)*.

swagger, *gloriari, se iactare*.

swallow, subst. *hirundo*.

swallow, v. (*ab*)*sorběre, (de)vorare*.

swamp, subst. *palus (-udis)*.

swamp, v. (*de*)*mergěre, immergěre*.

swampy, *paluster, paludosus*.

swan, *cygnus, olor*; of a —, *cygneus*.

swarm, subst. of bees, *examen*.

swarm, v. *congregari, confluěre*.

swarthy, *fuscus, adustus*.

sway, subst. *imperium, dominatio, dicio*.

sway, v., = move to and fro, *agitare, motare*; see also govern.

swear, *iurare*; — falsely, *peierare* or *periurare*.

sweat, subst. *sudor*.

sweat, v. *sudare*.

sweep, subst., = expanse, *ambitus (-ūs), spatium*.

sweep, v. *verrěre*.

sweepings, *quisquiliae (-arum)*.

sweet, *dulcis, suavis*; adv. *dulciter, suaviter*.

sweeten, *dulcem reddere* or *facere*.

sweetheart, *deliciae (-arum), amores (-um)*.

sweetness, *dulcedo, suavitas*.

swell, v.: transit., *tumefacěre, augěre*; intransit., *tuměre, tumescěre, crescěre* (= grow).

swelling, subst. *tumor, tuber*.

swerve, subst. *declinatio*.

swerve, v. *declinare*.

swift, *citus, velox, celer, pernix*; adv. *cito, celeriter, perniciter*.

swiftness, *celeritas, velocitas, pernicitas*.

swim, v. *nare, natare*; — across, *tranare*.

swimmer, *natator*.

swimming, subst. *natatio*.

swindle, subst. *fraus*.

swindle, v. *fraudare, circumvenire*.

swindler, *fraudator*.

swine, *sus, porcus*; adj., of —, *suillus*.

swineherd, *subulcus, suarius*.

swing, v.: transit., *agitare, vibrare, iactare.*
switch, subst. *virga, virgula.*
Switzerland, *Helvetia.*
swoon, v. *animo linqui, conlabi.*
swoop, subst. *impetus (-ūs).*
swoop, v. *impetum facĕre, incurrĕre.*
sword, *gladius, ensis, ferrum.*
sycophancy, *sycophantia, adsentatio, adulatio.*
sycophant, *sycophanta, adsentator, adulator.*
syllable, *syllaba.*
sylvan, *silvestris.*
symbol, *symbŏlum, signum.*
symmetrical, *aequalis, congruens;* adv. *pariter, aequaliter.*
symmetry, *convenientia, congruentia, aequalitas.*
sympathetic, *concors, humanus, misericors.*
sympathize, *congruĕre, consentire, miserēri* (= pity).
sympathy, *consensus (-ūs), concordia; humanitas.*
symphony, *symphonia, concentus (-ūs).*
symptom, (*morbi*) *indicium* or *signum.*
syndicate, *societas.*
synonymous, *idem significans.*
synopsis, *epitome* or *epitoma; breviarium.*
syntax, *syntaxis* (gram.); *verborum constructio.*
Syracuse, *Syracusae (-arum,* plur.).
system, *ratio, disciplina.*
systematic, *accuratus, compositus;* adv. *ordine, accurate, composite.*

T

tabernacle, *tabernaculum.*
table, *mensa;* = fare, *cena, victus (-ūs);* = list, *index.*
table-napkin, *mappa.*
tablet, *tabula, tabella, album.*
tacit, *tacitus;* adv. *tacite.*
taciturn, *taciturnus.*
taciturnity, *taciturnitas.*
tack, subst., = small nail, *clavulus.*
tack, v., in sailing, *reciprocare;* see also nail and sew.
tackle, subst. *instrumenta (-orum), armamenta (-orum).*
tackle, v. *tractare, obviam ire.*
tact, *dexteritas.*
tactful, *dexter;* adv. *dextere, dextre.*
tactics, *res militaris, belli ratio.*
tactless, *ineptus, insulsus, infacetus.*
tactlessness, *ineptiae (-arum).*
tail, *cauda.*
tailor, *textor.*
taint, subst. *contagio, vitium.*
taint, v. *inficĕre, contaminare, corrumpĕre.*
take, *capĕre, sumĕre, accipĕre* (= receive); — away, *auferre, demĕre, adimĕre;* — down, in writing, *litteris mandare;* — in, mentally, *percipĕre, comprehendĕre;* — on, *suscipĕre;* to —, = to move, by carrying, *ferre;* by leading, *ducĕre;* to — in good part, *in bonam partem accipĕre;* intransit., to — to, *se conferre ad,* with acc.

taking, subst. *acceptio, expugnatio* (of a city).
tale, *narratio, fabula, historia.*
tale-bearer, *delator, sycophanta.*
talent: = weight or coin, *talentum;* = faculty, *ingenium,* (*ingenii*) *facultas.*
talented, *ingeniosus, eximii ingenii.*
talk, subst. *sermo, conloquium.*
talk, (*con*)*loqui, sermocinari;* to — to, *adloqui, adfari.*
talkative, *loquax, garrulus;* adv. *loquaciter.*
talkativeness, *loquacitas.*
tall, *longus, procerus,* (*ex*)*celsus.*
tallness, *proceritas, statura procera.*
tally, v. *convenire.*
talon, *unguis, ungula.*
tame, adj. *cicur, mitis, mansuetus;* to grow —, *mitescĕre.* Transf., *demissus;* of language, *frigidus.* Adv. *demisse; frigide.*
tame, v. *mansuefacĕre, domare.*
tamer, *domitor;* f. *domitrix.*
taming, *domitus (-ūs).*
tamper; see meddle.
tan, v.: to — skins, *conficĕre;* of the sun, *colorare.*
tangible, *tractabilis; quod tangi potest.*
tangle, subst. *implicatio, nodus.*
tank, *lacus (-ūs).*
tantalize; see tease.
tap, v. *leviter ferire;* to — a cask, *relinĕre.*
tape; see ribbon.
taper, subst. *cereus, funalis.*
tapestry, *pictura acu facta, stragulum pictum.*
tar, *pix* (*liquida*).
Taranto, *Tarentum.*
tardiness, *tarditas.*
tardy, *tardus, lentus;* adv. *tarde, lente.*
target, *scopos.*
tarnish, v. transit., *inquinare.*
Tarragona, *Tarraco.*
tarry, (*com*)*morari, cunctari, cessare.*
tart, adj. *acerbus, amarus;* adv. *acerbe.*
tartness, *acerbitas.*
task, subst. *pensum, opus (-eris,* n.).
task-master, *operis exactor.*
taste, subst.: = sense of —, *gustatus (-ūs), palatum;* = flavour, *sapor, gustatus (-ūs).* Transf., critical —, *iudicium, intellegentia;* = liking, *gustatus (-ūs), studium.*
taste, v.: transit., (*de*)*gustare,* (*de*)*libare;* intransit., *sapĕre.*
tasteful, *elegans, scitus, concinnus;* adv. *eleganter, scite.*
tasteless, *sine sapore, insulsus; inelegans;* adv. *insulse, ineleganter.*
tastelessness, *insulsitas.*
tatter, *pannus.*
tattered, *pannosus.*
taunt, subst. *probrum, convicium.*
taunt, v. (*rem homini*) *obicĕre.*
taunting, *contumeliosus;* adv. *contumeliose.*
tavern, *caupona, taberna.*
tavern-keeper, *caupo.*
tawdry, *fucosus.*
tawny, *fulvus.*
tax, taxation, *vectigal, tributum.*

tax, v., *vectigal* or *tributum (homini) imponĕre.*
taxable, *vectigalis, stipendiarius.*
tax-collector, *(vectigalium) exactor.*
teach, *(e)docēre, instituĕre, erudire.*
teachable, *docilis.*
teachableness, *docilitas.*
teacher, *doctor, magister* (with f. *magistra*).
teaching, subst. *doctrina, disciplina, eruditio.*
team, (of horses or oxen), *iugum.*
tear, subst. *lacrima, fletus (-ūs,* = weeping).
tear, v. transit. *(di)scindĕre, (di)lacerare, (di)vellĕre;* — away, *avellĕre;* — down, *rescindĕre, revellĕre;* — out, *evellĕre.*
tearful, *lacrimans, lacrimabundus;* adv. *multis cum lacrimis.*
tearing, tear, subst. *scissura.*
tease, *fatigare, vexare, obtundĕre.*
tedious, *lentus, longus, molestus;* adv. *lente, moleste.*
tediousness, *molestia.*
teem, *scatēre.*
tell: = relate, say, *dicĕre, narrare, referre, (com)memorare, docēre* (= inform); = command, *iubēre, imperare;* = count, *numerare;* intransit., = have effect, *valēre.*
temerity, *temeritas.*
temper, subst. *ingenium, animus;* bad —, *iracundia, stomachus.*
temper, v. *temperare, miscēre, lenire.*
temperance, *temperantia, continentia, moderatio.*
temperate, *temperans, continens, moderatus;* adv. *continenter, moderate.*
temperateness, *temperantia.*
tempest, *tempestas, procella.*
tempestuous, *turbidus, violentus, vehemens;* adv. *turbide, violenter, vehementer.*
tempestuousness, *violentia.*
temple, *aedes, templum, fanum, delubrum;* of the head, *tempus (-oris, n.).*
temporal, *humanus.*
temporarily, *ad* or *in tempus.*
tempt, *(at)temptare, sollicitare, inlicere.*
temptation, *sollicitatio, inlecebra.*
ten, *decem;* — each, — at a time, *deni;* — times, *decie(n)s.*
tenacious, *tenax, pertinax;* adv. *tenaciter.*
tenacity, *tenacitas, pertinacia.*
tenant, *conductor, inquilinus, incola.*
tend: transit. *colĕre, curare;* intransit., *spectare, tendĕre.*
tendency, *inclinatio, proclivitas.*
tender, adj. *tener, mollis, indulgens* (= kind, fond); adv. *molliter, indulgenter.*
tender, v. *deferre.*
tenderness, *mollitia;* = affection, *indulgentia, amor.*
tendon, *nervus.*
tendril, *clavicula, pampinus.*
tenour, *tenor;* = drift, purport, *sententia.*
tense, subst. *tempus (-oris, n.).*
tense, adj. *intentus, attentus.*
tension, *intentio.*

tent, *tabernaculum;* general's —, *praetorium.*
tenth, *decimus.*
tenure, *possessio.*
tepid, *tepidus;* to become —, *tepescĕre;* to be —, *tepēre.*
term, subst.: = limited time, *spatium, dies;* = word, *verbum, vocabulum;* = condition, *condicio, lex;* to be on good —s with, *familiariter uti.*
term, v.: see call, name.
terminate; see end.
termination, *finis, exitus (-ūs), clausula.*
terrace, *solarium, ambulatio.*
terrestrial, *terrestris, terrenus, humanus.*
terrible, *terribilis, horribilis, atrox;* adv. *terribilem in modum, atrociter.*
terrific; see dreadful, terrible.
terrify, *(per)terrēre.*
territory, *fines, ager, regio, terra.*
terror, *terror, formido, metus (-ūs).*
terse, *pressus, brevis, angustus;* adv. *presse, breviter, anguste.*
terseness, *brevitas, oratio pressa.*
test, subst.; see trial, examination.
test, v. *temptare, experiri, explorare.*
testament, = will, *testamentum.*
testator, *testator.*
testify, *testari, testificari.*
testimonial, *litterae commendaticiae.*
testimony, *testimonium.*
testy, *morosus.*
text, *oratio, verba (-orum).*
textile, adj. *textilis.*
texture, *textura, textus (-ūs).*
Thames, *Tamesis* or *Tamesa.*
than, after comparative, *quam,* or abl. case.
thank, v. *gratias agĕre;* = feel gratitude, *gratiam habēre;* — you! or No — you! *benigne (dicis).*
thankful, *gratus;* adv. *grate, grato animo.*
thankfulness, *animus gratus.*
thankless, adj. *ingratus;* adv. *ingrate.*
thanks, subst. *gratia* or plur. *gratiae, grates.*
thanksgiving, *supplicatio.*
that, demonstr. pron. *ille, illa, illud,* or *is, ea, id,* or *iste, ista, istud.*
that, relat. pron. *qui, quae, quod.*
that, conj.: in indirect statement, render by acc. and infin; after verbs of fearing, *ne* followed by subj.; in final clauses, = in order —, *ut* followed by subj.; in consecutive clauses, *ut* followed by subj.
thatch, *stramentum.*
thaw, v.: transit., *(dis)solvĕre, liquefacĕre;* intransit., *(dis)solvi, liquescĕre.*
the, no regular equivalent in Latin; — famous, *ille, illa, illud;* — more people have, — more they want, *homines quo plura habent eo ampliora cupiunt.*
theatre, *theatrum, scaena* (= stage).
theatrical, *scaenicus, theatralis;* adv. *more histrionum.*
theft, *furtum.*
their, theirs, *suus* (= — own); *eorum, illorum.*
theme, *res, propositum, quaestio.*

then, *tum, tunc*; = therefore, *ergo, igitur.*

thence, *inde, illinc, istinc.*

thenceforth, *inde, ex eo tempore.*

theory, *ratio, doctrina, ars, scientia.*

there, *ibi, illic, istic*; to be —, *adesse*; — is, *est*; — are, *sunt*; = to that place, *eo, illuc.*

thereabouts, *prope* (= near), *fere* (= nearly).

thereafter, thereupon, *inde, deinde, postea.*

therefore, *igitur, ergo, itaque, ideo.*

therein, *in eo, in ea re.*

they, when emphatic, is rendered by nom. plur. of *is, ea, id* or of *ille, illa, illud.*

thick: = stout, *crassus, pinguis*; = closely packed, *densus, artus, confertus.* Adv. *confertim, crebro.*

thicken, v.: transit., *densare*; intransit., *densari, concrescĕre* (= curdle).

thicket, *dumetum, fruticetum.*

thickness, *crassitudo, crebritas.*

thief, *fur.*

thigh, *femur.*

thin, adj.: = slim, *gracilis, exilis, macer*; = rare, *tenuis, rarus.*

thin, v. *attenuare, extenuare.*

thine, *tuus.*

thing, *res, negotium*; often rendered by neuter of adj. or pron.

think, *cogitare*; = believe, suppose, *opinari, credĕre, putare*; to — about, (rem) *reputare,* (de re) *cogitare.*

thinness, *tenuitas, gracilitas, raritas, macies.*

third, *tertius.*

thirst, subst. *sitis.*

thirst, v. *sitire.*

thirsty, *sitiens, siccus.*

thirteen, *tredecim*; — each, — at a time, *terni deni*; — times, *terdecie(n)s.*

thirteenth, *tertius decimus.*

thirtieth, *trice(n)simus.*

thirty, *triginta*: — each, — at a time, *triceni*; — times, *tricie(n)s.*

this, *hic, haec, hoc*; on — side (of), *citra*; of — kind, *huiusmodi.*

thistle, *carduus.*

thither, *eo, illuc, istuc*; hither and —, *huc (et) illuc.*

thong, *lorum.*

thorn, *sentis, spina.*

thorn-bush, *vepres, dumus, sentis.*

thorny, *spinosus.* Transf., *arduus, impeditus.*

thorough; see complete. Adv. *penitus, prorsus, omnino.*

thoroughbred, *generosus.*

thoroughfare, *transitus (-ūs)*; = road through, *via (pervia).*

thou, *tu, tute, tutemet.*

though; see although.

thought, *cogitatio, animus* (= mind), *sententia* (= opinion), *opinio* (= supposition), *consilium* (= view, plan).

thoughtful, *in cogitatione defixus*; *prudens* (= sensible), *providus* (= farsighted). Adv. *prudenter.*

thoughtless, *neglegens, imprudens, temerarius* (= rash); adv. *neglegenter, imprudenter, temere.*

thoughtlessness, *neglegentia, temeritas* (= rashness).

thousand, *mille*; plur. *milia* (or *millia*); a — times, *millie(n)s.*

thousandth, *mille(n)simus.*

Thrace, *Thracia.*

thraldom, *servitūs (-ūtis).*

thrash: to — (or thresh) corn, *terĕre*; see also beat.

thrashing, threshing, *tritura.*

thrashing-floor, threshing-floor, *area.*

thrashing-machine, *tribulum.*

thread, subst. *filum, linea, linum.*

thread, v. *inserĕre.*

threadbare, *obsoletus, tritus.*

threat, *minae (-arum), (com)minatio.*

threaten, *(com)minari, minitari, denuntiare, intentare*; = impend, *(im)minēre, instare*; = seem likely to do, render by *vidēri* with fut. infin.

threatening, *minax, minitabundus*; = impending, *instans, imminens.* Adv. *minaciter.*

three, *tres*; — times, *ter*; — each, — at a time, *trini* or *terni*; in — parts, adj. *tripertitus* or *tripartitus.*

threefold, *triplus, triplex.*

three hundred, *trecenti*; — each, — at a time, *treceni*; — times, *trecentie(n)s.*

three hundredth, *trecente(n)simus.*

threshold, *limen.*

thrice, *ter.*

thrift, *frugalitas, parsimonia.*

thrifty, *frugi, parcus*; adv. *frugaliter, parce.*

thrill, subst.: of pleasure, *voluptas, gaudium*; of fear, *horror.*

thrill, v. *commovēre*; intransit., of sounds, *resonare.*

thrilling, *mirificus, mirus.*

thrive, *vigēre, virēre, florēre.*

throat, *fauces (-ium), iugulum, guttur.*

throb, v. *salire, palpitare, micare.*

throne, *(regale) solium, sedes regia*; = royal power, *regnum, imperium.*

throng, subst. *multitudo, frequentia.*

throng, v. *celebrare, stipare, frequentare.*

throttle, *suffocare, spiritum intercludĕre.*

through, prep. *per,* with acc.; = on account of, *propter,* or *ob,* with acc.

through, adv., render by compound verb with *trans-* or *per-*; — and —, *penitus, prorsus, omnino.*

throw, throwing, subst. *iactus (-ūs), coniectus (-ūs).*

throw, v. *iacĕre, conicĕre, mittĕre* (esp. of weapons); — away, *abicĕre*; — back, *reicĕre*; — down, *deicĕre, deturbare, proruĕre.*

thrower, *iaculator.*

thrust, v. *trudĕre*; see push, drive.

thumb, *(digitus) pollex.*

thunder, subst. *tonitrus (-ūs).*

thunder, v. *(in)tonare.*

thunder-bolt, *fulmen.*

thunder-struck, *attonitus, obstupefactus.*

thus, *ita, sic.*

thwart, subst. *transtrum.*

thwart, v.: see hinder, prevent.

thy, *tuus.*

thyme, *thymum.*

Tiber, river, *Tiberis.*

ticket, *tessera.*

tickle, titillare.

tide, (maritimus) aestus (-ūs); the turn of the —, commutatio aestūs.

tidiness, munditia.

tidings, nuntius.

tidy, mundus; adv. munde.

tie, subst. vinculum, nodus.

tie, v.; see bind; — a knot, nodum facère.

tier, ordo; see row.

tiger, tigris.

tight, strictus, a(d)strictus, artus; — rope, funis contentus.

tighten, v. stringère, contendère, adducère.

tile, tegula, testa; pan- —, imbrex.

till, prep. (usque) ad; — now, hactenus.

till, conj. dum, donec, quoad.

till, v. colere, arare.

tillage, cultus (-ūs), cultura.

tiller, (gubernaculi) clavus.

tilt, v. transit. (in)vertère.

timber, materia or materies.

time, subst. tempus (-oris, n.), dies, spatium (= space of —), saeculum (= age), otium (= leisure), occasio (= opportunity); — of life, aetas; for a —, ad or in tempus; on —, (in) tempore, temperi, tempestive; from the — when, ex quo (tempore); at —s, interdum; at the same —, simul, eodem tempore; — of day, hora; — in music, tempus, numerus.

timely: adj. tempestivus, opportunus; adv. ad tempus, tempestive, opportune.

timid, timidus, verecundus (= bashful), ignavus (= cowardly). Adv. timide.

timidity, timiditas, verecundia (= shyness).

tin, plumbum album, stannum.

tinder, fomes.

tinge, v. imbuère, colorare, inficère, tingère.

tinkle, v. tinnire.

tinkling, subst. tinnitus (-ūs).

tinkling, adj. tinnulus.

tinsel, = metal leaf, bractea.

tip, subst. cacumen, apex; or render by adj. extremus.

tip, v., = head, point, praefigère; — up, — over, (in)vertère, inclinare.

tipple, (per)potare.

tipsy, temulentus, ebrius.

tiptoe, on, suspenso gradu.

tire, v. transit., (de)fatigare.

tired, (de)fessus, fatigatus; I am — of saying, taedet me dicère.

tiresome, importunus, molestus.

tit-bits, cuppedia (-orum), scitamenta (-orum).

title, titulus, index (of a book), nomen (= name), praescriptio (= heading).

titled, nobilis.

titter, v.; see laugh.

Tivoli, Tibur.

to, commonly rendered by the Latin dative; for motion to, use ad with acc. (except with domus and rus and names of towns or small islands); —, or up —, a certain time, ad or in with acc.; to and fro, huc (et) illuc.

toad, bufo.

toadstool, fungus.

toast, v. torrère, frigère; — drink a health, (homini) propinare.

today: subst. hodiernus dies: of —, adj. hodiernus; adv. hodie.

toe, (pedis) digitus.

together, una, simul; all —, cuncti, universi.

toil, subst. labor, opera.

toil, v. (e)laborare, sudare.

toilsome, laboriosus, operosus.

token, signum.

Toledo, Toletum.

tolerable, tolerabilis, patibilis; = middling, tolerabilis, mediocris, modicus; adv. mediocriter, modice, satis (= sufficiently).

tolerance, toleration, tolerantia; indulgentia, lenitas, facilitas.

tolerate, tolerare, (aequo animo) ferre.

toll, subst. vectigal, portorium.

toll, v. sonare.

tomb, sepulcrum.

tomb-stone, lapis, cippus, monumentum.

tomorrow: subst. crastinus dies: of —, adj. crastinus; adv. cras.

tone, sonus, sonitus (-ūs), vox.

tongs, forceps.

tongue, lingua.

tonnage, expressed by numbers of amphorae.

too: = also, etiam, quoque, praeterea; = excessively, render by nimis or nimium or by comparative; — stupid to know, stultior quam qui sciat; — little, parum.

tool: an iron-, ferramentum; —s, plur., instrumentum.

tooth, dens.

top, subst.: = summit, cacumen, culmen; or render by adj. summus; a child's —, turbo.

top, adj. summus.

topic, res.

topical, hodiernus, hic.

topography, locorum descriptio.

torch, fax, taeda.

torment, subst. cruciatus (-ūs), tormentum.

torment, v. (ex)cruciare, torquère, vexare.

tormenter, vexator; or render by verb.

tornado, turbo, tempestas.

torpid, torpens, lentus, iners.

torpor, torpor.

torrent, torrens.

torrid, torridus.

tortoise, testudo.

torture, tormentum, cruciatus (-ūs), dolor, angor.

torture, v. (ex)cruciare, (ex)torquère.

torturer, tortor, carnifex.

toss, tossing, subst. iactus (-ūs), iactatio.

toss, v. iactare.

total, subst. summa, universitas.

total, adj. totus, omnis; adv. omnino, funditus, penitus.

totter, v. labare, vacillare, titubare.

touch, subst. (con)tactus (-ūs), tactio.

touch, v. tangère, attingère, contingère; = influence, affect, tangère. (com)movère.

touching, prep. de, with abl.

touchy, *inritabilis, iracundus,*
tough, *lentus, durus.*
toughness, *duritia.*
tour, *iter, peregrinatio, lustratio.*
tow, subst. *stuppa:* of —, adj. *stuppeus.*
tow, v. *trahĕre.*
toward, towards, prep.: of motion,
ad or *adversus* with acc.; of time, =
near to, *ad* or *sub*, with acc.; of
personal relations, *adversus, erga, in,*
with acc.
towel, *mantele.*
tower, subst. *turris;* fig., *arx, praesidium.*
tower, v. *eminēre, exstare;* — over,
imminēre, with dat.
towering, *arduus.*
town, *urbs, oppidum;* of a —, adj.,
urbanus.
town-hall, *curia.*
townsman, *civis, oppidanus.*
trace, subst. *vestigium, indicium.*
trace, v.: = draw, mark out, *designare,
describĕre, adumbrare;* = follow up,
track, *(in)vestigare.*
track, subst.; see path.
tract: = region, *tractus (-ūs), regio;*
= treatise, *libellus.*
tractable, *tractabilis, docilis, facilis.*
tractableness, *docilitas, facilitas.*
trade, subst., = commerce, *mercatura,
commercium;* = any occupation, *ars,
artificium.*
trade, v. *mercaturam facĕre, (com)mer-
cari, negotiari.*
trader, *mercator;* see also merchant.
tradition, *memoria, litterae (-arum,
documentary).*
traditional, *(a maioribus) posteris
traditus.*
tragedian: = writer, *tragicus;* = actor,
tragoedus, tragicus actor.
tragedy, *tragoedia;* fig. *casus (-ūs).*
tragic, *tragicus;* = sad, *tristis, miserabilis.* Adv. *tragice; miserabiliter.*
train, subst.: a robe with a —, *syrma;*
= procession, *pompa;* = any series,
ordo, series.
train, v. *(e)docēre, instituĕre;* = drill,
exercēre.
trainer, *magister;* of horses, *equorum
domitor.*
training, *disciplina, exercitatio.*
traitor, *proditor.*
tramp; see walk, march.
trample, *calcare, conculcare.*
trance, render by *animus a corpore
abstractus.*
tranquil, *tranquillus, placidus, quietus.*
tranquillity, *tranquillitas, quies.*
tranquillize, *tranquillare, pacare, sedare.*
transact, *gerĕre, agĕre, conficĕre.*
transaction, *res, negotium.*
transcend, *(ex)superare, excellĕre.*
transcendent, *praestans, singularis,
eximius.*
transcribe, *transcribĕre.*
transcript, *exemplum, exemplar.*
transfer, subst. *translatio, mancipium*
(of property).
transfer, v. *transferre, traducĕre.*
transference, *translatio.*
transfix, *transfigĕre, traicĕre, confodĕre.*
transform, *(con)vertĕre, (com)mutare.*

transgress, *transcendĕre, violare;* intransit., *delinquĕre, peccare.*
transgression, *delictum, peccatum.*
transient, adj. *brevis, fugax, caducus,
fluxus.*
transit, *transitus (-ūs).*
transition, *transitio, transgressio.*
transitive, *transitivus* (gram.).
translate, *(con)vertĕre, reddĕre.*
translator, *interpres.*
transmit, *transmittĕre, tradĕre.*
transparent, *perlucidus* (pell-), *perspicuus;* to be —, *perlucēre, lucem
transmittĕre.* Trans., *evidens, manifestus;* adv. *manifesto.*
transpire, of secrets, etc., *(di)vulgari,
pervulgari, percrebrescĕre.*
transplant, *transferre, traducĕre.*
transport, subst. as a ship, *navigium
vectorium, navis oneraria.*
transport, v. *transportare, transferre;*
for banishment, *relegare;* to be —ed
with rage, *iracundia exardescĕre,* with
delight, *gaudio efferri* or *exsultare.*
transpose, *traicĕre.*
transverse, *transversus, transversarius.*
trap, subst. *laqueus;* see also snare, net.
trap, v. *inretire;* see ensnare.
trappings, *ornamentum, insignia (-ium);*
of horses, *phalerae (-arum).*
trash, *quisquiliae (-arum), scruta (-orum).*
trashy, *vilis.*
travail, v. *parturire.*
travel, subst. *iter, peregrinatio* (abroad);
— through, see traverse.
traveller, *viator, vector, peregrinator.*
traverse, *obire, peragrare, (per)lustrare.*
tray, *ferculum.*
treacherous, *perfidus, perfidiosus;* adv.
perfidiose.
treachery, *perfidia, fraus.*
tread, subst. *(in)gressus (-ūs), gradus
(-ūs).*
tread, v. *ingredi, incedĕre, insistĕre.*
treason: in gen., *perfidia, proditio;*
high —, *maiestas, perduellio;* to commit —, *maiestatem minuĕre* or *laedĕre.*
treasure, subst. *thesaurus, gaza, opes
(-um).*
treasure, v.; see value: — up,
(re)condĕre.
treasure-house, *thesaurus.*
treasurer, *praefectus aerarii.*
treasury, *aerarium, fiscus.*
treat, v.: = discuss, *(rem) tractare, (de re)
disputare;* medically, *curare;* = entertain, *invitare;* = behave towards
(with adv.), *habēre, tractare;* — with,
= negotiate, *agĕre (cum).*
treatise, *liber, libellus.*
treatment, *tractatio, curatio;* kind —,
comitas; cruel —, *saevitia.*
treaty, *pactum, foedus (-eris,* n.).
Trebizond, *Trapezus (-untis).*
treble, adj., see triple; of voices,
acutus.
treble, v. *(rem) triplicem facĕre.*
tree, *arbor;* genealogical —, *stemma
(-atis,* n.).
tremble, *tremĕre, contremiscĕre, micare*
(= flicker); to cause to —, *tremefacĕre.*
trembling, subst. *tremor.*
trembling, adj. *tremebundus, tremulus.*

tremendous, *terribilis*; = huge, *ingens, immanis.*   Adv. *valde, magnopere, maxime.*

trench, subst. *fossa*; see also ditch.

trench, v. *fossam fodĕre* or *facĕre.*

Trent, *Tridentum.*

trepidation, *trepidatio.*

trial, *temptatio, experimentum, experientia*; = attempt, *conatus (-ūs)*; in court, *iudicium, quaestio.*

triangle, *triangulum.*

triangular, *triangulus, triquetrus.*

tribe, at *Rome, tribus (-ūs)*; by —s, *tributim*; in gen., *natio, gens.*

tribulation, *miseria, incommodum, aerumna.*

tribunal, *tribunal*; = law court, *iudicium.*

tribune, *tribunus.*

tributary, subst., render by verb *influĕre.*

tributary, adj. *vectigalis, stipendiarius.*

tribute, *tributum, vectigal, stipendium.*

trick, subst. *dolus, fraus, machina.*

trick, v.: see deceive.

trickery, *fallacia, astutia.*

trickle, v. *manare, rorare, stillare*

trident, *tridens.*

tried, *spectatus, cognitus, probatus.*

Trieste, *Tergeste.*

trifle, subst. *res parvi momenti; nugae (-arum).*

trifle, v. *nugari, ludĕre, ineptire.*

trifler, *nugator.*

trifling, subst. *iocus, ineptiae (-arum).*

trifling, adj. *levis, minutus, nugatorius.*

trim, v. *concinnare*; of hair, *comĕre*; = prune, *(am)putare.*

trimming, subst. *fimbriae (-arum).*

trio, = three together, *tres, tria.*

trip, v. transit., — up, *supplantare*; intransit., = stumble, *offendĕre.*

tripartite, *tripertitus* or *tripartitus.*

triple, *triplex.*

tripod, *tripūs (-podis).*

trite, *tritus, pervulgatus.*

triumph, subst. *triumphus*; = success, *victoria*, = rejoicing, *exsultatio.*

triumph, v. *triumphare, triumphum agĕre*; = exult, *exultare*; — over, = conquer, *superare, vincĕre.*

triumphal, *triumphalis.*

triumphant, *victor; elatus, exsultans.*

trivial, *levis.*

trochee, *trochaeus.*

Trojan, subst. *Tros*; adj. *Troianus.*

troop, subst. *caterva, grex, manus (ūs)*; of horsemen, *turma*; —s, *copiae.*

trooper, *eques.*

trophy, *tropaeum.*

tropics, *regiones torridae.*

trot, subst. *gradus (-ūs) citatus* or *tolutilis.*

troth, *fides*; to plight —, *fidem dare.*

trouble, subst.: = adversity, *molestia, incommodum, calamitas*; of mind, *sollicitudo, anxietas*; — taken, = effort, *opera, negotium, labor.*

trouble, v. *vexare, agitare, sollicitare*; to — oneself, *laborare*; — about, *curare.*

troublesome, *molestus, gravis, incommodus.*

trough, *alveus.*

trousers, *brac(c)ae (-arum).*

truce, *indutiae (-arum).*

truckle, *morem gerĕre, obtemperare.*

trudge; see walk.

true, *verus, sincerus, germanus*; = loyal, *fidus, fidelis.*   Adv. *vere, profecto, certe.*

trumpet, *tuba* (straight); *bucina, lituus, cornu* (curved); a — call, *classicum.*

trumpeter, *tubicen, bucinator.*

trump up, *fingĕre.*

truncheon, *scipio, fustis.*

trunk: of a tree, *truncus, stirps*; of the body, *truncus, corpus*; = chest, box, *arca*; of an elephant, *manus (-ūs), proboscis.*

trust, subst., = confidence, *fiducia, fides.*

trust, v.: = feel confidence, *(con)fidĕre, credĕre*; = entrust, *(con)credĕre, committĕre, mandare.*

trustee, *custos, procurator.*

trustworthiness, *constantia, fides.*

trustworthy, *certus, constans, fidus.*

truth, *veritas*; the —, = the fact(s), *verum, vera.*

truthful, *verus, verax, veridicus.*

truthfulness, *veritas.*

try, subst. *conatus (-ūs).*

try, v.: = make trial of, *temptare, experiri*; = attempt, *conari*; in court, to — a case, *iudicare, cognoscĕre, quaerĕre.*

trying, adj. *molestus, gravis, incommodus.*

tub, *dolium, labrum.*

tube, *tubus.*

tuck, v.: to — up, *succingĕre.*

tuft: of hair, *crinis*; of wool, *floccus*; of feathers, *crista.*

tufted, *cristatus.*

tug, v. *trahĕre.*

tumble, subst. *casus (-ūs), ruina.*

tumble, v. = disarrange, *(per)turbare, miscĕre*; intransit., see fall.

tumid, *tumidus, inflatus, turgidus.*

tumour, *tumor, tuber.*

tumult, *tumultus (-ūs), motus (-ūs), turba.*

tumultuous, *tumultuosus, turbulentus, turbidus*; adv. *tumultuose, turbulente.*

tune, *cantus (-ūs), carmen, modi (-orum)*; to keep in —, *concentum servare*; out of —, *absonus.*

tuneful, *canorus.*

tunic, *tunica.*

tunnel, *cuniculus.*

turban, *mitra.*

turbid, *turbidus.*

turbot, *rhombus.*

turbulent, *turbulentus, seditiosus, turbidus.*

turf, *caespes, herba.*

turgid, *tumidus.*

Turin, *Augusta Taurinorum.*

turmoil, *turba.*

turn, turning, *conversio, flexus (-ūs)*; of events, *vicissitudo, commutatio*; to take a — for the better, *in melius mutari*; of alternation, *sors* (= lot): by —s, *alternis, invicem*; a good —, *officium*; a — of speech, *genus dicendi.*

turn, v.: transit., (con)*vertĕre*, *advertĕre* (= turn towards), *versare*, *torquēre* (= twist), *flectĕre* (= bend); — aside, *deflectĕre*; — away, *avertĕre*; — round, *circumagĕre*, *rotare*, *volvĕre*;— one's attention to, *animum advertĕre*, *animadvertĕre*; intransit., (con)*verti*, *se* (con)*vertĕre*; — out, = issue, end, *evenire*, *evadĕre*, *cadĕre*; — up, *incidĕre*.

turnip, *rapum*.

turpitude, *turpitudo*, *dedecus* (*-oris*, n.).

turret, *turris*, *turricula*.

turtle, *turtle-dove, turtur*.

Tuscany, *Etruria*.

tusk, *dens*.

tutelage, *tutela*; see also protection.

tutor, *magister*, *praeceptor*.

tweak, *vellĕre*, *vellicare*.

twelfth, *duodecimus*.

twelve, *duodecim*; — each, — at a time, *duodeni*; — times, *duodecie(n)s*.

twelvemonth, *annus*.

twentieth, *vicesimus*.

twenty, *viginti*; — each, — at a time, *viceni*; — times, *vicie(n)s*.

twice, *bis*.

twig, *surculus*, *ramulus*, *virgula*.

twilight, evening, *crepusculum*; morning, *diluculum*.

twin, subst. and adj., *geminus*.

twinge, *dolor*.

twinkle, *micare*, *fulgēre*, *coruscare*.

twinkling, subst. *fulgor*; in the — of an eye, *temporis puncto*.

twist, v. : transit, (in)*torquēre*, (in)*flectĕre*.

twitch, v. *vellĕre*, *vellicare*.

two, *duo*; — each, — at a time, *bini*; in — parts, adj. *bipartitus*, adv. *bipartito*.

twofold, *duplex*.

two-footed, *bipes*.

two hundred., *ducenti*; — each, — at a time, *duceni*; — times, *ducentie(n)s*.

type: = model, *exemplar*, *exemplum*; = character, class, *forma*, *figura*, *genus* (*-eris*, n.).

tyrannical, adj. *tyrannicus*, *superbus*; adv. *tyrannice*, *superbe*, *regie*.

tyrannize, *dominari*.

tyranny, *dominatio*, *tyrannis*.

tyrant, *tyrannus* (= usurper or despot); *dominus superbus*.

U

udder, *uber*.

ugliness, *deformitas*, *foeditas*.

ugly, *deformis*, *turpis*, *foedus*.

ulcer, *vomica*, *ulcus* (*-eris*, n.).

ulterior, *ulterior*; see also further.

ultimate, *extremus*, *ultimus*; adv. *ad extremum*, *ad ultimum*, *postremo*.

umbrage: see shade, or offence.

umpire, *arbiter*, *disceptator*.

un-, as a negative prefix, is rendered by the Latin prefix *in-*, or else by *non* or *haud* or *sine*.

unabashed, = shameless, *impudens*.

unabated, *integer* (= whole).

unable, render by *non posse*.

unacceptable, *ingratus*, *iniucundus*.

unaccompanied, *solus*, *sine comitatu*.

unaccomplished, *imperfectus*, *infectus*.

unaccountable, *inexplicabilis*, *inenodabilis*.

unaccustomed, *insuetus*, *insolitus*.

unacquainted, *ignarus*, *imperitus*, *inscius*.

unadorned, *inornatus*, *incomptus*, *simplex*.

unadulterated, *sincerus*, *merus*, *integer*.

unadvised, *imprudens*, *inconsultus*; adv. *imprudenter*, *inconsulte*.

unaffected: = simple, *simplex*, *candidus*; = unmoved, *immotus*; to remain —, *non adfici*.

unafraid, *impavidus*, *intrepidus*, *interritus*.

unaided, *sine ope*, *sine auxilio*.

unalloyed, *purus*, *sincerus*, *merus*.

unalterable, *immutatus*.

unamiable, *morosus*, *difficilis*.

unanimity, *unanimitas*, *consensio*, *concordia*.

unanimous, *unanimus*, *concors*; adv. *uno consensu*, *una voce*.

unappeased, *non satiatus*, *implacatus*.

unapproachable: of place, *invius*; of persons, *rari aditūs*.

unarmed, *inermis*, *nudus*.

unasked, (sua) *sponte*, *ultro*.

unassuming, *modestus*, *modicus*.

unattempted: to leave nothing —, *nihil inexpertum omittĕre*, *omnia experiri*.

unattended, *incomitatus*, *sine comitibus*.

unauthorized, *inlicitus*, *inconcessus*.

unavailing, *inritus*, *futilis*, *vanus*.

unavenged, *inevitabilis*; *quod evitari non potest*.

unaware, adj. *inscius*, *nescius*, *ignarus*.

unaware, unawares, adv. (de) *improviso*, (ex) *inopinato*; often by adj. agreeing with the person surprised, e.g. *imprudens*, *necopinans*.

unbar, *reserare*.

unbearable: see intolerable.

unbeaten, *invictus*.

unbecoming, *indecorus*, *indignus*, *turpis*; adv. *indecore*, *turpiter*.

unbeliever, *qui non credit*.

unbelieving, *incredulus*.

unbend, *remittĕre*, (re)*laxare*.

unbending, *rigidus*, *durus*.

unbewailed, *in(de)fletus*, *indeploratus*.

unbiassed, *integer*; *neutro inclinatus*.

unbidden, *invocatus*, *iniussus*.

unbind, (dis)*solvere*, *laxare*.

unblemished, adj. *purus*, *integer*, *in(con)taminatus*.

unblushing, *impudens*; — effrontery, *os durissimum*.

unborn, *nondum natus*.

unbosom: to — oneself, *se patefacĕre*, (rem) *confiteri*.

unbought, *non emptus*, *inemptus*.

unbound, of hair, *passus*, *solutus*.

unbounded, *infinitus*, *immensus*.

unbribed, *incorruptus*, *integer*.

unbridled, *effrenatus*.

unbroken, *integer*, *sincerus*; in time *perpetuus*; of horses, *indomitus*.

unbuckle; see unfasten, untie.

unburden, *exonerare, liberare.*

unburied, *inhumatus, insepultus.*

uncalled, *invocatus;* — for, see unnecessary.

uncared for, *neglectus.*

unceasing, *perpetuus, continuus, adsiduus.*

unceremonious, *simplex* (= natural), *inurbanus* (= rude); adv. *simpliciter, inurbane.*

uncertain, *incertus, ambiguus, dubius, anceps;* to be —, *dubitare, haesitare.*

uncertainty, *dubitatio, dubium;* or render by adj.

unchain, *e vinculis eximĕre;* see loose.

unchangeable, *immutabilis, certus, constans;* adv. *constanter.*

unchangeableness, *immutabilitas, constantia.*

unchanged, *immutatus, integer; idem* (= same).

uncharitable, *durus, inhumanus, iniquus;* adv. *inhumaniter.*

uncharitableness, *inhumanitas.*

unchaste, *incestus, impudicus.*

unchastity, *incestum, impudicitia.*

unchecked, *liber.*

uncivil; see rude.

uncivilized, *ferus, barbarus, incultus.*

unclasp, *refibulare;* see also loose.

uncle, *patruus* (= father's brother), *avunculus* (= mother's brother).

unclean, *impurus, inquinatus.*

unclouded, *serenus, tranquillus.*

uncoil, *evolvĕre, explicare.*

uncombed, *impexus, horridus, incomptus.*

uncomfortable, *molestus, incommodus, gravis;* adv. *incommode.*

uncommanded; see unbidden.

uncommon, *rarus, insolitus, inusitatus;* adv. *plus solito, praeter solitum.*

uncommunicative; see silent.

uncomplaining, *patiens.*

uncompleted, *imperfectus.*

unconcerned, *securus, neglegens, incuriosus.*

unconditional, *simplex, purus;* adv. *simpliciter, sine ulla pactione.*

unconfined, *liber.*

uncongenial; see unpleasant.

unconquerable; see invincible.

unconquered, *invictus.*

unconscious: = insensible, (*omni*) *sensu carens;* = ignorant, *inscius, ignarus.*

unconsecrated, *profanus.*

unconsidered, *neglectus.*

unconstitutional, *non legitimus;* adv. *contra legem, contra rempublicam.*

unconstrained, *liber.*

unconsumed, *inconsumptus.*

uncontaminated, *in(con)taminatus.*

uncontrollable, *impotens.*

uncontrolled, *liber, effrenatus.*

uncooked, *crudus, incoctus.*

uncorrupt, *incorruptus, purus.*

uncouth, *rudis, incultus, rusticus.*

uncouthness, *inhumanitas.*

uncover, *detegĕre, recludĕre, aperire.*

uncultivated; of soil, *incultus, vastus;* of manners, etc., *inhumanus, rudis, agrestis.*

uncurbed; see unbridled.

uncut, *intonsus* (of hair); *integer* (= whole).

undamaged, *inviolatus, integer.*

undaunted, *impavidus, intrepidus.*

undeceive, *errorem (homini) eripĕre.*

undecided, *incertus, dubius, ambiguus, anceps.*

undefended, *indefensus, nudus.*

undefiled, *incorruptus, purus.*

undefined, *infinitus.*

undeniable, *evidens, haud dubius;* adv. *certe, sine dubio.*

under, prep. *sub* (to be —, *sub* with abl.; to go —, or go along —, *sub* with acc.); *subter; infra* (with acc.); — Teucer's leadership, *Teucro duce;* in size or number, *infra* or *intra* (with acc.) or render as 'less than'; — these circumstances, *quae cum ita sint.*

underestimate, *minoris facĕre* or *aestimare.*

under-garment, *subucula.*

undergo, *subire, sustinēre, pati;* to — punishment, *poenas dare.*

underground, adj. *subterraneus.*

undergrowth, *virgulta (-orum, plur.).*

underhand, *clandestinus, insidiosus.*

undermine, (*cuniculis*) *subruĕre, labefactare.*

undermost, *infimus, imus.*

underneath, adv. *infra, subter.*

underrate, *minoris facĕre* or *aestimare.*

undersell, *minoris (quam ceteri) vendĕre.*

understand, *intellegĕre* (*animo* or *mente*) *comprehendĕre.*

understanding, *mens, ingenium;* see also agreement.

undertake, *suscipĕre, (in se) recipĕre, incipĕre* (= begin).

undertaker, (of funerals), *libitinarius, vespillo.*

undertaking, subst. *inceptum, coeptum, res suscepta.*

undervalue, *minoris facĕre* or *aestimare.*

underwood; see undergrowth.

undeserved, *immeritus, iniustus* (= unjust); adv. *immerito.*

undeserving, *indignus, immerens.*

undesigned, *fortuitus.*

undesigning, *simplex, candidus.*

undesirable; see bad, worthless.

undeveloped, *immaturus, nondum adultus.*

undigested, *crudus, imperfectus.*

undiminished, *inlibatus, integer.*

undisciplined, *inexercitatus, inconditus.*

undisguised, *apertus;* adv. *palam.*

undistinguished, *mediocris, inglorius, ignobilis.*

undisturbed, *otiosus, tutus* (= safe).

undivided, *indivisus, totus, integer.*

undo: of knots, etc., (*dis*)*solvĕre, expedire;* see also ruin.

undone, *infectus;* to leave —, *omittĕre;* = ruined, *perditus.*

undoubted, *certus, haud dubius;* adv. *sine dubio.*

undress, v.: transit., *veste exuĕre* or *nudare;* intransit., *vestem exuĕre* or (*de*)*ponĕre.*

undressed, *nudus;* = unprocessed, *crudus, rudis.*

undue, *nimius, immodicus;* adv. *nimis, nimium.*

undulate, *fluctuare, vacillare.*

undutiful, *impius, officii immemor.*

unearth, *detegĕre, effodĕre.*

unearthly, *plus quam humanus.*

uneasiness, *sollicitudo,* (*animi*) *perturbatio.*

uneasy, in mind, *anxius, sollicitus, trepidus.*

uneducated, *indoctus, ineruditus, rudis.*

unemployed, *otiosus, vacuus.*

unencumbered, *liber, expeditus.*

unendowed, *indotatus.*

unenlightened, *indoctus, humanitatis expers.*

unenterprising, *iners, socors, piger.*

unenviable, *miser, tristis.*

unequal, *impar, dispar, dissimilis;* adv. *inaequaliter, impariter.*

unequalled, *summus, singularis.*

unerring, *certus.*

uneven, *iniquus, impar, inaequalis, asper* (= rough); adv. *inaequaliter.*

unevenness, *iniquitas, asperitas* (= roughness).

unexamined, *inexploratus.*

unexampled, *unicus, singularis, novus, inauditus.*

unexercised, *inexercitatus.*

unexhausted, *indefessus, integer* (= whole), *recens* (= fresh).

unexpected, *inexspectatus, insperatus, improvisus;* adv. (*ex*) *improviso, praeter spem, praeter opinionem.*

unexplored, *inexploratus.*

unfading, *immortalis, semper florens.*

unfailing, *perennis, perpetuus, certus.*

unfair, *iniquus, iniustus, immeritus;* adv. *inique, iniuste, iniuriâ.*

unfairness, *iniquitas, iniuria.*

unfaithful, *infidelis, infidus, perfidus;* adv. *infideliter.*

unfaithfulness, *infidelitas, perfidia.*

unfamiliar; see unaccustomed.

unfasten, (*re*)*solvĕre,* (*re*)*laxare, refigĕre.*

unfathomable, *immensus, infinitus.*

unfavourable, *iniquus, adversus;* of omens, *tristis, infaustus.* Adv. *male.*

unfavourableness, *iniquitas;* or render by adj.

unfed, *impastus.*

unfeeling, *durus, ferreus, inhumanus;* adv. *inhumane.*

unfeigned, *verus, sincerus;* adv. *vere, sincere, ex animo.*

unfilial, *impius* (*erga parentes*).

unfinished, *imperfectus;* = crude, *rudis, impolitus.*

unfit, *inutilis, incommodus, indignus.*

unfitness, *inutilitas.*

unfix, *refigĕre.*

unfledged, *implumis.*

unfold, v. transit. *explicare, aperire.*

unforeseen, *improvisus.*

unforgiving, *implacabilis, inexorabilis.*

unforgotten, render by phrase with *oblivio* (= oblivion) or *memoria* (= memory).

unformed, *informis, imperfectus.*

unfortified, *immunitus.*

unfortunate; see unlucky.

unfounded, *vanus, fictus, falsus.*

unfrequented, *avius, devius, desertus.*

unfriendliness, *inimicitia, simultas.*

unfriendly, *inimicus, iniquus, alienus.*

unfruitful, *sterilis, infecundus.*

unfruitfulness, *sterilitas, infecunditas.*

unfulfilled, *irritus, vanus.*

unfurl, of sails, *pandĕre, explicare.*

unfurnished, *imparatus.*

ungainly, *inhabilis.*

ungenerous, *inliberalis, sordidus;* adv. *inliberaliter.*

ungentlemanly, *inliberalis, indecorus.*

ungodly; see impious.

ungovernable, *indomitus, effrenatus, impotens.*

ungraceful, *invenustus, inelegans.*

ungracious, *iniquus, morosus, asper;* adv. *morose, aspere.*

ungrateful, *ingratus, beneficii immemor.*

ungrudging; see liberal.

unguarded, *incustoditus, indefensus;* = imprudent, *incautus, imprudens;* adv. *incaute, temere.*

unguent, *unguentum.*

unhallowed, *profanus.*

unhappiness, *miseria, aegrimonia.*

unhappy, *infelix, infortunatus, miser;* adv. *misere, infeliciter.*

unharmed, *salvus, incolumis.*

unharness, *disiungĕre, solvĕre.*

unhealthy, *infirmae valetudinis, infirmus;* = unwholesome, *pestilens, gravis.*

unheard, *inauditus.*

unheeded, *neglectus.*

unhesitating, *strenuus, confidens;* adv. *strenue, confidenter.*

unhewn, *rudis.*

unhindered, *liber, expeditus.*

unhinged, in mind, *mente, captus.*

unhistorical, *commenticius, fictus.*

unholy, *profanus;* see also impious.

unhonoured, *inhonoratus.*

unhoped for, *insperatus.*

unhurt, *integer, incolumis, salvus.*

uniform, adj. *constans, aequabilis; unius generis.* Adv. *constanter, aequabiliter.*

uniformity, *aequabilitas, constantia.*

unimpaired, *integer, intactus, inviolatus.*

unimpeachable, *sanctus, integer, locuples.*

unimportant, *lēvis; nullius momenti.*

uninformed, *indoctus.*

uninhabitable, *inhabitabilis.*

uninhabited, *desertus.*

uninitiated, *profanus.* Transf., *ignarus, imperitus.*

uninjured, *incolumis, integer, salvus.*

uninstructed, *indoctus, rudis.*

unintelligible, *obscurus;* adv. *obscure.*

unintentionally, *forte, non sponte;* or render by adj. agreeing with agent, such as *imprudens, insciens.*

uninteresting, *ieiunus, frigidus.*

uninterrupted, *continuus, perpetuus;* adv. *continenter, uno tenore.*

uninvited, *invocatus.*

union, (*con*)*iunctio, consociatio;* = united body, *societas, sodalitas.*

unique, *unicus, singularis.*

unison, *concordia vocum.*

unite, v.: transit., (*con*)*iungĕre,* (*con*)*sociare* (as partners), *miscēre* (= mix); intransit., *coniungi, coire, consentire* (= agree).

united, *coniunctus, consociatus, socius.*

unity, =agreement, *consensio, concordia.*

universal, *universus, communis, omnium* (= of all); adv. *universe, in universum.*

universe, *mundus, rerum natura.*

unjust, *iniustus, iniquus;* adv. *iniuste, inique, iniuria.*

unkempt, *neglectus, incomptus.*

unkind, *inhumanus, severus;* adv. *inhumane, severe.*

unkindness, *inhumanitas, severitas.*

unknowing, *inscius, insciens, ignarus.*

unknown, *ignotus, incognitus, inexploratus;* a person — to me, *nescio quis.*

unlamented, *infletus, indefletus.*

unlawful, *non legitimus, inlicitus;* adv. *contra legem* or *leges.*

unlearn, *dediscĕre.*

unlearned, *indoctus, inlitteratus.*

unless, *nisi* (contracted *ni*).

unlike, *dissimilis, dispar, diversus.*

unlikely; see improbable.

unlimited, *infinitus, immensus.*

unload, *exonerare, onere liberare.*

unlock, *recludĕre, reserare.*

unlooked-for, *inexspectatus, insperatus.*

unloose, *solvĕre.*

unlucky, *infelix;* adv. *infeliciter, secus.*

unmanageable; see ungovernable.

unmanly, *viro indignus, effeminatus, mollis.*

unmannerly, *male moratus, inurbanus.*

unmarried, *caelebs.*

unmask, *detegĕre, patefacĕre.*

unmatched, *unicus, singularis.*

unmentioned; to leave —, *omittĕre, praetermittĕre.*

unmerciful, *immisericors, inclemens, immitis;* adv. *immisericorditer, inclementer.*

unmindful, *immemor.*

unmistakable; see clear, certain.

unmitigated, often to be rendered by the superl. of an adj., e.g. a war of — cruelty, *bellum atrocissimum;* see also complete, absolute.

unmixed, *merus, simplex.*

unmolested, *incolumis, inviolatus.*

unmoved, *immotus.*

unnatural, *monstruosus, portentosus;* of character, *immanis, impius.* Adv. *contra naturam, praeter naturam.*

unnavigable, *innavigabilis.*

unnecessary, *non necessarius, supervacuus, vanus.* Adv. *cum non opus, ex supervacuo, praeter necessitatem;* sometimes *nimis* or *nimium.*

unnerve, *enervare, debilitare.*

unobserved; see unnoticed.

unorganized, *inconditus.*

unostentatious; see modest.

unpaid, *non solutus, residuus.*

unpalatable, *amarus.*

unparalleled, *unicus, singularis.*

unpardonable, *quod excusari non potest.*

unpatriotic, *patriae immemor.*

unpitied, *immiserabilis.*

unpitying, *immisericors, immitis.*

unpleasant, *molestus, ingratus, odiosus;* adv. *moleste, ingrate, odiose.*

unpleasantness, *incommodum, molestia.*

unploughed, *inaratus.*

unpolished, *impolitus, rudis.*

unpolluted, *impollutus, intemeratus, integer.*

unpopular, *invidiosus, ingratus, offensus.*

unpopularity, *invidia, offensio.*

unpractised, *inexercitatus, rudis.*

unprecedented, *novus, inauditus.*

unprejudiced, *integer;* see unbiassed.

unpremeditated, *subitus;* or use phrase *ex tempore.*

unprepared, *imparatus.*

unprepossessing; see unpleasant, ugly

unprincipled, *improbus, nequam.*

unproductive, *infecundus, sterilis.*

unprofitably, *inutiliter, frustra, incassum.*

unprovoked, *non laccessitus;* or render by *ultro.*

unpublished, *nondum editus.*

unpunished, *impunitus, inultus;* or render by adv. *impune.*

unqualified; see unsuitable or unconditional.

unquenchable, *inexstinctus.*

unquestionable, *certus, haud dubius;* adv. *sine dubio.*

unravel, *retexĕre.* Transf., *explicare, enodare.*

unreasonable, *absurdus* (= irrational), *iniquus* (= unfair); adv. *absurde, inique.*

unremitting, *continuus, adsiduus.*

unreserved, = frank, *liber, apertus, simplex;* see also unconditional. Adv. *absolute, sine ulla exceptione.*

unrest; see restlessness.

unrestrained, *effrenatus, effusus, impotens.*

unrevenged, *inultus.*

unrewarded, *sine praemio, inhonoratus.*

unrighteous, *improbus, iniustus, iniquus;* adv. *improbe, inuste, inique.*

unrighteousness, *improbitas.*

unripe, *immaturus, crudus.*

unrivalled, *eximius, unicus, singularis.*

unroll, *evolvĕre, explicare.*

unruffled, *tranquillus, immotus.*

unruly, *effrenatus, ferox, turbidus.*

unsafe, *infestus, intutus, periculosus.*

unsaid, *indictus.*

unsatisfactory, *non idoneus, malus;* adv. *male, minus bene, secus.*

unseal, *resignare.*

unseasonable, *intempestivus, importunus, immaturus;* adv. *intempestive.*

unseasoned, of food, *non conditus;* of wood, *viridis, humidus.*

unseemly; see indecorous.

unseen, *invisus.*

unselfish, *suae utilitatis immemor, liberalis* (= generous).

unserviceable, *inutilis.*

unsettle, *labefacĕre,* (*per*)*turbare.*

unsettled, *inconstans, varius, incertus.*

unshaken, *immotus, inlabefactus.*

unshaved, *intonsus.*

unsheathe, (*de*)*stringĕre, e vagina educĕre.*

unshod, *pedibus nudis.*

unsightly; see ugly.
unskilful, unskilled, *inscitus, imperitus*; adv. *inscite, imperite.*
unskilfulness, *imperitia.*
unsociable, *insociabilis, difficilis.*
unsophisticated, *simplex.*
unsound, *vitiosus, infirmus*; of unsound mind, *insanus.*
unspeakable, *infandus, inenarrabilis.*
unspoiled, *incorruptus, integer.*
unstable, *inconstans, instabilis, incertus.*
unstained, *purus, in(con)taminatus, integer.*
unsteadiness, *inconstantia.*
unstring; to — a bow, *arcum retendĕre.*
unstrung, of nerves, etc., *fractus, debilitatus.*
unstudied, (of style) *simplex.*
unsubdued, *indomitus.*
unsuccessful, *infelix, infaustus*; adv. *infeliciter.*
unsuitable, unsuited, *incommodus, alienus*; adv. *incommode.*
untainted, *incorruptus, non infectus.*
untamed, *indomitus, ferus.*
untasted, *ingustatus.*
untaught, *indoctus.*
unteachable, *indocilis.*
unthankful; see ungrateful.
unthinking; see thoughtless.
untie, (dis)solvĕre, *laxare.*
until, prep. *ad* or *in*, with acc.
until, conj. *dum, donec, quoad.*
untilled, *incultus, inaratus.*
untimely, *immaturus, intempestivus.*
untiring, *adsiduus, indefessus.*
unto; see to.
untouched, *intactus, integer.*
untoward, *adversus.*
untried, *inexpertus, intemptatus.*
untroubled, *tranquillus, placidus, quietus.*
untrue, *falsus*; adv. *falso.*
untruth, *falsum, mendacium.*
unused, see unaccustomed; = not yet used, *recens, integer.*
unusual, *inusitatus, insuetus, insolitus*; in an — manner, *inusitate.*
unutterable, *infandus, inenarrabilis.*
unvarnished, *simplex.*
unveil, *detegĕre, aperire, patefacĕre.*
unversed, *rudis, imperitus.*
unviolated, *inviolatus.*
unwariness, *imprudentia.*
unwarlike, *imbellis.*
unwarrantable, *iniquus, iniustus.*
unwary, *incautus, imprudens*; adv. *incaute, imprudenter.*
unwashed, *inlotus.*
unwatched, *incustoditus.*
unwavering; see firm.
unwearied, *indefessus, integer.*
unweave, *retexĕre.*
unwelcome, *ingratus.*
unwell, *aeger, invalidus, infirmus.*
unwholesome, *pestilens, gravis.*
unwieldy, *inhabilis.*
unwilling, *invitus*; to be —, *nolle.*
unwind, *retexĕre, explicare.*
unwise, *insipiens, stultus*; adv. *insipienter, stulte.*
unwitting, *inscius, insciens.*
unwonted; see unusual.
unworthiness, *indignitas.*

unworthy, *indignus*; adv. *indigne.*
unwounded, *invulneratus, integer.*
unwrap, *evolvĕre, explicare.*
unwrought, *rudis, infectus.*
unyielding; see inflexible.
unyoke, *disiungĕre.*
up, prep.: — the river, *adverso flumine*; — the mountain, *in adversum montem.*
up, adv. *sursum*; — to, *usque ad* (with acc.), *tenus* (after an abl. or genit.); to go —, *ascendĕre.*
upbraid, *reprehendĕre, obiurgare, exprobrare.*
upbraiding, *obiurgatio, exprobratio.*
uphill; adj. *adclivis, arduus*; adv. *adverso colle, adversus collem.*
uphold, *sustinēre, sustentare.*
upland, adj. *editus.*
upon, prep.: in space, *super, in*; in time, = directly after, *e* or *ex* (with abl.); — this subject, *de hac re.*
upper, *superus, superior*; to get the — hand, *superare, vincĕre.*
uppermost, *summus, supremus.*
upright, (e)rectus; morally, *probus, honestus*; adv. *recte, probe, honeste.*
uprightness, *probitas, honestas.*
uproar, *tumultus (-ūs)*; see noise.
uproarious, *tumultuosus.*
uproot, *radicitus tollĕre, evellĕre.*
upset, adj. *adflictus, perculsus.*
upset, v. *evertĕre, subvertĕre.*
upshot, *exitus (-ūs), eventus (-ūs).*
upstart, *novus homo.*
upwards, *sursum.*
urbane, *urbanus.*
urbanity, *urbanitas.*
urge, v. *impellĕre, incitare, urgēre.*
urgency, *gravitas, necessitas.*
urgent; of matters, *gravis, magni momenti*; of persons, *vehemens*; adv. *vehementer, magnopere.*
urn, *urna.*
usage, *mos, consuetudo.*
use, subst. *usus (-ūs), usurpatio, usura*; to make — of, (re) *uti.*
use, v.: = to make use of, *uti, usurpare, adhibēre*; = to treat, *tractare*; to — up, *consumĕre*; to — wrongly, *abuti.*
useful, *utilis, aptus, commodus*: to be —, *usui esse, prodesse.* Adv. *utiliter, apte, commode.*
usefulness, *utilitas, usus (-ūs), commoditas.*
useless, *inutilis, vanus, inritus*; adv. *frustra.*
usher, v.: to — in, *introducĕre.*
usual, *usitatus, solitus, consuetus*; more than —, *plus solito.* Adv. *ferme, fere, plerumque.*
usurer, *faenerator, toculio.*
usurp, *adsumĕre, occupare.*
usury, *faeneratio, usura*; to practise — *faenerari.*
utensils, *vasa (-orum), utensilia (-ium) supellex.*
utility; see usefulness.
utmost, *extremus, ultimus, summus*; to do one's —, *summis viribus contendĕre.*
utter, adj. *totus* (= whole). Adv. *omnino, penitus, funditus.*
utter, v. *dicĕre, pronuntiare, effari.*

utterance, *dictum* (= saying), *pronuntiatio* (= delivery).

V

vacancy: = empty space, *vacuum, inane, inanitas*; = unoccupied post, render ·by *vacuus*; — of mind, *stupiditas.*

vacant, *vacuus.*

vacate, *vacuefacĕre*; to — an office, *se magistratu abdicare.*

vacation, *feriae* (-*arum*).

vacillate, *vacillare.*

vacillating, *dubius, incertus.*

vacillation, *dubitatio.*

vagabond, vagrant: subst. *grassator*; adj. *vagus.*

vagary, *ineptiae* (-*arum*).

vague, *incertus, dubius, ambiguus*; adv. *incerte, dubie, ambigue.*

vain: = worthless, *inanis, levis*; = fruitless, *vanus, inritus*; = self-satisfied, *gloriosus*; to be —, *sibi placĕre.* Adv. —ly, or in —, *frustra, nequiquam.*

vainglorious, *vaniloquus, gloriosus.*

vale; see valley.

valiant, *fortis, animosus, acer*; adv. *fortiter, animose, acriter.*

valid, *gravis, certus*; of laws, *ratus.*

validity, *gravitas, pondus* (-*eris*, n.).

valley, (*con*)*vallis.*

valour, *virtus* (-*utis*), *fortitudo.*

valuable, *pretiosus, magni pretii.*

valuation, *aestimatio.*

value, subst. *aestimatio, pretium.*

value, v. *aestimare, ducĕre, pendĕre*; to — highly, *magni facĕre.*

valueless; see worthless.

van: of an army, *primum agmen*; as vehicle, see cart.

vanish, (*e*)*vanescĕre.*

vanity: = emptiness, *inanitas*; = self-satisfaction, *gloria, ostentatio.*

vanquish, (*de*)*vincĕre, superare.*

vanquisher, *victor* (f. *victrix*).

vapid, *vapidus, ieiunus, insulsus.*

vapour, *vapor, nebula, exhalatio.*

variable, *varius, mutabilis, inconstans.*

variableness, *mutabilitas*; see change.

variance, *discordia, dissensio, discrepantia*; to be at —, *dissidēre, discordare, discrepare.*

variation, *varietas, vicissitudo.*

variegated, *varius, versicolor.*

variety, *varietas, diversitas.*

various, *varius, diversus*; adv. *varie, diverse.*

vary, v.: transit.. *variare, mutare*; intransit., *variari, mutari.*

vase, *vas.*

vassal, *cliens.*

vassalage, *clientela.*

vast, *vastus, ingens, immanis*; adv. *magnopere, valde.*

vastness, *amplitudo, magnitudo.*

vat, *cupa, dolium.*

vault, subst., *fornix, camera*; a — underground, *hypogeum.*

vault, v., in building, *confornicare*; = leap, *salire.*

vaunt; see boast.

veal, (*caro*) *vitulina.*

veer, *se vertĕre, verti.*

vegetable, subst., *planta*; an edible —, *holus* (-*eris*, n.); — market, *forum holitorium.*

vegetate, v., fig., *hebescĕre.*

vegetation, *herbae, plantae* (-*arum*).

vehemence, *vis, contentio, impetus* (-*ūs*), *ardor.*

vehement, *vehemens, acer*; adv. *vehementer, acriter.*

vehicle: see carriage, waggon.

veil, subst. *rica*; bridal —, *flammeum, flammeolum.*

veil, v. *velare, tegĕre.*

vein, *vena.*

vellum, *membrana.*

velocity, *velocitas.*

venal, *venalis, nummarius.*

venality, *animus venalis.*

vend, *vendĕre.*

vendor, *venditor.*

venerable, *venerabilis.*

venerate, *colĕre, observare, venerari.*

veneration, *cultus* (-*ūs*), *veneratio.*

vengeance, *ultio, vindicta*; to take —, *ulcisci, vindicare.*

venial, *veniā dignus.*

venison, (*caro*) *ferina.*

venom, *venenum, virus.*

venomous, *venenatus.*

vent, subst. *foramen, spiramentum, emissarium*; to find —, *erumpĕre.*

vent, v.: to — anger, *stomachum effundĕre, evomĕre.*

ventilate, *ventilare* (= to fan); fig., *in medium proferre.*

venture, *periculum* (= risk); *alea* (= hazard); *facinus* (-*oris*, = bold act).

venture, v.: = dare, *audēre, periclitari*; = endanger, *periclitari.*

venturesome, venturous, *audax, temerarius*; adv., *audacter.*

venturousness, *audacia, temeritas.*

veracious, *verus, verax, veridicus.*

veracity, *veritas.*

veranda, *subdialia* (-*ium*), *porticus* (-*ūs*, f.).

verb, *verbum.*

verbal, render by *verbum* or *vox.*

verbatim, *ad verbum, totidem verbis.*

verbiage, *verba* (-*orum*).

verbose, *verbosus*; adv. *verbose.*

verbosity, *copia* or *ubertas verborum.*

verdant, *viridis, viridans.*

verdict, *sententia, iudicium*; to pronounce a —, *iudicare, sententiam dicĕre.*

verdure, *viriditas.*

verge, subst. *margo, ora*; fig., on the — of, render by fut. partic., or *instare*, or *prope.*

verge, v. *vergĕre, inclinare, appropinquare.*

verification, *confirmatio.*

verify, *confirmare, probare.*

verily, *profecto, sane, certe.*

verisimilitude, *verisimilitudo.*

veritable, *verus.*

vermilion: subst.. *minium*; adj. *miniatus.*

vernacular; — tongue, *sermo patrius.*

versatile, *versatilis, varius et multiplex.*

versatility, *facilitas, ingenium facile.*

verse, *versus (-ūs;* in sing. = line of poetry).

versed, *versatus, exercitatus, peritus.*

versification, *versuum ratio.*

versify, *versūs* (or *carmina*) *facĕre.*

vertex, *vertex,* or render by *summus.*

vertical, *(di)rectus;* a — line, *linea, perpendiculum;* adv. *recte, ad lineam, ad perpendiculum.*

vertigo, *vertigo.*

very, adj. *ipse;* see true, real.

very, adv.; render by superlative, or a special form with the prefix *per-,* or *maxime, summe, admodum;* not (so) —, *non ita, haud ita;* — much, with verbs, *magnopere, maxime, valde.*

vessel, *vas;* a blood —, *arteria, vena;* = ship, *navis.*

vest, v.: see clothe or invest.

vestal; a — virgin, *virgo vestalis.*

vestibule, *vestibulum.*

vestige, *vestigium, indicium.*

vetch, *vicia.*

veteran, subst. and adj. *veteranus.*

veto, subst. *intercessio* (of the tribunes).

veto, v. *intercedĕre, vetare.*

vex, *vexare, sollicitare;* to be —ed at, *aegre ferre,* or render by *piget.*

vexation, *indignatio, stomachus, molestia.*

vexatious, *molestus, gravis;* adv. *graviter.*

viands, *cibus.*

vibrate, *vibrare;* see also shake.

vibration, *motus (-ūs);* or render by verb.

vicarious, *vicarius;* adv. render by *loco* with genit., or *pro* with abl.

vice, *vitiositas, vitium, turpitudo.*

vicious, *vitiosus, turpis, flagitiosus;* adv. *turpiter, flagitiose.*

viciousness, *vitiositas;* see vice.

vicissitude, *vicissitudo, varietas, vices* (plur.).

victim, *victima, hostia.*

victor, *victor* (f. *victrix*).

victorious, *victor,* with f. *victrix;* adv. render by adj.

victory, *victoria;* to gain a —, *vincĕre, superare.*

victual, *rem frumentariam providēre* (with dat.).

vie, *certare, contendĕre, aemulari.*

Vienna, *Vindobona.*

view, subst.: = vision, *conspectus (-ūs);* *prospectus (-ūs);* mental —, = judgment, *sententia, iudicium;* in my —, *meo iudicio, me iudice.*

view, v. *adspicĕre, intuĕri, contemplari.*

vigil, *vigilia, pervigilatio, pervigilium.*

vigilance, *vigilantia, diligentia.*

vigilant, *vigilans, intentus, diligens;* adv. *vigilanter, intente, diligenter.*

vigorous, *strenuus, impiger, acer;* adv. *strenue, impigre, acriter.*

vigour, *vis, nervi (-orum).*

vile, *abiectus, nequam, turpis;* adv. *abiecte, nequiter, turpiter.*

vileness, *turpitudo.*

vilify; see slander.

villa, *villa* (= country-house).

village, *pagus, vicus.*

villager, *paganus, vicanus.*

villain, *homo scelestus;* colloq., *verbero, scelus (-eris,* n.).

villainous, *scelestus, sceleratus, flagitiosus.*

villainy: as disposition, *improbitas, pravitas, nequitia;* as act, *scelus (-eris,* n.), *flagitium.*

vindicate: = maintain, *tenēre, obtinēre, defendĕre;* = justify, *probare, purgare.*

vindication, *vindicta, defensio.*

vindicator, *vindex, defensor.*

vindictive, *ulciscendi cupidus.*

vine, *vitis.*

vine-dresser, *vinitor.*

vinegar, *acetum.*

vineyard, *vinea, vinetum.*

vintage, *vindemia.*

vintner, *vinarius.*

violate, *violare, rumpĕre.*

violation, *violatio.*

violator, *violator, ruptor.*

violence, *violentia, vis; ardor* (of passion, etc.); *gravitas* (of weather, etc.).

violent, *violentus, vehemens, gravis* (of illness, weather, etc.); adv. *vi, per vim, violenter, vehementer, graviter.*

violet, subst. *viola;* a bed of —s, *violarium.*

viper, *vipera, aspis;* of a —, adj., *vipereus.*

virgin, subst. *virgo.*

virginity, *virginitas.*

virile, *virilis;* see manly.

virility, *virilitas;* see manhood.

virtual, virtually, *re non verbo.*

virtue: moral —, *virtus (-utis,* f.), *probitas;* = chastity, *pudicitia, sanctimonia;* = efficacy, *virtus, vis,* or use verb, e.g. *posse, prodesse;* by — of, *per, ex, pro.*

virtuous, *virtute praeditus, honestus, probus;* = chaste, *pudicus, castus;* adv. *honeste.*

virulence, *vis;* of diseases, *gravitas;* of hostility, *acerbitas.*

virulent, *gravis, acerbus;* adv. *graviter, acerbe.*

viscera, *viscera (-um), exta (-orum).*

viscous, *lentus, tenax.*

visible, *manifestus;* to be —, *apparēre, in conspectu esse;* adv., *manifesto, quod cernĕre possis.*

vision: = faculty of sight, *visus (-ūs);* *aspectus (-ūs);* = thing seen, *visus (-ūs), species;* = apparition, *simulacrum, imago.*

visionary: of things, *inanis, fictus, vanus;* of character, *fanaticus.*

visit, subst. *salutatio.*

visit, v.: = go to see, *(in)visĕre, visitare, salutare;* = punish, *animadvertĕre, punire.*

visitation; see punishment.

visitor, *salutator, hospes, advena.*

visor, *buccula* (= cheek-piece).

vista, *prospectus (-ūs);* see view.

vital, *vitalis;* adv. *vitaliter;* see also essential.

vitality, *vis, animus.*

vitiate, *depravare, corrumpĕre, irritum facĕre* (= invalidate).

vitiation, *corruptio, depravatio.*

vituperate, *vituperare, reprehendĕre.*

vituperation, *vituperatio, reprehensio.*

vivacious, *vividus, alacer, acer*; adv. *acriter.*

vivacity, *alacritas, vigor.*

vivid; see lively.

vixen, *vulpes*; of women, *canis.*

vocabulary, *index verborum* (= list of words), *copia verborum* (= stock or flow of words).

vocation, *officium, munus (-eris, n.).*

vociferate, *vociferari, clamare.*

vociferation, *vociferatio, clamor.*

vociferous, vociferously, *magno clamore.*

vogue, *mos.*

voice, subst. *vox.*

voice, v.; see utter, express.

void, subst. *inanitas, inane, vacuum.*

void, adj.: = empty, *inanis, vacuus*; = invalid, *inritus, vanus.*

volatile, *volaticus, levis, mobilis.*

volatility, *levitas, mobilitas.*

volcano, *mons flammas eructans*; or refer to some specific volcano.

volition, *voluntas.*

volley, *tela (-orum) coniecta.*

voluble, *volubilis*; see also fluent.

volume: = book, *liber, volumen*; = size, *magnitudo, amplitudo*; = quantity, *copia.*

voluminous, *copiosus, magnus, amplus.*

voluntary, *voluntarius*; adv., *ultro, (mea, etc.) sponte.*

volunteer, subst. *voluntarius (miles).*

volunteer, v. *operam suam profitĕri.*

voluptuous, *voluptarius, luxuriosus, libidinosus.*

voluptuousness, *voluptas, luxuria.*

vomit, v. *(e)vomĕre.*

voracious, *edax, (cibi) avidus*; adv. *avide.*

voracity, *edacitas, (cibi) aviditas.*

vortex, *vertex, turbo.*

votary, *cultor.*

vote, subst. *suffragium, punctum, sententia.*

vote, v. *suffragium* or *sententiam ferre; censere.*

voter, *suffragator, qui suffragium fert.*

voting-tablet, *tabella, suffragium.*

votive, *votivus.*

vouch, v.: to — for a thing, *rem in se recipĕre*; = assert, warrant, *adseverare, testari.*

vouchsafe, *concedĕre.*

vow, subst. *votum, devotio, sponsio.*

vow, v. *(de)vovēre*; = to undertake, promise, *(de)spondĕre, promittĕre.*

vowel, *littera vocalis.*

voyage, subst. *navigatio, cursus (-ūs).*

voyage, v. *navigare.*

vulgar, *vulgaris, usitatus, plebeius.*

vulture, *vultur, vulturius.*

W

wade, *vado flumen transire.*

wag, subst. *ioculator, homo iocosus.*

wag, v. *movēre, quassare.*

wage; to — war, *bellum gerĕre.*

wager, subst. *sponsio, pignus (-oris).*

wager, v. *sponsionem facĕre, pignore certare.*

wages, *merces, stipendium.*

waggon, *plaustrum, vehiculum, carrus.*

wail, *plorare, plangĕre.*

wailing, subst. *ploratus (-ūs).*

wain, *plaustrum.*

wainscot, *paries* (= party-wall).

waist, *corpus (-oris, n.) medium.*

wait, subst. *mora* (= delay); to lie in — for, *aucupari, insidiari.*

wait, v. *manēre*; to — for, *opperiri, exspectare, praestolari*; to — at table, *ministrare.*

waiter, *famulus, minister, puer.*

waiting, subst.: = delay, *mora, commoratio*; at table, *ministerium.*

waive, *(rem) concedĕre, (de re) decedĕre.*

wake, subst. see watch; in the — of, *post.*

wake, v.: transit., *expergefacĕre, excitare*; intransit., *expergisci, excitari.*

wakefulness, *insomnia, vigilia.*

walk, subst.: a — as taken, *ambulatio*; to go for a —, *ire ambulatum*; = gait, *incessus (-ūs), ingressus (-ūs).*

walk, v. *pedibus ire, ambulare, ingredi, incedĕre.*

wall, subst. *murus, moenia (-ium*; of a town), *paries* (= partition).

wall, v. *muro cingĕre, munire.*

wallet, *saccus, crumena.*

wallow, *volutari.*

walnut, (fruit or tree), *iuglans.*

wan, *pallidus, exsanguis.*

wand, *virga, virgula.*

wander, *vagari, palari, errare*: to — through, *pervagari*; to — in mind, *delirare.*

wanderer, *erro, peregrinator.*

wandering, subst. *error, erratio.*

wandering, adj. *errabundus, vagus.*

wane, *decrescĕre, minui.*

want, subst. *penuria, inopia, egestas, desiderium* (— as felt), *defectio*; in —, adj. *inops, egenus, egens.*

want, v.: = lack, need, *egēre, indigēre, requirĕre, desiderare*; = wish, *velle, avēre, cupĕre.*

wanting, = defective, *vitiosus*; to be found —, *deesse, deficĕre.*

wanton, adj. *lascivus, petulans, protervus*; adv. *petulanter, proterve, ultro* (= without provocation).

wanton, v. *lascivire.*

wantonness, *lascivia, petulantia, protervitas.*

war, subst. *bellum*; civil —, *bellum intestinum, domesticum, civile*; a — of extermination, *bellum internecinum*; to declare —, *bellum indicĕre*; to make —, *bellum inferre*; to carry on a —, *bellum gerĕre.*

warble, *canĕre.*

war-cry, *clamor (bellicus), ululatus (-ūs).*

ward, subst.: = a quarter of a town, *regio, vicus*; = custody, *custodia*; = a minor, *pupillus.*

ward, v.: to — off, *arcēre, propulsare, avertere*; by prayers, *deprecari.*

warden, warder, *custos.*

wardrobe, *vestiarium.*

ware, wares, *merx.*

warehouse, *horreum, apotheca.*

warfare, *militia.*

wariness, *prudentia, cautio, circumspectio.*

warlike, *militaris, bellicus, ferox.*

warm, *calidus;* luke-—, *tepidus;* to be warm, *calēre.*

warm, v. *calefacēre.*

warmth, *calor, fervor.*

warn, (*ad*)*monēre;* in advance, *praemonēre.*

warning, subst. (*ad*)*monitio, monitus* (*-ūs*), *exemplum* (= object-lesson).

warp, subst., in weaving, *stamen.*

warp, v.: of timber, intransit., *pandari.* Transf., *depravare, torquēre;* see also distort.

warrant, subst.: = authority, *auctoritas, potestas;* = written authorization, *mandatum, diploma* (*-atis,* n.).

warrant, .v. (*con*)*firmare, promittēre* (= promise).

warranty, *satisdatio;* see guarantee.

warrior, *miles, homo* (or *vir*) *militaris.*

wary, *providus, circumspectus, cautus.*

wash, subst. *lavatio;* a colour-—, *fucus* (esp. red).

wash, v.: transit., *lavare;* to — out, — away, *abluēre;* intransit., *lavari.*

wasp, *vespa.*

waste, subst.: = unprofitable expenditure, *effusio, sumptus* (*-ūs*) *effusus, iactura;* = waste land, *vastitas, solitudo;* = discarded material, *ramenta* (*-orum*).

waste, adj. *vastus, incultus, desertus;* to lay —, *vastare,* (*de*)*populari.*

waste, v.: transit., = to spend unprofitably, *consumēre, perdēre;* intransit., to — away, (*con*)*tabescēre, consumi, confici.*

wasteful, *profusus, effusus;* adv. *profuse, effuse.*

wastefulness, *profusio, effusio.*

watch, subst.: = watching, *excubiae* (*-arum*), *vigilantia, vigilia:* to keep —, *vigilare;* concrete, the —, *vigilia, statio;* = quarter of a night, *vigilia;* = timepiece, *horologium.*

watch, v.: = observe or guard, (*ob*)*servare, tuēri;* = stay awake, *vigilare, excubare.*

watchful, *vigilans;* adv. *vigilanter.*

watchfulness, *vigilantia, vigilia.*

watchman, *vigil, excubitor, custos.*

watchtower, *specula.*

watchword, *tessera, signum.*

water, subst. *aqua;* fresh —, *aqua dulcis;* rain —, (*aqua*) *pluvia, aqua caelestis;* to go for —, *aquari;* of the —, adj., *aquatilis, aquarius.*

water, v. (*in*)*rigare, conspergēre* (= to sprinkle).

water-carrier, *aquator, aquarius.*

water-clock, *clepsydra.*

watering-place, *aquatio;* for bathing, etc., *aquae* (*-arum*).

water-jug, *hydria, urceus.*

water-snake, *hydrus.*

waterspout, *prester, typhon.*

waterworks, *aquae* or *aquarum ductus* (*-ūs*).

watery, *aquatilis, aquosus.*

wattle, subst.; = hurdle, *cratis;* of a cock, *palea.*

wave, subst. *fluctus* (*-ūs*), *unda.*

wave, v.: transit., *agitare, iactare, vibrare;* intransit., *fluctuare, undare.*

waver, *fluctuare, dubitare.*

wavering, subst. *dubitatio, fluctuatio.*

wavering, adj. *incertus, dubius.*

wax, subst. *cera.*

wax, v. = to cover with wax, (*in*)*cerare* intransit., = grow, *crescēre.*

waxen, *cereus.*

way. (1), abstract: = journey, *via, cursus* (*-ūs*), *iter:* — up to, *aditus* (*-ūs*); = manner, *modus, ratio, via;* in this —, *sic, ita;* = custom, *mos, institutum;* —s and means, *opes* (*-um;* plur.). (2), concrete, = road, *via;* a bye-—, *trames, semita, callis;* in the —, adj. *obvius;* out of the —, *devius, avius, remotus;* the milky —, *orbis lacteus.*

wayfarer, *viator.*

waylay, (*homini*) *insidiari.*

wayward; see wilful.

we, *nos;* but often not expressed.

weak, *infirmus, debilis, imbecillus, invalidus; hebes* (= dull, faint, etc.); *levis* (of character, etc.); adv. *infirme.*

weaken, v. transit. *debilitare, enervare, infirmare.*

weakness, *imbecillitas, infirmitas, debilitas; levitas* (of arguments. etc.); *vitium* (= fault).

weal: the public —, *respublica.*

wealth, *divitiae* (*-arum*), *opes* (*-um*), *copia.*

wealthy, *dives, locuples, opulentus.*

weapon, *arma* (*-orum;* defensive) *telum* (offensive).

wear, subst. *usus* (*-ūs*).

wear, v.: to — away, (*con*)*terēre;* = to have on the body, *gerēre, gestare;* = to last, *durare;* to — off, *evanescēre.*

weariness, *lassitudo, taedium.*

wearisome, *laboriosus, molestus.*

weary, adj. (*de*)*fatigatus,* (*de*)*fessus.*

weary, v.: transit., (*de*)*fatigare, obtundēre* (= to bore); intransit., use impersonal *taedet.*

weasel, *mustela.*

weather, subst. *caelum, tempestas.*

weather, v.: to — a cape, *promontorium circumvehi;* to — a storm *vim tempestatis perferre.*

weave, (*con*)*texēre*

weaver, *textor.*

web, *tela, textum.*

wed; see marry.

wedding, *nuptiae* (*-arum*).

wedge, subst. *cuneus;* —shaped, *cuneatus.*

week, *septem dies.*

week-days, *dies profesti.*

weep, *lacrimare, lacrimas fundēre, flēre;* to — for, (*de*)*plorare,* (*de*)*flēre, lamentari.*

weeping, subst. *fletus* (*-ūs*), *lamentatio.*

weigh, v.: transit. (lit. and fig.), (*ex*)*pendēre, pensare, examinare;* to

— down, *opprimĕre*, *gravare*; intransit., to — much, *magni ponderis esse*.

weight, *pondus* (*-eris*, n.), *gravitas*, *momentum*; to have great —, *multum valēre*.

weighty, *gravis* (lit. and fig.).

weir, *moles*, *agger*.

welcome, subst. *salutatio*.

welcome, adj. *acceptus*, *gratus*.

welcome! interj. *salve*.

welcome, v. *salutare*, *salvēre iubēre*.

welfare, *salūs* (*-ūtis*, f.), *commodum*, *utilitas*.

well, subst. *puteus*.

well, adj. *salvus*, *sanus*: to be —, (*bene*) *valēre*; to get —, *convalescĕre*.

well, adv. *bene*, *recte*; very —, *optime*, *praeclare*; it is —, *bene est*, *bene habet*.

well, v.: to — up, *scatēre*.

well-being, *salūs* (*-ūtis*, f.).

well-born, *nobilis*.

well-bred, *comis*, *urbanus*.

well-earned, *meritus*.

well-informed, *doctus*, *eruditus*.

well-known, (*omnibus*) *notus*, *celebratus*.

well-meaning, *benevolus*, *amicus*.

welter, subst. *congeries*.

west, subst. *occidens*, *solis occasus* (*-ūs*).

west, adj. *occidentalis*; — wind, *Zephyrus*, *Favonius*.

westwards, *ad occasum*, *ad occidentem*.

wet, adj. *umidus*, *madidus*; to be —, *madēre*.

wet, v. *madefacĕre*, (*in*)*rigare*.

wether, *vervex*.

whale, *balaena*, *cetus* or *cetos*.

wharf, *navale*, *crepido*.

what: interrog., as pronoun, *quid?*, as adj. *qui*, *quae*, *quod?*; of — sort? *qualis?*; of — size? *quantus?*; relative, = that which, (*id*) *quod*.

whatever, **whatsoever**: relat. pronoun or adj., *quisquis*, *quicunque*; indef., any —, *quivis*.

wheat, *triticum*; of —, adj., *triticeus*.

wheedle, (*e*)*blandiri*.

wheel, subst. *rota*.

wheel, v.: = turn round, transit., *convertĕre*, intransit., of troops, *signa convertĕre*; = push forward on wheels, *propulsare*.

wheeze, *anhelare*; see also pant.

whelp, *catulus*.

when: interrog., *quando?*; relat., *cum*, *ubi*, *quando*, *ut*, *postquam* (= after).

whence, *unde*.

whenever, *quandocumque*, *quoties*, *cum* (with indic).

where: interrog., *ubi?*; — from, *unde?*; — to, *quo?*; relat., *ubi*, *qua*.

whereas, *quoniam*, *quod*, *cum*.

whereby; render by relative.

wherefore: interrog., *cur?*; relat., *quare*, *quamobrem*, *quapropter*.

wherein, *in quo*, *in quibus*, *ubi*.

whereof, render by genit. of relat.

whereupon, *quo facto*.

wherever, *ubicumque*, *quacumque*.

whet, (*ex*)*acuĕre*.

whether, conj. In single indirect questions, *num*, *-ne* or *an*, followed by subj.; in disjunctive indirect

questions, *utrum . . . an*, *-ne . . . an*, followed by subj.; —. . . or not, *utrum . . . necne*. In disjunctive conditional sentences, when a thing is so in either of two conditions, —. . . or, is *sive* (or *seu*) . . . *sive* (or *seu*).

whetstone, *cos*.

whey, *serum*.

which: interrog., *quis?*; — of the two *uter?*; relat., *qui*, *quae*, *quod*.

whiff, *halitus* (*-ūs*; = breath).

while, subst.: for a —, *aliquamdiu*; in a little —, *brevi*, *mox*; for a little —, *parumper*, *paulisper*.

while, whilst, *dum*, *donec*, *quoad* (rare).

while, v.: to — away time, *tempus fallĕre*.

whim, *libido*.

whimsical, *levis* (= fickle).

whine, v. *vagire* (esp. of children).

whining, subst. *vagitus* (*-ūs*).

whinny, *hinnire*.

whip, *flagrum*, *flagellum*, *scutica*.

whip, v. *verberare*.

whirl, v. transit., (*con*)*torquēre*, *rotare*.

whirlpool, *vertex*, *vorago*, *gurges*.

whirlwind, *turbo*, *vertex*.

whirr, subst. *stridor*.

whirr, v. *stridēre* or *stridĕre*.

whisht, interj. *st! tace*, *tacete*.

whisper, subst. *susurrus*.

whisper, v. *susurrare*, *insusurrare*.

whistle, v. *sibilare*.

whit; not a —, *ne minimum quidem*, *minime*.

white, adj. *albus* (= dead —), *candidus* (= shining —), *canus* (= hoary); to be —, *albēre*.

whiten, **whitewash**, v. transit. *dealbare*.

whiteness, *candor*.

whither: interrog., *quo?*; relat., *quo*.

whithersoever, *quoquo*, *quocunque*.

who: interrog., *quis*, *quid?*; relat., *qui*, *quae*, *quod*.

whoever, *quicunque*, *quisquis*.

whole, subst.: the — of a thing, *tota res*; on the —, *plerumque*, *ferme*, *fere*.

whole, adj. *totus*, *omnis*, *universus*, *integer* (= unhurt).

wholesome, *salutaris*, *utilis*.

wholesomeness, *salubritas*, *utilitas*.

wholly, *omnino*, *prorsus*.

whose, *cuius*; plur. *quorum*, *quarum*, *quorum*.

why, *cur*, *quare*, *quamobrem*.

wicked, *improbus*, *malus*, *nefarius*; adv. *improbe*, *male*, *nefarie*.

wickedness, *improbitas*, *scelus* (*-eris*, n.).

wicker, *vimineus*; — work, *crates*.

wide, *latus*, *laxus*, *amplus*; adv. *late*.

widen, v.: transit. *amplificare*, *dilatare*; intransit., *patescĕre*.

widow, *vidua*.

widowed, *viduus*, *orbus*.

width, *latitudo*, *amplitudo*.

wield, *tractare*, *uti* (with abl.).

wife, *uxor*, *coniunx*.

Wight, Isle of, *Vectis*.

wild, adj. *ferus, incultus, ferox*; a — beast, *fera*; adv. *ferociter, saeve.*

wilderness, wilds, *loca (-orum) deserta, solitudo, vastitas.*

wildness, *feritas, ferocia.*

wile, *ars, dolus.*

wilful, *contumax, pervicax*; adv. *contumaciter, pervicaciter*; see also deliberately.

wilfulness, *contumacia, pervicacia.*

will, subst.: = volition, *voluntas, animus, arbitrium*; against one's —, *invitus,* adj.; = testament, *testamentum.*

will, v.: = wish, *velle*; = leave property by will, *legare, relinquĕre.*

willing, *libens, volens, paratus*; adv. *libenter,* or use adj. *libens.*

willingness, *voluntas.*

willow, *salix.*

wily, *vafer, astutus, versutus.*

win, v.: transit., see get, gain; intransit., *vincĕre, superare.*

wind, subst. *ventus.*

wind, v. = turn, twist, *volvĕre, torquĕre.*

winding, subst. *sinus (-ūs), flexus (-ūs).*

winding, adj. *flexuosus, tortuosus.*

windlass, *sucula, tormentum.*

window, *fenestra.*

windy, *ventosus.*

wine, *vinum*: sour —, *vappa*; undiluted, *merum*; the — god, *Bacchus.*

wine-cellar, *apotheca.*

wine-merchant, *vinarius.*

wing, subst. *ala*; of an army, *cornu, ala.*

wing, v.; to — one's way, *volare.*

winged, *alatus, aliger, pennatus.*

wink, v. *conivĕre, nictare.*

winner, *victor.*

winning, *venustus, suavis.*

winnow, *ventilare, evannĕre.*

winnowing-fan, *ventilabrum, vannus.*

winter, subst. *hiems, bruma* (lit. = shortest day).

winter, adj. *hiemalis, hibernus.*

winter, v. *hiemare, hibernare.*

winter-quarters, *castra (-orum) hiberna.*

wipe, *(abs)tergĕre, detergĕre*; to — out, *abolēre, delēre.*

wire, *filum (ferreum).*

wisdom, *sapientia, prudentia, consilium.*

wise, *sapiens, prudens* (= sensible); to be —, *sapĕre.* Adv. *sapienter, prudenter.*

wish, subst. *optatio, desiderium* (= longing), *votum* (= prayer).

wish, v. *velle, cupĕre, (ex)optare*; not to —, *nolle.*

wistful, render by *desiderium* (= longing).

wit: as a quality, *ingenium, (ingenii) acumen, facetiae (-arum), sal*; with one's —s about one, *sanus*; = witty person, *(homo) facetus.*

wit, v.: to —, *videlicet, scilicet, dico.*

witch, *venefica, saga.*

witchcraft, *veneficium, ars magica.*

with, prep., *cum* (with abl.); sometimes plain abl.

withal, *simul.*

withdraw, v.: transit., *avertĕre, revocare, removēre*; intransit., *(re)cedĕre,*

discedĕre, se recipĕre; to — from office, *magistratu se abdicare.*

wither, v.: transit., *urēre, corrumpĕre*; transit., *marcescĕre, marcēre.*

withered, *marcidus.*

withhold, *retinēre, recusare* (= to refuse).

within, prep. *intra* (with acc.), *in* (with abl.); — a period of time, render by plain abl.

within, adv. *intus, intro* (= to the inside).

without, prep. *sine* (with abl.), *extra* (with acc.); to be (or go) — a thing, *re carēre*; — going, — doing, etc., render by clause.

without, adv. *extra, foris* (= out of doors).

withstand, *resistĕre, obsistĕre* (with dat.).

witness, subst.: = one who gives evidence, *testis*; to call as a —, *testari, antestari*; = evidence, q.v.; = a party present, *arbiter, spectator*; before many —es, *coram multis.*

witness, v.: = give evidence, *testari*; = see, q.v.

witticism, *dictum, facetiae (-arum).*

witty, *dicax, facetus, salsus*; adv. *facete.*

wizard, *veneficus, magus.*

woad, *vitrum.*

woe, *dolor, luctus (-ūs)*; interj., *vae!*

wolf, *lupus, lupa*; of a —, adj. *lupinus.*

woman, *femina* (opp. *vir*), *mulier* (esp. a grown —); an old —, *anus (-ūs)*; a little —, *muliercula.*

womanish, *muliebris, mollis, effeminatus.*

womanly, *muliebris.*

womb, *alvus, uterus.*

wonder, subst.: as a feeling, *(ad)miratio*; = wonderful thing, *miraculum, res mira*; and no —, *nec mirum.*

wonder, v. *(ad)mirari*; I — whether, why, etc., *scire velim.*

wonderful, *mirus, mirificus, (ad)mirabilis*; adv. *mire, mirifice, (ad)mirabiliter.*

wont, subst. *mos, consuetudo.*

wont: to be —, *solēre, consuevisse.*

woo, *ambire, (in matrimonium) petĕre.*

wood: as substance, *lignum, materia (materies)*; to get —, *lignari*; = collection of trees, *silva, nemus (-oris, n.).*

wooden, *ligneus.*

woodland, *silvae (-arum), nemora (-um).*

woodman, *lignator.*

wood-nymph, *(hama)dryas.*

wood-pecker, *picus.*

wood-pigeon, *palumbes.*

woody, wooded, *silvestris, silvosus.*

wooer, *procus.*

woof, *subtemen, trama.*

wool, *lana.*

woollen, woolly, *laneus.*

word, subst. *verbum; vocabulum or nomen* (= name); *dictum* (= saying) = word of honour, *fides*: to keep one's —, *fidem servare*; to break one's —, *fidem fallĕre.*

word, v.; see express.

wordy, *verbosus.*

work, subst. *opus (-eris, n.)* = piece of —); *pensum* (= task); *opera,* labor (= effort); *liber* (= literary —); a small —, *opusculum*.

work, v.: intransit. (*e*)*laborare*, *operari*, to — at night, *lucubrare*; a —ing day, *dies profestus*; transit., = exercise, ply, *exercēre*, *exercitare*; = till, *colēre*; = effect, do, *facēre*, *efficēre*.

workman, *opifex*, *operarius*, *artifex*, *faber*.

workmanship, *ars*, *opus* (-*eris*, n.).

workshop, *officina*.

world, *rerum natura*, *mundus*; *orbis terrarum* or *terrae* (= the globe); *terrae* (-*arum*; = all countries); *gentes*, *homines*, *omnes* (all plur., = mankind); the ancient —, *antiquitas*, *veteres* (-*um*, plur.); a man of the —, *homo rerum peritus*; the lower —, *inferi* (-*orum*).

worm, subst. *vermis*, *vermiculus*, *tinea* (in wood, books, etc.).

worm, v.: to — one's way in, (*se*) *insinuare*.

worry, subst.; see anxiety.

worry, v.: = tear, maul, (*di*)*lacerare*, (*di*)*laniare*; = harass, *vexare*, *sollicitare*.

worse, adj. *peior*; to grow —, *degenerare*, *ingravescēre* (of troubles); adv. *peius*, *deterius*.

worship, subst. *veneratio*, *cultus* (-*ūs*): *divine* —, *cultus deorum*; to attend —, *sacris adesse*.

worship, v. *venerari*, *colēre*.

worshipper, *cultor*.

worst: adj. *pessimus*; adv. *pessime*.

worst, v. *vincēre*.

worth, subst., = merit, *virtūs* (-*ūtis*, f.), *dignitas*.

worth, adj.: render by genit. of value or by *valēre*; it is — while, *operae pretium est*.

worthless, *vilis*, *inutilis*, *nequam*.

worthy, *dignus* (with abl., or *qui* and subj.); adv. *digne*.

would: see will, wish; — that, in wishes, *utinam* and subj.

wound, subst. *vulnus* (-*eris*, n.), *cicatrix* (= scar).

wound, v. *vulnerare*, *sauciare*.

wounded, *vulneratus*, *saucius*.

wrangle; see quarrel.

wrap, *involvēre*, *velare*, *amicīre*.

wrapper, = cover, *involucrum*, *tegumentum*.

wrath, *ira*, *iracundia*, *indignatio*.

wrathful, *iratus*, *iracundus*, adv. *iracunde*, *per iram*.

wreath, *corona*, *serta* (-*orum*).

wreathe, *nectēre*, *contorquēre* (= twist).

wreck, wreckage, *naufragium*.

wrecked, *naufragus*.

wrench, wrest, (*rem homini*) *extorquēre* or *eripēre*.

wrestle, *luctari*.

wrestler, *luctator*, *athleta*.

wrestling, subst. *luctatio*.

wretch, *homo miser*.

wretched, = unfortunate, *miser*, *miserabilis*; = bad, *malus*, *nequam*; adv. *misere*, *miserabiliter*; *male* (= badly).

wretchedness, *miseria*, *aerumna*.

wriggle, *se torquēre*, *torquēri*.

wring; to — the neck, *gulam*, *frangēre*, wrinkle, subst. *ruga*.

wrinkle, v.; to — the forehead, *frontem contrahēre*.

wrinkled, *rugosus*.

wrist; render by *manus* (= hand).

writ: Holy —, *Litterae* (-*arum*) *Sanctae*; a legal —, *mandatum*, *praescriptum*.

write, *scribēre*; — out, *describēre*; — back, *rescribēre*; — often, *scriptitare*.

writer, *scriptor*, *scriba* (professional); *qui scribit*.

writhe, *torquēri*.

writing, subst.: as act, *scriptio*, *scriptura*; the art of —, *ars scribendi*; = thing written, *scriptum*, *litterae* (-*arum*).

writing-case, *scrinium*.

writing-tablet, *tabula*, *cera*.

wrong, subst.: = injury, *iniuria*; = wickedness, *nefas*; to do wrong, *peccare*, *delinquēre*.

wrong, adj. *falsus* (= false), *pravus* (= perverse), *iniquus* (= unfair); to be — (i.e. mistaken), *falli*, *errare*. Adv. *male*, *perperam*, *prave*, *falso*, *inique*, *iniuriā*.

wrong, v. *iniuriā adficēre*.

wroth, *iratus*.

wrought, *factus*, *confectus*.

wry, *distortus*, *perversus*, *pravus*.

Y

yacht, *celox*.

yard: the measure, *tres pedes* (-*um*); a — long, or wide, *tripedalis*: court —, *area*; sail—, *antenna*.

yawn, v. *oscitare*; = open wide, *scindi*, *hiare*.

ye; see you.

yea; see yes.

year, *annus*, *anni spatium*; lasting a —, adj. *annuus*; last —, *superiore* or *priore anno*; next —, *proximo anno*; every —, *singulis annis*; *quotannis*; every other —, *alternis annis*; a period of two —s, *biennium*.

yearly: adj., *annuus*, *anniversarius*; adv. *quotannis*, *singulis annis*.

yearn; to — for, *desiderare*.

yearning, *desiderium*.

yell, subst. *ululatus* (-*ūs*), *eiulatio*.

yell, v. *ululare*, *eiulare*.

yellow, *flavus*, *fulvus*, *aureus* (= golden), *croceus* (= saffron coloured).

yelp, yelping, subst. *gannitus* (-*ūs*).

yelp, v. *gannire*.

yes, *ita* (*est*), *certe*, *etiam*, *sane*; I say —, *aio*.

yesterday, adv. *heri*; of —, adj., *hesternus*.

yet: = nevertheless, (*at*)*tamen*, *at*; = even now, *etiamnunc*, *adhuc*; not —, *nondum*: with comparatives, = even, *etiam*.

yew, *taxus*.

yield, v.: transit., = produce, (*ef*)*ferre*; = give, *dare*, *praebēre*; = surrender, *dedēre*, (*con*)*cedēre*; intransit., (*con*)-*cedēre*, *obsequi*.

yielding, adj., *facilis, indulgens.*
yoke, subst. *iugum.*
yoke, v. *(con)iungĕre.*
yolk, (of an egg) *vitellus.*
yon, yonder, adj. *ille, iste.*
yonder, adv. *illic, istic* (= there, where you are).
yore: of —, *olim, quondam.*
York, *Eboracum.*
you, *tu, te,* etc. (sing.); *vos,* etc. (plur.); but often not expressed.
young, subst. *partus* (-*ūs*; = offspring), *fetus* (-*ūs*) or *proles* (= brood), *pullus* (= a single — animal).
young, adj. *parvus* or *parvulus* (= little), *adulescens* (= growing up), *novus* (= fresh, new); — child, *infans;* — lad, *puer;* — man, *adulescens adulescentulus, iuvenis.*
younger, *iunior,* (*natu*) *minor.*
youngest, (*natu*) *minimus.*
your, yours, *tuus* (of a sing. owner; = thy), *vester* (of plur. owner); that of —s, *iste.*
yourself, *tu ipse, tute, tutemet.*
yourselves, *vos ipsi, vosmet* (*ipsi*).

youth, *pueritia, adulescentia, iuventūs* (-*ūtis,* f.); from one's — up, *ab ineunte aetate, a puero;* collective, = young people, *iuventus* (-*utis,* f.), *iuvenes* (-*um*); = a young man, *puer, adulescens, iuvenis.*
youthful, *iuvenilis iuvenalis, puerilis;* adv. *iuveniliter, iuvenum more.*

Z

zeal, *studium, ardor, fervor, industria.*
zealous, *studiosus, acer;* adv. *studiose, acriter.*
zenith, *vertex.*
Zephyr, *Zephyrus, Favonius.*
zero, render by *nihil.*
zest, *studium.*
zodiac: girdle, *cingulum;* = region *orbis, regio, plaga.*
zoology, *animantium descriptio.*

FINIS